Collins easy learning
Italian
Dictionary

HarperCollins Publishers
Westerhill Road
Bishopbriggs
Glasgow
G64 2QT

Fourth Edition 2014

10 9 8 7 6 5 4

ISBN 978-0-00-753093-9
ISBN 978-0-06-279175-7

www.collins.co.uk
www.collinsdictionary.com

A catalogue record for this book is
available from the British Library

Typeset by Davidson Publishing Solutions,
Glasgow

Printed in Italy by Grafica Veneta S.p.A.

Acknowledgements
We would like to thank those authors and
publishers who kindly gave permission for
copyright material to be used in the Collins
Corpus. We would also like to thank Times
Newspapers Ltd for providing valuable data.

EDITOR
Mary O'Neill

CONTRIBUTORS
Daphne Day
Francesca Logi
Mery Martinelli
Loredana Riu
Teresa Álvarez García
Susie Beattie

FOR THE PUBLISHER
Gerry Breslin
Catherine Love
Kerry Ferguson
Sheena Shanks

FOR PREVIOUS EDITIONS
Gaëlle Amiot-Cadey
Gabriella Bachelli
Genevieve Gerrard
Ruth O'Donovan

CONCEPT DEVELOPMENT
Michela Clari
Ray Carrick

TECHNICAL SUPPORT
Thomas Callan
Agnieszka Urbanowicz

MIX
Paper from
responsible sources
FSC™ C007454

Contents

Contents

Introduction

Collins Easy Learning Italian Dictionary is an innovative dictionary designed specifically for anyone starting to learn Italian. We are grateful to all those teachers who have contributed to its development by advising us on how to tailor it to the needs of their students.

Following teachers' recommendations, we have incorporated the following features:

- Colour coding immediately distinguishes Italian and English content

- Thousands of set phrases and examples show words used in numerous structures and contexts

- The gender of nouns is made clear by the use of articles <u>and</u> the labels *masc* and *fem*

- All verbs are linked by reference numbers to verb tables in the middle of the book

- Extra notes alert learners to key language points (such as false friends) and inform about Italian life

- The colourful *Italian in Action* supplement contains the basic phrases a student needs to speak and write Italian confidently

We also gratefully acknowledge the help of the examining boards, whom we have consulted throughout this project, and whose word lists and exam papers we carefully studied when compiling this dictionary. As a result of this analysis, the dictionary contains all the words and structures a student needs.

Free downloadable resources are now available for teachers and learners of Italian at **www.collins.co.uk/easylearningresources**.

Dictionary skills

Using a dictionary is a skill you can improve with practice and by following some basic guidelines. This section gives you a detailed explanation of how to use the dictionary to ensure you get the most out of it.

The answers to the questions in this section are on page 19.

▶ **Make sure you look on the right side of the dictionary**

The Italian – English side comes first: you look there to find the meaning of an Italian word. The second part is English – Italian. That's what you need for translating into Italian. At the side of every page, you will see a tab with either **Italian – English** or **English – Italian**. The **Italian – English** side has a blue tab, the **English – Italian** side has a black tab, so you can see immediately if you've got the side you want.

1 **Which side of the dictionary would you need to look up to translate 'la strada'?**

▶ **Finding the word you want**

When you are looking for a word, for example **nuovo**, look at the first letter – **n** – and find the N section in the Italian – English side. Look at page 174. At the top of the page, you'll find the words **numeroso → nylon**. These are the first and last words on that page.

2 **Which comes first – 'filo' or 'fila'?**
3 **Does 'nuovo' come before or after 'nuotare'?**
4 **Does 'dopo' come before or after 'doppia'?**

▶ **Make sure you look at the right entry**

An entry is made up of a **word**, its translations and, often, example phrases to show you how to use the translations. If there is more

than one entry for the same word, then there is a note to tell you so.
Look at the following example entries:

flat ADJECTIVE
  ▷ *see also* **flat** NOUN
  piatto (FEM piatta)
  ▫ a flat surface una superficie piatta
  ▪ **flat shoes** scarpe basse
  ▪ **I've got a flat tyre.** Ho una gomma a terra.

flat NOUN
  ▷ *see also* **flat** ADJECTIVE
  l' appartamento *masc*

5 **Which of the two entries above will help you translate the phrase *'My car has a flat tyre'*? Look for the two clues which are there to help you:**
  > **an example similar to what you want to say**
  > **the word** ADJECTIVE

TIP
Look out too for information notes which have this shading on the left-hand side. They will give you guidance on grammatical points, and tell you about differences between Italian and British life.

▶ **Choosing the right translation**

The main translation of a word is shown on a new line and is underlined to make it stand out from the rest of the entry. If there is more than one main translation for a word, each one is numbered.

Often you will see a white square ▫ followed by a phrase in light blue. This shows you how the translation can be used. It also helps you choose the translation you want depending on the context.

6 **Use the dictionary to translate *'The exam is hard'*.**

Words often have more than one meaning and more than one translation: if you don't *get* to the station on time, you don't arrive on time, but if you say 'I don't *get* it', you mean you don't understand. When you are translating from English, be careful to choose the Italian word that has the particular meaning you want. The dictionary offers you a lot of help with this. Look at the following entry:

pool NOUN

▷ *see also* **pool** VERB

1 la pozza *fem*

   □ a pool of blood una pozza di sangue

2 lo stagno *masc (pond)*

3 la piscina *fem (swimming bath)*

4 il biliardo *masc*

   □ Let's play pool. Giochiamo a biliardo.

   ■ **the pools** il totocalcio

   ■ **to do the pools** giocare [18] la schedina

A **pool** can be a 'pool of blood', a pond or a swimming pool; **pool** can also be a game. Underlining highlights all the main translations, the numbers tell you that there is more than one possible translation and the words in brackets in *italics* after the translations help you choose the translation you want.

TIP

Never take the first translation you see without looking at the others. Always look to see if there is more than one translation underlined.

7 **How would you translate** *'I like playing pool'*?

Phrases in bold type preceded by a blue or black square ■/■ are phrases which are particularly common or important. Sometimes these phrases have a completely different translation from the main translation; sometimes the translation is the same. For example:

la **bomba** FEM NOUN

bomb

   □ È scoppiata una bomba alla stazione. A bomb went off at the station.

   ■ **bomba ad orologeria** time bomb

   ■ **bomba a mano** hand grenade

to **fulfil** VERB

realizzare [68]

   □ He fulfilled his dream. Ha realizzato il suo sogno.

   ■ **to fulfil a promise** mantenere [113] una promessa

TIP

When you look up a word, make sure you look beyond the main translations to see if the entry includes any bold phrases.

8 **In a job advert you read that applicants** 'devono fare una visita medica'. **What must they do?**

Look up 'visita' and find the answer as quickly as possible by skimming down the *bold phrases*.

▶ **Making use of phrases in the dictionary**

Sometimes when you look up a word you will find not only the word, but the exact phrase you want. For example, you might want to say '*What's the date today?*'. Look up **date** and you will find:

date NOUN
1 la data *fem*
  □ my date of birth la mia data di nascita
  ■ **What's the date today?** Quanti ne abbiamo oggi?

Sometimes you have to adapt what you find in the dictionary. If you want to say '*I bought a CD*' and look up **buy** you will find:

to **buy** VERB
  ▷ *see also* **buy** NOUN
  comprare [68]
  □ I've bought her some flowers. Le ho comprato dei fiori.

You have to substitute **ho comprato** for the infinitive form **comprare**. You will often have to adapt the infinitive in this way, adding the correct ending for **io**, **tu**, **lui** etc and choosing the present, future or past form. For help with this, look at the verb tables. On both sides of the dictionary, you will notice that verbs are followed by a number in square brackets, which correspond to verb tables on pages 22–29 in the middle section of this dictionary. **Comprare** is a verb ending in -**are** so it follows the same pattern as verb number [68] **parlare**, which is set out on page 41.

9 **How would you say '*I buy a lot of books*'?**

Phrases containing nouns and adjectives also need to be adapted. You may need to make the noun plural, or the adjective feminine or plural. Remember that some nouns and adjectives have irregular feminine or plural forms and that this is shown in the entry.

10 **How would you say '*The boys are tall*'?**

▶ Don't overuse the dictionary

It takes time to look up words so try to avoid using the dictionary unnecessarily, especially in exams. Think carefully about what you want to say and see if you can put it another way, using words you already know. To rephrase things you can:

- Use a word with a similar meaning. This is particularly easy with adjectives, as there are a lot of words which mean *good*, *bad*, *big* etc and you're sure to know at least one.

  To help you expand your vocabulary, we have suggested possible alternatives in the WORD POWER feature for the most common adjectives in English – for example, try looking up **big** on page 331 and learning some of the words you could use instead.

- Use negatives: if the cake you made was a total disaster, you could just say it wasn't very good.

- Use particular examples instead of general terms. If you are asked to describe the sports facilities in your area, and time is short, don't look up *facilities* – say something like *'In our town there is a swimming pool and a football ground.'*

11 **You want to ask *'Have you got any pets?'*. How could you avoid using the word *'pet'* if you don't know it?**

12 **How could you say *'The cathedral is huge'* without looking up the word *'huge'*?**

You can also often guess the meaning of an Italian word by using others to give you a clue. If you see the sentence *'Paul ascolta la musica'*, you may not know the meaning of the word **ascolta**, but you do know it's a verb because it is something Paul is doing. Therefore it must be something you can do to music: **listen**. So the translation is: *Paul listens to music.*

13 **In a description of a holiday centre you see a picture of bikes and read 'Noleggio bici: 10€ al giorno'. You may not know the meaning of 'noleggio', but you can see that you have to pay 10 euros, which gives you a clue to what it could mean. What can you do – ride bikes, borrow bikes or hire bikes?**

Parts of speech

There are two entries for **flat** because this word can be a noun or an adjective. Knowing how to recognize these different types of words helps you choose correctly between entries.

▶ Nouns and pronouns

Nouns often appear with words like *a, the, this, that, my, your* and *his*. They can be singular (abbreviated to SING in the dictionary):

*his **dog***   *her **cat***   *a **street***

or plural (abbreviated to PL in the dictionary):

*the **facts***   *those **people***   *his **shoes***   *our **holidays***

They can be the subject of a verb:

Vegetables *are good for you*

or the object of a verb:

*I play **tennis***

Words like *I, me, you, he, she, him, her* and *they* are pronouns. They can be used instead of nouns. You can refer to a person as *he* or *she* and to a thing as *it*.

> ***I bought my mother a box of chocolates.***

14 Which three words are nouns in this sentence?
15 Which of the nouns is plural?
16 Which word is a pronoun?

Italian nouns are either masculine or feminine. Masculine nouns are shown by **il, l'** (when followed by a noun beginning with a vowel or **h**), or **lo** (when the noun begins with **z**, **s**+consonant, **gn**, **pn**, **ps**, **x** or **y**) and the abbreviation *masc*:

il *giorno*   **l'***asino*   **lo** *zaino*

Feminine nouns are shown by **la** or **l'** (when followed by a noun beginning with a vowel or **h**) and the abbreviation *fem*:

la donna   *l'*ambulanza   *l'*handicappata

The plural form for **il** is **i**. For **l'** and **lo** it's **gli**. The **-o** ending changes to **-i**:

i giorni   *gli* asini   *gli* zaini

The plural form for **la** and **l'** is **le**. The **-a** ending changes to **-e**:

le donne   *le* ambulanze

If the noun ends in **-e** (it can be either masculine or feminine), the plural ending changes to **-i** in all cases:

il mare   *i* mari
la madre   *le* madri

Some nouns don't change ending in the plural. This is true of ones ending with an accent (**città**, **caffè**) and foreign words that are in common use (**sport**, **computer**, **euro**). This is shown in the entry:

la **città** (PL le **città**) FEM NOUN   **sport** NOUN
1 town   lo sport *masc* (PL gli sport)

Sometimes, however, the plural form is irregular and this is shown in the entry:

la **camicia** (PL le **camicie**) FEM NOUN   **shirt** NOUN
shirt   la camicia *fem* (PL le camicie)

Italian is written as it is spoken. It is therefore important to keep the same sound when nouns change from singular to plural. This might involve adjusting how the word is spelt. Where a noun ending in **-go** (with a hard 'guh' sound) changes to **-gi** in the plural, an **h** has to be inserted between the **g** and **i** to keep that hard sound. It is the same with **c**. Before **e** and **i**, both **g** and **c** are soft:

il lago   *i* laghi   *la* marca   *le* marche
il parco   *i* parchi   *la* paga   *le* paghe

Where it is necessary to soften **g** or **c**, an **i** is inserted. Compare:
gusto and **giusto**
casa and **ciabatta**

gonna and **giorno**
cura and **ciuffo**
cosa and **cioccolato**

Mangio la pasta tutti i giorni.

17 Two words in this sentence are nouns. Which ones?
18 Are they singular or plural?
19 What is the plural form of 'il cuore'?
20 Look in the dictionary to find the plural form of 'il braccio'.

▶ Adjectives

Flat can be an adjective as well as a noun. Adjectives describe nouns: your tyre can be **flat**, you can have a pair of **flat** shoes.

21 *'Dark'* is an adjective in one of these sentences and a noun in the other. Which is which?
I'm not afraid of the dark.
She's got dark hair.

Italian adjectives can be masculine or feminine, singular or plural, depending on the noun they describe:

un ragazzo **alto** (MASC SING)
una ragazza **alta** (FEM SING = replace -**o** of masculine singular with -**a**)
due ragazzi **alti** (MASC PL = replace -**o** of masculine singular with -**i**)
due ragazze **alte** (FEM PL = replace -**a** of feminine singular with -**e**)

The masculine and feminine singular forms of regular adjectives are shown on both sides of the dictionary.

So if you want to find out what sort of houses **le case vecchie** are, look under **vecchio**.

To form the plural of adjectives in Italian, you generally follow the same pattern as for making nouns plural (with the same spelling changes where necessary).

Adjectives that end in **-e** have the plural ending **-i** for both masculine and feminine.

MASC SING	FEM SING	MASC PL	FEM PL
alto	alta	alti	alte
verde	verde	verdi	verdi

Note the spelling changes when **c** or **g** are followed by **-e** or **-i**:

ricco	ricca	ricchi	ricche
lungo	lunga	lunghi	lunghe

This doesn't always happen and exceptions are shown in the entry.

Some adjectives remain the same whether they're masculine, feminine or plural. This is also shown in the dictionary:

rosa (FEM+PL **rosa**) ADJECTIVE
▷ *see also* **rosa** NOUN
pink

pink ADJECTIVE
rosa (FEM+PL rosa)

22 **What is the feminine singular form of 'nero'?**
23 **What is the masculine plural form of 'piccolo'?**
24 **What forms can 'giovane' be?**
25 **What is the masculine plural form of 'sporco'? And the feminine singular?**

▶ Verbs

> *She's going to record the programme for me.*
> *His time in the race was a new world record.*

Record in the first sentence is a verb. In the second, it is a noun.

One way to recognize a verb is that it frequently comes with a pronoun such as **I**, **you** or **she**, or with somebody's name. Verbs can relate to the present, the past or the future. They have a number of different forms to show this: **I'm going** (present), **he will go** (future), and **Nicola went by herself** (past). Often verbs appear with **to**: **they promised to go**. This basic form of the verb is called the infinitive.

In this dictionary, verbs are preceded by 'to', so you can identify them at a glance. No matter which of the four previous examples you want to translate, you should look up 'to **go**', not '**going**' or '**went**'.
If you want to translate '**I thought**', look up 'to **think**'.

26 **What would you look up to translate the verbs in these phrases?**

I *went*	*she's crying*	*he was lying*
I *did* it	*he is out*	*they've gone*

Verbs have different endings, depending on who is 'doing' the verb, I (**io**), we (**noi**), they (**loro**) etc: **io parlo**, **noi parliamo**, **loro parlono** etc. Unlike English, Italian doesn't need to include the subject such as I (**io**), we (**noi**), they (**loro**) etc, because the verb ending is enough to show who is the subject (for example, the ending -**o** for I and -**iamo** for we). Verbs also have different forms for the present, future, past etc. **Parliamo** (*we talk* = present), **abbiamo parlato** (*we talked* = past). **Parlare** is the infinitive and is the form that appears in the dictionary.

Sometimes the verb changes completely between the infinitive form and the **io**, **noi**, **loro** etc form. For example, *I go* is **vado**, but *to go* is **andare**, and **dico** (*I speak*) comes from **dire** (*to speak*).

On pages 30–45 of the middle section of this dictionary, you will find 16 of the most important Italian verbs shown in full. On both sides of the dictionary you will find a number beside all Italian verbs. When you look up that number in the verb tables on pages 22–29 in the middle section, you will be shown the verb forms for that type of verb. This will help you to work out which is the correct verb form you need, whether that verb is regular or irregular.

27 **Which verb form does the verb curare follow?**

The dictionary also reminds you which verbs use **essere**, rather than **avere**, as an auxiliary verb when forming particular tenses. On the Italian – English side, you will see the note 'aux **essere**' beside the verb number; on the English – Italian side, you will see a small capital letter **E**.

▶ Adverbs

An adverb is a word that describes a verb or an adjective:

*Write **soon**.*   *Check your work **carefully**.*
*They arrived **late**.*   *The film was **very** good.*

In the sentence '*The pool is open daily*', **daily** is an adverb describing the adjective **open**. In the phrase '*my daily routine*', **daily** is an adjective describing the noun **routine**. We use the same word in English but to get the right Italian translation, it is important to know if it's being used as an adjective or an adverb. When you look up **daily** you find:

daily ADJECTIVE
▷ *see also* **daily** ADVERB
<u>quotidiano</u> (FEM quotidiana)
□ It's part of my daily routine. Fa parte del mio tran tran quotidiano.
■ **a daily paper** un quotidiano

daily ADVERB
▷ *see also* **daily** ADJECTIVE
<u>ogni giorno</u>
□ The pool is open daily from nine until six. La piscina è aperta ogni giorno dalle nove alle diciotto.

The examples show you **daily** being used as an adjective and as an adverb and will help you choose the right Italian translation.

Take the sentence '*The menu changes daily*'.

28 **Does '*daily*' go with the noun '*menu*' or the verb '*changes*'?**
29 **Is it an adverb or an adjective?**
30 **How would you translate '*daily*' in this sentence?**

▶ Prepositions

Prepositions are words like **for**, **with** and **across**, which are followed by nouns or pronouns:

*I've got a present **for** David.   Come **with** me.   He ran **across** the road.*

31 **In one of these sentences 'over' is an adjective describing a noun, in the other it is a preposition followed by a noun. Which is which?**

The party's over.
The shop's just over the road.

Answers

1   the Italian side
2   **fila**
3   **nuovo** comes after **nuotare**
4   **dopo** comes before **doppia**
5   the first entry (the ADJECTIVE entry)
6   **L'esame è difficile.**
7   **Mi piace giocare a biliardo.**
8   they must have a **medical examination**
9   **Compro molti libri.**
10 **I ragazzi sono alti.**
11 you could ask 'Have you got a cat or a dog?'
12 you could say 'very big'
13 you can **hire** bikes
14 **mother**, **box** and **chocolates** are nouns
15 **chocolates** is plural
16 **I** is a pronoun
17 **pasta** and **giorni** are nouns
18 **pasta** is singular, **giorni** is plural
19 **i cuori**
20 **le braccia**
21 **dark** in the first sentence is a noun and in the second,
    it's an adjective
22 **nera**
23 **piccoli**
24 masculine or feminine singular
25 the masculine plural form is **sporchi** and the feminine singular
    form is **sporca**
26 to **go**, to **cry**, to **lie**, to **do**, to **be**, to **go**
27 **curare** follows the same verb form as **parlare**, number [68]
28 **daily** goes with the verb **changes**
29 it is an adverb
30 **ogni giorno**
31 in the first sentence, **over** is an adjective and in the second,
    it's a preposition

Pronouncing Italian

▶ Italian vowels

Italian vowels are always clearly pronounced.

a   like the a in apple
e   like the e in set
i   like the ee in sheep
o   like the o in orange
u   like the oo in soon

Remember that if a word ends with an accented vowel,
the stress is on this final syllable e.g. **univeristà**, **ragù**.

▶ Italian consonants

c   before e or i is pronounced **tch**
ch is pronounced like the **k** in kit
g   before e or i is pronounced like the **j** in jet
gh is pronounced like the **g** in get
gl before e or i is normally pronounced like the **lli** in million,
    and only in a few cases like the **gl** in glove
gn is pronounced like the **ny** in canyon
sc before e or i is pronounced **sh**
z   is pronounced like the **ts** in stetson or like the **d's** in bird's-eye

NB All double consonants in Italian are fully sounded e.g. the **tt** in
tutto is pronounced as in hat trick.

Aa

a PREPOSITION

1 at

□ Devo essere a casa alle quattro. **I've got to be home at four o'clock.** □ Scendo alla prossima fermata. **I'm getting off at the next stop.** □ Arriverò a mezzogiorno. **I'll arrive at midday.**

■ **A che ora parti?** What time are you leaving?

2 in

□ Abita a Bologna. **She lives in Bologna.** □ Sono nato a maggio. **I was born in May.** □ Era ancora a letto. **He was still in bed.**

3 to

□ Sei mai stato a New York? **Have you ever been to New York?** □ Andiamo al cinema? **Shall we go to the cinema?** □ Veramente l'ha dato a me. **Actually she gave it to me.** □ La cartolina era indirizzata a Paola. **The card was addressed to Paola.**

4 on

□ Abito al terzo piano. **I live on the third floor.** □ L'ho sentito alla radio. **I heard it on the radio.**

5 by

□ La lettera è stata recapitata a mano. **The letter was delivered by hand.** □ Sono entrati uno a uno. **They came in one by one.** □ È pagato a giornata. **He's paid by the day.**

■ **gelato alla fragola** strawberry ice-cream

■ **pentola a pressione** pressure cooker

■ **TV a colori** colour TV

■ **A domani!** See you tomorrow!

gli **abbaglianti** MASC PL NOUN
headlights

□ Aveva gli abbaglianti accesi. **He had his headlights on full beam.**

abbaiare VERB [17]
to bark

abbandonare VERB [68]

1 to abandon

□ I suoi genitori lo hanno abbandonato quando era piccolo. **His parents abandoned him when he was small.**

■ **Non mi abbandonare!** Don't leave me!

2 to give up

□ Hanno abbandonato tutte le speranze. **They gave up all hope.**

abbassare VERB [68]

1 to lower

□ Hanno abbassato i tassi di interesse. **They have lowered interest rates.**

2 to turn down

□ Ti dispiace abbassare il volume? **Would you mind turning down the volume?**

■ **Abbassa la voce!** Don't speak so loud!

■ **abbassarsi 1** (temperature, price, level) to fall **2** (person) to bend down

abbastanza ADVERB

1 quite

□ È abbastanza alto. **He's quite tall.** □ L'esame era abbastanza difficile. **The exam was quite difficult.**

2 enough

□ Non avevo studiato abbastanza. **I hadn't studied enough.** □ Non ho abbastanza soldi per comprarlo. **I haven't got enough money to buy it.**

LANGUAGE TIP abbastanza is sometimes translated as 'okay'.

□ Ti è piaciuto? — Sì, abbastanza. **Did you like it? — Yes, it was okay.** □ Vanno abbastanza d'accordo. **They get on okay.**

abbattere VERB [1]

1 to knock down

□ Hanno abbattuto molti edifici. **They've knocked down lots of buildings.**

2 to put down (animal)

abbattuto (FEM **abbattuta**) ADJECTIVE
depressed

□ Mi è sembrato un po' abbattuto. **He seemed a bit depressed.**

l' **abbazia** FEM NOUN
abbey

□ l'abbazia di Westminster **Westminster abbey**

l' **abbigliamento** MASC NOUN
clothes pl

□ Spende molto per l'abbigliamento. **He spends a lot on clothes.**

abboccare VERB [18]
to take the bait

l' **abbonamento** MASC NOUN

■ **abbonamento mensile** (for travel) monthly season ticket

■ **un abbonamento alla televisione** a television licence

■ **un abbonamento ad una rivista** a magazine subscription

abbonarsi – accalcarsi

abbonarsi VERB [56]
- ■ **abbonarsi a** to buy a season ticket for □ Vorrei abbonarmi a teatro. I'd like to buy a season ticket for the theatre.
- ■ **Mi sono abbonato ad una rivista di moto.** I've got a subscription to a motorbike magazine.

abbondante (FEM **abbondante**) ADJECTIVE
big
- □ un'abbondante colazione a big breakfast
- □ In quel ristorante le porzioni sono più abbondanti. The portions are bigger in that restaurant.
- ■ **Ne ho comprato un chilo abbondante.** I bought over a kilo.

l' **abbondanza** FEM NOUN
- ■ **in abbondanza** plenty □ Ne ho in abbondanza. I've got plenty. □ Dovresti mangiare frutta in abbondanza. You should eat plenty of fruit.

abbottonare VERB [68]
to button up
- □ Abbottonati il cappotto. Button your coat up.

abbracciarsi VERB [13, aux **essere**]
to hug

l' **abbraccio** MASC NOUN
- ■ **Ci siamo salutati con un abbraccio.** We hugged and said goodbye.
- ■ **Un abbraccio, Francesca** (on a letter, card, etc.) Lots of love, Francesca

l' **abbreviazione** FEM NOUN
abbreviation

l' **abbronzante** MASC NOUN
suntan lotion

abbronzarsi VERB [56]
to get tanned

abbronzato (FEM **abbronzata**) ADJECTIVE
tanned
- □ È abbronzatissima. She's very tanned.

abbuffarsi VERB [56]
- ■ **abbuffarsi di qualcosa** to stuff oneself with something

l' **abete** MASC NOUN
fir

abile (FEM **abile**) ADJECTIVE
skilful
- □ un abile politico a skilful politician
- ■ **essere abile in qualcosa** to be good at something □ È molto abile nel suo lavoro. He's very good at his job.

l' **abilità** (PL le **abilità**) FEM NOUN
skill
- □ Questo lavoro richiede una grande abilità. This work requires great skill.

l' **abitante** MASC/FEM NOUN
inhabitant

abitare VERB [68]
to live
- □ Dove abiti? Where do you live? □ Abito a Firenze. I live in Florence. □ Abito qui da sei anni. I've been living here for six years. □ Abito al numero quarantanove. I live at number forty nine.

l' **abitazione** FEM NOUN
house

l' **abito** MASC NOUN
1 suit
2 dress

abituarsi VERB [56]
- ■ **abituarsi a qualcosa** to get used to something
- ■ **abituarsi a fare qualcosa** to get used to doing something □ Dovrò abituarmi ad alzarmi presto. I'll have to get used to getting up early.

abituato (FEM **abituata**) ADJECTIVE
- ■ **essere abituato a qualcosa** to be used to something □ Sono abituato al caldo. I'm used to the heat.
- ■ **essere abituato a fare qualcosa** to be used to doing something □ Non sono abituato a cenare così presto. I'm not used to having dinner so early.

l' **abitudine** FEM NOUN
habit
- □ una brutta abitudine a bad habit
- ■ **Ha l'abitudine di dormire dopo pranzo.** He usually has a sleep after lunch.
- ■ **Ci ho fatto l'abitudine.** I've got used to it.

abolire VERB [51]
to abolish

l' **aborto** MASC NOUN
1 abortion
2 miscarriage

abusare VERB [68]
to take advantage
- □ Non vorrei abusare della tua gentilezza. I don't want to take advantage of your kindness.

abusivo (FEM **abusiva**) ADJECTIVE
illegal
- □ un altro esempio di edilizia abusiva another example of illegal building
- ■ **un taxi abusivo** an unlicensed taxi
  - **LANGUAGE TIP** Be careful! **abusivo** doesn't mean **abusive**.

l' **accademia** FEM NOUN
- ■ **accademia militare** military academy
- ■ **accademia di Belle Arti** art school
- ■ **accademia d'arte drammatica** drama school

accadere VERB [16]
to happen
- □ È accaduto l'anno scorso. It happened last year.

accalcarsi VERB [18, aux **essere**]
to crowd

accaldato (FEM **accaldata**) ADJECTIVE
hot
□ Ero stanco ed accaldato. I was tired and hot.

l' **accampamento** MASC NOUN
camp

accamparsi VERB [56]
to camp
□ Ci siamo accampati vicino al lago. We camped near the lake.

accanto ADVERB
near
□ Abita qui accanto. She lives near here.
■ **Abita nella casa accanto.** He lives next door.
■ **accanto a** next to □ La tua camera è accanto alla mia. Your room's next to mine. □ Siediti accanto a me. Sit next to me.

accantonare VERB [68]
1 to shelve
□ Ho accantonato il progetto per il momento. I've shelved the project for the moment.
2 to set aside
□ Sono riusciti ad accantonare una bella somma. They managed to set aside a considerable sum of money.

l' **accappatoio** MASC NOUN
bathrobe

accarezzare VERB [68]
to stroke
□ Stava accarezzando il gatto. He was stroking the cat.

accavallare VERB [68]
■ **accavallare le gambe** to cross one's legs

accelerare VERB [68]
to accelerate

l' **acceleratore** MASC NOUN
accelerator

accendere VERB [2]
1 to light
□ Abbiamo acceso le candeline. We lit the candles.
■ **Mi fai accendere?** Have you got a light?
2 to turn on (light, TV, gas)
□ Accendi la TV. Turn on the TV.

l' **accendino** MASC NOUN
lighter
□ Ho perso l'accendino. I've lost my lighter.

accennare VERB [68]
■ **accennare a** to mention □ Ti ha accennato al suo progetto? Did he mention his plan to you?
■ **Mi ha accennato qualcosa.** She mentioned something to me.

l' **accento** MASC NOUN
1 accent
□ Si scrive con l'accento sulla 'u'. It's spelled with an accent on the 'u'. □ Ha un forte accento scozzese. She's got a strong Scottish accent.
2 stress
□ L'accento cade sulla penultima sillaba. The stress is on the penultimate syllable.

accertarsi VERB [56]
to make sure
□ Accertati che Luca abbia chiuso bene la porta. Make sure that Luca shut the door properly.

acceso (FEM **accesa**) ADJECTIVE
1 on
□ C'era la luce accesa. The light was on.
2 burning (candle)
3 lit (cigarette)
■ **Quel fiammifero è ancora acceso.** That match is still alight.

l' **accesso** MASC NOUN
access
□ Nessuno aveva accesso all'edificio. Nobody had access to the building.
■ **Vietato l'accesso.** No entry.

gli **accessori** MASC PL NOUN
accessories

accettare VERB [68]
to accept
□ Ha accettato l'invito. She accepted the invitation.

l' **accettazione** FEM NOUN
reception (hotel, hospital)
■ **'accettazione bagagli'** 'check-in'

acchiappare VERB [68]
to catch
□ L'ho rincorso ma non sono riuscito ad acchiapparlo. I ran after him but couldn't catch him.

l' **acciaio** MASC NOUN
steel

accidenti EXCLAMATION (informal)
1 damn!
□ Accidenti a lui! Damn him!
2 wow!
□ Accidenti, che bella moto! Wow, what a great bike!

accingersi VERB [50, AUX **essere**]
■ **accingersi a fare qualcosa** to be about to do something □ Mi accingevo ad andare a letto. I was about to go to bed.

l' **acciuga** (PL le **acciughe**) FEM NOUN
anchovy

accludere VERB [3]
to enclose
□ Accludo una copia di... I enclose a copy of...

accogliente (FEM **accogliente**) ADJECTIVE
1 pleasant (house, room)
2 welcoming (atmosphere)

accogliere VERB [21]
to welcome
□ Mi ha accolto a braccia aperte. She welcomed me with open arms.
■ **Ci hanno accolto benissimo.** They gave us a warm welcome.

accoltellare VERB [68]
to stab
□ L'hanno accoltellato in una rissa. He was stabbed in a fight.

accomodarsi VERB [56]
to sit down
□ Si è accomodato sul divano. He sat down on the sofa.
■ **Prego, si accomodi!** 1 Please take a seat! 2 Please come in!

accompagnare VERB [14]
to take
□ Ti accompagno io all'aeroporto. I'll take you to the airport. □ Mi ha accompagnato a casa in macchina. She took me home in her car.

accontentare VERB [68]
to please
□ È molto difficile da accontentare. She's very difficult to please.
■ **Voleva lo scooter e i suoi l'hanno accontentato.** He wanted a moped and his parents got him one.
■ **accontentarsi di** to make do with □ Mi dovrò accontentare di vederlo in TV. I'll have to make do with seeing it on TV.

l' **acconto** MASC NOUN
deposit
□ Ho versato un acconto per il viaggio. I've paid a deposit for the trip.

accorciare VERB [13]
to shorten
□ Devo accorciare questi jeans. I need to shorten these jeans.
■ **accorciarsi** to get shorter □ Le giornate si stanno accorciando. The days are getting shorter.

accordare VERB [68]
to tune

l' **accordo** MASC NOUN
1 agreement
□ un accordo commerciale a trade agreement
■ **stringere un accordo** to sign an agreement
■ **essere d'accordo** to agree □ Su questo siamo tutti d'accordo. We all agree on this.
■ **D'accordo.** Okay.
■ **andare d'accordo con qualcuno** to get on well with somebody □ Non vado d'accordo con i miei. I don't get on well with my parents. □ Vanno abbastanza d'accordo. They get on quite well.
■ **mettersi d'accordo per fare qualcosa** to arrange to do something □ Ci siamo messi d'accordo per andare al cinema. We arranged to go to the cinema.
■ **rimanere d'accordo** to agree □ Siamo rimasti d'accordo che sarebbe venuto a

prendermi. We agreed that he'd come and pick me up.
2 chord

accorgersi VERB [4]
1 to notice
□ Non si sono accorti di niente. They didn't notice anything. □ Si è accorto del furto solo oggi. He only noticed it had been stolen today.
■ **L'ho urtato senza accorgermene.** I accidentally bumped into him.
2 to realize
□ Mi sono accorto subito che qualcosa non andava. I immediately realized something was wrong.

accudire VERB [51]
to look after

accurato (FEM **accurata**) ADJECTIVE
detailed
□ una descrizione accurata a detailed description
■ **un lavoro accurato** a careful piece of work

l' **accusa** FEM NOUN
accusation

accusare VERB [68]
to accuse
□ Mi ha accusato di avergli rotto lo stereo. He accused me of breaking his stereo.

acerbo (FEM **acerba**) ADJECTIVE
unripe

l' **aceto** MASC NOUN
vinegar

l' **acetone** MASC NOUN
nail varnish remover

l' **acido** MASC NOUN
▷ see also **acido** ADJECTIVE
acid

acido (FEM **acida**) ADJECTIVE
▷ see also **acido** NOUN
1 acid
□ Il vino è un po' acido. The wine is rather acid.
2 sour
□ latte acido sour milk

l' **acino** MASC NOUN
■ **acino d'uva** grape

l' **acne** FEM NOUN
acne

l' **acqua** FEM NOUN
water
□ Mi dai un bicchiere d'acqua, per favore? Could I have a glass of water please?
■ **acqua dolce** fresh water
■ **acqua gassata** fizzy water
■ **acqua minerale** mineral water
■ **acqua potabile** drinking water
■ **acqua del rubinetto** tap water
■ **acqua tonica** tonic water

l' **acquaio** MASC NOUN
sink

Acquario MASC NOUN
Aquarius
□ Sono dell'Acquario. I'm Aquarius.

l' **acquario** MASC NOUN
aquarium

l' **acquazzone** MASC NOUN
downpour

l' **acquerello** MASC NOUN
watercolour

acquistare VERB [68]
to buy
□ Abbiamo acquistato una casa nuova. We've bought a new house.

gli **acquisti** MASC PL NOUN
■ **andare a fare acquisti** to go shopping

l' **acquolina** FEM NOUN
■ **far venire l'acquolina in bocca a qualcuno** to make somebody's mouth water
□ Solo a vederlo ti fa venire l'acquolina in bocca! It makes your mouth water just to look at it!
■ **Mmm, ho già l'acquolina in bocca!** Mmm, my mouth's watering!

l' **acustica** FEM NOUN
▷ see also **acustico**
acoustics pl
□ La sala ha un'ottima acustica. The hall has excellent acoustics.

acustico (FEM **acustica**, MASC PL **acustici**, FEM PL **acustiche**) ADJECTIVE
▷ see also **acustica**
acoustic
□ una chitarra acustica an acoustic guitar
■ **un apparecchio acustico** a hearing aid

acutizzarsi VERB [56]
to become worse

acuto (FEM **acuta**) ADJECTIVE
1 high
□ Ha una voce acuta. She's got a high voice.
2 sharp
□ Ho sentito un dolore acuto al braccio. I felt a sharp pain in my arm.
3 acute (accent, angle)

adatto (FEM **adatta**) ADJECTIVE
right
□ È la persona adatta per quel lavoro. He's the right person for that job. □ Non è il momento adatto. It's not the right moment.

l' **addestramento** MASC NOUN
training
□ Il corso di addestramento dura un mese. The training course lasts a month.

addestrare VERB [68]
to train

l' **addio** MASC NOUN, EXCLAMATION
goodbye
■ **addio al celibato** stag night

addirittura ADVERB
even
□ Gli hanno addirittura proibito di uscire di casa. They've even forbidden him to leave the house.
■ **Addirittura?!** Really?! □ Gli hanno proibito di vedermi. — Addirittura?! They've forbidden him to see me. — Really?!

l' **addizione** FEM NOUN
sum

l' **addobbo** MASC NOUN
decoration
□ gli addobbi natalizi the Christmas decorations

addormentarsi VERB [56]
1 to go to sleep
□ Non voleva addormentarsi. He didn't want to go to sleep. □ Mi si è addormentato un piede. My foot has gone to sleep.
■ **Non riesco ad addormentarmi.** I can't get to sleep.
2 to fall asleep
□ Mi sono addormentato davanti alla TV. I fell asleep in front of the TV.

addormentato (FEM **addormentata**) ADJECTIVE
1 sleeping
□ un bambino addormentato a sleeping baby
2 asleep
□ Ero ancora mezzo addormentato. I was still half asleep.

addosso ADVERB
■ **avere addosso** to wear □ Aveva addosso un vecchio impermeabile. She was wearing an old raincoat.
■ **cadere addosso a qualcuno** to fall on top of somebody
■ **mettere le mani addosso a qualcuno** to hit somebody

aderente (FEM **aderente**) ADJECTIVE
tight

adesivo (FEM **adesiva**) ADJECTIVE
▷ see also **adesivo** NOUN
■ **nastro adesivo** sticky tape

l' **adesivo** MASC NOUN
▷ see also **adesivo** ADJECTIVE
sticker
□ Faccio collezione di adesivi. I collect stickers.

adesso ADVERB
now
□ Adesso non posso, sto studiando. I can't do it now, I'm studying. □ E me lo dici adesso? Now you tell me!
■ **È arrivato proprio adesso.** He's just arrived.
■ **Ho finito adesso.** I've just finished.

adirarsi VERB [56]
to get angry
□ Si è adirato moltissimo. He got very angry.

5

adolescente - affibbiare

l' **adolescente** MASC/FEM NOUN
  ▷ *see also* **adolescente** ADJECTIVE
  teenager

adolescente (FEM **adolescente**) ADJECTIVE
  ▷ *see also* **adolescente** NOUN
  teenage

adoperare VERB [68]
  to use

adorare VERB [68]
  to love
  □ Adoro le ciliegie! I love cherries!

adottare VERB [68]
1 to adopt
  □ È stato adottato. He was adopted.
2 to find
  □ Dovremo adottare un'altra soluzione. We'll have to find another solution.
3 to pass *(measure)*

adottivo (FEM **adottiva**) ADJECTIVE
1 adopted
2 adoptive

l' **ADSL** (PL gli **ADSL**) MASC NOUN
  broadband
  □ Hai l'ADSL? Have you got broadband?

adulto (FEM **adulta**) ADJECTIVE, MASC/FEM NOUN
  adult

aereo (FEM **aerea**) ADJECTIVE
  ▷ *see also* **aereo** NOUN
  ■ **per via aerea** by airmail

l' **aereo** MASC NOUN
  ▷ *see also* **aereo** ADJECTIVE
  plane
  □ L'aereo era in ritardo. The plane was late.
  ■ **viaggiare in aereo** to fly □ Mi piace viaggiare in aereo. I like flying.

l' **aerobica** FEM NOUN
  aerobics
  □ Faccio aerobica due volte alla settimana. I do aerobics twice a week.

l' **aeronautica** FEM NOUN
  ■ **aeronautica militare** air force

l' **aeroplano** MASC NOUN
  aeroplane

l' **aeroporto** MASC NOUN
  airport
  □ Ci vediamo in aeroporto. I'll meet you at the airport. □ l'aeroporto di Heathrow Heathrow airport

l' **afa** FEM NOUN
  ■ **C'è un'afa terribile.** It's terribly close.

affacciarsi VERB [13]
  ■ **affacciarsi alla finestra** to appear at the window

affamato (FEM **affamata**) ADJECTIVE
  ■ **essere affamato** to be starving

l' **affare** MASC NOUN
1 deal
  □ Mi ha proposto un affare interessante.

He offered me a good deal.
  ■ **Affare fatto!** It's a deal!
  ■ **affari** business □ Come vanno gli affari? How's business? □ un viaggio d'affari a business trip □ È via per affari. He's away on business. □ Sono affari miei. That's my business. □ Fatti gli affari tuoi! Mind your own business!
2 bargain
  □ A quel prezzo è proprio un affare. It's a real bargain at that price.
3 thing
  □ Come funziona quest'affare? How does this thing work?

affascinante (FEM **affascinante**) ADJECTIVE
1 very attractive *(person)*
2 fascinating *(experience)*

affaticato (FEM **affaticata**) ADJECTIVE
  tired

affatto ADVERB
  at all
  □ Non mi sono affatto divertita. I didn't enjoy myself at all.
  ■ **Niente affatto.** Not at all.

l' **affermazione** FEM NOUN
  statement

afferrare VERB [68]
1 to grab
  □ L'hanno afferrato per un braccio. They grabbed him by the arm.
2 to catch
  □ Non ho afferrato il tuo nome. I didn't catch your name.
  ■ **afferrare un concetto** to get an idea
  □ Afferri il concetto? Do you get the idea?

affettare VERB [68]
  to slice

l' **affetto** MASC NOUN
  affection
  □ Trova difficile dimostrare il suo affetto. He finds it difficult to show affection.
  ■ **Con affetto, Simona** *(in a letter)* Love, Simona

affettuoso (FEM **affettuosa**) ADJECTIVE
  affectionate
  □ Il mio gatto è molto affettuoso. My cat's very affectionate.
  ■ **Un saluto affettuoso, Roberta** *(in a letter, card)* Love, Roberta

affezionato (FEM **affezionata**) ADJECTIVE
  ■ **essere affezionato a** to be fond of
  □ Sono molto affezionato a mia zia. I'm very fond of my aunt.

affiatato (FEM **affiatata**) ADJECTIVE
  ■ **una squadra affiatata** a united team
  ■ **una coppia molto affiatata** a very close couple

affibbiare VERB [17]
  ■ **affibbiare un compito a qualcuno**

to saddle somebody with a task
■ **affibbiare un soprannome a qualcuno** to give somebody a nickname

affidabile (FEM **affidabile**) ADJECTIVE
reliable
□ una macchina affidabile a reliable car

l' **affidamento** MASC NOUN
■ **fare affidamento su** to rely on □ Sai che puoi fare affidamento su di me. You know you can rely on me. □ Non si può fare affidamento sui mezzi pubblici! You can't rely on public transport!

affidare VERB [68]
■ **affidare un incarico** to give a task □ Gli hanno affidato un incarico importante da svolgere. He's been given an important task to do.

affilato (FEM **affilata**) ADJECTIVE
sharp
□ Attento, quel coltello è affilato. Mind, that knife's sharp!

affinché CONJUNCTION
so that

affittare VERB [68]
to rent
□ Hanno affittato la casa a degli studenti. They've rented the house to students. □ Ho affittato una casa al mare. I rented a house at the seaside.
■ **'affittasi'** 'to let'

l' **affitto** MASC NOUN
rent
□ Quant'è l'affitto? How much is the rent?

affogare VERB [76, aux **essere**]
to drown
□ Per poco non affogavo. I nearly drowned.

affollato (FEM **affollata**) ADJECTIVE
crowded
□ La spiaggia era molto affollata. The beach was very crowded.

affondare VERB [68, aux **essere**]
to sink
□ La nave è affondata rapidamente. The ship sank quickly. □ Sono affondato nella neve fino al ginocchio. I sank up to my knees in the snow.

affrettarsi VERB [56]
to hurry up
□ Affrettati o perderai il treno. Hurry up, or you'll miss the train.

affrontare VERB [68]
1 to face up to
□ Cerchiamo di affrontare il problema. Let's try and face up to the problem.
2 to face
□ Affrontano domani la prova decisiva per il campionato. Tomorrow they face the decider for the championship.
3 to talk about

□ È un argomento difficile da affrontare. It's a difficult thing to talk about.

affumicato (FEM **affumicata**) ADJECTIVE
smoked

afoso (FEM **afosa**) ADJECTIVE
muggy
□ Oggi è una giornata afosa. It's muggy today.

l' **Africa** FEM NOUN
Africa

africano (FEM **africana**) ADJECTIVE,
MASC/FEM NOUN
African

l' **agenda** FEM NOUN
diary
□ L'ho segnato sull'agenda. I noted it in my diary.

> **LANGUAGE TIP** Be careful! **agenda** doesn't mean **agenda**.

l' **agendina** FEM NOUN
■ **agendina tascabile** pocket diary

l' **agente** MASC/FEM NOUN
officer (police)
■ **agente segreto** secret agent
■ **agente immobiliare** estate agent
■ **agente di cambio** stockbroker

l' **agenzia** FEM NOUN
1 agency
□ un'agenzia pubblicitaria an advertising agency
■ **agenzia di viaggi** travel agent's
■ **agenzia immobiliare** estate agent's
2 branch office

le **agevolazioni** FEM PL NOUN
■ **agevolazioni di pagamento** payment on easy terms
■ **agevolazioni fiscali** tax concessions

agganciare VERB [13]
1 to hook (fish)
2 to hang up

l' **aggeggio** MASC NOUN
thing
□ A cosa serve quest'aggeggio? What's this thing for?

l' **aggettivo** MASC NOUN
adjective

aggiornato (FEM **aggiornata**) ADJECTIVE
up-to-date
□ un orario aggiornato an up-to-date timetable
■ **tenersi aggiornato su qualcosa** to keep up to date with something □ Mi tengo aggiornato sulle novità discografiche. I keep up to date with the new releases.

aggiungere VERB [5]
to add
□ Aggiungi ancora un po' di latte. Add a bit more milk.

aggiustare VERB [68]
1 to mend

□ Mi ha aggiustato la bicicletta. He mended my bike for me.

2 to straighten

□ Si è aggiustato la cravatta. He straightened his tie.

aggrapparsi VERB [56]

■ **aggrapparsi a** to hold onto □ Si è aggrappato alla ringhiera. He held onto the banister. □ Aggrappati a me! Hold onto me!

aggravare VERB [68]

to make... worse

□ La pioggia ha aggravato ulteriormente la situazione. The rain has made the situation even worse.

■ **aggravarsi** to get worse □ La situazione si è aggravata. The situation got worse.

aggredire VERB [51]

to attack

□ È stato aggredito mentre tornava in albergo. He was attacked as he was going back to his hotel.

aggressivo (FEM **aggressiva**) ADJECTIVE

aggressive

l' **agguato** MASC NOUN

ambush

□ È stato ucciso in un agguato. He was killed in an ambush.

■ **tendere un agguato a qualcuno** to set a trap for somebody □ Ci hanno teso un agguato. They set a trap for us.

agile (FEM **agile**) ADJECTIVE

agile

l' **agio** MASC NOUN

ease

■ **sentirsi a proprio agio** to feel at ease □ Mi sono sentito subito a mio agio. I immediately felt at ease.

■ **mettere qualcuno a proprio agio** to put somebody at their ease □ Ha fatto del suo meglio per mettermi a mio agio. He did his best to put me at my ease.

agire VERB [51]

to act

□ Agisce senza riflettere. He acts without thinking.

agitare VERB [68]

to shake

□ Agitalo bene prima di aprirlo. Shake it well before you open it.

■ **agitarsi** to worry □ Non è il caso di agitarsi tanto. There's no need to worry so much.

agitato (FEM **agitata**) ADJECTIVE

nervous

□ Era molto agitato. He was very nervous.

l' **aglio** MASC NOUN

garlic

□ uno spicchio d'aglio a clove of garlic

l' **agnello** MASC NOUN

lamb

□ agnello arrosto roast lamb

l' **ago** (PL gli **aghi**) MASC NOUN

needle

l' **agopuntura** FEM NOUN

acupuncture

agosto MASC NOUN

August

> **LANGUAGE TIP** In Italian, months are not written with capital letters.

□ in agosto in August

l' **agricoltore** MASC NOUN

farmer

□ Fa l'agricoltore. He is a farmer.

l' **agricoltura** FEM NOUN

agriculture

l' **agriturismo** MASC NOUN

holiday accommodation on farms

l' **agrodolce** MASC NOUN

■ **in agrodolce** sweet and sour □ maiale in agrodolce sweet and sour pork

gli **agrumi** MASC PL NOUN

citrus fruit *sing*

l' **AIDS** MASC NOUN

Aids

□ Ha l'AIDS. He's got Aids.

l' **airone** MASC NOUN

heron

l' **aiuola** FEM NOUN

flower bed

aiutare VERB [68]

to help

□ Ha detto che ci avrebbe aiutati. He said he would help us. □ Mi puoi aiutare a compilare questo modulo? Can you help me to fill in this form?

l' **aiuto** MASC NOUN

help

□ Mi serve il tuo aiuto. I need your help. □ Aiuto! Help!

■ **essere d'aiuto** **1** to be of help □ Se posso esserti d'aiuto... If I can be of help to you... **2** to be useful □ La guida mi è stata di grande aiuto. The guidebook was very useful.

■ **gridare aiuto** to shout for help □ C'è qualcuno che grida aiuto. There's somebody shouting for help.

l' **ala** FEM NOUN

wing

□ Il piccione aveva un'ala spezzata. The pigeon had a broken wing. □ Gioco nel ruolo di ala destra. I play on the right wing.

l' **alba** FEM NOUN

dawn

□ Ci siamo alzati all'alba. We got up at dawn.

alberghiero (FEM **alberghiera**) ADJECTIVE
■ **scuola alberghiera** catering college □ Faccio la scuola alberghiera. I'm at catering college.

l' **albergo** (PL gli **alberghi**) MASC NOUN
hotel
□ Ho dormito in albergo. I spent the night in a hotel.

l' **albero** MASC NOUN
1 tree
□ un albero di mele an apple tree
■ **albero di Natale** Christmas tree
■ **albero genealogico** family tree
2 mast

l' **albicocca** (PL le **albicocche**) FEM NOUN
apricot
□ marmellata di albicocche apricot jam

l' **album** (PL gli **album**) MASC NOUN
album
□ Hai sentito il suo ultimo album? Have you heard her latest album? □ un album di fotografie a photograph album
■ **album da disegno** sketch book

l' **albume** MASC NOUN
egg white

l' **alcol** MASC NOUN
1 surgical spirit
2 alcohol

alcolico (FEM **alcolica**, MASC PL **alcolici**, FEM PL **alcoliche**) ADJECTIVE
▷ see also **alcolico** NOUN
alcoholic
□ È alcolico? Is it alcoholic?

l' **alcolico** (PL gli **alcolici**) MASC NOUN
▷ see also **alcolico** ADJECTIVE
alcoholic drink
■ **Non vendono alcolici.** They don't sell alcoholic drinks.

alcolizzato (FEM **alcolizzata**) ADJECTIVE, MASC/FEM NOUN
alcoholic

alcuno (FEM **alcuna**) ADJECTIVE, PRONOUN
■ **non... alcuno** no... □ Non c'è alcuna fretta. There's no hurry.
■ **alcuni** some □ Sono uscito con alcuni amici. I went out with some friends. □ Ne ho prese alcune. I took some.

alfabetico (FEM **alfabetica**, MASC PL **alfabetici**, FEM PL **alfabetiche**) ADJECTIVE
alphabetical
□ in ordine alfabetico in alphabetical order

l' **alfabeto** MASC NOUN
alphabet

l' **alfiere** MASC NOUN
bishop (in chess)

le **alghe** FEM PL NOUN
seaweed sing

l' **aliante** MASC NOUN
glider

l' **alibi** (PL gli **alibi**) MASC NOUN
alibi
□ Aveva un alibi di ferro. He had a cast-iron alibi.

l' **alimentari** MASC NOUN
■ **negozio di alimentari** grocer's □ C'è un negozio di alimentari qui vicino? Is there a grocer's near here?

l' **alimentazione** FEM NOUN
diet
□ un'alimentazione equilibrata a balanced diet

l' **aliscafo** MASC NOUN
hydrofoil

l' **alito** MASC NOUN
breath
□ Ha l'alito cattivo. He's got bad breath.

allacciare VERB [13]
1 to fasten
□ Allacciatevi la cintura di sicurezza. Fasten your seat belt.
2 to lace up
□ Allacciati le scarpe. Lace up your shoes.
3 to connect
□ Il telefono non è ancora allacciato. The phone hasn't been connected yet.

allagare VERB [76]
to flood
□ La pioggia aveva allagato le strade. The rain had flooded the roads. □ Si è allagato lo scantinato. The basement is flooded.

allargare VERB [76]
to widen
□ Stanno allargando la strada. They're widening the road.

allarmare VERB [68]
to alarm
□ Non volevo allarmarti. I didn't want to alarm you.

l' **allarme** MASC NOUN
alarm
□ I ladri hanno fatto scattare l'allarme. The burglars set off the alarm. □ un falso allarme a false alarm

allearsi VERB [56]
to join forces
□ Si sono alleate contro di me. They joined forces against me.

l' **alleato**, l' **alleata** MASC/FEM NOUN
ally

allegare VERB [76]
to enclose
□ Allego una copia di... I enclose a copy of...

l' **allegato** MASC NOUN
attachment
□ L'allegato può contenere un virus. The attachment may contain a virus.
■ **Le invio in allegato...** Please find enclosed...

allegro - altalena

allegro (FEM **allegra**) ADJECTIVE
cheerful
□ È un tipo sempre allegro. He's always cheerful.
■ **un colore allegro** a bright colour

l' **allenamento** MASC NOUN
training
□ Si è fatto male al braccio durante l'allenamento. He hurt his arm while training.
■ **essere fuori allenamento** to be out of practice □ Sono un po' fuori allenamento. I'm a bit out of practice.

allenare VERB [68]
to train
□ Ha allenato la squadra per due anni. He trained the team for two years. □ Ci alleniamo ogni giovedì. We train every Thursday.
■ **Si sta allenando per la maratona.** She's training for the marathon.

l' **allenatore**, l' **allenatrice** MASC/FEM NOUN
coach
□ l'allenatore della nazionale italiana the Italian coach

allergico (FEM **allergica**, MASC PL **allergici**, FEM PL **allergiche**) ADJECTIVE
■ **essere allergico a qualcosa** to be allergic to something □ Sono allergico alle fragole. I'm allergic to strawberries.

l' **allievo**, l' **allieva** MASC/FEM NOUN
pupil
□ È uno dei miei migliori allievi. He's one of my best pupils.

allineare VERB [68]
to line up
□ Ci ha allineati in fondo alla palestra. He lined us up at the back of the gym.

alloggiare VERB [58]
to stay
□ Ho alloggiato presso una famiglia scozzese. I stayed with a Scottish family.

l' **alloggio** MASC NOUN
accommodation
□ L'alloggio è compreso nel prezzo. Accommodation is included in the price.
■ **vitto e alloggio** board and lodging
■ **la crisi degli alloggi** the housing problem

allontanare VERB [68]
to move away
□ La polizia ha fatto allontanare tutti. The police moved everybody away.
■ **allontanarsi da** to move away from □ Allontanati dall'orlo, è pericoloso. Move away from the edge, it's dangerous.
■ **Ci eravamo allontanati troppo dalla riva.** We had got too far away from the shore.

allora ADVERB, CONJUNCTION
1 then
□ Allora non lo sapevo. I didn't know about it then. □ È stato allora che ho capito tutto. It was then that I understood everything.
■ **da allora** since then □ Da allora non l'ho più visto. I haven't seen him since then.
2 at that moment
□ Proprio allora ha squillato il telefono. Just at that moment the phone rang.
3 at that time
□ Allora aveva ancora i capelli lunghi. At that time she still had long hair.
4 so
□ Allora, che facciamo stasera? So, what are we going to do this evening? □ Allora? Com'è andata? So, how did it go?
■ **E allora?** So what?

l' **alloro** MASC NOUN
bay
□ una foglia d'alloro a bay leaf

l' **alluce** MASC NOUN
big toe

allucinante (FEM **allucinante**) ADJECTIVE
awful
□ uno spettacolo allucinante an awful sight
■ **C'era un freddo allucinante.** It was awfully cold.

l' **alluminio** MASC NOUN
aluminium

allungare VERB [76]
to lengthen
□ Basterebbe allungare un po' la gonna. The skirt just needs lengthening a bit.
■ **allungare le gambe** to stretch one's legs
□ Non c'era posto per allungare le gambe. There was no room to stretch one's legs.
■ **Su, allunga il passo.** Come on, hurry up.
■ **allungarsi** to get longer □ Le giornate si stanno allungando. The days are getting longer.

l' **allusione** FEM NOUN
hint
□ un'allusione velata a veiled hint

l' **alluvione** FEM NOUN
flood
□ L'alluvione ha causato molti danni. The flood caused a lot of damage.

almeno ADVERB
at least
□ Potevi almeno telefonare, no? You could at least have phoned, couldn't you? □ Dammene almeno uno! At least give me one! □ Ci saranno state almeno tremila persone. There must have been at least three thousand people.
■ **se almeno...** if only... □ Se almeno sapessi dov'è! If only I knew where it was!

l' **altalena** FEM NOUN
1 swing
2 seesaw

l' **altare** MASC NOUN
altar

l' **alternativa** FEM NOUN
alternative
□ Non abbiamo alternative. We have no alternative.

alternativo (FEM **alternativa**) ADJECTIVE
alternative
□ medicina alternativa alternative medicine

alterno (FEM **alterna**) ADJECTIVE
alternate
□ Ci vado a giorni alterni. I go on alternate days.

l' **altezza** FEM NOUN
height
□ È di altezza media. She's of medium height.
■ **avere un'altezza di...** to be... high □ Ha un'altezza di cinque centimetri. It's five centimetres high.
■ **all'altezza di** near □ L'albergo è all'altezza di piazza Verdi. The hotel is near Piazza Verdi.
■ **Non è all'altezza della situazione.** He's not equal to the situation.

alto (FEM **alta**) ADJECTIVE
▷ see also **alto** NOUN
1 high
□ un muro alto cinque metri a wall five metres high □ Aveva la febbre alta. She had a high temperature.
2 tall
□ un edificio alto a tall building □ Quanto sei alto? How tall are you? □ Marisa è più alta di me. Marisa's taller than me. □ Matteo è il più alto della famiglia. Matteo is the tallest in the family.
■ **Sono alto un metro e settanta.** I'm one metre seventy.
3 deep
□ In quel punto l'acqua è molto alta. The water's very deep there.
4 loud
□ a voce alta in a loud voice □ Abbassa un po', è troppo alto. Turn it down a bit, it's too loud.
■ **Leggilo a voce alta.** Read it out.

l' **alto** MASC NOUN
▷ see also **alto** ADJECTIVE
top
□ Dall'alto della torre si vede tutta la città. From the top of the tower you can see the whole city.
■ **È là in alto.** It's up there.
■ **alti e bassi** ups and downs □ La sua carriera ha avuto alti e bassi. His career has had its ups and downs.
■ **salto in alto** high jump

l' **altoparlante** MASC NOUN
loudspeaker

altrettanto PRONOUN
▷ see also **altrettanto** ADVERB
the same
□ Anna ne ha preso uno e io ho fatto altrettanto. Anna took one and I did the same.
□ Buon Natale! — Grazie, altrettanto. Merry Christmas! — Thank you, the same to you.

altrettanto ADVERB
▷ see also **altrettanto** PRONOUN
equally
□ Paolo è altrettanto bravo. Paolo is equally good.

altrimenti ADVERB
1 or
□ Sbrigati, altrimenti arriveremo in ritardo. Hurry up or we'll be late.
2 another way
□ È fatto altrimenti. It's done another way.

altro (FEM **altra**) ADJECTIVE, PRONOUN
other
□ Non trovo l'altra scarpa. I can't find the other shoe. □ L'ho visto l'altro giorno. I saw him the other day.
■ **un altro 1** another one □ Ne hanno inciso un altro. They've recorded another one. **2** a different one □ Quello era esaurito, ne ho preso un altro. That one was sold out, so I bought a different one.
■ **Tu o un altro è lo stesso.** You or somebody else, it doesn't matter.
■ **gli altri** other people □ Non m'interessa quello che dicono gli altri. I don't care what other people say.
■ **né l'uno né l'altro** neither of them
■ **l'altro ieri** the day before yesterday
■ **domani l'altro** the day after tomorrow
■ **Desidera altro?** Would you like anything else?
■ **Non fa altro che lamentarsi.** All he does is complain.

l' **alunno,** l' **alunna** MASC/FEM NOUN
pupil

alzare VERB [68]
to lift
□ È troppo pesante, non riesco nemmeno ad alzarla. It's too heavy, I can't even lift it. □ Non ha alzato un dito per aiutarmi. He didn't lift a finger to help me.
■ **alzare la voce** to speak up □ Alza la voce, non ti sento. Speak up, I can't hear you.
■ **Non alzare la voce con me!** Don't shout at me!
■ **alzarsi** to get up □ A che ora ti alzi la mattina? What time do you get up in the morning? □ Si è alzato e se n'è andato. He got up and went away.

l' **amante** MASC/FEM NOUN
▷ see also **amante** ADJECTIVE
lover
□ Sono amanti da anni. They've been lovers for years.

amante (FEM **amante**) ADJECTIVE
▷ *see also* **amante** NOUN
■ **essere amante di** to be very keen on
□ È amante del jazz. He's very keen on jazz.

amare VERB [68]
to love
□ Ti amo. I love you. □ Mi ami? Do you love me? □ Si amano. They love each other.
■ **Non amo i sapori forti.** I'm not fond of strong flavours.

amaro (FEM **amara**) ADJECTIVE
bitter
□ un sapore amaro a bitter taste
■ **Il caffè lo prendo amaro.** I take my coffee without sugar.

l' **ambasciata** FEM NOUN
embassy
□ l'ambasciata britannica the British Embassy

l' **ambasciatore**, l' **ambasciatrice** MASC/FEM NOUN
ambassador

ambedue (FEM **ambedue**) ADJECTIVE, PRONOUN
both
□ ambedue i ragazzi both boys

ambientare VERB [68]
to set
□ Il film è ambientato a Chicago. The film is set in Chicago.
■ **ambientarsi** to settle □ Ti stai ambientando nella nuova scuola? Are you settling into your new school?

l' **ambiente** MASC NOUN
environment
□ la difesa dell'ambiente the protection of the environment
■ **temperatura ambiente** room temperature

ambiguo (FEM **ambigua**) ADJECTIVE
ambiguous
□ una risposta ambigua an ambiguous answer

l' **ambizione** FEM NOUN
ambition
□ La mia ambizione è fare il giornalista. My ambition is to be a journalist.

l' **ambulanza** FEM NOUN
ambulance
□ Devo chiamare l'ambulanza? Shall I call an ambulance?

l' **ambulatorio** MASC NOUN
surgery
□ A che ora apre l'ambulatorio? What time does the surgery open?

l' **America** FEM NOUN
America

americano (FEM **americana**) ADJECTIVE, MASC/FEM NOUN
American

amichevole (FEM **amichevole**) ADJECTIVE
friendly
□ un sorriso amichevole a friendly smile

l' **amicizia** FEM NOUN
friendship
□ Ci tengo molto alla sua amicizia. Her friendship is very important to me.
■ **fare amicizia** to become friends
□ Abbiamo fatto subito amicizia. We immediately became friends.

l' **amico**, l' **amica** (MASC PL gli **amici**, FEM PL le **amiche**) MASC/FEM NOUN
friend
□ la mia migliore amica my best friend □ Ha molti amici. She's got a lot of friends. □ È un mio amico. He's a friend of mine.

l' **ammaccatura** FEM NOUN
dent
□ C'è un'ammaccatura sullo sportello. There's a dent in the door.

ammaestrato (FEM **ammaestrata**) ADJECTIVE
1 trained
□ È un cane ben ammaestrato. It's a well-trained dog.
2 performing
□ foche ammaestrate performing seals

ammalarsi VERB [56]
to get ill
□ Mi sono ammalato. I got ill.

ammalato (FEM **ammalata**) ADJECTIVE
ill
□ Metà della classe era ammalata. Half the class was ill.

ammazzare VERB [68]
to kill

ammettere VERB [59]
1 to admit
□ Ha ammesso di avere torto. She admitted she was wrong.
■ **ammettere qualcuno ad un club** to admit somebody to a club
■ **Sono ammessi solo i soci.** It's only open to members.
■ **Non mi hanno ammesso agli esami.** They didn't let me take the exams.
2 to suppose
□ Ammettiamo che... Let's suppose that...

amministrare VERB [68]
to run *(company, state)*

l' **ammiraglio** MASC NOUN
admiral

ammirare VERB [68]
to admire
□ Lo ammiro. I admire him.

l' **ammirazione** FEM NOUN
admiration

ammobiliato (FEM **ammobiliata**) ADJECTIVE
furnished

a

□ un appartamento ammobiliato a furnished flat

l' **ammoniaca** FEM NOUN
ammonia

ammonire VERB [51]
1 to reprimand
□ È stato ammonito dall'insegnante. He was reprimanded by the teacher.
2 to book
□ È stato ammonito dall'arbitro. He was booked by the referee.

l' **ammorbidente** MASC NOUN
fabric softener

l' **ammortizzatore** MASC NOUN
shock absorber

ammucchiare VERB [17]
to pile up
□ Ha ammucchiato le sue cose in un angolo. She piled up her things in a corner.

ammuffire VERB [51, aux **essere**]
to go mouldy
□ Il pane è ammuffito. The bread's gone mouldy.

l' **amo** MASC NOUN
fish hook

l' **amore** MASC NOUN
love
□ una canzone d'amore a love song
■ **Che amore questo gattino!** Isn't this kitten sweet!

ampio (FEM **ampia**) ADJECTIVE
1 spacious
2 loose (dress, sleeves)
■ **una gonna ampia** a full skirt

l' **amplificatore** MASC NOUN
amplifier

gli **anabbaglianti** MASC PL NOUN
dipped headlights
■ **mettere gli anabbaglianti** to dip one's headlights

analcolico (FEM **analcolica**, MASC PL **analcolici**, FEM PL **analcoliche**) ADJECTIVE
■ **bibita analcolica** soft drink
■ **birra analcolica** alcohol-free beer

l' **analfabeta** (MASC PL gli **analfabeti**, FEM PL le **analfabete**) MASC/FEM NOUN
illiterate

l' **analgesico** (PL gli **analgesici**) MASC NOUN
painkiller

l' **analisi** (PL le **analisi**) FEM NOUN
analysis
■ **analisi del sangue** blood test

l' **ananas** (PL gli **ananas**) MASC NOUN
pineapple

l' **anatra** FEM NOUN
duck
□ anatra all'arancia duck with orange sauce

l' **anatroccolo** MASC NOUN
duckling

anche CONJUNCTION
1 too
□ Parla italiano e anche francese. She speaks Italian and French too. □ Sono stanchissimo! — Anch'io! I'm really tired! — Me too! □ Vengo anch'io. I'll come too.
2 even
□ Lo saprebbe fare anche un bambino. Even a child could do it.

LANGUAGE TIP **anche** is sometimes not translated.

□ Vieni anche tu? Are you coming? □ Avresti anche potuto avvertirmi. You could have let me know.

ancora ADVERB, CONJUNCTION
1 still
□ Stava ancora dormendo. He was still asleep.
■ **non ancora** not yet □ Non è ancora arrivato. He hasn't arrived yet. □ È pronto? — No, non ancora. Is it ready? — No, not yet.
2 more
□ Mi dai ancora un po' di gelato? Could I have a bit more ice cream? □ Vorrei ancora latte. I'd like more milk.
3 again
□ Ancora tu! You again!
4 even
□ Oggi fa ancora più freddo. It's even colder today.

andare VERB [6]
to go
□ Andremo in Grecia quest'estate. We're going to Greece this summer. □ Dove vai in vacanza? Where are you going on holiday? □ Andiamo in macchina o a piedi? Shall we go by car or walk? □ Su, andiamo! Come on, let's go! □ Dove vanno questi bicchieri? Where do these glasses go? □ Com'è andata? How did it go? □ Come va con Jason? How are things going with Jason?
■ **Come va? — Bene, grazie!** How are you? — Fine thanks!
■ **Come va la scuola?** How's school?
■ **andare a sciare** to go skiing
■ **andare a cavallo** to ride
■ **andare in bicicletta** to cycle
■ **andarsene** to leave □ Si è alzato e se n'è andato. He got up and left.

l' **andata** FEM NOUN
■ **un biglietto di sola andata** a single ticket
■ **un biglietto di andata e ritorno** a return ticket
■ **All'andata ci ho messo due ore.** It took me two hours to get there.

l' **anello** MASC NOUN
ring
□ un anello d'oro a gold ring

anestesia – antico

l' **anestesia** FEM NOUN
anaesthesia

l' **angelo** MASC NOUN
angel

l' **angolo** MASC NOUN
1 corner
□ Il cinema è proprio dietro l'angolo. The cinema's just round the corner. □ È la casa all'angolo con via Verdi. It's the house on the corner of Via Verdi.
2 angle
□ Formano un angolo retto. They form a right angle.

l' **anguilla** FEM NOUN
eel

l' **anguria** FEM NOUN
watermelon

l' **anima** FEM NOUN
soul
□ Non c'era anima viva. There wasn't a soul there.

l' **animale** MASC NOUN
▷ see also **animale** ADJECTIVE
animal

animale (FEM **animale**) ADJECTIVE
▷ see also **animale** NOUN
animal
□ grasso animale animal fat

annaffiare VERB [17]
to water

annegare VERB [76, aux **essere**]
to drown
□ Non sapeva nuotare ed è annegato. He couldn't swim and drowned.

l' **anniversario** MASC NOUN
anniversary
□ È il loro anniversario di matrimonio. It's their wedding anniversary.

l' **anno** MASC NOUN
year
□ l'anno scorso last year □ l'anno prossimo next year
■ **Buon Anno!** Happy New Year!
■ **Quanti anni hai? — Ho sedici anni.** How old are you? — I'm sixteen.
■ **una ragazza di vent'anni** a girl of twenty
■ **gli anni novanta** the nineties

annoiare VERB [17]
to bore
□ Scusa, ti sto annoiando? Sorry, am I boring you?
■ **annoiarsi** to get bored □ A stare a casa mi annoio. I get bored staying at home.

LANGUAGE TIP Be careful! **annoiare** doesn't mean **to annoy**.

annotare VERB [68]
to note

annuale (FEM **annuale**) ADJECTIVE
annual

annullare VERB [68]
to cancel
□ Hanno annullato il viaggio. They cancelled the trip.

annunciare VERB [13]
to announce

l' **annuncio** MASC NOUN
announcement
□ Hanno dato l'annuncio ieri. They made the announcement yesterday.
■ **annunci economici** small ads

annusare VERB [68]
to sniff
□ Il cane mi ha annusato le mani. The dog sniffed my hands.

annuvolarsi VERB [56]
to cloud over
□ Si sta annuvolando. It's clouding over.

anonimo (FEM **anonima**) ADJECTIVE
anonymous
□ una telefonata anonima an anonymous phone call

anoressico (FEM **anoressica**, MASC PL **anoressici**, FEM PL **anoressiche**) ADJECTIVE
anorexic

Antartico MASC NOUN
■ **l'Antartico** the Antarctic

l' **antenna** FEM NOUN
aerial
□ Bisogna regolare l'antenna. The aerial needs adjusting.
■ **antenna parabolica** satellite dish

l' **anteprima** FEM NOUN
preview

anteriore (FEM **anteriore**) ADJECTIVE
front
□ lo sportello anteriore the front door

l' **antibiotico** (PL gli **antibiotici**) MASC NOUN
antibiotic

l' **anticipo** MASC NOUN
advance
□ Gli hanno dato un anticipo. They gave him an advance.
■ **pagare in anticipo** to pay in advance
■ **in anticipo** early □ Sei in anticipo. You're early.
■ **con mezz'ora di anticipo** half an hour early

l' **antico** (PL gli **antichi**) MASC NOUN
▷ see also **antico** ADJECTIVE
■ **gli antichi** the ancients

antico (FEM **antica**, MASC PL **antichi**, FEM PL **antiche**) ADJECTIVE
▷ see also **antico** NOUN
1 old
□ un'antica villa di campagna an old house in the country
■ **un mobile antico** an antique

2 ancient

□ gli antichi Romani the ancient Romans □ nei tempi antichi in ancient times

■ **un uomo all'antica** an old-fashioned man

l' **anticoncezionale** MASC NOUN
contraceptive

l' **antidoping** (PL gli **antidoping**) MASC NOUN
drugs test

■ **risultare positivo all'antidoping** to fail a drugs test

l' **antifona** FEM NOUN

■ **capire l'antifona** to take the hint □ Ha capito l'antifona e se n'è andato. He took the hint and left.

antiforfora (FEM+PL **antiforfora**) ADJECTIVE

■ **shampoo antiforfora** anti-dandruff shampoo

l' **antifurto** (PL gli **antifurto**) MASC NOUN
1 burglar alarm
2 car alarm

antincendio (FEM+PL **antincendio**)
ADJECTIVE

■ **scala antincendio** fire escape

gli **antinebbia** MASC PL NOUN
fog lights

antiorario (FEM **antioraria**) ADJECTIVE

■ **in senso antiorario** anticlockwise

l' **antipasto** MASC NOUN
starter

l' **antipatia** FEM NOUN

■ **prendere in antipatia** to take a dislike to □ L'ha preso subito in antipatia. She took an instant dislike to him.

■ **avere antipatia per** not to like □ Ho una certa antipatia per i viaggi in pullman. I don't really like travelling by coach.

antipatico (FEM **antipatica**, MASC PL **antipatici**, FEM PL **antipatiche**) ADJECTIVE
unpleasant

□ un tipo antipatico an unpleasant person

■ **Mi è proprio antipatica!** I really hate her!

antiproiettile (FEM **antiproiettile**)
ADJECTIVE

■ **giubbotto antiproiettile** bulletproof vest

l' **antiquariato** MASC NOUN

■ **negozio d'antiquariato** antique shop

l' **antiquario,** l' **antiquaria** MASC/FEM
NOUN
antique dealer

□ Fa l'antiquario. He is an antique dealer.

antiquato (FEM **antiquata**) ADJECTIVE
old-fashioned

l' **anulare** MASC NOUN
ring finger

anzi CONJUNCTION
in fact

□ Non mi dispiace, anzi sono contento. I don't mind, in fact I'm glad.

■ **Prendo un'aranciata, anzi una limonata.** I'll have an orangeade, no... a lemonade

anziano (FEM **anziana**) ADJECTIVE
▷ see also **anziano** NOUN
old

□ un signore anziano an old man

l' **anziano,** l' **anziana** MASC/FEM NOUN

■ **gli anziani** the elderly

anziché CONJUNCTION
1 rather than

□ Preferisco telefonare anziché scrivere. I prefer to phone rather than write. □ Ho comprato quello giallo anziché quello rosso. I bought the yellow one rather than the red one.

2 instead of

□ Quest'anno andiamo al mare anziché in montagna. This year we're going to the seaside instead of to the mountains.

l' **ape** FEM NOUN
bee

l' **aperitivo** MASC NOUN
aperitif

□ Prendiamo un aperitivo? Shall we have an aperitif?

apertamente ADVERB
frankly

□ Ne abbiamo parlato apertamente. We talked about it frankly.

aperto (FEM **aperta**) ADJECTIVE
▷ see also **aperto** NOUN
1 open

□ Hai lasciato la porta aperta. You've left the door open.

2 open-minded

□ I miei sono molto aperti. My parents are very open-minded.

l' **aperto** MASC NOUN

■ **all'aperto** outdoors □ Abbiamo dormito all'aperto. We slept outdoors.

l' **apertura** FEM NOUN
opening

□ orario di apertura opening times

l' **apnea** FEM NOUN

■ **immergersi in apnea** to dive without breathing apparatus

l' **apostrofo** MASC NOUN
apostrophe

l' **app** (PL le **app**) FEM NOUN
app

■ **un'app per il cellulare** a mobile app

appannarsi VERB [56]
1 to mist up

□ Il parabrezza si era appannato. The windscreen had misted up.

2 to steam up

□ Mi si sono appannati gli occhiali. My glasses steamed up.

apparecchiare VERB [17]
to set the table
  □ Ti aiuto ad apparecchiare? Shall I help you to set the table?

l' **apparecchio** MASC NOUN
1 device
  □ un complicato apparecchio elettronico a complex electronic device
2 brace *(for teeth)*
  □ Porta l'apparecchio. He wears a brace.
  ■ **apparecchio acustico** hearing aid

apparire VERB [7]
to appear

l' **appartamento** MASC NOUN
flat
  □ un appartamento ammobiliato a furnished flat

appartenere VERB [113, aux **essere**]
to belong
  □ Questa collana apparteneva a mia nonna. This necklace belonged to my grandma. □ A chi appartiene questo libro? Who does this book belong to?

appassionato (FEM **appassionata**)
ADJECTIVE
  ■ **essere appassionato di qualcosa** to love something □ È appassionato di musica jazz. He loves jazz.

appassito (FEM **appassita**) ADJECTIVE
dead
  □ fiori appassiti dead flowers

l' **appello** MASC NOUN
  ■ **fare l'appello** to take the register

appena ADVERB, CONJUNCTION
1 just
  □ Se n'è appena andato. He's just left. □ Latte? — Grazie, appena un goccio. Milk? — Yes please, just a drop.
2 only just
  □ L'indirizzo era appena leggibile. The address was only just legible. □ Sono appena le nove. It's only just nine o'clock. □ È appena tornato a casa. He's only just got home.
  ■ **Lo conosco appena.** I hardly know him.
3 as soon as
  □ Ha detto che sarebbe venuto appena possibile. He said he'd come as soon as possible. □ L'ho riconosciuto appena l'ho visto. I recognized him as soon as I saw him.

appendere VERB [8]
to hang
  □ Dove posso appendere il cappotto? Where can I hang my coat?

l' **appendicite** FEM NOUN
appendicitis
  □ Ha un'appendicite acuta. He's got acute appendicitis.

l' **appetito** MASC NOUN
appetite

  □ La camminata mi ha messo appetito. The walk has given me an appetite.
  ■ **Buon appetito!** Enjoy your meal!

appiccicare VERB [18]
to stick

appisolarsi VERB [56]
to doze off
  □ Mi ero appisolato un attimo. I dozed off for a moment.

applaudire VERB [41]
to clap
  □ Applaudivano tutti. Everybody was clapping.

l' **applauso** MASC NOUN
applause
  □ un applauso a round of applause □ Hanno ricevuto molti applausi. They got a lot of applause.

l' **applicazione** FEM NOUN
application
  ■ **un'applicazione per il cellulare** a mobile app

appoggiare VERB [58]
1 to put
  □ Puoi appoggiare il pacco sul tavolo. You can put the parcel on the table.
2 to lean
  □ Appoggia la scala al muro. Lean the ladder against the wall.
  ■ **appoggiarsi a** to lean against □ Si è dovuto appoggiare al muro per sostenersi. He had to lean against the wall for support.

l' **appoggio** MASC NOUN
support
  □ Ho bisogno di tutto il vostro appoggio. I need all your support.

apposta ADVERB
1 on purpose
  □ Scusa, non l'ho fatto apposta. I'm sorry, I didn't do it on purpose.
2 specially
  □ Siamo venuti apposta per parlare con te. We came specially to speak to you.

l' **apprendimento** MASC NOUN
learning

approfittare VERB [68]
  ■ **approfittare di qualcosa** to make the most of something □ Approfitta della bella giornata e vai al parco! Make the most of the weather and go to the park! □ Approfittane! Make the most of it!

approfondire VERB [51]
to study in depth
  □ Vorrei approfondire l'argomento. I'd like to study the subject in depth.

approfondito (FEM **approfondita**)
ADJECTIVE
thorough
  □ un'analisi approfondita a thorough analysis

approssimativo (FEM **approssimativa**)
ADJECTIVE
rough
□ È solo un calcolo approssimativo. It's only a rough estimate.

approvare VERB [68]
1 to approve of
□ Non approvo ciò che hai fatto. I don't approve of what you've done.
2 to approve
□ Hanno approvato il progetto. They approved the project.

l' **appuntamento** MASC NOUN
1 appointment
□ Venerdì ho un appuntamento dal dentista. I've got a dental appointment on Friday.
2 date
□ Stasera ho appuntamento con il mio ragazzo. I've got a date with my boyfriend tonight.
■ **darsi appuntamento** to arrange to meet
□ Ci siamo dati appuntamento alle otto. We arranged to meet at eight.

appuntito (FEM **appuntita**) ADJECTIVE
sharp
□ una matita appuntita a sharp pencil

l' **appunto** MASC NOUN
▷ see also **appunto** ADVERB
note
□ Non avevo preso appunti. I hadn't taken notes.

appunto ADVERB
▷ see also **appunto** NOUN
just
□ Parlavamo appunto di questo. We were just talking about that. □ Stavo appunto per chiederti di venire. I was just going to ask you to come.
■ **Appunto!** Exactly!

l' **apribottiglie** (PL gli **apribottiglie**) MASC NOUN
bottle-opener

aprile MASC NOUN
April

> **LANGUAGE TIP** In Italian, months are not written with capital letters.

□ in aprile in April
■ **Pesce d'aprile!** April Fool!

aprire VERB [9]
1 to open
□ Posso aprire la finestra? Can I open the window? □ Dai, non apri i regali? Come on, aren't you going to open your presents? □ A che ora apre la banca? What time does the bank open?
■ **Non ha aperto bocca.** She didn't say a word.
2 to turn on
□ Non riesco ad aprire il rubinetto. I can't turn the tap on.

l' **apriscatole** (PL gli **apriscatole**) MASC NOUN
tin opener

l' **aquila** FEM NOUN
eagle

l' **aquilone** MASC NOUN
kite
□ Facciamo volare l'aquilone! Let's fly the kite!

l' **Arabia Saudita** FEM NOUN
Saudi Arabia

arabo (FEM **araba**) ADJECTIVE, MASC/FEM NOUN
▷ see also **arabo** MASC NOUN
Arab

l' **arabo** MASC NOUN
▷ see also **arabo** ADJECTIVE, MASC/FEM NOUN
Arabic (language)
□ Parlano l'arabo. They speak Arabic.

l' **arachide** FEM NOUN
peanut

l' **aragosta** FEM NOUN
lobster

l' **arancia** (PL le **arance**) FEM NOUN
orange
□ succo d'arancia orange juice

l' **aranciata** FEM NOUN
orangeade

arancione (FEM **arancione**) ADJECTIVE, MASC/FEM NOUN
orange
□ una maglietta arancione an orange T-shirt

l' **arbitro** MASC NOUN
1 referee
2 umpire

l' **arbusto** MASC NOUN
shrub

l' **archeologia** FEM NOUN
archaeology
□ È laureata in archeologia. She's got a degree in archaeology.

l' **archeologo**, l' **archeologa** (MASC PL gli **archeologi**, FEM PL le **archeologhe**) MASC/FEM NOUN
archaeologist

l' **architetto** MASC NOUN
architect
□ Sua madre fa l'architetto. His mother is an architect.

l' **architettura** FEM NOUN
architecture
□ Studia architettura. He's studying architecture.

archiviare VERB [17]
to file
■ **archiviare un caso** to dismiss a case

l' **arco** (PL gli **archi**) MASC NOUN
1 arch
2 bow
□ arco e frecce bow and arrows
■ **nell'arco di tre settimane** within the space of three weeks

l' **arcobaleno** MASC NOUN
rainbow

l' **area** FEM NOUN
area

☐ un'area di due chilometri quadrati an area of two square kilometres

■ **area di rigore** penalty area

l' **argento** MASC NOUN
silver

☐ un anello d'argento a silver ring

l' **argilla** FEM NOUN
clay

☐ un vaso d'argilla a clay pot

l' **argomento** MASC NOUN
subject

☐ Cambiamo argomento. Let's change the subject. ☐ Visto che siamo in argomento... Since we're on the subject...

l' **aria** FEM NOUN
air

☐ un po' d'aria fresca a bit of fresh air

■ **aria condizionata** air conditioning

■ **all'aria aperta** in the open air

■ **avere l'aria allegra** to look happy

■ **avere l'aria stanca** to look tired

■ **Si dà un sacco di arie.** He thinks he's so important!

l' **Ariete** MASC NOUN
Aries

☐ Sono dell'Ariete. I'm Aries.

l' **aringa** (PL le **aringhe**) FEM NOUN
herring

☐ Le aringhe vivono in acque fredde. Herrings are cold water fish.

■ **un'aringa affumicata** a kipper

l' **arma** (PL le **armi**) FEM NOUN
weapon

☐ un'arma pericolosa a dangerous weapon

■ **essere alle prime armi** to have just started ☐ Come batterista sono ancora alle prime armi. I've just started playing the drums.

l' **armadietto** MASC NOUN

1 cabinet

☐ l'armadietto dei medicinali the medicine cabinet

2 locker

l' **armadio** MASC NOUN
wardrobe

armato (FEM **armata**) ADJECTIVE
armed

☐ Era armato di coltello. He was armed with a knife.

■ **rapina a mano armata** armed robbery

l' **armatura** FEM NOUN
armour

l' **armonica** (PL le **armoniche**) FEM NOUN
harmonica

☐ Suono l'armonica. I play the harmonica.

arrabbiare VERB [17]

■ **far arrabbiare qualcuno** to make somebody angry ☐ Mi ha fatto veramente arrabbiare. He really made me angry.

■ **arrabbiarsi** to get angry ☐ Non ti arrabbiare! Don't get angry!

arrabbiato (FEM **arrabbiata**) ADJECTIVE
angry

☐ Era molto arrabbiato. He was very angry. ☐ È più arrabbiato di lei. He's angrier than she is. ☐ Gianni era il più arrabbiato di tutti. Gianni was angriest of all.

arrampicarsi VERB [18, AUX **essere**]
to climb

☐ Ci siamo arrampicati sull'albero. We climbed the tree.

arrangiarsi VERB [58, AUX **essere**]
to manage

☐ In qualche modo ci arrangeremo. We'll manage somehow.

l' **arredamento** MASC NOUN
furniture

arredato (FEM **arredata**) ADJECTIVE
furnished

☐ un appartamento arredato a furnished flat

arrendersi VERB [83, AUX **essere**]
to surrender

☐ Si sono arresi alla polizia. They surrendered to the police.

arrestare VERB [68]
to arrest

☐ I rapinatori sono stati arrestati ieri. The robbers were arrested yesterday.

l' **arresto** MASC NOUN
arrest

☐ in stato d'arresto under arrest

gli **arretrati** MASC PL NOUN
back pay *sing*

arretrato (FEM **arretrata**) ADJECTIVE
backward

☐ un paese arretrato a backward country

■ **numero arretrato** (of newspaper, magazine) back number

■ **Ho un sacco di lavoro arretrato.** I've got a huge backlog of work.

arrivare VERB [68, AUX **essere**]
to arrive

☐ A che ora arrivi a scuola? What time do you arrive at school? ☐ Sono arrivato a Londra alle sette. I arrived in London at seven.

■ **arrivare in orario** to arrive on time

■ **arrivare in ritardo** to arrive late

■ **Come si arriva al castello?** How do you get to the castle?

■ **Aspettami, arrivo!** Wait for me, I'm coming!

■ **È troppo in alto, non ci arrivo.** It's too high, I can't reach it.

arrivederci EXCLAMATION
goodbye!
□ Arrivederci, Marco! Goodbye Marco!

l' **arrivo** MASC NOUN
arrival
□ al mio arrivo on my arrival
■ **essere in arrivo** to be arriving □ Il treno
per Roma è in arrivo al binario uno. The train to
Rome is arriving at platform one.
■ **'arrivi'** 'arrivals'

arrogante (FEM **arrogante**) ADJECTIVE
arrogant

arrossire VERB [51, AUX **essere**]
to go red
□ È arrossito per l'imbarazzo. He went red with
embarrassment.

l' **arrosto** MASC NOUN
▷ see also **arrosto** ADJECTIVE
roast meat
■ **arrosto di manzo** roast beef

arrosto (FEM+PL **arrosto**) ADJECTIVE
▷ see also **arrosto** NOUN
roast
□ pollo arrosto roast chicken

arrotondare VERB [68]
to supplement
□ Fa dei lavoretti extra per arrotondare lo
stipendio. He does part-time jobs to
supplement his salary.
■ **arrotondare una cifra 1** to round up a
figure **2** to round down a figure

arrugginito (FEM **arrugginita**) ADJECTIVE
rusty
□ un lucchetto arrugginito a rusty padlock

arruolarsi VERB [56]
to join
□ Si è arruolato in marina. He's joined the
navy.

l' **arte** FEM NOUN
art
□ una galleria d'arte an art gallery □ un'opera
d'arte a work of art

l' **articolo** MASC NOUN
article
□ un articolo sull'effetto serra an article about
the greenhouse effect
■ **negozio di articoli sportivi** sports shop

artificiale (FEM **artificiale**) ADJECTIVE
artificial

l' **artigianato** MASC NOUN
crafts *pl*
□ un negozio di artigianato locale a shop
selling local crafts
■ **fiera dell'artigianato** craft fair

l' **artista** (MASC PL gli **artisti**, FEM PL le **artiste**)
MASC/FEM NOUN
artist
□ È un artista. He's an artist.

artistico (FEM **artistica**, MASC PL **artistici**,
FEM PL **artistiche**) ADJECTIVE
artistic
□ Non ho nessuna inclinazione artistica. I'm
not at all artistic.
■ **liceo artistico** secondary school
specializing in arts subjects

l' **ascella** FEM NOUN
armpit

l' **ascensore** MASC NOUN
lift
□ L'ascensore è guasto. The lift's out of order.

l' **asciugacapelli** (PL gli **asciugacapelli**)
MASC NOUN
hair dryer

l' **asciugamano** MASC NOUN
towel

asciugare VERB [76]
to dry
□ Asciugati i capelli. Dry your hair.
■ **asciugarsi** to get dry □ La maglietta si è
asciugata in fretta. The T-shirt soon got dry.

asciutto (FEM **asciutta**) ADJECTIVE
dry
□ È asciutta la maglietta? Is the T-shirt dry?

ascoltare VERB [68]
to listen to
□ Mi stai ascoltando? Are you listening to me?

l' **Asia** FEM NOUN
Asia

asiatico (FEM **asiatica**, MASC PL **asiatici**, FEM
PL **asiatiche**) ADJECTIVE, MASC/FEM NOUN
Asian

l' **asilo** MASC NOUN
nursery school
□ Paolo va all'asilo. Paolo goes to nursery
school.
■ **asilo politico** political asylum □ Hanno
chiesto asilo politico. They've asked for political
asylum.

l' **asino** MASC NOUN
donkey

l' **asma** FEM NOUN
asthma

l' **asparago** (PL gli **asparagi**) MASC NOUN
asparagus
□ un mazzo di asparagi a bunch of asparagus
□ Gli asparagi sono buoni. Asparagus is nice.

aspettare VERB [68]
1 to wait
□ Aspetta un attimo! Wait a minute! □ È
un'ora che aspetto. I've been waiting for an
hour.
■ **aspettare qualcuno** to wait for
somebody □ Sto aspettando un'amica. I'm
waiting for a friend. □ Aspettami, vengo
anch'io! Wait for me, I'm coming too!
■ **fare aspettare qualcuno** to keep

19

somebody waiting □ Mi ha fatto aspettare un'ora. He kept me waiting for an hour.
2 to expect
□ Sto aspettando una telefonata importante. I'm expecting an important phone call. □ Era meglio di quanto mi aspettassi. It was better than I expected.

■ **aspettare un bambino** to be expecting a baby □ Mia sorella aspetta un bambino. My sister's expecting a baby.

l' **aspetto** MASC NOUN
appearance
□ Cura molto il suo aspetto. He takes great care of his appearance.

■ **di bell'aspetto** good-looking

l' **aspirapolvere** (PL gli **aspirapolvere**)
MASC NOUN
vacuum cleaner

■ **passare l'aspirapolvere** to vacuum

l' **aspirina®** FEM NOUN
aspirin
□ Prendi due aspirine. Take two aspirins.

aspro (FEM **aspra**) ADJECTIVE
sour
□ Questo pompelmo è molto aspro. This grapefruit is very sour.

assaggiare VERB [58]
to taste
□ Vuoi assaggiare? Would you like to taste it?

assai ADVERB
1 very
□ Sono assai contento. I'm very pleased.
2 much (in comparison)
□ È assai più giovane di me. He's much younger than me.

l' **assassino**, l' **assassina** MASC/FEM NOUN
1 murderer
2 assassin

l' **asse** FEM NOUN
board (plank)

■ **asse da stiro** ironing board

l' **assegno** MASC NOUN
cheque
□ Ha pagato con un assegno. He paid by cheque.

l' **assemblea** FEM NOUN
meeting

assente (FEM **assente**) ADJECTIVE
absent
□ Oggi sono assenti due scolari. Two pupils are absent today.

■ **La mia segretaria oggi è assente.** My secretary is not at work today.

■ **Sono stato assente da scuola per due settimane.** I was off school for two weeks.

l' **assenza** FEM NOUN
absence
□ in mia assenza in my absence

■ **Ho fatto molte assenze da scuola.** I've missed a lot of school.

assetato (FEM **assetata**) ADJECTIVE
thirsty

assicurare VERB [68]
1 to insure
□ La macchina non era assicurata contro il furto. The car wasn't insured against theft.
2 to assure
□ Mi ha assicurato che sarebbe venuto. He assured me that he'd come.

■ **assicurarsi** to make sure □ Assicurati che la porta sia chiusa. Make sure the door's closed.

l' **assicurazione** FEM NOUN
insurance
□ Ho fatto un'assicurazione sulla vita. I took out life insurance.

assieme ADVERB
together

l' **assistente** MASC/FEM NOUN
assistant
□ Il direttore ha chiamato sua assistente. The manager called his assistant.

■ **assistente di volo** flight attendant
■ **assistente sociale** social worker

assistere VERB [10]
to look after (ill person)
□ Assiste la madre ammalata. She's looking after her sick mother.

■ **assistere a 1** (show) to watch **2** (accident) to witness

l' **asso** MASC NOUN
ace
□ l'asso di picche the ace of spades □ È un asso del volante. He's an ace driver.

l' **associazione** FEM NOUN
association

assolutamente ADVERB
absolutely
□ È assolutamente incredibile. It's absolutely incredible.

■ **Devi assolutamente vedere quel film!** You really must see that film!

assolvere VERB [89]
to acquit
□ È stato assolto. He was acquitted.

assomigliare VERB [25, aux **avere** or **essere**]

■ **assomigliare a** to look like □ Assomiglia alla madre. She looks like her mother.

■ **assomigliarsi** to look alike □ Si assomigliano molto. They look very alike.

assonnato (FEM **assonnata**) ADJECTIVE
sleepy
□ Hai l'aria assonnata. You look sleepy.

assopirsi VERB [51]
to doze off
□ Mi sono assopito un attimo. I dozed off for a moment.

l' **assorbente** MASC NOUN
- **assorbente igienico** sanitary towel
- **assorbente interno** tampon

assordare VERB [68]
to deafen
□ Mi stai assordando! You're deafening me!

assortito (FEM **assortita**) ADJECTIVE
assorted
□ una scatola di cioccolatini assortiti a box of assorted chocolates

assumere VERB [11]
to take on
□ L'azienda assumerà due operai. The company is going to take on two workers.
- **essere assunto** to get a job □ È stata assunta come programmatrice. She's got a job as a programmer.

assurdo (FEM **assurda**) ADJECTIVE
ridiculous
□ Che idea assurda! What a ridiculous idea!
□ È assurdo! It's ridiculous!

l' **asta** FEM NOUN
pole
□ salto con l'asta pole vault
- **vendita all'asta** auction

astemio (FEM **astemia**) ADJECTIVE
teetotal

> **LANGUAGE TIP** Be careful! **astemio** doesn't mean **abstemious**.

l' **astenuto**, l' **astenuta** MASC/FEM NOUN
abstention
□ dieci a favore, tre contrari e due astenuti ten in favour, three against and two abstentions

l' **asterisco** (PL l' **asterischi**) MASC NOUN
asterisk

astratto (FEM **astratta**) ADJECTIVE
abstract

l' **astrologia** FEM NOUN
astrology

l' **astronauta** (MASC PL gli **astronauti**, FEM PL le **astronaute**) MASC/FEM NOUN
astronaut

l' **astronave** FEM NOUN
spacecraft

l' **astronomia** FEM NOUN
astronomy

astronomico (FEM **astronomica**, MASC PL **astronomici**, FEM PL **astronomiche**) ADJECTIVE
astronomical
□ prezzi astronomici astronomical prices

l' **astuccio** MASC NOUN
case
□ un astuccio portapenne a pencil case

astuto (FEM **astuta**) ADJECTIVE
cunning
□ È astuto come una volpe. He's cunning as a fox.

Atene FEM NOUN
Athens
□ Quest'estate andremo ad Atene. We're going to Athens this summer. □ Abita ad Atene. She lives in Athens.

l' **atleta** (MASC PL gli **atleti**, FEM PL le **atlete**)
MASC/FEM NOUN
athlete

l' **atletica** FEM NOUN
athletics sing
□ Guardo sempre l'atletica in TV. I always watch the athletics on TV.

l' **atmosfera** FEM NOUN
atmosphere
□ C'era una bella atmosfera. There was a nice atmosphere.

atomico (FEM **atomica**, MASC PL **atomici**, FEM PL **atomiche**) ADJECTIVE
atomic
□ la bomba atomica the atomic bomb

l' **atrio** MASC NOUN
1 entrance
2 concourse

atroce (FEM **atroce**) ADJECTIVE
terrible
□ un mal di testa atroce a terrible headache

l' **attaccante** MASC/FEM NOUN
forward
□ Gioca da attaccante. He's a forward.

l' **attaccapanni** (PL gli **attaccapanni**) MASC NOUN
hook
□ Appendi la giacca all'attaccapanni. Hang your jacket on the hook.

attaccare VERB [18]
1 to stick
□ Non so dove attaccare questo poster. I don't know where to stick this poster. □ Il sugo si sta attaccando. The sauce is sticking. □ Le pagine si sono attaccate. The pages are stuck together.
2 to sew on
□ Devo attaccare due bottoni. I've got to sew two buttons on.
3 to start
□ Quando attacca a lamentarsi non la smette più. Once she starts moaning she never stops.
4 to give (illness)
□ Non vorrei attaccarti il raffreddore. I wouldn't want to give you my cold.

l' **attacco** (PL gli **attacchi**) MASC NOUN
1 attack
□ un attacco d'asma an asthma attack
- **giocare in attacco** to play an attacking game
2 binding

l' **atteggiamento** MASC NOUN
attitude

□ Non mi piace il suo atteggiamento. I don't like his attitude.

l' **attentato** MASC NOUN
attack
□ un attentato terroristico a terrorist attack

l' **attentatore** MASC NOUN
■ **attentatore suicida** suicide bomber

attento (FEM **attenta**) ADJECTIVE
careful
□ Stai attento quando attraversi la strada. Be careful when you cross the road.
■ **Non sono stato attento alla lezione.** I didn't pay attention in class.
■ **Attento!** Watch out!
■ **Attento alle dita!** Mind your fingers!
■ **'attenti al cane'** 'beware of the dog'

l' **attenzione** FEM NOUN
attention
□ Gli piace essere al centro dell'attenzione. He likes to be the centre of attention. □ Cerca di richiamare l'attenzione del cameriere. Try and attract the waiter's attention.
■ **Attenzione al gradino!** Mind the step!

l' **atterraggio** MASC NOUN
landing
□ un atterraggio di fortuna an emergency landing

atterrare VERB [68]
to land
□ L'aereo ha appena atterrato. The plane has just landed.

l' **attesa** FEM NOUN
wait
□ dopo una lunga attesa after a long wait
■ **lista d'attesa** waiting list
■ **sala d'attesa** waiting room

attillato (FEM **attillata**) ADJECTIVE
tight

l' **attimo** MASC NOUN
minute
□ Aspetta un attimo. Wait a minute. □ Torno tra un attimo. I'll be back in a minute.

attirare VERB [68]
1 to attract
□ L'ha fatto per attirare la sua attenzione. He did it to attract her attention.
2 to appeal to
□ L'idea non mi attira per niente. The idea doesn't appeal to me at all.

l' **attività** (PL le **attività**) FEM NOUN
activity
□ Mi piacciono le attività all'aria aperta I like outdoor activities.

attivo (FEM **attiva**) ADJECTIVE
active

l' **atto** MASC NOUN
act
□ atti di sabotaggio acts of sabotage
□ durante il secondo atto during the second act

l' **attore** MASC NOUN
actor
□ un attore famoso a famous actor

attorno ADVERB
round
□ È entrato e si è guardato attorno. He came in and looked round. □ Erano seduti attorno al fuoco. They were sitting round the fire.

attraversare VERB [68]
1 to cross
□ Stai attento quando attraversi la strada. Be careful when you cross the road.
2 to go through
□ Sta attraversando un periodo difficile. She's going through a difficult time.

attraverso PREPOSITION
through
□ Sono entrati attraverso la finestra. They got in through the window.

attrezzato (FEM **attrezzata**) ADJECTIVE
■ **ben attrezzato** well-equipped □ una palestra ben attrezzata a well-equipped gym

l' **attrezzo** MASC NOUN
tool
□ attrezzi da giardinaggio gardening tools
■ **carro attrezzi** breakdown truck

l' **attrice** FEM NOUN
actress
□ un'attrice famosa a famous actress

attuale (FEM **attuale**) ADJECTIVE
1 present
□ al momento attuale at the present moment
□ l'attuale proprietario the present owner
2 current
□ l'attuale situazione politica the current political situation
> **LANGUAGE TIP** Be careful! **attuale** doesn't mean **actual**.

l' **attualità** FEM NOUN
current affairs pl
□ un programma di attualità a current affairs programme
■ **un problema di attualità** a topical issue

attualmente ADVERB
at the moment
□ Attualmente sono in tournée in America. They're on tour in America at the moment.
> **LANGUAGE TIP** Be careful! **attualmente** doesn't mean **actually**.

l' **audio** MASC NOUN
sound
□ Il video funziona ma l'audio no. There's a picture but no sound.

l' **audizione** FEM NOUN
audition

gli **auguri** MASC PL NOUN
■ **Auguri!** 1 Happy birthday! 2 Good luck!

■ **tanti auguri!** all the best!

■ **fare gli auguri di Natale a qualcuno** to wish somebody happy Christmas

l' **aula** FEM NOUN
classroom

aumentare VERB [68, AUX **avere** or **essere**]
to go up

□ Il prezzo della benzina è aumentato. The price of petrol has gone up. □ La disoccupazione è aumentata del dieci per cento. Unemployment's gone up by ten per cent. □ Gli hanno aumentato l'affitto. His rent's gone up.

■ **Gli hanno aumentato lo stipendio.** They've given him a pay rise.

l' **aumento** MASC NOUN
increase

□ C'è stato un aumento del tre per cento sul prezzo. There's been a three per cent increase in the price.

■ **essere in aumento** to rise □ I prezzi sono in aumento. Prices are rising.

■ **aumento di stipendio** pay rise

l' **Australia** FEM NOUN
Australia

□ Ti è piaciuta l'Australia? Did you like Australia? □ Quest'estate andremo in Australia. We're going to Australia this summer.

australiano (FEM **australiana**) ADJECTIVE, MASC/FEM NOUN
Australian

l' **Austria** FEM NOUN
Austria

□ Ti è piaciuta l'Austria? Did you like Austria? □ Quest'estate andremo in Austria. We're going to Austria this summer.

austriaco (FEM **austriaca**, MASC PL **austriaci**, FEM PL **austriache**) ADJECTIVE, MASC/FEM NOUN
Austrian

autentico (FEM **autentica**, MASC PL **autentici**, FEM PL **autentiche**) ADJECTIVE
genuine

□ La firma è autentica. The signature is genuine.

l' **autista** (MASC PL gli **autisti**, FEM PL le **autiste**) MASC/FEM NOUN
driver

□ Fa l'autista di autobus. He is a bus driver.

l' **auto** (PL le **auto**) FEM NOUN
car

□ Verremo in auto. We'll come by car.

autobiografico (FEM **autobiografica**, MASC PL **autobiografici**, FEM PL **autobiografiche**) ADJECTIVE
autobiographical

□ un romanzo autobiografico an autobiographical novel

l' **autobus** (PL gli **autobus**) MASC NOUN
bus

□ Vado a scuola in autobus. I go to school by bus. □ un autobus a due piani a double-decker bus

l' **autocarro** MASC NOUN
lorry

l' **autogol** (PL gli **autogol**) MASC NOUN
own goal

□ Ha fatto autogol. He scored an own goal.

l' **autografo** MASC NOUN
autograph

□ Mi ha fatto l'autografo! He gave me his autograph!

automatico (FEM **automatica**, MASC PL **automatici**, FEM PL **automatiche**) ADJECTIVE
automatic

□ porte a chiusura automatica automatic doors

l' **automobile** FEM NOUN
car

l' **automobilista** (MASC PL gli **automobilisti**, FEM PL le **automobiliste**) MASC/FEM NOUN
motorist

l' **autonoleggio** MASC NOUN
car hire place

□ C'è un autonoleggio da queste parti? Is there a car hire place near here?

l' **autoradio** (PL le **autoradio**) FEM NOUN
car radio

l' **autore** MASC NOUN
author

l' **autorità** (PL le **autorità**) FEM NOUN
authority

autorizzare VERB [68]

■ **autorizzare qualcuno a fare qualcosa** to give somebody permission to do something □ Mi hanno autorizzato ad aprire la corrispondenza. I was given permission to open correspondence.

■ **La manifestazione non era stata autorizzata.** Permission for the march had not been granted.

gli **autoscontri** MASC PL NOUN
Dodgems®

□ Facciamo un giro sugli autoscontri. Let's go on the dodgems.

l' **autoscuola** FEM NOUN
driving school

l' **autostop** MASC NOUN

■ **fare l'autostop** to hitchhike □ Abbiamo fatto l'autostop fino a Roma. We hitchhiked to Rome.

l' **autostoppista** (MASC PL gli **autostoppisti**, FEM PL le **autostoppiste**) MASC/FEM NOUN
hitchhiker

▢ Abbiamo dato un passaggio ad un autostoppista. We gave a hitchhiker a lift.

l' **autostrada** FEM NOUN
motorway

l' **autrice** FEM NOUN
author

l' **autunno** MASC NOUN
autumn
▢ in autunno in autumn

avanti ADVERB
forward
▢ Ho fatto un passo avanti. I took a step forward. ▢ Bisogna mettere l'orologio avanti di un'ora. You have to put the clock forward an hour.
■ **Il mio orologio è avanti.** My watch is fast.
■ **in avanti** forward ▢ Spostalo un po' in avanti. Move it forward a bit.
■ **andare avanti 1** to go on ▢ Non si può andare avanti così. We can't go on like this. **2** to go on ahead ▢ Vai pure avanti, ti raggiungo dopo. Go on ahead, I'll catch you up later.
■ **Avanti!** Come in!
■ **Avanti il prossimo!** Next please!
■ **Avanti, assaggialo!** Go on, taste it!
■ **avanti Cristo** BC ▢ nel cinquantacinque avanti Cristo in fifty-five BC

avanzare VERB [68, AUX **essere**]
to be left over
▢ È avanzato del pollo da ieri. There's some chicken left over from yesterday.
■ **Basta e avanza.** That's more than enough.

gli **avanzi** MASC PL NOUN
left-overs

avaro (FEM **avara**) ADJECTIVE
stingy
▢ È più avara di lui. She's stingier than him.
▢ È la persona più avara che abbia mai incontrato. He's the stingiest person I've ever met.

avere VERB [12]
1 to have
▢ Non sapevo che avessi una moto. I didn't know you had a motorbike. ▢ All'inizio ha avuto un sacco di problemi. He had a lot of problems at first.

┃ **LANGUAGE TIP** avere is used to form the perfect tense.

▢ Ho già mangiato. I've already eaten. ▢ Hai visto quel film? Have you seen that film? ▢ Se me l'avessi detto prima l'avrei portato. If you'd told me sooner I'd have brought it.

┃ **LANGUAGE TIP** avere is used to form the simple past tense.

▢ Gli ho parlato ieri. I spoke to him yesterday.

┃ **LANGUAGE TIP** If avere is used to show possession, 'got' is sometimes added.

▢ Ha la macchina nuova. She's got a new car. ▢ Ho due fratelli. I've got two brothers. ▢ Ha gli occhi azzurri. He's got blue eyes.
2 to be
▢ Ho diciassette anni. I'm seventeen. ▢ Aveva la mia età. He was the same age as me. ▢ Ho fame. I'm hungry.
■ **Cos'hai?** What's the matter?
■ **Quanti ne abbiamo oggi?** What's the date today?

aviario (FEM **aviaria**) ADJECTIVE
■ **influenza aviaria** bird flu

l' **avorio** MASC NOUN
ivory

avvelenare VERB [68]
to poison

l' **avvenimento** MASC NOUN
event
▢ i principali avvenimenti sportivi the main sporting events

avvenire VERB [120, AUX **essere**]
▷ see also **avvenire** NOUN
to happen
▢ È avvenuto nel 1999. It happened in 1999.

l' **avvenire** MASC NOUN
▷ see also **avvenire** VERB
future
▢ Fa progetti per l'avvenire. She's making plans for the future.

avventato (FEM **avventata**) ADJECTIVE
rash
▢ È stata una decisione avventata. It was a rash decision.

l' **avventura** FEM NOUN
1 adventure
▢ È la vacanza ideale per chi ama l'avventura. It's an ideal holiday for anyone who likes adventure.
2 affair (love)
▢ un'avventura con una donna sposata an affair with a married woman

avverarsi VERB [56]
to come true
▢ Il suo sogno si è avverato. Her dream came true.

l' **avverbio** MASC NOUN
adverb

avversario (FEM **avversaria**) ADJECTIVE
▷ see also **avversario** NOUN
opposing
▢ la squadra avversaria the opposing team

l' **avversario,** l' **avversaria** MASC/FEM NOUN
▷ see also **avversario** ADJECTIVE
opponent
▢ Ha battuto l'avversario. He beat his opponent.

avvertire VERB [41]
to tell
▢ Se mi avessi avvertito sarei arrivato prima.

If you'd told me I'd have come sooner.
□ Avresti anche potuto avvertirmi. You could have told me.
■ **Ti avverto, ogni tanto la doccia fa scherzi.** Watch out, the shower doesn't always work properly.

avvicinare VERB [68]
to move... closer
□ Avvicina la sedia al tavolo. Move your chair closer to the table. □ Ho avvicinato il tavolo alla finestra. I moved the table closer to the window.
■ **avvicinarsi** to come closer □ Mi ha fatto cenno di avvicinarmi. He beckoned to me to come closer. □ Avvicinati! Come closer!
■ **Non ti avvicinare troppo al cane, morde.** Don't go too near the dog, he bites.
■ **Si avvicina il giorno della partenza.** We'll soon be leaving.

l' **avviso** MASC NOUN
1 notice
□ Hai letto l'avviso in bacheca? Have you read the notice on the board? □ fino a nuovo avviso until further notice
2 opinion
□ A mio avviso è troppo complesso. In my opinion it's too complicated.

> **LANGUAGE TIP** Be careful! **avviso** doesn't mean **advice**.

avvitare VERB [68]
■ **avvitare una vite** to put in a screw
■ **avvitare una lampadina** to screw in a light bulb

l' **avvocato** MASC NOUN
lawyer
□ Suo padre fa l'avvocato. His father is a lawyer.

avvolgere VERB [91]
to wrap

□ Puoi avvolgere la scatola con questa carta. You can wrap the box in this paper.
■ **avvolgersi** to wrap oneself up □ Si è avvolto nella coperta. He wrapped himself up in the blanket.

l' **avvolgibile** MASC NOUN
roller blind

l' **azienda** FEM NOUN
business
□ È un'azienda familiare. It's a family business.

l' **azione** FEM NOUN
1 action
□ un film d'azione an action movie
2 deed
□ una buona azione a good deed
3 share (in a company)

azzardarsi VERB [56]
■ **azzardarsi a fare qualcosa** to dare to do something □ Nessuno si azzardò a parlare. Nobody dared to speak.

l' **azzardo** MASC NOUN
■ **gioco d'azzardo** gambling □ Gli piace il gioco d'azzardo. He likes gambling.

azzeccare VERB [18]
to get right
□ Non ne azzecca mai una! He never gets anything right!

azzuffarsi VERB [56]
to fight
□ S'azzuffa sempre col fratello. She's always fighting with her brother.

azzurro (FEM **azzurra**) ADJECTIVE
▷ see also **azzurro** NOUN
blue
□ occhi azzurri blue eyes

l' **azzurro** MASC NOUN
▷ see also **azzurro** ADJECTIVE
■ **gli azzurri** the Italian team

Bb

b

il **babbo** MASC NOUN
dad
□ È un regalo per il mio babbo. It's a present for my dad.
■ **Babbo Natale** Father Christmas

il/la **baby sitter** (PL i/le **baby sitter**) MASC/FEM NOUN
babysitter
□ Non sono riusciti a trovare una baby sitter. They couldn't find a babysitter.
■ **fare la baby sitter** to babysit □ Fa la baby sitter il sabato sera. She babysits on Saturday evenings.
■ **Durante le vacanze fa la baby sitter.** She looks after children during the holidays.

la **bacchetta** FEM NOUN
■ **bacchetta magica** magic wand
■ **bacchette 1** chopsticks **2** (for drums) drumsticks

la **bacheca** (PL le **bacheche**) FEM NOUN
1 notice board
□ Appendilo in bacheca. Put it on the notice board.
2 bulletin board

baciare VERB [13]
to kiss
□ L'ha baciato sulla guancia. She kissed him on the cheek.
■ **baciarsi** to kiss □ Ci siamo baciati. We kissed.

la **bacinella** FEM NOUN
bowl
□ una bacinella di plastica a plastic bowl

il **bacio** MASC NOUN
kiss
□ un bacio sulla guancia a kiss on the cheek
■ **Tanti baci, Anna** (in a letter) Lots of love, Anna

il **baco** (PL i **bachi**) MASC NOUN
1 worm
□ Questa mela ha il baco. There's a worm in this apple.
2 bug (computer)
■ **baco da seta** silkworm

la **badante** FEM NOUN
care worker

badare VERB [68]
1 to pay attention
□ Nessuno gli ha badato. Nobody paid any attention to him.
2 to mind
□ Bada a non cadere. Mind you don't fall.
□ È un tipo che non bada a spese. He doesn't mind how much he spends.

i **baffi** MASC PL NOUN
1 moustache sing
□ Ha i baffi. He's got a moustache.
2 whiskers
□ Non tirare i baffi al gatto. Don't pull the cat's whiskers.
■ **leccarsi i baffi** to lick one's lips

il **bagagliaio** MASC NOUN
boot
□ Metti la valigia nel bagagliaio. Put your case in the boot.

il **bagaglio** MASC NOUN
luggage
□ Hai molti bagagli? Have you got a lot of luggage? □ Ho lasciato i miei bagagli all'albergo. I left my luggage at the hotel.
■ **Dove si ritirano i bagagli?** Where's the baggage reclaim?
■ **bagaglio a mano** hand luggage
■ **fare i bagagli** to pack □ Hai già fatto i bagagli? Have you packed?

bagnare VERB [14]
1 to get wet
□ Non voglio bagnarmi le scarpe. I don't want to get my shoes wet.
2 to water
□ Hai bagnato le piante? Did you water the plants?
■ **bagnarsi** to get soaked □ Ci siamo bagnati anche se avevamo l'ombrello. We got soaked even though we had an umbrella.

bagnato (FEM **bagnata**) ADJECTIVE
wet
□ Ho i capelli bagnati. My hair's wet. □ Sei bagnato fradicio! You're soaking wet!

il **bagnino**, la **bagnina** MASC/FEM NOUN
lifeguard
□ Fa il bagnino. He is a lifeguard.

il **bagno** MASC NOUN
1 bathroom
□ il bagno e la camera da letto the bathroom and the bedroom
2 toilet
□ Scusi, dov'è il bagno? Where's the toilet, please?

3 bath

□ Preferisci il bagno o la doccia? **Which do you prefer, a bath or a shower?**

■ **fare il bagno 1** to have a bath **2** to go for a swim

il **bagnoschiuma** (PL i **bagnoschiuma**) MASC NOUN

bubble bath

la **baia** FEM NOUN

bay

balbettare VERB [68]

to stammer

il **balcone** MASC NOUN

balcony

□ Il balcone dà sul giardino. **The balcony looks onto the garden.**

la **balena** FEM NOUN

whale

ballare VERB [68]

to dance

□ Abbiamo ballato tutta la sera. **We danced all night.**

■ **andare a ballare** to go dancing

□ Andiamo a ballare? **Shall we go dancing?**

il **ballerino,** la **ballerina** MASC/FEM NOUN

dancer

□ un ottimo ballerino **a very good dancer** □ Vuole fare la ballerina. **She wants to be a dancer.**

■ **ballerino classico** ballet dancer

■ **ballerina classica** ballerina

il **ballo** MASC NOUN

dance

□ un ballo sudamericano **a Latin American dance**

■ **ballo mascherato** fancy-dress ball

il **balsamo** MASC NOUN

hair conditioner

la **bambina** FEM NOUN

little girl

il **bambino** MASC NOUN

1 child

□ Lo saprebbe fare anche un bambino! **A child could do it!** □ I bambini giocavano. **The children were playing.**

2 baby

□ Aspetta un bambino. **She's expecting a baby.**

3 little boy

□ Chi è quel bambino? **Who's that little boy?**

la **bambola** FEM NOUN

doll

banale (FEM **banale**) ADJECTIVE

1 minor

□ Si è trattato di un banale incidente. **It was a minor accident.**

2 ordinary

□ È solo un banale raffreddore. **It's just an ordinary cold.**

3 banal

□ La trama del libro era un po' banale. **The plot of the book was rather banal.**

la **banana** FEM NOUN

banana

la **banca** (PL le **banche**) FEM NOUN

bank

□ Devo andare in banca. **I need to go to the bank.**

la **bancarella** FEM NOUN

stall

□ L'ho comprato in una bancarella. **I bought it from a stall.**

la **banchina** FEM NOUN

quay

il **banco** (PL i **banchi**) MASC NOUN

1 desk

2 counter (in shop)

la **banconota** FEM NOUN

note

□ una banconota da cinque euro **a five euro note**

la **banda** FEM NOUN

1 gang

□ una banda di rapinatori **a gang of robbers**

2 band

□ Suona nella banda del paese. **She plays in the village band.**

la **bandiera** FEM NOUN

flag

□ la bandiera italiana **the Italian flag**

il **bar** (PL i **bar**) MASC NOUN

café

> **DID YOU KNOW...?**
> The main drink served in Italian **bars** is coffee, although alcoholic drinks are available. Many people go to a **bar** in the morning to have coffee and a cake for breakfast.

la **bara** FEM NOUN

coffin

la **baracca** (PL le **baracche**) FEM NOUN

hut

barare VERB [68]

to cheat

□ Hai barato! **You cheated!**

il **barattolo** MASC NOUN

1 jar

2 tin

3 pot

la **barba** FEM NOUN

beard

□ Ha la barba. **He's got a beard.**

■ **farsi la barba** to shave

la **barbabietola** FEM NOUN

beetroot

■ **barbabietola da zucchero** sugar beet

il **barbiere** MASC NOUN

barber

□ Fa il barbiere. **He is a barber.**

■ **Devo andare dal barbiere.** I need a haircut.

il **barboncino** MASC NOUN

poodle

il **barbone**, la **barbona** MASC/FEM NOUN
tramp

la **barca** (PL le **barche**) FEM NOUN
boat
□ Si è comprato una barca. He's bought himself a boat.
■ **barca a vela** sailing boat
■ **una barca di** loads of □ Ha una barca di soldi. She's got loads of money.

barcollare VERB [68]
to stagger
□ Ha barcollato ed è caduto. He staggered and fell.

la **barella** FEM NOUN
stretcher
□ L'hanno portato via in barella. He was carried away on a stretcher.

il/la **barista** (MASC PL i **baristi**, FEM PL le **bariste**) MASC/FEM NOUN
■ **Fa la barista.** She works in a bar.

barocco (FEM **barocca**, MASC PL **barocchi**, FEM PL **barocche**) ADJECTIVE, MASC NOUN
baroque

la **barzelletta** FEM NOUN
joke
□ una barzelletta molto divertente a very funny joke

basare VERB [68]
to base
□ Il film si basa su una storia vera. The film is based on a true story.
■ **Mi baso sulle esperienze precedenti.** I'm going on past experience.

la **base** FEM NOUN
1 base
□ la base della lampada the lamp base
2 basis
□ La fiducia sta alla base della nostra amicizia. Trust is the basis of our friendship.
■ **di base** basic □ Il suo stipendio di base è basso. Her basic salary is low.
■ **in base a** according to □ In base a questo depliant ci sono tre alberghi. According to this brochure there are three hotels.
■ **liquore a base di caffè** coffee liqueur

le **basette** FEM PL NOUN
sideburns

il **basilico** MASC NOUN
basil

il **basket** MASC NOUN
basketball
□ Gioco a basket. I play basketball.

il/la **bassista** (MASC PL i **bassisti**, FEM PL le **bassiste**) MASC/FEM NOUN
bass player

basso (FEM **bassa**) ADJECTIVE
▷ see also **basso** NOUN
1 low
□ Il volume è troppo basso. The sound's too

low. □ in bassa stagione in the low season
2 short
□ È basso e grasso. He's short and fat. □ È più bassa di me. She's shorter than me.
3 shallow
□ In quel punto l'acqua è bassa. The water's shallow there.

il **basso** MASC NOUN
▷ see also **basso** ADJECTIVE
bass guitar
■ **suonare il basso** to play bass guitar
■ **in basso** at the bottom □ Io sono quella in basso a destra nella foto. I'm the one in the bottom right of the photo.
■ **È là in basso.** It's down there.
■ **più in basso** lower down □ Mettilo un po' più in basso. Put it a bit lower down.

bastare VERB [68, aux **essere**]
to be enough
□ Sei sicuro che venti sterline bastino? Are you sure twenty pounds is enough? □ Questa pasta non basta per noi tutti. This pasta isn't enough for us all.
■ **Basta e avanza!** That's more than enough!
■ **Basta!** That's enough!
■ **Basta così?** Will that be all?
■ **Basta così, grazie.** That's all, thank you.
■ **Dimmi basta.** Say when.
■ **Basta chiedere a un poliziotto.** Just ask a policeman.

i **bastoncini** MASC PL NOUN
1 chopsticks
2 ski poles
■ **bastoncini di pesce** fish fingers

il **bastone** MASC NOUN
1 stick
□ L'ha picchiato con un bastone. He hit him with a stick.
2 walking stick

la **battaglia** FEM NOUN
battle

battere VERB [1]
1 to beat
□ Li abbiamo battuti due a zero. We beat them two nil. □ Gli batteva forte il cuore. His heart was beating fast. □ Ha battuto il record mondiale. She's beaten the world record.
2 to hit
□ Ha battuto il mento sul gradino. He hit his chin on the step.
■ **battere a macchina** to type
■ **battere un rigore** to take a penalty
■ **battersi** to fight

la **batteria** FEM NOUN
1 drums pl
□ Suona la batteria. He plays the drums.
2 battery
□ La batteria è scarica. The battery's flat.

il/la **batterista** (MASC PL i **batteristi**, FEM PL
le **batteriste**) MASC/FEM NOUN
drummer

il **battesimo** MASC NOUN
christening

■ **nome di battesimo** Christian name

la **battuta** FEM NOUN
joke
□ Era solo una battuta. It was only a joke.
■ **Ha sempre la battuta pronta.** He's
always ready with a witty remark.
■ **fare una battuta su qualcosa** to make
a joke about something

il **batuffolo** MASC NOUN
wad
□ un batuffolo di cotone a wad of cotton wool

il **baule** MASC NOUN
trunk

il **bavaglio** MASC NOUN
gag
□ Si è liberato del bavaglio. He got the gag off.

beato (FEM **beata**) ADJECTIVE
■ **Beato te!** Lucky you!

il **beauty case** (PL i **beauty case**) MASC NOUN
vanity case
□ Le ho regalato un beauty case. I gave her a
vanity case.

beccare VERB [18]
to catch
□ Mi sono beccato un raffreddore. I've caught a
cold. □ L'hanno beccato a rubare in un
negozio. They caught him shoplifting.

il **becco** (PL i **becchi**) MASC NOUN
beak

la **Befana** FEM NOUN
DID YOU KNOW...?
The **Befana** is an old woman who,
according to legend, brings children
presents at Epiphany (January 6).

belga (MASC PL **belgi**, FEM PL **belghe**) ADJECTIVE,
MASC/FEM NOUN
Belgian

il **Belgio** MASC NOUN
Belgium

la **bellezza** FEM NOUN
beauty
□ un istituto di bellezza a beauty salon
■ **Mi è costato la bellezza di trecento
euro.** I paid three hundred euros for it.
■ **Che bellezza!** Fantastic!

bello (FEM **bella**) ADJECTIVE
▷ see also **bello** NOUN
1 lovely
□ Che bella giornata! What a lovely day! □ Ha
dei bellissimi occhi. He's got really lovely eyes.
2 good-looking
□ Paolo è un bel ragazzo. Paolo is a good-
looking boy. □ È più bello di me. He's

better-looking than me.
3 good
□ un bel film a good film □ È troppo bello per
essere vero. It's too good to be true.
4 nice
□ una bella tazza di tè a nice cup of tea
■ **un bel niente** absolutely nothing
■ **bella copia** final copy

il **bello** MASC NOUN
▷ see also **bello** ADJECTIVE
■ **Il bello è che...** The best bit about it is that...
■ **Che fai di bello stasera?** What are you
doing this evening?
■ **proprio sul più bello** at that very moment

il **belvedere** (PL i **belvedere**) MASC NOUN
viewing point

la **benda** FEM NOUN
1 bandage
2 blindfold

bendare VERB [68]
1 to bandage
□ Mi ha bendato la mano. He bandaged my hand.
2 to blindfold
□ L'hanno bendato e imbavagliato. He was
blindfolded and gagged.

bene ADVERB
well
□ Parli molto bene l'italiano. You speak Italian
very well. □ Non mi sento troppo bene. I don't
feel very well.
■ **andare bene a** to fit □ Questi jeans non mi
vanno bene. These jeans don't fit me.
■ **Va bene.** OK. □ Va bene, ho capito. OK, I
understand. □ A che ora? — Va bene alle due?
What time? — Is two o'clock OK?
■ **stare bene** to be fine □ Sto bene, grazie.
I'm fine, thanks.
■ **Stai bene?** Are you OK?
■ **stare bene a** to suit □ Questi jeans ti
stanno molto bene. Those jeans really suit you.
■ **voler bene a qualcuno** to love somebody
□ Le voglio molto bene. I really love her.
■ **Hai fatto bene.** You did the right thing.
■ **La frutta fa bene.** Fruit is good for you.
■ **Bevi un po' d'acqua, ti farà bene.** Drink
some water, it'll make you feel better.
■ **Ben gli sta!** It serves him right!
■ **Lì si mangia molto bene.** The food is
excellent there.
■ **Sono pronta. — Bene, andiamo.** I'm
ready. — OK, let's go.

la **beneficenza** FEM NOUN
charity
□ un concerto di beneficenza a charity concert

benestante (FEM **benestante**) ADJECTIVE
well-off
□ una famiglia benestante a well-off family
□ Viene da una famiglia più benestante della
mia. His family is better off than mine.

b

benvenuto (FEM **benvenuta**) ADJECTIVE
welcome
□ Benvenuti a Roma! Welcome to Rome!

la **benzina** FEM NOUN
petrol
□ Siamo rimasti senza benzina. We ran out of
petrol.
■ **benzina verde** unleaded petrol

bere VERB [15]
to drink
□ Vuoi bere qualcosa? Would you like
something to drink?
■ **Chi porta da bere?** Who's going to bring
the drinks?

la **berlina** FEM NOUN
saloon car

i **bermuda** MASC PL NOUN
■ **un paio di bermuda** a pair of Bermuda
shorts

il **bernoccolo** MASC NOUN
bump
□ Ho un bernoccolo in fronte. I've got a bump
on my forehead.

il **berretto** MASC NOUN
cap
□ un berretto da baseball a baseball cap

il **bersaglio** MASC NOUN
target
□ Ha mancato il bersaglio. He missed the target.

la **besciamella** FEM NOUN
béchamel sauce

bestemmiare VERB [17]
to swear
□ Non l'ho mai sentito bestemmiare. I've never
heard him swear.

la **bestia** FEM NOUN
animal
□ Non voglio bestie in casa! I don't want
animals in the house!

bestiale (FEM **bestiale**) ADJECTIVE
■ **Fa un caldo bestiale.** It's absolutely boiling.
■ **Ho una fame bestiale!** I'm starving!

la **bevanda** FEM NOUN
drink
□ una bevanda alcolica an alcoholic drink

la **biancheria** FEM NOUN
sheets and towels pl
■ **biancheria intima** underwear

bianco (FEM **bianca**, MASC PL **bianchi**, FEM PL
bianche) ADJECTIVE, MASC NOUN
white
□ Ha i capelli bianchi. She's got white hair.
■ **TV in bianco e nero** black and white TV

la **Bibbia** FEM NOUN
Bible

la **bibita** FEM NOUN
soft drink
□ Vendono gelati e bibite. They sell ice

cream and soft drinks.

la **biblioteca** (PL le **biblioteche**) FEM NOUN
library

il **bicchiere** MASC NOUN
glass
□ un bicchiere di vino a glass of wine □ un
bicchiere da vino a wine glass
■ **un bicchiere di carta** a paper cup

la **bici** (PL le **bici**) FEM NOUN
bike

la **bicicletta** FEM NOUN
bike
□ Ci sono andato in bicicletta. I went there on
my bike.

il **bidé** (PL i **bidé**) MASC NOUN
bidet

il **bidello**, la **bidella** MASC/FEM NOUN
school caretaker

il **bidone** MASC NOUN
■ **bidone dell'immondizia** dustbin

la **bigiotteria** FEM NOUN
costume jewellery

la **biglietteria** FEM NOUN
booking office

il **biglietto** MASC NOUN
1 ticket
□ Hai fatto il biglietto? Have you bought a ticket?
■ **biglietto di andata e ritorno** return ticket
■ **il biglietto elettronico** e-ticket
2 card
□ Mi ha mandato un biglietto per il compleanno.
He sent me a card for my birthday.
3 note
□ Ho solo un biglietto da venti sterline. I've
only got a twenty-pound note.

il **bigodino** MASC NOUN
roller

il **bikini** (PL i **bikini**) MASC NOUN
bikini

Bilancia FEM NOUN
Libra
□ Sono della Bilancia. I'm Libra.

la **bilancia** (PL le **bilance**) FEM NOUN
scales pl
□ Hai una bilancia? Have you got scales?

il **biliardino** MASC NOUN
pinball
■ **giocare a biliardino** to play pinball

il **biliardo** MASC NOUN
pool
□ Sai giocare a biliardo? Can you play pool?
■ **sala da biliardo** poolroom

bilingue (FEM **bilingue**) ADJECTIVE
bilingual

il **binario** MASC NOUN
1 track
□ Camminava lungo il binario. He was walking
along the track.
2 platform

□ Da quale binario parte il treno per Roma? Which platform does the Rome train go from?

il **binocolo** MASC NOUN
1 binoculars *pl*
□ Guardava gli uccelli con il binocolo. She was looking at the birds through binoculars.
2 opera glasses *pl*

bio (FEM+PL **bio**) ADJECTIVE
organic

il **biocarburante** MASC NOUN
biofuel

biologico (FEM **biologica**, MASC PL **biologici**, FEM PL **biologiche**) ADJECTIVE
1 biological
■ **armi biologiche** biological weapons
2 organic

biondo (FEM **bionda**) ADJECTIVE
1 blond *(man)*
2 blonde *(woman)*

la **biro**® (PL le **biro**) FEM NOUN
Biro®

la **birra** FEM NOUN
beer
□ una birra alla spina a draught beer
■ **birra chiara** lager
■ **birra scura** stout

la **birreria** FEM NOUN
pub

il **bis** (PL i **bis**) MASC NOUN
■ **fare il bis di** to have some more □ Facciamo il bis di gelato? Shall we have some more ice cream?
■ **Bis!** Encore!

bisbigliare VERB [25]
to whisper
□ Mi ha bisbigliato qualcosa all'orecchio. He whispered something in my ear.

il **biscotto** MASC NOUN
biscuit

bisestile (FEM **bisestile**) ADJECTIVE
■ **anno bisestile** leap year

la **bisnonna** FEM NOUN
great-grandmother

il **bisnonno** MASC NOUN
great-grandfather
■ **i miei bisnonni** my great-grandparents

bisognare VERB [14]
■ **Bisogna prenotare?** Is it necessary to book?
■ **Bisogna arrivare un'ora prima.** You have to get there an hour beforehand.
■ **Bisognerebbe telefonargli.** We should phone him.

il **bisogno** MASC NOUN
need
□ Non c'è bisogno di prenotare. There's no need to book.
■ **aver bisogno di qualcosa** to need something □ Hai bisogno di qualcosa? Do you need anything?

■ **aver bisogno di fare qualcosa** to need to do something □ Ho bisogno di cambiare dei soldi. I need to change some money.

la **bistecca** (PL le **bistecche**) FEM NOUN
steak
□ una bistecca ai ferri a grilled steak

bisticciare VERB [13]
to quarrel
□ Bisticciano sempre. They're always quarrelling.

il **bivio** MASC NOUN
junction
□ Al bivio volta a destra. Go right at the junction.

bloccare VERB [18]
to block
□ La strada è bloccata da una frana. The road is blocked by a landslide.
■ **rimanere bloccato** to be stuck □ Siamo rimasti bloccati in un ingorgo. We were stuck in a traffic jam.
■ **bloccarsi** to get stuck □ L'ascensore si è bloccato. The lift got stuck.

il **blocchetto** MASC NOUN
notebook
■ **un blocchetto di biglietti per l'autobus** a book of tickets for the bus

il **blog** (PL i **blog**) MASC NOUN
blog
□ Scrive un blog. He writes a blog.

blu (FEM+PL **blu**) ADJECTIVE, MASC NOUN
navy
□ una maglietta blu a navy T-shirt

la **boa** FEM NOUN
buoy

la **bocca** (PL le **bocche**) FEM NOUN
mouth
□ Non ha aperto bocca. He didn't open his mouth.
■ **respirazione bocca a bocca** mouth-to-mouth resuscitation
■ **In bocca al lupo!** Good luck!

bocciare VERB [13]
■ **essere bocciato agli esami** to fail one's exams
■ **Andava male in tutte le materie ed è stato bocciato.** He did badly in all subjects and was kept down.

DID YOU KNOW...?
If Italian school students fail their end of year exams they have to retake them. They cannot move up into the next year until they have passed them.

la **bolla** FEM NOUN
bubble

bollente (FEM **bollente**) ADJECTIVE
1 boiling
□ Cuocere in acqua bollente. Cook in boiling water.
2 boiling hot
□ La minestra è bollente! The soup is boiling hot!

b

31

b

la **bolletta** FEM NOUN
bill
▫ la bolletta del telefono the phone bill

bollire VERB [41]
to boil
▫ L'acqua bolle. The water's boiling.

il **bollitore** MASC NOUN
kettle

la **bomba** FEM NOUN
bomb
▫ È scoppiata una bomba alla stazione. A bomb went off at the station.
■ **bomba ad orologeria** time bomb
■ **bomba a mano** hand grenade

la **bombetta** FEM NOUN
bowler hat
▫ la classica bombetta inglese the famous English bowler hat

la **bombola** FEM NOUN
cylinder
▫ una bombola di gas a gas cylinder

la **bomboletta** FEM NOUN
spray can

il **bordo** MASC NOUN
1 edge
▫ Eravamo seduti sul bordo della piscina. We were sitting on the edge of the pool.
2 border
▫ È nero, con un bordo rosso. It's black, with a red border.
■ **a bordo di** on board ▫ C'erano cento passeggeri a bordo dell'aereo. There were a hundred passengers on board the plane.
■ **salire a bordo** to get on ▫ Siamo saliti a bordo dell'aereo. We got on the plane.

borghese (FEM **borghese**) ADJECTIVE
middle-class
▫ una famiglia borghese a middle-class family
■ **un poliziotto in borghese** a plainclothes policeman

il **borotalco** MASC NOUN
talcum powder

la **borraccia** (PL le **borracce**) FEM NOUN
flask

la **borsa** FEM NOUN
bag
▫ una borsa nera a black bag
■ **borsa dell'acqua calda** hot water bottle
■ **borsa di studio** scholarship ▫ Ha vinto una borsa di studio. He won a scholarship.
■ **la Borsa** the Stock Exchange

il **borsellino** MASC NOUN
purse

la **borsetta** FEM NOUN
handbag

il **bosco** (PL i **boschi**) MASC NOUN
wood
▫ un bosco di querce an oak wood ▫ una passeggiata nel bosco a walk in the woods *pl*

la **Bosnia** FEM NOUN
Bosnia

bosniaco (FEM **bosniaca**, MASC PL **bosniaci**, FEM PL **bosniache**) ADJECTIVE, MASC/FEM NOUN
Bosnian

la **botta** FEM NOUN
■ **prendere una botta** to be hit ▫ Ha preso una botta sulla testa. He was hit on the head.
■ **fare a botte** to fight
■ **dare un sacco di botte a qualcuno**
1 to give somebody a hiding 2 to beat somebody up

la **bottiglia** FEM NOUN
bottle
▫ una bottiglia di vino a bottle of wine

il **botto** MASC NOUN
bang
▫ Abbiamo sentito un gran botto. We heard a loud bang.
■ **di botto** suddenly ▫ Si è fermato di botto. He stopped suddenly.

il **bottone** MASC NOUN
button

bovino (FEM **bovina**) ADJECTIVE, MASC NOUN
■ **carne bovina** beef
■ **bovini** cattle ▫ allevamento di bovini cattle farming

la **boxe** FEM NOUN
boxing
▫ un incontro di boxe a boxing match

i **boxer** MASC PL NOUN
■ **un paio di boxer** a pair of boxer shorts

braccetto MASC NOUN
■ **a braccetto** arm in arm ▫ Si tenevano a braccetto. They were arm in arm.

il **braccialetto** MASC NOUN
bracelet
▫ un braccialetto d'argento a silver bracelet

il **braccio** (PL le **braccia**) MASC NOUN
arm
▫ Mi fa male il braccio. My arm hurts.
■ **braccio di ferro** arm wrestling

il **bracciolo** MASC NOUN
armrest

il **Brasile** MASC NOUN
Brazil
▫ Mi è piaciuto molto il Brasile. I really liked Brazil. ▫ Andremo in Brasile quest'estate. We're going to Brazil this summer.

brasiliano (FEM **brasiliana**) ADJECTIVE, MASC/FEM NOUN
Brazilian

bravo (FEM **brava**) ADJECTIVE
good
▫ un attore molto bravo a very good actor
■ **il più bravo** the best ▫ È il più bravo della classe. He's the best in the class.
■ **essere bravo in qualcosa** to be good at

something □ Sono abbastanza bravo in inglese. I'm quite good at English.

■ **Bravo!** Well done!

le **bretelle** FEM PL NOUN

1 braces *(for trousers)*

2 straps *(of dress, bra)*

breve (FEM **breve**) ADJECTIVE

short

□ una breve visita a short visit

la **briciola** FEM NOUN

crumb

il **briciolo** MASC NOUN

bit

□ Non ha un briciolo di cervello. She hasn't got a bit of sense.

brillante (FEM **brillante**) ADJECTIVE

▷ *see also* **brillante** NOUN

bright

□ verde brillante bright green

il **brillante** MASC NOUN

▷ *see also* **brillante** ADJECTIVE

diamond

□ un anello con brillanti a diamond ring

brillare VERB [68]

to shine

□ Le stelle brillano in cielo. The stars are shining in the sky.

brillo (FEM **brilla**) ADJECTIVE

drunk

□ Era un po' brillo. He was a bit drunk.

la **brina** FEM NOUN

frost

□ C'è ancora la brina sui campi. There's still frost on the fields.

il **brindisi** (PL i **brindisi**) MASC NOUN

toast

□ Facciamo un brindisi! Let's drink a toast!

la **brioche** (PL le **brioche**) FEM NOUN

brioche

britannico (FEM **britannica**, MASC PL **britannici**, FEM PL **britanniche**) ADJECTIVE

British

□ le isole britanniche the British Isles

il **brivido** MASC NOUN

shiver

□ Ho i brividi. I've got the shivers.

■ **racconto del brivido** *(film)* thriller

la **brocca** (PL le **brocche**) FEM NOUN

jug

i **broccoli** MASC PL NOUN

broccoli *sing*

□ I broccoli fanno bene. Broccoli is good for you.

il **brodo** MASC NOUN

1 soup

□ brodo di pollo chicken soup

2 stock

■ **dadi da brodo** stock cubes

brontolare VERB [68]

to moan

□ Non fa altro che brontolare. He's always moaning.

■ **Mi brontola lo stomaco per la fame.** My stomach is rumbling.

il **bronzo** MASC NOUN

bronze

□ Ha vinto la medaglia di bronzo. She won the bronze medal.

bruciare VERB [13, AUX **avere** or **essere**]

to burn

□ Hai bruciato la torta! You've burnt the cake!

□ Mi sono bruciata un dito. I've burnt my finger.

■ **Mi bruciano gli occhi.** My eyes are smarting.

■ **bruciarsi** to burn oneself □ Mi sono bruciata! I've burnt myself!

il **bruciato** MASC NOUN

■ **Sento odore di bruciato.** I can smell burning.

il **brufolo** MASC NOUN

spot

bruno (FEM **bruna**) ADJECTIVE

■ **È bruno.** He's got dark hair.

brusco (FEM **brusca**, MASC PL **bruschi**, FEM PL **brusche**) ADJECTIVE

abrupt

□ È stato un po' brusco con me. He was a bit abrupt with me.

■ **Ha fatto una brusca frenata.** He braked suddenly.

brutto (FEM **brutta**) ADJECTIVE

1 ugly

□ È proprio brutto! He's really ugly. □ È il posto più brutto che abbia mai visto. It's the ugliest place I've ever seen.

2 bad

□ Ho un brutto raffreddore. I've got a bad cold.

□ Ho fatto un brutto sogno. I had a bad dream.

□ Ho preso un brutto voto in matematica. I got a bad mark in maths.

■ **Che brutta giornata!** What a horrible day!

Bruxelles FEM NOUN

Brussels

□ Vivo a Bruxelles. I live in Brussels.

la **buca** (PL le **buche**) FEM NOUN

hole

□ La strada è piena di buche. The road is full of holes.

■ **buca delle lettere** post box

bucare VERB [18]

to have a puncture

□ Abbiamo bucato. We had a puncture.

■ **bucarsi** to be on heroin

il **bucato** MASC NOUN

■ **fare il bucato** to do the washing

la **buccia** (PL le **bucce**) FEM NOUN

1 peel

□ bucce di patata potato peel *sing*

2 rind
- □ buccia di limone grattugiata grated lemon rind
- ■ **una buccia di banana** a banana skin

il **buco** (PL i **buchi**) MASC NOUN
hole
- □ C'è un buco nella tasca. There's a hole in the pocket.
- ■ **buco della serratura** keyhole

il **budino** MASC NOUN
pudding
- □ budino al cioccolato chocolate pudding

buffo (FEM **buffa**) ADJECTIVE
funny
- □ Pensa a qualcosa di più buffo. Think of something funnier. □ È la cosa più buffa che abbia mai sentito. It's the funniest thing I've ever heard.

la **bugia** (PL le **bugie**) FEM NOUN
lie
- □ Non dico mai le bugie. I never tell lies.

il **bugiardo**, la **bugiarda** MASC/FEM NOUN
▷ see also **bugiardo** ADJECTIVE
liar
- □ Mi ha dato del bugiardo. He called me a liar.

bugiardo (FEM **bugiarda**) ADJECTIVE
▷ see also **bugiardo** NOUN
- ■ **essere bugiardo** to be a liar

buio (FEM **buia**) ADJECTIVE
▷ see also **buio** NOUN
dark
- □ un vicolo buio a dark alley

il **buio** MASC NOUN
▷ see also **buio** ADJECTIVE
dark
- □ Ha paura del buio. She's afraid of the dark.

il **bullismo** MASC NOUN
bullying
- □ il bullismo verbale verbal bullying

il **bullo** MASC NOUN
bully
- □ comportarsi da bullo to be a bully

il **bullone** MASC NOUN
bolt

buonanotte EXCLAMATION
good night!

buonasera EXCLAMATION
1 good evening!
2 good afternoon!
3 goodbye!

buongiorno EXCLAMATION
1 good morning!
2 goodbye!

buono (FEM **buona**) ADJECTIVE
▷ see also **buono** NOUN
good
- □ un buon ristorante a good restaurant □ Ha

un buon sapore. It tastes good.
- ■ **Buona fortuna!** Good luck!
- ■ **Buon viaggio!** Have a good trip!
- ■ **Buon compleanno!** Happy birthday!
- ■ **Buon Natale!** Happy Christmas!
- ■ **Buone vacanze!** Have a good holiday!
- ■ **Buon divertimento!** Have a nice time!

il **buono** MASC NOUN
▷ see also **buono** ADJECTIVE
- ■ **i buoni e i cattivi** the goodies and the baddies
- ■ **C'è di buono che...** The good thing about it is that...
- ■ **buono sconto** coupon

il **buonsenso** MASC NOUN
common sense
- □ Non ha un briciolo di buonsenso. She hasn't a bit of common sense.

il **buonumore** MASC NOUN
- ■ **essere di buonumore** to be in a good mood □ Oggi sono di buonumore. I'm in a good mood today.

il **burattino** MASC NOUN
puppet

il **burro** MASC NOUN
butter
- □ pane e burro bread and butter

il **burrone** MASC NOUN
ravine

bussare VERB [68]
to knock
- □ Ho bussato alla porta. I knocked at the door.
- ■ **Hanno bussato.** There's somebody at the door.

la **bussola** FEM NOUN
compass

la **busta** FEM NOUN
envelope

la **bustarella** FEM NOUN
bribe
- □ lo scandalo delle bustarelle the bribes scandal

la **bustina** FEM NOUN
- ■ **una bustina di tè** a tea bag
- ■ **una bustina di zucchero** a sachet of sugar

buttare VERB [68]
to throw
- □ Ha buttato il cappotto sul letto. He threw his coat onto the bed.
- ■ **buttare via** to throw away □ Era rotto e l'ho buttato via. It was broken and I threw it away.
- ■ **buttare giù un muro** to knock down a wall
- ■ **buttare la pasta** to put the pasta on □ Hai già buttato la pasta? Have you put the pasta on?
- ■ **buttarsi in acqua** to jump into the water

Cc

la **cabina** FEM NOUN
cabin (on a ship)
□ una cabina di seconda classe a second-class cabin
■ **cabina telefonica** phone box
■ **cabina di pilotaggio** cockpit

il **cacao** MASC NOUN
cocoa

la **caccia** FEM NOUN
hunting
□ Sono contro la caccia. I'm against hunting.
■ **andare a caccia** to go hunting □ La domenica vanno a caccia. They go hunting on Sundays.
■ **dare la caccia a qualcuno** to go after somebody □ La polizia gli dava la caccia. The police went after him.
■ **caccia al tesoro** treasure hunt

cacciare VERB [13]
1 to hunt
□ Ha imparato a cacciare da bambino. He learned to hunt as a child.
2 to throw out
□ Lo cacceranno dalla squadra. They'll throw him out of the team.
3 to put
□ Dove hai cacciato quel libro? Where did you put that book?
■ **cacciarsi nei guai** to get into trouble □ Si caccia sempre nei guai. She's always getting into trouble.

il **cacciatore** MASC NOUN
hunter

il **cacciavite** (PL i **cacciavite**) MASC NOUN
screwdriver

il **cadavere** MASC NOUN
dead body

cadere VERB [16]
to fall
□ Ho inciampato e sono caduta. I tripped and fell. □ È caduto dalla bicicletta. He fell off his bike. □ Sono caduto dal letto. I fell out of bed.
■ **Il mio compleanno cade di lunedì.** My birthday is on a Monday.
■ **Ti è caduta la sciarpa.** You've dropped your scarf.
■ **far cadere** to knock over □ Attento che fai cadere il bicchiere. Mind you don't

knock over your glass.
■ **Ha fatto cadere il vassoio.** She dropped the tray.
■ **cadere dalle nuvole** to be very surprised
□ Quando gliel'ho detto è caduto dalle nuvole. When I told him about it he was very surprised.
■ **È caduta la linea.** We were cut off.

la **caduta** FEM NOUN
1 fall
□ Ha fatto una brutta caduta. He had a nasty fall.
2 loss
□ contro la caduta dei capelli against hair loss

il **caffè** (PL i **caffè**) MASC NOUN
1 coffee
□ un gelato al caffè a coffee ice cream
■ **caffè macchiato** coffee with a dash of milk
■ **caffè espresso** expresso
2 café
□ Si sono incontrati in un caffè. They met in a café.

il **caffellatte** (PL i **caffellatte**) MASC NOUN
milky coffee

la **caffettiera** FEM NOUN
coffee maker

il **calamaro** MASC NOUN
squid
□ calamari alla griglia grilled squid

la **calamita** FEM NOUN
magnet

calare VERB [68, aux **essere**]
1 to decrease
□ La popolazione è calata del dieci per cento. The population has decreased by ten percent.
■ **calare di peso** to lose weight
2 to fall
□ Il prezzo della benzina è calato. The price of petrol has fallen.
3 to drop
□ La temperatura è calata improvvisamente. The temperature suddenly dropped.
4 to lower
□ calare il sipario to lower the curtain

il **calcagno** MASC NOUN
heel

il **calcetto** MASC NOUN
table football

calciatore - cambiamento

il **calciatore** MASC NOUN
football player

il **calcio** (PL i **calci**) MASC NOUN
1 football
  □ una partita di calcio a football match
  □ Giochi a calcio? Do you play football?
2 kick
  □ Mi ha dato un calcio. He gave me a kick.
  ■ **calcio d'angolo** corner kick
  ■ **calcio di punizione** free kick
  ■ **calcio di rigore** penalty kick

calcolare VERB [68]
to work out
  □ Hai calcolato quanto viene a testa? Have you worked out how much it comes to each?

la **calcolatrice** FEM NOUN
calculator

il **calcolo** MASC NOUN
calculation
  □ Ho fatto un rapido calcolo. I did a quick calculation.
  ■ **fare il calcolo di** to work out □ Ho fatto il calcolo di quanto gli dovevo. I worked out how much I owed him.

la **caldaia** FEM NOUN
boiler

caldo (FEM **calda**) ADJECTIVE
  ▷ see also **caldo** NOUN
1 hot
  □ l'acqua calda hot water □ La minestra è troppo calda. The soup's too hot. □ È il mese più caldo. It's the hottest month.
2 warm
  □ una bella coperta calda a nice warm blanket
  □ Il tuo cappotto è più caldo del mio. Your coat is warmer than mine.

il **caldo** MASC NOUN
  ▷ see also **caldo** ADJECTIVE
heat
  □ Non sopporto il caldo. I can't stand the heat.
  ■ **avere caldo** to be hot □ Io ho caldo, e tu? I'm hot, what about you?
  ■ **fare caldo** to be hot □ Fa caldo qui, non trovi? It's hot here, isn't it?

il **calendario** MASC NOUN
calendar

la **calligrafia** FEM NOUN
handwriting
  □ Non capisco la sua calligrafia. I can't read her writing.

la **calma** FEM NOUN
peace
  □ Finalmente un po' di calma. A bit of peace at last.
  ■ **Fai pure con calma.** Take your time.
  ■ **Calma!** Steady on! □ Calma, non spingete! Steady on! Don't push.

calmare VERB [68]
1 to calm down
  □ Ho cercato di calmarlo. I tried to calm him down.
2 to relieve
  □ Non riusciva a calmare i dolori. He couldn't relieve the pain.
  ■ **calmarsi** to calm down □ Calmati e dimmi tutto. Calm down and tell me everything.

calmo (FEM **calma**) ADJECTIVE
calm
  □ Il mare è calmo, oggi. The sea's calm today.
  ■ **stare calmo** to keep calm □ State calmi, non c'è pericolo. Keep calm, there's no danger.

il **calo** MASC NOUN
drop
  □ un forte calo delle vendite a big drop in sales

il **calore** MASC NOUN
heat

il **calorifero** MASC NOUN
heater

caloroso (FEM **calorosa**) ADJECTIVE
warm
  □ un'accoglienza calorosa a warm welcome
  ■ **È un tipo caloroso.** He doesn't feel the cold.

calpestare VERB [68]
  ■ **'vietato calpestare l'erba'** 'keep off the grass'

calvo (FEM **calva**) ADJECTIVE
bald

la **calza** FEM NOUN
sock
  □ una calza bucata a sock with a hole in it
  ■ **calze** 1 socks 2 tights 3 stockings

la **calzamaglia** FEM NOUN
  ■ **una calzamaglia** a pair of tights □ una calzamaglia di lana a pair of woollen tights

il **calzettone** MASC NOUN
knee sock
  □ un paio di calzettoni a pair of knee socks

il **calzino** MASC NOUN
sock
  □ un paio di calzini a pair of socks

il **calzolaio** MASC NOUN
cobbler
  □ Mio padre fa il calzolaio. My father is a cobbler.

i **calzoncini** MASC PL NOUN
shorts
  □ Vorrei un paio di calzoncini rossi. I'd like a pair of red shorts.
  ■ **calzoncini da bagno** swimming trunks

i **calzoni** MASC PL NOUN
trousers
  □ un paio di calzoni rossi a pair of red trousers

il **cambiamento** MASC NOUN
change
  □ un cambiamento di orario a change in the timetable
  ■ **cambiamenti climatici** climate change

cambiare VERB [17]

to change

□Ultimamente è molto cambiato. He's changed a lot recently. □Cambiamo argomento. Let's change the subject. □Vorrei cambiare questi euro in sterline. I'd like to change these euros into pounds. □Se non va bene me lo cambia? If it's not right will you change it?

■ **cambiare idea** to change one's mind

□ Scusi, ho cambiato idea. Sorry, I've changed my mind.

■ **cambiare casa** to move house □ Ha cambiato casa il mese scorso. She moved house last month.

■ **cambiarsi** to get changed □ Devo andare a casa a cambiarmi. I've got to go home and get changed.

il **cambiavalute** (PL i **cambiavalute**) MASC NOUN

bureau de change

il **cambio** MASC NOUN

change

□ Ho portato solo un cambio d'abito. I've only brought one change of clothes.

■ **agenzia di cambio** bureau de change

■ **in cambio di** in exchange for □ Mi ha dato un CD in cambio del pallone. He gave me a CD in exchange for the football.

■ **dare il cambio a qualcuno** to take over from somebody □ Se sei stanco ti do il cambio. If you're tired I'll take over from you.

■ **il cambio della guardia** the changing of the guard

la **camera** FEM NOUN

1 room

□ una camera grande a big room

2 bedroom

□ È rimasto in camera sua tutto il pomeriggio. He stayed in his bedroom the whole afternoon.

■ **camera da letto** bedroom

■ **camera matrimoniale** double room

■ **camera singola** single room

LANGUAGE TIP Be careful! **camera** doesn't mean **camera**.

la **cameriera** FEM NOUN

1 waitress

2 chambermaid

il **cameriere** MASC NOUN

waiter

□ Fa il cameriere. He is a waiter. □ Scusi, cameriere! Waiter!

la **camicetta** FEM NOUN

blouse

la **camicia** (PL le **camicie**) FEM NOUN

shirt

□ una camicia rossa a red shirt

■ **camicia da notte** nightdress

il **caminetto** MASC NOUN

fireplace

il **camino** MASC NOUN

chimney

il **camion** (PL i **camion**) MASC NOUN

lorry

il/la **camionista** (MASC PL i **camionisti**, FEM PL le **camioniste**) MASC/FEM NOUN

lorry driver

□ Mio padre fa il camionista. My father is a lorry driver.

il **cammello** MASC NOUN

camel

camminare VERB [68]

to walk

□ Non sono abituato a camminare tanto. I'm not used to walking so much.

la **camomilla** FEM NOUN

camomile tea

la **campagna** FEM NOUN

1 country

□ Abita in campagna. She lives in the country. □ Siamo andati in campagna a passeggiare. We went for a walk in the country.

2 countryside

□ La campagna inglese è proprio bella. The English countryside is really beautiful.

3 campaign

□una campagna pubblicitaria a publicity campaign

la **campana** FEM NOUN

bell

■ **campana per la raccolta del vetro** bottle bank

il **campanello** MASC NOUN

bell

□ Hai suonato il campanello? Have you rung the bell?

il **campanile** MASC NOUN

bell tower

il **campeggio** MASC NOUN

camp site

□ C'è un campeggio qui vicino? Is there a camp site near here?

■ **andare in campeggio** to go camping

□ Quest'estate andremo in campeggio. We're going camping this summer.

il **camper** (PL i **camper**) MASC NOUN

camper van

il **campionato** MASC NOUN

championship

□il campionato di calcio the league championship

■**il campionato di serie A** the premier league

il **campione** MASC NOUN

1 champion

□ il campione del mondo di sci the world skiing champion

2 sample

□ un campione gratuito a free sample

37

la **campionessa** FEM NOUN
champion

il **campo** MASC NOUN
field
□ un campo di grano a field of wheat □ Nel suo campo è uno dei migliori. He's one of the best in his field.
■ **campo di calcio** football ground
■ **campo giochi** playground
■ **campo sportivo** sports ground
■ **campo da tennis** tennis court

il **Canada** MASC NOUN
Canada
□ Mi è piaciuto molto il Canada. I really liked Canada. □ Andremo in Canada quest'estate. We're going to Canada this summer.

canadese (FEM **canadese**) ADJECTIVE, MASC/
FEM NOUN
Canadian

il **canale** MASC NOUN
1 channel
□ Su che canale è il film? Which channel is the film on?
■ **il canale della Manica** the Channel
2 canal
□ i canali di Venezia the canals of Venice

il **canarino** MASC NOUN
canary

cancellare VERB [68]
1 to rub out
2 to cross out
3 to delete

il **cancello** MASC NOUN
gate

Cancro MASC NOUN
Cancer
□ Sono del Cancro. I'm Cancer.

il **cancro** MASC NOUN
cancer
□ cancro ai polmoni lung cancer

la **candeggina** FEM NOUN
bleach

la **candela** FEM NOUN
1 candle
2 spark plug

il **candidato**, la **candidata** MASC/
FEM NOUN
candidate

il **cane** MASC NOUN
dog
■ **cane da caccia** hunting dog
■ **cane da guardia** guard dog

il **canestro** MASC NOUN
basket (in basketball)
■ **fare canestro** to shoot a basket

il **canguro** MASC NOUN
kangaroo

il **canile** MASC NOUN
kennel

la **canna** FEM NOUN
reed
■ **canna da zucchero** sugar cane
■ **canna da pesca** fishing rod

la **cannuccia** (PL le **cannucce**) FEM NOUN
straw

la **canoa** FEM NOUN
canoe
■ **andare in canoa** to go canoeing

la **canottiera** FEM NOUN
vest

il **canotto** MASC NOUN
dinghy

il/la **cantante** MASC/FEM NOUN
singer

cantare VERB [68]
to sing
□ Ha cantato per tutta la sera. He sang all evening.

il **cantiere** MASC NOUN
shipyard

la **cantina** FEM NOUN
cellar
□ È in cantina. It's in the cellar.

> **LANGUAGE TIP** Be careful! **cantina** doesn't mean **canteen**.

la **canzone** FEM NOUN
song

capace (FEM **capace**) ADJECTIVE
1 able
□ un insegnante molto capace a very able teacher
■ **essere capace di** to be able to □ Sarai capace di farlo? Will you be able to do it?
■ **Sei capace di nuotare?** Can you swim?
■ **Non è stata capace di farlo.** She couldn't do it.
2 large
□ una stanza capace a large room
■ **La mia borsa è molto capace.** My bag holds a lot.

la **capanna** FEM NOUN
hut

il **capello** MASC NOUN
hair
□ C'è un capello nella minestra. There's a hair in the soup.
■ **i capelli** hair □ Ha i capelli corti. She's got short hair. □ Mi lavo i capelli ogni giorno. I wash my hair every day. □ Ho i capelli ancora bagnati. My hair is still wet.

capire VERB [51]
to understand
□ Va bene, capisco. OK, I understand. □ Non ho capito una parola. I didn't understand a word. □ Non ho capito, puoi ripetere? I don't understand, could you say it again?
■ **Fammi capire...** Let me get this straight...
■ **capire male** to misunderstand

la **capitale** FEM NOUN
capital

il **capitano** MASC NOUN
captain

capitare VERB [68, aux **essere**]
to happen
□ Sono cose che capitano. These things happen. □ Non mi è mai capitato. It's never happened to me.

il **capitello** MASC NOUN
capital (city)

il **capitolo** MASC NOUN
chapter

il **capo** MASC NOUN
1 head
  ■ **da capo a piedi** from head to foot
  □ Era coperto di fango da capo a piedi. He was covered in mud from head to foot.
  ■ **fare un discorso senza né capo né coda** to talk nonsense
2 boss
  □ Il mio capo è molto esigente. My boss is very demanding.
  ■ **il capo di stato** the head of state
3 end
  □ all'altro capo del tavolo at the other end of the table
  ■ **a capo** new paragraph
  ■ **da capo** all over again □ Ha dovuto ricominciare tutto da capo. He had to start all over again.

Capodanno MASC NOUN
New Year's Day
  ■ **il veglione di Capodanno** New Year's Eve

il **capogiro** MASC NOUN
  ■ **avere un capogiro** to feel dizzy □ Ho avuto un capogiro. I felt dizzy.

il **capolavoro** MASC NOUN
masterpiece

il **capolinea** (PL i **capolinea**) MASC NOUN
terminus

il **capostazione** (PL i **capistazione**) MASC NOUN
station master

il/la **capotavola** MASC/FEM NOUN
  ■ **sedere a capotavola** to sit at the head of the table

capovolgere VERB [91]
to turn upside down
  ■ **capovolgersi** 1 to overturn 2 to capsize 3 to be reversed

la **cappella** FEM NOUN
chapel

il **cappello** MASC NOUN
hat
  □ un cappello di paglia a straw hat

i **capperi** MASC PL NOUN
capers

cappottare VERB [68]
to overturn
  □ La macchina ha cappottato in curva. The car overturned on the bend.

il **cappotto** MASC NOUN
coat
  □ Infilati il cappotto. Put your coat on.

il **cappuccino** MASC NOUN
cappuccino

il **cappuccio** MASC NOUN
hood
  □ una felpa col cappuccio a sweatshirt with a hood

la **capra** FEM NOUN
goat
  □ formaggio di capra goat's cheese

il **capriccio** MASC NOUN
whim
  □ È solo un capriccio. It's just a whim.
  ■ **fare i capricci** to be naughty

capriccioso (FEM **capricciosa**) ADJECTIVE
naughty
  □ un bambino capriccioso a naughty boy

il **Capricorno** MASC NOUN
Capricorn
  □ Sono del Capricorno. I'm Capricorn.

la **capriola** FEM NOUN
somersault
  □ Sai fare le capriole? Can you do somersaults?

la **caraffa** FEM NOUN
carafe

la **caramella** FEM NOUN
sweet
  □ Vuoi una caramella? Would you like a sweet?
  ■ **una caramella alla menta** a mint

il **carattere** MASC NOUN
1 personality
  □ C'è una certa incompatibilità di carattere tra noi. There's a bit of a personality clash between us.
  ■ **avere un brutto carattere** to be bad-tempered
  ■ **avere un bel carattere** to be good-natured
2 letter

la **caratteristica** (PL le **caratteristiche**) FEM NOUN
feature

caratteristico (FEM **caratteristica**, MASC PL **caratteristici**, FEM PL **caratteristiche**) ADJECTIVE
1 special
  □ il sapore caratteristico del caviale the special taste of caviar
2 distinctive
  □ un elemento caratteristico dell'architettura locale a distinctive feature of the local architecture
3 traditional
  □ un ristorante caratteristico a traditional restaurant

il **carboidrato** MASC NOUN
carbohydrate

il **carburante** MASC NOUN
fuel
□ Siamo rimasti senza carburante. We ran out of fuel.

il **carburatore** MASC NOUN
carburettor

il **carcere** MASC NOUN
prison
□ Sono evasi dal carcere. They escaped from prison. □ Gli hanno dato dieci anni di carcere. He was sent to prison for ten years.

il **carciofo** MASC NOUN
artichoke

la **carestia** FEM NOUN
famine
□ Rischiano di morire a causa della carestia. They may die as a result of the famine.

cariarsi VERB [17, AUX **essere**]
■ Mi si è cariato un dente. I've got a hole in one of my teeth.

la **carica** (PL le **cariche**) FEM NOUN
■ in carica in office □ il presidente in carica the president in office
■ rimanere in carica per... to hold office for...
□ Il Presidente è rimasto in carica per cinque anni. The President held office for five years.

caricare VERB [18]
1 to load
□ Ho caricato le valigie in macchina. I've loaded the cases into the car. □ Hai caricato il programma? Have you loaded the program?
■ Come si carica questa macchina fotografica? How do you put the film in this camera?
2 to wind
□ Avevo dimenticato di caricare la sveglia. I'd forgotten to wind the alarm clock.
3 to charge
□ La polizia ha caricato i dimostranti. The police charged the demonstrators.
4 to upload
□ Ho caricato le foto delle vacanze su Flickr. I've uploaded the holiday pictures onto Flickr.

carico (FEM **carica**, MASC PL **carichi**, FEM PL **cariche**) ADJECTIVE
▷ see also **carico** NOUN
loaded
□ Il fucile era carico. The gun was loaded.
■ carico di loaded with □ È tornato carico di pacchi. He came back loaded with parcels.
■ un camion carico di mattoni a lorry with a load of bricks

il **carico** (PL i **carichi**) MASC NOUN
▷ see also **carico** ADJECTIVE
load
□ un carico di arance a load of oranges

la **carie** (PL le **carie**) FEM NOUN
■ Ho una carie. I've got a cavity in one of my teeth.

carino (FEM **carina**) ADJECTIVE
1 nice
□ Carina questa maglietta! That's a nice T-shirt! □ Ha una casa molto carina. She's got a very nice house. □ È stato molto carino da parte tua. It was really nice of you.
■ essere carino con qualcuno to be nice to somebody □ Sono stati molto carini con me. They were very nice to me.
2 nice-looking
□ È carino tuo fratello. Your brother's nice-looking.

la **carità** FEM NOUN
■ chiedere la carità to beg □ C'era uno che chiedeva la carità fuori dalla chiesa. There was a man begging outside the church.
■ Per carità! You're joking! □ Uscire con lui? Per carità! Go out with him? You're joking!

la **carnagione** FEM NOUN
complexion
□ Ha la carnagione chiara. She's got a fair complexion.

la **carne** FEM NOUN
meat
□ Preferisci la carne o il pesce? Which do you prefer, meat or fish?
■ carne di maiale pork
■ carne di manzo beef
■ carne tritata mince
■ in carne e ossa in the flesh □ Era proprio lui, in carne e ossa! It was really him, in the flesh!

il **carnevale** MASC NOUN
carnival
□ il carnevale di Venezia the Venice Carnival

DID YOU KNOW...?
Carnevale in Italy is a period when there are parties, often in costume, bonfires and processions. It begins at the end of January and ends on Shrove Tuesday, before the start of Lent.

caro (FEM **cara**) ADJECTIVE
1 dear
□ Caro Paul Dear Paul □ Carissima Cinzia Dearest Cinzia
■ cari saluti best wishes
2 expensive
□ È troppo caro, non lo compro. It's too expensive, I won't buy it.

la **carota** FEM NOUN
carrot

il **carrello** MASC NOUN
trolley

la **carriera** FEM NOUN
career
□ una carriera brillante a brilliant career

■ **fare carriera** to have a career □ Non è facile per loro far carriera. It's not easy for them to have a career.

■ **Farà sicuramente carriera.** He'll get on.

il **carro** MASC NOUN
cart

■ **carro attrezzi 1** breakdown truck **2** tow truck

■ **carro armato** tank

la **carrozza** FEM NOUN
carriage

la **carrozzina** FEM NOUN
1 pram
2 wheelchair

la **carta** FEM NOUN
paper
□ un foglio di carta a sheet of paper

■ **carta di credito** credit card

■ **carta geografica** map

■ **carta d'identità** identity card

■ **carta igienica** toilet paper

■ **carta d'imbarco** boarding card

■ **carta da lettere** writing paper

■ **carta da regalo** wrapping paper

■ **carte da gioco** playing cards

la **cartella** FEM NOUN
1 folder
2 briefcase
3 satchel

il **cartellino** MASC NOUN
price label

■ **timbrare il cartellino 1** to clock in **2** to clock out

il **cartello** MASC NOUN
sign
□ Cosa indica quel cartello? What does that sign say? □ Sul cartello c'era scritto 'Tutto esaurito'. The sign said 'Sold out'.

il **cartellone** MASC NOUN
hoarding

la **cartina** FEM NOUN
map

la **cartoleria** FEM NOUN
stationer's
□ Lo trovi in cartoleria. You'll get it at a stationer's.

la **cartolina** FEM NOUN
postcard
□ Mandami una cartolina. Send me a postcard.

■ **una cartolina virtuale** an e-card

il **cartone** MASC NOUN
1 cardboard
□ una scatola di cartone a cardboard box
2 carton
□ un cartone di latte a carton of milk

■ **cartone animato** cartoon □ i cartoni animati di Tom e Jerry Tom and Jerry cartoons

la **cartuccia** (PL le **cartucce**) FEM NOUN
cartridge

la **casa** FEM NOUN
1 house
□ una bella casa grande a nice big house □ una casa in campagna a house in the country □ Eravamo a casa mia. We were at my house. □ Andiamo a casa tua. Let's go to your house.

■ **casa editrice** publishing house

■ **casa popolare** council house
2 home
□ Sono stato in casa tutta la sera. I was at home all evening. □ Non è a casa. She isn't at home. □ Sarò a casa tra un'ora. I'll be home in an hour. □ Fai come se fossi a casa tua! Make yourself at home!

■ **andare a casa** to go home □ Io vado a casa. I'm going home.

■ **tornare a casa** to get home □ È tornato a casa tardi. He got home late.

■ **fatto in casa** home-made □ pane fatto in casa home-made bread
3 flat
□ Hanno una bella casa. They have a nice flat.

■ **'Tanti saluti a casa.'** 'Best wishes to all the family.'

■ **casa discografica** record company

■ **casa dello studente** hall of residence

la **casalinga** (PL le **casalinghe**) FEM NOUN
housewife
□ Fa la casalinga. She is a housewife.

cascare VERB [18, AUX **essere**]
to fall
□ È cascato dal letto. He fell out of bed.

■ **cascarci** to fall for it □ Gli ho detto che era mia e lui c'è cascato. I told him it was mine and he fell for it.

la **cascata** FEM NOUN
waterfall
□ Sono le cascate più alte del mondo. They're the biggest waterfalls in the world.

■ **le cascate del Niagara** the Niagara Falls

il **casco** (PL i **caschi**) MASC NOUN
crash helmet

■ **i Caschi blu** the Blue Helmets

la **caserma** FEM NOUN
barracks

il **casino** MASC NOUN
1 racket (noise)
□ Cos'è questo casino? What's this racket?
2 mess
□ In camera mia c'è un gran casino. My bedroom is in a terrible mess.
3 problem
□ In questo periodo ho tanti casini. I've got loads of problems at the moment.

■ **un casino di** loads of □ C'era un casino di gente. There were loads of people.

il **casinò** (PL i **casinò**) MASC NOUN
casino

il **caso** MASC NOUN
case

C

■ **in ogni caso** in any case □ In ogni caso non ci perdi niente. In any case you won't lose anything.

■ **in tal caso** in that case □ Be', in tal caso dovremo rimandare la partenza. Well, in that case we'll have to put off our departure.

■ **nel caso che** in case □ Ti do il mio numero, nel caso che tu venga a Roma. I'll give you my number, in case you come to Rome.

■ **per caso** by chance □ L'ho incontrato per caso. I met him by chance.

■ **a caso** at random □ Ho aperto il libro a caso. I opened the book at random.

■ **caso mai** if □ Caso mai non possiate venire, telefonate. If you can't come, phone. □ Dovrei essere lì alle cinque, caso mai aspetta. I should be there at five, if I'm not, wait for me.

■ **far caso a** to notice □ Hai fatto caso a come ti guardava? Did you notice how he was looking at you? □ Non ci ho fatto caso. I didn't notice.

■ **Non farci caso, è così con tutti.** Don't pay any attention, he's like that with everybody.

■ **I casi sono due...** There are two possibilities...

■ **mettiamo il caso che** supposing □ Mettiamo il caso che ti inviti: accetteresti? Supposing he invited you, would you go?

■ **non è il caso di** there's no point □ Non è il caso di prendersela! There's no point getting upset!

■ **Forse sarebbe il caso di andarcene.** Perhaps we'd better go.

caspita EXCLAMATION
1 wow!
2 for goodness' sake!

la **cassa** FEM NOUN
1 case
□ Ho comprato una cassa di birra. I bought a case of beer.
■ **cassa da imballaggio** packing case
2 cash desk
3 checkout

la **cassaforte** (PL le **casseforti**) FEM NOUN
safe
□ Hanno forzato la cassaforte. They forced open the safe.

la **cassetta** FEM NOUN
1 box
□ una cassetta di mele a box of apples
2 cassette
□ Ce l'ho sia su CD che su cassetta. I've got it on CD and on cassette.
3 post box
■ **cassetta delle lettere** letterbox

la **cassettiera** FEM NOUN
chest of drawers

il **cassetto** MASC NOUN
drawer
□ È nel primo cassetto. It's in the top drawer.

il **cassiere**, la **cassiera** MASC/FEM NOUN
1 cashier
2 checkout operator

il **cassonetto** MASC NOUN
wheelie bin

la **castagna** FEM NOUN
chestnut

castano (FEM **castana**) ADJECTIVE
brown
□ Ha gli occhi e i capelli castani. She's got brown eyes and brown hair.

il **castello** MASC NOUN
castle
□ un castello di sabbia a sand castle

il **castigo** (PL i **castighi**) MASC NOUN
punishment
□ per castigo as a punishment
■ **Sono in castigo e non posso uscire.** I'm being punished and I'm not allowed to go out.
■ **mettere in castigo** to punish

il **catalogo** (PL i **cataloghi**) MASC NOUN
catalogue

la **categoria** FEM NOUN
class

la **catena** FEM NOUN
chain

la **catenina** FEM NOUN
chain

il **catino** MASC NOUN
basin

il **catrame** MASC NOUN
tar

la **cattedra** FEM NOUN
teacher's desk

la **cattedrale** FEM NOUN
cathedral

la **cattiveria** FEM NOUN
■ **fare una cattiveria** to do something bad
■ **dire una cattiveria** to say something spiteful

cattivo (FEM **cattiva**) ADJECTIVE, MASC/FEM NOUN
1 bad
□ È sempre di cattivo umore. He's always in a bad mood.
2 nasty
□ Ha un cattivo odore. It's got a nasty smell.
□ È il ragazzo più cattivo della classe. He's the nastiest boy in the class.
■ **i cattivi** the baddies □ E quindi i cattivi sono finiti in prigione. And so the baddies ended up in prison.
■ **il cattivo** the villain □ Fa sempre la parte del cattivo. He always plays the villain.

cattolico (FEM **cattolica**, MASC PL **cattolici**, FEM PL **cattoliche**) ADJECTIVE, MASC/FEM NOUN
Catholic

la **causa** FEM NOUN
cause
▫ Quella è stata la causa principale. That was the main cause.
▪ **a causa di** because of ▫ L'aeroporto è chiuso a causa della nebbia. The airport is closed because of the fog.
▪ **fare causa a qualcuno** to take legal action against somebody ▫ Mi ha fatto causa. He took legal action against me.

causare VERB [68]
to cause
▫ Potrebbe causare dei problemi. It might cause problems.

cavalcare VERB [18]
to ride
▫ Sai cavalcare? Can you ride?
▪ **andare a cavalcare** to go riding

la **cavalcata** FEM NOUN
ride
▫ Abbiamo fatto una cavalcata nel bosco. We went for a ride in the woods.

il **cavalcavia** (PL i **cavalcavia**) MASC NOUN
flyover

cavalcioni ADVERB
▪ **a cavalcioni di** astride ▫ Era seduto a cavalcioni del muretto. He was sitting astride the wall.

la **cavalletta** FEM NOUN
grasshopper

il **cavalletto** MASC NOUN
1 tripod
2 easel

il **cavallo** MASC NOUN
1 horse
▫ Ti piacciono i cavalli? Do you like horses?
▪ **andare a cavallo** to ride ▫ Sai andare a cavallo? Can you ride?
▪ **cavallo a dondolo** rocking horse
▪ **cavallo da corsa** racehorse
2 knight (in chess)
3 crotch (of trousers)

cavarsi VERB [56]
▪ **cavarsela** to do all right ▫ Se l'è cavata all'esame. He did all right in the exam.
▪ **Se l'è cavata con qualche graffio.** He came out of it with only a few scratches.

il **cavatappi** (PL i **cavatappi**) MASC NOUN
corkscrew

la **cavia** FEM NOUN
guinea pig
▪ **fare da cavia** to be a guinea pig

la **caviglia** FEM NOUN
ankle
▫ Mi sono slogato la caviglia. I've sprained my ankle.

il **cavo** MASC NOUN
cable

▫ televisione via cavo cable television
▪ **cavo di traino** towrope

la **cavolata** FEM NOUN
▪ **fare una cavolata** to do something stupid
▪ **dire una cavolata** to talk rubbish

il **cavolfiore** MASC NOUN
cauliflower

il **cavolo** MASC NOUN
cabbage
▫ minestra di cavolo cabbage soup
▪ **Che cavolo vuoi?** What the hell do you want?
▪ **Non fa un cavolo tutto il giorno.** He doesn't do a damn thing all day.

ce ▷ see **ci**

i **ceci** MASC PL NOUN
chickpeas

ceco (FEM **ceca**, MASC PL **cechi**, FEM PL **ceche**)
ADJECTIVE, MASC/FEM NOUN
Czech

cedere VERB [27]
1 to give
▪ **cedere qualcosa a qualcuno** to give somebody something ▫ Le ho ceduto il posto. I gave her my seat.
2 to collapse
▫ La sedia ha ceduto sotto il suo peso. The chair collapsed under his weight.
3 to give in
▫ Ha insistito tanto che alla fine ho ceduto. She was so insistent that in the end I gave in.

celebre (FEM **celebre**) ADJECTIVE
famous

celeste (FEM **celeste**) ADJECTIVE, MASC NOUN
pale blue
▫ una gonna celeste a pale blue skirt
▪ **Ha gli occhi celesti.** She's got blue eyes.

celibe (FEM **celibe**) ADJECTIVE
unmarried
▫ un uomo celibe an unmarried man

la **cella** FEM NOUN
cell

il **cellulare** MASC NOUN
mobile phone

la **cellulite** FEM NOUN
cellulite
▫ una crema contro la cellulite an anti-cellulite cream

il **cemento** MASC NOUN
cement
▪ **cemento armato** reinforced concrete

la **cena** FEM NOUN
dinner
▫ Vieni a cena da noi? Would you like to come to dinner with us? ▫ Mi hanno invitato a cena.

cenare - cercare

They've invited me to dinner. □ Ti telefono all'ora di cena. I'll phone you at dinner time.

cenare VERB [68]
to have dinner
□ Hai cenato? Have you had dinner?

la **cenere** FEM NOUN
ash

Cenerentola FEM NOUN
Cinderella

il **cenno** MASC NOUN
1 nod
■ **far cenno di sì** to nod
■ **far cenno di no** to shake one's head
2 wave
■ **far cenno di no** to wag one's finger
■ **far cenno a qualcuno** to gesture to somebody □ Mi ha fatto cenno di avvicinarmi. He gestured to me to come closer.

il **centenario** MASC NOUN
centenary

il **centesimo** MASC NOUN
▷ see also **centesimo** ADJECTIVE
1 cent
□ Costa ottanta centesimi. It costs eighty cents.
2 hundredth
□ pochi centesimi di secondo a few hundredths of a second

centesimo (FEM **centesima**) ADJECTIVE
▷ see also **centesimo** NOUN
hundredth

centigrado (FEM **centigrada**) ADJECTIVE
centigrade
□ venti gradi centigradi twenty degrees centigrade

il **centimetro** MASC NOUN
centimetre
□ lungo venti centimetri twenty centimetres long

il **centinaio** (FEM PL le **centinaia**) MASC NOUN
■ **un centinaio di** about a hundred □ un centinaio di persone about a hundred people
■ **centinaia** hundreds □ Ci sono stato centinaia di volte. I've been there hundreds of times.
■ **diverse centinaia di sterline** several hundred pounds

cento NUMBER
a hundred
□ cento sterline a hundred pounds
■ **per cento** per cent □ cinque per cento five per cent
■ **al cento per cento** a hundred per cent □ Ne sono sicuro al cento per cento. I'm a hundred per cent sure.
■ **Cento di questi giorni!** Many happy returns!

centodieci NUMBER
one hundred and ten

■ **laurearsi con centodieci e lode** to get a first class degree

centomila NUMBER
a hundred thousand

centrale (FEM **centrale**) ADJECTIVE
▷ see also **centrale** NOUN
central
□ Dov'è la stazione centrale? Where's the central station? □ L'albergo è molto centrale. The hotel is very central.
■ **sede centrale** head office □ La sede centrale è a Roma. The head office is in Rome.

la **centrale** FEM NOUN
▷ see also **centrale** ADJECTIVE
■ **una centrale eolica** a wind farm
■ **centrale di polizia** police headquarters *sing*

il/la **centralinista** (MASC PL i **centralinisti**, FEM PL le **centraliniste**) MASC/FEM NOUN
switchboard operator

il **centralino** MASC NOUN
switchboard

centralizzato (FEM **centralizzata**) ADJECTIVE
central
■ **riscaldamento centralizzato** central heating
■ **chiusura centralizzata** central locking

il **centravanti** (PL i **centravanti**) MASC NOUN
centre forward

il **centro** MASC NOUN
1 centre
□ Al centro della piazza c'è una fontana. There's a fountain in the centre of the square.
■ **centro commerciale** shopping centre
■ **centro di permanenza temporanea** reception centre
2 town centre
□ Siamo andati in centro a fare spese. We went into the town centre to do some shopping.
□ Abiti in centro o in periferia? Do you live in the town centre or in the suburbs?

il **centrocampo** (PL i **centrocampo**) MASC NOUN
midfield

il **centrodestra** MASC NOUN
centre right

il **centrosinistra** MASC NOUN
centre left

la **cera** FEM NOUN
wax
■ **il museo delle cere** the waxworks

cercare VERB [18]
1 to look for
□ Le ho cercate dappertutto. I've looked for them everywhere. □ Stai cercando lavoro? Are you looking for a job?
2 to look up
□ Devo cercare la parola sul dizionario. I'll have to look the word up in the dictionary.

3 to try

□ Ho cercato di spiegargli il motivo. I tried to explain the reason to him. □ Cerca di non fare tardi. Try not to be late.

il **cerchietto** MASC NOUN
hairband

il **cerchio** MASC NOUN
circle

□ Eravamo seduti in cerchio. We were sitting in a circle.

i **cereali** MASC PL NOUN

1 cereals

□ la produzione annuale di cereali the annual production of cereals

2 cereal

□ A colazione mangio sempre cereali. I always have cereal for breakfast.

la **cerimonia** FEM NOUN
ceremony

il **cerino** MASC NOUN
wax match

□ una scatola di cerini a box of wax matches

la **cerniera** FEM NOUN
■ **cerniera lampo** zip

il **cerotto** MASC NOUN
sticking plaster

il **certificato** MASC NOUN
certificate

□ un certificato medico a medical certificate

certo (FEM **certa**) ADJECTIVE
▷ *see also* **certo** ADVERB

1 sure

□ Sono certo che verrà. I'm sure she'll come. □ Ne sono più che certo. I'm absolutely sure of it. □ Non sono certo di poter venire. I'm not sure I can come.

2 certain

□ un certo signor Smith a certain Mr Smith
■ **C'è un certo Sam che ti cerca.** Someone called Sam is looking for you.

3 some

□ Certi giorni l'ufficio apre più tardi. Some days the office opens later. □ Certa gente non è mai contenta. Some people are never satisfied. □ Non vado a vedere certi film. There are some films I don't go to see.
■ **certe volte** sometimes □ Certe volte non ti capisco proprio! Sometimes I just don't understand you!
■ **in un certo senso** in a way

certo ADVERB
▷ *see also* **certo** ADJECTIVE
of course

□ Posso portare un amico? — Ma certo! May I bring a friend? — Yes, of course! □ Certo che no! Of course not!

il **cervello** MASC NOUN
brain

il **cervo** MASC NOUN

1 deer

2 venison

il **cespuglio** MASC NOUN
bush

cessare VERB [68]
to stop

□ Non ha ancora cessato di piovere. It hasn't stopped raining yet.

il **cestino** MASC NOUN

1 basket

□ un cestino di vimini a wicker basket
■ **cestino dei rifiuti** litter bin

2 punnet

□ un cestino di fragole a punnet of strawberries

3 recycle bin

■ **trascinare nel cestino** to send to the recycle bin

il **cetriolo** MASC NOUN
cucumber

chattare VERB [68]
to chat *(online)*

che PRONOUN, ADJECTIVE, CONJUNCTION

1 what

□ Che giorno è oggi? What day is it today? □ Che ore sono? What time is it? □ Che tipo di musica ti piace? What sort of music do you like? □ A che ora parti? What time are you leaving?
■ **che cosa** what □ Che cosa fai? What are you doing? □ Che cosa vuoi? What do you want? □ A che cosa pensi? What are you thinking about?

2 which

□ Che gusto preferisci? Limone o cioccolato? Which flavour would you like? Lemon or chocolate? □ Che film hai visto? Which film did you see?

3 that

□ Ha detto che farà tardi. He said that he'll be late. □ la squadra che ha vinto il campionato the team that won the championship

4 who

□ il ragazzo che è seduto laggiù the boy who's sitting over there □ Ha un fratello che abita a Roma. She's got a brother who lives in Rome.
LANGUAGE TIP **che** is often not translated.
□ la ragazza che hai visto the girl you saw □ il libro che mi hai prestato the book you lent me □ la sera che ti ho visto the evening I saw you
LANGUAGE TIP In exclamations, when **che** is followed by a singular noun, it is translated by 'what a'. When it is followed by a plural noun, it is translated by 'what'.
□ Che bella ragazza! What a pretty girl! □ Che brutte scarpe! What horrible shoes!
LANGUAGE TIP When **che** is followed by an adjective, it is often translated by 'it's'.

□ Che buono! It's delicious! □ Che carino! It's lovely! □ Che freddo! It's freezing!

lo **chef** (PL **gli chef**) MASC NOUN
chef

chi PRONOUN
1 who
□ Chi è? Who is it? □ Ma chi crede di essere? Who does he think he is? □ Con chi desidera parlare? Who do you wish to speak to? □ Con chi parli? Who are you talking to? □ Di chi è? Who does it belong to?
■ **Di chi è l'idea?** Whose idea is it?
2 whoever
□ Chi arriva prima vince. Whoever gets there first is the winner. □ Esco con chi mi pare. I go out with whoever I like. □ Puoi invitare chi vuoi. You can invite whoever you like.
■ **Chi non vuole andarci non ci vada.** Anyone who doesn't want to go doesn't have to.

chiacchierare VERB [68]
to chat
□ Ci siamo fermati a chiacchierare sotto casa sua. We stopped to chat outside her house.

le **chiacchiere** FEM PL NOUN
■ **fare due chiacchiere** to have a chat

chiamare VERB [68]
1 to call
□ Hanno chiamato la polizia. They called the police.
2 to call to
□ L'ho chiamato ma non mi ha sentito. I called to him but he didn't hear me.
■ **chiamarsi** to be called □ Come si chiama il tuo amico? What is your friend called?
■ **Come ti chiami? — Mi chiamo Paolo.** What's your name? — My name's Paolo.
■ **Questa si chiama fortuna!** That's what I call luck!
3 to phone
□ Ha chiamato Loredana. Loredana phoned.

la **chiamata** FEM NOUN
call
□ una chiamata urbana a local call

chiarire VERB [51]
1 to get clear
□ Vorrei chiarire alcuni punti. I'd like to get some points clear.
2 to solve
□ Alla fine il mistero è stato chiarito. In the end the mystery was solved.

chiaro (FEM **chiara**) ADJECTIVE
1 clear
□ Non voglio andarci, è chiaro? I don't want to go, is that clear?
■ **Era chiaro che non se l'aspettava.** He clearly wasn't expecting it.
2 light
□ verde chiaro light green

3 fair
□ Ha i capelli chiari. She's got fair hair.

il **chiasso** MASC NOUN
noise
□ Cos'è tutto questo chiasso? What's all this noise?
■ **Smettetela di fare chiasso!** Be quiet!

la **chiave** FEM NOUN
key
□ Ho perso le chiavi di casa. I've lost my house keys.
■ **chiudere a chiave** to lock □ Mi raccomando, chiudi a chiave la porta. Make sure you lock the door.

la **chiavetta** FEM NOUN
1 key
□ la chiavetta d'accensione the ignition key
2 winder
■ **chiavetta USB** USB key

chiedere VERB [19]
1 to ask
□ Chiedi dov'è l'albergo. Ask where the hotel is.
■ **chiedere qualcosa a qualcuno** to ask somebody something □ Chiedi a Lidia come si chiama il suo cane. Ask Lidia what her dog's called. □ Mi ha chiesto l'ora. He asked me the time. □ Chiedi a Giulia di spostarsi un po'. Ask Giulia to move over a bit.
2 to ask for
■ **chiedere qualcosa a qualcuno** to ask somebody for something □ Ho chiesto il conto al cameriere. I asked the waiter for the bill.
□ Mi ha chiesto degli spiccioli. He asked me for some change.
■ **chiedere di qualcuno** to ask after somebody □ Tutti i miei amici chiedono di te. All my friends are asking after you.
■ **C'è un certo Andrea che chiede di te.** Someone called Andrea is looking for you.
■ **chiedere scusa a qualcuno** to apologize to somebody □ Ho chiesto scusa a Marco. I apologized to Marco.
■ **chiedersi** to wonder □ Mi chiedo cosa stia facendo. I wonder what she's doing.

la **chiesa** FEM NOUN
church
□ Va in chiesa ogni domenica. He goes to church every Sunday.

il **chilo** MASC NOUN
kilo
□ quarantacinque chili forty five kilos □ mezzo chilo di ciliegie half a kilo of cherries

il **chilometro** MASC NOUN
kilometre
□ cinquanta chilometri all'ora thirty miles per hour
■ **Abbiamo fatto chilometri a piedi.** We walked miles.

la **chimica** FEM NOUN
chemistry
□ la professoressa di chimica the chemistry teacher

il **chimico** (PL i **chimici**) MASC NOUN
chemist

chinarsi VERB [56]
to bend down
□ Si è chinata a raccogliere la borsa. She bent down to pick up the bag.

la **chiocciola** FEM NOUN
1 snail
2 @ sign
■ **scala a chiocciola** spiral staircase

il **chiodo** MASC NOUN
nail

il **chiosco** (PL i **chioschi**) MASC NOUN
kiosk

il **chirurgo** (PL i **chirurghi**) MASC NOUN
surgeon
□ Fa il chirurgo. He is a surgeon.

chissà ADVERB
I wonder
□ Chissà se verrà alla festa. I wonder if he'll come to the party. □ Chissà chi gliel'ha detto. I wonder who told him.

la **chitarra** FEM NOUN
guitar
□ una chitarra elettrica an electric guitar
□ Suona la chitarra. He plays the guitar.

il/la **chitarrista** (MASC PL i **chitarristi**, FEM PL le **chitarriste**) MASC/FEM NOUN
guitarist

chiudere VERB [20]
1 to close
□ Chiudi la finestra, per favore. Close the window please. □ A che ora chiude il negozio? What time does the shop close? □ La fabbrica ha chiuso due anni fa. The factory closed two years ago. □ Il centro è stato chiuso al traffico. The town centre is closed to traffic.
■ **Con lui ho chiuso.** I've finished with him.
■ **chiudersi** to close □ La porta si è chiusa. The door closed.
■ **chiudere a chiave** to lock □ Sei sicuro di aver chiuso a chiave? Are you sure you locked it?
2 to turn off
□ Ricordati di chiudere il gas. Remember to turn off the gas. □ Chiudi bene il rubinetto. Turn the tap off properly.

chiunque PRONOUN
1 whoever
□ Chiunque l'abbia fatto ha sbagliato. Whoever did it made a mistake.
■ **chiunque sia** whoever it is □ Chiunque sia, digli che non ci sono. Whoever it is, tell them I'm not here.
2 anyone

□ Attacca discorso con chiunque. She'll talk to anyone.

chiuso (FEM **chiusa**) ADJECTIVE
1 closed
□ una finestra chiusa a closed window □ La porta era chiusa. The door was closed. □ La banca è chiusa per sciopero. The bank is closed because of a strike.
■ **a occhi chiusi** with one's eyes closed □ Lo saprei fare ad occhi chiusi. I could do it with my eyes closed.
2 locked
□ La porta era chiusa. The door was locked.
□ Sono rimasto chiuso fuori. I was locked out.
■ **chiuso a chiave** locked
3 quiet
□ un ragazzo molto chiuso a very quiet boy
4 blocked-up
□ Ho il naso chiuso. I've got a blocked-up nose.

la **chiusura** FEM NOUN
■ **chiusura lampo** zip
■ **a chiusura ermetica** airtight □ un recipiente a chiusura ermetica an airtight container
■ **orario di chiusura** closing time

ci PRONOUN
▷ see also **ci** ADVERB

■ LANGUAGE TIP **ci** becomes **ce** before **lo, la, li, le** and **ne**.

1 us
□ Ci hanno visto. They saw us. □ Ci chiamava. He was calling to us. □ Ci sembrava una buona idea. It seemed a good idea to us. □ Ci ha sorriso. He smiled at us.
2 ourselves
□ Ci siamo preparati. We prepared ourselves.
■ LANGUAGE TIP **ci** is often not translated.
□ Ci siamo stancati. We got tired. □ Ci siamo lavati i denti. We brushed our teeth.
3 each other
□ Ci vogliamo bene. We love each other.
■ **Ci vediamo domani!** See you tomorrow!
4 it
□ Non ci credo. I don't believe it. □ Ci penserò. I'll think about it. □ Ci puoi scommettere. You can bet on it. □ Cosa c'entra? What's that got to do with it?

ci ADVERB
▷ see also **ci** PRONOUN
1 there
□ Ci sei mai stato? Have you ever been there?
■ LANGUAGE TIP **ci** is often not translated.
□ Ci andrò domani. I'll go tomorrow.
2 here
□ Qui non ci torno più! I'm not coming back here again!

la **ciabatta** FEM NOUN
1 slipper
2 ciabatta

ciao EXCLAMATION
1 hello!
2 goodbye!

ciascuno (FEM **ciascuna**) ADJECTIVE, PRONOUN
each
□ Ciascun candidato deve presentare un tema. Each candidate has to submit an essay.
□ Costano cinquanta euro ciascuno. They cost fifty euros each.

il **cibo** MASC NOUN
food

la **cicatrice** FEM NOUN
scar

il **ciccione**, la **cicciona** MASC/FEM NOUN
fatty

il **ciclamino** MASC NOUN
cyclamen

il **ciclismo** MASC NOUN
cycling

il/la **ciclista** (MASC PL i **ciclisti**, FEM PL le **cicliste**) MASC/FEM NOUN
cyclist
□ un ciclista professionista a professional cyclist

il **ciclo** MASC NOUN
1 series
□ un ciclo di film a series of films
2 cycle

la **cicogna** FEM NOUN
stork

la **cieca** (PL le **cieche**) FEM NOUN
blind woman

cieco (FEM **cieca**, MASC PL **ciechi**, FEM PL **cieche**) ADJECTIVE
▷ see also **cieco** NOUN
blind
□ Il mio cane è cieco da un occhio. My dog's blind in one eye.

il **cieco** (PL i **ciechi**) MASC NOUN
▷ see also **cieco** ADJECTIVE
blind man
■ **i ciechi** blind people

il **cielo** MASC NOUN
sky
□ un cielo azzurro a blue sky
■ **Santo cielo!** Good heavens!

la **cifra** FEM NOUN
figure
□ un numero di cinque cifre a five-figure number
■ **scrivere un numero in cifre** to write a number in figures
■ **L'ha pagato una bella cifra.** He paid a lot for it.

il **ciglio** MASC NOUN
1 eyelash
□ ciglia finte false eyelashes
2 edge
□ sul ciglio della strada at the edge of the road

il **cigno** MASC NOUN
swan

la **ciliegia** (PLle **ciliegie** or le **ciliege**) FEM NOUN
cherry
□ marmellata di ciliegie cherry jam

il **cilindro** MASC NOUN
1 cylinder
2 top hat

la **cima** FEM NOUN
1 top
□ sulla cima del monte on the top of the mountain □ Si è posato sulla cima dell'albero. It landed in the top of the tree. □ Sono in cima alla classifica. They're at the top of the league.
■ **da cima a fondo** from top to bottom
□ Hanno perquisito la casa da cima a fondo. They searched the house from top to bottom.
■ **L'ho letto da cima a fondo.** I read it from beginning to end.
■ **essere una cima** to be a genius □ Non è una cima, ma se la cava. He's not a genius, but he does OK.
2 peak

il **cimitero** MASC NOUN
graveyard

la **Cina** FEM NOUN
China

cincin EXCLAMATION
cheers!

il **cinema** (PL i **cinema**) MASC NOUN
cinema
□ Andiamo al cinema? Shall we go to the cinema? □ Cosa danno al cinema stasera? What's on at the cinema tonight?

cinese (FEM **cinese**) ADJECTIVE
▷ see also **cinese** MASC NOUN, FEM NOUN
Chinese

il **cinese** MASC NOUN
▷ see also **cinese** FEM NOUN, ADJECTIVE
1 Chinese man
■ **i cinesi** the Chinese
2 Chinese (language)
□ Parla cinese. She speaks Chinese.

la **cinese** FEM NOUN
▷ see also **cinese** MASC NOUN, ADJECTIVE
Chinese woman

la **cinghia** FEM NOUN
1 strap (on suitcase, rucksack)
2 belt

il **cinghiale** MASC NOUN
wild boar

cinquanta NUMBER
fifty
□ Ha cinquant'anni. He is fifty.

cinquantesimo (FEM **cinquantesima**) ADJECTIVE, MASC NOUN
fiftieth

la **cinquantina** FEM NOUN
about fifty

□ È sulla cinquantina. He's about fifty.

cinque NUMBER
five

□ Ha cinque anni. She is five. □ le cinque di sera five o'clock in the evening □ Eravamo in cinque. There were five of us.

■ **il cinque dicembre** the fifth of December

cinquecento NUMBER
five hundred

□ cinquecento sterline five hundred pounds

■ **il Cinquecento** the sixteenth century

la **cintura** FEM NOUN
belt

□ una cintura di pelle a leather belt

■ **cintura di sicurezza** seat belt □ Allacciati la cintura di sicurezza. Fasten your seat belt.

il **cinturino** MASC NOUN
strap *(of watch, shoe)*

ciò PRONOUN
this

□ Ciò significa che... This means that... □ Da ciò deduco che... From this I deduce that... □ Di ciò parleremo più tardi. We'll talk about this later.

■ **ciò che** what □ L'hanno sgridato per ciò che ha fatto. He got told off for what he did.

■ **ciò nonostante** anyway □ Aveva la febbre e ciò nonostante è uscito. He had a temperature, but went out anyway.

■ **E con ciò?** So what?

la **cioccolata** FEM NOUN
chocolate

□ una tavoletta di cioccolata a bar of chocolate □ Io vorrei una cioccolata calda. I'd like a hot chocolate.

il **cioccolatino** MASC NOUN
chocolate

□ una scatola di cioccolatini a box of chocolates

il **cioccolato** MASC NOUN
chocolate

■ **cioccolato al latte** milk chocolate

■ **cioccolato fondente** plain chocolate

cioè ADVERB
that is

□ Partirò il tredici, cioè domenica prossima. I'm leaving on the thirteenth, that's next Sunday.

■ **Vengo tra poco. — Cioè?** I'll come in a bit. — Meaning...?

la **ciotola** FEM NOUN
bowl

la **cipolla** FEM NOUN
onion

il **cipresso** MASC NOUN
cypress

circa ADVERB, PREPOSITION
about

□ Costerà circa venti sterline. It'll cost about twenty pounds. □ Sarà mezzogiorno circa. It must be about twelve o'clock. □ Non mi ha detto niente circa i suoi progetti. He didn't tell me anything about his plans.

il **circo** (PL i **circhi**) MASC NOUN
circus

circolare VERB [68, AUX **avere** OR **essere**]
▷ *see also* **circolare** ADJECTIVE, NOUN

1 to pass round

□ Ne ha fatto circolare una copia in classe. She passed a copy round the class.

2 to drive

□ Circolare in città diventa sempre più difficile. Driving in town is getting more and more difficult.

■ **Circola voce che...** There's a rumour going round that...

circolare (FEM **circolare**) ADJECTIVE
▷ *see also* **circolare** VERB, NOUN
circular

□ un movimento circolare a circular movement

la **circolare** FEM NOUN
▷ *see also* **circolare** VERB, ADJECTIVE
circular

□ Ha inviato una circolare. He's sent out a circular.

il **circolo** MASC NOUN

1 circle

■ **un circolo vizioso** a vicious circle

2 club

□ un circolo giovanile a youth club

circondare VERB [68]
to surround

□ La polizia aveva circondato il palazzo. The police had surrounded the building.

la **circonvallazione** FEM NOUN
ring road

la **circostanza** FEM NOUN
circumstance

□ Date le circostanze, è un buon risultato. In the circumstances, it's a good result.

il **circuito** MASC NOUN
circuit

□ televisione a circuito chiuso closed-circuit television

■ **fare corto circuito** to short-circuit

il **citofono** MASC NOUN

1 entry phone

2 intercom

la **città** (PL le **città**) FEM NOUN

1 town

□ Abiti in città o in campagna? Do you live in town or in the country? □ Ti faccio visitare la città. I'll show you round the town.

■ **la mia città** my home town

2 city
□ Firenze è una bella città. Florence is a beautiful city.

la **cittadinanza** FEM NOUN
citizenship
□ Ha la cittadinanza britannica. He has British citizenship.

il **cittadino**, la **cittadina** MASC/FEM NOUN
citizen

il **ciuccio** MASC NOUN
dummy

il **ciuffo** MASC NOUN
strand

la **civetta** FEM NOUN
owl

civile (FEM **civile**) ADJECTIVE
civil
■ **un paese civile** a civilized country

la **civiltà** (PL le **civiltà**) FEM NOUN
civilization
□ un'antica civiltà an ancient civilization

il **clacson** (PL i **clacson**) MASC NOUN
horn
■ **suonare il clacson** to sound the horn

la **classe** FEM NOUN
1 class
□ Che classe fai? What class are you in?
□ Viaggiano in prima classe? Do they travel first class? □ un mio compagno di classe a boy in my class
2 classroom
□ Siamo rimasti in classe durante l'intervallo. We stayed in the classroom during the break.

classico (FEM **classica**, MASC PL **classici**, FEM PL **classiche**) ADJECTIVE
▷ see also **classico** NOUN
classical
□ Non mi piace la musica classica. I don't like classical music.
■ **liceo classico** school specializing in classical subjects

il **classico** (PL i **classici**) MASC NOUN
▷ see also **classico** ADJECTIVE
classic
□ un classico del cinema francese a classic of the French cinema

la **classifica** (PL le **classifiche**) FEM NOUN
1 results pl
□ la classifica finale the final results
2 charts pl
3 league table
■ **essere primo in classifica** **1** to come first **2** to be number one in the charts **3** to be top of the league

la **clavicola** FEM NOUN
collarbone
□ Si è fratturato la clavicola. He broke his collarbone.

cliccare VERB [18]
■ **cliccare su** to click on

il/la **cliente** MASC/FEM NOUN
1 customer
□ Il negozio era pieno di clienti. The shop was full of customers.
2 client

il **clima** (PL i **climi**) MASC NOUN
climate

la **clinica** (PL le **cliniche**) FEM NOUN
1 private hospital
2 department

cloud (FEM+PL **cloud**) ADJECTIVE
cloud (in computing)
□ applicazioni cloud cloud applications

la **coca** FEM NOUN
coke

la **cocaina** FEM NOUN
cocaine

il/la **cocainomane** MASC/FEM NOUN
cocaine addict
□ È un cocainomane. He's a cocaine addict.

la **coccinella** FEM NOUN
ladybird

il **cocco** MASC NOUN
coconut
□ gelato al cocco coconut ice cream
■ **noce di cocco** coconut

il **coccodrillo** MASC NOUN
crocodile

le **coccole** FEM PL NOUN
■ **fare le coccole a qualcuno** to give somebody a cuddle

il **cocomero** MASC NOUN
watermelon

la **coda** FEM NOUN
1 tail
2 queue
■ **mettersi in coda** to join the queue
□ Prendi il vassoio e mettiti in coda. Take a tray and join the queue.
■ **fare la coda** to queue □ La coda si fa da questa parte. Queue this side.
■ **guardare con la coda dell'occhio** to look out of the corner of one's eye □ Mi guardava con la coda dell'occhio. She was looking at me out of the corner of her eye.
■ **coda di cavallo** ponytail □ Ha la coda di cavallo. She's got a ponytail.

il **codice** MASC NOUN
code
□ un messaggio in codice a message in code
■ **codice postale** postcode □ Sai qual è il codice postale? Do you know what the postcode is?
■ **codice della strada** highway code

il **codino** MASC NOUN
ponytail

c

□ Ha il codino. He's got a ponytail.

coetaneo (FEM **coetanea**) ADJECTIVE
■ **essere coetaneo di...** to be the same age as... □ Ma allora siamo coetanei! So we're the same age!

il **cofano** MASC NOUN
bonnet

cogliere VERB [21]
to pick
□ Ho colto una mela dall'albero. I picked an apple off the tree.
■ **cogliere qualcuno sul fatto** to catch somebody red-handed □ L'ho colto sul fatto. I caught him red-handed.

la **cognata** FEM NOUN
sister-in-law

il **cognato** MASC NOUN
brother-in-law

il **cognome** MASC NOUN
surname
□ Come ti chiami di cognome? What's your surname?

la **coincidenza** FEM NOUN
1 coincidence
□ Che coincidenza, vado anch'io a Bologna. What a coincidence, I'm going to Bologna too.
2 connection
□ Ho perso la coincidenza. I missed my connection.

coinvolgere VERB [91]
to involve
□ Non mi coinvolgere in questa storia. Don't involve me in this business.

il **colapasta** (PL i **colapasta**) MASC NOUN
colander

colare VERB [68]
1 to drain
□ Hai colato la pasta? Have you drained the pasta?
2 to strain

la **colazione** FEM NOUN
breakfast
□ Cosa mangi a colazione? What do you have for breakfast?
■ **fare colazione** to have breakfast
■ **colazione all'inglese** English breakfast

il **colino** MASC NOUN
strainer

la **colla** FEM NOUN
glue
□ un tubetto di colla a tube of glue

collaborare VERB [68]
1 to work together
□ Tu e Luca dovete cercare di collaborare. You and Luca must try to work together.
2 to work
□ Ho collaborato ad un progetto molto interessante. I worked on a very interesting project.

il **collaboratore**, la **collaboratrice**
MASC/FEM NOUN
1 member of a team
□ tutti i nostri collaboratori all the members of our team
■ **È uno dei nostri collaboratori più validi.** He's one of our best people.
■ **Stiamo cercando due collaboratori per questo progetto.** We're looking for two people to work on this project.
■ **collaboratrice domestica** home help
■ **collaboratore esterno** freelancer
2 contributor

la **collana** FEM NOUN
necklace

il **collant** (PL i **collant**) MASC NOUN
tights pl
□ un paio di collant a pair of tights

il **collare** MASC NOUN
collar

il **collasso** MASC NOUN
collapse
■ **avere un collasso** to collapse □ Ha avuto un collasso mentre giocava a pallone. He collapsed while playing football.

il/la **collega** (MASC PL i **colleghi**, FEM PL le **colleghe**) MASC/FEM NOUN
colleague
□ un suo collega a colleague of hers

il **collegamento** MASC NOUN
link

collegare VERB [76]
1 to connect
□ Devi collegare la stampante al computer. You have to connect the printer to the computer.
■ **collegarsi a** to connect to
2 to link
□ L'autostrada collega Bologna a Firenze. The motorway links Bologna and Florence.

il **collegio** (PL i **collegi**) MASC NOUN
boarding school

la **collera** FEM NOUN
■ **essere in collera con qualcuno** to be angry with somebody

la **colletta** FEM NOUN
collection
□ Abbiamo fatto una colletta per comprarle un regalo. We had a collection to buy her a present.

il **colletto** MASC NOUN
collar

collezionare VERB [68]
to collect
□ Colleziono cartoline da tutto il mondo. I collect postcards from all over the world.

la **collezione** FEM NOUN
collection

□ una collezione di francobolli a collection of stamps

■ **fare collezione di qualcosa** to collect something

la **collina** FEM NOUN
hill

il **collirio** MASC NOUN
eyedrops *pl*

□ Vorrei un collirio. I'd like some eyedrops.

il **collo** MASC NOUN
neck

□ Portava un foulard al collo. She had a scarf round her neck.

■ **essere nei guai fino al collo** to be in deep trouble

■ **maglione a collo alto** polo neck jumper

il **colloquio** MASC NOUN
interview

□ Domani ha un colloquio di lavoro. She's got a job interview tomorrow.

il **colombo** MASC NOUN
pigeon

la **colonia** FEM NOUN
colony

□ Era una colonia britannica. It was a British colony.

■ **colonia marina** seaside summer camp

la **colonna** FEM NOUN
column

□ le colonne di un tempio the columns of a temple

■ **colonna sonora** soundtrack

■ **colonna vertebrale** spine

il **colonnello** MASC NOUN
colonel

colorato (FEM **colorata**) ADJECTIVE
coloured

□ una camicia colorata a coloured shirt □ una maglietta molto colorata a brightly coloured T-shirt

il **colore** MASC NOUN
colour

□ Di che colore è? What colour is it? □ un cappotto color ruggine a rust-coloured coat

■ **TV a colori** colour TV

■ **di colore** black

■ **diventare di tutti i colori** to go red □ È diventato di tutti i colori per l'imbarazzo. He went red with embarrassment.

■ **farne di tutti i colori** to get up to all sorts of things □ In gita ne abbiamo fatte di tutti i colori. On the trip we got up to all sorts of things.

la **colpa** FEM NOUN

1 fault

□ Di chi è la colpa? Whose fault is it? □ È colpa mia. It's my fault. □ L'incidente è successo per colpa sua. The accident was his fault. □ Per

colpa sua non possiamo uscire. It's his fault we can't go out.

■ **sentirsi in colpa** to feel guilty □ Mi sento in colpa. I feel guilty.

2 blame

■ **addossarsi la colpa** to take the blame □ Si è addossato la colpa. He took the blame.

■ **dare la colpa a qualcuno** to blame somebody □ Non dare la colpa a me! Don't blame me!

colpevole (FEM **colpevole**) ADJECTIVE
▷ *see also* **colpevole** NOUN
guilty

□ colpevole di omicidio guilty of murder

il/la **colpevole** MASC/FEM NOUN
▷ *see also* **colpevole** ADJECTIVE
culprit

□ Non hanno trovato il colpevole. They haven't found the culprit.

colpire VERB [51]

1 to hit

□ È stata colpita alla testa. She was hit on the head.

■ **colpire qualcuno con un pugno** to punch somebody

2 to strike

□ Qual è la cosa che ti ha colpito di più? What's the thing that struck you most?

■ **rimanere colpito da qualcosa** to be shocked by something □ Sono rimasto colpito dalla sua reazione. I was shocked by his reaction.

il **colpo** MASC NOUN

1 blow

□ un colpo in testa a blow on the head □ Il divorzio dei suoi è stato un brutto colpo per lei. Her parents' divorce was a terrible blow for her.

■ **Mi hai fatto venire un colpo!** You gave me a fright!

■ **Ti venisse un colpo!** Drop dead!

■ **dare un colpo a qualcuno** to hit somebody □ Gli ha dato un colpo in testa. He hit him on the head.

■ **di colpo** suddenly □ Si è fermato di colpo. He stopped suddenly.

■ **sul colpo** instantly □ È morto sul colpo. He died instantly.

■ **fare colpo** to be a hit □ Hai fatto colpo sulla mia amica! You were a hit with my friend!

■ **colpo d'aria** chill □ Ho preso un colpo d'aria. I've caught a chill.

■ **colpo di fulmine** love at first sight □ È stato un colpo di fulmine. It was love at first sight.

■ **colpo di telefono** ring □ Ti do un colpo di telefono domani sera. I'll give you a ring tomorrow evening.

2 shot

□ Abbiamo sentito dei colpi. **We heard shots.**
  ■ **sparare un colpo** to fire □ Ha sparato dei colpi in aria. **He fired into the air.**
3 raid
  □ un colpo in banca **a bank raid**
il **coltello** MASC NOUN
  knife
coltivare VERB [68]
  to grow
  □ Coltivavano pomodori. **They grew tomatoes.**
colto (FEM **colta**) ADJECTIVE
  well-educated
  □ una persona molto colta **a very well-educated person**
il **coma** (PL i **coma**) MASC NOUN
  coma
  □ È entrato in coma. **He's gone into a coma.**
  ■ **Oggi sono in coma!** **I'm half dead today!**
il **comandante** MASC NOUN
  captain
comandare VERB [68]
1 to be the boss
  □ È lei che comanda in casa. **She's the boss in the house.**
2 to command
combattere VERB [1]
  to fight
  □ Hanno sempre combattuto contro l'ingiustizia. **They've always fought against injustice.**
combinare VERB [68]
  to do
  □ Che cosa stai combinando? **What are you doing?**
  ■ **Che cosa hai combinato?** **What have you gone and done?**
  ■ **Oggi non ho combinato nulla.** **I haven't got anything done today.**
combinato (FEM **combinata**) ADJECTIVE
  ■ **matrimonio combinato** arranged marriage
la **combinazione** FEM NOUN
1 combination
2 coincidence
  □ Che combinazione! **What a coincidence!**
  ■ **per combinazione** by chance □ Per combinazione era lì anche lui. **By chance he was there too.**
come ADVERB, CONJUNCTION
1 how
  □ Come stai? **How are you?** □ Com'è andato il viaggio? **How was the journey?** □ Com'è successo? **How did it happen?** □ Mi ha spiegato come l'ha conosciuto. **She told me how she met him.**
  ■ **Com'è carino!** **Isn't it pretty!**
  ■ **Come mai?** **1** How come? **2** Why?
2 what
  □ Scusa, come hai detto? **Sorry, what did you say?**

□ Ma come! Aveva detto che sarebbe venuto! **What! He said he'd come!** □ Come ti chiami? **What's your name?** □ Com'è la tua città? **What's your town like?** □ Com'è la cucina scozzese? **What's Scottish food like?** □ Come sarebbe a dire? **What do you mean?**
  ■ **Come?** Sorry?
3 like
  □ Ne ho uno come il tuo. **I've got one like yours.** □ Piangeva come un bambino. **He was crying like a child.**
4 as
  □ Ho fatto come hai detto tu. **I did as you said.** □ bianco come la neve **white as snow** □ Mi piace così com'è. **I like it as it is.** □ come puoi ben vedere **as you can see** □ come sai **as you know**
  ■ **come se** as if □ Sì, come se non lo sapessi! **Yes, as if you didn't know!**
  ■ **come se niente fosse** as if nothing had happened □ Si comportava come se niente fosse. **He behaved as if nothing had happened.**
  ■ **come non detto** let's forget it □ Va bene, come non detto. **OK, let's forget it.**
  ■ **A come Andrea** A for Andrew
comico (FEM **comica**, MASC PL **comici**, FEM PL **comiche**) ADJECTIVE
  ▷ see also **comico** NOUN
  funny
  □ una scena comica **a funny scene**
il **comico** (PL i **comici**) MASC NOUN
  ▷ see also **comico** ADJECTIVE
  comedian
  □ È un comico famoso. **He's a well-known comedian.**
cominciare VERB [13]
  to start
  □ Il film comincia con un'esplosione. **The film starts with an explosion.** □ Hai cominciato il libro che ti ho prestato? **Have you started the book I lent you?** □ La prima parola comincia per F. **The first word starts with F.** □ Ha cominciato a ridere. **She started to laugh.** □ Ha cominciato a piangere. **She started crying.**
  ■ **tanto per cominciare** in the first place □ Tanto per cominciare non sappiamo se funzionerà. **In the first place we don't know if it'll work.**
  ■ **Cominciamo bene!** This is a fine start!
la **comitiva** FEM NOUN
  group
  □ una comitiva di turisti **a group of tourists**
  ■ **sconto per comitive** group discount
la **commedia** FEM NOUN
1 play
2 comedy
commerciale (FEM **commerciale**) ADJECTIVE
  commercial

□ le attività industriali e commerciali industrial and commercial activities

■ **un'attività commerciale** a business

■ **avere rapporti commerciali con** to trade with

il/la **commerciante** MASC/FEM NOUN
shopkeeper

□ i commercianti del centro the shopkeepers in the town centre

■ **commerciante all'ingrosso** wholesaler

il **commercio** MASC NOUN
trade

□ commercio all'ingrosso wholesale trade

■ **economia e commercio** economics and business

il **commesso**, la **commessa** MASC/FEM
NOUN
shop assistant

□ Fa la commessa. She is a shop assistant.

il **commissario** (PL i **commissari**) MASC
NOUN

■ **commissario di polizia** police superintendent

■ **commissario tecnico** national team manager

la **commissione** FEM NOUN
commission

□ Ha una commissione sulle vendite. He gets commission on sales.

■ **la Commissione europea** the European Commission

■ **commissione esaminatrice** panel of examiners

commovente (FEM **commovente**)
ADJECTIVE
moving

□ una storia commovente a moving story

la **commozione** FEM NOUN
emotion

□ Non riusciva a nascondere la commozione. He couldn't hide his emotion.

■ **Si è messa a piangere per la commozione.** She got emotional and started to cry.

commuoversi VERB [62, aux essere]
to get emotional

□ Si è commossa. She got emotional.

il **comò** (PL i **comò**) MASC NOUN
chest of drawers

il **comodino** MASC NOUN
bedside table

la **comodità** (PL le **comodità**) FEM NOUN
convenience

□ la comodità di abitare in centro the convenience of living in the town centre

■ **Ho la comodità di avere la fermata sotto casa.** Conveniently for me, the stop is outside my house.

comodo (FEM **comoda**) ADJECTIVE

1 comfortable

□ una poltrona comoda a comfortable chair

□ Stai comodo lì? Are you comfortable there?

■ **State comodi!** Please don't get up!

2 easy

□ È comodo dare la colpa agli altri. It's easy to blame other people.

3 convenient

□ Sarebbe più comodo incontrarci qui. It would be more convenient to meet here.

■ **far comodo** to be a help □ Quei soldi mi hanno fatto proprio comodo. That money was a great help.

la **compagnia** FEM NOUN
company

□ Lavora in una compagnia di assicurazioni. He works in an insurance company.

■ **fare compagnia a qualcuno** to keep somebody company □ Quand'era malato andavo a fargli compagnia. When he was ill I used to go and keep him company.

■ **essere di compagnia** to be sociable

□ È un tipo di compagnia. He's a sociable kind of person.

il **compagno**, la **compagna** MASC/FEM
NOUN

1 classmate

□ È una mia compagna di scuola. She's one of my classmates.

■ **un mio compagno di classe** a boy in my class

■ **un compagno di squadra** a team-mate

2 partner

il **compenso** MASC NOUN
payment

■ **È brutto ma in compenso è molto simpatico.** He's not handsome, but he's very nice.

■ **Ha un lavoro noiosissimo. In compenso è pagato molto bene.** His job is very boring – the plus side is that it's very well paid.

le **compere** FEM PL NOUN

■ **andare a fare le compere** to go shopping

la **competizione** FEM NOUN
competition

compiere VERB [22]

■ **Quando compi gli anni?** When is your birthday?

■ **Quanti anni compi?** How old will you be?

■ **Ho compiuto sedici anni il mese scorso.** I was sixteen last month.

compilare VERB [68]
to fill in

□ Compila il modulo in stampatello. Fill in the form in block letters.

il **compito** MASC NOUN

1 test

□ Domani c'è il compito in classe di matematica. We've got a maths test tomorrow.

2 homework

■ **fare i compiti** to do one's homework

□ Non posso, devo fare i compiti. I can't, I've got to do my homework.

3 job

□ A me è toccato il compito di portare le bibite. It was my job to bring the drinks.

il **compleanno** MASC NOUN
birthday

□ Buon compleanno! Happy birthday!

complesso (FEM **complessa**) ADJECTIVE
▷ see also **complesso** NOUN
complex

□ un problema complesso a complex problem

il **complesso** MASC NOUN
▷ see also **complesso** ADJECTIVE

1 complex

□ un complesso d'inferiorità an inferiority complex □ Ha il complesso del naso grosso. She's got a complex about the size of her nose.

2 band

□ Suona in un complesso. He plays in a band.

■ **nel complesso** on the whole □ Nel complesso mi è piaciuto abbastanza. On the whole I quite liked it.

completamente ADVERB
completely

completo (FEM **completa**) ADJECTIVE
▷ see also **completo** NOUN
complete

□ È stato un disastro completo! It was a complete disaster! □ un frullatore completo di accessori a blender complete with accessories

■ **al completo** full □ L'albergo era al completo. The hotel was full.

il **completo** MASC NOUN
▷ see also **completo** ADJECTIVE
suit

□ Portava un completo grigio. He was wearing a grey suit.

■ **completo da sci** ski suit

complicato (FEM **complicata**) ADJECTIVE
complicated

□ una faccenda complicata a complicated affair □ È un po' complicato da spiegare. It's a bit complicated to explain.

il/la **complice** MASC/FEM NOUN
accomplice

la **complicità** (PL le **complicità**) FEM NOUN
collusion

il **complimento** MASC NOUN
compliment

■ **fare un complimento a qualcuno** to pay somebody a compliment

■ **Complimenti!** Congratulations!

□ Complimenti per la promozione!

Congratulations on your promotion!

┃ **LANGUAGE TIP complimenti** is sometimes not translated.

□ Complimenti, parli molto bene l'italiano! You speak very good Italian! □ Complimenti, che bella casa! Your house is lovely!

il **complotto** MASC NOUN
plot

comporre VERB [73]

1 to dial

□ Alzare il ricevitore e comporre il numero. Lift the receiver and dial the number.

2 to compose

□ Ha composto la colonna sonora. He composed the soundtrack.

■ **essere composto da** to consist of

□ La casa è composta da tre stanze. The house consists of three rooms.

il **comportamento** MASC NOUN
behaviour

□ Non capisco il suo comportamento. I don't understand her behaviour.

comportarsi VERB [56]
to behave

□ Si è comportato da vigliacco. He behaved like a coward. □ Non si è comportato molto bene con me. He didn't behave very well towards me.

comprare VERB [68]
to buy

□ Cosa hai comprato? What did you buy? □ Ho comprato un regalino per mia sorella. I bought a little present for my sister.

comprensivo (FEM **comprensiva**) ADJECTIVE
understanding

□ È molto comprensivo. He's very understanding.

┃ **LANGUAGE TIP** Be careful! **comprensivo** doesn't mean **comprehensive**.

compreso (FEM **compresa**) ADJECTIVE
inclusive

□ dall'otto al ventidue compreso from the eighth to the twenty-second inclusive

■ **È aperto tutta la settimana, domenica compresa.** It's open all week, including Sunday.

■ **tutto compreso** all-inclusive □ La vacanza, tutto compreso, costa mille euro. The holiday costs one thousand euros, all-inclusive.

comunale (FEM **comunale**) ADJECTIVE

■ **palazzo comunale** town hall

■ **Fa l'impiegato comunale.** He works for the council.

comune (FEM **comune**) ADJECTIVE
▷ see also **comune** NOUN
common

□ È un problema molto comune. It's a very common problem.

il comune MASC NOUN
▷ see also **comune** ADJECTIVE
1 council
□ Lavora per il comune. She works for the council.
2 town hall
□ Devi andare al comune per richiedere il certificato. You have to go to the town hall to get the certificate.
■ **avere in comune** to have in common
□ Non abbiamo niente in comune. We haven't got anything in common.
■ **Abbiamo un amico in comune.** We've got a mutual friend.

la comunione FEM NOUN
■ **prima comunione** first communion

la comunità (PL le **comunità**) FEM NOUN
community
□ C'è una grossa comunità britannica in Toscana. There's a big British community in Tuscany.
■ **Comunità Europea** European Community

comunque ADVERB, CONJUNCTION
anyway
□ I miei non vogliono, ma ci vado comunque. My parents don't want me to, but I'm going anyway. □ Comunque, avresti potuto telefonare. Anyway, you could have phoned.
■ **Comunque vada...** However it turns out...
□ Comunque vada, sono contento che sia finita. However it turns out, I'm glad it's over.

con PREPOSITION
1 with
□ Ci andrò con lei. I'll go with her. □ Con chi sei stato? Who were you with? □ un ragazzo con gli occhi azzurri a boy with blue eyes
■ **con la forza** by force
■ **Con questo freddo non potremo partire.** We can't set off in this cold weather.
■ **E con questo?** So what?
2 to
□ È sposata con uno scozzese. She's married to a Scot. □ Hai parlato con lui? Have you spoken to him? □ È gentile con tutti. She's nice to everybody.

concentrarsi VERB [56]
to concentrate
□ Non riuscivo a concentrarmi. I couldn't concentrate.

il concerto MASC NOUN
concert

il concetto MASC NOUN
idea
□ Non ho afferrato bene il concetto. I haven't quite got the idea.

la conchiglia FEM NOUN
shell

conciare VERB [13]
to make a mess of

□ Come hai conciato quei jeans! What a mess you've made of those jeans!
■ **Ma come ti sei conciato?** 1 What on earth have you got on? 2 How did you get into that state?

il/la concorrente MASC/FEM NOUN
1 competitor
2 contestant

la concorrenza FEM NOUN
competition

il concorso MASC NOUN
exam
■ **concorso a premi** competition □ Ha partecipato a un concorso a premi ed ha vinto. She went in for a competition and won.
■ **concorso di bellezza** beauty contest

concreto (FEM **concreta**) ADJECTIVE
concrete
□ una prova concreta concrete evidence
■ **in concreto** actually □ Ma cosa fa in concreto? What's he actually doing?

condannare VERB [68]
1 to sentence
□ L'hanno condannato a cinque anni di prigione. He's been sentenced to five years in prison.
■ **condannare qualcuno per** to convict somebody of □ Li hanno condannati per rapina a mano armata. They were convicted of armed robbery.
2 to condemn
□ Non me la sento di condannarlo. I don't condemn him.

condire VERB [51]
1 to dress (salad)
2 to season
■ **una salsa per condire la pasta** a sauce for pasta

condividere VERB [40]
to share
□ Condivide l'appartamento con il fratello. He shares the flat with his brother.
■ **condividere l'opinione di qualcuno** to agree with somebody □ Non condivido le tue opinioni. I don't agree with you.

la condizione FEM NOUN
condition
□ Lo farò ad una sola condizione. I'll do it on one condition.
■ **Non sei in condizione di guidare.** You're not in a fit state to drive.
■ **in buone condizioni** in good condition
□ La macchina è ancora in buone condizioni. The car is still in good condition.

il/la conducente MASC/FEM NOUN
driver
□ il conducente dell'autobus the bus driver

la conferenza FEM NOUN
1 conference

□ una conferenza sull'inquinamento atmosferico a conference on air pollution

■ **conferenza stampa** press conference

2 lecture

□ Terrà una conferenza nell'aula magna. He's going to give a lecture in the main hall.

confermare VERB [68]

to confirm

□ Devo confermare la prenotazione. I've got to confirm the booking. □ Ha confermato che verrà. He's confirmed that he's coming.

confessare VERB [68]

to confess

□ L'assassino ha confessato. The murderer has confessed. □ Ti confesso che... I must confess that...

■ **andare a confessarsi** to go to confession

il confetto MASC NOUN

sugared almond

la confettura FEM NOUN

jam

la confezione FEM NOUN

packet

□ una confezione di caramelle a packet of sweets

■ **confezione risparmio** economy size

■ **fare una confezione regalo** to giftwrap □ Mi può fare una confezione regalo? Can you giftwrap it for me?

conficcare VERB [18]

■ **conficcare in** to stick into □ Mi si è conficcata una spina nel dito. A thorn stuck into my finger.

confidare VERB [68]

■ **confidare qualcosa a qualcuno** to tell somebody something □ Ti voglio confidare un segreto. I want to tell you a secret.

■ **confidarsi con** to confide in □ Aveva bisogno di confidarsi con qualcuno. She needed to confide in somebody.

il confine MASC NOUN

border

□ Abbiamo passato il confine. We crossed the border.

il conflitto MASC NOUN

conflict

confondere VERB [23]

to mix up

□ Ho confuso le date. I mixed up the dates. □ Non starai confondendo i nomi? You're not mixing up the names, are you?

■ **confondersi** to get mixed up □ No, scusa, mi sono confuso: era ieri. No, sorry, I've got mixed up: it was yesterday.

■ **confondere le idee a qualcuno** to get somebody confused □ Tutti questi discorsi mi confondono le idee. All this talk is getting me confused.

confrontare VERB [68]

to compare

□ Abbiamo confrontato le nostre scuole. We compared our schools.

il confronto MASC NOUN

comparison

□ Non c'è confronto! There's no comparison!

■ **fare un confronto fra due cose** to compare two things

■ **in confronto a** compared to □ In confronto ai tuoi, i miei sono più piccoli. Mine are small, compared to yours.

■ **nei confronti di qualcuno** towards somebody □ Non ho risentimento nei suoi confronti. I don't feel any resentment towards him.

la confusione FEM NOUN

1 noise

□ Smettetela di fare confusione! Stop making all that noise!

2 confusion

□ Ha approfittato della confusione per scappare. He took advantage of the confusion to escape.

3 mess

□ Che confusione! What a mess!

■ **far confusione** to get mixed up

confuso (FEM **confusa**) ADJECTIVE

confused

□ Sono un po' confuso. I'm a bit confused. □ La situazione è ancora confusa. The situation is still confused.

il congegno MASC NOUN

device

congelato (FEM **congelata**) ADJECTIVE

frozen

□ Sono congelato! I'm frozen!

il congelatore MASC NOUN

freezer

congiungere VERB [5]

to link

□ Il ponte congiunge l'isola alla terraferma. The bridge links the island to the mainland.

il congiuntivo MASC NOUN

subjunctive

le congratulazioni FEM PL NOUN

congratulations

□ Congratulazioni per la promozione! Congratulations on your promotion!

il congresso MASC NOUN

1 conference

□ il congresso del partito socialista the Socialist Party conference

2 meeting

il coniglietto MASC NOUN

bunny

il coniglio MASC NOUN

rabbit

connessione – consumare

la **connessione** FEM NOUN
connection

connettere VERB [59]
1 to connect
  □ Non avevo connesso i due fatti. I hadn't connected the two facts.
2 to think straight
  □ La mattina non riesco a connettere. I can't think straight in the morning.

il **cono** MASC NOUN
cone
  □ un cono al cioccolato a chocolate cone

il/la **conoscente** MASC/FEM NOUN
acquaintance
  □ una mia conoscente an acquaintance of mine

conoscere VERB [24]
to know
  □ Non conosco bene la città. I don't know the town well.
  ■ **conoscere qualcuno di vista** to know somebody by sight □ Lo conosco solo di vista. I only know him by sight. □ Da quanto vi conoscete? How long have you known each other? □ Ci conosciamo da poco tempo. We haven't known each other long.
  ■ **conoscersi** (for the first time) to meet □ Ci siamo conosciuti in vacanza. We met on holiday. □ Ci siamo conosciuti a Firenze. We first met in Florence.

conosciuto (FEM **conosciuta**) ADJECTIVE
well-known
  □ un attore conosciuto a well-known actor

la **consegna** FEM NOUN
delivery
  □ La consegna è garantita in giornata. Same-day delivery is guaranteed.
  ■ **alla consegna** on delivery □ Si può pagare alla consegna. You can pay on delivery.
  ■ **consegna a domicilio** home delivery

consegnare VERB [14]
to deliver
  □ Mi hanno consegnato il pacco stamattina. The parcel was delivered this morning.

la **conseguenza** FEM NOUN
consequence
  □ Non aveva pensato alle conseguenze. He hadn't thought of the consequences.

conservare VERB [68]
to keep
  □ Lo conservo in una scatola. I keep it in a box.
  □ Si conserva bene per alcune settimane. It keeps well for several weeks.

il **conservatorio** MASC NOUN
music school
  □ Studio al conservatorio. I'm at music school.

considerare VERB [68]
1 to consider

□ Bisogna considerare i pro e i contro. You have to consider the pros and cons.
2 to regard as
  □ La considero un'amica. I regard her as a friend.
  ■ **considerarsi** to think oneself □ Puoi considerarti fortunato! You can think yourself lucky!
  ■ **Si considera il migliore.** He thinks he's the best.

considerato (FEM **considerata**) ADJECTIVE
  ■ **tutto considerato** all things considered □ Tutto considerato non è male. It's not bad, all things considered.
  ■ **considerato che** considering that □ Giochi bene, considerato che hai cominciato da poco. You play well, considering that you only started recently.

consigliare VERB [25]
1 to recommend
  □ Che cosa mi consigli? What do you recommend? □ Ti consiglio la pizza. I'd recommend the pizza.
2 to advise
  □ Gli ha consigliato di andarsene prima possibile. She advised him to leave as soon as possible. □ Ti consiglierei di sbrigarti. I'd advise you to get a move on.
  ■ **Ti consiglio di non accettare l'invito.** I don't advise you to accept the invitation.

il **consiglio** MASC NOUN
advice
  □ Mi ha chiesto un consiglio. She asked me for advice. □ Ho seguito i tuoi consigli. I followed your advice. □ Ti do due consigli... I'll give you two bits of advice...

consolare VERB [68]
to cheer up
  □ Ho cercato di consolarla un po'. I tried to cheer her up a bit.

il **consolato** MASC NOUN
consulate
  □ il consolato italiano the Italian consulate

la **consolazione** FEM NOUN
consolation
  □ L'unica consolazione è che... The only consolation is that...
  ■ **premio di consolazione** consolation prize

la **consonante** FEM NOUN
consonant

consumare VERB [68]
1 to wear out
  □ Ho consumato le suole delle scarpe. I've worn the soles of my shoes out.
2 to use
  □ Quanto consuma la tua macchina? How much petrol does your car use?

il **consumo** MASC NOUN
use
□ il consumo di energia energy use

il **contachilometri** (PL i **contachilometri**) MASC NOUN
mileometer

il **contadino**, la **contadina** MASC/FEM NOUN
peasant
□ A quel tempo i contadini erano molto poveri. At that time peasants were very poor.
■ **Mio zio è contadino.** My uncle works on the land.

contagioso (FEM **contagiosa**) ADJECTIVE
1 infectious
□ una malattia contagiosa an infectious disease
2 catching
□ Non preoccuparti, non è contagioso. Don't worry, it's not catching.

i **contanti** MASC PL NOUN
cash sing
□ mille euro in contanti a thousand euros in cash
■ **pagare in contanti** to pay cash

contare VERB [68]
to count
□ Li ho contati, sono quindici. I've counted them, there are fifteen. □ Conta fino a cinquanta e poi vieni a cercarci. Count to fifty and then come and look for us.
■ **senza contare** not counting □ Eravamo in dieci, senza contare i professori. There were ten of us, not counting the teachers.
■ **contare su qualcuno** to count on somebody □ Sai che puoi contare su di me. You know you can count on me.
■ **contare di** to think of □ Contavamo di partire nel pomeriggio. We were thinking of leaving in the afternoon.
■ **Conto di essere lì per mezzogiorno.** I think I'll be there by midday.

contattare VERB [68]
to contact
□ Mi ha contattato di recente. He contacted me recently.

il **contatto** MASC NOUN
contact
□ Il loro contatto negli Stati Uniti era Chris. Their contact in the United States was Chris.
■ **mettersi in contatto con** to contact □ Devo mettermi in contatto con John. I must contact John.
■ **mantenersi in contatto** to keep in touch □ Ci siamo mantenuti in contatto. We've kept in touch.

contemporaneamente ADVERB
at the same time
□ Sono arrivati contemporaneamente. They arrived at the same time.

contenere VERB [113]
to contain
□ Questo succo non contiene zucchero. This juice does not contain sugar.
■ **Lo stadio può contenere centomila spettatori.** The stadium can hold a hundred thousand spectators.

il **contenitore** MASC NOUN
container
□ un contenitore di plastica a plastic container

contento (FEM **contenta**) ADJECTIVE
1 happy
□ Sei contento adesso? Are you happy now? □ Oggi sono più contento. I'm happier today.
■ **far contento qualcuno** to make somebody happy □ Sono andato per far contenta la mamma. I went to make my mum happy.
2 glad
□ Sono contento di vederti. I'm glad to see you. □ Sono contenta che ti piaccia. I'm glad you like it.

il **contenuto** MASC NOUN
contents pl
□ Ha rovesciato sul tavolo il contenuto della borsa. He tipped the contents of the bag out onto the table.

il **continente** MASC NOUN
1 continent
2 mainland

continuamente ADVERB
nonstop
□ È piovuto continuamente. It rained nonstop.
■ **Cambia idea continuamente.** She keeps changing her mind.

continuare VERB [68]
1 to carry on
□ Per oggi basta, continueremo domani. That's enough for today, we'll carry on tomorrow. □ Se continua così... If he carries on like this...
■ **continuare a fare qualcosa** to go on doing something □ Ha continuato a dormire nonostante il chiasso. He went on sleeping despite the noise.
■ **Continua a piovere.** It's still raining.
■ **Continui pure.** Do go on.
2 to continue
□ Continuano le trattative. Negotiations are continuing. □ Continuava a credere in lei. He continued to believe in her.

continuo (FEM **continua**) ADJECTIVE
constant
□ Sono stufa delle sue continue lamentele. I'm fed up with her constant complaints.
■ **C'è un continuo viavai di gente.** There are people constantly coming and going.
■ **di continuo** nonstop □ Piove di continuo da tre giorni. It's been raining nonstop for three days.

C

conto - controllo

il conto MASC NOUN

1 bill

□ Il conto, per favore. Could I have the bill, please?

2 account

□ un conto corrente a current account

3 calculation

□ Ho fatto un rapido conto. I did a quick calculation.

■ **rendersi conto** to realize □ Non si era reso conto che c'ero anch'io. He hadn't realized I was there too. □ Non ti rendi conto delle conseguenze! You don't realize what will happen!

■ **tener conto di** to allow for □ Non avevo tenuto conto del fuso orario. I hadn't allowed for the time difference.

■ **per conto di** on behalf of □ Telefono per conto di Sara. I'm phoning on behalf of Sara.

■ **per conto mio 1** in my opinion □ Per conto mio la faccenda è un po' strana. In my opinion it's all rather strange. **2** on my own □ Ci vado per conto mio. I'm going on my own.

■ **in fin dei conti** after all □ In fin dei conti non ha tutti i torti. After all, he's quite right.

■ **sul conto di** about □ Girano voci sul tuo conto. People are saying things about you.

■ **Con te faccio i conti più tardi!** I'll sort you out later!

■ **conto alla rovescia** countdown

il contorno MASC NOUN

vegetables *pl*

> **DID YOU KNOW...?**
> In restaurants in Italy meat and fish dishes don't usually come with vegetables. These are ordered separately from the section of the menu headed **Contorni**.

□ Non prendo il contorno. I don't want any vegetables.

■ **Cosa prendi come contorno?** What would you like to go with it?

■ **arrosto con contorno di patate** roast meat and potatoes

il contrabbandiere MASC NOUN

smuggler

il contrabbando MASC NOUN

smuggling

□ contrabbando di droga drug smuggling

■ **sigarette di contrabbando** contraband cigarettes

il contrabbasso MASC NOUN

double bass

contraddire VERB [35]

to contradict

□ Mi contraddice sempre. He's always contradicting me.

contrario (FEM **contraria**) ADJECTIVE

▷ *see also* **contrario** NOUN

opposite

□ in direzione contraria in the opposite direction

■ **essere contrario a qualcosa** to be against something □ Sono contrario alla vivisezione. I'm against vivisection.

il contrario MASC NOUN

▷ *see also* **contrario** ADJECTIVE

opposite

□ Fa tutto il contrario di quello che dice. He does the complete opposite of what he says.

■ **al contrario di** contrary to □ Al contrario di quanto si crede, è piuttosto grande. Contrary to what people think, it's quite big.

■ **avere qualcosa in contrario** to have an objection □ Io avrei qualcosa in contrario. I have an objection. □ Se qualcuno ha qualcosa in contrario lo dica subito. If anyone has an objection they should say so at once. □ Non ho niente in contrario. I have no objection.

il contrattempo MASC NOUN

problem

□ Sono arrivato in ritardo per un contrattempo. There was a problem, and I arrived late.

il contratto MASC NOUN

contract

□ Il contratto sarà firmato domani. The contract will be signed tomorrow.

contribuire VERB [51]

to contribute

□ Abbiamo contribuito tutti alla spesa. We all contributed to the cost.

contro PREPOSITION, ADVERB

against

□ la lotta contro la droga the fight against drugs □ Non ho niente contro di lui. I've nothing against him. □ Hanno votato contro. They voted against it. □ Stava appoggiato contro la porta. He was leaning against the door.

■ **Si è schiantato contro un albero.** It crashed into a tree.

■ **Ho battuto la testa contro lo spigolo.** I banged my head on the corner.

■ **pastiglie contro la tosse** cough sweets

la controfigura FEM NOUN

stuntman

controllare VERB [68]

to check

□ Controlla che la porta sia ben chiusa. Check that the door is shut properly. □ Mi hanno controllato il passaporto. My passport was checked.

■ **controllarsi** to control oneself □ Non riuscivo a controllarmi. I couldn't control myself.

> **LANGUAGE TIP** Be careful! **controllare** doesn't mean **to control**.

il controllo MASC NOUN

1 control

□ Ha perso il controllo della macchina. He lost control of the car.

■ **sotto controllo** under control □ La situazione è sotto controllo. The situation is under control.

■ **Avevano il telefono sotto controllo.** Their phone was bugged.

2 check

□ un controllo di sicurezza a security check

■ **controllo bagagli** baggage check

■ **controllo passaporti** passport control

il **controllore** MASC NOUN
ticket inspector

□ Chiedi al controllore. Ask the ticket inspector.

■ **controllore di volo** air traffic controller

controluce ADVERB
against the light

□ Guardala controluce. Look at it against the light.

contromano ADVERB

■ **guidare contromano** 1 to drive on the wrong side of the road 2 to drive the wrong way along a one-way street

controvoglia ADVERB

■ **L'ho mangiato controvoglia.** I ate it, though I didn't want to.

■ **È andato alla festa controvoglia.** He went to the party, though he didn't want to.

convalidare VERB [68]
to stamp

conveniente (FEM **conveniente**) ADJECTIVE
cheap

> LANGUAGE TIP Be careful! **conveniente** doesn't mean **convenient**.

convenire VERB [120]
to be cheaper

□ Comprare al supermercato conviene sempre. It's always cheaper to shop at the supermarket.

■ **Converrebbe rimandare la gita.** We'd better put off the trip.

■ **Se vuoi evitare il traffico ti conviene partire presto.** If you want to avoid the traffic you'd better leave early.

il **convento** MASC NOUN
convent

la **conversazione** FEM NOUN
conversation

convertire VERB [41]
to convert

■ **Si è convertito al buddismo.** He has become a Buddhist.

convincente (FEM **convincente**) ADJECTIVE
convincing

□ una spiegazione convincente a convincing explanation

convincere VERB [121]
to convince

□ Va bene, mi hai convinto. OK, you've convinced me.

■ **convincere qualcuno a fare qualcosa**

to persuade somebody to do something □ Mi ha convinto a comprarlo. She persuaded me to buy it.

la **cooperativa** FEM NOUN
cooperative

il **coperchio** MASC NOUN
lid

la **coperta** FEM NOUN
blanket

□ una bella coperta calda a nice warm blanket

■ **stare sotto le coperte** to be in bed

la **copertina** FEM NOUN

1 cover

□ La sua faccia è sulla copertina di questa settimana. Her picture is on this week's cover.

2 jacket (of book)

coperto (FEM **coperta**) ADJECTIVE
▷ see also **coperto** NOUN

1 indoor

□ una piscina coperta an indoor pool

2 overcast

□ Il cielo è coperto. The sky is overcast.

■ **coperto di** covered with □ libri coperti di polvere books covered with dust □ una parete coperta di poster a wall covered with posters

■ **essere ben coperto** to be wearing warm clothes □ Sei ben coperto? Are you wearing warm clothes?

il **coperto** MASC NOUN
▷ see also **coperto** ADJECTIVE
cover charge

□ Il coperto è compreso nel conto. The cover charge is included in the bill.

■ **al coperto** indoors □ In caso di pioggia la festa si svolgerà al coperto. If it rains, the party will be held indoors.

la **copia** FEM NOUN

1 copy

□ Non è l'originale, è una copia. It's not the original, it's a copy. □ Hanno venduto un milione di copie dell'album. A million copies of the album have been sold.

■ **brutta copia** first draft

■ **bella copia** final draft

2 print

□ Vorrei due copie di ciascuna foto. I'd like two prints of each photo.

copiare VERB [17]
to copy

□ Non dovete copiare. You mustn't copy.

la **coppa** FEM NOUN

1 cup

□ La nostra squadra ha vinto la coppa. Our team won the cup.

2 tub

□ Prendi un cono o una coppa? Are you going to have a cone or a tub?

■ **una coppa di champagne** a glass of champagne

61

la **coppia** FEM NOUN
1 couple
  □ Sono una bella coppia. They're a nice-looking couple.
2 pair
  □ una coppia di canarini a pair of canaries

il **copriletto** MASC NOUN
  bedspread

coprire VERB [9]
  to cover
  □ Ho coperto la bici con un telo di plastica. I covered the bike with a plastic sheet.
  ■ **coprirsi** to cloud over

la **coque** FEM NOUN
  ■ **uovo alla coque** soft-boiled egg

il **coraggio** MASC NOUN
1 courage
  □ Ha dimostrato molto coraggio. She showed great courage.
  ■ **avere il coraggio di fare qualcosa** to be brave enough to do something □ Ha avuto il coraggio di dire la verità. He was brave enough to tell the truth.
  ■ **farsi coraggio** to pluck up courage □ Si è fatto coraggio e le ha chiesto di uscire con lui. He plucked up courage and asked her to go out with him.
  ■ **Coraggio!** Come on! □ Coraggio, siamo quasi arrivati! Come on, we're nearly there!
2 nerve
  □ Hai un bel coraggio! You've got a nerve!

il **corallo** MASC NOUN
  coral

la **corda** FEM NOUN
1 rope
  □ una corda per saltare a skipping rope
  ■ **saltare con la corda** to skip
2 string (guitar, racket)
  ■ **essere giù di corda** to feel down □ Oggi sono un po' giù di corda. I'm feeling a bit down today.

cordiale (FEM **cordiale**) ADJECTIVE
  friendly
  □ una persona molto cordiale a very friendly person □ È la ragazza più cordiale che abbia mai conosciuto. She's the friendliest girl I've ever met.

i **coriandoli** MASC PL NOUN
  confetti sing

coricarsi VERB [18]
  to go to bed
  □ Ieri mi sono coricato presto. I went to bed early yesterday.

la **cornacchia** FEM NOUN
  crow

la **cornamusa** FEM NOUN
  bagpipes pl

la **cornetta** FEM NOUN
  receiver

□ Sollevare la cornetta e comporre il numero. Lift the receiver and dial the number.

il **cornetto** MASC NOUN
1 croissant
2 cornet

la **cornice** FEM NOUN
  frame
  □ una cornice d'argento a silver frame

il **corno** MASC NOUN
  horn

la **Cornovaglia** FEM NOUN
  Cornwall
  □ Andremo in Cornovaglia a Pasqua. We're going to Cornwall at Easter. □ Mi è piaciuta molto la Cornovaglia. I really liked Cornwall.

il **coro** MASC NOUN
  choir
  □ Canta in un coro. He sings in a choir.
  ■ **un coro di proteste** a chorus of protests
  ■ **tutti in coro** all together

la **corona** FEM NOUN
  crown

il **corpo** MASC NOUN
  body

la **corporatura** FEM NOUN
  build
  □ di corporatura media of medium build

correggere VERB [82]
1 to correct
  □ Correggimi se faccio un errore. Correct me if I make a mistake.
2 to mark
  □ Deve ancora correggere i compiti. She hasn't marked the homework yet.

la **corrente** FEM NOUN
  ▷ see also **corrente** MASC NOUN, ADJECTIVE
1 power (electricity)
  □ È andata via la corrente. The electricity's gone off.
  ■ **presa di corrente** socket
2 current
  □ La corrente l'ha trascinato al largo. The current carried him out to sea.
3 draught
  □ Chiudi la porta, c'è corrente. Shut the door, there's a draught.

il **corrente** MASC NOUN
  ▷ see also **corrente** FEM NOUN, ADJECTIVE
  ■ **mettere qualcuno al corrente di qualcosa** to tell somebody about something
  □ Mi ha messo al corrente degli ultimi sviluppi. She told me about the latest developments.

corrente (FEM **corrente**) ADJECTIVE
  ▷ see also **corrente** FEM NOUN, MASC NOUN
  ■ **acqua corrente** running water

correntemente ADVERB
  ■ **parlare correntemente una lingua** to speak a language fluently □ Parla correntemente il francese. She speaks French fluently.

correre VERB [26]
1 to run
□ Abbiamo corso come pazzi per non perdere il treno. We ran like mad to catch the train.
□ Paolo vuole correre i cento metri. Paolo wants to run in the hundred metres.
■ **Sono corso subito fuori.** I immediately rushed outside.
■ **correre il rischio** to risk □ Non voglio correre il rischio di non trovare posto. I don't want to risk not getting a seat.
2 to go running
□ Oggi ho corso un'ora. I went running for an hour today.
■ **Corre troppo in macchina.** He drives too fast.

la **correzione** FEM NOUN
correction

la **corrida** FEM NOUN
bullfight

il **corridoio** MASC NOUN
1 corridor
2 aisle (in plane, cinema)

il **corridore** (PL i **corridori**) MASC NOUN
1 runner
2 racer

la **corriera** FEM NOUN
coach

il **corrimano** MASC NOUN
handrail

la **corrispondenza** FEM NOUN
correspondence
□ un corso per corrispondenza a correspondence course

corrispondere VERB [90]
to correspond
□ A ciascun numero corrisponde una lettera. Each number corresponds to a letter.

la **corsa** FEM NOUN
race
□ una corsa automobilistica a motor race
■ **da corsa** racing □ un'auto da corsa a racing car
■ **fare una corsa** to run □ Ho fatto una corsa per non perdere il treno. I ran to catch the train.
■ **fare qualcosa di corsa** to do something quickly □ Ho fatto i compiti di corsa e sono uscito. I did my homework quickly and went out.
■ **Ho mangiato di corsa un panino e sono uscito.** I had a quick sandwich and went out.
■ **arrivare di corsa** to rush in
■ **andarsene di corsa** to rush off
■ **A che ora c'è l'ultima corsa?** When's the last bus?

la **corsia** FEM NOUN
1 lane

□ la corsia di sorpasso the overtaking lane
■ **corsia di emergenza** hard shoulder
2 ward

il **corso** MASC NOUN
1 course
□ un corso d'inglese an English course
■ **nel corso di** during
2 main street
□ Ha un negozio sul corso. She's got a shop in the main street.

la **corte** FEM NOUN
court (of law, royal)

la **cortesia** FEM NOUN
favour
□ Mi faresti una cortesia? Would you do me a favour? □ Fammi la cortesia di star zitto! Do me a favour and shut up!
■ **Per cortesia...** Excuse me... □ Per cortesia, dov'è il bagno? Excuse me, where's the toilet?

il **cortile** MASC NOUN
courtyard

corto (FEM **corta**) ADJECTIVE
short
□ maniche corte short sleeves □ Questi pantaloni sono troppo corti. These trousers are too short.
■ **essere a corto di qualcosa** to be short of something □ Sono a corto di soldi. I'm short of money.

il **corvo** MASC NOUN
raven

la **cosa** FEM NOUN
1 thing
□ la cosa migliore the best thing □ E no, non è la stessa cosa! But that's not the same thing! □ Sono cose che capitano! These things happen! □ Le cose stanno così. That's how things are.
■ **Devo dirti una cosa.** I've got to tell you something.
■ **ogni cosa** everything □ Il terremoto ha distrutto ogni cosa. The earthquake destroyed everything.
■ **qualche cosa** something □ C'è qualche altra cosa da discutere. There's something else to discuss. □ Vuole qualche cosa da mangiare? Would you like something to eat?
2 what
□ Cosa stai facendo? What are you doing? □ Che cos'è? What is it? □ Che cosa ha detto? What did he say? □ Cosa?! What?!

la **coscia** (PL le **cosce**) FEM NOUN
1 thigh (of person)
2 leg
□ una coscia di pollo a chicken leg □ una coscia d'agnello a leg of lamb

così ADVERB, CONJUNCTION, ADJECTIVE
1 so

cosmetici - crampo

□ Pioveva, così siamo rimasti a casa. It was raining so we stayed at home. □ Com'era il concerto? — Così così. What was the concert like? — So-so. □ È così o no? Isn't that so? □ È così simpatica! She's so nice!

■ **È un ragazzo così simpatico.** He's such a nice boy.

■ **così... che...** so... that... □ Era così stanco che è andato subito a letto. He was so tired that he went to bed immediately.

2 like this

□ Devi ripiegarlo così. You have to fold it like this.

3 like that

□ Se lo tiri così lo rompi. If you pull it like that you'll break it. □ I tipi così mi danno ai nervi. People like that get on my nerves.

■ **Non ho detto così.** That's not what I said.

■ **Basta così!** That's enough!

■ **così... come...** as... as... □ Non è così lontano come credi. It isn't as far as you think.

i **cosmetici** MASC PL NOUN
cosmetics

la **costa** FEM NOUN
coast
□ una città sulla costa a town on the coast

■ **la Costa Azzurra** the French Riviera

costante (FEM **costante**) ADJECTIVE
constant

costare VERB [68, aux **essere**]
to cost
□ Quanto costa quell'anello? How much does that ring cost? □ È costato trenta euro. It cost thirty euros. □ Quanto t'è costato? How much did it cost you?

■ **costare caro** to be expensive □ Mangiare fuori tutte le sere costa caro. Eating out every evening is expensive.

■ **costare poco** to be cheap

il **costo** MASC NOUN
cost
□ il costo della vacanza the cost of the holiday

■ **a tutti i costi** at all costs □ Dev'essere evitato a tutti i costi. It must be avoided at all costs.

■ **L'ha voluto portare a tutti i costi.** He was determined to bring it, no matter what.

la **costola** FEM NOUN
rib
□ Mi sono rotto una costola. I broke a rib.

costoso (FEM **costosa**) ADJECTIVE
expensive
□ un albergo costoso an expensive hotel

costringere VERB [100]

■ **costringere qualcuno a fare qualcosa** to make somebody do something □ Mi ha costretto a dire la verità. She made me tell the truth.

■ **È stato costretto a ritirarsi dalla gara.** He had to withdraw from the competition.

costruire VERB [51]
to build
□ Qui costruiranno il nuovo stadio. They're going to build the new stadium here.

la **costruzione** FEM NOUN
building
□ una costruzione in vetro e acciaio a building made of glass and steel

■ **La costruzione del ponte è durata sette anni.** It took seven years to build the bridge.

■ **essere in costruzione** to be under construction □ L'autostrada è in costruzione. The motorway is under construction.

il **costume** MASC NOUN
custom
□ gli usi e i costumi di un paese the traditions and customs of a country

■ **costume da bagno** 1 swimsuit
2 swimming trunks *pl*

la **cotoletta** FEM NOUN
chop
□ una cotoletta di maiale a pork chop

■ **una cotoletta di vitello** a veal cutlet

il **cotone** MASC NOUN
cotton
□ una maglietta di cotone a cotton T-shirt

■ **cotone idrofilo** cotton wool

la **cotta** FEM NOUN

■ **prendersi una cotta per qualcuno** to get a crush on somebody

cotto (FEM **cotta**) ADJECTIVE

1 cooked
□ Cotta o cruda? Cooked or raw?

2 done
□ Sono cotti gli spaghetti? Is the spaghetti done?

■ **ben cotto** well done

■ **poco cotto** rare

■ **troppo cotto** overcooked

■ **mele cotte** stewed apples

■ **essere cotto di qualcuno** to have a crush on somebody

il **cotton fioc®** (PL i **cotton fioc**) MASC NOUN
cotton bud

la **cottura** FEM NOUN
cooking
□ Tempo di cottura: due ore. Cooking time: two hours.

la **cozza** FEM NOUN
mussel
□ spaghetti con le cozze spaghetti with mussels

il **crampo** MASC NOUN
cramp
□ Ho un crampo alla gamba. I've got cramp in my leg.

il **cranio** MASC NOUN
skull

la **cravatta** FEM NOUN
tie

creare VERB [68]
1 to create
□ Ha creato un personaggio molto divertente.
He created a very funny character.
2 to cause
□ La notizia ha creato il panico. The news
caused panic. □ Mi ha creato un sacco di
problemi. It's caused me a lot of problems.

credere VERB [27]
1 to believe
□ Non posso crederci! I can't believe it! □ Non
dirmi che credi ai fantasmi! Don't tell me you
believe in ghosts! □ Come puoi credere a una
cosa simile? How can you believe such a thing?
□ Non credeva ai suoi occhi. She couldn't
believe her eyes.
■ **credere a qualcuno** to believe somebody
□ Non ti credo. I don't believe you.
■ **Ti credo sulla parola.** I'll take your word
for it.
2 to think
□ Credo che arrivi domani. I think he's arriving
tomorrow. □ Credeva di aver perso le chiavi. She
thought she had lost her keys. □ Ma chi si crede di
essere? Who does she think she is? □ Ti credevo
meno ingenuo. I didn't think you were so naive.
□ Credo di sì. I think so. □ Credo di no. I don't think
so. □ Lo credo bene! I should think so too!

il **credito** MASC NOUN
credit
□ Non si fa credito. We do not give credit.

la **crema** FEM NOUN
1 cream
■ **crema idratante** moisturizing cream
■ **crema solare** sun cream
2 custard
□ una pasta con la crema a cake with a custard
filling
■ **un gelato alla crema** a vanilla ice cream

la **crepa** FEM NOUN
crack
□ una crepa sul muro a crack in the wall

la **crêpe** (PL le **crêpe**) FEM NOUN
pancake
□ una crêpe al cioccolato a chocolate pancake

crescere VERB [28, aux **essere**]
to grow
□ Com'è cresciuto tuo fratello! Hasn't your
brother grown!
■ **È cresciuto in campagna.** He grew up in
the country.
■ **farsi crescere i capelli** to grow one's hair
□ Si sta facendo crescere i capelli. She's
growing her hair.

la **cresima** FEM NOUN
■ **fare la cresima** to be confirmed

crespo (FEM **crespa**) ADJECTIVE
■ **capelli crespi** frizzy hair

la **creta** FEM NOUN
clay

la **cretinata** FEM NOUN
stupid thing

il **cretino,** la **cretina** MASC/FEM NOUN
▷ see also **cretino** ADJECTIVE
idiot
□ Quel cretino mi ha quasi investito. That idiot
nearly ran me over.

cretino (FEM **cretina**) ADJECTIVE
▷ see also **cretino** NOUN
stupid
□ Ma come sei cretina! You're so stupid!

il **cric** (PL i **cric**) MASC NOUN
jack (for changing tyre)

il **criceto** MASC NOUN
hamster

criminale (FEM **criminale**) ADJECTIVE, MASC/
FEM NOUN
criminal

il **crimine** MASC NOUN
crime

il **crisantemo** MASC NOUN
chrysanthemum

la **crisi** (PL le **crisi**) FEM NOUN
1 crisis
□ la crisi economica the economic crisis
■ **In questo periodo sono in crisi.** I've got
a lot of problems at the moment.
2 fit (epileptic, of nerves)

il **cristallo** MASC NOUN
crystal
□ un bicchiere di cristallo a crystal glass

cristiano (FEM **cristiana**) ADJECTIVE, MASC/FEM
NOUN
Christian

Cristo MASC NOUN
Christ

criticare VERB [18]
to criticize
□ Ha sempre qualcosa da criticare. She always
finds something to criticize.

critico (FEM **critica**, MASC PL **critici**, FEM PL
critiche) ADJECTIVE
▷ see also **critico** NOUN
critical
□ un momento critico a critical moment

il **critico** (PL i **critici**) MASC NOUN
▷ see also **critico** ADJECTIVE
critic
□ un critico cinematografico a film critic

croccante (FEM **croccante**) ADJECTIVE
1 crisp
□ un biscotto croccante a crisp biscuit

2 crusty
  □ un panino croccante a crusty roll

la **croce** FEM NOUN
  cross

la **crociera** FEM NOUN
  cruise
  □ Sono andati in crociera nel Mediterraneo.
  They went on a Mediterranean cruise.

il **crocifisso** MASC NOUN
  crucifix

crollare VERB [68, AUX **essere**]
  to collapse
  □ Il ponte è crollato. The bridge collapsed.
  □ È crollato sul letto, stanco morto. He
  collapsed onto the bed, absolutely
  exhausted.

il **crollo** MASC NOUN
  collapse

la **cronaca** (PL le **cronache**) FEM NOUN
  news *sing*
  □ un fatto di cronaca a news item
  ■ **la cronaca rosa** the gossip column

il **cronometro** MASC NOUN
  stopwatch

la **crosta** FEM NOUN
1 crust
2 scab

la **crostata** FEM NOUN
  tart
  □ una crostata di albicocche an apricot tart

il **crostino** MASC NOUN
1 crostino *(toasted bread appetizer)*
2 crouton

il **cruciverba** (PL i **cruciverba**) MASC NOUN
  crossword puzzle

crudele (FEM **crudele**) ADJECTIVE
  cruel
  □ Non essere così crudele! Don't be so cruel!

crudo (FEM **cruda**) ADJECTIVE
  raw
  □ Mangia carne cruda. He eats raw meat.
  ■ **La bistecca è un po' cruda.** The steak is
  rather underdone.

il **cruscotto** MASC NOUN
  dashboard

il **cubetto** MASC NOUN
  cube
  □ un cubetto di ghiaccio an ice cube

il **cubo** MASC NOUN
  cube

la **cuccetta** FEM NOUN
1 couchette
2 berth

il **cucchiaino** MASC NOUN
  teaspoon
  □ due cucchiaini di zucchero two teaspoons of
  sugar

il **cucchiaio** MASC NOUN
1 spoon

  □ forchetta, coltello e cucchiaio fork, knife and
  spoon
2 spoonful
  □ Aggiungere un cucchiaio di farina. Add a
  spoonful of flour. □ Ha mangiato qualche
  cucchiaio di minestra. She ate a few spoonfuls
  of soup.

la **cuccia** (PL le **cucce**) FEM NOUN
1 kennel
2 dog basket
  ■ **A cuccia!** Down!

la **cucciolata** FEM NOUN
  litter
  □ Era il più piccolo della cucciolata. It was the
  smallest of the litter.

il **cucciolo** MASC NOUN
1 puppy
2 cub *(of lion, of wolf)*

la **cucina** FEM NOUN
1 kitchen
  □ una cucina spaziosa a big kitchen
2 cooker
  □ una cucina a gas a gas cooker
3 food
  □ Mi piace la cucina cinese. I like Chinese food.

cucinare VERB [68]
  to cook
  □ Oggi cucino io! I'll cook today!

il **cucinino** MASC NOUN
  kitchenette

cucire VERB [41]
  to sew
  □ Non so cucire. I can't sew.

la **cucitrice** FEM NOUN
  stapler

il **cucù** (PL i **cucù**) MASC NOUN
  cuckoo
  □ un orologio a cucù a cuckoo clock

la **cuffia** FEM NOUN
1 headphones *pl*
2 bathing cap
3 shower cap

il **cugino**, la **cugina** MASC/FEM NOUN
  cousin

cui PRONOUN

  LANGUAGE TIP When **cui** comes after a
  preposition, it is not usually translated and
  the preposition goes to the end of the
  sentence.

  □ la persona a cui si riferiva the person he was
  referring to □ le ragazze di cui ti ho parlato the
  girls I told you about □ il ponte su cui
  camminavamo the bridge we were walking on
  □ la casa in cui abito the house I live in

  LANGUAGE TIP When **cui** shows possession,
  it is translated by 'whose'.

  □ un'attrice il cui nome mi sfugge an actress
  whose name I can't remember □ la persona di

cui ti ho dato il numero di telefono ieri the person whose phone number I gave you yesterday
- **per cui** so □ Io non c'ero, per cui non chiedere a me. I wasn't there, so don't ask me.
- **il motivo per cui non sono venuto** the reason why I didn't come

la **culla** FEM NOUN
cradle

il **culo** MASC NOUN
bum *(rude)*
- **aver culo** to be lucky

la **cultura** FEM NOUN
culture
□ la cultura occidentale Western culture
- **avere una certa cultura** to be educated
- **una donna di grande cultura** a well-educated woman
- **una persona di scarsa cultura** a person without much education
- **cultura generale** general knowledge
□ una domanda di cultura generale a general knowledge question

culturale (FEM **culturale**) ADJECTIVE
cultural
□ una serie di manifestazioni culturali a series of cultural events □ scambi culturali cultural exchanges

il **culturismo** MASC NOUN
body-building

la **cunetta** FEM NOUN
dip *(in road)*

la **cuoca** (PL le **cuoche**) FEM NOUN
cook
□ Tua madre è una cuoca eccezionale! Your mother is a wonderful cook!

cuocere VERB [29]
to cook
□ Lascialo cuocere per mezz'ora. Cook it for half an hour.
- **cuocere in umido** to stew
- **cuocere a vapore** to steam
- **cuocere al forno 1** to bake **2** to roast

il **cuoco** (PL i **cuochi**) MASC NOUN
cook

il **cuoio** MASC NOUN
leather
□ scarpe di cuoio leather shoes
- **cuoio capelluto** scalp

il **cuore** MASC NOUN
heart
□ La ginnastica fa bene al cuore. Exercise is good for your heart. □ un'operazione al cuore a

heart operation □ nel cuore della città in the heart of the city □ una scatola a forma di cuore a heart-shaped box
- **nel cuore della notte** in the middle of the night

la **cupola** FEM NOUN
dome

la **cura** FEM NOUN
cure
□ Non hanno ancora trovato una cura. They haven't found a cure yet.
- **fare una cura** to have treatment □ Sto facendo una cura contro l'acne. I'm having treatment for my acne.

curare VERB [68]
to treat

la **curiosità** FEM NOUN
curiosity
□ Siamo andati per curiosità. We went out of curiosity.
- **Per curiosità, quanto l'hai pagato?** As a matter of interest, how much did you pay for it?

curioso (FEM **curiosa**) ADJECTIVE
1 curious
□ Sono curioso di vedere cosa succederà. I'm curious to see what will happen.
2 nosy
□ È un po' troppo curioso. He's a bit too nosy.

la **curva** FEM NOUN
bend
□ Ha sorpassato in curva. He overtook on a bend.

curvo (FEM **curva**) ADJECTIVE
curved
□ una linea curva a curved line
- **stare curvo** to slouch □ Non stare curvo! Don't slouch!

il **cuscino** MASC NOUN
1 cushion
2 pillow

il/la **custode** MASC/FEM NOUN
1 attendant *(in museum)*
2 keeper *(in park)*

la **custodia** FEM NOUN
case
- **agente di custodia** prison warder

custodire VERB [51]
to keep
□ I gioielli sono custoditi in cassaforte. The jewels are kept in a safe.

il **cybercaffè** (PL i **cybercaffè**) MASC NOUN
cybercafé

Dd

da PREPOSITION
1 from
□ a tre chilometri da qui three kilometres from here □ Viene da Roma. He comes from Rome.
■ **scendere dalla macchina** to get out of the car
■ **uscire dalla finestra** to get out through the window
■ **cadere dal terrazzo** to fall off the balcony
2 to
□ Vado dal giornalaio. I'm going to the paper shop.
3 at
□ Sono da Pietro. I'm at Pietro's.
4 for
□ Vivo qui da un anno. I've been living here for a year.
5 since
□ È a Londra da martedì. He's been in London since Tuesday. □ Ti aspetto dalle tre. I've been waiting for you since three o'clock.
■ **da allora** since then
■ **d'ora in poi** from now on
■ **da... a** from... to □ dalle otto alle dieci from eight to ten
6 by
□ dipinto da un grande artista painted by a great artist
7 with
□ Tremava dal freddo. He was shivering with cold.
■ **qualcosa da bere** something to drink
■ **una ragazza dagli occhi azzurri** a girl with blue eyes
■ **un vestito da cento euro** a dress costing one hundred euros
■ **Da giovane andavo a ballare spesso.** When I was young I often went dancing.

daccapo ADVERB
■ **ricominciare daccapo** to start all over again

il **dado** MASC NOUN
1 dice
■ **giocare a dadi** to play dice
2 nut (for screw)
■ **dado da brodo** stock cube

il **daino** MASC NOUN
fallow deer
■ **pelle di daino** chamois leather

la **dama** FEM NOUN
1 draughts sing
■ **giocare a dama** to play draughts
2 partner (at a ball)

danese (FEM **danese**) ADJECTIVE
▷ see also **danese** MASC NOUN, FEM NOUN
Danish

il **danese** MASC NOUN
▷ see also **danese** FEM NOUN, ADJECTIVE
1 Dane (person)
□ i danesi the Danes
2 Danish (language)
□ Parli danese? Do you speak Danish?

la **danese** FEM NOUN
▷ see also **danese** MASC NOUN, ADJECTIVE
Dane

la **Danimarca** FEM NOUN
Denmark
□ Ti è piaciuta la Danimarca? Did you like Denmark? □ Andrò in Danimarca quest'estate. I'm going to Denmark this summer.

dannazione EXCLAMATION
damn!

danneggiare VERB [58]
to damage

il **danno** MASC NOUN
damage
□ Il danno ormai è fatto. The damage has been done. □ due milioni di risarcimento danni two million in damages
■ **Ho provocato un piccolo danno alla macchina.** I damaged the car slightly.
■ **fare danni** to do damage □ La grandine ha fatto molti danni. The hail did a lot of damage.
□ senza fare danni without doing any damage

dannoso (FEM **dannosa**) ADJECTIVE
harmful
□ una sostanza dannosa a harmful substance
■ **Il fumo è dannoso alla salute.** Smoking is bad for your health.

il **Danubio** MASC NOUN
Danube

la **danza** FEM NOUN
dance
□ una danza tribale a tribal dance
■ **danza classica** ballet

dappertutto ADVERB
everywhere

dare VERB [30]
to give
- **dare qualcosa a qualcuno** to give somebody something □ Gli ho dato un libro. I gave him a book. □ Gli ho dato la cartina. I gave the map to him. □ Dammelo. Give it to me.
- **dare su** to look onto □ La mia finestra dà sul giardino. My window looks onto the garden.
- **può darsi** maybe
- **Quanti anni mi dai?** How old do you think I am?
- **Danno ancora quel film?** Is that film still showing?
- **Devi darti da fare.** You'll have to get busy.

la **data** FEM NOUN
date
□ Che data è oggi? What's the date today? □ la mia data di nascita my date of birth

i **dati** MASC PL NOUN
data
□ I dati sono sbagliati. The data is wrong.
- **elaborazione dati** data processing
- **dati personali** personal details

dato (FEM **data**) ADJECTIVE
given
□ in un dato periodo at a given time □ dato che... given that...
- **entro quel dato giorno** by that particular day

il **datore** MASC NOUN
- **datore di lavoro** employer

il **dattero** MASC NOUN
date (fruit)

la **dattilografia** FEM NOUN
typing

il **dattilografo,** la **dattilografa** MASC/FEM NOUN
typist
□ Fa la dattilografa. She is a typist.

davanti ADVERB, PREPOSITION
▷ see also **davanti** ADJECTIVE
at the front
□ Posso sedermi davanti? Can I sit at the front?
- **davanti a 1** in front of □ Era seduto davanti a me. He was sitting in front of me.
2 opposite □ la casa davanti alla mia the house opposite mine

davanti ADJECTIVE
▷ see also **davanti** ADVERB, PREPOSITION
front
□ le file davanti the front rows

il **davanzale** MASC NOUN
windowsill

davvero ADVERB
really
□ È successo davvero. It really happened.

d.C. ABBREVIATION (= dopo Cristo)
AD

il **debito** MASC NOUN
debt
□ Ha molti debiti. He's got a lot of debts.
- **debito formativo** failure to achieve the required standard

debole (FEM **debole**) ADJECTIVE
▷ see also **debole** NOUN
1 weak
□ Mi sento debole. I feel weak.
2 faint
□ un debole suono a faint sound
3 dim
□ una luce debole a dim light

il **debole** MASC NOUN
▷ see also **debole** ADJECTIVE
weakness
□ Ha un debole per la cioccolata. He's got a weakness for chocolate.
- **Ha un debole per me.** She's got a soft spot for me.

la **debolezza** FEM NOUN
weakness

decaffeinato (FEM **decaffeinata**) ADJECTIVE, MASC/FEM NOUN
- **caffè decaffeinato** decaffeinated coffee
- **un decaffeinato** a cup of decaffeinated coffee

decappottabile (FEM **decappottabile**) ADJECTIVE
- **una macchina decappottabile** a convertible

il **decennio** MASC NOUN
decade

decente (FEM **decente**) ADJECTIVE
decent

decidere VERB [31]
to decide
□ Hai deciso? Have you decided?
- **decidere di fare qualcosa** to decide to do something □ Ho deciso di non andarci. I decided not to go.
- **decidersi** to decide □ Non so decidermi. I can't decide.

decifrare VERB [68]
1 to decode (message in code)
2 to decipher (handwriting)

decimo (FEM **decima**) ADJECTIVE, MASC NOUN
tenth

la **decina** FEM NOUN
- **una decina** about a dozen □ una decina di macchine about a dozen cars

la **decisione** FEM NOUN
decision
- **prendere una decisione** to make a decision
□ Ho preso una decisione. I've made a decision.
- **agire con decisione** to act decisively

decisivo (FEM **decisiva**) ADJECTIVE
decisive

□ Il suo voto è stato decisivo. His vote was decisive.

deciso (FEM **decisa**) ADJECTIVE
1 determined (person, character)
2 firm (tone)

declinare VERB [68]
1 to turn down
□ Ho declinato l'offerta. I turned down the offer.
2 to decline (in grammar)

il **declino** MASC NOUN
decline
□ in declino in decline

decollare VERB [68]
to take off
□ L'aereo è decollato alle otto. The plane took off at eight o'clock.

il **decollo** MASC NOUN
take-off

decorare VERB [68]
to decorate

la **decorazione** FEM NOUN
decoration

la **dedica** (PL le **dediche**) FEM NOUN
dedication

dedicare VERB [18]
to dedicate
□ Le ha dedicato una canzone. He dedicated a song to her.

dedurre VERB [85]
1 to deduce
□ Ne deduco che... I deduce from this that...
2 to deduct

il/la **deficiente** MASC/FEM NOUN
idiot

il **deficit** (PL i **deficit**) MASC NOUN
deficit

definire VERB [51]
1 to settle
□ Dobbiamo definire la questione. We must settle this matter.
2 to define (word)

definitiva FEM NOUN
■ in definitiva 1 in the end 2 all in all

definitivo (FEM **definitiva**) ADJECTIVE
1 definitive (reply, solution)
2 final (decision)

la **definizione** FEM NOUN
definition

deformare VERB [68]
1 to put out of shape (object)
2 to deform (body)
■ deformarsi to go out of shape

defunto (FEM **defunta**) ADJECTIVE
▷ see also **defunto** NOUN
late
□ il defunto presidente the late president

il **defunto**, la **defunta** MASC/FEM NOUN
▷ see also **defunto** ADJECTIVE

■ il **defunto** the deceased
■ i **defunti** the dead

il/la **degente** MASC/FEM NOUN
patient

deglutire VERB [51]
to swallow

degnare VERB [14]
■ **Non mi ha degnato di uno sguardo.** He didn't even look at me.
■ **Non si è degnato di rispondermi.** He didn't bother to answer me.

degno (FEM **degna**) ADJECTIVE
■ degno di fiducia trustworthy

il **degrado** MASC NOUN
■ degrado urbano urban decay

il **delfino** MASC NOUN
dolphin

delicato (FEM **delicata**) ADJECTIVE
delicate

il/la **delinquente** MASC/FEM NOUN
1 criminal
□ La polizia ha arrestato il delinquente. The police arrested the criminal.
2 scoundrel

la **delinquenza** FEM NOUN
crime
□ un aumento della delinquenza an increase in crime
■ la delinquenza minorile juvenile delinquency

il **delitto** MASC NOUN
crime
□ Ha commesso un terribile delitto. He committed a terrible crime.

delizioso (FEM **deliziosa**) ADJECTIVE
1 delicious (smell, food)
2 charming (person)

il **deltaplano** MASC NOUN
hang-glider
■ andare in deltaplano to hang-glide

deludente (FEM **deludente**) ADJECTIVE
disappointing
□ un film un po' deludente a rather disappointing film

deludere VERB [32]
to disappoint
□ Mi hai molto deluso. You've really disappointed me.
■ **Il suo ultimo film mi ha deluso.** His last film was disappointing.

la **delusione** FEM NOUN
disappointment
□ È stata una delusione. It was a disappointment.
□ Che delusione! What a disappointment!

deluso (FEM **delusa**) ADJECTIVE
disappointed
□ Sono deluso del voto che ho preso. I'm disappointed with the mark I got.

Italian-English

democratico (FEM **democratica**, MASC PL
democratici, FEM PL **democratiche**) ADJECTIVE
democratic

la **democrazia** FEM NOUN
democracy

demolire VERB [51]
to demolish

il **demonio** MASC NOUN
devil

il **denaro** MASC NOUN
money
□ Non ho molto denaro con me. I haven't got
much money with me.

denso (FEM **densa**) ADJECTIVE
thick
□ una minestra densa a thick soup

il **dente** MASC NOUN
tooth
□ Mi lavo i denti dopo ogni pasto. I clean my
teeth after every meal.
■ **denti del giudizio** wisdom teeth
■ **avere mal di denti** to have toothache
■ **mettere qualcosa sotto i denti** to have
a bite to eat
■ **al dente** al dente

la **dentiera** FEM NOUN
false teeth *pl*
□ Porta la dentiera. She's got false teeth.

il **dentifricio** MASC NOUN
toothpaste
□ dentifricio al fluoro fluoride toothpaste

il/la **dentista** (MASC PL i **dentisti**, FEM PL le
dentiste) MASC/FEM NOUN
dentist
□ Fa la dentista. She is a dentist.

dentro ADVERB
▷ *see also* **dentro** PREPOSITION
inside
□ Vai dentro. Go inside.
■ **qui dentro** in here
■ **tenere tutto dentro** to keep everything
bottled up

dentro PREPOSITION
▷ *see also* **dentro** ADVERB
in
□ È dentro l'armadio. It's in the wardrobe.

la **denuncia** (PL le **denunce**) FEM NOUN
■ **sporgere denuncia contro qualcuno**
to report somebody to the police
■ **denuncia dei redditi** tax return

denunciare VERB [13]
1 to report
□ Lo ha denunciato alla polizia. He reported
him to the police.
2 to expose
□ Ha denunciato la corruzione all'interno del
partito. He exposed the corruption within the
party.

denutrito (FEM **denutrita**) ADJECTIVE
undernourished

il **deodorante** MASC NOUN
deodorant

depilarsi VERB [56]
■ **depilarsi le gambe** to shave one's legs

depilatorio (FEM **depilatoria**) ADJECTIVE
■ **crema depilatoria** hair-removing cream

il **dépliant** (PL i **dépliant**) MASC NOUN
1 leaflet *(advertising)*
2 brochure

depositare VERB [68]
to deposit

il **deposito** MASC NOUN
1 warehouse
■ **deposito bagagli** left-luggage office
2 deposit *(of money)*

la **depressione** FEM NOUN
depression

depresso (FEM **depressa**) ADJECTIVE
depressed

deprimente (FEM **deprimente**) ADJECTIVE
depressing
□ una storia deprimente a depressing story

deprimere VERB [46]
to depress

il **deputato**, la **deputata** MASC/FEM NOUN
1 MP *(in Great Britain)*
2 congressman
congresswoman *(in USA)*

deragliare VERB [25]
to be derailed

deridere VERB [84]
to mock

la **deriva** FEM NOUN
■ **andare alla deriva** to drift

derivare VERB [68, aux **essere**]
to derive
□ 'Gas' deriva dalla parola greca 'chaos'. 'Gas'
derives from the Greek word 'chaos'.
■ **Questa parola deriva dal francese.**
This word is of French derivation.

il **dermatologo**, la **dermatologa** (MASC
PL i **dermatologi**, FEM PL le **dermatologhe**)
MASC/FEM NOUN
dermatologist

derubare VERB [68]
to rob
□ Lo hanno picchiato e derubato. He was
attacked and robbed.
■ **Mi hanno derubato del portafoglio.** I
had my wallet stolen.

descrivere VERB [99]
to describe
■ **descrivere qualcosa a qualcuno** to
describe something to somebody □ Mi ha
descritto ciò che aveva trovato. He described to
me what he had found.

d

descrizione - di

la **descrizione** FEM NOUN
description
■ **fare una descrizione** to give a description
deserto (FEM **deserta**) ADJECTIVE
▷ *see also* **deserto** NOUN
deserted
□ Le strade erano deserte. The streets were deserted.
■ **isola deserta** desert island
il **deserto** MASC NOUN
▷ *see also* **deserto** ADJECTIVE
desert
desiderare VERB [68]
to want
□ Desiderava migliorare il suo inglese. He wanted to improve his English. □ Sei desiderato al telefono. You're wanted on the phone.
■ **Desidero parlarvi subito.** I'd like to speak to you immediately.
■ **Cosa desidera? 1** *(in bar, café)* What would you like? **2** *(in shop)* Can I help you?
il **desiderio** MASC NOUN
1 wish
□ Esprimi un desiderio. Make a wish.
2 desire *(sexual)*
la **desinenza** FEM NOUN
ending
il **desktop** (PL i **desktop**) MASC NOUN
desktop *(computer)*
desolato (FEM **desolata**) ADJECTIVE
■ **Sono desolato!** I'm terribly sorry!
il **dessert** (PL i **dessert**) MASC NOUN
dessert
il **destinatario**, la **destinataria** MASC/
FEM NOUN
addressee
la **destinazione** FEM NOUN
destination
□ Sono giunti a destinazione. They reached their destination.
il **destino** MASC NOUN
destiny
□ il mio destino my destiny □ Era destino che ci incontrassimo. It was our destiny to meet.
la **destra** FEM NOUN
1 right
□ Sulla destra, nella foto... On the right of the photograph...
■ **voltare a destra** to turn right
■ **spostarsi verso destra** to move to the right
2 right hand
□ Scrivo con la destra. I write with my right hand.
■ **la destra** the right
■ **un partito di destra** a right-wing party
destro (FEM **destra**) ADJECTIVE
right

il **detenuto**, la **detenuta** MASC/FEM NOUN
prisoner
detergente (FEM **detergente**) ADJECTIVE
cleansing
□ latte detergente cleansing milk
> **LANGUAGE TIP** Be careful! **detergente** doesn't mean **detergent**.
determinativo (FEM **determinativa**)
ADJECTIVE
■ **articolo determinativo** definite article
determinato (FEM **determinata**) ADJECTIVE
1 certain
□ in determinate circostanze in certain circumstances
2 determined
□ È molto determinato. He's very determined.
il **detersivo** MASC NOUN
detergent
□ un detersivo neutro a mild detergent
■ **detersivo per bucato** washing powder
■ **detersivo per pavimenti** floor cleaner
■ **detersivo per i piatti** washing-up liquid
detestare VERB [68]
to detest
□ Lo detesto! I detest him!
■ **Detesto mentire.** I hate lying.
il **dettaglio** MASC NOUN
detail
□ in dettaglio in detail
■ **prezzo al dettaglio** retail price
dettare VERB [68]
to dictate
il **dettato** MASC NOUN
dictation
detto (FEM **detta**) ADJECTIVE
▷ *see also* **detto** NOUN
called
il **detto** MASC NOUN
▷ *see also* **detto** ADJECTIVE
saying
□ un detto cinese a Chinese saying
deviare VERB [17]
to divert
□ Il traffico è stato deviato. The traffic has been diverted.
la **deviazione** FEM NOUN
diversion
dezippare VERB [68]
to unzip
di PREPOSITION, ARTICLE
1 of
□ un gruppo di studenti a group of students
□ un bicchiere di vino a glass of wine □ È fatto di legno. It's made of wood. □ Era pieno di gente. It was full of people. □ Ho paura di volare. I'm afraid of flying.

LANGUAGE TIP **di** is often not translated. □ le chiavi della macchina the car keys □ un orologio d'oro a gold watch □ un bambino di tre anni a three-year-old child □ il professore di inglese the English teacher

■ **due milioni di euro** two thousand euros □ la moto di Gianni Gianni's bike □ i libri di mio padre my father's books □ la sorella di mia madre my mother's sister □ la reputazione di un'attrice an actress's reputation □ la casa dei miei genitori my parents' house

2 than
□ È più alto di me. He's taller than me. □ È più brava di lui. She's better than him.
■ **il migliore della classe** the best in the class

3 in
□ d'estate in the summer □ di mattina in the morning □ di sera in the evening
■ **di domenica** on Sundays
■ **di notte** at night

4 by
□ un poesia di Montale a poem by Montale
LANGUAGE TIP The article **del** (**della**, **dei**, **delle**) is translated by 'some'.
□ C'erano delle persone che aspettavano. There were some people waiting. □ Vuoi dei biscotti? Do you want some biscuits?

5 to (followed by infinitive)
□ Sto tentando di concentrarmi. I'm trying to concentrate. □ Ho dimenticato di fare l'esercizio. I forgot to do the exercise.
■ **Credo di capire.** I think I understand

il **diabete** MASC NOUN
diabetes sing

diabetico (FEM **diabetica**, MASC PL **diabetici**, FEM PL **diabetiche**) ADJECTIVE
diabetic

il **diaframma** (PL i **diaframmi**) MASC NOUN
diaphragm

la **diagnosi** (PL le **diagnosi**) FEM NOUN
diagnosis

il **dialetto** MASC NOUN
dialect

il **dialogo** (PL i **dialoghi**) MASC NOUN
dialogue (in book, at theatre)
■ **Non c'è più dialogo tra noi.** We don't talk to each other any more.

il **diamante** MASC NOUN
diamond
□ un anello con diamante a diamond ring

il **diametro** MASC NOUN
diameter

la **diapositiva** FEM NOUN
slide

il **diario** MASC NOUN
diary
■ **tenere un diario** to keep a diary

la **diarrea** FEM NOUN
diarrhoea

il **diavolo** MASC NOUN
devil
□ Povero diavolo! Poor devil!
■ **mandare qualcuno al diavolo** to tell somebody to go to hell (informal) □ L'ho mandato al diavolo. I told him to go to hell.
■ **Va al diavolo!** Go to hell! (informal)
■ **Cosa diavolo vuoi?** What the hell do you want?

il **dibattito** MASC NOUN
debate

dicembre MASC NOUN
December
LANGUAGE TIP In Italian, months are not written with capital letters.
□ in dicembre in December

la **diceria** FEM NOUN
rumour
□ Sono solo dicerie. They're only rumours.

dichiarare VERB [68]
1 to declare
□ Niente da dichiarare? Anything to declare?
2 to say
□ Il ministro ha dichiarato che... The minister said that...

la **dichiarazione** FEM NOUN
1 declaration
□ una dichiarazione d'indipendenza a declaration of independence
■ **Le ha fatto una dichiarazione d'amore.** He told her he loved her.
■ **dichiarazione dei redditi** tax return
2 statement
□ Ha rilasciato una dichiarazione. He made a statement.

diciannove NUMBER
nineteen
□ Ho diciannove anni. I'm nineteen.
■ **alle diciannove** at seven p.m.
■ **il diciannove maggio** the nineteenth of May

diciannovenne (FEM **diciannovenne**)
ADJECTIVE, MASC/FEM NOUN
nineteen-year-old

diciannovesimo (FEM **diciannovesima**)
ADJECTIVE
nineteenth

diciassette NUMBER
seventeen
□ Ho diciassette anni. I'm seventeen.
■ **alle diciassette** at five p.m.
■ **il diciassette maggio** the seventeenth of May

diciassettenne (FEM **diciassettenne**)
ADJECTIVE, MASC/FEM NOUN
seventeen-year-old

diciassettesimo (FEM **diciassettesima**)
ADJECTIVE
seventeenth

d

73

diciottenne (FEM **diciottenne**) ADJECTIVE, MASC/FEM NOUN
eighteen-year-old

diciottesimo (FEM **diciottesima**) ADJECTIVE
eighteenth

diciotto NUMBER
eighteen
□ Ho diciotto anni. I'm eighteen.
■ **alle diciotto** at six p.m.
■ **il diciotto maggio** the eighteenth of May

la **didascalia** FEM NOUN
1 caption (of illustration)
2 subtitle

dieci NUMBER
ten
□ Ho dieci anni. I'm ten. □ alle dieci at ten a.m.
■ **il dieci maggio** the tenth of May

diesel (FEM+PL **diesel**) ADJECTIVE
■ **motore diesel** diesel engine
■ **macchina diesel** diesel car

la **dieta** FEM NOUN
diet
■ **essere in dieta** to be on a diet

dietro ADVERB, PREPOSITION
▷ see also **dietro** ADJECTIVE
behind
□ dietro la porta behind the door □ Dev'essere qua dietro. It must be behind here.
■ **Abita qua dietro.** He lives round the corner.
■ **essere seduto dietro** 1 (of car) to be sitting in the back 2 (of bus) to be sitting at the back
■ **dietro l'angolo** round the corner
■ **dietro a** behind □ Era dietro alla scrivania. He was behind his desk.
■ **dietro di** behind □ Sono seduti dietro di me. They're sitting behind me.
■ **stare dietro a qualcuno** 1 to keep an eye on somebody 2 to be after somebody
■ **uno dietro l'altro** 1 one after the other 2 (in queue) one behind the other

dietro (FEM+PL **dietro**) ADJECTIVE
▷ see also **dietro** ADVERB, PREPOSITION
back
□ le file dietro the back rows

difendere VERB [33]
to defend
■ **difendersi** to defend oneself

il **difensore** MASC NOUN
1 lawyer for the defence
2 defender (in sport)

la **difesa** FEM NOUN
defence
□ giocare in difesa to play in defence
■ **per legittima difesa** in self-defence
■ **la difesa** (in court) the defence

il **difetto** MASC NOUN
fault
□ Ha molti difetti. He has many faults.

difettoso (FEM **difettosa**) ADJECTIVE
faulty

differente (FEM **differente**) ADJECTIVE
different

la **differenza** FEM NOUN
difference
□ Non c'è alcuna differenza. There's no difference.
■ **a differenza di** unlike □ A differenza del calcio qui il rugby non è molto diffuso. Unlike football, rugby isn't very popular here.

difficile (FEM **difficile**) ADJECTIVE
1 difficult
□ un esercizio difficile a difficult exercise
2 unlikely
□ È difficile che venga. It's unlikely he'll come.

la **difficoltà** (PL le **difficoltà**) FEM NOUN
difficulty
□ Non arrenderti alla prima difficoltà. Don't give up at the first difficulty.
■ **trovarsi in difficoltà** to have problems

diffidente (FEM **diffidente**) ADJECTIVE
suspicious
□ È diffidente nei miei confronti. He's suspicious of me.

la **diffidenza** FEM NOUN
■ **con diffidenza** suspiciously

diffondere VERB [23]
1 to spread (news, illness)
2 to give out (light, heat)
■ **diffondersi** to spread

diffuso (FEM **diffusa**) ADJECTIVE
common
□ un'usanza diffusa a common custom

la **diga** (PL le **dighe**) FEM NOUN
1 dam
2 breakwater

digerire VERB [51]
to digest
□ Ci vogliono otto ore per digerire. It takes eight hours to digest.
■ **Non ho digerito bene.** I've got indigestion.

la **digestione** FEM NOUN
digestion

il **digestivo** MASC NOUN
after-dinner liqueur

digitale (FEM **digitale**) ADJECTIVE
digital
□ un orologio digitale a digital watch □ TV digitale digital TV

il **digiuno** MASC NOUN
fasting
□ Alcune diete prevedono il digiuno. Some diets involve fasting.
■ **Sono a digiuno da ieri.** I haven't eaten since yesterday.
■ **stare a digiuno** to fast

la **dignità** FEM NOUN
dignity

dilettante (FEM **dilettante**) ADJECTIVE, MASC/
FEM NOUN
amateur
□ un fotografo dilettante an amateur
photographer

diligente (FEM **diligente**) ADJECTIVE
hard-working
□ un alunno diligente a hard-working student

diluviare VERB [17]
to pour
□ Sta diluviando. It's pouring

dimagrante (FEM **dimagrante**) ADJECTIVE
■ **fare una cura dimagrante** to go on a diet

dimagrire VERB [51, aux **essere**]
to lose weight
□ È dimagrita. She's lost weight.
■ **È dimagrito di dieci chili.** He's lost ten
kilos.

la **dimensione** FEM NOUN
dimension
□ la dimensione politica the political dimension
■ **dimensioni** size *sing* □ le dimensioni della
stanza the size of the room
■ **di piccole dimensioni** small
■ **di grandi dimensioni** big

la **dimenticanza** FEM NOUN
oversight
□ È stata una dimenticanza. It was an
oversight.

dimenticare VERB [18]
to forget
□ Ho dimenticato il tuo numero di telefono.
I've forgotten your phone number.
■ **Ho dimenticato a casa l'ombrello.** I
left my umbrella at home.
■ **dimenticarsi di qualcosa** to forget
something

dimettere VERB [59]
■ **dimettere qualcuno dall'ospedale** to
discharge somebody from hospital
■ **dimettersi** to resign □ Si è dimesso ieri. He
resigned yesterday.

diminuire VERB [51, aux **essere**]
1 to decrease
□ La popolazione è diminuita del dieci per
cento. The population has decreased by ten
percent.
■ **diminuire di peso** to lose weight
2 to fall
□ Il prezzo della carne è diminuito. The price of
meat has fallen.
3 to drop *(temperature, wind)*
4 to die down *(noise)*
5 to cut *(reduce)*
□ La ditta ha deciso di diminuire i prezzi. The
company has decided to cut its prices.

□ Dobbiamo diminuire le spese del venti per
cento. We must cut spending by twenty percent.

diminutivo (FEM **diminutiva**) ADJECTIVE,
MASC NOUN
diminutive

la **diminuzione** FEM NOUN
drop
□ una forte diminuzione della temperatura a
big drop in temperature
■ **essere in diminuzione** to be dropping
□ La temperatura è in diminuzione. The
temperature is dropping.

le **dimissioni** FEM PL NOUN
■ **dare le dimissioni** to hand in one's
resignation □ Ha dato le dimissioni. He
handed in his resignation.

dimostrare VERB [68]
1 to prove
□ Questo dimostra che hai ragione. This proves
you're right.
2 to show *(affection)*
■ **Non dimostra la sua età.** He doesn't
look his age.

la **dimostrazione** FEM NOUN
demonstration
□ una dimostrazione studentesca a student
demonstration
■ **una dimostrazione d'affetto** a show of
affection

la **dinamite** FEM NOUN
dynamite

il **dinosauro** MASC NOUN
dinosaur

i **dintorni** MASC PL NOUN
■ **nei dintorni** nearby □ Abita nei dintorni.
She lives nearby.
■ **nei dintorni di** *(city)* outside □ un paese
nei dintorni di Milano a village outside Milan

il **dio** (PL gli **dei**) MASC NOUN
god
□ gli dei the gods □ Credi in Dio? Do you
believe in God? □ Grazie a Dio! Thank God!
■ **Dio mio!** My goodness!

il/la **dipendente** MASC/FEM NOUN
▷ *see also* **dipendente** ADJECTIVE
employee
□ un dipendente della ditta an employee of the
firm

dipendente (FEM **dipendente**) ADJECTIVE
▷ *see also* **dipendente** NOUN
■ **essere dipendente da** to be addicted to

dipendere VERB [8, aux **essere**]
1 to depend
□ Dipende! It depends! □ Andiamo? — Non lo
so. Dipende da Mario. Are we going? — I don't
know. It depends on Mario.
■ **Puoi farlo o meno, dipende solo da te.**
You can do it or not, it's up to you.

d

dipingere – dirottare

2 to be dependent

□ Non voglio più dipendere dai miei. I don't want to be dependent on my parents any longer.

dipingere VERB [34]

to paint

il **dipinto** MASC NOUN

painting

il **diploma** (PL i **diplomi**) MASC NOUN

■ **diploma di laurea** degree

■ **diploma di maturità** school-leaving certificate

> **DID YOU KNOW...?**
> The education system in Italy is different, and students generally finish secondary school a year later than in Britain or America.

diplomatico (FEM **diplomatica**, MASC PL **diplomatici**, FEM PL **diplomatiche**)

ADJECTIVE

▷ see also **diplomatico** NOUN

diplomatic

□ Cerca di essere diplomatico. Try to be diplomatic.

il **diplomatico** (PL i **diplomatici**) MASC NOUN

▷ see also **diplomatico** ADJECTIVE

diplomat

diradare VERB [68]

■ **diradare le visite** to call less frequently

■ **diradarsi 1** (fog) to clear **2** (crowd) to disperse **3** (vegetation) to thin out

dire VERB [35]

1 to say

□ 'Grazie,' disse. 'Thank you,' she said. □ Ha detto che verrà. He said he'll come. □ Non disse una parola. She didn't say a word. □ Si dice che... They say that... □ Come si dice 'quadro' in inglese? How do you say 'quadro' in English?

■ **dire di sì** to say yes

■ **dire di no** to say no

■ **Come sarebbe a dire?** What do you mean?

■ **Che ne diresti di andarcene?** Shall we leave?

2 to tell

□ Hai detto troppe bugie. You've told too many lies.

■ **dire qualcosa a qualcuno** to tell somebody something □ Mi ha detto la verità. He told me the truth. □ Ti dirò un segreto. I'll tell you a secret. □ Dimmi dov'è. Tell me where it is.

■ **dire a qualcuno di fare qualcosa** to tell somebody to do something □ Gli ho detto di andarsene. I told him to go away.

la **diretta** FEM NOUN

■ **in diretta** live □ un incontro di calcio in diretta a live football match

diretto (FEM **diretta**) ADJECTIVE

direct

□ la strada più diretta the most direct route

■ **il mio diretto superiore** my immediate superior

■ **treno diretto** through train

il **direttore**, la **direttrice** MASC/FEM NOUN

1 manager (of bank, firm)

2 head (of school)

■ **direttore d'orchestra** conductor

■ **direttore tecnico** team manager

la **direzione** FEM NOUN

1 direction

□ È nella direzione opposta. It's in the opposite direction.

■ **In che direzione vai?** Which way are you going?

2 management (of company)

3 leadership (of political party)

il/la **dirigente** MASC/FEM NOUN

▷ see also **dirigente** ADJECTIVE

1 executive (of company)

2 leading figure (of political party)

dirigente (FEM **dirigente**) ADJECTIVE

▷ see also **dirigente** NOUN

■ **la classe dirigente** the ruling class

dirigere VERB [36]

■ **dirigere il traffico** to direct the traffic

■ **dirigere una ditta** to run a company

■ **dirigere un'orchestra** to conduct an orchestra

■ **dirigere i lavori** to be in charge of the work

■ **dirigersi verso** to make for □ Si è diretto verso la porta. He made for the door.

■ **essere diretti a nord** to be heading north

diritto (FEM **diritta**) ADJECTIVE

▷ see also **diritto** NOUN, ADVERB

straight

□ una strada diritta a straight road

diritto ADVERB

▷ see also **diritto** ADJECTIVE, NOUN

straight

□ Vai sempre diritto fino al semaforo. Keep straight on until you get to the traffic lights.

il **diritto** MASC NOUN

▷ see also **diritto** ADJECTIVE, ADVERB

1 right

□ Ho il diritto di sapere. I've got a right to know. □ il diritto di voto the right to vote

2 law

□ Studia diritto. He's studying law.

3 forehand (in tennis)

il **dirottamento** MASC NOUN

■ **dirottamento aereo** hijack

dirottare VERB [68]

1 to hijack

2 to divert (traffic)

il **dirottatore,** la **dirottatrice** MASC/FEM
NOUN
hijacker

dirotto (FEM **dirotta**) ADJECTIVE
  ■ **Piove a dirotto.** It's pouring.
  ■ **scoppiare in un pianto dirotto** to burst
into tears

disabitato (FEM **disabitata**) ADJECTIVE
uninhabited

il **disagio** MASC NOUN
  ■ **sentirsi a disagio** to feel ill at ease

disapprovare VERB [68]
  ■ **disapprovare qualcosa** to disapprove of
something □ Disapprovano il mio
comportamento. They disapprove of my
behaviour.

la **disapprovazione** FEM NOUN
disapproval

disarmato (FEM **disarmata**) ADJECTIVE
disarmed

il **disarmo** MASC NOUN
disarmament

il **disastro** MASC NOUN
disaster
  □ È il più grande disastro aereo mai avvenuto.
It's the worst air disaster there has ever been.
  ■ **Quel cameriere è un disastro!** That
waiter is awful!

disastroso (FEM **disastrosa**) ADJECTIVE
disastrous
  □ effetti disastrosi disastrous effects
  ■ **in condizioni disastrose** in a terrible state

disattento (FEM **disattenta**) ADJECTIVE
inattentive

la **disattenzione** FEM NOUN
  ■ **un errore di disattenzione** a careless
mistake

la **disavventura** FEM NOUN
misadventure

la **discarica** (PL le **discariche**) FEM NOUN
tip (for rubbish)

la **discesa** FEM NOUN
slope
  □ una discesa ripida a steep slope
  ■ **in discesa** downhill □ Da casa nostra al
paese la strada è in discesa. It's downhill from
our house to the village.
  ■ **discesa libera** downhill race

la **disciplina** FEM NOUN
discipline

il **disco** (PL i **dischi**) MASC NOUN
1 record
  □ uno dei miei dischi preferiti one of my
favourite records
2 disk
  □ il disco rigido the hard disk
3 discus (in sport)
  ■ **il lancio del disco** the discus □ Chi ha

vinto il lancio del disco? Who won the discus?
  ■ **disco orario** parking disc
  ■ **disco volante** flying saucer

discografico (FEM **discografica**, MASC PL
discografici, FEM PL **discografiche**) ADJECTIVE
  ■ **casa discografica** record company

il **discorso** MASC NOUN
speech
  ■ **fare un discorso** to make a speech
  ■ **discorso diretto** direct speech
  ■ **discorso indiretto** indirect speech

la **discoteca** (PL le **discoteche**) FEM NOUN
club
  □ una discoteca alla moda a popular club
  ■ **Vado in discoteca di sabato.** I go
clubbing on Saturdays.

discreto (FEM **discreta**) ADJECTIVE
1 reasonable
  □ un voto discreto a reasonable mark
2 discreet
  □ È una persona molto discreta. He's very
discreet.

la **discriminazione** FEM NOUN
discrimination
  □ la discriminazione razziale racial
discrimination

la **discussione** FEM NOUN
1 discussion (debate)
  ■ **fare una discussione** to have a
discussion
  ■ **mettere in discussione** to bring into
question
  ■ **È fuori discussione.** It's out of the question.
2 argument
  □ Abbiamo avuto una discussione. We had an
argument.

discutere VERB [37]
1 to discuss
  ■ **discutere di qualcosa** to discuss
something □ Discutono spesso di politica.
They often discuss politics.
  ■ **Ho discusso a lungo con lui.** I had a long
discussion with him.
2 to argue
  □ Non voglio mettermi a discutere con te. I
don't want to argue with you.
  ■ **Mi ha ubbidito senza discutere.** He
obeyed me without question.

disdire VERB [35]
to cancel (booking, appointment)

disegnare VERB [14]
1 to draw
  □ Mio fratello sta disegnando. My brother is
drawing.
2 to design
  □ Disegna mobili. He designs furniture.

il **disegnatore,** la **disegnatrice** MASC/FEM
NOUN
designer

il **disegno** MASC NOUN
1 drawing
□ un bel disegno a beautiful drawing
2 design
□ un disegno a fiori a floral design

disfare VERB [38]
to undo *(packet, knot, knitting)*
□ Ha disfatto il pacco. He undid the parcel.
■ **disfare la valigia** to unpack □ Ha disfatto
la valigia. He's unpacked.
■ **disfare il letto** to strip the bed

disfatto (FEM **disfatta**) ADJECTIVE
■ **un letto disfatto** an unmade bed

la **disgrazia** FEM NOUN
■ **È successa una disgrazia.** Something
terrible has happened.

disgustoso (FEM **disgustosa**) ADJECTIVE
disgusting

il **disinfettante** MASC NOUN
disinfectant

disinfettare VERB [68]
to disinfect

disinibito (FEM **disinibita**) ADJECTIVE
uninhibited

disintegrare VERB [68]
to disintegrate

il **disinteresse** MASC NOUN
indifference

disintossicante (FEM **disintossicante**)
ADJECTIVE
■ **una cura disintossicante** a detox

disintossicarsi VERB [18, aux **essere**]
■ **disintossicarsi dall'alcol** to be treated
for alcoholism
■ **disintossicarsi dalla droga** to be treated
for drug addiction

disinvolto (FEM **disinvolta**) ADJECTIVE
relaxed
□ Ha un modo di fare molto disinvolto. She's
got a very relaxed manner.

disobbediente (FEM **disobbediente**)
ADJECTIVE
disobedient

disobbedire VERB [28]
■ **disobbedire a qualcuno** to disobey
somebody □ Mi ha disobbedito. He disobeyed
me.

disoccupato (FEM **disoccupata**) ADJECTIVE,
MASC/FEM NOUN
unemployed
□ È ancora disoccupato. He's still unemployed.
■ **i disoccupati** the unemployed

la **disoccupazione** FEM NOUN
unemployment
□ La disoccupazione è in aumento.
Unemployment is rising.

disonesto (FEM **disonesta**) ADJECTIVE
dishonest

disordinato (FEM **disordinata**) ADJECTIVE
untidy
□ un ragazzo disordinato an untidy boy

il **disordine** MASC NOUN
mess
□ Non sopporto il disordine. I can't stand mess.
□ Che disordine! What a mess!
■ **essere in disordine** *(room, house)* to be in
a mess
■ **disordini** disturbances □ i disturbi della
settimana scorsa the disturbances of last
week

disorientato (FEM **disorientata**) ADJECTIVE
disorientated

dispari ADJECTIVE
■ **numeri dispari** odd numbers

disparte
■ **starsene in disparte** to stand by oneself
□ Se ne stava in disparte. He was standing by
himself.

la **dispensa** FEM NOUN
sideboard

disperato (FEM **disperata**) ADJECTIVE
desperate
□ un gesto disperato a desperate gesture
■ **Ho un disperato bisogno di soldi.** I
desperately need money.

la **disperazione** FEM NOUN
despair

il **disperso**, la **dispersa** MASC/FEM NOUN
missing person

il **dispetto** MASC NOUN
■ **fare dispetti a qualcuno** to tease
somebody □ Smettila di fargli dispetti. Stop
teasing him.
■ **per dispetto** out of spite

dispettoso (FEM **dispettosa**) ADJECTIVE
spiteful

il **dispiacere** MASC NOUN
▷ *see also* **dispiacere** VERB
■ **dare un dispiacere a qualcuno** to upset
someone □ Non voglio darti un dispiacere. I
don't want to upset you.
■ **Le ha dato molti dispiaceri.** He's made
her very unhappy.
■ **È un gran dispiacere dovervelo dire.**
I'm really sorry to have to tell you this.

dispiacere VERB [70]
▷ *see also* **dispiacere** NOUN
■ **Mi dispiace.** I'm sorry.
■ **Le dispiace se fumo?** Do you mind if I
smoke?
■ **Se non le dispiace** If you don't mind

disponibile (FEM **disponibile**) ADJECTIVE
1 available
□ È disponibile in molti colori. It's available in
many colours.
2 ready to help

□ Luca è sempre molto disponibile. Luca's always very ready to help.

il **dispositivo** MASC NOUN
device

□ un dispositivo di sicurezza a safety device

la **disposizione** FEM NOUN

1 order

□ Ho dato disposizioni precise. I gave precise orders.

■ **a tua disposizione** at your disposal

■ **avere a disposizione** to have at one's disposal □ Abbiamo a disposizione cinque computer nuovi. We've got five new computers at our disposal.

2 arrangement

□ la disposizione dei mobili the arrangement of the furniture

■ **Ha cambiato la disposizione dei mobili.** He rearranged the furniture.

disposto (FEM **disposta**) ADJECTIVE

■ **essere disposto a** to be prepared to □ Non sono disposta ad aiutarti. I'm not prepared to help you.

■ **essere ben disposto nei confronti di** to be well disposed towards

disprezzare VERB [68]
to despise

il **disprezzo** MASC NOUN
contempt

□ Mi ha guardato con disprezzo. He looked at me with contempt.

dissetante (FEM **dissetante**) ADJECTIVE
refreshing

□ una bevanda dissetante a refreshing drink

distaccare VERB [18]

■ **distaccare qualcuno** to leave somebody behind □ Li ha distaccati di parecchi metri. He left them several metres behind.

il **distacco** (PL i **distacchi**) MASC NOUN

■ **con distacco** coldly □ Mi guardava con distacco. He looked at me coldly.

■ **Il distacco dalla famiglia è spesso difficile.** Leaving home is often difficult.

■ **vincere con un distacco di cento metri** to win by a hundred metres

distante (FEM **distante**) ADVERB, ADJECTIVE
far away

□ Non abitano distante. They don't live far away.

■ **essere distante da** to be a long way from □ La casa è distante dal centro. The house is a long way from the centre. □ È distante da qui? Is it a long way from here?

la **distanza** FEM NOUN
distance

□ la distanza tra Roma e Milano the distance between Rome and Milan

■ **Era a due metri di distanza.** She was two metres away.

■ **a poca distanza da qui** not far from here

■ **a distanza di due giorni** two days later

■ **distanza di sicurezza** braking distance

distare VERB [68]
to be far

□ Dista molto da qui? Is it far from here?

■ **Dista pochi chilometri da Roma.** It's a few kilometres from Rome.

distendere VERB [112]
to stretch

□ Non c'era posto per distendere le gambe. There was no room to stretch your legs.

■ **distendere i nervi** to relax

■ **distendersi** 1 to lie down 2 to relax

disteso (FEM **distesa**) ADJECTIVE

■ **essere disteso** to be lying □ Era distesa sul letto. She was lying on the bed.

distinguere VERB [39]
to see

□ Non riesco a distinguere il numero dell'autobus. I can't see the number of the bus.

■ **distinguere tra** to tell the difference between □ Non li distinguo tra loro. I can't tell the difference between them.

■ **Si distingue per efficienza.** He's outstandingly efficient.

il **distintivo** MASC NOUN
badge

distinto (FEM **distinta**) ADJECTIVE

1 distinguished

□ un signore dall'aspetto distinto a distinguished-looking man

■ **modi distinti** excellent manners

2 distinct

□ due materie distinte two distinct subjects

■ **Distinti saluti** Yours sincerely

la **distorsione** FEM NOUN
sprain

distrarre VERB [115]
to distract

□ Non distrarlo dal lavoro. Don't distract him from his work.

■ **distrarsi** to take one's mind off things □ Ho bisogno di distrarmi un po'. I need to take my mind off things.

■ **Si distrae spesso durante le lezioni.** His mind often wanders during lessons.

■ **Non distrarti!** Pay attention!

distratto (FEM **distratta**) ADJECTIVE
absent-minded

□ È distratto. He's absent-minded.

■ **Scusa, ero distratta.** I'm sorry, I wasn't paying attention.

la **distrazione** FEM NOUN

■ **un errore di distrazione** a careless mistake

■ **Mi scusi, è stato un attimo di distrazione.** I'm sorry, I wasn't thinking.

distribuire – docile

distribuire VERB [51]
to hand out
  □ Distribuisci i quaderni. Hand out the exercise books.
  ■ **distribuire le carte** to deal the cards

il **distributore** MASC NOUN
pump *(petrol)*
  ■ **distributore automatico** vending machine

distruggere VERB [79]
to destroy

la **distruzione** FEM NOUN
destruction

disturbare VERB [68]
to disturb
  □ Ti disturbo? Am I disturbing you? □ 'non disturbare' 'do not disturb'
  ■ **La disturba se fumo?** Do you mind if I smoke?
  ■ **Grazie del regalo, ma non dovevi disturbarti!** Thank you for the present, but you shouldn't have!

il **disturbo** MASC NOUN
trouble
  □ Non è affatto un disturbo. It's no trouble at all.
  ■ **disturbi di stomaco** stomach trouble *sing*

disubbidiente (FEM **disubbidiente**) ADJECTIVE
disobedient

disubbidire VERB [51]
  ■ **disubbidire a qualcuno** to disobey somebody □ Mi ha disubbidito. He disobeyed me.

il **dito** (FEM PL le **dita**) MASC NOUN
1 finger
  □ Non ha mosso un dito per aiutarmi. He didn't lift a finger to help me.
2 toe

la **ditta** FEM NOUN
firm
  ■ **Spett. Ditta,...** *(in letter)* Dear Sirs,...

il **dittatore** MASC NOUN
dictator

la **dittatura** FEM NOUN
dictatorship

il **divano** MASC NOUN
sofa
  □ sul divano on the sofa
  ■ **divano letto** sofa-bed

diventare VERB [68, aux **essere**]
1 to become
  □ È diventato famoso. He became famous.
  □ La situazione è diventata pericolosa. The situation has become dangerous.
2 to go
  □ Il latte è diventato acido. The milk has gone sour. □ La maglietta è diventata rosa dopo il lavaggio. The T-shirt went pink in the wash.
  ■ **diventare vecchio** to grow old

diverso (FEM **diversa**) ADJECTIVE
different
  □ È diverso da me. He's different from me.
  ■ **diversi** several □ diversi amici several friends □ Gliel'ho detto diverse volte. I told him several times.

divertente (FEM **divertente**) ADJECTIVE
funny
  □ una barzelletta divertente a funny joke
  □ Mario è molto divertente. Mario is very funny.
  ■ **È un gioco molto divertente.** This game is really fun.

il **divertimento** MASC NOUN
  ■ **Buon divertimento!** Have fun!

divertire VERB [41]
to amuse
  □ Mi ha divertito molto la sua storia. I was very amused by her story.
  ■ **divertirsi** to have a good time □ Ti sei divertito? Did you have a good time?
  □ Divertiti! Have a good time!

dividere VERB [40]
to divide
  □ L'ho diviso in tre parti. I've divided it into three parts. □ otto diviso quattro fa due eight divided by four is two
  ■ **dividersi** to be divided □ Il libro si divide in tre parti. The book is divided into three parts.

il **divieto** MASC NOUN
  ■ **'divieto di accesso'** 'no entry'
  ■ **'divieto di sosta'** 'no parking'

la **divisa** FEM NOUN
uniform
  ■ **un ufficiale in divisa** a uniformed officer

la **divisione** FEM NOUN
division

il **divo**, la **diva** MASC/FEM NOUN
star
  □ un divo del cinema a film star

divorare VERB [68]
to devour

divorziare VERB [17]
to get divorced
  □ Hanno divorziato. They got divorced.

il **divorzio** MASC NOUN
divorce

il **dizionario** MASC NOUN
dictionary
  □ un dizionario di inglese an English dictionary

il **do** (PL i **do**) MASC NOUN
C *(musical note)*

doc (FEM+PL **doc**) ADJECTIVE
  ■ **vino doc** quality wine

la **doccia** (PL le **docce**) FEM NOUN
shower
  ■ **fare la doccia** to have a shower

docile (FEM **docile**) ADJECTIVE
docile

il **documentario** MASC NOUN
documentary

il **documento** MASC NOUN
- **documento di identità** proof of identity
- **documenti** papers □ È andato a ritirare i documenti. He went to pick up the papers. □ Il poliziotto mi ha chiesto i documenti. The policeman asked for my papers.

dodicenne (FEM **dodicenne**) ADJECTIVE, MASC/FEM NOUN
twelve-year-old

dodicesimo (FEM **dodicesima**) ADJECTIVE, MASC NOUN
twelfth

dodici NUMBER
twelve
□ Ha dodici anni. He's twelve. □ alle dodici at twelve o'clock
- **il dodici dicembre** the twelfth of December

la **dogana** FEM NOUN
customs pl
- **passare la dogana** to go through customs

il **doganiere** MASC NOUN
customs officer

dolce (FEM **dolce**) ADJECTIVE
▷ see also **dolce** NOUN
sweet
□ Il caffè è troppo dolce. The coffee's too sweet.
□ È molto dolce con me. He's very sweet to me.
- **un formaggio dolce** a mild cheese

il **dolce** MASC NOUN
▷ see also **dolce** ADJECTIVE
dessert
□ Hai ordinato il dolce? Have you ordered a dessert?

il **dolcificante** MASC NOUN
sweetener

il **dollaro** MASC NOUN
dollar

il **dolore** MASC NOUN
1 pain
□ un dolore acuto a sharp pain □ Ho un dolore al braccio. I've got a pain in my arm.
2 sorrow
□ È con grande dolore che annunciamo la scomparsa di... With great sorrow we announce the death of...
3 grief
- **morire di dolore** to die of grief

doloroso (FEM **dolorosa**) ADJECTIVE
1 painful
□ È un'operazione dolorosa. It's a painful operation.
2 sad
□ una notizia dolorosa a sad piece of news

la **domanda** FEM NOUN
1 question
- **fare una domanda a qualcuno** to ask somebody a question □ Ti ha fatto molte domande? Did he ask you a lot of questions?
2 application
□ Hai spedito la domanda? Have you sent off your application?
- **fare domanda per un lavoro** to apply for a job

domandare VERB [68]
to ask
- **domandare qualcosa a qualcuno** to ask somebody something □ Mi ha domandato l'ora. He asked me the time. □ Mi ha domandato se volevo andare alla festa. He asked me if I wanted to go to the party.
- **domandarsi** to wonder □ Mi domando dove possa essere. I wonder where it can be.
- **domandare di qualcuno** to ask after somebody □ Mi ha domandato di te. She asked after you.

domani ADVERB
tomorrow
□ Domani è sabato. Tomorrow's Saturday.
- **domani stesso** tomorrow
- **domani l'altro** the day after tomorrow
- **domani a otto** a week tomorrow
- **A domani!** See you tomorrow!

la **domenica** (PL le **domeniche**) FEM NOUN
Sunday
> LANGUAGE TIP In Italian, days are not written with capital letters.
□ L'ho visto domenica. I saw him on Sunday.
- **di domenica** on Sundays □ Di domenica vado al cinema. I go to the cinema on Sundays.
- **domenica scorsa** last Sunday
- **domenica prossima** next Sunday

la **domestica** (PL le **domestiche**) FEM NOUN
cleaning lady

il **domestico** (PL i **domestici**) MASC NOUN
▷ see also **domestico** ADJECTIVE
servant

domestico (FEM **domestica**, MASC PL **domestici**, FEM PL **domestiche**) ADJECTIVE
▷ see also **domestico** NOUN
- **lavori domestici** housework sing
- **animale domestico** pet

il **donatore**, la **donatrice** MASC/FEM NOUN
- **donatore di sangue** blood donor
- **donatore di organi** organ donor

dondolarsi VERB [56]
1 to rock (in chair)
2 to swing (on swing)

il **dondolo** MASC NOUN
- **cavallo a dondolo** rocking horse
- **sedia a dondolo** rocking chair

la **donna** FEM NOUN
1 woman
□ Ho visto due donne giovani. I saw two young women.
- **donna delle pulizie** cleaning lady
2 queen (in cards)

dopo - dovere

dopo ADVERB, PREPOSITION, CONJUNCTION
1 later
□ Ci vediamo dopo. See you later. □ un anno dopo a year later
2 then
□ Ora studia, e dopo potrai uscire. First do your homework, then you can go out.
3 after
□ il giorno dopo the day after □ Ci vediamo dopo le vacanze. See you after the holidays. □ È arrivato dopo di me. He arrived after me. □ Dopo aver telefonato è uscito. After making a phone call he went out. □ uno dopo l'altro one after the other
■ **dopo che** after □ dopo che è partito after he left

il **dopobarba** (PL i **dopobarba**) MASC NOUN
aftershave

dopodomani ADVERB
the day after tomorrow
□ Ci vediamo dopodomani. See you the day after tomorrow.

il **doposcì** (PL i **doposcì**) MASC NOUN
après-ski boot

doppiare VERB [17]
1 to dub (film)
2 to lap (in race)

doppio (FEM **doppia**) ADJECTIVE
▷ see also **doppio** NOUN, ADVERB
double
□ un doppio whisky a double whisky
■ **frase a doppio senso** double entendre
■ **doppi vetri** double-glazing
■ **strada a doppio senso** two-way street

doppio ADVERB
▷ see also **doppio** ADJECTIVE, NOUN
double
■ **vedere doppio** to see double

il **doppio** MASC NOUN
▷ see also **doppio** ADJECTIVE, ADVERB
■ **il doppio** twice as much □ Ho pagato il doppio. I paid twice as much.
■ **fare un doppio** (in tennis) to play a game of doubles

il **dormiglione**, la **dormigliona** MASC/FEM NOUN
sleepyhead
□ Sveglia, dormiglione! Wake up, sleepyhead!

dormire VERB [41]
to sleep
□ Sta dormendo. She's sleeping.
■ **andare a dormire** to go to bed □ Vado a dormire. I'm going to bed.
■ **dormire come un ghiro** to sleep like a log
■ **dormire in piedi** to be asleep on one's feet

la **dormita** FEM NOUN
■ **farsi una bella dormita** to have a good sleep

il **dorso** MASC NOUN
back
□ Sdraiati sul dorso. Lie on your back.
■ **nuotare a dorso** to do the backstroke

la **dose** FEM NOUN
dose

dotato (FEM **dotata**) ADJECTIVE
■ **un bambino dotato** a gifted child

il **dottorato** MASC NOUN
doctorate

il **dottore**, la **dottoressa** MASC/FEM NOUN
doctor

> **DID YOU KNOW...?**
> In Italy **dottore** is a title used by anyone who has a degree.

dove ADVERB
where
□ Dove abiti? Where do you live? □ Di dove sei? Where are you from? □ La città dove abito è sul mare. The town where I live is by the sea.
■ **Dov'è...?** Where is...? □ Dov'è la mia chiave? Where's my key?

il **dovere** MASC NOUN
▷ see also **dovere** VERB
duty
□ Credeva che fosse suo dovere. He thought it was his duty.
■ **Avevi il dovere di dirmelo.** You should have told me.
■ **Mi sono sentito in dovere di dirtelo.** I felt I should tell you.

dovere VERB [42]
▷ see also **dovere** NOUN
1 to have to
□ È dovuto partire. He had to leave. □ Devi tornare a casa presto stasera? Do you have to go home early this evening? □ Non devi andarci se non vuoi. You don't have to go if you don't want to.

> **LANGUAGE TIP** In the present tense, 'got' is sometimes added.

□ Ora devo andare. I've got to go now.
2 must
□ Devi farlo subito. You must do it at once. □ Devi finire i compiti prima di uscire. You must finish your homework before you go out. □ Non devi dirglielo per nessun motivo. You mustn't on any account tell him. □ Dev'essere tardi. It must be late. □ Devi essere stanco dopo un viaggio così lungo. You must be tired after such a long journey.

> **LANGUAGE TIP** **dovere** in the conditional is translated by 'should'.

□ Dovresti studiare di più. You should study more. □ Pensi che avrebbe dovuto dirmelo? Do you think he should have told me? □ Dovrebbe arrivare alle dieci. He should arrive at ten.

3 to owe
- **dovere qualcosa a qualcuno** to owe somebody something □ Gli devo quindici euro. I owe him fifteen euros.

dovunque ADVERB
1 wherever
□ Ti troverò dovunque tu vada. I'll find you wherever you go.
2 everywhere
□ L'ho cercato dovunque. I've looked for it everywhere.

dovuto (FEM **dovuta**) ADJECTIVE
- **essere dovuto a** to be due to □ Il ritardo è dovuto al maltempo. The delay is due to the bad weather.

la dozzina FEM NOUN
dozen
□ una dozzina di uova a dozen eggs

il dramma (PL i **drammi**) MASC NOUN
drama
- **fare un dramma di qualcosa** to make a drama out of something

drammatico (FEM **drammatica**, MASC PL **drammatici**, FEM PL **drammatiche**) ADJECTIVE
terrible (situation, moment)
- **arte drammatica** drama

drastico (FEM **drastica**, MASC PL **drastici**, FEM PL **drastiche**) ADJECTIVE
drastic

dritto = **diritto**

la droga (PL le **droghe**) FEM NOUN
drug
- **fare uso di droga** to be on drugs
- **droghe leggere** soft drugs
- **droghe pesanti** hard drugs

drogarsi VERB [76, aux **essere**]
to take drugs

il drogato, la drogata MASC/FEM NOUN
drug addict

il dromedario MASC NOUN
dromedary

il dubbio MASC NOUN
doubt
□ Ho i miei dubbi in proposito. I have my doubts about it.
- **mettere in dubbio qualcosa** to question something □ Ha messo in dubbio la mia onestà. He questioned my honesty.
- **avere il dubbio che...** to suspect that...
□ Ho il dubbio che sia stato lui. I suspect that it was him.
- **senza dubbio** undoubtedly □ È senza dubbio uno dei suoi quadri più belli. It's undoubtedly one of his finest paintings.

dubitare VERB [68]
to doubt
□ Pensi che telefonerà? — Dubito. Do you think he'll phone? — I doubt it. □ Dubito che

verrà. I doubt he'll come.
- **dubitare di** (honesty, capacity) to doubt
□ Nessuno dubita della tua onestà. Nobody doubts your honesty.

Dublino FEM NOUN
Dublin
□ Vive a Dublino. He lives in Dublin.

il duca (PL i **duchi**) MASC NOUN
duke

la duchessa FEM NOUN
duchess

due NUMBER
two
□ due bambini two children □ Ha due anni. She's two. □ alle due at two o'clock
- **il due dicembre** the second of December
- **Vorrei dire due parole.** I'd like to say a few words.
- **Ci metto due minuti.** It'll only take me a couple of minutes.
- **due volte** twice □ L'ho fatto due volte. I did it twice.

duecento NUMBER
two hundred
- **il Duecento** the thirteenth century

il duepezzi (PL i **duepezzi**) MASC NOUN
two-piece swimsuit

dunque CONJUNCTION
1 so
□ Ho sbagliato, dunque è giusto che paghi. It was my mistake, so it's fair I should pay.
2 well
□ Dunque, come dicevo... Well, as I was saying...

il duomo MASC NOUN
cathedral

il duplicato MASC NOUN
duplicate

durante PREPOSITION
during

durare VERB [68, aux **essere**]
to last
□ Le batterie non sono durate a lungo. The batteries didn't last long. □ Il film dura circa due ore. The film lasts about two hours.
- **Così non può durare!** This can't go on any longer!

duro (FEM **dura**) ADJECTIVE
▷ see also **duro** NOUN
hard
□ Il materasso è troppo duro per me. The mattress is too hard for me. □ Non essere troppo duro con lui. Don't be too hard on him.
- **duro d'orecchi** hard of hearing
- **fare il duro** to act tough

il duro MASC NOUN
▷ see also **duro** ADJECTIVE
- **fare il duro** to act tough

Ee

e CONJUNCTION
1 and
  □ Io e Davide ci andremo. Davide and I will go.
2 but
  □ Lo credevo onesto e non lo è. I thought he
  was honest but he isn't. □ Sapeva di sbagliare
  e l'ha fatto lo stesso. She knew she was making
  a mistake, but she did it all the same.
3 how about
  □ Io non ci vado, e tu? I'm not going, how
  about you?

▮ **LANGUAGE TIP** e is sometimes not translated.
  □ quattro sterline e cinquanta four pounds fifty
  □ A me piace molto, e a te? I like it a lot, do
  you? □ E smettila! Stop it!

l' **ebreo**, l' **ebrea** MASC/FEM NOUN
  ▷ see also **ebreo** ADJECTIVE
  Jew
  ▪ **gli ebrei** the Jews
ebreo (FEM **ebrea**) ADJECTIVE
  ▷ see also **ebreo** NOUN
  Jewish
  □ È ebreo. He's Jewish.
ecc. ABBREVIATION
  etc
  □ Vendono libri, dischi ecc. They sell books,
  records, etc.
eccellente (FEM **eccellente**) ADJECTIVE
  excellent
eccentrico (FEM **eccentrica**, MASC PL
  eccentrici, FEM PL **eccentriche**) ADJECTIVE
  eccentric
  □ Suo zio è un po' eccentrico. His uncle's a bit
  eccentric.
  ▪ **Si veste in modo eccentrico.** She wears
  unusual clothes.
eccessivo (FEM **eccessiva**) ADJECTIVE
  excessive
  □ Proibirgli di uscire mi sembra un po'
  eccessivo. I think it's a bit excessive to forbid
  him to go out.
l' **eccesso** MASC NOUN
  excess
  □ Devo smaltire il peso in eccesso. I must lose
  some excess weight.
  ▪ **eccesso di velocità** speeding □ Ha preso
  una multa per eccesso di velocità. She was
  fined for speeding.

eccetto PREPOSITION
  except
  □ Tutti lo sapevano, eccetto io. Everybody
  except me knew about it.
eccezionale (FEM **eccezionale**) ADJECTIVE
1 really good
  □ È un film eccezionale. It's a really good film.
2 exceptional
  □ in circostanze eccezionali in exceptional
  circumstances
l' **eccezione** FEM NOUN
  exception
  □ Va bene, ma lui è un'eccezione. Okay, but
  he's an exception. □ Non posso fare eccezioni.
  I can't make exceptions.
eccitato (FEM **eccitata**) ADJECTIVE
1 excited
2 aroused
ecco ADVERB
  ▪ **Ecco il treno!** Here's the train!
  ▪ **Eccomi!** Here I am!
  ▪ **Ecco, tieni.** Here you are.
  ▪ **Ah, ecco perché non è venuto!** So that's
  why he didn't come!
eccome ADVERB
  ▪ **Ti piace? — Eccome!** Do you like it? — Yes
  I do!
  ▪ **Era difficile? — Eccome!** Was it difficult?
  — Yes it was!
  ▪ **Ti sei divertito? — Eccome!** Did you
  enjoy yourself? — Yes I did!
l' **eclisse** FEM NOUN
  eclipse
l' **eco** (PL gli **echi**) MASC NOUN
  echo
ecologico (FEM **ecologica**, MASC PL
  ecologici, FEM PL **ecologiche**) ADJECTIVE
1 ecological
  □ una catastrofe ecologica an ecological
  disaster
2 environmentally friendly
  □ un detersivo ecologico an environmentally
  friendly detergent
l' **economia** FEM NOUN
1 economy
  □ L'economia è in crisi. The economy is in crisis.
2 economics sing
  □ Studia economia. He's studying economics.

economico (FEM **economica**, MASC PL **economici**, FEM PL **economiche**) ADJECTIVE
inexpensive

□ un albergo economico an inexpensive hotel

■ **più economico** cheaper □ È più economico viaggiare in pullman. It's cheaper to travel by coach.

■ **crisi economica** economic crisis

■ **viaggiare in classe economica** to travel economy class

l' **edera** FEM NOUN
ivy

l' **edicola** FEM NOUN
newspaper kiosk

l' **edificio** MASC NOUN
building

edile (FEM **edile**) ADJECTIVE

■ **un cantiere edile** a building site

■ **un operaio edile** a construction worker

Edimburgo FEM NOUN
Edinburgh

□ Domani andremo a Edimburgo. We're going to Edinburgh tomorrow. □ Abita ad Edimburgo. She lives in Edinburgh.

l' **editore** MASC NOUN
publisher

LANGUAGE TIP Be careful! **editore** doesn't mean **editor**.

l' **edizione** FEM NOUN
edition

□ la seconda edizione del libro the second edition of the book

■ **edizione economica** paperback □ Si trova anche in edizione economica. It's also available in paperback.

educato (FEM **educata**) ADJECTIVE
polite

□ È un ragazzo molto educato. He's a very polite boy.

■ **Non è educato fissare la gente.** It's rude to stare at people.

LANGUAGE TIP Be careful! **educato** doesn't mean **educated**.

l' **educazione** FEM NOUN
upbringing

□ Ha avuto un'educazione molto severa. He had a very strict upbringing.

■ **Ma che razza di educazione!** How rude!

■ **educazione fisica** physical education

effervescente (FEM **effervescente**) ADJECTIVE
fizzy

l' **effetto** MASC NOUN
effect

□ effetti speciali special effects □ La pastiglia farà effetto tra una mezz'ora. You'll feel the effect of the pill in about half an hour.

■ **Che effetto fa?** What's it like?

■ **in effetti** in fact □ In effetti non ha tutti i torti. In fact she's quite right.

■ **effetto serra** greenhouse effect

efficace (FEM **efficace**) ADJECTIVE
effective

□ un rimedio efficace contro il raffreddore an effective remedy for colds

efficiente (FEM **efficiente**) ADJECTIVE
efficient

□ un impiegato efficiente an efficient worker

l' **Egitto** MASC NOUN
Egypt

□ Mi è piaciuto molto l'Egitto. I really liked Egypt. □ Andremo in Egitto questa primavera. We're going to Egypt this spring.

egli PRONOUN
he

egoista (FEM **egoista**, MASC PL **egoisti**, FEM PL **egoiste**) ADJECTIVE
▷ see also **egoista** NOUN
selfish

□ Penso di essere stato molto egoista. I think I've been very selfish. □ Sei egoista! You're selfish!

l' **egoista** (MASC PL gli **egoisti**, FEM PL le **egoiste**) MASC/FEM NOUN
▷ see also **egoista** ADJECTIVE
selfish person

□ È un grande egoista. He's a very selfish person.

elasticizzato (FEM **elasticizzata**) ADJECTIVE
stretch

□ tessuto elasticizzato stretch material

l' **elastico** (PL gli **elastici**) MASC NOUN
▷ see also **elastico** ADJECTIVE
elastic band

elastico (FEM **elastica**, MASC PL **elastici**, FEM PL **elastiche**) ADJECTIVE
▷ see also **elastico** NOUN
elastic

l' **elefante** MASC NOUN
elephant

elegante (FEM **elegante**) ADJECTIVE
smart

□ una giacca elegante a smart jacket □ È sempre elegante. She's always smart.

eleggere VERB [57]
elect

□ Hanno eletto il nuovo presidente. They've elected the new president.

elementare (FEM **elementare**) ADJECTIVE
basic

□ alcune nozioni elementari di informatica some basic knowledge of computing

■ **scuola elementare** primary school

■ **la seconda elementare** the second year at primary school

l' **elemento** MASC NOUN
element

85

un elemento chimico a chemical element
- **Enrico è il miglior elemento della squadra.** Enrico's best player in the team.

l' **elemosina** FEM NOUN
- **chiedere l'elemosina** to beg □ Per strada tanti chiedevano l'elemosina. There were a lot of people begging in the street.

l' **elenco** (PL gli **elenchi**) MASC NOUN
list
□ un elenco di ostelli a list of hostels
- **fare un elenco di** to list
- **elenco telefonico** phone book □ L'ho cercato sull'elenco telefonico. I looked him up in the phone book.

elettorale (FEM **elettorale**) ADJECTIVE
- **campagna elettorale** election campaign
- **sistema elettorale** electoral system

l' **elettore**, l' **elettrice** MASC/FEM NOUN
voter

l' **elettricista** (PL gli **elettricisti**) MASC NOUN
electrician
□ Fa l'elettricista. He is an electrician.

l' **elettricità** FEM NOUN
electricity

elettrico (FEM **elettrica**, MASC PL **elettrici**, FEM PL **elettriche**) ADJECTIVE
electric
□ un filo elettrico an electric wire

elettrizzante (FEM **elettrizzante**) ADJECTIVE
thrilling

l' **elettrodomestico** (PL gli **elettrodomestici**) MASC NOUN
domestic appliance

elettronico (FEM **elettronica**, MASC PL **elettronici**, FEM PL **elettroniche**) ADJECTIVE
electronic
□ musica elettronica electronic music
- **posta elettronica** email

l' **elica** (PL le **eliche**) FEM NOUN
propeller

l' **elicottero** MASC NOUN
helicopter

eliminare VERB [68]
to eliminate
□ Siamo stati eliminati alle semifinali. We were eliminated in the semi-final.

gli **emarginati** MASC PL NOUN
- **gli emarginati** the socially excluded

l' **emergenza** FEM NOUN
emergency
□ È un'emergenza. It's an emergency.
- **in caso di emergenza** in case of emergency □ In caso di emergenza chiama questo numero. In case of emergency call this number.

l' **emicrania** FEM NOUN
migraine
□ Aveva l'emicrania. He had a migraine.

emigrare VERB [68, aux **essere**]
to emigrate
□ Erano emigrati in Germania. They emigrated to Germany.

l' **emittente** FEM NOUN
station
□ un'emittente radiofonica locale a local radio station □ un'emittente televisiva privata an independent television station

l' **emorragia** (PL le **emorragie**) FEM NOUN
bleeding
□ un'emorragia interna internal bleeding

le **emorroidi** FEM PL NOUN
piles

emotivo (FEM **emotiva**) ADJECTIVE
emotional
□ È molto emotiva. She's very emotional.

emozionante (FEM **emozionante**)
ADJECTIVE
exciting
□ È stata un'avventura emozionante. It was an exciting adventure.

emozionare VERB [68]
1 to move (emotionally)
2 to excite
- **emozionarsi** 1 to be moved 2 to be excited

emozionato (FEM **emozionata**) ADJECTIVE
1 moved
□ Era stupita ed emozionata per l'accoglienza ricevuta. She was amazed and moved by the welcome she got.
2 emotional
□ Ero troppo emozionato per fare un discorso. I was too emotional to make a speech.

l' **emozione** FEM NOUN
emotion
□ Le tremava la voce per l'emozione. Her voice trembled with emotion.
- **a caccia di emozioni** in search of excitement

l' **enciclopedia** FEM NOUN
encyclopaedia

l' **energia** FEM NOUN
energy
□ Come fai ad essere così pieno di energia? How do you manage to be so full of energy?
- **energia nucleare** nuclear energy

energico (FEM **energica**, MASC PL **energici**, FEM PL **energiche**) ADJECTIVE
energetic

enorme (FEM **enorme**) ADJECTIVE
huge
□ È un negozio enorme. It's a huge shop.
□ Ha avuto un enorme successo. It was a huge success.

entrambi ADJECTIVE, PRONOUN
both

□ su entrambi i lati della strada on both sides of the street □ Sono partiti entrambi. They've both left.

entrare VERB [68, AUX **essere**]

1 to go in

□ Ho bussato e sono entrato. I knocked and went in. □ Siamo entrati in aula. We went into the classroom.

2 to come in

□ Permesso? Posso entrare? Excuse me, can I come in?

3 to get in

□ I ladri sono entrati dalla finestra. The thieves got in through the window.

■ **Questo non c'entra.** That's got nothing to do with it.

■ **Io non c'entro.** It's got nothing to do with me.

■ **La matematica non mi entra in testa.** I can't understand maths.

l' **entrata** FEM NOUN

entrance

□ L'entrata principale è sulla via laterale. The main entrance is in the side street.

■ **'entrata libera'** 'admission free'

entro PREPOSITION

1 by

□ Devo pagare entro il dodici febbraio. I've got to pay by the twelfth of February. □ entro domani by tomorrow □ entro aprile by the end of April

2 within

□ Avremo i risultati entro un mese. We'll have the results within a month. □ entro quattro anni within four years

l' **entusiasmo** MASC NOUN

enthusiasm

□ All'inizio era pieno di entusiasmo. At the start he was full of enthusiasm.

entusiasta (MASC PL **entusiasti**, FEM PL **entusiaste**) ADJECTIVE

delighted

□ Non era troppo entusiasta, ma ha accettato. He wasn't exactly delighted, but he agreed.

■ **essere entusiasta di** to be extremely pleased with □ Sono entusiasta dei risultati. I'm extremely pleased with the results.

eolico (FEM **eolica**, MASC PL **eolici**, FEM PL **eoliche**) ADJECTIVE

wind

□ l'energia eolica wind power

l' **epidemia** FEM NOUN

epidemic

□ un'epidemia di influenza a flu epidemic

epilettico (FEM **epilettica**, MASC PL **epilettici**, FEM PL **epilettiche**) ADJECTIVE

epileptic

□ una crisi epilettica an epileptic fit

l' **episodio** MASC NOUN

episode

□ un episodio imbarazzante della sua vita an embarrassing episode in her life

■ **un grave episodio di razzismo** a serious instance of racism

l' **epoca** (PL le **epoche**) FEM NOUN

era

□ in epoca bizantina in the Byzantine era

■ **a quell'epoca** at that time □ A quell'epoca mi trovavo a Londra. At that time I was in London.

■ **mobili d'epoca** period furniture *sing*

eppure CONJUNCTION

and yet

□ Sembra impossibile, eppure è vero! It seems impossible, and yet it's true!

■ **Non è venuto all'appuntamento. Eppure aveva promesso.** He didn't come to the meeting, though he'd promised he would.

l' **equatore** MASC NOUN

equator

equatoriale (FEM **equatoriale**) ADJECTIVE

equatorial

□ clima equatoriale equatorial climate

l' **equilibrio** MASC NOUN

balance

□ Ha perso l'equilibrio ed è caduto. He lost his balance and fell.

l' **equipaggiamento** MASC NOUN

equipment

equipaggiato (FEM **equipaggiata**) ADJECTIVE

equipped

□ Erano ben equipaggiati per la montagna. They were well-equipped for climbing.

l' **equipaggio** MASC NOUN

crew

□ l'equipaggio dell'aereo the cabin crew

l' **equitazione** FEM NOUN

riding

□ C'è una scuola di equitazione qua vicino. There's a riding school near here.

l' **equivoco** (PL gli **equivoci**) MASC NOUN

▷ see also **equivoco** ADJECTIVE

misunderstanding

□ È stato tutto un equivoco. It was all a misunderstanding.

equivoco (FEM **equivoca**, MASC PL **equivoci**, FEM PL **equivoche**) ADJECTIVE

▷ see also **equivoco** NOUN

ambiguous

equo (FEM **equa**) ADJECTIVE

fair

□ un compenso equo fair payment

l' **erba** FEM NOUN

grass

□ Eravamo sdraiati sull'erba. We were lying on the grass.

■ **erbe aromatiche** herbs

l' **erbaccia** (PL le **erbacce**) FEM NOUN
weed

l' **erboristeria** FEM NOUN
herbalist's shop

l' **erede** MASC/FEM NOUN
heir

□ Lei è l'unica erede. She's the only heir.

l' **eredità** FEM NOUN
inheritance

□ Aveva paura di perdere l'eredità. He was afraid of losing his inheritance.

■ **lasciare in eredità** to leave □ Suo padre gli ha lasciato in eredità una bella casa. His father left him a beautiful house.

ereditare VERB [68]
to inherit

□ Ha ereditato la casa del nonno. She inherited her grandfather's house.

ereditario (FEM **ereditaria**) ADJECTIVE
hereditary

□ una malattia ereditaria a hereditary disease

l' **ergastolo** MASC NOUN
life sentence

□ Gli hanno dato l'ergastolo. He was given a life sentence.

l' **erica** FEM NOUN
heather

l' **eroe** MASC NOUN
hero

l' **eroina** FEM NOUN

1 heroine
□ l'eroina del romanzo the heroine of the novel

2 heroin
□ L'eroina è una droga pesante. Heroin is a hard drug.

errato (FEM **errata**) ADJECTIVE
wrong

l' **errore** MASC NOUN
mistake

□ Non ho fatto neanche un errore. I didn't make a single mistake. □ un errore di ortografia a spelling mistake

esagerare VERB [68]
to exaggerate

□ Non esagerare! Don't exaggerate!

■ **Ha esagerato un po' nel bere.** He had a bit too much to drink.

l' **esame** MASC NOUN

1 exam
□ dare un esame to take an exam □ Non ho passato l'esame. I didn't pass the exam. □ Quando saprai il risultato degli esami? When will you get your exam results?

2 test

■ **esame di guida** driving test
■ **esame del sangue** blood test

esaminare VERB [68]
to examine

esattamente ADVERB
exactly

□ È esattamente quello che intendevo. It's exactly what I meant.

esatto (FEM **esatta**) ADJECTIVE
exact

□ Non mi ricordo le parole esatte. I can't remember the exact words.

l' **esaurimento** MASC NOUN

■ **esaurimento nervoso** nervous breakdown

esaurire VERB [51]

1 to sell out
□ Vorrei una borsa di paglia. — Mi spiace, le abbiamo esaurite. I'd like a straw bag. — I'm sorry, we've sold out of them.

2 to run out of
□ L'aereo aveva esaurito il carburante. The plane had run out of fuel.

esaurito (FEM **esaurita**) ADJECTIVE

1 sold out
□ I biglietti erano tutti esauriti. All the tickets were sold out.

2 run-down
□ Sono un po' esaurito. I'm a bit run-down.

esausto (FEM **esausta**) ADJECTIVE
exhausted

□ Sono esausta! I'm exhausted!

l' **esca** (PL le **esche**) FEM NOUN
bait

eschimese (FEM **eschimese**) ADJECTIVE, MASC/FEM NOUN
Eskimo

esclamativo (FEM **esclamativa**) ADJECTIVE

■ **punto esclamativo** exclamation mark

l' **esclamazione** FEM NOUN
exclamation

escludere VERB [3]
to exclude

□ È stato escluso dalla gara. He was excluded from the competition.

esclusivamente ADVERB

1 entirely
□ La colpa è esclusivamente tua. The fault is entirely yours.

2 exclusively
□ una professione esclusivamente femminile an exclusively female profession

esclusivo (FEM **esclusiva**) ADJECTIVE
exclusive

□ un ristorante esclusivo an exclusive restaurant

escluso (FEM **esclusa**) ADJECTIVE
except

□ Tutti lo sapevano, escluso me. Everybody knew about it, except me.

■ **Le bevande sono gratuite, escluse**

quelle alcoliche. Drinks, apart from alcoholic ones, are free.

■ **Costa cinquecento sterline, escluso l'albergo.** It costs five hundred pounds, not including the hotel.

l' **esecuzione** FEM NOUN

1 execution *(of a task)*

■ **È responsabile dell'esecuzione dei lavori.** He's responsible for carrying out the work.

■ **esecuzione capitale** execution

2 performance *(musical)*

eseguire VERB [41]

1 to carry out

□ Stava solo eseguendo gli ordini. He was only carrying out orders.

2 to perform

□ Ha eseguito un valzer di Chopin. She performed a waltz by Chopin.

l' **esempio** MASC NOUN
example

□ Fammi un esempio. Give me an example.

■ **per esempio** for example

l' **esemplare** MASC NOUN
specimen

□ un esemplare rarissimo a very rare specimen

esercitare VERB [68]

1 to practise *(profession)*

2 to train *(body, mind)*

■ **esercitare il proprio controllo su qualcuno** to exert control over somebody

■ **esercitarsi** to practise □ esercitarsi nella guida to practise one's driving

l' **esercito** MASC NOUN
army

l' **esercizio** MASC NOUN
exercise

□ un esercizio di matematica a maths exercise
□ Questi esercizi sviluppano gli addominali. These exercises develop the abdominal muscles.

esigente (FEM **esigente**) ADJECTIVE
demanding

□ Il suo capo è molto esigente. His boss is very demanding.

esigere VERB [43]
to demand

□ Il proprietario esige il pagamento immediato. The owner is demanding immediate payment.
□ È un lavoro che esige molta concentrazione. It's a job which demands a lot of concentration.

l' **esilio** MASC NOUN
exile

□ Vive in esilio da alcuni anni. He's been living in exile for several years.

■ **mandare in esilio** to exile

esistere VERB [10, aux **essere**]
to exist

□ Babbo Natale non esiste. Santa Claus doesn't exist.

■ **Non esiste!** No way!

esitare VERB [68]
to hesitate

□ Ha esitato prima di rispondere. He hesitated before answering.

l' **esito** MASC NOUN
result

□ l'esito degli esami the exam results

l' **esodo** MASC NOUN
exodus

□ l'esodo delle vacanze estive the summer holiday exodus

l' **esordio** MASC NOUN
debut

□ il suo esordio in nazionale his debut in the national team

■ **La sua carriera è ancora agli esordi.** His career is just beginning.

esotico (FEM **esotica**, MASC PL **esotici**, FEM PL **esotiche**) ADJECTIVE
exotic

□ frutta esotica exotic fruit

espellere VERB [44]

1 to expel

□ L'hanno espulso dalla scuola. He was expelled from the school.

2 to send off

□ Il calciatore è stato espulso. The player was sent off.

l' **esperienza** FEM NOUN
experience

□ È stata un'esperienza molto utile. It was a very useful experience.

■ **parlare per esperienza** to speak from experience

l' **esperimento** MASC NOUN
experiment

□ esperimenti sugli animali experiments on animals

l' **esperto,** l' **esperta** MASC/FEM NOUN
expert

□ un esperto di computer a computer expert

esplicito (FEM **esplicita**) ADJECTIVE
explicit

esplodere VERB [45]
to explode

□ L'ordigno è esploso. The bomb exploded.

esplorare VERB [68]
to explore

□ Vorrei esplorare un po' la città. I'd like to explore the town a bit.

l' **esplosione** FEM NOUN
explosion

□ L'esplosione ha distrutto il palazzo. The explosion destroyed the building.

esporre VERB [73]

1 to display

□ Ha esposto la merce in vetrina. He displayed the goods in the window.

2 to explain

esportare – estremamente

□ Ha esposto i fatti con chiarezza. She explained the facts clearly.

3 to show

□ Espone i suoi quadri in una galleria d'arte. He's showing his paintings in an art gallery.

■ **esporsi al sole** to expose oneself to the sun

esportare VERB [68]
to export

esposto (FEM **esposta**) ADJECTIVE

■ **essere esposto a** to face □ La casa è esposta a nord. The house faces north.

l' **espressione** FEM NOUN
expression

□ libertà di espressione freedom of expression □ un'espressione volgare a coarse expression

l' **espresso** MASC NOUN

1 espresso

□ Un espresso e un cappuccino, per favore. An espresso and a cappuccino, please.

2 express train

□ Abbiamo preso l'espresso per Roma. We took the express train to Rome.

■ **per espresso** express □ Vorrei spedirlo per espresso. I'd like to send it express.

esprimere VERB [46]
to express

□ Sei libero di esprimere il tuo parere. You're free to express your opinion.

■ **esprimere un desiderio** to make a wish □ Dai, esprimi un desiderio! Go on, make a wish!

■ **esprimersi** to express oneself □ Trovo difficile esprimermi in inglese. I find it difficult to express myself in English.

■ **esprimersi a gesti** to communicate by gestures

l' **essenziale** MASC NOUN

■ **l'essenziale è...** the main thing is... □ L'essenziale è che tu sia arrivato sano e salvo. The main thing is that you got here safe and sound.

essenzialmente ADVERB
essentially

essere VERB [47]
▷ see also **essere** NOUN

1 to be

□ Sono italiana. I'm Italian. □ Sei sicuro? Are you sure? □ Chi è? Who is it? □ È l'una. It's one o'clock. □ Sono le otto. It's eight o'clock. □ Siamo in dieci. There are ten of us. □ È di Manchester. She's from Manchester. □ È di mio fratello. It's my brother's. □ Ce ne sono due. There are two of them. □ Cosa c'è che non va? What's wrong?

2 to have

□ Sono appena arrivato. I've just arrived. □ Mario è appena partito. Mario has just left.

l' **essere** MASC NOUN
▷ see also **essere** VERB

■ **essere umano** human being

essi (FEM **esse**) PRONOUN
they

esso (FEM **essa**) PRONOUN
it

est MASC NOUN
east

□ Il vento viene da est. The wind comes from the east.

■ **ad est** east □ ad est di Palermo east of Palermo

□ Il sole sorge ad est. The sun rises in the east.

■ **ad est di** east of □ Si trova ad est della città. It's east of the city.

■ **i paesi dell'Est** Eastern Europe

l' **estate** FEM NOUN
summer

□ d'estate in the summer

esteriore (FEM **esteriore**) ADJECTIVE

■ **La sua sicurezza è solo esteriore.** He seems confident, but he isn't really.

esterno (FEM **esterna**) ADJECTIVE, MASC NOUN
outside

□ il muro esterno the outside wall □ l'esterno del palazzo the outside of the building

estero (FEM **estera**) ADJECTIVE
▷ see also **estero** NOUN
foreign

□ Vendono giornali esteri? Do they sell foreign newspapers?

l' **estero** MASC NOUN
▷ see also **estero** ADJECTIVE

■ **all'estero** abroad □ Non è mai stato all'estero. He's never been abroad.

l' **estetista** FEM NOUN
beautician

□ Fa l'estetista. She is a beautician.

l' **estintore** MASC NOUN
fire extinguisher

l' **estinzione** FEM NOUN
extinction

□ una specie in via di estinzione a species on the verge of extinction

estivo (FEM **estiva**) ADJECTIVE
summer

□ le vacanze estive the summer holidays

■ **una giornata estiva** a summer's day

l' **estraneo**, l' **estranea** MASC/FEM NOUN
stranger

□ È difficile parlare di sé con un estraneo. It's difficult to talk about yourself to a stranger.

estrarre VERB [115]
to extract

estremamente ADVERB
extremely

□ È stato estremamente gentile. He was extremely kind.

l' **estremità** (PL le **estremità**) FEM NOUN
end
□ C'è una scala alle due estremità del corridoio.
There are stairs at both ends of the corridor.

estremo (FEM **estrema**) ADJECTIVE, MASC NOUN
extreme
□ l'estrema destra the extreme right □ Passa
da un estremo all'altro. She goes from one
extreme to the other.
■ **l'Estremo Oriente** the Far East

estroverso (FEM **estroversa**) ADJECTIVE
outgoing
□ Claudia è molto estroversa. Claudia's very
outgoing.

l' **età** (PL le **età**) FEM NOUN
age
□ Sandra ha la mia età. Sandra's the same age
as me.
■ **di mezza età** middle-aged

l' **eternità** FEM NOUN
eternity
□ Mi è sembrata un'eternità. It seemed like an
eternity.

l' **etichetta** FEM NOUN
label
□ Si è staccata l'etichetta. The label's come off.

l' **etto** MASC NOUN
one hundred grams
□ Ci vogliono tre etti di farina. You need three
hundred grams of flour.

l' **euro** (PL gli **euro**) MASC NOUN
euro
□ dieci euro ten euros

l' **euroconvertitore** MASC NOUN
euro-converter

l' **Europa** FEM NOUN
Europe

europeo (FEM **europea**) ADJECTIVE, MASC/FEM
NOUN
European
□ l'Unione Europea the European Union

evadere VERB [48]
to escape
□ Sono evasi dal carcere. They escaped from
prison.

eventuale (FEM **eventuale**) ADJECTIVE
any
□ Siamo assicurati contro eventuali danni.
We're insured against any damage. □ Per
eventuali domande rivolgersi a... If you have
any queries contact...

 LANGUAGE TIP Be careful! **eventuale**
 doesn't mean **eventual**.

eventualmente ADVERB
by any chance

□ Se eventualmente cambiassi idea, sai dove
trovarci. If by any chance you change your
mind, you know where to find us.
■ **Eventualmente potremmo sempre
andare in treno.** We could always go by
train.

 LANGUAGE TIP Be careful!
 eventualmente doesn't mean
 eventually.

evidente (FEM **evidente**) ADJECTIVE
obvious
□ Era evidente che non voleva venire. It was
obvious he didn't want to come.

evidentemente ADVERB
obviously
□ Era evidentemente seccato. He was
obviously annoyed. □ Evidentemente avevo
capito male. I obviously misunderstood.

evitare VERB [68]
to avoid
□ Passiamo di qui per evitare il traffico. We're
going this way to avoid the traffic.
■ **evitare di fare qualcosa** to avoid doing
something □ Evita di uscire da solo la notte.
Avoid going out alone at night.

evviva EXCLAMATION
hurrah!

ex (FEM+PL **ex**) ADJECTIVE, MASC/FEM NOUN
former
□ l'ex Primo ministro the former Prime
Minister
■ **il mio ex** my ex

extra (FEM+PL **extra**) ADJECTIVE
▷ see also **extra** NOUN
extra
□ una spesa extra an extra expense

l' **extra** (PL gli **extra**) MASC NOUN
▷ see also **extra** ADJECTIVE
□ Nel conto c'erano molti extra. There were a
lot of extras on the bill.

extracomunitario (FEM
extracomunitaria) ADJECTIVE
▷ see also **extracomunitario** NOUN
■ **i paesi extracomunitari** countries
outside the European Union

l' **extracomunitario, l'
extracomunitaria** MASC/FEM NOUN
▷ see also **extracomunitario** ADJECTIVE
■ **gli extracomunitari** people from outside
the European Union

extraterrestre (FEM **extraterrestre**)
ADJECTIVE, MASC/FEM NOUN
extraterrestrial

Ff

f

il **fa** (PL i **fa**) MASC NOUN
▷ see also **fa** ADVERB
F (musical note)

fa ADVERB
▷ see also **fa** NOUN
ago
□ L'ho incontrata due ore fa. I met her two hours ago.

la **fabbrica** (PL le **fabbriche**) FEM NOUN
factory

> **LANGUAGE TIP** Be careful! **fabbrica** doesn't mean **fabric**.

fabbricare VERB [18]
to make (produce)
□ È fabbricato in Cina. It's made in China.

la **faccenda** FEM NOUN
matter
□ È una faccenda complicata. It's a complicated matter.
■ **Devo sbrigare alcune faccende.** I've got a few things to do.
■ **faccende domestiche** housework sing

il **facchino** MASC NOUN
porter

la **faccia** (PL le **facce**) FEM NOUN
face
□ Cosa ti sei messa in faccia? What have you got on your face?
■ **faccia a faccia** face to face
■ **avere faccia tosta** to have a cheek □ Hai una bella faccia tosta! You've got a real cheek!

la **facciata** FEM NOUN
1 façade
2 side (of paper)
□ Scrivi su entrambe le facciate. Write on both sides.

la **faccina** MASC NOUN
emoticon (on computer)

facile (FEM **facile**) ADJECTIVE
1 easy
□ Non era facile come pensavo. It wasn't as easy as I thought. □ Il francese è più facile del tedesco. French is easier than German. □ È la lezione più facile del libro. It's the easiest exercise in the book.
2 likely
□ È facile che piova. It's likely to rain. □ È facile che venga. He's likely to come.

la **facoltà** (PL le **facoltà**) FEM NOUN
department
□ È iscritta alla facoltà di legge. She's a student in the law department.

facoltativo (FEM **facoltativa**) ADJECTIVE
optional
□ un corso facoltativo an optional course
■ **una fermata facoltativa** a request stop

il **faggio** MASC NOUN
beech

i **fagiolini** MASC PL NOUN
French beans

il **fagiolo** MASC NOUN
bean

il **fai-da-te** MASC NOUN
DIY (= do-it-yourself)

il **falco** (PL i **falchi**) MASC NOUN
hawk

il **falegname** MASC NOUN
carpenter
□ Mio padre fa il falegname. My father is a carpenter.

il **fallimento** MASC NOUN
1 bankruptcy
□ Molte aziende rischiavano il fallimento. Many firms were facing bankruptcy.
■ **andare in fallimento** to go bankrupt
2 failure
□ È stato un fallimento totale. It was a total failure.

fallire VERB [51, aux **avere** or **essere**]
1 to go bankrupt
□ La ditta è fallita. The firm has gone bankrupt.
2 to fail
□ Il nostro piano è destinato a fallire. Our plan is bound to fail.
3 to miss
□ Djokovic ha fallito il colpo. Djokovic missed the ball.

il **fallo** MASC NOUN
foul
□ un fallo sul portiere a foul on the goalkeeper
■ **mettere il piede in fallo** to lose one's footing □ Ha messo il piede in fallo ed è caduto. He lost his footing and fell.
■ **cogliere qualcuno in fallo** to catch somebody out □ Mi ha colto in fallo. He caught me out.

il **falò** (PL i **falò**) MASC NOUN
bonfire

falsificare VERB [18]
to forge (signature)

falso (FEM **falsa**) ADJECTIVE
▷ see also **falso** NOUN
1 false
  □ un nome falso a false name
2 forged
  □ Aveva un passaporto falso. He had a forged passport.
3 fake
  □ un diamante falso a fake diamond

il **falso** MASC NOUN
▷ see also **falso** ADJECTIVE
fake
  □ Il quadro era un falso. The painting was a fake.

la **fama** FEM NOUN
1 fame
  □ fama e successo fame and success
  ■ **un attore di fama mondiale** a world-famous actor
2 reputation
  □ Ha una cattiva fama. He's got a bad reputation.

la **fame** FEM NOUN
hunger
  □ la fame nel mondo hunger in the world
  ■ **avere fame** to be hungry □ Hai fame? Are you hungry?
  ■ **morire di fame** to be starving

la **famiglia** FEM NOUN
family
  □ una famiglia numerosa a large family

familiare (FEM **familiare**) ADJECTIVE
▷ see also **familiare** NOUN
familiar
  □ un viso familiare a familiar face

il/la **familiare** MASC/FEM NOUN
▷ see also **familiare** ADJECTIVE
relative
  □ Va in vacanza con dei familiari. He's going on holiday with relatives.

famoso (FEM **famosa**) ADJECTIVE
famous

fanatico (FEM **fanatica**, MASC PL **fanatici**, FEM PL **fanatiche**) ADJECTIVE
▷ see also **fanatico** NOUN
  ■ **essere fanatico di** to be mad about □ È fanatico di calcio. He's mad about football.

il **fanatico**, la **fanatica** (MASC PL i **fanatici**, FEM PL le **fanatiche**) MASC/FEM NOUN
▷ see also **fanatico** ADJECTIVE
fanatic
  □ È un fanatico della pallacanestro. He's a basketball fanatic.

il **fango** (PL i **fanghi**) MASC NOUN
mud

□ Ero coperto di fango. I was covered with mud.
  ■ **farsi i fanghi** to have a mud treatment

il **fannullone**, la **fannullona** MASC/FEM NOUN
layabout

la **fantascienza** FEM NOUN
science fiction
  □ un film di fantascienza a science fiction film

la **fantasia** FEM NOUN
1 imagination
  □ Non hai fantasia. You've got no imagination.
2 pattern (on fabric)
  □ Non mi piace questa fantasia. I don't like this pattern.
  ■ **camicia fantasia** patterned shirt

il **fantasma** (PL i **fantasmi**) MASC NOUN
ghost

i **fantasmini** MASC PL NOUN
trainer socks

fantastico (FEM **fantastica**, MASC PL **fantastici**, FEM PL **fantastiche**) ADJECTIVE
great
  □ È una festa fantastica. It's a great party.
  □ Fantastico! Great!

il **fantino** MASC NOUN
jockey

fare VERB [49]
1 to make
  □ Ho fatto un errore. I made a mistake.
  □ Posso fare una telefonata? Can I make a phone call? □ Due più due fa quattro. Two and two makes four.
2 to do
  □ Ho già fatto i compiti. I've already done my homework. □ Cosa fai stasera? What are you doing this evening? □ Cosa stai facendo? What are you doing? □ Cosa fa tuo padre? What does your father do? □ Abbiamo fatto cinque chilometri. We did five kilometres. □ Non farlo. Don't do it.
  ■ **andare a fare qualcosa** to go and do something □ Andiamo a fare la spesa. Let's go and do some shopping.
3 to be
  □ Fa il medico. He is a doctor. □ Fa caldo. It's hot. □ Fa freddo. It's cold. □ Le ha fatto da madre She was like a mother to her.
4 to have (holiday, dream, break)
  □ Vorrei fare una vacanza. I'd like to have a holiday.
  ■ **far fare qualcosa** to have something done □ Ho fatto riparare la macchina. I had the car repaired.
  ■ **far fare qualcosa a qualcuno** to make somebody do something □ Mi ha fatto riordinare la camera. She made me tidy up my room. □ Mi ha fatto ridere. He made me laugh.

■ **Lascia stare, lo farò fare a lui.** Don't bother, I'll get him to do it.
■ **farsi fare qualcosa** to have something done □ Mi sono fatta tagliare i capelli. I had my hair cut.
■ **fare un passeggiata** to go for a walk
■ **fare un viaggio** to go on a trip
■ **Fammi vedere.** Let me see.
■ **Non fa niente.** It doesn't matter.
■ **farcela** to do it □ Ce l'abbiamo fatta! We did it!
■ **Ce la fai?** Can you manage?
■ **Non ce la faremo ad arrivare in tempo.** We won't make it in time.
■ **Non ce la faccio più.** **1** *(walking)* I can't go on any further. **2** I can't take it any more.
■ **farsi** to do drugs *(informal)*

la **farfalla** FEM NOUN
butterfly
□ i cento metri farfalla the hundred metres butterfly

la **farina** FEM NOUN
flour

la **farmacia** (PL le **farmacie**) FEM NOUN
chemist's
□ Sto andando in farmacia. I'm going to the chemist's.
■ **farmacia di turno** duty chemist

il/la **farmacista** (MASC PL i **farmacisti**, FEM PL le **farmaciste**) MASC/FEM NOUN
chemist

il **faro** MASC NOUN
lighthouse
■ **fari** headlights □ Accendi i fari. Switch on your headlights.

la **fascia** (PL le **fasce**) FEM NOUN
bandage
□ una fascia elastica a crepe bandage

fasciare VERB [13]
to bandage
□ Gli hanno fasciato il ginocchio. They bandaged his knee.

il **fascicolo** MASC NOUN
file *(in office)*

il **fascino** MASC NOUN
charm
□ una donna di gran fascino a woman of great charm

la **fase** FEM NOUN
phase

il **fastidio** MASC NOUN
■ **dare fastidio a qualcuno** **1** to get on somebody's nerves □ Smettila! Mi dai fastidio! Stop it! You're getting on my nerves! **2** to bother somebody □ Ti dà fastidio il rumore? Is the noise bothering you? □ La caviglia mi dà ancora fastidio. My ankle is still bothering me.
■ **Il suo modo di fare mi dà fastidio.** I find his manner irritating.

■ **Le dà fastidio se fumo?** Do you mind if I smoke?

fastidioso (FEM **fastidiosa**) ADJECTIVE
annoying
□ È un bambino fastidioso. He's an annoying child.
■ **un dolore fastidioso** a nagging pain
■ LANGUAGE TIP Be careful! **fastidioso** doesn't mean **fastidious**.

la **fata** FEM NOUN
fairy

fatale (FEM **fatale**) ADJECTIVE
fatal
□ un errore fatale a fatal mistake

la **fatica** (PL le **fatiche**) FEM NOUN
effort
□ Ci vuole tempo e fatica. It takes time and effort.
■ **Che fatica!** It's hard work!
■ **L'ho convinto a fatica.** It was hard work convincing him.
■ **fare fatica a fare qualcosa** to find it difficult to do something □ Faccio fatica a capire la matematica. I find it difficult to understand maths.

faticoso (FEM **faticosa**) ADJECTIVE
tiring

fatto (FEM **fatta**) ADJECTIVE
▷ *see also* **fatto** NOUN
1 made
■ **fatto a mano** handmade
■ **fatto in casa** home-made
2 stoned *(high on drugs, drunk: informal)*
□ È completamente fatto. He's completely stoned.

il **fatto** MASC NOUN
▷ *see also* **fatto** ADJECTIVE
fact
□ I fatti parlano chiaro. The facts speak for themselves. □ Il fatto è che ha ragione lui. The fact is that he's right.
■ **È successo un fatto strano.** Something strange happened.
■ **un fatto di cronaca** a news item
■ **cogliere qualcuno sul fatto** to catch somebody red-handed □ Li hanno colti sul fatto. They caught them red-handed.
■ **Pensa ai fatti tuoi!** Mind your own business!

la **fattoria** FEM NOUN
farm
■ LANGUAGE TIP Be careful! **fattoria** doesn't mean **factory**.

il **fattorino** MASC NOUN
errand boy

la **fattura** FEM NOUN
invoice

la **fava** FEM NOUN
broad bean

la **favola** FEM NOUN
fairy tale

favoloso (FEM **favolosa**) ADJECTIVE
fabulous
□ una casa favolosa a fabulous house

il **favore** MASC NOUN
favour
■ **fare un favore a qualcuno** to do somebody a favour □ Mi faresti un favore? Would you do me a favour?
■ **chiedere un favore a qualcuno** to ask somebody a favour □ Posso chiederti un favore? Can I ask you a favour?
■ **per favore** please

il **fax** (PL i **fax**) MASC NOUN
fax
□ Gli ho mandato un fax. I sent him a fax.

il **fazzoletto** MASC NOUN
handkerchief
■ **fazzoletto di carta** tissue

il **febbraio** MASC NOUN
February

> LANGUAGE TIP In Italian, months are not written with capital letters.

□ in febbraio in February

la **febbre** FEM NOUN
temperature
■ **avere la febbre** to have a temperature
□ Hai la febbre? Have you got a temperature?

la **fede** FEM NOUN
1 faith
■ **in buona fede** in good faith □ Ho agito in buona fede. I acted in good faith.
2 wedding ring

fedele (FEM **fedele**) ADJECTIVE
faithful
□ un marito fedele a faithful husband
■ **essere fedele a** to be faithful to □ Gli è sempre stata fedele. She's always been faithful to him.

la **federa** FEM NOUN
pillowcase

il **fegato** MASC NOUN
liver
□ Non mi piace il fegato. I don't like liver.
■ **Ha fegato!** He's got guts!

la **felce** FEM NOUN
fern

felice (FEM **felice**) ADJECTIVE
happy
□ Adesso sono più felice. I'm happier now. □ il giorno più felice della mia vita the happiest day of my life

la **felicità** FEM NOUN
happiness

la **felpa** FEM NOUN
sweatshirt

la **femmina** FEM NOUN
▷ see also **femmina** ADJECTIVE
girl (daughter)
□ Ha un maschio e una femmina. She has a boy and a girl.

femmina ADJECTIVE
▷ see also **femmina** NOUN
female
□ una giraffa femmina a female giraffe

femminile (FEM **femminile**) ADJECTIVE
feminine
□ È molto femminile. She's very feminine.
■ **una rivista femminile** a women's magazine

il **femore** MASC NOUN
femur

il **fenomeno** MASC NOUN
phenomenon
□ un fenomeno inspiegabile an inexplicable phenomenon

feriale (FEM **feriale**) ADJECTIVE
■ **giorno feriale** week day

le **ferie** FEM PL NOUN
holiday sing
□ Ho due settimane di ferie. I have two weeks' holiday.
■ **un giorno di ferie** a day off
■ **andare in ferie** to go on holiday □ Dove vai in ferie? Where are you going on holiday?
■ **prendere un giorno di ferie** to take a day off □ Ho preso un giorno di ferie. I took a day off.

ferire VERB [51]
1 to injure
□ La bomba ha ferito tre persone. The bomb injured three people.
■ **Mi sono ferito ad una mano.** I've hurt my hand.
2 to wound
□ Il soldato è stato ferito ad una gamba. The soldier was wounded in the leg.

la **ferita** FEM NOUN
1 injury
□ La sue ferite non erano gravi. His injuries were not serious.
2 wound

il **ferito** MASC NOUN
casualty
□ Hanno portato i feriti all'ospedale. The casualties were taken to hospital.
■ **Nell'incidente ci sono stati due feriti.** Two people were injured in the accident.

il **fermaglio** MASC NOUN
1 clasp (for necklace, bracelet)
2 clip (for documents, hair)

fermare VERB [68]
to stop
□ Non cercare di fermarmi. Don't try and stop me.

95

- **fermarsi** to stop □ Fermati! Stop!
□ L'orologio si è fermato alle tre e cinque. The clock stopped at five past three. □ Mi sono fermato a salutarla. I stopped to say hello to her.

la **fermata** FEM NOUN
stop
□ la fermata dell'autobus the bus stop
- **una fermata a richiesta** a request stop

fermo (FEM **ferma**) ADJECTIVE
still
- **stare fermo** to keep still □ Non sta fermo un attimo. He can't keep still for a minute.
- **Fermo!** Don't move!
- **Ero fermo al semaforo.** I was waiting at the traffic lights.
- **La macchina era ferma in mezzo alla strada.** The car had stopped in the middle of the road.
- **Il treno era fermo in stazione.** The train was standing in the station.
- **Quell'orologio è fermo.** That clock has stopped.

il **ferragosto** MASC NOUN
August fifteenth

> **DID YOU KNOW...?**
> In Italy August 15 is a public holiday. Many shops, restaurants and businesses are closed on this day for a week or so.

il **ferro** MASC NOUN
iron
- **di ferro** iron □ una sbarra di ferro an iron bar
- **ferro battuto** wrought iron
- **ferro da stiro** iron
- **ai ferri** grilled □ una bistecca ai ferri a grilled steak
- **ferro di cavallo** horseshoe
- **Tocca ferro!** Touch wood!

> **DID YOU KNOW...?**
> Italians touch iron, rather than wood, when they are hoping for good luck.

la **ferrovia** FEM NOUN
railway

ferroviario (FEM **ferroviaria**) ADJECTIVE
railway
□ la stazione ferroviaria the railway station

il **ferroviere** MASC NOUN
railwayman

la **fessura** FEM NOUN
1 crack
2 slot (for coins)

la **festa** FEM NOUN
1 holiday
□ Oggi è festa. Today's a holiday.
2 party
□ Ha dato una festa per il suo compleanno. He gave a party for his birthday.

3 birthday
□ Quando è la tua festa? When is your birthday?
- **festa della mamma** Mother's Day
- **festa del papà** Father's Day

festeggiare VERB [58]
to celebrate

festivo (FEM **festiva**) ADJECTIVE
- **giorno festivo** holiday
- **'sabato e festivi'** 'Saturdays, Sundays and public holidays'

la **fetta** FEM NOUN
slice
□ una fetta di pane a slice of bread
- **tagliare a fette** to slice □ Può tagliarmelo a fette? Can you slice it for me?

la **fiaba** FEM NOUN
fairy tale

la **fiala** FEM NOUN
phial

la **fiamma** FEM NOUN
flame
□ La casa è andata in fiamme. The house went up in flames. □ È una sua vecchia fiamma. She's an old flame of his.
- **Morì tra le fiamme.** He died in the blaze.

il **fiammifero** MASC NOUN
match
□ una scatola di fiammiferi a box of matches

il **fianco** (PL i **fianchi**) MASC NOUN
1 hip
□ Ha i fianchi larghi. She's got wide hips.
2 side
□ Dormo sempre su un fianco. I always sleep on my side.
- **Starò sempre al tuo fianco.** I'll always stand by you.
- **fianco a fianco** side by side
- **a fianco di** next to □ Si trova a fianco della chiesa. It's next to the church.

il **fiasco** (PL i **fiaschi**) MASC NOUN
bottle
□ un fiasco di vino a bottle of wine
- **essere un fiasco** to be a fiasco □ La festa è stata un fiasco completo. The party was a complete fiasco.

fiatare VERB [68]
- **Non fiatate!** Don't say a word!

il **fiato** MASC NOUN
1 breath
□ Sono senza fiato. I'm out of breath.
- **riprendere fiato** to get one's breath back □ Mi sono fermato a riprendere fiato. I stopped to get my breath back.
- **rimanere senza fiato** to be speechless
□ Quando l'ho saputo sono rimasto senza fiato. I was speechless when I heard about it.
- **tutto d'un fiato** all in one go □ Bevilo tutto d'un fiato. Drink it all in one go.
- **strumenti a fiato** wind instruments

2 stamina

□ Non ho più molto fiato. I haven't got much stamina these days.

la **fibbia** FEM NOUN
buckle

la **fibra** FEM NOUN
fibre

ficcare VERB [18]

1 to put

□ Dove lo hai ficcato? Where did you put it?

■ **Ha ficcato tutti i libri in borsa.** She crammed all the books into her bag.

2 to stick

□ Mi ha ficcato un dito nell'occhio. He stuck his finger in my eye. □ Non ficcare il naso nei miei affari. Don't stick your nose into my business.

■ **ficcarsi** to get to □ Dove si sarà ficcato? Where's he got to?

il **fico** (PL i **fichi**) MASC NOUN

1 fig tree

2 fig

■ **fico d'India** prickly pear

■ **fico secco** dried fig

il **fidanzamento** MASC NOUN
engagement

fidanzarsi VERB [56]
to get engaged

□ Si sono appena fidanzati. They've just got engaged.

la **fidanzata** FEM NOUN
fiancée

il **fidanzato** MASC NOUN
fiancé

fidarsi VERB [56]

■ **fidarsi di qualcuno** to trust somebody

□ Mi fido di lui. I trust him.

■ **Non mi fido.** I'm not sure.

fidato (FEM **fidata**) ADJECTIVE
trustworthy

la **fiducia** FEM NOUN
trust

□ Ha tradito la nostra fiducia. He has betrayed our trust.

■ **avere fiducia in** to trust □ Ho fiducia in lui. I trust him.

■ **fiducia in se stesso** self-confidence

□ Devi avere più fiducia in te stesso. You should have more self-confidence.

■ **una persona di fiducia** a trustworthy person

la **fiera** FEM NOUN
fair (trade)

fiero (FEM **fiera**) ADJECTIVE
proud

■ **andare fiero di** to be proud of □ I suoi vanno molto fieri di lui. His parents are very proud of him.

la **fifa** FEM NOUN

■ **avere fifa** to have the jitters □ Ho fifa. I've got the jitters.

la **figlia** FEM NOUN
daughter

il **figlio** MASC NOUN

1 child (without specifying sex)

□ Aspetta il secondo figlio. She's expecting her second child. □ Ho due figli. I've got two children. □ Non vuole avere figli. She doesn't want to have children.

■ **figlio unico** only child

2 son

□ Mio figlio ha sette anni. My son is seven.

la **figura** FEM NOUN

1 picture

□ Questo libro ha molte figure. This book has lots of pictures.

2 impression

■ **fare una brutta figura** to make a bad impression □ Ho fatto una brutta figura al colloquio. I made a bad impression at the interview.

■ **fare una bella figura** to make a good impression

■ **Che figura!** How embarrassing!

figurarsi VERB [56]

■ **Ti disturbo? — Ma figurati!** Am I disturbing you? — Not at all!

la **figurina** FEM NOUN
picture card

la **fila** FEM NOUN

1 line

□ una fila di alberi a line of trees

■ **Ci hanno messo in fila per due.** They lined us up in twos.

■ **in fila indiana** in single file

2 row

□ Ero seduto in seconda fila. I was sitting in the second row.

3 queue

□ C'era una lunga fila alla cassa. There was a long queue at the till.

■ **fare la fila** to queue

la **filastrocca** (PL le **filastrocche**) FEM NOUN
nursery rhyme

il **filetto** MASC NOUN
fillet

la **filiale** FEM NOUN
branch (of bank, shop)

il **film** (PL i **film**) MASC NOUN
film

il **filo** MASC NOUN

1 thread

2 yarn

3 wire

■ **filo interdentale** dental floss

■ **filo spinato** barbed wire

il **filone** MASC NOUN
baguette (bread)

la **filosofia** FEM NOUN
philosophy

il **filosofo,** la **filosofa** MASC/FEM NOUN
philosopher

il **filtro** MASC NOUN
filter

finale (FEM **finale**) ADJECTIVE
▷ see also **finale** MASC NOUN, FEM NOUN
final

il **finale** MASC NOUN
▷ see also **finale** ADJECTIVE, FEM NOUN
ending
□ Non mi è piaciuto il finale. I didn't like the
ending.

la **finale** FEM NOUN
▷ see also **finale** ADJECTIVE, MASC NOUN
final
□ Sono entrati in finale. They reached the final.
■ **la finale di Coppa** the Cup Final

finalmente ADVERB
at last
□ Finalmente sei arrivato! You're here at last!

la **finanza** FEM NOUN
finance

finché CONJUNCTION
1 until
□ Aspetta finché non sarò tornato. Wait until I
come back.
2 as long as
□ Rimani finché vuoi. Stay as long as you like.

fine (FEM **fine**) ADJECTIVE
▷ see also **fine** MASC NOUN, FEM NOUN
1 thin (blade, paper)
2 fine (hair, dust)
3 good (sight, hearing)
4 refined (person)

il **fine** MASC NOUN
▷ see also **fine** ADJECTIVE, FEM NOUN
end
□ Il fine giustifica i mezzi. The end justifies the
means.
■ **a fin di bene** with good intentions □ L'ho
fatto a fin di bene. I did it with good intentions.
■ **a lieto fine** with a happy ending □ Mi
piacciono le storie a lieto fine. I like stories with
a happy ending.
■ **in fin dei conti** after all
■ **un secondo fine** an ulterior motive
■ **fine settimana** weekend

la **fine** FEM NOUN
▷ see also **fine** ADJECTIVE, MASC NOUN
end
□ verso la fine dell'anno towards the end of the
year □ dall'inizio alla fine from beginning to
end
■ **Che fine ha fatto?** What became of him?
■ **alla fine** in the end □ Alla fine lo ha
perdonato. In the end she forgave him.

la **finestra** FEM NOUN
window

il **finestrino** MASC NOUN
window (of car, train)

fingere VERB [50]
to pretend
□ Fingiamo di dormire. Let's pretend we're
asleep. □ Ha finto di non conoscermi. He
pretended he didn't recognize me. □ Si è finto
ubriaco. He pretended he was drunk.

finire VERB [51, aux **avere** or **essere**]
1 to finish
□ Non ho ancora finito i compiti. I haven't
finished my homework yet. □ Il film finisce alle
dieci. The film finishes at ten.
■ **finire di fare qualcosa** to finish doing
something □ Ho finito di leggere il libro. I've
finished reading the book.
2 to end
□ L'anno scolastico finisce a giugno. The
school year ends in June. □ Com'è finita la
partita? How did the match end?
3 to be over
□ La festa è finita. The party's over. □ Tra noi è
tutto finito. It's all over between us.
4 to run out of
□ Abbiamo finito il pane. We've run out of bread.
■ **andare a finire** to get to □ Dov'è andato a
finire quel libro? Where's that book got to?
■ **Com'è andata a finire?** What happened
in the end?
■ **Finiscila!** Stop it!

finlandese (FEM **finlandese**) ADJECTIVE
▷ see also **finlandese** MASC NOUN, FEM NOUN
Finnish

il **finlandese** MASC NOUN
▷ see also **finlandese** ADJECTIVE, FEM NOUN
1 Finn (person)
□ i finlandesi the Finns
2 Finnish (language)
□ Parli finlandese? Do you speak Finnish?

la **finlandese** FEM NOUN
▷ see also **finlandese** ADJECTIVE, MASC NOUN
Finn

la **Finlandia** FEM NOUN
Finland
□ Ti è piaciuta la Finlandia? Did you like
Finland? □ Andrò in Finlandia quest'estate. I'm
going to Finland this summer.

fino PREPOSITION
■ **fino a** 1 until □ Resto fino a venerdì. I'm
staying until Friday. 2 as far as □ Vengo con
te fino alla chiesa. I'll come with you as far as
the church.
■ **Fino a quando puoi rimanere?** How
long can you stay?

il **finocchio** MASC NOUN
fennel

finora ADVERB
1 yet

□ Finora non è arrivato. He hasn't arrived yet.

2 so far

□ Finora abbiamo fatto solo il presente. So far we've only studied the present tense.

la **finta** FEM NOUN
 ■ **far finta** to pretend □ Facciamo finta di dormire. Let's pretend we're asleep.
 ■ **L'ho detto per finta.** I was only joking.
 ■ **fare una finta** (in sport) to feint

finto (FEM **finta**) ADJECTIVE
1 false (teeth, beard)
2 artificial (flowers)
3 imitation (leather)
 □ una giacca in finta pelle an imitation leather jacket

il **fiocco** (PL i **fiocchi**) MASC NOUN
 bow (of ribbon)
 ■ **un fiocco di neve** a snowflake
 ■ **fiocchi di granturco** cornflakes

il **fioraio,** la **fioraia** MASC/FEM NOUN
 florist
 □ Sto andando dal fioraio. I'm going to the florist's.

il **fiore** MASC NOUN
 flower
 □ fiori di campo wild flowers
 ■ **a fiori** with a flower pattern □ una gonna a fiori a skirt with a flower pattern
 ■ **fiori** (in cards) clubs
 ■ **fior di latte** cream

la **fiorentina** FEM NOUN
1 Florentine (person)
2 T-bone steak

fiorentino (FEM **fiorentina**) ADJECTIVE, MASC NOUN
 Florentine
 ■ **i fiorentini** the people of Florence

Firenze FEM NOUN
 Florence
 □ Sto andando a Firenze. I'm going to Florence.
 □ Vive a Firenze. He lives in Florence.

la **firma** FEM NOUN
 signature

firmare VERB [68]
 to sign
 □ Dove devo firmare? Where shall I sign?

firmato (FEM **firmata**) ADJECTIVE
 ■ **un abito firmato** a designer dress

la **fisarmonica** (PL le **fisarmoniche**) FEM NOUN
 accordion

fiscale (FEM **fiscale**) ADJECTIVE
 ■ **evasione fiscale** tax evasion

fischiare VERB [17]
1 to whistle
 □ Sai fischiare? Can you whistle?
 ■ **fischiare un rigore** to give a penalty
2 to boo

□ Il pubblico lo ha fischiato. The audience booed him.

il **fischietto** MASC NOUN
 whistle

il **fischio** MASC NOUN
 whistle
 □ il fischio dell'arbitro the referee's whistle
 ■ **fare un fischio** to whistle

il **fisco** MASC NOUN
 tax authorities pl

la **fisica** FEM NOUN
 physics sing

fisico (FEM **fisica**, MASC PL **fisici**, FEM PL **fisiche**) ADJECTIVE
 ▷ see also **fisico** NOUN
 physical
 □ il contatto fisico physical contact
 ■ **educazione fisica** physical education
 ■ **aspetto fisico** appearance

il **fisico** (PL i **fisici**) MASC NOUN
 ▷ see also **fisico** ADJECTIVE
1 physique
 □ Ha un bel fisico. He has a good physique.
2 figure
 □ Ha un bel fisico. She has a good figure.
3 physicist
 □ un fisico nucleare a nuclear physicist

la **fisioterapia** FEM NOUN
 physiotherapy

il/la **fisioterapista** (MASC PL i **fisioterapisti**, FEM PL le **fisioterapiste**) MASC/FEM NOUN
 physiotherapist

fissare VERB [68]
1 to fix
 □ È fissato al muro. It's fixed to the wall. □ Hai fissato la data? Have you fixed the date?
2 to book
 □ Ho fissato una stanza per lunedì. I've booked a room for Monday.
3 to stare at
 □ Non fissarlo tutto il tempo. Don't keep staring at him.

fisso (FEM **fissa**) ADJECTIVE
 fixed
 □ prezzo fisso fixed price
 ■ **un lavoro fisso** a permanent job
 ■ **uno stipendio fisso** a regular income
 ■ **un ragazzo fisso** a steady boyfriend

la **fitta** FEM NOUN
 sharp pain
 □ Ho delle fitte al petto. I get sharp pains in my chest.

fitto (FEM **fitta**) ADJECTIVE
 thick (forest, fog)
 ■ **È buio fitto.** It's pitch dark.

il **fiume** MASC NOUN
 river

il **flagrante** MASC NOUN
■ **cogliere qualcuno in flagrante** to catch somebody red-handed □ Hanno colto il ladro in flagrante. They caught the burglar red-handed.

il **flauto** MASC NOUN
■ **flauto traverso** flute
■ **flauto dolce** recorder

flessibile (FEM **flessibile**) ADJECTIVE
flexible
■ **orario flessibile** flexitime

la **flessione** FEM NOUN
1 knee-bend (squat)
2 forward bend
3 sit-up
4 press-up

il **flipper** (PL i **flipper**) MASC NOUN
pinball machine

la **flotta** FEM NOUN
fleet

il **fluoro** MASC NOUN
■ **un dentifricio al fluoro** a fluoride toothpaste

la **foca** (PL le **foche**) FEM NOUN
seal

la **foce** FEM NOUN
mouth
□ la foce del Po the mouth of the Po

la **fodera** FEM NOUN
1 lining (of clothes)
2 cover (of settee, armchair)

la **foglia** FEM NOUN
leaf

il **foglio** MASC NOUN
sheet (of paper)
■ **un foglio a righe** a sheet of lined paper
■ **foglio elettronico** spreadsheet
■ **foglio rosa** (driving) provisional licence

la **fogna** FEM NOUN
sewer

il **föhn** (PL i **föhn**) MASC NOUN
hair dryer

la **folla** FEM NOUN
crowd

folle (FEM **folle**) ADJECTIVE
mad (person, idea)
■ **in folle** in neutral □ Assicurati che sia in folle. Make sure it's in neutral.

la **follia** FEM NOUN
madness
□ in un momento di follia in a moment of madness
■ **È una follia!** It's crazy!
■ **amare qualcuno alla follia** to be madly in love with somebody □ Lo amo alla follia. I'm madly in love with him.
■ **costare una follia** to cost the earth
□ Quella macchina dev'essere costata una follia. That car must have cost the earth.

il/la **follower** (PL i/le **follower**) MASC/FEM NOUN
follower
□ Ha moltissimi follower su Twitter. She has lots of followers on Twitter.

folto (FEM **folta**) ADJECTIVE
thick (hair, forest)

il **fon** (PL i **fon**) MASC NOUN
hair dryer

le **fondamenta** FEM PL NOUN
foundations

fondamentale (FEM **fondamentale**) ADJECTIVE
fundamental

fondente (FEM **fondente**) ADJECTIVE
■ **cioccolato fondente** plain chocolate

fondo (FEM **fonda**) ADJECTIVE
▷ see also **fondo** NOUN
deep
□ Qui l'acqua è fonda. The water is deep here.
□ una buca fonda tre metri a hole three metres deep
■ **un piatto fondo** a soup dish

il **fondo** MASC NOUN
▷ see also **fondo** ADJECTIVE
1 bottom
□ il fondo del bicchiere the bottom of the glass
■ **in fondo a** at the bottom of □ in fondo al mare at the bottom of the sea
■ **andare a fondo** to sink □ La nave è andata a fondo. The ship sank.
■ **in fondo alla strada** at the end of the street
■ **in fondo alla sala** at the back of the room
■ **laggiù in fondo** 1 (far off) over there
2 (deep down) down there
2 background
□ bianco su fondo nero white on a black background
3 fund
■ **in fondo** after all
■ **in fondo in fondo** deep down
■ **conoscere a fondo** to know inside out
□ Conosco a fondo la materia. I know this subject inside out.
■ **dar fondo a** to use up □ Abbiamo dato fondo alle provviste. We've used up all the food.
■ **sci di fondo** cross-country skiing

il **fondotinta** (PL i **fondotinta**) MASC NOUN
foundation

la **fonetica** FEM NOUN
phonetics sing

la **fontana** FEM NOUN
fountain

la **fonte** FEM NOUN
source
□ una fonte di informazioni a source of information

forare VERB [68]
to punch (ticket)
■ **Abbiamo forato.** We've got a puncture.

le **forbici** FEM PL NOUN
scissors
□ un paio di forbici a pair of scissors

la **forchetta** FEM NOUN
fork

la **forcina** FEM NOUN
hairpin

la **foresta** FEM NOUN
forest
□ foresta pluviale rain forest

la **forfora** FEM NOUN
dandruff

la **forma** FEM NOUN
1 shape
□ Di che forma è? What shape is it? □ a forma di cuore heart-shaped
2 form
□ una forma rara di cancro a rare form of cancer
■ **essere in forma** to be in good form □ Il giocatore era in ottima forma. The player was in great form.
■ **non essere in forma** to be off form □ La squadra non era in forma. The team was off form.
■ **tenersi in forma** to keep fit □ Mi tengo in forma nuotando tutti i giorni. I keep fit by swimming every day.

il **formaggio** MASC NOUN
cheese
□ un panino con il formaggio a cheese sandwich

formale (FEM **formale**) ADJECTIVE
formal

formare VERB [68]
1 to form
□ Abbiamo formato un gruppo. We formed a group.
■ **formare una famiglia** to start a family
■ **formarsi** to form □ Si è formata la fila allo sportello. A queue formed at the counter.
2 to dial
□ Solleva il ricevitore prima di formare il numero. Lift the receiver before dialling the number.

il **formato** MASC NOUN
size
□ formato A4 A4 size □ una confezione formato gigante a giant-size pack

la **formazione** FEM NOUN
1 training
□ un corso di formazione professionale a vocational training course
2 line-up (of team)

la **formica** (PL le **formiche**) FEM NOUN
ant

la **formula** FEM NOUN
formula

il **fornaio**, la **fornaia** MASC/FEM NOUN
baker

il **fornello** MASC NOUN
■ **fornello a gas** 1 gas ring 2 camping stove
■ **fornello elettrico** hotplate

fornire VERB [51]
■ **fornire qualcosa a qualcuno** to supply somebody with something □ Ci forniscono le materie prime. They supply us with raw materials.
■ **Ci ha fornito tutte le informazioni necessarie.** He gave us all the necessary information.

il **forno** MASC NOUN
1 oven
□ Metti la torta nel forno. Put the cake in the oven.
■ **pollo al forno** roast chicken
■ **forno a microonde** microwave oven
2 bakery

il **foro** MASC NOUN
hole

forse ADVERB
maybe
□ Forse hai ragione. Maybe you're right.
□ Forse dovremmo andarcene. Maybe we should leave. □ Verrà? — Non so. Forse. Will he come? — I don't know. Maybe.

forte (FEM **forte**) ADJECTIVE
▷ see also **forte** ADVERB
1 strong
□ un vento forte a strong wind □ È più forte di me. He's stronger than me.
■ **un forte fumatore** a heavy smoker
■ **il piatto forte** the main dish
2 hard
□ un forte colpo in testa a hard knock on the head
3 bad
□ Ho un forte mal di testa. I've got a bad headache.
4 loud
□ un rumore forte a loud noise
5 good
□ È proprio forte! He's really good!
■ **essere forte in qualcosa** to be good at something □ È forte in matematica. She's good at maths.

forte ADVERB
▷ see also **forte** ADJECTIVE
1 fast
□ Correva forte. He was running fast.
2 hard
□ Ha picchiato forte la testa. She hit her head hard.

3 loud
- □ Non parlare così forte. Don't speak so loud.
- □ Potresti parlare più forte? Could you speak louder?

4 tight
- □ Tieniti forte! Hold tight!

la **fortezza** FEM NOUN
fortress

la **fortuna** FEM NOUN
1 luck
- □ Buona fortuna! Good luck!
- ■ **portare fortuna** to bring good luck □ Mi ha sempre portato fortuna. It's always brought me good luck.
- ■ **avere fortuna** to be lucky
- ■ **per fortuna** luckily □ Per fortuna sei arrivato in tempo. Luckily, you arrived in time.
- ■ **atterraggio di fortuna** emergency landing
2 fortune
- □ Costa una fortuna. It costs a fortune.

fortunato (FEM **fortunata**) ADJECTIVE
lucky
- □ Sei più fortunato di me. You're luckier than me. □ È la persona più fortunata che conosca. She's the luckiest person I know.

il **foruncolo** MASC NOUN
boil

la **forza** FEM NOUN
1 force
- □ la forza dell'esplosione the force of the explosion
2 strength *sing*
- □ È per misurare la forza dei muscoli. It's to test the strength of the muscles. □ la forza del vento the strength of the wind □ Ha riacquistato presto le forze. He quickly regained his strength.
- ■ **Ha molta forza.** He's very strong.
- ■ **Forza!** Come on!
- ■ **Per forza!** Obviously!
- ■ **Mi ha costretto con la forza.** He forced me to do it.
- ■ **Lo ha fatto per forza.** He was forced to do it.
- ■ **Perderai la voce a forza di gridare.** You'll lose your voice if you shout so much.
- ■ **forza di volontà** willpower
- ■ **le forze armate** the armed forces

forzare VERB [68]
to force
- □ La serratura è stata forzata. The lock has been forced.

la **foschia** FEM NOUN
- ■ **Oggi c'è molta foschia.** It's very hazy today.

la **fossa** FEM NOUN
pit

la **fossetta** FEM NOUN
dimple

il **fosso** MASC NOUN
ditch

la **foto** (PL le **foto**) FEM NOUN
photo
- □ una foto in bianco e nero a black and white photo
- ■ **fare una foto** to take a photo □ Ha fatto molte foto. He took a lot of photos.

la **fotocopia** FEM NOUN
photocopy

fotocopiare VERB [17]
to photocopy

la **fotocopiatrice** FEM NOUN
photocopier

fotografare VERB [68]
to photograph

la **fotografia** FEM NOUN
photograph
- □ una fotografia a colori a colour photograph
- ■ **un corso di fotografia** a photography course

fotografico (FEM **fotografica**, MASC PL **fotografici**, FEM PL **fotografiche**) ADJECTIVE
- ■ **macchina fotografica** camera
- ■ **servizio fotografico** *(for a newspaper)* photo feature

il **fotografo**, la **fotografa** MASC/FEM NOUN
photographer

il **fotoromanzo** MASC NOUN
photo love story

la **fototessera** FEM NOUN
passport-size photo

fotovoltaico (FEM **fotovoltaica**, MASC PL **fotovoltaici**, FEM PL **fotovoltaiche**) ADJECTIVE
- ■ **i pannelli fotovoltaici** solar panels

il **foulard** (PL i **foulard**) MASC NOUN
scarf

fra PREPOSITION
1 between *(between two people, things)*
- □ Era seduto fra il padre e lo zio. He was sitting between his father and his uncle. □ Detto fra noi, non piace neanche a me. Between you and me, I don't like it either.
2 among *(for more than two)*
- □ Fra i feriti c'era anche il pilota dell'aereo. The pilot of the plane was among the injured.
3 in *(in expressions of time)*
- □ Torno fra un'ora. I'll be back in an hour. □ fra cinque giorni in five days
- ■ **fra poco** soon
- ■ **Fra venti chilometri c'è un'area di servizio.** It's twenty kilometres to the next services.

fradicio (FEM **fradicia**, MASC PL **fradici**, FEM PL **fradice**) ADJECTIVE
soaked
- □ Ho la camicia fradicia. My shirt is soaked.
- ■ **bagnato fradicio** soaking wet
- ■ **Era ubriaco fradicio.** He was blind drunk.

fragile (FEM **fragile**) ADJECTIVE
fragile

la **fragola** FEM NOUN
strawberry

fraintendere VERB [112]
to misunderstand
□ Mi hai frainteso. You misunderstood me.

la **frana** FEM NOUN
landslide

francese (FEM **francese**) ADJECTIVE
▷ see also **francese** MASC NOUN, FEM NOUN
French

il **francese** MASC NOUN
▷ see also **francese** ADJECTIVE, FEM NOUN
1 Frenchman (person)
■ **i Francesi** the French
2 French (language)
□ Parli francese? Do you speak French?

la **francese** FEM NOUN
▷ see also **francese** MASC NOUN, ADJECTIVE
Frenchwoman

la **Francia** FEM NOUN
France
□ Ti piace la Francia? Do you like France?
□ Andrò in Francia quest'estate. I'm going to France this summer.

franco (FEM **franca**, MASC PL **franchi**, FEM PL **franche**) ADJECTIVE
▷ see also **franco** NOUN
frank

il **franco** (PL i **franchi**) MASC NOUN
▷ see also **franco** ADJECTIVE
franc (currency)

il **francobollo** MASC NOUN
stamp

la **frangia** (PL le **frange**) FEM NOUN
fringe

il **frappé** (PL i **frappé**) MASC NOUN
milk shake

la **frase** FEM NOUN
sentence
□ Traduci questa frase. Translate this sentence.
■ **una frase fatta** a set phrase

il **frate** MASC NOUN
friar

il **fratello** MASC NOUN
brother
□ Questo è mio fratello. This is my brother.
■ **Hai fratelli?** Have you any brothers or sisters?
■ **Marina e Piero sono fratelli.** Marina and Piero are brother and sister.

frattempo MASC NOUN
■ **nel frattempo** in the meantime

la **frattura** FEM NOUN
fracture
□ una grave frattura a serious fracture

■ **Ha una frattura alla gamba.** He's broken his leg.

le **freccette** FEM PL NOUN
darts
□ Giochiamo a freccette. Let's play darts.

la **freccia** (PL le **frecce**) FEM NOUN
1 arrow
2 indicator (on car)
■ **mettere la freccia** to indicate □ Ha messo la freccia per voltare a destra. He indicated he was turning right.

freddo (FEM **fredda**) ADJECTIVE, MASC NOUN
cold
□ La minestra è fredda. The soup is cold.
■ **Fa freddo.** It's cold.
■ **avere freddo** to be cold □ Hai freddo? Are you cold?

freddoloso (FEM **freddolosa**) ADJECTIVE
■ **essere freddoloso** to feel the cold

fregare VERB [76]
1 to pinch
□ Mi ha fregato il portafoglio. He pinched my wallet.
2 to cheat
□ Ha cercato di fregarmi. He tried to cheat me.
3 to rub
□ Si fregava le mani. He was rubbing his hands.
■ **Chi se ne frega?** Who cares?

frenare VERB [68]
to brake
□ Ha frenato per evitare un cane. He braked to avoid a dog.
■ **Non riusciva a frenare le lacrime.** She couldn't hold back her tears.

il **freno** MASC NOUN
brake
■ **freno a mano** handbrake □ Tira il freno a mano. Put the handbrake on.

frequentare VERB [68]
1 to go to (school, course)
□ Frequento un corso di inglese. I go to English classes.
2 to see (person)
□ Non li frequento più. I don't see them any more.
□ La frequento poco. I don't see much of her.
■ **Non mi piace la gente che frequenta.** I don't like the people he mixes with.

frequentato (FEM **frequentata**) ADJECTIVE
popular
□ È la pizzeria più frequentata della città. It's the most popular pizzeria in town.

frequente (FEM **frequente**) ADJECTIVE
frequent
■ **di frequente** frequently

fresco (FEM **fresca**, MASC PL **freschi**, FEM PL **fresche**) ADJECTIVE
1 fresh
□ frutta fresca fresh fruit

f

2 cool

□ Fa fresco stasera. It's cool this evening.
- **mettere in fresco** to put in the fridge
□ Metti il vino in fresco. Put the wine in the fridge.
- **'vernice fresca'** 'wet paint'

la **fretta** FEM NOUN
hurry

□ Che fretta c'è? What's the hurry?
- **avere fretta** to be in a hurry □ Scusa ma ho un po' di fretta. I'm sorry but I'm in a bit of a hurry. □ Aveva fretta di andarsene. He was in a hurry to leave.
- **in fretta** quickly □ Fallo in fretta. Do it quickly.
- **Fa' in fretta!** Hurry up!
- **far fretta a qualcuno** to hurry somebody
□ Non farmi fretta. Don't hurry me.

friggere VERB [52]
to fry

il **frigo** (PL i **frigo**) MASC NOUN
fridge

□ Mettilo in frigo. Put it in the fridge.

la **frittata** FEM NOUN
omelette

fritto (FEM **fritta**) ADJECTIVE
▷ see also **fritto** NOUN
fried

□ pollo fritto fried chicken
- **patate fritte** chips

il **fritto** MASC NOUN
▷ see also **fritto** ADJECTIVE
- **fritto misto** mixed fried fish

la **frizione** FEM NOUN
clutch (in car)

frizzante (FEM **frizzante**) ADJECTIVE
sparkling

□ acqua minerale frizzante sparkling mineral water

frontale (FEM **frontale**) ADJECTIVE
- **uno scontro frontale** a head-on collision

la **fronte** FEM NOUN
▷ see also **fronte** MASC NOUN
forehead

□ Gli ha dato un bacio in fronte. She gave him a kiss on the forehead.
- **di fronte** opposite □ l'edificio di fronte the building opposite □ Abita qui di fronte. He lives in the house opposite.
- **di fronte a** opposite □ Si è seduto di fronte a me. He sat down opposite me. □ la casa di fronte alla mia the house opposite mine

il **fronte** MASC NOUN
▷ see also **fronte** FEM NOUN
front

la **frontiera** FEM NOUN
border

il **frullato** MASC NOUN
milk shake

il **frullatore** MASC NOUN
electric mixer

la **frusta** FEM NOUN
whip

la **frutta** FEM NOUN
fruit

□ frutta fresca fresh fruit □ Vuoi della frutta? Would you like some fruit? □ Mi piace molto la frutta. I love fruit.
- **frutta candita** candied fruit
- **frutta secca 1** (hazelnuts, almonds, etc.) nuts pl **2** dried fruit

il **fruttivendolo**, la **fruttivendola** MASC/FEM NOUN
greengrocer

il **frutto** MASC NOUN
fruit

□ un frutto tropicale a tropical fruit
- **frutti di mare** seafood sing

il **fucile** MASC NOUN
1 rifle
2 shotgun (for hunting)

la **fuga** (PL le **fughe**) FEM NOUN
escape

- **tentare la fuga** to try to escape
- **fuga di gas** gas leak

fuggire VERB [41, aux **essere**]
1 to escape

□ È fuggito di prigione. He escaped from jail.
2 to run away

□ È fuggita di casa. She ran away from home.

il **fulmine** MASC NOUN
lightning

□ È stato colpito da un fulmine. He was struck by lightning.
- **fulmini** lightning sing □ tuoni e fulmini thunder and lightning

fumare VERB [68]
to smoke

□ Ha smesso di fumare. She's given up smoking.
- **'è vietato fumare'** 'no smoking'

il **fumatore**, la **fumatrice** MASC/FEM NOUN
smoker

□ È un forte fumatore. He's a heavy smoker.
- **la sala fumatori** the room for smokers

il **fumetto** MASC NOUN
1 comic strip
2 comic

□ Le piacciono i fumetti. She likes comics.

il **fumo** MASC NOUN
1 smoke

□ Sento odore di fumo. I can smell smoke.
2 smoking

□ Il fumo fa male. Smoking is bad for you.
- **fumo passivo** passive smoking

la **fune** FEM NOUN
1 rope

□ Hanno tirato con forza e la fune si è spezzata. They pulled hard and the rope broke.

2 cable

il **funerale** MASC NOUN
funeral

il **fungo** (PL i **funghi**) MASC NOUN

1 mushroom

■ **fungo velenoso** toadstool

2 fungus

la **funivia** FEM NOUN
cable car

funzionare VERB [68]
to work

□ Come funziona? How does it work?
□ L'ascensore non funziona. The lift isn't working.

la **funzione** FEM NOUN
function

□ La funzione principale di... The main function of...

■ **essere in funzione** (machine) to be on
□ Non si apre quand'è in funzione. It won't open when it's on.

il **fuoco** (PL i **fuochi**) MASC NOUN
fire

■ **prendere fuoco** to catch fire □ La tenda ha preso fuoco. The curtain caught fire.

■ **dare fuoco a qualcosa** to set fire to something □ Ha dato fuoco alla casa. He set fire to the house.

■ **far fuoco** (shoot) to fire

■ **fuochi d'artificio** fireworks

fuori ADVERB, PREPOSITION

1 outside

□ Ti aspetto fuori. I'll wait for you outside.
□ Fuori è ancora buio. It's still dark outside.
□ Abito fuori Roma. I live outside Rome.

■ **fuori città** out of town

■ **fuori da** outside □ C'era molta gente fuori dal teatro. There were lots of people outside the theatre.

2 out

□ Cosa fai là fuori? What are you doing out there? □ Andiamo a mangiare fuori? Shall we eat out?

■ **Fuori!** Get out!

■ **Fuori dai piedi!** Get out of the way!

■ **Ha i denti in fuori.** Her teeth stick out.

■ **far fuori qualcuno** to kill somebody

■ **essere fuori di sé** to be furious

■ **fuori mano** out of the way

■ **fuori pasto** between meals

■ **fuori pericolo** out of danger

■ **fuori servizio** out of order

■ **fuori stagione** out of season

■ **fuori uso** out of use

il **fuorigioco** MASC NOUN

■ **in fuorigioco** offside □ Quando ha segnato era in fuorigioco. He was offside when he scored.

il **fuoristrada** (PL i **fuoristrada**) MASC NOUN
all-terrain vehicle

furbo (FEM **furba**) ADJECTIVE
▷ see also **furbo** NOUN
clever

□ un ragazzo furbo a clever boy

il **furbo**, la **furba** MASC/FEM NOUN
▷ see also **furbo** ADJECTIVE

■ **fare il furbo** to be clever □ Vuoi fare il furbo? Are you trying to be clever?

il **furgone** MASC NOUN
van

la **furia** FEM NOUN

■ **andare su tutte le furie** to fly into a rage

■ **Perderai la voce a furia di gridare.** You'll lose your voice if you shout so much.

furibondo (FEM **furibonda**) ADJECTIVE
furious

il **furto** MASC NOUN
theft

□ Vorrei denunciare un furto. I'd like to report a theft.

■ **furto con scasso** burglary

le **fusa** FEM PL NOUN

■ **fare le fusa** to purr

i **fuseaux** MASC PL NOUN
leggings

il **fuso** MASC NOUN

■ **fuso orario** time difference □ Non ho tenuto conto del fuso orario. I forgot about the time difference.

il **fustino** MASC NOUN
tub (of detergent)

futuro (FEM **futura**) ADJECTIVE, MASC NOUN
future

Gg

la **gabbia** FEM NOUN
cage

■ **gabbia toracica** rib cage

il **gabbiano** MASC NOUN
seagull

il **gabinetto** MASC NOUN
toilet

□ Dov'è il gabinetto? Where's the toilet? □ Posso andare al gabinetto? Can I go to the toilet, please?

la **gaffe** (PL le **gaffe**) FEM NOUN

■ **fare una gaffe** to put one's foot in it □ Ho fatto una gaffe. I've put my foot in it.

la **galera** FEM NOUN
prison

□ Ha fatto due anni di galera. He spent two years in prison.

■ **mandare qualcuno in galera** to send someone to prison □ Li hanno mandati in galera. They sent them to prison.

galla FEM NOUN

■ **venire a galla** to come to the surface
■ **stare a galla** to float □ Non so nuotare, ma sto a galla. I can't swim, but I can float.

galleggiare VERB [58]
to float

la **galleria** FEM NOUN

1 tunnel

□ la galleria del Monte Bianco the Mont Blanc tunnel

2 circle (in theatre)

□ due poltrone in galleria two seats in the circle

■ **galleria d'arte** art gallery

il **Galles** MASC NOUN
Wales

□ Mi è piaciuto molto il Galles. I really liked Wales. □ Andremo in Galles quest'estate. We're going to Wales this summer.

gallese (FEM **gallese**) ADJECTIVE
▷ see also **gallese** MASC NOUN, FEM NOUN
Welsh

□ la squadra gallese the Welsh team

il **gallese** MASC NOUN
▷ see also **gallese** ADJECTIVE, FEM NOUN

1 Welshman (person)

■ **i gallesi** the Welsh

2 Welsh (language)

la **gallese** FEM NOUN
▷ see also **gallese** ADJECTIVE, MASC NOUN
Welshwoman

la **gallina** FEM NOUN
hen

il **gallo** MASC NOUN
cock

il **galoppo** MASC NOUN

■ **andare al galoppo** to gallop

la **gamba** FEM NOUN
leg

□ Mi fa male la gamba. My leg hurts.

■ **in gamba** 1 clever □ Gloria è una ragazza in gamba. Gloria's a clever girl. 2 (at job) good □ Il nostro professore è molto in gamba. Our teacher's very good.

il **gamberetto** MASC NOUN
prawn

il **gambero** MASC NOUN

1 king prawn

2 crayfish

il **gambo** MASC NOUN
stem (of flower)

la **gamma** FEM NOUN
range

□ una vasta gamma di articoli sportivi a wide range of sports goods

il **gancio** MASC NOUN
hook

□ Le chiavi erano appese ad un gancio. The keys were hanging on a hook.

la **gara** FEM NOUN
competition

■ **partecipare a una gara** to take part in a competition
■ **gara di nuoto** swimming gala
■ **gara ciclistica** cycle race
■ **Facciamo a gara a chi arriva primo!** I'll race you!

il **garage** (PL i **garage**) MASC NOUN
garage

□ Hai messo la macchina in garage? Have you put the car in the garage?

garantire VERB [51]

1 to assure

□ Ti garantisco che... I assure you that...

2 to guarantee

□ Questo televisore è garantito tre anni. This television is guaranteed for three years.

la **garanzia** FEM NOUN
guarantee

□ una garanzia di un anno a one-year guarantee

■ **essere in garanzia 1** to be under guarantee **2** to be under warranty

il **garofano** MASC NOUN
carnation

il **gas** (PL i **gas**) MASC NOUN
gas

□ una stufa a gas a gas heater □ Hai spento il gas? Have you turned off the gas?

■ **gas lacrimogeno** tear gas

il **gasolio** MASC NOUN
diesel

gassato (FEM **gassata**) ADJECTIVE
fizzy

il **gattino** MASC NOUN
kitten

il **gatto**, la **gatta** MASC/FEM NOUN
cat

■ **gatto delle nevi** snow cat

gelare VERB [68, aux **essere**]
to freeze

□ Il lago gela durante l'inverno. The lake freezes in winter. □ Si gela qui dentro! It's freezing in here!

la **gelateria** FEM NOUN
ice-cream shop

il **gelato** MASC NOUN
▷ see also **gelato** ADJECTIVE
ice cream

□ un gelato alla fragola a strawberry ice cream

gelato (FEM **gelata**) ADJECTIVE
▷ see also **gelato** NOUN
frozen

□ Ho le mani gelate. My hands are frozen.

gelido (FEM **gelida**) ADJECTIVE
icy

□ un vento gelido an icy wind

la **gelosia** FEM NOUN
jealousy

geloso (FEM **gelosa**) ADJECTIVE
jealous

□ È geloso del fratellino. He's jealous of his baby brother.

la **gemella** FEM NOUN
twin

Gemelli MASC PL NOUN
Gemini

□ Sono dei Gemelli. I'm Gemini.

il **gemello** MASC NOUN

1 twin

□ Sono gemelli. They're twins.

2 cufflink

□ un paio di gemelli a pair of cufflinks

generale (FEM **generale**) ADJECTIVE
▷ see also **generale** NOUN
general

□ uno sciopero generale a general strike

■ **in generale** on the whole □ In generale le cose vanno bene. On the whole things are going well.

■ **In generale le ragazze sono più brave.** Girls are generally better.

il **generale** MASC NOUN
▷ see also **generale** ADJECTIVE
general

la **generazione** FEM NOUN
generation

il **genere** MASC NOUN

1 kind

□ È il genere di musica che mi piace. It's the kind of music I like.

■ **qualcosa del genere** something like that

■ **Non ho mai visto niente del genere!** I've never seen anything like it!

■ **in genere** usually □ In genere mi alzo alle sette. I usually get up at seven.

■ **generi di prima necessità** basic essentials

2 gender (in grammar)

il **genero** MASC NOUN
son-in-law

generoso (FEM **generosa**) ADJECTIVE
generous

□ un'offerta generosa a generous offer

la **gengiva** FEM NOUN
gum

geniale (FEM **geniale**) ADJECTIVE
brilliant

□ un'idea geniale a brilliant idea

il **genio** MASC NOUN
genius

□ Sei un genio! You're a genius!

■ **un colpo di genio** a brainwave □ Ho avuto un colpo di genio. I've had a brainwave.

il **genitore** MASC NOUN
parent

□ i miei genitori my parents

gennaio MASC NOUN
January

> LANGUAGE TIP In Italian, months are not written with capital letters.

□ in gennaio in January

Genova FEM NOUN
Genoa

□ Domani vado a Genova. I'm going to Genoa tomorrow. □ Abitiamo a Genova. We live in Genoa.

la **gente** FEM NOUN
people pl

□ C'era tanta gente. There were lots of people. □ C'era poca gente in spiaggia. There weren't many people on the beach. □ È gente molto simpatica. They're very nice people.

gentile (FEM **gentile**) ADJECTIVE
nice

gg

□ È molto gentile da parte vostra. It's very nice of you.

■ **Gent. Sig. Rossi** **1** *(on envelope)* Mr Rossi **2** *(in letter)* Dear Mr Rossi

la **geografia** FEM NOUN
geography

la **geometria** FEM NOUN
geometry

la **Germania** FEM NOUN
Germany
□ Mi è piaciuta molto la Germania. I really liked Germany. □ Andremo in Germania quest'estate. We're going to Germany this summer.

il **gerundio** MASC NOUN
gerund

il **gesso** MASC NOUN
1 chalk
2 plaster *(on arm, leg)*

la **gestione** FEM NOUN
management

gestire VERB [51]
to manage

il **gesto** MASC NOUN
gesture
□ un gesto di rabbia an angry gesture

Gesù MASC NOUN
Jesus
□ Gesù Bambino baby Jesus

gettare VERB [68]
to throw
□ Ha gettato il libro dalla finestra. He threw the book out of the window. □ Non gettare il giornale per terra. Don't throw the paper on the floor.
■ **gettarsi in acqua** to jump into water

il **gettone** MASC NOUN
token

ghiacciato (FEM **ghiacciata**) ADJECTIVE
1 frozen
□ Ho i piedi ghiacciati. My feet are frozen.
2 ice-cold
□ una birra ghiacciata an ice-cold beer

il **ghiaccio** MASC NOUN
ice
□ un cubetto di ghiaccio an ice cube

il **ghiacciolo** MASC NOUN
ice lolly
□ un ghiacciolo al limone a lemon ice lolly

la **ghiaia** FEM NOUN
gravel

la **ghiandola** FEM NOUN
gland

già ADVERB
already
□ Te l'ho già detto. I've already told you. □ Sei già di ritorno? Are you back already?
■ **Ma non ci conosciamo già?** Haven't we met before?

la **giacca** (PL le **giacche**) FEM NOUN
jacket
□ una giacca sportiva a sports jacket
■ **giacca a vento** anorak

il **giaccone** MASC NOUN
winter jacket

giallo (FEM **gialla**) ADJECTIVE, MASC NOUN
1 yellow
□ una sciarpa gialla a yellow scarf □ le Pagine gialle the Yellow Pages
2 amber
□ Non attraversare con il giallo. You mustn't cross on an amber light.
■ **romanzo giallo** detective story
■ **film giallo** thriller

il **Giappone** MASC NOUN
Japan
□ Mi è piaciuto molto il Giappone. I really liked Japan. □ Andremo in Giappone quest'estate. We're going to Japan this summer.

giapponese (FEM **giapponese**) ADJECTIVE
▷ *see also* **giapponese** MASC NOUN, FEM NOUN
Japanese

il **giapponese** MASC NOUN
▷ *see also* **giapponese** FEM NOUN, ADJECTIVE
1 Japanese man *(person)*
■ **i giapponesi** the Japanese
2 Japanese *(language)*
□ Parla giapponese. She speaks Japanese.

la **giapponese** FEM NOUN
▷ *see also* **giapponese** MASC NOUN, ADJECTIVE
Japanese woman

il **giardiniere** MASC NOUN
gardener

il **giardino** MASC NOUN
garden
□ Sono in giardino. They're in the garden.
■ **giardino pubblico** park

il **giga** (PL i **giga**) MASC NOUN
gig *(gigabyte)*

il **gigante** MASC NOUN
▷ *see also* **gigante** ADJECTIVE
giant

gigante (FEM **gigante**) ADJECTIVE
▷ *see also* **gigante** NOUN
giant
□ un cavolfiore gigante a giant cauliflower
■ **confezione gigante** economy-size packet

il **giglio** MASC NOUN
lily

il **gilè** (PL i **gilè**) MASC NOUN
waistcoat

il **ginecologo**, la **ginecologa** (MASC PL i **ginecologi**, FEM PL le **ginecologhe**) MASC/FEM NOUN
gynaecologist

Ginevra FEM NOUN
Geneva

□ Domani vado a Ginevra. I'm going to Geneva tomorrow. □ Abitano a Ginevra. They live in Geneva.

la **ginnastica** FEM NOUN
exercise

□ Dovresti fare un po' di ginnastica. You should do some exercise.

■ **Vado a fare ginnastica due volte alla settimana.** I go to the gym twice a week.

il **ginocchio** (FEM PL le **ginocchia**) MASC NOUN
knee

■ **mettersi in ginocchio** to kneel down

giocare VERB [18]
to play

□ Sai giocare a scacchi? Can you play chess?
□ Gioca nel Milan. He plays for Milan.

■ **giocare d'azzardo** to gamble

il **giocatore**, la **giocatrice** MASC/FEM NOUN
player

□ un giocatore di scacchi a chess player

■ **un giocatore d'azzardo** a gambler

il **giocattolo** MASC NOUN
toy

il **gioco** (PL i **giochi**) MASC NOUN
game

□ un gioco da tavolo a board game □ Facciamo un gioco. Let's play a game.

■ **i giochi olimpici** the Olympic Games

■ **È stato un gioco da ragazzi.** It was dead easy.

il **giocoliere** MASC NOUN
juggler

la **gioia** FEM NOUN
joy

la **gioielleria** FEM NOUN
jeweller's

il **gioiello** MASC NOUN

■ **un gioiello** a piece of jewellery

■ **i gioielli di mia madre** my mother's jewellery

la **Giordania** FEM NOUN
Jordan

il **giornalaio** MASC NOUN
newsagent's (shop)

il **giornale** MASC NOUN
newspaper

□ L'ho letto sul giornale. I read it in the newspaper.

■ **il giornale radio** the radio news sing

giornaliero (FEM **giornaliera**) ADJECTIVE
daily

il **giornalismo** MASC NOUN
journalism

il/la **giornalista** (MASC PL i **giornalisti**, FEM PL le **giornaliste**) MASC/FEM NOUN
journalist

□ Fa la giornalista. She is a journalist.

la **giornata** FEM NOUN
day

□ Bella giornata, vero? Lovely day, isn't it?

■ **giornata lavorativa** working day

il **giorno** MASC NOUN
day

□ due giorni fa two days ago □ uno di questi giorni one of these days

■ **di giorno** during the day □ Preferisco guidare di giorno. I prefer driving during the day.

■ **tre volte al giorno** three times a day

■ **Che giorno è oggi? 1** What day is it today? **2** What date is it today?

■ **al giorno d'oggi** nowadays

■ **un giorno feriale** a weekday

■ **un giorno festivo** a holiday

la **giostra** FEM NOUN
roundabout

■ **le giostre** funfair

giovane (FEM **giovane**) ADJECTIVE
▷ see also **giovane** MASC NOUN, FEM NOUN
young

□ Sei troppo giovane. You're too young. □ È più giovane di me. He's younger than me. □ È il più giovane della squadra. He's the youngest in the team.

il **giovane** MASC NOUN
▷ see also **giovane** ADJECTIVE, FEM NOUN
young man

□ da giovane when he was a young man

■ **i giovani** young people

la **giovane** FEM NOUN
▷ see also **giovane** ADJECTIVE, MASC NOUN
young woman

il **giovedì** (PL i **giovedì**) MASC NOUN
Thursday

> **LANGUAGE TIP** In Italian, days are not written with capital letters.

□ L'ho vista giovedì. I saw her on Thursday.

■ **di giovedì** on Thursdays □ Vado in piscina di giovedì. I go swimming on Thursdays.

■ **giovedì scorso** last Thursday

■ **giovedì prossimo** next Thursday

il **giradischi** (PL i **giradischi**) MASC NOUN
record player

la **giraffa** FEM NOUN
giraffe

girare VERB [68, aux **avere** or **essere**]
to turn

□ Gira a destra. Turn right.

■ **Mi gira la testa.** I feel dizzy.

■ **girarsi** to turn round □ Si è girata e mi ha guardato. She turned round and looked at me.

■ **girare un film** to make a film

■ **Ho girato tutta la città.** I've been all over town.

il **girasole** MASC NOUN
sunflower

girevole (FEM **girevole**) ADJECTIVE

■ **porta girevole** revolving door

■ **sedia girevole** swivel chair

il **giro** MASC NOUN
- **fare un giro 1** to go for a walk **2** *(on bike)* to go for a ride **3** to go for a drive
- **fare un giro in centro** to have a look round the city centre
- **guardarsi in giro** to look around
- **lasciare tutto in giro** to leave everything lying about
- **prendere in giro qualcuno** to make fun of somebody □ Mi prendono in giro perché sono grasso. They make fun of me because I'm fat.
- **Ma va', mi stai prendendo in giro!** Come on, you're pulling my leg!
- **giro turistico** sightseeing tour

il **girocollo** MASC NOUN
- **maglia a girocollo** crewneck sweater

il **girone** MASC NOUN
- **girone d'andata** first leg
- **girone di ritorno** second leg

la **gita** FEM NOUN
trip
□ una gita scolastica a school trip
- **fare una gita** to go on a trip

giù ADVERB
down
□ Vieni giù! Come down! □ Oggi sono un po' giù. I'm a bit down today.
- **più in giù** further down □ Spostalo più in giù. Move it further down.
- **bambini dai sette anni in giù** children of seven and under
- **Giù le mani!** Hands off!

il **giubbotto** MASC NOUN
bomber jacket
- **giubbotto salvagente** life jacket
- **giubbotto antiproiettile** bulletproof vest

giudicare VERB [18]
to judge
□ a giudicare da quello che dice judging by what he says

il **giudice** MASC NOUN
judge

il **giudizio** MASC NOUN
opinion
□ a mio giudizio in my opinion
- **denti del giudizio** wisdom teeth

il **giugno** MASC NOUN
June
> **LANGUAGE TIP** In Italian, months are not written with capital letters.
□ in giugno in June

la **giungla** FEM NOUN
jungle

giurare VERB [68]
to swear
□ È vero, te lo giuro! It's true, I swear! □ Ti giuro che non sono stato io. I swear it wasn't me. □ Mi pare di sì, ma non potrei giurarci. I think so, but I couldn't swear to it.

la **giuria** FEM NOUN
jury

giustificare VERB [18]
to excuse
□ Non lo giustifico, però capisco perché l'ha fatto. I don't excuse him but I understand why he did it.
- **Si è giustificato dicendo che era stanco.** His excuse was that he was tired.

la **giustificazione** FEM NOUN
excuse
□ Non c'è alcuna giustificazione per quello che hai fatto. There's no excuse for what you did.

la **giustizia** FEM NOUN
justice
□ In questo mondo non c'è giustizia! There's no justice in this world!
- **farsi giustizia da sé** to take the law into one's own hands

giustiziare VERB [17]
to execute

giusto (FEM **giusta**) ADJECTIVE
▷ see also **giusto** ADVERB
1 right
□ Dobbiamo aspettare il momento giusto. We'll have to wait for the right moment. □ Non trovo la parola giusta. I can't find the right word.
2 fair
□ Non è giusto! Vince sempre lui. It's not fair! He always wins.

giusto ADVERB
▷ see also **giusto** ADJECTIVE
just
□ Sono arrivato giusto in tempo. I arrived just in time. □ Volevo vedere giusto te. You're just the person I wanted to see.
- **Giusto!** Of course! □ Ah sì, giusto! Quasi mi dimenticavo. Yes, of course! I was nearly forgetting.
- **stare giusto** to fit perfectly □ I tuoi stivali mi stanno giusti. Your boots fit me perfectly.

gli ARTICLE
▷ see also **gli** PRONOUN
the
□ Gli spari provenivano dal parco. The shots came from the park.
> **LANGUAGE TIP** gli is often not translated.
□ Gli inglesi amano gli animali. English people love animals. □ Ti piacciono gli spaghetti? Do you like spaghetti? □ gli amici di Mario Mario's friends
> **LANGUAGE TIP** gli is sometimes translated by a possessive pronoun.
□ Si è tolto gli stivali. He took off his boots. □ Chiudi gli occhi. Close your eyes.

gli PRONOUN
▷ see also **gli** ARTICLE
1 him
□ Gli ho detto tutto. I told him everything.

□ Dagli qualcosa da mangiare. **Give him something to eat.** □ Scrivigli! **Write to him!** □ Gli sembrava una buona idea. **It seemed a good idea to him.** □ Gli ha sorriso. **He smiled at him.**

2 it

□ Dagli una lucidata. **Give it a polish.** □ Aggiungigli un po' di sale. **Add a bit of salt to it.** □ Dagli un'occhiata. **Have a look at it.**

> **LANGUAGE TIP glielo** is translated by 'him', 'her' or 'them', sometimes with a preposition.

□ Gabriele lo sa? — Sì, gliel'ho detto. **Does Gabriele know? — Yes, I've told him.** □ Lidia lo sa? — Sì, gliel'ho detto. **Does Lidia know? — Yes, I've told her.** □ I tuoi lo sanno? — Sì, gliel'ho detto. **Do your parents know? — Yes, I've told them.** □ Dagliela domani. **Give it to him tomorrow.** □ Glieli hai promessi. **You promised them to her.** □ Gliel'ha spedite. **He sent them to them.** □ Gliene ho parlato. **I spoke to her about it.**

la **gloria** FEM NOUN
glory
□ gloria e fama **glory and fame**

gli **gnocchi** MASC PL NOUN
gnocchi

la **goccia** (PL le **gocce**) FEM NOUN
drop
■ una goccia d'olio **a drop of oil**
■ gocce per gli occhi **eye drops**
■ **Questa è la goccia che fa traboccare il vaso!** That's the last straw!

il **goccio** MASC NOUN
drop
□ Vuoi un goccio di vino? **Would you like a drop of wine?**

gocciolare VERB [68, aux **avere** or **essere**]
to drip
□ Il rubinetto gocciola. **The tap's dripping.**
■ Mi gocciola il naso. **My nose is running.**

goffo (FEM **goffa**) ADJECTIVE
clumsy
□ È un po' goffo. **He's a bit clumsy.** □ È la persona la più goffa che abbia mai conosciuto. **He's the clumsiest person I've ever met.**

il **gol** (PL i **gol**) MASC NOUN
goal
□ fare un goal **to score a goal**

la **gola** FEM NOUN
throat
■ avere mal di gola **to have a sore throat**
□ Ho mal di gola. **I've got a sore throat.**

il **golf** (PL i **golf**) MASC NOUN
1 golf
■ giocare a golf **to play golf**
2 cardigan
3 jumper

il **golfo** MASC NOUN
gulf
■ il golfo del Messico **the Gulf of Mexico**
■ il golfo di Napoli **the Bay of Naples**
■ il golfo Persico **the Gulf**

goloso (FEM **golosa**) ADJECTIVE
■ essere goloso di dolci **to love sweets**
□ Sono golosa di dolci. **I love sweets.**

la **gomitata** FEM NOUN
■ dare una gomitata a qualcuno **to elbow somebody** □ Mi ha dato una gomitata nello stomaco. **He elbowed me in the stomach.**

il **gomito** MASC NOUN
elbow

il **gomitolo** MASC NOUN
■ un gomitolo di lana **a ball of wool**

la **gomma** FEM NOUN
1 rubber
□ Mi presti la gomma? **Can I borrow your rubber?**
■ gomma da masticare **chewing gum**
■ guanti di gomma **rubber gloves**
2 tyre
□ Ho una gomma a terra. **I've got a flat tyre.**

il **gommone** MASC NOUN
rubber dinghy

gonfiare VERB [17]
to blow up
□ Devo gonfiare le gomme della bici. **I need to blow up the tyres on my bike.**
■ gonfiarsi **to swell** □ Mi si è gonfiata la caviglia. **My ankle is swollen.**

gonfio (FEM **gonfia**) ADJECTIVE
1 swollen
□ Ho il piede gonfio. **My foot's swollen.**
2 puffy
□ Aveva gli occhi gonfi per il pianto. **Her eyes were puffy with crying.**

il **gonfiore** MASC NOUN
swelling

la **gonna** FEM NOUN
skirt
□ una gonna lunga **a long skirt**
■ una gonna pantalone **a pair of culottes**

googlare VERB [68]
to google

il **gorilla** (PL i **gorilla**) MASC NOUN
1 gorilla
2 bodyguard

gotico (FEM **gotica**, MASC PL **gotici**, FEM PL **gotiche**) ADJECTIVE
Gothic

il **governo** MASC NOUN
government
□ il governo britannico **the British government**
■ il partito al governo **the party in power**

il **GPS** MASC NOUN
GPS

g

Italian-English

la **gradinata** FEM NOUN
1 flight of steps
2 terraces pl
  □ Abbiamo seguito la partita dalla gradinata.
  We watched the match from the terraces.

il **gradino** MASC NOUN
  step
  □ Attento al gradino. Mind the step.

il **grado** MASC NOUN
  degree
  □ cinque gradi sotto zero five degrees below
  zero
  ■ **essere in grado di fare qualcosa** to be
  able to do something □ Presto sarà in grado di
  camminare di nuovo. He'll soon be able to walk
  again.
  ■ **Non sono in grado di farlo da solo.** I
  can't do it by myself.

graffiare VERB [17]
  to scratch
  □ Il gatto mi ha graffiato la mano. The cat
  scratched my hand.

il **graffio** MASC NOUN
  scratch

il **grafico** (PL i **grafici**) MASC NOUN
1 graph
  □ Il grafico illustra il calo nelle vendite. The
  graph shows the drop in sales.
2 graphic designer
  □ Fa il grafico. He is a graphic designer.

la **grammatica** (PL le **grammatiche**) FEM
  NOUN
  grammar
  □ un libro di grammatica a grammar book
  ■ **C'erano molti errori di grammatica.**
  There were lots of grammatical errors.

il **grammo** MASC NOUN
  gram

la **Gran Bretagna** FEM NOUN
  Great Britain
  □ Mi piace la Gran Bretagna. I like Great Britain.
  □ Andremo in Gran Bretagna quest'estate.
  We're going to Great Britain this summer.

il **granchio** MASC NOUN
  crab

grande (FEM **grande**) ADJECTIVE
  ▷ see also **grande** NOUN
1 big
  □ La stanza non è molto grande. The room isn't
  very big. □ Quant'è grande questa stanza?
  How big is this room? □ Come ti sei fatto
  grande! How big you've got! □ Milano è più
  grande di Genova. Milan is bigger than Genoa.
  □ lo stadio più grande d'Italia the biggest
  stadium in Italy
2 large
  □ un gran numero di macchine a large number
  of cars □ una grande quantità di materie prime

a large amount of raw materials □ Si è radunata
una gran folla. A large crowd gathered.
3 old
  □ Sei abbastanza grande per capire. You're old
  enough to understand. □ È più grande di me.
  He's older than me. □ Sono la più grande. I'm
  the oldest.
  ■ **Hanno due figli grandi.** They have two
  grown-up children.
4 great
  □ un grande poeta a great poet □ Sei stato di
  grande aiuto. You've been a great help.
  ■ **Ho una gran fame.** I'm starving.
  ■ **Fa un gran caldo oggi.** It's terribly hot today.
  ■ **con mia grande sorpresa...** to my great
  surprise...
  ■ **un gran bel film** an excellent film
  ■ **Sei un gran bugiardo!** You're such a liar!
  ■ **grandi magazzini** department store sing

il/la **grande** MASC/FEM NOUN
  ▷ see also **grande** ADJECTIVE
  grown-up
  □ Odio i grandi! I hate grown-ups!
  ■ **Cosa farai da grande?** What are you
  going to be when you grow up?

grandinare VERB [68, AUX **essere**]
  to hail
  □ Ieri è grandinato. It hailed yesterday.

la **grandine** FEM NOUN
  hail
  ■ **chicco di grandine** hailstone

il **granello** MASC NOUN
1 grain
  □ un granello di sabbia a grain of sand
2 speck
  □ un granello di polvere a speck of dust

il **grano** MASC NOUN
  wheat

il **granturco** MASC NOUN
  maize

il **grappolo** MASC NOUN
  ■ **grappolo d'uva** bunch of grapes

grasso (FEM **grassa**) ADJECTIVE
  ▷ see also **grasso** NOUN
1 fat
  □ un signore grasso a fat man □ È più grasso di
  te. He's fatter than you.
2 greasy
  □ Ho i capelli grassi. My hair is greasy. □ Ho i
  capelli più grassi dei tuoi. My hair is greasier
  than yours.
3 fatty
  □ Dovresti evitare i cibi grassi. You should avoid
  fatty food.

il **grasso** MASC NOUN
  ▷ see also **grasso** ADJECTIVE
1 fat
  □ grassi animali e vegetali animal and
  vegetable fats

g

2 grease

□ una macchia di grasso a grease stain

gratis ADVERB

free

□ I bambini viaggiano gratis. Children travel free.

■ **Me l'ha riparato gratis.** He repaired it for me for nothing.

il **grattacielo** MASC NOUN

skyscraper

grattarsi VERB [56]

to scratch

□ Smettila di grattarti! Stop scratching! □ Si grattava la schiena. He was scratching his back.

la **grattugia** (PL le **grattugie**) FEM NOUN

grater

grattugiare VERB [58]

to grate

gratuito (FEM **gratuita**) ADJECTIVE

free

□ L'ingresso è gratuito. Admission is free.

grave (FEM **grave**) ADJECTIVE

serious

□ Non è niente di grave. It's nothing serious. □ una malattia grave a serious illness

■ **un malato grave** a seriously-ill patient

gravemente ADVERB

seriously

□ È rimasto gravemente ferito. He was seriously injured.

la **gravidanza** FEM NOUN

pregnancy

□ una gravidanza difficile a difficult pregnancy

la **gravità** FEM NOUN

seriousness

□ la gravità della situazione the seriousness of the situation

■ **la legge di gravità** the law of gravity

■ **la forza di gravità** gravity

la **grazia** FEM NOUN

grace

□ la grazia di una ballerina the grace of a ballerina

■ **concedere la grazia a qualcuno** to pardon somebody

■ **ottenere la grazia** to be pardoned

grazie EXCLAMATION

1 thank you

□ Vuoi un caffè? — No grazie. Would you like a coffee? — No, thank you.

■ **Vuoi un tè? — Sì grazie.** Would you like some tea? — Yes, please.

2 thanks

□ Hai trovato i libri? — Sì grazie. Did you find the books? — Yes, thanks.

■ **mille grazie** many thanks*

■ **grazie a lui** thanks to him

■ **Grazie a Dio!** Thank God!

grazioso (FEM **graziosa**) ADJECTIVE

charming

la **greca** (PL le **greche**) FEM NOUN

Greek *(person)*

la **Grecia** FEM NOUN

Greece

□ Mi piace la Grecia. I like Greece. □ Andremo in Grecia quest'estate. We're going to Greece this summer.

greco (FEM **greca**, MASC PL **greci**, FEM PL **greche**) ADJECTIVE

▷ see also **greco** NOUN

Greek

il **greco** MASC NOUN

▷ see also **greco** ADJECTIVE

Greek *(person, language)*

□ Parla il greco? Do you speak Greek?

il **gregge** (FEM PL le **greggi**) MASC NOUN

flock

□ un gregge di pecore a flock of sheep

il **grembiule** MASC NOUN

1 apron

2 overall

il **grembo** MASC NOUN

lap

gridare VERB [68]

to shout

□ Smettila di gridare! Stop shouting!

■ **gridare aiuto** to shout for help □ C'era qualcuno che gridava aiuto. Someone was shouting for help.

il **grido** (FEM PL le **grida**) MASC NOUN

1 shout

□ le grida dei bambini the children's shouts

2 cry

□ le sue grida di aiuto his cries for help

grigio (FEM **grigia**, MASC PL **grigi**, FEM PL **grigie**) ADJECTIVE, MASC NOUN

grey

□ Ha i capelli grigi. She's got grey hair.

la **griglia** FEM NOUN

■ **alla griglia** grilled □ una bistecca alla griglia a grilled steak

il **grilletto** MASC NOUN

trigger

□ Ha premuto il grilletto. He pulled the trigger.

il **grillo** MASC NOUN

cricket

il **grissino** MASC NOUN

breadstick

la **grondaia** FEM NOUN

gutter

grosso (FEM **grossa**) ADJECTIVE

1 big

□ un grosso macigno a big rock □ È più grossa della mia. It's bigger than mine. □ È il più grosso del mondo. It's the biggest in the world.

■ **Stavolta l'hai fatta grossa.** This time you're in big trouble.

■ **Ti sbagli di grosso.** You're very much mistaken.

Italian-English

2 thick
- □ una grossa fune a thick rope

3 large
- □ una grossa somma a large sum

4 serious
- □ Sarebbe un grosso errore. It would be a serious mistake.

la **grotta** FEM NOUN
cave

la **gru** (PL le **gru**) FEM NOUN
crane (bird, machine)

la **gruccia** (PL le **grucce**) FEM NOUN
1 crutch
2 coat hanger

il **grumo** MASC NOUN
lump
- □ C'erano dei grumi nella besciamella. There were lumps in the béchamel sauce.

il **gruppo** MASC NOUN
group
- □ Dividiamoli in gruppi di tre. Let's divide them into groups of three.
- ■ **Sono arrivati a gruppi di tre.** They came in threes.
- ■ **gruppo sanguigno** blood group

guadagnare VERB [14]
1 to earn
- □ Guadagna bene. He earns a lot. □ Quanto guadagni al mese? How much do you earn per month?
- ■ **E io che cosa ci guadagno?** What's in it for me?

2 to gain
- □ Non ci guadagni niente a fare così. There's nothing to be gained by doing that.
- ■ **guadagnare tempo** to gain time □ L'ha detto per guadagnare tempo. He said it to gain time.

il **guadagno** MASC NOUN
earnings pl

guai EXCLAMATION
- ■ **Guai a te!** Don't you dare!
- ■ **Guai a te se lo fai un'altra volta!** Don't you dare do that again!

il **guaio** MASC NOUN
trouble
- □ Il guaio è che sono già partiti. The trouble is that they've already left.
- ■ **Sono in un bel guaio.** I'm in a real mess.

la **guancia** (PL le **guance**) FEM NOUN
cheek

il **guanto** MASC NOUN
glove
- □ un paio di guanti di lana a pair of woollen gloves

il **guardalinee** (PL i **guardalinee**) MASC NOUN
linesman

guardare VERB [68]
1 to look
- □ Guarda qui! Look here! □ Guarda cos'hai combinato! Look what you've done! □ Guarda chi si vede! Look who's here! □ Si guardavano negli occhi. They were looking into each other's eyes.

2 to look at
- □ Si girò a guardarlo. She turned to look at him. □ Cos'hai da guardare? What are you looking at? □ Si guardò allo specchio. He looked at himself in the mirror.

3 to watch
- □ Hai guardato la partita ieri sera? Did you watch the match last night? □ Stasera guardo la tivù. I'm going to watch TV tonight. □ L'ho guardata mentre correva giù per le scale. I watched her run down the stairs.

il **guardaroba** (PL i **guardaroba**) MASC NOUN
1 wardrobe
- □ Metti in ordine il tuo guardaroba! Tidy up your wardrobe!

2 cloakroom
- □ Ho lasciato l'impermeabile al guardaroba. I left my raincoat in the cloakroom.

la **guardia** FEM NOUN
- ■ **guardia carceraria** prison warder
- ■ **guardia del corpo** bodyguard
- ■ **Guardia di Finanza** financial police
- ■ **guardia giurata** security guard
- ■ **guardia medica** emergency doctor service
- ■ **il cambio della guardia** the changing of the guard
- ■ **fare la guardia** to keep watch □ Stavo facendo la guardia. I was keeping watch.
- ■ **essere di guardia** to be on duty □ Al cancello c'era un poliziotto di guardia. There was a policeman on duty at the gate.
- ■ **cane da guardia** guard dog

il **guardiano** MASC NOUN
caretaker
- □ il guardiano della scuola the school caretaker
- ■ **guardiano notturno** night watchman

la **guarigione** FEM NOUN
recovery
- □ Auguri di pronta guarigione! Best wishes for a speedy recovery!

guarire VERB [51, aux **avere** or **essere**]
1 to be better
- □ Spero che tu guarisca presto. I hope you'll be better soon. □ Non sono ancora completamente guarito. I'm not completely better yet.

2 to cure
- □ I medici non sono riusciti a guarirlo. The doctors couldn't cure him.

3 to heal up
- □ La ferita guarirà in dieci giorni. The wound will heal up in ten days.

g

il/la **guastafeste** MASC/FEM NOUN
killjoy
□ Non fare il guastafeste! Don't be such a killjoy!

guastarsi VERB [56]
to break down
□ Mi si è guastata la macchina in autostrada. My car broke down on the motorway.
■ **Speriamo che il tempo non si guasti.** Let's hope the weather doesn't change for the worse.

guasto (FEM **guasta**) ADJECTIVE
▷ *see also* **guasto** NOUN
1 not working
□ Il mio televisore è guasto. My television isn't working.
■ **'guasto'** 'out of order'
2 bad
□ Quella mela è guasta. That apple is bad.

il **guasto** MASC NOUN
▷ *see also* **guasto** ADJECTIVE
failure
□ L'aereo è precipitato per un guasto al motore. The plane crashed because of engine failure
■ **Il meccanico ha riparato un guasto al motore.** The mechanic repaired a fault in the engine.

la **guerra** FEM NOUN
war
□ la guerra del Vietnam the Vietnam war
■ **guerra civile** civil war
■ **guerra mondiale** world war □ la seconda guerra mondiale the Second World War
■ **guerra chimica** chemical warfare

il **gufo** MASC NOUN
owl

la **guida** FEM NOUN
1 guide
□ Ho comprato una guida di Londra. I bought a guide to London. □ Fa la guida turistica. He is a tourist guide.
■ **la guida telefonica** the phone book
2 driving
□ Ha preso la multa per guida in stato di ebbrezza. He was fined for drink-driving.
□ lezioni di guida driving lessons
■ **una macchina con la guida a destra** a right-hand drive car

guidare VERB [68]
1 to drive
□ Sai guidare? Can you drive? □ Ha guidato per tutta la notte. She drove all night. □ Ha mai guidato in Gran Bretagna? Have you ever driven in Britain?
2 to lead
□ Ha guidato una spedizione in Antartide. He led an expedition to Antarctica.
■ **Lasciati guidare dall'istinto.** Let your instinct be your guide.

il **guidatore**, la **guidatrice** MASC/FEM NOUN
driver

il **guinzaglio** MASC NOUN
lead
□ un cane al guinzaglio a dog on a lead

il **guscio** (PL i **gusci**) MASC NOUN
shell *(of egg, nut)*

il **gusto** MASC NOUN
1 flavour
□ disponibile in tre nuovi gusti available in three new flavours
■ **al gusto di fragola** strawberry-flavoured
2 taste
□ un gusto amaro a bitter taste □ Veste con gusto. She's got good taste in clothes. □ uno scherzo di cattivo gusto a joke in bad taste
□ Abbiamo gusti diversi in fatto di musica. We have different tastes in music.
■ **Abbiamo gli stessi gusti.** We like the same things.
■ **Ci ha preso gusto.** He got to like it.
■ **Per i miei gusti tu corri un po' troppo.** You drive too fast for my liking.
■ **Lo fa per il gusto di farlo.** He does it for the fun of it.

gustoso (FEM **gustosa**) ADJECTIVE
tasty
□ un piatto gustoso a tasty dish □ La carne è più gustosa cucinata così. Meat is tastier when it's cooked like this.

g

h

l' **handicappato**, l' **handicappata**
MASC/FEM NOUN
▷ *see also* **handicappato** ADJECTIVE
disabled person

handicappato (FEM **handicappata**)
ADJECTIVE
▷ *see also* **handicappato** NOUN
disabled

l' **hascisc** MASC NOUN
hashish

l' **hashtag** (PL gli **hashtag**) MASC NOUN
hashtag

l' **hi-fi** (PL gli **hi-fi**) MASC NOUN
hi-fi

l' **hobby** (PL gli **hobby**) MASC NOUN
hobby

l' **hockey** MASC NOUN
hockey

■ **hockey su ghiaccio** ice hockey

la **hostess** (PL le **hostess**) FEM NOUN
air hostess

l' **hotel** (PL gli **hotel**) MASC NOUN
hotel

Ii

i ARTICLE
the
□ I bambini erano già a letto. The children were already in bed. □ Chi ha preso i libri? Who's taken the books?

LANGUAGE TIP i is often not translated.
□ I bambini viaggiano gratis. Children travel free. □ Non mi piacciono i funghi. I don't like mushrooms. □ i genitori di Mario Mario's parents

LANGUAGE TIP i is sometimes translated by a possessive adjective.
□ Si è tolto i guanti. He took off his gloves.
□ Lavarti i denti. Brush your teeth.

ibrido (FEM **ibrida**) ADJECTIVE
hybrid
□ un'auto ibrida a hybrid car

l' **iceberg** (PL gli **iceberg**) MASC NOUN
iceberg
□ la punta dell'iceberg the tip of the iceberg

l' **idea** FEM NOUN
idea
□ È un'idea geniale! It's a brilliant idea! □ Non hai idea del traffico che c'era. You've no idea how much traffic there was. □ Non ne ho la più pallida idea. I haven't the faintest idea.
■ **Neanche per idea!** No way! □ Pensi di andarci? — Neanche per idea! Are you thinking of going? — No way!
■ **cambiare idea** to change one's mind
□ Ho cambiato idea. I've changed my mind.

ideale (FEM **ideale**) ADJECTIVE
▷ see also **ideale** NOUN
ideal
□ la soluzione ideale the ideal solution

l' **ideale** MASC NOUN
▷ see also **ideale** ADJECTIVE
ideal
□ Hanno fatto sacrifici per i loro ideali. They have made sacrifices for their ideals.
■ **L'ideale sarebbe andarsene adesso.** The best thing would be to leave now.

identico (FEM **identica**, MASC PL **identici**, FEM PL **identiche**) ADJECTIVE
identical
□ Sono identici. They're identical.
■ **essere identico a** to be exactly the same as □ È identico al mio. It's exactly the same as mine.

l' **identità** (PL le **identità**) FEM NOUN
identity
□ la carta d'identità the identity card

idiomatico (FEM **idiomatica**, MASC PL **idiomatici**, FEM PL **idiomatiche**) ADJECTIVE
■ **una frase idiomatica** an idiom

idiota (MASC PL **idioti**, FEM PL **idiote**) ADJECTIVE
▷ see also **idiota** NOUN
stupid

l' **idiota** (MASC PL gli **idioti**, FEM PL le **idiote**)
MASC/FEM NOUN
▷ see also **idiota** ADJECTIVE
idiot

idratante (FEM **idratante**) ADJECTIVE
■ **crema idratante** moisturizing cream

l' **idraulico** (PL gli **idraulici**) MASC NOUN
plumber
□ Fa l'idraulico. He is a plumber.

la **iena** FEM NOUN
hyena

ieri ADVERB
yesterday
□ Sono tornato ieri. I got back yesterday. □ il giornale di ieri yesterday's paper □ ieri mattina yesterday morning □ ieri sera yesterday evening
■ **ieri notte** last night
■ **ieri l'altro** the day before yesterday

igienico (FEM **igienica**, MASC PL **igienici**, FEM PL **igieniche**) ADJECTIVE
1 hygiene (*regulations*)
2 hygienic (*conditions*)
■ **carta igienica** toilet paper

ignorante (FEM **ignorante**) ADJECTIVE
ignorant
□ Non ho fatto domande per paura di sembrare ignorante. I didn't ask any questions for fear of appearing ignorant.
■ **Come sei ignorante!** Don't you know anything!

ignorare VERB [68]
1 to ignore
□ Mi ha ignorato completamente. She completely ignored me.
2 to be unaware
□ Ignoravo che tu fossi qui. I was unaware that you were here.

il ARTICLE
the

illegale - imbrogliare

□ Il bambino ha fame. The baby is hungry.
□ il Tamigi the Thames

LANGUAGE TIP il is often not translated.
□ Il nuoto è il mio sport preferito. Swimming is my favourite sport. □ Non mi piace il riso. I don't like rice. □ Il Milan gioca in casa. A.C. Milan is playing at home. □ il padre di Mario Mario's father

LANGUAGE TIP il is sometimes translated by a possessive adjective.
□ Si è tolto il cappotto. He took off his coat.
□ Soffiati il naso. Blow your nose.

illegale (FEM **illegale**) ADJECTIVE
illegal

illeggibile (FEM **illeggibile**) ADJECTIVE
illegible

illeso (FEM **illesa**) ADJECTIVE
unhurt
□ È uscito illeso dall'incidente. He escaped unhurt from the accident.

illudersi VERB [32, aux **essere**]
to deceive oneself
□ Ti illudi se pensi di riavere i soldi. You're deceiving yourself if you think you'll get the money back.
■ **Si illudeva di trovare qualcuno pronto ad aiutarlo.** He mistakenly thought he might find somebody ready to help him.

illuminare VERB [68]
to light
□ La stanza era illuminata da un'unica lampada. The room was lit by a single lamp.
■ **illuminare a giorno** to floodlight □ Lo stadio era illuminato a giorno. The stadium was floodlit.

l' **illuminazione** FEM NOUN
lighting

l' **illusione** FEM NOUN
illusion
□ un'illusione ottica an optical illusion
■ **Non farti illusioni, non è sicuro che vengano.** Don't get your hopes up, it's not certain they're coming.

l' **illuso**, l' **illusa** MASC/FEM NOUN
■ **Sei un illuso!** You're fooling yourself!

illustrare VERB [68]
to illustrate

l' **illustrazione** FEM NOUN
illustration

l' **imballaggio** MASC NOUN
packing
□ una cassa da imballaggio a packing case
■ **carta da imballaggio** brown paper

imbarazzante (FEM **imbarazzante**) ADJECTIVE
1 awkward
□ una domanda imbarazzante an awkward question
2 embarrassing

□ una situazione imbarazzante an embarrassing situation

imbarazzato (FEM **imbarazzata**) ADJECTIVE
embarrassed
□ Ero imbarazzato. I was embarrassed.

l' **imbarazzo** MASC NOUN
embarrassment
□ Cercò di mascherare il suo imbarazzo. He tried to hide his embarrassment.
■ **mettere in imbarazzo** to embarrass
□ La sua domanda mi ha messo in imbarazzo. Her question embarrassed me.
■ **avere solo l'imbarazzo della scelta** to be spoilt for choice

l' **imbarcazione** FEM NOUN
boat

l' **imbarco** (PL gli **imbarchi**) MASC NOUN
boarding
□ È già cominciato l'imbarco del mio volo? Has boarding started for my flight yet?
■ **carta d'imbarco** boarding card

imbattibile (FEM **imbattibile**) ADJECTIVE
unbeatable

imbavagliare VERB [25]
to gag
□ L'hanno imbavagliato. They gagged him.

imbecille (FEM **imbecille**) ADJECTIVE
▷ see also **imbecille** NOUN
stupid

l' **imbecille** MASC/FEM NOUN
▷ see also **imbecille** ADJECTIVE
idiot

imbiancare VERB [18]
1 to whitewash
2 to paint

l' **imbianchino** MASC NOUN
painter and decorator
□ Fa l'imbianchino. He is a painter and decorator.

l' **imboscata** FEM NOUN
ambush

imbottire VERB [51]
1 to fill (sandwich)
2 to pad (jacket)
3 to stuff (cushion, pillow)
■ **imbottirsi di** (food) to stuff oneself with

imbottito (FEM **imbottita**) ADJECTIVE
1 filled
□ un panino imbottito a filled roll
2 padded
□ un reggiseno imbottito a padded bra

imbranato (FEM **imbranata**) ADJECTIVE
hopeless
□ Con le ragazze è proprio imbranato. He's hopeless with girls. □ Quell'imbranata non ne combina una giusta! She's hopeless, she never does anything right!

imbrogliare VERB [25]
to cheat

▢ Non imbrogliare! Don't cheat!

imbroglione (FEM **imbrogliona**) ADJECTIVE, MASC/FEM NOUN
cheat *(at game)*

▢ Sei un imbroglione! You're a cheat!

■ **un affarista imbroglione** a dishonest businessman

imbronciato (FEM **imbronciata**) ADJECTIVE
sulky

imbucare VERB [18]
to post

imburrare VERB [68]
1 to grease
2 to butter *(bread)*

l' **imbuto** MASC NOUN
funnel

imitare VERB [68]
to imitate

immaginare VERB [68]
1 to imagine

▢ Non riesco ad immaginarlo. I can't imagine it. ▢ Immagina di essere su un'isola deserta... Imagine you're on a desert island...
2 to think

▢ Me lo immaginavo più giovane. I thought he was younger. ▢ Me lo immaginavo! I thought so!

■ **Grazie mille! — S'immagini!** Thank you very much! — Don't mention it!

l' **immaginazione** FEM NOUN
imagination

l' **immagine** FEM NOUN
picture

immangiabile (FEM **immangiabile**) ADJECTIVE
inedible

▢ Il cibo era immangiabile. The food was inedible.

immaturo (FEM **immatura**) ADJECTIVE
immature

▢ un ragazzo immaturo an immature boy

immediatamente ADVERB
immediately

▢ Vai immediatamente dal medico! Go and see the doctor immediately!

immenso (FEM **immensa**) ADJECTIVE
huge

▢ un giardino immenso a huge garden

immergere VERB [54]
to plunge

▢ Ha immerso il viso nell'acqua. He plunged his face into the water.

■ **immergersi 1** *(swimmer)* to plunge
2 *(frogman)* to dive

■ **immergersi in** to immerse oneself in

immigrato (FEM **immigrata**) ADJECTIVE, MASC/FEM NOUN
immigrant

immischiarsi VERB [17, AUX **essere**]
to interfere

▢ Non t'immischiare, non sono fatti tuoi. Don't interfere, it's nothing to do with you.

immobile (FEM **immobile**) ADJECTIVE
motionless

▢ È rimasto lì, immobile. He stood there, motionless.

immobiliare (FEM **immobiliare**) ADJECTIVE
■ **agenzia immobiliare** estate agent's

le **immondizie** FEM PL NOUN
rubbish *sing*

▢ L'ha gettato nelle immondizie. He threw it in the rubbish.

impacchettare VERB [68]
to wrap up

▢ Devo impacchettare il regalo. I've got to wrap up the present.

impacciato (FEM **impacciata**) ADJECTIVE
awkward

▢ Mi sentivo un po' impacciato. I felt a bit awkward.

l' **impacco** (PL gli **impacchi**) MASC NOUN
compress

▢ Dovrai fare degli impacchi freddi. You'll have to apply cold compresses.

impalato (FEM **impalata**) ADJECTIVE
■ **Non stare lì impalato, fa' qualcosa!** Don't just stand there, do something!

l' **impalcatura** FEM NOUN
scaffolding

impallidire VERB [51, AUX **essere**]
to go pale

▢ È impallidito per la paura. He went pale with fear.

impanato (FEM **impanata**) ADJECTIVE
fried in breadcrumbs

▢ una cotoletta di vitello impanata a veal cutlet fried in breadcrumbs

impantanarsi VERB [56]
to get stuck in the mud

▢ La nostra macchina si è impantanata. Our car got stuck in the mud.

impappinarsi VERB [56]
to stammer

▢ Si è impappinata per l'emozione. She stammered with emotion.

imparare VERB [68]
to learn

▢ Sto imparando a suonare la chitarra. I'm learning to play the guitar. ▢ L'ha imparata a memoria. He's learnt it by heart.

imparziale (FEM **imparziale**) ADJECTIVE
impartial

impasticcarsi VERB [18, AUX **essere**]
to pop pills

l' **impatto** MASC NOUN
impact

impaurire VERB [51]
to frighten
□ Mi hai impaurito. You frightened me.

impaziente (FEM **impaziente**) ADJECTIVE
impatient

impazzire VERB [51, aux **essere**]
to go mad
□ Ma sei impazzito? Have you gone mad?
■ **far impazzire qualcuno** to drive
somebody mad □ Questo compito mi sta
facendo impazzire. This homework is driving
me mad.
■ **Ho un prurito da impazzire.** I've got an
itch that's driving me mad.

impeccabile (FEM **impeccabile**) ADJECTIVE
impeccable
□ Ha un gusto impeccabile. She's got
impeccable taste.
■ **in modo impeccabile** impeccably □ Si
veste sempre in modo impeccabile. He's
always impeccably dressed.

impedire VERB [51]
■ **impedire a qualcuno di fare qualcosa**
to stop somebody doing something □ Il
rumore mi ha impedito di dormire. The noise
stopped me sleeping. □ Serve per impedire alle
macchine di parcheggiare. It's there to stop
cars parking.
■ **Chi ti impedisce di farlo?** Who's
stopping you?

impegnarsi VERB [14, aux **essere**]
■ **impegnarsi a fare qualcosa** to promise
to do something □ Si è impegnato a darmi una
mano. He promised to give me a hand.
■ **impegnarsi nello studio** to study hard
□ Non s'impegna abbastanza nello studio. She
doesn't study hard enough.

impegnativo (FEM **impegnativa**) ADJECTIVE
demanding
□ un lavoro impegnativo a demanding job

impegnato (FEM **impegnata**) ADJECTIVE
busy
□ Oggi sono impegnato. I'm busy today. □ Mi
sembra che sia più impegnato di te. I think he's
busier than you.
■ **Mi dispiace, stasera sono già
impegnata.** I'm sorry, I'm already doing
something tonight.

l' **impegno** MASC NOUN
1 engagement
□ un impegno precedente a previous
engagement
■ **Domani non posso, ho un impegno.**
I can't tomorrow, I've got something on.
2 commitment
□ Ha molti impegni di lavoro. She has a lot of
work commitments.
■ **studiare con impegno** to study hard

impellente (FEM **impellente**) ADJECTIVE
urgent
□ un bisogno impellente an urgent need

l' **imperativo** MASC NOUN
imperative

l' **imperatore** MASC NOUN
emperor

l' **imperatrice** FEM NOUN
empress

imperfetto (FEM **imperfetta**) MASC NOUN,
ADJECTIVE
imperfect

impermeabile (FEM **impermeabile**)
ADJECTIVE
▷ see also **impermeabile** NOUN
waterproof
□ tessuto impermeabile waterproof material

l' **impermeabile** MASC NOUN
▷ see also **impermeabile** ADJECTIVE
raincoat

l' **impero** MASC NOUN
empire
□ l'impero romano the Roman Empire

impertinente (FEM **impertinente**) ADJECTIVE
impertinent

impiantarsi VERB [56]
to hang (computer, program)

l' **impianto** MASC NOUN
system
□ l'impianto di riscaldamento the heating
system
■ **impianti di risalita** ski lifts

impiccare VERB [18]
to hang
□ L'hanno impiccato. He was hanged.
■ **impiccarsi** to hang oneself □ Si è
impiccato. He hanged himself.

impicciarsi VERB [13, aux **essere**]
■ **Non t'impicciare!** Keep out of this!
■ **Impicciati degli affari tuoi!** Mind your
own business!

impiegare VERB [76]
■ **Ho impiegato più di due ore a fare i
compiti.** It took me more than two hours to
do my homework.
■ **Quanto ci impieghi per arrivare a
scuola?** How long does it take you to get to
school?

l' **impiegato**, l' **impiegata** MASC/FEM NOUN
clerk
□ un'impiegata di banca a bank clerk
■ **un impiegato statale** a clerical worker in
the public sector

l' **impiego** (PL gli **impieghi**) MASC NOUN
job
□ un impiego fisso a permanent job

impigliarsi VERB [25, aux **essere**]
to get caught

□ Mi si è impigliato il vestito in un chiodo.
My dress got caught on a nail.

impolverato (FEM **impolverata**) ADJECTIVE
dusty

□ È impolverato. It's dusty.

imponente (FEM **imponente**) ADJECTIVE
impressive

□ un edificio imponente an impressive building

impopolare (FEM **impopolare**) ADJECTIVE
unpopular

□ un provvedimento impopolare an unpopular
measure

importante (FEM **importante**) ADJECTIVE
▷ see also **importante** NOUN
important

□ Questo è importante. This is very important.
■ una partita importante a big match

l' **importante** MASC NOUN
▷ see also **importante** ADJECTIVE
important thing

□ L'importante è arrivare entro domani. The
important thing is to get there by tomorrow.

l' **importanza** FEM NOUN
importance

□ un fatto della massima importanza a matter
of the greatest importance

■ **dare importanza a qualcosa** to think
something is important □ Danno molta
importanza all'abbigliamento. They think
clothes are very important.

■ **avere importanza** to matter □ Che
importanza ha sapere chi è stato? What does it
matter who it was?

importare VERB [68, aux **avere** or **essere**]
1 to matter

□ Oggi o domani non importa. Today or
tomorrow, it doesn't matter. □ Non preoccuparti,
non importa. Don't worry, it doesn't matter.
□ Non m'importa niente di quello che pensano. It
doesn't matter to me what they think.

■ **Sembra che non gli importi degli esami.**
He doesn't seem to care about the exams.
2 to import

□ La vodka viene importata dalla Russia. Vodka
is imported from Russia.

l' **importo** MASC NOUN
amount

impossibile (FEM **impossibile**) ADJECTIVE
impossible

□ Ma va', è impossibile! Come off it, it's
impossible!

■ **È impossibile che lo sappia.** She can't
know about it.

l' **imposta** FEM NOUN
1 shutter (on window)
2 tax

le **impostazioni** FEM PL NOUN
settings

impraticabile (FEM **impraticabile**) ADJECTIVE
1 impassable (road)
2 unplayable (pitch)

l' **imprecazione** FEM NOUN
■ **lanciare un'imprecazione** to curse

l' **imprenditore** MASC NOUN
entrepreneur

l' **imprenditrice** FEM NOUN
entrepreneur

l' **impresa** FEM NOUN
business

□ Lavora nell'impresa del padre. He works in
his father's business. □ le piccole e medie
imprese small and medium-sized businesses
■ **un'impresa edile** a building firm
■ **Sarà un'impresa riuscire a
convincerlo!** It'll be hard work persuading
him!

impressionante (FEM **impressionante**)
ADJECTIVE
1 terrible

□ una scena impressionante a terrible scene
2 amazing

□ una velocità impressionante an amazing
speed

l' **impressione** FEM NOUN
1 feeling

□ Ho l'impressione che non si fidi di me. I have
a feeling you don't trust me.
2 impression

□ Che impressione ti ha fatto? What was your
impression of him?

■ **Il sangue mi fa impressione.** I can't
stand the sight of blood.

imprevedibile (FEM **imprevedibile**)
ADJECTIVE
unpredictable

imprevisto (FEM **imprevista**) ADJECTIVE
▷ see also **imprevisto** NOUN
unexpected

□ una spesa imprevista an unexpected
expense

l' **imprevisto** MASC NOUN
▷ see also **imprevisto** ADJECTIVE
something unexpected

□ salvo imprevisti unless something
unexpected happens

improbabile (FEM **improbabile**) ADJECTIVE
unlikely

□ È improbabile che venga. He's unlikely to
come.

l' **impronta** FEM NOUN
print (of foot, hand)

■ **impronte digitali** fingerprints

improvvisamente ADVERB
1 suddenly

□ Improvvisamente si è messo a piovere.
It suddenly started to rain.

Italian-English

2 unexpectedly

□ È arrivato improvvisamente. He arrived unexpectedly.

improvvisare VERB [68]
1 to improvise *(in music, at theatre)*
2 to put together

□ Abbiamo improvvisato una cenetta alla buona. We put together a simple meal.

improvviso (FEM **improvvisa**) ADJECTIVE
sudden

□ un improvviso cambiamento di programma a sudden change of plan

■ **all'improvviso** suddenly □ All'improvviso si è spalancata la porta. The door suddenly opened. □ È partita all'improvviso. She left suddenly.

imprudente (FEM **imprudente**) ADJECTIVE
careless

□ un guidatore imprudente a careless driver

impugnare VERB [14]
to hold *(arms, racket)*

impulsivo (FEM **impulsiva**) ADJECTIVE
impulsive

□ Ha un carattere impulsivo. He's got an impulsive nature.

l' **impulso** MASC NOUN
impulse

□ Ho agito d'impulso. I acted on impulse.

l' **imputato**, l' **imputata** MASC/FEM NOUN
defendant

in PREPOSITION
1 in

□ Vive in Canada. He lives in Canada. □ È nel cassetto. It's in the drawer. □ nel millenovecentonovantanove in nineteen-ninety nine □ in estate in summer □ L'ha fatto in sei mesi. He did it in six months. □ Camminavano in silenzio. They walked in silence. □ Parlavano in tedesco. They were speaking in German. □ L'ha tagliato in due. She cut it in two.

2 to

□ Andrò in Germania quest'estate. I'm going to Germany this summer. □ È andato in ufficio. He's gone to the office.

3 into

□ Su, sali in macchina. Come on, get into the car. □ Come sono penetrati nella banca? How did they get into the bank? □ L'ha gettato in acqua. He threw it into the water.

4 by

□ Siamo andati in treno. We went by train.

■ **essere in vacanza** to be on holiday
■ **andare in vacanza** to go on holiday

inabitabile (FEM **inabitabile**) ADJECTIVE
uninhabitable

inaccettabile (FEM **inaccettabile**) ADJECTIVE
unacceptable

inacidirsi VERB [51, AUX **essere**]
to go sour

inaffidabile (FEM **inaffidabile**) ADJECTIVE
unreliable

□ È totalmente inaffidabile. He's totally unreliable.

l' **inalatore** MASC NOUN
inhaler

inamidato (FEM **inamidata**) ADJECTIVE
starched

inaspettato (FEM **inaspettata**) ADJECTIVE
unexpected

□ una visita inaspettata an unexpected visit

inaudito (FEM **inaudita**) ADJECTIVE
■ **È inaudito!** It's outrageous!

inaugurare VERB [68]
to open

□ Il nuovo stadio sarà inaugurato domani. The new stadium is being opened tomorrow.

■ **Oggi ho inaugurato le scarpe nuove.** I wore my new shoes for the first time today.

l' **inaugurazione** FEM NOUN
opening

□ l'inaugurazione di una mostra the opening of an exhibition

incamminarsi VERB [56]
to set off

□ Ci siamo incamminati verso la spiaggia. We set off towards the beach.

incantevole (FEM **incantevole**) ADJECTIVE
lovely

□ un paesaggio incantevole lovely scenery
□ È ancora più incantevole del solito. It's even lovelier than usual.

l' **incanto** MASC NOUN
■ **Questo paesino è un incanto!** This village is lovely!

■ **come per incanto** as if by magic
□ L'eczema è scomparso come per incanto. The eczema disappeared as if by magic.

incapace (FEM **incapace**) ADJECTIVE
■ **essere incapace di** to be incapable of □ È incapace di mentire. She's incapable of lying.

incaricare VERB [18]
■ **incaricare qualcuno di fare qualcosa** to ask somebody to do something □ Mi hanno incaricato di rispondere al telefono. They asked me to answer the phone.

■ **Me ne incarico io.** I'll see to it.

l' **incarico** (PL gli **incarichi**) MASC NOUN
job

□ un incarico importante an important job
■ **Chi aveva l'incarico di comprare i biglietti?** Who was supposed to get the tickets?

incarnita ADJECTIVE
■ **unghia incarnita** ingrown toenail

incartare VERB [68]
to wrap

□ Devo ancora incartare i regali. I still have to wrap the presents. □ Me lo incarta, per favore? Could you wrap it for me please?

incasinare VERB [68]
to mess up
□ Mio fratello ha incasinato i miei CD. My brother has messed up my CDs.

incasinato (FEM **incasinata**) ADJECTIVE
in a mess
□ In questo periodo sono proprio incasinata. I'm in a real mess at the moment.

incassare VERB [68]
to cash
□ Puoi incassare l'assegno in qualunque banca. You can cash the cheque at any bank.

l' **incasso** MASC NOUN
takings *pl*
□ I ladri sono fuggiti con l'incasso della giornata. The thieves escaped with the day's takings.
■ **Il film ha battuto ogni record d'incasso.** The film has been a great box office success.

incastrare VERB [68]
to frame
□ Era ovvio che l'avevano incastrato. It was obvious that he'd been framed.
■ **incastrarsi 1** to get stuck □ La chiave si è incastrata nella serratura. The key got stuck in the lock.
2 to fit □ Quel pezzo si incastra qui. That piece fits here.

incatenare VERB [68]
to chain
□ Erano incatenati al muro. They were chained to the wall.

incavato (FEM **incavata**) ADJECTIVE
1 hollow *(cheeks)*
2 sunken *(eyes)*

incavolarsi VERB [56]
to get angry
□ S'incavola per ogni sciocchezza. She gets angry about the slightest thing. □ Non t'incavolare! Don't get angry!

incendiare VERB [17]
to set fire to
□ Dei vandali hanno incendiato la scuola. Vandals set fire to the school.

l' **incendio** MASC NOUN
fire
□ I vigili del fuoco hanno domato l'incendio. The firefighters have got the fire under control.

l' **inceneritore** MASC NOUN
incinerator

l' **incenso** MASC NOUN
incense
□ odore d'incenso smell of incense
■ **bastoncini d'incenso** joss sticks

incepparsi VERB [56]
to jam
□ La serratura si è inceppata. The lock jammed.

l' **incertezza** FEM NOUN
uncertainty
□ un periodo di incertezza politica a period of political uncertainty
■ **Ha avuto un momento d'incertezza nel rispondere.** He hesitated for a moment before answering.

incerto (FEM **incerta**) ADJECTIVE
uncertain
□ La situazione è ancora incerta. The situation is still uncertain. □ Ero incerto se dirglielo o no. I was uncertain whether to tell him or not.

l' **inchiesta** FEM NOUN
1 inquiry
□ È stata aperta un'inchiesta. An inquiry has been opened.
2 special report
□ un'inchiesta sui giovani e la droga a special report on young people and drugs

l' **inchiostro** MASC NOUN
ink
□ una macchia d'inchiostro an ink stain

inciampare VERB [68, AUX **avere** or **essere**]
to trip
□ Sono inciampato nel tappeto. I tripped over the carpet.

l' **incidente** MASC NOUN
accident
□ Sono rimasti feriti in un incidente d'auto. They were injured in a car accident.
■ **incidente aereo** plane crash □ È il terzo incidente aereo in un mese. It's the third plane crash in a month.
■ **un incidente ferroviario** a train crash

incinta ADJECTIVE
pregnant
□ È incinta di cinque mesi. She's five months pregnant.
■ **rimanere incinta** to get pregnant

incirca ADVERB
■ **all'incirca** about □ È grande all'incirca così. It's about this big. □ Saranno all'incirca le tre. It must be about three.

incivile (FEM **incivile**) ADJECTIVE
rude
□ una persona incivile a rude person
■ **Che modi incivili!** What bad manners!

inclinare VERB [68]
to tilt
□ Inclina un po' il tavolo. Tilt the table a bit.

includere VERB [3]
to include

incluso (FEM **inclusa**) ADJECTIVE
1 included
□ È inclusa la colazione? Is breakfast included?
2 including
□ Tutti lo sapevano, incluso John. Everyone, including John, knew about it.

da pagina cinque a pagina sette inclusa from page five to the end of page seven

incollare VERB [68]
to stick
□ Ha incollato le sue foto sul diario. She stuck the photos of him into her diary.

incollato (FEM **incollata**) ADJECTIVE
glued
□ Passa il pomeriggio incollata al computer. She spends the afternoon glued to the computer.

incolpare VERB [68]
to blame
□ Hanno incolpato me. They blamed me.
■ **Mi ha incolpato di avergli rotto il motorino.** He accused me of damaging his bike.

incolume (FEM **incolume**) ADJECTIVE
unhurt
□ È uscito incolume dall'incidente. He escaped from the accident unhurt.

incominciare VERB [13, aux **avere** or **essere**]
to start
□ La partita incomincia alle sette. The match starts at seven. □ La prima parola incomincia per F. The first word starts with F. □ Ha incominciato a ridere. She started to laugh. □ Ha incominciato a piangere. She started crying.

incompetente (FEM **incompetente**)
ADJECTIVE
▷ see also **incompetente** NOUN
incompetent

l' **incompetente** MASC/FEM NOUN
▷ see also **incompetente** ADJECTIVE
incompetent person

incompiuto (FEM **incompiuta**) ADJECTIVE
unfinished
□ una sinfonia incompiuta an unfinished symphony

incomprensibile (FEM **incomprensibile**)
ADJECTIVE
incomprehensible

inconcepibile (FEM **inconcepibile**)
ADJECTIVE
incredible
□ È inconcepibile! It's incredible!

inconfondibile (FEM **inconfondibile**)
ADJECTIVE
unmistakable
□ Il suo stile è inconfondibile. His style is unmistakable.

inconsueto (FEM **inconsueta**) ADJECTIVE
unusual

incontrare VERB [68]
1 to meet
□ Incontriamoci davanti al cinema. Let's meet in front of the cinema. □ Ci siamo incontrati ad una festa. We met at a party.

2 to bump into
□ L'ho incontrato per strada. I bumped into him in the street.

3 to play
□ L'Inter incontrerà la Juve. Inter Milan are playing Juventus.

l' **incontro** MASC NOUN
▷ see also **incontro** PREPOSITION
1 meeting
□ un incontro casuale a chance meeting
2 match
□ un incontro di pugilato a boxing match

incontro PREPOSITION
▷ see also **incontro** NOUN
■ **incontro a** towards □ Mi è venuto incontro sorridente. He came towards me smiling.

l' **inconveniente** MASC NOUN
1 drawback
□ Ha un unico inconveniente: è troppo piccolo. It's only got one drawback: it's too small.
2 problem
□ Ho avuto qualche inconveniente con la moto. I had some problems with my motorbike.

incoraggiare VERB [58]
to encourage
□ I suoi l'hanno incoraggiato a studiare musica. His parents encouraged him to study music.

incorniciare VERB [13]
to frame
□ Ho incorniciato la foto. I've framed the photo.

incosciente (FEM **incosciente**) ADJECTIVE
▷ see also **incosciente** NOUN
1 unconscious
□ È rimasto incosciente per alcuni minuti. He was unconscious for several minutes.
2 reckless
□ un automobilista incosciente a reckless driver

l' **incosciente** MASC/FEM NOUN
▷ see also **incosciente** ADJECTIVE
reckless person

incredibile (FEM **incredibile**) ADJECTIVE
incredible
□ È incredibile! That's incredible!

incrinare VERB [68]
to crack
□ Non l'ho rotto, l'ho solo incrinato. I didn't break it, I just cracked it.

incrociare VERB [13]
1 to cross
□ Ha incrociato le braccia. He crossed his arms.
2 to meet
□ Ci siamo incrociati nel corridoio. We met in the corridor.

l' **incrocio** (PL gli **incroci**) MASC NOUN
1 junction
□ All'incrocio gira a destra. Turn right at the junction.

2 cross

□ un incrocio tra un collie e un labrador a cross between a collie and a labrador

l' **incubo** MASC NOUN

nightmare

□ Stanotte ho avuto un incubo. I had a nightmare last night.

incurabile (FEM **incurabile**) ADJECTIVE

incurable

□ un male incurabile an incurable disease

l' **incursione** FEM NOUN

raid

□ un'incursione aerea an air raid

incustodito (FEM **incustodita**) ADJECTIVE

unattended

□ Il parcheggio è incustodito. The car park is unattended. □ Non lasciare il bagaglio incustodito. Don't leave your luggage unattended.

indaffarato (FEM **indaffarata**) ADJECTIVE

busy

□ Era indaffarato a riparare la bici. He was busy mending his bike. □ È sempre più indaffarato. He's busier and busier.

indagare VERB [76]

■ **indagare su** to investigate □ La polizia sta indagando sul delitto. The police are investigating the crime.

l' **indagine** FEM NOUN

investigation

□ le indagini della polizia police investigations

indebitarsi VERB [56]

■ **indebitarsi con** to borrow money from □ Si è indebitato con la banca. He borrowed money from the bank.

indebolirsi VERB [51, AUX **essere**]

1 to get weak

□ Si è molto indebolito. He's got very weak.

2 to deteriorate (sight)

indecente (FEM **indecente**) ADJECTIVE

indecent

□ Quella minigonna è indecente! That mini skirt is indecent!

indeciso (FEM **indecisa**) ADJECTIVE

■ **Sono indeciso tra questi due.** I can't decide between these two.

■ **Era indeciso su cosa regalarle.** He couldn't decide what to give her.

indeterminativo (FEM **indeterminativa**) ADJECTIVE

■ **articolo indeterminativo** indefinite article

l' **India** FEM NOUN

India

□ Mi è piaciuta molto l'India. I really liked India. □ Andremo in India quest'estate. We're going to India this summer.

indiano (FEM **indiana**) ADJECTIVE, MASC/FEM NOUN

Indian

□ un ristorante indiano an Indian restaurant □ gli indiani the Indians

indicare VERB [18]

to show

□ Gli indicherò la strada. I'll show him the way.

■ **indicare qualcosa** to point to something

l' **indicativo** MASC NOUN

indicative

le **indicazioni** FEM PL NOUN

1 directions

□ Mi ha dato le indicazioni per arrivarci. She gave me directions to get here.

2 signs

□ Segui le indicazioni. Follow the signs.

l' **indice** MASC NOUN

1 index finger

2 index (of book)

indietro ADVERB

back

□ Ho fatto un passo indietro. I took a step back. □ Ha voluto indietro i soldi. She wanted her money back.

■ **tornare indietro** to turn back □ Torniamo indietro? Shall we turn back?

■ **all'indietro** backwards □ È caduta all'indietro. She fell backwards.

■ **essere indietro 1** to be slow □ Il mio orologio è indietro di 10 minuti. My watch is 10 minutes slow. **2** (in studies, etc) to be behind

indifeso (FEM **indifesa**) ADJECTIVE

defenceless

□ un povero bambino indifeso a poor defenceless child

indifferente (FEM **indifferente**) ADJECTIVE

▷ see also **indifferente** NOUN

■ **A piedi o in auto, per me è indifferente.** We can walk or drive, I don't mind which.

■ **lasciare indifferente** to leave cold □ La notizia mi ha lasciato del tutto indifferente. The news left me completely cold.

l' **indifferente** MASC/FEM NOUN

▷ see also **indifferente** ADJECTIVE

■ **fare l'indifferente** to act casual □ Cerca di fare l'indifferente quando la vedi. Try to act casual when you see her.

■ **Non fare l'indifferente.** Don't pretend you don't understand.

l' **indigestione** FEM NOUN

■ **Ho fatto un'indigestione di dolci.** I've eaten too many cakes.

indimenticabile (FEM **indimenticabile**) ADJECTIVE

unforgettable

□ una vacanza indimenticabile an unforgettable holiday

indipendente (FEM **indipendente**) ADJECTIVE

independent

□ Ha un carattere molto indipendente. She's got a very independent nature.

■ **essere economicamente indipendente** to be financially independent
□ Non sono ancora economicamente indipendente. I'm not yet financially independent.

indiretto (FEM **indiretta**) ADJECTIVE
indirect
□ discorso indiretto indirect speech
□ **per vie indirette** indirectly

indirizzare VERB [68]
1 to address
□ La lettera era indirizzata a me. The letter was addressed to me.
2 to send
□ Mi hanno indirizzato qui. They sent me here.

l' **indirizzo** MASC NOUN
address
□ Mi dai il tuo indirizzo? Can I have your address?
■ **indirizzo di posta elettronica** email address
■ **indirizzo Internet** web address

indispensabile (FEM **indispensabile**)
ADJECTIVE
▷ see also **indispensabile** NOUN
essential
□ È uno strumento indispensabile. It's an essential tool. □ Non è indispensabile che ci sia anche tu. It's not essential for you to be here.

l' **indispensabile** MASC NOUN
▷ see also **indispensabile** ADJECTIVE
what's necessary
□ Ho portato solo l'indispensabile per una notte. I've just brought what's necessary for one night.

individuale (FEM **individuale**) ADJECTIVE
personal
□ libertà individuale personal freedom
■ **lezioni individuali** one-to-one tuition sing

l' **indizio** MASC NOUN
clue
□ La polizia non ha trovato alcun indizio. The police haven't found any clues.

indolenzito (FEM **indolenzita**) ADJECTIVE
aching
□ Sono tutto indolenzito. I'm aching all over.

l' **indomani** MASC NOUN
■ **l'indomani** the next day □ Ha detto che sarebbe tornata l'indomani. She said she'd come back the next day.

indossare VERB [68]
to wear

l' **indossatore**, l' **indossatrice** MASC/FEM NOUN
model
□ Fa l'indossatrice. She is a model.

indovinare VERB [68]
to guess

□ Indovina chi ho incontrato ieri! Guess who I met yesterday!
■ **Bravo, hai indovinato!** Well done, you've got it right!
■ **tirare a indovinare** to have a guess
□ Non lo sapevo, quindi ho tirato a indovinare. I didn't know, so I had a guess.

l' **indovinello** MASC NOUN
riddle
□ Sai risolvere questo indovinello? Do you know the answer to this riddle?

indubbiamente ADVERB
definitely
□ È indubbiamente uno dei migliori. It's definitely one of the best.

indurire VERB [51]
to harden
□ Viene usato per indurire l'acciaio. It's used to harden steel.
■ **indurirsi** to go hard □ Il terreno si è indurito. The ground has gone hard.

l' **industria** FEM NOUN
industry
□ Lavora nell'industria automobilistica. He works in the car industry.

industriale (FEM **industriale**) ADJECTIVE
▷ see also **industriale** NOUN
industrial
□ una città industriale an industrial town

l' **industriale** MASC/FEM NOUN
▷ see also **industriale** ADJECTIVE
industrialist
□ È un industriale. He is an industrialist.

inedito (FEM **inedita**) ADJECTIVE
unpublished

l' **inesperienza** FEM NOUN
inexperience
□ un errore dovuto all'inesperienza a mistake caused by inexperience

inesperto (FEM **inesperta**) ADJECTIVE
inexperienced
□ un giovane medico inesperto an inexperienced young doctor

inevitabile (FEM **inevitabile**) ADJECTIVE
inevitable

infallibile (FEM **infallibile**) ADJECTIVE
1 excellent
□ un rimedio infallibile contro il raffreddore an excellent remedy for colds
2 infallible
□ Nessuno è infallibile. Nobody is infallible.

infangato (FEM **infangata**) ADJECTIVE
covered with mud
□ Ho le scarpe infangate. My shoes are covered with mud.

infantile (FEM **infantile**) ADJECTIVE
childish
□ comportamento infantile childish behaviour
■ **asilo infantile** nursery school

l' **infarinatura** FEM NOUN
■ **Ho solo un'infarinatura di informatica.**
I only know a bit about computing.

l' **infarto** MASC NOUN
heart attack
□ Ha avuto un infarto. He had a heart attack.

infatti CONJUNCTION
■ **Mi aveva promesso un regalo e infatti me l'ha portato.** She'd promised me a present and she brought me one.
■ **Penso che sia uscito. — Infatti non risponde nessuno.** I think he's out. — Yes, no one's answering.
■ **Ha detto che avrebbe telefonato. — Sì, infatti...** She said she'd phone. — Yes, well...
LANGUAGE TIP Be careful! **infatti** doesn't mean **in fact**.

infedele (FEM **infedele**) ADJECTIVE
unfaithful

infelice (FEM **infelice**) ADJECTIVE
unhappy
□ il giorno più infelice della mia vita the unhappiest day of my life

inferiore (FEM **inferiore**) ADJECTIVE
1 lower
□ il labbro inferiore the lower lip
2 inferior
□ un prodotto di qualità inferiore a product of inferior quality
■ **i bambini di età inferiore ai cinque anni** children under five

l' **inferiorità** FEM NOUN
inferiority
□ un complesso d'inferiorità an inferiority complex

l' **infermiere**, l' **infermiera** MASC/FEM NOUN
nurse
□ Fa l'infermiere. He is a nurse.

infernale (FEM **infernale**) ADJECTIVE
terrible
□ C'era un chiasso infernale. There was a terrible noise.
■ **Qui dentro fa un caldo infernale!** It's terribly hot in here!

l' **inferno** MASC NOUN
hell

l' **inferriata** FEM NOUN
railings pl

l' **infezione** FEM NOUN
infection

infiammabile (FEM **infiammabile**) ADJECTIVE
inflammable

l' **infiammazione** FEM NOUN
inflammation

infilare VERB [68]
to put
□ Ho infilato la chiave nella serratura. I put the key into the lock.

■ **infilarsi** 1 to put on □ Si è infilato la giacca ed è uscito. He put on his jacket and went out. 2 to get □ Il gatto si è infilato sotto il letto. The cat got under the bed.

infine ADVERB
finally
□ Vorrei dire, infine... Finally I would like to say...

infinito (FEM **infinita**) ADJECTIVE
▷ see also **infinito** NOUN
endless
□ Ha una pazienza infinita. She has endless patience.
■ **Grazie infinite!** Many thanks!

l' **infinito** MASC NOUN
▷ see also **infinito** ADJECTIVE
infinitive (in grammar)

l' **influenza** FEM NOUN
flu
□ Ho l'influenza. I've got flu.
■ **influenza suina** swine flu

influenzare VERB [68]
to influence
□ Si lascia influenzare troppo dagli amici. She's too easily influenced by her friends.

influire VERB [51]
■ **influire su** to influence □ Non ha influito sulla sua decisione. It didn't influence his decision.

infondato (FEM **infondata**) ADJECTIVE
unfounded
□ un sospetto infondato an unfounded suspicion

informare VERB [68]
to inform
□ Avete informato la polizia? Have you informed the police?
■ **informarsi su qualcosa** to ask about something □ Mi sono informato sugli orari dei treni. I asked about train times.

l' **informatica** FEM NOUN
computing
□ un corso d'informatica a computing course

informato (FEM **informata**) ADJECTIVE
informed
□ Tienimi informato. Keep me informed.
■ **È sempre informato sulle novità discografiche.** He always knows about the latest releases.

l' **informatore**, l' **informatrice** MASC/FEM NOUN
informer

l' **informazione** FEM NOUN
information
□ Scusi, può darmi un'informazione? Excuse me, can you give me some information? □ Mi ha dato un'informazione utile. He gave me some useful information. □ Per ulteriori informazioni telefonare al numero... For

further information call... ▢ Dov'è l'ufficio informazioni? Where's the information office?

infortunato (FEM **infortunata**) ADJECTIVE
injured

l' **infortunio** MASC NOUN
accident
▢ Ha avuto un infortunio sul lavoro. He had an accident at work.

infreddolito (FEM **infreddolita**) ADJECTIVE
cold
▢ Sono un po' infreddolito. I'm a bit cold.

infuori ADVERB
out
▢ Sporge un po' infuori. It sticks out a bit.
■ **all'infuori di** except ▢ Lo sapevano tutti all'infuori di lui. They all knew except him.

ingaggiare VERB [58]
■ **essere ingaggiato** to sign ▢ È stato ingaggiato per la prossima stagione. He's signed for next season.

ingannare VERB [68]
1 to deceive
▢ Mi hai ingannato! You deceived me!
■ **Le apparenze spesso ingannano.** Appearances are often deceptive.
2 to take in
▢ Non lasciarti ingannare dalla sua aria innocente. Don't be taken in by his air of innocence.
■ **ingannarsi** to be mistaken
■ **ingannare il tempo** to while away the time

ingarbugliarsi VERB [25, aux **essere**]
1 to get tangled
2 to get complicated
▢ A questo punto la faccenda s'ingarbuglia. At this point things get complicated.

l' **ingegnere** MASC NOUN
engineer
▢ Fa l'ingegnere. He is an engineer.

l' **ingegneria** FEM NOUN
engineering
▢ È laureata in ingegneria. She's got a degree in engineering.

ingelosire VERB [51]
to make jealous
▢ L'ha fatto solo per farlo ingelosire. She just did it to make him jealous.

ingenuo (FEM **ingenua**) ADJECTIVE
▷ see also **ingenuo** NOUN
naïve
▢ È molto ingenua. She's very naïve. ▢ Ma come fai ad essere così ingenuo? How can you be so naïve?

LANGUAGE TIP Be careful! **ingenuo** doesn't mean **ingenious**.

l' **ingenuo**, l' **ingenua** MASC/FEM NOUN
▷ see also **ingenuo** ADJECTIVE
■ **fare l'ingenuo** to act the innocent ▢ Non fare l'ingenuo, sai benissimo di cosa parlo.

Don't act the innocent, you know perfectly well what I'm talking about.

ingessare VERB [68]
to put in plaster
▢ Gli hanno ingessato il braccio. They put his arm in plaster.

l' **ingessatura** FEM NOUN
plaster
▢ Mi hanno tolto l'ingessatura. They took off the plaster.

l' **Inghilterra** FEM NOUN
England
▢ Mi è piaciuta molto l'Inghilterra. I really liked England. ▢ Andrò in Inghilterra quest'estate. I'm going to England this summer.

DID YOU KNOW...?
Italians often refer to Britain as a whole as **l'Inghilterra**.

inghiottire VERB [51]
to swallow

inginocchiarsi VERB [17, aux **essere**]
to kneel down
▢ Si è inginocchiato accanto al cane. He knelt down beside the dog.

ingiusto (FEM **ingiusta**) ADJECTIVE
unfair
▢ Questo è profondamente ingiusto. This is utterly unfair.

inglese (FEM **inglese**) ADJECTIVE
▷ see also **inglese** MASC NOUN, FEM NOUN
English
▢ la squadra inglese the English team

l' **inglese** MASC NOUN
▷ see also **inglese** FEM NOUN, ADJECTIVE
1 Englishman
■ **gli inglesi** English people
2 English (language)
▢ Parli inglese? Do you speak English?

l' **inglese** FEM NOUN
▷ see also **inglese** MASC NOUN, ADJECTIVE
Englishwoman

ingoiare VERB [17]
to swallow

ingolfarsi VERB [56]
to flood
▢ Il motore si è ingolfato. The engine has flooded.

ingombrante (FEM **ingombrante**) ADJECTIVE
cumbersome
▢ una valigia ingombrante a cumbersome case

ingombrare VERB [68]
to block
▢ Si prega di non ingombrare il corridoio. Please don't block the corridor.
■ **I bagagli ingombravano la stanza.** The room was full of luggage.

ingordo (FEM **ingorda**) ADJECTIVE
greedy
▢ Non essere ingordo! Don't be greedy! ▢ È più ingordo di me. He's greedier than me.

l' **ingorgo** (PL gli **ingorghi**) MASC NOUN
hold-up

□ C'era un ingorgo all'incrocio. There was a
hold-up at the junction.

ingranare VERB [68]

■ **ingranare la marcia** to get into gear
□ Non riesco a ingranare la marcia. I can't get
into gear.

l' **ingrandimento** MASC NOUN
enlargement

□ Vorrei un ingrandimento di questa foto.
I'd like an enlargement of this photo.

■ **far fare un ingrandimento** to get an
enlargement

■ **una lente d'ingrandimento** a
magnifying glass

ingrandire VERB [51]

1 to enlarge (photo)
2 to extend

□ Ho deciso di ingrandire la casa. I've decided
to extend my house.

■ **ingrandirsi** to get bigger □ La città si sta
ingrandendo. The town is getting bigger.

ingrassare VERB [68, AUX **essere**]
to put on weight

□ Sei un po' ingrassata. You've put on a bit of
weight.

■ **ingrassare di** to put on □ Sono ingrassato
di due chili. I've put on two kilos.

■ **far ingrassare** to be fattening □ I dolci
fanno ingrassare. Puddings are fattening.

l' **ingrediente** MASC NOUN
ingredient

l' **ingresso** MASC NOUN

1 entrance

□ L'ingresso principale è sulla via laterale. The
main entrance is in the side street.

2 doorway

□ Non stare qui nell'ingresso, accomodati.
Don't stand there in the doorway, come in.

■ **'ingresso libero'** 'admission free'
■ **'vietato l'ingresso'** 'no admittance'

ingrosso ADVERB

■ **all'ingrosso** wholesale

l' **inguine** MASC NOUN
groin

inibito (FEM **inibita**) ADJECTIVE
inhibited

□ Non pensavo che fossi così inibito! I didn't
think you were so inhibited!

l' **iniezione** FEM NOUN
injection

■ **fare un'iniezione** to give an injection
□ Mi hanno fatto un'iniezione di penicillina.
They gave me an injection of penicillin.

■ **motore a iniezione** fuel injection engine

ininterrottamente ADVERB
non-stop

□ Ha parlato ininterrottamente per tre ore.
He talked non-stop for three hours.

iniziale (FEM **iniziale**) ADJECTIVE
▷ see also **iniziale** NOUN
initial

□ la fase iniziale the initial phase

■ **lo stipendio iniziale** the starting salary

l' **iniziale** FEM NOUN
▷ see also **iniziale** ADJECTIVE
initial

□ un accendino con le sue iniziali a lighter with
his initials

iniziare VERB [17]
to start

□ Il film sta per iniziare. The film is about to start.

■ **iniziare a fare qualcosa** to start doing
something □ Hai iniziato a cucinare? Have you
started cooking?

l' **iniziativa** FEM NOUN
initiative

□ È venuta di propria iniziativa. She came on
her own initiative.

■ **prendere l'iniziativa** to take the initiative
□ Devi prendere tu l'iniziativa. You need to take
the initiative.

■ **una serie di iniziative culturali** a series
of arts events

l' **inizio** MASC NOUN
beginning

□ Ho riletto l'inizio della lettera. I re-read the
beginning of the letter. □ all'inizio del secondo
tempo at the beginning of the second half

■ **L'inizio dei lavori è previsto per la
fine del mese.** Work will begin at the end of
the month.

■ **avere inizio** to begin □ Il film ha inizio con
una scena d'azione. The film begins with an
action scene.

■ **all'inizio** at first □ All'inizio pensavo che
scherzasse. At first I thought he was joking.

■ **all'inizio di** at the beginning of □ Abito
proprio all'inizio della strada. I live at the
beginning of the street.

innaffiare VERB [17]
to water

innamorarsi VERB [56]
to fall in love

□ Si è subito innamorato di lei. He instantly fell
in love with her.

innamorato (FEM **innamorata**) ADJECTIVE
in love

□ È innamorata persa. She's madly in love.

■ **essere innamorato di qualcuno** to be
in love with someone □ Sei innamorato di lei?
Are you in love with her?

innanzitutto ADVERB
first of all

□ Innanzitutto bisogna informarsi degli orari.
First of all you need to ask about the times.

129

innervosire VERB [51]
- ■ **innervosire qualcuno** to get on somebody's nerves □ Il traffico mi innervosisce. The traffic gets on my nerves.
- ■ **Si è innervosito per il rumore.** The noise got on his nerves.

l' **inno** MASC NOUN
- ■ **inno nazionale** national anthem

innocente (FEM **innocente**) ADJECTIVE
innocent
- □ Secondo me è innocente. In my opinion he's innocent.
- ■ **dichiararsi innocente** to maintain one's innocence □ Si è sempre dichiarato innocente. He has always maintained his innocence.
- ■ **uno scherzo innocente** a harmless joke

inodore (FEM **inodore**) ADJECTIVE
odourless
- □ un gas inodore an odourless gas

inoltre ADVERB
besides

inosservato (FEM **inosservata**) ADJECTIVE
unnoticed
- □ L'errore non è passato inosservato. The mistake didn't go unnoticed.

inossidabile (FEM **inossidabile**) ADJECTIVE
- ■ **acciaio inossidabile** stainless steel

l' **inquilino**, l' **inquilina** MASC/FEM NOUN
tenant

l' **inquinamento** MASC NOUN
pollution
- □ la lotta contro l'inquinamento the fight against pollution

inquinare VERB [68]
to pollute
- □ Le fabbriche hanno inquinato il mare. The factories have polluted the sea.

l' **insalata** FEM NOUN
1 salad
- □ un'insalata verde a green salad □ un'insalata di pomodori a tomato salad □ un'insalata di mare a seafood salad
2 lettuce
- □ Hai lavato l'insalata? Have you washed the lettuce?

l' **insalatiera** FEM NOUN
salad bowl

insaputa FEM NOUN
- ■ **all'insaputa di qualcuno** without somebody's knowledge □ L'ha comprato all'insaputa dei suoi. She bought it without her parents' knowledge.

l' **insegna** FEM NOUN
sign
- □ un'insegna al neon a neon sign

l' **insegnamento** MASC NOUN
teaching
- □ il suo metodo d'insegnamento her way of teaching

l' **insegnante** MASC/FEM NOUN
teacher
- □ Fa l'insegnante. She is a teacher.
- □ l'insegnante d'inglese the English teacher
- ■ **insegnante di sostegno** teaching assistant

insegnare VERB [14]
to teach
- ■ **insegnare qualcosa a qualcuno** to teach somebody something □ Ha insegnato ai bambini i nomi delle piante. She taught the children the names of plants.
- ■ **insegnare a qualcuno a fare qualcosa** to teach somebody to do something □ Mi ha insegnato a suonare la chitarra. He taught me to play the guitar.

inseguire VERB [41]
to chase
- □ La polizia ha inseguito i rapinatori. The police chased the robbers.

l' **insenatura** FEM NOUN
inlet

inserire VERB [51]
to put
- □ Bisogna inserire la vite nel foro. You need to put the screw in the hole.
- ■ **inserire la spina della TV** to plug in the TV
- ■ **inserirsi in** to settle into □ Non si è ancora inserito bene nella nuova scuola. He hasn't settled into his new school yet.

l' **inserzione** FEM NOUN
advert
- □ Ho messo un'inserzione sul giornale. I put an advert in the paper.

l' **insetticida** (PL gli **insetticidi**) MASC NOUN
- ■ **una bomboletta d'insetticida** a can of fly spray

l' **insetto** MASC NOUN
insect

insicuro (FEM **insicura**) ADJECTIVE
insecure

insieme ADVERB
▷ see also **insieme** NOUN
together
- □ Da quanto tempo state insieme? How long have you been together? □ colori che stanno bene insieme colours that go well together
- □ Forza, spingete tutti insieme! Come on, everyone push together!
- ■ **Non parlate tutti insieme, per favore.** Don't all speak at the same time, please.
- ■ **mettersi insieme** to start going out together □ Si sono messi insieme due anni fa. They started going out together two years ago.
- ■ **insieme a** with □ Ha cenato insieme a noi. He had dinner with us.

l' **insieme** MASC NOUN
▷ see also **insieme** ADVERB
- ■ **nell'insieme** on the whole □ Nell'insieme mi sembra buono. It seems okay on the whole.

■ **nel suo insieme** as a whole □ Bisogna considerarlo nel suo insieme. It needs to be considered as a whole.

insignificante (FEM **insignificante**) ADJECTIVE
insignificant
□ un particolare insignificante an insignificant detail

insinuare VERB [68]
to insinuate
□ Cosa vorresti insinuare? What are you insinuating?

insipido (FEM **insipida**) ADJECTIVE
insipid

insistere VERB [10]
1 to insist
□ Se proprio insisti, vengo. If you really insist, I'll come.
2 to keep on
□ Non insistere, tanto non te lo presto. Don't keep on, I'm not going to lend it to you.
□ È inutile insistere su quell'argomento. There's no point keeping on about this.

l' **insolazione** FEM NOUN
sunstroke
□ Ho preso un'insolazione. I got sunstroke.

insolito (FEM **insolita**) ADJECTIVE
unusual

insomma ADVERB, EXCLAMATION
1 well
□ Insomma, sei pronta o no? Well, are you ready or not? □ Insomma, cosa ti hanno detto? Well, what did they say to you?
2 all in all
□ Era sporco e caro, insomma un disastro! It was dirty and expensive – all in all, a disaster!
■ **Come stai? — Insomma.** How are you? — Not too bad.
■ **Insomma, basta!** That's enough!

l' **insonnia** FEM NOUN
■ **soffrire d'insonnia** not to be able to sleep
□ Da un po' di tempo soffro d'insonnia. I haven't been able to sleep lately.

insonnolito (FEM **insonnolita**) ADJECTIVE
sleepy
□ È sempre più insonnolito. He's getting sleepier and sleepier.

insopportabile (FEM **insopportabile**)
ADJECTIVE
horrible
□ una puzza insopportabile a horrible smell
■ **È una ragazza proprio insopportabile.** That girl is a real pain.

insospettire VERB [51]
to make suspicious
□ Il suo atteggiamento mi ha insospettito. Her behaviour made me suspicious.
■ **insospettirsi** to become suspicious □ Si è insospettito e ha chiamato la polizia. He became suspicious and called the police.

instabile (FEM **instabile**) ADJECTIVE
1 unstable
□ Il situazione politica è un po' instabile. The political situation is rather unstable.
2 unsettled
□ Il tempo è ancora instabile. The weather is still unsettled.
3 unsteady
□ La sedia è un po' instabile. The chair is a bit unsteady.

insufficiente (FEM **insufficiente**) ADJECTIVE
1 unsatisfactory (grade)
2 below standard (homework)
■ **Il cibo è insufficiente.** There's not enough food.

l' **insufficienza** FEM NOUN
■ **prendere un'insufficienza in** to fail
□ Ho preso un'insufficienza in chimica. I failed chemistry.
■ **insufficienza di prove** lack of evidence
□ L'hanno assolto per insufficienza di prove. He was acquitted because of lack of evidence.

l' **insulto** MASC NOUN
insult

intanto ADVERB
1 for now
□ Intanto prendi questo, poi ti darò il resto. Take this for now, I'll give you the rest later.
2 but
□ Sì, sì, intanto tocca sempre a me farlo! Yes, yes, but it's always me who has to do it!
■ **Mettiti il cappotto, io intanto chiamo un taxi.** Put on your coat while I get a taxi.

intasarsi VERB [56]
to be blocked
□ Si è intasato il lavandino. The sink's blocked.

intascare VERB [18]
to pocket

integrale (FEM **integrale**) ADJECTIVE
■ **pane integrale** wholemeal bread
■ **abbronzatura integrale** all-over tan
■ **edizione integrale** unabridged edition
■ **auto a trazione integrale** four-wheel drive vehicle

intellettuale (FEM **intellettuale**) ADJECTIVE, MASC/FEM NOUN
intellectual

intelligente (FEM **intelligente**) ADJECTIVE
intelligent

intendere VERB [112]
to mean
□ Cosa intendi? What did you mean?
□ Dipende da cosa intendi per 'giustizia'. It depends what you mean by 'justice'.
■ **intendersi** to understand each other
□ Cominciamo a intenderci. We're beginning to understand each other.
■ **Ci siamo intesi?** Is that clear?

■ **intendersi di qualcosa** to know about something □ Si intende di fotografia. She knows about photography.

l' **intenditore,** l' **intenditrice** MASC/FEM NOUN
expert

intenso (FEM **intensa**) ADJECTIVE
1 intense
□ un calore intenso intense heat
2 bright
□ una luce intensa a bright light
3 heavy
□ Il traffico è più intenso attorno alle otto. The traffic is heaviest around eight.

l' **intenzione** FEM NOUN
intention
□ Non so quali sono le sue intenzioni. I don't know what her intentions are.
■ **avere intenzione di fare qualcosa** to mean to do something □ Avevo intenzione di andare ma poi ho cambiato idea. I meant to go but then I changed my mind. □ Non avevo intenzione di offenderti. I didn't mean to offend you.

interessante (FEM **interessante**) ADJECTIVE
interesting

interessare VERB [68]
■ **Se ti interessa ti posso dare il suo indirizzo.** If you're interested I can give you his address.
■ **Non mi interessa dove sei stato.** I'm not interested where you've been.
■ **interessarsi di qualcosa** to be interested in something □ Non mi interesso di politica. I'm not interested in politics.

l' **interesse** MASC NOUN
interest
□ Ha ascoltato con grande interesse. She listened with great interest. □ un interesse del cinque percento five per cent interest
■ **Lo dico nel tuo interesse.** I'm saying this for your own good.

l' **interferenza** FEM NOUN
interference
□ Ci sono delle interferenze sulla linea. There's interference on the line.

interferire VERB [51]
to interfere
□ Non interferire in questa faccenda! Don't interfere in this!

l' **intermezzo** MASC NOUN
interval

internazionale (FEM **internazionale**) ADJECTIVE
international

Internet MASC NOUN
the internet
□ L'ho trovato su Internet. I've found it on the internet.

■ **navigare in Internet** to surf the net

il **Internet cafè** (PL i **Internet cafè**) MASC NOUN
internet café

interno (FEM **interna**) ADJECTIVE
▷ see also **interno** NOUN
inside
□ la tasca interna della giacca the inside pocket of the jacket

l' **interno** MASC NOUN
▷ see also **interno** ADJECTIVE
1 inside
□ L'interno della scatola è rosso. The inside of the box is red.
■ **dall'interno di** from inside □ Le urla provenivano dall'interno della casa. The screams were coming from inside the house.
■ **all'interno di** inside □ all'interno della discoteca inside the club
2 extension
□ Vorrei l'interno trentadue. Can I have extension thirty two, please?

intero (FEM **intera**) ADJECTIVE
whole
□ Ho trascorso l'intera settimana a studiare. I spent the whole week studying.
■ **latte intero** full-cream milk

interpretare VERB [68]
1 to interpret
□ Non so come interpretare il suo comportamento. I don't know how to interpret his behaviour.
■ **interpretare male** to misunderstand
□ Forse hai interpretato male quello che ha detto. Perhaps you misunderstood what he said.
2 to play
□ Ha interpretato il ruolo di Robin Hood. He played the part of Robin Hood.

l' **interprete** MASC/FEM NOUN
1 interpreter
□ Fa l'interprete. She is an interpreter.
2 actor
3 performer

interrogare VERB [76]
1 to test
□ L'insegnante di inglese mi ha interrogato sul futuro. The English teacher tested me on the future tense.
■ **essere interrogato** to have an oral test
□ Sono stato interrogato in matematica oggi. I had an oral test in maths today.
2 to question
□ La polizia vuole interrogarlo. The police want to question him.

l' **interrogazione** FEM NOUN
oral test

interrompere VERB [92]
to interrupt

□ Scusa se t'interrompo. Excuse me for interrupting.

l' interruttore MASC NOUN
switch
□ l'interruttore della luce the light switch

l' interurbana FEM NOUN
long-distance call
□ Posso fare un'interurbana? Can I make a long-distance call?

l' intervallo MASC NOUN
1 interval
□ nell'intervallo in the interval
2 half-time
□ nell'intervallo at half-time
3 break
□ nell'intervallo during break

intervenire VERB [120]
to intervene
□ È intervenuto nella discussione. He intervened in the discussion.
■ **intervenire a** to take part in □ Tutti possono intervenire alla riunione. Everybody can take part in the meeting.

l' intervento MASC NOUN
1 operation
□ Ha subito un intervento delicato. He's had a complicated operation.
2 speech
□ un intervento interessante an interesting speech

l' intervista FEM NOUN
interview
□ Non concede interviste. She doesn't give interviews.

intervistare VERB [68]
to interview
□ È stato intervistato alla TV. He was interviewed on TV.

intestato (FEM **intestata**) ADJECTIVE
■ **essere intestato** to be registered □ La macchina è intestata a lui. The car is registered in his name.

l' intestino MASC NOUN
intestine

l' intimità FEM NOUN
privacy
□ nell'intimità della propria casa in the privacy of one's own home

intimo (FEM **intima**) ADJECTIVE
intimate
□ una cenetta intima an intimate dinner
■ **amico intimo** close friend
■ **biancheria intima** underwear

intitolare VERB [68]
to call
□ Questo quadro l'ho intitolato 'Mattina e Sera'. I've called this picture 'Morning and Evening'.

■ **intitolarsi** to be called □ Come s'intitola il film? What's the film called?

l' intolleranza FEM NOUN
intolerance
□ intolleranza religiosa religious intolerance
□ intolleranza al glutine gluten intolerance

l' intonaco (PL gli **intonaci**) MASC NOUN
plaster

intonato (FEM **intonata**) ADJECTIVE
matching
□ Portava una cravatta intonata alla camicia. He was wearing a shirt and matching tie.
■ **essere intonato** to be in tune

intorno ADVERB
round
□ Qui intorno non c'è neanche un giornalaio. There's isn't even a paper shop round here.
□ un giardino con una siepe intorno a garden with a hedge round it
■ **intorno a** round □ Erano seduti intorno al tavolo. They were sitting round the table.

intorpidito (FEM **intorpidita**) ADJECTIVE
■ **Ho la gamba intorpidita.** My leg's gone to sleep.

l' intossicazione FEM NOUN
■ **intossicazione alimentare** food poisoning

intransitivo (FEM **intransitiva**) ADJECTIVE
intransitive

intraprendente (FEM **intraprendente**) ADJECTIVE
enterprising
□ un giovane intraprendente an enterprising young man

intrattabile (FEM **intrattabile**) ADJECTIVE
awkward
□ Oggi sei proprio intrattabile. You're being really awkward today.

intravedere VERB [119]
to catch sight of
□ L'ho intravisto tra la folla. I caught sight of him in the crowd.

introdurre VERB [85]
to put
□ Introdurre la moneta nella fessura. Put the coin in the slot.

l' introduzione FEM NOUN
introduction
□ Dobbiamo leggere solo l'introduzione. We only have to read the introduction.

intromettersi VERB [59, aux **essere**]
to interfere
□ S'intromette sempre nei fatti degli altri. She's always interfering in other people's business.

intuire VERB [51]
to realize
□ Ha intuito la verità. She realized the truth.
□ Ho intuito subito che c'era qualcosa che non

i

andava. I realized at once that something was wrong.

l' **intuito** MASC NOUN
intuition

inumano (FEM **inumana**) ADJECTIVE
inhuman

inutile (FEM **inutile**) ADJECTIVE
1 useless
□ un aggeggio inutile a useless gadget □ Mi sento inutile qui. I feel useless here.
2 pointless
□ È inutile, tanto non lo convinci. It's pointless, you won't persuade him.
■ **È inutile arrabbiarsi!** There's no point getting angry!

inutilmente ADVERB
unnecessarily
□ Non volevo preoccuparti inutilmente. I didn't want to worry you unnecessarily.

invadente (FEM **invadente**) ADJECTIVE
interfering
□ un vicino di casa invadente an interfering neighbour

invadere VERB [55]
to invade
□ I tifosi hanno invaso il campo. The fans invaded the pitch.

invalido (FEM **invalida**) ADJECTIVE
▷ see also **invalido** NOUN
disabled

l' **invalido**, l' **invalida** MASC/FEM NOUN
▷ see also **invalido** ADJECTIVE
disabled person

invecchiare VERB [17]
to get old
□ Molti hanno paura di invecchiare. A lot of people are afraid of getting old.

invece ADVERB
but
□ Pensavo di farcela e invece ho dovuto arrendermi. I thought I could do it, but I had to give up.

> LANGUAGE TIP **invece** is often not translated.

□ A me piace il rock, a Luca invece il rap. I like rock, Luca likes rap.
■ **invece di** instead of □ Potresti aiutarmi invece di stare lì impalato. You could help me instead of just sitting there. □ Prendo un tè invece del caffè. I'll have tea instead of coffee.

inventare VERB [68]
1 to make up
□ Ho inventato una scusa per uscire prima. I made up an excuse to leave early.
2 to invent
□ Ha inventato un nuovo gioco. He invented a new game.

invernale (FEM **invernale**) ADJECTIVE
winter

□ una giornata invernale a winter's day

l' **inverno** MASC NOUN
winter
■ **d'inverno** in winter

l' **inversione** FEM NOUN
■ **inversione di marcia** U-turn

inverso (FEM **inversa**) ADJECTIVE
opposite
□ un'auto che veniva in senso inverso a car coming in the opposite direction

l' **investigatore**, l' **investigatrice**
MASC/FEM NOUN
detective
□ un investigatore privato a private detective

l' **investimento** MASC NOUN
investment
□ un buon investimento a good investment

investire VERB [41]
1 to run over
□ È stato investito da un camion. He was run over by a lorry.
2 to invest
□ Ha investito i suoi risparmi in titoli di stato. He has invested his savings in government bonds.

inviare VERB [55]
to send

l' **inviato**, l' **inviata** MASC/FEM NOUN
correspondent
□ un inviato speciale a special correspondent

l' **invidia** FEM NOUN
envy
□ Sta morendo d'invidia. He's green with envy.
■ **È tutta invidia, la tua.** You're just jealous.

invidiare VERB [17]
to envy
□ L'ha sempre invidiato. He's always envied him.

invidioso (FEM **invidiosa**) ADJECTIVE
jealous
□ È invidioso perché io ce l'ho e lui no. He's jealous because I've got one and he hasn't.

l' **invio** MASC NOUN
return (on keyboard)

invitare VERB [68]
to invite
□ Mi hanno invitato ad una festa. They've invited me to a party.
■ **invitare qualcuno a ballare** to ask someone to dance

l' **invitato**, l' **invitata** MASC/FEM NOUN
guest

l' **invito** MASC NOUN
invitation
□ Hai ricevuto l'invito? Did you get the invitation?

l' **involtini** MASC PL NOUN
■ **involtini di manzo** beef olives

inzuppare VERB [68]
  to dip
  □ Inzuppo sempre il pane nel latte. I always dip my bread in my milk.

io PRONOUN
  I

> **LANGUAGE TIP** In Italian, **io** is not written with a capital letter like 'I'.

  □ Io ci vado, tu fai come vuoi. I'm going, you do what you like. □ Fallo tu, io non ci riesco. You do it, I can't. □ Ho fame. — Anch'io. I'm hungry. — So am I. □ Vengo anch'io. I'll come too.
  ■ **Non lo sapevo nemmeno io.** I didn't even know it myself.
  ■ **Chi è? — Sono io, apri.** Who's that? — It's me, open the door.
  ■ **Pronto, c'è Paola? — Sì, sono io.** Hello, is Paola there? — Yes, speaking.

lo **iodio** MASC NOUN
  iodine

lo **Ionio** MASC NOUN
  ■ **il mar Ionio** the Ionian Sea

l' **iPad**® (PL gli **iPad**) MASC NOUN
  iPad®

l' **ipertesto** MASC NOUN
  hypertext

l' **iPhone**® (PL gli **iPhone**) MASC NOUN
  iPhone®

ipnotizzare VERB [68]
  to hypnotize
  □ L'hanno ipnotizzato. He was hypnotized.

l' **ipocrita** (MASC PL gli **ipocriti**, FEM PL le **ipocrite**) MASC/FEM NOUN
  hypocrite

l' **iPod**® (PL gli **iPod**) MASC NOUN
  iPod®

l' **ipotesi** (PL le **ipotesi**) FEM NOUN
  possibility
  □ Le ipotesi sono due. There are two possibilities.
  ■ **Facciamo l'ipotesi che non venga.** Supposing he doesn't come.
  ■ **nella migliore delle ipotesi** at best
  □ Nella migliore delle ipotesi lo finirò sabato. At best I'll finish it on Saturday.
  ■ **nella peggiore delle ipotesi** if the worst comes to the worst

l' **ippica** FEM NOUN
  horse-racing

l' **ippodromo** MASC NOUN
  racecourse

l' **ippopotamo** MASC NOUN
  hippo

la **ipsilon** (PL le **ipsilon**) FEM NOUN
  y
  □ Si scrive con la 'i' o con la 'ipsilon'? Do you spell it with an 'i' or with a 'y'?

iracheno (FEM **irachena**) ADJECTIVE, MASC/FEM NOUN
  Iraqi

l' **Irak** MASC NOUN
  Iraq

l' **Iran** MASC NOUN
  Iran

iraniano (FEM **iraniana**) ADJECTIVE, MASC/FEM NOUN
  Iranian

l' **Irlanda** FEM NOUN
  Ireland
  □ Mi è piaciuta molto l'Irlanda. I really liked Ireland. □ Andremo in Irlanda quest'estate. We're going to Ireland this summer.
  ■ **l'Irlanda del Nord** Northern Ireland
  ■ **il mar d'Irlanda** the Irish Sea

irlandese (FEM **irlandese**) ADJECTIVE
  ▷ see also **irlandese** MASC NOUN, FEM NOUN
  Irish
  □ la squadra irlandese the Irish team

l' **irlandese** MASC NOUN
  ▷ see also **irlandese** ADJECTIVE, FEM NOUN
  1 Irishman
  ■ **gli irlandesi** the Irish
  2 Irish (language)

l' **irlandese** FEM NOUN
  ▷ see also **irlandese** ADJECTIVE, MASC NOUN
  Irishwoman

ironico (FEM **ironica**, MASC PL **ironici**, FEM PL **ironiche**) ADJECTIVE
  ironic
  □ un sorrisetto ironico an ironic smile

irregolare (FEM **irregolare**) ADJECTIVE
  1 irregular
  □ un verbo irregolare an irregular verb
  □ lineamenti irregolari irregular features
  2 uneven (ground)

irritare VERB [68]
  to irritate (throat, eyes)
  ■ **irritare qualcuno** to get on somebody's nerves □ Il suo modo di ridere mi irrita. His laugh gets on my nerves.
  ■ **irritarsi** to get annoyed □ Si irrita moltissimo se qualcuno lo interrompe. He gets very annoyed if anyone interrupts him.

l' **iscritto**, l' **iscritta** MASC/FEM NOUN
  1 student
  □ gli iscritti al primo anno di università first year university students
  2 competitor
  3 member (of club)
  ■ **mettere per iscritto** to put something in writing

iscriversi VERB [99, AUX **essere**]
  1 to register
  □ Si è iscritto all'università. He's registered at the university.

135

2 to enrol
□ Mi iscriverò ad un corso di lingue. I'm going to enrol on a language course.

3 to join
□ Non si è mai iscritto a un partito. He never joined a political party.

l' **iscrizione** FEM NOUN
■ **tassa di iscrizione 1** *(at university)* registration fee **2** *(of club)* membership fee

l' **Islam** MASC NOUN
Islam

l' **Islanda** FEM NOUN
Iceland

l' **isola** FEM NOUN
island
□ un'isola deserta a desert island
■ **le isole britanniche** the British Isles
■ **isola pedonale** pedestrian precinct

l' **isolamento** MASC NOUN
isolation
□ È ricoverata nel reparto d'isolamento. She's been admitted to the isolation ward.

isolare VERB [68]
to cut off
□ La bufera di neve ha isolato il paese. The village was cut off by the snowstorm.
■ **isolarsi** to cut oneself off □ Non isolarti, frequenta un po' di gente. Don't cut yourself off, go out and meet people.

isolato (FEM **isolata**) ADJECTIVE
▷ *see also* **isolato** NOUN
isolated
□ un caso isolato di epatite an isolated case of hepatitis
■ **Vivono isolati, in campagna.** They live in a remote place in the country.
■ **rimanere isolato** to be cut off □ Il paese è rimasto isolato a causa della neve. The village was cut off by the snow.

l' **isolato** MASC NOUN
▷ *see also* **isolato** ADJECTIVE
block
□ Ho fatto il giro dell'isolato. I went round the block. □ Il cinema è a due isolati da qui. The cinema is two blocks from here.

l' **ispettore**, l' **ispettrice** MASC/FEM NOUN
inspector

ispirare VERB [68]
to inspire
□ Non mi ha ispirato fiducia. He didn't inspire confidence.
■ **L'idea non mi ispira.** The idea doesn't attract me.
■ **ispirarsi a** to get one's idea from □ Per il romanzo si è ispirato a un fatto di cronaca. He got the idea for the novel from a news story.

Israele MASC NOUN
Israel
□ Andremo in Israele quest'estate. We're going

to Israel this summer.

israeliano (FEM **israeliana**) ADJECTIVE, MASC/ FEM NOUN
Israeli

l' **istante** MASC NOUN
moment
□ Sarò pronta tra un istante. I'll be ready in a moment. □ In quell'istante è entrata Paola. At that moment Paola came in.

l' **istinto** MASC NOUN
instinct
□ Ho seguito il mio istinto. I followed my instinct.

l' **istituto** MASC NOUN
college
□ un istituto tecnico a technical college
■ **istituto d'arte** art school
■ **istituto di bellezza** beauty salon

istruito (FEM **istruita**) ADJECTIVE
well-educated
□ una persona molto istruita a very well-educated person

l' **istruttore**, l' **istruttrice** MASC/FEM NOUN
instructor
□ un istruttore di nuoto a swimming instructor
□ un istruttore di scuola guida a driving instructor

l' **istruzione** FEM NOUN
education
□ Ha avuto una buona istruzione. He had a good education.
■ **Ministero della pubblica istruzione** Ministry of Education
■ **istruzioni** instructions □ Siamo in attesa di istruzioni. We're waiting for instructions.
□ istruzioni per l'uso instructions for use

l' **Italia** FEM NOUN
Italy
□ Ti è piaciuta l'Italia? Did you like Italy?
□ Verranno in Italia quest'estate. They're coming to Italy this summer.

l' **italiana** FEM NOUN
Italian

italiano (FEM **italiana**) ADJECTIVE
▷ *see also* **italiano** NOUN
Italian

l' **italiano** MASC NOUN
▷ *see also* **italiano** ADJECTIVE
Italian *(person, language)*
□ gli italiani the Italians □ Parli italiano? Do you speak Italian? □ l'insegnante di italiano the Italian teacher

l' **itinerario** MASC NOUN
itinerary

la **Iugoslavia** FEM NOUN
■ **la ex Iugoslavia** the former Yugoslavia

IVA ABBREVIATION
VAT (= Value Added Tax)
□ cento euro + IVA one hundred euros plus VAT

Jj

il **jazz** MASC NOUN
  jazz
i **jeans** MASC PL NOUN
  jeans
la **jeep** (PL le **jeep**) FEM NOUN
  Jeep®
il **jogging** MASC NOUN
  jogging
  ■ **fare jogging** to go jogging

il **jolly** (PL i **jolly**) MASC NOUN
  joker
il **judo** MASC NOUN
  judo
la **Jugoslavia** FEM NOUN
  ■ **la ex Jugoslavia** the former Yugoslavia
il **jukebox** (PL i **jukebox**) MASC NOUN
  jukebox

Kk

il **karatè** MASC NOUN
karate

il **kayak** (PL i **kayak**) MASC NOUN
kayak

il **koala** (PL i **koala**) MASC NOUN
koala

il **krapfen** (PL i **krapfen**) MASC NOUN
doughnut

la ARTICLE

▷ *see also* **la** PRONOUN, NOUN

the

□ La bambina ha fame. **The baby is hungry.**
□ Chi ha rotto la finestra? **Who broke the window?** □ la Senna **the Seine**

LANGUAGE TIP **la** is often not translated.

□ La pallacanestro è il mio sport preferito. **Basketball is my favourite sport.** □ Non mi piace la pastasciutta. **I don't like pasta.** □ La Juventus gioca in casa. **Juventus is playing at home.** □ la madre di Mario **Mario's mother**

LANGUAGE TIP **la** is sometimes translated by a possessive adjective.

□ Si è tolto la giacca. **He took off his jacket.**
□ Dammi la mano. **Give me your hand.** □ Mi fa male la gamba. **My leg hurts.**

la PRONOUN

▷ *see also* **la** ARTICLE, NOUN

1 her

□ La chiamerò domani mattina. **I'll call her tomorrow morning.** □ Chiamala! **Call her!**

2 it

□ La compro io. **I'll buy it.** □ Riesci ad alzarla? **Can you lift it?**

3 you *(polite form)*

□ La ringrazio molto, signore. **Thank you very much, sir.** □ Lieto di conoscerla. **Pleased to meet you.**

il **la** (PL i **la**) MASC NOUN

▷ *see also* **la** ARTICLE, PRONOUN

A *(musical note)*

là ADVERB

there

□ Mettilo là. **Put it there.** □ Vieni via di là. **Come away from there.**

■ **Mia madre è di là.** My mother's in the other room.

■ **per di là** that way □ Non passo mai per di là. I never go that way.

■ **più in là** **1** further on □ La mia casa è un po' più in là. My house is a bit further on.
2 later on □ Deciderò più in là. I'll decide later on.

■ **Potresti sederti un po' più in là?** Could you move along a bit?

■ **là dentro** in there

■ **là fuori** out there

■ **là sopra** up there

■ **là sotto** under there

il **labbro** (FEM PL le **labbra**) MASC NOUN

lip

il **labirinto** MASC NOUN

maze

il **laboratorio** MASC NOUN

laboratory

■ **laboratorio linguistico** language laboratory

la **lacca** (PL le **lacche**) FEM NOUN

1 hair spray

2 nail varnish

i **lacci** MASC PL NOUN

■ **lacci per scarpe** shoelaces

la **lacrima** FEM NOUN

tear

□ con le lacrime agli occhi **with tears in his eyes**

■ **scoppiare in lacrime** to burst into tears
□ È scoppiata in lacrime. She burst into tears.

lacrimogeno (FEM **lacrimogena**) ADJECTIVE

■ **gas lacrimogeno** tear gas

la **lacuna** FEM NOUN

■ **Ho molte lacune in matematica.** My knowledge of maths is rather sketchy.

il **ladro**, la **ladra** MASC/FEM NOUN

1 thief

■ **Al ladro!** Stop thief!

2 burglar

laggiù ADVERB

1 down there

2 over there

il **lago** (PL i **laghi**) MASC NOUN

lake

□ il lago di Garda **Lake Garda**

la **laguna** FEM NOUN

lagoon

la **lama** FEM NOUN

blade

lamentarsi VERB [56, AUX **essere**]

to complain

□ Si sono lamentati del cibo. **They complained about the food.** □ Non mi lamento! **I can't complain!**

la **lamentela** FEM NOUN

complaint

□ Ci sono state molte lamentele sul servizio.

There have been a lot of complaints about the service.

la **lametta** FEM NOUN
razor blade

la **lampada** FEM NOUN
lamp
□ Accendi quella lampada. Switch that lamp on.

il **lampadario** MASC NOUN
chandelier

la **lampadina** FEM NOUN
light bulb
□ una lampadina da cento watt a hundred watt light bulb
■ **lampadina tascabile** torch

il **lampeggiatore** MASC NOUN
indicator *(on car)*

il **lampione** MASC NOUN
street lamp

il **lampo** MASC NOUN
▷ *see also* **lampo** ADJECTIVE
flash of lightning
■ **tuoni e lampi** thunder and lightning
■ **un lampo di luce** a flash of light

lampo (FEM+PL **lampo**) ADJECTIVE
▷ *see also* **lampo** NOUN
■ **cerniera lampo** zip

il **lampone** MASC NOUN
raspberry

la **lana** FEM NOUN
wool
□ un maglione di lana a wool sweater
■ **pura lana vergine** pure new wool

la **lancetta** FEM NOUN
1 hand *(of clock)*
2 needle *(of instrument)*

lanciare VERB [13]
1 to throw
□ Ho lanciato la palla a Piero. I threw the ball to Piero. □ Mi ha lanciato un sasso. He threw a stone at me.
2 to launch
□ La NASA ha lanciato un razzo la settimana scorsa. NASA launched a rocket last week.
3 to start
□ Hanno lanciato una nuova moda. They've started a new fashion.
■ **lanciare un grido** to let out a cry □ Ha lanciato un grido di dolore. He let out a cry of pain.

lancinante (FEM **lancinante**) ADJECTIVE
■ **un dolore lancinante** a shooting pain

il **lancio** MASC NOUN
■ **lancio del disco** discus
■ **lancio del giavellotto** javelin
■ **lancio del peso** shot put

la **lapide** FEM NOUN
tombstone

il **lapsus** (PL i **lapsus**) MASC NOUN
slip
□ un lapsus freudiano a Freudian slip

larga FEM NOUN
■ **stare alla larga** to keep away □ Stai alla larga da casa mia! Keep away from my house!

la **larghezza** FEM NOUN
width
□ Larghezza: 20 cm. Width: 20 cm.
■ **La stanza ha tre metri di larghezza.** The room is three metres wide.

largo (FEM **larga**, MASC PL **larghi**, FEM PL **larghe**) ADJECTIVE
▷ *see also* **largo** NOUN
1 wide
□ Il corridoio è largo due metri. The corridor is two metres wide. □ Ha i fianchi larghi. She's got wide hips.
■ **Ha le spalle larghe.** He's got broad shoulders.
2 loose
□ Questa gonna è troppo larga. This skirt is too loose.

largo MASC NOUN
▷ *see also* **largo** ADJECTIVE
■ **Fate largo!** Make way!
■ **farsi largo tra la folla** to push one's way through the crowd □ Si è fatta larga tra la folla ed è salita sul palco. She pushed her way through the crowd and went up on the stage.
■ **al largo di Genova** off the coast of Genoa

le **lasagne** FEM PL NOUN
lasagne *sing*

lasciare VERB [13]
to leave
□ Il marito l'ha lasciata per un'altra. Her husband left her for another woman. □ Hai lasciato a casa il maglione? Did you leave your jumper at home? □ Non lasciare la finestra aperta. Don't leave the window open.
■ **lasciare fare qualcosa a qualcuno** to let somebody do something □ Mio padre non mi lascia uscire fino a tardi. My father doesn't let me stay out late. □ Lascia fare a me. Let me do it.
■ **lasciar stare qualcuno** to leave somebody alone □ Lascia stare mia sorella! Leave my sister alone!
■ **Lascialo stare, non vale la pena arrabbiarsi.** Just ignore him, it's not worth getting annoyed.
■ **Lasciami in pace!** Leave me alone!
■ **lasciarsi** to split up □ I miei si sono lasciati un anno fa. My parents split up a year ago.

laser (FEM+PL **laser**) ADJECTIVE
laser
□ una stampante laser a laser printer

il **lassativo** MASC NOUN
laxative

lassù ADVERB
up there
□ Guarda lassù! Look up there!

la **lastra** FEM NOUN
1 slab (of stone)
2 sheet (of ice, glass)
3 X-ray
   ▪ **Ho fatto una lastra alla gamba.** I had my leg X-rayed.

laterale (FEM **laterale**) ADJECTIVE
   side
   □ una strada laterale a side street

latino (FEM **latina**) ADJECTIVE, MASC NOUN
   Latin

il **lato** MASC NOUN
1 side
   □ l'altro lato della strada the other side of the street
2 aspect
   □ Questo è un lato essenziale del problema. This is a key aspect of the problem.
   ▪ **da un lato... dall'altro...** on the one hand... on the other hand...

la **latta** FEM NOUN
   tin
   □ un barattolo di latta a tin can

il **latte** MASC NOUN
   milk
   ▪ **latte intero** full-cream milk
   ▪ **latte scremato** skimmed milk
   ▪ **latte parzialmente scremato** semi-skimmed milk
   ▪ **latte detergente** cleansing milk

i **latticini** MASC PL NOUN
   dairy products
   □ Sono allergico ai latticini. I'm allergic to dairy products.

la **lattina** FEM NOUN
   can
   □ una lattina di birra a can of beer

la **lattuga** (PL le **lattughe**) FEM NOUN
   lettuce

la **laurea** FEM NOUN
   degree

laurearsi VERB [56, aux **essere**]
   to graduate

il **laureato**, la **laureata** MASC/FEM NOUN
   graduate

il **lavabo** MASC NOUN
   washbasin

il **lavaggio** MASC NOUN
   washing
   □ istruzioni per il lavaggio washing instructions
   ▪ **fare il lavaggio del cervello a qualcuno** to brainwash somebody □ Gli hanno fatto il lavaggio del cervello. He's been brainwashed.

la **lavagna** FEM NOUN
   blackboard
   □ Scrivilo sulla lavagna. Write it on the blackboard.

   ▪ **lavagna interattiva** interactive whiteboard
   ▪ **lavagna luminosa** overhead projector

la **lavanda** FEM NOUN
   lavender
   ▪ **Gli hanno fatto una lavanda gastrica.** He had his stomach pumped.

la **lavanderia** FEM NOUN
   ▪ **lavanderia automatica** Launderette®
   ▪ **lavanderia a secco** dry-cleaner's

il **lavandino** MASC NOUN
1 sink
2 washbasin

lavare VERB [68]
   to wash
   □ Lava la macchina tutte le domeniche. He washes his car every Sunday.
   ▪ **lavare a secco** to dry-clean
   ▪ **lavare i piatti** to wash up
   ▪ **lavarsi le mani** to wash one's hands □ Si è lavata le mani. She washed her hands.
   ▪ **lavarsi i capelli** to wash one's hair □ Mi lavo i capelli ogni mattina. I wash my hair every morning.
   ▪ **lavarsi i denti** to brush one's teeth
   □ Lavati i denti prima di andare a letto. Brush your teeth before you go to bed.

la **lavastoviglie** (PL le **lavastoviglie**) FEM NOUN
   dishwasher

la **lavatrice** FEM NOUN
   washing machine

lavorare VERB [68]
   to work
   □ Lavoro dalle otto alle cinque. I work from eight to five.
   ▪ **andare a lavorare** to go to work □ Vado a lavorare alle sette. I go to work at seven.

lavorativo (FEM **lavorativa**) ADJECTIVE
   ▪ **giorno lavorativo** working day

il **lavoratore**, la **lavoratrice** MASC/FEM NOUN
   worker

il **lavoro** MASC NOUN
1 work
   □ Ho molto lavoro da fare. I've got a lot of work to do. □ Il papà è al lavoro. Dad is at work.
2 job
   □ Ho un buon lavoro. I've got a good job.
   □ È rimasto senza lavoro. He's lost his job.
   ▪ **lavori di casa** housework sing
   ▪ **lavori stradali** roadworks

le ARTICLE
   ▷ see also **le** PRONOUN
   the
   □ Le ragazze erano già a letto. The girls were already in bed. □ Chi ha preso le forbici? Who's taken the scissors?
   ▨ **LANGUAGE TIP le** is often not translated.

141

□ Le macchine nuove costano troppo. New cars cost too much. □ Non mi piacciono le melanzane. I don't like aubergines. □ le sorelle di Mario Mario's sisters

> **LANGUAGE TIP** le is sometimes translated by a possessive adjective.

□ Si è tolto le scarpe. He took off his shoes. □ Va' a lavarti le mani. Go and wash your hands.

le PRONOUN

▷ *see also* **le** ARTICLE

1 her

□ Le ho detto tutto. I told her everything. □ Dalle qualcosa da mangiare. Give her something to eat. □ Le ho già scritto. I've already written to her. □ Le ho spiegato il motivo. I explained the reason to her. □ Le ha sorriso. He smiled at her.

2 you *(polite form)*

□ Le posso offrire qualcosa da bere? Can I get you something to drink? □ Le ho prenotato una stanza nello stesso albergo. I've booked you a room at the same hotel.

3 them

□ Mettile nel frigo. Put them in the fridge. □ Guardale! Look at them!

leale (FEM **leale**) ADJECTIVE
loyal

il **lecca lecca** (PL i **lecca lecca**) MASC NOUN
lollipop

leccare VERB [18]
to lick

■ **leccarsi i baffi** to lick one's lips

legale (FEM **legale**) ADJECTIVE
legal

legalizzare VERB [68]
to legalize

il **legame** MASC NOUN
link

□ Dev'esserci un legame tra i due episodi. There must be a link between the two events.

■ **C'è un legame molto forte tra di loro.** They're very close.

■ **legame di parentela** family tie

legare VERB [76]
to tie

□ Hai legato bene il pacco? Have you tied the parcel securely? □ Legali le mani. Tie his hands. □ Lo hanno legato ad una sedia. They tied him to a chair.

■ **Non ho mai legato con lui.** I've never been very friendly with him.

■ **essere legato a qualcuno** to be close to somebody □ Sono molto legato a mia madre. I'm very close to my mother.

■ **essere legato a qualcosa** to be attached to something □ È molto legato alla sua vecchia bici. He's very attached to his old bike.

■ **legarsi le scarpe** to do up one's shoes

□ Non sa ancora legarsi le scarpe. He doesn't know how to do up his shoes yet.

la **legge** FEM NOUN
law

□ una nuova legge a new law □ Studia legge. He's studying law.

la **leggenda** FEM NOUN
legend

leggere VERB [57]
to read

□ Non ho ancora letto quel libro. I haven't read that book yet.

leggero (FEM **leggera**) ADJECTIVE

1 light

□ un pacco leggero a light parcel □ un pasto leggero a light meal

■ **Questo caffè è un po' troppo leggero.** This coffee is a bit weak.

2 slight

□ Ho un leggero mal di testa. I've got a slight headache. □ Ha un leggero accento francese. She's got a slight French accent.

la **legna** FEM NOUN
wood

□ una stufa a legna a wood stove

il **legno** MASC NOUN
wood

□ un pezzo di legno a piece of wood

■ **di legno** wooden □ un tavolo di legno a wooden table

lei PRONOUN

1 she

□ Lei è molto bella. She's very beautiful. □ Viene anche lei? Is she coming too?

■ **Non lo sapeva nemmeno lei.** She didn't even know it herself.

2 her

□ Vado alla festa con lei. I'm going to the party with her. □ Dimmi qualcosa di lei. Tell me something about her. □ È lei, apri la porta. It's her, open the door. □ senza di lei without her

3 you *(polite form)*

□ Posso venire con lei? May I come with you?

lentamente ADVERB
slowly

la **lente** FEM NOUN
lens

■ **lenti a contatto** contact lenses □ Porto le lenti a contatto. I wear contact lenses.

■ **lenti morbide** soft lenses

■ **lenti rigide** hard lenses

■ **lente d'ingrandimento** magnifying glass

le **lenticchie** FEM PL NOUN
lentils

le **lentiggini** FEM PL NOUN
freckles

lento (FEM **lenta**) ADJECTIVE
slow

□ Il mio computer è troppo lento. My computer is too slow. □ È molto più lenta di me. She's much slower than me. □ È il ragazzo più lento della squadra. He's the slowest boy in the team.

la **lenza** FEM NOUN
fishing line

il **lenzuolo** (FEM PL le **lenzuola**) MASC NOUN
sheet (for bed)

Leone MASC NOUN
Leo
■ **essere del Leone** to be Leo

il **leone** MASC NOUN
lion

la **lepre** FEM NOUN
hare

lercio (FEM **lercia**) ADJECTIVE
filthy

la **lesbica** (PL le **lesbiche**) FEM NOUN
lesbian

lesso (FEM **lessa**) ADJECTIVE
boiled
□ carne lessa boiled meat

il **letame** MASC NOUN
manure

il **letargo** MASC NOUN
hibernation
□ Gli orsi vanno in letargo d'inverno. Bears go into hibernation in the winter.

la **lettera** FEM NOUN
letter
□ Hai ricevuto la mia lettera? Did you get my letter? □ una lettera d'amore a love letter □ Era scritto a lettere minuscole. It was written in tiny letters.
■ **lettere** arts □ Fa lettere all'università. She's doing arts at university.

letteralmente ADVERB
literally

la **letteratura** FEM NOUN
literature

il **letto** MASC NOUN
bed
■ **andare a letto** to go to bed □ Ieri sera sono andato a letto molto tardi. I went to bed very late last night.
■ **letto a castello** bunk bed
■ **letto a una piazza** single bed
■ **letto matrimoniale** double bed

il **lettore**, la **lettrice** MASC/FEM NOUN
reader
□ un avido lettore di fantascienza an avid reader of science fiction
■ **lettore universitario** language assistant
■ **lettore CD** CD player
■ **lettore DVD** DVD reader
■ **lettore MP3/MP4** MP3/MP4 player

la **lettura** FEM NOUN
reading

LANGUAGE TIP Be careful! **lettura** doesn't mean **lecture**.

la **leva** FEM NOUN
lever
□ Ha premuto una leva. He pressed a lever.
■ **la leva del cambio** the gear lever

levare VERB [68]
to take off
□ Leva i tuoi libri dal tavolo. Take your books off the table. □ Leva il coperchio dalla pentola. Take the lid off the saucepan.
■ **levare un dente** to take a tooth out □ Il dentista mi ha levato un dente. The dentist took one of my teeth out.
■ **levarsi** to take off □ Levati il maglione. Take your jumper off.
■ **Levati di mezzo!** Get out of the way!

il **levriero** MASC NOUN
greyhound

la **lezione** FEM NOUN
1 lesson
□ una lezione di inglese an English lesson
□ Do lezioni private. I give private lessons.
2 lecture

li PL PRONOUN
them
□ Li ho visti ieri. I saw them yesterday.
□ Guardali! Look at them!

lì ADVERB
there
□ Mettilo lì. Put it there. □ Vieni via di lì. Come away from there.
■ **lì dentro** in there
■ **lì fuori** out there
■ **lì sopra** up there
■ **lì sotto** under there

il **Libano** MASC NOUN
Lebanon
□ Andremo in Libano. We're going to Lebanon.

la **libellula** FEM NOUN
dragonfly

liberale (FEM **liberale**) ADJECTIVE
liberal

liberalizzare VERB [68]
to liberalize

liberare VERB [68]
to set free
□ Hanno curato il cigno e poi l'hanno liberato. They treated the swan and then set it free.
■ **liberare un prigioniero** to release a prisoner
■ **liberare una stanza** to vacate a room □ Dobbiamo liberare la stanza entro le undici. We have to vacate the room by eleven.
■ **liberarsi** to get away □ Finalmente mi sono liberata di lui. I finally got away from him.
□ Spero di liberarmi per le cinque. I hope to get away by five o'clock.

I

143

■ **È riuscito a liberarsi ed è scappato.** He managed to get free and escaped.

libero (FEM **libera**) ADJECTIVE

free

□ Sei libera domani sera? Are you free tomorrow evening? □ Siete liberi di andarvene. You're free to go. □ L'ingresso è libero. Admission is free. □ Finalmente è libero! *(telephone)* The line is free at last! □ È libero questo posto? Is this seat free?

■ **Avete una camera libera per questa sera?** Have you got a room available for tonight?

■ **La strada è libera.** The road is clear.

■ **tempo libero** spare time □ Cosa fai nel tempo libero? What do you do in your spare time?

la libertà (PL le **libertà**) FEM NOUN

1 freedom

□ libertà di scelta freedom of choice

2 liberty

□ le libertà civili civil liberties

■ **libertà provvisoria** bail

la Libia FEM NOUN

Libya

il libraio MASC NOUN

bookseller

la libreria FEM NOUN

1 bookshop

2 bookcase

> **LANGUAGE TIP** Be careful! **libreria** doesn't mean **library**.

il libretto MASC NOUN

little book

□ un libretto di proverbi a little book of proverbs

■ **libretto d'istruzioni** instruction booklet

■ **libretto degli assegni** chequebook

il libro MASC NOUN

book

■ **libro elettronico** e-book

■ **libro di testo** textbook

la licenza FEM NOUN

licence *(fishing, hunting)*

■ **andare in licenza** *(from army)* to go on leave

licenziare VERB [17]

1 to sack

□ Ha minacciato di licenziarla. He threatened to sack her.

2 to make redundant

□ Mio padre è stato licenziato. My father has been made redundant.

■ **licenziarsi** to give up one's job □ Si è licenziata per occuparsi del bambino. She gave up her job to look after her little boy.

il liceo MASC NOUN

secondary school

> **DID YOU KNOW...?**
> The two main types of **liceo** are the **liceo classico**, which specializes in classical subjects, and the **liceo scientifico**, which specializes in science subjects.

lieto (FEM **lieta**) ADJECTIVE

happy

□ una storia a lieto fine a story with a happy ending

■ **Molto lieto!** Pleased to meet you!

il lievito MASC NOUN

yeast

lilla (FEM+PL **lilla**) ADJECTIVE, MASC NOUN

lilac

il lillà (PL i **lillà**) MASC NOUN

lilac

la lima FEM NOUN

■ **lima da unghie** nailfile

il limite MASC NOUN

▷ see also **limite** ADJECTIVE

limit

■ **limite di velocità** speed limit

■ **nei limiti del possibile** as far as possible □ Ti aiuterò nei limiti del possibile. I'll help you as far as possible.

■ **al limite** if necessary □ Non portare l'ombrello; al limite te ne presto uno. Don't bring your umbrella; if necessary I'll lend you one.

■ **Hai passato ogni limite!** You've gone too far!

limite (FEM+PL **limite**) ADJECTIVE

▷ see also **limite** NOUN

■ **un caso limite** an extreme case

la limonata FEM NOUN

1 lemonade

2 lemon squash

il limone MASC NOUN

lemon

limpido (FEM **limpida**) ADJECTIVE

clear *(water, sky)*

la linea FEM NOUN

line

□ linea di partenza starting line

■ **È caduta la linea.** I've been cut off.

■ **in linea d'aria** as the crow flies □ È a dieci chilometri da qui in linea d'aria. It's ten kilometres from here as the crow flies.

■ **in linea di massima** on the whole □ In linea di massima penso che tu abbia ragione. On the whole I think you're right.

■ **linea aerea** airline

■ **volo di linea** scheduled flight

i lineamenti MASC PL NOUN

features

la lineetta FEM NOUN

1 hyphen

2 dash *(in sentence)*

la lingua FEM NOUN

1 tongue

□ Ce l'ho sulla punta della lingua. It's on the tip of my tongue.

2 language

□ Parla tre lingue. He speaks three languages. □ Studio lingue all'università. I'm studying languages at university.

■ **paesi di lingua inglese** English-speaking countries

il **lino** MASC NOUN
linen

□ una giacca di lino a linen jacket

liofilizzato (FEM **liofilizzata**) ADJECTIVE
freeze-dried

□ caffè liofilizzato freeze-dried coffee granules

liquefatto (FEM **liquefatta**) ADJECTIVE
melted

□ Aggiungere il burro liquefatto all'impasto. Add the melted butter to the mixture.

la **liquidazione** FEM NOUN
clearance sale

■ **in liquidazione** in a sale □ Ho comprato questa gonna in liquidazione. I bought this skirt in a sale.

liquido (FEM **liquida**) ADJECTIVE
▷ *see also* **liquido** NOUN
liquid

□ un gas liquido a liquid gas

■ **denaro liquido** cash

il **liquido** MASC NOUN
▷ *see also* **liquido** ADJECTIVE

1 liquid

□ un liquido verde a green liquid

2 cash

la **liquirizia** FEM NOUN
liquorice

□ un bastoncino di liquirizia a stick of liquorice

il **liquore** MASC NOUN
liqueur

la **lira** FEM NOUN
lira

■ **lira sterlina** pound sterling

lirico (FEM **lirica**, MASC PL **lirici**, FEM PL **liriche**)
ADJECTIVE

■ **musica lirica** opera □ una cantante lirica an opera singer

Lisbona FEM NOUN
Lisbon

□ Andrò a Lisbona quest'estate. I'm going to Lisbon this summer. □ Abita a Lisbona. He lives in Lisbon.

la **lisca** (PL le **lische**) FEM NOUN
fishbone

liscio (FEM **liscia**, MASC PL **lisci**, FEM PL **lisce**)
ADJECTIVE
▷ *see also* **liscio** ADVERB
smooth

□ Ha la pelle liscia. She's got smooth skin.

■ **passarla liscia** to get away with it

□ Questa volta non la passerà liscia. He won't get away with it this time.

■ **Un whisky. — Liscio o con ghiaccio?** A whisky. — Neat or with ice?

■ **avere i capelli lisci** to have straight hair

liscio ADVERB
▷ *see also* **liscio** ADJECTIVE
smoothly

□ È andato tutto liscio. It went smoothly.

la **lista** FEM NOUN
list

□ la lista della spesa the shopping list □ la lista degli invitati the guest list

■ **lista elettorale** electoral register

■ **lista delle vivande** menu

la **lite** FEM NOUN
quarrel

litigare VERB [76]
to quarrel

□ Litigo spesso con il mio ragazzo. I often quarrel with my boyfriend.

■ **Ho litigato con il mio capo.** I had an argument with my boss.

il **litigio** MASC NOUN
quarrel

il **litro** MASC NOUN
litre

□ un litro d'acqua a litre of water

il **livello** MASC NOUN
level

□ allo stesso livello at the same level

il **livido** MASC NOUN
bruise

lo ARTICLE
▷ *see also* **lo** PRONOUN
the

□ Chiudi lo sportello. Close the door. □ Mi passeresti lo zucchero? Could you pass me the sugar, please?

▌ **LANGUAGE TIP lo** is often not translated. □ Lo sci è il mio sport preferito. Skiing is my favourite sport. □ Non metto mai lo zucchero nel caffè. I never take sugar in my coffee. □ lo zio di Mario Mario's uncle

▌ **LANGUAGE TIP lo** is sometimes translated by a possessive adjective. □ Si è tolto lo stivale. He took off his boot.

lo PRONOUN
▷ *see also* **lo** ARTICLE

1 him

□ Lo chiamerò domani mattina. I'll call him tomorrow morning. □ Vuoi conoscerlo? Would you like to meet him? □ Guardalo! Look at him!

2 it

□ Lo compro io. I'll buy it. □ Riesci ad alzarlo? Can you lift it?

locale (FEM **locale**) ADJECTIVE
▷ *see also* **locale** NOUN
local

I

145

locale - lottare

□ il giornale locale the local paper
- **treno locale** stopping train

il **locale** MASC NOUN
▷ see also **locale** ADJECTIVE
place *(public place)*
□ È un locale molto costoso. It's a very expensive place.
- **locale notturno** nightclub

la **località** (PL le **località**) FEM NOUN
- **località turistica** holiday resort
- **località balneare** seaside resort

lodare VERB [68]
to praise

la **lode** FEM NOUN
- **laurearsi con centodieci e lode** to graduate with first-class honours

loggarsi VERB [56]
to log in

il **loggione** MASC NOUN
- **il loggione** the gods *(in theatre)*

logicamente ADVERB
obviously

logico (FEM **logica**, MASC PL **logici**, FEM PL **logiche**) ADJECTIVE
logical
□ Quello che dici non è molto logico. What you're saying isn't very logical.

logoro (FEM **logora**) ADJECTIVE
threadbare
□ un tappeto logoro a threadbare rug
- **un cappotto logoro** a shabby overcoat

il/la **londinese** MASC/FEM NOUN
▷ see also **londinese** ADJECTIVE
Londoner

londinese (FEM **londinese**) ADJECTIVE
▷ see also **londinese** NOUN
London
□ il traffico londinese London traffic
- **la vita londinese** life in London

Londra FEM NOUN
London
□ Domani vado a Londra. I'm going to London tomorrow. □ Abita a Londra. He lives in London.

la **lontananza** FEM NOUN
- **in lontananza** in the distance □ Vedo una casa in lontananza. I can see a house in the distance.
- **La lontananza da casa lo faceva soffrire.** Being away from home made him unhappy.

lontano (FEM **lontana**) ADJECTIVE
▷ see also **lontano** ADVERB
1 a long way
□ È lontano. It's a long way.

> LANGUAGE TIP **lontano** is translated by 'far' in questions and negative phrases.

□ Il mare non è lontano da qui. The sea isn't far from here. □ È lontana la casa? Is the house far

from here? □ la città più lontana dal mare the city farthest from the sea
- **La città è ancora molto lontana.** The city is still a long way off.
2 distant
□ paesi lontani distant countries □ Sento delle voci lontane. I can hear distant voices.

lontano ADVERB
▷ see also **lontano** ADJECTIVE
far
□ Abiti lontano dalla scuola? Do you live far from school? □ È più lontano di quanto pensassi. It's farther than I thought.
- **Abita lontano.** He lives a long way from here.
- **da lontano** from a distance □ Da lontano mi sembravi tuo fratello. From a distance you looked like your brother.

lordo (FEM **lorda**) ADJECTIVE
gross *(weight, salary)*

loro PRONOUN
▷ see also **loro** ADJECTIVE
1 they
□ Loro abitano qui. They live here. □ Vengono anche loro? Are they coming too?
- **Non lo sapevano nemmeno loro.** They didn't even know it themselves.
- **Sono loro, apri la porta.** It's them, open the door.
2 them
□ Vado alla festa con loro. I'm going to the party with them. □ Dimmi qualcosa di loro. Tell me something about them. □ Ho spedito loro una cartolina. I sent them a postcard. □ senza di loro without them
3 theirs
□ La nostra casa è più grande della loro. Our house is bigger than theirs. □ Di chi è questo? — È loro. Whose is this? — It's theirs.

loro (FEM+PL **loro**) ADJECTIVE
▷ see also **loro** PRONOUN
their
□ i loro libri their books □ Verranno con la loro macchina. They'll come in their car. □ È colpa loro. It's their fault.
- **un loro amico** a friend of theirs

losco (FEM **losca**, MASC PL **loschi**, FEM PL **losche**) ADJECTIVE
- **un tipo losco** a shady character

la **lotta** FEM NOUN
struggle
□ la lotta per la sopravvivenza the struggle for survival □ la lotta politica the political struggle
- **la lotta contro la droga** the fight against drugs
- **lotta libera** all-in wrestling

lottare VERB [68]
to fight
□ Dobbiamo lottare per i nostri diritti. We must

fight for our rights. □ Ha sempre lottato contro il razzismo. She's always fought against racism.

la **lotteria** FEM NOUN
lottery
■ **vincere alla lotteria** to win the lottery □ Hai mai vinto alla lotteria? Have you ever won the lottery?

la **lozione** FEM NOUN
lotion

il **lucchetto** MASC NOUN
padlock

luccicare VERB [18]
1 to sparkle (crystal, diamond, eyes)
2 to glitter (gold)
3 to twinkle (star)

la **lucciola** FEM NOUN
glow-worm

la **luce** FEM NOUN
light
□ Accendi la luce. Switch the light on.
■ **luce del sole** sunlight
■ **luci di posizione** sidelights

la **lucertola** FEM NOUN
lizard

il **lucidalabbra** (PL i **lucidalabbra**) MASC NOUN
lip gloss

lucidare VERB [68]
to polish

lucido (FEM **lucida**) ADJECTIVE
▷ see also **lucido** NOUN
1 shiny
□ una camicia di raso nero lucido a shiny black satin blouse □ Ha le scarpe più lucide delle tue. His shoes are shinier than yours.
2 lucid
□ È ancora lucido. He's still lucid.

il **lucido** MASC NOUN
▷ see also **lucido** ADJECTIVE
■ **lucido per scarpe** shoe polish

il **lucro** MASC NOUN
■ **a scopo di lucro** for money □ Non lo fa a scopo di lucro. He doesn't do it for money.
■ **organizzazione senza scopo di lucro** non-profit organization

luglio MASC NOUN
July

LANGUAGE TIP In Italian, months are not written with capital letters.

□ in luglio in July

lugubre (FEM **lugubre**) ADJECTIVE
gloomy
□ un'atmosfera lugubre a gloomy atmosphere □ sempre più lugubre gloomier and gloomier

lui PRONOUN
1 he

□ Ha ragione lui. He's right. □ Viene anche lui? Is he coming too?
■ **Non lo sapeva nemmeno lui.** He didn't even know it himself.
2 him
□ Vado alla festa con lui. I'm going to the party with him. □ Dimmi qualcosa di lui. Tell me something about him. □ È lui, apri la porta. It's him, open the door. □ senza di lui without him

la **lumaca** (PL le **lumache**) FEM NOUN
1 slug
2 snail

luminoso (FEM **luminosa**) ADJECTIVE
1 bright
□ Il soggiorno è molto luminoso. The living room is very bright.
2 luminous
■ **un'insegna luminosa** a neon sign

la **luna** FEM NOUN
moon
□ il sole e la luna the sun and the moon
■ **avere la luna** to be in a bad mood □ Oggi ha la luna. He's in a bad mood today.
■ **luna di miele** honeymoon

il **luna park** (PL i **luna park**) MASC NOUN
funfair

il **lunario** MASC NOUN
■ **sbarcare il lunario** to make ends meet □ Riesco a malapena a sbarcare il lunario. I can only just make ends meet.

lunatico (FEM **lunatica**, MASC PL **lunatici**, FEM PL **lunatiche**) ADJECTIVE
temperamental

il **lunedì** (PL i **lunedì**) MASC NOUN
Monday

LANGUAGE TIP In Italian, days are not written with capital letters.

□ L'ho vista lunedì. I saw her on Monday.
■ **di lunedì** on Mondays □ Vado in piscina di lunedì. I go swimming on Mondays.
■ **lunedì scorso** last Monday
■ **lunedì prossimo** next Monday

lunga FEM NOUN
■ **di gran lunga** far and away □ È di gran lunga il migliore. It's far and away the best.
■ **alla lunga** in the end □ Alla lunga si stuferà. He'll get fed up with it in the end.

la **lunghezza** FEM NOUN
length
□ Lunghezza: 20 cm. Length: 20 cm.
■ **La stanza ha tre metri di lunghezza.** The room is three metres long.

lungo (FEM **lunga**, MASC PL **lunghi**, FEM PL **lunghe**) ADJECTIVE, MASC NOUN
▷ see also **lungo** PREPOSITION
long
□ È lungo quattro metri. It's four metres long.
□ Questa gonna è troppo lunga. This skirt is

too long. □ Hanno fatto una lunga passeggiata. They went for a long walk.

■ **a lungo** for a long time □ Abbiamo parlato a lungo. We talked for a long time.

■ **un caffè lungo** a weak coffee

■ **a lungo andare** in the end □ A lungo andare si stuferà. He'll get fed up with it in the end.

■ **in lungo e in largo** everywhere □ L'ho cercato in lungo e in largo. I looked for it everywhere.

lungo PREPOSITION

▷ see also **lungo** ADJECTIVE, NOUN

along

□ Camminava lungo la riva del fiume. He was walking along the river bank.

il **luogo** (PL i **luoghi**) MASC NOUN

place

□ È un luogo sicuro. It's a safe place.

■ **in primo luogo** in the first place

■ **aver luogo** to take place □ L'incontro ha avuto luogo in maggio. The meeting took place in May.

■ **luogo del delitto** scene of the crime

■ **luogo di villeggiatura** holiday resort

■ **luogo comune** cliché

il **lupo** MASC NOUN

wolf

□ Ho visto un lupo. I saw a wolf.

■ **cane lupo** Alsatian

■ **lupo mannaro** werewolf

■ **Ho una fame da lupi.** I'm starving.

■ **In bocca al lupo!** Good luck!

lurido (FEM **lurida**) ADJECTIVE

filthy

□ sempre più lurido filthier and filthier

il **lusso** MASC NOUN

luxury

□ Non posso permettermi il lusso di una vacanza. I can't afford the luxury of a holiday.

■ **di lusso** luxury □ un'auto di lusso a luxury car

lussuoso (FEM **lussuosa**) ADJECTIVE

luxury

□ un albergo lussuoso a luxury hotel

il **lutto** MASC NOUN

loss

□ È stato un grave lutto per il paese. It was a great loss to the country.

■ **essere in lutto** to be in mourning □ È ancora in lutto per suo marito. She's still in mourning for her husband.

Mm

ma CONJUNCTION
but
□ Strano, ma vero. Strange, but true.
■ **Ti dispiace? — Ma no!** Do you mind?
— Of course I don't!
■ **Ma insomma! Vuoi smetterla?** Stop it, for heaven's sake!

macché EXCLAMATION
■ **Sei innamorata di lui? — Macché! È solo un amico.** Are you in love with him?
— Of course not! He's just a friend.
■ **Hai finito il compito? — Macché! Sono ancora a metà.** Have you finished your homework? — You're joking! I've only done half of it.

i **maccheroni** MASC PL NOUN
macaroni *sing*
□ Sono buoni i maccheroni? Is the macaroni nice?

la **macchia** FEM NOUN
stain
□ una macchia di caffè a coffee stain

macchiare VERB [17]
■ **Hai macchiato la tovaglia di caffè.** You've got coffee on the tablecloth.
■ **Mi sono macchiata il vestito.** I've got a mark on my dress.

macchiato (FEM **macchiata**) ADJECTIVE
■ **macchiato di** stained with □ I suoi vestiti erano macchiati di fango. His clothes were stained with mud.
■ **caffè macchiato** espresso coffee with a dash of milk

la **macchina** FEM NOUN
1 car
□ Sali in macchina! Get into the car!
■ **andare in macchina** to go by car □ Ci andate in macchina o in treno? Are you going there by car or by train?
2 machine
□ La macchina funziona premendo il pulsante. The machine works when you press the button.
■ **macchina da cucire** sewing machine
■ **macchina fotografica** camera
■ **macchina da scrivere** typewriter

il **macchinario** MASC NOUN
machinery
■ **macchinari** machinery *sing*

il **macchinista** (PL i **macchinisti**) MASC NOUN
engine driver

la **macedonia** FEM NOUN
fruit salad

il **macellaio,** la **macellaia** MASC/FEM NOUN
butcher

la **macelleria** FEM NOUN
butcher's
□ Sono andato in macelleria. I went to the butcher's.

le **macerie** FEM PL NOUN
rubble *sing*

il **macigno** MASC NOUN
rock

macinare VERB [68]
1 to grind
□ caffè macinato ground coffee
2 to mince *(meat)*
■ **carne macinata** mince

macrobiotico (FEM **macrobiotica**, MASC PL **macrobiotici**, FEM PL **macrobiotiche**) ADJECTIVE
macrobiotic

madornale (FEM **madornale**) ADJECTIVE
■ **un errore madornale** a huge mistake

la **madre** FEM NOUN
mother
□ mia madre my mother □ la madre dei due bambini the mother of the two children □ la madre di Matteo Matteo's mother

la **madrelingua** FEM NOUN
mother tongue
□ Non è di madrelingua inglese. English isn't his mother tongue.

maestà FEM NOUN
■ **Sua Maestà la regina** Her Majesty the Queen

la **maestra** FEM NOUN
teacher
□ maestra di scuola primary school teacher
□ maestra d'asilo nursery school teacher
■ **Scusi, signora maestra...** Excuse me, Miss...

il **maestro** MASC NOUN
teacher
□ maestro di scuola primary school teacher
■ **Scusi, signor maestro...** Excuse me, sir...

m

■ **maestro di sci** ski instructor
■ **maestro d'orchestra** conductor

la **maga** (PL le **maghe**) FEM NOUN
sorceress

magari EXCLAMATION, ADVERB
1 if only
□ Magari fosse vero! If only it were true!
■ **Ti piacerebbe andare a Londra? —
Magari!** Would you like to go to London? —
I certainly would!
2 maybe
□ Saremo in cinque, magari in sei. There will be
five of us, or maybe six.

il **magazzino** MASC NOUN
warehouse
□ Lo tengono in un magazzino. They keep it in
a warehouse.
■ **grandi magazzini** department store *sing*

> LANGUAGE TIP Be careful! **magazzino**
doesn't mean **magazine**.

maggio MASC NOUN
May

> LANGUAGE TIP In Italian, months are not
written with capital letters.

□ in maggio in May

la **maggioranza** FEM NOUN
majority

maggiore (FEM **maggiore**) ADJECTIVE
▷ *see also* **maggiore** NOUN
1 more
□ con maggiore entusiasmo with more
enthusiasm
■ **Le spese sono state maggiori del
previsto.** Costs were higher than expected.
■ **la maggior parte di** most of □ la maggior
parte dei miei amici most of my friends
■ **la maggior parte della gente** most people
■ **la maggiore industria
automobilistica d'Italia** the biggest car
maker in Italy
■ **il maggiore poeta francese del secolo**
the most important French poet of the century
2 older
□ il mio fratello maggiore my older brother
3 major
□ in re maggiore in D major

il/la **maggiore** MASC/FEM NOUN
▷ *see also* **maggiore** ADJECTIVE
1 older *(of two)*
□ la maggiore delle due sorelle the older of the
two sisters
2 oldest *(of more than two)*
□ il maggiore dei tre fratelli the oldest of the
three brothers

maggiorenne (FEM **maggiorenne**) ADJECTIVE
of age
□ Adesso sono maggiorenne. Now I'm of age.
■ **diventare maggiorenne** to come of age

■ **Quando sarai maggiorenne...** When
you're eighteen...

la **magia** FEM NOUN
magic
□ Scomparve come per magia. It disappeared
as if by magic.

magico (FEM **magica**, MASC PL **magici**, FEM PL
magiche) ADJECTIVE
magic

il **magistrato** MASC NOUN
magistrate

la **maglia** FEM NOUN
1 sweater
2 T-shirt
■ **maglia intima** vest
■ **lavorare a maglia** to knit □ Mi piace
lavorare a maglia. I like knitting.

la **maglietta** FEM NOUN
T-shirt

il **maglione** MASC NOUN
sweater

magnetico (FEM **magnetica**, MASC PL
magnetici, FEM PL **magnetiche**) ADJECTIVE
magnetic

magnifico (FEM **magnifica**, MASC PL
magnifici, FEM PL **magnifiche**) ADJECTIVE
wonderful
□ uno scenario magnifico wonderful scenery

il **mago** (PL i **maghi**) MASC NOUN
magician

magro (FEM **magra**) ADJECTIVE
thin
□ È alta e magra. She's tall and thin. □ È più
magra di me. She's thinner than me.
■ **formaggio magro** low-fat cheese

mai ADVERB
never
□ Non esco mai. I never go out. □ Non l'ho mai
visto. I've never seen it.
■ **il più bello che abbia mai visto** the best
I've ever seen

> LANGUAGE TIP **mai** is translated by 'ever' in
questions and negative phrases.

□ Sei mai stato in Russia? Have you ever been
to Russia? □ Non lo aveva mai visto nessuno.
Nobody had ever seen it.
■ **quasi mai** hardly ever □ Non esco quasi
mai. I hardly ever go out. □ Mai, o quasi mai.
Never, or hardly ever.
■ **mai più** never again □ Non lo farò mai più.
I'll never do it again.
■ **Come mai?** Why? □ Come mai sei arrivato
in ritardo? Why were you late? □ Hai fatto
molti errori nel tema, come mai? You made a
lot of mistakes in your essay, why was that?

il **maiale** MASC NOUN
1 pig *(animal, person)*
□ Sei proprio un maiale! You're a real pig!

2 pork
□ una cotoletta di maiale a pork chop

la **mail** (PL le **mail**) FEM NOUN
email

la **maionese** FEM NOUN
mayonnaise

il **mais** MASC NOUN
1 corn
2 sweetcorn

maiuscolo (FEM **maiuscola**) ADJECTIVE
▷ see also **maiuscolo** NOUN
capital
□ a lettere maiuscole in capital letters

il **maiuscolo** MASC NOUN
▷ see also **maiuscolo** ADJECTIVE
■ **in maiuscolo** in capital letters

la **malafede** FEM NOUN
■ **È sicuramente in malafede.** He's
certainly not sincere.
■ **Questo dimostra la tua malafede.** This
shows you aren't sincere.

il **malanno** MASC NOUN
■ **prendersi un malanno** to catch
something □ Mi devo essere preso un
malanno. I must have caught something.

malapena ADVERB
■ **a malapena** hardly □ Ti vedo a malapena.
I can hardly see you.

la **malaria** FEM NOUN
malaria

malato (FEM **malata**) ADJECTIVE
▷ see also **malato** NOUN
1 ill
□ Mio nonno è molto malato. My grandfather
is very ill.
■ **È malata di cuore.** She has heart trouble.
■ **È malato di cancro.** He's got cancer.
2 sick
□ un bambino malato a sick child

il **malato,** la **malata** MASC/FEM NOUN
▷ see also **malato** ADJECTIVE
patient
□ un malato di cancro a cancer patient
■ **i malati di mente** mentally ill people

la **malattia** FEM NOUN
1 illness
□ È morto dopo una lunga malattia. He died
after a long illness.
2 disease
□ una malattia infettiva an infectious disease
□ L'AIDS è una malattia terribile. Aids is a
terrible disease.
■ **mettersi in malattia** to go off sick

la **malavita** FEM NOUN
■ **la malavita** the underworld

malavoglia ADVERB
■ **di malavoglia** reluctantly □ Lo fece di
malavoglia. She did it reluctantly.

maldestro (FEM **maldestra**) ADJECTIVE
clumsy

□ È la persona più maldestra che conosca.
He's the clumsiest person I know.

male ADVERB
▷ see also **male** NOUN
badly
□ Oggi ho giocato male. I played badly today.
■ **Male! Non avresti dovuto farlo.** That
was wrong of you. You shouldn't have done it.
■ **sentirsi male** to feel ill □ Mi sono sentita
male. I felt ill.
■ **capire male** to misunderstand □ Hai
capito male. You've misunderstood.
■ **Mi ha parlato male di te.** He said bad
things about you.

il **male** MASC NOUN
▷ see also **male** ADVERB
evil
□ Questo è il male minore. This is the lesser
evil. □ il bene e il male good and evil
■ **far male** to hurt □ Mi fa male una gamba.
My leg hurts. □ Ahi! Mi hai fatto male! Ouch!
You've hurt me!
■ **Fumare fa male.** Smoking is bad for you.
■ **Ho mal di testa.** I've got a headache.
■ **Ho mal di stomaco.** I've got a stomach ache.
■ **Ho mal di gola.** I've got a sore throat.
■ **soffrire di mal di mare** to get sea sick
■ **soffrire di mal d'auto** to get car sick

maledetto (FEM **maledetta**) ADJECTIVE
damn
□ Spegni quella maledetta radio! Turn off that
damn radio!

maledire VERB [35]
to curse

la **maledizione** FEM NOUN
curse
□ la maledizione del faraone the curse of the
Pharaoh
■ **Maledizione!** Damn!

maleducato (FEM **maleducata**) ADJECTIVE
rude

la **maleducazione** FEM NOUN
bad manners
□ È maleducazione parlare con la bocca piena.
It's bad manners to speak with your mouth full.

il **malessere** MASC NOUN
■ **Ho avuto un leggero malessere.** I didn't
feel very well.

malfamato (FEM **malfamata**) ADJECTIVE
■ **un quartiere malfamato** a rough area

malgrado PREPOSITION
in spite of
□ Malgrado tutto sono ancora amici. They're
still friends, in spite of everything.

maligno (FEM **maligna**) ADJECTIVE
malicious
□ delle insinuazioni maligne malicious gossip
■ **un tumore maligno** a malignant tumour

m

la **malinconia** FEM NOUN
melancholy

malinconico (FEM **malinconica**, MASC PL
malinconici, FEM PL **malinconiche**)
ADJECTIVE
sad
□ Cantava una canzone malinconica. She was
singing a sad song. □ sempre più malinconico
sadder and sadder

malincuore ADVERB
■ **a malincuore** reluctantly □ Gliel'ho dato a
malincuore. I gave it to him reluctantly.

il **malinteso** MASC NOUN
misunderstanding

malizioso (FEM **maliziosa**) ADJECTIVE
mischievous

il **malore** MASC NOUN
■ **È stato colto da malore.** He was
suddenly taken ill.

la **malta** FEM NOUN
mortar

il **maltempo** MASC NOUN
bad weather

maltrattare VERB [68]
to ill-treat
□ Gli ostaggi non sono stati maltrattati. The
hostages weren't ill-treated.

il **malumore** MASC NOUN
■ **di malumore** in a bad mood □ Oggi il capo
è di malumore. The boss is in a bad mood
today.

la **malva** FEM NOUN
mallow

malvagio (FEM **malvagia**, MASC PL **malvagi**,
FEM PL **malvagie**) ADJECTIVE
wicked

malvolentieri ADVERB
unwillingly

la **mamma** FEM NOUN
mum
□ Me l'ha detto la mamma. Mum told me that.
□ la mia mamma my mum
■ **Mamma mia!** Good heavens!

il **mammifero** MASC NOUN
mammal

la **mancanza** FEM NOUN
lack
□ per mancanza di soldi because of lack of
money
■ **sentire la mancanza di qualcuno** to
miss somebody □ Sento la tua mancanza. I
miss you.

mancare VERB [18, AUX **avere** or **essere**]
to be missing
□ Quanti pezzi mancano? How many pieces
are missing?
■ **Mancano ancora dieci sterline.** We're
still ten pounds short.

■ **Fammi sapere se ti manca qualcosa.**
Let me know if you need anything.
■ **Mi manchi.** I miss you.
■ **Manca un quarto alle due.** It's a quarter
to two.

la **mancia** (PL le **mance**) FEM NOUN
tip
■ **dare la mancia a qualcuno** to tip
somebody □ Ha dato la mancia al cameriere.
He tipped the waiter.

la **manciata** FEM NOUN
handful

mancino (FEM **mancina**) ADJECTIVE
left-handed

mandare VERB [68]
to send
■ **mandare qualcosa a qualcuno** to send
somebody something □ Manderò una
cartolina a Loredana. I'll send Loredana a
postcard. □ Mi puoi mandare un po' di denaro?
Can you send me some money?
■ **Glielo manderò.** I'll send it to him.
■ **Mando sempre una cartolina a tutti i
miei amici.** I always send postcards to all my
friends.
■ **mandare in onda** to broadcast

il **mandarino** MASC NOUN
mandarin

il **mandato** MASC NOUN
■ **mandato di arresto** arrest warrant
■ **mandato di perquisizione** search
warrant

la **mandibola** FEM NOUN
jaw

la **mandorla** FEM NOUN
almond

la **mandria** FEM NOUN
herd

il **maneggio** (PL i **maneggi**) MASC NOUN
riding school

le **manette** FEM PL NOUN
handcuffs
■ **mettere le manette a qualcuno** to
handcuff somebody

il **mangianastri** (PL i **mangianastri**) MASC
NOUN
cassette recorder

mangiare VERB [58]
to eat
□ Non mangio carne. I don't eat meat. □ Vuoi
mangiare qualcosa? Would you like something
to eat?
■ **Si mangia bene in quel ristorante.** The
food is good in that restaurant.
■ **fare da mangiare** to cook □ La mamma
sta facendo da mangiare. Mum is cooking.

il **mangime** MASC NOUN
birdseed

2 fish food

la **mania** FEM NOUN
 ■ **Ha la mania dell'ordine.** He's
 obsessively tidy.
 ■ **una delle sue manie** one of his strange
 habits

il **maniaco**, la **maniaca** (MASC PL i
 maniaci, FEM PL le **maniache**) MASC/FEM
 NOUN
 maniac

la **Manica** FEM NOUN
 the Channel
 ■ **il Canale della Manica** the Channel

la **manica** (PL le **maniche**) FEM NOUN
 sleeve
 □ Le maniche sono troppo corte. The sleeves
 are too short.
 ■ **una maglia con le maniche lunghe** a
 long-sleeved sweater

il **manichino** MASC NOUN
 dummy

il **manico** (PL i **manici**) MASC NOUN
1 handle
2 neck *(of guitar)*

il **manicomio** MASC NOUN
 psychiatric hospital

la **maniera** FEM NOUN
 way
 □ in maniera strana in an odd way
 ■ **maniere** manners □ Non conosce le buone
 maniere. Her manners are awful.

la **manifestazione** FEM NOUN
1 demonstration
 □ una manifestazione contro il governo a
 demonstration against the government
2 event
 □ una manifestazione sportiva a sporting event

il **manifesto** MASC NOUN
 poster

la **maniglia** FEM NOUN
 handle

la **mano** (PL le **mani**) FEM NOUN
 hand
 □ Mi sono scottato la mano. I've burnt my
 hand.
 ■ **Mani in alto!** Hands up!
 ■ **stringersi la mano** to shake hands □ I
 due ministri si strinsero la mano. The two
 ministers shook hands.
 ■ **tenersi per mano** to hold hands □ Si
 tenevano per mano. They were holding hands.
 ■ **dare una mano a qualcuno** to give
 somebody a hand □ Dammi una mano, per
 favore. Give me a hand, please.
 ■ **a portata di mano** within reach □ Tienilo
 sempre a portata di mano. Always keep it
 within reach.
 ■ **fatto a mano** handmade
 ■ **di seconda mano** second-hand □ una

macchina di seconda mano a second-hand car
 ■ **una mano di vernice** a coat of paint

la **manodopera** FEM NOUN
 labour

manomettere VERB [59]
 to tamper with

la **manopola** FEM NOUN
1 knob
 □ Girò la manopola per cercare il canale. He
 turned the knob to find the station.
2 mitten

il **manovale** MASC NOUN
 labourer

la **manovella** FEM NOUN
 handle

la **manovra** FEM NOUN
 manoeuvre

la **mansarda** FEM NOUN
 attic

il **mantello** MASC NOUN
 cloak

mantenere VERB [113]
1 to keep
 □ Pensi che manterrà la promessa? Do you
 think she'll keep her promise? □ Cerca di
 mantenere la calma. Try to keep calm.
2 to support
 □ Ha una famiglia da mantenere. He's got a
 family to support.
 ■ **Lavora per mantenersi.** She works for a
 living.

Mantova FEM NOUN
 Mantua
 □ Abito a Mantova. I live in Mantua.

manuale (FEM **manuale**) ADJECTIVE,
 MASC NOUN
 manual
 □ il lavoro manuale manual work □ il manuale
 di istruzioni the instructions manual

il **manubrio** MASC NOUN
 handlebars *pl*

la **manutenzione** FEM NOUN
 maintenance

il **manzo** MASC NOUN
1 beef
 □ uno spezzatino di manzo a beef stew
2 steer *(animal)*

il **mappamondo** MASC NOUN
 globe

la **maratona** FEM NOUN
 marathon

la **marca** (PL le **marche**) FEM NOUN
1 make
 □ Di che marca è il tuo stereo? What make is
 your stereo?
 ■ **capi di marca** designer clothes
2 brand

marcare VERB [18]
1 to mark

m

□ Devi marcare il numero otto. Mark number eight.

2 to score

□ La squadra ha marcato all'ultimo minuto. The team scored in the final minute.

la **marchesa** FEM NOUN
marchioness

la **marcia** (PL le **marce**) FEM NOUN

1 march

2 walking *(sport)*

3 gear

□ Cambiò marcia. She changed gear.
■ **fare marcia indietro** to reverse
■ **Mettiamoci in marcia.** Let's get going.

il **marciapiede** MASC NOUN
pavement

marciare VERB [13]
to march

marcio (FEM **marcia**, MASC PL **marci**, FEM PL **marce**) ADJECTIVE
rotten *(egg, fruit, wood)*

marcire VERB [51, aux **essere**]
to go rotten

il **mare** MASC NOUN

1 sea

□ Il mare era mosso. The sea was rough. □ È morto in mare. He died at sea.
■ **il Mar Adriatico** the Adriatic

2 seaside

□ una casa al mare a house at the seaside
■ **andare al mare** to go to the seaside
□ Sono andati al mare. They went to the seaside.

la **marea** FEM NOUN
■ **alta marea** high tide
■ **bassa marea** low tide □ C'era bassa marea. It was low tide.

la **margarina** FEM NOUN
margarine

la **margherita** FEM NOUN
daisy

il **margine** MASC NOUN
margin

la **marina** FEM NOUN
marina
■ **la marina militare** the navy
■ **la marina mercantile** the merchant navy

il **marinaio** MASC NOUN
sailor

marinare VERB [68]
■ **marinare la scuola** to play truant

la **marionetta** FEM NOUN
puppet

il **marito** MASC NOUN
husband

□ suo marito her husband □ il marito di mia sorella my sister's husband

la **marmellata** FEM NOUN
jam

□ marmellata di fragole strawberry jam
■ **marmellata di arance** marmalade

la **marmitta** FEM NOUN
silencer
■ **marmitta catalitica** catalytic converter

il **marmo** MASC NOUN
marble

□ una statua di marmo a marble statue

marocchino (FEM **marocchina**) ADJECTIVE, MASC/FEM NOUN
Moroccan

il **Marocco** MASC NOUN
Morocco

□ Mi è piaciuto molto il Marocco. I really liked Morocco. □ Andremo in Marocco quest'estate. We're going to Morocco this summer.

marrone (FEM **marrone**) ADJECTIVE
brown

> **LANGUAGE TIP** Be careful! **marrone** doesn't mean **maroon**.

il **marsupio** MASC NOUN

1 pouch *(of kangaroo)*

2 bumbag

il **martedì** (PL i **martedì**) MASC NOUN
Tuesday

> **LANGUAGE TIP** In Italian, days are not written with capital letters.

□ L'ho vista martedì. I saw her on Tuesday.
■ **di martedì** on Tuesdays □ Vado in piscina di martedì. I go swimming on Tuesdays.
■ **martedì scorso** last Tuesday
■ **martedì prossimo** next Tuesday
■ **martedì grasso** Shrove Tuesday

> **DID YOU KNOW...?**
> **martedì grasso** is the last day of the Italian **Carnevale**, which begins at the end of January.

il **martello** MASC NOUN
hammer

il **marzapane** MASC NOUN
marzipan

marzo MASC NOUN
March

> **LANGUAGE TIP** In Italian, months are not written with capital letters.

□ in marzo in March

il **mascara** (PL i **mascara**) MASC NOUN
mascara

la **mascella** FEM NOUN
jaw

la **maschera** FEM NOUN
mask

□ una maschera di carnevale a carnival mask □ Ho comprato la maschera e le pinne. I bought a mask and flippers.
■ **vestirsi in maschera** to wear fancy dress
■ **un ballo in maschera** a fancy dress ball

mascherare VERB [68]
to hide *(feelings, fear)*

Italian-English

maschile (FEM **maschile**) ADJECTIVE

1 male
□ una voce maschile a male voice □ Sesso: maschile. Sex: male.

2 masculine
□ un nome maschile a masculine noun

il **maschilista** (PL i **maschilisti**) MASC NOUN
male chauvinist

il **maschio** MASC NOUN
▷ see also **maschio** ADJECTIVE

1 boy
□ Hanno un maschio e una femmina. They've got a boy and a girl.

2 male
□ un maschio bianco a white male
■ **i maschi** the men

maschio (FEM **maschia**) ADJECTIVE
▷ see also **maschio** NOUN
male
□ i miei colleghi maschi my male colleagues

la **massa** FEM NOUN
■ **una massa di** masses of □ una massa di persone masses of people
■ **di massa** mass □ turismo di massa mass tourism

il **massacro** MASC NOUN
massacre

il **massaggio** MASC NOUN
massage

massiccio (FEM **massiccia**, MASC PL **massicci**, FEM PL **massicce**) ADJECTIVE
■ **oro massiccio** solid gold
■ **legno massiccio** solid wood

massimo (FEM **massima**) ADJECTIVE
▷ see also **massimo** NOUN
maximum
□ la temperatura massima the maximum temperature
■ **È una questione della massima importanza.** It's a question of the greatest importance.

il **massimo** MASC NOUN
▷ see also **massimo** ADJECTIVE
■ **al massimo** at the most □ Può portare al massimo cinque persone. It can take five people at the most.
■ **Cerca di impegnarti al massimo.** Try to do your best.

il **masso** MASC NOUN
rock
□ 'Attenzione! Caduta massi.' 'Beware! Falling rocks.'

masticare VERB [18]
to chew
■ **gomma da masticare** chewing gum

la **matematica** FEM NOUN
maths sing
□ È brava in matematica. She's good at maths.

il **materassino** MASC NOUN
mat (for sport)
■ **materassino gonfiabile** airbed

il **materasso** MASC NOUN
mattress

la **materia** FEM NOUN

1 subject
□ È una materia difficile. It's a difficult subject.

2 material
■ **materie prime** raw materials

il **materiale** MASC NOUN
material
□ Sto raccogliendo materiale per il mio progetto. I'm collecting material for my project.
■ **materiale da costruzione** building materials pl

la **maternità** FEM NOUN
maternity
□ reparto maternità maternity ward
■ **essere in maternità** to be on maternity leave

materno (FEM **materna**) ADJECTIVE
maternal
□ l'istinto materno the maternal instinct
■ **i miei nonni materni** my mother's parents
■ **la mia lingua materna** my mother tongue
■ **scuola materna** nursery school

la **matita** FEM NOUN
pencil
■ **a matita** in pencil □ Scrivi le note a matita. Write your notes in pencil. □ un disegno a matita a pencil drawing

la **matrigna** FEM NOUN
stepmother

matrimoniale (FEM **matrimoniale**) ADJECTIVE
■ **una camera matrimoniale** a double room
■ **un letto matrimoniale** a double bed

il **matrimonio** MASC NOUN

1 marriage
□ dopo dieci anni di matrimonio after ten years of marriage

2 wedding
□ Non mi hanno invitato al matrimonio. They didn't invite me to the wedding.

la **mattina** FEM NOUN
morning
■ **di mattina** in the morning □ alle sette di mattina at seven in the morning
■ **domani mattina** tomorrow morning
■ **ogni mattina** every morning

matto (FEM **matta**) ADJECTIVE
mad
□ Sei matto! You're mad! □ sempre più matto madder and madder

m

■ **diventare matto** to go mad □ Sto
diventando matta! I'm going mad!

■ **far diventare matto qualcuno** to drive
somebody mad □ Mi ha fatto diventare matto.
He drove me mad.

■ **andare matto per** to be mad about □ Va
matto per il calcio. He's mad about football.

il **mattone** MASC NOUN
brick

□ un muro di mattoni a brick wall

■ **Questo libro è un mattone.** This book is
really hard going.

la **mattonella** FEM NOUN
tile

la **maturità** FEM NOUN

■ **esame di maturità** school-leaving
examination

maturo (FEM **matura**) ADJECTIVE
1 ripe

□ una pesca matura a ripe peach
2 mature

□ È molto matura per la sua età. She's very
mature for her age.

la **mazza** FEM NOUN
1 bat (baseball)
2 club (golf)

la **mazzetta** FEM NOUN
1 bundle (of banknotes)
2 bribe

il **mazzo** MASC NOUN
bunch

□ un mazzo di fiori a bunch of flowers □ un
mazzo di chiavi a bunch of keys

■ **un mazzo di carte** a pack of cards

me PRONOUN
me

□ Vieni con me! Come with me! □ senza di me
without me □ Dopo di me tocca a te. It's your
turn after me. □ È alta come me. She's as tall
as me. □ Me la dai? Will you give it to me?

il **meccanico** (PL i **meccanici**) MASC NOUN
mechanic

□ Fa il meccanico. He is a mechanic.

■ **Devo portare la macchina dal
meccanico.** I've got to take my car to the
garage.

il **meccanismo** MASC NOUN
mechanism

la **medaglia** FEM NOUN
medal

□ Ha vinto una medaglia d'oro. He won a gold
medal.

medesimo (FEM **medesima**) ADJECTIVE
same

□ Mi ha detto le medesime cose. He said the
same things to me.

la **media** FEM NOUN
average

□ al di sopra della media above average □ al di
sotto della media below average □ con la media
dell'otto with an average of eight out of ten

■ **in media** on average □ Guadagna in media
mille euro al mese. On average she earns a
thousand euros a month.

■ **Abbiamo fatto in media settanta
chilometri all'ora.** We did an average of
seventy kilometres an hour.

mediante PREPOSITION
by means of

medicare VERB [18]
1 to treat (patient)

□ La medicò e la rimandò a casa. He treated
her and sent her home.
2 to dress (wound)

□ Gli medicò la ferita. She dressed his wound.

la **medicina** FEM NOUN
medicine

□ una medicina contro la tosse a cough
medicine □ Voglio studiare medicina. I want to
study medicine.

il **medico** (PL i **medici**) MASC NOUN
▷ see also **medico** ADJECTIVE
doctor

□ il medico di famiglia the family doctor □ Chi
è il tuo medico curante? Who's your doctor?

medico (FEM **medica**, MASC PL **medici**, FEM PL
mediche) ADJECTIVE
▷ see also **medico** NOUN
medical sing

□ cure mediche medical treatment

■ **fare una visita medica** to have a medical
examination □ Ha fatto una visita medica. He
had a medical examination.

medio (FEM **media**) ADJECTIVE
average

□ una persona di statura media a person of
average height

■ **il dito medio** the middle finger

■ **il Medio Oriente** the Middle East

mediocre (FEM **mediocre**) ADJECTIVE
mediocre

□ Il suo ultimo disco è mediocre. His latest
record is mediocre.

■ **un prodotto di qualità mediocre** a
poor quality product

il **medioevo** MASC NOUN
Middle Ages pl

□ nel medioevo in the Middle Ages

mediterraneo (FEM **mediterranea**)
ADJECTIVE
Mediterranean

■ **il mar Mediterraneo** the Mediterranean

la **medusa** FEM NOUN
jellyfish

il **mega** (PL i **mega**) MASC NOUN
meg (megabyte)

meglio ADVERB, ADJECTIVE
  better
    □ Sto meglio. I feel better. □ È molto meglio così. It's much better like this. □ Franca gioca meglio di lui. Franca plays better than him. □ È meglio che tu te ne vada. You'd better leave. □ meglio tardi che mai better late than never

la **mela** FEM NOUN
  apple
    □ una torta di mele an apple tart
    ■ **mela cotogna** quince

la **melagrana** FEM NOUN
  pomegranate

la **melanzana** FEM NOUN
  aubergine

il **melo** MASC NOUN
  apple tree

la **melodia** FEM NOUN
  tune

il **melone** MASC NOUN
  melon

il **membro** MASC NOUN
  member
    □ un membro del partito socialista a member of the Socialist Party

la **memoria** FEM NOUN
  memory
    □ Ho una buona memoria. I've got a good memory. □ Non ho molta memoria. I haven't got a good memory. □ Il mio computer non ha abbastanza memoria. My computer hasn't got enough memory.
    ■ **imparare qualcosa a memoria** to learn something by heart □ Ha imparato a memoria la poesia. She learnt the poem by heart.

il/la **mendicante** MASC/FEM NOUN
  beggar

meno ADVERB, ADJECTIVE
  ▷ see also **meno** PREPOSITION
  1 less
    □ Dovresti mangiare meno. You should eat less. □ La birra costa meno in Italia. Beer costs less in Italy. □ C'è meno lavoro. There's less work.
    ■ **di meno** less □ Ho speso di meno. I spent less.
    ■ **quello che mi è piaciuto di meno** the one I liked least
    ■ **più o meno** more or less
    ■ **meno... di** less... than □ Sono meno stanca di lei. I'm less tired than her.
    ■ **Ha due anni meno di me.** He's two years younger than me.
    ■ **Sono meno brava di te in matematica.** I'm not as good at maths as you.
    ■ **il meno intelligente** the least intelligent
  2 fewer
    □ Quest'anno ci sono meno turisti. There are fewer tourists this year.

  3 minus
    □ Quattro meno uno fa tre. Four minus one makes three. □ meno tre gradi minus three degrees
    ■ **Sono le tre meno un quarto.** It's a quarter to three.
    ■ **Meno male!** Thank goodness!

meno PREPOSITION
  ▷ see also **meno** ADVERB, ADJECTIVE
  except
    □ Ci siamo tutti meno lui. Everybody's here except him.
    ■ **a meno che** unless □ Ci andrò, a meno che non piova. I'll go, unless it rains.

la **menopausa** FEM NOUN
  menopause
    ■ **essere in menopausa** to be going through the menopause

la **mensa** FEM NOUN
  canteen

mensile (FEM **mensile**) ADJECTIVE
  monthly
    □ un abbonamento mensile a monthly ticket

la **mensola** FEM NOUN
  shelf

la **menta** FEM NOUN
  mint
    ■ **una caramella alla menta** a mint

mentale (FEM **mentale**) ADJECTIVE
  mental

la **mentalità** (PL le **mentalità**) FEM NOUN
    ■ **Ha una mentalità aperta.** He's open-minded.
    ■ **Ha una mentalità ristretta.** He's narrow-minded.

la **mente** FEM NOUN
  mind
    □ Ha una mente logica. He's got a logical mind. □ Ha qualcosa in mente. He's got something in mind.
    ■ **Ma cosa ti salta in mente?** You must be crazy!

mentire VERB [41]
  to lie
    □ Mente. He's lying.

il **mento** MASC NOUN
  chin

mentre CONJUNCTION
  while
    □ È successo mentre eri fuori. It happened while you were out.

il **menù** (PL i **menù**) MASC NOUN
  menu
    □ menù turistico tourist menu □ Potrei avere il menù? Could I have the menu?

la **menzogna** FEM NOUN
  lie
    □ dire menzogne to tell lies

la **meraviglia** FEM NOUN
surprise
□ con mia grande meraviglia to my great
surprise
■ **Tutto va a meraviglia.** Everything is going
perfectly.
■ **È una meraviglia!** It's wonderful!

meravigliarsi VERB [25, aux **essere**]
to be surprised
□ Mi meraviglio di te! I'm surprised at you!

meraviglioso (FEM **meravigliosa**) ADJECTIVE
wonderful

il **mercatino** MASC NOUN
local street market

il **mercato** MASC NOUN
market
□ Vado al mercato. I'm going to the market.

la **merce** FEM NOUN
goods pl

il **mercoledì** (PL i **mercoledì**) MASC NOUN
Wednesday

> **LANGUAGE TIP** In Italian, days are not
> written with capital letters.

□ L'ho vista mercoledì. I saw her on
Wednesday.
■ **di mercoledì** on Wednesdays □ Vado in
piscina di mercoledì. I go swimming on
Wednesdays.
■ **mercoledì scorso** last Wednesday
■ **mercoledì prossimo** next Wednesday

la **merenda** FEM NOUN
snack
□ Ragazzi, venite a fare merenda. Children,
come and have a snack.

meridionale (FEM **meridionale**) ADJECTIVE
▷ see also **meridionale** NOUN
southern

il/la **meridionale** MASC/FEM NOUN
▷ see also **meridionale** ADJECTIVE
■ **i meridionali** people from Southern Italy

il **meridione** MASC NOUN
■ **il meridione** Southern Italy

la **meringa** (PL le **meringhe**) FEM NOUN
meringue

meritare VERB [68]
1 to deserve
□ Meriti un premio. You deserve a prize.
2 to be worth
□ Non merita neanche parlarne. It's not worth
talking about.

il **merito** MASC NOUN
■ **È merito suo se hanno vinto.** It's thanks
to him that they won.
■ **in merito a** with regard to

il **merletto** MASC NOUN
lace

il **merlo** MASC NOUN
blackbird

il **merluzzo** MASC NOUN
cod

meschino (FEM **meschina**) ADJECTIVE
mean
■ **fare una figura meschina** to look silly

mescolare VERB [68]
to mix
□ Mescolate la farina e lo zucchero. Mix the
flour and sugar.

il **mese** MASC NOUN
month
□ fra due mesi in two months
□ alla fine del mese at the end of the
month

la **messa** FEM NOUN
Mass
□ Andiamo a messa di domenica. We go to
Mass on Sundays.

messaggiarsi VERB [56]
to text
□ Messaggiamoci. We'll text each other.

il **messaggio** MASC NOUN
message
□ Vuole lasciare un messaggio? Would you like
to leave a message?
■ **messaggio di posta elettronica** email

il **Messico** MASC NOUN
Mexico
□ Mi è piaciuto molto il Messico. I really liked
Mexico.
□ Quest'estate andremo in Messico. We're
going to Mexico this summer.

il **mestiere** MASC NOUN
job
□ un mestiere difficile a difficult job
■ **Cosa fa tuo padre di mestiere?** What
does your father do?

il **mestolo** MASC NOUN
ladle

le **mestruazioni** FEM PL NOUN
period sing
□ Ho le mestruazioni. I've got my period.

la **meta** FEM NOUN
destination
□ Finalmente giunsero alla meta. They finally
reached their destination.
■ **senza meta** aimlessly □ Vagava senza
meta. He was wandering aimlessly.

la **metà** (PL le **metà**) FEM NOUN
half
□ Dammene metà. Give me half. □ Dividilo a
metà. Divide it in half. □ Lo vendono a metà
prezzo. They're selling it at half price. □ le due
metà the two halves □ Facciamo a metà. Let's
go halves.
■ **a metà strada** halfway □ Incontriamoci a
metà strada. Let's meet halfway.

il **metallo** MASC NOUN
metal
□ un portacenere di metallo a metal ashtray

il **metano** MASC NOUN
methane *(gas)*
■ **riscaldamento a metano** gas heating

il **metodo** MASC NOUN
method

il **metro** MASC NOUN
1 metre
□ un metro quadrato a square metre □ un metro cubo a cubic metre
2 tape measure

la **metropolitana** FEM NOUN
underground
□ Ha preso la metropolitana. He took the underground.

mettere VERB [59]
1 to put
□ Dove hai messo la mia penna? Where did you put my pen? □ Hai messo i bambini a letto? Have you put the children to bed? □ Metterò un annuncio sul giornale. I'll put an advert in the paper.
■ **Mettiti là e aspetta.** Wait there.
■ **Quanto tempo ci hai messo?** How long did it take you?
■ **mettersi a sedere** to sit down
2 to put on
□ Mettiti il maglione. Put your jumper on.
□ Si mise le scarpe. He put his shoes on.
■ **Non metto più quelle scarpe.** I don't wear those shoes any more.
3 to set
□ Hai messo la sveglia? Have you set the alarm?
■ **mettersi a fare qualcosa** to start to do something □ Si mise a piangere. She started to cry.

la **mezzanotte** FEM NOUN
midnight
□ a mezzanotte at midnight

mezzo (FEM **mezza**) ADJECTIVE
▷ *see also* **mezzo** NOUN
half
□ mezza bottiglia di vino half a bottle of wine □ un chilo e mezzo one and a half kilos □ Sono le due e mezza. It's half past two. □ mezz'ora half an hour
■ **un uomo di mezza età** a middle-aged man

il **mezzo** MASC NOUN
▷ *see also* **mezzo** ADJECTIVE
1 middle
□ Era in mezzo alla strada. He was in the middle of the road. □ il sedile di mezzo the middle seat
2 means *sing*

□ un mezzo di trasporto a means of transport
■ **i mezzi pubblici** public transport
■ **per mezzo di** by means of □ per mezzo della nuova tecnologia by means of new technology

il **mezzogiorno** MASC NOUN
midday
□ a mezzogiorno at midday
■ **È mezzogiorno e mezzo.** It's half past twelve.
■ **Il Mezzogiorno** the South of Italy

mi PRONOUN
▷ *see also* **mi** NOUN
1 me
□ Mi aiuti? Could you help me? □ Dammi quel libro. Give me that book. □ Mi scusi! Excuse me! □ Puoi prestarmi la penna? Could you lend me your pen? □ Mi chiamava. He was calling to me. □ Mi sembrava una buona idea. It seemed a good idea to me. □ Mi ha sorriso. He smiled at me. □ Aspettami! Wait for me!
2 myself
□ Mi sono divertita. I enjoyed myself. □ Mi sono fatto male. I've hurt myself. □ Mi guardai allo specchio. I looked at myself in the mirror.
■ **Mi sono lavato i denti.** I brushed my teeth.

il **mi** (PL i **mi**) MASC NOUN
▷ *see also* **mi** PRONOUN
E *(musical note)*

miagolare VERB [68]
to miaow

mica ADVERB
■ **Non ci crederai mica!** You won't believe it!
■ **Non sono mica stanco.** I'm not a bit tired.
■ **Non sarà mica partito?** He wouldn't have left, would he?

la **miccia** (PL le **micce**) FEM NOUN
fuse
■ **accendere la miccia** to light the fuse

il **microblog** (PL i **microblog**) MASC NOUN
microblog

il **microfono** MASC NOUN
microphone

il **microscopio** MASC NOUN
microscope

il **midollo** MASC NOUN
■ **midollo osseo** bone marrow
■ **midollo spinale** spinal cord

il **miele** MASC NOUN
honey

il **migliaio** (FEM PL le **migliaia**) MASC NOUN
about a thousand
□ un migliaio di persone about a thousand people □ due migliaia di persone about two thousand people

m

■ **parecchie migliaia di copie** several thousand copies

■ **L'ho fatto migliaia di volte.** I've done it thousands of times.

il **miglio** (FEM PL le **miglia**) MASC NOUN
mile

□ Camminò per miglia e miglia. She walked for miles and miles.

■ **miglio marino** nautical mile

il **miglioramento** MASC NOUN
improvement

□ Non c'è ancora nessun miglioramento. There hasn't been any improvement yet.

migliorare VERB [68, aux **avere** or **essere**]
to improve

□ Partiremo domani, se il tempo migliora. We'll set off tomorrow, if the weather improves. □ Fa un corso per migliorare il suo inglese. He's doing a course to improve his English.

migliore (FEM **migliore**) ADJECTIVE, MASC/FEM NOUN

1 better

□ molto migliore much better □ Il libro è migliore del film. The book is better than the film.

2 best

□ la migliore della classe the best in the class □ Questo è il miglior ristorante della città. This is the best restaurant in town.

il **mignolo** MASC NOUN

1 little finger

2 little toe

-mila SUFFIX
thousand

■ **tremila sterline** three thousand pounds

■ **seicentomila** six hundred thousand

Milano FEM NOUN
Milan

□ Domani vado a Milano. I'm going to Milan tomorrow. □ Abitiamo a Milano. We live in Milan.

miliardario (FEM **miliardaria**) ADJECTIVE
billionaire

□ È miliardario. He's a billionaire.

il **miliardo** MASC NOUN
thousand million

□ un miliardo di euro one thousand million euros □ tre miliardi di euro three thousand million euros

■ **miliardi di persone** millions of people

il **milione** MASC NOUN
million

□ un milione di dollari one million dollars □ due milioni di sterline two million pounds □ parecchi milioni di euro several million euros

■ **milioni di persone** millions of people

militare (FEM **militare**) ADJECTIVE
▷ see also **militare** NOUN
military

□ il servizio militare military service

DID YOU KNOW...?
Until recently young men in Italy had to do military service.

■ **un ufficiale militare** an army officer

il **militare** MASC NOUN
▷ see also **militare** ADJECTIVE
serviceman

□ due militari two servicemen

■ **fare il militare** to do one's military service

□ Non ho fatto il militare. I didn't do military service.

mille (FEM **mille**) ADJECTIVE
a thousand

□ mille persone a thousand people

■ **Grazie mille.** Thank you very much.

il **millimetro** MASC NOUN
millimetre

la **milza** FEM NOUN
spleen

mimetizzarsi VERB [56]
to camouflage oneself

il **mimo** MASC NOUN
mime

la **mimosa** FEM NOUN
mimosa

la **mina** FEM NOUN
mine

la **minaccia** (PL le **minacce**) FEM NOUN
threat

□ una minaccia per l'ambiente a threat to the environment

■ **fare delle minacce a qualcuno** to threaten somebody

minacciare VERB [13]
to threaten

□ Mi minacciò con la pistola. He threatened me with a gun. □ Lo hanno minacciato di morte. They threatened to kill him.

■ **Minaccia di piovere.** It looks like rain.

il **minatore** MASC NOUN
miner

minerale (FEM **minerale**) ADJECTIVE, MASC NOUN
mineral

□ acqua minerale mineral water □ un minerale a mineral

la **minestra** FEM NOUN
soup

□ minestra di verdura vegetable soup

la **miniera** FEM NOUN
mine

□ una miniera d'oro a gold mine □ una miniera di carbone a coal mine

la **minigonna** FEM NOUN
miniskirt

minimo (FEM **minima**) ADJECTIVE
▷ see also **minimo** NOUN

1 minimum
□ la temperatura minima the minimum temperature

2 minimal
□ ad un costo minimo at a minimal cost
■ **La differenza è minima.** There's hardly any difference.

3 slightest
□ Non ne ho la minima idea. I haven't the slightest idea. □ Non c'è stato il minimo cambiamento. There hasn't been the slightest change.

il **minimo** MASC NOUN
▷ see also **minimo** ADJECTIVE
minimum
□ il minimo indispensabile the bare minimum
■ **È il minimo che tu possa fare.** It's the least you can do.

il **ministero** MASC NOUN
ministry

il **ministro** MASC NOUN
minister
■ **il ministro della Pubblica Istruzione** the Minister of Education

la **minoranza** FEM NOUN
minority

minore (FEM **minore**) ADJECTIVE
▷ see also **minore** NOUN

1 less
□ con minore entusiasmo with less enthusiasm

2 lower
□ Le spese sono state minori del previsto. Costs were lower than expected.
■ **un numero minore di studenti** a smaller number of students

3 younger
□ il mio fratello minore my younger brother

4 minor
□ le opere minori di Shakespeare Shakespeare's minor works □ in do minore in C minor

il/la **minore** MASC/FEM NOUN
▷ see also **minore** ADJECTIVE

1 younger (between two)
□ la minore delle due sorelle the younger of the two sisters

2 youngest (between more than two)
□ il minore dei tre fratelli the youngest of the three brothers

3 minor (underage)
■ **vietato ai minori di 18 anni** 18 certificate

minorenne (FEM **minorenne**) ADJECTIVE
under age
□ Mia sorella è minorenne. My sister is under age.

minuscolo (FEM **minuscola**) ADJECTIVE
▷ see also **minuscolo** NOUN

1 small
□ a lettere minuscole in small letters

2 tiny
□ un appartamento minuscolo a tiny flat

il **minuscolo** MASC NOUN
▷ see also **minuscolo** ADJECTIVE
■ **in minuscolo** in small letters

il **minuto** MASC NOUN
minute
□ tra pochi minuti in a few minutes

mio (FEM **mia**, MASC PL **miei**, FEM PL **mie**)
ADJECTIVE
▷ see also **mio** PRONOUN
my
□ i miei libri my books □ È colpa mia. It's my fault.
■ **un mio amico** a friend of mine

mio (FEM **mia**, MASC PL **miei**, FEM PL **mie**)
PRONOUN
▷ see also **mio** ADJECTIVE
mine
□ È questo il tuo cappotto? — No, il mio è nero. Is this your coat? — No, mine's black. □ La tua casa è più grande della mia. Your house is bigger than mine. □ Di chi è questo? — È mio. Whose is this? — It's mine.
■ **i miei** my parents □ Vivo con i miei. I live with my parents.

miope (FEM **miope**) ADJECTIVE
short-sighted

la **mira** FEM NOUN
■ **prendere la mira** to take aim
■ **prendere di mira qualcuno** to target somebody

il **miracolo** MASC NOUN
miracle

mirare VERB [68]
■ **mirare a qualcosa** to aim at something
□ Mirai al bersaglio e sparai. I aimed at the target and fired.

il **mirino** MASC NOUN
1 viewfinder
2 sight (on firearm)

il **mirtillo** MASC NOUN
bilberry

la **miseria** FEM NOUN
poverty
□ Vivono nella miseria. They live in poverty.
■ **Porca miseria!** Bloody hell! (informal)

il **missile** MASC NOUN
missile

il **missionario,** la **missionaria** MASC/FEM
NOUN
missionary

misterioso (FEM **misteriosa**) ADJECTIVE
mysterious

il **mistero** MASC NOUN
mystery

misto (FEM **mista**) ADJECTIVE
mixed
□ un'insalata mista a mixed salad □ una

m

grigliata mista a mixed grill □ una scuola mista a mixed school

la **misura** FEM NOUN

1 size
□ Ha una misura più piccola? Have you got a smaller size?

2 measurement
□ Può prendermi le misure? Can you take my measurements?
■ **fatto su misura** made-to-measure □ un completo fatto su misura a made-to-measure suit
■ **unità di misura** unit of measurement

3 measure
□ misure di sicurezza safety measures

misurare VERB [68]
to measure
□ Misura la distanza fra questi due punti. Measure the distance between these two points.
■ **Quanto misura questa stanza?** How big is this room?

mite (FEM **mite**) ADJECTIVE
mild
□ un clima mite a mild climate

il **mito** MASC NOUN
myth

la **mitologia** FEM NOUN
mythology

il **mitra** (PL i **mitra**) MASC NOUN
machine gun

il/la **mittente** MASC/FEM NOUN
sender
□ Rispedire al mittente. Return to sender.

il **mobile** MASC NOUN
■ **un mobile** a piece of furniture
■ **i mobili** the furniture sing □ un negozio di mobili a furniture shop

la **moda** FEM NOUN
fashion
□ una sfilata di moda a fashion show
■ **essere di moda** to be in fashion □ È di moda il nero. Black is in fashion.
■ **essere fuori moda** to be out of fashion

il **modello**, la **modella** MASC/FEM NOUN
model

moderno (FEM **moderna**) ADJECTIVE
modern

modesto (FEM **modesta**) ADJECTIVE
modest

la **modifica** (PL le **modifiche**) FEM NOUN

1 modification
□ Sono necessarie alcune modifiche. Some modifications need to be made.

2 alteration

modificare VERB [18]
to modify

il **modo** MASC NOUN

1 way
□ Lo farò a modo mio. I'll do it my own way.

□ in modo strano in an odd way
■ **in modo eccessivo** excessively
■ **in questo modo** this way □ Fallo in questo modo. Do it this way.
■ **ad ogni modo** anyway □ Ad ogni modo, non ha importanza. Anyway, it doesn't matter.
■ **in qualche modo** somehow □ In qualche modo riuscirò a farlo. I'll manage it somehow.
■ **in modo da** so as to □ Entrai in punta di piedi in modo da non disturbarlo. I went in on tiptoe so as not to disturb him.
■ **fare in modo di** to try to □ Fate in modo di tornare per le cinque. Try to be back by five o'clock.
■ **Che modi!** What bad manners!
■ **un modo di dire** an expression

2 mood (in grammar)

il **modulo** MASC NOUN
form
□ Riempite il modulo in stampatello. Fill in the form in block letters.

la **moglie** FEM NOUN
wife
□ Questa è mia moglie Anna. This is my wife Anna.

il **molare** MASC NOUN
molar

molestare VERB [68]

1 to torment
□ Non molestare quel povero cane. Don't torment that poor dog.

2 to sexually harass

le **molestie** FEM PL NOUN
■ **molestie sessuali** sexual harassment sing

la **molla** FEM NOUN
spring
□ una molla rotta a broken spring

mollare VERB [68]

1 to chuck
□ Ha mollato il lavoro. She's chucked her job.

2 to dump
□ Ha mollato il suo ragazzo. She's dumped her boyfriend.

3 to give up
□ Non mollare proprio adesso! Don't give up now!
■ **mollare un ceffone a qualcuno** to give somebody a slap □ Gli mollò un ceffone. She gave him a slap.

molle (FEM **molle**) ADJECTIVE
soft

la **molletta** FEM NOUN

1 clothes peg

2 hairgrip

la **mollica** FEM NOUN
soft part (of bread)

il **molo** MASC NOUN
jetty

moltiplicare VERB [18]
  to multiply
    □ Moltiplicate otto per cinque. Multiply eight by five.

la **moltiplicazione** FEM NOUN
  multiplication

molto (FEM **molta**) ADJECTIVE
  ▷ see also **molto** ADVERB
1 a lot of
    □ Hai molti libri. You've got a lot of books.
    □ Bevo molta acqua. I drink a lot of water.
    □ C'era molta gente. There were a lot of people.
2 much
    □ Non ho molto denaro. I haven't got much money. □ Hai ancora molto lavoro da fare? Have you got much work left to do?
3 many
    □ Non ha molti amici. He hasn't got many friends. □ Hai visto molti film ultimamente? — Non molti. Have you seen many films lately? — No, not many.

molto ADVERB
  ▷ see also **molto** ADJECTIVE
1 a lot
    □ Leggo molto. I read a lot. □ Viaggi molto? Do you travel a lot?
    ■ **Ci vorrà molto?** Will it take long?
2 much
    □ Non esco molto. I don't go out much.
    □ Chiara è molto più alta di me. Chiara is much taller than me.
    ■ **molto meglio** much better □ Ora mi sento molto meglio. I feel much better now.
3 very
    □ L'ha fatto molto bene. He did it very well.
    □ Sono molto stanco. I'm very tired.
    ■ **moltissimo** very much □ Mi sono divertita moltissimo. I enjoyed myself very much.
    ■ **Mi dispiace moltissimo.** I'm terribly sorry.

momentaneamente ADVERB
  at the moment
    □ È momentaneamente assente. She's not here at the moment.

il **momento** MASC NOUN
  moment
    □ Un momento, per favore! Just a moment please!
    ■ **in questo momento** at the moment □ In questo momento è al telefono. He's on the phone at the moment.
    ■ **da un momento all'altro** any moment now □ Può arrivare da un momento all'altro. He'll be here any moment now.
    ■ **È un momento difficile.** It's a difficult time.

la **monaca** (PL le **monache**) FEM NOUN
  nun

Monaco FEM NOUN
    ■ **Monaco di Baviera** Munich
    ■ **il Principato di Monaco** Monaco

il **monaco** (PL i **monaci**) MASC NOUN
  monk

la **monarchia** FEM NOUN
  monarchy

il **monastero** MASC NOUN
1 monastery
2 convent

mondiale (FEM **mondiale**) ADJECTIVE
  world
    □ la seconda guerra mondiale the Second World War
    ■ **i mondiali di calcio** the World Cup

il **mondo** MASC NOUN
  world
    □ il migliore del mondo the best in the world
    □ in tutto il mondo all over the world

la **moneta** FEM NOUN
1 coin
    □ una moneta da due euro a two euro coin
2 change
    □ Non ho moneta. I haven't got any change.
3 currency
    □ La sterlina è una moneta forte. The pound is a strong currency.

la **mongolfiera** FEM NOUN
  hot-air balloon

il **monitor** (PL i **monitor**) MASC NOUN
  monitor

il **monolocale** MASC NOUN
  studio flat

il **monopattino** MASC NOUN
  scooter

il **monopolio** MASC NOUN
  monopoly

monotono (FEM **monotona**) ADJECTIVE
  monotonous

il **montaggio** (PL i **montaggi**) MASC NOUN
1 assembly (of pieces)
2 editing (of film)

la **montagna** FEM NOUN
1 mountain
    □ È la montagna più alta della Scozia. It's the highest mountain in Scotland. □ un paesino di montagna a mountain village
2 mountains pl
    □ Mi piace la montagna. I like the mountains.
    □ Andremo in vacanza in montagna. We're going to the mountains for our holiday. □ Ha una casa in montagna. He's got a house in the mountains.
    ■ **montagne russe** roller coaster sing

montare VERB [68, aux **avere** or **essere**]
1 to assemble
    □ Ha montato l'armadio da solo. He assembled the wardrobe himself.

163

■ **Montarono la tenda vicino al lago.** They pitched their tent near the lake.

2 to whip *(cream)*

■ **montare a neve** to whisk until stiff

□ Montate a neve gli albumi. Whisk the egg whites until stiff.

■ **montare in 1** *(car)* to get into **2** *(train, bike)* to get on

■ **montare su una scala** to climb a ladder

■ **montarsi la testa** to get big-headed □ Si è montato la testa. He's got big-headed.

la **montatura** FEM NOUN
frames *pl (of glasses)*

il **monte** MASC NOUN
mountain

□ Qual è il monte più alto d'Europa? Which is the highest mountain in Europe?

■ **il monte Everest** Mount Everest

il **montone** MASC NOUN

1 ram

2 mutton

■ **una giacca di montone** a sheepskin jacket

montuoso (FEM **montuosa**) ADJECTIVE
mountainous

il **monumento** MASC NOUN

■ **visitare i monumenti** to go sightseeing

■ **un monumento ai caduti** a war memorial

la **moquette** (PL le **moquette**) FEM NOUN
carpet

la **mora** FEM NOUN

1 blackberry

2 mulberry

il **morale** MASC NOUN
▷ *see also* **morale** ADJECTIVE, FEM NOUN
morale

□ Bisogna tenere alto il morale della squadra. We must keep the team's morale high.

■ **Sono giù di morale.** I'm feeling down.

■ **Su col morale!** Cheer up!

la **morale** FEM NOUN
▷ *see also* **morale** ADJECTIVE, MASC NOUN

1 moral

□ la morale della favola the moral of the story

2 morals *pl*

□ Non hanno morale. They haven't got any morals.

morale (FEM **morale**) ADJECTIVE
▷ *see also* **morale** MASC NOUN, FEM NOUN
moral

morbido (FEM **morbida**) ADJECTIVE
soft

□ Ha la pelle morbida. She's got soft skin.

▮ LANGUAGE TIP Be careful! **morbido** doesn't mean **morbid**.

il **morbillo** MASC NOUN
measles *sing*

□ Ho il morbillo. I've got measles.

il **morbo** MASC NOUN
disease

mordere VERB [60]
to bite

□ Il cane mi ha morso la gamba. The dog bit my leg.

morire VERB [61]
to die

□ Morì nel 1857. He died in 1857. □ Muoio di sete. I'm dying of thirst.

■ **Muoio di fame.** I'm starving.

■ **Fa un caldo da morire.** It's terribly hot.

■ **morire dalla voglia di fare qualcosa** to be dying to do something □ Moriva dalla voglia di raccontarle tutto. He was dying to tell her everything.

mormorare VERB [68]
to mutter

morsicare VERB [18]
to bite

il **morso** MASC NOUN
bite

□ Mi dai un morso del tuo panino? Can I have a bite of your roll?

■ **dare un morso a qualcosa** to bite into something □ Diede un morso al panino. He bit into his roll.

mortale (FEM **mortale**) ADJECTIVE

1 fatal *(accident)*

2 deadly *(poison)*

la **morte** FEM NOUN
death

il **morto** MASC NOUN
▷ *see also* **morto** ADJECTIVE

■ **i morti** the dead □ Il due novembre commemoriamo i morti. We remember the dead on November the second.

■ **Ci sono stati tre morti nella sparatoria.** Three people were killed in the shooting.

■ **fare il morto** *(swimming)* to float

morto (FEM **morta**) ADJECTIVE
▷ *see also* **morto** NOUN
dead

□ il loro fratello morto their dead brother

■ **essere morto di paura** to be scared to death

■ **essere stanco morto** to be knackered

■ **essere morto di freddo** to be frozen stiff

il **mosaico** (PL i **mosaici**) MASC NOUN
mosaic

Mosca FEM NOUN
Moscow

□ Vado a Mosca. I'm going to Moscow.
□ Abitano a Mosca. They live in Moscow.

la **mosca** (PL le **mosche**) FEM NOUN
fly

il **moscerino** MASC NOUN
midge

la **moschea** FEM NOUN
mosque

la **mossa** FEM NOUN
move
□ Ha fatto una mossa sbagliata. He made a bad move.

mosso (FEM **mossa**) ADJECTIVE
1 rough
□ Oggi c'è mare mosso. The sea's rough today.
2 wavy
□ Ha i capelli mossi. He's got wavy hair.
3 blurred
□ La fotografia è un po' mossa. The photo is a bit blurred.

la **mostarda** FEM NOUN
mustard

la **mostra** FEM NOUN
exhibition
□ una mostra d'arte an art exhibition
■ **mostra canina** dog show
■ **Le piace mettersi in mostra.** She likes to be the centre of attention.

mostrare VERB [68]
to show
■ **mostrare qualcosa a qualcuno** to show somebody something □ Ho mostrato le foto a Paolo. I showed Paolo the photos. □ Le ho mostrato il mio vestito nuovo. I showed her my new dress. □ Mi mostri come si fa? Will you show me how to do it?
■ **mostrare la lingua a** to stick out one's tongue at

il **mostro** MASC NOUN
monster

mostruoso (FEM **mostruosa**) ADJECTIVE
terrible
□ un delitto mostruoso a terrible crime
■ **Ha una cultura mostruosa.** She knows an awful lot.

il **motel** (PL i **motel**) MASC NOUN
motel

il **motivo** MASC NOUN
reason
□ Ho un motivo valido per farlo. I've got a good reason for doing it. □ per motivi personali for personal reasons
■ **Per quale motivo?** Why?
■ **senza motivo** for no reason

la **moto** (PL le **moto**) FEM NOUN
▷ see also **moto** MASC NOUN
motorbike
□ Vado a scuola in moto. I go to school on my motorbike.

il **moto** MASC NOUN
▷ see also **moto** FEM NOUN
exercise

□ Devi fare un po' di moto. You should take some exercise.
■ **mettere in moto la macchina** to start the car

il/la **motociclista** (MASC PL i **motociclisti**, FEM PL le **motocicliste**) MASC/FEM NOUN
motorcyclist

il **motore** MASC NOUN
engine
□ Spegni il motore. Switch off the engine.
□ un motore diesel a diesel engine
■ **motore di ricerca** search engine
■ **a motore** motor □ una barca a motore a motor boat

il **motorino** MASC NOUN
moped
□ Vado a scuola in motorino. I go to school on my moped.

il **motoscafo** MASC NOUN
motorboat

il **movente** MASC NOUN
motive
□ Avevano un movente per ucciderlo. They had a motive for killing him.

il **movimento** MASC NOUN
movement
□ un movimento politico a political movement
□ un movimento brusco a sudden movement
■ **È sempre in movimento.** She's always on the go.

il **mozzicone** MASC NOUN
butt (of cigarette)

la **mucca** (PL le **mucche**) FEM NOUN
cow

il **mucchio** MASC NOUN
heap
□ un mucchio di sassi a heap of stones
■ **un mucchio di** loads of □ Ho un mucchio di cose da fare. I've got loads of things to do. □ Ha detto un mucchio di sciocchezze. He talked a load of rubbish.

la **muffa** FEM NOUN
mould
■ **fare la muffa** to go mouldy

il **mulino** MASC NOUN
mill
■ **un mulino a vento** a windmill

il **mulo** MASC NOUN
mule

la **multa** FEM NOUN
fine
□ una multa di cinquanta euro a fine of fifty euros
■ **Ho preso una multa per divieto di sosta.** I got a parking ticket.
■ **dare la multa a qualcuno** to fine somebody □ Il controllore le ha dato la multa. The inspector fined her.

il **municipio** MASC NOUN
town hall

le **munizioni** FEM PL NOUN
ammunition *sing*

muovere VERB [62]
to move
□ Non riesco a muovere la gamba. I can't move my leg.
■ **muoversi** to move □ Non si muove. It won't move.
■ **Muoviti!** Hurry up! □ Muoviti, o perdiamo il treno! Hurry up, or we'll miss the train!

le **mura** FEM PL NOUN
walls
□ le mura della città the city walls

il **muratore** MASC NOUN
bricklayer
□ Fa il muratore. He is a bricklayer.

il **muro** MASC NOUN
wall
□ un muro alto a high wall
■ **un armadio a muro** a built-in cupboard

il **muschio** MASC NOUN
moss

il **muscolo** MASC NOUN
muscle
□ muscoli forti strong muscles
■ **scaldare i muscoli** to warm up

il **museo** MASC NOUN
museum

la **museruola** FEM NOUN
muzzle
■ **mettere la museruola a un cane** to muzzle a dog
■ **I cani devono avere la museruola.** Dogs have to be muzzled.

la **musica** FEM NOUN
music
□ Mi piace la musica classica. I like classical music.

musicale (FEM **musicale**) ADJECTIVE
musical

il/la **musicista** (MASC PL i **musicisti**, FEM PL le **musiciste**) MASC/FEM NOUN
1 musician
□ Fa il musicista. He is a musician.
2 player
□ uno dei musicisti dell'orchestra one of the players in the orchestra

il **muso** MASC NOUN
1 muzzle
2 face
□ Gli diede un pugno sul muso. He punched him in the face.
■ **fare il muso** to sulk □ Fa il muso. She's sulking.

mussulmano (FEM **mussulmana**)
ADJECTIVE, MASC/FEM NOUN
Muslim

la **muta** FEM NOUN
■ **una muta subacquea** a wet suit

le **mutande** FEM PL NOUN
1 underpants
□ È in mutande. He's in his underpants.
2 pants *(women's)*

muto (FEM **muta**) ADJECTIVE
silent
□ il cinema muto the silent cinema □ La h è muta. The h is silent.
■ **Giuro che sarò muto come un pesce.** I swear I won't say a word.

il **mutuo** MASC NOUN
mortgage
■ **fare un mutuo** to take out a mortgage
□ Ho fatto un mutuo per comprare la casa. I took out a mortgage to buy the house.

Nn

la **nafta** FEM NOUN
diesel

la **nanna** FEM NOUN
■ **andare a nanna** to go to beddy-byes
□ Andiamo a nanna. Let's go to beddy-byes.
■ **Fai la nanna, ora.** Go to sleep now.

il **nano,** la **nana** MASC/FEM NOUN
dwarf

Napoli FEM NOUN
Naples
□ Domani vado a Napoli. I'm going to Naples tomorrow. □ Abitiamo a Napoli. We live in Naples.

la **narice** FEM NOUN
nostril

la **narrativa** FEM NOUN
fiction
□ uno dei capolavori della narrativa europea one of the greatest works of European fiction

nasale (FEM **nasale**) ADJECTIVE
nasal

nascere VERB [63]
to be born
□ È nato nel 1997. He was born in 1997. □ Sono nata il 28 aprile. I was born on the 28th of April.

la **nascita** FEM NOUN
birth
□ dopo la nascita della bambina after the baby's birth □ È cieco dalla nascita. He has been blind from birth.

nascondere VERB [64]
to hide
□ Dove hai nascosto la lettera? Where have you hidden the letter?
■ **nascondersi** to hide □ Si è nascosto dietro al divano. He hid behind the sofa.

il **nascondiglio** MASC NOUN
hiding place

il **nascondino** MASC NOUN
■ **giocare a nascondino** to play hide-and-seek

nascosto (FEM **nascosta**) ADJECTIVE
hidden
□ un pericolo nascosto a hidden danger
■ **di nascosto** secretly □ L'abbiamo fatto di nascosto. We did it secretly.

il **naso** MASC NOUN
nose

□ Si è soffiato il naso. He blew his nose.
■ **Ha naso per gli affari.** He has a flair for business.

il **nastro** MASC NOUN
1 ribbon
□ un nastro di seta a silk ribbon
2 tape
□ Ha fatto tornare indietro il nastro. He rewound the tape.
■ **nastro adesivo** adhesive tape
■ **nastro trasportatore** conveyor belt

il **Natale** MASC NOUN
Christmas
□ Cosa fai a Natale? What are you doing at Christmas? □ albero di Natale Christmas tree
□ Buon Natale! Merry Christmas!

natalizio (FEM **natalizia**) ADJECTIVE
Christmas
□ gli addobbi natalizi Christmas decorations

la **natica** (PL le **natiche**) FEM NOUN
buttock

nato (FEM **nata**) ADJECTIVE
■ **un attore nato** a born actor

la **natura** FEM NOUN
nature
□ gli amanti della natura nature lovers □ la natura umana human nature
■ **È allegra di natura.** She's got a cheerful personality.
■ **una natura morta** a still life

naturale (FEM **naturale**) ADJECTIVE
1 natural
□ risorse naturali natural resources
■ **acqua minerale naturale** still mineral water
2 of course
□ Posso venire anch'io? — Naturale! Can I come with you? — Of course!

naturalmente ADVERB
of course
□ Mi telefonerai? — Sì, naturalmente. Will you phone me? — Yes, of course.

naturista (FEM **naturista**, MASC PL **naturisti**, FEM PL **naturiste**) ADJECTIVE, MASC/FEM NOUN
nudist

naufragare VERB [76]
1 to be wrecked

n

□ La nave è naufragata a causa della tempesta. The ship was wrecked in the storm.

2 to be shipwrecked

□ Naufragarono poco lontano dall'isola. They were shipwrecked not far from the island.

il **naufrago**, la **naufraga** (MASC PL i **naufraghi**, FEM PL le **naufraghe**) MASC/FEM NOUN

1 shipwrecked person

2 castaway

la **nausea** FEM NOUN

■ **avere la nausea** to feel sick □ Avevo un po' di nausea. I felt a bit sick.

nauseante (FEM **nauseante**) ADJECTIVE
disgusting

□ un odore nauseante a disgusting smell

la **navata** FEM NOUN

■ **navata centrale** nave

■ **navata laterale** aisle

la **nave** FEM NOUN
ship

■ **nave da guerra** warship

■ **nave da crociera** cruise liner

la **navicella** FEM NOUN

■ **una navicella spaziale** a spaceship

navigare VERB [76]
to sail

□ Navigarono per tre mesi prima di raggiungere la costa. They sailed for three months before they reached land.

■ **navigare in Internet** to surf the Net

il **navigatore** MASC NOUN

■ **navigatore satellitare** satnav □ Hai il navigatore satellitare? Have you got satnav?

la **navigazione** FEM NOUN

■ **dopo una settimana di navigazione** after a week at sea

nazionale (FEM **nazionale**) ADJECTIVE
▷ see also **nazionale** NOUN
national

□ l'inno nazionale the national anthem □ un parco nazionale a national park

la **nazionale** FEM NOUN
▷ see also **nazionale** ADJECTIVE

■ **la nazionale azzurra** the Italian team

la **nazionalità** (PL le **nazionalità**) FEM NOUN
nationality

□ Nazionalità: Italiana. Nationality: Italian.

■ **È di nazionalità britannica.** She's British.

la **nazione** FEM NOUN
nation

ne ADVERB, PRONOUN

LANGUAGE TIP **ne** is often not translated.

□ È meglio che tu te ne vada. You'd better leave. □ Dammene uno, per favore. Give me one, please. □ Ne voglio ancora un po'. I want a bit more. □ Hai del pane? — No, non ne ho.

Have you got any bread? — No, I haven't.

□ Quanti anni hai? — Ne ho diciassette. How old are you? — I'm seventeen.

LANGUAGE TIP When **ne** means 'regarding', it is translated by 'about it'.

□ Non parliamone più! Let's not talk about it any more! □ Non me ne importa niente. I couldn't care less about it.

né CONJUNCTION

■ **né... né...** neither... nor... □ Non verranno né Chiara né Donatella. Neither Chiara nor Donatella are coming.

LANGUAGE TIP In negative translations, use 'either... or'.

□ Non parla né l'italiano né il tedesco. He doesn't speak either Italian or German.

■ **Non l'ho più vista né sentita.** I didn't see or hear from her again.

■ **né l'uno né l'altro** neither of them □ Né l'uno né l'altro gioca a tennis. Neither of them plays tennis.

■ **Non conosco né l'uno né l'altro.** I don't know either of them.

neanche ADVERB, CONJUNCTION

1 not even

□ Neanche un bambino ci crederebbe. Not even a child would believe it.

■ **non... neanche** not even... □ Non mi ha neanche pagato. She didn't even pay me.

■ **neanche se** even if □ Non potrebbe venire neanche se volesse. He couldn't come even if he wanted to.

2 neither

□ Non l'ho visto. — Neanch'io. I didn't see him. — Neither did I. □ Non ne ero sicuro. — Neanche lei. I wasn't sure. — Neither was she.

■ **Neanche per idea!** Certainly not!

■ **Non ci penso neanche!** I wouldn't dream of it!

la **nebbia** FEM NOUN
fog

□ Odio la nebbia. I hate fog.

■ **Oggi c'è nebbia.** It's foggy today.

necessario (FEM **necessaria**) ADJECTIVE
▷ see also **necessario** NOUN
necessary

□ Porta i documenti necessari. Bring the necessary documents.

■ **È necessario far presto.** We've got to hurry.

il **necessario** MASC NOUN
▷ see also **necessario** ADJECTIVE

■ **lo stretto necessario** the bare essentials pl □ Ha messo in valigia lo stretto necessario. She packed the bare essentials.

la **necessità** (PL le **necessità**) FEM NOUN
necessity

□ Non è un lusso, è una necessità. It isn't a luxury, it's a necessity.

■ **L'ho fatto per necessità.** I did it because I had to.

■ **in caso di necessità** if necessary

negare VERB [76]
to deny

□ Non puoi negarlo. You can't deny it.

■ **negare di aver fatto qualcosa** to deny doing something □ Ha negato di aver preso i soldi. He denied taking the money.

■ **negare qualcosa a qualcuno** to refuse to give somebody something □ Mi ha negato il suo appoggio. He refused to give me his support.

la negativa FEM NOUN
negative (of photograph)

negativo (FEM **negativa**) ADJECTIVE
negative

□ Il risultato del test è stato negativo. The result of the test was negative.

negato (FEM **negata**) ADJECTIVE

■ **essere negato per** to be no good at
□ Sono negato per lo sport. I'm no good at sport.

il/la negoziante MASC/FEM NOUN
shopkeeper

il negoziato MASC NOUN

■ **negoziati per la pace** peace talks

il negozio MASC NOUN
shop

□ un negozio di scarpe a shoe shop
□ un negozio di abbigliamento a clothes shop

negro (FEM **negra**) ADJECTIVE
black

nemico (FEM **nemica**, MASC PL **nemici**, FEM PL **nemiche**) ADJECTIVE, MASC/FEM NOUN
enemy

□ Ha molti nemici. He's got a lot of enemies.
□ territorio nemico enemy territory

nemmeno ADVERB, CONJUNCTION

1 not even

□ Nemmeno un bambino ci crederebbe. Not even a child would believe it.

■ **non... nemmeno** not even... □ Non mi ha nemmeno pagato. She didn't even pay me.

■ **nemmeno se** even if □ Non potrebbe venire nemmeno se volesse. He couldn't come even if he wanted to.

2 neither

□ Non l'ho visto. — Nemmeno io. I didn't see him. — Neither did I. □ Non ne ero sicuro. — Nemmeno lei. I wasn't sure. — Neither was she.

■ **Nemmeno per idea!** Certainly not!

■ **Non ci penso nemmeno!** I wouldn't dream of it!

il neo MASC NOUN
mole

il neon MASC NOUN
neon

□ una luce al neon a neon light

il neonato, la **neonata** MASC/FEM NOUN
newborn baby

neozelandese (FEM **neozelandese**)
ADJECTIVE
▷ see also **neozelandese** NOUN
New Zealand

□ la squadra neozelandese the New Zealand team

il/la neozelandese MASC/FEM NOUN
▷ see also **neozelandese** ADJECTIVE
New Zealander

neppure = **nemmeno**

nero (FEM **nera**) ADJECTIVE, MASC NOUN
black

□ Ha i capelli neri. She's got black hair.
□ È vestita di nero. She's dressed in black.

■ **essere di umore nero** to be in a very bad mood □ Oggi sono di umore nero. I'm in a very bad mood today.

■ **mercato nero** black market

■ **lavoro nero** work in the black economy

il nervo MASC NOUN
nerve

■ **dare sui nervi a qualcuno** to get on somebody's nerves □ Mi dà proprio sui nervi. It really gets on my nerves.

■ **avere i nervi saldi** to be calm

■ **avere i nervi a fior di pelle** to be edgy

nervoso (FEM **nervosa**) ADJECTIVE

1 irritable

□ È sempre nervoso e si arrabbia spesso. He's always irritable and often loses his temper.

2 stressed

■ **essere nervoso** to feel stressed □ Ero nervoso e gli ho risposto male. I was feeling stressed and didn't give him a proper answer.

3 nervous

□ Sono sempre un po' nervoso prima di un compito in classe. I'm always a bit nervous before a test at school.

nessuno (FEM **nessuna**) PRONOUN
▷ see also **nessuno** ADJECTIVE

| **LANGUAGE TIP** When **nessuno** is the subject and the English verb is not in the negative, use 'nobody' or 'no one'.

□ Non è venuto nessuno. Nobody came.
□ Nessuno mi crede. No one believes me.
□ Non c'era nessuno. There was no one there.

| **LANGUAGE TIP** In negative translations, use 'anybody' or 'anyone'.

□ Non c'era nessuno. There wasn't anyone there. □ Non dirlo a nessuno. Don't tell that to anybody.

| **LANGUAGE TIP** In questions, use 'anybody' or 'anyone'.

n

□ Ha telefonato nessuno? Did anybody phone? □ Hai visto nessuno? Did you see anyone?

■ **nessuno di loro** none of them □ Non è venuto nessuno di loro. None of them came.

nessuno (FEM **nessuna**) ADJECTIVE
▷ *see also* **nessuno** PRONOUN

1 no
□ Non c'è nessun bisogno di andare. There's no need to go.

> **LANGUAGE TIP** In negative translations, use 'any'.

□ Non ha fatto nessun commento. He didn't make any comment.

2 any
□ Nessuna obiezione? Any objections?

■ **nessun altro** no one else □ Nessun altro voleva andarci. No one else wanted to go.

■ **Non ho incontrato nessun altro.** I didn't meet anyone else.

■ **da nessuna parte** not... anywhere
□ Non riesco a trovarlo da nessuna parte. I can't find it anywhere.

netto (FEM **netta**) ADJECTIVE

1 clear
□ una netta vittoria a clear victory

2 net
□ peso netto net weight

il **netturbino** MASC NOUN
dustman

neutrale (FEM **neutrale**) ADJECTIVE
neutral

neutro (FEM **neutra**) ADJECTIVE

1 neutral *(colour)*

2 neuter *(grammatical gender)*

la **neve** FEM NOUN
snow
□ Mi piace camminare sulla neve. I like walking in the snow.

■ **È caduta tanta neve ieri.** It snowed a lot yesterday.

nevicare VERB [18]
to snow
□ Nevica. It's snowing.

la **nevicata** FEM NOUN
snowfall

il **nevischio** MASC NOUN
sleet

la **nicotina** FEM NOUN
nicotine

il **nido** MASC NOUN

1 nest

2 crèche

niente PRONOUN, ADVERB
nothing
□ Cos'hai comprato? — Niente. What did you buy? — Nothing. □ Cosa c'è? — Niente. What's the matter? — Nothing. □ Non è

successo niente. Nothing happened.

> **LANGUAGE TIP** In negative translations and in questions, use 'anything'.

□ Non ho visto niente. I didn't see anything.
□ Hai bisogno di niente? Do you need anything?

■ **Non mi sono fatto niente.** I didn't hurt myself.

■ **poco o niente** next to nothing

■ **Nient'altro?** *(in shop)* Will that be all?

■ **Grazie. — Di niente.** Thanks. — You're welcome.

■ **niente affatto** not at all □ Le dispiace se fumo? — Niente affatto. Do you mind if I smoke? — Not at all.

■ **non... per niente** not... at all □ Non mi sono divertito per niente. I didn't enjoy it at all.

■ **Niente male!** Not bad at all!

■ **Niente paura!** Don't worry!

■ **Non fa niente.** It doesn't matter.

la **ninnananna** FEM NOUN
lullaby

il/la **nipote** MASC/FEM NOUN

■ **il nipote** 1 grandson 2 nephew

■ **la nipote** 1 granddaughter 2 niece

■ **nipoti** 1 grandchildren 2 nieces and nephews

nitido (FEM **nitida**) ADJECTIVE
sharp
□ un'immagine nitida a sharp image

no ADVERB

1 no
□ Vieni? — No. Are you coming? — No, I'm not. □ Ti piace? — No. Do you like it? — No, I don't. □ Ne vuoi ancora? — No, grazie. Would you like some more? — No thank you.

2 not
□ Perché no? Why not? □ Vieni o no? Are you coming or not? □ Spero di no. I hope not.

> **LANGUAGE TIP** To translate **..., no?** at the end of a sentence, see the examples below.

□ Mi scriverai, no? You'll write to me, won't you? □ Può venire, no? He can come, can't he? □ Vieni anche tu, no? You're coming too, aren't you? □ Hai finito, no? You've finished, haven't you?

nobile (FEM **nobile**) ADJECTIVE
▷ *see also* **nobile** NOUN

1 aristocratic
□ una famiglia nobile an aristocratic family

2 noble
□ nobili sentimenti noble sentiments

il/la **nobile** MASC/FEM NOUN
▷ *see also* **nobile** ADJECTIVE

1 aristocrat

2 nobleman
noblewoman

■ **i nobili** the aristocracy

la **nocca** (PL le **nocche**) FEM NOUN
knuckle

la **nocciola** FEM NOUN
▷ see also **nocciola** ADJECTIVE
hazelnut

□ gelato alla nocciola hazelnut ice cream

nocciola (FEM+PL **nocciola**) ADJECTIVE
▷ see also **nocciola** NOUN
hazel (colour)

la **nocciolina** FEM NOUN
■ **nocciolina americana** peanut

il **nocciòlo** MASC NOUN
hazel (tree)

il **nòcciolo** MASC NOUN
stone

□ un nocciolo di pesca a peach stone

■ **Il nocciolo della questione è...** The main point is...

la **noce** FEM NOUN
▷ see also **noce** MASC NOUN
walnut

■ **noce di cocco** coconut

■ **noce moscata** nutmeg

il **noce** MASC NOUN
▷ see also **noce** FEM NOUN
walnut tree

nocivo (FEM **nociva**) ADJECTIVE
harmful

□ Non contiene sostanze nocive. It doesn't contain any harmful substances.

il **nodo** MASC NOUN

1 knot

■ **fare un nodo** to tie a knot

■ **sciogliere un nodo** to untie a knot

2 tangle (in hair)

noi PRONOUN

1 we

□ Noi andiamo al cinema. We're going to the cinema.

■ **Non lo sapevamo nemmeno noi.** We didn't even know it ourselves.

2 us

□ Chi viene con noi? Who's coming with us? □ Sono più giovani di noi. They are younger than us. □ Chi è? — Siamo noi. Who is it? — It's us.

la **noia** FEM NOUN
boredom

□ Stavano morendo di noia. They were dying of boredom.

■ **Che noia, quel film!** The film was so boring!

■ **noie** trouble sing □ Ha avuto delle noie con i vicini. She had trouble with the neighbours. □ Ha avuto delle noie con la polizia. He was in trouble with the police.

■ **dare noia a qualcuno** to bother somebody □ Finiscila di dar noia a tua sorella.

Stop bothering your sister.

■ **Le dà noia se fumo?** Do you mind if I smoke?

■ **Mi è venuto a noia.** I'm tired of it.

noioso (FEM **noiosa**) ADJECTIVE
boring

> LANGUAGE TIP Be careful! **noioso** doesn't mean **noisy**.

noleggiare VERB [58]

1 to hire

□ Dove possiamo noleggiare una macchina? Where can we hire a car?

2 to hire out

□ Noleggiano biciclette ai turisti. They hire out bikes to tourists.

il **noleggio** MASC NOUN
hire (of car, bike, skis)

■ **prendere a noleggio** to hire

□ Prenderemo gli sci a noleggio. We're going to hire skis.

il/la **nomade** MASC/FEM NOUN
nomad

il **nome** MASC NOUN

1 name

□ Che bel nome! What a nice name! □ Lo conosco di nome. I know the name. □ Li conosce tutti per nome. She knows them all by name. □ Posso chiamarti per nome? Can I call you by your first name?

■ **Gli hanno dato il nome del nonno.** He is named after his grandfather.

■ **a nome di** in the name of □ La macchina è a nome di mio marito. The car is in my husband's name.

■ **Tanti saluti anche a nome di mia moglie.** My wife asked me to give you her regards.

■ **nome di battesimo** Christian name

■ **nome utente** username □ Inserisci il nome utente e la password. Type your username and password.

2 noun

la **nomina** FEM NOUN
appointment

nominare VERB [68]

1 to mention

□ L'ha nominata nel suo discorso. He mentioned her in his speech.

■ **Non l'ho mai sentito nominare.** I've never heard of it.

2 to appoint

□ È stato nominato segretario generale. He has been appointed secretary-general.

non ADVERB
not

□ La legge non è stata ancora approvata. The law has not yet been passed.

> LANGUAGE TIP 'not' is often abbreviated to **n't**.

□ Mario non c'è. Mario isn't here. □ Non sono inglesi. They aren't English. □ Non ci sono andato. I didn't go. □ Non lo so. I don't know. □ Non andarci! Don't go! □ Non avresti dovuto farlo. You shouldn't have done that.

la **nonna** FEM NOUN
grandmother

il **nonno** MASC NOUN
grandfather

■ **i miei nonni** my grandparents

nono (FEM **nona**) ADJECTIVE, MASC NOUN
ninth

□ Abita al nono piano. He lives on the ninth floor.

nonostante PREPOSITION
▷ *see also* **nonostante** CONJUNCTION
in spite of

□ Ci è riuscita nonostante tutto. She succeeded in spite of everything.

nonostante CONJUNCTION
▷ *see also* **nonostante** PREPOSITION
even though

□ Ha voluto alzarsi nonostante fosse ancora malato. He wanted to get up even though he was still ill.

il **nord** MASC NOUN
north

□ La sua famiglia è del nord. His family comes from the north.

■ **a nord** north □ Si è diretto a nord. He headed north. □ Piove di più a nord. It rains more in the north.

■ **a nord di** north of □ Si trova a nord della città. It's north of the city.

■ **l'America del Nord** North America

■ **l'Italia del nord** Northern Italy

il **nordest** MASC NOUN
north-east

■ **a nordest di** north-east of

il **nordovest** MASC NOUN
north-west

■ **a nordovest di** north-west of

la **norma** FEM NOUN
norm

□ le norme sociali social norms

■ **di norma** as a rule □ Di norma chiudo a chiave la porta. I lock the door as a rule.

■ **norme di sicurezza** safety regulations

■ **norme per l'uso** instructions for use

normale (FEM **normale**) ADJECTIVE
normal

norvegese (FEM **norvegese**) ADJECTIVE
▷ *see also* **norvegese** MASC NOUN, FEM NOUN
Norwegian

il **norvegese** MASC NOUN
▷ *see also* **norvegese** ADJECTIVE, FEM NOUN
Norwegian *(person, language)*

□ Parla norvegese. He speaks Norwegian.
□ i norvegesi the Norwegians

la **norvegese** FEM NOUN
▷ *see also* **norvegese** ADJECTIVE, MASC NOUN
Norwegian

la **Norvegia** FEM NOUN
Norway

□ Ti è piaciuta la Norvegia? Did you like Norway? □ Andremo in Norvegia quest'estate. We're going to Norway this summer.

la **nostalgia** FEM NOUN

■ **Ho nostalgia di casa.** I'm homesick.

■ **Ho nostalgia dei vecchi tempi.** I'm nostalgic for the good old days.

nostro (FEM **nostra**) ADJECTIVE
▷ *see also* **nostro** PRONOUN
our

□ il nostro giardino our garden □ la nostra macchina our car □ i nostri libri our books □ nostro padre our father □ È colpa nostra. It's our fault.

■ **un nostro amico** a friend of ours

■ **Alla nostra!** To us!

nostro (FEM **nostra**) PRONOUN
▷ *see also* **nostro** ADJECTIVE
ours

□ È questa la vostra macchina? — No, la nostra è nera. Is this your car? — No, ours is black. □ Le sue foto sono più belle delle nostre. His pictures are better than ours. □ Di chi è questo? — È nostro. Whose is this? — It's ours.

la **nota** FEM NOUN
note

□ la nota a pagina dieci the note on page fifty six

■ **prendere nota di qualcosa** to make a note of something □ Ho preso nota di tutto quello che ha detto. I made a note of everything she said.

■ **degno di nota** noteworthy

■ **una nota musicale** a note

■ **note a piè di pagina** footnotes

il **notaio** MASC NOUN
notary

notare VERB [68]
to notice

□ Hai notato com'era strano? Did you notice how strange he was?

■ **Gli ho fatto notare che l'errore era suo.** I pointed out that it was his mistake.

■ **farsi notare** to draw attention to oneself □ Le piace farsi notare. She likes to draw attention to herself.

notevole (FEM **notevole**) ADJECTIVE

■ **Quell'anello ha un valore notevole.** That ring is very valuable.

■ **una donna di notevole bellezza** a very beautiful woman

la **notizia** FEM NOUN
news *sing*

□ Questa è una notizia interessante. That's

interesting news. □ Ho sentito la notizia della sua morte per radio. I heard the news of his death on the radio. □ La notizia è stata uno shock per lui. The news was a shock to him.

■ **notizie** news □ Ho delle buone notizie per te. I've got some good news for you. □ Brutte notizie, purtroppo! Bad news, unfortunately! □ Non abbiamo sue notizie da un anno. It's a year since we had any news of her.

■ **Fammi avere tue notizie!** Keep in touch!

il **notiziario** MASC NOUN
news sing
□ L'hanno detto al notiziario delle otto. It was on the eight o'clock news.

noto (FEM **nota**) ADJECTIVE
well-known
□ un noto politico a well-known politician □ Suo fratello è più noto. His brother is better known.

la **notte** FEM NOUN
night

■ **di notte** at night □ Ha paura di uscire di notte. She's afraid to go out at night.

■ **È successo di notte.** It happened during the night.

■ **questa notte 1** last night **2** tonight

notturno (FEM **notturna**) ADJECTIVE
night
□ Non c'è un servizio notturno. There is no night service.

novanta NUMBER
ninety

novantesimo (FEM **novantesima**)
ADJECTIVE, MASC NOUN
ninetieth

nove NUMBER
nine
□ Ho nove anni. I'm nine. □ le nove di sera nine o'clock in the evening

■ **il nove dicembre** the ninth of December

novecento NUMBER
nine hundred

■ **il Novecento** the twentieth century

novembre MASC NOUN
November

> **LANGUAGE TIP** In Italian, months are not written with capital letters.

□ in novembre in November

la **novità** (PL le **novità**) FEM NOUN
news sing
□ Ci sono novità? Is there any news?

■ **Questa è una novità!** That's something new!

■ **l'ultima novità in fatto di lettori CD** the latest thing in CD players

le **nozze** FEM PL NOUN
wedding sing
□ un regalo di nozze a wedding present

■ **nozze d'argento** silver wedding

■ **nozze d'oro** golden wedding

■ **viaggio di nozze** honeymoon □ Dove andrete in viaggio di nozze? Where are you going on your honeymoon?

nubile (FEM **nubile**) ADJECTIVE
unmarried
□ una donna nubile an unmarried woman

la **nuca** (PL le **nuche**) FEM NOUN
nape of the neck

nucleare (FEM **nucleare**) ADJECTIVE
nuclear
□ l'energia nucleare nuclear energy

il **nucleo** MASC NOUN

■ **il nucleo familiare** the family unit

■ **il nucleo antidroga** the anti-drugs squad

nudista (FEM **nudista**, MASC PL **nudisti**, FEM PL **nudiste**) ADJECTIVE, MASC/FEM NOUN
nudist

nudo (FEM **nuda**) ADJECTIVE
naked
□ un uomo nudo a naked man □ Era completamente nuda. She was completely naked.

■ **a piedi nudi** barefoot □ Camminava a piedi nudi in giardino. He was walking barefoot in the garden.

■ **a occhio nudo** to the naked eye □ È invisibile a occhio nudo. It's not visible to the naked eye.

nulla PRONOUN, ADVERB
nothing
□ Cos'hai comprato? — Nulla. What did you buy? — Nothing. □ Cosa c'è? — Nulla. What's the matter? — Nothing. □ Non è successo nulla. Nothing happened.

> **LANGUAGE TIP** In negative translations and in questions, use 'anything'.

□ Non ho visto nulla. I didn't see anything.
□ Hai bisogno di nulla? Do you need anything?

■ **Non mi sono fatto nulla.** I didn't hurt myself.

■ **Grazie. — Di nulla.** Thanks. — You're welcome.

■ **non... per nulla** not... at all □ Non mi sono divertito per nulla. I didn't enjoy it at all.

il **numero** MASC NOUN
1 number
□ Abito al numero sei. I live at number six.
□ Qual è il tuo numero di telefono? What's your phone number?

2 size
□ Che numero di scarpe porti? What size shoe do you take?

> **DID YOU KNOW...?**
> Italian shoe sizes are different: for example, 38 is the equivalent of a British size 5, and 40 is the equivalent of size 6½.

3 act
□ Il suo numero è stato molto divertente. His act was very entertaining.

numeroso (FEM **numerosa**) ADJECTIVE

1 numerous

□ Ci sono stati numerosi casi di morbillo. There have been numerous cases of measles.

2 large

□ Ha una famiglia numerosa. He's got a large family.

nuocere VERB [65]

■ **nuocere a** to be bad for □ Il fumo nuoce alla salute. Smoking is bad for your health.

la **nuora** FEM NOUN
daughter-in-law

nuotare VERB [68]
to swim

□ Sai nuotare? Can you swim?

■ **nuotare a rana** to do the breast stroke

■ **nuotare a dorso** to do the backstroke

il **nuotatore,** la **nuotatrice** MASC/FEM NOUN
swimmer

□ È un bravo nuotatore. He's a good swimmer.

il **nuoto** MASC NOUN
swimming

□ una gara di nuoto a swimming gala

■ **Ho attraversato il lago a nuoto.** I swam across the lake.

nuovamente ADVERB
again

□ Si è nuovamente ammalato. He's ill again.

la **Nuova Zelanda** FEM NOUN
New Zealand

□ Ti è piaciuta la Nuova Zelanda? Did you like New Zealand? □ Andremo in Nuova Zelanda. We're going to New Zealand.

nuovo (FEM **nuova**) ADJECTIVE
new

□ un vestito nuovo a new dress □ Sono nuovo di qui. I'm new here.

■ **Il suo volto non mi è nuovo.** I know his face.

■ **nuovo di zecca** brand-new □ Ha una macchina nuova di zecca. He's got a brand-new car.

■ **di nuovo** again □ È successo di nuovo. It happened again. □ Sei di nuovo tu? Is it you again?

■ **Che c'è di nuovo?** What's new?

■ **Non c'è niente di nuovo.** There's nothing new.

nutriente (FEM **nutriente**) ADJECTIVE
nourishing

□ una crema nutriente a nourishing cream

nutrire VERB [41]
to feed

□ La madre nutriva i piccoli. The mother was feeding her young.

■ **nutrirsi di** to eat □ I leoni si nutrono esclusivamente di carne. Lions only eat meat.

la **nuvola** FEM NOUN
cloud

■ **avere la testa fra le nuvole** to have one's head in the clouds □ Ha sempre la testa tra le nuvole. He always has his head in the clouds.

■ **cadere dalle nuvole** to be astonished □ Quando gliel'ho detto è caduto dalle nuvole. When I told him he was astonished.

nuvoloso (FEM **nuvolosa**) ADJECTIVE
cloudy

□ Oggi è più nuvoloso di ieri. It's cloudier today than it was yesterday.

nuziale (FEM **nuziale**) ADJECTIVE
wedding

□ la cerimonia nuziale the wedding ceremony

il **nylon** MASC NOUN
nylon

Oo

O CONJUNCTION
   or
   □ due o tre volte two or three times
   ■ **o... o...** either... or... □ o oggi o domani
   either today or tomorrow

obbediente (FEM **obbediente**) ADJECTIVE
   obedient

obbedire VERB [51]
   to obey
   □ Ha obbedito subito alla madre. He obeyed
   his mother at once.

obbligare VERB [76]
   ■ **obbligare qualcuno a fare qualcosa** to
   make somebody do something □ Mi ha obbligato
   a fare i compiti. She made me do my homework.
   ■ **essere obbligato a fare qualcosa** to
   have to do something □ Non sei obbligato a
   farlo. You don't have to do it.

obbligatorio (FEM **obbligatoria**) ADJECTIVE
   compulsory

l' **obbligo** (PL gli **obblighi**) MASC NOUN
   obligation
   □ Ho degli obblighi nei confronti dei miei.
   I've got obligations to my parents.
   ■ **Non ho l'obbligo di timbrare il**
   cartellino. I don't have to clock in.
   ■ **la scuola dell'obbligo** compulsory
   education

obiettare VERB [68]
   ■ **Non ho nulla da obiettare.** I haven't got
   any objections.

l' **obiettivo** MASC NOUN
   ▷ see also **obiettivo** ADJECTIVE
1 lens sing (of camera)
2 aim
   □ Il suo obiettivo è quello di vincere. His aim is
   to win.

obiettivo (FEM **obiettiva**) ADJECTIVE
   ▷ see also **obiettivo** NOUN
   objective

l' **obiettore** MASC NOUN
   ■ **obiettore di coscienza** conscientious
   objector

l' **obiezione** FEM NOUN
   objection
   □ Ci sono obiezioni? Any objections?

obliquo (FEM **obliqua**) ADJECTIVE
   oblique

□ una linea obliqua an oblique line

obliterare VERB [68]
   to stamp
   □ Il biglietto va obliterato prima di partire. The
   ticket must be stamped before you start your
   journey.

l' **obliteratrice** FEM NOUN
   stamping machine

l' **oblò** (PL gli **oblò**) MASC NOUN
   porthole

l' **oca** (PL le **oche**) FEM NOUN
   goose

l' **occasione** FEM NOUN
1 opportunity
   □ Lo farò alla prima occasione. I'll do it at the
   first opportunity.
2 occasion
   □ in occasione del suo compleanno on the
   occasion of his birthday
3 bargain
   □ Compralo! È un'occasione. Buy it! It's a
   bargain.
   ■ **comprare qualcosa d'occasione** to get
   something cheap

le **occhiaie** FEM PL NOUN
   bags under one's eyes
   □ Ho le occhiaie. I've got bags under my eyes.

gli **occhiali** MASC PL NOUN
   glasses
   □ Porto gli occhiali. I wear glasses.
   ■ **occhiali da sole** sunglasses

l' **occhiata** FEM NOUN
   ■ **dare un'occhiata a qualcosa** to have a
   look at something □ Vorrei dare un'occhiata a
   quel libro. I'd like to have a look at that book.
   ■ **Potresti dare un'occhiata alle mie**
   valigie? Could you keep an eye on my cases?

l' **occhio** MASC NOUN
   eye
   □ Ha gli occhi azzurri. He's got blue eyes.
   ■ **tenere d'occhio** to keep an eye on □ Per
   favore, tieni d'occhio le mie valigie. Please
   could you keep an eye on my cases?
   ■ **chiudere un occhio** to turn a blind eye
   □ Per questa volta chiuderò un occhio. I'll turn
   a blind eye this once.
   ■ **dare nell'occhio** to attract attention
   □ Vestiti in modo da non dare troppo nell'occhio.

o

Dress so as not to attract too much attention.
- **a occhio e croce** round about □ A occhio e croce costerà cento euro. It'll cost round about one hundred euros.
- **Costa un occhio della testa.** It costs an arm and a leg.
- **Occhio!** Watch out!

l' **occhiolino** MASC NOUN
- **fare l'occhiolino a qualcuno** to wink at somebody □ Le fece l'occhiolino. He winked at her.

occidentale (FEM **occidentale**) ADJECTIVE
western
□ i paesi occidentali western countries
- **la costa occidentale della Francia** the west coast of France

l' **occidente** MASC NOUN
west
- **a occidente** in the west □ Il sole tramonta ad occidente. The sun sets in the west.

occorrere VERB [26]
- **Ti occorre qualcosa?** Do you need anything?
- **Mi occorre del denaro.** I need some money.
- **Non occorre che mi telefoni.** You don't need to phone me.
- **Occorre farlo subito.** It should be done at once.

> LANGUAGE TIP Be careful! **occorrere** doesn't mean **to occur**.

occupare VERB [68]
1 to take up
□ L'armadio occupa tutta la parete. The cupboard takes up the whole wall. □ Lo sport mi occupa tutto il tempo libero. Sport takes up all my spare time.
2 to occupy
□ Gli studenti hanno occupato la scuola. The students have occupied the school. □ La città è stata occupata durante la guerra. The city was occupied during the war.
- **occuparsi di** to look after □ Potresti occuparti dei bambini? Could you look after the children?
- **Si occupa di computer.** He's in computers.
- **Occupati dei fatti tuoi!** Mind your own business!

occupato (FEM **occupata**) ADJECTIVE
1 occupied
□ La scuola è ancora occupata. The school is still occupied. □ una città occupata an occupied city
2 busy
□ In questo momento sono molto occupato. I'm very busy at the moment. □ Domani sarò ancora più occupato. I'll be even busier tomorrow.

3 taken
□ È occupato quel posto? Is that seat taken?
4 engaged
□ La toilette è occupata. The toilet is engaged.
□ Non riesco a telefonargli. È sempre occupato. I can't get through to him. The line's always engaged.

l' **occupazione** FEM NOUN
1 job
□ Sto cercando un'occupazione. I'm looking for a job.
2 occupation
□ Occupazione: Infermiere Occupation: Nurse

l' **oceano** MASC NOUN
ocean

l' **oculista** (MASC PL gli **oculisti**, FEM PL le **oculiste**) MASC/FEM NOUN
eye specialist
□ Devo andare dall'oculista. I need to go to the eye specialist.

odiare VERB [17]
to hate
□ Ti odio! I hate you! □ Odio le persone egoiste. I hate selfish people.
- **odiare fare qualcosa** to hate doing something □ Odio alzarmi presto al mattino. I hate getting up early in the morning.
- **odiarsi** to hate each other □ Marco e Matteo si odiano. Marco and Matteo hate each other.

l' **odio** MASC NOUN
hatred

odioso (FEM **odiosa**) ADJECTIVE
horrible
□ Sei odioso. You're horrible.

l' **odore** MASC NOUN
smell
□ un buon odore a nice smell □ un cattivo odore a bad smell
- **Ha un buon odore.** It smells nice.
- **Ha un cattivo odore.** It smells awful.
- **sentire odore di qualcosa** to smell something □ Sento odore di pesce. I can smell fish.
- **gli odori** (in cookery) herbs

offendere VERB [33]
to insult
□ Non avevo intenzione di offenderti. I didn't mean to insult you.
- **offendersi** to take offence □ Se non vieni mi offendo. I'll be offended if you don't come. □ Si è offeso per non essere stato invitato. He took offence because they didn't invite him.

l' **offerta** FEM NOUN
offer
□ Mi ha fatto un'offerta generosa. He made me a generous offer. □ È in offerta speciale. It's on special offer. □ Ho accettato la sua offerta di lavoro. I've accepted his offer of a job.
- **'offerte d'impiego'** 'situations vacant'

l' **offesa** FEM NOUN
insult

offeso (FEM **offesa**) ADJECTIVE
offended

□ È terribilmente offesa per quello che hai detto. She's terribly offended about what you said.

l' **officina** FEM NOUN
garage

□ Devo portare la macchina in officina. I have to take the car to the garage.

offrire VERB [66]
to offer

■ **offrire qualcosa a qualcuno** to offer somebody something □ Mi ha offerto un passaggio. He offered me a lift. □ Le hanno offerto un lavoro. They've offered her a job. □ Mi ha offerto un caffè. She offered me a coffee. □ L'ha offerto prima a me. He offered it to me first.

■ **Mi offri una sigaretta?** Could I have a cigarette?

■ **Vieni, ti offro da bere.** Come on, I'll buy you a drink.

■ **Offro io, questa volta!** I'll pay this time!

■ **offrirsi volontario** to volunteer
□ Nessuno si è offerto volontario. Nobody volunteered.

■ **offrirsi di fare qualcosa** to offer to do something □ Si è offerto di aiutarci. He offered to help us.

l' **oggetto** MASC NOUN
object

□ un oggetto rotondo a round object

■ **oggetti smarriti** lost property *sing*
□ Dov'è l'ufficio oggetti smarriti? Where's the lost property office?

oggi ADVERB
today

□ Oggi è venerdì. It's Friday today. □ il giornale di oggi today's paper

■ **oggi stesso** today □ Lo farò oggi stesso. I'll do it today.

■ **dall'oggi al domani** from one day to the next □ Potrebbe cambiare tutto dall'oggi al domani. Everything could change from one day to the next.

■ **oggi a otto** a week today

oggigiorno ADVERB
nowadays

ogni (FEM+PL **ogni**) ADJECTIVE
every

□ Lo vedo ogni giorno. I see him every day. □ Viene ogni due giorni. He comes every two days.

■ **C'era gente di ogni tipo.** There were all sorts of people.

■ **in ogni caso** anyway □ Dovresti

telefonargli in ogni caso. You should phone him anyway.

■ **ogni tanto** every so often □ Ogni tanto le scrivo. I write to her every so often.

ognuno (FEM **ognuna**) PRONOUN
1 each

□ Ad ognuno di voi verrà dato un questionario. Each of you will be given a questionnaire.
2 everybody

□ Ognuno ha il diritto di dire quello che pensa. Everybody has the right to say what they think.

l' **Olanda** FEM NOUN
Holland

□ Mi è piaciuta molto l'Olanda. I liked Holland very much. □ Andrò in Olanda in giugno. I'm going to Holland in June.

olandese (FEM **olandese**) ADJECTIVE
▷ see also **olandese** MASC NOUN, FEM NOUN
Dutch

l' **olandese** MASC NOUN
▷ see also **olandese** ADJECTIVE, FEM NOUN
1 Dutchman *(person)*

■ **gli olandesi** the Dutch
2 Dutch *(language)*

□ Parla olandese. He speaks Dutch.

l' **olandese** FEM NOUN
▷ see also **olandese** ADJECTIVE, MASC NOUN
Dutchwoman

l' **oleandro** MASC NOUN
oleander

l' **oliera** FEM NOUN
oil and vinegar set

le **Olimpiadi** FEM PL NOUN
the Olympic Games

olimpico (FEM **olimpica**, MASC PL **olimpici**, FEM PL **olimpiche**) ADJECTIVE
Olympic

l' **olio** MASC NOUN
oil

□ un quadro a olio an oil painting □ una lampada ad olio an oil lamp

■ **olio d'oliva** olive oil

■ **olio di semi** vegetable oil

■ **olio solare** suntan oil

■ **olio dei freni** brake fluid

■ **sott'olio** in oil □ funghi sott'olio mushrooms in oil

l' **oliva** FEM NOUN
olive

l' **olivo** MASC NOUN
olive tree

oltre PREPOSITION, ADVERB
over

□ L'ho gettato oltre il muro. I threw it over the wall. □ gli uomini oltre i cinquant'anni men over fifty □ Non la vedo da oltre tre mesi. I haven't seen her for over three months.

■ **Non posso aspettare oltre.** I can't wait any longer.

177

■ **oltre a** apart from □ Oltre a te non voglio vedere nessuno. Apart from you, I don't want to see anyone.

■ **È anche piccola, oltre ad essere cara.** It's small as well as being expensive.

oltrepassare VERB [68]
to cross

□ Oltrepassarono il confine. They crossed the border.

■ **Questa volta hai oltrepassato ogni limite!** This time you've gone too far!

l' **omaggio** MASC NOUN
▷ *see also* **omaggio** ADJECTIVE
gift

□ Ecco un piccolo omaggio per le signore. Here's a little gift for the ladies.

omaggio (FEM+PL **omaggio**) ADJECTIVE
▷ *see also* **omaggio** NOUN
free

□ un biglietto omaggio a free ticket

l' **ombelico** (PL gli **ombelichi**) MASC NOUN
navel

l' **ombra** FEM NOUN
1 shade

□ Mi sedetti all'ombra. I sat down in the shade.
2 shadow

□ l'ombra di un grattacielo the shadow of a skyscraper

■ **senza ombra di dubbio** without a shadow of a doubt

l' **ombrello** MASC NOUN
umbrella

l' **ombrellone** MASC NOUN
beach umbrella

l' **ombretto** MASC NOUN
eyeshadow

l' **omelette** (PL le **omelette**) FEM NOUN
omelette

□ un'omelette al prosciutto a ham omelette

l' **omeopata** (MASC PL gli **omeopati**, FEM PL le **omeopate**) MASC/FEM NOUN
homeopath

l' **omeopatia** FEM NOUN
homeopathy

l' **omicida** (MASC PL gli **omicidi**, FEM PL le **omicide**) MASC/FEM NOUN
murderer

l' **omicidio** MASC NOUN
murder

■ **commettere un omicidio** to commit a murder

gli **omogeneizzati** MASC PL NOUN
baby food *sing*

omonimo (FEM **omonima**) ADJECTIVE, MASC/FEM NOUN

■ **È un mio omonimo.** He's got the same name as me.

■ **il film tratto dall'omonimo romanzo** the film based on the novel of the same name

omosessuale (FEM **omosessuale**)
ADJECTIVE, MASC/FEM NOUN
homosexual

l' **onda** FEM NOUN
wave

□ Si è tuffato tra le onde. He dived into the waves.

■ **andare in onda** to be on □ Il programma va in onda alle sei. The programme is on at six o'clock.

■ **mandare in onda** to broadcast

l' **onestà** FEM NOUN
honesty

onesto (FEM **onesta**) ADJECTIVE
1 honest

□ È una persona onesta. He's an honest person.
2 fair

□ Mi sembra un prezzo onesto. It seems a fair price.

l' **onomastico** (PL gli **onomastici**) MASC NOUN
name day

□ Oggi è il mio onomastico. Today's my name day.

> **DID YOU KNOW...?**
> In Italy people celebrate their 'name day' – that is, the day of the saint with the same name. For someone called Giorgio, for example, this would be April 23, which is St George's Day.

l' **onore** MASC NOUN
honour

□ È un onore per me. It's an honour for me.

■ **fare gli onori di casa** to act as host
□ Paolo ha fatto gli onori di casa. Paolo acted as host.

■ **farsi onore** to do well □ Si è fatto onore agli esami. He did well in the exams.

l' **O.N.U.** FEM NOUN
the UN (= the United Nations)

opaco (FEM **opaca**, MASC PL **opachi**, FEM PL **opache**) ADJECTIVE
1 opaque (glass)
2 matt (paper)

l' **opera** FEM NOUN
work

□ le opere più importanti di Dante Dante's most important works

■ **mettersi all'opera** to get down to work
■ **opera d'arte** work of art
■ **opera lirica** opera

l' **operaio**, l' **operaia** MASC/FEM NOUN
▷ *see also* **operaio** ADJECTIVE
worker

operaio (FEM **operaia**) ADJECTIVE
▷ *see also* **operaio** NOUN

■ **il movimento operaio** the labour movement

■ **un quartiere operaio** a working-class district

■ **la classe operaia** the working class

operare VERB [68]

to do an operation

□ Hanno dovuto operare d'urgenza. They had to do an emergency operation.

■ **Sono stato operato allo stomaco.** I had an operation on my stomach.

■ **operarsi** to have an operation □ Dovrò operarmi la prossima settimana. I'm going to have an operation next week.

■ **Si è operato d'appendicite.** He had his appendix removed.

l' **operazione** FEM NOUN

operation

l' **opinione** FEM NOUN

opinion

□ Vorrei sapere qual è la tua opinione su di lui. I'd like to know your opinion of him.

■ **l'opinione pubblica** public opinion

opporre VERB [73]

■ **opporre resistenza** to put up a struggle

□ Si sono arresi senza opporre resistenza. They surrendered without putting up a struggle.

■ **opporsi** to object □ Ci siamo opposti alla proposta. We objected to the proposal.

l' **opportunista** (MASC PL gli **opportunisti**, FEM PL le **opportuniste**) MASC/FEM NOUN

opportunist

□ È un opportunista. He's an opportunist.

l' **opportunità** FEM NOUN

opportunity

□ Non ho avuto l'opportunità di parlargli. I didn't have the opportunity to speak to him.

opportuno (FEM **opportuna**) ADJECTIVE

right

□ il momento opportuno the right moment

l' **opposizione** FEM NOUN

opposition

□ i partiti dell'opposizione the opposition parties

opposto (FEM **opposta**) ADJECTIVE, MASC NOUN

opposite

□ Veniva dalla direzione opposta. She was coming from the opposite direction.

□ l'opposto the opposite

■ **Hanno opinioni opposte.** They have very different ideas.

oppure CONJUNCTION

or

□ Possiamo guardare la TV oppure noleggiare un video. We can watch TV or rent a video.

l' **opuscolo** MASC NOUN

booklet

■ **opuscolo pubblicitario** brochure

l' **ora** FEM NOUN

▷ see also **ora** ADVERB

1 hour

□ Aspetto da un'ora. I've been waiting for an hour. □ tre ore e mezza three and a half hours

■ **mezz'ora** half an hour

■ **all'ora** an hour □ Lo pagano trenta euro all'ora. They pay him thirty euros an hour. □ 70 km all'ora 70 km an hour

■ **ora di punta** rush hour □ il traffico dell'ora di punta the rush hour traffic

■ **di buon'ora** early

■ **Non vedo l'ora di dirglielo.** I can't wait to tell him.

2 time

□ Che ora è? What time is it? □ A che ora parti? What time are you leaving? □ È ora di partire. It's time we went. □ domani a quest'ora this time tomorrow

■ **ora di pranzo** lunchtime

■ **ora legale** summer time

■ **ora locale** local time

ora ADVERB

▷ see also **ora** NOUN

now

□ Ora sto meglio. I'm better now.

■ **Ora sono molto occupata.** I'm very busy at the moment.

LANGUAGE TIP **ora** is sometimes translated as 'just'.

□ È uscito proprio ora. He's just gone out. □ Ora arrivo. I'm just coming.

■ **d'ora in avanti** from now on

■ **per ora** for now

orale (FEM **orale**) ADJECTIVE

oral

□ un esame orale an oral exam

orario (FEM **oraria**) ADJECTIVE

▷ see also **orario** NOUN

time

□ il segnale orario the time signal

■ **in senso orario** clockwise

■ **la tariffa oraria** the hourly rate

l' **orario** MASC NOUN

▷ see also **orario** ADJECTIVE

1 timetable

□ l'orario ferroviario the railway timetable

2 hours pl

□ l'orario di lavoro working hours □ orario di ufficio business hours

3 time

□ Qual è l'orario delle visite? When's visiting time?

■ **l'orario di apertura** opening time

■ **l'orario di chiusura** closing time

■ **in orario** on time

l' **orbita** FEM NOUN

orbit

□ Il razzo fu lanciato in orbita. The rocket was launched into orbit.

le **Orcadi** FEM PL NOUN
the Orkneys

l' **orchestra** FEM NOUN
orchestra

l' **orchidea** FEM NOUN
orchid

l' **ordigno** MASC NOUN
■ **un ordigno esplosivo** an explosive device

ordinale (FEM **ordinale**) ADJECTIVE
ordinal

ordinare VERB [68]
to order
□ Hai già ordinato? Have you already ordered?
■ **ordinare a qualcuno di fare qualcosa**
to order somebody to do something □ Gli hanno ordinato di andarsene subito. They ordered him to leave immediately.
■ **Il medico mi ha ordinato di riposare.**
The doctor told me to rest.

ordinato (FEM **ordinata**) ADJECTIVE
tidy
□ È la persona la più ordinata che abbia mai conosciuto. He's the tidiest person I've ever met.

l' **ordine** MASC NOUN
order
□ in ordine alfabetico in alphabetical order □ in ordine d'importanza in order of importance □ per ordine del preside by order of the headmaster
■ **Ho l'ordine di non farvi entrare.** I've been told not to let you in.
■ **mettere in ordine** to tidy up □ Stavano mettendo in ordine la loro camera. They were tidying up their room.
■ **in ordine** tidy □ La casa è in ordine. The house is tidy.
■ **le forze dell'ordine** the police

l' **orecchino** MASC NOUN
earring
□ un paio di orecchini d'oro a pair of gold earrings

l' **orecchio** (FEM PL le **orecchie**) MASC NOUN
ear
■ **farsi fare i buchi nelle orecchie** to have one's ears pierced □ Mi sono fatta fare i buchi nelle orecchie. I've had my ears pierced.
■ **Ha orecchio.** He's got a good ear.
■ **Mi fa male un orecchio.** I've got earache.

gli **orecchioni** MASC PL NOUN
mumps *sing*

l' **orefice** MASC/FEM NOUN
jeweller

l' **oreficeria** FEM NOUN
jeweller's

l' **orfano**, l' **orfana** MASC/FEM NOUN
▷ see also **orfano** ADJECTIVE
orphan

orfano (FEM **orfana**) ADJECTIVE
▷ see also **orfano** NOUN
■ **rimanere orfano** to be orphaned □ È rimasto orfano a dieci anni. He was orphaned at the age of ten.
■ **È orfano di madre.** His mother is dead.

organizzare VERB [68]
to organize
□ Hanno organizzato un concerto. They organized a concert.
■ **Abbiamo organizzato una gita in campagna.** We've arranged a trip to the country.

l' **organizzazione** FEM NOUN
organization
□ un'organizzazione studentesca a student organization
■ **Ci occuperemo dell'organizzazione della festa.** We'll organize the party.

l' **organo** MASC NOUN
organ
□ trapianto d'organi organ transplants
□ Suona l'organo. She plays the organ.

l' **orgoglio** MASC NOUN
pride

orgoglioso (FEM **orgogliosa**) ADJECTIVE
proud

orientale (FEM **orientale**) ADJECTIVE
1 eastern
□ l'Europa orientale eastern Europe
■ **la costa orientale della Gran Bretagna** the east coast of Britain
2 oriental
□ un tappeto orientale an oriental carpet

l' **orientamento** MASC NOUN
■ **perdere l'orientamento** to lose one's bearings □ Ho perso l'orientamento. I've lost my bearings.
■ **senso di orientamento** sense of direction

orientarsi VERB [56]
to know one's way
□ Si orientava bene in città. He knew his way around the city.

l' **oriente** MASC NOUN
east
□ a oriente in the east
■ **il Medio Oriente** the Middle East
■ **l'Estremo Oriente** the Far East

l' **origano** MASC NOUN
oregano

originale (FEM **originale**) ADJECTIVE, MASC NOUN
original
□ un'idea originale an original idea □ Vuoi una copia o l'originale? Do you want a copy, or the original?
■ **È un tipo originale.** He's a bit eccentric.

l' **origine** FEM NOUN
origin

origliare VERB [25]
to eavesdrop

orizzontale (FEM **orizzontale**) ADJECTIVE
horizontal

l' **orizzonte** MASC NOUN
horizon

■ **all'orizzonte** on the horizon
□ Improvvisamente compare un'isola all'orizzonte. **Suddenly an island appeared on the horizon.**

l' **orlo** MASC NOUN
1 edge
□ sull'orlo del precipizio **on the edge of the precipice**
2 brink
□ È sull'orlo della rovina. **He's on the brink of ruin.**
3 brim
□ Ha riempito il bicchiere fino all'orlo. **She filled the glass to the brim.**
4 hem
□ L'orlo della tovaglia si è scucito. **The hem of the tablecloth has come unstitched.**

l' **orma** FEM NOUN
1 track
□ Segui le orme della volpe. **Follow the fox's tracks.**
2 footprint
□ Ho trovato delle orme in giardino. **I found footprints in the garden.**

■ **seguire le orme di qualcuno** to follow in somebody's footsteps □ Ha seguito le orme del padre. **He followed in his father's footsteps.**

ormai ADVERB
by now
□ Ormai dovrebbe essere partito. **He must have left by now.**

> **LANGUAGE TIP** ormai is sometimes not translated.

□ Non fermarti! Ormai siamo quasi arrivati. **Don't stop! We're nearly there.**

l' **ormone** MASC NOUN
hormone

l' **oro** MASC NOUN
gold

■ **d'oro** gold □ un orologio d'oro **a gold watch** □ Ha vinto la medaglia d'oro. **He won the gold medal.**

■ **un'occasione d'oro** a golden opportunity
■ **Ha un cuore d'oro.** He has a heart of gold.
■ **È un affare d'oro.** It's a real bargain.

l' **orologio** MASC NOUN
1 clock
2 watch

■ **un orologio da polso** a wristwatch

l' **oroscopo** MASC NOUN
horoscope

orrendo (FEM **orrenda**) ADJECTIVE
awful

orribile (FEM **orribile**) ADJECTIVE
horrible

l' **orrore** MASC NOUN
horror
□ un film dell'orrore **a horror film**
■ **I ragni mi fanno orrore.** I hate spiders.

l' **orsacchiotto** MASC NOUN
teddy bear

l' **orso** MASC NOUN
bear
■ **un orso bianco** a polar bear
■ **un orso bruno** a brown bear

l' **ortica** (PL le **ortiche**) FEM NOUN
nettle
□ Mi sono punto con le ortiche. **I stung myself on the nettles.**

l' **orticaria** FEM NOUN
nettle rash

l' **orto** MASC NOUN
vegetable garden

l' **ortografia** FEM NOUN
spelling
□ un errore di ortografia **a spelling mistake**

l' **ortopedico** (PL gli **ortopedici**) MASC NOUN
orthopaedic specialist

l' **orzaiolo** MASC NOUN
stye

l' **orzo** MASC NOUN
barley

osare VERB [68]
to dare

■ **osare fare qualcosa** to dare to do something □ Ha osato sfidarlo. **She dared to defy him.** □ Non osavo dirlo. **I didn't dare to say it.** □ Oserei dire che... **I dare say...**
■ **Come osi?** How dare you?

osceno (FEM **oscena**) ADJECTIVE
obscene

oscillare VERB [68]
1 to swing to and fro
2 to fluctuate (temperature)

l' **oscurità** FEM NOUN
darkness
□ La stanza piombò nell'oscurità. **The room was plunged into darkness.**

oscuro (FEM **oscura**) ADJECTIVE
▷ see also **oscuro** NOUN
unclear
□ Ci sono alcuni punti oscuri nel suo racconto. **There are some unclear points in his account.**
■ **È morto in circostanze oscure.** He died in mysterious circumstances.

l' **oscuro** MASC NOUN
▷ see also **oscuro** ADJECTIVE
■ **all'oscuro** in the dark □ Mi hanno sempre tenuto all'oscuro della faccenda. **They've always kept me in the dark about this.**

o

181

l' **ospedale** MASC NOUN
hospital

■ **essere ricoverato in ospedale** to be
admitted to hospital

■ **essere all'ospedale** to be in hospital
□ Luigi è all'ospedale da una settimana. Luigi's
been in hospital for a week.

ospitale (FEM **ospitale**) ADJECTIVE
hospitable

ospitare VERB [68]
to put up
□ Mi hanno ospitato per una settimana. They
put me up for a week.

l' **ospite** MASC/FEM NOUN
1 guest
□ Ero l'unico ospite dell'albergo. I was the only
guest at the hotel.

■ **la stanza degli ospiti** the guest room
2 host
hostess

l' **ospizio** MASC NOUN
old people's home

osservare VERB [68]
1 to watch
□ Osservava quello che stavo facendo. He
watched what I was doing.
2 to notice
□ Hai osservato che zoppica un po'? Have you
noticed that she limps a bit?

■ **far osservare qualcosa a qualcuno** to
point something out to somebody □ Vorrei
farvi osservare alcune cose. I'd like to point out
a few things to you.

l' **osservazione** FEM NOUN
1 observation
□ L'hanno tenuto sotto osservazione per due
giorni. He was kept under observation for two
days.
2 remark
□ Questa è un'osservazione molto acuta.
That's a very intelligent remark.

■ **Nessuno ha delle osservazioni da
fare?** Has anyone got any comments?

■ **Il professore mi ha fatto
un'osservazione ingiusta.** The teacher
criticized me unfairly.

l' **ossigeno** MASC NOUN
oxygen

l' **osso** (FEM PL le **ossa**) MASC NOUN
bone
□ le ossa della gamba the bones of the leg

■ **essere bagnato fino all'osso** to be
soaked to the skin

■ **rompersi l'osso del collo** to break one's
neck

■ **essere un osso duro** to be a tough nut

ostacolare VERB [68]
to hinder

□ Le gonne strette ostacolano i movimenti.
Tight skirts hinder one's movements.

■ **Hai cercato di ostacolare il mio piano.**
You tried to spoil my plan.

■ **Hanno cercato di ostacolarmi.** They
tried to make things difficult for me.

■ **ostacolare la giustizia** to obstruct justice

l' **ostacolo** MASC NOUN
1 difficulty
□ Ha superato molti ostacoli. She has
overcome many difficulties.
2 hurdle
□ i quattrocento metri a ostacoli the four
hundred meter hurdles
3 jump (in horse-riding)

l' **ostaggio** MASC NOUN
hostage

■ **prendere qualcuno in ostaggio** to take
somebody hostage □ I dirottatori hanno preso
in ostaggio due donne. The hijackers have
taken two women hostage.

l' **ostello** MASC NOUN
■ **ostello della gioventù** youth hostel

l' **osteria** FEM NOUN
inn

l' **ostetrica** (PL le **ostetriche**) FEM NOUN
midwife
□ Mia madre fa l'ostetrica. My mother is a
midwife.

ostile (FEM **ostile**) ADJECTIVE
hostile

ostinarsi VERB [56]
■ **ostinarsi a fare qualcosa** to keep on
doing something □ È inutile che ti ostini a
negarlo. It's no use keeping on denying it.

ostinato (FEM **ostinata**) ADJECTIVE
stubborn

l' **ostrica** (PL le **ostriche**) FEM NOUN
oyster

> LANGUAGE TIP Be careful! **ostrica** doesn't
mean **ostrich**.

ostruire VERB [51]
to block
□ C'è qualcosa che ostruisce il tubo. There's
something blocking the pipe.

l' **otite** FEM NOUN
ear infection
□ Ho l'otite. I've got an ear infection.

l' **otorino** MASC NOUN
ear, nose and throat specialist

ottanta NUMBER
eighty

ottantesimo (FEM **ottantesima**) ADJECTIVE
eightieth

ottavo (FEM **ottava**) ADJECTIVE
> see also **ottavo** NOUN
eighth
□ Abita all'ottavo piano. He lives on the eighth
floor.

l' **ottavo** MASC NOUN
▷ *see also* **ottavo**
eighth

■ **superare gli ottavi di finale** to reach the quarter-finals

ottenere VERB [113]
to get
□ Ha ottenuto il permesso di uscire. **She got permission to go out.** □ Abbiamo ottenuto un buon risultato. **We got a good result.**

ottico (FEM **ottica**, MASC PL **ottici**, FEM PL **ottiche**) ADJECTIVE
▷ *see also* **ottico** NOUN

■ **un'illusione ottica** an optical illusion

l' **ottico** (PL gli **ottici**) MASC NOUN
▷ *see also* **ottico** ADJECTIVE
optician

l' **ottimismo** MASC NOUN
optimism

l' **ottimista** (MASC PL gli **ottimisti**, FEM PL le **ottimiste**) MASC/FEM NOUN
▷ *see also* **ottimista** ADJECTIVE
optimist

ottimista (FEM **ottimista**, MASC PL **ottimisti**, FEM PL **ottimiste**) ADJECTIVE
▷ *see also* **ottimista** NOUN
optimistic

ottimo (FEM **ottima**) ADJECTIVE
excellent
□ risultati ottimi **excellent results**

■ **La cena è stata ottima.** The dinner was delicious.

otto NUMBER
eight
□ Ha otto anni. **He is eight.** □ le otto di sera eight o'clock in the evening

■ **l'otto dicembre** the eighth of December

ottobre MASC NOUN
October

> **LANGUAGE TIP** In Italian, months are not written with capital letters.

□ in ottobre in October

ottocento NUMBER
eight hundred

■ **l'Ottocento** the nineteenth century

l' **ottone** MASC NOUN
brass
□ un campanello di ottone **a brass bell**

otturare VERB [68]
1 to seal
□ Bisogna otturare la falla. **We need to seal the leak.**
2 to block
□ C'è qualcosa che ottura il lavandino. **There's something blocking the sink.**
3 to fill
□ Il dentista mi ha otturato due denti. **The dentist has filled two of my teeth.**

l' **otturatore** MASC NOUN
shutter

l' **otturazione** FEM NOUN
filling

ovale (FEM **ovale**) ADJECTIVE
oval

l' **ovatta** FEM NOUN
cotton wool

l' **ovest** MASC NOUN
west
□ Il vento viene da ovest. **The wind comes from the west.**

■ **ad ovest** west □ Si è diretto ad ovest. **He headed west.**

■ **Il sole tramonta ad ovest.** The sun sets in the west.

■ **L'Italia confina ad ovest con la Francia.** Italy has a border to the west with France.

■ **ad ovest di** west of □ Si trova ad ovest della città. **It's west of the city.**

ovunque ADVERB
1 wherever
□ Ti troverò ovunque tu vada. **I'll find you wherever you go.**
2 everywhere
□ L'ho cercato ovunque. **I've looked for it everywhere.**

ovvio (FEM **ovvia**) ADJECTIVE
obvious

l' **ozio** MASC NOUN
■ **Se ne sta tutto il giorno in ozio.** He sits around doing nothing all day.

l' **ozono** MASC NOUN
ozone
□ il buco dell'ozono **the hole in the ozone layer**

Pp

il **pacchetto** MASC NOUN
1 packet
□ un pacchetto di sigarette a packet of cigarettes
2 parcel
□ Le ho spedito un pacchetto. I sent her a parcel.
■ **un pacchetto software** a software package
■ **un pacchetto turistico** a package holiday

il **pacco** (PL i **pacchi**) MASC NOUN
parcel
□ un grosso pacco marrone a large brown parcel
□ C'era un grosso pacco per lui sotto l'albero. There was a big parcel for him under the tree.
■ **un pacco di zucchero** a packet of sugar

la **pace** FEM NOUN
peace
□ un trattato di pace a peace treaty
■ **fare la pace con qualcuno** to make it up with somebody □ Ho fatto la pace con Luciana. I've made it up with Luciana.
■ **Lasciami in pace!** Leave me alone!

pacifico (FEM **pacifica**, MASC PL **pacifici**, FEM PL **pacifiche**) ADJECTIVE
peaceful (demonstration, protest)
■ **l'Oceano Pacifico** the Pacific Ocean

pacifista (FEM **pacifista**, MASC PL **pacifisti**, FEM PL **pacifiste**) ADJECTIVE, MASC/FEM NOUN
pacifist
□ È pacifista. He's a pacifist.

la **padella** FEM NOUN
frying pan

il **padre** MASC NOUN
father
□ mio padre my father □ il padre di Roberto Roberto's father

il **padrone**, la **padrona** MASC/FEM NOUN
owner
□ Chi è il padrone di questo cane? Who's the owner of this dog?
■ **padrone di casa** landlord
■ **padrona di casa** landlady

il **paesaggio** MASC NOUN
landscape

il **paese** MASC NOUN
1 country
□ i paesi in via di sviluppo developing countries
2 village
□ Vivo in un paese. I live in a village.
■ **i Paesi Bassi** the Netherlands

la **paga** (PL le **paghe**) FEM NOUN
pay
□ La paga non è molto alta. The pay's not very good.
LANGUAGE TIP paga can also be translated as 'wages'.
□ Dava tutta la paga alla moglie. He gave all his wages to his wife.

il **pagamento** MASC NOUN
payment
■ **fare un pagamento** to make a payment

pagare VERB [76]
to pay
□ Hai pagato il conto? Have you paid the bill?
□ Posso pagare con la carta di credito? Can I pay by credit card? □ Te la farò pagare! You'll pay for this! □ Quanto l'hai pagato? How much did you pay for it? □ L'ho pagato venti euro. I paid twenty euros for it.
■ **Pago io.** (at bar) I'll get it.

la **pagella** FEM NOUN
school report

la **pagina** FEM NOUN
page
□ Fate l'esercizio due a pagina dieci. Do exercise two on page ten. □ Andate a pagina cinque. Turn to page five. □ Ha scritto un tema di tre pagine. He wrote a three-page essay.
■ **pagina web** webpage

la **paglia** FEM NOUN
straw
□ un cappello di paglia a straw hat

il **pagliaccio** MASC NOUN
clown

il **paio** (FEM PL le **paia**) MASC NOUN
pair
□ un paio di occhiali a pair of glasses □ un paio di guanti a pair of gloves
■ **un paio di** a couple of □ un paio di giorni a couple of days

la **pala** FEM NOUN
shovel
■ **pala eolica** wind turbine

il **palato** MASC NOUN
palate

il **palazzo** MASC NOUN
1 building
2 palace
  ■ **palazzo dello sport** sports centre

il **palco** (PL i **palchi**) MASC NOUN
  box *(at theatre)*

il **palcoscenico** (PL i **palcoscenici**) MASC NOUN
  stage

la **palestra** FEM NOUN
  gym
  □ Vado in palestra due volte alla settimana. I go to the gym twice a week.
  ■ **fare palestra** to work out □ Fa palestra un'ora al giorno. He works out for an hour every day.

la **paletta** FEM NOUN
1 spade *(toy)*
2 dustpan

il **palio** MASC NOUN
  ■ **mettere qualcosa in palio** to offer something as a prize

la **palla** FEM NOUN
  ball
  □ una palla da tennis a tennis ball
  ■ **giocare a palla** to play ball
  ■ **una palla di neve** a snowball

la **pallacanestro** FEM NOUN
  basketball

la **pallamano** FEM NOUN
  handball

la **pallanuoto** FEM NOUN
  water polo

la **pallavolo** FEM NOUN
  volleyball

pallido (FEM **pallida**) ADJECTIVE
  pale
  □ Sei pallida. You're pale.
  ■ **Non ne ho la più pallida idea.** I haven't the faintest idea.

i **pallini** MASC PL NOUN
  spots
  □ rosso a pallini bianchi red with white spots

il **palloncino** MASC NOUN
  balloon

il **pallone** MASC NOUN
  ball
  ■ **giocare a pallone** to play football

la **pallottola** FEM NOUN
  bullet

la **palma** FEM NOUN
  palm

il **palmo** MASC NOUN
  palm
  ■ **restare con un palmo di naso** to be very disappointed

il **palo** MASC NOUN
1 pole

□ un palo della luce a telegraph pole
2 goalpost
  ■ **fare il palo** *(in robbery)* to act as look-out

la **palpebra** FEM NOUN
  eyelid

la **palude** FEM NOUN
  marsh

la **pancetta** FEM NOUN
  bacon

la **panchina** FEM NOUN
  bench

la **pancia** (PL le **pance**) FEM NOUN
  belly
  □ Mio padre ha un po' di pancia. My dad's got a bit of a belly.
  ■ **avere mal di pancia** to have stomach ache

il **panciotto** MASC NOUN
  waistcoat

la **pandemia** FEM NOUN
  pandemic
  □ una pandemia di influenza a flu pandemic

il **pane** MASC NOUN
  bread
  □ una fetta di pane a slice of bread
  ■ **pane a cassetta** sliced bread
  ■ **pane di segale** rye bread
  ■ **pane integrale** wholemeal bread
  ■ **pane tostato** toast □ una fetta di pane tostato a slice of toast

la **panetteria** FEM NOUN
  bakery
  □ la panetteria all'angolo the bakery on the corner
  ■ **Vado in panetteria.** I'm going to the baker's.

il **panettiere** MASC NOUN
  baker
  □ Fa il panettiere. He is a baker.

il **pangrattato** MASC NOUN
  breadcrumbs *pl*

il **panico** MASC NOUN
  panic
  ■ **essere in preda al panico** to panic
  ■ **farsi prendere dal panico** to panic
  □ Si è fatta prendere dal panico. She panicked.

il **panificio** MASC NOUN = **panetteria**

il **panino** MASC NOUN
  roll
  □ un panino al prosciutto a ham roll

la **panna** FEM NOUN
  cream
  ■ **panna da cucina** single cream
  ■ **panna montata** whipped cream

la **panne** FEM NOUN
  ■ **rimanere in panne** to break down
  □ Siamo rimasti in panne sull'autostrada. We broke down on the motorway.

il **pannello** MASC NOUN
panel
- **pannello di controllo** control panel
- **pannello solare** solar panel

il **panno** MASC NOUN
cloth
□ un panno umido a damp cloth
- **Mettiti nei miei panni.** Put yourself in my shoes.

il **pannolino** MASC NOUN
nappy

il **panorama** (PL i **panorami**) MASC NOUN
view
□ Che bel panorama! What a lovely view!

i **pantaloni** MASC PL NOUN
trousers
□ un paio di pantaloni nuovi a pair of new trousers

le **pantofole** FEM PL NOUN
slippers
□ Era in pantofole. He was in his slippers.

il **Papa** MASC NOUN
Pope
□ Papa Benedetto XVI Pope Benedict XVI

il **papà** (PL i **papà**) MASC NOUN
dad
□ il mio papà my dad □ il papà di Claudio Claudio's father

il **papavero** MASC NOUN
poppy

la **pappa** FEM NOUN
baby food

il **pappagallo** MASC NOUN
parrot

parabolico (FEM **parabolica**) ADJECTIVE
- **antenna parabolica** satellite dish

il **parabrezza** (PL i **parabrezza**) MASC NOUN
windscreen

il **paracadute** (PL i **paracadute**) MASC NOUN
parachute

il **paradiso** MASC NOUN
heaven

i **paraggi** MASC PL NOUN
- **nei paraggi di** near □ nei paraggi della stazione near the station
- **Dev'essere qui nei paraggi.** It's around here somewhere.

paragonare VERB [68]
to compare
□ Paragonate le due frasi. Compare the two sentences.
- **paragonare a** to compare with □ Lo paragona sempre al fratello. She's always comparing him with his brother.

il **paragone** MASC NOUN
- **fare un paragone tra** to compare □ Se facciamo un paragone tra le due macchine... If we compare the two cars...

il **paragrafo** MASC NOUN
paragraph

paralizzato (FEM **paralizzata**) ADJECTIVE
paralyzed

le **parallele** FEM PL NOUN
parallel bars

parallelo (FEM **parallela**) ADJECTIVE, MASC NOUN
parallel

paranoico (FEM **paranoica**, MASC PL **paranoici**, FEM PL **paranoiche**) ADJECTIVE
paranoid

il **parapetto** MASC NOUN
parapet

parare VERB [68]
to save
□ Ha parato il rigore. He saved the penalty.

la **parata** FEM NOUN
save (in football)
- **una parata militare** a military parade

il **paraurti** (PL i **paraurti**) MASC NOUN
bumper

parcheggiare VERB [58]
to park

il **parcheggio** MASC NOUN
1 car park
□ Hanno costruito un nuovo parcheggio. A new car park has been built.
2 parking space
□ Non riesco a trovare parcheggio. I can't find a parking space.
- **Qui c'è divieto di parcheggio.** You can't park here.

il **parchimetro** MASC NOUN
parking meter

il **parco** (PL i **parchi**) MASC NOUN
park
- **parco dei divertimenti** amusement park
- **parco giochi** playground

parecchio (FEM **parecchia**) PRONOUN
▷ see also **parecchio** ADJECTIVE
quite a lot
□ Mi è costato parecchio. It cost me quite a lot.
□ Ce n'è parecchio. There's quite a lot.
- **parecchi di noi** quite a few of us

parecchio (FEM **parecchia**) ADJECTIVE
▷ see also **parecchio** PRONOUN
quite a lot of
□ C'era parecchia gente alla festa. There were quite a lot of people at the party. □ C'erano parecchie ragazze. There were quite a lot of girls.
- **Non lo vedo da parecchio tempo.** I haven't seen him for ages.
- **parecchio tempo fa** a long time ago

pareggiare VERB [58]
to draw (in sport)
□ Hanno pareggiato due a due. They drew two all.

il **pareggio** MASC NOUN
draw *(in sport)*

il/la **parente** MASC/FEM NOUN
relative
□ È un mio parente. He's a relative of mine.
> **LANGUAGE TIP** Be careful! **parente** doesn't mean **parent**.

la **parentesi** (PL le **parentesi**) FEM NOUN
bracket
□ parentesi tonde round brackets
■ **tra parentesi** in brackets

il **parere** MASC NOUN
▷ *see also* **parere** VERB
opinion
□ Vuoi il mio parere? Do you want my opinion?
■ **a mio parere** in my opinion

parere VERB [67]
▷ *see also* **parere** NOUN
■ **Mi pare che...** I think that... □ Mi pare che sia già arrivato. I think he's already here.
■ **Fa' come ti pare!** Do as you like!
■ **Mi pare di sì.** I think so.
■ **Mi pare di no.** I don't think so.
■ **Che te ne pare?** What do you think?
■ **pare che** apparently □ Pare che voglia cambiare squadra. Apparently he wants to change teams. □ Pare che sia stato lui. Apparently it was him.
■ **Ma ti pare!** Not at all. □ Disturbo? — Ma ti pare! Am I disturbing you? — Not at all.

la **parete** FEM NOUN
wall

pari (FEM+PL **pari**) ADJECTIVE
1 even
□ numeri pari even numbers
2 equal
□ pari diritti e doveri equal rights and duties
■ **La partita è finita pari.** The match was a draw.
■ **Siamo pari.** It's a draw.
■ **Hanno vinto a pari merito.** They were joint winners.
■ **rimettersi in pari** to catch up □ Cercherò di rimettermi in pari. I'll try to catch up.
■ **una ragazza alla pari** an au pair girl

Parigi FEM NOUN
Paris
□ Vado a Parigi quest'estate. I'm going to Paris this summer. □ Vive a Parigi. He lives in Paris.

parlamentare (FEM **parlamentare**)
ADJECTIVE
▷ *see also* **parlamentare** NOUN
parliamentary

il/la **parlamentare** MASC/FEM NOUN
▷ *see also* **parlamentare** ADJECTIVE
Member of Parliament

il **parlamento** MASC NOUN
parliament

□ il parlamento europeo the European Parliament

la **parlantina** FEM NOUN
■ **avere la parlantina** to have the gift of the gab

parlare VERB [68]
1 to speak
□ Sai parlare l'inglese? Can you speak English? □ Parla più forte. Speak louder. □ Pronto, chi parla? Hello, who's speaking? □ Posso parlare con Marina? Can I speak to Marina? □ Voglio parlare con il direttore! I want to speak to the manager!
■ **Ne ho sentito parlare.** I've heard about it.
■ **Non parliamone più.** Let's just forget about it.
2 to talk
□ Abbiamo parlato per ore. We talked for hours. □ Non parlate tutti insieme. Don't all talk at once. □ Non sa ancora parlare. He can't talk yet.
■ **parlare di qualcosa** to talk about something □ Di che cosa avete parlato? What did you talk about? □ Parliamone. Let's talk about it.
■ **parlare a qualcuno** to talk to somebody □ Lascia che gli parli io. Let me talk to him. □ Gli parlerò di te. I'll talk to him about you.
■ **parlare del più e del meno** to talk about this and that
■ **parlare male di qualcuno** to say nasty things about somebody
■ **parlare bene di qualcuno** to say nice things about somebody
3 to be about *(book, film)*
□ Di cosa parla quel libro? What is that book about?
■ **Ne parlano tutti i giornali.** It's in all the newspapers.

il **parmigiano** MASC NOUN
Parmesan cheese

la **parola** FEM NOUN
word
□ una parola difficile a difficult word
■ **rivolgere la parola a qualcuno** to speak to somebody
■ **dare la propria parola a qualcuno** to give somebody one's word □ Gli ho dato la mia parola. I gave him my word.
■ **mantenere la parola** to keep one's word □ Ho mantenuto la parola. I've kept my word.
■ **rimangiarsi la parola** to break one's promise □ Si è rimangiato la parola. He broke his promise.
■ **parola d'ordine** password
■ **parole incrociate** crossword *sing* □ Sta facendo le parole incrociate. She's doing the crossword.

P

187

la **parolaccia** (PL le **parolacce**) FEM NOUN
swearword
■ **dire le parolacce** to swear

la **parrucca** (PL le **parrucche**) FEM NOUN
wig

il **parrucchiere**, la **parrucchiera** MASC/
FEM NOUN
hairdresser
□ Fa la parrucchiera. She is a hairdresser.

la **parte** FEM NOUN
1 part
□ la prima parte del libro the first part of the book
2 side
□ È dall'altra parte della strada. It's on the other side of the road.
3 share
□ Ognuno ebbe la sua parte. Everyone had their share.
■ **la maggior parte di** most of □ la maggior parte dei ragazzi most of the boys
■ **fare parte di** to belong to □ Fa parte di un club sportivo. He belongs to a sports club.
■ **prendere parte a** to take part in □ Non ha preso parte alla discussione. He didn't take part in the discussion.
■ **mettere da parte** (money) to save up □ Ha messo da parte del denaro. He's saved up some money.
■ **a parte questo** apart from that
■ **d'altra parte** on the other hand
■ **da parte di** (on the part of) from □ Questo è da parte di Giorgio. This is from Giorgio.
■ **da qualche parte** somewhere
■ **da nessuna parte** not... anywhere □ Non riesco a trovarlo da nessuna parte. I can't find it anywhere.
■ **da questa parte** this way
■ **prendere le parti di qualcuno** to side with somebody □ Hanno preso le sue parti. They sided with him.
■ **scherzi a parte** but, seriously

partecipare VERB [68]
■ **partecipare a** (race, demonstration) to take part in □ Parteciperai alla gara? Are you going to take part in the competition?
■ **Posso partecipare alle spese?** Can I help pay?

la **partenza** FEM NOUN
1 departure
□ il tabellone delle partenze the departure board
■ **Dobbiamo decidere prima della mia partenza.** We must decide before I leave.
■ **essere in partenza** to be about to leave
□ Fa' presto, il treno è in partenza. Hurry up, the train is about to leave.
■ **I passeggeri in partenza per...** Passengers travelling to...

2 start (in race)
□ una falsa partenza a false start

il **participio** MASC NOUN
participle
□ participio passato past participle

particolare (FEM **particolare**) ADJECTIVE
▷ see also **particolare** NOUN
1 particular
□ in questo caso particolare in this particular case
2 distinctive
□ Ha un sapore particolare. It has a distinctive flavour.

il **particolare** MASC NOUN
▷ see also **particolare** ADJECTIVE
detail
□ Vorrei sapere i particolari. I'd like to know the details.
■ **in particolare** in particular

partire VERB [41]
to leave
□ A che ora parte il treno? What time does the train leave? □ Il volo parte da Ciampino. The flight leaves from Ciampino. □ Sono partita da Roma alle sei. I left Rome at six.
■ **La macchina non parte.** The car won't start.
■ **partendo da** from □ È la seconda partendo da destra. It's the second from the right.

la **partita** FEM NOUN
1 match
□ una partita di calcio a football match
2 game
□ una partita a carte a game of cards
□ Facciamo una partita a tennis. Let's have a game of tennis.

il **partito** MASC NOUN
party (political)

il **parto** MASC NOUN
birth
□ È stato un parto difficile. It was a difficult birth.
■ **parto cesareo** Caesarean
■ **parto naturale** natural childbirth

parziale (FEM **parziale**) ADJECTIVE
partial
□ un successo parziale a partial success

il **pascolo** MASC NOUN
pasture

la **Pasqua** FEM NOUN
Easter
□ Cosa fai per Pasqua? What are you doing at Easter? □ le vacanze di Pasqua the Easter holidays □ il lunedì di Pasqua Easter Monday □ un uovo di Pasqua an Easter egg

il **passaggio** MASC NOUN
1 lift (in car)
□ Può darmi un passaggio? Can you give me a lift?
2 pass (in sport)
□ un passaggio indietro a back pass

3 passage

□ uno stretto passaggio tra le rocce a narrow passage between the rocks □ un passaggio da I Promessi Sposi a passage from I Promessi Sposi

■ **passaggio a livello** level crossing
■ **passaggio pedonale** pedestrian crossing

il/la **passante** MASC/FEM NOUN
▷ see also **passante** NOUN
passer-by

il **passante** MASC NOUN
▷ see also **passante** NOUN
loop (of belt)

il **passaporto** MASC NOUN
passport

passare VERB [68]

1 to pass

□ Hai passato l'esame? Did you pass the exam? □ Ha passato la palla a Enrico. He passed the ball to Enrico. □ Potresti passarmi il sale? Could you pass me the salt, please? □ Sono passati molti anni dalla fine della guerra. Many years have passed since the end of the war.

■ **Non è passata neanche una macchina.** Not one car went by.
■ **Mi hai passato l'influenza.** You gave me the flu.
■ **Può passarmi Daniela?** (on phone) Can I speak to Daniela?
■ **Ti passo Michele.** Here's Michele.
■ **lasciar passare qualcuno** to let somebody through □ Non mi hanno lasciato passare. They didn't let me through.
■ **passare davanti a** to go past □ Siamo passati davanti a casa tua. We went past your house.

2 to call in

□ Passa quando vuoi. Call in whenever you like. □ Passo da te dopo cena. I'll call in after dinner.
■ **Devo passare in banca.** I've got to go to the bank.
■ **passare a prendere qualcuno** to come and pick somebody up □ Ti passo a prendere alle otto. I'll come and pick you up at eight o'clock.

3 to spend (time)

□ Ho passato due giorni in montagna. I spent two days in the mountains.

4 to be over

□ Il peggio è passato. The worst is over.
■ **Ti è passato il mal di testa?** Has your headache gone?

il **passatempo** MASC NOUN
pastime

passato (FEM **passata**) ADJECTIVE
▷ see also **passato** NOUN
last

□ l'anno passato last year
■ **Sono le otto passate.** It's past eight o'clock.
■ **participio passato** past participle

il **passato** MASC NOUN
▷ see also **passato** ADJECTIVE
past

■ **in passato** in the past
■ **passato prossimo** present perfect
■ **passato remoto** simple past

il **passeggero,** la **passeggera** MASC/FEM NOUN
passenger

passeggiare VERB [58]
to stroll

la **passeggiata** FEM NOUN
■ **fare una passeggiata** to go for a walk

il **passeggino** MASC NOUN
pushchair

la **passerella** FEM NOUN

1 catwalk
2 gangway

il **passero** MASC NOUN
sparrow

la **passione** FEM NOUN
passion

□ amore e passione love and passion
■ **Il giardinaggio è la mia più grande passione.** Gardening is my greatest pleasure.

passivo (FEM **passiva**) ADJECTIVE
passive

il **passo** MASC NOUN

1 step

□ un passo di danza a dance step □ Fai un passo avanti. Take a step forward.
■ **Camminava con passo veloce.** He was walking fast.
■ **fare due passi** to go for a walk
■ **di questo passo** at this rate □ Di questo passo non finiremo mai. We'll never finish at this rate.

2 pass (mountain)

la **pasta** FEM NOUN

1 pasta
2 cake
3 dough

■ **pasta frolla** shortcrust pastry
■ **pasta sfoglia** puff pastry

il **pastello** MASC NOUN
pastel

la **pasticceria** FEM NOUN
cake shop

il **pasticciere,** la **pasticciera** MASC/FEM NOUN
baker

□ Fa il pasticciere. He is a baker.

il **pasticcino** MASC NOUN
cake

il **pasticcio** MASC NOUN

1 pie

□ un pasticcio di carne a meat pie

2 mess

□ È proprio un bel pasticcio. It's a real mess.
■ **mettersi nei pasticci** to get into trouble

P

pastiglia – pazienza

la **pastiglia** FEM NOUN
tablet
- **pastiglie per il mal di gola** throat sweets

il **pasto** MASC NOUN
meal

il **pastore** MASC NOUN
shepherd
- **cane da pastore** sheepdog
- **pastore tedesco** Alsatian

la **patata** FEM NOUN
potato
□ patate arrosto roast potatoes
- **patate fritte** chips

le **patatine** FEM PL NOUN
1 crisps
2 chips

la **patente** FEM NOUN
driving licence
□ Ho perso la patente. I've lost my driving licence.
- **Mio fratello non ha la patente.** My brother doesn't drive.

LANGUAGE TIP Be careful! **patente** doesn't mean **patent**.

patetico (FEM **patetica**, MASC PL **patetici**, FEM PL **patetiche**) ADJECTIVE
pathetic
□ Non essere patetico! Don't be pathetic!

il **patito**, la **patita** MASC/FEM NOUN
fan
□ È un patito del calcio. He's a football fan.
- **un patito di musica classica** a classical music lover

la **patria** FEM NOUN
country

il **patrigno** MASC NOUN
stepfather

il **patrimonio** MASC NOUN
1 fortune
□ Mi è costato un patrimonio. It cost me a fortune.
2 heritage
□ il nostro patrimonio artistico our artistic heritage

il **pattinaggio** MASC NOUN
skating
- **fare pattinaggio** to go skating
- **pattinaggio a rotelle** roller skating
- **pattinaggio su ghiaccio** ice skating

pattinare VERB [68]
to skate

il **pattinatore**, la **pattinatrice** MASC/FEM NOUN
skater

il **pattino** MASC NOUN
skate
- **pattini a rotelle** roller skates
- **pattini da ghiaccio** ice skates
- **pattini in linea** Rollerblades®

il **patto** MASC NOUN
pact
- **fare un patto** to make a pact
- **a patto che** on condition that

la **pattuglia** FEM NOUN
patrol

la **pattumiera** FEM NOUN
bin

la **paura** FEM NOUN
fear
□ Stava tremando dalla paura. She was trembling with fear.
- **Era morto di paura.** He was scared to death.
- **avere paura** to be scared □ Avevo molta paura. I was really scared.
- **aver paura di qualcosa** to be scared of something □ Ho paura dei ragni. I'm scared of spiders.

LANGUAGE TIP You can also use 'to be afraid of'.

□ Hai paura del buio? Are you afraid of the dark?
- **aver paura di fare qualcosa** to be scared of doing something □ Ha paura di volare. He's scared of flying.
- **Ho paura di uscire da sola la sera.** I'm afraid to go out alone at night.
- **far paura a qualcuno** to frighten somebody □ Mi hai fatto paura. You frightened me.
- **Ho paura di sì.** I'm afraid so.
- **Ho paura di no.** I'm afraid not.

pauroso (FEM **paurosa**) ADJECTIVE
awful
□ un pauroso incidente stradale an awful road accident
- **essere pauroso** to get scared easily □ È pauroso. He gets scared easily.

la **pausa** FEM NOUN
1 break
□ una pausa di un'ora an hour's break
□ Facciamo una pausa. Let's have a break.
2 pause (in speaking)
□ dopo una pausa after a pause

il **pavimento** MASC NOUN
floor

LANGUAGE TIP Be careful! **pavimento** doesn't mean **pavement**.

il **pavone** MASC NOUN
peacock

paziente (FEM **paziente**) ADJECTIVE, MASC/FEM NOUN
patient

la **pazienza** FEM NOUN
patience
□ Ha perso la pazienza e se n'è andato. He lost patience and left.
- **avere pazienza** to be patient
- **Pazienza!** Never mind!

P

pazzesco (FEM **pazzesca**, MASC PL **pazzeschi**, FEM PL **pazzesche**) ADJECTIVE
1 crazy
□ un'idea pazzesca a crazy idea □ Quest'idea è ancora più pazzesca. This idea is even crazier.
2 incredible
□ una somma pazzesca an incredible amount of money

la **pazzia** FEM NOUN
madness
□ È stata una pazzia! It was madness!
■ **Ho paura che possa fare una pazzia.** I'm afraid he'll do something crazy.

pazzo (FEM **pazza**) ADJECTIVE
▷ see also **pazzo** NOUN
crazy
□ È pazzo! He's crazy! □ È pazzo di lei. He's crazy about her. □ È il ragazzo più pazzo che abbia mai conosciuto. He's the craziest boy I've ever known.
■ **essere innamorato pazzo** to be madly in love
■ **essere pazzo da legare** to be raving mad

il **pazzo,** la **pazza** MASC/FEM NOUN
▷ see also **pazzo** ADJECTIVE
madman
madwoman
□ Guidava come un pazzo. He was driving like a madman.
■ **Dovremo lavorare come pazzi per finire in tempo.** We'll have to work like mad to finish in time.

il **peccato** MASC NOUN
1 shame
□ È un peccato che non sia potuto venire. It's a shame that he couldn't come. □ Che peccato! What a shame!
2 sin
□ un peccato mortale a mortal sin

la **pecora** FEM NOUN
sheep
□ C'erano solo due pecore nel campo. There were only two sheep in the field.
■ **la pecora nera della famiglia** the black sheep of the family

il **pedaggio** MASC NOUN
toll

pedalare VERB [68]
to pedal

il **pedale** MASC NOUN
pedal

la **pedata** FEM NOUN
■ **dare una pedata a** to kick □ Mi ha dato una pedata. He kicked me.

il/la **pediatra** (MASC PL i **pediatri**, FEM PL le **pediatre**) MASC/FEM NOUN
paediatrician
□ Fa il pediatra. He is a paediatrician.

pedonale (FEM **pedonale**) ADJECTIVE
pedestrian
□ una zona pedonale a pedestrian precinct

il **pedone** MASC NOUN
pedestrian

peggio ADVERB
▷ see also **peggio** NOUN
worse
□ Luca è andato peggio di me all'esame. Luca did worse than me in the exam. □ Sta sempre peggio. He's getting worse and worse.
■ **Peggio per te.** That's your loss. □ Non vuoi venire? Peggio per te. You don't want to come? That's your loss.

la **peggio** FEM NOUN
▷ see also **peggio** ADVERB
■ **alla peggio** if the worst comes to the worst
■ **avere la peggio** to come off worst
□ Hanno litigato e Gigi ha avuto la peggio. They had an argument and Gigi came off worst.

peggiorare VERB [68, AUX **avere** or **essere**]
to get worse

peggiore (FEM **peggiore**) ADJECTIVE
▷ see also **peggiore** NOUN
worse
□ È peggiore di lui. She's worse than him.

il/la **peggiore** MASC/FEM NOUN
▷ see also **peggiore** ADJECTIVE
worst
□ È il peggiore della classe. He's the worst in the class.
■ **nel peggiore dei casi** if the worst comes to the worst

il **pegno** MASC NOUN
■ **dare in pegno** to leave as security □ Posso darle in pegno l'orologio. I can leave you my watch as security.
■ **un pegno d'amore** a token of love

pelare VERB [68]
to peel

pelato (FEM **pelata**) ADJECTIVE
bald
□ È pelato. He's bald.
■ **pomodori pelati** peeled tomatoes

la **pelle** FEM NOUN
1 skin
□ Ho la pelle secca. I've got dry skin.
■ **avere la pelle d'oca** to have goose pimples
2 leather
□ una giacca di pelle a leather jacket

il/la **pellerossa** (PL i/le **pellirosse**) MASC/FEM NOUN
Indian

la **pelliccia** (PL le **pellicce**) FEM NOUN
fur coat

la **pellicola** FEM NOUN
film

pelo - penultimo

il **pelo** MASC NOUN
1 fur
    □ Il gatto ha il pelo morbido. The cat has soft fur.
2 hair *(on body)*
    ■ **per un pelo** nearly □ Per un pelo non ho perso il treno. I nearly missed the train.
    ■ **L'ha mancato per un pelo.** He just missed him.

peloso (FEM **pelosa**) ADJECTIVE
    hairy

il **peluche** MASC NOUN
    ■ **un pupazzo di peluche** a cuddly toy

la **pena** FEM NOUN
    ■ **essere in pena per qualcuno** to worry about somebody □ Ero in pena per te. I was worried about you.
    ■ **Mi fa pena.** I feel sorry for him.
    ■ **valere la pena** to be worth it □ Non ne vale la pena. It's not worth it. □ Vale la pena farlo. It's worth doing.
    ■ **la pena di morte** the death penalty □ Sono contrario alla pena di morte. I'm against the death penalty.
    ■ **È stato condannato alla pena di morte.** He was sentenced to death.

penale (FEM **penale**) ADJECTIVE
    ■ **codice penale** penal code
    ■ **precedenti penali** criminal record *sing*

pendere VERB [8]
    to hang
    □ la lampada che pende dal soffitto the lamp that hangs from the ceiling

il **pendio** (PL i **pendii**) MASC NOUN
    slope

il/la **pendolare** MASC/FEM NOUN
    commuter
    ■ **fare il pendolare** to commute

penetrare VERB [68, aux **essere**]
    ■ **penetrare in** to go into □ Il proiettile gli è penetrato nel cuore. The bullet went into his heart.
    ■ **I ladri sono penetrati in casa di notte.** The thieves entered the house at night.

la **penisola** FEM NOUN
    peninsula

la **penna** FEM NOUN
1 pen
    ■ **penna a sfera** ballpoint pen
    ■ **penna stilografica** fountain pen
2 feather

il **pennarello** MASC NOUN
    felt-tip pen

il **pennello** MASC NOUN
    paintbrush
    ■ **pennello da barba** shaving brush
    ■ **stare a pennello** to fit perfectly □ Quel vestito ti sta a pennello. That dress fits you perfectly.

la **pennetta** FEM NOUN
    ■ **pennetta USB** memory stick

la **penombra** FEM NOUN
    ■ **in penombra** in the half-light □ Ho visto qualcuno nella penombra. I saw someone in the half-light.

pensare VERB [68]
    to think
    □ Penso che I think that □ Cosa ne pensi? What do you think of it?
    ■ **Penso di sì.** I think so.
    ■ **Penso di no.** I don't think so.
    ■ **a pensarci bene** on second thoughts
    ■ **pensare a** to think about □ A chi stai pensando? Who are you thinking about? □ Non voglio nemmeno pensarci. I don't even want to think about it.
    ■ **Vorrei pensarci su.** I'd like to think it over.
    ■ **Ci penso io.** I'll see to it.
    ■ **pensare di fare qualcosa** to think of doing something □ Pensavo di invitare anche lui. I was thinking of inviting him too.

il **pensiero** MASC NOUN
1 thought
    □ libertà di pensiero freedom of thought
    □ È un pensiero gentile. It's a kind thought.
    □ Era immerso nei suoi pensieri. He was deep in thought.
2 worry
    □ Ha tanti pensieri. He has so many worries.
    ■ **stare in pensiero per qualcuno** to be worried about somebody

pensieroso (FEM **pensierosa**) ADJECTIVE
    thoughtful

il **pensionato**, la **pensionata** MASC/FEM NOUN
    pensioner

la **pensione** FEM NOUN
1 pension
    ■ **andare in pensione** to retire
    ■ **essere in pensione** to be retired
2 boarding house
    ■ **mezza pensione** half board
    ■ **pensione completa** full board

pentirsi VERB [41, aux **essere**]
    ■ **pentirsi di qualcosa** to regret something □ Vieni con noi e non te ne pentirai. If you come with us you won't regret it.
    ■ **pentirsi di aver fatto qualcosa** to regret doing something □ Mi pento di averglielo detto. I regret telling him.

la **pentola** FEM NOUN
    pot
    □ Metti la pentola sul fuoco. Put the pot on the gas.
    ■ **pentola a pressione** pressure cooker

penultimo (FEM **penultima**) ADJECTIVE
    second from last

□ È arrivato penultimo. He arrived second from last.

il **pepe** MASC NOUN
pepper

il **peperoncino** MASC NOUN
chilli pepper

il **peperone** MASC NOUN
pepper

□ un peperone rosso a red pepper □ peperoni ripieni stuffed peppers

■ **rosso come un peperone** as red as a beetroot

per PREPOSITION

1 for

□ Questo è per te. This is for you. □ un poster per la mia stanza a poster for my room □ È troppo difficile per lui. It's too difficult for him. □ È partito per l'Inghilterra. He left for England. □ L'ho comprato per trenta centesimi. I bought it for thirty cents. □ Ho guidato per dieci chilometri. I drove for ten kilometres. □ per molto tempo for a long time

■ **per tutto il giorno** all day long

2 through

□ I ladri sono passati per la finestra. The thieves got in through the window. □ Sono passata per Londra. I came through London.

■ **L'ho incontrato per le scale.** I met him on the stairs.

3 by

□ per posta by post □ per ferrovia by rail □ L'ho preso per mano. I took him by the hand.

■ **Abbiamo parlato per telefono.** We spoke on the phone.

4 out of

□ per abitudine out of habit □ per curiosità out of curiosity □ Non l'ho fatto per pigrizia. I didn't do it out of laziness.

■ **per errore** by mistake

■ **Tremava per il freddo.** She was shivering with cold.

5 to

□ L'ho fatto per aiutarti. I did it to help you.

■ **uno per uno** one by one

■ **giorno per giorno** day by day

■ **moltiplicare due per tre** to multiply two by three

■ **Due per tre fa sei.** Two times three equals six.

■ **uno per volta** one at a time

■ **per cento** per cent □ il dieci per cento ten per cent

■ **sedersi per terra** to sit on the ground

■ **L'ha fatto per gioco.** He did it as a joke.

la **pera** FEM NOUN
pear

perbene (FEM **perbene**) ADJECTIVE
respectable

□ gente perbene respectable people

la **percentuale** FEM NOUN
percentage

perché ADVERB

1 why

□ Perché? Why? □ Perché l'hai fatto? Why did you do it? □ Spiegami perché sei arrabbiato. Tell me why you're angry. □ Non so perché. I don't know why.

2 because

□ Perché vai via? — Perché è tardi. Why are you going? — Because it's late. □ Non posso uscire perché ho molto da fare. I can't go out because I've got a lot to do.

3 so that

□ Ho telefonato perché non si preoccupassero. I phoned so that they wouldn't worry.

perciò CONJUNCTION
so

percorrere VERB [26]
to cover

□ Abbiamo percorso venti chilometri al giorno. We covered twenty kilometres a day.

il **percorso** MASC NOUN
route

□ Ho seguito il percorso più breve. I took the shortest route.

■ **lungo il percorso** along the way

perdere VERB [69]

1 to lose

□ Ho perso il portafoglio. I've lost my wallet. □ Non perdere la speranza. Don't lose hope. □ Non ho niente da perdere. I've got nothing to lose. □ Il libro è andato perso. The book got lost.

■ **perdere di vista qualcuno** to lose sight of somebody □ L'ho perso di vista dopo mezzora. I lost sight of him after half an hour.

■ **Dopo la scuola si sono persi di vista.** They lost touch after leaving school.

■ **Lascia perdere!** Forget it!

■ **Lascialo perdere!** Don't listen to him.

2 to miss *(train, bus, plane)*

□ Ho perso il treno. I've missed the train.

■ **È un'occasione da non perdere.** It's an opportunity not to be missed.

3 to waste

□ Hai perso tempo e denaro. You've wasted time and money.

4 to leak

□ Il tubo perde. The pipe is leaking.

■ **perdersi** to get lost □ Ci siamo persi. We got lost.

la **perdita** FEM NOUN

1 loss

□ È una grave perdita. It's a great loss.

2 waste

□ È una perdita di tempo. It's a waste of time.

P

perdonare VERB [68]
   to forgive
      □ Mi perdoni? Do you forgive me? □ Non glielo perdonerò mai. I'll never forgive him for that.
      ■ **Le ha comprato dei fiori per farsi perdonare.** He bought her flowers as a peace offering.

perfettamente ADVERB
   perfectly
      □ Funziona perfettamente. It works perfectly.
      □ Sai perfettamente che... You know perfectly well that...

perfetto (FEM **perfetta**) ADJECTIVE
   perfect

il **perfezionamento** MASC NOUN
      ■ **un corso di perfezionamento di inglese** a course to improve one's English

perfezionare VERB [68]
   to improve

perfino ADVERB
   even

pericolante (FEM **pericolante**) ADJECTIVE
   unsafe

il **pericolo** MASC NOUN
   danger
      ■ **essere in pericolo** to be in danger
      ■ **essere fuori pericolo** to be out of danger

pericoloso (FEM **pericolosa**) ADJECTIVE
   dangerous

la **periferia** FEM NOUN
   outskirts pl
      □ la periferia di Milano the outskirts of Milan
      ■ **Vivo in periferia.** I live on the edge of town.

il **periodico** (PL i **periodici**) MASC NOUN
   periodical

il **periodo** MASC NOUN
   period
      □ un periodo di tre anni a period of three years
      □ un periodo di prova a trial period

il **perito** MASC NOUN
      ■ **È perito chimico.** He has a qualification in chemistry.

la **perla** FEM NOUN
   pearl
      □ una collana di perle a pearl necklace

la **perlina** FEM NOUN
   bead

permaloso (FEM **permalosa**) ADJECTIVE
   touchy

la **permanente** FEM NOUN
      ▷ see also **permanente** ADJECTIVE
   perm
      □ Ha la permanente. She's got a perm.
      ■ **farsi fare la permanente** to have one's hair permed □ Mi sono fatta fare la permanente. I had my hair permed.

permanente (FEM **permanente**) ADJECTIVE
      ▷ see also **permanente** NOUN
   permanent

la **permanenza** FEM NOUN
   stay
      □ Buona permanenza! Enjoy your stay!

il **permesso** MASC NOUN
1   permission
      □ Ho chiesto il permesso di uscire. I asked permission to leave the room.
2   permit
      ■ **permesso di lavoro** work permit
      ■ **permesso di soggiorno** residence permit

permettere VERB [59]
   to allow
      ■ **permettere a qualcuno di fare qualcosa** to allow somebody to do something
      □ Non mi ha permesso di vederla. He didn't allow me to see her.
      ■ **Permettete che mi presenti.** Let me introduce myself.
      ■ **Permesso?** 1 May I come in? 2 *(to get past)* Excuse me.
      ■ **permettersi** 1 to afford □ Non può permettersi una macchina nuova. He can't afford a new car. 2 to dare □ Come ti permetti? How dare you?

la **pernacchia** FEM NOUN
   raspberry *(informal)*
      ■ **fare una pernacchia** to blow a raspberry

pernottare VERB [68]
   to spend the night

però CONJUNCTION
   but
      □ Mi piace, però è troppo caro. I like it, but it's too expensive.

perplesso (FEM **perplessa**) ADJECTIVE
   puzzled

perquisire VERB [51]
   to search
      □ All'aeroporto siamo stati perquisiti. We were searched at the airport.

la **perquisizione** FEM NOUN
   search
      □ un mandato di perquisizione a search warrant

la **persiana** FEM NOUN
   shutter *(on window)*

persino ADVERB
   even

perso (FEM **persa**) ADJECTIVE
      ■ **a tempo perso** in one's spare time
      □ Dipinge a tempo perso. She paints in her spare time.
      ■ **È tempo perso.** It's a waste of time.

la **persona** FEM NOUN
   person
      □ una persona intelligente an intelligent person
      ■ **persone** people pl □ C'erano molte persone. There were a lot of people.

il **personaggio** MASC NOUN
character
□ i personaggi del romanzo the characters in
the novel
■ **un importante personaggio politico**
an important political figure

personale (FEM **personale**) ADJECTIVE
▷ see also **personale** NOUN
personal

il **personale** MASC NOUN
▷ see also **personale** ADJECTIVE
staff
□ il personale dell'azienda the staff of the
company
■ **ufficio personale** personnel office

la **personalità** (PL le **personalità**) FEM NOUN
personality
□ Ha una forte personalità. He's got a strong
personality.

perspicace (FEM **perspicace**) ADJECTIVE
shrewd

pertanto CONJUNCTION
therefore

la **pertica** (PL le **pertiche**) FEM NOUN
pole (in gym)

la **pertosse** FEM NOUN
whooping cough

perverso (FEM **perversa**) ADJECTIVE
perverse

il **pervertito,** la **pervertita** MASC/FEM NOUN
pervert

p.es. ABBREVIATION (= per esempio)
e.g.

pesante (FEM **pesante**) ADJECTIVE
1 heavy
□ Quella valigia è troppo pesante. That suitcase
is too heavy. □ La mia è la più pesante. Mine is
the heaviest.
2 heavy going
□ Il film era un po' pesante. The film was rather
heavy going.
■ **droghe pesanti** hard drugs

pesare VERB [68]
to weigh
□ Quanto pesa? How much does it weigh?
□ L'ho già pesato. I've already weighed it.
■ **Come pesa!** It weighs a ton!
■ **pesarsi** to weigh oneself

la **pesca** (PL le **pesche**) FEM NOUN
1 peach
2 fishing
■ **andare a pesca** to go fishing
■ **pesca subacquea** underwater fishing
■ **pesca con la lenza** angling
■ **pesca di beneficenza** lucky dip

pescare VERB [18]
1 to fish
□ Ti insegnerò a pescare. I'll teach you how to fish.

■ **Ho pescato un pesce enorme.** I caught
an enormous fish.
2 to get (find)
□ Dove diavolo hai pescato quella giacca?
Where on earth did you get that jacket?

il **pescatore** MASC NOUN
fisherman

il **pesce** MASC NOUN
fish
□ Ho pescato due pesci. I caught two fish.
□ Ti piace il pesce? Do you like fish?
■ **pesce rosso** goldfish
■ **pesce spada** swordfish
■ **pesce d'aprile** April Fool

il **pescecane** MASC NOUN
shark

il **peschereccio** (PL i **pescherecci**) MASC
NOUN
fishing boat

la **pescheria** FEM NOUN
fishmonger's

Pesci MASC PL NOUN
Pisces
□ Sono dei Pesci. I'm Pisces.

il **peso** MASC NOUN
weight
■ **peso lordo** gross weight
■ **peso netto** net weight
■ **dar peso a qualcosa** to attach importance
to something □ Non ho dato molto peso alle
sue parole. I didn't attach much importance to
his words.
■ **essere di peso a qualcuno** to be a
burden to somebody □ Non voglio essere di
peso a nessuno. I don't want to be a burden to
anybody.
■ **portare qualcuno via di peso** to carry
somebody away bodily
■ **avere due pesi e due misure** to have
double standards
■ **fare pesi** to do weight training
■ **sollevamento pesi** weightlifting
■ **lancio del peso** shot put

pessimista (FEM **pessimista**, MASC PL
pessimisti, FEM PL **pessimiste**) ADJECTIVE
▷ see also **pessimista** NOUN
pessimistic

il/la **pessimista** (MASC PL i **pessimisti**, FEM
PL le **pessimiste**) MASC/FEM NOUN
▷ see also **pessimista** ADJECTIVE
pessimist

pessimo (FEM **pessima**) ADJECTIVE
1 very bad
□ un pessimo insegnante a very bad teacher
2 terrible
□ un odore pessimo a terrible smell
■ **essere di pessimo umore** to be in a very
bad mood

pestare VERB [68]
1 to beat
  □ Suo marito la pesta. Her husband beats her.
2 to crush (garlic, etc)

la **peste** FEM NOUN
1 plague
2 pest
  □ Sei una peste! You're a pest!

il **petalo** MASC NOUN
  petal

il **petardo** MASC NOUN
  firecracker

la **petroliera** FEM NOUN
  oil tanker

il **petrolio** MASC NOUN
  oil

  LANGUAGE TIP Be careful! **petrolio** doesn't
  mean **petrol**.

il **pettegolezzo** MASC NOUN
  gossip
  □ Sono solo pettegolezzi. It's just gossip.
  □ Vuoi sentire un pettegolezzo? Do you want to
  hear a bit of gossip?
  ■ **fare pettegolezzi** to gossip

pettegolo (FEM **pettegola**) ADJECTIVE,
MASC/FEM NOUN
  gossip
  □ Lucia è un po' pettegola. Lucia is a bit of a
  gossip.

pettinare VERB [68]
  to comb
  □ Le ho pettinato i capelli. I combed her hair.
  ■ **pettinarsi** to comb one's hair □ Ti sei
  pettinata? Have you combed your hair?

la **pettinatura** FEM NOUN
  hairstyle

il **pettine** MASC NOUN
  comb

il **pettirosso** MASC NOUN
  robin

il **petto** MASC NOUN
  chest
  □ Ho un dolore al petto. I've got a pain in my
  chest.
  ■ **petto di pollo** chicken breast
  ■ **giacca a doppio petto** double-breasted
  jacket

la **pezza** FEM NOUN
  patch
  □ Ha una pezza sui pantaloni. He has a patch
  on his trousers.
  ■ **una bambola di pezza** a rag doll

il **pezzo** MASC NOUN
1 piece
  □ un pezzo di pane a piece of bread
2 part (of car, engine)
  □ Ha cambiato un pezzo. He's replaced a part.
  ■ **un pezzo di ricambio** a spare part

  ■ **andare in pezzi** to break □ Il bicchiere è
  andato in pezzi. The glass broke.
  ■ **essere a pezzi** (person) to be shattered
  □ Ho lavorato tutto il giorno e sono a pezzi.
  I've been working all day and I'm shattered.
  ■ **un due pezzi** a bikini
  ■ **da un pezzo** for a while □ È qui da un
  pezzo. He has been here for a while.

photoshoppare VERB [68]
  to Photoshop

piacere VERB [70]
  ▷ see also **piacere** NOUN
  ■ **Mi piace.** I like it.
  ■ **Questa musica non mi piace.** I don't
  like this music.
  ■ **Cosa ti piacerebbe fare?** What would
  you like to do?

il **piacere** MASC NOUN
  ▷ see also **piacere** VERB
1 pleasure
  □ È un viaggio d'affari o di piacere? Is this trip
  for business or for pleasure? □ Con piacere!
  With pleasure!
  ■ **Mi farebbe piacere rivederlo.** It would
  be nice to see him again.
  ■ **Mi fa piacere per lui.** I'm pleased for him.
  ■ **'Piacere!'** 'Pleased to meet you!'
  ■ **Che piacere vederti!** How nice to see you!
2 favour
  □ Mi faresti un piacere? Would you do me a
  favour?
  ■ **per piacere** please

piacevole (FEM **piacevole**) ADJECTIVE
  pleasant

la **piaga** (PL le **piaghe**) FEM NOUN
  sore
  ■ **piaghe da decubito** bedsores

piagnucolare VERB [68]
  to whimper

il **pianerottolo** MASC NOUN
  landing

il **pianeta** (PL i **pianeti**) MASC NOUN
  planet

piangere VERB [71]
  to cry

il/la **pianista** (MASC PL i **pianisti**, FEM PL le
  pianiste) MASC/FEM NOUN
  pianist

piano ADVERB
  ▷ see also **piano** NOUN
1 slowly
  □ Guida piano! Drive slowly!
  ■ **Fai piano, è fragile!** Be careful, it's fragile!
2 quietly
  □ Parla più piano. Speak more quietly.
  ■ **pian piano** little by little

il **piano** MASC NOUN
  ▷ see also **piano** ADVERB

1 floor

□ Abito al terzo piano. I live on the third floor. □ all'ultimo piano on the top floor □ al piano terra on the ground floor □ al piano di sopra on the floor above □ al piano di sotto on the floor below

■ **una casa di tre piani** a three-storey house

■ **autobus a due piani** double-decker bus

2 plan

□ un piano di pace a peace plan □ Tutto va secondo i piani. Everything's going according to plan.

3 piano (musical instrument)

■ **in primo piano** in the foreground □ una figura in primo piano a figure in the foreground

■ **primo piano** (photograph) close-up

il **pianoforte** MASC NOUN
piano

la **pianta** FEM NOUN

1 plant

□ una pianta d'appartamento a house plant

■ **pianta grassa** succulent

2 map

□ una pianta della città a map of the city

■ **pianta del piede** sole of the foot

piantare VERB [68]

1 to plant

□ Ho piantato un albero in giardino. I've planted a tree in the garden.

■ **piantare una tenda** to put up a tent

2 to dump

□ Ha piantato il ragazzo. She's dumped her boyfriend.

■ **piantare qualcuno in asso** to leave somebody in the lurch □ Mi ha piantata in asso. He left me in the lurch.

■ **Piantala!** Stop it!

la **pianura** FEM NOUN
plain

la **piastra** FEM NOUN
slab (of stone)

■ **piastra per capelli** hair straighteners pl

■ **una piastra di registrazione** a tape deck

la **piastrella** FEM NOUN
tile

la **piattaforma** FEM NOUN
platform

il **piattino** MASC NOUN
saucer

piatto (FEM **piatta**) ADJECTIVE
▷ see also **piatto** NOUN
flat

□ Questa zona è più piatta. This area is flatter.

il **piatto** MASC NOUN
▷ see also **piatto** ADJECTIVE

1 dish

□ Lavo io i piatti. I'll wash the dishes. □ un piatto tipico spagnolo a traditional Spanish dish

■ **piatto del giorno** dish of the day

2 plate

□ un piatto di carne a plate of meat □ Metti più piselli nel mio piatto. Put more peas on my plate.

■ **un piatto di minestra** a bowl of soup

■ **piatto fondo** soup plate

■ **piatto piano** dinner plate

■ **i piatti** the cymbals

la **piazza** FEM NOUN
square

□ Piazza San Marco St Mark's Square

■ **scendere in piazza** to take to the streets

□ Gli operai sono scesi in piazza. The workers took to the streets.

■ **a una piazza** single □ un lenzuolo ad una piazza a single sheet

■ **a due piazze** double

il **piazzale** MASC NOUN
square

piccante (FEM **piccante**) ADJECTIVE

1 hot (spicy)

□ È molto piccante? Is it very hot? □ A me piace più piccante. I like it hotter.

2 risqué

□ una barzelletta piccante a risqué joke

le **picche** FEM PL NOUN
spades (in cards)

il **picchetto** MASC NOUN
peg (for tent)

picchiare VERB [17]

1 to hit

□ È lui che mi ha picchiato! It was him who hit me!

2 to beat

□ Picchia la moglie. He beats his wife.

3 to bang

□ Ho picchiato la testa. I banged my head.

4 to knock

□ Qualcuno picchiava alla porta. Somebody was knocking at the door.

picchiata FEM NOUN

■ **scendere in picchiata** (plane) to nosedive

piccino (FEM **piccina**) ADJECTIVE
tiny

□ Ha preso in braccio il più piccino. He took the tiniest one in his arms.

il **piccione** MASC NOUN
pigeon

il **picco** (PL i **picchi**) MASC NOUN
peak (in graph)

■ **una roccia a picco sul mare** a sheer cliff

■ **colare a picco** (ship) to sink

piccolo (FEM **piccola**) ADJECTIVE
▷ see also **piccolo** NOUN

1 small

□ una macchina molto piccola a very small car □ Me ne dia uno più piccolo. Give me a smaller

P

197

one. □ la stanza più piccola della casa the smallest room in the house

2 little

□ una piccola casetta in campagna a little house in the country □ un bambino piccolo a little boy

3 young

□ È ancora troppo piccolo. He's still too young. □ i bambini piccoli young children □ mio fratello più piccolo my younger brother □ Paolo è il più piccolo dei fratelli. Paolo is the youngest of the brothers.

il **piccolo,** la **piccola** MASC/FEM NOUN
▷ see also **piccolo** ADJECTIVE
small child

■ **da piccolo** as a child □ Da piccola ero molto timida. I was very shy as a child.

il **picnic** (PL i **picnic**) MASC NOUN
picnic

■ **fare un picnic** to have a picnic

il **pidocchio** (PL i **pidocchi**) MASC NOUN
louse

il **piede** MASC NOUN
foot

□ Mi fanno male i piedi. My feet are sore.

■ **andare a piedi** to walk □ Ci andrò a piedi. I'll walk.

■ **a piedi nudi** barefoot

■ **stare in piedi** to be standing □ Stava in piedi in un angolo. He was standing in a corner.

■ **tra i piedi** in the way □ È sempre tra i piedi. He's always in the way.

■ **Fuori dai piedi!** Get out of the way!

la **piega** (PL le **pieghe**) FEM NOUN

1 fold (in paper)

2 pleat (of skirt)

3 crease (in trousers)

piegare VERB [76]

1 to fold

□ Piega la cartina e mettila via. Fold the map and put it away.

2 to bend (arms, legs)

□ Piegate le braccia. Bend your arms.

3 to bow

■ **piegarsi** (person) to bend

pieghevole (FEM **pieghevole**) ADJECTIVE
folding

□ una sedia pieghevole a folding chair

il **Piemonte** MASC NOUN
Piedmont

la **piena** FEM NOUN

■ **essere in piena** to be in flood □ Il fiume è in piena. The river is in flood.

pieno (FEM **piena**) ADJECTIVE
▷ see also **pieno** NOUN
full

□ La mia valigia è piena. My suitcase is full.

■ **pieno di** full of □ una borsa piena di libri a bag full of books

■ **Sono pieno di lavoro.** I have a lot of work to do.

■ **pieno zeppo** packed □ Il cinema era pieno zeppo. The cinema was packed.

■ **a tempo pieno** full-time □ Cerco un lavoro a tempo pieno. I'm looking for a full-time job.

■ **in pieno giorno** in broad daylight

■ **in pieno inverno** in the depths of winter

■ **in piena notte** in the middle of the night

il **pieno** MASC NOUN
▷ see also **pieno** ADJECTIVE

■ **Mi fa il pieno per favore?** Can you fill it up, please?

il **piercing** (PL i **piercing**) MASC NOUN
piercing

□ Ha molti piercing. He's got lots of piercings.

■ **Voglio farmi un piercing sull'ombelico.** I want to get my navel pierced.

la **pietà** FEM NOUN
pity

□ Non voglio la vostra pietà. I don't want your pity.

pietoso (FEM **pietosa**) ADJECTIVE
pitiful

□ uno spettacolo pietoso a pitiful sight □ È in uno stato pietoso. It's in a pitiful state.

la **pietra** FEM NOUN
stone

■ **una pietra preziosa** a precious stone

■ **Mettiamoci una pietra sopra.** Let bygones be bygones.

■ **di pietra** stone □ una casa di pietra a stone house

il **pigiama** (PL i **pigiami**) MASC NOUN
pyjamas pl

□ Questo pigiama mi è un po' stretto. These pyjamas are a bit tight on me.

■ **essere in pigiama** to be in one's pyjamas □ Siamo ancora in pigiama. We're still in our pyjamas.

la **pigna** FEM NOUN
pine cone

pignolo (FEM **pignola**) ADJECTIVE
fussy

□ È più pignolo di me. He's fussier than me.

la **pigrizia** FEM NOUN
laziness

□ Non l'ho fatto per pigrizia. I didn't do it out of laziness.

pigro (FEM **pigra**) ADJECTIVE
lazy

□ È il ragazzo più pigro che abbia mai conosciuto. He's the laziest boy I've ever known.

la **pila** FEM NOUN

1 pile

□ una pila di libri a pile of books

2 battery

□ Funziona a pile. It works on batteries.

3 torch

il **pilastro** MASC NOUN
pillar

la **pillola** FEM NOUN
pill

■ **prendere la pillola** to be on the pill

il **pilone** MASC NOUN
1 pylon
2 pier

il/la **pilota** (MASC PL i **piloti**, FEM PL le **pilote**)
MASC/FEM NOUN
1 pilot
2 driver

■ **pilota automatico** automatic pilot

la **pinacoteca** (PL le **pinacoteche**) FEM NOUN
art gallery

la **pineta** FEM NOUN
pinewood

il **ping-pong** MASC NOUN
table tennis

il **pinguino** MASC NOUN
penguin

la **pinna** FEM NOUN
1 fin
2 flipper *(for swimming)*

il **pino** MASC NOUN
pine tree

il **pinolo** MASC NOUN
pine kernel

la **pinza** FEM NOUN
pliers *pl*

le **pinzette** FEM PL NOUN
tweezers

la **pioggia** (PL le **piogge**) FEM NOUN
rain
□ sotto la pioggia in the rain
■ **pioggia acida** acid rain

il **piolo** MASC NOUN
rung
□ un piolo rotto a broken rung
■ **scala a pioli** ladder

il **piombo** MASC NOUN
lead
■ **benzina senza piombo** unleaded petrol

il **pioniere**, la **pioniera** MASC/FEM NOUN
pioneer

il **pioppo** MASC NOUN
poplar

piovere VERB [72]
to rain
□ Piove. It's raining.

piovigginare VERB [68]
to drizzle

piovoso (FEM **piovosa**) ADJECTIVE
rainy

la **pipa** FEM NOUN
pipe
□ Fuma la pipa. He smokes a pipe.

la **pipì** FEM NOUN
■ **fare pipì** to have a pee

il **pipistrello** MASC NOUN
bat

il **pirata** (PL i **pirati**) MASC NOUN
pirate
■ **un pirata della strada** a hit-and-run
driver

la **piscina** FEM NOUN
swimming pool

i **piselli** MASC PL NOUN
peas

il **pisolino** MASC NOUN
nap
■ **fare un pisolino** to have a nap

la **pista** FEM NOUN
1 track
□ I corridori erano in pista. The runners were
on the track.
■ **Pista!** Out of the way!
■ **pista ciclabile** cycle track
■ **pista da sci** ski run
■ **pista da pattinaggio** skating rink
■ **pista da ballo** dance floor
2 lead
□ La polizia sta seguendo una pista. The police
are following a lead.
3 runway

il **pistacchio** (PL i **pistacchi**) MASC NOUN
pistachio

la **pistola** FEM NOUN
gun

il **pittore**, la **pittrice** MASC/FEM NOUN
painter

pittoresco (FEM **pittoresca**, MASC PL
pittoreschi, FEM PL **pittoresche**) ADJECTIVE
picturesque

la **pittura** FEM NOUN
painting
□ la pittura astratta abstract painting
■ **pittura fresca** wet paint

pitturare VERB [68]
to paint

più ADVERB
more
□ Quella gonna è più costosa. That skirt is
more expensive. □ Può parlare più
lentamente? Could you speak more slowly?
□ Lucia è più carina. Lucia is prettier.
□ Quella stanza è più luminosa. That room is
brighter.
■ **più di** more than □ Paolo le piace più di
Marco. She likes Paolo more than Marco. □ Ho
speso più di 10 sterline. I spent more than 10
pounds. □ Studia più di me. She studies more
than I do.
■ **più... di** more... than □ È più intelligente
di me. He's more intelligent than me.
□ Ho più compiti di te. I've got more homework
than you.

■ **È più veloce di me.** He's quicker than me.
■ **il più** the most □ il ristorante più caro della città the most expensive restaurant in the town □ Sono le ragazze più belle della classe. They're the most attractive girls in the class. □ Questa è la cabina telefonica più vicina. This is the nearest phone box.
■ **non... più** not... any more □ Non lavora più. He doesn't work any more. □ Non ce n'è più. There isn't any more.

> **LANGUAGE TIP** If the English verb is not in the negative, use 'no more'.

□ Non c'è più birra. There's no more beer.
■ **Non c'è più nessuno.** There's no one left.
■ **Non c'è più niente da fare.** There's nothing else to do.
■ **di più** more □ Costa molto di più. It costs a lot more.
■ **È la persona che odio di più.** He's the person I hate most.
■ **in più** more □ Ci sono tre persone in più. There are three more people.
■ **più o meno** more or less
■ **più che mai** more than ever
■ **mai più** never again
■ **per lo più** mostly
■ **al più presto** as soon as possible
■ **al più tardi** at the latest
■ **il più delle volte** more often than not
■ **sempre più veloce** faster and faster
■ **due più due fa quattro** two plus two equals four

la **piuma** FEM NOUN
feather

il **piumino** MASC NOUN
1 duvet
2 quilted jacket

piuttosto ADVERB
rather
□ Prenderei piuttosto un'acqua minerale. I'd rather have some mineral water. □ Fa piuttosto caldo. It's rather hot.

la **pizza** FEM NOUN
pizza

la **pizzeria** FEM NOUN
pizzeria

pizzicare VERB [18]
1 to pinch
□ Gli ho pizzicato un braccio. I pinched his arm.
■ **Mi sono pizzicato un dito nella porta.** I caught my finger in the door.
2 to itch
□ Mi pizzica il naso. My nose is itching.

il **pizzico** (PL i **pizzichi**) MASC NOUN
pinch
□ un pizzico di sale a pinch of salt

il **pizzicotto** MASC NOUN
pinch

il **pizzo** MASC NOUN
lace (fabric)

il **plaid** (PL i **plaid**) MASC NOUN
travelling rug

la **plastica** FEM NOUN
plastic
■ **di plastica** plastic □ un piatto di plastica a plastic plate
■ **farsi fare la plastica** to have plastic surgery

il **platano** MASC NOUN
plane tree

la **platea** FEM NOUN
1 the stalls pl (in theatre)
□ un posto in platea a seat in the stalls
2 audience
□ La platea ha applaudito. The audience applauded.

plausibile (FEM **plausibile**) ADJECTIVE
plausible

il **plico** (PL i **plichi**) MASC NOUN
parcel

il **plotone** MASC NOUN
platoon
■ **plotone d'esecuzione** firing squad

plurale (FEM **plurale**) ADJECTIVE, MASC NOUN
plural

lo **pneumatico** (PL gli **pneumatici**) MASC NOUN
tyre

po' ADVERB, MASC NOUN
■ **un po'** a bit □ Sono un po' stanco. I'm a bit tired. □ Zoppica un po'. He limps a bit.
■ **un po' di** some □ Potrei avere ancora un po' di tè? Could I have some more tea? □ Mettici un po' di zucchero. Put some sugar in it. □ un po' di soldi some money
■ **un bel po'** quite a lot □ un bel po' di soldi quite a lot of money
■ **tra un po'** shortly

poco (FEM **poca**, MASC PL **pochi**, FEM PL **poche**) ADJECTIVE, ADVERB, MASC NOUN
1 not much (for quantity)
□ Bevo poco vino. I don't drink much wine. □ C'è poco spazio. There's not much room.
2 not many (for number)
□ C'erano poche ragazze alla festa. There weren't many girls at the party. □ Questa macchina ha fatto pochi chilometri. This car hasn't done many kilometres. □ Pochi ci crederebbero. Not many people would believe that.
■ **È poco più alta di lui.** She's a bit taller than him.
■ **Studia troppo poco.** He doesn't study enough.
■ **a poco a poco** little by little
■ **poco fa** a short time ago

■ **per poco** nearly □ Per poco non cadevo. I nearly fell.

■ **poco dopo** shortly afterwards

■ **poco prima** shortly before

■ **fra poco** soon

■ **poco spesso** not very often

■ **Sono arrivato da poco.** I have just arrived.

■ **Sta poco bene.** He's not very well.

il **podio** MASC NOUN
podium

la **poesia** FEM NOUN
1 poem
  □ una poesia di Foscolo a poem by Foscolo
2 poetry
  □ la poesia e la prosa poetry and prose

il **poeta,** la **poetessa** MASC/FEM NOUN
poet

poggiare VERB [58]
1 to put (on top of something)
  □ Puoi poggiare il pacco sul tavolo. You can put the parcel on the table.
2 to lean (against something)
  □ Poggia la scala al muro. Lean the ladder against the wall.
  ■ **poggiarsi a** to lean against □ Si è dovuto poggiare al muro per sostenersi. He had to lean against the wall for support.

il **poggiatesta** (PL i **poggiatesta**) MASC NOUN
headrest

poi ADVERB
1 then
  □ E poi cos'è successo? And then what happened?
2 later
  □ Poi te lo dico. I'll tell you later.
  ■ **prima o poi** sooner or later
  ■ **d'ora in poi** from now on
  ■ **da domani in poi** from tomorrow onwards

poiché CONJUNCTION
since

la **polacca** (PL le **polacche**) FEM NOUN
Pole (person)

polacco (FEM **polacca**, MASC PL **polacchi**, FEM PL **polacche**) ADJECTIVE
▷ see also **polacco** NOUN
Polish

il **polacco** (PL i **polacchi**) MASC NOUN
▷ see also **polacco** ADJECTIVE
1 Pole (person)
  □ i polacchi the Poles
2 Polish (language)
  □ Parli polacco? Do you speak Polish?

la **polemica** (PL le **polemiche**) FEM NOUN
controversy

polemico (FEM **polemica**, MASC PL **polemici**, FEM PL **polemiche**) ADJECTIVE
argumentative

il **polipo** MASC NOUN
polyp

il **polistirolo** MASC NOUN
polystyrene

la **politica** (PL le **politiche**) FEM NOUN
1 politics sing
  □ Si interessa di politica. He's interested in politics.
2 policy
  □ la politica economica del governo the government's economic policy

politico (FEM **politica**, MASC PL **politici**, FEM PL **politiche**) ADJECTIVE
political
  □ la situazione politica the political situation
  ■ **elezioni politiche** general election
  ■ **un uomo politico** a politician

la **polizia** FEM NOUN
police pl
  □ È arrivata la polizia? Have the police arrived?
  □ Chiama la polizia! Call the police!

poliziesco (FEM **poliziesca**, MASC PL **polizieschi**, FEM PL **poliziesche**) ADJECTIVE
  ■ **un film poliziesco** a detective film

la **poliziotta** FEM NOUN
policewoman

il **poliziotto** MASC NOUN
policeman
  ■ **cane poliziotto** police dog

il **pollaio** MASC NOUN
henhouse

il **pollice** MASC NOUN
1 thumb
  ■ **girarsi i pollici** to twiddle one's thumbs
2 inch (= 2.45 cm)
  □ un televisore a 24 pollici a 24-inch TV

il **polline** MASC NOUN
pollen
  ■ **Sono allergico al polline.** I suffer from hay fever.

il **pollo** MASC NOUN
chicken

il **polmone** MASC NOUN
lung

la **polmonite** FEM NOUN
pneumonia

il **polo** MASC NOUN
  ■ **il Polo nord** the North Pole
  ■ **il Polo sud** the South Pole

la **Polonia** FEM NOUN
Poland
  □ Ti è piaciuta la Polonia? Did you like Poland?
  □ Sei mai stato in Polonia? Have you ever been to Poland?

il **polpaccio** MASC NOUN
calf

il **polpastrello** MASC NOUN
fingertip

la **polpetta** FEM NOUN
meatball

il **polpo** MASC NOUN
octopus

il **polsino** MASC NOUN
cuff

il **polso** MASC NOUN
wrist

□ Ha un braccialetto al polso. She's got a
bracelet on her wrist.

■ **avere polso** to be firm

poltrire VERB [51]
to laze about

la **poltrona** FEM NOUN
armchair

la **polvere** FEM NOUN
dust

□ uno strato di polvere a layer of dust

■ **polvere da sparo** gunpowder

la **pomata** FEM NOUN
ointment

il **pomeriggio** MASC NOUN
afternoon

■ **nel pomeriggio** in the afternoon

■ **alle due del pomeriggio** at two o'clock in
the afternoon

■ **domani pomeriggio** tomorrow afternoon

■ **ogni pomeriggio** every afternoon

il **pomodoro** MASC NOUN
tomato

■ **spaghetti al pomodoro** spaghetti with
tomato sauce

la **pompa** FEM NOUN
pump

□ una pompa da bicicletta a bicycle pump

■ **pompa antincendio** fire hose

■ **pompa di benzina** petrol pump

pompare VERB [68]
to pump up

□ Devo pompare il materassino. I need to
pump up my airbed.

il **pompelmo** MASC NOUN
grapefruit

il **pompiere** MASC NOUN
firefighter

□ Fa il pompiere. He is a firefighter.

■ **i pompieri** the fire brigade *sing* □ Chiamate
i pompieri! Call the fire brigade!

il **ponte** MASC NOUN

1 bridge

□ È dell'altra parte del ponte. It's across the
bridge.

■ **ponte levatoio** drawbridge

2 deck

■ **fare ponte** to have a long weekend

popolare (FEM **popolare**) ADJECTIVE
popular

□ un cantante molto popolare a very popular

singer □ la stampa popolare the popular press

■ **un quartiere popolare** a poor area

■ **una casa popolare** a council house

la **popolazione** FEM NOUN
population

il **popolo** MASC NOUN
people *pl*

la **porcellana** FEM NOUN
porcelain

il **porcellino** MASC NOUN
piglet

■ **porcellino d'India** guinea pig

la **porcheria** FEM NOUN
rubbish

□ Mangia un sacco di porcherie. He eats a lot of
rubbish.

il **porcino** MASC NOUN
cep *(mushroom)*

il **porco** (PL i **porci**) MASC NOUN
pig

il **porcospino** MASC NOUN
porcupine

porno (FEM+PL **porno**) ADJECTIVE

■ **un film porno** a porn film

la **pornografia** FEM NOUN
pornography

porre VERB [73]

1 to put

2 to place

3 to lay down

■ **Poniamo che...** Let's suppose that...

■ **porre una domanda a qualcuno** to ask
somebody a question

■ **porre fine a** to put an end to

■ **porsi in salvo** to save oneself

il **porro** MASC NOUN
leek

□ una minestra di porri leek soup

la **porta** FEM NOUN

1 door

□ Chiudi la porta, per favore. Close the door,
please.

■ **mettere qualcuno alla porta** to throw
somebody out □ Lo hanno messo alla porta.
They threw him out.

■ **vendita porta a porta** door-to-door
selling

2 goal *(in football)*

il **portabagagli** (PL i **portabagagli**) MASC
NOUN
boot

il **portacenere** (PL i **portacenere**) MASC
NOUN
ashtray

il **portachiavi** (PL i **portachiavi**) MASC NOUN

1 key ring

2 key case

la **portaerei** (PL le **portaerei**) FEM NOUN
aircraft carrier

la **portafinestra** (PL le **portefinestre**) FEM
NOUN
French window

il **portafoglio** MASC NOUN
wallet

il **portafortuna** (PL i **portafortuna**) MASC
NOUN
lucky charm

il **portamatite** (PL i **portamatite**) MASC
NOUN
pencil case

il **portamonete** (PL i **portamonete**) MASC
NOUN
purse

il **portaombrelli** (PL i **portaombrelli**) MASC
NOUN
umbrella stand

il **portapacchi** (PL i **portapacchi**) MASC
NOUN
luggage rack

portare VERB [68]
1 to take
□ Sta portando i bambini a scuola. She's taking
the children to school. □ Puoi portarlo laggiù?
Can you take it down? □ Porta questa lettera a
Lucia. Take this letter to Lucia.
2 to bring
□ Portalo qui. Bring it here. □ Puoi portarmi
quel libro? Can you bring me that book?
3 to carry
□ Portava un pacco sottobraccio. He was
carrying a parcel under his arm.
4 to wear
□ Portava un bel vestito. She was wearing a
beautiful dress.
5 to lead
□ Dove porta questa strada? Where does this
street lead?
■ **portare fortuna** to bring good luck

il **portariviste** (PL i **portariviste**) MASC NOUN
magazine rack

il **portasigarette** (PL i **portasigarette**)
MASC NOUN
cigarette case

la **portata** FEM NOUN
course (of meal)
□ la portata principale the main course
■ **a portata di mano** within reach

il **portatelefonino** MASC NOUN
mobile phone case

portatile (FEM **portatile**) ADJECTIVE
portable
□ una TV portatile a portable TV □ un
computer portatile a laptop

portato (FEM **portata**) ADJECTIVE
■ **essere portato per qualcosa** to have a
gift for something □ È portato per le lingue. He
has a gift for languages.

il **portauovo** (PL i **portauova**) MASC NOUN
egg cup

il/la **portavoce** (MASC/FEM i/le **portavoce**)
MASC/FEM NOUN
spokesperson

la **portiera** FEM NOUN
door (of car, etc)

il **portiere** MASC NOUN
1 goalkeeper
2 porter
3 concierge

il **porto** MASC NOUN
1 harbour
□ un porto riparato a sheltered harbour
2 port
□ un importante porto fluviale an important
river port
■ **porto d'armi** gun licence

il **Portogallo** MASC NOUN
Portugal
□ Ti è piaciuto il Portogallo? Did you like
Portugal? □ Sei mai stato in Portogallo? Have
you ever been to Portugal?

portoghese (FEM **portoghese**) ADJECTIVE,
MASC/FEM NOUN
Portuguese
■ **i portoghesi** the Portuguese

il **portone** MASC NOUN
main entrance

la **porzione** FEM NOUN
portion
□ una porzione abbondante a big portion

la **posa** FEM NOUN
1 exposure
□ un rullino a 24 pose a 24 exposure film
2 pose
■ **mettersi in posa** to pose
■ **lavorare senza posa** to work without a break

posare VERB [68]
to put
□ Ha posato la penna sul tavolo. He put the
pen on the table.

le **posate** FEM PL NOUN
cutlery sing

positivo (FEM **positiva**) ADJECTIVE
positive

la **posizione** FEM NOUN
position
□ una posizione scomoda an uncomfortable
position
■ **Si è fatto una posizione.** He's done well.
■ **luci di posizione** sidelights

posporre VERB [73]
to postpone

possedere VERB [101]
1 to have
□ Quasi tutti possiedono una macchina. Most
people have a car.

P

203

Italian-English

2 to own
□ Possiede una casa in campagna. She owns a house in the country.

possessivo (FEM **possessiva**) ADJECTIVE
possessive

possibile (FEM **possibile**) ADJECTIVE, MASC NOUN
possible
□ Pensi che sia possibile? Do you think it's possible?
■ **fare tutto il possibile** to do everything possible
■ **il più presto possibile** as soon as possible

la **possibilità** (PL le **possibilità**) FEM NOUN
1 possibility
□ Ci sono varie possibilità. There are various possibilities.
2 opportunity
□ Non ha avuto la possibilità di viaggiare. He didn't have the opportunity to travel.

il **post** (PL i **post**) MASC NOUN
post

la **posta** FEM NOUN
1 post
□ C'è posta per me? Is there any post for me?
■ **per posta** by post □ Mandalo per posta. Send it by post.
■ **posta aerea** airmail
■ **posta elettronica** email
2 post office
□ Sto andando alla posta. I'm going to the post office.

postale (FEM **postale**) ADJECTIVE
postal
□ servizio postale postal service
■ **impiegato postale** post office employee
■ **timbro postale** postmark

postare VERB [68]
to post
□ Ha postato il messaggio su Facebook. She posted the message on Facebook.

posteggiare VERB [58]
to park

il **posteggio** MASC NOUN
1 car park
□ un posteggio gratuito a free car park
2 parking space
□ Non riesco a trovare posteggio. I can't find a parking space.
■ **posteggio taxi** taxi rank

il **poster** (PL i **poster**) MASC NOUN
poster

posteriore (FEM **posteriore**) ADJECTIVE
back
□ il sedile posteriore the back seat

posticipare VERB [68]
to postpone

la **postina** FEM NOUN
postwoman

il **postino** MASC NOUN
postman

il **posto** MASC NOUN
1 place
□ È un posto magnifico. It's a beautiful place.
□ Rimetti il libro al suo posto. Put the book back in its place.
2 room (space)
□ Non c'è più posto in macchina. There's no more room in the car.
3 seat (in theatre, on train)
□ Vorrei prenotare due posti. I'd like to book two seats.
■ **un posto a sedere** a seat
■ **posti in piedi** standing room
■ **a posto** tidy □ La casa era a posto. The house was tidy.
■ **Tutto a posto?** Is everything OK?
■ **mettere a posto** to tidy □ Metti a posto la tua camera. Tidy your room.
■ **al posto di** instead of □ C'è un film al posto della partita. There's a film instead of the match.
□ Andrò io al suo posto. I'll go instead of him.
■ **Se fossi al tuo posto ci andrei.** If I were you I would go.
■ **posto di blocco** roadblock
■ **posto di lavoro** job

potabile (FEM **potabile**) ADJECTIVE
■ **acqua potabile** drinking water

potente (FEM **potente**) ADJECTIVE
powerful
□ un motore potente a powerful engine

la **potenza** FEM NOUN
power

potere VERB [74]
▷ see also **potere** NOUN
1 can
□ Non posso venire. I can't come. □ Posso entrare? Can I come in? □ Si può entrare gratis di domenica. You can get in free on Sundays.
2 could
□ Non è potuto venire. He couldn't come. □ Potresti aprire la finestra? Could you open the window?
3 to be able to
□ Non potrò venire domani. I won't be able to come tomorrow. □ Dovresti potercela fare da solo. You should be able to do it by yourself.

LANGUAGE TIP To express a possibility, use 'may' or 'might'.

□ Può aver avuto un incidente. He may have had an accident. □ Potrebbe essere vero. It might be true.
■ **può darsi** perhaps □ Pensi di andarci? — Può darsi. Do you think you'll go? — Perhaps.
■ **Può darsi che non venga.** He may not come.
■ **Non ne posso più!** I can't take any more!

p

il **potere** MASC NOUN
▷ *see also* **potere** VERB
power
□ una lotta per il potere a power struggle
■ **essere al potere** to be in power

povero (FEM **povera**) ADJECTIVE, MASC/FEM NOUN
poor
□ Sono molto poveri. They're very poor.
■ **i poveri** the poor

la **povertà** FEM NOUN
poverty

la **pozzanghera** FEM NOUN
puddle

il **pozzo** MASC NOUN
well
■ **pozzo petrolifero** oil well

pranzare VERB [68]
to have lunch
□ Abbiamo appena pranzato. We've just had lunch.
■ **pranzare fuori** to go out for lunch

il **pranzo** MASC NOUN
lunch
□ un pranzo di lavoro a business lunch □ Vieni a pranzo da me? Will you come and have lunch with me?

la **pratica** (PL le **pratiche**) FEM NOUN
1 practice
□ Devi solo fare un po' di pratica. You only need a bit of practice. □ la pratica e la teoria practice and theory
■ **in pratica** in practice
■ **mettere in pratica** to put into practice
□ Cercate di mettere in pratica questa idea. Try to put this idea into practice.
2 experience
□ Non ho molta pratica di queste cose. I haven't got much experience in these things.
3 file
□ Può cercarmi quella pratica? Can you get that file for me?
■ **fare le pratiche per** to do the paperwork for

praticamente ADVERB
practically

praticare VERB [18]
1 to do
□ Pratica molti sport. He does a lot of different sports.
2 to play

pratico (FEM **pratica**, MASC PL **pratici**, FEM PL **pratiche**) ADJECTIVE
1 practical
□ un metodo pratico a practical method
2 handy
□ un aggeggio molto pratico a very handy tool
□ l'aggeggio più pratico the handiest tool
3 convenient

□ Mi è più pratico venire di pomeriggio. It's more convenient for me to come in the afternoon.
■ **essere pratico di qualcosa** to know something □ È pratico del mestiere. He knows the job. □ Non sono pratica di queste parti. I don't know this area very well.

il **prato** MASC NOUN
1 meadow
□ Giocavano sul prato. They were playing in the meadow.
2 lawn
□ Giocavano sul prato. They were playing on the lawn.
■ **prato all'inglese** lawn

la **precauzione** FEM NOUN
precaution
■ **prendere delle precauzioni** to take precautions

precedente (FEM **precedente**) ADJECTIVE
previous
□ il giorno precedente the previous day

la **precedenza** FEM NOUN
■ **avere la precedenza** to have the right of way
■ **dare la precedenza** 1 to give way 2 to give priority

precedere VERB [27]
to precede

precipitare VERB [68, aux **essere**]
to fall
□ Sono precipitati in un burrone. They fell into a ravine.
■ **La situazione sta precipitando.** The situation is getting out of control.

precipitoso (FEM **precipitosa**) ADJECTIVE
rash
□ È un po' troppo precipitoso. He's a bit too rash.
■ **una fuga precipitosa** a hasty escape

il **precipizio** MASC NOUN
precipice
□ È caduto da un precipizio. He fell over a precipice.

precisamente ADVERB
precisely
□ È precisamente quello che intendevo. That's precisely what I meant.

precisare VERB [68]
to point out
□ Vorrei precisare che... I'd like to point out that...

preciso (FEM **precisa**) ADJECTIVE
1 precise
□ le sue precise parole his precise words □ in quel preciso istante at that precise moment
■ **Non ho un'idea precisa di come funzioni.** I don't know precisely how it works.

P

205

■ **Sono le nove precise.** It's exactly 9 o'clock.

2 careful

  □ È molto preciso nel suo lavoro. He's very careful in his work.

il **preconcetto** MASC NOUN
  prejudice

la **preda** FEM NOUN
  prey

  ■ **essere in preda al panico** to panic □ Era in preda al panico. He was panicking.

predire VERB [35]
  to predict

  □ Aveva predetto che sarebbe successo. He had predicted it would happen.

  ■ **predire il futuro** to tell the future

la **predisposizione** FEM NOUN

  ■ **avere predisposizione a** to have a gift for □ Ha predisposizione alla musica. He has a gift for music.

la **prefazione** FEM NOUN
  preface

la **preferenza** FEM NOUN
  preference

  □ Non ho preferenze. I have no preference.

  ■ **Qui non si fanno preferenze.** There is no favouritism here.

preferire VERB [51]
  to prefer

  □ Preferisco il caffè al tè. I prefer coffee to tea.
  □ Preferisce spendere i suoi soldi in vestiti. He prefers to spend his money on clothes.

  ■ **Cosa preferisci, caffè o tè?** Which would you like, coffee or tea?

  ■ **Preferirei un'insalata.** I'd rather have a salad.

  | LANGUAGE TIP If **preferire** is followed by a verb, use 'would rather'.

  □ Preferisco non parlarne. I would rather not talk about it. □ Preferirei lavorare a casa. I'd rather work at home.

preferito (FEM **preferita**) ADJECTIVE
  favourite

prefiggersi VERB [75]

  ■ **prefiggersi uno scopo** to set oneself a goal □ Questo era lo scopo che mi ero prefissa. This was the goal that I had set myself.

il **prefisso** MASC NOUN

1 code (for phone)

  □ Qual è il prefisso di Londra? What's the code for London?

2 prefix

pregare VERB [76]
  to pray

  □ Stava pregando. She was praying.

  ■ **pregare qualcuno di fare qualcosa** to ask somebody to do something □ L'ho pregata di venire. I asked her to come.

■ **I passeggeri sono pregati di...** Passengers are kindly requested to...

  ■ **Ti prego!** Please! □ Ti prego, lasciami in pace. Please leave me alone.

la **preghiera** FEM NOUN
  prayer

pregiato (FEM **pregiata**) ADJECTIVE
  valuable

  □ un tappeto pregiato a valuable carpet

il **pregio** MASC NOUN
  good quality

  □ Ha molti pregi. He has a lot of good qualities.

  ■ **i pregi e i difetti** the good points and the bad points

il **pregiudizio** MASC NOUN
  prejudice

  □ pregiudizio razziale racial prejudice

  ■ **avere dei pregiudizi nei confronti di qualcuno** to be prejudiced against somebody

prego EXCLAMATION
  you're welcome

  □ Grazie dell'aiuto. — Prego! Thank you for your help. — You're welcome!

  ■ **Prego, si accomodi. 1** Please come in.

  2 Please take a seat.

  ■ **Prego?** Pardon?

prelevare VERB [68]
  to withdraw

  □ Vorrei prelevare cinquanta sterline. I'd like to withdraw fifty pounds, please.

il **prelievo** MASC NOUN
  withdrawal (of money)

  ■ **fare un prelievo di sangue** to take a blood sample

premere VERB [27]
  to press

  □ Premi forte! Press hard!

  ■ **premere il grilletto** to pull the trigger

premiare VERB [17]
  to give a prize to

  □ Il preside ha premiato due studenti. The headmaster gave prizes to two students.

  ■ **essere premiato** to win a prize □ Il film è stato premiato. The film won a prize.

la **premiazione** FEM NOUN

1 prize-giving (at school)

2 award ceremony (film, book)

il **premio** MASC NOUN
  prize

  □ Ho ricevuto un premio. I was given a prize.

  ■ **premio di consolazione** consolation prize

  ■ **premio Nobel** Nobel prize

la **premura** FEM NOUN

  ■ **aver premura** to be in a hurry □ Svelto, che ho premura! Quick, I'm in a hurry!

  ■ **fare premura a qualcuno** to hurry somebody □ Mi dispiace farti premura, ma devo andare. I'm sorry to hurry you, but I have to go.

■ **circondare qualcuno di premure** to make a fuss of somebody

premuroso (FEM **premurosa**) ADJECTIVE
thoughtful

prendere VERB [77]

1 to take
□ Prendi quella borsa. Take that bag. □ Hai preso l'ombrello? Have you taken your umbrella? □ Ho preso il treno delle dieci. I took the ten o'clock train.

2 to get (obtain)
□ Ho preso un bel voto. I got a good mark.
■ **andare a prendere qualcosa** to go and get something □ Vai a prendermi gli occhiali. Go and get my glasses.
■ **venire a prendere qualcuno** to come and get somebody □ Potresti venire a prendermi alla stazione? Could you come and get me at the station?
■ **prendere paura** to get a fright

3 to have (at bar, restaurant)
□ Prendo un caffè. I'll have a coffee.
■ **Prende qualcosa da bere?** Would you like something to drink?

4 to earn
□ Quanto prende al mese? How much does he earn a month?

5 to charge
□ Quanto prende per un taglio di capelli? How much do you charge for a haircut?

6 to catch
□ Ho preso un grosso pesce. I caught a huge fish.

7 to handle
□ So come prenderlo. I know how to handle him.
■ **prendere l'influenza** to catch the flu
■ **prendere fuoco** to catch fire
■ **prendere qualcuno per** to mistake somebody for □ Mi ha preso per mio fratello. He mistook me for my brother.
■ **Per chi mi prendi?** Who do you think I am?
■ **prendersi a calci** to kick each other
■ **prendersi a pugni** to punch each other
■ **prendersela 1** to get annoyed **2** to get upset
■ **Perché te la prendi sempre con me?** Why do you always pick on me?
■ **Cosa ti prende?** What's got into you?

prenotare VERB [68]
to book

la **prenotazione** FEM NOUN
booking
■ **fare una prenotazione** to make a booking

preoccupare VERB [68]
to worry

■ **preoccuparsi** to worry □ Non preoccuparti. Don't worry.
■ **preoccuparsi per qualcosa** to worry about something

preoccupato (FEM **preoccupata**) ADJECTIVE
worried

la **preoccupazione** FEM NOUN
worry
□ Ha molte preoccupazioni. He has a lot of worries.

preparare VERB [68]
to prepare
■ **preparare da mangiare** to prepare a meal
■ **prepararsi** (dressed) to get ready
■ **prepararsi ad un esame** to prepare for an exam

i **preparativi** MASC PL NOUN
preparations
□ i preparativi per la festa the preparations for the party

la **preposizione** FEM NOUN
preposition

prepotente (FEM **prepotente**) ADJECTIVE,
MASC/FEM NOUN
bully
□ È un prepotente. He's a bully.
■ **un ragazzo prepotente** a bully

la **presa** FEM NOUN
grip
□ Ha allentato la presa. He loosened his grip.
■ **presa di corrente** socket
■ **macchina da presa** cine camera

presbite (FEM **presbite**) ADJECTIVE
long-sighted

prescrivere VERB [99]
to prescribe

presentare VERB [68]

1 to introduce
□ L'ha presentata ai suoi amici. He introduced her to his friends.

2 to present (show, programme, etc)
□ Chi ha presentato lo spettacolo? Who presented the show?

3 to put in
□ Ha presentato una domanda di assunzione. He put in a job application.
■ **presentarsi 1** to introduce oneself
2 (opportunity) to arise

presente (FEM **presente**) ADJECTIVE, MASC NOUN
present
□ Erano tutti presenti alla lezione. Everybody was present at the class.
■ **Presente!** Here!
■ **il presente** the present tense
■ **i presenti** those present
■ **aver presente qualcosa** to know something □ Hai presente la casa vicino alla

P

207

mia? You know the house next to mine?

■ **tener presente qualcosa** to remember something □ Tieni presente che non ho molto tempo libero. Remember I don't have much spare time.

il **presentimento** MASC NOUN
■ **Ho il presentimento che...** I've a feeling that...

la **presenza** FEM NOUN
presence

il **presepio** MASC NOUN
crib

il **preservativo** MASC NOUN
condom

il/la **preside** MASC/FEM NOUN
1 head *(of school)*
2 dean *(of faculty)*

il/la **presidente** MASC/FEM NOUN
1 president
2 chairman
chairwoman

pressappoco ADVERB
about
□ Ha pressappoco quarant'anni. He's about forty.

pressi MASC PL NOUN
■ **nei pressi di** near □ Si trova nei pressi della stazione. It's near the station.

la **pressione** FEM NOUN
1 pressure
■ **pentola a pressione** pressure cooker
2 blood pressure
□ Ha la pressione alta. He's got high blood pressure.
■ **far pressione su qualcuno** to put pressure on somebody
■ **essere sotto pressione** to be under pressure

presso PREPOSITION
c/o
□ Lucia Micoli, presso fam. Bianchi Lucia Micoli, c/o Mr and Mrs Bianchi
■ **Abita presso una zia.** He lives with an aunt.
■ **Lavora presso di noi.** He works for us.

prestare VERB [68]
■ **prestare qualcosa a qualcuno** to lend somebody something □ Mi ha prestato venticinque euro. He lent me twenty five euros. □ Gliel'ho prestato. I lent it to him.
■ **farsi prestare qualcosa da qualcuno** to borrow something from somebody □ Mi sono fatto prestare una penna da Luca. I borrowed a pen from Luca.
■ **prestare attenzione** to pay attention

la **prestazione** FEM NOUN
performance *(of car, athlete)*

il **prestigiatore** MASC NOUN
conjurer

il **prestigio** MASC NOUN
prestige
□ una questione di prestigio a matter of prestige
■ **gioco di prestigio** conjuring trick

il **prestito** MASC NOUN
loan
□ un prestito bancario a bank loan
■ **dare in prestito qualcosa a qualcuno** to lend somebody something □ Gli ho dato in prestito la mia bici. I lent him my bike.
■ **prendere in prestito qualcosa da qualcuno** to borrow something from somebody □ Ha preso in prestito cento euro da sua madre. She borrowed a hundred euros from her mother.
■ **fare un prestito** to give a loan □ Mi faresti un prestito? Could you give me a loan?

presto ADVERB
1 soon
□ Arriverà presto. He'll be here soon. □ il più presto possibile as soon as possible
■ **presto o tardi** sooner or later
■ **Presto!** Hurry up!
■ **A presto!** See you soon!
2 early
□ Mi alzo sempre presto. I always get up early. □ Mi alzo più presto di te. I get up earlier than you. □ Sono arrivato troppo presto. I arrived too early.

presumere VERB [11]
to presume

presuntuoso (FEM **presuntuosa**) ADJECTIVE
conceited

il **prete** MASC NOUN
priest

pretendere VERB [112]
to expect
□ Pretende di essere pagato in anticipo. He expects to be paid in advance.
■ **Pretende di aver sempre ragione.** He thinks he's always right.

> **LANGUAGE TIP** Be careful! pretendere doesn't mean **to pretend**.

la **pretesa** FEM NOUN
■ **Non ho molte pretese.** I'm easily pleased.
■ **senza pretese** unpretentious

il **pretesto** MASC NOUN
pretext
■ **con il pretesto di** on the pretext of

prevedere VERB [78]
1 to foresee
□ Non possiamo prevedere cosa succederà. We can't foresee what will happen.
■ **come previsto** as expected
2 to plan
□ È previsto per martedì. It's planned for Tuesday.

3 to forecast

□ È previsto maltempo per il fine settimana. Bad weather is forecast for the weekend.

il **preventivo** MASC NOUN
estimate

■ **fare un preventivo** to give an estimate

la **prevenzione** FEM NOUN
prevention

□ prevenzione degli infortuni prevention of accidents

la **previdenza** FEM NOUN

■ **la previdenza sociale** social security

le **previsioni** FEM PL NOUN

■ **previsioni del tempo** weather forecast *sing* □ Cosa dicono le previsioni del tempo per domani? What is the weather forecast for tomorrow?

previsto MASC NOUN

■ **più del previsto** more than expected

■ **prima del previsto** earlier than expected

prezioso (FEM **preziosa**) ADJECTIVE

1 precious

□ una pietra preziosa a precious stone

2 invaluable

□ Il loro consiglio mi è stato prezioso. Their advice was invaluable to me.

il **prezzemolo** MASC NOUN
parsley

il **prezzo** MASC NOUN
price

□ il prezzo della benzina the price of petrol □ a metà prezzo half price □ a prezzo scontato at a reduced price

la **prigione** FEM NOUN
prison

il **prigioniero,** la **prigioniera** MASC/FEM
NOUN
prisoner

prima ADVERB, CONJUNCTION
▷ *see also* **prima** NOUN

1 before

□ due giorni prima two days before □ Prima non lo sapevo. I didn't know that before.

■ **prima di** before □ Sono andati via prima di noi. They left before us. □ Mi sono alzato prima delle sette. I got up before seven. □ Dobbiamo decidere prima della mia partenza. We must decide before I leave. □ prima d'ora before now

2 earlier

□ È arrivato prima del previsto. He arrived earlier than expected. □ Domani devo alzarmi un po' prima. Tomorrow I have to get up a bit earlier.

■ **prima o poi** sooner or later

■ **prima possibile** as soon as possible

3 in advance

□ La prossima volta dimmelo prima. Next time let me know in advance.

la **prima** FEM NOUN
▷ *see also* **prima** ADVERB, CONJUNCTION

1 opening night *(of play)*

2 première *(of film)*

■ **prima elementare** first year at primary school

■ **prima media** first year at secondary school

■ **prima superiore** fourth year at secondary school

il **primario** MASC NOUN
consultant

il/la **primatista** (MASC PL i **primatisti**, FEM PL le **primatiste**) MASC/FEM NOUN
record holder

□ il primatista mondiale del salto in lungo the world record holder for the long jump

il **primato** MASC NOUN
record

la **primavera** FEM NOUN
spring

□ in primavera in spring

primitivo (FEM **primitiva**) ADJECTIVE
primitive

primo (FEM **prima**) ADJECTIVE, MASC/FEM NOUN
first

□ le prime due pagine the first two pages □ il primo luglio the first of July □ Prendi la prima strada a destra. Take the first street on the right.

■ **le prime ore del mattino** the early hours of the morning

■ **prima classe** first class □ un biglietto di prima classe a first class ticket □ viaggiare in prima classe to travel first-class

■ **essere primo in classifica 1** to be top of the league **2** to be number one in the charts

■ **in prima pagina** on the front page

■ **ai primi di maggio** at the beginning of May

■ **per prima cosa** firstly

■ **in primo luogo** first of all

■ **di prima qualità** first-class

■ **in un primo momento** at first

la **primula** FEM NOUN
primrose

principale (FEM **principale**) ADJECTIVE
▷ *see also* **principale** NOUN
main

□ È questa la strada principale? Is this the main road? □ proposizione principale main clause

il/la **principale** MASC/FEM NOUN
▷ *see also* **principale** ADJECTIVE
boss *(informal)*

□ Il principale ti vuole parlare. The boss wants to speak to you.

principalmente ADVERB
mainly

il **principe** MASC NOUN
prince

la **principessa** FEM NOUN
princess

il/la **principiante** MASC/FEM NOUN
beginner

il **principio** MASC NOUN
1 beginning
□ dal principio alla fine from beginning to end
■ **al principio** at first
■ **fin dal principio** right from the start
2 principle
□ una questione di principio a matter of principle □ per principio on principle

privato (FEM **privata**) ADJECTIVE, MASC NOUN
private
□ la proprietà privata private property
■ **in privato** in private

privilegiato (FEM **privilegiata**) ADJECTIVE
privileged

il **privilegio** MASC NOUN
privilege

privo (FEM **priva**) ADJECTIVE
■ **privo di** without □ un albero privo di foglie a tree without leaves
■ **parole prive di significato** meaningless words
■ **essere privo di** to have no □ È privo di scrupoli. He's got no scruples.
■ **privo di sensi** unconscious

i **pro** MASC PL NOUN
□ i pro e i contro the pros and cons

probabile (FEM **probabile**) ADJECTIVE
probable

la **probabilità** (PL le **probabilità**) FEM NOUN
chance
□ Che probabilità hanno di vincere? What are their chances of winning? □ Ha buone probabilità di ottenere il lavoro. He's got a good chance of getting the job. □ una probabilità su mille a chance in a thousand
■ **una probabilità su due** a fifty-fifty chance
■ **con molta probabilità** very probably

probabilmente ADVERB
probably

il **problema** (PL i **problemi**) MASC NOUN
problem

la **proboscide** FEM NOUN
trunk

procedere VERB [27, aux **avere** or **essere**]
to get on
□ Come procede il lavoro? How's the work getting on?
■ **Gli affari procedono bene.** Business is going well.
■ **Il traffico procede lentamente.** The traffic is moving slowly.

processare VERB [68]
to try

il **processo** MASC NOUN
trial
□ un processo per omicidio a murder trial
■ **essere sotto processo** to be on trial

procurare VERB [68]
to get
□ Hai procurato i biglietti? Did you get the tickets?

il **prodotto** MASC NOUN
product
□ È un buon prodotto. It's a good product.
■ **prodotti agricoli** farm produce *sing*
■ **prodotti alimentari** foodstuffs
■ **prodotti di bellezza** cosmetics
■ **prodotti chimici** chemicals

produrre VERB [85]
to produce

la **produzione** FEM NOUN
production

professionale (FEM **professionale**)
ADJECTIVE
professional

la **professione** FEM NOUN
occupation
□ Professione: infermiera. Occupation: nurse.
■ **la professione medica** the medical profession

professionista (FEM **professionista**, MASC
PL **professionisti**, FEM PL **professioniste**)
ADJECTIVE, MASC/FEM NOUN
professional
□ un fotografo professionista a professional photographer
■ **i liberi professionisti** the self-employed

il **professore**, la **professoressa** MASC/
FEM NOUN
1 teacher
2 lecturer
3 professor

il **profilo** MASC NOUN
profile
■ **di profilo** in profile

il **profitto** MASC NOUN
profit
□ un profitto di ottomila euro an eight thousand euro profit

la **profondità** (PL le **profondità**) FEM NOUN
depth
□ la profondità del mare the depth of the sea
■ **avere una profondità di...** to be...deep
□ Il fiume qui ha una profondità di cinque metri. The river here is five metres deep.

profondo (FEM **profonda**) ADJECTIVE
deep
□ È profondo otto metri. It's eight metres deep.

il **profugo,** la **profuga** (MASC PL i **profughi,** FEM PL le **profughe**) MASC/FEM NOUN
refugee

profumato (FEM **profumata**) ADJECTIVE
1 fragrant
2 scented

la **profumeria** FEM NOUN
perfume shop

> **DID YOU KNOW...?**
> As well as perfume a **profumeria** sells cosmetics, jewellery and gift items.

il **profumo** MASC NOUN
perfume
- **mettersi il profumo** to put perfume on
- **Questi fiori hanno un buon profumo.** These flowers smell lovely.
- **Questa saponetta ha un profumo di limone.** This soap smells of lemon.

progettare VERB [68]
to plan

il **progetto** MASC NOUN
plan
□ i miei progetti per il futuro my plans for the future □ il progetto della casa the plan of the house
- **progetto di legge** bill

il **programma** (PL i **programmi**) MASC NOUN
1 programme
- **Hai programmi per stasera?** Have you anything planned for this evening?
2 program (computer)
3 syllabus

programmare VERB [68]
1 to plan
2 to program (on computer)

il **programmatore,** la **programmatrice** MASC/FEM NOUN
computer programmer

il **progresso** MASC NOUN
progress
□ i progressi della scienza scientific progress
- **fare progressi** to make progress □ Sta facendo progressi in matematica. She's making progress in maths.

proibire VERB [51]
to forbid
□ Mi ha proibito di uscire. She has forbidden me to go out.

il **proiettile** MASC NOUN
bullet

il **proiettore** MASC NOUN
projector

la **prolunga** (PL le **prolunghe**) FEM NOUN
extension (electrical)

il **promemoria** (PL i **promemoria**) MASC NOUN
note

la **promessa** FEM NOUN
promise

- **fare una promessa** to make a promise
- **mantenere una promessa** to keep a promise

promettere VERB [59]
to promise
□ Promettimi che scriverai. Promise me that you'll write.
- **Promette bene.** It looks promising.

promuovere VERB [62]
- **essere promosso agli esami** to pass one's exams
- **essere promosso** to be promoted

il **pronome** MASC NOUN
pronoun

pronto (FEM **pronta**) ADJECTIVE
ready
□ È pronto il pranzo? Is lunch ready? □ Sono pronto a tutto. I'm ready for anything.
- **Pronto?** (on phone) Hello!
- **pronto soccorso** first aid
- **Pronti? Attenti! Via!** Ready, steady, go!

la **pronuncia** FEM NOUN
pronunciation

pronunciare VERB [13]
to pronounce

proporre VERB [73]
to suggest
- **proporre di fare qualcosa** to suggest doing something □ Ho proposto di andare al cinema. I suggested going to the cinema.
- **proporre un brindisi** to propose a toast

proporzionale (FEM **proporzionale**) ADJECTIVE
proportional

il **proposito** MASC NOUN
intention
□ È pieno di buoni propositi. He's full of good intentions.
- **di proposito** on purpose □ L'ha fatto di proposito. He did it on purpose.
- **a proposito** by the way □ A proposito, come sta tua madre? By the way, how's your mother?
- **A proposito di Roberto...** Speaking of Roberto...

la **proposizione** FEM NOUN
clause (in grammar)
- **proposizione principale** main clause
- **proposizione secondaria** subordinate clause

la **proposta** FEM NOUN
suggestion
□ Ha fatto una proposta. He made a suggestion.

la **proprietà** (PL le **proprietà**) FEM NOUN
property
□ la proprietà privata private property

il proprietario, la proprietaria MASC/FEM
NOUN
owner

proprio (FEM **propria**) ADJECTIVE, MASC/FEM
NOUN
▷ *see also* **proprio** ADVERB
own

□ L'ha visto con i propri occhi. He saw it with
his own eyes. □ Ognuno è arrivato con la
propria macchina. Everybody arrived in their
own car.

■ **Ognuno è tornato a casa propria.**
Everybody went back home.

■ **un nome proprio** a proper noun

■ **mettersi in proprio** to set up one's own
business □ Si è messo in proprio. He set up his
own business.

proprio ADVERB
▷ *see also* **proprio** ADJECTIVE, NOUN
1 just
□ Le cose sono andate proprio così. That's just
how things went.
2 really
□ Sono proprio stanco. I'm really tired.

■ **non... proprio** not... at all □ Non mi piace
proprio. I don't like it at all.

la prosa FEM NOUN
prose
□ la prosa e la poesia prose and poetry

■ **un attore di prosa** a theatre actor

il prosciutto MASC NOUN
ham

■ **prosciutto cotto** cooked ham

■ **prosciutto crudo** Parma ham

proseguire VERB [41]
to continue
□ Decise di proseguire il viaggio. He decided to
continue his journey.

la prospettiva FEM NOUN
1 prospect
□ Non ci sono molte prospettive di lavoro.
There aren't many job prospects.
2 perspective *(in painting)*
□ in prospettiva in perspective

prossimo (FEM **prossima**) ADJECTIVE, MASC/FEM
NOUN
next
□ Ci vediamo venerdì prossimo. See you next
Friday. □ Scende alla prossima fermata? Are
you getting off at the next stop? □ Avanti il
prossimo. Next please.

■ **un parente prossimo** a close relative

■ **passato prossimo** perfect tense

la prostituta FEM NOUN
prostitute

il/la protagonista (MASC PL **i protagonisti**,
FEM PL **le protagoniste**) MASC/FEM NOUN
protagonist

proteggere VERB [79]
to protect

la protesta FEM NOUN
protest

protestante (FEM **protestante**) ADJECTIVE,
MASC/FEM NOUN
Protestant

protestare VERB [68]
to protest

protetto (FEM **protetta**) ADJECTIVE
sheltered
□ un porto protetto a sheltered harbour

■ **una specie protetta** a protected species

la protezione FEM NOUN
protection

la prova FEM NOUN
1 test
□ un giro di prova a test run

■ **Facciamo una prova.** Let's try it.

■ **prova scritta** written test

■ **prova orale** oral exam

■ **in prova** on a trial basis
2 proof
□ Ho la prova che è stato lui. I've got proof that
it was him.
3 evidence
□ Non ci sono abbastanza prove per
incriminarlo. There isn't enough evidence to
charge him.
4 rehearsal

■ **prova generale** dress rehearsal

provare VERB [68]
1 to try
□ Ho provato una nuova crema. I've tried a new
cream. □ Prova questo gelato, ti piacerà. Try
this ice cream. You'll like it. □ Ho provato il suo
motorino. I tried out his moped. □ Perché non
provi a parlargli? Why don't you try talking to
him?
2 to try on
□ Provati questo maglione. Try this jumper on.
3 to feel
□ Ho provato rabbia quando l'ho saputo. I felt
angry when I found out.
4 to prove
□ Posso provare che ero a casa. I can prove
I was at home.

provenire VERB [120]
to come
□ Proviene dagli Stati Uniti. It comes from the
United States.

il proverbio MASC NOUN
proverb

la provetta FEM NOUN
test tube

■ **bambino in provetta** test-tube baby

il provider (PL **i provider**) MASC NOUN
provider

la **provincia** (PL le **province**) FEM NOUN
province

il **provino** MASC NOUN
1 screen test
  □ Ha fatto un provino. She did a screen test.
2 trailer *(before film)*

provocare VERB [18]
1 to cause
  □ La nebbia ha provocato molti incidenti. The fog caused a lot of accidents.
2 to provoke
  □ Non provocarmi! Don't provoke me!

la **provocazione** FEM NOUN
provocation

il **provvedimento** MASC NOUN
measure
  □ un provvedimento disciplinare a disciplinary measure

provvisorio (FEM **provvisoria**) ADJECTIVE
  ■ **orario provvisorio** provisional timetable
  ■ **un lavoro provvisorio** a temporary job
  ■ **un governo provvisorio** an interim government

le **provviste** FEM PL NOUN
provisions
  □ Abbiamo abbastanza provviste. We've got enough provisions.
  ■ **fare provviste** to stock up

la **prua** FEM NOUN
bow

prudente (FEM **prudente**) ADJECTIVE
careful
  □ un guidatore prudente a careful driver □ Sii prudente! Be careful!
  ■ **Non è prudente guidare quando si è stanchi.** It's not a good idea to drive when you're tired.
  ■ **È più prudente aspettare qui.** It would be better to wait here.

la **prudenza** FEM NOUN
  ■ **Guida con prudenza!** Drive carefully!
  ■ **per prudenza** as a precaution

prudere VERB [27]
to itch
  □ Mi prude il naso. My nose is itching.

la **prugna** FEM NOUN
plum
  ■ **prugna secca** prune

il **prurito** MASC NOUN
  ■ **Ho prurito alla mano.** My hand is itching.

lo/la **psicanalista** (MASC PL gli **psicanalisti**, FEM PL le **psicanaliste**) MASC/FEM NOUN
psychoanalyst

lo/la **psichiatra** (MASC PL gli **psichiatri**, FEM PL le **psichiatre**) MASC/FEM NOUN
psychiatrist

psichiatrico (FEM **psichiatrica**, MASC PL **psichiatrici**, FEM PL **psichiatriche**)
ADJECTIVE
psychiatric

la **psicologia** FEM NOUN
psychology

psicologico (FEM **psicologica**, MASC PL **psicologi**, FEM PL **psicologhe**) ADJECTIVE
psychological

lo **psicologo**, la **psicologa** (MASC PL gli **psicologi**, FEM PL le **psicologhe**) MASC/FEM NOUN
psychologist

pubblicare VERB [18]
to publish

la **pubblicazione** FEM NOUN
publication
  ■ **le pubblicazioni** *(for wedding)* the banns

la **pubblicità** (PL le **pubblicità**) FEM NOUN
1 advert
  □ Ho visto la pubblicità sul giornale. I saw the advert in the paper.
2 adverts *pl*
  □ C'è troppa pubblicità in TV. There are too many adverts on TV.
  ■ **fare pubblicità a qualcosa** to advertise something □ Fa pubblicità ad uno shampoo. She advertises a shampoo.
3 advertising
  □ Si occupa di pubblicità. He's in advertising.

pubblico (FEM **pubblica**, MASC PL **pubblici**, FEM PL **pubbliche**) ADJECTIVE
  ▷ *see also* **pubblico** NOUN
public
  □ la pubblica amministrazione public administration □ pubbliche relazioni public relations
  ■ **una scuola pubblica** a state school

il **pubblico** MASC NOUN
  ▷ *see also* **pubblico** ADJECTIVE
1 public
  □ È aperto al pubblico? Is it open to the public?
  ■ **in pubblico** in public
2 audience

pudico (FEM **pudica**, MASC PL **pudichi**, FEM PL **pudiche**) ADJECTIVE
modest

il **pugilato** MASC NOUN
boxing
  □ un incontro di pugilato a boxing match

il **pugile** MASC NOUN
boxer

pugnalare VERB [68]
to stab

il **pugnale** MASC NOUN
dagger

il **pugno** MASC NOUN
fist

□ con i pugni stretti with clenched fists
■ **dare un pugno a qualcuno** to punch somebody □ Gli ho dato un pugno sul naso. I punched him on the nose.

la **pulce** FEM NOUN
flea

il **pulcino** MASC NOUN
chick

pulire VERB [51]
to clean
□ Stava pulendo il fornello. She was cleaning the cooker.
■ **pulirsi i piedi** to wipe one's feet
■ **far pulire qualcosa** to have something cleaned □ Ho fatto pulire la macchina. I had my car cleaned.
■ **pulire a secco** to dry-clean

pulito (FEM **pulita**) ADJECTIVE
clean
□ un pavimento pulito a clean floor
■ **avere la coscienza pulita** to have a clear conscience

la **pulitura** FEM NOUN
■ **pulitura a secco** dry cleaner's

le **pulizie** FEM PL NOUN
■ **fare le pulizie** to do the cleaning

il **pullman** (PL i **pullman**) MASC NOUN
coach

il **pulmino** MASC NOUN
minibus

il **pulsante** MASC NOUN
button
□ Premi il pulsante. Press the button.

pungere VERB [80]
to sting
□ L'ha punto una vespa. A wasp stung him.
■ **pungersi un dito** to prick one's finger

punire VERB [51]
to punish

la **punizione** FEM NOUN
punishment
□ una punizione severa a harsh punishment
■ **calcio di punizione** free kick

la **punta** FEM NOUN
1 point (of pencil, needle, knife)
■ **fare la punta alla matita** to sharpen a pencil
2 top (of steeple, tree, mountain)
3 touch
□ una punta di invidia a touch of envy
■ **a punta** pointed □ un paio di scarpe a punta a pair of pointed shoes
■ **in punta di piedi** on tiptoe
■ **ore di punta** peak hours
■ **doppie punte** split ends

puntare VERB [68]
to point
□ Le ha puntato un fucile contro. He pointed a gun at her.

■ **puntare su** to bet on □ Ha puntato su quel cavallo. He bet on that horse.

la **puntata** FEM NOUN
1 episode
□ Hai visto la prima puntata? Did you see the first episode?
2 flying visit
□ Farò una puntata a Parigi. I'm going to pay a flying visit to Paris.

la **punteggiatura** FEM NOUN
punctuation

il **punteggio** MASC NOUN
score
□ Qual è il punteggio? What's the score?

la **puntina** FEM NOUN
■ **puntina da disegno** drawing pin

il **puntino** MASC NOUN
dot
■ **cotto a puntino** cooked to perfection

il **punto** MASC NOUN
1 point
□ Ha segnato tre punti. He scored three points.
□ Su questo punto siamo d'accordo. We agree on this point.
■ **A che punto sei?** How are you getting on?
■ **alle sei in punto** at six o'clock sharp
■ **di punto in bianco** suddenly
■ **punto debole** weak point
■ **punto di partenza** starting point
■ **punto d'incontro** meeting place
■ **punto di vista** point of view
■ **punti neri** blackheads
2 stitch
3 full stop
■ **due punti** colon
■ **punto e virgola** semicolon
■ **punto esclamativo** exclamation mark
■ **punto interrogativo** question mark

puntuale (FEM **puntuale**) ADJECTIVE
punctual
□ È sempre puntuale. He's always punctual.
■ **arrivare puntuale** to arrive on time

la **puntura** FEM NOUN
1 injection
□ Gli ha fatto una puntura sul braccio. She gave him an injection in his arm.
2 sting
3 bite (from mosquito)
▌ LANGUAGE TIP Be careful! **puntura** doesn't mean **puncture**.

il **pupazzo** MASC NOUN
puppet
■ **pupazzo di neve** snowman

la **pupilla** FEM NOUN
pupil

purché CONJUNCTION
as long as
□ Verrò con te purché non piova. I'll come with you as long as it doesn't rain.

pure CONJUNCTION, ADVERB
1 <u>too</u>
  □ È venuto pure lui. He came too.
2 <u>even though</u>
  □ Pur non volendolo ho dovuto farlo. I had to do it even though I didn't want to.
  ■ **Faccia pure!** Please do!

il **purè** MASC NOUN
  ■ **purè di patate** mashed potatoes

il **purgante** MASC NOUN
  laxative

puro (FEM **pura**) ADJECTIVE
  <u>pure</u>
  □ pura lana vergine pure new wool
  ■ **È la pura verità.** It's the honest truth.
  ■ **per puro caso** by sheer chance
  ■ **per pura curiosità** out of sheer curiosity

il/la **purosangue** (PL i/le **purosangue**)
  MASC/FEM NOUN
  <u>thoroughbred</u>

purtroppo ADVERB
  <u>unfortunately</u>

il **pus** MASC NOUN
  <u>pus</u>

la **puzza** FEM NOUN
  <u>stink</u>

puzzare VERB [68]
  <u>to stink</u>
  □ Puzza di fumo. It stinks of smoke.
  ■ **La faccenda puzza d'imbroglio.** There's something fishy about the whole thing.

puzzolente (FEM **puzzolente**) ADJECTIVE
  <u>stinking</u>

Qq

qua ADVERB
here

□ Vieni qua. Come here. □ Eccomi qua. Here I am.

■ **qua dentro** in here □ Le penne sono qua dentro. The pens are in here.

■ **qua sotto** under here □ Qua sotto c'è la tua camicia. Your shirt is under here.

■ **Abita qua sotto.** She lives on the floor below.

■ **Vieni più in qua.** Come closer.

■ **di qua** this way □ Passavo di qua. I was passing this way.

■ **al di qua del fiume** on this side of the river

■ **Da quando in qua?** Since when? □ Da quando in qua ti interessi di politica? Since when have you been interested in politics?

il **quaderno** MASC NOUN
exercise book

il **quadrante** MASC NOUN
face (on clock)

quadrare VERB [68, aux **avere** or **essere**]
■ **Qui c'è qualcosa che non quadra.** There's something wrong here.

quadrato (FEM **quadrata**) ADJECTIVE
▷ see also **quadrato** NOUN
square

□ una tovaglia quadrata a square tablecloth
□ due metri quadrati two square metres

il **quadrato** MASC NOUN
▷ see also **quadrato** ADJECTIVE
1 square

□ un quadrato rosso a red square
2 ring (in boxing)

il **quadrifoglio** MASC NOUN
four-leaf clover

il **quadrimestre** MASC NOUN
term (school)

il **quadro** MASC NOUN
painting

□ un quadro di Van Gogh a painting by Van Gogh □ un quadro a olio an oil painting

■ **dipingere un quadro** to paint a picture

■ **quadri** (in cards) diamonds

■ **a quadri** checked □ una giacca a quadri a checked jacket

quaggiù ADVERB
down here

la **quaglia** FEM NOUN
quail

qualche (FEM **qualche**) ADJECTIVE

LANGUAGE TIP If **qualque** is followed by a singular noun, it is translated by 'some' with a plural noun.

□ Ho comprato qualche CD. I've bought some CDs. □ Ha qualche amico a Londra. He has some friends in London.

LANGUAGE TIP In questions, use 'any' with a plural noun.

□ Hai qualche sigaretta? Have you got any cigarettes? □ Mi ha chiesto se c'era qualche problema. He asked me if there were any problems.

LANGUAGE TIP When offering or asking for something, use 'some'.

□ Vuole qualche rivista mentre aspetta? Would you like some magazines while you're waiting? □ Posso prendere in prestito qualche CD? Can I borrow some CDs?

■ **qualche volta** sometimes □ Qualche volta si sente un po' giù. She sometimes feels a bit down.

■ **Vieni a trovarmi qualche volta.** Come and see me some time.

■ **L'ho incontrato qualche volta.** I've met him a couple of times.

■ **fra qualche mese** in a few months

■ **per qualche giorno** for a few days

■ **in qualche modo** somehow □ In qualche modo riuscirò a trovarlo. I'll manage to find him somehow.

qualcosa PRONOUN

LANGUAGE TIP In affirmative sentences, use 'something'.

□ Ci dev'essere qualcosa che non va. There must be something wrong. □ Voglio fare qualcos'altro. I'd like to do something else.

LANGUAGE TIP In questions, use 'anything'.

□ Qualcosa da dichiarare? Anything to declare? □ Vedi qualcosa? Can you see anything? □ Hai bisogno di qualcosa? Do you need anything?

LANGUAGE TIP When offering or asking for something, use 'something'.

□ Vuole qualcosa da mangiare? Would you like something to eat? □ Mi dai qualcosa da bere, per favore? Can I have something to drink, please?

q

LANGUAGE TIP qualcosa di is translated by 'something' or 'anything' without a preposition.

□ Vorrei qualcosa di nuovo. I'd like something new. □ Hai visto qualcosa di bello? Did you see anything nice?

qualcuno PRONOUN

1 somebody
someone

□ Ha telefonato qualcuno per te. Somebody phoned for you. □ Chiedilo a qualcun altro. Ask somebody else. □ Cosa fai qui? Aspetti qualcuno? What are you doing here? Are you waiting for somebody? □ Qualcuno ha perso la sua borsa. Somebody has lost their bag. □ C'è qualcuno alla porta. There's someone at the door.

LANGUAGE TIP In questions, use 'anybody' or 'anyone'.

□ C'è qualcuno in casa? Is there anybody at home? □ Qualcuno ha visto il mio ombrello? Has anyone seen my umbrella? □ Hai incontrato qualcun altro alla festa? Did you meet anybody else at the party?

2 some

□ Prendine ancora qualcuno. Take some more. □ Hai visto i suoi film? — Ne ho visto qualcuno. Have you seen his films? — I've seen some of them.

quale (FEM **quale**) ADJECTIVE, PRONOUN

1 what

□ Qual è il tuo colore preferito? What's your favourite colour? □ Quali programmi hai? What are your plans?

■ **Per quale ragione?** Why?

2 who

□ Qual è il tuo cantante preferito? Who's your favourite singer?

3 which

□ Quale dei due vuoi? Which one do you want? □ Quali giocatori hanno scelto per la squadra? Which players have they chosen for the team?

LANGUAGE TIP il quale is often not translated.

□ La ragione per la quale sono venuto è semplice. The reason why I came is simple. □ Il ragazzo con il quale esco è molto alto. The boy I go out with is very tall. □ Questi sono gli amici con i quali siamo andati in vacanza. These are the friends we went on holiday with. □ La signora alla quale ho telefonato è un'amica di mia madre. The lady I phoned is a friend of my mother's.

la **qualifica** (PL le **qualifiche**) FEM NOUN
qualification

qualificarsi VERB [18, AUX **essere**]
to qualify

□ La squadra si è qualificata per i mondiali. The team has qualified for the World Cup.

qualificato (FEM **qualificata**) ADJECTIVE

1 qualified

□ È qualificato per quel lavoro. He's qualified for that job.

2 skilled

□ un operaio qualificato a skilled worker

la **qualificazione** FEM NOUN

■ **una partita di qualificazione** a qualifying match

■ **un corso di qualificazione professionale** a vocational training course

la **qualità** (PL le **qualità**) FEM NOUN
quality

□ Preferisco la qualità alla quantità. I prefer quality to quantity.

■ **di qualità** quality

■ **di ottima qualità** top-quality

qualsiasi ADJECTIVE
any

□ in qualsiasi momento at any time

■ **qualsiasi cosa** anything □ Farei qualsiasi cosa per lei. I'd do anything for her.

■ **Qualsiasi cosa accada, telefonami.** Whatever happens, phone me.

■ **Mettiti un vestito qualsiasi.** Wear anything you like.

■ **a qualsiasi costo** no matter what □ Ci riuscirò a qualsiasi costo. I'll manage it no matter what.

qualunque = **qualsiasi**

quando CONJUNCTION, ADVERB
when

□ Quando vai in vacanza? When are you going on holiday? □ Quando arriverà? When's he arriving? □ Non so quando abbia telefonato. I don't know when he phoned. □ Passerò a trovarti, ma non so quando. I'll come and see you, but I don't know when. □ Quando finirò verrò da te. When I finish I'll come to your place. □ Lo comprerò quando avrò abbastanza denaro. I'll buy it when I have enough money. □ Quando avrò finito verrò da te. When I've finished I'll come to your place.

■ **da quando** since □ Abita qui da quando era piccola. She has lived here since she was a child.

■ **Da quando sei qui?** How long have you been here?

■ **di quando in quando** from time to time □ Ci penso di quando in quando. I think about it from time to time.

la **quantità** (PL le **quantità**) FEM NOUN
quantity

□ Preferisco la qualità alla quantità. I prefer quality to quantity.

■ **in grande quantità** in large quantities

■ **una quantità di** lots of □ Hanno invitato una quantità di gente. They invited lots of

q

people. □ Ho una quantità di cose da fare. I've got lots of things to do.

quanto (FEM **quanta**) ADJECTIVE, PRONOUN, ADVERB

1 how much

□ Quanto pane hai comprato? How much bread did you buy? □ Quanto costa? How much does it cost? □ Quanto pesi? How much do you weigh? □ Quant'è? How much is it?

■ **Quanti?** How many? □ Quanti ne vuoi? How many do you want?

■ **Quanti anni hai?** How old are you?

■ **Quante?** How many? □ Quante ragazze ci sono in classe? How many girls are there in the class?

2 how long

□ Quanto starai via? How long will you be away? □ Da quanto sei qui? How long have you been here? □ Quanto tempo ci vorrà? How long will it take?

3 what a (in exclamations)

□ Quanto tempo sprecato! What a waste of time! □ Quante storie! What a fuss!

■ **Quanta gente!** What a lot of people!

■ **Quanti ne abbiamo oggi?** What's the date today?

■ **per quanto ne sappia** as far as I know

quaranta NUMBER

forty

quarantesimo (FEM **quarantesima**) ADJECTIVE, MASC NOUN

fortieth

quarantina NUMBER

■ **È sulla quarantina.** He's about forty.

la **quaresima** FEM NOUN

Lent

la **quarta** FEM NOUN

▷ see also **quarto** NOUN, ADJECTIVE

fourth gear

■ **quarta elementare** fourth year at primary school

■ **quarta superiore** seventh year at secondary school

il **quartiere** MASC NOUN

area

□ un quartiere malfamato a rough area

■ **quartier generale** headquarters pl

quarto (FEM **quarta**) ADJECTIVE

▷ see also **quarto** NOUN

fourth

□ Abito al quarto piano. I live on the fourth floor. □ È arrivato quarto nella gara. He came fourth in the competition. □ La squadra è quarta in classifica. The team is fourth in the league.

il **quarto** MASC NOUN

▷ see also **quarto** ADJECTIVE

quarter

□ un quarto della miscela a quarter of the mixture □ un quarto di vino a quarter-litre

bottle of wine □ un quarto di pollo a quarter chicken □ un quarto d'ora a quarter of an hour □ tre quarti d'ora three quarters of an hour □ Sono le tre e un quarto. It's a quarter past three. □ Sono le due meno un quarto. It's a quarter to two. □ Sono le otto e tre quarti. It's a quarter to nine.

■ **quarti di finale** quarterfinals

il **quarzo** MASC NOUN

quartz

quasi ADVERB

1 nearly

□ Ha quasi vent'anni. He's nearly twenty.

2 hardly

□ Non è venuto quasi nessuno. Hardly anybody came. □ Non sento quasi niente. I can hardly hear anything.

■ **quasi mai** hardly ever □ Non lo vedo quasi mai. I hardly ever see him.

quassù ADVERB

up here

quattordicenne (FEM **quattordicenne**) ADJECTIVE

fourteen-year-old

quattordicesimo (FEM **quattordicesima**) ADJECTIVE

fourteenth

quattordici NUMBER

fourteen

□ Ho quattordici anni. I'm fourteen.

■ **le quattordici** two p.m.

■ **il quattordici dicembre** the fourteenth of December

quattro NUMBER

four

□ Ha quattro anni. He's four. □ le quattro del pomeriggio four o'clock in the afternoon

■ **il quattro maggio** the fourth of May

■ **fare quattro chiacchiere** to have a chat □ Abbiamo fatto quattro chiacchiere. We had a chat.

■ **fare quattro passi** to go for a little walk

■ **a quattr'occhi** face to face □ Vorrei parlarti a quattr'occhi. I'd like to speak to you face to face.

quattrocento NUMBER

four hundred

□ quattrocento sterline four hundred pounds

■ **il Quattrocento** the fifteenth century

quello (FEM **quella**) ADJECTIVE, PRONOUN

1 that

□ Dammi quel libro. Give me that book. □ Chi è quella donna? Who's that woman? □ Cos'è quello? What's that?

2 that one

□ Preferisci questo o quello? Do you prefer this one or that one?

■ **il mio cappotto e quello di Sara** my coat and Sara's

■ **quello là** that □ Quello là è il mio professore. That's my teacher.

■ **Prendo quello là.** I'll take that one.

■ **quelli** those □ Dove hai comprato quei pantaloni? Where did you buy those trousers? □ Quelle ragazze abitano qui vicino. Those girls live near here. □ Penso che quelle siano le mie scarpe. I think those are my shoes. □ Prendo quelli. I'll have those.

■ **quello che** what □ Ho fatto quello che potevo. I did what I could. □ Da quello che ho sentito sei molto bravo a tennis. From what I've heard you're very good at tennis.

la **quercia** (PL le **querce**) FEM NOUN
oak

il **questionario** MASC NOUN
questionnaire

la **questione** FEM NOUN
matter
□ Si tratta di una questione personale. It's a personal matter. □ È solo questione di tempo. It's only a matter of time. □ È una questione di vita o di morte. It's a matter of life and death.

questo (FEM **questa**) ADJECTIVE, PRONOUN
this
□ Questa gonna è troppo stretta. This skirt is too tight. □ Cos'è questo? What's this? □ Questo è il tuo posto. This is your seat.

■ **Dove hai comprato questo quadro?** Where did you buy that picture?

■ **questi** these □ Queste scarpe sono comode. These shoes are comfortable.

■ **questo qua** this □ Questo qua è il mio migliore amico. This is my best friend.

■ **Prendo questo qua.** I'll have this one.

■ **E con questo?** So what?

■ **Questo è quanto.** That's all.

la **questura** FEM NOUN
police headquarters *sing*

qui ADVERB
here
□ Vieni qui. Come here. □ Eccomi qui. Here I am.

■ **qui dentro** in here □ Non c'è molto spazio qui dentro. There's not much room in here.

■ **qui sotto** under here □ Qui sotto c'è la tua camicia. Your shirt's under here.

■ **Abita qui sotto.** She lives on the floor below.

quindi ADVERB, CONJUNCTION

1 then
□ Ho cenato e quindi sono andato al cinema. I had dinner and then went to the cinema.

2 so
□ Avevo freddo e quindi mi sono messo il maglione. I was cold, so I put on a sweater.

quindicenne (FEM **quindicenne**) ADJECTIVE
fifteen-year-old

quindicesimo (FEM **quindicesima**) ADJECTIVE
fifteenth

quindici NUMBER
fifteen
□ Ho quindici anni. I'm fifteen.

■ **le quindici** three p.m.

■ **il quindici dicembre** the fifteenth of December

■ **quindici giorni** a fortnight

la **quindicina** FEM NOUN
■ **una quindicina** about fifteen □ C'erano una quindicina di persone. There were about fifteen people.

■ **una quindicina di giorni** a fortnight

la **quinta** FEM NOUN
▷ *see also* **quinto** ADJECTIVE, NOUN
fifth gear

■ **quinta elementare** fifth year at primary school

■ **quinta superiore** final year at secondary school

il **quintale** MASC NOUN
one hundred kilos
□ Questa cassa pesa più di un quintale. This box weighs more than a hundred kilos.

■ **Pesa un quintale!** It weighs a ton!

quinto (FEM **quinta**) ADJECTIVE, MASC NOUN
fifth
□ Abito al quinto piano. I live on the fifth floor. □ È arrivato quinto nella gara. He came fifth in the competition. □ La squadra è quinta in classifica. The team is fifth in the league. □ un quinto a fifth □ un quinto della popolazione a fifth of the population

il **quiz** (PL i **quiz**) MASC NOUN
question
□ i quiz della patente the questions for the driving test

■ **gioco a quiz** quiz show

la **quota** FEM NOUN
■ **L'aereo volava a bassa quota.** The plane was flying low.

■ **prendere quota** to gain height

■ **quota d'iscrizione** *(to a club)* membership fee

quotidiano (FEM **quotidiana**) ADJECTIVE
▷ *see also* **quotidiano** NOUN
daily
□ la vita quotidiana daily life

il **quotidiano** MASC NOUN
▷ *see also* **quotidiano** ADJECTIVE
daily paper

q

Rr

la rabbia FEM NOUN

1 rage

□ Urlava dalla rabbia. **He howled with rage.**

■ **Mi fanno una rabbia!** They make me so angry!

■ **Che rabbia!** That's so annoying!

2 rabies *sing*

rabbrividire VERB [51, AUX **essere**]
to shiver

raccapricciante (FEM **raccapricciante**)
ADJECTIVE
horrifying

□ una scena raccapricciante **a horrifying scene**

il raccattapalle (PL i **raccattapalle**) MASC
NOUN
ballboy

la racchetta FEM NOUN

1 racket *(tennis)*

2 bat *(table tennis)*

raccogliere VERB [21]

1 to pick up

□ Mi ero chinato a raccogliere la penna. **I had bent down to pick up the pen.**

2 to pick

□ Abbiamo raccolto un mazzo di fiori. **We picked a bunch of flowers.**

3 to collect

□ Stiamo raccogliendo libri usati per la biblioteca. **We're collecting second-hand books for the library.**

la raccolta FEM NOUN
collection

□ la mia raccolta di CD **my CD collection**

■ **fare raccolta di** to collect □ Faccio raccolta di cartoline. **I collect postcards.**

■ **fare la raccolta differenziata** to sort waste □ Quanti di voi fanno la raccolta differenziata? **How many of you sort your waste?**

il raccolto MASC NOUN
harvest

raccomandabile (FEM **raccomandabile**)
ADJECTIVE

■ **poco raccomandabile** not to be trusted
□ È un tipo poco raccomandabile. **He's not to be trusted.**

raccomandare VERB [68]
to recommend

□ L'albergo è raccomandato dalla guida.

The hotel is recommended by the guide.

■ **mi raccomando** please □ Mi raccomando, scrivimi! **Please write to me!**

■ **Non perderlo, mi raccomando!** Please don't lose it!

la raccomandata FEM NOUN
recorded delivery

□ Spediscilo per raccomandata. **Send it by recorded delivery.**

raccontare VERB [68]
to tell

□ Mi ha raccontato una barzelletta molto divertente. **He told me a very funny joke.** □ Dai, raccontami tutto. **Come on, tell me all about it.**

il racconto MASC NOUN
short story

□ un racconto di Calvino **a short story by Calvino**

■ **racconti per bambini** children's stories

il radar (PL i **radar**) MASC NOUN
radar

raddoppiare VERB [17, AUX **essere**]
to double

□ Il prezzo del biglietto è raddoppiato. **The price of the ticket has doubled.**

raddrizzare VERB [68]
to straighten

radere VERB [81]
to shave

□ S'è fatto radere i capelli a zero. **He's had his head shaved.**

■ **radersi** to shave □ Si rade ogni mattina. **He shaves every morning.**

il radiatore MASC NOUN
radiator

la radiazione FEM NOUN
radiation

radicale (FEM **radicale**) ADJECTIVE
radical

□ un cambiamento radicale **a radical change**

la radice FEM NOUN
root

la radio (PL le **radio**) FEM NOUN
radio

□ L'ho sentito alla radio. **I heard it on the radio.**

radioattivo (FEM **radioattiva**) ADJECTIVE
radioactive

□ scorie radioattive **radioactive waste**

la **radiocronaca** (PL le **radiocronache**)
FEM NOUN
commentary
□ la radiocronaca della partita the commentary
on the match

la **radiografia** FEM NOUN
X-ray

il **radioregistratore** MASC NOUN
radio cassette player

la **radiosveglia** FEM NOUN
radio alarm

rado (FEM **rada**) ADJECTIVE
thin
□ sempre più radi thinner and thinner
■ **di rado** rarely □ Vanno di rado al ristorante.
They rarely go to a restaurant.

la **raffica** (PL le **raffiche**) FEM NOUN
■ **una raffica di vento** a gust of wind
■ **una raffica di mitra** a burst of
machine-gun fire

raffigurare VERB [68]
to show
□ Il quadro raffigura la Vergine con Bambino.
The picture shows the Virgin and Child.

raffinato (FEM **raffinata**) ADJECTIVE
sophisticated
□ una donna raffinata a sophisticated woman

il **raffreddamento** MASC NOUN
cooling
□ raffreddamento ad aria air cooling

raffreddare VERB [68]
to cool
□ Lascia raffreddare la torta. Leave the cake to
cool.
■ **raffreddarsi** to get cold □ Non lasciare
che la minestra si raffreddi. Don't let the soup
get cold.

raffreddato (FEM **raffreddata**) ADJECTIVE
■ **essere raffreddato** to have a cold □ Sono
raffreddata. I've got a cold.

il **raffreddore** MASC NOUN
cold
□ Prenderai un raffreddore! You'll get a cold!
□ Ha il raffreddore. He's got a cold.
■ **raffreddore da fieno** hay fever

la **ragazza** FEM NOUN
1 girl
□ una ragazza alta e bionda a tall blonde girl
2 girlfriend
□ È la mia ragazza. She's my girlfriend.
■ **ragazza alla pari** au pair □ È una ragazza
alla pari. She's an au pair.

il **ragazzo** MASC NOUN
1 boy
□ un ragazzo irlandese an Irish boy
2 boyfriend
□ Ha litigato con il suo ragazzo. She's
quarrelled with her boyfriend.

LANGUAGE TIP **ragazzi** can also be
translated by 'children'.
□ È in vacanza con sua moglie e i ragazzi. He's
on holiday with his wife and children.

LANGUAGE TIP **ragazzi** is sometimes not
translated.
□ Dai ragazzi, andiamo via. Come on, let's go!

il **raggio** MASC NOUN
ray
□ un raggio di sole a ray of sunlight
■ **raggi X** X-rays

raggiungere VERB [5]
to reach
□ La temperatura può raggiungere i quaranta
gradi. The temperature can reach forty
degrees.
■ **Vi raggiungo più tardi.** I'll join you later.

ragionare VERB [68]
to think
□ Ragionaci su! Think about it! □ Quando ho
fame non ragiono più. I can't think when I'm
hungry.

la **ragione** FEM NOUN
reason
□ Avrà le sue buone ragioni per rifiutare. He
must have his reasons for refusing.
■ **aver ragione** to be right □ Sì, hai
perfettamente ragione. Yes, you're quite right.

la **ragioneria** FEM NOUN
accounting
□ Studia ragioneria. She's studying accounting

ragionevole (FEM **ragionevole**) ADJECTIVE
1 sensible
□ Sii ragionevole! Be sensible!
2 reasonable
□ Il prezzo mi sembra ragionevole. The price
seems reasonable.

il **ragioniere**, la **ragioniera** MASC/FEM
NOUN
accountant
□ È ragioniere. He is an accountant.

la **ragnatela** FEM NOUN
cobweb
□ C'erano un sacco di ragnatele. There were
lots of cobwebs.

il **ragno** MASC NOUN
spider
□ Ho paura dei ragni. I'm scared of spiders.

il **ragù** (PL i **ragù**) MASC NOUN
meat sauce
□ spaghetti al ragù spaghetti with meat sauce

rallegrare VERB [68]
1 to cheer up
□ La notizia ha rallegrato tutti. The news
cheered everyone up.
2 to brighten up
□ Quel bel tappeto giallo rallegra la stanza.
That lovely yellow carpet brightens up the
room.

r

221

rallentare VERB [68, aux **essere**]
to slow down
□ Rallenta, c'è un passaggio pedonale. Slow down, there's a pedestrian crossing.

il **rallentatore** MASC NOUN
■ **al rallentatore** in slow motion

il **rally** (PL i **rally**) MASC NOUN
rally
□ il rally di Montecarlo the Monte Carlo rally

il **rame** MASC NOUN
copper

rammendare VERB [68]
1 to darn
2 to mend

il **ramo** MASC NOUN
1 branch (of tree)
2 field (area of expertise)
□ Non è il suo ramo. It's not his field.

il **ramoscello** MASC NOUN
twig

la **rampa** FEM NOUN
■ **rampa di scale** flight of stairs
■ **rampa d'accesso** ramp

il **rampicante** MASC NOUN
climber

la **rana** FEM NOUN
frog
■ **nuotare a rana** to do the breaststroke
□ Sai nuotare a rana? Can you do the breaststroke?

rancido (FEM **rancida**) ADJECTIVE
rancid

randagio (FEM **randagia**, MASC PL **randagi**, FEM PL **randage**) ADJECTIVE
stray
□ un cane randagio a stray dog

rannicchiarsi VERB [17, aux **essere**]
to crouch
□ Era rannicchiato dietro la macchina. He was crouching behind the car.

la **rapa** FEM NOUN
turnip

rapace (FEM **rapace**) ADJECTIVE
■ **uccello rapace** bird of prey

rapidamente ADVERB
quickly
□ L'incendio si è esteso rapidamente. The fire spread quickly.

rapido (FEM **rapida**) ADJECTIVE
quick
□ Gli ho dato solo una rapida occhiata. I just had a quick look at it.

il **rapimento** MASC NOUN
kidnapping
□ Il rapimento è avvenuto in pieno giorno. The kidnapping happened in broad daylight.

la **rapina** FEM NOUN
robbery
□ C'è stata una rapina in banca ieri. There was a bank robbery yesterday.

rapinare VERB [68]
to rob
□ Quella banca è stata rapinata tre volte. That bank has been robbed three times.

il **rapinatore**, la **rapinatrice** MASC/FEM NOUN
robber
□ I rapinatori sono fuggiti a piedi. The robbers ran away.

rapire VERB [51]
to kidnap
□ L'hanno rapito due mesi fa. He was kidnapped two months ago.

il **rapitore**, la **rapitrice** MASC/FEM NOUN
kidnapper
□ I rapitori hanno minacciato di uccidere l'ostaggio. The kidnappers threatened to kill the hostage.

il **rapporto** MASC NOUN
1 relationship
□ Abbiamo un ottimo rapporto. We have a very good relationship.
■ **avere rapporti sessuali** to have intercourse
2 report
□ Scrivi un rapporto sulla situazione. Write a report on the situation.

il/la **rappresentante** MASC/FEM NOUN
1 representative
□ il rappresentante di classe the class representative
2 rep (sales)
□ Fa il rappresentante. He is a rep.

rappresentare VERB [68]
to represent
□ Questo rappresenta un passo avanti nella scienza. This represents a step forward in science.

la **rappresentazione** FEM NOUN
1 representation
2 play (at theatre)

raramente ADVERB
rarely
□ Ci vediamo raramente. We rarely see each other.

raro (FEM **rara**) ADJECTIVE
rare
□ una pianta rara a rare plant

rasare VERB [68]
to shave off
□ Si è rasato la barba. He's shaved his beard off.

raschiare VERB [17]
to scrape
■ **raschiarsi la gola** to clear one's throat

raso (FEM **rasa**) ADJECTIVE, ADVERB
▷ see also **raso** NOUN

■ **un cucchiaio raso di farina** a level spoonful of flour

■ **raso terra** close to the ground □ Volava raso terra. It flew close to the ground.

il **raso** MASC NOUN
▷ *see also* **raso** ADJECTIVE, ADVERB
satin
□ una camicetta di raso a satin blouse

il **rasoio** MASC NOUN
razor
□ un rasoio radi e getta a disposable razor
■ **rasoio elettrico** electric shaver

la **rassegna** FEM NOUN
■ **una rassegna del cinema latino-americano** a season of Latin American films

rassegnarsi VERB [14, aux **essere**]
■ **rassegnarsi a qualcosa** to accept something □ Si è rassegnato alla decisione del padre. He accepted his father's decision. □ È stato difficile ma alla fine si è rassegnata. It was difficult, but she eventually accepted it.

rassicurare VERB [68]
to reassure
□ Il medico ci ha rassicurati sulla sua salute. The doctor reassured us about his health.
□ Ho cercato di rassicurarla. I tried to reassure her.

rassodare VERB [68]
to tone
□ Il nuoto aiuta a rassodare i muscoli. Swimming helps to tone the muscles.

rassomigliare VERB [25, aux **avere** or **essere**]
to look like
□ Rassomigli molto a tua madre. You look very like your mother.
■ **rassomigliarsi** to look alike □ Vi rassomigliate moltissimo. You look very alike.

il **rastrello** MASC NOUN
rake

la **rata** FEM NOUN
instalment
□ Si può pagare a rate. You can pay by instalments.

il **ratto** MASC NOUN
rat

rattoppare VERB [68]
to patch
□ Devo rattoppare i jeans. I need to patch my jeans.

rattrappito (FEM **rattrappita**) ADJECTIVE
stiff
□ Ho le gambe rattrappite. My legs are stiff.

rauco (FEM **rauca**, MASC PL **rauchi**, FEM PL **rauche**) ADJECTIVE
hoarse

il **ravanello** MASC NOUN
radish

i **ravioli** MASC PL NOUN
ravioli *sing*

ravvicinato (FEM **ravvicinata**) ADJECTIVE
■ **a distanza ravvicinata** at close range
□ Gli hanno sparato a distanza ravvicinata. He was shot at close range.

razionale (FEM **razionale**) ADJECTIVE
rational
□ una spiegazione razionale a rational explanation

il **razionamento** MASC NOUN
rationing
□ il razionamento della benzina petrol rationing

razionare VERB [68]
to ration
□ Stanno razionando l'acqua. Water is being rationed.

la **razza** FEM NOUN
1 race
□ studenti di tutte le razze students of all races
2 breed
□ Di che razza è il tuo cane? What breed is your dog?
3 sort
□ Ma che razza di discorso è? What sort of argument is that?
■ **Che razza di cretino!** What an idiot!

il **razzismo** MASC NOUN
racism

razzista (FEM **razzista**, MASC PL **razzisti**, FEM PL **razziste**) ADJECTIVE, MASC/FEM NOUN
racist

il **razzo** MASC NOUN
rocket

il **re** (PL i **re**) MASC NOUN
1 king
□ Re Artù King Arthur
2 D *(musical note)*
□ in re maggiore in D major

reagire VERB [51]
to react
□ Come hai reagito alla notizia? How did you react to the news?

reale (FEM **reale**) ADJECTIVE
1 true
□ È basato su un fatto reale. It's based on a true story.
2 royal
□ la famiglia reale the royal family

il **reality** (PL i **reality**) MASC NOUN
reality show *(TV)*

realizzare VERB [68]
1 achieve
□ Ho realizzato il mio sogno di viaggiare. I've achieved my ambition to travel.
■ **realizzarsi** to come true
2 to realize

□ Quando Luca ha realizzato quello che era successo... When Luca realized what had happened...

realmente ADVERB
really

□ È un fatto realmente accaduto? Did it really happen?

la **realtà** (PL le **realtà**) FEM NOUN
reality

□ La realtà era molto diversa. The reality was very different.

■ **realtà virtuale** virtual reality

■ **in realtà** in fact □ Sembra un ragazzino, in realtà ha quasi quarant'anni. He looks very young, but in fact he's nearly forty.

il **reato** MASC NOUN
crime

la **reazione** FEM NOUN
reaction

□ La sua prima reazione è stata scappare. Her immediate reaction was to run away.

il **rebus** (PL i **rebus**) MASC NOUN
picture puzzle

recapitare VERB [68]
to deliver

il **recapito** MASC NOUN
address

□ Puoi lasciarmi il tuo recapito? Can you give me your address?

■ **recapito telefonico** telephone number

la **recensione** FEM NOUN
review

□ Il film ha avuto delle ottime recensioni. The film has had excellent reviews.

recente (FEM **recente**) ADJECTIVE
recent

□ una scoperta recente a recent discovery

■ **di recente** recently □ Questo ristorante è stato aperto di recente. This restaurant opened recently.

recentemente ADVERB
recently

□ Ha cominciato a lavorare lì solo recentemente. She started working there only recently.

recintare VERB [68]

■ **recintare qualcosa** to put a fence round something □ Hanno recintato il giardino. They've put a fence round the garden.

il **recinto** MASC NOUN
fence

il **recipiente** MASC NOUN
container

□ recipienti di plastica plastic containers

reciproco (FEM **reciproca**, MASC PL **reciproci**, FEM PL **reciproche**) ADJECTIVE
mutual

□ È chiaro che la adora, e l'affetto è reciproco.

He obviously adores her, and the affection is mutual.

recitare VERB [68]
to act

□ Non sa recitare. He can't act. □ Mi piace recitare. I like acting.

■ **Recita molto bene.** He's a very good actor.

■ **recitare una parte** to play a part □ Ha recitato la parte di Giulietta. She played the part of Juliet.

il **reclamo** MASC NOUN

■ **fare reclamo** to complain □ Hanno presentato reclamo alla direzione per il chiasso. They complained to the manager about the noise.

reclinabile (FEM **reclinabile**) ADJECTIVE

■ **sedile reclinabile** reclining seat

la **reclusione** FEM NOUN
imprisonment

□ dieci anni di reclusione ten years' imprisonment

■ **L'hanno condannato a un anno di reclusione.** He was sentenced to a year in prison.

il **record** (PL i **record**) MASC NOUN
record

□ Ha battuto il record mondiale del salto in alto. He beat the world record for the high jump.

■ **a tempo di record** in record time

recuperare VERB [68]
1 to recover

□ Parte della refurtiva è stata recuperata. Some of the stolen goods have been recovered.

2 to get back

□ Ho recuperato la borsa che avevo smarrito. I've got back the bag I lost.

■ **recuperare il tempo perduto** to make up for lost time

redditizio (FEM **redditizia**) ADJECTIVE
profitable

□ un'attività redditizia a profitable business

il **reddito** MASC NOUN
income

le **redini** FEM PL NOUN
reins

□ Tiene le redini dell'azienda He holds the reins of the company

le **referenze** FEM PL NOUN
references

□ Martin aveva delle buone referenze. Martin had good references.

regalare VERB [68]
to give

□ Mia sorella mi ha regalato un suo CD. My sister gave me one of her CDs.

il **regalo** MASC NOUN
present

□ regali di Natale Christmas presents

□ Ho ricevuto un sacco di regali. I got lots of presents.

■ **fare un regalo a qualcuno** to give somebody a present

■ **Mi può fare una confezione regalo?** Could you gift-wrap it for me?

reggere VERB [82]

to hold

□ Reggi questa borsa, per favore. Hold this bag, please.

■ **reggersi** to hold on □ Reggiti a me. Hold on to me. □ Reggiti forte. Hold on tight.

■ **Non mi reggo in piedi dalla stanchezza.** I'm so tired I can hardly stand.

il **reggimento** MASC NOUN

regiment

il **reggiseno** MASC NOUN

bra

il **regime** MASC NOUN

regime

□ un regime totalitario a totalitarian regime

la **regina** FEM NOUN

queen

□ la regina Elisabetta Queen Elizabeth □ la regina madre the Queen Mother

regionale (FEM **regionale**) ADJECTIVE

regional

la **regione** FEM NOUN

region

□ L'Italia è suddivisa in venti regioni. Italy is divided into twenty regions.

il/la **regista** (MASC PL i **registi**, FEM PL le **registe**) MASC/FEM NOUN

director

registrare VERB [68]

to record

□ Voglio registrare questo programma. I want to record this programme.

il **registratore** MASC NOUN

tape recorder

■ **registratore di cassa** till

il **registro** MASC NOUN

register

□ il registro di classe the class register

regnare VERB [14]

to reign

il **regno** MASC NOUN

kingdom

■ **il Regno Unito** the United Kingdom

la **regola** FEM NOUN

rule

□ le regole del gioco the rules of the game

■ **essere in regola** to be in order □ Tutti i documenti erano in regola. All the papers were in order.

il **regolamento** MASC NOUN

rules pl

■ **essere proibito dal regolamento** to be against the rules □ Fumare è proibito dal regolamento scolastico. Smoking is against the school rules.

regolare (FEM **regolare**) ADJECTIVE

▷ see also **regolare** VERB

regular

□ a intervalli regolari at regular intervals

regolare VERB [68]

▷ see also **regolare** ADJECTIVE

to adjust

□ Non riesco a regolare il volume. I can't adjust the sound.

■ **Ricordati di regolare l'orologio.** Remember to set the clock.

■ **Non so come regolarmi.** I don't know what to do.

relativo (FEM **relativa**) ADJECTIVE

relative

□ un pronome relativo a relative pronoun

■ **relativo a** relating to

la **relazione** FEM NOUN

1 relationship

□ La loro relazione è un po' in crisi. Their relationship isn't going well.

2 affair

□ Ha scoperto che il marito ha una relazione. She's discovered that her husband is having an affair.

3 report

□ Devo scrivere una relazione sulla visita al museo. I've got to write a report on our visit to the museum.

la **religione** FEM NOUN

religion

remare VERB [68]

to row

□ Ora tocca a te remare. It's your turn to row now.

il **remo** MASC NOUN

oar

■ **barca a remi** rowing boat

rendere VERB [83]

1 to give back

□ Potresti rendermi la penna? Could you give me back my pen?

2 to make

□ Un po' di diplomazia renderebbe tutto più facile. A bit of diplomacy would make everything easier.

■ **rendersi utile** to make oneself useful □ Posso rendermi utile? Can I make myself useful?

■ **rendersi conto di qualcosa** to realize something □ Forse non ti rendi conto di quanto sia pericoloso. Maybe you don't realize how dangerous it is.

il **rene** MASC NOUN

kidney

renna - restringere

la **renna** FEM NOUN
1 reindeer
2 suede
   □ una giacca di renna a suede coat

il **reparto** MASC NOUN
1 department (in large stores)
   □ Scusi, dov'è il reparto casalinghi? Excuse me, where's the household department?
2 ward
   □ il reparto maternità the maternity ward

la **replica** (PL le **repliche**) FEM NOUN
   repeat
   □ Domani trasmettono la replica dell'ultima puntata. The repeat of the final episode is on tomorrow.

la **repressione** FEM NOUN
   repression

la **repubblica** (PL le **repubbliche**) FEM NOUN
   republic

la **reputazione** FEM NOUN
   reputation
   □ Si è rovinato la reputazione. He has ruined his reputation.

il **requisito** MASC NOUN
   requirement
   □ Uno dei requisiti era la conoscenza del tedesco. One of the requirements was a knowledge of German.

il/la **residente** MASC/FEM NOUN
   ▷ see also **residente** ADJECTIVE
   resident
   □ per i residenti dell'unione europea for the residents of the European Union

residente (FEM **residente**) ADJECTIVE
   ▷ see also **residente** NOUN
   ■ **È residente a Londra.** He lives in London.
   ■ **Sono residenti all'estero.** They live abroad.

residenziale (FEM **residenziale**) ADJECTIVE
   residential
   · □ un quartiere residenziale a residential area

la **resina** FEM NOUN
   resin

resistente (FEM **resistente**) ADJECTIVE
   strong
   □ un tessuto molto resistente a very strong material

resistere VERB [10]
   to resist
   □ Non ho saputo resistere alla tentazione! I couldn't resist the temptation!

respingere VERB [106]
   to reject
   □ La sua domanda è stata respinta. His application was rejected.

respirare VERB [68]
   to breathe
   □ Non riuscivo a respirare. I couldn't breathe.

la **respirazione** FEM NOUN
   breathing
   □ esercizi di respirazione breathing exercises
   ■ **respirazione bocca a bocca** mouth-to-mouth resuscitation □ Gli hanno fatto la respirazione bocca a bocca. He was given mouth-to-mouth resuscitation.

il **respiro** MASC NOUN
   breath
   □ Prova a trattenere il respiro. Try to hold your breath.

responsabile (FEM **responsabile**) ADJECTIVE
   ▷ see also **responsabile** NOUN
   responsible
   □ È un tipo molto responsabile. He's a very responsible person. □ Si sente responsabile dell'accaduto. She feels responsible for what happened.

il/la **responsabile** MASC/FEM NOUN
   ▷ see also **responsabile** ADJECTIVE
   person in charge
   □ Vorrei parlare con il responsabile. I'd like to speak to the person in charge.

la **responsabilità** (PL le **responsabilità**) FEM NOUN
   responsibility
   □ Non voglio responsabilità. I don't want responsibilities.

restare VERB [68, AUX **essere**]
1 to stay
   □ Dai, resta ancora un po'. Go on, stay a bit longer. □ Sono restato a casa tutto il giorno. I stayed at home all day.
2 to be left
   □ Ne restano solo due. There are only two left.
   ■ **Mi restano solo cinquanta sterline.** I've only got fifty pounds left.

restaurare VERB [68]
   to restore
   □ Stanno restaurando il quadro. The painting is being restored.

restituire VERB [51]
   to give... back
   □ Me lo presti? Te lo restituisco domani. Will you lend it to me? I'll give it back to you tomorrow.

il **resto** MASC NOUN
1 rest
   □ Dove mettiamo il resto della roba? Where shall we put the rest of the stuff?
2 change
   □ Tenga pure il resto. Keep the change.
   □ Signora, ha dimenticato il resto! You've forgotten your change!

restringere VERB [109]
   to take in
   ■ **restringersi** 1 (material, clothes) to shrink
   2 (road) to narrow

la **rete** FEM NOUN
net
□ La pallina ha toccato la rete. The ball touched the net.
■ **collegarsi in rete** to get connected to the Net
■ **segnare una rete** to score a goal

il **retro** MASC NOUN
back
□ Sul retro c'è un giardino. There's a garden at the back.

retrocedere VERB [27, aux **avere** or **essere**]
to relegate
□ La squadra è stata retrocessa in serie B. The team has been relegated to the second division.

la **retromarcia** FEM NOUN
reverse
■ **mettere la retromarcia** to go into reverse □ Ha messo la retromarcia. He went into reverse.
■ **fare retromarcia** to reverse □ Ho sbattuto facendo retromarcia. I bumped the car when I was reversing.

retrovisore (FEM **retrovisore**) ADJECTIVE
■ **specchietto retrovisore** rear-view mirror

la **retta** FEM NOUN
1 straight line
■ **dar retta a** to listen to □ Non dargli retta, quello s'inventa le cose! Don't listen to him, he makes things up! □ Dammi retta, non vale la pena. Listen to me, it's not worth it.
2 fee

rettangolare (FEM **rettangolare**) ADJECTIVE
rectangular

il **rettile** MASC NOUN
reptile

retto (FEM **retta**) ADJECTIVE
■ **linea retta** straight line
■ **angolo retto** right angle

il **retweet** (PL i **retweet**) MASC NOUN
retweet

retwittare VERB [68]
to retweet

il **reumatismo** MASC NOUN
rheumatism
□ Soffre di reumatismi. She suffers from rheumatism.

la **revisione** FEM NOUN
1 revision (of document, book)
2 service (of car)

il **revival** (PL i **revival**) MASC NOUN
revival
□ un revival degli anni settanta a Seventies revival

riabbracciare VERB [13]
■ **Spero di riabbracciarvi presto.** Hope to see you again soon.

la **riabilitazione** FEM NOUN
rehabilitation

riaddormentarsi VERB [56]
to go back to sleep
□ Ho spento la sveglia e mi sono riaddormentata. I switched off the alarm and went back to sleep.

riagganciare VERB [13]
to hang up
□ Non riagganciare, premi il pulsante e rifai il numero. Don't hang up, press the button and redial.

rialzarsi VERB [56]
to get up
□ È caduto ma si è rialzato subito. He fell, but got up immediately.

la **rianimazione** FEM NOUN
■ **in rianimazione** in intensive care

riaprire VERB [9]
to reopen
□ Quando riaprono le scuole? When do the schools reopen? □ Il cinema ha riaperto dopo l'incendio. The cinema has reopened after the fire.

riassumere VERB [11]
to summarize

il **riassunto** MASC NOUN
summary

riattaccare VERB [18]
to hang up
□ Ha riattaccato senza lasciarmi finire. He hung up without letting me finish.

ribaltare VERB [68]
to turn over
■ **ribaltarsi** to turn over

ribassare VERB [68]
to cut
□ Hanno ribassato i prezzi. They've cut the prices.

ribellarsi VERB [56]
to rebel
□ Si è ribellato alla decisione del padre. He rebelled against his father's decision.

ribelle (FEM **ribelle**) ADJECTIVE, MASC/FEM NOUN
rebel

il **ribes** (PL i **ribes**) MASC NOUN
■ **ribes nero** blackcurrants
■ **ribes rosso** redcurrants

la **ricaduta** FEM NOUN
■ **avere una ricaduta** to relapse

ricamare VERB [68]
to embroider

ricamato (FEM **ricamata**) ADJECTIVE
embroidered

ricambiare VERB [17]
to return
□ Bisogna ricambiare l'invito. We must return the invitation.

il **ricambio** MASC NOUN
■ **pezzi di ricambio** spare parts

ricapitolare VERB [68]
to sum up
□ Dunque, ricapitolando... So, to sum up...

ricaricabile (FEM **ricaricabile**) ADJECTIVE
rechargeable

ricaricare VERB [18]
1 to reload (gun, camera)
2 to wind up (toy, clock)
3 to refill (pen)
4 to recharge (battery)

ricattare VERB [68]
to blackmail
□ Lo stavano ricattando. They were blackmailing him.

il **ricatto** MASC NOUN
blackmail
□ Ma questo è un ricatto! This is blackmail!

la **ricca** (PL le **ricche**) FEM NOUN
rich woman

riccio (FEM **riccia**, MASC PL **ricci**, FEM PL **ricce**) ADJECTIVE
▷ see also **riccio** NOUN
curly
□ Ho i capelli ricci. I've got curly hair. □ I suoi capelli sono più ricci dei miei. His hair is curlier than mine.

il **riccio** MASC NOUN
▷ see also **riccio** ADJECTIVE
1 hedgehog
2 sea urchin

il **ricciolo** MASC NOUN
curl

ricco (FEM **ricca**, MASC PL **ricchi**, FEM PL **ricche**) ADJECTIVE
▷ see also **ricco** NOUN
rich
□ Viene da una famiglia ricca. He comes from a rich family. □ Le arance sono ricche di vitamina C. Oranges are rich in vitamin C.

il **ricco** (PL i **ricchi**) MASC NOUN
▷ see also **ricco** ADJECTIVE
rich man
□ Ha sposato un ricco. She married a rich man.
■ **i ricchi e i poveri** the rich and the poor

la **ricerca** (PL le **ricerche**) FEM NOUN
1 search
□ Hanno abbandonato le ricerche. The search has been abandoned.
■ **essere alla ricerca di qualcosa** to be looking for something □ Mia sorella è alla ricerca di un lavoro. My sister is looking for a job.
2 research
□ la ricerca scientifica scientific research
3 project
□ Devo fare una ricerca sulla Pop Art. I've got to do a project on Pop Art.

ricercato (FEM **ricercata**) ADJECTIVE
■ **È ricercato dalla polizia.** He's wanted by the police.

il **ricercatore**, la **ricercatrice** MASC/FEM NOUN
researcher

la **ricetta** FEM NOUN
1 recipe
□ Mi dai la ricetta della torta di mele? Could I have the recipe for apple pie?
2 prescription
□ Puoi comprare l'aspirina senza ricetta. You can buy aspirin without a prescription.

ricevere VERB [27]
to get
□ Cara Denise, ho ricevuto ieri la tua lettera... Dear Denise, I got your letter yesterday... □ Non ha ancora ricevuto lo stipendio. He hasn't got his pay yet.

il **ricevimento** MASC NOUN
reception
□ un ricevimento di nozze a wedding reception

il **ricevitore** MASC NOUN
receiver

la **ricevuta** FEM NOUN
receipt
□ Mi dà la ricevuta, per favore? Could you give me a receipt please?

richiamare VERB [68]
to call back
□ Richiamerò tra un quarto d'ora. I'll call back in a quarter of an hour.

richiedere VERB [19]
1 to ask for
□ Ha richiesto il parere di un avvocato. He has asked for a lawyer's opinion.
2 to apply for
□ Ha richiesto il passaporto più d'un mese fa. He applied for a passport more than a month ago.
3 to require
□ un lavoro che richiede concentrazione a job that requires concentration

la **richiesta** FEM NOUN
request
□ una fermata a richiesta a request stop

riciclare VERB [68]
to recycle
□ carta riciclata recycled paper

ricominciare VERB [13]
to start again
□ Ho ricominciato tutto da capo. I started all over again.
■ **ricominciare a fare qualcosa** to start doing something again □ Ha ricominciato a fumare. He's started smoking again.

la **ricompensa** FEM NOUN
reward

riconoscente (FEM **riconoscente**)
ADJECTIVE
grateful

riconoscere VERB [24]
1 to recognize
□ L'ho riconosciuto appena l'ho visto.
I recognized him as soon as I saw him.
2 to admit
□ Devo riconoscere che hai ragione. I must
admit you're right.

ricoperto (FEM **ricoperta**) ADJECTIVE
covered
□ una torta ricoperta di panna a cake covered
with cream

ricordare VERB [68]
1 to remember
□ Il mio numero è facile da ricordare. My
number is easy to remember. □ Ti ricordi di
Laura? Do you remember Laura? □ Non mi
ricordo. I can't remember.
2 to remind
■ **ricordare a qualcuno qualcosa** to
remind somebody of something □ Mi ricorda
un po' la Scozia. It reminds me a bit of
Scotland.
■ **ricordare a qualcuno di fare qualcosa**
to remind somebody to do something
□ Ricordami di spedire la lettera. Remind me to
post the letter.

il **ricordo** MASC NOUN
1 memory
□ Ho dei bellissimi ricordi dell'Irlanda. I have
very happy memories of Ireland.
2 souvenir
□ Questo è un ricordo del viaggio in Marocco.
This is a souvenir of my trip to Morocco.

ricostruire VERB [51]
1 to rebuild
2 to reconstruct

la **ricotta** FEM NOUN
ricotta

ricoverare VERB [68]
■ **È stato ricoverato in ospedale.** He's
been admitted to hospital.

la **ricreazione** FEM NOUN
break
□ Facciamo quindici minuti di ricreazione.
We have a fifteen minute break.

ricredersi VERB [27, aux **essere**]
to change one's mind
□ Mi sono ricreduto sul suo conto. I've
changed my mind about him.

ridare VERB [30]
to give... back
□ Me lo presti? Te lo ridò domani. Will you lend
it to me? I'll give it back to you tomorrow.

ridere VERB [84]
to laugh
□ Perché ridi? Why are you laughing? □ Tutti
sono scoppiati a ridere. They all burst out
laughing.
■ **Che c'è da ridere?** What's so funny?
■ **Non c'è niente da ridere.** It's not funny.

ridicolo (FEM **ridicola**) ADJECTIVE
1 funny
□ Era così ridicolo con quel cappello! He was so
funny in that hat! □ ancora più ridicolo even
funnier
2 ridiculous
□ Non essere ridicolo! Io non c'entro niente!
Don't be ridiculous! It's nothing to do with me!

ridire VERB [35]
■ **trovare da ridire su** to criticize □ Trova
sempre da ridire sui miei amici. She's always
criticizing my friends.

ridotto (FEM **ridotta**) ADJECTIVE
reduced
□ L'ho comprata a prezzo ridotto. I bought it at
a reduced price.

ridurre VERB [85]
to cut
□ Hanno ridotto il prezzo a trenta sterline.
They've cut the price to thirty pounds. □ Ho
dovuto ridurre la lunghezza del tema. I had to
cut the length of the essay.
■ **Guarda come hai ridotto quei jeans!**
Look at the state of your jeans!
■ **Ma come ti sei ridotto?** What a state
you're in!
■ **essere ridotto proprio male** to be in a
terrible state

riempire VERB [86]
1 to fill
□ Ho riempito il termos di caffè. I've filled the
flask with coffee.
2 to fill in (form)
□ Riempi il modulo, per favore. Fill in the form,
please.

rientrare VERB [68, aux **essere**]
to get back
□ Sono rientrato molto tardi. I got back very
late.
■ **Non è ancora rientrata.** She isn't back
yet.

riepilogare VERB [76]
to sum up
□ Dunque, riepilogando... So, to sum up...

rifare VERB [49]
to do again
□ Lo devo rifare da capo. I've got to do it all over
again. □ Stai tranquillo, non lo rifarà. Don't
worry, she won't do it again.
■ **rifarsi il trucco** to redo one's make-up
■ **rifare il letto** to make the bed

il **riferimento** MASC NOUN
reference

□ Nell'articolo si fa riferimento allo scandalo. There's a reference to the scandal in the article.

■ **punto di riferimento** reference point
□ Ho preso la stazione come punto di riferimento. I took the station as my reference point.

■ **in riferimento alla Vostra del...** with reference to your letter of the...

riferire VERB [51]
to tell
□ È andato a riferire tutto al professore. He went and told the teacher everything.

■ **riferirsi a** to refer to □ Non ho capito a cosa si riferisse. I didn't understand what he was referring to.

rifinito (FEM **rifinita**) ADJECTIVE
■ **ben rifinito** well finished

rifiutare VERB [68]
to refuse
□ Ha rifiutato di pagare la sua parte. He refused to pay his share.

il **rifiuto** MASC NOUN
refusal
□ un secco rifiuto a flat refusal

■ **rifiuti** rubbish sing □ L'ha buttato nei rifiuti. She threw it in the rubbish.

la **riflessione** FEM NOUN
1 remark
□ Ha fatto alcune riflessioni interessanti. He made some interesting remarks.
2 thought (reflection)
□ Ha risposto dopo un attimo di riflessione. She replied after a moment's thought.

riflessivo (FEM **riflessiva**) ADJECTIVE
reflexive

il **riflesso** MASC NOUN
1 reflection
□ il riflesso della luce sui vetri the reflection of the light on the windows □ il riflesso della luna sul mare the reflection of the moon in the sea
2 reflex
□ Quando si beve non si ha i riflessi pronti. Your reflexes are slower when you've been drinking.

riflettere VERB [87]
to think
□ Agisce senza riflettere. He does things without thinking. □ Rifletticci su. Think about it.

il **riflettore** MASC NOUN
floodlight

la **riforma** FEM NOUN
reform
□ la riforma del sistema sanitario the reform of the health service

■ **la riforma della scuola** educational reforms

il **riformatorio** MASC NOUN
community home

il **rifornimento** MASC NOUN
■ **fare rifornimento 1** to get petrol □ Dove possiamo fare rifornimento? Where can we get petrol? **2** to stock up

il **rifugiato,** la **rifugiata** MASC/FEM NOUN
refugee

il **rifugio** MASC NOUN
shelter

la **riga** (PL le **righe**) FEM NOUN
1 line
□ Ne ho letto solo poche righe. I just read a few lines.

■ **un foglio a righe** a piece of lined paper
■ **mettersi in riga** to line up
2 stripe
□ giallo a righe rosse yellow with red stripes
■ **una camicia a righe** a striped shirt
3 parting (of hair)

rigare VERB [76]
■ **rigare dritto** to behave □ Ti conviene rigare dritto! You'd better behave!

rigido (FEM **rigida**) ADJECTIVE
1 stiff (collar, card)
2 harsh (climate)
3 hard (winter)
4 strict (discipline, education)

il **rigore** MASC NOUN
1 penalty (in football)
2 rigour

riguardare VERB [68]
to concern
□ È un problema che ci riguarda tutti. It's a problem which concerns us all.

■ **Sono cose che non mi riguardano.** It's none of my business.

■ **per quel che mi riguarda** as far as I'm concerned □ Per quel che mi riguarda la faccenda è chiusa. As far as I'm concerned the matter is closed.

il **riguardo** MASC NOUN
consideration
□ Non ha alcun riguardo per gli altri. He has no consideration for other people.

■ **riguardo a** about □ Cos'hai deciso di fare riguardo all'offerta di lavoro? What have you decided to do about the job offer?

rilasciare VERB [13]
to release
□ Gli ostaggi sono stati rilasciati ieri. The hostages were released yesterday.

■ **rilasciare un'intervista** to give an interview
■ **rilasciare una dichiarazione** to make a statement

rilassarsi VERB [56]
to relax
□ Rilassati! Andrà tutto bene. Relax! Everything will be all right.

rileggere VERB [57]
to read through
□ Ho consegnato il compito senza rileggerlo. I gave in my homework without reading it through.

la **rima** FEM NOUN
■ **fare rima** to rhyme □ 'Head' fa rima con 'red'. 'Head' rhymes with 'red'.

rimandare VERB [68]
to put off
□ Abbiamo rimandato la gita di qualche giorno. We put off the trip for a few days.

rimanere VERB [88]
1 to stay
□ Sono rimasto a casa tutto il giorno. I stayed at home all day. □ Mi piacerebbe rimanere qualche altro giorno. I'd like to stay a few more days.
2 to be left
□ Ne è rimasto solo uno. There's only one left. □ È rimasto indietro. He was left behind.
■ **rimanere senza qualcosa** to run out of something □ Siamo rimasti senza benzina. We ran out of petrol.
■ **Sono rimasto senza parole.** I was speechless.
■ **rimanere male** to be hurt □ C'è rimasta molto male. She was really hurt.
■ **rimanere ferito** to be injured □ È rimasto ferito in un incidente stradale. He was injured in a car accident.

rimangiarsi VERB [58, aux **essere**]
■ **rimangiarsi la parola** to go back on one's word □ Aveva promesso e poi s'è rimangiato la parola. He promised, and then went back on his word.

rimbalzare VERB [68]
to bounce
□ La palla ha rimbalzato un paio di volte. The ball bounced a couple of times.

rimborsare VERB [68]
to refund
□ Mi hanno rimborsato il biglietto. They refunded the price of my ticket.

rimediare VERB [17]
■ **rimediare a qualcosa** to try and find a solution to something

il **rimedio** MASC NOUN
cure
□ un ottimo rimedio contro il raffreddore an excellent cure for a cold
■ **Non c'è rimedio.** There's no way out.
■ **porre rimedio a** to remedy □ Occorre porre rimedio alla situazione. We must remedy the situation.

rimettere VERB [59]
1 to put back
□ L'ho rimesso subito sul tavolo. I put it back on the table immediately.

2 to bring up (vomit)
■ **rimettersi** to recover □ Non si è ancora rimesso dall'operazione. He hasn't yet recovered from the operation.
■ **rimettersi in cammino** to set off again □ Dopo un breve sosta ci siamo rimessi in cammino. After a short stop we set off again.
■ **rimetterci** to lose □ Ci ho rimesso un sacco di soldi. I lost a lot of money.

rimodernare VERB [68]
to modernize

rimorchiare VERB [17]
to tow
□ Ci può rimorchiare fino all'officina? Could you tow us to the garage?

il **rimorchio** MASC NOUN
trailer

il **rimorso** MASC NOUN
remorse
□ Non ha dimostrato alcun rimorso. He showed no remorse.

rimpiangere VERB [71]
to be sorry
□ Ora rimpiange di non essere andato all'università. He's sorry now that he didn't go to university.

il **rimpianto** MASC NOUN
regret
□ Non ho rimpianti. I have no regrets.

rimpinzarsi VERB [56]
■ **rimpinzarsi di** to stuff oneself with □ Mi sono rimpinzato di biscotti. I stuffed myself with biscuits.

rimproverare VERB [68]
to tell off
□ L'hanno rimproverato per essere tornato tardi. He was told off for coming home late.

il **Rinascimento** MASC NOUN
Renaissance

rincarare VERB [68, aux **essere**]
to go up
□ La benzina è rincarata. Petrol has gone up.

rincasare VERB [68, aux **essere**]
to get home
□ È rincasato molto tardi. He got home very late.
■ **No, Maria non è ancora rincasata.** No, Maria isn't back yet.

rinchiudere VERB [20]
to lock up
□ Dovrebbero rinchiuderlo in galera. He should be locked up.
■ **Si è rinchiuso in camera.** He shut himself up in his bedroom.

rincorrere VERB [26]
to run after
□ L'ho rincorso ma non sono riuscito ad acchiapparlo. I ran after him but I couldn't catch him.

r

■ **giocare a rincorrersi** to play tag □ Dei bambini giocavano a rincorrersi. Some children were playing tag.

la **rincorsa** FEM NOUN
run-up
□ Ha preso la rincorsa prima di saltare. She took a run-up before she jumped.

rincrescere VERB [28, AUX **essere**]
■ **Mi rincresce che tu non stia bene.** I'm sorry you're not well.
■ **Mi rincresce di non poter venire.** I'm sorry I can't come.
■ **Se non ti rincresce vorrei pensarci su.** If you don't mind I'd like to think it over.

rinforzare VERB [68]
to reinforce

rinfrescare VERB [18]
to freshen
□ Il temporale ha rinfrescato l'aria. The storm freshened the air.
■ **rinfrescarsi** to freshen up □ Vorrei rinfrescarmi un po'. I'd like to freshen up a bit.

il **rinfresco** (PL i **rinfreschi**) MASC NOUN
reception
□ un rinfresco di nozze a wedding reception
■ **rinfreschi** refreshments

la **ringhiera** FEM NOUN
1 railing
2 banisters *pl*

ringiovanire VERB [51]
to make look younger
□ Quella pettinatura la ringiovanisce molto. That hair style makes her look much younger.

ringraziare VERB [17]
to thank
□ Non so proprio come ringraziarvi! I don't know how to thank you!
■ **ringraziare qualcuno per aver fatto qualcosa** to thank somebody for doing something □ Vi ringrazio per avermi ospitato a Edimburgo. Thank you for putting me up in Edinburgh.
■ **Ti ringrazio.** Thank you.

rinnovare VERB [68]
to renew
□ Devo rinnovare l'abbonamento ferroviario. I need to renew my season ticket. □ Quest'anno non gli hanno rinnovato il contratto. His contract hasn't been renewed this year.

il **rinoceronte** MASC NOUN
rhino

rintracciare VERB [13]
to find
□ Stanno cercando di rintracciare i testimoni. They're trying to find the witnesses.

rinunciare VERB [13]
■ **rinunciare a** to give up □ Ho dovuto rinunciare al viaggio. I had to give up my trip.

□ È troppo difficile, ci rinuncio! It's too difficult, I give up!

rinviare VERB [17]
to postpone
□ La riunione è stata rinviata a fine mese. The meeting has been postponed till the end of the month.

il **rinvio** MASC NOUN
postponement

riordinare VERB [68]
to tidy
□ Devo riordinare la mia camera. I must tidy my room.

riparare VERB [68]
to repair
□ Me l'ha riparato in un attimo. He repaired it for me in no time.
■ **far riparare qualcosa** to get something repaired □ Ho fatto riparare il videoregistratore. I got the video repaired.
■ **ripararsi da** to shelter from □ Siamo entrati in un bar per ripararci dalla pioggia. We went into a bar to shelter from the rain.

la **riparazione** FEM NOUN
repair

riparlare VERB [68]
■ **Ne riparleremo domani.** We'll talk about it tomorrow.

il **riparo** MASC NOUN
shelter
□ Dobbiamo trovare un riparo. We need to find shelter.
■ **Siamo al riparo!** We're safe!

ripartire VERB [41, AUX **essere**]
to leave
□ È arrivato ieri e riparte domani. He arrived yesterday and is leaving tomorrow.

ripassare VERB [68, AUX **avere** or **essere**]
1 to come back
□ Sara non c'è, può ripassare più tardi? Sara's not here, could you come back later?
2 to revise
□ Devo ripassare, domani ho l'esame. I've got to revise, I've got the exam tomorrow.

ripensare VERB [68]
1 to think
□ Quando ci ripenso mi vergogno un po'. When I think about it I feel rather ashamed.
2 to change one's mind
□ Ci ho ripensato, non vengo. I've changed my mind, I'm not coming.

ripetere VERB [1]
to repeat
□ Scusi, può ripetere? Excuse me, could you repeat that?
■ **Non se l'è fatto ripetere due volte!** He didn't need to be asked twice!

il **ripetitore** MASC NOUN
relay *(radio, TV)*

■ **un ripetitore per telefoni cellulari** a mobile phone mast

la **ripetizione** FEM NOUN
private lesson

□ Malcom dà ripetizioni di inglese. Malcom gives private English lessons.

■ **andare a ripetizione** to have private lessons □ Vado a ripetizione di matematica. I have private maths lessons.

il **ripiano** MASC NOUN
shelf

□ L'ho messo sull'ultimo ripiano. I put it on the top shelf.

la **ripicca** (PL le **ripicche**) FEM NOUN
■ **per ripicca** out of spite □ L'ha fatto solo per ripicca. She did it just out of spite.

ripido (FEM **ripida**) ADJECTIVE
steep

□ C'è una salita ripida per andare al castello. It's a steep climb up to the castle.

ripiegare VERB [76]
to fold up

□ Ho ripiegato per bene il giornale. I folded the newspaper up neatly.

■ **ripiegare su qualcosa** to make do with something □ Era troppo caro, ho ripiegato su uno più economico. It was too expensive, I made do with a cheaper one.

ripieno (FEM **ripiena**) ADJECTIVE
stuffed

□ peperoni ripieni stuffed peppers

riportare VERB [68]
1 to take back

□ Riportalo in cucina. Take it back to the kitchen. □ Mi ha riportato all'albergo a mezzanotte. He took me back to the hotel at midnight.

2 to bring back

□ Tieni, ti ho riportato il CD. Here, I've brought you back your CD.

riposare VERB [68]
1 to rest

□ Sta riposando in camera sua. She's resting in her room.

2 to sleep

□ Avete riposato bene? Did you sleep well?

il **riposo** MASC NOUN
rest

□ cinque minuti di riposo five minutes' rest

■ **giorno di riposo** day off □ Oggi ha preso un giorno di riposo. He's taken a day off today.

il **ripostiglio** MASC NOUN
junk room

riprendere VERB [77]
to take back

□ Si è ripreso tutte le sue foto. He's taken back all his photos.

■ **Puoi riprenderlo, non mi serve più.**

You can have it back, I don't need it any more.

■ **riprendere sonno** to get back to sleep □ Non sono riuscito a riprendere sonno. I couldn't get back to sleep.

■ **riprendersi** to recover □ Si è appena ripreso dalla polmonite. He's just recovered from pneumonia.

la **ripresa** FEM NOUN
1 second half

□ Ha segnato al 15° della ripresa. He scored in the fifteenth minute of the second half.

2 round (in boxing)

□ un incontro in 10 riprese a ten-round fight

3 acceleration (of car)

□ Questa macchina non ha ripresa. This car hasn't got any acceleration.

4 shot (with camcorder, etc)

□ Ho fatto delle belle riprese nel Galles. I got some nice shots in Wales.

■ **ripresa economica** economic recovery

riprovare VERB [68]
to try again

□ Riproverò più tardi. I'll try again later.

risalire VERB [93]
to date from

□ Il palazzo risale al Cinquecento. The palace dates from the sixteenth century.

risaputo (FEM **risaputa**) ADJECTIVE
■ **È risaputo che...** Everyone knows that...

il **risarcimento** MASC NOUN
compensation

□ un risarcimento di diecimila euro ten thousand euros compensation

la **risata** FEM NOUN
laugh

□ Ci siamo fatti una bella risata. We had a good laugh.

il **riscaldamento** MASC NOUN
1 heating

□ Il riscaldamento non funziona. The heating isn't working.

2 warm-up

□ Prima della partita facciamo riscaldamento. Before a match we do a warm-up.

riscaldare VERB [68]
1 to warm up

□ Il pollo dev'essere solo riscaldato. The chicken just needs warming up.

2 to heat

□ Un caminetto riscaldava la stanza. The room was heated by an open fire.

il **riscatto** MASC NOUN
ransom

rischiare VERB [17]
to risk

□ Ha rischiato la vita. He risked his life.

■ **rischiare di fare qualcosa** to risk doing something □ Non voglio rischiare di arrivare in ritardo. I don't want to risk arriving late.

r

il **rischio** MASC NOUN
risk
■ **correre il rischio di fare qualcosa** to
risk doing something □ Ha corso il rischio di
essere licenziato. He risked being sacked.

rischioso (FEM **rischiosa**) ADJECTIVE
risky
□ un'impresa rischiosa a risky enterprise
□ l'operazione più rischiosa del secolo the
century's riskiest operation

risciacquare VERB [68]
to rinse

la **riserva** FEM NOUN
reserve
□ Domenica scorsa ho giocato come riserva.
Last Sunday I played as reserve.
■ **di riserva** spare □ Ne tengo sempre uno di
riserva. I've always got a spare one.
■ **riserva naturale** nature reserve

riservare VERB [68]
to book
□ Vorrei riservare un tavolo per stasera. I'd like
to book a table for this evening.

riservato (FEM **riservata**) ADJECTIVE
reserved

il **riso** (PL le **risa**) MASC NOUN
1 rice
□ riso integrale brown rice
2 laughter
□ il riso e il pianto laughter and tears □ risa
allegre cheerful laughter

risolto (FEM **risolta**) ADJECTIVE
solved

risolvere VERB [89]
to solve
□ Ho risolto l'indovinello! I've solved the riddle!

le **risorse** FEM PL NOUN
■ **risorse naturali** natural resources
■ **È una donna di grandi risorse.** She's a
very resourceful woman.

il **risotto** MASC NOUN
risotto

risparmiare VERB [17]
to save
□ Sto risparmiando per comprare un
videogame. I'm saving to buy a video game.
■ **far risparmiare tempo** to save time

il **risparmio** MASC NOUN
saving
□ un grosso risparmio di tempo a big saving in
time □ Ha speso tutti i suoi risparmi. He spent
all his savings.

rispettare VERB [68]
to respect
□ Bisogna rispettare le opinioni altrui. You have
to respect other people's opinions.

il **rispetto** MASC NOUN
respect
□ Non ha alcun rispetto per le cose altrui. She
has no respect for other people's things.
■ **rispetto a** compared to □ Rispetto all'anno
scorso è molto più caro. Compared to last year
it's much more expensive.

rispondere VERB [90]
to answer
□ Ho telefonato ma non ha risposto nessuno.
I phoned, but nobody answered.
■ **rispondere a** to answer □ Sai rispondere
alla mia domanda? Can you answer my
question? □ Ha risposto alla tua lettera? Has
he answered your letter?
■ **rispondere di sì** to say yes
■ **rispondere di no** to say no
■ **rispondere di qualcosa** to be
accountable for something

la **risposta** FEM NOUN
answer
□ la risposta esatta the right answer

la **rissa** FEM NOUN
brawl
□ Ieri c'è stata una rissa nel bar. There was a
brawl in the bar yesterday.

il **ristorante** MASC NOUN
restaurant
□ Abbiamo mangiato al ristorante. We ate in a
restaurant.

ristretto (FEM **ristretta**) ADJECTIVE
■ **caffè ristretto** extra strong coffee
■ **una persona di idee ristrette** a
narrow-minded person

risultare VERB [68, AUX **essere**]
to emerge
□ Dalle indagini è risultato che... It emerged
from the inquiry that...
■ **La tue previsioni sono risultate
errate.** Your predictions proved to be wrong.
■ **Non mi risulta che...** I don't think...
□ Non mi risulta che sia partito. I don't think
he's left.

il **risultato** MASC NOUN
result
□ Domani sapremo il risultato degli esami.
We'll get the exam results tomorrow.

ritagliare VERB [25]
to cut out
□ Ho ritagliato l'articolo dal giornale. I cut the
article out of the paper.

il **ritardo** MASC NOUN
delay
□ un ritardo di due ore a two hour delay
■ **Il volo ha avuto un ritardo di due ore.**
The flight was two hours late.
■ **in ritardo** late □ Il treno è in ritardo. The
train is late. □ Miriam arriva sempre in ritardo.
Miriam always arrives late.
■ **Scusa il ritardo!** Sorry I'm late!

r

ritirare VERB [68]

1 to take out

□ Ha ritirato dei soldi. He took out some money.

■ **ritirare lo stipendio** to get paid

□ Quando ritira lo stipendio? When does he get paid?

2 to collect

□ È andata alla posta a ritirare un pacco. She's gone to the post office to collect a parcel.

■ **Dove si ritirano i bagagli?** Where is the baggage reclaim?

3 to take away (permit, passport)

■ **Gli hanno ritirato la patente.** He lost his licence.

il **ritmo** MASC NOUN

rhythm

ritornare VERB [68, aux **essere**]

1 to get back

□ È appena ritornata da New York. She's just got back from New York. □ Parto il cinque e ritorno il dieci. I leave on the fifth and get back on the tenth.

2 to go back

□ Mi piacerebbe ritornare in Irlanda. I'd like to go back to Ireland.

il **ritornello** MASC NOUN

chorus (of song)

il **ritorno** MASC NOUN

■ **essere di ritorno** to be back □ Sarò di ritorno venerdì prossimo. I'll be back next Friday.

■ **al ritorno** on the way back □ Al ritorno siamo passati per Bristol. We went through Bristol on the way back.

■ **il viaggio di ritorno** the return journey □ Il viaggio di ritorno è stato più breve. The return journey was shorter.

■ **due ore andata e ritorno** two hours there and back

■ **un biglietto di andata e ritorno** a return ticket

il **ritratto** MASC NOUN

portrait

ritrovare VERB [68]

to find

□ Ho ritrovato la mia agendina. I've found my diary.

■ **ritrovarsi 1** (in a situation) to find oneself **2** to meet again

ritto (FEM **ritta**) ADJECTIVE

upright

□ Non riusciva a stare ritto. He couldn't stand upright.

la **riunione** FEM NOUN

meeting

□ essere in riunione to be in a meeting

riunirsi VERB [51, aux **essere**]

to meet

□ Il consiglio si riunisce di giovedì. The council meets on Thursdays. □ Ci siamo riuniti a casa di Roberto. We met at Roberto's house.

riuscire VERB [117, aux **essere**]

■ **riuscire a fare qualcosa** to manage to do something □ Siamo riusciti a convincerla. We managed to persuade her.

■ **Non riesco ad aprirlo.** I can't open it.

■ **Spostalo un po'. — Non ci riesco.** Move it a bit. — I can't.

■ **riuscire bene** to go well □ La festa è riuscita bene. The party went well.

la **riva** FEM NOUN

1 shore

■ **in riva al mare** on the seashore

2 bank (of river)

rivale (FEM **rivale**) ADJECTIVE, MASC/FEM NOUN

rival

□ Come stilista non ha rivali. As a designer he has no rivals. □ Appartengono a bande rivali. They belong to rival gangs.

la **rivalità** (PL le **rivalità**) FEM NOUN

rivalry

rivedere VERB [119]

to see again

□ Non mi dispiacerebbe rivedere quel film. I wouldn't mind seeing that film again.

■ **Dalla scorsa estate non li ho più rivisti.** I haven't seen them since last summer.

rivelare VERB [68]

to reveal

□ Non ha voluto rivelare il nome dell'informatore. She wouldn't reveal the name of her informant.

■ **rivelarsi** to prove to be □ Si è rivelato un ottimo portiere. He proved to be an excellent goalkeeper.

la **rivelazione** FEM NOUN

revelation

□ Come ballerina è stata una rivelazione! Her dancing was a revelation!

riversarsi VERB [56]

to pour out

□ La folla si è riversata nelle strade. The crowd poured out into the streets.

il **rivestimento** MASC NOUN

covering

□ un rivestimento di plastica a plastic covering

la **rivincita** FEM NOUN

rematch

□ Mi ha chiesto la rivincita. He challenged me to a rematch.

la **rivista** FEM NOUN

magazine

□ una rivista di moda a fashion magazine

rivolgere VERB [91]

■ **rivolgere la parola a qualcuno** to speak to somebody □ Sono due giorni che non mi

235

rivolge la parola. She hasn't spoken to me for two days.

■ **rivolgersi a** to go and ask □ Dovrebbe rivolgersi all'impiegato laggiù. You should go and ask the man over there.

la **rivolta** FEM NOUN
revolt

la **rivoltella** FEM NOUN
revolver

rivoluzionare VERB [68]
to revolutionize

rivoluzionario (FEM **rivoluzionaria**)
ADJECTIVE, MASC/FEM NOUN
revolutionary

la **rivoluzione** FEM NOUN
revolution

la **roba** FEM NOUN
1 things pl
□ Ho ancora un sacco di roba da fare. I've still got lots of things to do.

2 stuff
□ Cos'è quella roba sul tavolo? What's that stuff on the table?

■ **roba da mangiare** food □ C'era un sacco di roba da mangiare. There was lots of food.

■ **roba da lavare** washing □ Metti in lavatrice la roba da lavare. Put the washing in the machine.

■ **Roba da matti!** It's just incredible!

robusto (FEM **robusta**) ADJECTIVE
strong
□ un ramo robusto a strong branch □ un uomo robusto a strong man

■ **È un po' robusta.** She's quite a big woman.

la **roccia** (PL le **rocce**) FEM NOUN
rock

roco (FEM **roca**, MASC PL **rochi**, FEM PL **roche**)
ADJECTIVE
hoarse

il **rodaggio** MASC NOUN

■ **essere in rodaggio** to be being run in
□ La macchina è ancora in rodaggio. The car is still being run in.

il **rognone** MASC NOUN
kidney

Roma FEM NOUN
Rome
□ Domani andremo a Roma. We're going to Rome tomorrow. □ Abita a Roma. She lives in Rome.

la **Romania** FEM NOUN
Romania

romano (FEM **romana**) ADJECTIVE
Roman

romantico (FEM **romantica**, MASC PL **romantici**, FEM PL **romantiche**) ADJECTIVE
romantic

il **romanzo** MASC NOUN
novel

□ Leggo soprattutto romanzi. I mainly read novels.

■ **romanzo giallo** detective story

rompere VERB [92]
to break
□ Ho rotto un bicchiere! I've broken a glass!

■ **Uffa quanto rompi!** What a pain you are! (informal)

■ **rompersi 1** to break □ Il piatto si è rotto. The plate broke. □ Si è rotto una gamba. He broke a leg. **2** to break down □ La macchina si è rotta sull'autostrada. The car broke down on the motorway.

il/la **rompiscatole** (PL i/le **rompiscatole**)
MASC/FEM NOUN

■ **È un vero rompiscatole!** He's a real pain! (informal)

la **rondine** FEM NOUN
swallow

la **rosa** FEM NOUN
▷ see also **rosa** ADJECTIVE
rose
□ un mazzo di rose a bunch of roses

rosa (FEM+PL **rosa**) ADJECTIVE
▷ see also **rosa** NOUN
pink
□ calzini rosa pink socks

■ **un romanzo rosa** a romantic novel

rosato (FEM **rosata**) ADJECTIVE
rosé
□ vino rosato rosé wine

il **rosmarino** MASC NOUN
rosemary

il **rospo** MASC NOUN
toad

il **rossetto** MASC NOUN
lipstick

rosso (FEM **rossa**) ADJECTIVE
▷ see also **rosso** NOUN
red
□ Ha i capelli rossi. She's got red hair.

il **rosso** MASC NOUN
▷ see also **rosso** ADJECTIVE
yolk
□ rosso d'uovo egg yolk

la **rosticceria** FEM NOUN
delicatessen

la **rotaia** FEM NOUN
rail

la **rotella** FEM NOUN
wheel
□ una valigia con le rotelle a case with wheels

■ **pattini a rotelle** roller skates

■ **Gli manca una rotella!** He's got a screw loose!

rotolare VERB [68, AUX **essere**]
to roll
□ Il pallone è rotolato giù per le scale. The ball rolled down the steps.

r

il **rotolo** MASC NOUN
roll
□ un rotolo di carta igienica a roll of toilet paper
rotondo (FEM **rotonda**) ADJECTIVE
round
il **rottame** MASC NOUN
wreck
□ Questa macchina è un rottame! This car is a wreck!
rotto (FEM **rotta**) ADJECTIVE
broken
□ Il videoregistratore è rotto. The video is broken. □ Betty ha un braccio rotto. Betty has a broken arm.
la **roulotte** (PL le **roulotte**) FEM NOUN
caravan
il **rovere** MASC NOUN
oak
□ una botte di rovere an oak barrel
la **rovescia** FEM NOUN
■ **alla rovescia 1** upside down **2** inside out **3** back to front
rovesciare VERB [13]
1 to knock over
□ Mi sono alzato di scatto e ho rovesciato la sedia. I got up in a hurry and knocked over the chair.
2 to spill
□ Ha rovesciato il latte per terra. She spilled the milk on the floor.
■ **rovesciarsi** (car) to overturn
il **rovescio** (PL i **rovesci**) MASC NOUN
1 wrong side
□ Stirala dal rovescio. Iron it on the wrong side.
2 backhand (in tennis)
□ Ha un rovescio potentissimo. She has a very powerful backhand.
rovinare VERB [68, aux **avere** or **essere**]
to ruin
□ Si è rovinata il vestito. She's ruined her dress.
rubare VERB [68]
to steal
□ Mi hanno rubato la macchina fotografica. My camera has been stolen.
il **rubinetto** MASC NOUN
tap
il **rubino** MASC NOUN
ruby

la **rubrica** (PL le **rubriche**) FEM NOUN
■ **rubrica telefonica** address book
la **ruga** (PL le **rughe**) FEM NOUN
wrinkle
la **ruggine** FEM NOUN
rust
la **rugiada** FEM NOUN
dew
il **rullino** MASC NOUN
film
□ un rullino da ventiquattro foto a twenty-four exposure film
il **rum** MASC NOUN
rum
rumeno (FEM **rumena**) ADJECTIVE
Romanian
il **rumore** MASC NOUN
noise
□ Cos'è questo rumore? What's that noise?
■ **fare rumore** to make a noise □ Cerca di non far rumore. Try not to make a noise.
■ **un rumore di passi** a sound of footsteps
  LANGUAGE TIP Be careful! **rumore** doesn't mean **rumour**.
rumoroso (FEM **rumorosa**) ADJECTIVE
noisy
□ una strada rumorosa a noisy street □ Mi ha dato una stanza ancora più rumorosa. He gave me an even noisier room.
il **ruolo** MASC NOUN
part
□ Recita nel ruolo di Capitan Uncino. He's playing the part of Captain Hook.
la **ruota** FEM NOUN
wheel
□ la ruota di scorta the spare wheel
il **ruscello** MASC NOUN
stream
russare VERB [68]
to snore
la **Russia** FEM NOUN
Russia
russo (FEM **russa**) ADJECTIVE, MASC/FEM NOUN
Russian
il **rutto** MASC NOUN
■ **fare un rutto** to burp
ruvido (FEM **ruvida**) ADJECTIVE
rough

r

Ss

il **sabato** MASC NOUN
Saturday
□ L'ho visto sabato. I saw him on Saturday.
■ **di sabato** on Saturdays □ Vado in piscina di sabato. I go swimming on Saturdays.
■ **sabato scorso** last Saturday
■ **sabato prossimo** next Saturday

la **sabbia** FEM NOUN
sand
□ sulla sabbia on the sand
■ **sabbie mobili** quicksand *sing*

sabbioso (FEM **sabbiosa**) ADJECTIVE
sandy

la **sacca** (PL le **sacche**) FEM NOUN
bag
□ una sacca da viaggio a travel bag

il **sacchetto** MASC NOUN
bag
□ un sacchetto di carta a paper bag □ un sacchetto di plastica a plastic bag

il **sacco** (PL i **sacchi**) MASC NOUN
sack
□ un sacco di patate a sack of potatoes
■ **sacco a pelo** sleeping bag
■ **un sacco di** lots of □ C'era un sacco di gente. There were lots of people.

il **sacerdote** MASC NOUN
priest

il **sacrificio** MASC NOUN
sacrifice
■ **fare dei sacrifici** to make sacrifices

sacro (FEM **sacra**) ADJECTIVE
sacred

sadico (FEM **sadica**, MASC PL **sadici**, FEM PL **sadiche**) ADJECTIVE
sadistic

saggio (FEM **saggia**, MASC PL **saggi**, FEM PL **sagge**) ADJECTIVE
▷ *see also* **saggio** NOUN
wise

il **saggio** (PL i **saggi**) MASC NOUN
▷ *see also* **saggio** ADJECTIVE
essay
□ un saggio su Dante an essay on Dante
■ **un saggio di ginnastica** a gymnastics display
■ **un saggio di musica** a recital

il **Sagittario** MASC NOUN
Sagittarius
□ Sono del Sagittario. I'm Sagittarius.

la **sagoma** FEM NOUN
1 outline
□ la sagoma di una nave the outline of a ship
2 shape
□ Ha una sagoma irregolare. It has an irregular shape.

la **sala** FEM NOUN
1 room
□ C'era un tavolo in mezzo alla sala. There was a table in the middle of the room.
■ **sala da pranzo** dining room
■ **sala d'attesa** waiting room
■ **sala di lettura** reading room
2 hall
□ L'enorme sala era piena zeppa. The enorme hall was packed.
■ **sala giochi** amusement arcade
■ **sala operatoria** operating theatre

il **salame** MASC NOUN
salami

la **salamoia** FEM NOUN
brine
□ olive in salamoia olives in brine

salato (FEM **salata**) ADJECTIVE
salty
□ È troppo salato. It's too salty. □ Questo è più salato. This one is saltier.
■ **acqua salata** salt water

saldare VERB [68]
1 to settle
□ Devo saldare il conto. I must settle the bill.
2 to solder

i **saldi** MASC PL NOUN
sales
□ I saldi cominciano a gennaio. The sales start in January.

saldo (FEM **salda**) ADJECTIVE
■ **Tieniti saldo!** Hold tight!
■ **Non è più molto saldo sulle gambe.** He's not very steady on his feet any more.

il **sale** MASC NOUN
salt
□ C'è troppo sale. There's too much salt in it.
■ **sotto sale** salted □ acciughe sotto sale salted anchovies

- ■ **sale fino** table salt
- ■ **sale grosso** cooking salt
- ■ **sali da bagno** bath salts

il **salice** MASC NOUN

willow

- ■ **salice piangente** weeping willow

salire VERB [93]

to go up

□ I prezzi sono saliti. Prices have gone up. □ È appena salito in camera sua. He's just gone up to his room.

> **LANGUAGE TIP** **salire** can also by translated by 'to come up'.

□ Sali tu o scendo io? Are you coming up or shall I come down?

- ■ **salire su** to climb □ È salito sull'albero per raccogliere ciliege. He climbed the tree to pick some cherries.
- ■ **salire in** *(train, bus, plane)* to get on □ È già salito in aereo? Has he already got on the plane?
- ■ **salire in macchina** to get into the car

la **salita** FEM NOUN

1 climb

□ La salita è stata molto faticosa. The climb was very tiring.

2 hill

□ Abbiamo dovuto fermarci a metà della salita. We had to stop halfway up the hill.

- ■ **una strada in salita** a road going uphill

la **saliva** FEM NOUN

saliva

il **salmone** MASC NOUN

salmon

il **salone** MASC NOUN

1 lounge

2 show *(exhibition)*

- ■ **salone dell'automobile** motor show
- ■ **salone di bellezza** beauty salon

il **salotto** MASC NOUN

sitting room

la **salsa** FEM NOUN

sauce

□ spaghetti con salsa di pomodoro spaghetti with tomato sauce

la **salsiccia** (PL le **salsicce**) FEM NOUN

sausage

saltare VERB [68]

1 to jump

□ Il gatto è saltato sul tavolo. The cat jumped on the table. □ È saltato giù dal treno. He jumped off the train.

- ■ **Ma che ti salta in mente?** What on earth are you thinking of?
- ■ **saltare fuori** *(reappear)* to turn up □ Il libro è saltato fuori dopo una settimana. The book turned up a week later.
- ■ **Da dove salta fuori questa camicia?**

Where has this shirt appeared from?

- ■ **saltare in aria** to blow up □ Ha fatto saltare in aria l'edificio. He blew up the building.

2 to skip

□ Hai saltato il pranzo oggi? Did you skip lunch today? □ Ho saltato una riga. I've skipped a line.

- ■ **saltare con la corda** to skip

il **salto** MASC NOUN

jump

□ un salto in avanti a jump forward

- ■ **fare un salto** to jump
- ■ **fare un salto da qualcuno** to drop in on somebody □ Faccio un salto da te questo pomeriggio. I'll drop in on you this afternoon.
- ■ **salto con l'asta** pole vault
- ■ **salto in alto** high jump
- ■ **salto in lungo** long jump
- ■ **salto mortale** somersault

saltuario (FEM **saltuaria**) ADJECTIVE

- ■ **lavoro saltuario** occasional work

la **salumeria** FEM NOUN

delicatessen

i **salumi** MASC PL NOUN

cold meats

salutare VERB [68]

1 to say hello to

□ Non mi saluta mai. He never says hello to me. □ Salutami Giulia. Say hello to Giulia for me.

- ■ **Mi saluti sua moglie.** Give my regards to your wife.

2 to say goodbye to

□ È uscito senza salutare nessuno. He left without saying goodbye to anybody.

la **salute** FEM NOUN

health

□ Fumare fa male alla salute. Smoking is bad for your health.

- ■ **godere di buona salute** to be in good health
- ■ **Salute!** **1** *(to someone who has sneezed)* Bless you! **2** Cheers!

il **saluto** MASC NOUN

- ■ **tanti saluti** *(on postcard, in letter)* best wishes
- ■ **Cordiali saluti.** *(in letter)* Yours sincerely,...

il **salvadanaio** MASC NOUN

money box

il **salvagente** MASC NOUN

1 rubber ring

□ Sai nuotare senza il salvagente? Can you swim without a rubber ring?

2 lifebelt

3 life jacket

salvare VERB [68]

1 to save *(protect)*

□ La cintura di sicurezza lo ha salvato. The seat belt saved him.

■ **salvare la vita a qualcuno** to save somebody's life □ Una volta mi ha salvato la vita. He once saved my life.

2 to rescue

□ I pompieri hanno salvato due bambini. The firemen rescued two children.

■ **Non si è salvato nessuno nell'incidente.** Nobody survived the accident.

il **salvataggio** MASC NOUN
rescue

□ durante le operazioni di salvataggio during the rescue operation

■ **scialuppa di salvataggio** lifeboat
■ **giubbotto di salvataggio** life jacket

salve! EXCLAMATION
hello!

la **salvia** FEM NOUN
sage

la **salvietta** FEM NOUN
serviette

■ **salviette umidificate per bambini** baby wipes

salvo (FEM **salva**) ADJECTIVE, MASC NOUN
▷ see also **salvo** PREPOSITION
safe

□ Sono salvo! I'm safe!

■ **essere in salvo** to be safe □ Non preoccuparti, ora sei in salvo. Don't worry, you're safe now.

■ **mettersi in salvo** to reach safety

salvo PREPOSITION
▷ see also **salvo** ADJECTIVE, NOUN
except

□ Sono libero tutti i giorni salvo il lunedì. I'm free every day except Monday.

■ **Ci vediamo domani, salvo imprevisti.** I'll see you tomorrow, all being well.

San ADJECTIVE
Saint

□ San Francesco Saint Francis

il **sandalo** MASC NOUN
1 sandal
2 sandalwood

il **sangue** MASC NOUN
blood

□ Devo fare le analisi del sangue. I've got to have a blood test.

■ **una bistecca al sangue** a rare steak

sanguinare VERB [68]
to bleed

la **sanità** FEM NOUN

■ **Ministero della Sanità** Department of Health

sano (FEM **sana**) ADJECTIVE
healthy

□ un bambino sano a healthy child □ È più sana di lui. She's healthier than him. □ la dieta più sana di tutte the healthiest diet of all

■ **sano e salvo** safe and sound □ È tornata a casa sana e salva. She got home safe and sound.

■ **sano come un pesce** fit as a fiddle
■ **sano di mente** sane

San Silvestro MASC NOUN
New Year's Eve

□ Cosa fai per San Silvestro? What are you doing on New Year's Eve?

santo (FEM **santa**) ADJECTIVE
▷ see also **santo** NOUN
holy

il **santo,** la **santa** MASC/FEM NOUN
▷ see also **santo** ADJECTIVE
saint

□ Non è un santo. He's no saint.

il **santuario** MASC NOUN
sanctuary

sapere VERB [94]
1 to know

□ Sai dove abita? Do you know where he lives? □ Lo so, non è colpa tua. I know, it's not your fault. □ Non ne so nulla. I don't know anything about it.

■ **far sapere qualcosa a qualcuno** to let somebody know something □ Fagli sapere che lo sto cercando. Let him know I'm looking for him.

2 to be able to

□ È utile saper guidare. It's useful to be able to drive.

> **LANGUAGE TIP** 'can' and 'could' are also used.

□ Sai nuotare? Can you swim? □ Non so guidare. I can't drive. □ Non sapeva andare in bicicletta. He couldn't ride a bike.

■ **sapere di 1** to taste of □ Sa di fragola. It tastes of strawberries. **2** to smell of □ Sa di pesce. It smells of fish.

il **sapone** MASC NOUN
soap

il **sapore** MASC NOUN
taste

□ Non ha nessun sapore. It doesn't have any taste.

■ **avere un buon sapore** to taste good

saporito (FEM **saporita**) ADJECTIVE
tasty

□ un piatto saporito a tasty dish □ È più saporito cucinato così. It's tastier when it's cooked like this.

la **saracinesca** FEM NOUN
shutter

la **Sardegna** FEM NOUN
Sardinia

□ Mi è piaciuta molto la Sardegna. I really liked Sardinia. □ Andrò in Sardegna quest'estate. I'm going to Sardinia this summer.

le **sardine** FEM PL NOUN
  sardines
  □ una scatoletta di sardine a tin of sardines

la **sarta** FEM NOUN
  dressmaker

il **sarto** MASC NOUN
  tailor

il **sasso** MASC NOUN
  stone

il **sassofono** MASC NOUN
  saxophone

il **satellite** MASC NOUN
  satellite
  □ la TV via satellite satellite TV

la **sauna** FEM NOUN
  sauna
  □ Abbiamo fatto la sauna. We had a sauna.

sazio (FEM **sazia**) ADJECTIVE
  ■ essere sazio to be full □ Sono sazio. I'm full.

sbadato (FEM **sbadata**) ADJECTIVE
  careless

sbadigliare VERB [25]
  to yawn

lo **sbadiglio** MASC NOUN
  yawn
  ■ fare uno sbadiglio to yawn

sbagliare VERB [25]
  to make a mistake
  □ Mi dispiace, ho sbagliato. I'm sorry, I've
  made a mistake.
  ■ sbagliare numero to get the wrong
  number □ Scusi, ho sbagliato numero. Sorry,
  I've got the wrong number.
  ■ sbagliare strada to take the wrong road
  ■ sbagliarsi to be wrong □ Pensavo fosse lei,
  ma mi sono sbagliato. I thought it was her, but
  I was wrong.
  ■ Sbagliando s'impara. You learn by your
  mistakes.

sbagliato (FEM **sbagliata**) ADJECTIVE
  wrong

lo **sbaglio** MASC NOUN
  mistake
  □ È stato uno sbaglio. It was a mistake.
  ■ fare uno sbaglio to make a mistake

sbalordire VERB [51]
  to stun
  □ La notizia mi ha sbalordito. I was stunned by
  the news.

sbalzare VERB [68]
  to throw
  □ È stato sbalzato fuori dall'auto. He was
  thrown out of the car.

sbandare VERB [68]
  to skid (car)

sbarazzarsi VERB [56]
  ■ sbarazzarsi di to get rid of □ Mi sono
  sbarazzata di quei vecchi dischi. I got rid of

those old records.

sbarcare VERB [18, AUX **avere** or **essere**]
1 to disembark
  □ I passeggeri stavano sbarcando. The
  passengers were disembarking.
2 to unload (goods)

la **sbarra** FEM NOUN
  bar (metal)

sbarrare VERB [68]
  to block
  □ Una macchina gli ha sbarrato la strada. A car
  blocked his way.

sbattere VERB [1]
1 to slam
  □ Se n'è andato sbattendo la porta. He went
  out slamming the door.
2 to bang
  □ La finestra sbatte per il vento. The window is
  banging in the wind. □ Ho sbattuto il
  ginocchio. I banged my knee.
  ■ sbattere contro to bump into □ Era buio
  e ho sbattuto contro l'armadio. It was dark and
  I bumped into the wardrobe.
  ■ sbattere fuori qualcuno to throw
  somebody out

la **sberla** FEM NOUN
  ■ dare una sberla a qualcuno to slap
  somebody

sbiadito (FEM **sbiadita**) ADJECTIVE
  faded (material, painting)

sbocciare VERB [13, AUX **essere**]
  to bloom (flower)

la **sbornia** FEM NOUN
  ■ prendersi una sbornia to get drunk
  ■ smaltire la sbornia to sober up

sborsare VERB [68]
  to pay out

sbottonare VERB [68]
  to unbutton
  □ Si è sbottonato la camicia. He unbuttoned
  his shirt.

sbriciolare VERB [68]
  to crumble
  ■ sbriciolarsi to crumble □ La pietra mi si è
  sbriciolata in mano. The stone crumbled in my
  hand.
  ■ La torta s'è tutta sbriciolata. The cake
  got all broken.

sbrigare VERB [76]
  to do
  □ Ho ancora alcune faccende da sbrigare. I've
  still got a few things to do.
  ■ sbrigarsi to hurry □ Devi sbrigarti se non
  vuoi perdere il treno. You'll have to hurry if you
  don't want to miss the train.
  ■ Sbrigatevi! Hurry up!

la **sbronza** FEM NOUN
  ■ prendersi una sbronza to get drunk
  ■ smaltire la sbronza to sober up

sbronzarsi – scansarsi

sbronzarsi VERB [56]
to get drunk

sbronzo (FEM **sbronza**) ADJECTIVE
drunk

sbucciare VERB [13]
1 to peel (fruit, potatoes)
2 to shell (peas)
 ■ **sbucciarsi un ginocchio** to graze
 one's knee □ Mi sono sbucciato un ginocchio.
 I grazed my knee.

sbuffare VERB [68]
1 to pant
 □ Saliva le scale sbuffando per la fatica. He was
 panting with the effort of climbing the stairs.
2 to grumble
 □ Sbuffa sempre quando deve lavare i piatti. He
 always grumbles when he has to wash the
 dishes.

gli **scacchi** MASC PL NOUN
chess sing
 □ Sai giocare a scacchi? Can you play chess?
 ■ **a scacchi** checked □ una camicia a scacchi
 a checked shirt

scadente (FEM **scadente**) ADJECTIVE
poor-quality
 □ un prodotto scadente a poor-quality product

la **scadenza** FEM NOUN
1 expiry date
2 sell-by date
3 use-by date

scadere VERB [16, aux **essere**]
to expire
 □ Il mio passaporto è scaduto. My passport has
 expired.
 ■ **Il latte è scaduto.** The milk is past its
 sell-by date.

lo **scaffale** MASC NOUN
bookcase

scagliare VERB [25]
to hurl

la **scala** FEM NOUN
1 ladder
2 staircase
 ■ **scale** 1 (within building) stairs 2 (outside
 building) steps
 ■ **salire le scale** to go upstairs
 ■ **scendere le scale** to go downstairs
 ■ **scala a chiocciola** spiral staircase
 ■ **scala mobile** escalator
 ■ **scala antincendio** fire escape
3 scale
 □ una riproduzione in scala a reproduction to
 scale

scalare VERB [68]
to climb

lo **scaldabagno** (PL gli **scaldabagno**)
MASC NOUN
water heater

scaldare VERB [68]
to heat
 □ Scalda un po' di latte. Heat some milk.
 ■ **scaldare il motore** to warm up the engine
 ■ **scaldarsi** 1 to warm oneself 2 to warm up

la **scalinata** FEM NOUN
1 staircase
2 flight of steps

lo **scalino** MASC NOUN
step

lo **scalo** MASC NOUN
 ■ **fare scalo a** 1 to make a stopover at 2 (by
 boat) to call at

la **scaloppina** FEM NOUN
escalope
 □ una scaloppina di vitello a veal escalope

scalzo (FEM **scalza**) ADJECTIVE
barefoot
 □ Era scalzo. He was barefoot.

scambiare VERB [17]
to exchange
 □ Ho scambiato un CD con un libro. I
 exchanged a CD for a book.
 ■ **scambiare qualcuno per** to mistake
 somebody for □ L'ho scambiato per suo
 fratello. I mistook him for his brother.

lo **scambio** MASC NOUN
exchange
 □ uno scambio di prigionieri an exchange of
 prisoners □ scambi culturali cultural
 exchanges □ uno scambio di opinioni an
 exchange of views
 ■ **fare uno scambio** to do a swap
 □ Facciamo uno scambio? Shall we do a swap?

la **scampagnata** FEM NOUN
 ■ **fare una scampagnata** to go for a day
 out in the country

scampare VERB [68]
 ■ **scamparla bella** to have a narrow escape

gli **scampi** MASC PL NOUN
scampi sing

scampo MASC NOUN
 ■ **Non c'è scampo.** There's no way out.

scandalizzarsi VERB [56]
to be shocked
 □ Si scandalizza per un nonnulla. She's easily
 shocked.

lo **scandalo** MASC NOUN
scandal

lo/la **scansafatiche** (PL gli/le
 scansafatiche) MASC/FEM NOUN
layabout

scansarsi VERB [56]
to dodge
 □ Si è scansato per evitare il colpo. He dodged
 to avoid the blow.
 ■ **Potresti scansarti un po'?** Could you
 move over a bit?

lo **scantinato** MASC NOUN
basement

la **scapola** FEM NOUN
shoulder blade

lo **scapolo** MASC NOUN
bachelor

lo **scappamento** MASC NOUN
■ **tubo di scappamento** exhaust pipe

scappare VERB [68]
to get away
□ I ladri sono scappati. The thieves got away.
■ **scappare di prigione** to escape from
prison
■ **scappare di casa** to run away from home
■ **Scusa, ma devo scappare.** I'm sorry, but
I must dash.
■ **Non lasciarti scappare l'occasione.**
Don't miss this opportunity.
■ **Mi è scappato da ridere.** I burst out
laughing.
■ **Mi è scappato di mente.** It slipped my
mind.
■ **Mi scappa la pipì.** I'm bursting.

la **scappatoia** FEM NOUN
way out

lo **scarabeo** MASC NOUN
1 beetle
2 Scrabble®

scarabocchiare VERB [17]
to scribble

lo **scarabocchio** MASC NOUN
scribble

lo **scarafaggio** MASC NOUN
cockroach

la **scaramanzia** FEM NOUN
■ **Incrocia le dita per scaramanzia.** Cross
your fingers for luck.
■ **Non gliel'ho ancora detto per
scaramanzia.** I haven't told him yet, just in
case.

scaricare VERB [18]
1 to unload
□ Stanno scaricando il camion. They're
unloading the lorry.
2 to download
□ Ci vuole un'ora per scaricare il file. It takes an
hour to download the file.
■ **scaricarsi** 1 *(car battery)* to go flat
2 *(battery, torch)* to run out 3 *(relax)* to unwind

scarico (FEM **scarica**, MASC PL **scarichi**, FEM PL
scariche) ADJECTIVE
1 not loaded *(firearm)*
2 dead *(battery, torch)*
3 flat *(car battery)*

la **scarlattina** FEM NOUN
scarlet fever

la **scarpa** FEM NOUN
shoe

□ Mettiti le scarpe. Put on your shoes.
□ scarpe coi tacchi alti high-heeled shoes
□ scarpe coi tacchi bassi flat shoes
■ **scarpe da ginnastica** trainers

la **scarpiera** FEM NOUN
shoe rack

lo **scarpone** MASC NOUN
boot
■ **scarponi da sci** ski boots
■ **scarponi da montagna** climbing boots

scarseggiare VERB [58]
to be in short supply
□ I viveri scarseggiavano. Food was in short
supply.
■ **Cominciano a scarseggiare i
medicinali.** Supplies of medicine are starting
to run low.

scarso (FEM **scarsa**) ADJECTIVE
1 rather small
□ Le porzioni erano scarse. The portions were
rather small.
■ **un chilo scarso** just under a kilo
■ **di scarso interesse** of little interest
2 few
□ Hanno scarse risorse a disposizione. They
have few resources at their disposal.
3 poor
□ scarsa visibilità poor visibility

scartare VERB [68]
1 to unwrap
□ Hai scartato i regali? Have you unwrapped
your presents?
2 to reject
□ Hanno scartato tutte le mie proposte. They
rejected all my suggestions.

scassinare VERB [68]
to force *(door, lock, safe)*

la **scatola** FEM NOUN
1 box
□ una scatola di cioccolatini a box of
chocolates
2 can
□ una scatola di fagioli a can of beans
■ **cibi in scatola** canned foods

scattare VERB [68]
to go off
□ È scattato l'allarme. The alarm went off.
■ **far scattare l'allarme** to set off the alarm
■ **scattare una fotografia** to take a picture
■ **scattare in piedi** to spring to one's feet
□ Sono scattati in piedi. They sprang to their
feet.

lo **scatto** MASC NOUN
1 click *(noise)*
□ Ho sentito lo scatto della serratura. I heard
the click of the lock.
2 spurt
□ Ha sorpassato gli altri corridori con uno scatto. 243

He put on a spurt and overtook the other
runners.
■ **alzarsi di scatto** to jump up □ Si è alzato
di scatto ed è uscito. He jumped up and went
out.

scavalcare VERB [18]
to climb over
□ Abbiamo scavalcato il muro. We climbed
over the wall.

scavare VERB [68]
to dig

scegliere VERB [95]
to choose
□ Hai scelto il suo regalo? Have you chosen her
present?

la **scelta** FEM NOUN
choice
□ Non ho scelta, devo accettare. I've got no
choice, I have to agree.
■ **fare una scelta** to make a choice □ Hai
fatto la scelta giusta. You made the right
choice.
■ **di prima scelta** top-quality □ verdura di
prima scelta top-quality vegetables

scemo (FEM **scema**) ADJECTIVE
stupid

la **scena** FEM NOUN
scene
□ Compare nella prima scena. He appears in
the first scene.
■ **Ha fatto scena muta.** He didn't open his
mouth.
■ **mettere in scena una commedia** to
stage a play

lo **scenario** MASC NOUN
scenery
□ un magnifico scenario wonderful scenery

la **scenata** FEM NOUN
■ **fare una scenata** to make a scene □ Ha
fatto una scenata al ristorante. She made a
scene at the restaurant.

scendere VERB [96]
1 to go down
□ Sono arrivati. Scendi ad aprire la porta.
They're here. Go down and open the door.
2 to come down
□ Sali tu o scendo io? Are you coming up or
shall I come down?
■ **Scendo subito!** I'm coming!
■ **scendere da** 1 (car) to get out of 2 (train,
plane, bus) to get off
3 to fall (prices, temperature)
□ La temperatura è scesa di due gradi. The
temperature fell by two degrees.

lo **sceneggiato** MASC NOUN
TV drama

scettico (FEM **scettica**, MASC PL **scettici**,
FEM PL **scettiche**) ADJECTIVE
sceptical

la **scheda** FEM NOUN
card
■ **scheda elettorale** ballot paper
■ **scheda di memoria** memory card
■ **scheda telefonica** phonecard

lo **schedario** MASC NOUN
1 card index
2 filing cabinet

la **schedina** FEM NOUN
■ **giocare la schedina** to do the football pools

la **scheggia** (PL le **schegge**) FEM NOUN
splinter

lo **scheletro** MASC NOUN
skeleton

lo **schema** (PL gli **schemi**) MASC NOUN
diagram
□ Ha disegnato lo schema alla lavagna. He
drew the diagram on the board.
■ **uno schema riassuntivo** an outline of
the main points

la **scherma** FEM NOUN
fencing
□ Faccio scherma. I do fencing.

lo **schermo** MASC NOUN
screen
□ il grande schermo the big screen □ il piccolo
schermo the small screen □ TV a schermo
panoramico widescreen TV

scherzare VERB [68]
to joke
□ Stavo solo scherzando. I was only joking.

lo **scherzo** MASC NOUN
joke
■ **per scherzo** as a joke □ L'ho detto per
scherzo. I said it as a joke.
■ **fare uno scherzo a qualcuno** to play a
trick on somebody □ Facciamo uno scherzo a
Daniele! Let's play a trick on Daniele!
■ **scherzi a parte** seriously □ Scherzi a
parte, penso che sia una ragazza intelligente.
Seriously, I think she's a clever girl.

schiacciare VERB [13]
1 to squash
□ Si è seduta sul mio cappello e l'ha
schiacciato. She sat on my hat and squashed it.
2 to crush
□ La macchina gli ha schiacciato un piede. The
car crushed his foot.
3 to crack (nuts)
4 to press (button)
■ **schiacciare la palla** (at tennis, volleyball)
to smash the ball
■ **schiacciare un pisolino** to have a nap

lo **schiaffo** MASC NOUN
■ **dare uno schiaffo a qualcuno** to slap
somebody's face
■ **prendere a schiaffi qualcuno** to slap
somebody's face

schiantarsi VERB [56]
to crash
□ La macchina si è schiantata contro un albero. The car crashed into a tree.

schiarirsi VERB [51, aux **essere**]
■ **schiarirsi i capelli** to dye one's hair blonde □ Si è schiarita i capelli. She's dyed her hair blonde.
■ **schiarirsi la voce** to clear one's throat

lo **schiavo**, la **schiava** MASC/FEM NOUN
slave

la **schiena** FEM NOUN
back
□ Mi voltava la schiena. She had her back to me. □ Mi ha voltato la schiena proprio quando avevo bisogno di lui. He turned his back on me just when I needed him.
■ **mal di schiena** backache □ Ho mal di schiena. I've got backache.

lo **schienale** MASC NOUN
back (of chair)

lo **schifo** MASC NOUN
■ **fare schifo 1** (insect, food) to be disgusting **2** (film, book) to be awful
■ **Mi fai proprio schifo!** You really make me sick!
■ **Che schifo!** It's disgusting!

schifoso (FEM **schifosa**) ADJECTIVE
disgusting (insect, food)

la **schiuma** FEM NOUN
1 foam
□ schiuma da barba shaving foam
2 lather

schizzare VERB [68, aux **avere** or **essere**]
to splash
□ Finiscila di schizzarmi. Stop splashing me.
■ **Ti sei schizzato la giacca di vino.** You've got wine on your jacket.
■ **schizzare via** (car, motorbike) to speed off

schizzinoso (FEM **schizzinosa**) ADJECTIVE
fussy
□ È più schizzinosa di me. She's fussier than me.

lo **schizzo** MASC NOUN
1 splash
□ uno schizzo d'acqua a splash of water
2 sketch

lo **sci** (PL gli **sci**) MASC NOUN
1 ski
□ un nuovo paio di sci a new pair of skis
□ una gara di sci a ski race
2 skiing
□ Lo sci mi piace molto. I love skiing.
■ **sci da fondo** cross-country skiing
■ **sci nautico** water-skiing

sciacquare VERB [68]
to rinse

la **sciagura** FEM NOUN
disaster
□ una sciagura aerea an air disaster

lo **scialle** MASC NOUN
shawl

la **scialuppa** FEM NOUN
■ **scialuppa di salvataggio** lifeboat

lo **sciame** MASC NOUN
swarm

sciare VERB [55]
to ski
□ Sai sciare? Can you ski?
■ **andare a sciare** to go skiing

la **sciarpa** FEM NOUN
scarf

lo **sciatore**, la **sciatrice** MASC/FEM NOUN
skier

scientifico (FEM **scientifica**, MASC PL **scientifici**, FEM PL **scientifiche**) ADJECTIVE
scientific
□ la ricerca scientifica scientific research
■ **una materia scientifica** a science subject
■ **Ha scelto il ramo scientifico.** He chose science.

la **scienza** FEM NOUN
science
□ la scienza e la tecnologia science and technology
■ **scienze** (at school) science sing

lo **scienziato**, la **scienziata** MASC/FEM NOUN
scientist

la **scimmia** FEM NOUN
monkey

lo **scimpanzé** (PL gli **scimpanzé**) MASC NOUN
chimpanzee

scintillare VERB [68]
to sparkle

la **sciocchezza** FEM NOUN
■ **fare una sciocchezza** to do something silly □ Mi raccomando, non fare sciocchezze! Make sure you don't do anything silly!
■ **dire sciocchezze** to talk nonsense
■ **Sciocchezze!** Nonsense!

sciocco (FEM **sciocca**, MASC PL **sciocchi**, FEM PL **sciocche**) ADJECTIVE
silly
□ È l'idea più sciocca che abbia mai sentito. It's the silliest idea I've ever heard.

sciogliere VERB [97]
1 to melt
□ Il sole ha sciolto il neve. The sun has melted the snow.
■ **sciogliersi** to melt
2 to dissolve (sugar, salt)
■ **sciogliersi** (sugar, salt) to dissolve
3 to untie
■ **sciogliersi** (knot) to come undone

245

S

scioglilingua - sconcio

4 to undo (hair)

- **esercizi per sciogliere i muscoli** warm-up exercises

lo **scioglilingua** (PL gli **scioglilingua**) MASC NOUN
tongue-twister

lo **sciopero** MASC NOUN
strike

- **essere in sciopero** to be on strike
- **fare sciopero** to strike
- **sciopero della fame** hunger strike □ Sta facendo lo sciopero della fame. He is on hunger strike.

la **sciovia** FEM NOUN
ski tow

scippare VERB [68]

- **scippare qualcuno** to snatch somebody's bag □ Mi hanno scippato. My bag was snatched.

lo **sciroppo** MASC NOUN
syrup

□ sciroppo per la tosse cough syrup

sciupare VERB [68]
to ruin

□ Le scarpe nuove si sono sciupate. My new shoes were ruined.

scivolare VERB [68, aux **essere**]
to slip

□ È scivolato ed è caduto giù dalle scale. He slipped and fell down the stairs.

- **Attento, si scivola!** Be careful, it's slippery!
- **scivolare sul ghiaccio** **1** (person) to slip on the ice **2** (car) to skid on the ice

lo **scivolo** MASC NOUN
slide (in playpark)

scivoloso (FEM **scivolosa**) ADJECTIVE
slippery

la **scodella** FEM NOUN
bowl

la **scogliera** FEM NOUN

1 cliff

□ le bianche scogliere di Dover the white cliffs of Dover

2 rocks pl

□ La nave è finita sulla scogliera. The ship went onto the rocks.

lo **scoglio** MASC NOUN
rock (at sea)

lo **scoiattolo** MASC NOUN
squirrel

lo **scolapasta** (PL gli **scolapasta**) MASC NOUN
colander

lo **scolapiatti** (PL gli **scolapiatti**) MASC NOUN
plate rack

scolare VERB [68]
to drain

□ Puoi scolare la pasta, per favore? Can you drain the pasta, please?

lo **scolaro**, la **scolara** MASC/FEM NOUN
pupil

> **LANGUAGE TIP** Be careful! **scolaro** doesn't mean **scholar**.

scolastico (FEM **scolastica**, MASC PL **scolastici**, FEM PL **scolastiche**) ADJECTIVE
school

□ l'anno scolastico the school year

scollato (FEM **scollata**) ADJECTIVE
low-cut

□ un abito scollato a low-cut dress

la **scollatura** FEM NOUN
neckline

scollegarsi VERB [76, aux **essere**]

1 to disconnect (from internet)

2 to log off (from chatline)

scolorirsi VERB [51, aux **essere**]
to fade

□ La camicia si è scolorita. The shirt has faded.

scolorito (FEM **scolorita**) ADJECTIVE
faded

scolpire VERB [51]
to carve (wood, marble)

la **scommessa** FEM NOUN
bet

□ Ho mangiato dieci panini per scommessa. I ate ten rolls for a bet.

- **fare una scommessa** to make a bet □ Ho fatto una scommessa con Martina. I made a bet with Martina.

scommettere VERB [59]
to bet

□ Ha scommesso ottanta euro su un cavallo. He bet eighty euros on a horse.

- **Scommettiamo che...?** I bet you...
  □ Scommettiamo che Paola arriva in ritardo? I bet you Paola will be late.

scomodo (FEM **scomoda**) ADJECTIVE

1 uncomfortable

□ una sedia scomoda an uncomfortable chair

- **stare scomodo** to be uncomfortable

2 difficult

□ Mi è un po' scomodo venire di pomeriggio. It's a bit difficult for me to come in the afternoon.

- **L'orario della banca mi è scomodo.** The opening hours of the bank are inconvenient for me.

scomparire VERB [7]
to disappear

□ La nave è scomparsa all'orizzonte. The ship disappeared over the horizon.

- **Dov'eri scomparso?** Where did you get to?

lo **scompartimento** MASC NOUN
compartment (of train)

sconcio (FEM **sconcia**, MASC PL **sconci**, FEM PL **sconce**) ADJECTIVE

- **una barzelletta sconcia** a dirty joke

sconfiggere VERB [98]
  to defeat
la **sconfitta** FEM NOUN
  defeat
scongelare VERB [68]
  to defrost
scongiurare VERB [68]
  to beg
  □ Ti scongiuro, aiutami. I beg you, help me.
  ■ **Il pericolo è scongiurato.** We're out of
  danger.
lo **scongiuro** MASC NOUN
  ■ **Facciamo gli scongiuri!** Touch wood!
sconosciuto (FEM **sconosciuta**) ADJECTIVE
  ▷ see also **sconosciuto** NOUN
  unknown
  □ un attore sconosciuto an unknown actor
  ■ **È una zona sconosciuta.** It's a
  little-known area.
lo **sconosciuto**, la **sconosciuta** MASC/
  FEM NOUN
  ▷ see also **sconosciuto** ADJECTIVE
  stranger
  □ Non parlare agli sconosciuti. Don't talk to
  strangers.
sconsigliare VERB [25]
  ■ **sconsigliare a qualcuno di fare
  qualcosa** to advise somebody not to do
  something □ Ti ho sconsigliato di telefonarle.
  I advised you not to phone her.
  ■ **Ti sconsiglio di telefonarle.** I wouldn't
  advise you to phone her.
  ■ **Voleva dirtelo, ma l'ho sconsigliato.**
  He wanted to tell you, but I advised him not to.
scontare VERB [68]
  ■ **scontare due anni di prigione** to serve
  two years in prison
scontato (FEM **scontata**) ADJECTIVE
1 reduced
  □ tutto a prezzi scontati everything at reduced
  prices
2 predictable
  □ Il finale del film era scontato. The ending of
  the film was predictable.
  ■ **essere scontato che** to be bound to □ Era
  scontato che finisse così. It was bound to end
  that way.
  ■ **dare qualcosa per scontato** to assume
  something □ Davo per scontato che venissi.
  I assumed that you would come.
scontento (FEM **scontenta**) ADJECTIVE
  unhappy
  □ È sempre scontento. He's always unhappy.
  □ Ora è più scontento. He's unhappier now.
  ■ **essere scontento di** to be unhappy with
  □ Sono molto scontento della squadra. I'm very
  unhappy with the team.
lo **sconto** MASC NOUN
  discount

  □ uno sconto del dieci per cento a ten per cent
  discount □ Mi ha fatto uno sconto. He gave
  me a discount.
scontrarsi VERB [56]
  to crash (vehicles)
  □ La macchina si è scontrata con un autobus.
  The car crashed into a bus.
lo **scontrino** MASC NOUN
  receipt
lo **scontro** MASC NOUN
1 crash (of vehicles)
  □ È rimasto ferito nello scontro. He was injured
  in the crash.
  ■ **uno scontro frontale** a head-on collision
2 clash
  □ Ci sono stati scontri tra la polizia e i
  manifestanti. There have been clashes
  between the police and the demonstrators.
  ■ **uno scontro a fuoco** a shoot-out
sconvolgere VERB [91]
  to upset
  □ La notizia mi ha sconvolto. The news upset
  me.
sconvolto (FEM **sconvolta**) ADJECTIVE
  upset
  □ Era sconvolto. He was upset. □ Grazia aveva
  una faccia sconvolta. Grazia looked upset.
la **scopa** FEM NOUN
  broom
scopare VERB [68]
  to sweep
  □ Ho scopato la cucina. I've swept the kitchen.
la **scoperta** FEM NOUN
  discovery
scoperto (FEM **scoperta**) ADJECTIVE
1 bare (arms, shoulders)
  ■ **a capo scoperto** bare-headed
2 uncovered (pan)
  ■ **una macchina scoperta** an open car
  ■ **un assegno scoperto** a dud cheque
lo **scopo** MASC NOUN
  aim
  □ lo scopo di questo studio the aim of this
  research
  ■ **A che scopo?** What for? □ A che scopo
  lavori tanto? What are you working so
  hard for?
  ■ **a scopo di lucro** for money
scoppiare VERB [17, AUX **essere**]
1 to go off
  □ La bomba è scoppiata alle 11 precise. The
  bomb went off at exactly 11 o'clock.
2 to burst
  □ Mi è scoppiata una gomma sull'autostrada.
  My tyre burst on the motorway.
  ■ **scoppiare a piangere** to burst into tears
  ■ **scoppiare dal caldo** to be boiling
3 to break out (war, revolt)

□ La guerra è scoppiata nel 1939. War broke out in 1939.

lo **scoppio** MASC NOUN

1 explosion

2 bang

scoprire VERB [9]

1 to find out

□ Ha scoperto la verità. He's found out the truth.

2 to discover

□ Chi ha scoperto l'America? Who discovered America?

scoraggiarsi VERB [58, aux **essere**]

to get discouraged

la **scorciatoia** FEM NOUN

short cut

□ Ho preso una scorciatoia. I took a short cut.

scordare VERB [68]

to forget

□ Ho scordato il tuo numero di telefono. I've forgotten your phone number.

■ **Ho scordato a casa l'ombrello.** I left my umbrella at home.

■ **scordarsi di fare qualcosa** to forget to do something □ Mi sono scordato di telefonargli. I forgot to phone him.

■ **scordarsi di qualcuno** to forget about somebody

le **scorie** FEM PL NOUN

■ **scorie radioattive** radioactive waste *sing*

Scorpione MASC NOUN

Scorpio

□ Sono dello Scorpione. I'm Scorpio.

lo **scorpione** MASC NOUN

scorpion

scorrere VERB [26, aux **essere**]

to run *(liquid, river)*

□ Lascia scorrere l'acqua. Let the water run.

scorretto (FEM **scorretta**) ADJECTIVE

1 incorrect

□ un uso scorretto an incorrect use

2 unfair

□ È stato scorretto da parte tua. It was unfair of you.

scorrevole (FEM **scorrevole**) ADJECTIVE

■ **porta scorrevole** sliding door

scorso (FEM **scorsa**) ADJECTIVE

last

□ lo scorso mese last month

la **scorta** FEM NOUN

police escort

□ Il ministro è arrivato con la scorta. The minister arrived with a police escort.

■ **di scorta** spare □ la ruota di scorta the spare wheel

■ **fare scorta di** to stock up with

scortese (FEM **scortese**) ADJECTIVE

rude *(impolite)*

■ **in modo scortese** rudely

la **scorza** FEM NOUN

peel

la **scossa** FEM NOUN

electric shock

□ Ho preso la scossa accendendo la lampada. I got an electric shock when I switched on the lamp.

■ **una scossa di terremoto** an earth tremor

scosso (FEM **scossa**) ADJECTIVE

shaken

□ Sono ancora scosso. I'm still shaken.

■ **Ho i nervi scossi.** I'm still in a nervous state.

lo **scotch®** MASC NOUN

Sellotape®

scottare VERB [68]

to be hot

□ Attento che scotta. Be careful, it's hot. □ Il sole scotta in agosto. The sun is hot in August.

■ **scottarsi 1** to burn oneself **2** *(in sun)* to get burnt

la **scottatura** FEM NOUN

1 burn

□ Ho una scottatura sulla mano. I've got a burn on my hand.

2 sunburn

scotto (FEM **scotta**) ADJECTIVE

overcooked

la **Scozia** FEM NOUN

Scotland

□ Mi è piaciuta molto la Scozia. I really liked Scotland. □ Andremo in Scozia quest'estate. We're going to Scotland this summer.

lo/la **scozzese** MASC/FEM NOUN

▷ *see also* **scozzese** ADJECTIVE

Scot

□ gli scozzesi the Scots

scozzese (FEM **scozzese**) ADJECTIVE

▷ *see also* **scozzese** NOUN

Scottish

□ le isole scozzesi the Scottish islands

scremato (FEM **scremata**) ADJECTIVE

skimmed

□ latte scremato skimmed milk □ latte parzialmente scremato semi-skimmed milk

screpolato (FEM **screpolata**) ADJECTIVE

chapped

□ Ho le labbra screpolate. My lips are chapped.

scricchiolare VERB [68]

to creak

lo **scrittore**, la **scrittrice** MASC/FEM NOUN

writer

la **scrittura** FEM NOUN

writing

□ Non riesco a leggere la sua scrittura. I can't read his writing.

la **scrivania** FEM NOUN

desk

s

scrivere VERB [99]

1 to write

□ Scrivimi presto. Write to me soon.

■ **scrivere qualcosa a qualcuno** to write somebody something □ Ho scritto una lettera a Luca. I wrote Luca a letter. □ Gli hai scritto una cartolina? Have you written him a postcard?

■ **Scrivo sempre cartoline a tutti i miei amici.** I always write postcards to all my friends.

■ **scrivere a macchina** to type

■ **scrivere a penna** to write in pen

2 to spell

□ Come si scrive? How do you spell it? □ Si scrive con la K. It's spelt with a K.

lo scroccone, la scroccona MASC/FEM NOUN

scrounger

scrollare VERB [68]

■ **scrollare la testa** to shake one's head □ Ha scrollato la testa. He shook his head.

■ **scrollare le spalle** to shrug one's shoulders

lo scrupolo MASC NOUN

scruple

□ Non mi farei degli scrupoli a chiederglielo. I wouldn't have any scruples about asking him.

■ **essere senza scrupoli** to be unscrupulous

scrupoloso (FEM **scrupolosa**) ADJECTIVE

conscientious

scucirsi VERB [41, aux **essere**]

to come unstitched

□ Mi si è scucita una tasca. One of my pockets has come unstitched.

la scuderia FEM NOUN

stable

lo scudetto MASC NOUN

■ **vincere lo scudetto** to win the championship □ Il Milan ha vinto lo scudetto. AC Milan has won the championship.

lo scudo MASC NOUN

shield

sculacciare VERB [13]

to spank

lo scultore, la scultrice MASC/FEM NOUN

sculptor

la scultura FEM NOUN

sculpture

la scuola FEM NOUN

school

■ **andare a scuola** to go to school □ Vado a scuola ogni giorno. I go to school every day. □ I miei devono andare a scuola a parlare con i professori. My parents have to go to the school to talk to the teachers.

■ **scuola materna** nursery school

■ **scuola primaria** primary school

■ **scuola secondaria di primo grado** secondary school

■ **scuola secondaria di secondo grado** secondary school

> **DID YOU KNOW...?**
> Secondary school in Italy comprises three years at the **scuola secondaria di primo grado**, informally called **scuola media**, and four or five years at the **scuola secondaria di secondo grado**, informally called **scuola superiore**.

■ **scuola privata** private school

■ **scuola pubblica** state school

■ **la scuola dell'obbligo** compulsory education

■ **scuola serale** night school

■ **scuola guida** driving school

scuotere VERB [100]

to shake

□ Ha scosso la testa. He shook his head.

scuro (FEM **scura**) ADJECTIVE

dark

□ un colore scuro a dark colour □ una gonna verde scuro a dark green skirt

la scusa FEM NOUN

excuse

□ Era solo una scusa per andarsene. It was just an excuse to leave.

■ **chiedere scusa a qualcuno** to apologize to somebody □ Devi chiedere scusa all'insegnante. You must apologize to the teacher.

■ **Vi prego di accettare le mie scuse.** Please accept my apologies.

■ **una lettera di scuse** a letter of apology

scusare VERB [68]

to excuse

□ Scusate un attimo, torno subito. Excuse me, I'll be back in a minute.

■ **scusarsi** to apologize □ Si è scusato del ritardo. He apologized for being late. □ Ti sei scusato con lui? Did you apologize to him?

■ **Scusi!** 1 I'm sorry! (formal) 2 (to get attention) Excuse me! (formal)

■ **Scusa!** 1 I'm sorry! 2 (to get attention) Excuse me!

sdraiarsi VERB [17, aux **essere**]

to lie down

□ Si è sdraiato sul letto. He lay down on the bed.

la sdraio (PL le **sdraio**) FEM NOUN

deck chair

se CONJUNCTION

1 if

□ Fammi sapere se c'è qualche problema. Let me know if there are any problems. □ Guarda se è lì. See if it's there. □ Se fosse più furbo verrebbe. If he had more sense he would come. □ Se fossi in te... If I were you...

2 whether

□ Sono indecisa se scrivere o telefonare. I'm not sure whether to write or to phone. □ Non so se dirglielo o no. I don't know whether to tell him or not.

■ **se no** or else □ Rispondigli, se no si arrabbia. Answer him, or else he'll get angry.

sé PRONOUN

> LANGUAGE TIP **sé** can be translated by 'himself', 'herself', 'itself' or 'themselves', depending on the context.

□ L'ha fatto da sé. He did it himself. □ Hanno tenuto la notizia per sé. They kept the news to themselves. □ È piena di sé. She's full of herself.

■ **L'ha portato con sé.** He took it with him.

■ **sé stesso** himself

■ **sé stessa** herself □ Pensa solo a sé stessa. She only thinks of herself.

seccare VERB [18]

1 to dry

□ Il vento secca la pelle. Wind dries the skin.

■ **seccarsi** to dry up

2 to annoy

□ Mi secca dover aspettare. It annoys me to have to wait.

■ **Smettila di seccarmi!** Stop bothering me!

■ **seccarsi** to get annoyed

3 to mind

□ Ti secca se ti faccio una domanda? Do you mind if I ask you a question? □ Ti secca abbassare il volume? Would you mind turning down the volume?

seccato (FEM **seccata**) ADJECTIVE
annoyed

la seccatura FEM NOUN

1 nuisance

□ Che seccatura! What a nuisance!

2 bother

□ Non voglio seccature! I don't want any bother!

il secchiello MASC NOUN
bucket

il secchio MASC NOUN
bucket

□ un secchio d'acqua a bucket of water

■ **secchio della spazzatura** dustbin

secco (FEM **secca**, MASC PL **secchi**, FEM PL **secche**) ADJECTIVE

1 dry

□ Ho la pelle molto secca. I've got very dry skin. □ La mia pelle è più secca della tua. My skin is drier than yours.

■ **frutta secca 1** nuts pl **2** dried fruit

■ **avere la gola secca** to be parched

□ Potrei avere qualcosa da bere? Ho la gola

secca. Could I have something to drink please, I'm parched.

■ **far lavare a secco qualcosa** to get something dry-cleaned □ Devo far lavare a secco la giacca. I need to get my jacket dry-cleaned.

2 hard

□ Devi dare un colpo secco. You need to give it a hard bang.

il secolo MASC NOUN
century

□ nel XX secolo in the 20th century

la seconda FEM NOUN

1 second year (at school)

■ **seconda elementare** second year at primary school

■ **seconda media** second year at secondary school

■ **seconda superiore** fifth year at secondary school

2 second gear

□ mettere in seconda to go into second gear

■ **a seconda di** according to □ Le tariffe cambiano a seconda dell'ora del giorno. Charges vary according to the time of day.

secondo (FEM **seconda**) ADJECTIVE
▷ see also **secondo** NOUN, PREPOSITION
second

□ in seconda fila in the second row □ Prendi la seconda strada a destra. Take the second street on the right. □ È arrivato secondo. He came second.

■ **Il suo disco è secondo in classifica.** His record is number two in the charts.

■ **di seconda mano** second-hand □ una moto di seconda mano a second-hand motorbike

■ **seconda classe** second class □ un biglietto di seconda classe a second class ticket

■ **viaggiare in seconda classe** to travel second-class

il secondo MASC NOUN
▷ see also **secondo** ADJECTIVE, PREPOSITION

1 second

□ un minuto e dieci secondi one minute and ten seconds

■ **Un secondo, arrivo subito!** I won't be a minute!

2 main course (of meal)

□ Come secondo vorrei una bistecca. I'd like a steak for my main course.

secondo PREPOSITION
▷ see also **secondo** ADJECTIVE, NOUN
according to

□ Tutto sta andando secondo i piani. Everything's going according to plan.

□ Secondo il giornale quel film è da non perdere. According to the paper that film shouldn't be missed.

■ **secondo me** in my opinion □ Secondo me dovresti scrivergli. In my opinion you should write to him.

il **sedano** MASC NOUN
celery

la **sede** FEM NOUN
office *(of company, bank)*
■ **sede centrale** head office

sedere VERB [101]
▷ *see also* **sedere** NOUN
to be sitting
□ Era seduta accanto a me. She was sitting beside me.
■ **sedersi** to sit □ Si è seduto per terra. He sat on the floor. □ Siediti qui! Sit here! □ Sono così stanca che non vedo l'ora di sedermi! I'm so tired I can't wait to sit down!
■ **un posto a sedere** a seat

il **sedere** MASC NOUN
▷ *see also* **sedere** VERB
bottom

la **sedia** FEM NOUN
chair
■ **sedia a rotelle** wheelchair
■ **sedia elettrica** electric chair

sedicenne (FEM **sedicenne**) ADJECTIVE
sixteen-year-old

sedicesimo (FEM **sedicesima**) ADJECTIVE
sixteenth

sedici NUMBER
sixteen
□ Ha sedici anni. She's sixteen.
■ **alle sedici** at four p.m.
■ **il sedici dicembre** the sixteenth of December

il **sedile** MASC NOUN
seat

sedurre VERB [85]
to seduce

la **seduta** FEM NOUN
sitting
□ una seduta del parlamento a parliamentary sitting
■ **seduta spiritica** seance

la **sega** (PL le **seghe**) FEM NOUN
saw

segare VERB [76]
to saw

il **seggio** MASC NOUN
■ **seggio elettorale** polling station

la **seggiola** FEM NOUN
chair

il **seggiolone** MASC NOUN
highchair

la **seggiovia** FEM NOUN
chair lift

segnalare VERB [68]
1 to report

□ Ho segnalato il fatto alla polizia. I reported the incident to the police. □ Niente da segnalare. Nothing to report.
2 to recommend
□ Potresti segnalarci un buon albergo? Could you recommend a good hotel?
■ **L'insegnante ha segnalato alcuni nomi per la borsa di studio.** The teacher suggested a few names for the scholarship.

il **segnale** MASC NOUN
signal
□ Al mio segnale spegnete la luce. When I give the signal switch the light off.
■ **segnale stradale** road sign
■ **segnale orario** time signal
■ **Lasciate un messaggio dopo il segnale acustico.** Leave a message after the tone.

il **segnalibro** MASC NOUN
bookmark

segnare VERB [14]
1 to mark
□ Gli errori sono segnati in rosso. The mistakes are marked in red.
2 to show
□ Non segna la velocità giusta. It's not showing the right speed.
3 to score *(in football)*
□ Ha segnato nella ripresa. He scored in the second half.
4 to make a note of
□ Segna quanto ti devo. Make a note of what I owe you.

il **segno** MASC NOUN
1 sign
□ È un brutto segno. It's a bad sign. □ Di che segno sei? What sign are you?
2 mark
□ Aveva dei segni rossi sul viso. She had red marks on her face.

il **segretario**, la **segretaria** MASC/FEM NOUN
secretary

la **segreteria** FEM NOUN
secretary's office
■ **segreteria telefonica** answering machine

segreto (FEM **segreta**) ADJECTIVE, MASC NOUN
secret
□ un passaggio segreto a secret passage
■ **mantenere un segreto** to keep a secret
□ Sai mantenere un segreto? Can you keep a secret?
■ **in segreto** in secret

il/la **seguace** NOUN
follower

seguente (FEM **seguente**) ADJECTIVE
following
□ il giorno seguente the following day

S

251

seguire VERB [41]
to follow
□ Mi ha seguita fino a casa. He followed me home. □ Mi segui o vado troppo veloce? Are you following me or am I going too fast?
□ Lo seguo su Twitter. I follow him on Twitter.
■ **Perché non segui i miei consigli?** Why don't you take my advice?
■ **seguire un corso** to attend a course

il **seguito** MASC NOUN
■ **in seguito** then □ Ora leggete; in seguito vi farò delle domande. Now read it, then I'll ask you some questions.
■ **di seguito** non-stop □ È piovuto per tre giorni di seguito. It rained non-stop for three days.

sei NUMBER
six
□ Ha sei anni. She's six. □ alle sei at six o'clock
■ **il sei dicembre** the sixth of December

seicento NUMBER
six hundred
■ **il Seicento** the seventeenth century

selezionare VERB [68]
to select

la **sella** FEM NOUN
saddle

il **sellino** MASC NOUN
saddle (of bike)

la **selvaggina** FEM NOUN
game

selvaggio (FEM **selvaggia**, MASC PL **selvaggi**, FEM PL **selvagge**) ADJECTIVE
wild

selvatico (FEM **selvatica**, MASC PL **selvatici**, FEM PL **selvatiche**) ADJECTIVE
wild

il **semaforo** MASC NOUN
traffic lights pl
□ Attento! Il semaforo è rosso. Watch out! The traffic lights are red.

sembrare VERB [68, aux **essere**]
1 to look
□ Ha quarant'anni, ma sembra più giovane. She's forty, but she looks younger.
2 to seem
□ Non è facile come sembra. It's not as easy as it seems. □ Non mi sembra possibile. It doesn't seem possible.
■ **Mi sembra che...** I think... □ Mi sembra che tu abbia ragione. I think you're right.
■ **Non mi sembra vero!** I can't believe it!

il **seme** MASC NOUN
1 seed
2 pip (of apple, pear, etc)
■ **olio di semi** vegetable oil

la **semifinale** FEM NOUN
semifinal

il **semifreddo** MASC NOUN
frozen dessert

il **seminario** MASC NOUN
seminar
□ Ho seguito un seminario di storia. I attended a history seminar.

il **seminterrato** MASC NOUN
basement

semplice (FEM **semplice**) ADJECTIVE
simple
□ L'esercizio è molto semplice. The exercise is very simple. □ Conduce una vita semplice. He lives a simple life.
■ **una semplice formalità** a mere formality

sempre ADVERB
1 always
□ È sempre in ritardo. He's always late.
□ Crede di avere sempre ragione. He thinks he's always right.
■ **per sempre** for ever □ La situazione non durerà per sempre. The situation won't last for ever.
■ **una volta per sempre** once and for all
■ **sempre più** more and more □ Diventa sempre più difficile. It's getting more and more difficult.
■ **Diventa sempre più raro.** It's getting rarer and rarer.
■ **sempre meno** less and less □ L'attività è sempre meno redditizia. The business is getting less and less profitable.
2 still
□ Esci sempre con lui? Are you still going out with him? □ È pur sempre tuo fratello. He's still your brother.

la **senape** FEM NOUN
mustard

il **Senato** MASC NOUN
the Italian Senate

il **senatore,** la **senatrice** MASC/FEM NOUN
senator

il **seno** MASC NOUN
breast

sensazionale (FEM **sensazionale**) ADJECTIVE
sensational

la **sensazione** FEM NOUN
feeling
□ Ho la sensazione di averlo già incontrato. I've a feeling I've met him before.

sensibile (FEM **sensibile**) ADJECTIVE
1 sensitive
□ È un ragazzo sensibile. He's a sensitive boy.
■ **essere sensibile al freddo** to feel the cold
2 considerable
□ un sensibile aumento della temperatura a considerable rise in the temperature

LANGUAGE TIP Be careful! **sensibile** doesn't mean **sensible**.

il **senso** MASC NOUN

1 sense

□ i cinque sensi the five senses

■ **avere senso** to make sense □ Questo non ha senso. This doesn't make sense.

■ **Che senso ha?** What's the sense in it?

■ **Non capisco il senso della frase.** I can't understand the sentence.

■ **un discorso senza senso** a meaningless speech

■ **avere senso pratico** to be practical

□ Ha molto senso pratico. She's very practical.

■ **senso dell'umorismo** sense of humour

■ **senso di colpa** sense of guilt

■ **riprendere i sensi** to regain consciousness

■ **Mi fa senso.** It disgusts me.

2 direction

□ Veniva in senso contrario. He was coming in the opposite direction.

■ **in senso orario** clockwise

■ **in senso antiorario** anticlockwise

■ **una via a senso unico** a one-way street

sensuale (FEM **sensuale**) ADJECTIVE

1 sensual (person)

2 sensuous (voice)

il **sentiero** MASC NOUN

path

sentimentale (FEM **sentimentale**)
ADJECTIVE

sentimental

il **sentimento** MASC NOUN

feeling

□ Aveva sempre nascosto i suoi sentimenti per lei. He had always hidden his feelings for her.

sentire VERB [41]

1 to hear

□ Mi sentite? Can you hear me? □ Sento dei passi. I can hear footsteps. □ Ho sentito dire che... I've heard that...

■ **Ci sentiamo spesso.** We often talk on the phone.

■ **Fatti sentire.** Keep in touch.

■ **Stammi a sentire!** Listen to me!

2 to feel

□ Sento freddo. I feel cold. □ Non sento niente per lui. I don't feel anything for him.

■ **Sento che succederà qualcosa.** I've got a feeling that something is going to happen.

■ **sentirsi bene** to feel well

■ **sentirsi male** to feel ill

■ **Come ti senti?** How do you feel?

■ **sentirsela di fare qualcosa** to feel like doing something □ Non me la sento di continuare. I don't feel like going on.

senza PREPOSITION

without

□ È uscito senza ombrello. He went out

without an umbrella. □ È andato via senza dire niente. He left without saying anything.

□ senza di te without you

■ **senz'altro** of course □ Mi scriverai? — Senz'altro! Will you write to me? — Of course!

■ **Lo farò senz'altro domani.** I'll do it tomorrow without fail.

separare VERB [68]

1 to separate

2 to distinguish

■ **separarsi** to split up □ I miei genitori si sono separati quando ero piccolo. My parents split up when I was little.

■ **Si è separata dal marito un anno fa.** She and her husband split up a year ago.

separato (FEM **separata**) ADJECTIVE

1 separate

□ Abbiamo chiesto conti separati. We asked for separate bills.

2 separated

□ I miei genitori sono separati. My parents are separated.

seppellire VERB [51]

to bury

la **seppia** FEM NOUN

cuttlefish

sequestrare VERB [68]

to confiscate

□ I miei mi hanno sequestrato il motorino. My parents have confiscated my moped.

il **sequestro** MASC NOUN

■ **sequestro di persona** kidnapping

la **sera** FEM NOUN

evening

■ **di sera** in the evening

■ **domani sera** tomorrow evening

■ **questa sera** this evening

serale (FEM **serale**) ADJECTIVE

evening

□ un corso serale an evening class

■ **scuola serale** night school

la **serata** FEM NOUN

evening

□ Grazie per la bella serata. Thanks for the lovely evening.

il **serbatoio** MASC NOUN

tank

serbo (FEM **serba**) ADJECTIVE, MASC/FEM NOUN

Serb

sereno (FEM **serena**) ADJECTIVE

1 calm

2 clear (sky)

la **serie** (PL le **serie**) FEM NOUN

series

□ una serie di furti a series of robberies

■ **serie A** first division □ Gioca in serie A. He plays in the first division.

■ **serie B** second division

■ **produzione in serie** mass production

serio (FEM **seria**) ADJECTIVE
1 serious
□ È una faccenda seria. It's a serious matter.
□ Aveva un'espressione molto seria. He looked very serious.
2 reliable
□ È una ditta seria. It's a reliable firm.
■ **sul serio** really □ Sul serio vuoi andarci? Do you really want to go?
■ **Dico sul serio.** I'm serious.
■ **Faccio sul serio.** I mean it.
■ **prendere qualcosa sul serio** to take something seriously □ Prende lo studio molto sul serio. He takes his schoolwork very seriously.

il **serpente** MASC NOUN
snake

la **serra** FEM NOUN
greenhouse
□ l'effetto serra the greenhouse effect

la **serratura** FEM NOUN
lock

il **server** (PL i **server**) MASC NOUN
server

servire VERB [41, aux **avere** or **essere**]
to serve (lunch, dinner, coffee)
□ Dopo la cena ha servito il caffè. After dinner she served coffee.
■ **Serviti pure!** Help yourself!
■ **servire a qualcosa** to be for something
□ A che cosa serve? What's it for?
■ **servire per qualcosa** to be for something
□ Serve per tagliare il formaggio. It's for cutting cheese.
■ **Non mi serve più.** I don't need it any more.

il **servizio** MASC NOUN
1 service
□ Il servizio è compreso? Is service included?
■ **servizio assistenza** helpline
■ **un servizio assistenza clienti** a customer helpline
■ **servizio militare** military service
■ **i servizi segreti** the secret service sing
■ **fuori servizio** out of order
■ **una casa con doppi servizi** a house with two bathrooms
2 report (article)
□ un servizio sul terremoto in Afghanistan a report on the earthquake in Afghanistan
3 serve (in tennis)
□ Ha un servizio potentissimo. She has a very powerful serve.
4 set
□ un servizio di posate a set of cutlery □ un servizio da tè a tea set

sessanta NUMBER
sixty

sessantesimo (FEM **sessantesima**)
ADJECTIVE, MASC NOUN
sixtieth

il **sesso** MASC NOUN
sex
■ **fare sesso** to have sex

sessuale (FEM **sessuale**) ADJECTIVE
sexual

sesto (FEM **sesta**) ADJECTIVE, MASC NOUN
sixth
□ Abito al sesto piano. I live on the sixth floor.
□ È arrivato sesto nella gara. He came sixth in the competition. □ un sesto a sixth □ un sesto della popolazione a sixth of the population

la **seta** FEM NOUN
silk
□ una camicia di seta a silk shirt

la **sete** FEM NOUN
thirst
□ Muoio di sete. I'm dying of thirst.
■ **avere sete** to be thirsty

settanta NUMBER
seventy

settantesimo (FEM **settantesima**)
ADJECTIVE, MASC NOUN
seventieth

sette NUMBER
seven
□ Ha sette anni. She's seven. □ alle sette di sera at seven p.m.
■ **il sette dicembre** the seventh of December

settecento NUMBER
seven hundred
■ **il Settecento** the eighteenth century

il **settembre** MASC NOUN
September

> **LANGUAGE TIP** In Italian, months are not written with capital letters.

□ in settembre in September

settentrionale (FEM **settentrionale**)
ADJECTIVE
northern
□ l'Italia settentrionale northern Italy

la **settimana** FEM NOUN
week
□ la settimana scorsa last week □ la settimana prossima next week □ tra due settimane in two weeks □ Ho preso tre settimane di ferie. I took three weeks' holiday.

settimanale (FEM **settimanale**) ADJECTIVE,
MASC NOUN
weekly

settimo (FEM **settima**) ADJECTIVE, MASC NOUN
seventh
□ Abito al settimo piano. I live on the seventh floor. □ un settimo della popolazione a seventh of the population

il **settore** MASC NOUN
sector

severo (FEM **severa**) ADJECTIVE
1 strict
2 severe *(punishment)*

la **sezione** FEM NOUN
section

la **sfacchinata** FEM NOUN
■ **È stata una bella sfacchinata!** It was really exhausting!

sfacciato (FEM **sfacciata**) ADJECTIVE
cheeky
□ È la ragazza più sfacciata della classe. She's the cheekiest girl in the class.

sfasciare VERB [13]
to smash up *(car, motorbike)*

la **sfera** FEM NOUN
■ **sfera di cristallo** crystal ball
■ **penna a sfera** ballpoint pen

la **sfida** FEM NOUN
challenge

sfidare VERB [68]
to challenge
□ L'ho sfidato a scacchi. I challenged him to a game of chess.
■ **Sfido io!** No wonder! □ Ho fame! — Sfido io, non hai mangiato niente oggi. I'm hungry! — No wonder, you've eaten nothing today.

sfilare VERB [68, aux **avere** or **essere**]
1 to march
2 to slip off
■ **sfilarsi** to take off *(clothes, shoes)* □ Si è sfilata il vestito. She took her dress off.

la **sfilata** FEM NOUN
■ **sfilata di moda** fashion show

sfinito (FEM **sfinita**) ADJECTIVE
exhausted

sfiorare VERB [68]
1 to brush against
□ Qualcosa mi ha sfiorato la gamba. Something brushed against my leg.
■ **Il proiettile l'ha solo sfiorato.** The bullet only grazed him.
2 to touch on
□ Non ha neppure sfiorato l'argomento. He didn't even touch on the subject.

sfocato (FEM **sfocata**) ADJECTIVE
out of focus

sfogarsi VERB [76, aux **essere**]
■ **sfogarsi con qualcuno** to confide in someone □ Avevo proprio bisogno di sfogarmi con qualcuno. I really needed to confide in someone.
■ **Non sfogarti su di me!** Don't take it out on me!

sfogliare VERB [25]
to leaf through
□ Stava sfogliando una rivista. She was leafing through a magazine.

sfondare VERB [68]
1 to break down
□ Ha sfondato la porta. He broke down the door.
2 to be successful
□ È difficile sfondare nel cinema. It's difficult to be successful in the film world.

lo **sfondo** MASC NOUN
background
□ bianco su sfondo rosso white on a red background

la **sfortuna** FEM NOUN
bad luck
□ Che sfortuna! What bad luck!
■ **portare sfortuna** to be unlucky □ Passare sotto una scala porta sfortuna. It's unlucky to walk under a ladder.
■ **avere sfortuna** to be unlucky □ Ho avuto sfortuna ieri sera, non ho vinto niente. I was unlucky last night, I didn't win anything.

sfortunato (FEM **sfortunata**) ADJECTIVE
unlucky

sforzarsi VERB [56]
■ **sforzarsi di fare qualcosa** to try to do something □ Sforzati di ricordare! Try to remember!

lo **sforzo** MASC NOUN
effort
■ **fare uno sforzo** to make an effort

sfrattare VERB [68]
to evict

lo **sfratto** MASC NOUN
■ **dare lo sfratto a qualcuno** to give somebody notice to quit □ Ci hanno dato lo sfratto. We've been given notice to quit.

sfregare VERB [76]
to rub
□ Si sfregava gli occhi. He was rubbing his eyes.

lo **sfruttamento** MASC NOUN
exploitation

sfruttare VERB [68]
1 to make the most of
□ Dobbiamo sfruttare lo spazio che abbiamo. We have to make the most of the space we have.
2 to exploit
3 to take advantage of

sfuggire VERB [41, aux **essere**]
to escape
□ Mi sfugge il nome. His name escapes me.
■ **È sfuggita alla polizia.** She got away from the police.
■ **sfuggire di mano a qualcuno** to slip out of somebody's hands □ Il vaso mi è sfuggito di mano. The vase slipped out of my hands.
■ **Mi è sfuggito di mente.** It slipped my mind.
■ **lasciarsi sfuggire** to miss □ Non lasciarti sfuggire l'occasione. Don't miss this opportunity.

S

la **sfumatura** FEM NOUN
shade (of colour, meaning)

lo **sgabello** MASC NOUN
stool

lo **sgabuzzino** MASC NOUN
junk room

lo **sgambetto** MASC NOUN
■ **fare lo sgambetto a qualcuno** to trip
somebody up

sganciare VERB [13]
to undo

sgarbato (FEM **sgarbata**) ADJECTIVE
rude (person)

sgargiante (FEM **sgargiante**) ADJECTIVE
gaudy

sgobbare VERB [68]
1 to swot
2 to slog

sgomberare VERB [68]
1 to clear
□ Stanno sgomberando la stanza. They're
clearing the room.
2 to move out
□ Dobbiamo sgomberare entro lunedì. We
have to move out by Monday.

lo **sgombro** MASC NOUN
mackerel

sgonfiare VERB [17]
to let down
□ Sgonfia il materassino. Let down the airbed.
■ **sgonfiarsi 1** (airbed) to deflate **2** (tyre) to
go flat
■ **La sua caviglia si è sgonfiata.** Her ankle
is no longer swollen.

sgonfio (FEM **sgonfia**) ADJECTIVE
flat (tyre, ball)
□ Hai una gomma sgonfia. You've got a flat
tyre.

sgradevole (FEM **sgradevole**) ADJECTIVE
unpleasant

sgranchirsi VERB [51, AUX **essere**]
■ **sgranchirsi le gambe** to stretch one's
legs □ Ho bisogno di sgranchirmi le gambe.
I need to stretch my legs.

sgranocchiare VERB [17]
to munch

sgraziato (FEM **sgraziata**) ADJECTIVE
clumsy
□ Luigi è ancora più sgraziato. Luigi is even
clumsier.

sgridare VERB [68]
■ **sgridare qualcuno** to tell somebody off
□ Perché mi sgridi? Why are you telling me off?

sgualcire VERB [51]
to crease
□ Attenta a non sgualcire il vestito. Mind you
don't crease your dress.
■ **sgualcirsi** to get creased

lo **sguardo** MASC NOUN
look
□ Mi ha lanciato uno sguardo d'intesa. He gave
me a knowing look.
■ **Aveva lo sguardo triste.** He looked sad.
■ **sollevare lo sguardo** to look up

sguazzare VERB [68]
to splash about

lo **shampoo** MASC NOUN
shampoo

si PRONOUN
▷ see also **si** NOUN

█ **LANGUAGE TIP si** can be translated by
'oneself', 'herself', 'himself', 'itself' or
'themselves', depending on the context.
□ Si è scottata. She's burned herself. □ Si è
tagliato. He's cut himself. □ Si sono già
presentati. They've already introduced
themselves.

█ **LANGUAGE TIP si** is often not translated.
□ Si sta lavando le mani. She's washing her
hands. □ Si è pettinato prima di uscire. He
combed his hair before going out. □ Si è
dimenticato l'ombrello a casa. He left his
umbrella at home. □ L'orologio si è fermato.
The clock has stopped. □ Si sono incontrati alle
cinque. They met at five o'clock.
■ **Si odiano.** They hate each other.
■ **Si stanno baciando?** Are they kissing?

il **sì** (PL i **sì**) MASC NOUN
▷ see also **sì** PRONOUN
B (musical note)

sì ADVERB
yes
□ Vuoi un caffè? — Sì, grazie. Would you like a
coffee? — Yes, please. □ Gli hai telefonato?
— Sì. Have you phoned him? — Yes, I have.
□ Siete andati al cinema ieri? — Sì. Did you go
to the cinema yesterday? — Yes, we did.
■ **dire di sì** to say yes
■ **Penso di sì.** I think so.
■ **Spero di sì.** I hope so.
■ **un giorno sì e uno no** every other day

sia CONJUNCTION
■ **sia... che...** both... and... □ Verranno sia
Luigi che suo fratello. Both Luigi and his
brother will be coming.

la **siccità** FEM NOUN
drought

siccome CONJUNCTION
since
□ Siccome era tardi ho deciso di tornare a casa.
Since it was late I decided to go home.

la **Sicilia** FEM NOUN
Sicily
□ Mi è piaciuta molto la Sicilia. I really liked
Sicily. □ Vado in Sicilia quest'estate. I'm going
to Sicily this summer.

S

la **sicura** FEM NOUN
safety catch

la **sicurezza** FEM NOUN
safety
□ una campagna per la sicurezza sulle strade a
road safety campaign
■ **di sicurezza** safety
■ **cintura di sicurezza** seat belt □ Mettiti la
cintura di sicurezza. Fasten your seat belt.
■ **per sicurezza** just in case □ Per sicurezza
portati l'ombrello. Take your umbrella, just in
case.
■ **con sicurezza** confidently □ Ha risposto
con molta sicurezza. He answered very
confidently.
■ **Lo so con sicurezza.** I'm quite certain.

sicuro (FEM **sicura**) ADJECTIVE
▷ see also **sicuro** NOUN, ADVERB
1 safe
□ Questo non è un luogo sicuro. This isn't a
safe place. □ Non mi sento sicuro qui. I don't
feel safe here.
2 sure
□ Sono sicuro che ce la farai. I'm sure you'll
manage it. □ Sei sicuro? Are you sure?
■ **Ne ero sicuro!** I knew it!
■ **L'ho saputo da fonte sicura.** I heard
about it from a reliable source.
■ **di sicuro** for sure □ Non sappiamo di
sicuro cosa sia successo. We don't know for
sure what happened.
■ **sicuro di sé** self-confident □ È molto
sicuro di sé. He's very self-confident.

sicuro MASC NOUN
▷ see also **sicuro** ADJECTIVE, ADVERB
■ **essere al sicuro** to be safe □ Non
preoccuparti, qui siamo al sicuro. Don't worry,
we're safe here.
■ **mettere qualcosa al sicuro** to put
something in a safe place □ Ho messo il tuo
anello al sicuro. I've put your ring in a safe
place.

sicuro ADVERB
▷ see also **sicuro** ADJECTIVE, NOUN
of course
□ Verrai? — Sicuro! Will you come? — Of
course I will!

la **siepe** FEM NOUN
hedge

sieronegativo (FEM **sieronegativa**)
ADJECTIVE
HIV-negative

sieropositivo (FEM **sieropositiva**) ADJECTIVE
HIV-positive

la **sigaretta** FEM NOUN
cigarette

il **sigaro** MASC NOUN
cigar

la **sigla** FEM NOUN
acronym

significare VERB [18]
to mean
□ Cosa significa questa parola? What does this
word mean?

il **significato** MASC NOUN
meaning

la **signora** FEM NOUN
lady
□ È una signora molto simpatica. She's a very
nice lady. □ Signore e signori! Ladies and
Gentlemen!
■ **la signora Rossi** Mrs Rossi
■ **Gentile Signora,...** (in a letter) Dear
Madam,...
■ **Gentile Signora Rossi,...** Dear Mrs Rossi,...

il **signore** MASC NOUN
gentleman
□ C'è un signore che ti cerca. There's a
gentleman looking for you. □ Signore e signori!
Ladies and Gentlemen!
■ **il signor Rossi** Mr Rossi
■ **Gentile Signore,...** (in a letter) Dear Sir,...
■ **Gentile Signor Rossi,...** Dear Mr Rossi,...
■ **i signori Bianchi** Mr and Mrs Bianchi
■ **il Signore** the Lord

la **signorina** FEM NOUN
young woman
□ la signorina che abita al piano di sotto the
young woman who lives downstairs
■ **la signorina Rossi** Miss Rossi
■ **Gentile Signorina,...** (in a letter) Dear
Madam,...
■ **Gentile Signorina Rossi,...** Dear Miss
Rossi,...

il **silenzio** MASC NOUN
silence
■ **Fate silenzio!** Be quiet!
■ **in silenzio** in silence □ Ascoltavano in
silenzio. They listened in silence.

silenzioso (FEM **silenziosa**) ADJECTIVE
quiet
□ È un ragazzo silenzioso. He's a quiet boy.

la **sillaba** FEM NOUN
syllable

il **simbolo** MASC NOUN
symbol

simile (FEM **simile**) ADJECTIVE
similar
□ Abbiamo gusti simili. We've got similar
tastes. □ Ha una gonna simile alla mia. She's
got a skirt similar to mine.
■ **Non ho mai visto niente di simile.** I've
never seen anything like it.

la **simpatia** FEM NOUN
■ **provare simpatia per qualcuno** to like
somebody

257

simpatico (FEM **simpatica**, MASC PL **simpatici**, FEM PL **simpatiche**) ADJECTIVE
nice
□ È una ragazza simpatica. She's a nice girl.
■ **Mi è molto simpatico.** I really like him.

| LANGUAGE TIP Be careful! **simpatico** doesn't mean **sympathetic**.

sincero (FEM **sincera**) ADJECTIVE
1 honest
□ Sii sincero con me. Be honest with me.
■ **un ragazzo sincero** a truthful boy
2 sincere

il **sindacato** MASC NOUN
trade union

il **sindaco** (PL i **sindaci**) MASC NOUN
mayor

la **sinfonia** FEM NOUN
symphony

singhiozzare VERB [68]
to sob

il **singhiozzo** MASC NOUN
■ **avere il singhiozzo** to have hiccups

singolare (FEM **singolare**) ADJECTIVE, MASC NOUN
singular
□ la prima persona singolare the first person singular □ al singolare in the singular

singolo (FEM **singola**) ADJECTIVE
▷ see also **singolo** NOUN
single
□ una camera singola a single room

il **singolo** MASC NOUN
▷ see also **singolo** ADJECTIVE
singles
□ il singolo maschile the men's singles pl

la **sinistra** FEM NOUN
1 left (side)
□ sulla sinistra, nella foto on the left of the photo
■ **voltare a sinistra** to turn left
■ **spostarsi verso sinistra** to move to the left
2 left hand
□ Scrive con la sinistra. He writes with his left hand.
■ **la sinistra** (in politics) the left □ Ha vinto la sinistra. The left won the election.
■ **un partito di sinistra** a left-wing party

sinistro (FEM **sinistra**) ADJECTIVE
left (hand, arm)

il **sinonimo** MASC NOUN
synonym

sintetico (FEM **sintetica**, MASC PL **sintetici**, FEM PL **sintetiche**) ADJECTIVE
synthetic
□ materiali sintetici synthetic materials

il **sintomo** MASC NOUN
symptom

sintonizzarsi VERB [56]
■ **sintonizzarsi su una stazione radio** to tune in to a radio station

la **sirena** FEM NOUN
siren

la **siringa** (PL le **siringhe**) FEM NOUN
syringe

il **sistema** (PL i **sistemi**) MASC NOUN
1 system
□ un sistema operativo an operating system
□ il sistema nervoso the nervous system □ il sistema solare the solar system
2 way
□ È un nuovo sistema per imparare le lingue. It's a new way to learn languages.

sistemare VERB [68]
1 to arrange
□ Ha sistemato tutti i libri sullo scaffale. He arranged all the books on the shelf.
2 to settle
□ Abbiamo ancora una questione da sistemare. We've still got one question to settle.
■ **sistemarsi 1** to settle down **2** to find a job
■ **Vedrai, tutto si sistemerà.** You'll see, everything will work out.

la **sistemazione** FEM NOUN
accommodation
□ È solo una sistemazione provvisoria. It's only temporary accommodation.

il **sito** MASC NOUN
site
□ un sito web a web site

situato (FEM **situata**) ADJECTIVE
situated
□ La casa è situata nel centro del paese. The house is situated in the middle of the village.

la **situazione** FEM NOUN
situation

Skype® MASC NOUN
Skype®
□ parlare su Skype to talk on Skype

slacciare VERB [13]
to undo

slavo (FEM **slava**) ADJECTIVE
Slav
■ **lingue slave** Slavonic languages

sleale (FEM **sleale**) ADJECTIVE
1 disloyal
2 unfair
□ concorrenza sleale unfair competition

slegare VERB [76]
to untie

gli **slip** MASC PL NOUN
briefs
□ un paio di slip nuovi a new pair of briefs

la **slitta** FEM NOUN
1 sledge
2 sleigh

slittare VERB [68]
1 to slip *(person)*
2 to skid *(car)*

slogarsi VERB [76, aux **essere**]
to sprain
□ Mi sono slogato la caviglia. I've sprained my ankle.

la **Slovenia** FEM NOUN
Slovenia

sloveno (FEM **slovena**) ADJECTIVE, MASC/FEM NOUN
Slovene

lo **smacchiatore** MASC NOUN
stain remover

smagliante (FEM **smagliante**) ADJECTIVE
■ un sorriso smagliante a dazzling smile

la **smagliatura** FEM NOUN
1 ladder *(in tights)*
2 stretch mark *(on skin)*

lo **smaltimento** MASC NOUN
■ lo smaltimento dei rifiuti waste disposal

smaltire VERB [51]
■ smaltire la sbornia to sober up

lo **smalto** MASC NOUN
■ smalto per unghie nail varnish □ Mi sto mettendo lo smalto. I'm putting my nail varnish on.

smarrire VERB [51]
to lose
□ Ho smarrito il portafoglio. I've lost my wallet.
■ smarrirsi to get lost □ Si sono smarriti nel bosco. They got lost in the woods.

smentire VERB [51]
to deny
□ Il ministro ha smentito le voci. The minister denied the rumours.

lo **smeraldo** MASC NOUN
emerald
□ un anello con smeraldo an emerald ring

smettere VERB [59]
to stop
□ Smettila subito! Stop it at once!
■ smettere di fare qualcosa to stop doing something □ Quando sono entrato hanno smesso di parlare. When I came in they stopped talking. □ Sta cercando di smettere di fumare. He's trying to stop smoking.

smistare VERB [68]
to sort *(packets, letters)*

smontare VERB [68, aux **avere** or **essere**]
1 to take apart *(car, furniture, etc)*
2 to get off *(train, bike, bus)*
□ Stava smontando dall'autobus. He was getting off the bus.

■ smontare dalla macchina to get out of the car

la **smorfia** FEM NOUN
grimace
□ una smorfia di dolore a grimace of pain
■ fare smorfie to make faces

snello (FEM **snella**) ADJECTIVE
slim
□ È la più snella. She's the slimmest.

snervante (FEM **snervante**) ADJECTIVE
■ un lavoro snervante a stressful job
■ L'attesa è stata snervante. It was a strain having to wait.

lo/la **snob** (PL gli/le **snob**) MASC/FEM NOUN
▷ see also **snob** ADJECTIVE
snob

snob (FEM+PL **snob**) ADJECTIVE
▷ see also **snob** NOUN
snobbish

snobbare VERB [68]
to snub

snodare VERB [68]
to untie

sobrio (FEM **sobria**) ADJECTIVE
sober

socchiudere VERB [20]
1 to leave ajar
□ Ha socchiuso la porta. He left the door ajar.
2 to half-close
□ Ha socchiuso gli occhi. He half-closed his eyes.

socchiuso (FEM **socchiusa**) ADJECTIVE
1 ajar
□ Lascia la porta socchiusa. Leave the door ajar.
2 half-closed
□ Aveva gli occhi socchiusi. His eyes were half-closed.

soccorrere VERB [26]
to help

il **soccorritore**, la **soccorritrice** MASC/FEM NOUN
rescuer

il **soccorso** MASC NOUN
■ prestare soccorso to help □ Nessuno si è fermato a prestare soccorso. Nobody stopped to help.
■ pronto soccorso casualty
■ soccorso stradale breakdown service
■ soccorsi aid *sing* □ Stanno organizzando i soccorsi per i terremotati. They are organizing aid for the earthquake victims.

sociale (FEM **sociale**) ADJECTIVE
social

la **società** (PL le **società**) FEM NOUN
1 society
□ la società dei consumi the consumer society
2 company

259

□ una società di assicurazioni an insurance company

■ **mettersi in società con qualcuno** to go into business with somebody □ Si è messo in società con suo fratello. He went into business with his brother.

■ **società sportiva** sports club

sociévole (FEM **sociévole**) ADJECTIVE
sociable

il **socio**, la **socia** MASC/FEM NOUN
1 partner (of firm)
2 member (of association, club)

soddisfacente (FEM **soddisfacente**)
ADJECTIVE
satisfactory

soddisfare VERB [38]
to satisfy
□ Il mio lavoro non mi soddisfa. My job doesn't satisfy me.

soddisfatto (FEM **soddisfatta**) ADJECTIVE
pleased
□ Sono soddisfatto del risultato. I'm pleased with the result.

la **soddisfazione** FEM NOUN
satisfaction

sodo (FEM **soda**) ADJECTIVE
▷ see also **sodo** ADVERB, NOUN
■ **un uovo sodo** a hard-boiled egg

sodo ADVERB
▷ see also **sodo** ADJECTIVE, NOUN
■ **lavorare sodo** to work hard
■ **dormire sodo** to sleep soundly

sodo MASC NOUN
▷ see also **sodo** ADJECTIVE, ADVERB
■ **venire al sodo** to come to the point
□ Vieni al sodo! Come to the point!

sofferto (FEM **sofferta**) ADJECTIVE
■ **una vittoria sofferta** a hard-won victory
■ **una decisione sofferta** a painful decision

soffiare VERB [17]
to blow
□ Soffiava un forte vento. A strong wind was blowing.
■ **soffiarsi il naso** to blow one's nose □ Si è soffiata il naso rumorosamente. She blew her nose loudly.

la **soffiata** FEM NOUN
■ **fare una soffiata alla polizia** to tip off the police

soffice (FEM **soffice**) ADJECTIVE
soft

il **soffio** MASC NOUN
breath
□ Non c'era neanche un soffio di vento. There wasn't a breath of wind.

la **soffitta** FEM NOUN
attic

il **soffitto** MASC NOUN
ceiling

soffocante (FEM **soffocante**) ADJECTIVE
stifling

soffocare VERB [18]
to suffocate
□ Ho rischiato di soffocare. I nearly suffocated.
■ **Qua dentro si soffoca.** It's stifling in here.

soffrire VERB [66]
1 to suffer
□ Sta soffrendo molto. He's suffering a lot.
■ **soffrire la fame** to suffer from hunger
■ **soffrire la sete** to suffer from thirst
■ **soffrire di** to suffer from □ Soffre di frequenti mal di testa. He suffers from frequent headaches.
2 to stand
□ Non lo posso soffrire. I can't stand him.

sofisticato (FEM **sofisticata**) ADJECTIVE
sophisticated

il **soggetto** MASC NOUN
subject

la **soggezione** FEM NOUN
■ **avere soggezione di qualcuno** to be in awe of somebody □ Aveva soggezione del fratello maggiore. He was in awe of his older brother.

il **soggiorno** MASC NOUN
1 living room
2 stay
□ un soggiorno di due settimane a Londra a two-week stay in London

la **sogliola** FEM NOUN
sole

sognare VERB [14]
to dream
□ Ho sognato di essere sulla luna. I dreamt I was on the moon. □ Ho sempre sognato una casa così. I've always dreamt of a house like this. □ Stanotte ti ho sognato. I dreamt about you last night.
■ **Te lo puoi sognare!** In your dreams!
■ **sognare a occhi aperti** to daydream

il **sogno** MASC NOUN
dream
□ un brutto sogno a bad dream
■ **fare un sogno** to have a dream □ Ho fatto uno strano sogno. I had a strange dream.
■ **Neanche per sogno!** No way!

la **soia** FEM NOUN
soya

il **sol** (PL i **sol**) MASC NOUN
G (musical note)

solamente ADVERB
only

solare (FEM **solare**) ADJECTIVE
solar
□ l'energia solare solar power
■ **crema solare** sun cream

S

il **soldato** MASC NOUN
soldier
- **soldato di leva** conscript
- **fare il soldato** to serve in the army

i **soldi** MASC PL NOUN
money *sing*
□ Mi presteresti dei soldi? Could you lend me some money? □ È pieno di soldi. He's got lots of money.
- **È roba da quattro soldi.** It's cheap stuff.

il **sole** MASC NOUN
sun
□ Preferirei stare al sole. I'd rather stay in the sun. □ Oggi c'è il sole. The sun is shining today.
- **una giornata di sole** a sunny day
- **prendere il sole** to sunbathe

solenne (FEM **solenne**) ADJECTIVE
solemn

la **solidarietà** FEM NOUN
solidarity

solido (FEM **solida**) ADJECTIVE
1 solid
2 substantial

solitario (FEM **solitaria**) ADJECTIVE
▷ see also **solitario** NOUN
lonely
□ una strada buia e solitaria a dark, lonely road □ una strada ancora più solitaria an even lonelier road
- **È un tipo solitario.** He's a loner.

il **solitario** MASC NOUN
▷ see also **solitario** ADJECTIVE
patience *(card game)*
□ Sto facendo un solitario. I'm playing patience.

solito (FEM **solita**) ADJECTIVE
usual
□ più tardi del solito later than usual □ come al solito as usual
- **di solito** usually □ Di solito mi alzo alle sette. I usually get up at seven o'clock.

la **solitudine** FEM NOUN
loneliness
□ La solitudine è un problema per gli anziani. Loneliness is a problem for old people.
- **Soffre di solitudine.** He feels lonely.

il **solletico** MASC NOUN
- **fare il solletico a qualcuno** to tickle somebody □ Mi ha fatto il solletico. He tickled me.
- **soffrire il solletico** to be ticklish □ Soffro molto il solletico. I'm very ticklish.

il **sollevamento** MASC NOUN
- **sollevamento pesi** weightlifting

sollevare VERB [68]
to lift
□ Non riesco a sollevare la valigia. I can't lift the suitcase.

- **Ha sollevato gli occhi dal libro.** She raised her eyes from the book.
- **sollevarsi 1** *(smoke, dust)* to rise **2** *(fog)* to lift
- **sentirsi sollevato** to feel relieved

il **sollievo** MASC NOUN
relief
□ Ho tirato un sospiro di sollievo. I heaved a sigh of relief.

solo (FEM **sola**) ADJECTIVE
▷ see also **solo** ADVERB
1 just one
□ Hanno un solo figlio. They've just got one child.
2 lonely
□ Mi sento solo. I feel lonely. □ sempre più solo lonelier and lonelier
3 alone
□ Vuole stare sola. She wants to be alone.
- **da solo** on one's own
- **Vive da solo.** He lives on his own.
- **L'hai fatto da solo?** Did you do it on your own?
- **Ci vado da sola.** I'll go on my own.

solo ADVERB
▷ see also **solo** ADJECTIVE
only
□ L'ho incontrato solo due volte. I've only met him twice.
- **Mancavi solo tu.** You were the only one who wasn't there.

soltanto ADVERB
only

solubile (FEM **solubile**) ADJECTIVE
instant *(coffee)*

la **soluzione** FEM NOUN
solution
□ Non riesco a trovare una soluzione. I can't find a solution.

il **somaro** MASC NOUN
donkey
- **Sei un somaro!** You're an idiot!

somigliare VERB [25]
- **somigliare a** to look like □ Somiglio moltissimo a mia madre. I look very like my mother.

la **somma** FEM NOUN
sum
□ una grossa somma di denaro a large sum of money
- **fare le somme** to add up □ Sai fare le somme? Can you add up?

sommare VERB [68]
to add together
□ Somma i due numeri. Add the two numbers together.
- **tutto sommato** all in all □ Tutto sommato sono contento di essere venuto. All in all I'm glad I came.

il **sommario** MASC NOUN
summary

il **sommergibile** MASC NOUN
submarine

la **sommossa** FEM NOUN
uprising

il **sondaggio** MASC NOUN
■ **sondaggio d'opinioni** opinion poll

il **sonnambulo**, la **sonnambula**
MASC/FEM NOUN
sleepwalker

il **sonnellino** MASC NOUN
■ **fare un sonnellino** to have a nap

il **sonnifero** MASC NOUN
sleeping pill

il **sonno** MASC NOUN
sleep
□ Parli durante il sonno. You talk in your sleep.
■ **aver sonno** to be sleepy
■ **prendere sonno** to fall asleep

sonoro (FEM **sonora**) ADJECTIVE
loud
□ una risata sonora a loud laugh
■ **colonna sonora** soundtrack

sopportare VERB [68]
1 to stand
□ Non lo sopporto. I can't stand him. □ Non sopporto il dolore fisico. I can't stand physical pain.
2 to put up with
□ Hanno dovuto sopportare molte umiliazioni. They had to put up with a great deal of humiliation.

> **LANGUAGE TIP** Be careful! **sopportare** doesn't mean **to support**.

sopprimere VERB [46]
to withdraw
□ Il servizio di autobus è stato soppresso. The bus service has been withdrawn.

sopra PREPOSITION, ADVERB
1 over
□ Indossava un maglione sopra la camicia. He was wearing a jumper over his shirt. □ le donne sopra i sessant'anni women over sixty
2 above
□ L'aereo volava sopra le nuvole. The plane was flying above the clouds. □ cento metri sopra il livello del mare a hundred metres above sea level □ cinque gradi sopra lo zero five degrees above zero
3 on top of
□ Il dizionario è sopra quella pila di libri. The dictionary is on top of that pile of books.
■ **là sopra** up there
■ **qua sopra** up here
■ **di sopra** upstairs □ Abito di sopra. I live upstairs.

il **soprabito** MASC NOUN
coat

il **sopracciglio** (FEM PL le **sopracciglia**)
MASC NOUN
eyebrow

il **soprammobile** MASC NOUN
ornament

soprannaturale (FEM **soprannaturale**)
ADJECTIVE
supernatural

il **soprannome** MASC NOUN
nickname

il/la **soprano** MASC/FEM NOUN
soprano

soprappensiero ADVERB
■ **essere soprappensiero** to be miles away

soprassalto MASC NOUN
■ **di soprassalto** with a start □ Mi sono svegliata di soprassalto. I woke up with a start.

soprattutto ADVERB
1 mainly
□ Dipende soprattutto da lui. It depends mainly on him.
2 especially
□ Firenze è piena di turisti, soprattutto d'estate. Florence is full of tourists, especially in the summer.

il **sopravvissuto**, la **sopravvissuta**
MASC/FEM NOUN
survivor

sopravvivere VERB [122]
to survive
□ Riuscirà a sopravvivere? Will he survive?
□ È sopravvissuto all'incidente. He survived the accident.

il **sorbetto** MASC NOUN
sorbet

sordo (FEM **sorda**) ADJECTIVE
deaf
□ È sordo da un orecchio. He's deaf in one ear.
■ **un rumore sordo** a dull sound

la **sorella** FEM NOUN
sister
□ mia sorella my sister □ la sorella di Nadia Nadia's sister

sorgere VERB [102]
to rise (sun)

sorpassare VERB [68]
to overtake

sorprendente (FEM **sorprendente**)
ADJECTIVE
surprising

sorprendere VERB [77]
1 to catch
□ Mia madre mi ha sorpreso a fumare. My mother caught me smoking. □ Sono stati sorpresi dal temporale. They were caught in the storm.

2 to surprise
□ Mi ha sorpreso molto la sua risposta. His answer really surprised me.

la **sorpresa** FEM NOUN
surprise
□ Voglio fargli una sorpresa. I want to give him a surprise.

sorpreso (FEM **sorpresa**) ADJECTIVE
surprised
□ Sono sorpreso di vederti qui. I'm surprised to see you here.

sorridente (FEM **sorridente**) ADJECTIVE
smiling
□ un viso sorridente a smiling face □ È sempre sorridente. He's always smiling.

sorridere VERB [84]
to smile
□ Mi sorrideva. She was smiling at me.

il **sorriso** MASC NOUN
smile

il **sorso** MASC NOUN
sip
□ Vuoi un sorso? Do you want a sip?
■ **tutto d'un sorso** all in one gulp □ L'ho bevuto tutto d'un sorso. I drank it all in one gulp.

la **sorte** FEM NOUN
fate
□ Non sappiamo quale sarà la sua sorte. We don't know what his fate will be.
■ **tirare a sorte** to draw lots □ Hanno tirato a sorte. They drew lots.

sorvegliare VERB [25]
to watch
□ La polizia sorveglia la casa. The police are watching the house.

il/la **sosia** (PL i/le **sosia**) MASC/FEM NOUN
double
□ È un tuo sosia! He's your double!

sospendere VERB [8]
to suspend
□ La partita è stata sospesa. The match was suspended.

sospettare VERB [68]
to suspect
□ Nessuno sospettava niente. Nobody suspected anything.
■ **sospettare di qualcuno** to suspect somebody □ La polizia sospettava di loro. The police suspected them.

il **sospetto** MASC NOUN
suspicion
□ Avevo dei sospetti su di lui. I had my suspicions about him.

sospettoso (FEM **sospettosa**) ADJECTIVE
suspicious

sospirare VERB [68]
to sigh

il **sospiro** MASC NOUN
sigh

□ Ho tirato un sospiro di sollievo. I heaved a sigh of relief.

la **sosta** FEM NOUN
■ **fare una sosta** to stop □ Abbiamo fatto una sosta a Torino. We stopped in Turin.
■ **senza sosta** non-stop □ Oggi abbiamo lavorato senza sosta. We've worked non-stop today.
■ **Qui è divieto di sosta.** You can't stop here.

il **sostantivo** MASC NOUN
noun

la **sostanza** FEM NOUN
substance

sostare VERB [68]
to stop

sostenere VERB [113]
1 to support
□ L'albero è sostenuto da una sbarra di ferro. The tree is supported by an iron bar. □ Il partito è sostenuto dall'industria. The party is supported by industry.
2 to claim
□ Sostiene di essere un tuo amico. He claims to be a friend of yours.
■ **Ha sempre sostenuto la propria innocenza.** He's always maintained his innocence.
■ **sostenere che** to insist that □ Sostiene che Paolo ha ragione. He insists that Paolo is right.
■ **sostenere gli esami** to sit one's exams □ Ho sostenuto gli esami in giugno. I sat my exams in June.

sostituire VERB [51]
1 to change
□ Devo sostituire la cartuccia. I need to change the cartridge.
2 to take somebody's place
□ Era stanco e il suo collega l'ha sostituito. He was tired and his colleague took his place.

la **sostituzione** FEM NOUN
substitution

i **sottaceti** MASC PL NOUN
pickles

sotterraneo (FEM **sotterranea**) ADJECTIVE
underground
□ un fiume sotterraneo an underground river

sotterrare VERB [68]
to bury

sottile (FEM **sottile**) ADJECTIVE
thin (object, layer, slice)
□ Le voglio più sottili. I want them thinner.
■ **capelli sottili** fine hair

sottinteso (FEM **sottintesa**) ADJECTIVE
understood
□ Il verbo è sottinteso. The verb is understood.
■ **È sottinteso che...** It goes without saying that...

sotto PREPOSITION
1 under
□ La cartina è sotto quel libro. The map is under that book. □ Si è nascosto sotto il letto. He hid under the bed. □ Ha un maglione verde sotto il cappotto. She's wearing a green sweater under her coat. □ Non è adatto ai bambini sotto i tre anni. It's not suitable for children under three.
2 below
□ È sotto il livello del mare. It's below sea level. □ Abita sotto di noi. He lives below us. □ cinque gradi sotto zero five degrees below zero
■ **al piano di sotto** downstairs
■ **là sotto** down there
■ **qua sotto** down here
■ **sotto la pioggia** in the rain
■ **sotto il sole** in the sun

il **sottofondo** MASC NOUN
■ **sottofondo musicale** background music

sottolineare VERB [68]
1 to underline
□ Hai sottolineato le parole che non conosci? Have you underlined the words you don't know?
2 to stress
□ Vorrei sottolineare l'importanza di quello che ha detto. I'd like to stress the importance of what he said.

il **sottomarino** MASC NOUN
submarine

il **sottopassaggio** MASC NOUN
underpass

sottoporre VERB [73]
to submit
□ Gli ho sottoposto la mia richiesta. I submitted my request to him.

sottosopra ADVERB
upside down
□ Hanno messo la casa sottosopra. They turned the house upside down.

sottoterra ADVERB
underground

i **sottotitoli** MASC PL NOUN
subtitles
□ un film coi sottotitoli a film with subtitles

sottovalutare VERB [68]
to underestimate

la **sottoveste** FEM NOUN
slip

sottovoce ADVERB
in a low voice

sottovuoto (FEM+PL **sottovuoto**) ADJECTIVE
■ **confezione sottovuoto** vacuum pack

sottrarre VERB [115]
to subtract (in maths)
■ **sottrarsi alle proprie responsabilità**

to avoid one's responsibilities □ Cerca di sottrarsi alle sue responsabilità. He's trying to avoid his responsibilities.

la **sottrazione** FEM NOUN
subtraction

il **souvenir** (PL i **souvenir**) MASC NOUN
souvenir

sovietico (FEM **sovietica**, MASC PL **sovietici**, FEM PL **sovietiche**) ADJECTIVE
Soviet

sovraccarico (FEM **sovraccarica**, MASC PL **sovraccarichi**, FEM PL **sovraccariche**) ADJECTIVE
overloaded

sovraffollato (FEM **sovraffollata**) ADJECTIVE
overcrowded

la **sovvenzione** FEM NOUN
subsidy

spaccare VERB [18]
to break
□ Ho spaccato il vaso. I broke the vase.
■ **spaccarsi** to break □ Per poco non mi spaccavo un dente. I nearly broke a tooth.
■ **spaccarsi la testa** to cut one's head open
□ È caduto e si è spaccato la testa. He fell and cut his head open.

la **spaccatura** FEM NOUN
split

spacciare VERB [13]
■ **spacciare droga** to sell drugs
■ **spacciarsi per qualcuno** to pretend to be somebody □ Si è spacciata per tua cugina. She pretended to be your cousin.

lo **spacciatore**, la **spacciatrice** MASC/FEM NOUN
drug dealer

lo **spaccio** MASC NOUN
■ **spaccio di droga** drug dealing

lo **spacco** (PL gli **spacchi**) MASC NOUN
slit (in skirt, dress)

la **spada** FEM NOUN
sword

spaesato (FEM **spaesata**) ADJECTIVE
lost
□ Si sentiva spaesato nella grande città. He felt lost in the big city.
■ **Mi sentivo spaesato tra quella gente.** I didn't feel comfortable with those people.

gli **spaghetti** MASC PL NOUN
spaghetti sing
□ Sono buoni gli spaghetti? Is the spaghetti nice?

la **Spagna** FEM NOUN
Spain
□ Mi è piaciuta molto la Spagna. I really liked Spain. □ Andrò in Spagna quest'estate. I'm going to Spain this summer.

la **spagnola** FEM NOUN
Spanish woman

spagnolo (FEM **spagnola**) ADJECTIVE
▷ see also **spagnolo** NOUN
Spanish

lo **spagnolo** MASC NOUN
▷ see also **spagnolo** ADJECTIVE
1 Spaniard (person)
  ■ **gli spagnoli** the Spanish
2 Spanish (language)
  □ Parli spagnolo? Do you speak Spanish? □ un insegnante di spagnolo a Spanish teacher

lo **spago** (PL gli **spaghi**) MASC NOUN
string

la **spalla** FEM NOUN
shoulder
  □ Mi fa male una spalla. One of my shoulders hurts. □ Ha le spalle curve. He's got round shoulders.
  ■ **alle mie spalle** behind me
  ■ **voltare le spalle a qualcuno** to turn one's back on somebody □ Mi ha voltato le spalle proprio quando avevo bisogno di lui. He turned his back on me just when I needed him.

la **spalliera** FEM NOUN
1 back (of seat)
2 headboard (of bed)
3 wall bars pl (in gym)

la **spallina** FEM NOUN
strap (of dress)

spalmare VERB [68]
1 to spread
  □ Spalma il burro sul pane. Spread the butter on the bread.
2 to rub
  □ Stava spalmandosi la crema sulle gambe. She was rubbing cream on her legs.

lo **spam** (PL gli **spam**) MASC NOUN
spam

sparare VERB [68]
  ■ **sparare a qualcuno** to shoot somebody
  □ Le ha sparato. He shot her.
  ■ **sparare un colpo** to fire a shot

la **sparatoria** FEM NOUN
shoot-out

sparecchiare VERB [17]
to clear the table
  □ Ti aiuto a sparecchiare? Shall I help you clear the table?

lo **spareggio** MASC NOUN
play-off

spargere VERB [103]
to scatter
  □ I miei fogli erano sparsi sulla scrivania. My papers were scattered over the desk.
  ■ **Si è sparsa una voce sul suo conto.** There's a rumour going round about him.

sparire VERB [104]
to disappear

□ La nave è sparita all'orizzonte. The ship disappeared over the horizon.
  ■ **Dov'è sparita la mia penna?** Where has my pen gone?

sparlare VERB [68]
  ■ **sparlare di qualcuno** to say nasty things about somebody □ Sparla sempre di lei con i suoi amici. He's always saying nasty things about her to his friends.

lo **sparo** MASC NOUN
shot

sparpagliato (FEM **sparpagliata**) ADJECTIVE
scattered
  □ I giocattoli erano sparpagliati sul pavimento. The toys were scattered over the floor.

spartire VERB [51]
to share out

lo **spartito** MASC NOUN
score (musical)

lo **spasso** MASC NOUN
  ■ **andare a spasso** to go for a walk
  ■ **portare a spasso il cane** to take the dog for a walk

spavaldo (FEM **spavalda**) ADJECTIVE
cocky
  □ Ora è più spavaldo che mai. Now he's cockier than ever.

spaventare VERB [68]
to scare
  □ L'idea mi spaventa un po'. The idea scares me a bit.
  ■ **spaventarsi** to be scared □ Si è spaventato molto vedendo la pistola. He was very scared when he saw the gun.

lo **spavento** MASC NOUN
  ■ **far spavento a qualcuno** to scare somebody

spaventoso (FEM **spaventosa**) ADJECTIVE
terrible

spazientirsi VERB [51, AUX **essere**]
to lose patience
  □ Si è spazientito e se n'è andato. He lost patience and left.

lo **spazio** MASC NOUN
1 room
  □ Occupa molto spazio. It takes up a lot of room. □ Non c'è più spazio nell'armadio. There's no more room in the wardrobe.
2 space
  □ grandi spazi aperti wide open spaces □ Hanno lanciato un satellite nello spazio. They've launched a satellite into space. □ È riuscita a parcheggiare in uno spazio piccolissimo. She managed to park in a tiny space.

spazioso (FEM **spaziosa**) ADJECTIVE
spacious

lo **spazzaneve** (PL gli **spazzaneve**) MASC NOUN
snowplough

spazzare VERB [68]
to sweep

la **spazzatura** FEM NOUN
rubbish
□ Puoi portare fuori la spazzatura? Can you
take the rubbish out?
■ **il secchio della spazzatura** the dustbin

lo **spazzino** MASC NOUN
road sweeper

la **spazzola** FEM NOUN
brush
■ **spazzola per capelli** hairbrush
■ **spazzola per abiti** clothes brush

spazzolare VERB [68]
to brush

lo **spazzolino** MASC NOUN
■ **spazzolino da denti** toothbrush

lo **specchietto** MASC NOUN
pocket mirror
■ **specchietto retrovisore** rear-view mirror
■ **specchietto laterale** wing mirror

lo **specchio** MASC NOUN
mirror
□ Mi sono guardata allo specchio. I looked at
myself in the mirror.

speciale (FEM **speciale**) ADJECTIVE
special

lo/la **specialista** (MASC PL gli **specialisti**,
FEM PL le **specialiste**) MASC/FEM NOUN
specialist

la **specialità** (PL le **specialità**) FEM NOUN
speciality
□ la specialità della casa the house speciality
(in a restaurant)

specialmente ADVERB
especially

la **specie** (PL le **specie**) FEM NOUN
1 sort
□ È una specie di piatto con grandi manici. It's
a sort of dish with big handles.
2 species
□ una specie in via di estinzione an endangered
species □ alcune specie rare di piante some
rare species of plants

specificare VERB [18]
to specify

la **speculazione** FEM NOUN
speculation

spedire VERB [51]
to send
□ Non ho ancora spedito la lettera. I haven't
sent the letter yet.
■ **spedire qualcosa a qualcuno** to send
somebody something □ Gli ho spedito un
pacco. I sent him a parcel. □ Spedisco sempre
una cartolina a Lucia. I always send a postcard
to Lucia. □ Gliel'ho già spedito. I've already
sent it to him.

spegnere VERB [105]
1 to put out (fire, cigarette)
2 to turn off (light, electrical device, gas, engine)
■ **spegnersi** 1 (light, electrical device) to go
off □ La luce si è spenta all'improvviso. The
light went off suddenly. 2 (engine) to stall
□ Il motore si è spento al semaforo. The engine
stalled at the traffic lights. 3 (flame, cigarette)
to go out

spellarsi VERB [56]
to peel
□ Mi si sta spellando la schiena. My back's
peeling.

spendere VERB [8]
to spend
□ Quanto hai speso? How much did you
spend?
■ **Si mangia bene e si spende poco.** The
food's good and it doesn't cost much.

spensierato (FEM **spensierata**) ADJECTIVE
carefree

spento (FEM **spenta**) ADJECTIVE
off (light, electrical device, engine)

la **speranza** FEM NOUN
hope
□ Hai qualche speranza di rivederlo? Do you
have any hope of seeing him again?

sperare VERB [68]
to hope
□ Spero che Luca arrivi in tempo. I hope Luca
arrives in time.
■ **sperare di fare qualcosa** to hope to do
something □ Spero di trovare un lavoro presto.
I hope to find a job soon.
■ **Spero di sì.** I hope so.
■ **Spero di no.** I hope not.
■ **Speriamo bene!** Let's hope it'll be okay.

la **spesa** FEM NOUN
expense
□ una grossa spesa a big expense □ Le spese ti
verranno rimborsate. Your expenses will be
reimbursed. □ Sono andata a Parigi a spese
della ditta. I went to Paris at the company's
expense.
■ **fare la spesa** to do the shopping
■ **Adoro fare spese.** I love shopping.
■ **ridurre le spese** to spend less □ Stiamo
cercando di ridurre le spese del riscaldamento.
We're trying to spend less on heating.
■ **spesa pubblica** public expenditure

spesso (FEM **spessa**) ADJECTIVE
▷ see also **spesso** ADVERB
thick
□ È spesso cinque millimetri. It's five
millimetres thick.

spesso ADVERB
▷ see also **spesso** ADJECTIVE
often

□ Vai spesso al cinema? Do you go to the cinema often?

lo **spessore** MASC NOUN
■ **avere uno spessore di...** to be... thick
□ Ha uno spessore di due centimetri. It's two centimetres thick.

Spett. ABBREVIATION
■ **Spett. Ditta, ...** *(in a letter)* Dear Sirs, ...
DID YOU KNOW...?
Letters to companies also have **Spett.** before the name of the company on the envelope.

lo **spettacolo** MASC NOUN
show
□ uno spettacolo televisivo a TV show
■ **il primo spettacolo** *(at cinema)* the first showing □ Andremo al primo spettacolo. We'll go to the first showing.

spettare VERB [68, aux **essere**]
■ **spettare a qualcuno** 1 *(decision)* to be up to □ Spetta a te decidere. It's up to you to decide.
2 *(money)* to be due to □ Voglio solo quello che mi spetta. I only want what's due to me.

lo **spettatore**, la **spettatrice** MASC/FEM NOUN
1 viewer
2 spectator
■ **gli spettatori** the audience *sing*

spettegolare VERB [68]
to gossip

spettinato (FEM **spettinata**) ADJECTIVE
■ **Sono tutta spettinata.** My hair's in a mess.

le **spezie** FEM PL NOUN
spices

spezzare VERB [68]
to break
□ Basta, mi spezzi il braccio! Stop it! You're breaking my arm!
■ **spezzarsi** to break □ La fune si è spezzata. The rope broke.

spezzato (FEM **spezzata**) ADJECTIVE
broken

la **spia** FEM NOUN
1 spy
■ **Non fare la spia.** Don't be a sneak.
2 light
□ la spia dell'olio the oil light

spiacente (FEM **spiacente**) ADJECTIVE
sorry
□ Spiacente, ma... Sorry, but...

spiacevole (FEM **spiacevole**) ADJECTIVE
unpleasant

la **spiaggia** (PL le **spiagge**) FEM NOUN
beach
□ una spiaggia sabbiosa a sandy beach

spiare VERB [55]
■ **spiare qualcuno** to spy on somebody □ Ci stava spiando da dietro la porta. He was spying on us from behind the door.

lo **spiazzo** MASC NOUN
1 piece of ground
□ Giocano in uno spiazzo davanti alla casa. They play on a piece of ground in front of the house.
2 clearing
□ Si fermarono in uno spiazzo nel bosco. They stopped in a clearing in the forest.

lo **spicchio** MASC NOUN
1 segment *(of fruit)*
2 clove *(of garlic)*

spicciarsi VERB [13, aux **essere**]
to hurry up
□ Digli di spicciarsi. Tell him to hurry up.

gli **spiccioli** MASC PL NOUN
change *sing*
□ Hai spiccioli per il caffè? Have you got change for a coffee?
■ **Mi dispiace, ma non ho spiccioli.** I'm sorry, but I haven't got anything smaller.

lo **spiedino** MASC NOUN
1 kebab
2 skewer

lo **spiedo** MASC NOUN
spit
■ **allo spiedo** spit-roasted □ un pollo allo spiedo a spit-roasted chicken

spiegare VERB [76]
1 to explain
□ Potresti spiegarci il motivo? Could you explain the reason to us? □ Gli ho spiegato la situazione. I explained the situation to him.
■ **spiegarsi** to make oneself understood
□ Era così agitato che non riusciva a spiegarsi. He was so upset that he couldn't make himself understood.
■ **Mi sono spiegato?** Do you understand?
■ **Non mi spiego come sia potuto accadere.** I can't understand how it could have happened.
2 to unfold *(tablecloth, map)*

la **spiegazione** FEM NOUN
explanation

spiegazzato (FEM **spiegazzata**) ADJECTIVE
creased

spietato (FEM **spietata**) ADJECTIVE
ruthless

lo **spiffero** MASC NOUN
draught
□ Questa stanza è piena di spifferi. This room is full of draughts.

lo **spigolo** MASC NOUN
edge

la **spilla** FEM NOUN
brooch
□ una spilla d'oro a gold brooch

lo **spillo** MASC NOUN
pin
- **tacchi a spillo** stiletto heels

spilorcio (FEM **spilorcia**, MASC PL **spilorci**,
FEM PL **spilorce**) ADJECTIVE
mean

la **spina** FEM NOUN
1 plug (electric)
2 thorn
3 bone (fish)
- **spina dorsale** backbone
- **birra alla spina** draught beer

gli **spinaci** MASC PL NOUN
spinach sing
□ Gli spinaci fanno bene. Spinach is good for
you.

lo **spinello** MASC NOUN
joint (cannabis)

spingere VERB [106]
1 to push
□ Non spingete! Don't push!
2 to drive
□ È stato spinto dalla gelosia. He was driven by
jealousy.

la **spinta** FEM NOUN
push
□ Mi aiuta a dare una spinta alla macchina?
Could you help me give the car a push?

lo **spioncino** MASC NOUN
peephole

spiritico (FEM **spiritica**, MASC PL **spiritici**,
FEM PL **spiritiche**) ADJECTIVE
- **seduta spiritica** séance

lo **spirito** MASC NOUN
spirit
□ Ha preso lo scherzo con lo spirito giusto.
He took the joke in the right spirit.
- **È una persona di spirito.** He's got a
sense of humour.
- **lo Spirito Santo** the Holy Spirit

spiritoso (FEM **spiritosa**) ADJECTIVE
witty
□ È il più spiritoso del gruppo. He's the wittiest
in the group.

splendere VERB [27]
to shine
□ Il sole splende. The sun's shining.

splendido (FEM **splendida**) ADJECTIVE
wonderful

spogliare VERB [25]
to undress
□ Ha spogliato il bambino e l'ha messo a letto.
She undressed the baby and put him to bed.
- **spogliarsi** to get undressed

lo **spogliarello** MASC NOUN
striptease

lo **spogliatoio** MASC NOUN
changing room

spolverare VERB [68]
to dust

spontaneo (FEM **spontanea**) ADJECTIVE
spontaneous
□ È stato un gesto spontaneo da parte sua.
It was a spontaneous gesture on his part.
- **I bambini sono sempre spontanei.**
Children always act naturally.
- **di sua spontanea volontà** of his own
free will

sporcare VERB [18]
to dirty
□ Attento a non sporcare il tappeto. Mind you
don't dirty the carpet.
- **sporcarsi** to get dirty □ Deve essersi
sporcato in giardino. He must have got dirty in
the garden. □ Mi sono sporcato la camicia
riparando la moto. I got my shirt dirty when I
was fixing the motorbike.
- **Si è sporcato la camicia di sugo.** He's
got sauce on his shirt.

sporco (FEM **sporca**, MASC PL **sporchi**, FEM PL
sporche) ADJECTIVE
dirty
□ Il fazzoletto è sporco. The handkerchief is
dirty. □ sempre più sporco dirtier and dirtier
- **Il fazzoletto è sporco di sangue.**
There's blood on the handkerchief.
- **avere la coscienza sporca** to have a
guilty conscience

sporgere VERB [107]
to stick out
□ Sporge un po' troppo. It sticks out a bit too
much.
- **sporgersi** to lean out □ Non sporgerti dal
finestrino. Don't lean out of the window.

lo **sport** (PL gli **sport**) MASC NOUN
sport
□ Fa diversi sport. He does various sports.

lo **sportello** MASC NOUN
1 door (of train, car)
2 window (in bank, office)
- **sportello automatico** cash machine

sportivo (FEM **sportiva**) ADJECTIVE
1 sports
□ una macchina sportiva a sports car □ la
pagina sportiva the sports page
2 sporty
□ È molto sportiva. She's very sporty. □ Sei
molto più sportiva di me. You're much sportier
than I am.
- **abbigliamento sportivo** casual clothes

la **sposa** FEM NOUN
bride
□ una bella sposa a beautiful bride
- **un abito da sposa** a wedding dress

sposare VERB [68]
to marry

□ Le ha chiesto di sposarlo. He asked her to marry him.

■ **sposarsi** to get married □ Si sono sposati in giugno. They got married in June.

■ **sposarsi con qualcuno** to marry somebody □ Si è sposato con Paola. He married Paola.

sposato (FEM **sposata**) ADJECTIVE
married

lo **sposo** MASC NOUN
bridegroom

□ un giovane sposo a young bridegroom

■ **gli sposi** the newlyweds

■ **Viva gli sposi!** To the bride and groom!

spostare VERB [68]
to move

□ Mi aiuti a spostare il tavolo? Can you help me move the table?

■ **Hanno spostato la data.** They've changed the date.

■ **spostarsi** to move □ Potresti spostarti più in là? Could you move along a bit?

sprecare VERB [18]
to waste

□ Stai sprecando tempo. You're wasting time.

spremere VERB [58]
to squeeze (orange, lemon)

■ **spremersi le meningi** to rack one's brains

lo **spremiagrumi** (PL gli **spremiagrumi**) MASC NOUN
lemon squeezer

la **spremuta** FEM NOUN

■ **spremuta d'arancia** freshly-squeezed orange juice

sproporzionato (FEM **sproporzionata**) ADJECTIVE
out of proportion

□ Il suo peso è sproporzionato all'altezza. His weight is out of proportion to his height.

lo **sproposito** MASC NOUN

■ **parlare a sproposito** to go off the point

la **sprovvista** FEM NOUN

■ **prendere qualcuno alla sprovvista** to catch somebody unawares

sprovvisto (FEM **sprovvista**) ADJECTIVE

■ **sprovvisto di** without □ I passeggeri sprovvisti di biglietto saranno multati. Passengers without tickets will be fined.

■ **Ne siamo rimasti sprovvisti.** (in shop) We're out of it at the moment.

spruzzare VERB [68]
to spray

la **spugna** FEM NOUN
sponge

□ una spugna saponata a soapy sponge

■ **di spugna** towelling □ un accappatoio di spugna a towelling bathrobe

spuntare VERB [68, aux **essere**]
1 to sprout
2 to rise (sun)
3 to appear

□ È spuntato da chissà dove. Heaven knows where he appeared from.

■ **spuntarla** to get one's own way □ La spunta sempre lui. He always gets his own way.

lo **spuntino** MASC NOUN
snack

■ **fare uno spuntino** to have a snack

lo **spunto** MASC NOUN

■ **prendere spunto da qualcosa** to take inspiration from something □ Il regista ha preso spunto da un fatto realmente accaduto. The director took his inspiration from a real life story.

sputare VERB [68]
to spit

la **squadra** FEM NOUN
team

□ una squadra di calcio a football team

■ **squadra del buon costume** vice squad

■ **squadra mobile** flying squad

squagliarsi VERB [25, aux **essere**]
to melt

squalificare VERB [18]
to disqualify

squallido (FEM **squallida**) ADJECTIVE
1 dingy

□ una squallida stanza d'albergo a dingy hotel room
2 miserable

□ una vita squallida a miserable life

lo **squalo** MASC NOUN
shark

squarciagola ADVERB

■ **a squarciagola** at the top of one's voice □ Gridava a squarciagola. He was shouting at the top of his voice.

squilibrato (FEM **squilibrata**) ADJECTIVE
deranged

■ **una dieta squilibrata** an unbalanced diet

squillare VERB [68, aux **avere** or **essere**]
to ring (doorbell, phone)

lo **squillo** MASC NOUN
ring

squisito (FEM **squisita**) ADJECTIVE
delicious

srotolare VERB [68]
to unroll

stabile (FEM **stabile**) ADJECTIVE
▷ see also **stabile** NOUN
stable

■ **un'occupazione stabile** a steady job

■ **La scala non è stabile.** The ladder's shaky.

lo **stabile** MASC NOUN
  ▷ *see also* **stabile** ADJECTIVE
  building

lo **stabilimento** MASC NOUN
  ■ **uno stabilimento industriale** an industrial plant

stabilire VERB [51]
  to fix (prices, date)
  ■ **stabilirsi** to settle □ Si sono stabiliti qui tre anni fa. They settled here three years ago.

staccare VERB [18]
1 to remove
  □ Hai staccato l'etichetta dal dischetto? Did you remove the label from the disk?
  ■ **staccarsi** to come off □ Mi si è staccato un bottone della camicia. A button has come off my shirt.
2 to pull away
  □ Stacca la sedia dal muro. Pull the chair away from the wall.
3 to tear out
  □ Ha staccato una pagina dal quaderno. He tore a page out of the exercise book.
4 disconnect
  □ Se non paghi ti staccheranno il telefono. If you don't pay they'll disconnect your phone.
  ■ **Ho staccato il telefono perché la bambina dormiva.** I took the phone off the hook because the baby was sleeping.
  ■ **staccare la presa** to take the plug out of the socket
  ■ **staccare la presa di** (TV, electrical devices) to unplug

lo **stadio** MASC NOUN
1 stadium
2 stage (phase)
  □ durante l'ultimo stadio della malattia during the final stage of the illness

la **staffetta** FEM NOUN
  relay race

stagionato (FEM **stagionata**) ADJECTIVE
  ■ **formaggio stagionato** mature cheese

la **stagione** FEM NOUN
  season
  □ l'alta stagione the high season □ la bassa stagione the low season
  ■ **la bella stagione** the summer months *pl*

lo **stagno** MASC NOUN
1 pond
2 tin (metal)

la **stagnola** FEM NOUN
  tinfoil

la **stalla** FEM NOUN
1 cowshed
2 stable

stamattina ADVERB
  this morning

la **stampa** FEM NOUN
  print
  ■ **la stampa** (newspapers) the press
  ■ **'stampe'** (on envelope) 'printed matter'

la **stampante** FEM NOUN
  printer
  □ una stampante laser a laser printer

stampare VERB [68]
  to print

lo **stampatello** MASC NOUN
  block letters *pl*
  □ Scrivi il tuo nome in stampatello. Write your name in block letters.

la **stampella** FEM NOUN
  crutch

stancare VERB [18]
  to tire
  □ Non stancare i bambini con troppi giochi. Don't tire the children with too many games. □ Il viaggio lo ha stancato molto. The journey tired him out.
  ■ **Mi hai stancato con le tue lamentele.** I'm fed up of your complaining.
  ■ **stancarsi** to get tired □ Non stancarti troppo. Don't get too tired. □ Mi sono stancato di aspettare. I got tired of waiting.

stanco (FEM **stanca**, MASC PL **stanchi**, FEM PL **stanche**) ADJECTIVE
  tired
  □ Sei stanco? Are you tired? □ Sono stanco di ripetere la stessa cosa. I'm tired of repeating the same thing. □ Sono stanco morto. I'm dead tired.

la **stanghetta** FEM NOUN
  leg (of spectacles)

stanotte ADVERB
1 tonight
  □ Stanotte ci saranno i fuochi d'artificio. There are going to be fireworks tonight.
2 last night
  □ Stanotte non ho dormito bene. I didn't sleep well last night.

la **stanza** FEM NOUN
  room
  ■ **stanza da letto** bedroom

stappare VERB [68]
  to open

stare VERB [108]
1 to be
  □ Sei mai stato in Francia? Have you ever been to France? □ La casa sta sulla collina. The house is on the hill. □ Come stai? How are you? □ Sto bene, grazie. I'm fine, thanks. □ Sta studiando. He's studying. □ Stavo andando a casa. I was going home.
2 to stay
  □ Stai ancora un po'! Stay a bit longer!
3 to live

□ Sto con i miei. I live with my parents.
□ Dove stai? Where do you live?
■ **A Londra starò da amici.** I'll be staying with friends in London.
■ **stare in piedi** to stand
■ **stare seduto** to be sitting
■ **stare fermo** to keep still
■ **stare zitto** to be quiet
■ **stare per fare qualcosa** to be about to do something □ Stavo per uscire quando ha squillato il telefono. I was about to go out when the phone rang.
■ **stare bene a qualcuno** to suit somebody □ Quel vestito ti sta bene. That dress suits you.
■ **Nel bagagliaio non ci sta più niente.** There's no room for anything more in the boot.
■ **Staremo a vedere.** Let's wait and see.
■ **Sta a te decidere.** It's up to you to decide.
■ **Ci sto!** OK!

starnutire VERB [51]
to sneeze

lo **starnuto** MASC NOUN
sneeze

stasera ADVERB
this evening

statale (FEM **statale**) ADJECTIVE
state
□ un impiegato statale a state employee
■ **un'industria statale** a state-owned industry

lo **stato** MASC NOUN
state
□ uno stato totalitario a totalitarian state □ un capo di stato a head of state □ Guarda in che stato si è ridotto! Look at the state he's in!
■ **La macchina è in buono stato.** The car is in good condition.
■ **stato civile** status
■ **gli Stati Uniti d'America** the United States of America
■ **in stato interessante** pregnant

la **statua** FEM NOUN
statue

la **statura** FEM NOUN
■ **essere alto di statura** to be tall
■ **essere basso di statura** to be short

stavolta ADVERB
this time

la **stazione** FEM NOUN
station
□ la stazione ferroviaria the railway station
□ la stazione degli autobus the bus station
■ **una stazione di servizio** a petrol station

la **stecca** (PL le **stecche**) FEM NOUN
■ **una stecca di sigarette** a two hundred pack of cigarettes

lo **steccato** MASC NOUN
fence

la **stella** FEM NOUN
star
□ Stanotte si vedono le stelle. You can see the stars tonight. □ una stella cadente a shooting star □ una stella del cinema a film star
■ **stella alpina** edelweiss
■ **stella di mare** starfish

lo **stemma** (PL gli **stemmi**) MASC NOUN
coat of arms

stempiato (FEM **stempiata**) ADJECTIVE
■ **essere stempiato** to have a receding hairline

stendere VERB [112]
1 to stretch (arms, legs)
■ **stendersi** to lie down □ Si è steso sul letto. He lay down on the bed.
2 to spread out (tablecloth)
3 to hang out (washing)

la **stenografia** FEM NOUN
shorthand

stentare VERB [68]
■ **stentare a fare qualcosa** to find it hard to do something □ Stentavo a crederlo. I found it hard to believe.

lo **stento** MASC NOUN
■ **Riesco a stento a pagare l'affitto.** I only just manage to pay the rent.

lo **stereo** (PL gli **stereo**) MASC NOUN
stereo

sterile (FEM **sterile**) ADJECTIVE
sterile

la **sterlina** FEM NOUN
pound

sterminare VERB [68]
to exterminate

sterminato (FEM **sterminata**) ADJECTIVE
immense

lo **sterzo** MASC NOUN
steering wheel

stesso (FEM **stessa**) ADJECTIVE, PRONOUN
same
□ Aveva addosso lo stesso vestito. She was wearing the same dress. □ Abbiamo gli stessi gusti. We have the same tastes. □ Sei la stessa di sempre. You're the same as ever. □ In quello stesso istante ha suonato il campanello. That same moment the bell rang.
■ **L'ho sentito con le mie stesse orecchie.** I heard it with my own ears.
■ **lo stesso** all the same □ Per me fa lo stesso. It's all the same to me. □ Parto lo stesso. I'm leaving all the same.

> **LANGUAGE TIP** **stesso** can be translated by 'myself', 'himself', 'herself', 'ourselves', 'yourselves' or 'themselves', depending on the context.

□ L'ho visto io stesso. I saw it myself. □ Lei stessa è venuta a dirmelo. She came and told me herself.

stile - strada

lo **stile** MASC NOUN
style
  □ gli stili architettonici architectural styles
  □ Bisogna ammettere che ha stile! You have to admit he's got style!
  ■ **Non è nel suo stile.** It's not like him.
  ■ **stile libero** crawl □ Sai nuotare a stile libero? Can you do the crawl?
  ■ **i cento metri stile libero** the hundred metres freestyle
  ■ **mobili in stile** period furniture *sing*

lo/la **stilista** (MASC PL gli **stilisti**, FEM PL le **stiliste**) MASC/FEM NOUN
fashion designer

la **stilografica** (PL le **stilografiche**) FEM NOUN
fountain pen

la **stima** FEM NOUN
respect
  □ Ho molta stima di lui. I have great respect for him.

stimare VERB [68]
to respect
  □ La stimo molto. I really respect her.

stimolare VERB [68]
to stimulate

stinto (FEM **stinta**) ADJECTIVE
faded

lo **stipendio** MASC NOUN
salary

stirare VERB [68]
to iron

la **stitichezza** FEM NOUN
constipation

lo **stivale** MASC NOUN
boot

la **stoffa** FEM NOUN
material

lo **stomaco** (PL gli **stomaci**) MASC NOUN
stomach
  □ Ho mal di stomaco. I've got stomach ache.
  ■ **dare di stomaco** to vomit

stonato (FEM **stonata**) ADJECTIVE
1 tone-deaf
2 out of tune

lo **stop** (PL gli **stop**) MASC NOUN
1 stop sign
2 brake-light
  ■ **Stop!** Stop!

storcere VERB [100]
  ■ **storcere il naso** to turn up one's nose
  ■ **storcersi la caviglia** to twist one's ankle

stordire VERB [51]
to stun

stordito (FEM **stordita**) ADJECTIVE
stunned

la **storia** FEM NOUN
1 story
  □ una storia d'amore a love story □ Mi racconti una storia? Will you tell me a story? □ È sempre la stessa storia. It's the same old story.
  ■ **Non voglio più saperne di questa storia!** I don't want to hear any more about this!
2 history
  □ l'insegnante di storia the history teacher
  ■ **storie** 1 fuss *sing* □ Non ha fatto storie. He didn't make a fuss. 2 nonsense *sing*
  □ Racconta un sacco di storie. He talks a lot of nonsense.

storico (FEM **storica**, MASC PL **storici**, FEM PL **storiche**) ADJECTIVE
1 historical
  □ un personaggio storico a historical figure
2 historic (*memorable*)
  □ È stato un momento storico. It was a historic moment.

lo **stormo** MASC NOUN
flock

la **storta** FEM NOUN
  ■ **prendersi una storta alla caviglia** to sprain one's ankle

storto (FEM **storta**) ADJECTIVE
1 crooked
2 bent
  ■ **avere gli occhi storti** to be cross-eyed
  ■ **Mi va tutto storto.** Everything's going wrong for me.

le **stoviglie** FEM PL NOUN
dishes

strabico (FEM **strabica**, MASC PL **strabici**, FEM PL **strabiche**) ADJECTIVE
  ■ **essere strabico** to have a squint

stracciare VERB [13]
to tear up
  □ Ho stracciato la lettera. I tore up the letter.

lo **straccio** MASC NOUN
  ▷ see also **straccio** ADJECTIVE
cloth (*for cleaning*)

straccio (FEM **straccia**) ADJECTIVE
  ▷ see also **straccio** NOUN
  ■ **carta straccia** waste paper

la **strada** FEM NOUN
1 road
  □ Ho attraversato la strada. I crossed the road.
2 way
  □ C'è tanta strada da fare? Is it a long way?
  □ Ti faccio strada. I'll show you the way.
  ■ **Sono tre ore di strada in macchina.** It's three hours' drive.
  ■ **Facciamo la strada insieme?** Shall we walk along together?
3 track
  ■ **essere sulla buona strada** to be on the right track
  ■ **essere fuori strada** to be on the wrong track

■ **portare qualcuno sulla cattiva strada**
to lead somebody astray

stradale (FEM **stradale**) ADJECTIVE
road
□ un cartello stradale a road sign

la **strage** FEM NOUN
massacre

strambo (FEM **stramba**) ADJECTIVE
odd
□ un tipo strambo an odd person

strangolare VERB [68]
to strangle

straniero (FEM **straniera**) ADJECTIVE
▷ see also **straniero** NOUN
foreign
□ un paese straniero a foreign country

lo **straniero**, la **straniera** MASC/FEM NOUN
▷ see also **straniero** ADJECTIVE
foreigner

  LANGUAGE TIP Be careful! **straniero**
  doesn't mean **stranger**.

strano (FEM **strana**) ADJECTIVE
strange

straordinario (FEM **straordinaria**)
ADJECTIVE
▷ see also **straordinario** NOUN
extraordinary

lo **straordinario** MASC NOUN
▷ see also **straordinario** ADJECTIVE
overtime
□ Ho fatto tre ore di straordinario. I did three
hours' overtime.

strappare VERB [68]
to tear up
□ Ha strappato la lettera. She tore up the letter.
■ **Ho strappato una pagina dal
quaderno.** I tore a page out of the exercise
book.
■ **strappare qualcosa a qualcuno** to
snatch something from somebody □ Mi ha
strappato la borsa. He snatched the bag from
me.
■ **strapparsi** to tear □ La camicia si è
strappata sulla manica. The sleeve of the shirt
is torn.
■ **strapparsi un muscolo** to tear a muscle

lo **strappo** MASC NOUN
1 tear
□ C'è uno strappo nella camicia. There's a tear
in the shirt.
■ **strappo muscolare** torn muscle
2 lift (in car)
□ Mi dai uno strappo? Could you give me a lift?

straripare VERB [68, AUX **avere** or **essere**]
to overflow

lo **stratagemma** (PL gli **stratagemmi**)
MASC NOUN
stratagem

strategico (FEM **strategica**, MASC PL
strategici, FEM PL **strategiche**) ADJECTIVE
strategic

lo **strato** MASC NOUN
layer
□ uno strato di polvere a layer of dust
■ **uno strato di pittura** a coat of paint

lo **strattone** MASC NOUN
■ **Mi ha dato uno strattone.** He tugged at
me.

stravagante (FEM **stravagante**) ADJECTIVE
eccentric

stravolto (FEM **stravolta**) ADJECTIVE
distraught
□ Era stravolto. He was distraught.
■ **Era stravolto dalla stanchezza.** He was
shattered.

lo **strazio** MASC NOUN
■ **È uno strazio!** It's dead boring!

la **strega** (PL le **streghe**) FEM NOUN
witch

stremato (FEM **stremata**) ADJECTIVE
exhausted

strepitoso (FEM **strepitosa**) ADJECTIVE
■ **un successo strepitoso** a huge success

stressante (FEM **stressante**) ADJECTIVE
stressful
□ Fa un lavoro stressante. He has a stressful job.

stressato (FEM **stressata**) ADJECTIVE
stressed
□ È un po' stressato ultimamente. He's been
rather stressed lately.

la **stretta** FEM NOUN
■ **stretta di mano** handshake

stretto (FEM **stretta**) ADJECTIVE
1 narrow
□ La strada diventa stretta in quel punto. The
road gets narrow there.
2 tight
□ Questa gonna mi è stretta. This skirt's tight
on me. □ Tienti stretto! Hold on tight!
■ **un parente stretto** a close relative
■ **lo stretto necessario** the bare minimum

la **strettoia** FEM NOUN
bottleneck

stridulo (FEM **stridula**) ADJECTIVE
shrill

strillare VERB [68]
to scream

lo **strillo** MASC NOUN
scream

stringere VERB [109]
to be tight
□ Queste scarpe mi stringono. These shoes are
tight on me.
■ **stringere qualcosa** 1 to clench
something 2 to tighten something 3 (dress,
skirt) to take something in

S

273

■ **stringersi la mano** to shake hands
□ Ci siamo stretti la mano. We shook hands.
■ **stringersi** to squeeze up
□ Se vi stringete un po' posso sedermi anch'io. If you squeeze up a bit I'll be able to sit down.

la **striscia** (PL le **strisce**) FEM NOUN
strip (of paper, material)
■ **a strisce** striped □ una maglia a strisce blu e bianche a blue and white striped jumper
■ **strisce pedonali** zebra crossing sing

strisciare VERB [13]
1 to crawl
□ Stava strisciando sul pavimento. He was crawling on the floor.
2 to scratch
□ Scusami, ti ho strisciato la macchina. I'm sorry, I've scratched your car.

lo **striscione** MASC NOUN
banner

strizzare VERB [68]
to wring out
■ **strizzare l'occhio** to wink □ Mi ha strizzato l'occhio. She winked at me.

lo **strofinaccio** MASC NOUN
1 duster
2 dishcloth

strofinare VERB [68]
to rub

strozzare VERB [68]
to strangle

struccarsi VERB [18, aux **avere** or **essere**]
to take off one's make-up
□ Mi sono struccata e sono andata a letto. I took off my make-up and went to bed.

lo **strumento** MASC NOUN
■ **strumento musicale** musical instrument

la **struttura** FEM NOUN
structure

lo **struzzo** MASC NOUN
ostrich

lo **stucco** MASC NOUN
1 plaster (on walls)
2 stucco
□ una stanza piena di stucchi a room full of stucco work

lo **studente**, la **studentessa** MASC/FEM NOUN
student

studiare VERB [17]
to study

lo **studio** MASC NOUN
1 study
□ Ha interrotto gli studi per un anno. He took a break from his studies for a year. □ Il nonno legge nello studio. Grandpa's reading in the study.

■ **un recente studio sull'inquinamento** a recent piece of research on pollution
2 office (of professional person)
□ uno studio legale a lawyer's office
■ **studio fotografico** photographer's studio

studioso (FEM **studiosa**) ADJECTIVE
▷ see also **studioso** NOUN
studious

lo **studioso**, la **studiosa** MASC/FEM NOUN
▷ see also **studioso** ADJECTIVE
scholar

la **stufa** FEM NOUN
■ **stufa elettrica** electric heater
■ **stufa a gas** gas heater

stufare VERB [68]
■ **stufarsi di** to get fed up with □ Mi sono stufato di loro. I got fed up with them.
■ **stufarsi di fare qualcosa** to get fed up of doing something □ Mi sono stufato di aspettarlo. I got fed up of waiting for him.
■ **Mi hai proprio stufato!** I'm really fed up with you!

stufo (FEM **stufa**) ADJECTIVE
■ **essere stufo** to be fed up □ Sei già stufa? Are you fed up already?
■ **essere stufo di fare qualcosa** to be fed up of doing something □ Sono stufo di studiare. I'm fed up of studying.

stupefacente (FEM **stupefacente**)
ADJECTIVE
■ **sostanze stupefacenti** drugs

stupefatto (FEM **stupefatta**) ADJECTIVE
astonished

stupendo (FEM **stupenda**) ADJECTIVE
wonderful

la **stupidaggine** FEM NOUN
■ **Ho fatto una stupidaggine.** I did something stupid.
■ **Non dire stupidaggini!** Don't talk nonsense!

stupido (FEM **stupida**) ADJECTIVE
stupid

stupire VERB [51]
to amaze
□ La sua risposta mi ha stupito molto. His answer really amazed me.
■ **stupirsi di qualcosa** to be amazed at something □ Mi sono stupito del suo coraggio. I was amazed at his courage.
■ **Non c'è da stupirsi.** It's not surprising.

lo **stupore** MASC NOUN
amazement
□ Con mio grande stupore ho scoperto che... Much to my amazement I discovered that...

stuprare VERB [68]
to rape

lo **stupro** MASC NOUN
rape

lo **stuzzicadenti** (PL gli **stuzzicadenti**)
MASC NOUN
  toothpick
stuzzicare VERB [18]
  to tease
  □ Smettila di stuzzicarlo. Stop teasing him.
  ■ **stuzzicare l'appetito** to whet the
  appetite
su PREPOSITION
1 on
  □ Il libro è sul tavolo. The book's on the table.
  □ Mettilo sulla sedia. Put it on the chair. □ È
  sulla destra. It's on the right. □ un libro sulla
  seconda guerra mondiale a book on the Second
  World War
  ■ **L'ho letto sul giornale.** I read it in the
  paper.
  ■ **in tre casi su dieci** in three cases out of
  ten
  ■ **Su, avanti!** Come on!
2 up
  □ Guarda su! Look up!
  ■ **Era su che aspettava.** She was waiting
  upstairs.
  ■ **andare su e giù** to go up and down
  ■ **dai venti anni in su** from the age of
  twenty onwards
  ■ **100 metri sul livello del mare** 100
  metres above sea level
3 about
  □ È costata sui cinquemila euro. It cost about
  five thousand euros.
il **subacqueo**, la **subacquea** MASC/FEM
NOUN
  ▷ see also **subacqueo** ADJECTIVE
  skin-diver
subacqueo (FEM **subacquea**) ADJECTIVE
  ▷ see also **subacqueo** NOUN
  underwater
  □ esplorazione subacquea underwater
  exploration
  ■ **una muta subacquea** a wetsuit
subire VERB [51]
1 to suffer
  □ Dovrai subirne le conseguenze. You'll have to
  suffer the consequences. □ Ha subito un torto.
  He suffered an injustice.
2 to undergo
  □ Il progetto ha subito alcune modifiche. The
  project has undergone some modifications.
subito ADVERB
  immediately
  □ È arrivato subito dopo di te. He arrived
  immediately after you. □ Fallo subito! Do it
  immediately!
  ■ **Torno subito.** I'll be right back.
subordinato (FEM **subordinata**) ADJECTIVE
  subordinate

  ■ **proposizione subordinata** subordinate
  clause
succedere VERB [110]
  to happen
  □ Cos'è successo? What happened?
  □ Dev'essergli successo qualcosa. Something
  must have happened to him. □ Sono cose che
  succedono. These things happen.
successivo (FEM **successiva**) ADJECTIVE
  following
  □ il giorno successivo the following day
il **successo** MASC NOUN
  success
  □ È stato un successo! It was a success! □ Ho
  provato ma senza successo. I tried, but without
  success.
  ■ **di successo** successful □ un film di
  successo a successful film
  ■ **avere successo** to be successful
succhiare VERB [17]
  to suck
il **succhiotto** MASC NOUN
  dummy
il **succo** (PL i **succhi**) MASC NOUN
  juice
  □ succo di frutta fruit juice □ succo di
  pomodoro tomato juice
il **sud** MASC NOUN
  south
  □ La sua famiglia è del sud. His family is from
  the south. □ Il vento viene da sud. The wind
  comes from the south.
  ■ **a sud** south □ Si è diretto a sud. He headed
  south.
  ■ **La Svizzera confina a sud con l'Italia.**
  To the south Switzerland has a border with
  Italy.
  ■ **a sud di** south of □ Si trova a sud della città.
  It's south of the city.
  ■ **l'Italia del Sud** Southern Italy
  ■ **l'America del Sud** South America
sudare VERB [68]
  to sweat
sudato (FEM **sudata**) ADJECTIVE
  sweaty
  □ sempre più sudato sweatier and sweatier
  ■ **una vittoria sudata** a hard-won
  victory
sudicio (FEM **sudicia**, MASC PL **sudici**, FEM PL
  sudice) ADJECTIVE
  dirty
  □ sempre più sudicio dirtier and dirtier
il **sudoku** (PL i **sudoku**) MASC NOUN
  sudoku
il **sudore** MASC NOUN
  sweat
  □ Si è asciugato il sudore dalla fronte. He wiped
  the sweat off his forehead.

sufficiente (FEM **sufficiente**) ADJECTIVE
enough
□ Pensi che il pane sia sufficiente? Do you think there's enough bread? □ È più che sufficiente. It's more than enough.

la **sufficienza** FEM NOUN
pass mark
□ Ho preso la sufficienza. I got a pass mark.
■ **a sufficienza** enough □ Ne hai a sufficienza? Have you got enough?

il **suggerimento** MASC NOUN
suggestion
□ Qualcuno ha altri suggerimenti? Has anyone got any other suggestions?

suggerire VERB [51]
to suggest
□ Cosa suggerisci? What do you suggest? □ Gli ho suggerito di dire tutto ai suoi. I suggested he told his parents everything.
■ **Non suggerite!** (in class) Don't help!

il **sughero** MASC NOUN
cork

il **sugo** (PL i **sughi**) MASC NOUN
sauce
■ **sugo di carne** gravy

suicidarsi VERB [56]
to commit suicide

il **suicidio** MASC NOUN
suicide

suo (FEM **sua**) ADJECTIVE
▷ see also **suo** PRONOUN
1 his
□ Fabio ha preso i suoi libri. Fabio took his books. □ È colpa sua. Si è dimenticato i biglietti. It's his fault. He forgot the tickets.
■ **un suo amico** a friend of his
■ **i suoi genitori** his parents
2 her
□ Luciana e le sue amiche Luciana and her friends
3 its
□ Il cane dorme nella sua cuccia. The dog is sleeping in its kennel.
4 your (polite form)
□ Mi presta il suo ombrello? Could you lend me your umbrella?

suo (FEM **sua**) PRONOUN
▷ see also **suo** ADJECTIVE
1 his
□ La mia casa è più grande della sua. My house is bigger than his.
2 hers
□ È di Roberta questa macchina? — Sí, è sua. Is this Roberta's car? — Yes, it's hers.
3 yours (polite form)
□ Scusi signore, È suo questo? Excuse me sir, is this yours?

la **suocera** FEM NOUN
mother-in-law

il **suocero** MASC NOUN
father-in-law
■ **i miei suoceri** my in-laws

la **suola** FEM NOUN
sole (of shoe)

suonare VERB [68]
1 to play (musical instrument)
□ Sai suonare la chitarra? Can you play the guitar?
■ **suonare il clacson** to hoot
2 to ring
□ Sta suonando il telefono. The phone is ringing.
3 to sound
□ Mi suona strano. It sounds strange to me.

la **suoneria** FEM NOUN
1 alarm
2 ringtone

il **suono** MASC NOUN
sound

la **suora** FEM NOUN
nun
□ Vuole farsi suora. She wants to become a nun.
■ **Suor Maria** Sister Maria

la **super** FEM NOUN
four-star petrol

superare VERB [68]
1 to exceed
□ Il risultato ha superato le aspettative. The result exceeded expectations.
■ **Ha superato il limite di velocità.** He broke the speed limit.
2 to overcome
□ Sono certo che riusciremo a superare queste difficoltà. I'm sure we can overcome these difficulties.
3 to pass (exam)
□ Ha superato l'esame di guida. He's passed his driving test.
■ **superare per primo il traguardo** to be first to cross the finishing line
■ **aver superato la cinquantina** to be over fifty

superbo (FEM **superba**) ADJECTIVE
haughty

superficiale (FEM **superficiale**) ADJECTIVE
superficial
□ una ferita superficiale a superficial wound
□ È un po' superficiale. She's a bit superficial.

la **superficie** (PL le **superfici**) FEM NOUN
surface

superfluo (FEM **superflua**) ADJECTIVE
superfluous

superiore (FEM **superiore**) ADJECTIVE
▷ see also **superiore** NOUN
1 upper
□ la parte superiore del corpo the upper part of the body

2 above

□ La temperatura è superiore alla media. The temperature is above average. □ Sono superiore a queste cose. I'm above such things.

■ **scuola superiore** secondary school

il/la **superiore** MASC/FEM NOUN

▷ *see also* **superiore** ADJECTIVE

superior

□ È il mio superiore. He's my superior.

superlativo (FEM **superlativa**) ADJECTIVE, MASC NOUN

superlative

il **supermercato** MASC NOUN

supermarket

il/la **superstite** MASC/FEM NOUN

survivor

la **superstizione** FEM NOUN

superstition

superstizioso (FEM **superstiziosa**)

ADJECTIVE

superstitious

supplementare (FEM **supplementare**)

ADJECTIVE

extra

■ **tempi supplementari** extra time *sing*

□ Hanno segnato nei tempi supplementari. They scored in extra time.

il **supplemento** MASC NOUN

supplement

il/la **supplente** MASC/FEM NOUN

supply teacher

supplicare VERB [18]

to implore

supporre VERB [73]

to suppose

□ Supponiamo che... Let's suppose that...

□ Suppongo di sì. I suppose so. □ Suppongo di no. I suppose not.

la **supposta** FEM NOUN

suppository

surgelato (FEM **surgelata**) ADJECTIVE

frozen

□ cibo surgelato frozen food

suscettibile (FEM **suscettibile**) ADJECTIVE

touchy

□ È molto suscettibile. She's very touchy. □ È più suscettibile di me. She's touchier than me.

la **susina** FEM NOUN

plum

il **sussidio** MASC NOUN

■ **sussidi audiovisivi** audio-visual aids

■ **sussidio di disoccupazione**

unemployment benefit

sussurrare VERB [68]

to whisper

il **sussurro** MASC NOUN

whisper

il **SUV** (PL i **SUV**) MASC NOUN

SUV *(car)*

svagarsi VERB [76, aux **essere**]

to take one's mind off things

□ Ho bisogno di svagarmi un po'. I need to take my mind off things a bit.

svaligiare VERB [58]

■ **svaligiare una banca** to rob a bank

■ **svaligiare una casa** to burgle a house

la **svalutazione** FEM NOUN

devaluation

svanire VERB [51, aux **essere**]

to disappear

svantaggiato (FEM **svantaggiata**) ADJECTIVE

disadvantaged

□ i bambini svantaggiati disadvantaged children

lo **svantaggio** MASC NOUN

disadvantage

□ i vantaggi e gli svantaggi della situazione the advantages and disadvantages of the situation

■ **essere in svantaggio di due punti** to be two points down

svedese (FEM **svedese**) ADJECTIVE

▷ *see also* **svedese** MASC NOUN, FEM NOUN

Swedish

□ il governo svedese the Swedish government

lo **svedese** MASC NOUN

▷ *see also* **svedese** FEM NOUN, ADJECTIVE

1 Swede *(person)*

□ gli svedesi the Swedes

2 Swedish *(language)*

□ Parla svedese. He speaks Swedish.

la **svedese** FEM NOUN

▷ *see also* **svedese** MASC NOUN, ADJECTIVE

Swede

la **sveglia** FEM NOUN

alarm clock

□ Hai puntato la sveglia? Have you set the alarm clock? □ Non ho sentito la sveglia stamattina. I didn't hear the alarm clock this morning.

svegliare VERB [25]

■ **svegliare qualcuno** to wake somebody up □ Svegliami alle sette. Wake me up at seven.

■ **svegliarsi** to wake up □ Mi sveglio sempre presto. I always wake up early.

sveglio (FEM **sveglia**, MASC PL **svegli**, FEM PL **sveglie**) ADJECTIVE

1 awake

□ Ero sveglio quando ha telefonato. I was awake when he phoned.

2 bright

□ un ragazzo sveglio a bright boy

svelare VERB [68]

to reveal

svelto (FEM **svelta**) ADJECTIVE

quick

□ Svelto, vieni qua! Quick, come here!

la **svendita** FEM NOUN
  sale
  □ una svendita di fine stagione an end-of-season sale
  ■ **in svendita** in a sale □ Ho comprato questo cappotto in svendita. I bought this coat in a sale.

svenire VERB [120]
  to faint

sventolare VERB [68]
  to wave
  □ Sulla torre sventolavano delle bandiere. Flags were waving on the tower.

svestirsi VERB [41, AUX **essere**]
  to get undressed

la **Svezia** FEM NOUN
  Sweden
  □ Ti è piaciuta la Svezia? Did you like Sweden?
  □ Andrò in Svezia quest'estate. I'm going to Sweden this summer.

sviluppare VERB [68]
  to develop
  □ Hai già fatto sviluppare le foto? Have you had the photos developed yet?
  ■ **svilupparsi** to develop

lo **sviluppo** MASC NOUN
  development
  ■ **paesi in via di sviluppo** developing countries

la **svista** FEM NOUN
  oversight

svitare VERB [68]
  to unscrew

la **Svizzera** FEM NOUN
  Switzerland

□ Ti è piaciuta la Svizzera? Did you like Switzerland? □ Andrò in Svizzera quest'inverno. I'm going to Switzerland this winter.

la **svizzera** FEM NOUN
  Swiss woman

svizzero (FEM **svizzera**) ADJECTIVE
  ▷ see also **svizzero** NOUN
  Swiss
  □ il formaggio svizzero Swiss cheese

lo **svizzero** MASC NOUN
  ▷ see also **svizzero** ADJECTIVE
  Swiss man
  ■ **gli svizzeri** the Swiss

svolgere VERB [91]
  ■ **svolgere un tema** to write an essay
  ■ **Che attività svolge?** What do you do?
  ■ **svolgersi** to happen □ Tutto si è svolto rapidamente. Everything happened quickly.
  □ Come si sono svolti veramente i fatti? How did it actually happen?

la **svolta** FEM NOUN
  turn
  □ C'è un divieto di svolta a sinistra. There's a no left turn sign.
  ■ **Prendi la prima svolta a destra.** Take the first turning on the right.

svoltare VERB [68]
  to turn
  □ All'incrocio svolta a destra. Turn right at the junction.

svuotare VERB [68]
  to empty
  □ Ho dovuto svuotare tutti i cassetti per trovarlo. I had to empty all the drawers to find it.

Tt

la **tabaccheria** FEM NOUN
tobacconist's shop

> **DID YOU KNOW...?**
> In Italy tobacco is a state monopoly.

il **tabacco** (PL i **tabacchi**) MASC NOUN
tobacco

la **tabella** FEM NOUN
table

il **tabellone** MASC NOUN
timetable

il **tablet** (PL i **tablet**) MASC NOUN
tablet (computer)

il **tacchino** MASC NOUN
turkey

il **tacco** (PL i **tacchi**) MASC NOUN
heel
□ tacchi alti high heels

tacere VERB [111]
to be quiet
□ Taci! Be quiet!

la **taglia** FEM NOUN
size
□ Che taglia porti? What size do you take?
□ taglia unica one size

il **tagliando** MASC NOUN
coupon

tagliare VERB [25]
to cut
□ Taglialo in due. Cut it in two.
■ **tagliarsi** to cut oneself □ Mi sono tagliato.
I've cut myself.
■ **Mi sono tagliato un dito.** I've cut my finger.
■ **tagliarsi i capelli** to have one's hair cut
□ Devo tagliarmi i capelli. I need to get my hair
cut. □ Ti sei tagliato i capelli? Have you had
your hair cut?

le **tagliatelle** FEM PL NOUN
tagliatelle sing

tagliente (FEM **tagliente**) ADJECTIVE
sharp

il **taglio** MASC NOUN
cut
□ Ha un taglio sulla fronte. He's got a cut on
his forehead.
■ **taglio di capelli** hairstyle □ Questo taglio
di capelli ti dona. That hairstyle suits you.

il **tailleur** (PL i **tailleur**) MASC NOUN
suit

il **talco** MASC NOUN
talcum powder

tale (FEM **tale**) ADJECTIVE
such
□ Dice tali sciocchezze. He says such stupid
things. □ Mi son preso un tale spavento! I got
such a fright!
■ **essere tale quale** to be exactly like
□ Il tuo vestito è tale quale il mio. Your dress
is exactly like mine.

il **talismano** MASC NOUN
talisman

il **tallone** MASC NOUN
heel

talmente ADVERB
1 so much
□ L'Irlanda mi è talmente piaciuta che ci
tornerei domani. I liked Ireland so much that
I'd go back there tomorrow.
2 so
□ È talmente noioso! It's so boring!

la **talpa** FEM NOUN
mole

il **tamburo** MASC NOUN
drum

il **Tamigi** MASC NOUN
Thames

tamponare VERB [68]
to crash into
□ Abbiamo tamponato un furgone. We crashed
into a van.

il **tampone** MASC NOUN
tampon

la **tangente** FEM NOUN
kickback (bribe)

la **tangenziale** FEM NOUN
bypass (road)

tanto (FEM **tanta**) ADJECTIVE, PRONOUN
▷ see also **tanto** ADVERB
1 a lot of
□ Mangio sempre tanta pasta. I always eat a lot
of pasta. □ Alla festa c'erano tante ragazze.
There were a lot of girls at the party.
■ **da tanto tempo** for a long time □ Non lo
vedevo da tanto tempo. I hadn't seen him for a
long time.
■ **Tanti saluti ai tuoi!** Give my regards to
your family!

■ **Ho ancora tanta strada da fare.** I've still got a long way to go.

2 so much

□ Ho mangiato tanta pasta che sono stato male. I ate so much pasta that I felt ill. □ Non credevo che costasse tanto. I didn't think it cost so much.

■ **tanti** so many □ Non pensavo che ce ne sarebbero stati tanti. I didn't think there would be so many.

■ **ogni tanto** every so often

■ **È da tanto che aspetti?** Have you been waiting long?

■ **tanto vale che tu** you may as well □ Se lo devi fare, tanto vale che lo faccia subito. If you're going to do it, you may as well do it at once.

tanto ADVERB

▷ see also **tanto** ADJECTIVE, PRONOUN

1 so

□ È tanto simpatico! He's so nice!

2 so much

□ Non capisco come hai speso tanto. I don't understand how you spent so much.

■ **tanto ... quanto** as ... as □ Non è tanto semplice quanto sembra. It's not as simple as it seems.

■ **tanto per cambiare** just for a change □ Tanto per cambiare è in ritardo. She's late, just for a change.

■ **Parla tanto per parlare.** He just talks for the sake of talking.

■ **L'abbiamo fatto così, tanto per ridere.** We just did it for a laugh.

la **tappa** FEM NOUN
stop

□ la prima tappa del nostro viaggio the first stop on our journey

■ **fare tappa** to stop off

■ **Abbiamo fatto tappa a Bath.** We stopped off at Bath.

tappare VERB [68]
to put the cork in

□ Potresti tappare la bottiglia? Could you put the cork in the bottle, please?

■ **tapparsi il naso** to hold one's nose

■ **tapparsi le orecchie** to cover one's ears

la **tapparella** FEM NOUN
shutter

il **tappetino** MASC NOUN
mat

■ **tappetino del mouse** mouse pad

il **tappeto** MASC NOUN
rug

□ un tappeto persiano a Persian rug

la **tappezzeria** FEM NOUN
wallpaper

□ In camera da letto c'era la tappezzeria rosa. There was pink wallpaper in the bedroom.

il **tappo** MASC NOUN

1 cork

2 plug *(for sink, bath)*

tardare VERB [68]
to be late

□ Come mai hai tardato tanto? How come you're so late?

■ **Scusa se ho tardato a rispondere alla tua lettera, ma...** I'm sorry I've taken so long to reply to your letter, but...

tardi ADVERB
late

□ Oggi mi sono alzato tardi. I got up late today. □ Ormai è troppo tardi. It's too late now. □ Vi raggiungo più tardi. I'll join you later.

■ **A più tardi!** See you later!

■ **Meglio tardi che mai!** Better late than never!

■ **fare tardi** to be late □ Scusa se ho fatto tardi. I'm sorry I'm late.

■ **Non devo fare tardi stasera.** I mustn't stay up late tonight.

■ **presto o tardi** sooner or later □ Presto o tardi se ne pentirà. Sooner or later he'll be sorry.

la **targa** (PL le **targhe**) FEM NOUN
number plate

□ Non sono riuscito a leggere la targa. I couldn't read the number plate.

la **targhetta** FEM NOUN

1 nameplate

2 name tag

la **tariffa** FEM NOUN

1 fare

□ le tariffe ferroviarie train fares □ C'è una tariffa ridotta per i bambini. There are reduced fares for children.

2 rate *(for postage)*

3 charge *(for telephone)*

il **tarlo** MASC NOUN
woodworm

la **tarma** FEM NOUN
moth

i **tarocchi** MASC PL NOUN
tarot cards

la **tartaruga** (PL le **tartarughe**) FEM NOUN

1 tortoise

2 turtle

la **tartina** FEM NOUN
canapé

la **tasca** (PL le **tasche**) FEM NOUN
pocket

□ L'ho messo nella tasca della giacca. I put it in my jacket pocket.

tascabile (FEM **tascabile**) ADJECTIVE
pocket

□ una calcolatrice tascabile a pocket calculator □ un'edizione tascabile a pocket edition

la **tassa** FEM NOUN
tax
□ Non aveva pagato le tasse. He hadn't paid his taxes.
■ **tasse scolastiche** school fees

il/la **tassista** (MASC PL i **tassisti**, FEM PL le **tassiste**) MASC/FEM NOUN
taxi driver
□ Fa il tassista. He is a taxi driver.

il **tasso** MASC NOUN
■ **tasso di cambio** rate of exchange
■ **tasso di interesse** rate of interest

la **tastiera** FEM NOUN
keyboard

il/la **tastierista** (MASC PL i **tastieristi**, FEM PL le **tastieriste**) MASC/FEM NOUN
1 keyboard player
2 keyboarder (on computer)

il **tasto** MASC NOUN
key

il **tatuaggio** MASC NOUN
tattoo
□ Ha un tatuaggio sul braccio. He's got a tattoo on his arm.

la **tavola** FEM NOUN
table
□ Apparecchio la tavola? Shall I set the table?
■ **A tavola!** Dinner's ready!

la **tavola calda** (PL le **tavole calde**) FEM NOUN
snack bar

la **tavoletta** FEM NOUN
■ **una tavoletta di cioccolata** a bar of chocolate

il **tavolino** MASC NOUN
table
□ un bar con i tavolini all'aperto a café with tables outside

il **tavolo** MASC NOUN
table
□ Vieni a sedere al nostro tavolo. Come and sit at our table.

il **taxi** (PL i **taxi**) MASC NOUN
taxi

la **tazza** FEM NOUN
1 cup
2 mug

te PRONOUN
you
□ È alto come te. He's as tall as you.
□ Parlavamo di te. We were talking about you.

il **tè** (PL i **tè**) MASC NOUN
tea

il **teatro** MASC NOUN
theatre
□ Qualche volta vanno a teatro. They sometimes go to the theatre.

la **tecnica** (PL le **tecniche**) FEM NOUN
technique

tecnico (FEM **tecnica**, MASC PL **tecnici**, FEM PL **tecniche**) ADJECTIVE
▷ see also **tecnico** NOUN
technical
□ Fa l'istituto tecnico. He goes to the technical college.

il **tecnico** (PL i **tecnici**) MASC NOUN
▷ see also **tecnico** ADJECTIVE
1 technician
2 repair man
□ È venuto il tecnico per riparare la TV. The repair man's come to fix the TV.

la **tedesca** (PL le **tedesche**) FEM NOUN
German

tedesco (FEM **tedesca**, MASC PL **tedeschi**, FEM PL **tedesche**) ADJECTIVE
▷ see also **tedesco** NOUN
German
□ È tedesca. She's German.

il **tedesco** (PL i **tedeschi**) MASC NOUN
▷ see also **tedesco** ADJECTIVE
German (person, language)
□ i tedeschi the Germans □ Parli tedesco? Do you speak German?

il **tegame** MASC NOUN
pan

la **teiera** FEM NOUN
teapot

la **tela** FEM NOUN
cloth
□ una pezza di tela a piece of cloth
■ **pantaloni di tela** cotton trousers
■ **borsa di tela** canvas bag

la **telecamera** FEM NOUN
TV camera

il **telecomando** MASC NOUN
remote control

telefonare VERB [68]
to phone
□ Stamattina ha telefonato tua madre. Your mother phoned this morning.
■ **telefonare a qualcuno** to phone somebody □ Ieri ho telefonato a Richard. I phoned Richard yesterday.

la **telefonata** FEM NOUN
phone call
□ Posso fare una telefonata? Can I make a phone call?

telefonico (FEM **telefonica**, MASC PL **telefonici**, FEM PL **telefoniche**) ADJECTIVE
phone
■ **cabina telefonica** phone box
■ **elenco telefonico** phone book
■ **scheda telefonica** phone card

il **telefonino** MASC NOUN
mobile phone
■ **telefonino con fotocamera** camera phone

il **telefono** MASC NOUN
phone

□ È al telefono. She's on the phone.

■ **dare un colpo di telefono a qualcuno** to give somebody a ring □ Ti do un colpo di telefono più tardi. I'll give you a ring later.

■ **numero di telefono** phone number

■ **telefono cellulare** mobile

■ **telefono fisso** landline

■ **telefono a monete** pay phone

■ **telefono pubblico** public phone

■ **telefono a scheda** cardphone

il **telegiornale** MASC NOUN
news *sing*

□ L'hanno detto al telegiornale. It was on the news. □ Il telegiornale è alle otto. The news is at eight.

il **telegramma** (PL i **telegrammi**) MASC NOUN
telegram

il **telespettatore,** la **telespettatrice**
MASC/FEM NOUN
viewer

la **televendita** FEM NOUN
teleshopping

la **televisione** FEM NOUN
television

□ L'ho visto alla televisione. I saw it on television.

il **televisore** MASC NOUN
television set

□ un televisore nuovo a new television set

il **tema** (PL i **temi**) MASC NOUN
essay

□ Ho consegnato il tema senza rileggerlo. I handed in my essay without reading it through.

il **temperamatite** (PL i **temperamatite**)
MASC NOUN
pencil sharpener

la **temperatura** FEM NOUN
temperature

il **temperino** MASC NOUN
penknife

la **tempesta** FEM NOUN
tempest

le **tempie** FEM PL NOUN
temples

il **tempio** MASC NOUN
temple

il **tempo** MASC NOUN

1 time

□ Scusa, adesso non ho tempo. Sorry, I haven't got time at the moment. □ Rilassati, abbiamo ancora tempo! Relax, we've still got time!

■ **al tempo stesso** at the same time

■ **tempo libero** spare time □ Cosa fai nel tempo libero? What do you do in your spare time?

■ **un po' di tempo** a while □ Non lo vedo da un po' di tempo. I haven't seen him for a while. □ Era qui un po' di tempo fa. She was here a while ago.

■ **tempi supplementari** extra time *sing*

2 weather

□ Che tempo fa? What's the weather like?
□ brutto tempo bad weather □ bel tempo good weather

■ **le previsioni del tempo** the weather forecast *sing*

3 half *(of match)*

□ Ha segnato nel secondo tempo. He scored in the second half.

4 part *(of film, play)*

□ Il primo tempo era un po' noioso. The first part was a bit boring.

il **temporale** MASC NOUN
thunderstorm

temporaneo (FEM **temporanea**) ADJECTIVE
temporary

□ una sistemazione temporanea temporary accommodation

le **tenaglie** FEM PL NOUN
pincers

la **tenda** FEM NOUN

1 tent

2 awning

■ **tende** curtains

■ **tirare le tende** to draw the curtains

tendere VERB [112]
to stretch

□ Hanno teso una corda tra due alberi. They stretched a rope between two trees.

■ **tendere a** to tend to □ Tende ad ingrassare. She tends to put on weight.

■ **blu che tende al verde** blue-green

il **tenente** MASC NOUN
lieutenant

tenere VERB [113]

1 to hold

□ Tiene la racchetta con la sinistra. He holds the racket with his left hand.

■ **tenere in braccio un bambino** to hold a baby

■ **tenersi a** to hold onto □ Tieniti al corrimano. Hold onto the rail.

■ **Tieniti forte!** Hold on tight!

■ **tenersi per mano** to hold hands □ Si tenevano per mano. They were holding hands.

■ **Tieniti pronta per le cinque.** Be ready by five.

2 to keep

□ Non mi serve, puoi tenerlo. I don't need it, you can keep it. □ Mi tieni il posto? Torno subito. Will you keep my seat for me. I'll be right back.

■ **tenere la destra** to keep to the right

■ **Tieni!** Here! □ Tieni, usa il mio. Here, use mine. □ Tieni, questo è per te. Here, this is for you.

tenero (FEM **tenera**) ADJECTIVE

1 soft

□ Il materasso è troppo tenero. The mattress is too soft.

2 tender *(meat)*

il **tennis** MASC NOUN
tennis
▫ Giochi a tennis? Do you play tennis?
■ **tennis da tavolo** table tennis

il/la **tennista** (MASC PL i **tennisti**, FEM PL le **tenniste**) MASC/FEM NOUN
tennis player

tentare VERB [68]
to try
▫ Tenterà di battere il record. She's going to try to beat the record. ▫ Le ho tentate tutte per convincerli. I tried everything to persuade them.

il **tentativo** MASC NOUN
attempt

la **tentazione** FEM NOUN
temptation
▫ Non ho saputo resistere alla tentazione! I couldn't resist the temptation!

la **teoria** FEM NOUN
theory
■ **in teoria** in theory

il **teppista** (PL i **teppisti**) MASC NOUN
hooligan

la **terapia** FEM NOUN
therapy

il **tergicristallo** MASC NOUN
windscreen wiper

terminare VERB [68, aux essere]
to finish
▫ A che ora termina il film? What time does the film finish?

il **termine** MASC NOUN
end
■ **avere termine** to end

il **termometro** MASC NOUN
thermometer

il **termos** (PL i **termos**) MASC NOUN
flask

il **termosifone** MASC NOUN
radiator

il **termostato** MASC NOUN
thermostat

la **terra** FEM NOUN
ground
▫ La terra è bagnata. The ground's wet.
■ **per terra 1** on the ground **2** on the floor
■ **cadere per terra** to fall down
■ **la Terra** the Earth

la **terrazza** FEM NOUN
terrace
▫ Erano seduti in terrazza. They were sitting on the terrace.

il **terrazzo** MASC NOUN
balcony

il **terremoto** MASC NOUN
earthquake

il **terreno** MASC NOUN
1 land

▫ una casa con 500 ettari di terreno a house with 500 hectares of land ▫ Hanno dei terreni in Toscana. They've got land in Tuscany.
2 ground
▫ Il terreno è bagnato. The ground's wet.

terribile (FEM **terribile**) ADJECTIVE
terrible

il **territorio** MASC NOUN
territory

il **terrore** MASC NOUN
■ **avere il terrore di** to be terrified of ▫ Anna ha il terrore dei ragni. Anna's terrified of spiders.
■ **avere il terrore di fare qualcosa** to be terrified of doing something ▫ Sergio ha il terrore di volare. Sergio's terrified of flying.

il **terrorismo** MASC NOUN
terrorism

il/la **terrorista** (MASC PL i **terroristi**, FEM PL le **terroriste**) MASC/FEM NOUN
terrorist

terrorizzato (FEM **terrorizzata**) ADJECTIVE
■ **essere terrorizzato** to be terrified

la **terza** FEM NOUN
▷ see also **terzo** ADJECTIVE, NOUN
third gear
■ **terza elementare** third year at primary school
■ **terza media** third year at secondary school
■ **terza superiore** sixth year at secondary school

il **terzino** MASC NOUN
back
▫ Gioca da terzino sinistro. He plays left back.

terzo (FEM **terza**) ADJECTIVE, MASC NOUN
third
▫ Abito al terzo piano. I live on the third floor.
▫ un terzo della classe a third of the class

il **teschio** MASC NOUN
skull

la **tesi** (FEM le **tesi**) FEM NOUN
dissertation
▫ una tesi su Jane Austen a dissertation on Jane Austen

teso (FEM **tesa**) ADJECTIVE
tense

il **tesoro** MASC NOUN
treasure
▫ caccia al tesoro treasure hunt
■ **Grazie tesoro!** Thank you darling!

la **tessera** FEM NOUN
1 card
▫ una tessera magnetica a swipe card
2 membership card
▫ Ho la tessera del Milan. I've got a membership card for AC-Milan.
■ **tessera dell'autobus** bus pass

il **tessuto** MASC NOUN
fabric

la **testa** FEM NOUN
head
□ Ho battuto la testa. I banged my head.
■ **dalla testa ai piedi** from head to foot
■ **a testa** a head □ quindici euro a testa
fifteen euros a head
■ **Testa o croce?** Heads or tails?
■ **Facciamo a testa o croce?** Shall we toss
for it?
■ **essere in testa alla classifica 1** (racing
driver, record) to be number one **2** (team) to be
top of the league

il **testamento** MASC NOUN
will
□ Ha deciso di fare testamento. He decided to
make his will.

testardo (FEM **testarda**) ADJECTIVE
stubborn

il/la **testimone** MASC/FEM NOUN
witness
□ Non c'erano testimoni. There weren't any
witnesses.

testimoniare VERB [17]
to give evidence
□ Era disposta a testimoniare contro di lui.
She was ready to give evidence against him.

la **testina** FEM NOUN
head

il **testo** MASC NOUN
text
□ un testo difficile a difficult text
■ **un libro di testo** a textbook

il **tetto** MASC NOUN
roof

la **tettoia** FEM NOUN
1 canopy
2 roof (of station)

il **tettuccio** MASC NOUN
■ **tettuccio apribile** sunroof

il **Tevere** MASC NOUN
Tiber

ti PRONOUN
1 you
□ Ti telefono più tardi. I'll phone you later. □ Ti
piace? Do you like it? □ Ti ha parlato? Did she
speak to you? □ Ti ha sorriso. He smiled at you.
2 yourself
□ Ti sei divertito? Did you enjoy yourself?
■ **Ti sei lavato i denti?** Have you brushed
your teeth?
■ **Ti ricordi?** Do you remember?

tiepido (FEM **tiepida**) ADJECTIVE
lukewarm
□ acqua tiepida lukewarm water

il **tifo** MASC NOUN
■ **fare il tifo per** to support □ Faccio il tifo
per la Juventus. I support Juventus.

il **tifoso**, la **tifosa** MASC/FEM NOUN
supporter
□ i tifosi del Liverpool the Liverpool supporters

la **tigre** FEM NOUN
tiger

timbrare VERB [68]
to stamp
□ Hai timbrato il biglietto? Have you stamped
your ticket?

il **timbro** MASC NOUN
stamp
■ **mettere il timbro su qualcosa** to stamp
something □ Gli hanno messo il timbro sul
passaporto. They stamped his passport.
■ **timbro postale** postmark

timido (FEM **timida**) ADJECTIVE
shy

il **timone** MASC NOUN
rudder

la **tinta** FEM NOUN
1 paint
□ un barattolo di tinta a tin of paint
2 colour
□ una tinta vivace a bright colour
■ **in tinta unita** plain □ un vestito giallo in
tinta unita a plain yellow dress

la **tintoria** FEM NOUN
dry cleaner's
□ Devo portare il cappotto in tintoria. I need to
take my coat to the dry cleaner's.

tipico (FEM **tipica**, MASC PL **tipici**, FEM PL
tipiche) ADJECTIVE
1 typical
□ un esempio tipico a typical example
2 traditional
□ un tipico pub inglese a traditional English
pub □ un tipico piatto scozzese a traditional
Scottish dish

il **tipo** MASC NOUN
1 sort
□ Che tipo di bici hai? What sort of bike have
you got? □ piante di tutti i tipi all sorts of plants
2 type
□ Non è il mio tipo. He's not my type.
■ **Chi era quel tipo?** Who was that?
■ **Mi sembra un tipo simpatico.** He
seems nice.

tirare VERB [68]
1 to pull
□ Tira! Pull! □ Mi ha tirato i capelli. She pulled
my hair.
2 to throw
□ Tirami la palla! Throw me the ball! □ Ha
tirato un sasso nell'acqua. He threw a stone in
the water.
■ **tirare un pugno a qualcuno** to punch
somebody
■ **tirare uno schiaffo a qualcuno** to slap
somebody
■ **tirare un calcio** to kick
■ **tirarsi indietro** to back out □ Aveva

t

promesso di aiutarmi ma poi si è tirato indietro. He promised to help me and then backed out.

tirchio (FEM **tirchia**) ADJECTIVE
mean
□ Quant'è tirchio! He's so mean!

il titolo MASC NOUN
title
□ Qual è il titolo di quella canzone? What's the title of that song? □ Ha conservato il titolo mondiale. He retained the world title.
■ **i titoli** (of news) the headlines

la tivù (PL le **tivù**) FEM NOUN
TV
□ Cosa c'è in tivù stasera? What's on TV tonight?

il toast (PL i **toast**) MASC NOUN
toastie

toccare VERB [18, AUX **avere** or **essere**]
to touch
□ Non toccarlo! Don't touch it! □ Non vuole che si tocchi la sua roba. He doesn't like people touching his things.
■ **A chi tocca?** Whose turn is it?
■ **Tocca a David.** It's David's turn.
■ **Perché tocca sempre a me farlo?** Why do I always have to do it?
■ **Mi è toccato pagare per tutti.** I had to pay for everybody.

togliere VERB [114]
1 to take off
□ Togliti il cappotto. Take off your coat. □ Ho tolto il poster dalla parete. I took the poster off the wall.
2 to take out
□ Mi hanno tolto due denti. I had two teeth taken out.

la toilette (PL le **toilette**) FEM NOUN
toilet
□ Dov'è la toilette? Where's the toilet?

la tomba FEM NOUN
grave

la tombola FEM NOUN
bingo
■ **giocare a tombola** to play bingo

tondo (FEM **tonda**) ADJECTIVE
round
□ un cuscino tondo a round cushion
□ parentesi tonde round brackets
■ **chiaro e tondo** bluntly □ Gli ho detto chiaro e tondo quello che pensavo. I told him bluntly what I thought.

la tonnellata FEM NOUN
ton
□ Questa valigia pesa una tonnellata! This suitcase weighs a ton!

il tonno MASC NOUN
tuna
□ un tramezzino al tonno a tuna sandwich

il tono MASC NOUN
tone
□ Dal tono di voce si capiva che era seccata. You could tell she was annoyed by her tone of voice.

il topo MASC NOUN
1 mouse
2 rat

il torace MASC NOUN
chest

la torcia (PL le **torce**) FEM NOUN
■ **torcia elettrica** torch

il torcicollo MASC NOUN
stiff neck
□ Ho il torcicollo. I've got a stiff neck.

il torero MASC NOUN
bullfighter

Torino FEM NOUN
Turin
□ Domani andremo a Torino. We're going to Turin tomorrow. □ Abita a Torino. She lives in Turin.

tormentare VERB [68]
to torment
□ Smettila di tormentare quel povero cane. Stop tormenting that poor dog.

il tornante MASC NOUN
hairpin bend

tornare VERB [68, AUX **essere**]
1 to get back
□ Quando sei tornato? When did you get back?
□ Sono tornato domenica mattina. I got back on Sunday morning.
■ **tornare a casa** to get home
■ **A che ora torni da scuola?** What time do you get home from school?
2 to be back
□ Non sono ancora tornati dalle vacanze. They're not back from their holidays yet.
□ Torno tra un attimo. I'll be back in a minute.

il torneo MASC NOUN
tournament
□ un torneo di tennis a tennis tournament

Toro MASC NOUN
Taurus
□ Sono del Toro. I'm Taurus.

il toro MASC NOUN
bull

la torre FEM NOUN
1 tower
□ la torre pendente di Pisa the Leaning Tower of Pisa
2 rook (in chess)

il torrente MASC NOUN
torrent

il torrone MASC NOUN
nougat

il torsolo MASC NOUN
core
□ un torsolo di mela an apple core

la **torta** FEM NOUN
cake
▫ una fetta di torta a slice of cake

i **tortellini** MASC PL NOUN
tortellini *sing*

il **torto** MASC NOUN
■ **avere torto** to be wrong ▫ Mi dispiace, ma hai torto. I'm sorry, but you're wrong.
■ **In effetti non ha tutti i torti.** In fact she's quite right.
■ **Tutti mi hanno dato torto.** Everybody said I was wrong.

la **tortura** FEM NOUN
torture

torturare VERB [68]
1 to torture
2 to torment
▫ Smetti di torturare quel povero gatto! Stop tormenting that poor cat!

Toscana FEM NOUN
Tuscany
▫ Andrò in Toscana quest'estate. I'm going to Tuscany this summer. ▫ Ti è piaciuta la Toscana? Did you like Tuscany?

la **tosse** FEM NOUN
cough
▫ Ho la tosse. I've got a cough.

il/la **tossicodipendente** MASC/FEM NOUN
drug addict

tossire VERB [51]
to cough

il **tostapane** (PL i **tostapane**) MASC NOUN
toaster

tostato (FEM **tostata**) ADJECTIVE
■ **pane tostato** toast ▫ una fetta di pane tostato a piece of toast

totale (FEM **totale**) ADJECTIVE, MASC NOUN
total
▫ La festa è stata un fallimento totale. The party was a total failure. ▫ Il totale è di sessanta sterline. The total is sixty pounds.

il **totocalcio** MASC NOUN
the pools *pl*
▫ Gioco al totocalcio ogni settimana. I do the pools every week.

la **tournée** (PL le **tournée**) FEM NOUN
tour
▫ Sono in tournée in Italia. They're on tour in Italy.

la **tovaglia** FEM NOUN
tablecloth

il **tovagliolo** MASC NOUN
napkin

tra PREPOSITION
1 between
▫ Era seduto tra il padre e lo zio. He was sitting between his father and his uncle. ▫ Detto tra noi, non piace neanche a me. Between you and me, I don't like it either.

2 among
▫ Tra i feriti c'era anche il pilota dell'aereo. The pilot of the plane was among the injured.
3 in
▫ Torno tra un'ora. I'll be back in an hour. ▫ tra cinque giorni in five days
■ **tra poco** soon
■ **Tra venti chilometri c'è un'area di servizio.** It's twenty kilometres to the next service area.

la **traccia** (PL le **tracce**) FEM NOUN
trace
▫ Sul bicchiere c'erano tracce di rossetto. There were traces of lipstick on the glass.
■ **sparire senza lasciar traccia** to vanish without trace

la **tracolla** FEM NOUN
■ **borsa a tracolla** shoulder bag

tradire VERB [51]
1 to be unfaithful to
▫ Ha tradito suo marito. She was unfaithful to her husband.
2 to betray
▫ Hai tradito la mia fiducia. You betrayed my trust.

tradizionale (FEM **tradizionale**) ADJECTIVE
traditional

la **tradizione** FEM NOUN
tradition

tradurre VERB [85]
to translate
▫ Ho dovuto tradurlo dall'inglese in italiano. I had to translate it from English into Italian.

la **traduzione** FEM NOUN
translation

il/la **trafficante** MASC/FEM NOUN
■ **trafficante di droga** drug trafficker

il **traffico** MASC NOUN
traffic
▫ C'è un traffico pazzesco. The traffic's terrible.
■ **traffico di droga** drug trafficking

la **tragedia** FEM NOUN
tragedy
▫ una tragedia greca a Greek tragedy
■ **Non è il caso di farne una tragedia!** There's no need to make such a fuss about it!

il **traghetto** MASC NOUN
ferry
▫ Siamo andati in Irlanda col traghetto. We went to Ireland by ferry.

tragico (FEM **tragica**, MASC PL **tragici**, FEM PL **tragiche**) ADJECTIVE
tragic

il **tragitto** MASC NOUN
journey
▫ un breve tragitto a short journey
■ **lungo il tragitto** on the way ▫ È scomparso lungo il tragitto verso la scuola. He disappeared on the way to school.

t

il **traguardo** MASC NOUN
finishing line
□ È stato il primo a tagliare il traguardo. He was the first to cross the finishing line.

trainare VERB [68]
to tow
□ Il carro attrezzi ha trainato la macchina fino all'officina. The breakdown van towed the car to the garage.

il **tram** (PL i **tram**) MASC NOUN
tram

la **trama** FEM NOUN
plot
□ La trama del film è un po' complicata. The plot of the film is rather complicated.

il **tramezzino** MASC NOUN
sandwich
□ un tramezzino al prosciutto a ham sandwich

il **tramonto** MASC NOUN
sunset

il **trampolino** MASC NOUN
diving board

tranne PREPOSITION
except
□ Ha invitato tutti tranne me. He invited everybody except me.

il **tranquillante** MASC NOUN
tranquillizer

tranquillizzare VERB [68]
to reassure
□ L'ho detto per tranquillizzarla. I said it to reassure her.

> **LANGUAGE TIP** Be careful! **tranquillizzare** doesn't mean **to tranquillize**.

tranquillo (FEM **tranquilla**) ADJECTIVE
quiet
□ Cerchiamo un angolo tranquillo. Let's find a quiet corner. □ È un tipo molto tranquillo. He's very quiet.
■ **Sta' tranquillo!** Don't worry!

transitivo (FEM **transitiva**) ADJECTIVE
transitive

il **trapano** MASC NOUN
drill

il **trapianto** MASC NOUN
transplant

la **trappola** FEM NOUN
trap
□ Sono caduti nella trappola della polizia. They fell into the police trap.

la **trapunta** FEM NOUN
quilt

trarre VERB [115]
to draw
■ **trarre le conclusioni** to draw conclusions □ Sta a te trarre le conclusioni. You can draw your own conclusions.
■ **trarre in inganno** to be misleading □ Il

suo modo di fare trae in inganno. His manner is misleading.
■ **trarre in salvo** to rescue □ Sono stati tratti in salvo dai vigili del fuoco. They were rescued by the firemen.
■ **un film tratto da un romanzo di A. Christie** a film based on a novel by A. Christie

trasandato (FEM **trasandata**) ADJECTIVE
■ **È trasandato nel vestire.** He wears scruffy clothes.

trascinare VERB [68]
to drag

trascorrere VERB [26]
1 to spend
□ Trascorrono sempre le vacanze al mare. They always spend their holidays at the seaside.
2 to pass
□ Sono già trascorsi sei giorni da allora. Six days have passed since then.

il **trasferimento** MASC NOUN
transfer
□ Ha chiesto il trasferimento. He's asked for a transfer.

trasferire VERB [51]
to transfer
□ È stato trasferito a Milano. He's been transferred to Milan.
■ **trasferirsi** to move □ Il mese prossimo ci trasferiamo a Firenze. We're moving to Florence next month.

la **trasferta** FEM NOUN
■ **giocare in trasferta** to play away from home □ La prossima settimana giochiamo in trasferta. We're playing away from home next week.

trasformare VERB [68]
1 to transform
□ Il soggiorno in America l'ha trasformato. His stay in America has transformed him.
2 to convert
□ Hanno trasformato la stalla in un ristorante. They converted the stable into a restaurant.
■ **trasformarsi** to convert □ un tavolo che si trasforma in asse da stiro a table that converts into an ironing board

traslocare VERB [18]
to move

il **trasloco** (PL i **traslochi**) MASC NOUN
removal
□ una ditta di traslochi a removal firm
■ **fare un trasloco** to move house □ Li ho aiutati a fare il trasloco. I helped them to move house.

trasmettere VERB [59]
to broadcast
■ **trasmettere in diretta** to broadcast live □ Il concerto sarà trasmesso in diretta. The concert will be broadcast live.

la **trasmissione** FEM NOUN
programme

□ una trasmissione radiofonica a radio programme

trasparente (FEM **trasparente**) ADJECTIVE
transparent

trasportare VERB [68]
to carry

□ Il camion trasportava un carico di arance. The lorry was carrying a load of oranges.

il **trasporto** MASC NOUN
transport

□ un sistema di trasporti efficiente an efficient transport system

■ **i trasporti pubblici** public transport *sing* □ Qui i trasporti pubblici funzionano molto bene. Public transport is very efficient here.

trattare VERB [68]
to treat

□ Lo tratta come un cane. She treats him like a dog.

■ **trattare con qualcuno** to deal with somebody □ Ho trattato direttamente con il proprietario. I dealt directly with the owner.

■ **trattare di** to be about □ Di cosa tratta il libro? What's the book about? □ Ti ha detto di cosa si tratta? Did he tell you what it's about?

■ **Si tratterebbe di poche ore.** It would just be a few hours.

trattenere VERB [113]
1 to hold

□ Prova a trattenere il respiro. Try to hold your breath.

2 to hold back

□ Se non l'avessimo trattenuto l'avrebbe picchiato. If we hadn't held him back he would have hit him.

■ **trattenersi** **1** to stay □ Quanto ti trattieni? How long are you staying? **2** to stop □ Non sono più riuscito a trattenermi. I just couldn't stop myself.

il **trattino** MASC NOUN
hyphen

□ Si scrive con il trattino. It's spelt with a hyphen.

il **tratto** MASC NOUN
stretch

□ È un tratto di strada molto pericoloso. It's a very dangerous stretch of road.

■ **C'è ancora un bel tratto da fare.** We've still got a long way to go.

■ **tutt'a un tratto** suddenly □ Tutt'a un tratto ha cominciato a piovere. It suddenly started to rain.

la **trattoria** FEM NOUN
restaurant

il **trauma** (PL i **traumi**) MASC NOUN
shock

□ La morte del padre è stata un trauma per lui. His father's death was a shock to him.

■ **trauma cranico** concussion

la **traversa** FEM NOUN
1 sidestreet

□ Abita in una traversa di Via Roma. She lives in a sidestreet off Via Roma.

■ **Prendi la seconda traversa a destra.** Take the second right.

2 crossbar

□ La palla ha colpito la traversa. The ball hit the crossbar.

la **traversata** FEM NOUN
crossing

□ la traversata dell'Atlantico the crossing of the Atlantic

traverso ADVERB

■ **di traverso** sideways □ Mettilo di traverso. Put it sideways.

■ **andare di traverso** to go down the wrong way □ Il latte mi è andato di traverso. The milk went down the wrong way.

travestirsi VERB [41, AUX **essere**]
to disguise oneself

□ Si erano travestiti da infermieri. They were disguised as nurses.

tre NUMBER
three

□ Ha tre anni. He is three. □ alle tre at three o'clock

■ **il tre dicembre** the third of December

la **treccia** (PL le **trecce**) FEM NOUN
plait

□ Anita ha le trecce. Anita has plaits.

trecento NUMBER
three hundred

■ **il Trecento** the fourteenth century

tredicenne (FEM **tredicenne**) ADJECTIVE
thirteen-year-old

tredicesimo (FEM **tredicesima**) ADJECTIVE
thirteenth

tredici NUMBER
thirteen

□ Ha tredici anni. He is thirteen.

■ **le tredici** one p.m.

■ **il tredici dicembre** the thirteenth of December

■ **fare tredici al totocalcio** to win the pools

tremare VERB [68]
to shake

□ Tremavo di paura. I was shaking with fear. □ Mi tremavano le mani. My hands were shaking.

■ **Tremava di freddo.** She was shivering with cold.

tremendo (FEM **tremenda**) ADJECTIVE
terrible

□ Aveva un mal di testa tremendo. He had a terrible headache.

■ **Ho una sete tremenda.** I'm terribly thirsty.

LANGUAGE TIP Be careful! **tremendo** doesn't mean **tremendous**.

remila NUMBER
three thousand

treno MASC NOUN
train
□ Ho perso il treno. I missed the train. □ Siamo andati in treno. We went by train.

renta NUMBER
thirty

rentesimo (FEM **trentesima**) ADJECTIVE
thirtieth

a **trentina** FEM NOUN
about thirty
□ Eravamo una trentina. There were about thirty of us. □ Sarà sulla trentina. He must be about thirty.

triangolo MASC NOUN
triangle

tribunale MASC NOUN
court

triciclo MASC NOUN
tricycle

trimestre MASC NOUN
term

a **trincea** FEM NOUN
trench

trionfo MASC NOUN
triumph
□ il trionfo della nazionale italiana the triumph of the Italian team

triplo MASC NOUN
three times as much
□ Guadagna il triplo di lei. He earns three times as much as her.

triste (FEM **triste**) ADJECTIVE
sad
□ Aveva un'aria molto triste. He looked very sad. □ una notizia ancora più triste even sadder news

tritato (PL **tritata**) ADJECTIVE
chopped
□ cipolle tritate chopped onions
■ **carne tritata** minced meat

a **tromba** FEM NOUN
trumpet
□ Suono la tromba. I play the trumpet.
■ **tromba d'aria** whirlwind

l **tronco** (PL i **tronchi**) MASC NOUN
trunk

l **trono** MASC NOUN
throne

tropicale (FEM **tropicale**) ADJECTIVE
tropical

troppo (FEM **troppa**) ADJECTIVE, PRONOUN
▷ see also **troppo** ADVERB
■ too much
□ Questa pasta è troppa per me. This pasta is too much for me. □ Ne vorrei ancora un po', ma

non troppo. I'd like a bit more, but not too much. □ Ho mangiato troppo. I've eaten too much.
2 too many
□ C'erano troppi bambini. There were too many children. □ Siamo in troppi. There are too many of us.

troppo ADVERB
▷ see also **troppo** ADJECTIVE, PRONOUN
too
□ Fa troppo caldo. It's too hot.
■ **È troppo poco.** It's not enough.

la **trota** FEM NOUN
trout

la **trottola** FEM NOUN
spinning top

trovare VERB [68]
1 to find
□ Ha trovato lavoro. She's found a job. □ Non riesco a trovare le chiavi. I can't find my keys.
2 to think
□ L'ho trovato molto cambiato. I thought he'd changed a lot. □ Fa caldo, non trovi? It's hot, don't you think?
■ **trovarsi 1** to be □ L'albergo si trova proprio al centro. The hotel's right in the town centre. □ In quel periodo mi trovavo a Napoli. At that time I was in Naples. **2** to meet □ Troviamoci alle cinque davanti al cinema. Let's meet at five in front of the cinema.
■ **trovarsi bene con qualcuno** to get on well with somebody □ Mi sono trovata benissimo con i suoi. I got on very well with his parents.
■ **andare a trovare qualcuno** to go to see somebody □ Ieri sono andato a trovare Chris. I went to see Chris yesterday.

truccarsi VERB [18, aux **essere**]
to do one's make-up
□ Passa delle ore a truccarsi. She spends hours doing her make-up.
■ **Si trucca pochissimo.** She doesn't wear much make-up.

il **trucco** (PL i **trucchi**) MASC NOUN
1 make-up
□ Aveva un trucco pesante. She was wearing heavy make-up.
2 trick
□ un trucco che riesce sempre a trick that always works

truffa FEM NOUN
swindle

truffare VERB [68]
to swindle
□ Sono stato truffato. I've been swindled.

il **truffatore,** la **truffatrice** MASC/FEM NOUN
swindler

tu PRONOUN
you

t

289

il **tubo** MASC NOUN
pipe *(for water, gas, etc)*
- **i tubi dell'acqua** the pipes
- **un tubo di cartone** a cardboard tube

tuffarsi VERB [56]
to dive

il **tuffo** MASC NOUN
dive
- **fare un tuffo** to dive

il **tulipano** MASC NOUN
tulip

il **tumore** MASC NOUN
tumour

tuo (FEM **tua**) ADJECTIVE
▷ *see also* **tuo** PRONOUN
your
□ tuo fratello your brother □ la tua bici your bike
- **una tua amica** a friend of yours

tuo (FEM **tua**) PRONOUN
▷ *see also* **tuo** ADJECTIVE
yours
□ È questo il tuo? Is this one yours? □ La tua è più bella della mia. Yours is nicer than mine.
- **i tuoi** your parents □ Cosa hanno detto i tuoi? What did your parents say?

il **tuono** MASC NOUN
thunder

il **tuorlo** MASC NOUN
yolk

il **turbante** MASC NOUN
turban

turbato (FEM **turbata**) ADJECTIVE
upset
□ Era molto turbato. He was very upset.

la **turca** (PL le **turche**) FEM NOUN
Turk

la **Turchia** FEM NOUN
Turkey
□ Mi è piaciuta molto la Turchia. I really liked Turkey. □ Andremo in Turchia quest'estate. We're going to Turkey this summer.

turco (FEM **turca**, MASC PL **turchi**, FEM PL **turche**) ADJECTIVE
▷ *see also* **turco** NOUN
Turkish
□ È turca. She's Turkish.

il **turco** (PL i **turchi**) MASC NOUN
▷ *see also* **turco** ADJECTIVE
1 Turk
□ i turchi the Turks
2 Turkish
□ Parla turco? Does he speak Turkish?

il **turismo** MASC NOUN
tourism

il/la **turista** (MASC PL i **turisti**, FEM PL le **turiste**) MASC/FEM NOUN
tourist

turistico (FEM **turistica**, MASC PL **turistici**, FEM PL **turistiche**) ADJECTIVE
tourist
□ una località turistica a tourist resort

il **turno** MASC NOUN
1 turn
□ È il tuo turno. It's your turn.
- **fare a turno a fare qualcosa** to take turns to do something □ Abbiamo fatto a turno a guidare. We took turns to drive.
2 shift
□ il turno di notte the night shift □ un turno di sei ore a six-hour shift

la **tuta** FEM NOUN
- **tuta da meccanico** overalls *pl*
- **tuta da ginnastica** tracksuit

il/la **tutor** (PL i/le **tutor**) MASC/FEM NOUN
▷ *see also* **tutor** NOUN
tutor

il **tutor** (PL i **tutor**) MASC NOUN
▷ *see also* **tutor** NOUN
speed cameras *pl*

tuttavia ADVERB
but
□ Il compito era difficile, tuttavia ce l'ho fatta. The homework was difficult, but I managed to do it.

tutto (FEM **tutta**) ADJECTIVE
▷ *see also* **tutto** PRONOUN
all
□ Ho bevuto tutto il latte. I've drunk all the milk. □ L'ho bevuto tutto. I've drunk it all.
□ Sei tutto bagnato! You're all wet! □ tutto il giorno all day
- **tutti** every □ tutti i venerdì every Friday
□ tutte le sere every evening

tutto PRONOUN
▷ *see also* **tutto** ADJECTIVE
everything
□ Va tutto bene? Is everything okay? □ Mi hai detto tutto? Have you told me everything?
- **In tutto sono venti sterline.** That's twenty pounds in all.
- **tutti** everybody □ Vengono tutti. Everybody's coming. □ Lo sanno tutti tranne me. Everybody knows except me.
- **tutti e due** both □ Ci siamo andati tutti e due. We both went. □ Sbagliate tutti e due. You're both wrong.

la **TV** (PL le **TV**) FEM NOUN
TV
□ L'hanno detto alla TV. It was on TV.

Uu

ubriacarsi VERB [18, AUX **essere**]
to get drunk
□ Gli basta una birra per ubriacarsi. He gets drunk if he has just one beer.

ubriaco (FEM **ubriaca**, MASC PL **ubriachi**, FEM PL **ubriache**) ADJECTIVE, MASC/FEM NOUN
drunk
□ Era un po' ubriaco. He was a bit drunk. □ Un ubriaco cantava a squarciagola. A drunk was singing at the top of his voice.

l' **uccello** MASC NOUN
bird

uccidere VERB [31]
to kill
□ È rimasto ucciso in un incidente stradale. He was killed in a road accident.

l' **udito** MASC NOUN
hearing

ufficiale (FEM **ufficiale**) ADJECTIVE
▷ see also **ufficiale** NOUN
official
□ È in visita ufficiale in Italia. He's on an official visit to Italy.

l' **ufficiale** MASC NOUN
▷ see also **ufficiale** ADJECTIVE
officer
□ un ufficiale di marina a naval officer

l' **ufficio** MASC NOUN
office
□ Oggi non è andata in ufficio. She didn't go to the office today.
■ **ufficio postale** post office
■ **ufficio informazioni** information desk

uguagliare VERB [25]
to equal
□ Ha uguagliato il record mondiale. He equalled the world record.

uguale (FEM **uguale**) ADJECTIVE
the same
□ Sono esattamente uguali. They're exactly the same.
■ **uguale a** the same as □ Il tuo maglione è uguale al mio. Your sweater's the same as mine.
■ **per me è uguale** it doesn't matter to me
□ Che venga oppure no, per me è uguale. It doesn't matter to me whether he comes or not.
■ **Decidi tu, per me è uguale.** You decide, I don't mind.

■ **due più due è uguale a quattro** two and two equals four

ultimamente ADVERB
lately
□ Non hanno giocato bene ultimamente. They haven't been playing well lately.

ultimo (FEM **ultima**) ADJECTIVE
▷ see also **ultimo** NOUN
1 last
□ Quella è stata l'ultima volta che l'ho vista. That was the last time I saw her.
■ **all'ultimo momento** at the last moment
□ Ha cambiato idea all'ultimo momento. He changed his mind at the last moment.
■ **arrivare per ultimo** to arrive last □ Marco è arrivato per ultimo. Marco arrived last.
■ **arrivare ultimo** (in a race) to come last
□ Chiara è arrivata ultima. Chiara came last.
■ **l'ultimo anno** the final year □ Fa l'ultimo anno dell'università. She is in her final year at university.
■ **l'ultimo piano** the top floor □ Abito all'ultimo piano. I live on the top floor.
■ **negli ultimi tempi** recently □ Ci vediamo poco, negli ultimi tempi. We haven't seen each other much recently.
2 latest
□ Hai visto l'ultimo film di Spielberg? Have you seen Spielberg's latest film? □ Il loro ultimo album è in testa alla classifica. Their latest album is at the top of the charts.

l' **ultimo**, l' **ultima** MASC/FEM NOUN
▷ see also **ultimo** ADJECTIVE
last one
□ Lei è stata l'ultima ad arrivare. She was the last one to arrive. □ Questi sono gli ultimi. These are the last ones.
■ **È l'ultima della classe.** She's bottom of the class.

umano (FEM **umana**) ADJECTIVE
human
□ il corpo umano the human body

l' **umidità** FEM NOUN
■ **Nella casa c'era molta umidità.** The house was very damp.

umido (FEM **umida**) ADJECTIVE
1 damp
□ un clima caldo e umido a hot, damp climate

2 wet

□ L'erba è un po' umida. **The grass is a bit wet.**
□ ancora più umido **even wetter**

umile (FEM **umile**) ADJECTIVE
humble

□ Era di umili origini. **He was of humble origins.**
■ **i lavori più umili** the most menial tasks

l' **umore** MASC NOUN
mood

□ Di che umore è, oggi? **What mood is he in today?**
■ **essere di buon umore** to be in a good mood
■ **essere di cattivo umore** to be in a bad mood

l' **umorismo** MASC NOUN
■ **avere il senso dell'umorismo** to have a sense of humour

umoristico (FEM **umoristica**, MASC PL **umoristici**, FEM PL **umoristiche**) ADJECTIVE
funny

□ un racconto più umoristico **a funnier story**

unanime (FEM **unanime**) ADJECTIVE
unanimous

□ una decisione unanime **a unanimous decision**

l' **uncino** MASC NOUN
hook

undicenne (FEM **undicenne**) ADJECTIVE, MASC/FEM NOUN
eleven-year-old

undicesimo (FEM **undicesima**) ADJECTIVE, MASC NOUN
eleventh

undici NUMBER
eleven

□ Ha undici anni. **He's eleven.** □ alle undici **at eleven o'clock**
■ **l'undici dicembre** the eleventh of December

ungere VERB [116]

1 to oil

□ Devo ungere la catena della bici. **I need to oil the chain of my bike.**

2 to grease

□ Ungi bene la teglia. **Grease the tin well.**

ungherese (FEM **ungherese**) ADJECTIVE, MASC/FEM NOUN
▷ see also **ungherese** NOUN
Hungarian

l' **ungherese** MASC NOUN
▷ see also **ungherese** ADJECTIVE, NOUN
Hungarian (language)

l' **Ungheria** FEM NOUN
■ **l'Ungheria** Hungary □ Ti è piaciuta l'Ungheria? **Did you like Hungary?** □ Andrò in Ungheria quest'estate. **I'm going to Hungary this summer.**

l' **unghia** FEM NOUN

1 nail

□ Marina si mangia le unghie. **Marina bites her nails.**
■ **unghie delle mani** fingernails
■ **unghie dei piedi** toenails

2 claw (of cat)

unico (FEM **unica**, MASC PL **unici**, FEM PL **uniche**) ADJECTIVE
▷ see also **unico** NOUN
only

□ È stata l'unica volta che l'ho visto. **It was the only time I saw him.** □ Robert è figlio unico. **Robert's an only child.**

l' **unico**, l' **unica** (MASC PL gli **unici**, FEM PL le **uniche**) MASC/FEM NOUN
▷ see also **unico** ADJECTIVE
the only one

□ Lei è stata l'unica a capire. **She was the only one who understood.**

l' **unificazione** FEM NOUN
unification

□ dopo l'unificazione della Germania **after the unification of Germany**

l' **uniforme** FEM NOUN
uniform

□ l'uniforme della marina **naval uniform**

l' **unione** FEM NOUN
union

□ l'Unione Europea **the European Union**

unire VERB [51]

1 to put together

□ Se uniamo i due tavoli ci stiamo tutti. **If we put the two tables together there'll be room for all of us.**

2 to join

□ Abbiamo deciso di unire i nostri sforzi. **We decided to join forces.**
■ **unirsi a** to join □ Due ragazzi svizzeri si sono uniti a noi. **Two Swiss boys joined us.**

l' **unità** (PL le **unità**) FEM NOUN
unity

□ un passo avanti verso l'unità europea **a step towards European unity**
■ **unità di misura** unit of measurement

unito (FEM **unita**) ADJECTIVE

1 close

□ La mia è una famiglia molto unita. **My family's very close.**

2 united (team, political party)
■ **in tinta unita** plain □ una cravatta in tinta unita **a plain tie**

l' **università** (PL le **università**) FEM NOUN
university

□ L'ho visto uscire dall'università. **I saw him coming out of the university.** □ Fa l'università. **She's at university.** □ Andrai all'università? **Are you going to go to university?**

l' **universo** MASC NOUN
universe

uno (FEM **una**) ARTICLE

▷ *see also* **uno** PRONOUN, NUMBER

1 a

□ Era una giornata splendida. It was a beautiful day. □ un mio amico a friend of mine

2 an

□ È un artista. He's an artist. □ un programma interessante an interesting programme

uno (FEM **una**) NUMBER

▷ *see also* **uno** PRONOUN, ARTICLE

one

□ Ne ho comprato uno stamattina. I bought one this morning. □ Ce n'è uno a testa. There's one each. □ una camera solo per una notte a room for one night only □ a uno a uno one by one □ Che ore sono? — È l'una. What time is it? — It's one o'clock.

uno (FEM **una**) PRONOUN

▷ *see also* **uno** NUMBER, ARTICLE

someone

□ Ho incontrato uno che ti conosce. I met someone who knows you.

■ **o l'uno o l'altro** either of them □ O l'uno o l'altro per me va bene. Either of them will be fine.

■ **né l'uno né l'altro** neither of them □ Quale prendi? — Né l'uno né l'altro. Which one are you going to take? — Neither of them.

■ **Non prendo né l'uno né l'altro.** I'm not going to take either of them.

unto (FEM **unta**) ADJECTIVE

greasy

□ ancora più unti even greasier

l' **uomo** (PL gli **uomini**) MASC NOUN

man

□ un uomo di mezz'età a middle-aged man □ C'erano due uomini nell'ufficio. There were two men in the office.

■ **scarpe da uomo** men's shoes

l' **uovo** (FEM PL le **uova**) MASC NOUN

egg

■ **uovo alla coque** soft-boiled egg

■ **uovo fritto** fried egg

■ **uovo sodo** hard-boiled egg

■ **uova strapazzate** scrambled eggs

■ **uovo di Pasqua** Easter egg

l' **uragano** MASC NOUN

hurricane

urgente (FEM **urgente**) ADJECTIVE

urgent

□ Ha detto che era urgente. He said it was urgent.

l' **urgenza** FEM NOUN

hurry

□ Non c'è urgenza. There's no hurry.

■ **Questo lavoro va fatto con molta urgenza.** This work is very urgent.

■ **essere ricoverato d'urgenza** to be

rushed into hospital □ È stato ricoverato d'urgenza. He's been rushed into hospital.

urlare VERB [68]

to shout

□ Ho dovuto urlare per farmi sentire. I had to shout to make myself heard.

■ **urlare di dolore** to scream with pain

l' **urlo** (FEM PL le **urla**) MASC NOUN

scream

□ urla di terrore screams of terror

■ **lanciare un urlo** to scream □ Quando l'ha visto ha lanciato un urlo. She screamed when she saw him.

urtare VERB [68]

to bump into

□ L'ha urtata senza volere. He accidentally bumped into her.

l' **usanza** FEM NOUN

custom

□ È un'usanza del posto. It's a local custom.

usare VERB [68]

to use

□ Non mi lascia usare il suo computer. He doesn't let me use his computer. □ Come si usa questo coso? How do you use this thing?

■ **Quest'anno si usano le gonne lunghe.** This year long skirts are in fashion.

usato (FEM **usata**) ADJECTIVE

second-hand

□ una macchina usata a second-hand car

uscire VERB [117]

1 to go out

□ È uscito senza dire una parola. He went out without saying a word. □ È uscita a comprare il giornale. She's gone out to buy a newspaper. □ Ieri sono uscita con degli amici. I went out with friends yesterday.

2 to come out

□ Uscirà dall'ospedale domani. He's coming out of hospital tomorrow. □ L'ho incontrata che usciva dalla farmacia. I met her coming out of the chemist's. □ La rivista esce di lunedì. The magazine comes out on Mondays. □ È appena uscito il loro ultimo album. Their latest album has just come out.

■ **uscire di strada** to leave the road □ La macchina è uscita di strada. The car left the road.

l' **uscita** FEM NOUN

exit

□ Dov'è l'uscita? Where's the exit?

■ **Ho incontrato Claudia all'uscita di scuola.** I met Claudia when we were coming out of school.

■ **uscita di sicurezza** emergency exit

l' **usignolo** MASC NOUN

nightingale

l' **uso** MASC NOUN

1 use

□ per uso personale for personal use

u

293

Italian-English

2 usage
□ l'uso corretto di quell'espressione the correct usage of that expression
■ **gli usi e i costumi degli antichi romani** the customs of the ancient Romans

l' **ustione** FEM NOUN
burn
□ ustioni di terzo grado third-degree burns

l' **utensile** MASC NOUN
tool

utile (FEM **utile**) ADJECTIVE
useful
□ Grazie per la guida, mi è stata molto utile.

Thanks for the guide book, it was very useful.
■ **rendersi utile** to make oneself useful
□ Posso rendermi utile? Can I make myself useful?

utilizzare VERB [68]
to use
□ Ho utilizzato ritagli di stoffa. I used scraps of material.

l' **uva** FEM NOUN
grapes pl
□ un grappolo d'uva a bunch of grapes
■ **uva passa** raisins pl

Vv

la **vacanza** FEM NOUN
holiday
□ Ho fatto una lunga vacanza. I had a long
holiday. □ le vacanze scolastiche the school
holidays □ Trascorriamo sempre le vacanze al
mare. We always spend our holidays at the
seaside.
- **andare in vacanza** to go on holiday
□ Dove andrai in vacanza quest'anno? Where
are you going on holiday this year?
- **essere in vacanza** to be on holiday

LANGUAGE TIP Be careful! **vacanza** doesn't
mean **vacancy**.

vaccinare VERB [68]
to vaccinate
- **farsi vaccinare** to get vaccinated □ Si è
fatto vaccinare contro l'influenza. He got
vaccinated against flu.

il **vagabondo,** la **vagabonda** MASC/FEM NOUN
tramp

vagare VERB [76]
to wander
□ Vagava senza meta per la città. He was
wandering aimlessly around the town.

il **vaglia** (PL i **vaglia**) MASC NOUN
- **vaglia postale** postal order

vago (FEM **vaga**, MASC PL **vaghi**, FEM PL **vaghe**)
ADJECTIVE
vague

il **vagone** MASC NOUN
1 carriage (of train)
- **vagone letto** sleeping car
- **vagone ristorante** restaurant car
2 truck (for goods)

la **valanga** (PL le **valanghe**) FEM NOUN
avalanche

valere VERB [118]
to be worth
□ L'auto vale tremila euro. The car is worth
three thousand euros.
- **non valere niente** to be worthless
- **valere la pena** to be worth it □ Non ne
vale la pena. It's not worth it. □ Non vale la
pena arrabbiarsi tanto. It's not worth getting so
angry.
- **vale a dire** that is to say
- **Tanto vale che te lo dica.** I might as well
tell you.

- **Questo vale anche per te.** This applies to
you, too.
- **Così non vale!** That's not fair!

il **valico** (PL i **valichi**) MASC NOUN
pass
- **valico di frontiera** border crossing

valido (FEM **valida**) ADJECTIVE
valid
□ Il suo passaporto non è più valido. Your
passport is no longer valid.

la **valigia** (PL le **valigie** or le **valige**) FEM NOUN
suitcase
- **fare le valigie** to pack
- **disfare le valigie** to unpack

la **valle** FEM NOUN
valley

il **valore** MASC NOUN
value
□ il valore di un anello the value of a ring
□ valori morali moral values □ Questo
documento non ha valore legale. This
document has no legal value.
- **È un anello di gran valore.** It's a very
valuable ring.

la **valuta** FEM NOUN
- **valuta estera** foreign currency

valutare VERB [68]
1 to value
□ La casa è stata valutata centomila euro. The
house has been valued at a hundred thousand
euros.
2 to assess
□ I danni sono valutati attorno a cinquecentomila
euro. The damage has been assessed at about
five hundred thousand euros.
3 to weigh up
□ Bisogna valutare i pro e i contro. We need to
weigh up the pros and cons.

la **valvola** FEM NOUN
valve
□ una valvola di sicurezza a safety valve

il **valzer** (PL i **valzer**) MASC NOUN
waltz
□ Sai ballare il valzer? Can you do the waltz?

il **vampiro** MASC NOUN
vampire

il **vandalismo** MASC NOUN
vandalism
□ un atto di vandalismo an act of vandalism

vangelo – vedere

il **vangelo** MASC NOUN
gospel

la **vaniglia** FEM NOUN
vanilla
▫ un gelato alla vaniglia a vanilla ice cream

vanitoso (FEM **vanitosa**) ADJECTIVE
vain

vano (FEM **vana**) ADJECTIVE
vain
▫ vane speranze vain hopes
■ **Tutti i nostri sforzi sono stati vani.**
All our efforts were useless.

il **vantaggio** MASC NOUN
advantage
▫ i vantaggi e gli svantaggi di vivere in città the advantages and disadvantages of living in a city
▫ Sei in una posizione di vantaggio. You're at an advantage.
■ **essere in vantaggio** (in sport) to be in the lead ▫ Siamo in vantaggio. We're in the lead.
■ **Sono in vantaggio di due punti sugli avversari.** They have a two-point lead over their opponents.

vantaggioso (FEM **vantaggiosa**) ADJECTIVE
good
▫ Mi ha fatto un'offerta molto vantaggiosa. He made me a very good offer. ▫ un prezzo vantaggioso a good price

vantarsi VERB [56]
to boast
▫ Si vanta sempre del proprio successo. He's always boasting about his success.

vanvera FEM NOUN
■ **parlare a vanvera** to talk nonsense

il **vapore** MASC NOUN
steam
■ **a vapore** steam ▫ un ferro a vapore a steam iron
■ **al vapore** steamed ▫ verdure al vapore steamed vegetables

varare VERB [68]
■ **varare una nave** to launch a ship
■ **varare una legge** to pass a law

la **varechina** FEM NOUN
bleach

variabile (FEM **variabile**) ADJECTIVE
1 variable
▫ La qualità del prodotto è molto variabile. The quality of the product is very variable.
2 unsettled
▫ Il tempo si manterrà variabile. The weather will continue to be unsettled.

la **varicella** FEM NOUN
chickenpox

la **varietà** (PL le **varietà**) FEM NOUN
variety
▫ Hanno una grande varietà di piatti. They have a great variety of dishes.

vario (FEM **varia**) ADJECTIVE
varied
▫ Il paesaggio è molto vario. The landscape is very varied.
■ **vari** various ▫ Devo vedere varie persone oggi. I've got to see various people today.

la **vasca** (PL le **vasche**) FEM NOUN
tub
■ **vasca da bagno** bathtub
■ **vasca dei pesci** fish tank

la **vaschetta** FEM NOUN
tub
▫ una vaschetta di gelato a tub of ice cream

la **vaselina** FEM NOUN
Vaseline®

il **vasetto** MASC NOUN
jar
▫ un vasetto di marmellata a jar of jam

il **vaso** MASC NOUN
1 vase
2 flowerpot

il **vassoio** MASC NOUN
tray

vasto (FEM **vasta**) ADJECTIVE
vast
▫ una vasta area a vast area
■ **su vasta scala** on a huge scale

ve ▷ see **vi**

la **vecchia** FEM NOUN
old woman

vecchio (FEM **vecchia**, MASC PL **vecchi**, FEM PL **vecchie**) ADJECTIVE
▷ see also **vecchio** NOUN
old
▫ Ho una macchina vecchia. I've got an old car. ▫ È un mio vecchio amico. He's an old friend of mine. ▫ È più vecchio di me. He's older than me. ▫ la casa più vecchia della via the oldest house in the street

il **vecchio** (PL i **vecchi**) MASC NOUN
▷ see also **vecchio** ADJECTIVE
old man
■ **i vecchi** the old

vedere VERB [119]
to see
▫ Non ci vedo senza occhiali. I can't see without my glasses. ▫ Fammi vedere il tuo tema. Let me see your essay. ▫ Non lo vedo da molto tempo. I haven't seen him for a long time.
■ **Ci vediamo domani!** See you tomorrow!
■ **farsi vedere** to be seen ▫ Da quella volta non si è fatto più vedere. He hasn't been seen since.
■ **Si fa vedere ogni tanto.** He comes to see us from time to time.
■ **Non lo posso vedere.** I can't stand him.
■ **Non vedo l'ora di conoscerlo.** I can't wait to meet him.

la **vedova** FEM NOUN
widow
□ Mia madre è vedova. My mother is a widow.
■ **rimanere vedova** to be widowed

il **vedovo** MASC NOUN
widower
□ Mio padre è vedovo. My father is a widower.
■ **rimanere vedovo** to be widowed

la **veduta** FEM NOUN
view
□ Da quassù si ha una stupenda veduta sul mare. You get a wonderful view of the sea from up here.
■ **di larghe vedute** broad-minded □ I miei sono di larghe vedute. My parents are broad-minded.
■ **di vedute ristrette** narrow-minded

vegetale (FEM **vegetale**) ADJECTIVE
vegetable

vegetariano (FEM **vegetariana**) ADJECTIVE, MASC/FEM NOUN
vegetarian

la **vegetazione** FEM NOUN
vegetation

il **veglione** MASC NOUN
party
□ il veglione di Capodanno New Year's Eve party

il **veicolo** MASC NOUN
vehicle

la **vela** FEM NOUN
1 sail *(on boat)*
2 sailing
■ **barca a vela** sailing boat
■ **Tutto va a gonfie vele.** Everything's going perfectly.

il **veleno** MASC NOUN
poison

velenoso (FEM **velenosa**) ADJECTIVE
poisonous

la **velina** FEM NOUN
■ **carta velina** tissue paper

il **velluto** MASC NOUN
velvet
□ un paio di pantaloni di velluto a pair of velvet trousers
■ **velluto a coste** corduroy

il **velo** MASC NOUN
veil

veloce (FEM **veloce**) ADJECTIVE, ADVERB
fast
□ È una macchina veloce. It's a fast car. □ Guidi troppo veloce. You drive too fast. □ La mia moto è più veloce della tua. My motorbike is faster than yours. □ È uno dei corridori più veloci del mondo. He's one of the fastest drivers in the world.
■ **Su, veloce, corri a casa!** Quick, go home!

la **velocità** (PL le **velocità**) FEM NOUN
speed
□ Guidava a tutta velocità. He was driving at full speed.

la **vena** FEM NOUN
vein
□ le vene e le arterie veins and arteries
■ **Oggi non sono in vena.** I'm not in the mood today.

la **vendemmia** FEM NOUN
grape harvest

vendere VERB [27]
to sell
□ L'ho venduto per dieci euro. I sold it for ten euros.
■ **'vendesi'** 'for sale'

la **vendetta** FEM NOUN
revenge
■ **farsi vendetta** to take one's revenge □ Ha deciso di farsi vendetta da solo. He decided to take his revenge.

vendicarsi VERB [18, AUX **essere**]
to take revenge
□ Vuole vendicarsi di loro. He wants to take revenge on them.
■ **Voglio vendicarmi.** I want revenge.

la **vendita** FEM NOUN
sale
□ reparto vendite sales department □ I biglietti saranno in vendita da venerdì. Tickets will be on sale from Friday. □ Hanno messo in vendita la casa. They have put their house up for sale.
■ **vendita al minuto** retail
■ **vendita all'ingrosso** wholesale

il **venerdì** MASC NOUN
Friday

    LANGUAGE TIP In Italian, days are not
    written with capital letters.

□ L'ho vista venerdì. I saw her on Friday.
■ **di venerdì** on Fridays □ Vado in piscina di venerdì. I go swimming on Fridays.
■ **venerdì scorso** last Friday
■ **venerdì prossimo** next Friday
■ **venerdì santo** Good Friday

Venezia FEM NOUN
Venice
□ Abito a Venezia. I live in Venice.
□ Domani vado a Venezia. I'm going to Venice tomorrow.

venire VERB [120]
1 to come
□ È venuto in macchina. He came by car. □ Da dove vieni? Where do you come from? □ Vieni a trovarci. Come and see us! □ È venuto il momento di dire la verità. The time has come to tell the truth.
■ **Quanto viene?** How much is it?
■ **Mi è venuta un'idea!** I've had an idea!

■ **Gli è venuto il mal di testa.** He's got a headache.

■ **Mi viene da piangere.** I feel like crying.

2 to turn out

□ Il dolce è venuto bene. The cake turned out well.

3 to be

□ Viene venduto al chilo. It's sold by the kilo.

il **ventaglio** MASC NOUN

fan

ventenne (FEM **ventenne**) ADJECTIVE, MASC/FEM NOUN

twenty-year-old

ventesimo (FEM **ventesima**) ADJECTIVE

twentieth

□ il ventesimo secolo the twentieth century

venti NUMBER

twenty

□ Ha vent'anni. He is twenty.

■ **alle venti** at eight p.m.

■ **il venti dicembre** the twentieth of December

il **ventilatore** MASC NOUN

fan

il **vento** MASC NOUN

wind

□ contro vento against the wind

■ **C'è vento.** It's windy.

la **vera** FEM NOUN

wedding ring

veramente ADVERB

1 really

□ È veramente bella. She's really beautiful.

2 actually

□ Veramente non ne sapevo niente. Actually, I didn't know anything about it.

la **veranda** FEM NOUN

1 veranda

2 conservatory

il **verbo** MASC NOUN

verb

□ un verbo transitivo a transitive verb

verde (FEM **verde**) ADJECTIVE, MASC NOUN

green

□ una camicia verde scuro a dark green shirt

■ **essere al verde** to be broke

■ **i Verdi** (political party) the Greens

la **verdura** FEM NOUN

vegetables pl

□ Non mi piace la verdura. I don't like vegetables.

■ **negozio di frutta e verdura** greengrocer's

vergine (FEM **vergine**) ADJECTIVE

▷ see also **vergine** NOUN

virgin

■ **essere vergine** to be a virgin

■ **pura lana vergine** pure new wool

la **vergine** FEM NOUN

▷ see also **vergine** ADJECTIVE

virgin

■ **Vergine** Virgo □ Sono della Vergine. I'm Virgo.

la **vergogna** FEM NOUN

embarrassment

□ È arrossito per la vergogna. He went red with embarrassment.

■ **È una vergogna!** It's a disgrace!

vergognarsi VERB [14, aux **essere**]

1 to be ashamed

□ Non ti vergogni di aver copiato all'esame? Aren't you ashamed that you copied in the exam?

■ **Vergognati!** You should be ashamed!

2 to be embarrassed

□ Dai, suonaci qualcosa. — No, mi vergogno. Come on, play something. — No, I'm embarrassed.

vergognoso (FEM **vergognosa**) ADJECTIVE

terrible

□ È vergognoso che debbano ancora succedere cose simili! It's terrible that such things still happen!

verificare VERB [18]

to check

■ **verificarsi** to happen

la **verità** (PL le **verità**) FEM NOUN

truth

□ Hai detto la verità? Did you tell the truth? □ a dire la verità to tell the truth

il **verme** MASC NOUN

worm

la **vernice** FEM NOUN

1 varnish

2 paint

□ vernice fresca wet paint

3 patent leather

□ una borsetta di vernice a patent leather bag

verniciare VERB [13]

1 to varnish

2 to paint

vero (FEM **vera**) ADJECTIVE

▷ see also **vero** NOUN

1 true

□ Vero o falso? True or false? □ Questa è una storia vera. This is a true story. □ Magari fosse vero! If only it were true!

2 real

□ Quei fiori sembrano veri. Those flowers look real. □ Il vero problema è... The real problem is...

■ **vero e proprio** real □ Questo è un vero e proprio affare. This is a real bargain.

3 genuine

□ perle vere genuine pearls □ È un vero Picasso. It's a genuine Picasso.

LANGUAGE TIP To translate ..., **vero?** at the end of a sentence, see the examples below.
□ Questa è la tua macchina, vero? **This is your car, isn't it?** □ Hai finito i compiti, vero? **You've finished your homework, haven't you?** □ Ti piace la cioccolata, vero? **You like chocolate, don't you?**

il **vero** MASC NOUN
▷ *see also* **vero** ADJECTIVE
truth
□ a dire il vero **to tell the truth**

la **verruca** (PL le **verruche**) FEM NOUN
1 wart
2 verruca

la **versamento** FEM NOUN
deposit

versare VERB [68]
1 to pour
□ Mi versi un po' d'acqua? **Can you pour me some water?**
2 to spill
□ Ho versato un po' di vino sulla tovaglia. **I spilt some wine on the tablecloth.**
3 to pay in
□ Vorrei versare mille euro nel mio conto corrente. **I'd like to pay a thousand euros into my current account.**

la **versione** FEM NOUN
version
□ Vorrei sentire la sua versione dell'accaduto. **I'd like to hear her version of what happened.**
■ **una versione più aggiornata della guida** a more up-to-date edition of the guide
■ **in versione originale** *(film)* in the original language

il **verso** MASC NOUN
▷ *see also* **verso** PREPOSITION
1 line *(of poetry)*
2 noise *(of animal)*
□ Che verso fa il maiale? **What noise does a pig make?**
■ **fare il verso a qualcuno** to mimic somebody □ Faceva il verso al professore. **He mimicked the teacher.**
■ **Non c'è verso di fargli cambiare idea.** There's no way of making him change his mind.

verso PREPOSITION
▷ *see also* **verso** NOUN
1 towards
□ Veniva verso di me. **He was coming towards me.** □ Stavo camminando verso la stazione quando l'ho visto. **I was walking towards the station when I saw him.**
■ **È tardi. Faremo bene ad avviarci verso casa.** It's late. We'd better head for home.
■ **verso l'alto** upwards □ Tirare l'anello verso l'alto. **Pull the ring upwards.**
■ **verso il basso** downwards

2 around
□ Ci rivediamo verso la fine di novembre. **I'll see you around the end of November.**
□ Arriverò verso le sette. **I'll be there at around seven.**

vertebrale (FEM **vertebrale**) ADJECTIVE
■ **colonna vertebrale** spine

verticale (FEM **verticale**) ADJECTIVE
vertical

le **vertigini** FEM PL NOUN
■ **soffrire di vertigini** to be afraid of heights
□ Non vengo lassù perché soffro di vertigini. **I'm not coming up because I'm afraid of heights.**

la **vescica** (PL le **vesciche**) FEM NOUN
1 blister
□ Ho una vescica sul piede. **I've got a blister on my foot.**
2 bladder

il **vescovo** MASC NOUN
bishop

la **vespa** FEM NOUN
wasp

la **vestaglia** FEM NOUN
dressing gown

vestirsi VERB [41, aux **essere**]
1 to get dressed
□ Si è vestito in fretta ed è uscito. **He got dressed quickly and went out.** □ Vestiti, che usciamo. **Get dressed, we're going out.**
2 to dress
□ Si veste bene. **She dresses well.**
■ **vestirsi da** to dress up as □ Si è vestito da donna. **He dressed up as a woman.**

il **vestito** MASC NOUN
1 dress
2 suit *(men's)*
■ **vestiti** clothes □ Ho messo alcuni vestiti in valigia. **I put some clothes in a suitcase.**

il **veterinario**, la **veterinaria** MASC/FEM NOUN
vet

il **vetraio** MASC NOUN
glazier

la **vetrata** FEM NOUN
1 big window
2 stained-glass window

vetrato (FEM **vetrata**) ADJECTIVE
glazed *(door)*
■ **carta vetrata** sandpaper

la **vetrina** FEM NOUN
window *(shop)*
□ C'è una gonna che mi piace in vetrina. **There's a skirt I like in the window.**

il/la **vetrinista** (MASC PL i **vetrinisti**, FEM PL le **vetriniste**) MASC/FEM NOUN
window dresser
□ Fa la vetrinista. **She is a window dresser.**

il **vetro** MASC NOUN
glass
□ un vaso di vetro a glass vase
■ **pulire i vetri** to clean the windows

la **vetta** FEM NOUN
summit
□ Abbiamo raggiunto la vetta in quattro ore. We reached the summit in four hours.

vi PRONOUN
▷ see also **vi** ADVERB

> LANGUAGE TIP **vi** becomes **ve** before **lo**, **la**, **li**, **le** and **ne**.

1 you
□ Vi darò un consiglio. I'll give you some advice. □ Vorrebbero aiutarvi. They'd like to help you. □ Vi scriverò. I'll write to you. □ Vi ha salutato? Did he say hello to you? □ Ve lo do subito. I'll give it to you in a moment. □ Vi ha sorriso. He smiled at you. □ Vi stava cercando. She was looking for you.

2 yourselves
□ Vi siete fatti male? Did you hurt yourselves? □ Vi siete divertiti? Did you enjoy yourselves?
■ **Pettinatevi.** Comb your hair.

vi ADVERB
▷ see also **vi** PRONOUN
there
□ Vi sono stato parecchie volte. I've been there several times. □ Vi sono molti modi per farlo. There are many ways of doing it.

la **via** FEM NOUN
▷ see also **via** MASC NOUN, ADVERB
street
□ Abito in una via molto stretta. I live in a very narrow street.
■ **Non c'è via d'uscita.** There's no way out.
■ **spedire per via aerea** to send by airmail

il **via** MASC NOUN
▷ see also **via** FEM NOUN, ADVERB
starting signal
□ Quando darai il via? When are you going to give the starting signal?

via ADVERB
▷ see also **via** MASC NOUN, FEM NOUN
away
□ Vai via! Go away! □ L'ho buttato via. I threw it away.
■ **Pronti, attenti, via!** Ready, steady, go!

viaggiare VERB [58]
to travel
□ Viaggi spesso per lavoro? Do you travel much for your job? □ Mi piace viaggiare. I like travelling.

il **viaggiatore,** la **viaggiatrice** MASC/FEM NOUN
traveller

il **viaggio** MASC NOUN
1 journey

□ un viaggio faticoso a tiring journey □ Avete fatto buon viaggio? Did you have a good journey?
■ **Vorrei fare un viaggio in Cina.** I'd like to visit China.

2 trip (shorter)
□ Buon viaggio! Have a good trip!
■ **viaggio d'affari** business trip □ Papà è in viaggio d'affari. Dad's on a business trip.
■ **spese di viaggio** travelling expenses
■ **agenzia di viaggi** travel agency
■ **viaggio di nozze** honeymoon □ Dove andranno in viaggio di nozze? Where are they going on their honeymoon?
■ **viaggio organizzato** package tour □ Sono andato a Praga con un viaggio organizzato. I went to Prague on a package tour.

il **viale** MASC NOUN
avenue

la **vicenda** FEM NOUN
1 event
□ le vicende che hanno portato alla guerra the events that led up to the war

2 story
□ È una vicenda estremamente complicata. It's an extremely complicated story.
■ **a vicenda** each other □ Ci siamo aiutati a vicenda. We helped each other.

viceversa ADVERB
vice versa

vicino (FEM **vicina**) ADJECTIVE, ADVERB
▷ see also **vicino** NOUN
near
□ Abitiamo qui vicino. We live near here. □ La stazione è abbastanza vicina. The station is quite near. □ La mia macchina è più vicina della tua. My car is nearer than yours. □ Dov'è il telefono più vicino? Where's the nearest phone?
■ **un paese vicino** a nearby village
■ **Vieni più vicino.** Come closer.
■ **Mi sono stati molto vicini.** They were very supportive towards me.
■ **vicino a** near □ Il campanello è vicino alla porta. The bell is near the door.
■ **Era seduta vicino a me.** She was sitting next to me.
■ **guardare qualcosa da vicino** to take a close look at something □ Guardalo da vicino! Take a close look at it!

il **vicino,** la **vicina** MASC/FEM NOUN
▷ see also **vicino** ADJECTIVE, ADVERB
neighbour
□ i miei vicini di casa my next-door neighbours

il **vicolo** MASC NOUN
alley
■ **vicolo cieco** blind alley

il **video** (PL i **video**) MASC NOUN
video

la **videocamera** FEM NOUN
camcorder

la **videocassetta** FEM NOUN
video
□ Abbiamo noleggiato una videocassetta.
We rented a video.

videochiamare VERB [68]
to video call

il **videofonino** MASC NOUN
videophone

il **videogioco** (PL i **videogiochi**) MASC NOUN
video game

il **videoregistratore** MASC NOUN
video recorder

vietare VERB [68]
to forbid
□ Il dottore gli ha vietato di fumare. The doctor
has forbidden him to smoke.
■ **Fallo, se vuoi. Chi te lo vieta?** Do it if you
like. Who's stopping you?

vietato (FEM **vietata**) ADJECTIVE
■ **Qui è vietato fumare.** Smoking is not
allowed here.
■ **'Vietato fumare'** 'No smoking'
■ **È un film vietato ai minori di 18 anni.**
You have to be eighteen to see that film.

il **vigile** MASC NOUN
traffic warden
□ Il vigile mi ha dato la multa. The traffic
warden gave me a ticket.
■ **vigile del fuoco** firefighter
■ **i vigili del fuoco** the fire brigade *sing*
□ Qualcuno ha chiamato i vigili del fuoco.
Somebody called the fire brigade.

la **vigilia** FEM NOUN
eve
□ la vigilia di Natale Christmas Eve □ alla vigilia
di on the eve of

il **vigliacco,** la **vigliacca** (MASC PL i **vigliacchi**,
FEM PL le **vigliacche**) MASC/FEM NOUN
coward

il **vigneto** MASC NOUN
vineyard

la **vignetta** FEM NOUN
1 cartoon
2 motorway pass

il **vigore** MASC NOUN
■ **essere in vigore** *(law)* to be in force
■ **entrare in vigore** to come into force

la **villa** FEM NOUN
house

il **villaggio** MASC NOUN
village
□ un villaggio africano an African village

la **villetta** FEM NOUN
house with a garden

vimini MASC PL NOUN
■ **una sedia di vimini** a wicker chair

vincere VERB [121]
to win
□ Ieri abbiamo vinto la partita. We won the
match yesterday.

il **vincitore,** la **vincitrice** MASC/FEM NOUN
winner

il **vino** MASC NOUN
wine
□ vino bianco white wine □ vino rosso red
wine

viola (FEM+PL **viola**) ADJECTIVE
▷ *see also* **viola** NOUN
purple

la **viola** FEM NOUN
▷ *see also* **viola** ADJECTIVE
violet *(flower)*

violentare VERB [68]
to rape

violento (FEM **violenta**) ADJECTIVE
violent

la **violenza** FEM NOUN
violence
■ **violenza carnale** rape

violetto (FEM **violetta**) ADJECTIVE, MASC NOUN
violet *(colour)*

il/la **violinista** (MASC PL i **violinisti**, FEM PL
le **violiniste**) MASC/FEM NOUN
violinist

il **violino** MASC NOUN
violin

il **violoncello** MASC NOUN
cello

la **vipera** FEM NOUN
viper

virale (FEM **virale**) ADJECTIVE
viral
□ marketing virale viral marketing

la **virgola** FEM NOUN
1 comma
2 point
□ 5,7% 5.7%

le **virgolette** FEM PL NOUN
inverted commas
□ una parola scritta tra virgolette a word
written in inverted commas

virtuale (FEM **virtuale**) ADJECTIVE
■ **realtà virtuale** virtual reality

il **virus** (PL i **virus**) MASC NOUN
virus

viscido (FEM **viscida**) ADJECTIVE
slimy
□ ancora più viscido even slimier

la **visione** FEM NOUN
vision
□ una visione della Madonna a vision of the
Madonna
■ **film in prima visione** newly released
film

la **visita** FEM NOUN

visit

■ **fare visita a qualcuno** to visit somebody □ Andiamo a fargli visita. Let's go and visit him.

■ **orario delle visite** visiting hours

■ **visita medica** medical □ Devi fare una visita medica. You have to have a medical.

■ **visita di controllo** check-up □ Ho fatto una visita di controllo. I had a check-up.

■ **visita guidata** guided tour □ Quanto costa la visita guidata della città? How much is a guided tour of the city?

visitare VERB [68]

1 to visit

□ Hai già visitato la National Gallery? Have you visited the National Gallery? □ Visitate il nostro sito Internet. Visit our web site.

2 to examine

□ Il dottore l'ha visitata subito. The doctor examined her immediately.

il **visitatore**, la **visitatrice** MASC/FEM NOUN

visitor

il **viso** MASC NOUN

face

□ Si è spalmata la crema sul viso. She rubbed the cream into her face.

il **visone** MASC NOUN

mink

□ una pelliccia di visone a mink coat

la **vista** FEM NOUN

1 sight

□ La vista mi si sta indebolendo. My sight is deteriorating.

■ **Ha la vista buona.** He has good eyesight.

■ **a prima vista** at first sight □ È stato amore a prima vista. It was love at first sight.

■ **conoscere qualcuno di vista** to know somebody by sight □ Lo conosco solo di vista. I only know him by sight.

■ **perdere qualcuno di vista** to lose sight of somebody □ Correva così veloce che l'ho perso di vista. He was running so fast that I lost sight of him.

■ **Dopo aver finito l'università si sono persi di vista.** They lost touch after they left university.

2 view

□ una camera con vista sul lago a room with a view of the lake

il **visto** MASC NOUN

1 visa

2 tick (on form)

la **vita** FEM NOUN

1 life

□ Ha rischiato la vita per aiutarla. He risked his life to help her. □ È piena di vita. She's full of life.

■ **essere in vita** to be alive □ Quando sono arrivati era ancora in vita. When they got there he was still alive.

2 waist

□ Mi è un po' largo in vita. It's a bit loose round the waist.

la **vitamina** FEM NOUN

vitamin

la **vite** FEM NOUN

1 screw

2 vine

il **vitello** MASC NOUN

1 calf

2 veal

□ una scaloppina di vitello a veal escalope

la **vittima** FEM NOUN

victim

il **vitto** MASC NOUN

■ **vitto e alloggio** board and lodging

la **vittoria** FEM NOUN

victory

viva EXCLAMATION

■ **Viva gli sposi!** To the bride and groom!

■ **Viva l'Italia!** Hooray for Italy!

vivace (FEM **vivace**) ADJECTIVE

lively

□ una ragazza vivace a lively girl □ È più vivace della sorella. She's livelier than her sister.

■ **un colore vivace** a bright colour

vivere VERB [122]

to live

□ Mi piacerebbe vivere in Scozia. I'd like to live in Scotland.

■ **modo di vivere** way of life

la **vivisezione** FEM NOUN

vivisection

vivo (FEM **viva**) ADJECTIVE

1 alive

□ Il pesce era ancora vivo. The fish was still alive.

2 live

□ esperimenti su animali vivi experiments on live animals

■ **un colore vivo** a bright colour

■ **farsi vivo** to keep in touch □ Fatti vivo! Keep in touch!

■ **È da tanto che non si fa viva.** She hasn't been in touch for a long time.

viziato (FEM **viziata**) ADJECTIVE

1 spoilt

□ un bambino viziato a spoilt child

2 stale

□ aria viziata stale air

il **vizio** MASC NOUN

1 bad habit

□ Il mio unico vizio è quello di mangiarmi le unghie. Biting my nails is my only bad habit.

■ **Ha il vizio del gioco.** He's addicted to gambling.

2 vice

□ i vizi e le virtù vices and virtues

il **vocabolario** MASC NOUN

dictionary

□ un vocabolario di italiano an Italian dictionary

il **vocabolo** MASC NOUN
word

la **vocale** FEM NOUN
vowel

la **voce** FEM NOUN
voice

□ Ho perso la voce. I've lost my voice.

■ **parlare ad alta voce** to speak loudly
■ **parlare a bassa voce** to speak quietly
■ **Leggi il brano ad alta voce.** Read the passage aloud.
■ **voci di corridoio** rumours □ Sono solo voci di corridoio. They're only rumours.

la **voglia** FEM NOUN

■ **aver voglia di fare qualcosa** to feel like doing something □ Adesso non ho voglia di mangiare. I don't feel like eating just now.
■ **morire dalla voglia di fare qualcosa** to be dying to do something □ Muoio dalla voglia di vederlo. I'm dying to see him.

voi PRONOUN
you

□ Io ci vado, voi fate come volete. I'm going, you do what you like. □ Venite anche voi? Are you coming too? □ Sono più giovani di voi. They are younger than you.

■ **Non lo sapevate nemmeno voi.** You didn't even know it yourselves.

il **volante** MASC NOUN
steering wheel

il **volantino** MASC NOUN
leaflet

volare VERB [68, aux **avere** or **essere**]
to fly

volenteroso (FEM **volenterosa**) ADJECTIVE
willing

□ un alunno volenteroso a willing pupil

volentieri ADVERB
willingly

□ L'ho fatto volentieri. I did it willingly.

■ **Volentieri!** 1 Certainly! □ Mi aiuti? — Volentieri! Will you help me? — Certainly!
2 *(in reply to invitation)* I'd love to! □ Vieni da noi stasera? — Grazie, volentieri! Would you like to come over this evening? — Yes, I'd love to!

volere VERB [123]
to want

□ Voglio comprare una macchina nuova. I want to buy a new car. □ Che cosa vuoi che faccia? What do you want me to do? □ Quanto vuole per quel quadro? How much do you want for that picture?

■ **Devo pagare subito o posso pagare domani? — Come vuole.** Do I have to pay now or can I pay tomorrow? — As you prefer.

LANGUAGE TIP When something is being offered or in conditional sentences, use 'would like'.

□ Vuole un po' di caffè? Would you like some coffee? □ Adesso vorrei andarmene. I'd like to go now. □ Vorrebbe andare in America. She'd like to go to America.

■ **volerci** 1 to take □ Quanto ci vuole per andare da Roma a Firenze? How long does it take to get from Rome to Florence? 2 to need □ Per una giacca ci vogliono quattro metri di stoffa. You need four metres of material to make a jacket. □ Ci vuole il pane. We need bread.

■ **volere dire** to mean □ Cosa vuol dire questa parola? What does this word mean?

■ **senza volere** accidentally □ L'ho spinto senza volere. I accidentally pushed him.

volgare (FEM **volgare**) ADJECTIVE
vulgar

il **volo** MASC NOUN
flight

□ due ore di volo a two-hour flight

■ **volo charter** charter flight
■ **volo di linea** scheduled flight
■ **prendere al volo** to only just catch □ Ho preso il treno al volo. I only just caught the train.
■ **capire al volo** to understand immediately □ Ha capito al volo la situazione. He understood the situation immediately.

la **volontà** FEM NOUN
will

□ L'ha fatto di sua spontanea volontà. He did it of his own free will.

il **volontario,** la **volontaria** MASC/FEM NOUN
volunteer

□ C'è qualche volontario? Are there any volunteers?

■ **Lavoro come volontario.** I'm a voluntary worker.

la **volpe** FEM NOUN
fox

la **volta** FEM NOUN
time

□ La prima volta che l'ho visto... The first time I saw him... □ Ti ricordi quella volta che... Do you remember the time when...
□ Questa volta ci vado io. I'll go this time.
□ Gli telefonerò un'altra volta, adesso non ne ho voglia. I'll phone him some other time, I don't feel like it now. □ Tre volte quattro fa dodici. Three times four makes twelve.

■ **una volta** once □ Le ho scritto una volta sola. I wrote to her only once.
■ **Una volta si camminava di più.** People used to walk more.
■ **una volta alla settimana** once a week

■ **due volte** twice □ Gli ho telefonato due volte. I phoned him twice.

■ **tre volte** three times

■ **certe volte** sometimes □ Certe volte sono un po' triste. I feel a bit down sometimes.

■ **una volta tanto** just for once □ Una volta tanto potresti pagare tu. You could pay, just for once.

■ **una volta o l'altra** one of these days □ Una volta o l'altra glielo dirò. I'll tell him one of these days.

■ **una volta per tutte** once and for all □ Deciditi una volta per tutte. Make up your mind once and for all.

■ **di volta in volta** as we go □ Decideremo di volta in volta cosa fare. We'll decide what to do as we go.

■ **una cosa per volta** one thing at a time □ Facciamo una cosa per volta. Let's do one thing at a time.

■ **C'era una volta...** Once upon a time there was...

voltare VERB [68]
to turn

□ Volta a sinistra e poi va' dritto. Turn left and then go straight on. □ Voltate pagina. Turn the page.

■ **voltarsi** to turn □ Voltati dall'altra parte. Turn the other way.

■ **Si è allontanato senza voltarsi indietro.** He went off without looking back.

il **voltastomaco** MASC NOUN

■ **dare il voltastomaco a qualcuno** to make somebody sick □ Mi dà il voltastomaco. It makes me sick.

il **volume** MASC NOUN
volume

□ Potresti abbassare il volume? Could you turn down the volume, please?

vomitare VERB [68]
to vomit

il **vomito** MASC NOUN
vomit

la **vongola** FEM NOUN
clam

vostro (FEM **vostra**) ADJECTIVE
▷ see also **vostro** PRONOUN
your

□ i vostri libri your books □ È colpa vostra. It's your fault.

■ **un vostro amico** a friend of yours

vostro (FEM **vostra**) PRONOUN
▷ see also **vostro** ADJECTIVE
yours

□ La nostra casa è più grande della vostra. Our house is bigger than yours. □ Di chi è questo? — È vostro. Whose is this? — It's yours.

votare VERB [68]
to vote

□ Ho votato per loro. I voted for them.

il **voto** MASC NOUN

1 mark (at school)
□ Ho preso un bel voto in matematica. I got a good mark in maths.

2 vote (in elections)
□ Hanno vinto per pochi voti. They won by a few votes.

il **vulcano** MASC NOUN
volcano

vuotare VERB [68]
to empty

vuoto (FEM **vuota**) ADJECTIVE
▷ see also **vuoto** NOUN
empty

□ un appartamento vuoto an empty flat

■ **a mani vuote** empty-handed □ È arrivato a mani vuote. He arrived empty-handed.

il **vuoto** MASC NOUN
▷ see also **vuoto** ADJECTIVE

1 gap
□ La sua morte ha lasciato un vuoto tra di noi. His death has left a real gap.

■ **guardare nel vuoto** to gaze into space

■ **avere paura del vuoto** to be afraid of heights

■ **assegno a vuoto** dud cheque

■ **vuoto d'aria** air pocket

■ **Ho fatto un viaggio a vuoto.** It was a wasted journey.

2 empty (bottle)

Ww

il **wafer** (PL i **wafer**) MASC NOUN
wafer

il **water** (PL i **water**) MASC NOUN
toilet
□ L'ho gettato nel water. I threw it in the toilet.

il **watt** (PL i **watt**) MASC NOUN
watt

il **W.C.** (PL i **W.C.**) MASC NOUN
W.C.

la **webcam** (PL le **webcam**) FEM NOUN
webcam

western (FEM+PL **western**) ADJECTIVE, MASC NOUN

■ un film western a western
■ un western all'italiana a spaghetti western

il **windsurf** (PL i **windsurf**) MASC NOUN
1 windsurfer
2 windsurfing
■ **fare windsurf** to go windsurfing

il **würstel** (PL i **würstel**) MASC NOUN
frankfurter
□ un würstel con la senape a frankfurter with mustard
■ **un panino con il würstel** a hot dog

xenofobo (FEM **xenofoba**) ADJECTIVE
<u>xenophobic</u>

lo **xilofono** MASC NOUN
<u>xylophone</u>

Yy

lo **yacht** (PL gli **yacht**) MASC NOUN
yacht

lo **yoga** MASC NOUN
yoga

■ **fare yoga** to do yoga

lo **yogurt** (PL gli **yogurt**) MASC NOUN
yoghurt

□ uno yogurt alla fragola a strawberry yoghurt

Zz

lo **zafferano** MASC NOUN
saffron

lo **zaino** MASC NOUN
rucksack

la **zampa** FEM NOUN
1 leg *(of animal)*
2 paw
3 foot *(of elephant)*
■ **a quattro zampe** on all fours
■ **zampe di gallina** crow's feet

la **zanzara** FEM NOUN
mosquito

la **zanzariera** FEM NOUN
mosquito net

la **zattera** FEM NOUN
raft

la **zebra** FEM NOUN
zebra

la **zecca** (PL le **zecche**) FEM NOUN
1 tick *(insect)*
2 mint *(for money)*

zeppo (FEM **zeppa**) ADJECTIVE
■ **zeppo di...** crammed with... □ Era zeppo di gente. It was crammed with people.

lo **zerbino** MASC NOUN
doormat

lo **zero** MASC NOUN
1 zero
□ tre, due, uno, zero three, two, one, zero □ trenta gradi sotto zero thirty degrees below zero
2 O *(in telephone numbers)*
3 nil
□ Hanno vinto tre a zero. They won three-nil.
4 love *(in tennis)*
□ trenta a zero thirty love
■ **partire da zero** to start from scratch

la **zia** FEM NOUN
aunt

lo **zigomo** MASC NOUN
cheekbone

lo **zigzag** (PL gli **zigzag**) MASC NOUN
■ **andare a zigzag** to zigzag

lo **zingaro**, la **zingara** MASC/FEM NOUN
gypsy

lo **zio** MASC NOUN
uncle
■ **i miei zii** my aunt and uncle

zippare VERB [68]
to zip

la **zitella** FEM NOUN
spinster

zitto (FEM **zitta**) ADJECTIVE
quiet
□ Sta' zitto! Be quiet!

lo **zoccolo** MASC NOUN
1 clog
2 hoof

zodiacale (FEM **zodiacale**) ADJECTIVE
■ **segno zodiacale** sign of the zodiac

lo **zodiaco** MASC NOUN
zodiac

la **zolletta** FEM NOUN
sugar lump

la **zona** FEM NOUN
area
□ una zona malfamata a rough area
■ **zona pedonale** pedestrian precinct

lo **zoo** (PL gli **zoo**) MASC NOUN
zoo

zoppicare VERB [18]
to limp

zoppo (FEM **zoppa**) ADJECTIVE
lame

la **zucca** (PL le **zucche**) FEM NOUN
pumpkin

zuccherare VERB [68]
to sugar

zuccherato (FEM **zuccherata**) ADJECTIVE
sweetened

la **zuccheriera** FEM NOUN
sugar bowl

lo **zucchero** MASC NOUN
sugar
■ **zucchero a velo** icing sugar
■ **zucchero filato** candy floss

la **zucchina** FEM NOUN
courgette

la **zuppa** FEM NOUN
soup
□ una zuppa di verdura a vegetable soup

zuppo (FEM **zuppa**) ADJECTIVE
soaked
□ Sono zuppo. I'm soaked.

Italian in Action

- With an area of about 300,000 km², Italy is seventh in size among the countries of Western Europe. Italy's population is about 61 million.

- The Po is the longest river in Italy, and is around 650 km long.

- Italy has four active volcanoes: Etna, Vesuvius, Stromboli and Vulcano. Etna is Europe's most active volcano.

- Italy's map outline has often been compared to a boot, kicking the unfortunate island of Sicily as if it were a football. Italy also includes the island of Sardinia.

- Italy encloses two very much smaller independent countries – the Vatican City, within Rome, and San Marino.

Some useful phrases

Questo è il mio ragazzo.	This is my boyfriend.
Questa è la mia ragazza.	This is my girlfriend.
Questa è mia moglie.	This is my wife.
Le presento mio marito.	I'd like to introduce you to my husband.
Ho due bambini.	I have two children.
Mio figlio/Mia figlia ha dieci anni.	My son/My daughter is ten years old.
I miei figli sono grandi.	My children are grown up.
Ho due nipoti.	I have two grandchildren.
Sono divorziato/divorziata.	I'm divorced.
Sono separato/separata.	I'm separated.
Questa è mia suocera.	This is my mother-in-law.
Questo è mio suocero.	This is my father-in-law.
È mio genero.	He is my son-in-law.
È mia nuora.	She is my daughter-in-law.

Rapporti	Relationships
Andiamo molto d'accordo.	We get on very well.
Litighiamo sempre.	We are always quarrelling.
Ho molti amici.	I have a lot of friends.
I nostri amici vivono a ...	Our friends live in ...
Siamo in vacanza con degli amici.	We are on holiday with friends.
Vado d'accordo con il mio papà.	I get on well with my dad.
Vedo il mio papà durante il fine settimana.	I see my dad at weekends.
Abbiamo litigato.	We've quarrelled.
Ci occupiamo dei nostri nipoti.	We look after our grandchildren.
I nostri genitori/nonni sono molto severi.	Our parents/ grandparents are very strict.
John ed io ci siamo separati.	John and I have split up.
È un ragazzo simpatico.	He is a nice boy.
È simpaticissima.	She's really nice.
Paolo mi è molto simpatico.	I really like Paolo.
Non la posso soffrire!	I can't stand her!

Componenti della famiglia	Members of the family
mio padre, il mio papà	my father, my dad
mia madre, la mia mamma	my mother, my mum
mio fratello	my brother
mia sorella	my sister
mio zio	my uncle
mia zia	my aunt
mio nipote	my nephew/ my grandson
mia nipote	my niece/ my granddaughter
mio nonno	my grandfather, my granddad
mia nonna	my grandmother, my gran
i miei nonni	my grandparents
mia suocera	my mother-in-law
mio suocero	my father-in-law
i miei suoceri	my in-laws (i.e. parents-in-law)
mio genero	my son-in-law
mia nuora	my daughter-in-law
mio cognato	my brother-in-law
mia cognata	my sister-in-law
il mio patrigno/ la mia matrigna	my stepfather/ my stepmother
il mio fratellastro/ la mia sorellastra	my stepbrother/ my stepsister

Emozioni	Emotions
essere ...	**to be ...**
triste	sad
contento/contenta	pleased
felice	happy
arrabbiato/arrabbiata	angry
annoiato/annoiata	bored
innamorato/innamorata	in love
sorpreso/sorpresa	surprised
Sono innamorata di Adriano.	I'm in love with Adriano.
Sono contento che tu venga.	I'm pleased you're coming.
Sono così triste!	I'm so sad!
Perché sei arrabbiato?	Why are you angry?
Spero che tu non sia troppo arrabbiato.	I hope you're not too angry.

At home

Da casa in città	From home into town
Il centro è abbastanza lontano da casa mia.	The town centre is quite a long way from my house.
Sto a cinque minuti dal centro.	I live five minutes from the centre of town.
Devo prendere l'autobus per andare in città.	I have to catch a bus into town.
È molto difficile parcheggiare in città.	It is very difficult to park in town.
In genere vado in città a piedi.	I usually walk into town.

Dove vivi?	Where do you live?
Vivo ...	**I live ...**
in un paese	in a village
in una cittadina	in a small town
in centro	in the town centre
nella periferia di Londra	on the outskirts of London
in campagna	in the country
sul mare	by the sea
a 100 km da Manchester	100 km from Manchester
a nord di Birmingham	north of Birmingham
in una villetta	in a detached house
in una villetta bifamiliare	in a semi-detached house
in una casa a due piani	in a two-storey house
in un condominio	in a block of flats
Vivo in un appartamento ...	**I live in a flat ...**
al piano terra	on the ground floor
al primo piano	on the first floor
al secondo piano	on the second floor
all'ultimo piano	on the top floor
in un edificio nuovo	in a new building
in un bel palazzo storico	in a beautiful old building

A casa	At home
Al piano terra c'è ...	**On the ground floor there is ...**
la cucina	the kitchen
il salotto	the living room
la sala da pranzo	the dining room
la sala	the lounge
Al piano di sopra c'è ...	**Upstairs there is ...**
la mia/nostra camera	my/our bedroom
la camera di mio figlio	my son's bedroom
la camera di mia figlia	my daughter's bedroom
la camera degli ospiti	the spare bedroom
il bagno	the bathroom
uno studio	a study
un giardino	a garden
un campo di calcio	a football pitch
un campo da tennis	a tennis court
un vicino	a neighbour
le persone che stanno qui di fronte	the people opposite
i vicini di casa	the next-door neighbours

Some useful phrases

La mia casa è molto piccola.	My house is very small.
C'è un giardino.	There is a garden.
Mi piace la mia camera.	I like my bedroom.
Non abbiamo il garage.	We don't have a garage.
Vivo in una zona tranquilla.	I live in a quiet area.
C'è un centro sportivo vicino a casa mia.	There's a sports centre near to my house.
Non ci sono molti negozi nel mio paese.	There aren't many shops in my village.
Traslochiamo il mese prossimo.	We're moving next month.

Nelle vicinanze	In the local area
un cinema	a cinema
un teatro	a theatre
un museo	a museum
un parco	a park
un sportello automatico	a cash machine
un caffè	a café
un Internet cafè	an internet café
l'ufficio turistico	the tourist office
una cattedrale	a cathedral
una chiesa	a church
una moschea	a mosque
un centro commerciale	a shopping centre
una banca	a bank
la piscina	the swimming pool
la pista da pattinaggio su ghiaccio	the ice rink
la biblioteca	the library
il municipio	the town hall
il mercato	the market

Mezzi di trasporto	Means of transport
un autobus	a bus
una corriera	a coach
un battello	a boat
un traghetto	a ferry
un vaporetto	a waterbus (Venice)
la metropolitana	the underground
il tram	the tram
il treno	the train
la stazione	the station
la stazione delle corriere	the bus station
una fermata della metropolitana	an underground station
A che ora è il prossimo treno per Milano?	What time is the next train to Milan?
Vorrei un biglietto di sola andata per Latina.	I'd like a single to Latina.
Un biglietto di andata e ritorno per Lecco.	A return to Lecco, please.

Città o campagna? — Town or country?

È più interessante vivere in città.	It's more interesting to live in a town.
In campagna c'è meno inquinamento.	In the country there's less pollution.
Preferisco la campagna perché ho due cani.	I prefer the country because I've got two dogs.
In città è più facile incontrarsi con gli amici.	In a town it's easier to meet your friends.

Indicazioni	Directions
di fronte	opposite
vicino a	next to
vicino	near
tra ... e ...	between ... and ...
Dov'è la stazione delle corriere?	Where's the bus station?
Sto cercando l'ufficio turistico.	I'm looking for the tourist office.
Vada fino alla fine della strada.	Go right to the end of the street.
Giri a destra.	Turn right.
Attraversi il ponte.	Cross the bridge.
Prenda la prima strada a sinistra.	Take the first street on the left.
È sulla sua destra.	It's on your right.
È di fronte al cinema.	It's opposite the cinema.
È vicino all'ufficio postale.	It's next to the post office.
Che autobus va alla stazione ferroviaria?	Which bus goes to the train station?

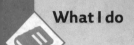

What I do

Lavoro	Work
Ho studiato ...	**I studied ...**
medicina	medicine
legge	law
sociologia	sociology
psicologia	psychology
lingue	languages
architettura	architecture
Vorrei ...	**I'd like to ...**
guadagnare molti soldi	earn lots of money
viaggiare in Sudamerica	travel in South America
scrivere un libro	write a book
lavorare con i bambini	work with children
vincere alla lotteria	win the lottery
Faccio ...	**I am ...**
l'insegnante	a teacher
il/la dentista	a dentist
l'attore/l'attrice	an actor
il/la cantante	a singer
la parrucchiera	a hairdresser
il/la giornalista	a journalist
l'avvocato	a solicitor
Sono ...	**I am ...**
uno studente/una studentessa	a student
un calciatore professionista	a professional footballer
un politico	a politician
Penso che sia ...	**I think it's ...**
interessante	interesting
noioso/noiosa	boring
stancante	tiring
stressante	stressful
facile	easy
troppo difficile	too difficult

Ambizioni	Ambitions
Vorrei ottenere dei buoni risultati agli esami e andare all'università.	I'd like to get good results in my exams and go to university.
Vorrei prendere un anno sabbatico prima di andare all'università.	I'd like to have a gap year before going to university.
Vorremmo andare a vivere in Italia.	We would like to go and live in Italy.
Vorrei trovare un lavoro a Roma.	I want to get a job in Rome.

Lavoro	Work
un curriculum vitae	a CV
un annuncio di lavoro	a job advert
un modulo di richiesta di lavoro	an application form
un colloquio	an interview
un lavoro estivo/un lavoro fisso	a holiday job/a permanent job
un lavoro temporaneo	a temporary job
Lavoro a tempo pieno/a tempo parziale.	I work full-time/part-time.
Ha esperienza?	Do you have any experience?
Lavoro dal lunedì al venerdì, dalle 9 alle 5.	I work Monday to Friday, from 9am to 5pm.
Sto cercando lavoro come segretaria.	I'm looking for a secretarial job.
Sto cercando un lavoro part-time.	I'm looking for a part-time job.

Sport	Sports
Gioco a ...	**I play ...**
calcio	football
pallacanestro	basketball
golf	golf
rugby	rugby
tennis	tennis
ping-pong	table tennis
Scio.	I ski.
Vado in canoa.	I canoe.
Vado in mountain-bike.	I go mountain-biking.
Faccio skateboard.	I go skateboarding.
Vado in palestra.	I go to the gym.
Faccio danza classica.	I do ballet.
Nuoto.	I swim.
Vado a cavallo.	I go horse riding.
Ho intenzione di fare un corso di vela quest'estate.	I'm going to do a sailing course this summer.
Non ho mai sciato.	I've never been skiing.
Ho intenzione di imparare ad andare in canoa.	I'm going to learn how to canoe.

Tempo libero	Leisure
A mio marito piace andare a vela.	My husband loves sailing.
Mi piace ascoltare musica.	I love listening to music.
Mi piace andare a fare compere con i miei amici/i miei nipoti.	I love shopping with my friends/my grandchildren.
Trascorro molto tempo in giardino.	I spend a long time in my garden.
Preferirei fare giardinaggio piuttosto che guardare la televisione.	I'd rather garden than watch television.
Odio i videogame.	I hate video games.

Strumenti musicali	Musical instruments
Suono ...	**I play ...**
il piano	the piano
la chitarra	the guitar
il flauto	the flute
Ho imparato a suonare il piano a scuola.	I learnt to play the piano at school.
Suoni qualche strumento?	Do you play any instruments?
Suono in un gruppo.	I play in a band.
Mio figlio/Mia figlia suona in un gruppo.	My son/My daughter plays in a band.

Cucinare in casa	Cooking at home
Mi piace cucinare.	I like cooking.
Non so cucinare.	I can't cook.
Vieni a cena da noi!	Come and have dinner at ours!

Sogni e desideris	Daydreams
Vorrei comprare una casa in Italia.	I would like to buy a house in Italy.
Vorrei andare in pensione il prossimo anno e viaggiare.	I'd like to retire next year and travel.
Vorrei trovare una ragazza italiana e sposarmi.	I would like to meet an Italian girl and get married.
Vorrei trovare un lavoro migliore.	I would like to get a better job.
Vorrei comprare una casa più grande.	I would like to buy a bigger house.
Vorremmo avere molti bambini.	We would like to have lots of children.
Vorrebbe diventare un astronauta.	He would like to become an astronaut.
Vuole diventare una celebrità.	She wants to become a celebrity.

Describing someone

Personalità	Personality
È ...	**He/She is ...**
divertente	funny
simpatico/simpatica	nice
timido/timida	shy
calmo/calma	quiet
irritante	annoying
generoso/generosa	generous
chiacchierone/ chiacchierona	talkative
intelligente	intelligent
stupido/stupida	stupid
avaro/avara	stingy
strano/strana	strange
pigro/pigra	lazy
severo/severa	strict
giusto/giusta	fair

Penso che abbia un bel carattere. — I think he's got a nice personality.
Secondo me è troppo sicura di sé. — In my opinion she's too self-confident.

Colori	Colours
giallo/gialla	yellow
arancione (masc, fem, pl)	orange
rosso/rossa	red
rosa (masc, fem, pl)	pink
viola (masc, fem, pl)	purple
azzurro/azzurra	blue
verde	green
marrone	brown
grigio/grigia	grey
nero/nera	black
bianco/bianca	white
bordeaux (masc, fem, pl)	burgundy
blu scuro (masc, fem, pl)	navy (blue)
turchese	turquoise
beige (masc, fem, pl)	beige
crema (masc, fem, pl)	cream

Occhi: — **Eyes:**
nocciola (masc, fem, pl) — hazel
chiari/scuri — light/dark

Capelli: — **Hair:**
color rame (masc, fem, pl) — auburn
biondi — blonde
castani — brown
castano chiaro (masc, fem, pl) — light brown
castano scuro (masc, fem, pl) — dark brown
lisci/crespi — straight/frizzy
rossi — red

Ho gli occhi nocciola. — I've got hazel eyes.
Ha i capelli castani. — He's got brown hair.
Ha i capelli corti grigi. — She's got short grey hair.
Ha i capelli neri. — She's got black hair.
È calvo. — He's bald.
Ha lunghi capelli ricci e biondi. — She's got long curly blonde hair.

Describing someone

Caratteristiche	Characteristics
Com'è?	What's he/she like?
È ...	**He/She is ...**
alto/alta	tall
piccolo/piccola	small
basso/bassa	short
grasso/grassa	fat
bello/bella	good-looking
giovane	young
vecchio/vecchia	old
brutto/brutta	ugly
Ha circa trent'anni.	He's about thirty.
È piccola, magra e bionda.	She is small, thin and blonde.
Assomiglia a sua madre.	She looks like her mother.

Abbigliamento	Clothes
un maglione	a jumper
pantaloni	trousers
jeans	jeans
fuseaux	leggings
una camicetta	a blouse
una maglietta	a T-shirt
un cappotto	a coat
una giacca	a jacket
un cardigan	a cardigan
un vestito	a dress
una gonna	a skirt
una cravatta	a tie
una camicia	a shirt
scarpe	shoes
scarpe da ginnastica	trainers
infradito	flip-flops
stivali	boots (knee-high)
Porta una maglietta azzurro chiaro.	She's wearing a light blue T-shirt.
Porta un vestito grigio scuro.	He's wearing a dark grey suit.
A scuola porto un blazer nero.	I wear a black blazer at school.
Indossa un vestito blu scuro, una camicia bianca, una cravatta a strisce grigie e bordeaux, calzini grigi e scarpe nere.	He is wearing a navy blue suit, a white shirt, a tie with burgundy and grey stripes, grey socks and black shoes.

9

Keeping fit and healthy

Pasti	Meals
colazione	breakfast
pranzo	lunch
merenda	snack
spuntino	bite to eat
cena	dinner (in the evening)

Mi piace ...	**I love ...**
la pasta	pasta
l'insalata	salad
il pesce	fish
il risotto	risotto

Mi piacciono ...	**I like ...**
le fragole	strawberries
i biscotti	biscuits

Non mi piace ...	**I don't like ...**
il succo d'arancia	orange juice
l'acqua minerale	mineral water

Non mi piacciono ...	**I don't like ...**
le banane	bananas

Odio ...	**I hate...**
i broccoli	broccoli
il latte	milk

Non mangio maiale.	I don't eat pork.
Mangio molta frutta.	I eat a lot of fruit.
I miei figli vogliono sempre bibite gassate.	My children always want fizzy drinks.
Sono vegetariano/ vegetariana.	I'm a vegetarian.
È allergico alle noccioline americane.	He is allergic to peanuts.

Com'è il cibo?	What's the food like?
È ottimo.	It's excellent.
Non è molto buono.	It's not very nice.
È delizioso.	It's delicious.
È molto piccante.	It's very spicy.
Fa ingrassare.	It's fattening.

Piccoli problemi di salute	Ailments
Mi fa male ...	**I have a sore ...**
lo stomaco	stomach
la schiena	back
un ginocchio	knee
il piede	foot
il collo	neck
la testa	head
la gola	throat
la gamba	leg

Ho mal di denti.	I've got toothache.
Ho mal d'orecchi.	I've got earache.
Mi bruciano gli occhi.	My eyes are hurting.
Ho il raffreddore.	I've got a cold.
Ho l'influenza.	I've got flu.
Ho la nausea.	I feel sick.
Sono stanco/ stanca.	I'm tired.
Sono malato/ malata.	I'm ill.

Altri problemi	Other problems
avere ...	**to be ...**
freddo	cold
caldo	hot
sete	thirsty
fame	hungry

Mantenersi in forma	Keeping fit
Faccio molto sport.	I do a lot of sport.
Non fumo.	I don't smoke.
Vado a letto presto.	I go to bed early.
Vado al lavoro a piedi.	I walk to work.
Fa bene alla salute.	It's good for your health.
L'alcol fa male.	Alcohol is bad for your health.

> **Writing a personal letter**
> In Italian, the address of the sender (mittente) is written on the envelope. You would only include the address of the sender in a business letter, not a personal one.

Angela e Claudio Botta
Via Manzoni, 16
22019 Tremezzo (CO)
Italia

Mittente: John e Joyce Nichols
18 Scotland Road
Lancaster LA1 5EF
UK

Writing a letter

14 febbraio 2014

Cari Angela e Claudio,
vi scrivo per ringraziarvi ancora una volta delle splendide giornate che abbiamo trascorso con voi a Tremezzo. Ci ha fatto veramente molto piacere rivedervi e speriamo che possiate venirci a trovare presto. Ora che i ragazzi sono via, a casa nostra c'è tanto spazio!

Vi prego di salutarci tanto i genitori di Angela. Sono stati veramente gentili ad invitarci a casa loro, e la cena è stata ottima. Come sapete, io e John apprezziamo molto la cucina italiana, specialmente quando si tratta di cucina casalinga!

Tremezzo è un paese bellissimo, e siamo stati fortunati ad avere sempre bel tempo. La prossima volta cercheremo di andare a nuotare al lago.

Grazie ancora della vostra gentilezza!

Tanti cari saluti,

John e Joyce

Starting a personal letter

Ti ringrazio della tua lettera.	Thank you for your letter.
Mi ha fatto piacere sentirti.	It was lovely to hear from you.
Mi dispiace di non averti scritto prima.	I'm sorry I didn't write sooner.

Common terms and abbreviations used in letters

Egregio Signore (Egr. Sig.) — Dear Sir
  (can also be followed by name: *Egr. Sig. Rossi*)
Gentile Signore/Signora — Dear Sir/Madam
  (Gent. Sig./Sig.ra)
  (can also be followed by name: *Gent. Sig.ra Rossi*)
Sig. — Mr
Sig.ra — Mrs/Ms

Ending a personal letter

Scrivi presto!	Write soon!
Salutami Federico!	Give my love to Federico!
Saluti da Paul.	Paul sends his best wishes.

Alternative endings for a personal letter

Ciao	Bye
Un abbraccio	Love
Tanti baci	Lots of love

Email, texting

Writing an email						
File	Modifica	Visualizza	Strumenti	**Componi**	?	Invia ✉

Componi messaggio
Rispondi all'autore
Rispondi a tutti
Inoltra
Inserisci file

A: diana@yahoo.it
Cc: diego@yahoo.it
Ccn: cat44@yahoo.co.uk
Oggetto: viaggio a Milano

Ciao Diana,
come stai? Penso di venire a Milano per lavoro la prossima settimana. Sarai in città? Sarebbe carino se riuscissimo ad incontrarci e ad andare a mangiare una pizza, magari insieme a Diego. O almeno potremmo andare a bere un aperitivo da qualche parte vicino al Duomo, cosa dici? Ho un sacco di cose da raccontarti…

Fammi sapere!
Ciao, Caroline

Saying your email address
To give your email address to someone in Italian, say:
"Diana chiocciola yahoo punto it(eet)"

Italian	English
a	to
oggetto	subject
data	date
cc (copia carbone)	cc (carbon copy)
ccn (copia carbone nascosta)	bcc (blind carbon copy)
inserisci file	attach file
invia	send
file	file
modifica	edit
visualizza	view
strumenti	tools
componi messaggio	new message
?	help
rispondi all'autore	reply to sender
rispondi a tutti	reply to all
inoltra	forward
invia	send

You'll notice that just as the numbers 2,4 and 8 are used in English text messages (C U 2moro; R U coming 4 Xmas?; Gr8!), Italian texts use 1 for un or uno (qualcuno = qlk1), 6 for 'sei' (you are), 3 for tre (treno = 3no), 8 for otto (baciotto= baci8). The letter x replaces 'per' (persona = xsona, spero = sxo), k replaces 'ch' which is a kuh sound in Italian (chi = ki), q replaces 'qu' (quando = qnd).

SMS	Italian	English
baci8	*baciotto*	little kiss
c sent	*ci sentiamo*	speak soon
d	*di*	of
doma	*domani*	tomorrow
dp	*dopo*	later
dv 6?	*dove sei?*	where are you?
k	*che*	that, what
ke	*che*	what
k fai?	*che fai?*	what are you doing?
ki	*chi*	who
nm	*numero*	number
nn	*non*	not
pome	*pomeriggio*	afternoon
qd	*quando*	when
qlk1	*qualcuno*	someone
qlk	*qualche*	some
qlks	*qualcosa*	something
qnd	*quando*	when
qnt	*quanto*	how much/many
qst	*questo/questa*	this
rsp	*rispondi*	reply
scs	*scusa*	sorry
sxo	*spero*	I hope
t tel	*ti telefono*	I'll phone you
trp	*troppo*	too much
tu 6	*tu sei*	you are
tvb	*ti voglio bene*	I love you
tvtb	*ti voglio tanto bene*	I love you so much
x	*per*	for
xke	*perché*	because
xke?	*perché?*	why?
xò	*però*	because
xsona	*persona*	person
3no	*treno*	train
+ tardi	*più tardi*	later
+o-	*più o meno*	more or less

On the phone and online

When your number answers

Pronto! Potrei parlare con Valentina, per favore?	Hello! Could I speak to Valentina, please?
Può chiedergli/chiederle di richiamarmi, per favore?	Would you ask him/ask her to call me back, please?
Richiamo fra una mezz'ora.	I'll call back in half an hour.

Answering the telephone

Pronto, sono Jane.	Hello! It's Jane speaking.
Sono io.	Speaking.
Chi parla?	Who's speaking?

Difficulties

Non riesco a prendere la linea.	I can't get through.
Scusi, ho sbagliato numero.	I'm sorry, I dialled the wrong number.
Qui non c'è campo.	I can't get a signal (*for mobile*).
Hanno il cellulare spento.	Their mobile is switched off.
Non ti sento bene.	I can't hear you very well.
Non ho più credito sul cellulare.	I've no credit left on my mobile phone.

Su Internet — On the internet

Chatto con gli amici.	I chat online with my friends.
Parlo con gli amici su Skype.	I talk to my friends on Skype.
Puoi scaricare gratis questa app.	You can download this app for nothing.
Qui c'è il WiFi gratuito.	There's free Wi-Fi here.

Dates, festivals and holidays

Giorni della settimana	Days of the week
lunedì	Monday
martedì	Tuesday
mercoledì	Wednesday
giovedì	Thursday
venerdì	Friday
sabato	Saturday
domenica	Sunday
lunedì	on Monday
lunedì scorso	last Monday
lunedì prossimo	next Monday
ieri	yesterday
oggi	today
domani	tomorrow

Mesi dell'anno	Months of the year
gennaio	January
febbraio	February
marzo	March
aprile	April
maggio	May
giugno	June
luglio	July
agosto	August
settembre	September
ottobre	October
novembre	November
dicembre	December
Che giorno è oggi?	What date is it today?
È il 16 giugno.	It's the 16th of June.
Che giorno è il tuo compleanno?	What date is your birthday?
È il 22 maggio.	It's the 22nd of May.

Vacanze	Holidays
le vacanze estive	the summer holidays
le vacanze di Natale	the Christmas holidays
le vacanze di Pasqua	the Easter holidays
le vacanze scolastiche	the school holidays
la settimana bianca	skiing holiday
Facciamo ponte.	We're having a long weekend. *(usually Thur/Fri or Mon/Tue plus weekend)*
un weekend lungo	a long weekend
la Vigilia di Natale	Christmas Eve
(il giorno di) Natale	Christmas Day
Santo Stefano	Boxing Day
San Silvestro	New Year's Eve
Capodanno	New Year's Day
(il giorno di) San Valentino	Valentine's Day
martedì grasso	Pancake Day
Carnevale	Carnival
il primo aprile	April Fools' Day
Pasqua	Easter
la festa della mamma	Mother's Day
la festa del papà	Father's Day
Ognissanti	All Saints' Day
Halloween	Halloween
Buon compleanno!	Happy Birthday!
Buon Natale!	Happy Christmas!
Pesce d'Aprile!	April fool!

Vacanze	Holidays
Cosa fai per il tuo compleanno?	What are you doing for your birthday?
Dai una festa?	Are you having a party?
Vuoi venire ad una festa per Capodanno?	Would you like to come to a New Year's Eve party?
Cosa fai il giorno di Natale?	What do you do on Christmas Day?
Andiamo dai nostri cugini per Capodanno.	We go to our cousins' for New Year.
Cos'hai intenzione di fare durante le vacanze?	What are you going to do in the holidays?
Andremo in Italia per una settimana quest'estate.	We're going to Italy for a week this summer.
Andiamo sempre a sciare in febbraio.	We always go skiing in February.
Starò con mia zia per una settimana.	I'm going to stay with my aunt for a week.
L'anno scorso sono andata negli Stati Uniti.	Last summer I went to the United States.

Time

Che ora sono?	What time is it?
È…/Sono…	It's… (for one o'clock)/It's… (for all other times)

È l'una

Sono le quattro e dieci

Sono le quattro e un quarto

Sono le quattro e mezza

Sono le cinque meno venti

Sono le cinque meno un quarto

A che ora?	At what time?

a mezzanotte

a mezzogiorno

all'una (di pomeriggio)

alle otto (di sera)

alle undici e quindici

alle venti e quarantacinque

In Italian times are often given in the twenty-four hour clock.

15

Numbers

24

Numbers

1	*uno(a)*
2	*due*
3	*tre*
4	*quattro*
5	*cinque*
6	*sei*
7	*sette*
8	*otto*
9	*nove*
10	*dieci*
11	*undici*
12	*dodici*
13	*tredici*
14	*quattordici*
15	*quindici*
16	*sedici*
17	*diciassette*
18	*diciotto*
19	*diciannove*
20	*venti*
21	*ventuno*
22	*ventidue*
30	*trenta*
40	*quaranta*
50	*cinquanta*
60	*sessanta*
70	*settanta*
80	*ottanta*
90	*novanta*
100	*cento*
101	*centouno*
300	*trecento*
301	*trecentouno*
1,000	*mille*
2,000	*duemila*
1,000,000	*un milione*

Italian puts a full stop where English would use a comma (2.000) and Italian puts a comma where English would use a full stop (0,60 €).

Examples

a pagina diciannove	on page nineteen
nel capitolo sette	in chapter seven

Years

1700	*millesettecento*
1998	*millenovecentonovantaotto*
2014	*duemilaquattordici*

Fractions etc

½	*un mezzo*
⅓	*un terzo*
⅔	*due terzi*
¼	*un quarto*
⅕	*un quinto*
0.5	*zero virgola cinque (0,5)*
3.4	*tre virgola quattro (3,4)*
10%	*il dieci per cento*
100%	*il cento per cento*
1st	*primo (1º)*
2nd	*secondo (2º)*
3rd	*terzo (3º)*
4th	*quarto (4º)*
5th	*quinto (5º)*
6th	*sesto (6º)*
7th	*settimo (7º)*
8th	*ottavo (8º)*
9th	*nono (9º)*
10th	*decimo (10º)*
11th	*undicesimo (11º)*
12th	*dodicesimo (12º)*
13th	*tredicesimo (13º)*
14th	*quattordicesimo (14º)*
15th	*quindicesimo (15º)*
16th	*sedicesimo (16º)*
17th	*diciassettesimo (17º)*
18th	*diciottesimo (18º)*
19th	*diciannovesimo (19º)*
20th	*ventesimo (20º)*
21st	*ventunesimo (21º)*
22nd	*ventiduesimo (22º)*
30th	*trentesimo (30º)*
100th	*centesimo (100º)*
101st	*centunesimo (101º)*
1000th	*millesimo (1000º)*

Examples

Abita al quinto piano.	He lives on the fifth floor.
È arrivato terzo.	He came in third.
È la seconda volta che vengo qui.	This is the second time I've been here.

Contents

Italian verb tables

This section is designed to help you find all the verb forms you need in Italian. From page 22 to 29 you will find a list of 123 regular and irregular verbs (with those tenses that are irregular set out in full), followed on pages 30 to 45 by some very common regular and irregular verbs shown in full, with example phrases.

How to find the verb you need

Most of the Italian verbs on both sides of the dictionary are followed by a number in square brackets. Each of these numbers corresponds to a verb in this section.

> **guardare** VERB [68]
> **1** to look

In this example, the number [68] after the verb **guardare** means that **guardare** follows the same pattern as verb number 68 in the list, which is **parlare**.

> **comporre** VERB [73]
> **1** to dial

For other verbs, a summary of the main forms is given. In the example above, **comporre** follows the same pattern as verb number [73] in the list, which is **porre**. When you look it up, you can see that the main forms of **porre** are given to show you how this verb and others like it work.

In the full verb tables, you will find examples of regular verbs: a regular –**are** verb (**parlare**), a regular –**ere** verb (**credere**) and regular –**ire** verbs (**dormire** and **finire**). Note that although **finire** follow the same endings as **dormire**, –**isc**– is added to the stem for a number of forms. Regular verbs follow one of these set patterns. When you have learnt these patterns, you will be able to form any regular verb.

You will also find **avere** (to have) and **essere** (to be) in the full verb tables. These are very important verbs which are also used to make up other tenses. The present tense of **avere** or **essere** is used to form the **perfect tense**. In most cases **avere** is used, but reflexive verbs like **lavarsi** (to wash oneself) and verbs of movement like **andare** (to go) and **venire** (to come) use **essere** – e.g. the Italian for both 'he's gone' and 'he went' is **è andato**, not **ha andato**. **Avere** and **essere** are known as auxiliary verbs. When the auxiliary verb is **essere**, this is shown in the verb tables or after the verb number as a superscript [E] on the English side.

> **arrivare** VERB [68, AUX **essere**]   to **arrive** VERB
> to be left over   arrivare [68[E]]

Here **arrivare** follows the same pattern as **parlare** but forms the perfect tense with **essere**.

Verb tenses

The present tense

The present tense is used to talk about what is true at the moment, what happens regularly and what is happening now, for example, 'I'm a student'; 'he works as a consultant'; 'I'm studying Italian'.

There is more than one way to express the present tense in English. For example, you can either say 'I speak, 'I'm speaking' or occasionally 'I do speak'. In Italian, you use the same form **parlo** for all these.

It is also possible to use another form: **sto parlando**, which is the exact equivalent of 'I am speaking', but this form is much less common in Italian than in English. It is used to stress that something is happening just at that point:

Stanno arrivando!	**They're coming.**
Cosa **stai facendo**?	What **are you doing**?

In English you can also use the present to talk about something that is going to happen in the near future. You can do the same in Italian.

Parto domani alle undici.	**I'm leaving** tomorrow at eleven.
Arriva la settimana prossima.	**She's coming** next week.

The future tense

The future tense is used to talk about something that will happen or will be true. There are several ways to express the future tense in English: you can use the future tense ('I'll ask him on Tuesday'), the present tense ('I'm not working tomorrow'), or 'going to' followed by an infinitive ('she's going to study in Italy for a year'). In Italian you can use the future tense or the present tense.

Quando **saranno** pronti i documenti?	When **will** the documents **be** ready?
Se non le dispiace **ripasso** sabato.	If you don't mind **I'll come back** on Saturday.
Vedo Gianni giovedì.	**I'm seeing** Gianni on Thursday.
Pensi di rivederlo?	**Are you going to** see him again?

The imperfect tense

The imperfect tense is one of the tenses used to talk about the past, especially in descriptions, and to say what used to happen, for example 'I used to work in Manchester'; 'it was sunny yesterday'.

Ieri mi **sentivo** bene.	I **felt** fine yesterday.
Tu gli hai detto che **andava** bene, no?	You told him it **was** okay, didn't you?
Ci **trovavamo** ogni venerdì.	**We used to meet** every Friday.

The perfect tense

In English the perfect tense is made with the verb *have* and the past participle:
I have done; he has gone.

In Italian the perfect tense is also made up of two parts: the present tense of **avere** or **essere** (known as auxiliary verbs) and the past participle, as in (*I have done, she has spoken*).

The past participles of regular verbs are formed as follows:

With –**are** verbs, replace the –**are** of the infinitive with –**ato** (–ata/–ati/–ate).
With –**ere** verbs, replace the –**ere** of the infinitive with –**uto** (–uta/–uti/–ute).
With –**ire** verbs, replace the –**ire** of the infinitive with –**ito** (–ita/–iti/–ite).

Many irregular verbs have an irregular past participle. These are shown in the verb list and full verb tables.

Most verbs form the perfect tense with **avere**. There are two main groups of verbs which form their perfect tense with **essere** instead of **avere**: all reflexive verbs (see **lavarsi** page 40) and a group of verbs that are mainly used to talk about movement or a change of some kind, including:

andare	to go
venire	to come
succedere	to happen
partire	to leave, to go
scendere	to go down, to come down, to get off
salire	to go up, to come up
entrare	to go in, to come in
uscire	to go out, to come out
morire	to die
nascere	to be born
diventare	to become
restare	to stay
cadere	to fall

When **essere** is used to form the perfect tense, then the past participle agrees with the subject of the verb.

Si è rotto una gamba.	**He's broken** his leg.
Sono partita prima di lui.	**I left** before him.
Carla **è uscita**.	Carla has gone out.

The past historic

This is equivalent to English simple past (*I did, he went, she ate*). While in Italian the perfect past is most commonly used in newspapers and in everyday conversation to convey this tense (though not in the south of Italy), the past historic is extensively used in Italian literature.

The imperative

An imperative is a form of the verb used when giving orders and instructions, for example, 'Be quiet!', 'Don't forget your passport!', 'Please fill in this form'.

In Italian, you give instructions or orders to someone by adding the appropriate endings to the verb stem, depending on whether the infinitive ends in **-are**, **-ere**, or **-ire**.

To make suggestions ('let's'; 'shall we?'), the **noi** form of the imperative is used.

Parlami del tuo nuovo ragazzo.	**Tell** me about your new boyfriend.
Aiutate mi!	**Help** me!
Prendiamo prima un aperitivo?	**Shall we** have a drink first?

To tell someone not to do something, **non** is used with the imperative, except in the case of a person you call **tu**, when **non** is used with the infinitive.

Non preoccuparti!	**Don't** worry!

The conditional

The conditional is used to talk about things that would happen or could be true under certain conditions, for instance, 'I would help you if I could'. It is also used to express wishes and desires, even for something as basic as, 'I would like a coffee'. It is often used with the verbs: **volere** (to want), **potere** (to be able) and **dovere** (to have to – 'should' in the conditional).

Vorrei un caffè.	**I'd like** a coffee.
Potrebbe venire domani.	**He could** come tomorrow.
Carla **dovrebbe** imparare inglese.	Carla **should** learn English.

The subjunctive

The subjunctive is used in unreal or hypothetical situations, often after certain impersonal expressions and after verbs expressing desire, will, preference, opinions and feelings (when the subject of the desire, wish, etc, is different to the subject of the verb). Usually there will be **che** 'that' between the expressions and the subjunctive.

Penso **che siano** pronti.	I think that they are ready.
Bisogna **che** Luca **parta** subito.	Luca needs to leave now.
Preferisce **che stiamo** in casa.	He prefers us to stay at home.

Italian verb forms

1 abbattere
Verbs ending in **-tere** don't have alternative forms **-etti**, **-ette**, **-ettero** for past historic

2 accendere
PAST PARTICIPLE acceso
PAST HISTORIC accesi, accendesti, accese, accendemmo, accendeste, accesero

3 accludere
PAST PARTICIPLE accluso
PAST HISTORIC acclusi, accludesti, accluse, accludemmo, accludeste, acclusero

4 accorgersi (*auxiliary* essere)
PAST PARTICIPLE accorto
PAST HISTORIC mi accorsi, ti accorgesti, si accorse, ci accorgemmo, vi accorgeste, si accorsero

5 aggiungere
PAST PARTICIPLE aggiunto
PAST HISTORIC aggiunsi, aggiungesti, aggiunse, aggiungemmo, aggiungeste, aggiunsero

6 andare (*auxiliary* essere)
see full verb table on page 30

7 apparire (*auxiliary* essere)
PAST PARTICIPLE apparso
PRESENT appaio, appari *or* apparisci, appare *or* apparisce, appariamo, apparite, appaiono *or* appariscono
PAST HISTORIC apparvi, appraisti, apparve, apparimmo, appariste, apparvero
PRESENT SUBJUNCTIVE appaia, appaia, appaia, appariamo, appariate, appaiano

8 appendere
PAST PARTICIPLE appeso
PAST HISTORIC appesi, appendesti, appese, appendemmo, appendeste, appesero

9 aprire
PAST PARTICIPLE aperto
PAST HISTORIC aprii, apristi, aprì, aprimmo, apriste, aprirono

10 assistere
PAST PARTICIPLE assistito
PAST HISTORIC assistei *or* assistetti, assistesti, assistette, assistemmo, assisteste, assisterono *or* assistettero

11 assumere
PAST PARTICIPLE assunto
PAST HISTORIC assunsi, assumesti, assunse, assumemmo, assumeste, assunsero

12 avere
see full verb table on page 31

13 baciare
When the verb ending begins with e, the **-i-** of the root is dropped → **bacerò** (*not* **bacierò**)

14 bagnare
PRESENT bagniamo, bagniate
PRESENT SUBJUNCTIVE bagniamo, bagniate (*not* **bagnamo, bagnate**)

15 bere
PAST PARTICIPLE bevuto
GERUND bevendo
PRESENT bevo, bevi, beve, beviamo, bevete, bevono
FUTURE berrò, berrai, berrà, berremo, berrete, berranno
IMPERFECT bevevo, bevevi, beveva, bevevamo, bevevate, bevevano
PRESENT SUBJUNCTIVE beva, beva, beva, beviamo, beviate, bevano
PAST HISTORIC bevvi *or* bevetti, bevesti, bevve *or* bevette, bevemmo, beveste, bevvero *or* bevettero
PRESENT CONDITIONAL berrei, berresti, berrebbe, berremmo, berreste, berrebbero
IMPERATIVE bevi!, beva!, beviamo!, bevete!, bevano!

16 cadere (*auxiliary* essere)
FUTURE cadrò, cadrai, cadrà, cadremo, cadrete, cadranno
PAST HISTORIC caddi, cadesti, cadde, cademmo, cadeste, caddero
CONDITIONAL cadrei, cadresti, cadrebbe, cadremmo, cadreste, cadrebbero

17 cambiare (*auxiliary* essere/avere)
When 1st person sing. of present doesn't have a stress on the -i- of the root and an ending starts with i (as in the past historic), then the verb drops the -i- of the root (**cambi**, **cambino** and *not* **cambii**, **cambiino** [cf. **inviare**])

18 caricare
When -c- in the root is followed by i *or* e, an **h** should be inserted to retain the hard 'kuh' sound (ie **carichi**, **carichiamo**, **caricherò**)

19 chiedere
PAST PARTICIPLE chiesto
PAST HISTORIC chiesi, chiedesti, chiese, chiedemmo, chiedeste, chiesero

20 chiudere
PAST PARTICIPLE chiuso
PAST HISTORIC chiusi, chiudesti, chiuse, chiudemmo, chiudeste, chiusero

21 cogliere
PAST PARTICIPLE colto
PRESENT colgo, cogli, coglie, cogliamo, cogliete, colgono
PAST HISTORIC colsi, cogliesti, colse, cogliemmo, coglieste, colsero
PRESENT SUBJUNCTIVE colga, colga, colga, cogliamo, cogliate, colgan
IMPERATIVE cogli!, colga!, cogliamo!, cogliete!, colgano!

22 compiere
PAST PARTICIPLE compiuto
PAST HISTORIC compii, compisti, compì, compimmo, compiste, compirono

23 confondere
PAST PARTICIPLE confuso
PAST HISTORIC confusi, confondesti, confuse, confondemmo, confondeste, confusero

24 conoscere
PAST PARTICIPLE conosciuto
PAST HISTORIC conobbi, conoscesti, conobbe, conoscemmo, conosceste, conobbero

25 consigliare
When the ending begins with i, then the -i- of the root is dropped → **consigli** (*not* **consiglii**)

26 correre (*auxiliary* essere/avere)
PAST PARTICIPLE corso
PAST HISTORIC corsi, corresti, corse, corremmo, correste, corsero

27 credere
see full verb table on page 32

28 crescere (*auxiliary* essere)
PAST PARTICIPLE cresciuto
PAST HISTORIC crebbi, crescesti, crebbe, crescemmo, cresceste, crebbero

29 cuocere
PAST PARTICIPLE cotto
PAST HISTORIC cossi, cuocesti, cosse, cuocemmo, cuoceste, cossero

30 dare
see full verb table on page 33

31 decidere
PAST PARTICIPLE deciso
PAST HISTORIC decisi, decidesti, decise, decidemmo, decideste, decisero**

32 deludere
PAST PARTICIPLE deluso
PAST HISTORIC delusi, deludesti, deluse, deludemmo, deludeste, delusero

33 difendere
PAST PARTICIPLE difeso
PAST HISTORIC difesi, difendesti, difese, difendemmo, difendeste, difesero

34 dipingere
PAST PARTICIPLE dipinto
PAST HISTORIC dipinsi, dipingesti, dipinse, dipingemmo, dipingeste, dipinsero

35 dire
see full verb table on page 34

36 dirigere
PAST PARTICIPLE diretto
PAST HISTORIC diressi, dirigesti, diresse, dirigemmo, dirigeste, diressero

37 discutere
PAST PARTICIPLE discusso
PAST HISTORIC discussi, discutesti, discusse, discutemmo, discuteste, discussero

38 disfare
Although it follows the conjugation of fare, it follows the -are verb form in the present (disfo, etc), future (disferò), and in the subjunctive (disfi)

39 distinguere
PAST PARTICIPLE distinto
PAST HISTORIC distinsi, distinguesti, distinse, distinguemmo, distingueste, distinsero

40 dividere
PAST PARTICIPLE diviso
PAST HISTORIC divisi, dividesti, divise, dividemmo, divideste, divisero

41 dormire
see full verb table on page 35

42 dovere
see full verb table on page 36

43 esigere
PAST PARTICIPLE esatto (*not common*)
PAST HISTORIC esigei *or* esigetti, esigesti, esigette, esigemmo, esigeste, esigettero

44 espellere
PAST PARTICIPLE espulso
PAST HISTORIC espulsi, espellesti, espulse, espellemmo, espelleste, espulsero

45 esplodere (*auxiliary* essere)
PAST PARTICIPLE esploso
PAST HISTORIC esplosi, esplodesti, esplose, esplodemmo, esplodeste, esplosero

46 esprimere
PAST PARTICIPLE espresso
PAST HISTORIC espressi, esprimesti, espresse, esprimemmo, esprimeste, espressero

47 essere
see full verb table on page 37

48 evadere (*auxiliary* essere)
PAST PARTICIPLE evaso
PAST HISTORIC evasi, evadesti, evase, evademmo, evadeste, evasero

49 fare
see full verb table on page 38

50 fingere
PAST PARTICIPLE finto
PAST HISTORIC finsi, fingesti, finse, fingemmo, fingeste, finsero

51 finire
see full verb table on page 39

52 friggere
PAST PARTICIPLE fritto
PAST HISTORIC frissi, friggesti, frisse, friggemmo, friggeste, frissero

53 immergere
PAST PARTICIPLE immerso
PAST HISTORIC immersi, immergesti, immerse, immergemmo, immergeste, immersero

54 invadere
PAST PARTICIPLE invaso
PAST HISTORIC invasi, invadesti, invase, invademmo, invadeste, invasero

55 inviare
When 1st person sing of present has a stress on the -i- of the root, the verb keeps the -i- of the root even if the ending starts with i (invii, inviino)

56 lavarsi (*auxiliary* essere)
see full verb table on page 40

57 leggere
PAST PARTICIPLE letto
PAST HISTORIC lessi, leggesti, lesse, leggemmo, leggeste, lessero

58 mangiare
When the ending begins with e, the -i- of the root is no longer needed to soften the g and is dropped
→ mangerò (*not* mangierò)

59 mettere
PAST PARTICIPLE messo
PAST HISTORIC misi, mettesti, mise, mettemmo, metteste, misero

60 mordere
PAST PARTICIPLE morso
PAST HISTORIC morsi, mordesti, morse, mordemmo, mordeste, morsero

61 morire (*auxiliary* essere)
PAST PARTICIPLE morto
PRESENT muoio, muori, muore, moriamo, morite, muoiono
PRESENT SUBJUNCTIVE muoia, muoia, muoia, moriamo, moriate, muoiano

62 muovere
PAST PARTICIPLE mosso
PAST HISTORIC mossi, muovesti, mosse, muovemmo, muoveste, mossero

63 nascere (*auxiliary* essere)
PAST PARTICIPLE nato
PAST HISTORIC nacqui, nascesti, nacque, nascemmo, nasceste, nacquero

64 nascondere
PAST PARTICIPLE nascosto
PAST HISTORIC nascosi, nascondesti, nascose, nascondemmo, nascondeste, nascosero

65 nuocere
PAST PARTICIPLE nociuto *or* nuociuto
GERUND nocendo *or* nuocendo
PRESENT nuoccio, nuoci, nuoce, nuociamo, nuocete, nuocciono
PAST HISTORIC nocqui, nuocesti, nocque, nuocemmo, nuoceste, nocquero

66 offrire
PAST PARTICIPLE offerto
PAST HISTORIC offrii, offristi, offrì, offrimmo, offriste, offrirono

67 parere (*auxiliary* essere)
PAST PARTICIPLE parso
PRESENT pare, paiono
FUTURE parrà, parranno
PAST HISTORIC parve, parvero
PRESENT SUBJUNCTIVE paia, paiano

68 parlare
see full verb table on page 41

69 perdere
PAST PARTICIPLE perso *or* perduto
PAST HISTORIC persi, perdesti, perse, perdemmo, perdeste, persero

70 piacere (*auxiliary* essere)
PAST PARTICIPLE piaciuto
PRESENT piaccio, piaci, piace, piacciamo *or* piaciamo, piacete, piacciono
PAST HISTORIC piacqui, piacesti, piacque, piacemmo, piaceste, piacquero
PRESENT SUBJUNCTIVE piaccia, piaccia, piaccia, piacciamo, piacciate, piacciano

71 piangere
PAST PARTICIPLE pianto
PAST HISTORIC piansi, piangesti, pianse, piangemmo, piangeste, piansero

72 piovere
PAST PARTICIPLE piovuto
PAST HISTORIC piovve

73 porre
PAST PARTICIPLE posto
PRESENT pongo, poni, pone, poniamo, ponete, pongono
FUTURE porrò, porrai, porrà, porremo, porrete, porranno
PAST HISTORIC posi, ponesti, pose, ponemmo, poneste, posero
PRESENT SUBJUNCTIVE ponga, ponga, ponga, poniamo, poniate, pongano

74 potere
see full verb table on page 42

75 prefiggersi (*auxiliary* essere)
PAST PARTICIPLE prefisso
PAST HISTORIC mi prefissi, ti prefiggesti, si prefisse, ci prefiggemmo, vi prefiggeste, si prefissero

76 pregare
When -g- in the root is followed by i *or* e an h should be inserted to keep the hard 'guh' sound (ie **preghi**, **preghiamo, pregherò**)

77 prendere
PAST PARTICIPLE preso
PAST HISTORIC presi, prendesti, prese, prendemmo, prendeste, presero

78 prevedere
This verb is conjugated like **vedere** except in the future → **prevederò, prevederai** etc (*not* prevedrò, prevedrai etc) and in the conditional → **prevederei** (*not* prevedrei etc)

79 proteggere
PAST PARTICIPLE protetto
PAST HISTORIC protessi, proteggesti, protesse, proteggemmo, proteggeste, protessero

80 pungere
PAST PARTICIPLE punto
PAST HISTORIC punsi, pungesti, punse, pungemmo, pungeste, punsero

81 radere
PAST PARTICIPLE raso
PAST HISTORIC rasi, radesti, rase, rademmo, radeste, rasero

82 reggere
PAST PARTICIPLE retto
PAST HISTORIC ressi, reggesti, resse, reggemmo, reggeste, ressero

83 rendere
PAST PARTICIPLE reso
PAST HISTORIC resi, rendesti, rese, rendemmo, rendeste, resero

84 ridere
PAST PARTICIPLE riso
PAST HISTORIC risi, ridesti, rise, ridemmo, rideste, risero

85 ridurre
PAST PARTICIPLE ridotto
GERUND riducendo
PRESENT riduco, riduci, riduce, riduciamo, riducete, riducono
FUTURE ridurrò, ridurrai, ridurrà, ridurremo, ridurrete, ridurranno
IMPERFECT riducevo, riducevi, riduceva, riducevamo, riducevate, riducevano
PAST HISTORIC ridussi, riducesti, ridusse, riducemmo, riduceste, ridussero
PRESENT SUBJUNCTIVE riduca, riduca, riduca, riduciamo, riduciate, riducano

86 riempire
GERUND riempiendo
PRESENT riempio, riempi, riempie, riempiamo, riempite, riempiono

87 riflettere
PAST PARTICIPLE riflettuto *or* riflesso

88 rimanere (*auxiliary* essere)
PAST PARTICIPLE rimasto
PRESENT rimango, rimani, rimane, rimaniamo, rimanete, rimangono
FUTURE rimarrò, rimarrai, rimarrà, rimarremo, rimarrete, rimarranno
PAST HISTORIC rimasi, rimanesti, rimase, rimanemmo, rimaneste, rimasero
PRESENT SUBJUNCTIVE rimanga, rimanga, rimanga, rimaniamo, rimaniate, rimangano

89 risolvere
PAST PARTICIPLE risolto
PAST HISTORIC risolsi, risolvesti, risolse, risolvemmo, risolveste, risolsero

90 rispondere
PAST PARTICIPLE risposto
PAST HISTORIC risposi, rispondesti, rispose, rispondemmo, rispondeste, risposero

91 rivolgere
PAST PARTICIPLE rivolto
PAST HISTORIC rivolsi, rivolgesti, rivolse, rivolgemmo, rivolgeste, rivolsero

92 rompere
PAST PARTICIPLE rotto
PAST HISTORIC ruppi, rompesti, ruppe, rompemmo, rompeste, ruppero

93 salire (*auxiliary* essere/avere)
PRESENT salgo, sali, sale, saliamo, salite, salgono
PRESENT SUBJUNCTIVE salga, salga, salga, saliamo, saliate, salgano
IMPERATIVE sali!, salga!, saliamo!, salite!, salgano!

94 sapere
see full verb table on page 43

95 scegliere
PAST PARTICIPLE scelto
PRESENT scelgo, scegli, sceglie, scegliamo, scegliete, scelgono
PAST HISTORIC scelsi, scegliesti, scelse, scegliemmo, sceglieste, scelsero
PRESENT SUBJUNCTIVE scelga, scelga, scelga, scegliamo, scegliate, scelgano
IMPERATIVE scegli!, scelga!, scegliamo!, scegliete!, scelgano!

96 scendere (*auxiliary* essere)
PAST PARTICIPLE sceso
PAST HISTORIC scesi, scendesti, scese, scendemmo, scendeste, scesero

97 sciogliere
PAST PARTICIPLE sciolto
PRESENT sciolgo, sciogli, scioglie, sciogliamo, sciogliete, sciolgono
PAST HISTORIC sciolsi, sciogliesti, sciolse, sciogliemmo, scioglieste, sciolsero
PRESENT SUBJUNCTIVE sciolga, sciolga, sciolga, sciogliamo, sciogliate, sciolgano
IMPERATIVE sciogli!, sciolga!, sciogliamo!, sciogliete!, sciolgano!

98 sconfiggere
PAST PARTICIPLE sconfitto
PAST HISTORIC sconfissi, sconfiggesti, sconfisse, sconfiggemmo, sconfiggeste, sconfissero

99 scrivere
PAST PARTICIPLE scritto
PAST HISTORIC scrissi, scrivesti, scrisse, scrivemmo, scriveste, scrissero

100 scuotere
PAST PARTICIPLE scosso
PAST HISTORIC scossi, scuotesti, scosse, scuotemmo, scuoteste, scossero

101 sedere
PRESENT siedo, siedi, siede, sediamo, sedete, siedono
PRESENT SUBJUNCTIVE sieda, sieda, sieda, sediamo, sediate, siedano

102 sorgere (*auxiliary* essere)
PAST PARTICIPLE sorto
PAST HISTORIC sorse, sorsero

103 spargere
PAST PARTICIPLE sparso
PAST HISTORIC sparsi, spargesti, sparse, spargemmo, spargeste, sparsero

104 sparire (*auxiliary* essere)
PAST HISTORIC sparii, sparisti, sparì, sparimmo, spariste, sparirono

105 spegnere
PAST PARTICIPLE spento
PRESENT spengo, spegni, spegne, spegniamo, spegnete, spengono
PAST HISTORIC spensi, spegnesti, spense, spegnemmo, spegneste, spensero
PRESENT SUBJUNCTIVE spenga, spenga, spenga, spegniamo, spegniate, spengano

106 spingere
PAST PARTICIPLE spinto
PAST HISTORIC spinsi, spingesti, spinse, spingemmo, spingeste, spinsero

107 sporgersi (*auxiliary* essere)
PAST PARTICIPLE sporto
PAST HISTORIC mi sporsi, ti sporgesti, si sporse, ci sporgemmo, vi sporgeste, si sporsero

108 stare
see full verb table on page 44

109 stringere
PAST PARTICIPLE stretto
PAST HISTORIC strinsi, stringesti, strinse, stringemmo, stringeste, strinsero

110 succedere (*auxiliary* essere)
PAST PARTICIPLE successo
PAST HISTORIC successi, succedesti, successe, succedemmo, succedeste, successero

111 tacere
PAST PARTICIPLE taciuto
PRESENT taccio, taci, tace, tacciamo, tacete, tacciono
PAST HISTORIC tacqui, tacesti, tacque, tacemmo, taceste, tacquero
PRESENT SUBJUNCTIVE taccia, taccia, taccia, tacciamo, tacciate, tacciano

112 tendere

PAST PARTICIPLE teso
PAST HISTORIC tesi, tendesti, tese, tendemmo, tendeste, tesero

113 tenere

PAST PARTICIPLE tenuto
PRESENT tengo, tieni, tiene, teniamo, tenete, tengono
FUTURE terrò, terrai, terrà, terremo, terrete, terranno
PAST HISTORIC tenni, tenesti, tenne, tenemmo, teneste, tennero
PRESENT SUBJUNCTIVE tenga, tenga, tenga, teniamo, teniate, tengano
CONDITIONAL terrei, terresti, terrebbe, terremmo, terreste, terrebbero

114 togliere

PAST PARTICIPLE tolto
PRESENT tolgo, togli, toglie, togliamo, togliete, tolgono
PAST HISTORIC tolsi, togliesti, tolse, togliemmo, toglieste, tolsero
PRESENT SUBJUNCTIVE tolga, tolga, tolga, togliamo, togliate, tolgano
IMPERATIVE togli!, tolga!, togliamo!, togliete!, tolgano!

115 trarre

PAST PARTICIPLE tratto
GERUND traendo
PRESENT traggo, trai, trae, traiamo, traete, traggono
FUTURE trarrò, trarrai, trarrà, trarremo, trarrete, trarranno
IMPERFECT traevo, traevi, traeva, traevamo, traevate, traevano
PAST HISTORIC trassi, traesti, trasse, traemmo, traeste, trassero
PRESENT SUBJUNCTIVE tragga, tragga, tragga, traiamo, traiate, traggano

116 ungere

PAST PARTICIPLE unto
PAST HISTORIC unsi, ungesti, unse, ungemmo, ungeste, unsero

117 uscire (*auxiliary* essere)

PRESENT esco, esci, esce, usciamo, uscite, escono
PRESENT SUBJUNCTIVE esca, esca, esca, usciamo, usciate, escano

118 valere (*auxiliary* essere)

PAST PARTICIPLE valso
PRESENT valgo, vali, vale, valiamo, valete, valgono
FUTURE varrò, varrai, varrà, varremo, varrete, varranno
PAST HISTORIC valsi, valesti, valse, valemmo, valeste, valsero
PRESENT SUBJUNCTIVE valga, valga, valga, valiamo, valiate, valgano

119 vedere

PAST PARTICIPLE visto
FUTURE vedrò, vedrai, vedrà, vedremo, vedrete, vedranno
PAST HISTORIC vidi, vedesti, vide, vedemmo, vedeste, videro

120 venire (*auxiliary* essere)

PAST PARTICIPLE venuto
PRESENT vengo, vieni, viene, veniamo, venite, vengono
FUTURE verrò, verrai, verrà, verremo, verrete, verranno
PAST HISTORIC venni, venisti, venne, venimmo, veniste, vennero
PRESENT SUBJUNCTIVE venga, venga, venga, veniamo, veniate, vengano
IMPERATIVE vieni!, venga!, veniamo!, venite!, vengano!

121 vincere

PAST PARTICIPLE vinto
PAST HISTORIC vinsi, vincesti, vinse, vincemmo, vinceste, vinsero

122 vivere (*auxiliary* essere)

PAST PARTICIPLE vissuto
PAST HISTORIC vissi, vivesti, visse, vivemmo, viveste, vissero

123 volere

see full verb table on page 45

andare (to go)

	PRESENT		FUTURE
io	**vado**	io	**andrò**
tu	**vai**	tu	**andrai**
lui/lei/Lei	**va**	lui/lei/Lei	**andrà**
noi	**andiamo**	noi	**andremo**
voi	**andate**	voi	**andrete**
loro	**vanno**	loro	**andranno**

	IMPERFECT		CONDITIONAL
io	**andavo**	io	**andrei**
tu	**andavi**	tu	**andresti**
lui/lei/Lei	**andava**	lui/lei/Lei	**andrebbe**
noi	**andavamo**	noi	**andremmo**
voi	**andavate**	voi	**andreste**
loro	**andavano**	loro	**andrebbero**

	PERFECT		PRESENT SUBJUNCTIVE
io	**sono andato/a**	io	**vada**
tu	**sei andato/a**	tu	**vada**
lui/lei/Lei	**è andato/a**	lui/lei/Lei	**vada**
noi	**siamo andati/e**	noi	**andiamo**
voi	**siete andati/e**	voi	**andiate**
loro	**sono andati/e**	loro	**vadano**

	PAST HISTORIC	GERUND
io	**andai**	**andando**
tu	**andasti**	
lui/lei/Lei	**andò**	**PAST PARTICIPLE**
noi	**andammo**	**andato**
voi	**andaste**	
loro	**andarono**	**IMPERATIVE**

va' or **vai** / **andiamo** / **andate**

....

EXAMPLE PHRASES

Ci **vado** spesso. I go there often.
Andate via! Go away!
Spero che **vada** bene. I hope it goes well.

Remember that subject pronouns are not used very often in Italian.

avere (to have)

	PRESENT		FUTURE
io	ho	io	avrò
tu	hai	tu	avrai
lui/lei/Lei	ha	lui/lei/Lei	avrà
noi	abbiamo	noi	avremo
voi	avete	voi	avrete
loro	hanno	loro	avranno

	IMPERFECT		CONDITIONAL
io	avevo	io	avrei
tu	avevi	tu	avresti
lui/lei/Lei	aveva	lui/lei/Lei	avrebbe
noi	avevamo	noi	avremmo
voi	avevate	voi	avreste
loro	avevano	loro	avrebbero

	PERFECT		PRESENT SUBJUNCTIVE
io	ho avuto	io	abbia
tu	hai avuto	tu	abbia
lui/lei/Lei	ha avuto	lui/lei/Lei	abbia
noi	abbiamo avuto	noi	abbiamo
voi	avete avuto	voi	abbiate
loro	hanno avuto	loro	abbiano

	PAST HISTORIC
io	ebbi
tu	avesti
lui/lei/Lei	ebbe
noi	avemmo
voi	aveste
loro	ebbero

GERUND

avendo

PAST PARTICIPLE

avuto

IMPERATIVE

abbi / abbiamo / abbiate

EXAMPLE PHRASES

Ha un fratello e una sorella. He has a brother and a sister.
Avevo la febbre. I had a temperature.
Domani **avranno** più tempo. They'll have more time tomorrow.

Remember that subject pronouns are not used very often in Italian.

credere (to believe)

	PRESENT		FUTURE
io	credo	io	crederò
tu	credi	tu	crederai
lui/lei/Lei	crede	lui/lei/Lei	crederà
noi	crediamo	noi	crederemo
voi	credete	voi	crederete
loro	credono	loro	crederanno

	IMPERFECT		CONDITIONAL
io	credevo	io	crederei
tu	credevi	tu	crederesti
lui/lei/Lei	credeva	lui/lei/Lei	crederebbe
noi	credevamo	noi	crederemmo
voi	credevate	voi	credereste
loro	credevano	loro	crederebbero

	PERFECT		PRESENT SUBJUNCTIVE
io	ho creduto	io	creda
tu	hai creduto	tu	creda
lui/lei/Lei	ha creduto	lui/lei/Lei	creda
noi	abbiamo creduto	noi	crediamo
voi	avete creduto	voi	crediate
loro	hanno creduto	loro	credano

	PAST HISTORIC
io	credei or credetti
tu	credesti
lui/lei/Lei	credè or credette
noi	credemmo
voi	credeste
loro	credettero

GERUND

credendo

PAST PARTICIPLE

creduto

IMPERATIVE

credi / crediamo / credete

EXAMPLE PHRASES

Credo di sì. I think so.
Gli **ho creduto**. I believed him.
Non ci posso **credere**! I can't believe it!

Remember that subject pronouns are not used very often in Italian.

dare (to give)

PRESENT

io	**do**
tu	**dai**
lui/lei/Lei	**dà**
noi	**diamo**
voi	**date**
loro	**danno**

FUTURE

io	**darò**
tu	**darai**
lui/lei/Lei	**darà**
noi	**daremo**
voi	**darete**
loro	**daranno**

IMPERFECT

io	**davo**
tu	**davi**
lui/lei/Lei	**dava**
noi	**davamo**
voi	**davate**
loro	**davano**

CONDITIONAL

io	**darei**
tu	**daresti**
lui/lei/Lei	**darebbe**
noi	**daremmo**
voi	**dareste**
loro	**darebbero**

PERFECT

io	**ho dato**
tu	**hai dato**
lui/lei/Lei	**ha dato**
noi	**abbiamo dato**
voi	**avete dato**
loro	**hanno dato**

PRESENT SUBJUNCTIVE

io	**dia**
tu	**dia**
lui/lei/Lei	**dia**
noi	**diamo**
voi	**diate**
loro	**diano**

PAST HISTORIC

io	**diedi** or **detti**
tu	**desti**
lui/lei/Lei	**diede** or **dette**
noi	**demmo**
voi	**deste**
loro	**diedero** or **dettero**

GERUND

dando

PAST PARTICIPLE

dato

IMPERATIVE

da' or **dai** / **diamo** / **date**

EXAMPLE PHRASES

Zia Maria ci **dà** le caramelle. Aunt Maria gives us sweets.

Mi **ha dato** un libro. He gave me a book.

Mi **daranno** una risposta domani. They'll give me an answer tomorrow.

Remember that subject pronouns are not used very often in Italian.

dire (to say)

	PRESENT		FUTURE
io	dico	io	dirò
tu	dici	tu	dirai
lui/lei/Lei	dice	lui/lei/Lei	dirà
noi	diciamo	noi	diremo
voi	dite	voi	direte
loro	dicono	loro	diranno

	IMPERFECT		CONDITIONAL
io	dicevo	io	direi
tu	dicevi	tu	diresti
lui/lei/Lei	diceva	lui/lei/Lei	direbbe
noi	dicevamo	noi	diremmo
voi	dicevate	voi	direste
loro	dicevano	loro	direbbero

	PERFECT		PRESENT SUBJUNCTIVE
io	ho detto	io	dica
tu	hai detto	tu	dica
lui/lei/Lei	ha detto	lui/lei/Lei	dica
noi	abbiamo detto	noi	diciamo
voi	avete detto	voi	diciate
loro	hanno detto	loro	dicano

	PAST HISTORIC	GERUND
io	dissi	dicendo
tu	dicesti	
lui/lei/Lei	disse	PAST PARTICIPLE
noi	dicemmo	detto
voi	diceste	
loro	dissero	IMPERATIVE
		di / diciamo / dite

EXAMPLE PHRASES

Dice sempre quello che pensa. She always says what she thinks.

Mi **ha detto** una bugia. He told me a lie.

Diranno che è colpa mia. They'll say it's my fault.

Remember that subject pronouns are not used very often in Italian.

dormire (to sleep)

	PRESENT		**FUTURE**
io	dormo	io	dormirò
tu	dormi	tu	dormirai
lui/lei/Lei	dorme	lui/lei/Lei	dormirà
noi	dormiamo	noi	dormiremo
voi	dormite	voi	dormirete
loro	dormono	loro	dormiranno

	IMPERFECT		**CONDITIONAL**
io	dormivo	io	dormirei
tu	dormivi	tu	dormiresti
lui/lei/Lei	dormiva	lui/lei/Lei	dormirebbe
noi	dormivamo	noi	dormiremmo
voi	dormivate	voi	dormireste
loro	dormivano	loro	dormirebbero

	PERFECT		**PRESENT SUBJUNCTIVE**
io	ho dormito	io	dorma
tu	hai dormito	tu	dorma
lui/lei/Lei	ha dormito	lui/lei/Lei	dorma
noi	abbiamo dormito	noi	dormiamo
voi	avete dormito	voi	dormiate
loro	hanno dormito	loro	dormano

	PAST HISTORIC
io	dormii
tu	dormisti
lui/lei/Lei	dormì
noi	dormimmo
voi	dormiste
loro	dormirono

GERUND

dormendo

PAST PARTICIPLE

dormito

IMPERATIVE

dormi / dormiamo / dormite

EXAMPLE PHRASES

I bambini **dormono**. The children are sleeping.
Quando ha telefonato **dormivo**. I was sleeping when he phoned.
Hai dormito bene? Did you sleep well?

Remember that subject pronouns are not used very often in Italian.

dovere (to have to)

	PRESENT			FUTURE
io	**devo**		io	**dovrò**
tu	**devi**		tu	**dovrai**
lui/lei/Lei	**deve**		lui/lei/Lei	**dovrà**
noi	**dobbiamo**		noi	**dovremo**
voi	**dovete**		voi	**dovrete**
loro	**dovono**		loro	**dovranno**

	IMPERFECT			CONDITIONAL
io	**dovevo**		io	**dovrei**
tu	**dovevi**		tu	**dovresti**
lui/lei/Lei	**doveva**		lui/lei/Lei	**dovrebbe**
noi	**dovevamo**		noi	**dovremmo**
voi	**dovevate**		voi	**dovreste**
loro	**dovevano**		loro	**dovrebbero**

	PERFECT			PRESENT SUBJUNCTIVE
io	**ho dovuto**		io	**deva** or **debba**
tu	**hai dovuto**		tu	**deva** or **debba**
lui/lei/Lei	**ha dovuto**		lui/lei/Lei	**deva** or **debba**
noi	**abbiamo dovuto**		noi	**dobbiamo**
voi	**avete dovuto**		voi	**dobbiate**
loro	**hanno dovuto**		loro	**devano** or **debbano**

	PAST HISTORIC			
io	**dovetti**		**GERUND**	
tu	**dovesti**		**dovendo**	
lui/lei/Lei	**dovette**			
noi	**dovemmo**		**PAST PARTICIPLE**	
voi	**deveste**		**dovuto**	
loro	**dovettero**			
			IMPERATIVE	
			not used	

EXAMPLE PHRASES

Ho **dovuto** dirglielo. I had to tell him.
Dev'essere tardi. It must be late.
Dovresti aiutarlo. You should help him.

Remember that subject pronouns are not used very often in Italian.

essere (to be)

	PRESENT			**FUTURE**
io	**sono**		io	**sarò**
tu	**sei**		tu	**sarai**
lui/lei/Lei	**è**		lui/lei/Lei	**sarà**
noi	**siamo**		noi	**saremo**
voi	**siete**		voi	**sarete**
loro	**sono**		loro	**saranno**

	IMPERFECT			**CONDITIONAL**
io	**ero**		io	**sarei**
tu	**eri**		tu	**saresti**
lui/lei/Lei	**era**		lui/lei/Lei	**sarebbe**
noi	**eravamo**		noi	**saremmo**
voi	**eravate**		voi	**sareste**
loro	**erano**		loro	**sarebbero**

	PERFECT			**PRESENT SUBJUNCTIVE**
io	**sono stato/a**		io	**sia**
tu	**sei stato/a**		tu	**sia**
lui/lei/Lei	**è stato/a**		lui/lei/Lei	**sia**
noi	**siamo stati/e**		noi	**siamo**
voi	**siete stati/e**		voi	**siate**
loro	**sono stati/e**		loro	**siano**

	PAST HISTORIC
io	**fui**
tu	**fosti**
lui/lei/Lei	**fu**
noi	**fummo**
voi	**foste**
loro	**furono**

GERUND

essendo

PAST PARTICIPLE

stato

IMPERATIVE

sii / siamo / siate

EXAMPLE PHRASES

Sono italiana. I'm Italian.
Siete mai **stati** in Africa? Have you ever been to Africa?
Quando è arrivato **erano** le quattro in punto. When he arrived it was exactly four o'clock.
Spero che **sia** vero. I hope it is true.

Remember that subject pronouns are not used very often in Italian.

fare (to do, to make)

	PRESENT			**FUTURE**
io	faccio		io	farò
tu	fai		tu	farai
lui/lei/Lei	fa		lui/lei/Lei	farà
noi	facciamo		noi	faremo
voi	fate		voi	farete
loro	fanno		loro	faranno

	IMPERFECT			**CONDITIONAL**
io	facevo		io	farei
tu	facevi		tu	faresti
lui/lei/Lei	faceva		lui/lei/Lei	farebbe
noi	facevamo		noi	faremmo
voi	facevate		voi	fareste
loro	facevano		loro	farebbero

	PERFECT			**PRESENT SUBJUNCTIVE**
io	ho fatto		io	faccia
tu	hai fatto		tu	faccia
lui/lei/Lei	ha fatto		lui/lei/Lei	faccia
noi	abbiamo fatto		noi	facciamo
voi	avete fatto		voi	facciate
loro	hanno fatto		loro	facciano

	PAST HISTORIC
io	feci
tu	facesti
lui/lei/Lei	fece
noi	facemmo
voi	faceste
loro	fecero

GERUND

facendo

PAST PARTICIPLE

fatto

IMPERATIVE

fa' *or* fai / facciamo / fate

EXAMPLE PHRASES

Cosa stai **facendo**? What are you doing?
Ho fatto i letti. I've made the beds.
Ieri non **abbiamo fatto** niente. We didn't do anything yesterday.

Remember that subject pronouns are not used very often in Italian.

finire (to finish)

	PRESENT		**FUTURE**
io	**finisco**	io	**finirò**
tu	**finisci**	tu	**finirai**
lui/lei/Lei	**finisce**	lui/lei/Lei	**finirà**
noi	**finiamo**	noi	**finiremo**
voi	**finite**	voi	**finirete**
loro	**finiscono**	loro	**finiranno**

	IMPERFECT		**CONDITIONAL**
io	**finivo**	io	**finirei**
tu	**finivi**	tu	**finiresti**
lui/lei/Lei	**finiva**	lui/lei/Lei	**finirebbe**
noi	**finivamo**	noi	**finiremmo**
voi	**finivate**	voi	**finireste**
loro	**finivano**	loro	**finirebbero**

	PERFECT		**PRESENT SUBJUNCTIVE**
io	**ho finito**	io	**finisca**
tu	**hai finito**	tu	**finisca**
lui/lei/Lei	**ha finito**	lui/lei/Lei	**finisca**
noi	**abbiamo finito**	noi	**finiamo**
voi	**avete finito**	voi	**finiate**
loro	**hanno finito**	loro	**finiscano**

	PAST HISTORIC	**GERUND**
io	**finii**	**finendo**
tu	**finisti**	
lui/lei/Lei	**finì**	**PAST PARTICIPLE**
noi	**finimmo**	**finito**
voi	**finiste**	
loro	**finirono**	**IMPERATIVE**
		finisci / finiamo / finite

EXAMPLE PHRASES

Le lezioni **finiscono** alle tre. Classes finish at three.
Finisci i compiti! Finish your homework!
Ho finito. I've finished.

Remember that subject pronouns are not used very often in Italian.

lavarsi (to wash oneself)

PRESENT

io	mi lavo
tu	ti lavi
lui/lei/Lei	si lava
noi	ci laviamo
voi	vi lavate
loro	si lavano

FUTURE

io	mi laverò
tu	ti laverai
lui/lei/Lei	si laverà
noi	ci laveremo
voi	vi laverete
loro	si laveranno

IMPERFECT

io	mi lavavo
tu	ti lavavi
lui/lei/Lei	si lavava
noi	ci lavavamo
voi	vi lavavate
loro	si lavavano

CONDITIONAL

io	mi laverei
tu	ti laveresti
lui/lei/Lei	si laverebbe
noi	ci laveremmo
voi	vi lavereste
loro	si laverebbero

PERFECT

io	mi sono lavato/a
tu	ti sei lavato/a
lui/lei/Lei	si è lavato/a
noi	ci siamo lavati/e
voi	vi siete lavati/e
loro	si sono lavati/e

PRESENT SUBJUNCTIVE

io	mi lavi
tu	ti lavi
lui/lei/Lei	si lavi
noi	ci laviamo
voi	vi laviate
loro	si lavino

PAST HISTORIC

io	mi lavai
tu	ti lavasti
lui/lei/Lei	si lavò
noi	ci lavammo
voi	vi lavaste
loro	si lavarono

GERUND

lavandosi

PAST PARTICIPLE

lavatosi

IMPERATIVE

lavati / laviamoci / lavatevi

EXAMPLE PHRASES

Si sta **lavando**. He's washing.
Ti sei lavato le mani? Did you wash your hands?
Lavati i denti. Brush your teeth.

Remember that subject pronouns are not used very often in Italian.

parlare (to speak)

	PRESENT		FUTURE
io	**parlo**	io	**parlerò**
tu	**parli**	tu	**parlerai**
lui/lei/Lei	**parla**	lui/lei/Lei	**parlerà**
noi	**parliamo**	noi	**parleremo**
voi	**parlate**	voi	**parlerete**
loro	**parlano**	loro	**parleranno**

	IMPERFECT		CONDITIONAL
io	**parlavo**	io	**parlerei**
tu	**parlavi**	tu	**parleresti**
lui/lei/Lei	**parlava**	lui/lei/Lei	**parlerebbe**
noi	**parlavamo**	noi	**parleremmo**
voi	**parlavate**	voi	**parlereste**
loro	**parlavano**	loro	**parlerebbero**

	PERFECT		PRESENT SUBJUNCTIVE
io	**ho parlato**	io	**parli**
tu	**hai parlato**	tu	**parli**
lui/lei/Lei	**ha parlato**	lui/lei/Lei	**parli**
noi	**abbiamo parlato**	noi	**parliamo**
voi	**avete parlato**	voi	**parliate**
loro	**hanno parlato**	loro	**parlino**

	PAST HISTORIC
io	**parlai**
tu	**parlasti**
lui/lei/Lei	**parlò**
noi	**parlammo**
voi	**parlaste**
loro	**parlarono**

GERUND

parlando

PAST PARTICIPLE

parlato

IMPERATIVE

parla / parliamo / parlate

EXAMPLE PHRASES

Non **parlo** francese. I don't speak French.
Ho parlato con tuo fratello ieri. I spoke to your brother yesterday.
Parlerò con lei stasera. I'll speak to her this evening.

Remember that subject pronouns are not used very often in Italian.

potere (to be able)

	PRESENT		**FUTURE**
io	posso	io	potrò
tu	puoi	tu	potrai
lui/lei/Lei	può	lui/lei/Lei	potrà
noi	possiamo	noi	potremo
voi	potete	voi	potrete
loro	possono	loro	potranno

	IMPERFECT		**CONDITIONAL**
io	potevo	io	potrei
tu	potevi	tu	potresti
lui/lei/Lei	poteva	lui/lei/Lei	potrebbe
noi	potevamo	noi	potremmo
voi	potevate	voi	potreste
loro	potevano	loro	potrebbero

	PERFECT		**PRESENT SUBJUNCTIVE**
io	ho potuto	io	possa
tu	hai potuto	tu	possa
lui/lei/Lei	ha potuto	lui/lei/Lei	possa
noi	abbiamo potuto	noi	possiamo
voi	avete potuto	voi	possiate
loro	hanno potuto	loro	possano

	PAST HISTORIC		
io	potei		**GERUND**
tu	potesti		potendo
lui/lei/Lei	potè		
noi	potemmo		**PAST PARTICIPLE**
voi	poteste		potuto
loro	poterono		

IMPERATIVE

not used

EXAMPLE PHRASES

Puoi venire con noi? Can you come with us?
Potrebbe succedere. It could happen.
Non **ho potuto** farlo ieri. I couldn't do it yesterday.

Remember that subject pronouns are not used very often in Italian.

sapere (to know)

	PRESENT		FUTURE
io	**so**	io	**saprò**
tu	**sai**	tu	**saprai**
lui/lei/Lei	**sa**	lui/lei/Lei	**saprà**
noi	**sappiamo**	noi	**sapremo**
voi	**sapete**	voi	**saprete**
loro	**sanno**	loro	**sapranno**

	IMPERFECT		CONDITIONAL
io	**sapevo**	io	**saprei**
tu	**sapevi**	tu	**sapresti**
lui/lei/Lei	**sapeva**	lui/lei/Lei	**saprebbe**
noi	**sapevamo**	noi	**sapremmo**
voi	**sapevate**	voi	**sapreste**
loro	**sapevano**	loro	**saprebbero**

	PERFECT		PRESENT SUBJUNCTIVE
io	**ho saputo**	io	**sappia**
tu	**hai saputo**	tu	**sappia**
lui/lei/Lei	**ha saputo**	lui/lei/Lei	**sappia**
noi	**abbiamo saputo**	noi	**sappiamo**
voi	**avete saputo**	voi	**sappiate**
loro	**hanno saputo**	loro	**sappiano**

	PAST HISTORIC
io	**seppi**
tu	**sapesti**
lui/lei/Lei	**seppe**
noi	**sapemmo**
voi	**sapeste**
loro	**seppero**

GERUND

sapendo

PAST PARTICIPLE

saputo

IMPERATIVE

sappi / sappiamo / sappiate

EXAMPLE PHRASES

Non lo **so**. I don't know.
Non ne **sapeva** niente. He didn't know anything about it.
Non **ha saputo** cosa fare. He didn't know what to do.

Remember that subject pronouns are not used very often in Italian.

stare (to be)

	PRESENT		FUTURE
io	sto	io	starò
tu	stai	tu	starai
lui/lei/Lei	sta	lui/lei/Lei	starà
noi	stiamo	noi	staremo
voi	state	voi	starete
loro	stanno	loro	staranno

	IMPERFECT		CONDITIONAL
io	stavo	io	starei
tu	stavi	tu	staresti
lui/lei/Lei	stava	lui/lei/Lei	starebbe
noi	stavamo	noi	staremmo
voi	stavate	voi	stareste
loro	stavano	loro	starebbero

	PERFECT		PRESENT SUBJUNCTIVE
io	sono stato/a	io	stia
tu	sei stato/a	tu	stia
lui/lei/Lei	è stato/a	lui/lei/Lei	stia
noi	siamo stati/e	noi	stiamo
voi	siete stati/e	voi	stiate
loro	sono stati/e	loro	stiano

	PAST HISTORIC
io	stetti
tu	stesti
lui/lei/Lei	stette
noi	stemmo
voi	steste
loro	stettero

GERUND

stando

PAST PARTICIPLE

stato

IMPERATIVE

sta' *or* stai / stiamo / state

EXAMPLE PHRASES

Come **stai**? How are you?
Sto leggendo un libro. I'm reading a book.
Sei mai **stato** a Firenze? Have you ever been to Florence?

Remember that subject pronouns are not used very often in Italian.

volere (to want)

	PRESENT		**FUTURE**
io	voglio	io	vorrò
tu	vuoi	tu	vorrai
lui/lei/Lei	vuole	lui/lei/Lei	vorrà
noi	vogliamo	noi	vorremo
voi	volete	voi	vorrete
loro	vogliono	loro	vorranno

	IMPERFECT		**CONDITIONAL**
io	volevo	io	vorrei
tu	volevi	tu	vorresti
lui/lei/Lei	voleva	lui/lei/Lei	vorrebbe
noi	volevamo	noi	vorremmo
voi	volevate	voi	vorreste
loro	volevano	loro	vorrebbero

	PERFECT		**PRESENT SUBJUNCTIVE**
io	ho voluto	io	voglia
tu	hai voluto	tu	voglia
lui/lei/Lei	ha voluto	lui/lei/Lei	voglia
noi	abbiamo voluto	noi	vogliamo
voi	avete voluto	voi	vogliate
loro	hanno voluto	loro	vogliano

	PAST HISTORIC
io	volli
tu	volesti
lui/lei/Lei	volle
noi	volemmo
voi	voleste
loro	vollero

GERUND

volendo

PAST PARTICIPLE

voluto

IMPERATIVE

not used

EXAMPLE PHRASES

Cosa **vuoi**? What do you want?
Vorrei andare in Australia. I'd like to go to Australia.
Non **ha voluto** ammetterlo. He didn't want to admit it.

Remember that subject pronouns are not used very often in Italian.

Aa

A NOUN
1 la A *fem (letter)*
2 ottimo *(school mark)*
   □ I got an A for my essay. Nel compito ho preso ottimo.
3 il la *masc* (PL i la) *(musical note)*
   □ It's in A flat. È in la bemolle.

a ARTICLE
1 un *masc*
   □ a book un libro □ He's a friend. È un amico.
   LANGUAGE TIP When the article comes before a masculine noun starting with impure s, gn, pn, ps, x, y or z use **uno**.
   □ an uncle uno zio
2 una *fem*
   □ a letter una lettera
   LANGUAGE TIP When the article comes before a feminine noun starting with a vowel use **un'**.
   □ She's a friend. È un'amica. □ a herring un'aringa
   LANGUAGE TIP 'a' is sometimes translated by the Italian definite article.
   □ He's a butcher. Fa il macellaio. □ I haven't got a car. Non ho la macchina. □ once a week una volta alla settimana □ seventy kilometres an hour settanta chilometri all'ora
   ■ **a hundred pounds** cento sterline

aback ADVERB
   ■ **to be taken aback** rimanere [88ᴱ] sconcertato □ I was taken aback by his reaction. Sono rimasto sconcertato dalla sua reazione.

to **abandon** VERB
   abbandonare [68]

abbey NOUN
   l' abbazia *fem*

abbreviation NOUN
   l' abbreviazione *fem*

ability NOUN
   la capacità *fem* (PL le capacità)
   □ Ian's got plenty of ability, but he doesn't work. Ian ha le capacità ma non si applica.

able ADJECTIVE
   ■ **to be able to do something** poter [74] fare qualcosa

to **abolish** VERB
   abolire [51]

abortion NOUN
   l' aborto *masc*
   ■ **to have an abortion** abortire [51]

about PREPOSITION, ADVERB
1 a proposito di
   □ I'm phoning you about Tina. Ti chiamo a proposito di Tina.
2 su
   □ a book about London un libro su Londra
   ■ **I don't know anything about it.** Non ne so niente.
   ■ **What's it about?** Di che si tratta?
3 circa
   □ It takes about ten hours. Ci vogliono circa dieci ore.
   ■ **at about eleven o'clock** verso le undici
   ■ **to be about to do something** stare [108ᴱ] per fare qualcosa □ I was about to go out. Stavo per uscire.
   ■ **What about me?** E io?
   ■ **How about?** E se? □ How about going to the cinema? E se andassimo al cinema?

above PREPOSITION, ADVERB
   sopra
   □ He raised his hands above his head. Ha sollevato le mani sopra la testa.
   ■ **the flat above** l'appartamento al piano di sopra
   ■ **above all** soprattutto

abroad ADVERB
   all'estero
   □ They decided to go abroad. Hanno deciso di andare all'estero.

abrupt ADJECTIVE
1 brusco (FEM brusca, MASC PL bruschi, FEM PL brusche)
   □ He was a bit abrupt with me. È stato un po' brusco con me.
2 improvviso (FEM improvvisa)
   □ His abrupt departure aroused suspicion. La sua improvvisa partenza ha sollevato dei sospetti.

abruptly ADVERB
   di scatto

absence NOUN
1 l' assenza *fem*
   □ in my absence in mia assenza
2 la mancanza *fem*

absent ADJECTIVE
assente (FEM assente)

absent-minded ADJECTIVE
distratto (FEM distratta)

absolutely ADVERB
assolutamente

□ Jill's absolutely right. Jill ha assolutamente
ragione.

■ **Absolutely!** Altroché! □ Do you think it's a
good idea? — Absolutely! Ti sembra una buona
idea? — Altroché!

absorbed ADJECTIVE

■ **to be absorbed in something** essere [47ᴱ]
assorto in qualcosa

absorbent cotton NOUN (US)
il cotone idrofilo masc

absurd ADJECTIVE
assurdo (FEM assurda)

abuse NOUN

▷ see also **abuse** VERB

■ **child abuse** la violenza sui minori

■ **drug abuse** l'abuso di sostanze stupefacenti

to **abuse** VERB

▷ see also **abuse** NOUN

■ **to abuse drugs** far [49] uso di stupefacenti

■ **to be abused** subire [51] violenza

□ Children who have been abused... I bambini
che hanno subito violenza...

abusive ADJECTIVE

1 ingiurioso (FEM ingiuriosa) (language)

2 violento (FEM violenta) (person, husband)

academic ADJECTIVE

1 scolastico (FEM scolastica, MASC PL scolastici,
FEM PL scolastiche)

□ his academic performance il suo
rendimento scolastico

2 accademico (FEM accademica, MASC PL
accademici, FEM PL accademiche)

□ the academic year l'anno accademico

3 portato per gli studi (FEM portata)

□ I'm not very academic. Non sono molto
portato per gli studi.

academy NOUN
l' accademia fem

to **accelerate** VERB
accelerare [68]

accelerator NOUN
l' acceleratore masc

accent NOUN
l' accento masc

□ He hasn't got an accent. Non ha alcun
accento.

to **accept** VERB
accettare [68]

□ I decided to accept the offer. Ho deciso di
accettare l'offerta.

■ **to accept responsibility for something**
assumersi [11ᴱ] la responsabilità di qualcosa

acceptable ADJECTIVE
accettabile (FEM accettabile)

access NOUN
l' accesso masc

□ wheelchair access accesso per disabili

■ **Her ex-husband has access to the
children.** Il suo ex marito ha diritto a vedere i
bambini.

■ **to gain access to something** (files,
documents) riuscire [117ᴱ] ad accedere a qualcosa

accessible ADJECTIVE
accessibile (FEM accessibile)

accessory NOUN
l' accessorio masc

accident NOUN
l' incidente masc

□ The fog caused several accidents. La nebbia
ha provocato diversi incidenti.

■ **by accident** per caso □ They made the
discovery by accident. La scoperta è avvenuta
per caso.

■ **The burglar killed him by accident.** Il
ladro lo ha ucciso per errore.

accidental ADJECTIVE
involontario (FEM involontaria, MASC PL
involontari, FEM PL involontarie)

to **accommodate** VERB
alloggiare [58]

accommodation (US **accommodations**)
NOUN
l' alloggio masc

to **accompany** VERB
accompagnare [14]

accord NOUN

■ **of his own accord** spontaneamente

accordingly ADVERB
di conseguenza

according to PREPOSITION
secondo

□ According to him, everyone had left. Secondo
lui erano tutti andati via.

accordion NOUN
la fisarmonica fem (PL le fisarmoniche)

account NOUN

1 il conto masc

□ I've just opened an account. Ho appena
aperto un conto.

■ **a bank account** un conto in banca

■ **the account number** il numero di conto

■ **to do the accounts** tenere [113] la
contabilità

2 il resoconto masc

□ He gave a detailed account of what
happened. Ha fatto un resoconto
particolareggiato dell'accaduto.

■ **to take something into account** prendere
[77] in considerazione qualcosa

■ **by all accounts** a detta di tutti

■ **on account of** a causa di □ We couldn't go out on account of the bad weather. Non siamo potuti uscire a causa del maltempo.

to **account for** VERB
spiegare [76]
□ If she was ill, that would account for her poor results. Se fosse malata si spiegherebbero gli scarsi risultati.

accountable ADJECTIVE
■ **to be accountable to someone** dover [42] rendere conto a qualcuno

accountancy NOUN
la ragioneria fem

accountant NOUN
1 il/la commercialista masc/fem (graduate)
2 il ragioniere masc
la ragioniera fem (bookkeeper)

accuracy NOUN
l' accuratezza fem

accurate ADJECTIVE
accurato (FEM accurata)

accurately ADVERB
accuratamente

accusation NOUN
l' accusa fem

to **accuse** VERB
■ **to accuse somebody of something** accusare [68] qualcuno di qualcosa

ace NOUN
1 l' asso masc (in cards)
2 l' ace masc (PL gli ace) (in tennis)

ache NOUN
▷ see also **ache** VERB
il dolore masc
■ **to have stomach ache** avere [12] mal di stomaco

to **ache** VERB
▷ see also **ache** NOUN
far [49] male
□ My leg's aching. Mi fa male la gamba.

to **achieve** VERB
ottenere [113]
□ You won't achieve anything. Non otterrai nulla.

achievement NOUN
il risultato masc
□ It was a fantastic achievement for our team. È stato un risultato meraviglioso per la nostra squadra.

acid NOUN
l' acido masc
□ acid rain pioggia acida

acne NOUN
l' acne fem

acre NOUN
l' acro masc

acrobat NOUN
l' acrobata masc/fem

across PREPOSITION, ADVERB
dall'altra parte di
□ the shop across the road il negozio dall'altra parte della strada
■ **an expedition across the Sahara** una spedizione nel Sahara
■ **to run across the road** attraversare [68] di corsa la strada
■ **across from** di fronte a □ He sat down across from her. Si è seduto di fronte a lei.

to **act** VERB
▷ see also **act** NOUN
1 agire [51]
□ The police acted quickly. La polizia ha agito prontamente.
■ **to act as** fare [49] da □ She acts as his interpreter. Lei gli fa da interprete.
2 recitare [68]
□ She's acting the part of Juliet. Recita il ruolo di Giulietta.

act NOUN
▷ see also **act** VERB
1 l' atto masc
□ in the first act nel primo atto
2 la scena fem
□ It was all an act. Era tutta una scena.

action NOUN
l' azione fem
□ The film was full of action. Nel film c'erano molte scene d'azione.
■ **to take firm action against** prendere [77] misure energiche contro

active ADJECTIVE
attivo (FEM attiva)

activity NOUN
l' attività fem (PL le attività)
□ outdoor activities attività all'aria aperta

actor NOUN
l' attore masc

actress NOUN
l' attrice fem

actual ADJECTIVE
effettivo (FEM effettiva)
□ What's the actual amount? Qual è la cifra effettiva?

> **LANGUAGE TIP** Be careful not to translate **actual** by **attuale**.

actually ADVERB
1 effettivamente
□ You only pay for the electricity you actually use. Si paga solo per l'elettricità effettivamente consumata.

> **LANGUAGE TIP** 'actually' is sometimes not translated.

□ I was so bored I actually fell asleep! Ero così annoiato che mi sono addormentato! □ I'm not a student, I'm a doctor, actually. Non sono uno studente, sono un medico.

2 veramente

▫ Fiona's awful, isn't she? — Actually, I quite like her. Fiona è odiosa, no? — Veramente a me è abbastanza simpatica.

▌ **LANGUAGE TIP** Be careful not to translate **actually** by **attualmente**.

acupuncture NOUN
l' agopuntura *fem*

AD ABBREVIATION (= *Anno Domini*)
d.C. (= *dopo Cristo*)

▫ in 800 AD nell'anno 800 d.C.

ad NOUN

1 l' annuncio *masc*

▫ He put an ad in the paper. Ha messo un annuncio sul giornale.

2 la pubblicità *fem* (PL le pubblicità)

▫ I saw an ad for the concert. Ho visto la pubblicità del concerto.

to **adapt** VERB
adattare [68]

■ **to adapt to something** adattarsi [56E] a qualcosa

adaptor NOUN

1 il riduttore *masc (for plug)*

2 la presa multipla *fem (with several sockets)*

to **add** VERB
aggiungere [5]

▫ Add a bit of sugar. Aggiungi un po' di zucchero.

to **add up** VERB
sommare [68]

▫ If you add up the numbers... Se sommi i numeri...

addict NOUN
il/la tossicomane *masc/fem*

addicted ADJECTIVE

■ **to be addicted to drugs** essere [47E] tossicodipendente

■ **She's addicted to soaps.** È appassionata di telenovelas.

addition NOUN

■ **in addition** inoltre

■ **in addition to** oltre a

address NOUN
l' indirizzo *masc*

adjective NOUN
l' aggettivo *masc*

to **adjust** VERB
regolare [68]

▫ You can adjust the height of the seat. Si può regolare l'altezza della sedia.

■ **to adjust to something** adattarsi [56E] a qualcosa

adjustable ADJECTIVE
regolabile (FEM regolabile)

administration NOUN
l' amministrazione *fem*

admiral NOUN
l' ammiraglio *masc*

to **admire** VERB
ammirare [68]

admission NOUN
l' ingresso *masc*

▫ 'admission free' 'ingresso gratuito'

to **admit** VERB

1 ammettere [59]

▫ I must admit that... Devo ammettere che...

2 confessare [68]

▫ He admitted that he'd done it. Ha confessato di averlo fatto.

admittance NOUN

■ 'no admittance' 'vietato l'ingresso'

adolescent NOUN
l' adolescente *masc/fem*

to **adopt** VERB
adottare [68]

adopted ADJECTIVE
adottivo (FEM adottiva)

adoption NOUN
l' adozione *fem*

to **adore** VERB
adorare [68]

Adriatic NOUN

■ **the Adriatic** l'Adriatico

adult NOUN
l' adulto *masc*

■ **adult education** i corsi per adulti

to **advance** VERB
▷ *see also* **advance** NOUN

1 avanzare [68]

▫ The troops are advancing. Le truppe avanzano.

2 fare [49] progressi

▫ Technology has advanced a great deal. La tecnologia ha fatto grandi progressi.

advance NOUN
▷ *see also* **advance** VERB
l' anticipo *masc*

■ **in advance** in anticipo

advance booking NOUN
la prenotazione *fem*

advanced ADJECTIVE
avanzato (FEM avanzata)

advantage NOUN
il vantaggio *masc*

▫ This is an advantage. Questo è un vantaggio.

■ **to take advantage of something** approfittare [68] di qualcosa

■ **to take advantage of somebody** approfittarsi [56E] di qualcuno

adventure NOUN
l' avventura *fem*

adverb NOUN
l' avverbio *masc*

advert NOUN

1 l' annuncio *masc*

▫ He put an advert in the paper. Ha messo un annuncio sul giornale.

2 la pubblicità *fem*
□ I saw an advert for the concert. Ho visto la pubblicità del concerto.

to **advertise** VERB
fare [49] pubblicità
□ They're advertising the new model. Stanno facendo pubblicità per il nuovo modello.
■ **Jobs are advertised in the paper.** Il giornale pubblica annunci di lavoro.

advertisement NOUN
1 l' annuncio *masc*
□ an advertisement in the paper un annuncio sul giornale
2 la pubblicità *fem*
□ an advertisement for the concert una pubblicità del concerto

advertising NOUN
la pubblicità *fem*

advice NOUN
il consiglio *masc*
□ Take my advice and stay away from him! Segui il mio consiglio, tieniti alla larga da lui!

> **LANGUAGE TIP** Unlike 'advice', **consiglio** is used with an article, and can be made plural.

■ **some advice** dei consigli □ He gave me some good advice. Mi ha dato dei buoni consigli.

to **advise** VERB
consigliare [25]
□ He advised me to wait. Mi ha consigliato di aspettare.

aerial NOUN
l' antenna *fem*

aerobics NOUN PL
l' aerobica *fem sing*

aeroplane (US **airplane**) NOUN
l' aeroplano *masc*

aerosol NOUN
l' aerosol *masc*

affair NOUN
1 la faccenda *fem*
□ They mishandled the affair. Hanno gestito male la faccenda.
2 la relazione *fem*
□ She's having an affair with Shaun. Ha una relazione con Shaun.

to **affect** VERB
avere [12] un impatto su

affectionate ADJECTIVE
affettuoso (FEM affettuosa)

to **afford** VERB
permettersi [59E]
□ I can't afford a new pair of jeans. Non mi posso permettere un altro paio di jeans.

afraid ADJECTIVE
■ **to be afraid of something** aver [12] paura di qualcosa □ I'm afraid of spiders. Ho paura dei ragni.

■ **I'm afraid I can't come.** Mi dispiace ma non posso venire.
■ **I'm afraid so.** Temo di sì.
■ **I'm afraid not.** Temo di no.

Africa NOUN
l' Africa *fem*

African ADJECTIVE
▷ *see also* **African** NOUN
africano (FEM africana)

African NOUN
▷ *see also* **African** ADJECTIVE
l' africano *masc*
l' africana *fem*
□ the Africans gli africani

after PREPOSITION, ADVERB, CONJUNCTION
1 dopo
□ after dinner dopo cena □ after I'd had a rest dopo essermi riposato □ the day after il giorno dopo
2 dietro
□ He ran after me. Mi è corso dietro. □ Shut the door after you. Chiudi la porta dietro di te.
■ **after all** dopotutto

afternoon NOUN
il pomeriggio *masc*
□ in the afternoon nel pomeriggio □ at four o'clock in the afternoon alle quattro del pomeriggio

afters NOUN
il dessert *masc*
□ What's for afters? Cosa c'è per dessert?

aftershave NOUN
il dopobarba *masc* (PL i dopobarba)

afterwards ADVERB
dopo

again ADVERB
di nuovo
□ They're friends again. Sono di nuovo amici.
■ **not... again** non... più □ I won't go there again. Lì non ci torno più.
■ **again and again** ripetutamente

against PREPOSITION
contro
□ I'm against hunting. Sono contro la caccia.

age NOUN
l' età *fem* (PL le età)
□ at the age of sixteen all'età di sedici anni
□ the age limit il limite d'età
■ **the 40 to 50 age group** le persone fra i quaranta e i cinquant'anni
■ **I haven't been to the cinema for ages.** Sono secoli che non vado al cinema.

aged ADJECTIVE
■ **aged ten** di dieci anni

agenda NOUN
l' ordine del giorno *masc*

agent NOUN
l' agente *masc/fem*

□ an estate agent un agente immobiliare □ a travel agent un agente di viaggio

aggressive ADJECTIVE
aggressivo (FEM aggressiva)

agitated ADJECTIVE
turbato (FEM turbata)

ago ADVERB
fa
□ two days ago due giorni fa □ not long ago poco tempo fa

agony NOUN
■ to be in agony soffrire [66] moltissimo
■ It was agony! È stata una tortura!

to **agree** VERB
essere [47ᴱ] d'accordo
□ I don't agree! Non sono d'accordo!
■ to agree to do something accettare [68] di fare qualcosa □ He agreed to go and pick her up. Ha accettato di andare a prenderla.
■ to agree that ammettere [59] che □ I agree that it's difficult. Ammetto che è difficile.
■ Garlic doesn't agree with me. L'aglio mi è indigesto.

agreed ADJECTIVE
stabilito (FEM stabilita)
□ at the agreed time all'ora stabilita

agreement NOUN
l' accordo masc
■ to be in agreement essere [47ᴱ] d'accordo

agricultural ADJECTIVE
agricolo (FEM agricola)

agriculture NOUN
l' agricoltura fem

ahead ADVERB
davanti
□ She looked straight ahead. Guardava dritto davanti a sé.
■ ahead of time in anticipo
■ to plan ahead pianificare [18]
■ to be ahead (in sport) essere [47ᴱ] in vantaggio □ Italy is five points ahead. L'Italia è in vantaggio di cinque punti.
■ Go ahead! Fai pure!

aid NOUN
gli aiuti masc pl
□ humanitarian aid aiuti umanitari
■ in aid of charity a scopo di beneficenza

AIDS NOUN
l' AIDS fem

to **aim** VERB
▷ see also **aim** NOUN
puntare [68]
□ He aimed the gun at me. Mi ha puntato contro la pistola.
■ to be aimed at essere [47ᴱ] diretto a □ It's aimed at a young audience. È diretto ad un pubblico giovane.
■ to aim to do something avere [12] intenzione di fare qualcosa

aim NOUN
▷ see also **aim** VERB
l' obiettivo masc

air NOUN
l' aria fem
□ in the open air all'aria aperta
■ to travel by air viaggiare [58] in aereo

air-conditioned ADJECTIVE
con l'aria condizionata

air conditioning NOUN
l' aria condizionata fem

Air Force NOUN
l' aviazione militare fem

air hostess NOUN
la hostess fem (PL le hostess)

airline NOUN
la compagnia aerea fem

airmail NOUN
■ by airmail per via aerea

airplane NOUN (US)
l' aeroplano masc

airport NOUN
l' aeroporto masc

aisle NOUN
1 il corridoio masc
□ an aisle seat un posto sul corridoio
2 la navata fem
□ the central aisle of the church la navata centrale della chiesa

alarm NOUN
l' allarme masc
□ He raised the alarm. Ha dato l'allarme.
■ a fire alarm un allarme antincendio

alarm clock NOUN
la sveglia fem

album NOUN
l' album masc (PL gli album)

alcohol NOUN
1 gli alcolici masc pl (drinks)
2 l'alcol masc (substance)

alcoholic NOUN
▷ see also **alcoholic** ADJECTIVE
l' alcolizzato masc
l' alcolizzata fem

alcoholic ADJECTIVE
▷ see also **alcoholic** NOUN
alcolico (FEM alcolica, MASC PL alcolici, FEM PL alcoliche)
□ alcoholic drinks bevande alcoliche fem pl

alert ADJECTIVE
1 sveglio (FEM sveglia, MASC PL svegli, FEM PL sveglie)
□ He's a very alert baby. È un bambino molto sveglio.
2 all'erta
□ Stay alert! Stai all'erta!

A level NOUN
■ I did French at A level. Il francese è una delle materie che ho studiato per la matura.

Algeria NOUN
l' Algeria *fem*

alike ADVERB
■ **to look alike** assomigliarsi [25ᴱ] □ They look alike. Si assomigliano.

alive ADJECTIVE
vivo (FEM viva)

all ADJECTIVE, PRONOUN, ADVERB
tutto (FEM tutta)
□ all alone tutto solo □ That's all I can remember. È tutto ciò che ricordo.
■ **after all** dopotutto
■ **not at all** per niente □ I'm not at all tired. Non sono per niente stanco.
■ **all the time** tutto il tempo □ We can't be together all the time. Non possiamo stare assieme tutto il tempo.
■ **She talks all the time.** Parla in continuazione.
■ **The score is five all.** Il punteggio è di cinque a cinque.

allergic ADJECTIVE
allergico (FEM allergica, MASC PL allergici, FEM PL allergiche)

allergy NOUN
l' allergia *fem* (PL le allergie)
■ **a nut allergy** un'allergia alla frutta secca

alley NOUN
il vicolo *masc*

to **allow** VERB
permettere [59]
□ Smoking is not allowed. Non è permesso fumare.
■ **to allow somebody to do something** permettere [59] a qualcuno di fare qualcosa □ His mum allowed him to go out. Sua madre gli ha permesso di uscire.
■ **to be allowed to do something** avere [12] il permesso di fare qualcosa □ He's not allowed to go out at night. Non ha il permesso di uscire la sera.

all right ADVERB, ADJECTIVE
bene
□ Everything turned out all right. Tutto è andato bene.
■ **All right!** Va bene!
■ **to be all right 1** (*person*) stare [108ᴱ] bene □ I'm all right. Sto bene. **2** (*thing*) andare [6ᴱ] bene □ Is that all right with you? Per te va bene?
■ **The film was all right.** Il film non era male.

almond NOUN
la mandorla *fem*

almost ADVERB
quasi

alone ADJECTIVE, ADVERB
solo (FEM sola)

□ The flight alone costs £500. Solo il volo costa cinquecento sterline.
■ **She lives alone.** Vive da sola.
■ **Leave her alone!** Lasciala in pace!
■ **Leave my things alone!** Lascia stare le mie cose!

along PREPOSITION, ADVERB
lungo
□ Chris was walking along the beach. Chris passeggiava lungo la spiaggia.
■ **all along** fin dall'inizio □ He was lying to me all along. Mi ha mentito fin dall'inizio.

aloud ADVERB
ad alta voce

alphabet NOUN
l' alfabeto *masc*

Alps NOUN PL
le Alpi *fem pl*

already ADVERB
già
□ Liz had already gone. Liz se n'era già andata.

also ADVERB
anche

altar NOUN
l' altare *masc*

to **alter** VERB
cambiare [17]

alternate ADJECTIVE
■ **on alternate days** a giorni alterni

alternative NOUN
▷ *see also* **alternative** ADJECTIVE
l' alternativa *fem*
□ You have no alternative. Non hai alternative.

alternative ADJECTIVE
▷ *see also* **alternative** NOUN
alternativo (FEM alternativa)
□ an alternative solution una soluzione alternativa
■ **They made alternative plans.** Hanno fatto altri piani.
■ **alternative medicine** medicina alternativa

alternatively ADVERB
altrimenti
□ Alternatively, we could stay at home. Altrimenti potremmo stare a casa.

although CONJUNCTION
nonostante
□ Although she was tired, she stayed up late. Nonostante fosse stanca è rimasta alzata fino a tardi.

altogether ADVERB
1 in tutto
□ You owe me twenty pounds altogether. In tutto mi devi venti sterline.
2 del tutto
□ I'm not altogether sure. Non sono del tutto sicuro.

aluminium – angry

aluminium (us **aluminum**) NOUN
l' alluminio *masc*

always ADVERB
sempre
□ He's always moaning. Si lamenta sempre.

am VERB ▷ *see* **be**

a.m. ADVERB (= *ante meridiem*)
del mattino
□ at four a.m. alle quattro del mattino

amateur NOUN
il/la dilettante *masc/fem*

amazed ADJECTIVE
stupefatto (FEM stupefatta)
□ I was amazed that I managed to do it. Io
stesso ero stupefatto di esserci riuscito.

amazing ADJECTIVE
1 incredibile (FEM incredibile)
□ That's amazing news! È una notizia
incredibile!
2 eccezionale (FEM eccezionale)
□ an amazing cook una cuoca eccezionale

ambassador NOUN
l' ambasciatore *masc*
l' ambasciatrice *fem*

amber ADJECTIVE
giallo (FEM gialla)
□ The light is amber! È giallo!

ambition NOUN
l' ambizione *fem*

ambitious ADJECTIVE
ambizioso (FEM ambiziosa)

ambulance NOUN
l' ambulanza *fem*

amenities NOUN PL
■ The hotel has very good amenities.
L'albergo è molto ben attrezzato dal punto di
vista ricreativo.

America NOUN
l' America *fem*

American ADJECTIVE
▷ *see also* **American** NOUN
americano (FEM americana)

American NOUN
▷ *see also* **American** ADJECTIVE
l' americano *masc*
l' americana *fem*
□ the Americans gli americani

among PREPOSITION
tra
□ I was among friends. Ero tra amici.

amount NOUN
1 la quantità *fem* (PL le quantità)
□ a huge amount of rice una grossa quantità
di riso
2 la somma *fem*
□ a large amount of money una grossa
somma di denaro

amp NOUN
1 l' ampere *masc* (PL gli ampere) (*electricity*)
2 l' amplificatore *masc* (*amplifier*)

amplifier NOUN
l' amplificatore *masc*

to **amuse** VERB
divertire [41]
□ He was most amused by the story. La storia
lo divertì molto.

amusement arcade NOUN
la sala giochi *fem*

an ARTICLE ▷ *see* **a**

anaemic (us **anemic**) ADJECTIVE
anemico (FEM anemica, MASC PL anemici, FEM PL
anemiche)

to **analyse** (us **analyze**) VERB
analizzare [68]

analysis NOUN
l' analisi *fem* (PL le analisi)

to **analyze** VERB (US)
analizzare [68]

ancestor NOUN
l' antenato *masc*
l' antenata *fem*

anchor NOUN
l' ancora *fem*

ancient ADJECTIVE
antico (FEM antica, MASC PL antichi, FEM PL
antiche)
□ ancient Greece la Grecia antica
■ an ancient monument un monumento
storico

and CONJUNCTION
e
□ you and me tu ed io
■ Please try and come! Cerca di venire!
■ better and better sempre meglio

anemic ADJECTIVE (US)
anemico (FEM anemica, MASC PL anemici, FEM PL
anemiche)

angel NOUN
l' angelo *masc*

anger NOUN
la rabbia *fem*

angle NOUN
l' angolo *masc*
■ a right angle un angolo retto

angler NOUN
il pescatore *masc*

angling NOUN
la pesca con la lenza *fem*

angry ADJECTIVE
arrabbiato (FEM arrabbiata)
□ Your father looks very angry. Tuo padre ha
l'aria molto arrabbiata.
■ You're making me angry. Mi stai facendo
arrabbiare.
■ to get angry arrabbiarsi [17E]

animal NOUN
l' animale *masc*

ankle NOUN
la caviglia *fem*
□ I've twisted my ankle. Mi sono slogato la caviglia.

anniversary NOUN
l' anniversario *masc*
□ It's their wedding anniversary. È il loro anniversario di matrimonio.

to **announce** VERB
annunciare [13]

announcement NOUN
l' annuncio *masc*
□ an announcement about our flight un annuncio riguardo al nostro volo

to **annoy** VERB
dare [30] fastidio
□ He's really annoying me. Mi sta veramente dando fastidio.
■ **to get annoyed** arrabbiarsi [17ᴱ] □ He got annoyed and put the phone down. Si arrabbiò e mise giù il ricevitore.
■ **Don't get so annoyed!** Non prendertela tanto!

annoying ADJECTIVE
seccante (FEM seccante)

annual ADJECTIVE
annuale (FEM annuale)

anonymous ADJECTIVE
anonimo (FEM anonima)

anorak NOUN
la giacca a vento *fem* (PL le giacche a vento)

anorexic ADJECTIVE
anoressico (FEM anoressica, MASC PL anoressici, FEM PL anoressiche)

another ADJECTIVE
un altro
un'altra
□ I've got another T-shirt in my bag. Ho un'altra maglietta nella borsa.

to **answer** VERB
▷ *see also* **answer** NOUN
rispondere [90]
□ Could you answer the phone? Potresti rispondere al telefono?
■ **to answer the door** andare [6ᴱ] ad aprire

answer NOUN
▷ *see also* **answer** VERB
la risposta *fem*
□ We need an answer by Tuesday. Dobbiamo avere una risposta entro martedì.
■ **the answer to the problem** la soluzione del problema

answering machine NOUN
la segreteria telefonica *fem* (PL le segreterie telefoniche)

ant NOUN
la formica *fem* (PL le formiche)

Antarctic NOUN
l' Antartide *fem*

anthem NOUN
■ **the national anthem** l'inno nazionale

antibiotic NOUN
l' antibiotico *masc* (PL gli antibiotici)

antidepressant NOUN
l' antidepressivo *masc*

antique NOUN
il pezzo d'antiquariato *masc*
□ I bought an antique. Ho comprato un pezzo d'antiquariato.

antique shop NOUN
il negozio d'antiquario *masc*

antiseptic NOUN
il disinfettante *masc*

any ADJECTIVE, PRONOUN
1 qualche
□ Have you got any comment? Hai qualche commento?
2 qualunque *(any at all)*
□ You can make the tart with any fruit you like. Puoi fare la crostata con qualunque tipo di frutta.
■ **any time you like** quando vuoi
  LANGUAGE TIP 'any' is sometimes not translated.
□ I haven't got any money. Non ho soldi.
  LANGUAGE TIP 'any' is sometimes translated by **ne**.
□ I haven't got any. Non ne ho.
■ **any more** più □ I don't love him any more. Non lo amo più.

anybody PRONOUN
1 qualcuno
□ Has anybody got a pen? Qualcuno ha una penna?
2 nessuno
  LANGUAGE TIP Use **nessuno** in negative sentences.
□ I can't see anybody. Non vedo nessuno.
3 chiunque *(anybody at all)*
□ Anybody can learn to swim. Chiunque può imparare a nuotare.

anyhow ADVERB
comunque
□ He doesn't want to go out and anyhow he's not allowed. Non vuole uscire e comunque non ha il permesso di farlo.

anyone PRONOUN
1 qualcuno
□ Has anyone got a pen? Qualcuno ha una penna?
2 nessuno
  LANGUAGE TIP Use **nessuno** in negative sentences.
□ I can't see anyone. Non vedo nessuno.

317

English-Italian

a

3 chiunque *(anyone at all)*
□ Anyone can learn to swim. Chiunque può imparare a nuotare.

anything PRONOUN

1 qualcosa
□ Do you need anything? Ti serve qualcosa?

2 niente

> **LANGUAGE TIP** Use **niente** in negative sentences.

□ I can't hear anything. Non sento niente.

3 qualunque cosa *(anything at all)*
□ Anything could happen. Potrebbe succedere qualunque cosa.

anyway ADVERB

comunque
□ He doesn't want to go out and anyway he's not allowed. Non vuole uscire e comunque non ha il permesso di farlo.

■ **What business is it of yours, anyway?** E tu di che t'impicci?

anywhere ADVERB

1 da qualche parte
□ Have you seen my coat anywhere? Hai visto il mio cappotto da qualche parte?

2 da nessuna parte

> **LANGUAGE TIP** Use **da nessuna parte** in negative sentences.

□ I can't find it anywhere. Non riesco a trovarlo da nessuna parte.

3 dovunque *(anywhere at all)*
□ You can buy stamps almost anywhere. Puoi comprare i francobolli dovunque.

apart ADVERB

■ **The towns are ten kilometres apart.** Le città distano dieci chilometri.

■ **Nothing will keep them apart.** Niente li terrà lontani l'uno dall'altra.

■ **apart from** a parte □ Apart from that, everything's fine. A parte quello, va tutto bene.

apartment NOUN

l' appartamento *masc*
□ a small apartment un piccolo appartamento

to **apologize** VERB

chiedere [19] scusa

> **LANGUAGE TIP** Word for word, this means 'to ask for pardon'.

□ I apologize! Chiedo scusa!

apology NOUN

le scuse *fem pl*
□ I owe you an apology. Ti devo delle scuse.

apostrophe NOUN

l' apostrofo *masc*

app NOUN

l' app *fem*
□ a mobile app un'app per il cellulare

apparatus NOUN

1 le apparecchiature *fem pl*
□ the apparatus in the chemistry lab le apparecchiature del laboratorio chimico

2 l' attrezzatura *fem*
□ the apparatus in the gym l'attrezzatura della palestra

apparent ADJECTIVE

apparente (FEM apparente)

apparently ADVERB

■ **Apparently…** A quanto pare… □ Apparently he was abroad when it happened. A quanto pare era all'estero quando è successo il fatto.

to **appeal** VERB

▷ *see also* **appeal** NOUN

chiedere [19]
□ They appealed for help. Hanno chiesto aiuto.

■ **Greece doesn't appeal to me.** La Grecia non mi attira.

appeal NOUN

▷ *see also* **appeal** VERB

l' appello *masc*
□ They've launched an appeal. Hanno lanciato un appello.

to **appear** VERB

1 apparire [7E]
□ The bus appeared around the corner. L'autobus è apparso all'angolo della strada.

2 sembrare [68E]
□ She appeared to be asleep. Sembrava che dormisse.

appearance NOUN

l' aspetto *masc*
□ She takes great care over her appearance. Cura molto il suo aspetto.

■ **to make an appearance** fare [49] un'apparizione

■ **to put in an appearance** fare [49] atto di presenza

appendicitis NOUN

l' appendicite *fem*

appetite NOUN

l' appetito *masc*
□ He has a big appetite. Ha molto appetito.

to **applaud** VERB

applaudire [41]

applause NOUN

gli applausi *masc pl*
□ laughter and applause risa e applausi

■ **a round of applause** un applauso

apple NOUN

la mela *fem*

applicant NOUN

■ **There were a hundred applicants.** Hanno fatto domanda cento persone.

■ **They're interviewing four applicants this week.** Hanno colloqui con quattro candidati questa settimana.

application NOUN

la domanda *fem*
□ a job application una domanda di lavoro

application form NOUN

il modulo *masc*

to **apply** VERB
- **to apply for a job** fare [49] domanda per un posto di lavoro
- **to apply to** riguardare [68] □ This rule doesn't apply to us. Questa norma non ci riguarda.

to **appoint** VERB
nominare [68]

appointment NOUN
l' appuntamento *masc*
□ a dental appointment un appuntamento dal dentista

to **appreciate** VERB
- **to appreciate something** essere [47ᴱ] riconoscente di qualcosa □ I really appreciate your help. Ti sono veramente riconoscente dell'aiuto.

apprentice NOUN
l' apprendista *masc/fem*

to **approach** VERB
1 avvicinarsi [56ᴱ] a
□ He approached the house. Si è avvicinato alla casa.
2 affrontare [68]
□ I'm not sure how to approach the problem. Non so come affrontare il problema.

appropriate ADJECTIVE
1 adatto (FEM adatta)
□ an appropriate outfit un abbigliamento adatto
2 apposito (FEM apposita)
□ Tick the appropriate box. Barrare l'apposita casella.
3 corretto (FEM corretta)
□ appropriate behaviour comportamento corretto

approval NOUN
l' approvazione *fem*

to **approve** VERB
- **to approve of** approvare [68] □ I don't approve of his choice. Non approvo la sua scelta.

approximate ADJECTIVE
approssimativo (FEM approssimativa)

apricot NOUN
l' albicocca *fem* (PL le albicocche)

April NOUN
aprile
□ in April in aprile
- **April Fools' Day** il primo aprile

apron NOUN
il grembiule da cucina *masc*

aquarium NOUN
l' acquario *masc*

Aquarius NOUN
l' Acquario *masc*
□ I'm Aquarius. Sono dell'Acquario.

Arab ADJECTIVE
▷ see also **Arab** NOUN
arabo (FEM araba)

Arab NOUN
▷ see also **Arab** ADJECTIVE
l' arabo *masc*
l' araba *fem*
□ the Arabs gli arabi

Arabic NOUN
l' arabo *masc* (language)

arch NOUN
l' arcata *fem*

archaeologist NOUN
l' archeologo *masc*
l' archeologa *fem*

archaeology NOUN
l' archeologia *fem*

archbishop NOUN
l' arcivescovo *masc*

archeologist NOUN (US)
l' archeologo *masc*
l' archeologa *fem*

archeology NOUN (US)
l' archeologia *fem*

architect NOUN
l' architetto *masc*

architecture NOUN
l' architettura *fem*

Arctic NOUN
- **the Arctic** l'Artico

are VERB ▷ see **be**

area NOUN
1 la zona *fem*
□ He lives in the Sheffield area. Abita nella zona di Sheffield.
2 il quartiere *masc*
□ My favourite area of London is Chelsea. Il quartiere londinese che preferisco è Chelsea.
3 la superficie *fem*
□ an area of 2000 square metres una superficie di duemila metri quadri

area code NOUN (US)
il prefisso *masc* (for telephone)

Argentina NOUN
l' Argentina *fem*

Argentinian NOUN
l' argentino *masc*
l' argentina *fem*

to **argue** VERB
1 litigare [76]
□ They're always arguing. Litigano sempre.
2 sostenere [113]
□ She argued that her client had been misled. Sosteneva che il suo cliente era stato tratto in inganno.

argument NOUN
1 il motivo *masc*
□ There are strong arguments against lowering the price. Ci sono motivi validi per non abbassare il prezzo.

319

Aries – ashtray

2 la discussione *fem*

□ a heated argument un'accesa discussione

■ **to have an argument** litigare [76]

Aries NOUN

l' Ariete *masc*

□ I'm Aries. Sono dell'Ariete.

arm NOUN

il braccio *masc* (FEM PL le braccia) *(limb)*

armchair NOUN

la poltrona *fem*

armour (US **armor**) NOUN

l' armatura *fem*

army NOUN

l' esercito *masc*

around PREPOSITION, ADVERB

1 intorno

□ She ignored the people around her. Ha ignorato la gente che aveva intorno.

2 circa

□ It costs around a hundred pounds. Costa circa cento sterline.

3 verso

□ Let's meet at around eight o'clock. Troviamoci verso le otto.

■ **around here** da queste parti □ Is there a chemist's around here? C'è una farmacia da queste parti?

to arrange VERB

1 organizzare [68]

□ She arranged the trip. Ha organizzato il viaggio.

■ **to arrange to do something** mettersi [59ᴱ] d'accordo per fare qualcosa □ They arranged to go out together on Friday. Si sono messi d'accordo per uscire venerdì.

■ **an arranged marriage** un matrimonio combinato

2 sistemare [68]

□ The chairs were arranged in a circle. Le sedie erano sistemate in cerchio.

arrangement NOUN

■ **We have an arrangement.** Siamo d'accordo.

■ **arrangements** preparativi □ Pamela is in charge of the travel arrangements. Pamela si occupa dei preparativi del viaggio.

to arrest VERB

▷ *see also* **arrest** NOUN

arrestare [68]

arrest NOUN

▷ *see also* **arrest** VERB

l' arresto *masc*

□ You're under arrest! La dichiaro in arresto!

arrival NOUN

l' arrivo *masc*

to arrive VERB

arrivare [68ᴱ]

□ We arrived at eight. Siamo arrivati alle otto.

arrogant ADJECTIVE

arrogante (FEM arrogante)

arrow NOUN

la freccia *fem* (PL le frecce)

art NOUN

1 l' arte *fem*

□ Greek art l'arte greca

2 le materie artistiche *fem pl*

□ He's good at art. È bravo nelle materie artistiche.

artery NOUN

l' arteria *fem*

art gallery NOUN

la galleria d'arte *fem*

article NOUN

l' articolo *masc*

artificial ADJECTIVE

artificiale (FEM artificiale)

artist NOUN

l' artista *masc/fem*

artistic ADJECTIVE

artistico (FEM artistica, MASC PL artistici, FEM PL artistiche)

as CONJUNCTION, ADVERB

1 quando

□ He came in as I was leaving. È arrivato quando stavo uscendo.

2 visto che

□ As it's Sunday, you can have a lie-in. Visto che è domenica puoi restare a letto fino a tardi.

3 come

□ He works as a waiter. Lavora come cameriere.

> **LANGUAGE TIP** There are various ways of translating 'as ... as' when used in comparisons.

□ Peter's as tall as Michael. Peter è alto come Michael. □ I haven't got as much money as you. Non ho tanti soldi quanti ne hai tu. □ Her coat cost twice as much as mine. Il suo cappotto è costato il doppio del mio.

■ **as soon as possible** prima possibile

■ **as from tomorrow** a partire da domani

■ **as if** come se

■ **as though** come se □ She acted as though she hadn't seen me. Si comportava come se non mi avesse visto.

asap ABBREVIATION (= *as soon as possible*)

prima possibile

ash NOUN

la cenere *fem* (*from fire, cigarette*)

ashamed ADJECTIVE

■ **to be ashamed** vergognarsi [14ᴱ] □ You should be ashamed of yourself! Dovresti vergognarti!

ashtray NOUN

il portacenere *masc* (PL i portacenere)

Asia NOUN
l' Asia fem

Asian ADJECTIVE
▷ see also **Asian** NOUN
asiatico (FEM asiatica, MASC PL asiatici, FEM PL asiatiche)

Asian NOUN
▷ see also **Asian** ADJECTIVE
l' asiatico masc
l' asiatica fem
□ the Asians gli asiatici

to **ask** VERB
1 chiedere [19]
□ 'Have you finished?' she asked. 'Hai finito?' chiese.
■ to ask for something chiedere [19] qualcosa □ He asked for a cup of tea. Ha chiesto una tazza di tè.
■ to ask about something informarsi [56ᴱ] su qualcosa □ I asked about train times to Leeds. Mi sono informato sugli orari dei treni per Leeds.
■ to ask somebody a question fare [49] una domanda a qualcuno
2 invitare [68]
□ Have you asked Matthew to the party? Hai invitato Matthew alla festa?
■ to ask somebody out chiedere [19] a qualcuno di uscire □ Peter asked her out. Peter le ha chiesto di uscire con lui.

asleep ADJECTIVE
■ to be asleep dormire [41] □ He's asleep. Dorme.
■ to fall asleep addormentarsi [56ᴱ] □ I fell asleep. Mi sono addormentato.

asparagus NOUN
gli asparagi masc noun

aspect NOUN
l' aspetto masc

aspirin NOUN
l' aspirina fem

asset NOUN
il vantaggio masc
□ Her experience will be an asset to the firm. La sua esperienza sarà di grande vantaggio per la ditta.

assignment NOUN
il compito masc
□ We have to do three written assignments. Dobbiamo fare tre compiti scritti.

assistance NOUN
l' aiuto masc

assistant NOUN
1 il commesso masc
la commessa fem (in shop)
2 l' assistente masc/fem (helper)

association NOUN
l' associazione fem

assortment NOUN
l' assortimento masc

to **assume** VERB
1 supporre [73]
□ I assume so. Suppongo di sì.
2 dare [30] per scontato
□ I assumed he was coming. Ho dato per scontato che venisse.

to **assure** VERB
assicurare [68]
□ He assured me he was coming. Mi ha assicurato che sarebbe venuto.

asthma NOUN
l' asma fem

to **astonish** VERB
stupire [51]

astonishing ADJECTIVE
stupefacente (FEM stupefacente)

astrology NOUN
l' astrologia fem

astronaut NOUN
l' astronauta masc/fem

astronomy NOUN
l' astronomia fem

asylum seeker NOUN
■ seven per cent of asylum seekers il sette per cento di chi chiede asilo politico

at PREPOSITION
a
□ at four o'clock alle quattro □ two at a time due alla volta □ at school a scuola
■ at the office in ufficio
■ at night di notte

ate VERB ▷ see **eat**

Athens NOUN
Atene fem

athlete NOUN
l' atleta masc/fem

athletic ADJECTIVE
atletico (FEM atletica, MASC PL atletici, FEM PL atletiche)

athletics NOUN SING
l' atletica fem

Atlantic NOUN
■ the Atlantic l'Atlantico

atlas NOUN
l' atlante masc

atmosphere NOUN
l' atmosfera fem

atom NOUN
l' atomo masc

atomic ADJECTIVE
atomico (FEM atomica, MASC PL atomici, FEM PL atomiche)

to **attach** VERB
attaccare [18]
□ They attached a rope to the car. Hanno attaccato una corda alla macchina.

attached – avalanche

attached ADJECTIVE
■ **to be attached to somebody** essere [47ᴱ]
affezionato a qualcuno
■ **Please find attached...** Allego...

attachment NOUN
1 l' allegato *masc (to email)*
2 l' attaccamento *masc*
□ his attachment to his mother il suo
attaccamento alla madre

to **attack** VERB
▷ *see also* **attack** NOUN
aggredire [51]

attack NOUN
▷ *see also* **attack** VERB
1 l' aggressione *fem*
□ a savage attack una feroce aggressione
2 l' attacco *masc (PL gli attacchi)*
□ a surprise attack un attacco a sorpresa
■ **to be under attack** essere [47ᴱ] attaccato

attempt NOUN
▷ *see also* **attempt** VERB
il tentativo *masc*
□ after several attempts dopo diversi tentativi

to **attempt** VERB
▷ *see also* **attempt** NOUN
■ **to attempt to do something** tentare [68] di
fare qualcosa □ I attempted to write a song.
Ho tentato di scrivere una canzone.

to **attend** VERB
essere [47ᴱ] presente a
□ He attended the meeting. Era presente alla
riunione.
┃ **LANGUAGE TIP** Be careful not to translate
┃ **to attend** by **attendere**.

attention NOUN
l' attenzione *fem*
■ **to pay attention** fare [49] attenzione

attic NOUN
la mansarda *fem*

attitude NOUN
l' atteggiamento *masc*

attorney NOUN (US)
l' avvocato *masc*

to **attract** VERB
attirare [68]
□ London attracts lots of tourists. Londra
attira molti turisti.

attraction NOUN
l' attrazione *fem*

attractive ADJECTIVE
attraente (FEM attraente)

aubergine NOUN
la melanzana *fem*

auction NOUN
l' asta *fem*

audience NOUN
il pubblico *masc*
□ a huge audience un grandissimo pubblico

audition NOUN
l' audizione *fem*

August NOUN
agosto
□ in August in agosto

aunt NOUN
la zia *fem*

aunty NOUN
la zia *fem*

au pair NOUN
la ragazza alla pari *fem*

Australia NOUN
l' Australia *fem*

Australian ADJECTIVE
▷ *see also* **Australian** NOUN
australiano (FEM australiana)

Australian NOUN
▷ *see also* **Australian** ADJECTIVE
l' australiano *masc*
l' australiana *fem*
□ the Australians gli australiani

Austria NOUN
l' Austria *fem*

Austrian ADJECTIVE
▷ *see also* **Austrian** NOUN
austriaco (FEM austriaca, MASC PL austriaci,
FEM PL austriache)

Austrian NOUN
▷ *see also* **Austrian** ADJECTIVE
l' austriaco *masc*
l' austriaca *fem*
□ the Austrians gli austriaci

author NOUN
l' autore *masc*
l' autrice *fem*

autobiography NOUN
l' autobiografia *fem*

autograph NOUN
l' autografo *masc*

automatic ADJECTIVE
automatico (FEM automatica, MASC PL
automatici, FEM PL automatiche)

automatically ADVERB
automaticamente

autumn NOUN
l' autunno *masc*
□ in autumn in autunno □ last autumn lo
scorso autunno

availability NOUN
la disponibilità *fem*

available ADJECTIVE
1 disponibile (FEM disponibile)
□ the amount of money available la cifra
disponibile
2 libero (FEM libera)
□ Is Mr Cooke available today? Il signor Cooke
è libero oggi?

avalanche NOUN
la valanga *fem* (PL le valanghe)

avenue NOUN
il viale *masc*

average NOUN
▷ *see also* **average** ADJECTIVE
la media *fem*
□ on average in media

average ADJECTIVE
▷ *see also* **average** NOUN
medio (FEM media)
□ the average price il prezzo medio

avocado NOUN
l' avocado *masc* (PL gli avocado)

to **avoid** VERB
evitare [68]
□ Avoid going out on your own at night. Evita di uscire da sola di sera.

awake ADJECTIVE
■ **to be awake** essere [47^E] sveglio

award NOUN
il premio *masc*

aware ADJECTIVE
■ **aware of** conscio di □ They're aware of the danger. Sono consci del pericolo.
■ **to become aware of** accorgersi [4^E] di

away ADJECTIVE, ADVERB
1 via
□ Jason was away on a business trip. Jason era via per lavoro. □ He's away for a week. È andato via per una settimana.
■ **Go away!** Vattene!
2 di distanza

□ two kilometres away a due chilometri di distanza □ two hours away by car a due ore di distanza in macchina
■ **The holiday was two weeks away.** Mancavano due settimane alla vacanza.
■ **away from his family and friends** lontano dalla famiglia e dagli amici
■ **He was still working away in the library.** Stava ancora lavorando in biblioteca.

away match NOUN
la partita in trasferta *fem*

awful ADJECTIVE
orribile (FEM orribile)
□ The weather's awful. Il tempo è orribile.
■ **I feel awful.** Mi sento malissimo.
■ **an awful lot of...** un sacco di...

> **LANGUAGE TIP** Word for word, this means 'a sack of ...'.

awfully ADVERB
terribilmente
□ I'm awfully sorry. Sono terribilmente spiacente.

awkward ADJECTIVE
1 imbarazzante (FEM imbarazzante)
□ It's an awkward situation. È una situazione imbarazzante.
2 scomodo (FEM scomoda)
□ It's a bit awkward for me to come and see you. Mi è un po' scomodo passare da te.

axe NOUN
l' ascia *fem* (PL le asce)

Bb

BA NOUN (= *Bachelor of Arts*)
la laurea *fem*
□ a BA in History una laurea in storia

baby NOUN
il bambino *masc*
la bambina *fem*

baby carriage NOUN (US)
la carrozzina *fem*

to **babysit** VERB
fare [49] la babysitter

babysitter NOUN
il/la babysitter *masc/fem*

babysitting NOUN
■ **to go babysitting** fare [49] la babysitter

bachelor NOUN
lo scapolo *masc*

back NOUN
▷ *see also* **back** ADJECTIVE, ADVERB, VERB
1 la schiena *fem*
□ He's got a bad back. Ha problemi alla schiena.
2 la groppa *fem*
□ on the horse's back sulla groppa del cavallo
3 il retro *masc*
□ on the back of the cheque sul retro dell'assegno □ at the back of the house sul retro della casa
4 il fondo *masc*
□ at back of the class in fondo alla classe
■ **the back of a chair** lo schienale della sedia
■ **in the back of the car** nel sedile posteriore dell'auto

back ADJECTIVE, ADVERB
▷ *see also* **back** NOUN, VERB
posteriore (FEM posteriore)
□ the back seat il sedile posteriore
■ **the back door** la porta sul retro
■ **to be back** tornare [68ᴱ] □ He's not back yet. Non è ancora tornato.
■ **We went there by bus and walked back.** Siamo andati in autobus e siamo ritornati a piedi.
■ **to call somebody back** richiamare [68] qualcuno

to **back** VERB
▷ *see also* **back** NOUN, ADJECTIVE, ADVERB
1 appoggiare [58]
□ The union is backing him. Il sindacato lo appoggia.

■ **to back a horse** puntare [68] su un cavallo
2 fare [49] marcia indietro
□ The road was blocked so I had to back up. La strada era bloccata e ho dovuto fare marcia indietro.
■ **She backed into the parking space.** È entrata in parcheggio in retromarcia.

to **back out** VERB
tirarsi [56ᴱ] indietro
□ They promised to help us and then backed out. Avevano promesso di aiutarci, ma si sono tirati indietro.
■ **He backed the car out of the garage.** È uscito in retromarcia dal garage.

to **back up** VERB
appoggiare [58]
□ She complained, and her colleagues backed her up. Ha fatto reclamo e i suoi colleghi l'hanno appoggiata.
■ **There's no evidence to back up his theory.** Non ci sono prove a sostegno della sua teoria.

backache NOUN
il mal di schiena *masc*
□ I have backache. Ho mal di schiena.

backbone NOUN
la spina dorsale *fem*

to **backfire** VERB
avere [12] effetto contrario

background NOUN
lo sfondo *masc*
□ a house in the background una casa sullo sfondo
■ **background noise** rumori di fondo
■ **his family background** il suo ambiente familiare

backhand NOUN
il rovescio *masc (tennis)*

backing NOUN
l' appoggio *masc*
□ They promised their backing. Hanno garantito il loro appoggio.

backpack NOUN
lo zaino *masc*

backpacker NOUN
il saccopelista *masc*

back pay NOUN
gli arretrati *masc pl*

backside NOUN
il sedere *masc*

backstroke NOUN
il dorso *masc*

backup NOUN
la riserva *fem*
□ They've got a generator as an emergency backup. Hanno un generatore di riserva per le emergenze.
■ **a backup file** un file di backup

backwards ADVERB
indietro
□ He took a step backwards. Ha fatto un passo indietro.
■ **to fall backwards** cadere [16^E] all'indietro

back yard NOUN
il cortile sul retro *masc (paved)*

bacon NOUN
la pancetta *fem*
□ bacon and eggs uova con pancetta

bad ADJECTIVE
1 cattivo (FEM cattiva)
□ He's in a bad mood. È di cattivo umore.
□ You bad boy! Cattivo!

WORD POWER
You can use a number of other words instead of **bad** to mean 'terrible':
awful orribile
□ an awful day un giorno orribile
dreadful terribile
□ a dreadful mistake un terribile errore
shocking vergognoso
□ a shocking situation una situazione vergognosa
terrible terribile
□ a terrible nightmare un terribile incubo

---

2 brutto (FEM brutta)
□ bad weather brutto tempo
3 grave (FEM grave)
□ a bad accident un grave incidente
■ **to go bad** *(food)* andare [6^E] a male
■ **I feel bad about it.** Mi sento un po' in colpa.
■ **not bad** niente male □ That's not bad at all. Non è niente male.
■ **to be bad at something** non essere [47^E] bravo in qualcosa □ I'm really bad at maths. Non sono bravo in matematica.
■ **bad language** parolacce *fem pl*

badge NOUN
il distintivo *masc*

badly ADVERB
male
□ She behaved badly. Si è comportata male.
□ badly paid mal pagato
■ **badly wounded** gravemente ferito

■ **He badly needs a rest.** Ha assolutamente bisogno di riposare.

badminton NOUN
il badminton *masc*

bad-tempered ADJECTIVE
■ **to be bad-tempered** 1 *(always)* avere [12^E] un brutto carattere 2 *(at a particular time)* essere [47^E] di malumore

to **baffle** VERB
lasciare [13] perplesso

bag NOUN
la borsa *fem*

baggage NOUN
i bagagli *masc pl*
■ **baggage allowance** il peso consentito di bagaglio

baggy ADJECTIVE
sformato (FEM sformata) *(jumper, trousers)*

bagpipes NOUN PL
la cornamusa *fem sing*

to **bake** VERB
cuocere [29] al forno *(potatoes, fish)*
■ **to bake a cake** fare [49] un dolce

baked ADJECTIVE
cotto al forno
□ baked potatoes patate cotte al forno con la buccia

baked beans NOUN PL
i fagioli in salsa rossa *masc pl*

baker NOUN
il fornaio *masc*

bakery NOUN
la panetteria *fem*

baking ADJECTIVE
■ **It's baking in here!** Qui dentro si muore di caldo!

balance NOUN
l' equilibrio *masc*
■ **to lose one's balance** perdere [69] l'equilibrio

balanced ADJECTIVE
equilibrato (FEM equilibrata)

balcony NOUN
il terrazzo *masc*

bald ADJECTIVE
calvo (FEM calva)

ball NOUN
1 la palla *fem*
□ Pass the ball to me! Passami la palla!
2 la pallina *fem*
□ a tennis ball una pallina da tennis
3 il pallone *masc*
□ a rugby ball un pallone da rugby

ballet NOUN
il balletto *masc*
□ We went to a ballet. Siamo andati a vedere un balletto.
■ **ballet lessons** corso di danza classica 325

b

ballet dancer NOUN
il ballerino classico *masc*
la ballerina classica *fem*

balloon NOUN
il palloncino *masc*
□ Lucy was holding a balloon. Lucy teneva in mano un palloncino.
■ **a hot-air balloon** una mongolfiera

ballpoint pen NOUN
la penna a sfera *fem*

ban NOUN
▷ *see also* **ban** VERB
il divieto *masc*

to **ban** VERB
▷ *see also* **ban** NOUN
vietare [68]

banana NOUN
la banana *fem*
□ a banana skin una buccia di banana

band NOUN
1 il gruppo *masc*
□ He plays the guitar in a band. Suona la chitarra in un gruppo.
2 la banda *fem*
□ The procession was led by a band. La processione era preceduta da una banda.

bandage NOUN
▷ *see also* **bandage** VERB
la fascia *fem* (PL le fasce)

to **bandage** VERB
▷ *see also* **bandage** NOUN
fasciare [13]

Band-Aid® NOUN (US)
il cerotto *masc*

bandit NOUN
il bandito *masc*

bang NOUN
▷ *see also* **bang** VERB
1 lo scoppio *masc*
□ I heard a loud bang. Ho sentito un forte scoppio.
2 il colpo *masc*
□ a bang on the head un colpo sulla testa
■ **bangs** (US) la frangetta *fem sing*

to **bang** VERB
▷ *see also* **bang** NOUN
sbattere [1]
□ I banged my head. Ho sbattuto la testa.
■ **to bang on the door** picchiare [17] alla porta

banger NOUN
la salsiccia *fem* (PL le salsicce)
□ bangers and mash salsicce e purè di patate

bank NOUN
1 la banca *fem* (PL le banche)
□ The bank is closed. La banca è chiusa.
2 la riva *fem*
□ We walked along the bank. Abbiamo camminato lungo la riva.

to **bank on** VERB
contare [68] su
□ He was banking on a pay rise. Contava su un aumento. □ I wouldn't bank on it. Non ci conterei.

bank account NOUN
il conto in banca *masc*

bank card NOUN
la carta assegni *fem*

banker NOUN
il banchiere *masc*

bank holiday NOUN
la festa *fem*
□ Monday's a bank holiday. Lunedì è festa.

banknote NOUN
la banconota *fem*

bankrupt ADJECTIVE
fallito (FEM fallita)
■ **to go bankrupt** fallire [51]

bar NOUN
1 il bar *masc* (PL i bar) *(pub)*
2 il banco *masc* (PL i banchi)
□ Please order meals at the bar. Si prega di ordinare le consumazioni al banco.
■ **a bar of chocolate** una tavoletta di cioccolata
■ **a bar of soap** una saponetta

barbaric ADJECTIVE
barbaro (FEM barbara)

barbecue NOUN
1 la grigliata all'aperto *fem* *(party)*
2 la griglia *fem* *(equipment)*

barber NOUN
il barbiere *masc*

bar code NOUN
il codice a barre *masc*

bare ADJECTIVE
nudo (FEM nuda)

barefoot ADJECTIVE, ADVERB
scalzo (FEM scalza)
□ The children go around barefoot. I bambini vanno in giro scalzi.

barely ADVERB
a malapena
□ I could barely hear her. La sentivo a malapena.

bargain NOUN
l' affare *masc*
□ It was a real bargain! È stato un vero affare!

barge NOUN
il barcone *masc*

to **bark** VERB
abbaiare [17]

barmaid NOUN
la barista *fem*

barman NOUN
il barista *masc*

barn NOUN
il fienile *masc*

barrel NOUN
1   il barile masc
    □ a barrel of beer un barile di birra
2   la canna fem (of gun)

barrier NOUN
    la barriera fem

bartender NOUN (US)
    il barista masc

base NOUN
    ▷ see also **base** VERB
    la base fem

to **base** VERB
    ▷ see also **base** NOUN
    ■ **to base on** basare [68] su □ The film is
    based on a play by Shakespeare. Il film è basato
    su una commedia di Shakespeare.
    ■ **I'm based in London.** Vivo a Londra.

baseball NOUN
    il baseball masc
    ■ **a baseball cap** un berretto da baseball

basement NOUN
    il seminterrato masc
    □ a basement flat un appartamento nel
    seminterrato

to **bash** VERB
    ▷ see also **bash** NOUN
    pestare [68]

bash NOUN
    ▷ see also **bash** VERB
    ■ **I'll have a bash.** Ci proverò.

basic ADJECTIVE
1   fondamentale (FEM fondamentale)
    □ It's one of the basic requirements. È uno dei
    requisiti fondamentali.
2   base (FEM+PL base)
    □ It's a basic model. È un modello base.
3   modesto
    □ The accommodation is pretty basic.
    L'alloggio è piuttosto modesto.

basically ADVERB
    fondamentalmente

basics NOUN PL
    i principi fondamentali masc pl

basil NOUN
    il basilico masc

basin NOUN
1   la terrina fem
    □ Put the ingredients in a basin. Mettete gli
    ingredienti in una terrina.
2   il lavandino masc
    □ He let the water out of the basin. Ha fatto
    uscire l'acqua dal lavandino.

basis NOUN
    ■ **on a daily basis** quotidianamente
    ■ **on a regular basis** regolarmente

basket NOUN
    il cestino masc

basketball NOUN
    la pallacanestro fem

bass NOUN
    il basso masc
    ■ **double bass** contrabbasso

bass drum NOUN
    la grancassa fem

bassoon NOUN
    il fagotto masc

bastard NOUN
    il bastardo masc

bat NOUN
1   la mazza fem (for baseball, cricket)
2   la racchetta fem (for ping pong)
3   il pipistrello masc (animal)

bath NOUN
1   il bagno masc
    □ I'll have a bath. Farò un bagno.
2   la vasca da bagno fem (PL le vasche da bagno)
    □ There's a spider in the bath. C'è un ragno
    nella vasca da bagno.

to **bathe** VERB
    fare [49] il bagno
    □ It was too cold to bathe. Era troppo freddo
    per fare il bagno.

bathing suit NOUN (US)
    il costume da bagno masc

bathroom NOUN
    il bagno masc

baths NOUN PL
    ■ **swimming baths** la piscina fem sing

batter NOUN
    la pastella fem

battery NOUN
1   la pila fem (for torch, toy)
2   la batteria fem (in car)

battle NOUN
    la battaglia fem

battleship NOUN
    la corazzata fem

bay NOUN
    la baia fem
    □ San Francisco Bay la baia di San Francisco

bay leaf NOUN
    la foglia d'alloro fem

BC ABBREVIATION (= before Christ)
    a.C. (= avanti Cristo)

to **be** VERB
1   essere [47E]
    □ I'm tired. Sono stanco. □ I was very happy.
    Ero molto felice. □ You're late. Sei in ritardo.
    □ He is very tall. È molto alto. □ Aren't we
    lucky? Non siamo fortunati? □ They are very
    nice. Sono molto gentili. □ They were at
    home yesterday. Ieri erano in casa. □ It's a
    nice day, isn't it? È una bella giornata, no?
    □ It's one o'clock. È l'una.

LANGUAGE TIP Use **sono** for all times except one o'clock.

□ It's four o'clock. Sono le quattro.

LANGUAGE TIP 'to be' + the present participle is often translated by a simple tense in Italian.

□ Are you coming? Vieni?

2 fare [49]

LANGUAGE TIP **fare** is used when talking about jobs and the weather.

□ She's a doctor. Fa il medico. □ It was cold. Faceva freddo.

3 avere [12]

□ I'm not cold. Non ho freddo.

LANGUAGE TIP Use **avere** when saying how old you are.

□ I'm fourteen. Ho quattordici anni. □ How old are you? Quanti anni hai?

4 stare [108ᴱ]

□ I've never been to Paris. Non sono mai stato a Parigi.

LANGUAGE TIP Use **stare** to say what you're doing at the moment, and how you're feeling.

□ What are you doing? Cosa stai facendo? □ How are you? Come stai? □ I'm fine. Sto bene.

beach NOUN
la spiaggia *fem* (PL le spiagge)

bead NOUN
la perlina *fem*

beak NOUN
il becco *masc* (PL i becchi)

beam NOUN
1 il raggio *masc*
□ a beam of light un raggio di luce
2 la trave *fem* (of wood)

bean NOUN
il fagiolo *masc*
■ **beans on toast** fagioli in salsa rossa sopra una fetta di pane tostato
■ **green beans** fagiolini

bear NOUN
▷ *see also* **bear** VERB
l' orso *masc*

to **bear** VERB
▷ *see also* **bear** NOUN
sopportare [68]
□ I can't bear it! Non lo sopporto! □ He bore his sufferings bravely. Ha sopportato con coraggio la sofferenza.
■ **If you would bear with me for a moment...** Se ha la cortesia di attendere un attimo...

beard NOUN
la barba *fem*

bearded ADJECTIVE
barbuto (FEM barbuta)

beat NOUN
▷ *see also* **beat** VERB
il ritmo *masc*

to **beat** VERB
▷ *see also* **beat** NOUN
battere [1]
□ We beat them three-nil. Li abbiamo battuti tre a zero. □ We were beaten. Siamo stati battuti.
■ **Beat it!** Fila!

to **beat up** VERB
picchiare [17]

beautiful ADJECTIVE
bello (FEM bella, MASC PL belli, FEM PL belle)
□ The weather was really beautiful. Il tempo è stato proprio bello. □ His sisters are beautiful. Le sue sorelle sono belle.

LANGUAGE TIP Use **bel** before a masculine noun starting with a consonant.

□ Thank you for the beautiful present. Grazie del bel regalo.

LANGUAGE TIP Use **bell'** before a masculine noun starting with a vowel.

□ a beautiful old watch un bell'orologio antico

LANGUAGE TIP Use **bello** before a masculine noun starting with impure s, gn, pn, ps, x, y or z.

□ a beautiful sapphire un bello zaffiro

LANGUAGE TIP Use **bei** before a plural masculine noun starting with a consonant.

□ Thanks for the beautiful flowers. Grazie dei bei fiori.

LANGUAGE TIP Use **begli** before a plural masculine noun starting with a vowel, or with impure s, gn, pn, ps, x, y or z.

□ He's got beautiful eyes. Ha begli occhi.

beauty NOUN
la bellezza *fem*

beauty spot NOUN
la località pittoresca *fem* (PL le località pittoresche)

became VERB ▷ *see* **become**

because CONJUNCTION
perché
□ I ate it because I was hungry. L'ho mangiato perché ero affamato.
■ **because of** a causa di

to **become** VERB
diventare [68ᴱ]
□ He has become a professional footballer. È diventato un calciatore professionista. □ It became increasingly difficult to cover costs. È diventato sempre più difficile far fronte ai costi.

bed NOUN
il letto *masc*
□ in bed a letto
■ **to go to bed with somebody** andare [6ᴱ] a letto con qualcuno

bed and breakfast NOUN
la pensione familiare *fem* (place)
■ **How much is it for bed and breakfast?** Quanto costa la camera con prima colazione?

bedclothes NOUN PL
■ **the bedclothes** le coperte e le lenzuola
bedding NOUN
■ **the bedding** le coperte e le lenzuola
bedroom NOUN
la camera da letto *fem*
■ **a three-bedroom house** una casa con tre camere da letto
bedsit NOUN
il monolocale *masc*
bedspread NOUN
il copriletto *masc*
bedtime NOUN
■ **Bedtime!** A nanna!
■ **Ten o'clock is my usual bedtime.** Generalmente vado a letto alle dieci.
bee NOUN
l' ape *fem*
beef NOUN
il manzo *masc*
■ **roast beef** arrosto di manzo
beefburger NOUN
l' hamburger *masc* (PL gli hamburger)
been VERB ▷ *see* **be**
beer NOUN
la birra *fem*
beetle NOUN
lo scarabeo *masc*
beetroot NOUN
la barbabietola *fem*
before PREPOSITION, CONJUNCTION, ADVERB
1 prima
□ before Tuesday prima di martedì
□ Before opening the packet, read the instructions. Prima di aprire il pacchetto leggi le istruzioni.
2 già
□ I've seen this film before. Questo film l'ho già visto.
beforehand ADVERB
prima
to **beg** VERB
1 chiedere [19] l'elemosina
□ She was begging. Chiedeva l'elemosina.
2 pregare [76]
□ He begged me to stop. Mi ha pregato di smettere.
began VERB ▷ *see* **begin**
beggar NOUN
il/la mendicante *masc/fem*
to **begin** VERB
iniziare [17]

    LANGUAGE TIP Both **essere** and **avere** can be used as auxiliaries.

□ It began to rain. Ha iniziato a piovere. □ The match began at 10 a.m. La partita è iniziata alle dieci del mattino. □ The film has just begun. Il film è appena iniziato.

beginner NOUN
il/la principiante *masc/fem*
beginning NOUN
l' inizio *masc*
■ **in the beginning** all'inizio
begun VERB ▷ *see* **begin**
behalf NOUN
■ **on behalf of...** per conto di...
to **behave** VERB
comportarsi [56ᴱ]
□ He behaved like an idiot. Si è comportato da stupido.
■ **to behave oneself** comportarsi [56ᴱ] bene
□ Did the children behave themselves? Si sono comportati bene i bambini?
■ **Behave!** Comportati bene!
behaviour (US **behavior**) NOUN
il comportamento *masc*
behind PREPOSITION, ADVERB
▷ *see also* **behind** NOUN
dietro
□ behind the television dietro il televisore
■ **to be behind** essere [47ᴱ] indietro □ I'm behind with my revision. Sono indietro con il ripasso.
behind NOUN
▷ *see also* **behind** PREPOSITION, ADVERB
il didietro *masc*
beige ADJECTIVE
beige (FEM+PL beige)
Belgian ADJECTIVE
▷ *see also* **Belgian** NOUN
belga (FEM belga, MASC PL belgi, FEM PL belghe)
Belgian NOUN
▷ *see also* **Belgian** ADJECTIVE
il/la belga *masc/fem*
■ **the Belgians** i belgi
Belgium NOUN
il Belgio *masc*
to **believe** VERB
credere [27]
□ Do you believe in ghosts? Credi ai fantasmi?
bell NOUN
1 il campanello *masc*
□ I rang the bell, but nobody came. Ho suonato il campanello, ma non è arrivato nessuno.
2 la campana *fem*
□ the church bell la campana della chiesa
3 la campanella *fem*
□ The bell goes at three. La campanella suona alle tre.
4 il sonaglio *masc*
□ Our cat has a bell on its collar. Il nostro gatto ha un sonaglio al collare.
belly NOUN
la pancia *fem* (PL le pance)

belong – better

to **belong** VERB
1 essere [47E] di
□ This ring belonged to my grandmother. Quest'anello era di mia nonna. □ Who does it belong to? Di chi è? □ That belongs to me. È mio.
2 far [49] parte
□ Do you belong to any clubs? Fai parte di qualche club?
■ **Where does this belong?** Dove va questo?

belongings NOUN PL
le cose fem pl
□ I collected my belongings and left. Ho raccolto le mie cose e me ne sono andato.
■ **your personal belongings** i suoi effetti personali

below PREPOSITION, ADVERB
sotto
□ ten degrees below freezing dieci gradi sotto zero
■ **on the floor below** al piano di sotto

belt NOUN
la cintura fem

beltway NOUN (US)
1 la circonvallazione fem
2 l' autostrada fem (motorway)

bench NOUN
la panchina fem

bend NOUN
▷ see also **bend** VERB
la curva fem

to **bend** VERB
▷ see also **bend** NOUN
1 piegare [76]
□ I can't bend my arm. Non riesco a piegare il braccio.
2 curvarsi [56E]
□ It bends easily. Si curva facilmente.

to **bend down** VERB
chinarsi [56E]
□ She bent down to pick a flower. Si è chinata a raccogliere un fiore.

to **bend over** VERB
chinarsi [56E]

beneath PREPOSITION
sotto

benefit NOUN
▷ see also **benefit** VERB
il beneficio masc
□ the benefits of this treatment i benefici di questa terapia
■ **unemployment benefit** l'indennità di disoccupazione
■ **state benefits** sussidi statali
■ **to live on benefit** vivere [122] di sussidi

to **benefit** VERB
▷ see also **benefit** NOUN
■ **He'll benefit from the change.** Il cambiamento gli farà bene.

■ **The scheme benefits children.** Il programma si rivolge ai bambini.

bent VERB ▷ see **bend**

bent ADJECTIVE
curvo (FEM curva)

beret NOUN
il berretto masc

berserk ADJECTIVE
■ **to go berserk** andare [6E] in bestia

berth NOUN
la cuccetta fem

beside PREPOSITION
accanto
□ beside the television accanto al televisore
■ **to be beside oneself** essere [47E] fuori di sé
□ He was beside himself. Era fuori di sé.
■ **That's beside the point.** Questo non c'entra affatto.

besides ADVERB
inoltre
□ Besides, it's too expensive. E inoltre è troppo caro.
■ **... and much more besides.** ... e altro ancora.

best ADJECTIVE, ADVERB
1 migliore (FEM migliore)
□ He's the best player in the team. È il migliore giocatore della squadra. □ the best artist of his generation il miglior artista della sua generazione
2 meglio
□ Emma sings best. È Emma che canta meglio.
■ **to do one's best** fare [49] del proprio meglio □ It's not perfect, but I did my best. Non è perfetto, ma ho fatto del mio meglio.
■ **to make the best of it** accontentarsi [68E]
□ We'll have to make the best of it. Dovremo accontentarci.

best man NOUN
il testimone dello sposo masc

bet NOUN
▷ see also **bet** VERB
la scommessa fem

to **bet** VERB
▷ see also **bet** NOUN
scommettere [59]
■ **I bet you...** Scommetti...? □ I bet you he won't come. Scommetti che non viene?

to **betray** VERB
tradire [51]

better ADJECTIVE, ADVERB
1 migliore (FEM migliore)
□ This one's better than that one. Questo è migliore di quello.
2 meglio
□ That's better! Così va meglio! □ Are you feeling better now? Ti senti meglio ora?

LANGUAGE TIP 'had better' is usually translated by the conditional of **dovere**.
□ You had better do it straight away. Dovresti farlo subito. □ I'd better go home. Dovrei proprio tornare a casa.
- **better still** meglio ancora
- **to get better 1** *(weather)* migliorare [68]
2 *(person)* rimettersi [59ᴱ]
- **better off** più benestante □ They're better off than us. Sono più benestanti di noi.

betting shop NOUN
la sala corse *fem* (PL le sale corse)

between PREPOSITION
tra
□ between fifteen and twenty minutes tra i quindici e i venti minuti

to **beware** VERB
- **Beware!** Attento!
- **to beware of...** stare [108ᴱ] attento a...

to **bewilder** VERB
sconcertare [68]

beyond PREPOSITION, ADVERB
1 oltre
□ I heard footsteps beyond the door. Ho sentito dei passi oltre la porta.
2 più in là
□ the wheat fields and the mountains beyond... i campi di grano e le montagne più in là...
- **beyond belief** incredibile
- **beyond repair** irreparabile

biased ADJECTIVE
parziale (FEM parziale)

Bible NOUN
la Bibbia *fem*

bicycle NOUN
la bicicletta *fem*

bifocals NOUN PL
gli occhiali bifocali *masc pl*

big ADJECTIVE
1 grande (FEM grande)
□ a big house una casa grande

WORD POWER
You can use a number of other words instead of **big** to mean 'large':
enormous enorme
□ an enormous cake una torta enorme
gigantic gigantesco
□ a gigantic building un palazzo gigantesco
huge enorme
□ a huge garden un giardino enorme
massive enorme
□ a massive change un enorme cambiamento

---

2 grosso (FEM grossa)
□ Taiwan's biggest companies le più grosse aziende di Taiwan
- **my big brother** il mio fratello maggiore

- **Big deal!** Capirai!
- **It's no big deal.** Non è importante.

bigheaded ADJECTIVE
- **to be bigheaded** darsi [30ᴱ] un sacco di arie

bike NOUN
la bici *fem* (PL le bici)

bikini NOUN
il bikini *masc* (PL i bikini)

bilingual ADJECTIVE
bilingue (FEM bilingue)

bill NOUN
1 il conto *masc*
□ Can we have the bill, please? Il conto, per favore.
2 la bolletta *fem*
□ the gas bill la bolletta del gas
3 la banconota *fem* (US)
□ a five-dollar bill una banconota da cinque dollari

billiards NOUN
il biliardo *masc*

billion NOUN
il miliardo *masc*

bin NOUN
il bidone *masc*

bingo NOUN
la tombola *fem*

binoculars NOUN PL
il binocolo *masc sing*
- **a pair of binoculars** un binocolo

biochemistry NOUN
la biochimica *fem*

biofuel NOUN
il biocarburante *masc*

biography NOUN
la biografia *fem*

biology NOUN
la biologia *fem*

bird NOUN
l' uccello *masc*

bird flu NOUN
l' influenza aviaria *fem*

bird-watching NOUN
il bird-watching *masc*

Biro® NOUN
la biro® *fem*

birth NOUN
la nascita *fem*
□ date of birth data di nascita

birth certificate NOUN
il certificato di nascita *masc*

birth control NOUN
il controllo delle nascite *masc*

birthday NOUN
il compleanno *masc*
□ a birthday cake una torta di compleanno
□ a birthday party una festa di compleanno
- **a birthday card** un biglietto d'auguri

biscuit – bleach

biscuit NOUN
il biscotto *masc*

bishop NOUN
il vescovo *masc*

bit VERB ▷ see bite

bit NOUN
■ **a bit** **1** un pezzo □ a bit of cake un pezzo di torta □ Would you like another bit? Ne vuoi un altro pezzo? **2** un po' □ a bit of music un po' di musica □ He's a bit mad. È un po' matto.
■ **It's a bit of a nuisance.** È un po' una scocciatura.
■ **Wait a bit!** Aspetta un attimo!
■ **to fall to bits** cadere [16ᴱ] a pezzi
■ **to take something to bits** smontare [68] qualcosa
■ **bit by bit** a poco a poco

bitch NOUN
la cagna *fem*
□ a bitch with three puppies una cagna con tre cuccioli

to **bite** VERB
▷ see also bite NOUN
1 mordere [60]
□ The dog bit him. Il cane lo ha morso.
□ My dog's never bitten anyone. Il mio cane non ha mai morso nessuno.
2 pungere [80]
□ I got bitten by mosquitoes. Mi hanno punto le zanzare.
■ **to bite one's nails** mangiarsi [58ᴱ] le unghie

> LANGUAGE TIP Word for word, this means 'to eat one's nails'.

bite NOUN
▷ see also bite VERB
1 la puntura *fem*
□ lots of mosquito bites molte punture di zanzara
2 il morso *masc*
□ a dog bite il morso di un cane
■ **to have a bite to eat** mangiare [58] un boccone

bitten VERB ▷ see bite

bitter ADJECTIVE
▷ see also bitter NOUN
amaro (FEM amara)
□ It tastes bitter. Ha un sapore amaro.
■ **It's bitter today.** Oggi si gela.

bitter NOUN
▷ see also bitter ADJECTIVE
la birra rossa *fem*

black ADJECTIVE
nero (FEM nera)
□ black coffee caffè nero

blackberry NOUN
la mora di rovo *fem*

blackbird NOUN
il merlo *masc*

blackboard NOUN
la lavagna *fem*

blackcurrant NOUN
il ribes nero *masc sing*
□ blackcurrant jam marmellata di ribes nero
■ **blackcurrants** il ribes nero *masc sing*

blackmail NOUN
▷ see also blackmail VERB
il ricatto *masc*

to **blackmail** VERB
▷ see also blackmail NOUN
ricattare [68]

black market NOUN
il mercato nero *masc*

blackout NOUN
il black-out *masc* (PL i black-out)
■ **to have a blackout** *(faint)* perdere [69] conoscenza

black pudding NOUN
il sanguinaccio *masc*

blacksmith NOUN
il fabbro *masc*

blade NOUN
la lama *fem*

to **blame** VERB
dare [30] la colpa a
□ Don't blame me! Non dare la colpa a me!

blank ADJECTIVE
▷ see also blank NOUN
1 bianco (FEM bianca, MASC PL bianchi, FEM PL bianche)
□ a blank sheet of paper un foglio di carta bianca
2 vergine (FEM vergine)
■ **My mind went blank.** Ho avuto un vuoto di memoria.

blank NOUN
▷ see also blank ADJECTIVE
lo spazio in bianco *masc*
□ Fill in the blanks. Riempi gli spazi in bianco.

blank cheque NOUN
l' assegno in bianco *masc*

blanket NOUN
la coperta *fem*

blast NOUN
■ **a bomb blast** un'esplosione

blatant ADJECTIVE
palese (FEM palese)
□ a blatant lie una bugia palese

blaze NOUN
l' incendio *masc*

blazer NOUN
il blazer *masc* (PL i blazer)

bleach NOUN
la candeggina *fem*

bleached ADJECTIVE
- **bleached hair** capelli ossigenati *masc pl*

bleak ADJECTIVE
1 poco promettente (FEM poco promettente)
  □ The future looks bleak. Il futuro sembra poco promettente.
2 desolato (FEM desolata)
  □ a bleak area un'area desolata

to bleed VERB
sanguinare [68]
  □ My hand is bleeding. Mi sanguina una mano.
- **to bleed to death** morire [61E] dissanguato

bleeper NOUN
il cercapersone *masc* (PL i cercapersone)

blender NOUN
il frullatore *masc*

to bless VERB
benedire [35]
  □ The priest blessed the children. Il prete ha benedetto i bambini.
- **Bless you!** *(after sneezing)* Salute!

blew VERB ▷ *see* **blow**

blind ADJECTIVE
  ▷ *see also* **blind** NOUN
cieco (FEM cieca, MASC PL ciechi, FEM PL cieche)

blind NOUN
  ▷ *see also* **blind** ADJECTIVE
l' avvolgibile *masc*

blindfold NOUN
  ▷ *see also* **blindfold** VERB
la benda per occhi *fem*

to blindfold VERB
  ▷ *see also* **blindfold** NOUN
bendare [68]

to blink VERB
strizzare [68] gli occhi

bliss NOUN
- **It was bliss!** È stato fantastico!

blister NOUN
la vescica *fem* (PL le vesciche)

blizzard NOUN
la bufera di neve *fem*

blob NOUN
la goccia *fem* (PL le gocce)
  □ a blob of glue una goccia di colla

block NOUN
  ▷ *see also* **block** VERB
1 il palazzo *masc*
  □ He lives in our block. Abita nel nostro palazzo.
2 l' isolato *masc*
  □ He walked around the block three times. Ha fatto tre volte il giro dell'isolato.
- **a block of flats** un caseggiato

to block VERB
  ▷ *see also* **block** NOUN
bloccare [18]

blockage NOUN
l' ingorgo *masc* (PL gli ingorghi)

blog NOUN
  ▷ *see also* **blog** VERB
il blog *masc* (PL i blog)
  □ She has her own blog. Ha un suo blog.

to blog VERB
  ▷ *see also* **blog** NOUN
scrivere [99] un blog
  □ He blogs about his school. Scrive un blog sulla sua scuola.

blogger NOUN
il/la blogger *masc/fem* (PL i/le blogger)

bloke NOUN
il tipo *masc*
  □ He's a really nice bloke. È un tipo veramente simpatico.

blonde ADJECTIVE
biondo (FEM bionda)

blood NOUN
il sangue *masc*

blood pressure NOUN
la pressione del sangue *fem*

blood sports NOUN PL
gli sport cruenti *masc pl*

blood test NOUN
l' analisi del sangue *fem* (PL le analisi del sangue)

bloody ADJECTIVE
maledetto (FEM maledetta) *(informal)*
  □ that bloody television quel maledetto televisore
- **bloody difficult** maledettamente difficile
- **Bloody hell!** Porca miseria!

blouse NOUN
la camicetta *fem*

blow NOUN
  ▷ *see also* **blow** VERB
il colpo *masc*

to blow VERB
  ▷ *see also* **blow** NOUN
soffiare [17]
  □ A cold wind was blowing. Soffiava un vento freddo.
- **They were one-all when the whistle blew.** Erano uno a uno quando l'arbitro ha fischiato la fine.
- **to blow one's nose** soffiarsi [17E] il naso
  □ He blew his nose. Si è soffiato il naso.

to blow out VERB
spegnere [105]
  □ Blow out the candles! Spegni le candeline!

to blow up VERB
1 far [49] saltare
  □ They blew up a plane. Hanno fatto saltare un aereo.
2 saltare [68E] in aria
  □ The house blew up. La casa è saltata in aria.

3 gonfiare [17]
□ We've blown up the balloons. Abbiamo gonfiato i palloncini.

blow-dry NOUN
la messa in piega con il fon *fem*

blown VERB ▷ see **blow**

blue ADJECTIVE
azzurro (FEM azzurra)
□ a blue dress un vestito azzurro
■ navy blue blu
■ out of the blue all'improvviso

blues NOUN PL
■ the blues il blues

to **bluff** VERB
▷ see also **bluff** NOUN
bluffare [68]

bluff NOUN
▷ see also **bluff** VERB
il bluff *masc* (PL i bluff)

blunder NOUN
l'errore *masc*

blunt ADJECTIVE
1 brusco (FEM brusca, MASC PL bruschi, FEM PL brusche)
□ He was blunt. È stato brusco.
2 spuntato (FEM spuntata)
□ The knife was blunt. Il coltello era spuntato.

to **blush** VERB
arrossire [51ᴱ]

board NOUN
1 l'asse *fem* (plank)
2 la lavagna *fem*
□ Write it on the board. Scrivilo sulla lavagna.
3 la bacheca *fem* (PL le bacheche)
□ There's a notice on the board. C'è un avviso in bacheca.
4 la scacchiera *fem*
□ There were six pawns on the board. C'erano sei pedoni sulla scacchiera.
■ a chopping board un tagliere
■ on board a bordo
■ full board pensione completa

boarder NOUN
il/la collegiale *masc/fem*

board game NOUN
il gioco da tavolo *masc* (PL i giochi da tavolo)

boarding card NOUN
la carta d'imbarco *fem*

boarding school NOUN
il collegio *masc*

to **boast** VERB
vantarsi [56ᴱ]
■ to boast about something vantarsi [56ᴱ] di qualcosa

boat NOUN
la barca *fem* (PL le barche)

body NOUN
il corpo *masc*

bodybuilding NOUN
il culturismo *masc*

bodyguard NOUN
la guardia del corpo *fem*

bog NOUN
la palude *fem*

boil NOUN
▷ see also **boil** VERB
il foruncolo *masc*

to **boil** VERB
▷ see also **boil** NOUN
1 far [49] bollire
□ Boil some water. Fai bollire dell'acqua.
2 bollire [41]
□ The water's boiling. L'acqua bolle.

to **boil over** VERB
traboccare [18ᴱ]

boiled ADJECTIVE
bollito (FEM bollita)
□ boiled rice riso bollito
■ boiled potatoes patate lesse
■ a boiled egg un uovo alla coque

boiling ADJECTIVE
■ It's boiling in here! Qui dentro si soffoca!
■ a boiling hot day una giornata torrida

bolt NOUN
1 il catenaccio *masc*
□ There was a heavy bolt on the door. C'era un pesante catenaccio alla porta.
2 il bullone *masc*
□ nuts and bolts dadi e bulloni

bomb NOUN
▷ see also **bomb** VERB
la bomba *fem*

to **bomb** VERB
▷ see also **bomb** NOUN
bombardare [68]

bomber NOUN
1 il bombardiere *masc* (plane)
2 il dinamitardo *masc*
la dinamitarda *fem* (person)

bombing NOUN
il bombardamento *masc*

bond NOUN
il legame *masc*

bone NOUN
1 l'osso *masc* (FEM PL le ossa)
LANGUAGE TIP The plural of **osso** is feminine when the bone is human.
□ a broken bone un osso rotto
2 la lisca *fem* (PL le lische) (fishbone)

bone dry ADJECTIVE
asciuttissimo (FEM asciuttissima)

bonfire NOUN
il falò *masc* (PL i falò)

bonnet NOUN
il cofano *masc* (of car)

bonus NOUN
la gratifica *fem* (PL le gratifiche)

book NOUN
▷ *see also* **book** VERB
il libro *masc*

to **book** VERB
▷ *see also* **book** NOUN
prenotare [68]

bookcase NOUN
la libreria *fem*

booklet NOUN
l' opuscolo *masc*

bookmark NOUN
1 il segnalibro *masc (of book)*
2 il bookmark *masc* (PL i bookmark) *(internet)*

bookshelf NOUN
la mensola per libri *fem*

bookshop NOUN
la libreria *fem*

to **boost** VERB
dare [30] una spinta a
□ They're trying to boost the economy. Stanno cercando di dare una spinta all'economia.
■ **to boost somebody's morale** sollevare [68] il morale di qualcuno □ The win boosted the team's morale. La vittoria ha sollevato il morale della squadra.

boot NOUN
1 il bagagliaio *masc (of car)*
2 lo stivale *masc (knee-high boot)*
3 lo stivaletto *masc (ankle boot)*
4 lo scarpone *masc (hiking boot)*
■ **football boots** scarpe da calcio

booze NOUN
gli alcolici *masc pl*

border NOUN
il confine *masc*

bore VERB ▷ *see* **bear**

bore NOUN
la noia *fem*
□ What a bore! Che noia!
■ **John's a bore.** John è noioso.

bored ADJECTIVE
annoiato (FEM annoiata)
■ **to get bored** annoiarsi [17ᴱ]

boredom NOUN
la noia *fem*

boring ADJECTIVE
noioso (FEM noiosa)

born ADJECTIVE
nato (FEM nata)
■ **to be born** nascere [63ᴱ] □ I was born in 1995. Sono nato nel 1995.

borne VERB ▷ *see* **bear**

to **borrow** VERB
■ **Can I borrow your pen?** Mi presti la penna?
■ **to borrow something from somebody** farsi [49ᴱ] prestare qualcosa da qualcuno

Bosnia NOUN
la Bosnia *fem*

Bosnian ADJECTIVE
bosniaco (FEM bosniaca, MASC PL bosniaci, FEM PL bosniache)

boss NOUN
il capo *masc*

to **boss around** VERB
■ **to boss somebody around** comandare [68] a bacchetta qualcuno

bossy ADJECTIVE
prepotente (FEM prepotente)

both ADJECTIVE, PRONOUN, ADVERB
tutt'e due
□ We both went. Ci siamo andati tutt'e due.
■ **Emma and Jane both went.** Sono andate sia Emma che Jane.

to **bother** VERB
▷ *see also* **bother** NOUN
1 preoccupare [68]
□ What's bothering you? Cosa c'è che ti preoccupa?
2 disturbare [68]
□ I'm sorry to bother you. Scusa se ti disturbo.
■ **Don't bother!** Lascia perdere!
■ **to bother to do something** darsi [30ᴱ] la pena di fare qualcosa □ He didn't bother to tell me about it. Non si è dato la pena di farmelo sapere.

bother NOUN
▷ *see also* **bother** VERB
■ **No bother!** Nessun problema!
■ **Sliced bread is less bother.** Il pane già affettato è più comodo.
■ **No bother.** Non c'è problema.

bottle NOUN
la bottiglia *fem*

bottle bank NOUN
il contenitore per la raccolta del vetro *masc*

bottle-opener NOUN
l' apribottiglie *masc* (PL gli apribottiglie)

bottom NOUN
▷ *see also* **bottom** ADJECTIVE
1 il fondo *masc*
□ at the bottom of the page in fondo alla pagina
■ **to be bottom of** essere [47ᴱ] l'ultimo di
□ He was always bottom of the class. Era sempre l'ultimo della classe.
2 il sedere *masc*
□ Do these trousers make my bottom look big? Questi pantaloni mi fanno il sedere grosso?

bottom ADJECTIVE
▷ *see also* **bottom** NOUN
inferiore (FEM inferiore)
□ the bottom shelf il ripiano inferiore

bought VERB ▷ *see* **buy**

to **bounce** VERB
rimbalzare [68]
□ The ball bounced. La palla è rimbalzata.

bouncer NOUN
il buttafuori masc (PL i buttafuori)

bound ADJECTIVE
■ **He's bound to fail.** Fallirà sicuramente.
■ **There are bound to be price rises.** Ci sarà sicuramente un aumento dei prezzi.

boundary NOUN
il confine masc

bow NOUN
▷ see also **bow** VERB
1 il fiocco masc (PL i fiocchi)
■ **to tie a bow** fare [49] un fiocco
2 l' arco masc (PL gli archi)
□ a bow and arrows arco e frecce

to **bow** VERB
▷ see also **bow** NOUN
fare [49] un inchino

bowels NOUN PL
l' intestino masc sing

bowl NOUN
▷ see also **bowl** VERB
la scodella fem

to **bowl** VERB
▷ see also **bowl** NOUN
lanciare [13] la palla (in cricket)

bowler NOUN
il lanciatore masc
la lanciatrice fem (in cricket)

bowling NOUN
il bowling masc
■ **to go bowling** andare [6ᴱ] a giocare a bowling
■ **a bowling alley** una pista da bowling

bowls NOUN SING
le bocce fem pl
□ He plays bowls. Gioca a bocce.

bow tie NOUN
la cravatta a farfalla fem

box NOUN
1 la scatola fem
□ a box of matches una scatola di fiammiferi
2 la casella fem
□ Tick the appropriate box. Barrare l'apposita casella.

boxer NOUN
il pugile masc

boxer shorts NOUN PL
i boxer masc pl

boxing NOUN
il pugilato masc

Boxing Day NOUN
■ **on Boxing Day** il ventisei dicembre

box office NOUN
la biglietteria fem

boy NOUN
1 il ragazzo masc
□ a boy of fifteen un ragazzo di quindici anni
2 il bambino masc

□ a boy of seven un bambino di sette anni
3 il maschio masc
□ She has two boys and a girl. Ha due maschi e una femmina.
■ **a baby boy** un maschietto

boyfriend NOUN
il ragazzo masc

bra NOUN
il reggiseno masc

brace NOUN
l' apparecchio masc (for teeth)
□ Richard wears a brace. Richard porta l'apparecchio.

bracelet NOUN
il braccialetto masc

brackets NOUN PL
le parentesi fem pl
■ **in brackets** tra parentesi

brain NOUN
il cervello masc

brainy ADJECTIVE
intelligente (FEM intelligente)

brake NOUN
▷ see also **brake** VERB
il freno masc
□ The brakes failed. I freni non hanno funzionato.

to **brake** VERB
▷ see also **brake** NOUN
frenare [68]

branch NOUN
1 il ramo masc (of tree)
2 la filiale fem (of bank)

brand NOUN
la marca fem (PL le marche)
□ a famous brand una marca famosa

brand name NOUN
la marca fem (PL le marche)

brand-new ADJECTIVE
nuovo di zecca

brandy NOUN
il brandy masc (PL i brandy)

brass NOUN
l' ottone masc

brass band NOUN
la banda fem

brat NOUN
il moccioso masc
□ He's a spoiled brat. È un moccioso viziato.

brave ADJECTIVE
coraggioso (FEM coraggiosa)

Brazil NOUN
il Brasile masc

bread NOUN
il pane masc
□ brown bread pane integrale

break NOUN
▷ see also **break** VERB

1 la pausa *fem*
□ Let's take a break. Facciamo una pausa.
2 la ricreazione *fem* (at school)
■ **the Christmas break** le vacanze di Natale
■ **Give me a break!** Ma per carità!

to **break** VERB
▷ *see also* **break** NOUN
1 rompere [92]
□ Careful, you'll break something! Attento, o romperai qualcosa! □ I've broken a glass. Ho rotto un bicchiere.
2 rompersi [92ᴱ]
□ Careful, it'll break! Stai attento che si rompe!
■ **to break a promise** mancare [18] a una promessa
■ **to break a record** battere [1] un record
□ He broke the world record. Ha battuto il record mondiale.

to **break down** VERB
rimanere [88ᴱ] in panne

to **break in** VERB
entrare [68ᴱ]
□ The thief had broken in through a window. Il ladro era entrato forzando una finestra.

to **break into** VERB
entrare [68ᴱ] in
□ Thieves broke into the house. Dei ladri sono entrati in casa.

to **break off** VERB
rompere [92]

to **break out** VERB
scoppiare [17ᴱ] (war, fight)
■ **to break out in a rash** coprirsi [9ᴱ] di brufoli

to **break up** VERB
1 disperdere [69]
□ Police broke up the demonstration. La polizia ha disperso i dimostranti.
2 finire [51ᴱ]
□ Their marriage broke up. Il loro matrimonio è finito.
3 lasciarsi [13ᴱ]
□ Richard and Marie have broken up. Richard e Marie si sono lasciati.
■ **to break up a fight** sedare [68] una lite
■ **We break up next Wednesday.** Mercoledì cominciano le vacanze.

breakdown NOUN
1 la fine *fem*
□ the breakdown of their marriage la fine del loro matrimonio
2 l' esaurimento *masc*
□ He had a breakdown because of the stress. Ha avuto un esaurimento dovuto allo stress.
3 l' analisi *fem*
□ a breakdown of the costs un'analisi dei costi
4 la panne *fem*
■ **to have a breakdown** rimanere [88ᴱ] in panne □ We had a breakdown near Leeds. Siamo rimasti in panne vicino a Leeds.
■ **a breakdown truck** un carro attrezzi

breakfast NOUN
la colazione *fem*

break-in NOUN
il furto con scasso *masc*

breast NOUN
il seno *masc* (woman's)
■ **chicken breast** il petto di pollo

to **breast-feed** VERB
allattare [68]

breaststroke NOUN
la rana *fem*

> **LANGUAGE TIP** Word for word, this means 'the frog'.

breath NOUN
1 l' alito *masc*
□ bad breath l'alito cattivo
2 il fiato *masc*
□ I'm out of breath. Sono senza fiato.

to **breathe** VERB
respirare [68]

to **breathe in** VERB
inspirare [68]

to **breathe out** VERB
espirare [68]

to **breed** VERB
▷ *see also* **breed** NOUN
riprodursi [85ᴱ]
□ They rarely breed in captivity. In cattività si riproducono raramente.
■ **to breed dogs** allevare [68] cani

breed NOUN
▷ *see also* **breed** VERB
la razza *fem*

breeze NOUN
la brezza *fem*

brewery NOUN
la fabbrica di birra *fem* (PL le fabbriche di birra)

bribe NOUN
▷ *see also* **bribe** VERB
la bustarella *fem*

> **LANGUAGE TIP** Word for word, this means 'little envelope'.

to **bribe** VERB
▷ *see also* **bribe** NOUN
corrompere [92]

brick NOUN
il mattone *masc*

bricklayer NOUN
il muratore *masc*

bride NOUN
la sposa *fem*

bridegroom NOUN
lo sposo *masc*

bridesmaid NOUN
la damigella d'onore *fem*

bridge NOUN
1 il ponte *masc*
□ a suspension bridge un ponte sospeso

2 il bridge *masc*
□ He plays bridge. Gioca a bridge.

brief ADJECTIVE
breve (FEM breve)

briefcase NOUN
la valigetta ventiquattr'ore *fem*

briefly ADVERB
brevemente

briefs NOUN PL
gli slip *masc pl*
■ **a pair of briefs** un paio di slip

bright ADJECTIVE
1 vivace (FEM vivace)
□ a bright colour un colore vivace
■ **bright red** rosso vivo
2 sveglio (FEM sveglia)
□ He's not very bright. Non è molto sveglio.

brilliant ADJECTIVE
1 fantastico (FEM fantastica, MASC PL fantastici, FEM PL fantastiche)
□ It's a brilliant idea! È un'idea fantastica!
■ **We had a brilliant time!** Ci siamo divertiti moltissimo!
2 geniale (FEM geniale)
□ a brilliant scientist uno scienziato geniale

to **bring** VERB
portare [68]
□ Bring warm clothes. Porta vestiti pesanti.
□ Can I bring a friend? Posso portare un amico?
□ I've brought you a present. Ti ho portato un regalo.

to **bring about** VERB
causare [68]

to **bring back** VERB
riportare [68]
□ He's taken your drill. He'll bring it back tomorrow. Ha preso il trapano. Lo riporterà domani.
■ **That song brings back memories.** Quella canzone mi fa tornare in mente tanti ricordi.

to **bring forward** VERB
anticipare [68]
□ The meeting was brought forward. La riunione è stata anticipata.

to **bring up** VERB
allevare [68]
□ She brought up five children on her own. Ha allevato cinque figli da sola.

Britain NOUN
la Gran Bretagna *fem*

British ADJECTIVE
britannico (FEM britannica, MASC PL britannici, FEM PL britanniche)
■ **the British** i britannici
DID YOU KNOW...?
Italians often refer to the British as 'gli inglesi'.
■ **the British Isles** le Isole Britanniche

broad ADJECTIVE
largo (FEM larga, MASC PL larghi, FEM PL larghe)
□ He's got broad shoulders. Ha le spalle larghe.
■ **in broad daylight** in pieno giorno

broadband NOUN
la banda larga *fem*

broad bean NOUN
la fava *fem*

broadcast NOUN
▷ see also **broadcast** VERB
la trasmissione *fem*

to **broadcast** VERB
▷ see also **broadcast** NOUN
trasmettere [59]
■ **to broadcast live** trasmettere [59] in diretta

broad-minded ADJECTIVE
di larghe vedute

broccoli NOUN SING
i broccoli *masc pl*
□ The broccoli is delicious. I broccoli sono buonissimi.

brochure NOUN
il dépliant *masc* (PL i dépliant)

broke VERB ▷ see **break**

broke ADJECTIVE
■ **to be broke** essere [47E] al verde

broken VERB ▷ see **break**

broken ADJECTIVE
rotto (FEM rotta)
□ a broken glass un bicchiere rotto

bronchitis NOUN
la bronchite *fem*

bronze NOUN
il bronzo *masc*
□ the bronze medal la medaglia di bronzo

brooch NOUN
la spilla *fem*

broom NOUN
la scopa *fem*

brother NOUN
il fratello *masc*

brother-in-law NOUN
il cognato *masc*

brought VERB ▷ see **bring**

brown ADJECTIVE
1 marrone (FEM+PL marrone) *(shoes, eyes)*
2 castano (FEM castana) *(hair)*
3 abbronzato (FEM abbronzata) *(tanned)*
■ **brown bread** pane integrale
■ **brown sugar** zucchero di canna

Brownie NOUN
la giovane esploratrice *fem*

to **browse** VERB
curiosare [68] *(in bookshop)*
■ **to browse on the internet** fare [49] una ricerca in Internet

browser NOUN
il browser *masc* (PL i browser)

bruise NOUN
il livido *masc*

brush NOUN
▷ *see also* **brush** VERB
1 la spazzola *fem (for hair)*
2 il pennello *masc (for painting)*

to **brush** VERB
▷ *see also* **brush** NOUN
spazzolare [68]
■ **to brush one's hair** spazzolarsi [56ᴱ] i capelli
■ **to brush one's teeth** lavarsi [56ᴱ] i denti
■ **to brush up one's English** rispolverare [68] il proprio inglese

Brussels NOUN
la Bruxelles *fem*

Brussels sprouts NOUN PL
i cavoletti di Bruxelles *masc pl*

brutal ADJECTIVE
brutale (FEM brutale)

BSc NOUN (= *Bachelor of Science*)
la laurea in scienze *fem*

BSE NOUN (= *bovine spongiform encephalopathy*)
l' encefalite bovina spongiforme *fem*

bubble NOUN
la bolla *fem*

bubble bath NOUN
il bagnoschiuma *masc* (PL i bagnoschiuma)

bubble gum NOUN
la gomma da masticare *fem*

bucket NOUN
il secchio *masc*

buckle NOUN
la fibbia *fem*

Buddhism NOUN
il buddismo *masc*

Buddhist ADJECTIVE
buddista (FEM buddista)

buddy NOUN (US)
l' amico *masc*

budget NOUN
▷ *see also* **budget** ADJECTIVE, VERB
il budget *masc* (PL i budget)
□ the defence budget il budget per la Difesa
■ **the Budget** la legge finanziaria
■ **to be on a tight budget** avere [12] un budget limitato

budget ADJECTIVE
▷ *see also* **budget** NOUN, VERB
■ **budget prices** prezzi ridotti

to **budget** VERB
▷ *see also* **budget** NOUN, ADJECTIVE
gestire [51] le proprie finanze
□ I'm learning how to budget. Sto imparando a gestire le mie finanze.

budgie NOUN
il pappagallino *masc*

buffet NOUN
il buffet *masc* (PL i buffet)

□ a cold buffet un buffet freddo
■ **a buffet lunch** un buffet

buffet car NOUN
il servizio ristoro *masc*

bug NOUN
1 l' insetto *masc (insect)*
2 il virus *masc* (PL i virus)
□ There's a bug going round. C'è in giro un virus.
■ **a stomach bug** una gastroenterite
3 il baco *masc* (PL i bachi) *(in computer)*

bugged ADJECTIVE
■ **The room was bugged.** C'erano delle microspie nella stanza.

to **build** VERB
costruire [51]
□ They're going to build houses here. Qui costruiranno delle case.

to **build up** VERB
1 mettere [59] insieme
□ He has built up a huge collection of stamps. Ha messo insieme una vasta collezione di francobolli.
2 accumularsi [56ᴱ]
□ Debts are building up. Si stanno accumulando i debiti.

builder NOUN
1 l' imprenditore edile *masc (boss)*
2 il muratore *masc (worker)*

building NOUN
l' edificio *masc*

building society NOUN
la società immobiliare e finanziaria *fem*

built VERB ▷ *see* **build**

bulb NOUN
1 la lampadina *fem*
□ I'll change the bulb. Cambierò la lampadina.
2 il bulbo *masc (of plant)*

bull NOUN
il toro *masc*

bullet NOUN
la pallottola *fem*

bulletin board NOUN
la bacheca elettronica *fem* (PL le bacheche elettroniche)

bullfighting NOUN
la corrida *fem*

bullied VERB ▷ *see* **bully**

bullring NOUN
l' arena *fem*

bully NOUN
▷ *see also* **bully** VERB
il/la prepotente *masc/fem*
□ He's a big bully. È un grande prepotente.

to **bully** VERB
▷ *see also* **bully** NOUN
fare [49] il prepotente con

bullying – busy

bullying NOUN
il bullismo *masc*

bum NOUN
il sedere *masc*

bum bag NOUN
il marsupio *masc*

bump NOUN
▷ *see also* **bump** VERB
1 il bernoccolo *masc*
□ I've got a bump on my forehead. Ho un bernoccolo sulla fronte.
2 la scossa *fem*
□ We felt a sudden bump. Abbiamo sentito una scossa improvvisa.

to **bump** VERB
▷ *see also* **bump** NOUN
sbattere [1]
□ I bumped my head. Ho sbattuto la testa.

to **bump into** VERB
incontrare [68] per caso
□ I bumped into Paul yesterday. Ho incontrato per caso Paul, ieri.

bumper NOUN
il paraurti *masc* (PL i paraurti)

bumpy ADJECTIVE
accidentato (FEM accidentata)

bun NOUN
il panino dolce *masc*

bunch NOUN
■ a bunch of flowers un mazzo di fiori
■ a bunch of grapes un grappolo d'uva
■ a bunch of bananas un casco di banane

bunches NOUN PL
le codine *fem pl*

bungalow NOUN
la villetta ad un piano *fem*

bunk NOUN
il letto a castello *masc*

burger NOUN
l' hamburger *masc* (PL gli hamburger)

burglar NOUN
lo scassinatore *masc*
la scassinatrice *fem*

burglar alarm NOUN
l' antifurto *masc* (PL gli antifurto)

to **burglarize** VERB (US)
svaligiare [58]

burglary NOUN
il furto con scasso *masc*

to **burgle** (US **burglarize**) VERB
svaligiare [58]

buried VERB ▷ *see* **bury**

burn NOUN
▷ *see also* **burn** VERB
la bruciatura *fem*

to **burn** VERB
▷ *see also* **burn** NOUN
bruciare [13]

□ I burned the cake. Ho bruciato la torta.
■ to burn oneself bruciarsi [13ᴱ]
■ I've burned my hand. Mi sono bruciato la mano.

to **burn down** VERB
■ The factory burned down. La fabbrica è andata distrutta in un incendio.

to **burst** VERB
scoppiare [17ᴱ]
□ The balloon burst. Il palloncino è scoppiato.
■ to burst out laughing scoppiare [17ᴱ] a ridere
■ to burst into tears scoppiare [17ᴱ] in lacrime
■ to burst into flames prendere [77] fuoco

to **bury** VERB
seppellire [51]

bus NOUN
l' autobus *masc* (PL gli autobus)
□ the bus stop la fermata dell'autobus
■ the school bus il pulmino della scuola

bush NOUN
il cespuglio *masc*

business NOUN
1 l' impresa *fem*
□ He's got his own business. Ha un'impresa in proprio.
2 gli affari *masc pl*
□ He's away on business. È via per affari.
□ It's none of my business. Non sono affari miei.
■ a business trip un viaggio d'affari

businessman NOUN
1 l' uomo d'affari *masc* (gli uomini d'affari) (in general)
2 l' imprenditore *masc* (entrepreneur)

businesswoman NOUN
1 la donna d'affari *fem* (in general)
2 l' imprenditrice *fem* (entrepreneur)

busker NOUN
il suonatore ambulante *masc*
la suonatrice ambulante *fem*

bus pass NOUN
la tessera ridotta dell'autobus *fem*

bus shelter NOUN
la pensilina *fem*

bus station NOUN
la stazione delle corriere *fem*

bust NOUN
il petto *masc*

busy ADJECTIVE
1 impegnato (FEM impegnata)
□ She's a very busy woman. È una donna molto impegnata.
2 intenso (FEM intensa)
□ I've had a busy day. Ho avuto una giornata intensa.

3 animato (FEM animata)

□ The Strand is one of London's busiest streets. Lo Strand è una delle vie più animate di Londra.

busy signal NOUN (US)

il segnale di occupato *masc*

but CONJUNCTION

ma

□ strange but true strano ma vero

■ **all but** tutti tranne □ They won all but two of their matches. Hanno vinto tutte le partite tranne due.

■ **the last but one** il penultimo

butcher NOUN

il macellaio *masc*

butcher's NOUN

la macelleria *fem*

butter NOUN

il burro *masc*

butterfly NOUN

la farfalla *fem*

buttocks NOUN PL

le natiche *fem pl*

button NOUN

1 il bottone *masc*

2 il distintivo *masc* (US: *badge*)

to **buy** VERB

▷ *see also* **buy** NOUN

comprare [68]

□ I've bought her some flowers. Le ho comprato dei fiori.

buy NOUN

▷ *see also* **buy** VERB

l' affare *masc*

□ It was a good buy. È stato un buon affare.

by PREPOSITION

1 da

□ They were caught by the police. Sono stati catturati dalla polizia.

2 di

□ a painting by Picasso un quadro di Picasso

3 in

□ by car in macchina

4 vicino a

□ Where's the bank? — It's by the post office. Dov'è la banca? — È vicino all'ufficio postale.

5 entro

□ We have to be there by 4 o'clock. Dobbiamo essere lì entro le 4.

■ **by the time** quando □ By the time I got there it was too late. Quando sono arrivato era troppo tardi. □ It'll be ready by the time you get back. Sarà pronto per quando ritorni.

■ **That's fine by me.** Per me va benissimo.

■ **all by himself** da solo

■ **I did it all by myself.** L'ho fatto tutto da solo.

■ **by the way** a proposito

bye EXCLAMATION

ciao

bypass NOUN

la circonvallazione *fem*

Cc

cab NOUN
il taxi *masc* (PL i taxi)

cabbage NOUN
il cavolo *masc*

cabin NOUN
la cabina *fem (on ship)*

cabin crew NOUN
l' equipaggio di bordo *masc*

cabinet NOUN
l' armadietto *masc*
□ a bathroom cabinet un armadietto del bagno
■ **the Cabinet** il Consiglio dei Ministri

cable NOUN
il cavo *masc*

cable car NOUN
la funivia *fem*

cable television NOUN
la televisione via cavo *fem*

cadet NOUN
■ **a police cadet** un allievo poliziotto
■ **a cadet officer** un allievo ufficiale

café NOUN
il caffè *masc* (PL i caffè)

cafeteria NOUN
1 la mensa *fem (in school, hospital)*
2 il self-service *masc* (PL i self-service) *(in store)*

cage NOUN
la gabbia *fem*

cagoule NOUN
il K-Way® *masc* (PL i K-Way)

cake NOUN
1 la torta *fem (large)*
□ a chocolate cake una torta al cioccolato
2 la pasta *fem (small)*
□ a coffee and a cake un caffè e una pasta
■ **It's a piece of cake.** È un gioco da ragazzi.

to **calculate** VERB
calcolare [68]
□ They are calculating the cost. Stanno calcolando il costo.

calculation NOUN
il calcolo *masc*

calculator NOUN
la calcolatrice *fem*

calendar NOUN
il calendario *masc*

calf NOUN
1 il vitello *masc*
□ a cow and her calf una mucca e il suo vitello
2 il polpaccio *masc (of leg)*

call NOUN
▷ *see also* **call** VERB
1 la chiamata *fem*
□ Thanks for your call. Grazie per la chiamata.
2 la visita *fem*
□ He decided to pay a call on Tom. Ha deciso di far visita a Tom.
■ **a phone call** una telefonata
■ **to be on call** *(doctor)* essere [47E] reperibile

to **call** VERB
▷ *see also* **call** NOUN
1 chiamare [68]
□ We called the police. Abbiamo chiamato la polizia.
■ **to be called** chiamarsi [56E] □ What's she called? Come si chiama?
2 telefonare [68]
□ I'll tell him you called. Gli dirò che hai telefonato.

to **call back** VERB
1 richiamare [68]
□ Can I call you back? Ti posso richiamare?
2 ripassare [68E]
□ I'll call back later. Ripasso più tardi.

to **call for** VERB
1 passare [68E] a prendere
□ Shall I call for you at seven? Passo a prenderti alle sette?
2 richiedere [19]
□ This job calls for strong nerves. Questo lavoro richiede nervi saldi.

to **call in** VERB
passare [68E]
□ I'll call in at the office later. Passerò più tardi in ufficio.

to **call off** VERB
annullare [68]
□ The match was called off. La partita è stata annullata.

to **call on** VERB
invitare [68]
□ He was called on to give a speech. Fu invitato a fare un discorso.

call box NOUN
la cabina telefonica *fem*

call centre NOUN
il call centre *masc* (PL i call centre)

calm ADJECTIVE
calmo (FEM calma)

to **calm down** VERB
1 calmarsi [56E]
□ Calm down! Calmati!
2 calmare [68]
□ He calmed her down. L'ha calmata.

Calor gas® NOUN
il liquigas® *masc*

calorie NOUN
la caloria *fem*

calves NOUN ▷ see **calf**

camcorder NOUN
la videocamera *fem*

came VERB ▷ see **come**

camel NOUN
1 il cammello *masc (with two humps)*
2 il dromedario *masc (with one hump)*

camera NOUN
1 la macchina fotografica *fem (for photos)*
2 la cinepresa *fem (for filming, TV)*

cameraman NOUN
il cameraman *masc* (PL i cameraman)

camera phone NOUN
il telefonino con fotocamera *masc*

to **camp** VERB
▷ see also **camp** NOUN
accamparsi [56E]

camp NOUN
▷ see also **camp** VERB
1 il campeggio *masc*
□ a summer camp un campeggio estivo
■ a camp bed una brandina
2 il campo *masc*
□ a refugee camp un campo profughi

campaign NOUN
▷ see also **campaign** VERB
la campagna *fem*
□ an advertising campaign una campagna pubblicitaria

to **campaign** VERB
▷ see also **campaign** NOUN
fare [49] una campagna
□ They are campaigning for a change in the law. Stanno facendo una campagna per cambiare la legge.

camper NOUN
il campeggiatore *masc*
la campeggiatrice *fem*

camper van NOUN
il camper *masc* (PL i camper)

camping NOUN
il campeggio *masc*
■ to go camping andare [6E] in campeggio
□ We went camping in Cornwall. Siamo andati in campeggio in Cornovaglia.

camping gas NOUN
il butano *masc*

campsite NOUN
il campeggio *masc*
□ It's a nice campsite by the sea. È un bel campeggio sul mare.

campus NOUN
il campus *masc* (PL i campus)

can VERB
▷ see also **can** NOUN, **could** VERB
1 potere [74] *(be able, be allowed to)*
□ Can I use your phone? Posso usare il telefono? □ I'll do it as soon as I can. Lo farò appena posso. □ I can't do that. Non posso farlo. □ That can't be true! Non può essere vero! □ Our company cannot be held responsible for this. La nostra ditta non può essere ritenuta responsabile di questo.
□ You can come to the party, can't you? Puoi venire alla festa, vero?

> LANGUAGE TIP 'can' is sometimes not translated.

□ I can't hear you. Non ti sento. □ I can't remember. Non ricordo. □ Can you speak French? Parli francese?
2 sapere [94] *(know how to)*
□ I can swim. So nuotare. □ He can't drive. Non sa guidare.

can NOUN
▷ see also **can** VERB
il barattolo *masc (tin)*
□ a can of peas un barattolo di piselli
■ a can of beer una lattina di birra
■ a spray can una bomboletta

Canada NOUN
il Canada *masc*

Canadian NOUN
▷ see also **Canadian** ADJECTIVE
il/la canadese *masc/fem*

Canadian ADJECTIVE
▷ see also **Canadian** NOUN
canadese (FEM canadese)

canal NOUN
il canale *masc*

Canaries NOUN PL
■ the Canaries le Canarie

canary NOUN
il canarino *masc*

to **cancel** VERB
1 annullare [68]
□ Why did they cancel their booking? Perché hanno annullato la prenotazione?
2 disdire [35]
□ I had to cancel my appointment. Ho dovuto disdire l'appuntamento.
3 cancellare [68]
□ Our flight was cancelled. Il nostro volo è stato cancellato.

4 sopprimere [46]
□ The train has been cancelled. Il treno è stato soppresso.

cancellation NOUN
1 la disdetta *fem (of appointment)*
2 l' annullamento *masc (of order, booking)*
3 la cancellazione *fem (of flight)*
4 la soppressione *fem (of train)*

Cancer NOUN
Cancro
□ I'm Cancer. Sono del Cancro.

cancer NOUN
il cancro *masc*
□ He's got cancer. Ha il cancro.

candidate NOUN
il candidato *masc*
la candidata *fem*

candle NOUN
1 la candela *fem*
□ He lit a candle. Ha acceso una candela.
2 la candelina *fem*
□ a cake with fifteen candles una torta con quindici candeline

candy NOUN (US)
1 la caramella *fem (sweet)*
2 i dolciumi *masc pl (confectionery)*

candyfloss NOUN
lo zucchero filato *masc*

cannabis NOUN
la canapa indiana *fem*

canned ADJECTIVE
in scatola *(food)*

cannot VERB = can not

to **canoe** VERB
▷ *see also* **canoe** NOUN
andare [6ᴱ] in canoa
□ On holiday we canoed. In vacanza siamo andati in canoa.

canoe NOUN
▷ *see also* **canoe** VERB
la canoa *fem*

canoeing NOUN
il canottaggio *masc*
■ We went canoeing. Siamo andati in canoa.

can opener NOUN
l' apriscatole *masc* (PL gli apriscatole)

can't VERB ▷ *see* can

canteen NOUN
la mensa *fem*
□ I eat in the canteen. Mangio in mensa.
LANGUAGE TIP Be careful not to translate **canteen** by **cantina**.

to **canter** VERB
andare [6ᴱ] a piccolo galoppo

canvas NOUN
la tela *fem*

cap NOUN
1 il tappo *masc*
□ Please put the cap back on the toothpaste. Rimetti il tappo al dentifricio, per favore.

2 il berretto *masc (with peak)*
■ This is his second cap for Scotland. È la seconda volta che veste la maglia della nazionale scozzese.

capable ADJECTIVE
capace (FEM capace)
□ He was capable of murder. Era capace di uccidere.
■ She's capable of achieving much more. È in grado di ottenere molto di più.

capacity NOUN
la capacità *fem*
□ a capacity of 40 litres una capacità di 40 litri
■ to have a capacity for hard work essere [47ᴱ] un gran lavoratore
■ to work at full capacity lavorare [68] a pieno ritmo
■ to be filled to capacity essere [47ᴱ] pieno

cape NOUN
il capo *masc*
■ Cape Horn capo Horn

capital NOUN
1 la capitale *fem*
□ Cardiff is the capital of Wales. Cardiff è la capitale del Galles.
2 la maiuscola *fem (letter)*
□ with a capital C con la C maiuscola
■ in capitals in stampatello

capitalism NOUN
il capitalismo *masc*

capital punishment NOUN
la pena capitale *fem*

Capricorn NOUN
il Capricorno *masc*
□ I'm Capricorn. Sono del Capricorno.

to **capsize** VERB
capovolgersi [91ᴱ]
□ The boat capsized. La barca si è capovolta.

captain NOUN
il capitano *masc*

caption NOUN
la didascalia *fem*

to **capture** VERB
catturare [68]

car NOUN
1 la macchina *fem*
□ We went by car. Siamo andati in macchina.
■ a car bomb un'autobomba
■ a car crash un incidente stradale
■ a car ferry un traghetto
■ car hire l'autonoleggio *masc*
■ a car park un parcheggio
■ car rental l'autonoleggio *masc*
■ a car radio un autoradio
■ a car wash un lavaggio auto
2 la carrozza *fem (carriage)*
■ the dining car la carrozza ristorante

caramel NOUN
la caramella gommosa *fem*

caravan NOUN
la roulotte *fem* (PL le roulotte)
□ **a caravan site** un campeggio per roulotte

carbohydrate NOUN
il carboidrato *masc*

carbon footprint NOUN
l' impronta di carbonio *fem*
□ **We need to reduce our carbon footprint.**
Dobbiamo ridurre la nostra impronta di carbonio.

card NOUN
1 il biglietto *masc* (greetings card)
□ **I'd like to send him a card for his birthday.**
Vorrei spedirgli un biglietto per il suo compleanno.
2 la cartolina *fem*
□ **I sent all my friends cards from New York.**
Ho mandato una cartolina da New York a tutti i miei amici.
3 la carta *fem*
□ **a card game** un gioco di carte
■ **a credit card** una carta di credito
■ **a membership card** una tessera

cardboard NOUN
il cartone *masc*
□ **a cardboard box** una scatola di cartone

cardigan NOUN
il cardigan *masc* (PL i cardigan)

cardphone NOUN
il telefono a scheda *masc*

care NOUN
▷ *see also* **care** VERB
la cura *fem*
□ **with care** con cura
■ **children in care** bambini sotto la custodia dello stato
■ **to take care of** occuparsi [68ᴱ] di □ **I take care of the children on Saturdays.** Io mi occupo dei bambini di sabato.
■ **Take care!** 1 (be careful) Stai attento!
2 (look after yourself) Stammi bene!

to care VERB
▷ *see also* **care** NOUN

> **LANGUAGE TIP** 'care' is often translated by **importare**, which is an impersonal verb. This means that in Italian you say 'it matters to me' rather than 'I care about it.'

□ **I don't care!** Non mi importa! □ **Of course I care about him.** Certo che m'importa di lui.
□ **Who cares?** Chi se ne importa?
■ **They don't care about their image.** Non si curano della loro immagine.

to care for VERB
1 voler [123] bene a (love)
□ **I still care a lot for you.** Ti voglio ancora tanto bene.
2 prendersi [77ᴱ] cura di (look after)
□ **A nurse cared for her.** Un'infermiera si prendeva cura di lei.

career NOUN
la carriera *fem*
□ **She had a successful career in journalism.**
Ha fatto una brillante carriera come giornalista.

careful ADJECTIVE
attento (FEM attenta)
□ **Be careful!** Sta' attento!

carefully ADVERB
1 accuratamente
□ **She avoided talking about it.** Ha evitato di parlarne.
2 attentamente
□ **Think carefully!** Pensaci attentamente!
3 con prudenza
□ **Drive carefully!** Guida con prudenza!

careless ADJECTIVE
1 sbadato (FEM sbadata) (person)
□ **She's very careless.** È molto sbadata.
2 fatto con poco impegno (work)
■ **a careless driver** un guidatore distratto
■ **a careless mistake** un errore di distrazione

caretaker NOUN
il custode *masc* (of building)
■ **a school caretaker** un bidello

cargo NOUN
il carico *masc* (PL i carichi)

Caribbean ADJECTIVE
▷ *see also* **Caribbean** NOUN
caraibico (FEM caraibica, MASC PL caraibici, FEM PL caraibiche)

Caribbean NOUN
▷ *see also* **Caribbean** ADJECTIVE
■ **the Caribbean** i Caraibi □ **We're going to the Caribbean.** Andremo ai Caraibi.

caring ADJECTIVE
premuroso (FEM premurosa) (person)

carnation NOUN
il garofano *masc*

carnival NOUN
il carnevale *masc* (public celebration)

carol NOUN
■ **a Christmas carol** un canto natalizio

carpenter NOUN
il carpentiere *masc*

carpentry NOUN
la carpenteria *fem*

carpet NOUN
1 la moquette *fem* (PL le moquette) (fitted)
2 il tappeto *masc*
□ **a Persian carpet** un tappeto persiano

carriage NOUN
la carrozza *fem*

carrier bag NOUN
la borsa di plastica *fem*

carrot NOUN
la carota *fem*

to carry VERB
1 portare [68]
□ **I'll carry your bag.** Porto io la tua borsa.

carry on – casually

2 transportare [68]

□ A plane carrying 100 passengers has crashed. È caduto un aereo che trasportava 100 passeggeri.

to **carry on** VERB

continuare [68]

□ She carried on talking. Continuò a parlare.

■ **Carry on!** Va avanti! ■ Am I boring you? — No, carry on! Ti annoio? — No, va' avanti!

to **carry out** VERB

1 eseguire [41]

□ See that he carries out my orders. Assicurati che esegua i miei ordini.

2 mettere [59] in pratica

□ I don't believe he'll carry out his threat. Non penso che metterà in pratica la sua minaccia.

carrycot NOUN

il porte-enfant *masc* (PL i porte-enfant)

cart NOUN

1 il carro *masc*

□ a horse and cart un cavallo e un carro

2 il carrello *masc* (US)

carton NOUN

il cartone *masc* (of milk, fruit juice)

cartoon NOUN

1 il cartone animato *masc* (film)

2 la vignetta *fem* (in newspaper)

■ **a strip cartoon** un fumetto

cartridge NOUN

la cartuccia *fem* (PL le cartucce)

to **carve** VERB

tagliare [25]

□ Dad carved the roast. Il papà ha tagliato l'arrosto.

■ **a carved oak chair** una sedia di quercia intagliata

case NOUN

1 la valigia *fem* (PL le valigie or le valige)

□ I've packed my case. Ho fatto la valigia.

2 la cassa *fem*

□ a case of wine una cassa di vini

3 il caso *masc*

□ in some cases in alcuni casi □ in any case in ogni caso □ in case of emergency in caso di emergenza □ The police are investigating the case. La polizia sta indagando sul caso.

■ **There's a case for taxing airplane fuel.** Ci sono ottime ragioni per tassare il carburante degli aerei.

■ **just in case** per sicurezza □ Take some money, just in case. Prendi un po' di soldi per sicurezza.

■ **in case it rains** caso mai dovesse piovere

■ **a case in point** un tipico esempio

■ **If this is the case...** Se è così...

cash NOUN

i soldi *masc pl*

□ I'm a bit short of cash. Sono un po' a corto di soldi.

■ **in cash** in contanti □ £200 in cash 200 sterline in contanti

■ **to pay cash** pagare [76] in contanti

cash card NOUN

il tesserino per i prelievi automatici *masc*

cash desk NOUN

la cassa *fem*

cashew nut NOUN

l' anacardio *masc*

cash flow NOUN

la liquidità *fem* (PL le liquidità)

cashier NOUN

il cassiere *masc*

la cassiera *fem*

cash machine NOUN

lo sportello automatico *masc*

cashmere NOUN

il cashmere *masc*

□ a cashmere jumper un maglione di cashmere

cash register NOUN

il registratore di cassa *masc*

casino NOUN

il casinò *masc* (PL i casinò)

casserole NOUN

la casseruola *fem*

□ chicken casserole pollo in casseruola

■ **to make a casserole** fare [49] uno spezzatino

■ **a casserole dish** una casseruola

cassette NOUN

la cassetta *fem*

■ **a cassette player** un riproduttore a cassette

■ **a cassette recorder** un registratore a cassette

cast NOUN

il cast *masc* (PL i cast)

□ After the play we met the cast. Dopo la commedia abbiamo incontrato il cast.

castle NOUN

il castello *masc*

casual ADJECTIVE

1 sportivo (FEM sportiva)

□ I prefer casual clothes. Preferisco i vestiti sportivi.

2 noncurante (FEM noncurante)

□ a casual attitude un atteggiamento noncurante

3 poco importante

□ a casual affair una storia poco importante

4 saltuario (FEM saltuaria)

□ It's just a casual job. È solo un lavoro saltuario.

■ **a casual remark** un'osservazione buttata là

casually ADVERB

■ **to dress casually** vestirsi [41ᴱ] sportivo

casualty NOUN
1 il pronto soccorso *masc (ward)*
2 il ferito *masc (injured person)*
□ There were no casualties. Non c'è stato nessun ferito.
3 la vittima *fem*
□ The casualties include a young boy. Tra le vittime c'è un ragazzo giovane.

cat NOUN
il gatto *masc*
la gatta *fem*

catalogue NOUN
il catalogo *masc* (PL i cataloghi)

catalytic converter NOUN
la marmitta catalitica *fem* (PL le marmitte catalitiche)

catastrophe NOUN
la catastrofe *fem*

to **catch** VERB
1 catturare [68]
□ They caught the thief. Hanno catturato il ladro.
2 prendere [77]
□ We caught the last train. Abbiamo preso l'ultimo treno.
■ **to catch a cold** prendere [77] il raffreddore
3 afferrare [68]
□ I didn't catch his name. Non ho afferrato il suo nome.
4 sorprendere [77]
□ He caught her stealing. L'ha sorpresa a rubare.

to **catch up** VERB
1 rimettersi [59ᴱ] in pari
□ I've got to catch up on my work. Devo rimettermi in pari col lavoro.
2 raggiungere [5]
□ She caught me up. Mi ha raggiunto.

catching ADJECTIVE
contagioso (FEM contagiosa)
□ Don't worry, it's not catching! Non preoccuparti, non è contagioso!

catering NOUN
il servizio ristorazione *masc*

cathedral NOUN
la cattedrale *fem*

Catholic ADJECTIVE
▷ see also **Catholic** NOUN
cattolico (FEM cattolica, MASC PL cattolici, FEM PL cattoliche)

Catholic NOUN
▷ see also **Catholic** ADJECTIVE
il cattolico *masc* (PL i cattolici)
la cattolica *fem* (PL le cattoliche)
□ I'm a Catholic. Sono cattolico.

cattle NOUN PL
il bestiame *masc*

caught VERB ▷ see **catch**

cauliflower NOUN
il cavolfiore *masc*

cause NOUN
▷ see also **cause** VERB
la causa *fem*

to **cause** VERB
▷ see also **cause** NOUN
causare [68]

cautious ADJECTIVE
cauto (FEM cauta)

cautiously ADVERB
con cautela

cave NOUN
la grotta *fem*

caviar NOUN
il caviale *masc*

CCTV NOUN (= *closed circuit television*)
la televisione a circuito chiuso *fem*

CCTV camera NOUN
la telecamera a circuito chiuso *fem*

CD NOUN
il CD *masc* (PL i CD)

CD player NOUN
il lettore CD *masc*

CD-ROM NOUN
il CD-ROM *masc* (PL i CD-ROM)

ceasefire NOUN
il cessate il fuoco *masc* (PL i cessate il fuoco)

ceiling NOUN
il soffitto *masc*

to **celebrate** VERB
festeggiare [58]
□ I celebrated my birthday last week. Ho festeggiato il mio compleanno la settimana scorsa.

celebrity NOUN
la celebrità *fem* (PL le celebrità)

celery NOUN
il sedano *masc*

cell NOUN
1 la cella *fem*
□ Prisoners spend many hours in their cells. I prigionieri trascorrono molte ore in cella.
2 la cellula *fem (in biology)*

cellar NOUN
la cantina *fem*
■ **in the cellar** in cantina
■ **a wine cellar** una cantina

cello NOUN
il violoncello *masc*

cement NOUN
il cemento *masc*

cemetery NOUN
il cimitero *masc*

cent NOUN
il centesimo *masc (coin)*
■ **per cent** per cento

centenary NOUN
il centenario *masc*

center – change

center NOUN (US)
il centro *masc*

centigrade ADJECTIVE
centigrado
□ 20 degrees centigrade 20 gradi centigradi

centimetre (US **centimeter**) NOUN
il centimetro *masc*

central ADJECTIVE
centrale (FEM centrale)

central heating NOUN
il riscaldamento autonomo *masc*

central reservation NOUN
la banchina spartitraffico *fem* (PL le banchine spartitraffico)

centre NOUN
il centro *masc*
□ a sports centre un centro sportivo □ the city centre il centro della città

century NOUN
il secolo *masc*
□ the twenty first century il ventunesimo secolo

cereal NOUN
i cereali *masc pl*
□ I have cereal for breakfast. Mangio cereali per colazione.

ceremony NOUN
la cerimonia *fem*

certain ADJECTIVE
certo (FEM certa)
□ a certain person una certa persona □ I am certain he's not coming. Sono certo che non verrà.
■ **for certain** per certo

certainly ADVERB
sicuramente
□ I shall certainly be there. Ci sarò sicuramente.
■ **Certainly not!** No di certo!

certificate NOUN
il certificato *masc*

CFCs NOUN PL
i CFC *masc pl*

chain NOUN
1 la catena *fem*
□ The gate was fastened with a chain. Il cancello era chiuso con una catena.
2 la catenina *fem*
□ a gold chain una catenina d'oro
■ **a chain of events** una serie di avvenimenti

chair NOUN
1 la sedia *fem*
□ a table and four chairs un tavolo e quattro sedie
2 la poltrona *fem*
□ a sofa and two chairs un divano e due poltrone

chairlift NOUN
la seggiovia *fem*

chairman NOUN
il presidente *masc*

chalet NOUN
1 lo chalet *masc* (PL gli chalet) *(in ski resort)*
2 il bungalow *masc* (PL i bungalow) *(in holiday camp)*

chalk NOUN
il gesso *masc*

challenge NOUN
▷ see also **challenge** VERB
la sfida *fem*

to **challenge** VERB
▷ see also **challenge** NOUN
sfidare [68]
□ She challenged me to a race. Mi ha sfidato ad una gara.

challenging ADJECTIVE
impegnativo (FEM impegnativa)
□ a challenging job un lavoro impegnativo

chambermaid NOUN
la cameriera *fem*

champagne NOUN
lo champagne *masc*

champion NOUN
il campione *masc*
la campionessa *fem*

championship NOUN
il campionato *masc*

chance NOUN
▷ see also **chance** ADJECTIVE
1 la possibilità *fem* (PL le possibilità)
□ the team's chances of winning le possibilità di vittoria della squadra
■ **No chance!** Impossibile!
2 l' opportunità *fem* (PL le opportunità)
□ I'll write when I get the chance. Scriverò quando ne avrò l'opportunità.
■ **by chance** per caso
■ **to take a chance** rischiare [17] □ I'm taking no chances! Non intendo rischiare!

chance ADJECTIVE
▷ see also **chance** NOUN
casuale (FEM casuale)
□ a chance meeting un incontro casuale

Chancellor of the Exchequer NOUN
il Cancelliere dello Scacchiere *masc*

chandelier NOUN
il lampadario *masc*

to **change** VERB
▷ see also **change** NOUN
cambiare [17]
□ The town has changed a lot. La città è molto cambiata. □ I'd like to change fifty pounds. Vorrei cambiare 50 sterline. □ He wants to change his job. Vuole cambiare lavoro.
■ **to change one's mind** cambiare [17] idea
□ I've changed my mind. Ho cambiato idea.
■ **to change places** scambiarsi [17^E] di posto

□ We changed places. Ci siamo scambiati di posto.

change NOUN

▷ *see also* **change** VERB

1 il cambiamento *masc*

□ a change of plan un cambiamento di programma

■ **a change of clothes** un cambio di vestiti

■ **for a change** tanto per cambiare

2 gli spiccioli *masc pl*

□ I haven't got any change. Non ho spiccioli.

■ **Can you give me change for a pound?** Mi può cambiare una sterlina?

3 il resto *masc*

□ Here's your change. Ecco il resto.

changeable ADJECTIVE

1 variabile (FEM variabile)

□ The weather's very changeable. Il tempo è molto variabile.

2 incostante (FEM incostante) *(person)*

change purse NOUN (US)

il portamonete *masc* (PL i portamonete)

changing room NOUN

1 il camerino *masc*

□ Three garments only allowed in the changing room. Si possono portare solo tre articoli nel camerino.

2 lo spogliatoio *masc (in gym)*

Channel NOUN

■ **the Channel** il canale della Manica

■ **the Channel Islands** le isole della Manica

■ **the Channel Tunnel** il tunnel sotto la Manica

channel NOUN

il canale *masc (on TV)*

chaos NOUN

il caos *masc*

chap NOUN

il tipo *masc*

□ He's a nice chap. È un tipo simpatico.

chapel NOUN

la cappella *fem*

chapter NOUN

il capitolo *masc*

character NOUN

1 il carattere *masc*

□ Can you give me some idea of his character? Puoi descrivermi un po' il suo carattere?

■ **She's quite a character.** È un tipo originale.

2 il personaggio *masc (in film, book)*

■ **a character reference** una referenza

characteristic NOUN

la caratteristica *fem* (PL le caratteristiche)

charcoal NOUN

1 il carbone *masc (for barbecue)*

2 il carboncino *masc (for sketching)*

charge NOUN

▷ *see also* **charge** VERB

■ **Is there a charge for delivery?** C'è qualcosa da pagare per la spedizione?

■ **an extra charge** un supplemento

■ **free of charge** gratuito

■ **I'd like to reverse the charges.** Vorrei fare una chiamata a carico del destinatario.

■ **to be on a charge of** essere [47ᴱ] accusato di □ He's on a charge of murder. È stato accusato di omicidio.

■ **to be in charge** essere [47ᴱ] responsabile

□ She was in charge of the group. Era responsabile per il gruppo.

to **charge** VERB

▷ *see also* **charge** NOUN

far [49] pagare a

□ How much did he charge you? Quanto ti ha fatto pagare?

■ **to charge somebody with...** accusare [68] qualcuno di... □ The police have charged him with murder. La polizia lo ha accusato di omicidio.

charge card NOUN

la carta acquisti *fem*

charity NOUN

la beneficenza *fem*

□ He gave the money to charity. Ha dato il denaro in beneficenza.

■ **to collect for charity** raccogliere [21] denaro per beneficenza

■ **a cancer charity** un'associazione per la raccolta di fondi contro il cancro

charm NOUN

il fascino *masc*

□ the charm of this region il fascino di questa regione

charming ADJECTIVE

delizioso (FEM deliziosa)

□ She's a charming girl. È una ragazza deliziosa.

■ **Prince Charming** il Principe azzurro

chart NOUN

il grafico *masc* (PL i grafici)

□ The chart shows the rise of unemployment. Il grafico mostra l'aumento della disoccupazione.

■ **the charts** la Hit Parade □ His record has been in the charts for ten weeks. Il suo disco è rimasto nella classifica dei dischi più venduti per dieci settimane.

charter flight NOUN

il volo charter *masc* (PL i voli charter)

chase NOUN

▷ *see also* **chase** VERB

l' inseguimento *masc*

□ a car chase un inseguimento in macchina

to **chase** VERB

▷ *see also* **chase** NOUN

chase away - chemist

1 inseguire [41]
□ The policeman chased the thief. Il poliziotto ha inseguito il ladro.
2 correre [26ᴱ] dietro a
□ He's always chasing the girls. Corre sempre dietro alle ragazze.

to **chase away** VERB
cacciare [13] via

chat NOUN
▷ see also **chat** VERB
la chiacchierata *fem*
■ **to have a chat** fare [49] una chiacchierata

to **chat** VERB
▷ see also **chat** NOUN
chiacchierare [68]
□ I was chatting to Claire. Stavo chiacchierando Claire.
■ **to chat online** chattare [68] in Internet

to **chat up** VERB
abbordare [68]
□ He's not very good at chatting up girls. Non è molto bravo ad abbordare le ragazze.

chatroom NOUN
la chatline *fem* (ᴘʟ le chatline)

chat show NOUN
il talk show *masc* (ᴘʟ i talk show)

chauvinist NOUN
■ **a male chauvinist** un maschilista

cheap ADJECTIVE
1 economico (ғᴇᴍ economica, ᴍᴀsᴄ ᴘʟ economici, ғᴇᴍ ᴘʟ economiche)
□ a cheap flight un volo economico □ The bus is cheaper. L'autobus è più economico. □ The cheapest seats are five pounds. I posti più economici vengono cinque sterline.
2 scadente (ғᴇᴍ scadente) (poor quality)
□ a dress made of a cheap material un vestito di stoffa scadente □ This stuff is cheap and nasty. Questa roba è proprio scadente.

to **cheat** VERB
▷ see also **cheat** NOUN
1 imbrogliare [25] (at cards, in games)
□ You're cheating! Stai imbrogliando!
2 copiare [17] (in exam)

cheat NOUN
▷ see also **cheat** VERB
l' imbroglione *masc*
l' imbrogliona *fem*

check NOUN
▷ see also **check** VERB
1 il controllo *masc*
□ a thorough check un controllo accurato
2 l' assegno *masc* (ᴜs: cheque)

to **check** VERB
▷ see also **check** NOUN
controllare [68]
□ Could you check the oil, please? Può controllare l'olio, per favore?
■ **to check with somebody** chiedere [19]

a qualcuno □ I'll check with Ian what time the bus leaves. Chiederò a Ian quando parte l'autobus.

to **check in** VERB
1 fare [49] il check-in (at airport)
2 arrivare [68] (in hotel)

to **check out** VERB
lasciare [13] la camera e saldare [68] il conto (in hotel)
■ **Check it out.** Vedi di che si tratta.

checked ADJECTIVE
a quadretti

checkers NOUN (ᴜs)
la dama *fem*

check-in NOUN
il banco del check-in *masc*

checking account NOUN (ᴜs)
il conto corrente *masc*

checkout NOUN
la cassa *fem*

check-up NOUN
il check-up *masc* (ᴘʟ i check-up)

cheddar NOUN
il cheddar *masc*

cheek NOUN
la guancia *fem* (ᴘʟ le guance)
□ a kiss on the cheek un bacio sulla guancia
■ **What a cheek!** Che faccia tosta!

cheeky ADJECTIVE
sfacciato (ғᴇᴍ sfacciata)
□ Don't be cheeky! Non essere sfacciato!

cheer NOUN
▷ see also **cheer** VERB
l' urrà *masc* (ᴘʟ gli urrà)
□ Three cheers for the winner! Tre urrà per il vincitore!
■ **Cheers!** 1 (when drinking) Cin cin! 2 (thank you) Grazie!

to **cheer** VERB
▷ see also **cheer** NOUN
applaudire [41]
■ **to cheer somebody up** tirare [68] qualcuno su di morale □ I was trying to cheer him up. Cercavo di tirarlo su di morale.
■ **Cheer up!** Coraggio!

cheerful ADJECTIVE
allegro (ғᴇᴍ allegra)

cheerio EXCLAMATION
ciao

cheese NOUN
il formaggio *masc*

chef NOUN
lo chef *masc* (ᴘʟ gli chef)

chemical NOUN
il prodotto chimico *masc* (ᴘʟ i prodotti chimici)

chemist NOUN
1 il/la farmacista *masc/fem* (person)
2 la farmacia *fem* (ᴘʟ le farmacie) (shop)

□ You get it from the chemist. Si compra in
farmacia.
3 il chimico *masc* (PL i chimici) *(scientist)*
chemistry NOUN
la chimica *fem*
□ the chemistry lab il laboratorio di chimica
cheque NOUN
l' assegno *masc*
□ He wrote a cheque. Ha fatto un assegno.
□ Can I pay by cheque? Posso pagare con un
assegno?
chequebook NOUN
il libretto degli assegni *masc*
cherry NOUN
la ciliegia *fem* (PL le ciliegie *or* le ciliege)
chess NOUN
gli scacchi *masc pl*
□ He likes playing chess. Gli piace giocare a
scacchi.
chessboard NOUN
la scacchiera *fem*
chest NOUN
il petto *masc*
□ I've got a pain in my chest. Ho un dolore al
petto.
■ **a chest of drawers** una cassettiera
chestnut NOUN
1 la castagna *fem (nut)*
2 il castagno *masc (tree)*
to **chew** VERB
masticare [18]
chewing gum NOUN
la gomma da masticare *fem*
chick NOUN
il pulcino *masc*
chicken NOUN
il pollo *masc*
□ a chicken leg una coscia di pollo
chickenpox NOUN
la varicella *fem*
chickpeas NOUN PL
i ceci *masc pl*
chief NOUN
▷ *see also* **chief** ADJECTIVE
il capo *masc*
□ the chief of security il capo della sicurezza
chief ADJECTIVE
▷ *see also* **chief** NOUN
principale (FEM principale)
□ his chief reason for resigning la ragione
principale per cui si è licenziato
child NOUN
1 il bambino *masc*
la bambina *fem*
□ a child of six un bambino di sei anni □ I like
children. Mi piacciono i bambini.
2 il figlio *masc*
la figlia *fem*

□ Susan is our eldest child. Susan è la nostra
figlia maggiore. □ They've got three children.
Hanno tre figli.
childish ADJECTIVE
infantile (FEM infantile)
child minder NOUN
la bambinaia *fem*
children NOUN PL ▷ *see* **child**
Chile NOUN
il Cile *masc*
to **chill** VERB
▷ *see also* **chill** NOUN
mettere [59] in fresco *(wine, food)*
■ **serve chilled** servire fresco
chill NOUN
▷ *see also* **chill** VERB
■ **to catch a chill** prendere [77] un colpo di
freddo
chilli NOUN
il peperoncino *masc*
■ **chilli con carne** piatto di carne macinata e
fagioli con il peperoncino
chilly ADJECTIVE
freddo (FEM fredda)
chimney NOUN
il camino *masc*
chin NOUN
il mento *masc*
China NOUN
la Cina *fem*
china NOUN
la porcellana *fem*
□ a china plate un piatto di porcellana
Chinese ADJECTIVE
▷ *see also* **Chinese** NOUN
cinese (FEM cinese)
Chinese NOUN
▷ *see also* **Chinese** ADJECTIVE
il cinese *masc (language)*
■ **the Chinese** i cinesi
chip NOUN
1 la patatina fritta *fem (to eat)*
2 il chip *masc* (PL i chip) *(in computer)*
■ **potato chips** (US) le patatine
chiropodist NOUN
il/la callista *masc/fem*
chives NOUN PL
l' erba cipollina *fem*
chocolate NOUN
1 il cioccolato *masc*
□ a chocolate cake una torta al cioccolato
2 il cioccolatino *masc*
□ a box of chocolates una scatola di
cioccolatini
■ **hot chocolate** la cioccolata calda
choice NOUN
la scelta *fem*
□ I had no choice. Non avevo scelta.

351

choir NOUN
il coro *masc*

to **choke** VERB
soffocare [18]
□ Help him, he's choking! Aiutatelo, sta soffocando!

to **choose** VERB
scegliere [95]
□ I don't know which to choose. Non so quale scegliere. □ She chose a pale pink skirt. Ha scelto una gonna rosa pallido. □ Have you already chosen? Hai già scelto?

to **chop** VERB
▷ *see also* **chop** NOUN
1 tagliare [25] a pezzetti *(meat, vegetables)*
2 tritare [68] *(onion)*

chop NOUN
▷ *see also* **chop** VERB
la cotoletta *fem*
□ a pork chop una cotoletta di maiale

chopsticks NOUN PL
i bastoncini *masc pl*

chose, chosen VERB ▷ *see* **choose**

Christ NOUN
Cristo

christening NOUN
il battesimo *masc*

Christian NOUN
▷ *see also* **Christian** ADJECTIVE
il cristiano *masc*
la cristiana *fem*

Christian ADJECTIVE
▷ *see also* **Christian** NOUN
cristiano (FEM cristiana)

Christian name NOUN
il nome di battesimo *masc*

Christmas NOUN
il Natale *masc*
□ Happy Christmas! Buon Natale!
■ **a Christmas card** un biglietto di auguri natalizi
■ **Christmas Day** il giorno di Natale
■ **Christmas Eve** la vigilia di Natale

chunk NOUN
il grosso pezzo *masc*
□ Cut the meat into chunks. Taglia la carne a grossi pezzi.

church NOUN
la chiesa *fem*
■ **the Church of England** la chiesa anglicana

cider NOUN
il sidro *masc*

cigar NOUN
il sigaro *masc*

cigarette NOUN
la sigaretta *fem*
□ He's smoking a cigarette. Sta fumando una sigaretta.
■ **a cigarette end** un mozzicone

cigarette lighter NOUN
l' accendino *masc*

cinema NOUN
il cinema *masc* (PL i cinema)

cinnamon NOUN
la cannella *fem*

circle NOUN
il cerchio *masc*

circular ADJECTIVE
circolare (FEM circolare)

circulation NOUN
1 la circolazione *fem*
□ She has poor circulation. Ha una cattiva circolazione.
2 la tiratura *fem* *(of newspaper)*

circumstances NOUN PL
le circostanze *fem pl*
□ in the circumstances date le circostanze
■ **under no circumstances** in nessun caso

circus NOUN
il circo *masc* (PL i circhi)

citizen NOUN
il cittadino *masc*
la cittadina *fem*

citizenship NOUN
la cittadinanza *fem*

City NOUN
■ **the City** la City di Londra

city NOUN
la città *fem* (PL le città)
■ **the city centre** il centro

city technology college NOUN
l' istituto tecnico *masc* (PL gli istituti tecnici)

civilization NOUN
la civiltà *fem*

civil servant NOUN
il funzionario dello Stato *masc*

civil war NOUN
la guerra civile *fem* (PL le guerre civili)

to **claim** VERB
▷ *see also* **claim** NOUN
1 sostenere [113]
□ He claims he found the money. Sostiene di aver trovato il denaro.
2 chiedere [19]
□ He's claiming compensation from the company. Chiede un risarcimento da parte della società.
3 ricevere [27]
□ She's claiming benefit. Riceve un sussidio.

claim NOUN
▷ *see also* **claim** VERB
1 l' affermazione *fem*
□ These claims are untrue. Queste affermazioni sono false.
2 la richiesta di risarcimento *fem*
□ We sent in a claim to our insurance company. Abbiamo mandato una richiesta

di risarcimento alla nostra assicurazione.

■ **a claim form** un modulo di richiesta di risarcimento

■ **to put in a claim for a pay rise** chiedere [19] un aumento di stipendio

to **clap** VERB
applaudire [41]

□ Everybody clapped. Tutti applaudirono.

■ **to clap one's hands** battere [1] le mani

□ Clap your hands. Batti le mani.

clarinet NOUN
il clarinetto *masc*

to **clash** VERB
1 stonare [68]

□ Red clashes with orange. Il rosso stona con l'arancio.

2 coincidere [31]

□ The date of the party clashes with the meeting. La data della festa coincide con quella della riunione.

clasp NOUN
il fermaglio *masc (of necklace, handbag)*

class NOUN
1 la classe *fem*

□ We're in the same class. Siamo in classe insieme.

2 la lezione *fem*

□ I go to dancing classes. Vado a lezione di ballo.

classic ADJECTIVE
▷ *see also* **classic** NOUN
classico (FEM classica, MASC PL classici, FEM PL classiche)

□ a classic example un esempio classico

classic NOUN
▷ *see also* **classic** ADJECTIVE
il classico *masc (PL* i classici)

□ This song is a classic. Questa canzone è un classico.

classical ADJECTIVE
classico (FEM classica, MASC PL classici, FEM PL classiche)

□ classical music la musica classica

classmate NOUN
il compagno di classe *masc*
la compagna di classe *fem*

classroom NOUN
la classe *fem*

classroom assistant NOUN
l' insegnante di sostegno *masc/fem*

clause NOUN
la proposizione *fem*

claw NOUN
l' artiglio *masc (of dog, cat, bird)*

clean ADJECTIVE
▷ *see also* **clean** VERB
pulito (FEM pulita)

to **clean** VERB
▷ *see also* **clean** ADJECTIVE
pulire [51]

□ He never cleans the bath. Non pulisce mai la vasca da bagno.

■ **to clean one's teeth** lavarsi [56ᴱ] i denti

┃ LANGUAGE TIP Word for word, this means 'to wash one's teeth'.

cleaner NOUN
1 l' addetto alle pulizie *masc*
l' addetta alle pulizie *fem (person)*

2 il detersivo *masc (product)*

cleaner's NOUN
la tintoria *fem*

□ He took his coat to the cleaner's. Ha portato il cappotto in tintoria.

cleaning lady NOUN
la donna delle pulizie *fem*

cleansing lotion NOUN
il latte detergente *masc*

clear ADJECTIVE
▷ *see also* **clear** VERB
1 chiaro (FEM chiara)

□ a clear explanation una spiegazione chiara
□ Have I made myself clear? Sono stato chiaro?

2 libero (FEM libera)

□ Wait till the road is clear. Aspetta finché la strada sarà libera.

3 trasparente (FEM trasparente)

□ a clear plastic bottle una bottiglia di plastica trasparente

■ **a clear day** una giornata limpida

to **clear** VERB
▷ *see also* **clear** ADJECTIVE
1 liberare [68]

□ They are clearing the road. Stanno liberando la strada.

2 diradarsi [56ᴱ] *(mist)*

■ **to be cleared of...** essere [47ᴱ] scagionato dall'accusa di... □ She was cleared of murder. È stata scagionata dall'accusa di omicidio.

■ **to clear the table** sparecchiare [17] la tavola

to **clear off** VERB
andarsene [6ᴱ]

□ Clear off and leave me alone! Vattene e lasciami in pace!

to **clear up** VERB
1 mettere [59] in ordine

□ Who's going to clear all this up? Chi metterà tutto in ordine?

2 chiarire [51]

□ I'm sure we can clear up this problem. Sono sicuro che possiamo chiarire il problema.

3 schiarire [51ᴱ] *(weather)*

□ I think it's going to clear up. Penso che schiarirà.

clearly ADVERB
chiaramente

□ Clearly this project will cost money.

Chiaramente il progetto avrà un costo.
- **to speak clearly** parlare [68] chiaro

clementine NOUN
la clementina *fem*

to **clench** VERB
stringere [109]
□ She clenched her fists. Strinse i pugni.

clerk NOUN
l' impiegato *masc*
l' impiegata *fem*

clever ADJECTIVE
1 intelligente (FEM intelligente)
□ She's very clever. È molto intelligente.
2 ingegnoso
□ a clever system un sistema ingegnoso
3 geniale
□ What a clever idea! Che idea geniale!

click NOUN
▷ see also **click** VERB
il click *masc* (PL i click)

to **click** VERB
▷ see also **click** NOUN
- **to click on** cliccare [18] su

client NOUN
il/la cliente *masc/fem*

cliff NOUN
la scogliera *fem*

climate NOUN
il clima *masc*

climate change NOUN
i cambiamenti climatici *masc pl*
□ the fight against climate change la lotta contro i cambiamenti climatici

to **climb** VERB
1 scalare [68]
□ Her ambition is to climb Mount Everest. La sua ambizione è quella di scalare l'Everest.
2 salire [93ᴱ]
□ We had to climb three flights of stairs. Abbiamo dovuto salire tre rampe di scale.
3 salire [93ᴱ] su
□ They climbed a tree. Sono saliti su un albero.

climber NOUN
l' alpinista *masc/fem*

climbing NOUN
l' alpinismo *masc*
- **to go climbing** andare [6ᴱ] a fare roccia

cling film NOUN
la pellicola trasparente *fem*

clinic NOUN
la clinica *fem* (PL le cliniche)

clip NOUN
1 il fermaglio *masc* (for hair)
2 la sequenza *fem*
□ some clips from her latest film alcune sequenze del suo ultimo film

clippers NOUN
- **nail clippers** il tagliaunghie

cloakroom NOUN
1 il guardaroba *masc* (PL i guardaroba) (for coats)
2 la toilette *fem* (PL le toilette) (toilet)

clock NOUN
l' orologio *masc*
- **an alarm clock** una sveglia
- **a clock-radio** una radiosveglia
- **It's seven o'clock.** Sono le sette.

clockwork NOUN
- **to go like clockwork** funzionare [68] alla perfezione

clog NOUN
lo zoccolo *masc*

clone NOUN
▷ see also **clone** VERB
il clone *masc*

to **clone** VERB
▷ see also **clone** NOUN
clonare [68]

close ADJECTIVE, ADVERB
▷ see also **close** VERB
1 vicino (FEM vicina)
□ The shops are very close. I negozi sono molto vicini. □ Come closer. Vieni più vicino.
- **She was close to tears.** Stava per piangere.
2 stretto (FEM stretta)
□ We're just inviting close relations. Invitiamo solo i parenti più stretti.
3 intimo (FEM intima)
□ She's a close friend of mine. È una mia amica intima.
- **I'm very close to my sister.** Io e mia sorella siamo molto unite.
4 combattuto (FEM combattuta)
□ It was a very close contest. È stata una gara molto combattuta.
- **It's close this afternoon.** C'è afa questo pomeriggio.

to **close** VERB
▷ see also **close** ADJECTIVE, ADVERB
1 chiudere [20]
□ The shops close at five thirty. I negozi chiudono alle cinque e mezza. □ Please close the door. Chiudi la porta, per favore.
2 chiudersi [20ᴱ]
□ The doors close automatically. Le porte si chiudono automaticamente.

closed ADJECTIVE
chiuso (FEM chiusa)

closely ADVERB
da vicino (look, examine)
- **a closely fought race** una gara molto combattuta

cloth NOUN
la stoffa *fem*
□ five metres of cloth cinque metri di stoffa
- **a cloth** uno straccio □ Wipe it with a damp cloth. Puliscilo con uno straccio umido.

clothes NOUN PL
  i vestiti *masc pl*
  □ smart clothes vestiti eleganti
  ■ **a clothes line** una corda per il bucato
  ■ **a clothes horse** uno stendibiancheria
  ■ **a clothes peg** una molletta

cloud NOUN
  ▷ *see also* **cloud** ADJECTIVE
  la nuvola *fem*

cloud ADJECTIVE
  ▷ *see also* **cloud** NOUN
  cloud (FEM+PL cloud) *(in computing)*
  ■ **cloud applications** le applicazioni cloud

cloudy ADJECTIVE
  nuvoloso (FEM nuvolosa)

clove NOUN
  ■ **a clove of garlic** uno spicchio d'aglio

clown NOUN
  il clown *masc* (PL i clown)

club NOUN
1 la mazza *fem*
  □ a golf club una mazza da golf
2 il circolo *masc*
  □ the youth club il circolo giovanile
3 la discoteca *fem* (PL le discoteche)
  □ We had dinner and went on to a club.
  Abbiamo cenato e poi siamo andati in
  discoteca.
  ■ **clubs** *(in cards)* i fiori

to **club together** VERB
  fare [49] colletta
  □ We clubbed together to buy her a present.
  Abbiamo fatto colletta per comprarle un
  regalo.

clubbing NOUN
  ■ **to go clubbing** andare [6ᴱ] in discoteca

clue NOUN
  l' indizio *masc*
  □ an important clue un indizio importante
  ■ **I haven't a clue.** Non ne ho la minima idea.

clumsy ADJECTIVE
  maldestro (FEM maldestra)

cluster NOUN
  il gruppo *masc*

clutch NOUN
  ▷ *see also* **clutch** VERB
  la frizione *fem (of car)*

to **clutch** VERB
  ▷ *see also* **clutch** NOUN
  afferrare [68]
  □ She clutched my arm. Mi ha afferrato il
  braccio.

clutter NOUN
  il disordine *masc*
  □ There's so much clutter in here. C'è un gran
  disordine qua dentro.

coach NOUN
1 la corriera *fem*

  □ by coach in corriera □ the coach station la
  stazione delle corriere
  ■ **a coach trip** un viaggio in pullman
2 l' allenatore *masc (of team)*

coal NOUN
  il carbone *masc*
  ■ **a coal mine** una miniera di carbone
  ■ **a coal miner** un minatore

coarse ADJECTIVE
1 ruvido (FEM ruvida)
  □ The bag was made of coarse black cloth.
  La borsa era fatta di una stoffa nera ruvida.
2 grosso (FEM grossa)
  □ coarse sand sabbia grossa

coast NOUN
  la costa *fem*

coastguard NOUN
  la guardia costiera *fem*

coat NOUN
  il cappotto *masc*
  □ a nice warm coat un bel cappotto caldo
  ■ **a coat of paint** una mano di pittura
    LANGUAGE TIP Word for word, this means
    'a hand of paint'.

coat hanger NOUN
  la gruccia *fem* (PL le grucce)

cobweb NOUN
  la ragnatela *fem*

cocaine NOUN
  la cocaina *fem*

cock NOUN
  il gallo *masc (bird)*

cockerel NOUN
  il gallo *masc*

cockney NOUN
  ■ **He's got a cockney accent.** Ha un accento
  cockney.

cocoa NOUN
  il cacao *masc*

coconut NOUN
  la noce di cocco *fem*

cod NOUN
  il merluzzo *masc*

code NOUN
1 il codice *masc*
  □ It's written in code. È scritto in codice.
2 il prefisso *masc (for telephone)*
  □ What's the code for York? Qual è il prefisso
  di York?

coffee NOUN
  il caffè *masc* (PL i caffè)
  □ a cup of coffee una tazza di caffè

coffeepot NOUN
  la caffettiera *fem*

coffee table NOUN
  il tavolino *masc*

coffin NOUN
  la bara *fem*

coin NOUN
la moneta *fem*
- □ a 50p coin una moneta da 50 pence

coincidence NOUN
la coincidenza *fem*

coinphone NOUN
il telefono a monete *masc*

Coke® NOUN
la Coca® *fem*

colander NOUN
il colapasta *masc* (PL i colapasta)

> **LANGUAGE TIP** Word for word, this means 'pasta drainer'.

cold ADJECTIVE
▷ *see also* **cold** NOUN
freddo (FEM fredda)
- □ It's cold. Fa freddo.
- ■ **to be cold** avere [12] freddo □ Are you cold? Hai freddo?

cold NOUN
▷ *see also* **cold** ADJECTIVE
1 il freddo *masc*
- □ I can't stand the cold. Non sopporto il freddo.
2 il raffreddore *masc*
- ■ **to catch a cold** prendere [77] un raffreddore
- ■ **to have a cold** avere [12] il raffreddore

cold sore NOUN
la febbre *fem*

coleslaw NOUN
insalata di cavolo, carote e maionese

to collapse VERB
1 crollare [68E]
- □ The bridge collapsed last year. Il ponte è crollato l'anno scorso.
2 avere [12] un collasso
- □ He collapsed while playing tennis. Ha avuto un collasso mentre giocava a tennis.

collar NOUN
1 il colletto *masc* (of coat, shirt)
2 il collare *masc* (for animal)

collarbone NOUN
la clavicola *fem*

colleague NOUN
il/la collega *masc/fem*

to collect VERB
1 raccogliere [21]
- □ The teacher collected the exercise books. L'insegnante ha raccolto i quaderni.
2 fare [49] collezione di
- □ He collects stamps. Fa collezione di francobolli.
3 andare [6E] a prendere
- □ Their mother collects them from school. La mamma li va a prendere a scuola.
4 fare [49] una colletta
- □ I'm collecting for UNICEF. Faccio una colletta per l'UNICEF.

collect call NOUN (US)
la telefonata con addebito al ricevente *fem*

collection NOUN
1 la collezione *fem*
- □ my CD collection la mia collezione di CD
2 la colletta *fem*
- □ a collection for charity una colletta per beneficenza

collector NOUN
il/la collezionista *masc/fem*

college NOUN
1 l' università *fem* (PL le università)
- □ I want to go to college. Voglio andare all'università.
- ■ **college students** gli studenti universitari
2 il collegio *masc* (PL i collegi) (boarding school)
3 la scuola *fem* (school)

to collide VERB
scontrarsi [56E]

collie NOUN
il collie *masc* (PL i collie)

colliery NOUN
la miniera di carbone *fem*

collision NOUN
la collisione *fem*

colon NOUN
i due punti *masc pl* (punctuation mark)

colonel NOUN
il colonnello *masc*

colour (US color) NOUN
il colore *masc*
- □ What colour is it? Di che colore è? □ It doesn't matter what colour you are. Non importa il colore della tua pelle.
- ■ **a colour TV** un televisore a colori

colourful (US colorful) ADJECTIVE
colorato (FEM colorata)

colouring (US coloring) NOUN
il colorante *masc* (for food)

comb NOUN
▷ *see also* **comb** VERB
il pettine *masc*

to comb VERB
▷ *see also* **comb** NOUN
- ■ **to comb one's hair** pettinarsi [56E] □ You haven't combed your hair. Non ti sei pettinato.

combination NOUN
la combinazione *fem*

to combine VERB
1 unire [51]
- □ The film combines humour with suspense. Il film unisce umorismo e suspense.
2 conciliare [17]
- □ It's difficult to combine a career with a family. È difficile conciliare la carriera con la famiglia.

to come VERB
1 venire [120E]

□ Can I come too? Posso venire anch'io?
□ Come home. Vieni a casa. □ Come and see us soon. Vieni a trovarci presto. □ Helen came with me. Helen è venuta con me.

2 arrivare [68ᴱ]
□ They came late. Sono arrivati tardi. □ The letter came this morning. La lettera è arrivata stamattina.

to come across VERB
trovare [68] per caso *(by chance)*
□ I came across an old photo. Ho trovato per caso una vecchia foto.

■ **to come across as** dare [30] l'impressione di essere □ She comes across as a nice girl. Dà l'impressione di essere una ragazza simpatica.

to come apart VERB
scucirsi [41ᴱ]
□ My jacket is coming apart. La mia giacca si sta scucendo.

to come at VERB
avventarsi [56ᴱ] su
□ He came at me with a knife. Si è avventato su di me con un coltello.

to come back VERB
tornare [68ᴱ]
□ He came back an hour later. È tornato un'ora dopo.

■ **Can I come back to you on that one?** Possiamo discuterne più tardi?

to come down VERB
scendere [96ᴱ]

to come for VERB
passare [68ᴱ] a prendere
□ I'll come for you at seven. Passo a prenderti alle sette.

to come forward VERB
farsi [49ᴱ] avanti

to come in VERB
entrare [68ᴱ]
□ They came in together. Entrarono insieme.
■ **Come in!** Avanti!

to come off VERB
1 staccarsi [18ᴱ]
□ A button came off my coat. Mi si è staccato un bottone dal cappotto.

2 andare [6ᴱ] via
□ I don't think this stain will come off. Non penso che la macchia andrà via.

to come on VERB
■ **Come on! 1** *(encouragement)* Avanti!
2 *(protest)* Ma dai!

■ **I've got a cold coming on.** Mi sta venendo un raffreddore.

to come out VERB
1 uscire [117ᴱ]
□ We came out of the cinema at 10. Siamo usciti dal cinema alle dieci. □ Her book comes out in May. Il suo libro esce in maggio.

2 venire [120ᴱ]
□ None of my photos came out. Non è venuta nessuna delle mie foto.

to come round VERB
1 passare [68]
□ He is coming round to see us. Passa a trovarci.

2 riprendere [77] conoscenza
□ He came round after about ten minutes. Ha ripreso conoscenza dopo circa dieci minuti.

to come through VERB
superare [68]
□ They came through a difficult time. Hanno superato un periodo difficile.

to come to VERB
riprendere [77] conoscenza
□ She came to in a hospital bed. Ha ripreso conoscenza in un letto d'ospedale.

to come up VERB
1 saltare [68] fuori
□ Something has come up. È saltato fuori un problema.

2 avvicinarsi [56ᴱ]
□ She came up to me and kissed me. Mi si è avvicinata e mi ha baciato.

comedian NOUN
il comico *masc* (PL i comici)

comedy NOUN
la commedia *fem*

comfortable ADJECTIVE
1 comodo (FEM comoda)
□ comfortable shoes scarpe comode
□ Are you comfortable sitting there? Sei seduto comodo?
■ **Make yourself comfortable.** Mettiti a tuo agio.

2 confortevole
□ Their house is small but comfortable. La loro casa è piccola ma confortevole.

comic NOUN
il giornalino *masc* *(magazine)*

comic strip NOUN
la striscia *fem* (PL le strisce)

coming ADJECTIVE
prossimo (FEM prossima)
□ in the coming weeks nelle prossime settimane

comma NOUN
la virgola *fem*

command NOUN
il comando *masc*

comment NOUN
▷ *see also* **comment** VERB
il commento *masc*
□ He made no comment. Non fece commenti.

to comment VERB
▷ *see also* **comment** NOUN
fare [49] commenti
□ The police have not commented on these

357

rumours. La polizia non ha fatto commenti sulle voci.

commentary NOUN
1 la telecronaca *fem* (PL le telecronache) *(on TV)*
2 la radiocronaca *fem* (PL le radiocronache) *(on radio)*

commentator NOUN
1 il/la telecronista *masc/fem (on TV)*
2 il/la radiocronista *masc/fem (on radio)*

commercial NOUN
▷ *see also* **commercial** ADJECTIVE
lo spot pubblicitario *masc* (PL gli spot pubblicitari)

commercial ADJECTIVE
▷ *see also* **commercial** NOUN
commerciale (FEM commerciale)

commission NOUN
1 la commissione *fem*
□ a commission of 1% una commissione dell'uno per cento
□ A commission has been set up to investigate the tragedy. È stata nominata una commissione per indagare sulla tragedia.
2 la provvigione *fem (on sales)*
□ He gets commission on top of his basic salary. Oltre allo stipendio base prende una provvigione.
■ **to work on commission** lavorare [68] a provvigione

to **commit** VERB
■ **to commit a crime** commettere [59] un delitto
■ **to commit suicide** suicidarsi [56ᴱ]
■ **to commit oneself** impegnarsi [14ᴱ]
□ I don't want to commit myself. Non voglio impegnarmi.

committee NOUN
la commissione *fem*

common ADJECTIVE
▷ *see also* **common** NOUN
comune (FEM comune)
□ It's a common name. È un nome comune.

common NOUN
▷ *see also* **common** ADJECTIVE
il parco comunale *masc*
□ a walk on the common una passeggiata nel parco comunale
■ **in common** in comune □ We've got a lot in common. Abbiamo molto in comune.

Commons NOUN PL
■ **the House of Commons** la Camera dei Comuni

common sense NOUN
il buonsenso *masc*

to **communicate** VERB
comunicare [18]

communication NOUN
la comunicazione *fem*

communion NOUN
la comunione *fem*

communism NOUN
il comunismo *masc*

communist NOUN
▷ *see also* **communist** ADJECTIVE
il/la comunista *masc/fem*

communist ADJECTIVE
▷ *see also* **communist** NOUN
comunista (FEM comunista)

community NOUN
la comunità *fem* (PL le comunità)

to **commute** VERB
fare [49] il pendolare
□ She commutes between Oxford and London. Fa la pendolare tra Oxford e Londra.

compact disc NOUN
il compact disc *masc* (PL i compact disc)

compact disc player NOUN
il lettore di compact disc *masc*

companion NOUN
il compagno *masc*
la compagna *fem*

company NOUN
1 la società *fem* (PL le società)
□ He works for a big company. Lavora per una grossa società.
2 la compagnia *fem*
□ an insurance company una compagnia di assicurazione
□ a theatre company una compagnia teatrale
■ **to keep somebody company** fare [49] compagnia a qualcuno □ I'll keep you company. Ti farò compagnia.

comparatively ADVERB
relativamente
□ a comparatively easy exercise un esercizio relativamente facile

to **compare** VERB
1 paragonare [68]
□ They compared his work to that of Joyce. Hanno paragonato la sua opera a quella di Joyce. □ People always compare him with his brother. Tutti lo paragonano sempre a suo fratello.
2 mettere [59] a confronto
□ Compare the two illustrations. Mettete a confronto le due illustrazioni.
■ **compared with** rispetto a □ Oxford is small compared with London. Oxford è piccola rispetto a Londra.

comparison NOUN
il paragone *masc*

compartment NOUN
1 lo scompartimento *masc*
□ a first class compartment uno scompartimento di prima classe
2 lo scomparto *masc (in fridge, drawer)*

compass NOUN
la bussola *fem (magnetic)*
■ **compasses** compasso *masc sing*
compelling ADJECTIVE
1 avvincente (FEM avvincente)
□ It's a compelling film. È un film avvincente.
2 convincente (FEM convincente)
□ a compelling argument un argomento
convincente
compensation NOUN
l' indennizzo *masc (money)*
compere NOUN
il presentatore *masc*
la presentatrice *fem*
to **compete** VERB
■ **to compete in** partecipare [68] a □ I'm
competing in the marathon. Partecipo alla
maratona.
■ **to compete for something** concorrere [26]
per qualcosa □ There are fifty students
competing for six places. Ci sono cinquanta
studenti che concorrono per sei posti.
competent ADJECTIVE
competente (FEM competente)
competition NOUN
1 la gara *fem*
□ a singing competition una gara di canto
2 la concorrenza *fem (in business)*
□ Competition is fierce. C'è una concorrenza
spietata.
competitive ADJECTIVE
competitivo (FEM competitiva)
□ I'm a very competitive person. Sono molto
competitivo.
competitor NOUN
il/la concorrente *masc/fem*
to **complain** VERB
1 presentare [68] un reclamo
□ We're going to complain to the manager.
Presenteremo un reclamo al direttore.
2 lamentarsi [56E]
□ She's always complaining about her husband.
Si lamenta in continuazione di suo marito.
complaint NOUN
la lamentela *fem*
complete ADJECTIVE
completo (FEM completa)
completely ADVERB
completamente
complexion NOUN
la carnagione *fem*
complicated ADJECTIVE
complicato (FEM complicata)
compliment NOUN
▷ *see also* **compliment** VERB
il complimento *masc*
□ Thanks for the compliment. Grazie del
complimento.

■ **to pay somebody a compliment** fare [49]
un complimento a qualcuno □ He's always
paying her compliments. Le fa sempre
complimenti.
■ **with our compliments** con i nostri omaggi
■ **compliments of the season** auguri per le
festività
to **compliment** VERB
▷ *see also* **compliment** NOUN
complimentarsi [56E]
□ They complimented me on my Italian. Si
sono complimentati con me per il mio italiano.
complimentary ADJECTIVE
■ **a complimentary ticket** un biglietto
omaggio
composer NOUN
il compositore *masc*
la compositrice *fem*
comprehension NOUN
la comprensione *fem*
comprehensive ADJECTIVE
completo (FEM completa)
□ a comprehensive guide to Rome una guida
completa di Roma
> LANGUAGE TIP Be careful not to translate
> **comprehensive** by the Italian word
> **comprensivo**.
comprehensive school NOUN
la scuola secondaria *fem*
compromise NOUN
▷ *see also* **compromise** VERB
il compromesso *masc*
to **compromise** VERB
▷ *see also* **compromise** NOUN
accettare [68] un compromesso
compulsory ADJECTIVE
obbligatorio (FEM obbligatoria, MASC PL
obbligatori, FEM PL obbligatorie)
computer NOUN
il computer *masc* (PL i computer)
computer game NOUN
il gioco per il computer *masc* (PL i giochi per il
computer)
computer programmer NOUN
il programmatore *masc*
la programmatrice *fem*
computer science NOUN
l' informatica *fem*
computing NOUN
l' informatica *fem*
to **concentrate** VERB
concentrarsi [56E]
□ I couldn't concentrate. Non riuscivo a
concentrarmi.
concentration NOUN
la concentrazione *fem*
concept NOUN
il concetto *masc*

concern – congratulations

concern NOUN
▷ see also **concern** VERB
la preoccupazione *fem*
□ They expressed concern about the situation. Hanno espresso la loro preoccupazione per la situazione.

to **concern** VERB
▷ see also **concern** NOUN
1 preoccupare [68]
□ what most concerns me ciò che mi preoccupa di più □ They are more concerned to save money than to save lives. Ciò che li preoccupa maggiormente è risparmiare denaro e non salvare vite umane.
2 riguardare [68]
□ This does not concern you. Questo non ti riguarda.
■ **as far as I'm concerned** per quanto mi riguarda □ As far as I'm concerned, you can come any time you like. Per quanto mi riguarda, puoi venire quando vuoi.
■ **As far as I'm concerned he's an idiot.** Secondo me è un idiota.
■ **It was tragic for everyone concerned.** È stato tragico per tutti.

concerned ADJECTIVE
preoccupato (FEM preoccupata)
□ His mother is concerned about him. Sua madre è preoccupata per lui.

concerning NOUN
il riguardo a *masc*
□ For further information concerning the job, contact Mr Ross. Per maggiori informazioni riguardo al lavoro, contatti il signor Ross.

concert NOUN
il concerto *masc*

concrete NOUN
il calcestruzzo *masc*

to **condemn** VERB
condannare [68]
□ The government has condemned the decision. Il governo ha condannato la decisione.

condition NOUN
la condizione *fem*
□ I'll do it, on one condition... Lo farò, ma ad una condizione... □ in good condition in buone condizioni

conditional NOUN
il condizionale *masc*

conditioner NOUN
il balsamo *masc* (for hair)

condom NOUN
il preservativo *masc*

to **conduct** VERB
dirigere [36] (orchestra)

conductor NOUN
1 il direttore d'orchestra *masc* (musician)
2 il bigliettaio *masc* (on bus)

cone NOUN
il cono *masc*
□ an ice-cream cone un cono di gelato

conference NOUN
la conferenza *fem*

to **confess** VERB
confessare [68]
□ He confessed to the murder. Ha confessato di aver commesso l'omicidio.

confession NOUN
la confessione *fem*

confetti NOUN SING
i coriandoli *masc pl*

> **LANGUAGE TIP** Be careful not to translate **confetti** by the Italian word **confetti**.

confidence NOUN
1 la fiducia *fem*
□ I've got a lot of confidence in him. Ho molta fiducia in lui.
2 la fiducia in se stessi *fem*
□ She lacks confidence. Non ha fiducia in se stessa.
■ **in confidence** in via confidenziale □ I'm telling you this in confidence. Te lo dico in via confidenziale.

confident ADJECTIVE
1 sicuro (FEM sicura)
□ I'm confident everything will be okay. Sono sicuro che tutto andrà bene.
2 sicuro di sé
□ She seems very confident. Sembra molto sicura di sé.

confidential ADJECTIVE
confidenziale (FEM confidenziale)

to **confirm** VERB
confermare [68]

confirmation NOUN
la conferma *fem*

conflict NOUN
il conflitto *masc*

to **confuse** VERB
confondere [23]

confused ADJECTIVE
confuso (FEM confusa) (person, situation)

confusing ADJECTIVE
confuso (FEM confusa)
□ It's all very confusing. È tutto molto confuso.
■ **All these messages are confusing for young people.** Tutti questi messaggi confondono i giovani.

confusion NOUN
la confusione *fem*

to **congratulate** VERB
congratularsi [56E] con
□ My friends congratulated me. I miei amici si sono congratulati con me.

congratulations NOUN PL
le congratulazioni *fem pl*

□ Congratulations on your new job!
Congratulazioni per il tuo nuovo lavoro!
conjunction NOUN
la congiunzione *fem*
conjurer NOUN
il prestigiatore *masc*
connection NOUN
1 il rapporto *masc*
□ There's no connection between the two
events. Non c'è rapporto tra i due fatti.
2 la coincidenza *fem*
□ We missed our connection. Abbiamo perso
la coincidenza.
■ **connection to the internet** collegamento
ad Internet
■ **a loose connection** un filo staccato
to **conquer** VERB
1 conquistare [68] *(country)*
2 vincere [121] *(enemy)*
conscience NOUN
la coscienza *fem*
■ **to have a clear conscience** avere [12]
la coscienza pulita
■ **to have a guilty conscience** avere [12]
la coscienza sporca
conscious ADJECTIVE
1 consapevole (FEM consapevole)
□ She was conscious of it. Ne era consapevole.
■ **to make a conscious decision to** decidere
[31] deliberatamente di □ He made a
conscious decision to tell nobody. Ha deciso
deliberatamente di non dirlo a nessuno.
2 in sé
□ He was still conscious when the doctor arrived.
Era ancora in sé quando è arrivato il dottore.
consciousness NOUN
la conoscenza *fem*
□ I lost consciousness. Ho perso conoscenza.
consequence NOUN
la conseguenza *fem*
consequently ADVERB
di conseguenza
conservation NOUN
1 la tutela *fem*
□ the conservation of rain forests la tutela
delle foreste pluviali
2 la salvaguardia ambientale *fem*
□ a conservation project un progetto di
salvaguardia ambientale
■ **People are aware of the need for
conservation.** La gente sa che è necessario
salvaguardare l'ambiente.
■ **energy conservation** risparmio energetico
conservative ADJECTIVE
▷ *see also* **conservative** NOUN
conservatore (FEM conservatrice, MASC PL
conservatori, FEM PL conservatrici)
□ the Conservative Party il partito conservatore

conservative NOUN
▷ *see also* **conservative** ADJECTIVE
il conservatore *masc*
la conservatrice *fem (person)*
□ He votes Conservative. Vota per i conservatori.
conservatory NOUN
la veranda chiusa *fem*
to **consider** VERB
1 prendere [77] in considerazione
□ I'm considering the idea. Sto prendendo in
considerazione l'idea.
2 ritenere [113]
□ He considers it a waste of time. La ritiene
una perdita di tempo.
considerate ADJECTIVE
premuroso (FEM premurosa)
considering PREPOSITION
1 dato che
□ Considering we were there for a month...
Dato che ci siamo rimasti per un mese...
2 tutto sommato
□ I got a good mark, considering. Tutto
sommato ho preso un bel voto.
to **consist** VERB
■ **to consist of** consistere [10ᴱ] di
consistent ADJECTIVE
dal rendimento costante
□ a consistent player un giocatore dal
rendimento costante
■ **to be consistent with** essere [47ᴱ] coerente
con □ It is consistent with his views. È
coerente con il suo modo di pensare.
consonant NOUN
la consonante *fem*
constant ADJECTIVE
costante (FEM costante)
□ a constant temperature una temperatura
costante
constantly ADVERB
in continuazione
constipated ADJECTIVE
stitico (FEM stitica, MASC PL stitici, FEM PL stitiche)
to **construct** VERB
costruire [51]
construction NOUN
la costruzione *fem*
consulate NOUN
il consolato *masc*
to **consult** VERB
consultare [68]
consumer NOUN
il consumatore *masc*
la consumatrice *fem*
contact NOUN
▷ *see also* **contact** VERB
il contatto *masc*
□ I'm in contact with her. Sono in contatto
con lei.

■ **your contact details** il tuo indirizzo e numero di telefono

■ **a contact number** un numero di telefono

to **contact** VERB

▷ *see also* **contact** NOUN

contattare [68]

contact lenses NOUN PL

le lenti a contatto *fem pl*

to **contain** VERB

contenere [113]

container NOUN

il contenitore *masc*

contempt NOUN

il disprezzo *masc*

contents NOUN PL

il contenuto *masc sing*

■ **the table of contents** l'indice *masc*

contest NOUN

1 la gara *fem*

□ a fishing contest una gara di pesca

2 la lotta *fem*

□ He won the leadership contest. Ha vinto la lotta per la leadership.

■ **a beauty contest** un concorso di bellezza

contestant NOUN

il/la concorrente *masc/fem*

context NOUN

il contesto *masc*

continent NOUN

il continente *masc*

■ **the Continent** l'Europa continentale

continental breakfast NOUN

la colazione *fem*

to **continue** VERB

1 continuare [68]

□ She continued talking. Ha continuato a parlare.

2 riprendere [77] *(after a break)*

□ We continued working after lunch. Abbiamo ripreso a lavorare dopo pranzo.

continuous ADJECTIVE

continuo (FEM continua)

contraceptive NOUN

il contraccettivo *masc*

contract NOUN

il contratto *masc*

to **contradict** VERB

contraddire [35]

contrary NOUN

il contrario *masc*

■ **on the contrary** al contrario

■ **contrary to** contrariamente a □ Contrary to what you may have heard, I am not resigning. Contrariamente a quello che potete aver sentito, non mi dimetto.

contrast NOUN

il contrasto *masc*

to **contribute** VERB

1 contribuire [51]

□ Everyone contributed to the success of the play. Tutti hanno contribuito al successo della commedia.

2 contribuire [51] con

□ She contributed £10. Ha contribuito con dieci sterline.

3 partecipare [68]

□ He didn't contribute to the discussion. Non ha partecipato alla discussione.

contribution NOUN

il contributo *masc*

control NOUN

▷ *see also* **control** VERB

il controllo *masc*

□ Everything is under control. Tutto è sotto controllo.

■ **He always seems to be in control.** Non perde mai il controllo della situazione.

■ **to lose control** *(of car, oneself)* perdere [69^E] il controllo

■ **to keep control of** tenere [113] sotto controllo □ She can't keep control of the class. Non riesce a tenere la classe sotto controllo.

■ **to be out of control** *(child)* essere [47^E] scatenato

■ **the controls** *(of car, plane)* i comandi

to **control** VERB

▷ *see also* **control** NOUN

1 dirigere [36] *(country, organization)*

2 tenere [113] sotto controllo

□ He can't control the class. Non riesce a tenere la classe sotto controllo.

3 controllare [68]

□ Control yourself! Controllati!

controversial ADJECTIVE

controverso (FEM controversa)

□ a controversial subject un argomento controverso

convenient ADJECTIVE

1 vicino (FEM vicina) *(place)*

□ The hotel's convenient for the airport. L'albergo è vicino all'aeroporto.

2 comodo (FEM comoda)

□ It is more convenient to eat in the kitchen. È più comodo mangiare in cucina.

■ **It's not a convenient time for me.** Non sono libero a quell'ora.

■ **Would Monday be convenient for you?** Ti andrebbe bene lunedì?

⎮ **LANGUAGE TIP** Be careful not to translate **convenient** by the Italian word **conveniente**.

conventional ADJECTIVE

1 tradizionalista (FEM tradizionalista)

□ My parents are very conventional. I miei genitori sono molto tradizionalisti.

2 tradizionale (FEM tradizionale)
□ a conventional method un metodo tradizionale
■ **conventional weapons** le armi convenzionali

conversation NOUN
la conversazione *fem*
□ We had a long conversation. Abbiamo fatto una lunga conversazione.

to **convert** VERB
trasformare [68]
□ We've converted the loft into a bedroom. Abbiamo trasformato la soffitta in una camera da letto.

to **convict** VERB
▷ *see also* **convict** NOUN
dichiarare [68] colpevole
□ He was convicted of the crime. È stato dichiarato colpevole del delitto.

convict NOUN
▷ *see also* **convict** VERB
il carcerato *masc*
la carcerata *fem*

conviction NOUN
1 la convinzione *fem*
□ She spoke with great conviction. Ha parlato con grande convinzione.
2 la condanna *fem*
□ He has three previous convictions for robbery. Ha tre precedenti condanne per furto.

to **convince** VERB
convincere [121]

to **cook** VERB
▷ *see also* **cook** NOUN
1 cucinare [68]
□ I can't cook. Non so cucinare. □ The chicken isn't cooked. Il pollo non è cotto.
2 preparare [68]
□ She's cooking lunch. Sta preparando il pranzo.

cook NOUN
▷ *see also* **cook** VERB
il cuoco *masc* (PL i cuochi)
la cuoca *fem* (PL le cuoche)

cookbook NOUN
il libro di cucina *masc*

cooker NOUN
il fornello *masc*
□ a gas cooker un fornello a gas

cookery NOUN
la cucina *fem*

cookie NOUN (US)
il biscotto *masc*

cooking NOUN
la cucina *fem*
□ French cooking la cucina francese
■ **I like cooking.** Mi piace cucinare.

cool ADJECTIVE
▷ *see also* **cool** VERB

1 fresco (FEM fresca, MASC PL freschi, FEM PL fresche)
□ a cool place un luogo fresco □ It's cool. Fa fresco.
2 leggero (FEM leggera)
□ a cool top una maglietta leggera
3 figo (FEM figa, MASC PL fighi, FEM PL fighe)
□ They think it's cool to do drugs. Pensano che sia figo drogarsi.
■ **Keep your cool!** Calma!

to **cool** VERB
▷ *see also* **cool** ADJECTIVE
raffreddare [68] *(food)*
■ **Just cool it!** Calmati!

cooperation NOUN
la cooperazione *fem*

cop NOUN
il poliziotto *masc*

to **cope** VERB
farcela [49]
□ It was hard, but we coped. È stato difficile ma ce l'abbiamo fatta.
■ **to cope with** affrontare [68] □ She's got a lot of problems to cope with. Ha molti problemi da affrontare.

copied VERB ▷ *see* **copy**

copper NOUN
1 il rame *masc*
□ a copper bracelet un braccialetto di rame
2 il poliziotto *masc*
□ our friendly neighbourhood copper il cordiale poliziotto del nostro quartiere

copy NOUN
▷ *see also* **copy** VERB
la copia *fem*
■ **rough copy** la brutta copia
■ **fair copy** la bella copia

to **copy** VERB
▷ *see also* **copy** NOUN
copiare [17]

core NOUN
il torsolo *masc (of apple)*

cork NOUN
1 il tappo *masc (of bottle)*
2 il sughero *masc (material)*

corkscrew NOUN
il cavatappi *masc* (PL i cavatappi)

corn NOUN
1 il grano *masc (wheat)*
□ fields of corn campi di grano
2 il granturco *masc (maize)*
■ **corn on the cob** la pannocchia bollita

corner NOUN
l'angolo *masc*
□ the shop on the corner il negozio all'angolo
□ He lives just round the corner. Abita qua dietro l'angolo.
■ **a corner kick** un calcio d'angolo

cornet NOUN
1 la cornetta *fem (instrument)*
2 il cornetto *masc (ice cream)*

cornflakes – council

cornflakes NOUN PL
i fiocchi di granturco *masc pl*

cornstarch NOUN (US)
la fecola di patate *fem*

Cornwall NOUN
la Cornovaglia *fem*

corporal punishment NOUN
la punizione corporale *fem*

corpse NOUN
il cadavere *masc*

correct ADJECTIVE
▷ *see also* **correct** VERB
giusto (FEM giusta)
□ That's correct. È giusto.
■ **the correct answer** la risposta esatta
■ **to be correct** avere [12] ragione □ You're absolutely correct. Hai proprio ragione.

to **correct** VERB
▷ *see also* **correct** ADJECTIVE
correggere [82]

correction NOUN
la correzione *fem*
■ **correction fluid** bianchetto

correctly ADVERB
correttamente

correspondent NOUN
il/la corrispondente *masc/fem* (on paper)

corridor NOUN
il corridoio *masc*

corruption NOUN
la corruzione *fem*

Corsica NOUN
la Corsica *fem*

cosmetics NOUN PL
i cosmetici *masc pl*

cosmetic surgery NOUN
la chirurgia estetica *fem*

to **cost** VERB
▷ *see also* **cost** NOUN
costare [68ᴱ]
□ How much does it cost? Quanto costa?

cost NOUN
▷ *see also* **cost** VERB
il costo *masc*
□ the cost of living il costo della vita
■ **at all costs** a tutti i costi
■ **cost price** il prezzo all'ingrosso

costume NOUN
il costume *masc*

cosy ADJECTIVE
accogliente (FEM accogliente)
□ a cosy room una stanza accogliente
■ **to be cosy** (person) stare [108ᴱ] bene
□ I'm very cosy here. Sto proprio bene qui.

cot NOUN
1 il lettino *masc* (for baby)
2 la brandina *fem* (us: camp bed)

cottage NOUN
la villetta *fem*

cottage cheese NOUN
i fiocchi di latte *masc pl*

cotton NOUN
il cotone *masc*
□ a cotton shirt una camicia di cotone

cotton candy NOUN
lo zucchero filato *masc*

cotton wool NOUN
l' ovatta *fem*

couch NOUN
il divano *masc*
□ He was sitting on the couch. Era seduto sul divano.
■ **couch potato** pigrone teledipendente

couchette NOUN
la cuccetta *fem*

to **cough** VERB
▷ *see also* **cough** NOUN
tossire [51]

cough NOUN
▷ *see also* **cough** VERB
la tosse *fem*
□ I've got a cough. Ho la tosse.
■ **a cough mixture** uno sciroppo per la tosse

could VERB
▷ *see also* **can** VERB

> **LANGUAGE TIP** 'could' is often translated by conditional tenses of **potere**.

□ Could you please close the window? Potresti chiudere la finestra per favore? □ You could be right. Potresti avere ragione. □ You could have killed me. Avresti potuto uccidermi. □ We couldn't wait. Non abbiamo potuto aspettare.

> **LANGUAGE TIP** When it means 'couldn't manage to' **couldn't** is often translated by the appropriate tense of **riuscire**.

□ He couldn't concentrate because of the noise. Non riusciva a concentrarsi a causa del rumore. □ He said that he couldn't do it by next Friday. Ha detto che non sarebbe riuscito a farlo per il venerdì seguente.

> **LANGUAGE TIP** When it means 'knew how to' **could** is often translated by the appropriate tense of **sapere**.

□ I thought you could drive. Pensavo che sapessi guidare.

> **LANGUAGE TIP** 'could' is sometimes not translated.

□ I could see that something was wrong. Capivo che c'era qualcosa che non andava.

council NOUN
il consiglio comunale *masc* (in town)
□ He's on the council. Fa parte del consiglio comunale.
■ **a council estate** un complesso di case popolari
■ **a council house** una casa popolare

councillor NOUN
- ■ **a local councillor** un consigliere comunale

to **count** VERB
contare [68]
- □ You can count on me. Puoi contare su di me.

counter NOUN
1. il banco masc (PL i banchi) (in shop)
2. lo sportello masc (in post office, bank)
3. il gettone masc (for game)

country NOUN
1. il paese masc
   - □ the border between the two countries il confine tra i due paesi
2. la campagna fem
   - □ I live in the country. Vivo in campagna.
   - ■ **a country house** una villa in campagna
   - ■ **country dancing** danza popolare

countryside NOUN
la campagna fem

county NOUN
la contea fem
- ■ **the county council** il consiglio di contea

couple NOUN
1. la coppia fem
   - □ the couple who live next door la coppia che vive qui accanto
2. il paio masc
   - □ a couple of hours un paio d'ore

courage NOUN
il coraggio masc

courgette NOUN
la zucchina fem

courier NOUN
1. l' accompagnatore turistico masc
   l' accompagnatrice turistica fem (for tourists)
2. il corriere masc (delivery service)
   - □ They sent it by courier. L'hanno spedito con il corriere.

course NOUN
1. il corso masc
   - □ a French course un corso di francese
2. la portata fem
   - □ the main course la portata principale
   - ■ **the first course** il primo piatto
3. il campo masc
   - □ a golf course un campo da golf
   - ■ **of course** certo □ Do you love me? — Of course I do! Mi ami? — Ma certo!

court NOUN
la corte fem (legal, royal)
- ■ **a tennis court** un campo da tennis

courtyard NOUN
il cortile masc

cousin NOUN
il cugino masc
la cugina fem

cover NOUN
▷ see also **cover** VERB

1. la copertina fem (of book)
2. la coperta fem (on bed)

to **cover** VERB
▷ see also **cover** NOUN
coprire [9]
- □ He covered his face. Si coprì il viso.

to **cover up** VERB
tenere [113] nascosto
- □ The government tried to cover up the details. Il governo ha cercato di tenere nascosti i particolari.

cover charge NOUN
il coperto masc

cover-up NOUN
l' occultamento di informazioni masc

cow NOUN
la mucca fem (PL le mucche)

coward NOUN
il codardo masc
la codarda fem

cowardly ADJECTIVE
vigliacco (FEM vigliacca, MASC PL vigliacchi, FEM PL vigliacche)

cowboy NOUN
il cowboy masc (PL i cowboy)

crab NOUN
il granchio masc

crack NOUN
▷ see also **crack** VERB
1. la crepa fem (in wall)
2. l' incrinatura fem (in cup, plate)
3. il crack masc (drug)
   - ■ **to open the door a crack** aprire [9] la porta lasciandola accostata
   - ■ **I'll have a crack at it.** Ci proverò.

to **crack** VERB
▷ see also **crack** NOUN
1. rompere [92] (egg, nut)
2. sbattere [1]
   - □ He cracked his head on the pavement. Ha sbattuto la testa sul marciapiede.
   - ■ **I think we've cracked it!** Penso che ci siamo!
   - ■ **to crack a joke** fare [49] una battuta

to **crack down on** VERB
prendere [77] serie misure contro
- □ The police are cracking down on graffiti. La polizia sta prendendo serie misure contro i graffitari.

cracked ADJECTIVE
incrinato (FEM incrinata) (cup, plate, window)

cracker NOUN
il cracker masc (PL i cracker) (biscuit)
- ■ **a Christmas cracker** un mortaretto con sorpresa

cradle NOUN
la culla fem

craft NOUN
l' artigianato masc

■ **a craft shop** un negozio che vende prodotti d'artigianato

craftsman NOUN
l' artigiano *masc*

to **cram** VERB
1 stipare [68]
□ We crammed our stuff into the boot. Abbiamo stipato la nostra roba nel bagagliaio.
2 riempire [86]
□ She crammed her bag with books. Ha riempito la borsa di libri.
■ **to cram for an exam** studiare [17] come un pazzo per un esame

crammed ADJECTIVE
■ **to be crammed with** essere [47ᴱ] pieno zeppo di □ Her house was crammed with furniture. La casa era piena zeppa di mobili.

crane NOUN
la gru *fem* (PL le gru)

to **crash** VERB
▷ *see also* **crash** NOUN
1 scontrarsi [56ᴱ]
□ The two cars crashed. Le due macchine si sono scontrate.
■ **He's crashed his car.** Ha avuto un incidente con la macchina.
2 precipitare [68ᴱ]
□ The plane crashed. L'aereo è precipitato.
3 impiantarsi [56ᴱ]
□ I'd nearly finished when my computer crashed. Avevo quasi finito quando il computer si è impiantato.

crash NOUN
▷ *see also* **crash** VERB
1 l' incidente *masc* (car crash)
2 la caduta *fem* (plane crash)

crash course NOUN
il corso intensivo *masc*

crash helmet NOUN
il casco di protezione *masc* (PL i caschi di protezione)

crash landing NOUN
l' atterraggio di fortuna *fem*

to **crawl** VERB
▷ *see also* **crawl** NOUN
andare [6ᴱ] gattoni *(baby)*

crawl NOUN
▷ *see also* **crawl** VERB
lo stile libero *masc*
■ **to do the crawl** nuotare [68] a stile libero

crazy ADJECTIVE
pazzo (FEM pazza)
□ She's crazy about him. È pazza di lui.
□ Paul is crazy about football. Paul va pazzo per il calcio.

cream ADJECTIVE
▷ *see also* **cream** NOUN
crema (FEM+PL crema)
□ a cream silk blouse una camicetta di seta crema

cream NOUN
▷ *see also* **cream** ADJECTIVE
1 la panna *fem*
□ strawberries and cream fragole con panna
□ a cream cake una torta alla panna
■ **cream cheese** formaggio cremoso
2 la crema *fem* (for skin)
□ sun cream crema solare

crease NOUN
la piega *fem* (PL le pieghe)

creased ADJECTIVE
spiegazzato (FEM spiegazzata)

to **create** VERB
creare [68]

creation NOUN
la creazione *fem*

creative ADJECTIVE
creativo (FEM creativa)

creature NOUN
la creatura *fem*

crèche NOUN
l' asilo nido *masc*

  LANGUAGE TIP Word for word, this means 'nest nursery'.

credit NOUN
il credito *masc*
■ **on credit** a credito

credit card NOUN
la carta di credito *fem*

creep NOUN
■ **He's a creep.** È un tipo viscido.
■ **It gives me the creeps.** Mi fa venire la pelle d'oca.

  LANGUAGE TIP Word for word, this means 'it makes me have goose skin'.

to **creep up** VERB
■ **to creep up on somebody** avvicinarsi [68ᴱ] quatto quatto a qualcuno

crept VERB ▷ *see* **creep up**

cress NOUN
il crescione *masc*

crew NOUN
l' equipaggio *masc* (of ship, plane)
■ **a film crew** una troupe cinematografica

crew cut NOUN
il taglio a spazzola *masc*

cricket NOUN
1 il cricket *masc*
□ I play cricket. Gioco a cricket.
2 il grillo *masc* (insect)

cried VERB ▷ *see* **cry**

crime NOUN
1 il crimine *masc*

□ He committed a crime. Ha commesso un crimine.

■ **the scene of the crime** la scena del delitto

2 la criminalità *fem*

□ Crime is rising. La criminalità è in aumento.

criminal NOUN

▷ *see also* **criminal** ADJECTIVE

il/la criminale *masc/fem*

□ a dangerous criminal un pericoloso criminale

criminal ADJECTIVE

▷ *see also* **criminal** NOUN

■ **a criminal offence** un reato

■ **to have a criminal record** avere [12] precedenti penali

crippled ADJECTIVE

■ **to be crippled in an accident** rimanere [88ᴱ] invalido in un incidente

■ **to be crippled with arthritis** soffrire [66] di una grave forma di artrite

crisis NOUN

la crisi *fem* (PL le crisi)

crisp ADJECTIVE

croccante (FEM croccante) *(food)*

crisps NOUN PL

le patatine *fem pl*

□ a bag of crisps un sacchetto di patatine

criterion NOUN

1 il criterio *masc*

□ I don't understand what their criteria were. Non riesco a capire i criteri che hanno seguito.

■ **Price was the only criterion.** Il prezzo era l'unico criterio di scelta.

2 il requisito *masc*

□ Only one candidate met all the criteria. Un solo candidato soddisfaceva tutti i requisiti.

critic NOUN

il critico *masc* (PL i critici)

critical ADJECTIVE

critico (FEM critica, MASC PL critici, FEM PL critiche)

criticism NOUN

la critica *fem* (PL le critiche)

to criticize VERB

criticare [18]

Croatia NOUN

la Croazia *fem*

to crochet VERB

lavorare [68] all'uncinetto

crocodile NOUN

il coccodrillo *masc*

crook NOUN

l' imbroglione *masc*

□ He's a crook. È un imbroglione.

■ **a petty crook** un piccolo delinquente

crop NOUN

il raccolto *masc*

cross NOUN

▷ *see also* **cross** ADJECTIVE, VERB

la croce *fem*

cross ADJECTIVE

▷ *see also* **cross** NOUN, VERB

arrabbiato (FEM arrabbiata)

□ He was cross about something. Era arrabbiato per qualcosa.

to cross VERB

▷ *see also* **cross** ADJECTIVE, NOUN

attraversare [68] *(street, bridge)*

to cross out VERB

cancellare [68]

cross-country NOUN

■ **a cross-country race** una corsa campestre

■ **cross-country skiing** sci da fondo *masc*

crossing NOUN

1 la traversata *fem*

□ a ten-hour crossing una traversata di dieci ore

2 il passaggio pedonale *masc*

□ Always cross at the crossing. Attraversa sempre sul passaggio pedonale.

crossroads NOUN SING

l' incrocio *masc*

crossword NOUN

le parole crociate *fem pl*

crow NOUN

la cornacchia *fem* (PL le cornacchie)

crowd NOUN

▷ *see also* **crowd** VERB

la folla *fem*

to crowd VERB

▷ *see also* **crowd** NOUN

affollarsi [56ᴱ]

□ The children crowded round. I bambini si sono affollati lì attorno.

crowded ADJECTIVE

affollato (FEM affollata)

crown NOUN

la corona *fem*

■ **the crown jewels** i gioielli della Corona

crucifix NOUN

il crocefisso *masc*

crude ADJECTIVE

volgare (FEM volgare)

□ crude language linguaggio volgare

cruel ADJECTIVE

crudele (FEM crudele)

cruise NOUN

la crociera *fem*

crumb NOUN

la briciola *fem*

to crush VERB

▷ *see also* **crush** NOUN

1 schiacciare [13] *(can)*

2 tritare [68]

□ Crush two cloves of garlic. Tritate due spicchi d'aglio.

crush NOUN

▷ *see also* **crush** VERB

■ **to have a crush on somebody** avere[12] una cotta per qualcuno □ She's had a crush on him for months. Ha una cotta per lui da mesi.

crutch NOUN
la stampella *fem*

to **cry** VERB
▷ *see also* **cry** NOUN
1 piangere[71]
□ The baby's crying. Il bambino sta piangendo.
2 gridare[68]
□ 'You're wrong,' he cried. 'Hai torto,' gridò.

cry NOUN
▷ *see also* **cry** VERB
1 il pianto *masc*
□ After he left she had a good cry. Dopo che lui è partito lei si è fatta un bel pianto.
2 il grido *masc* (FEM PL le grida)

| LANGUAGE TIP The plural of **grido** is usually feminine.

□ With a cry, she rushed forward. Con un grido si lanciò in avanti.

crystal NOUN
il cristallo *masc*

CTC NOUN (= city technology college)
l' istituto tecnico *masc* (PL gli istituti tecnici)

cub NOUN
1 il cucciolo *masc (animal)*
2 il lupetto *masc (scout)*

cube NOUN
1 il cubetto *masc*
□ Cut the meat into cubes. Tagliate la carne a cubetti.
2 la zolletta *fem (of sugar)*
3 il cubo *masc (in geometry)*

cubic ADJECTIVE
■ **a cubic metre** un metro cubo

cucumber NOUN
il cetriolo *masc*
□ tomatoes and cucumbers pomodori e cetrioli
■ **to be as cool as a cucumber** essere[47E] imperturbabile

cuddle NOUN
▷ *see also* **cuddle** VERB
la carezza *fem*
□ kisses and cuddles baci e carezze
■ **Give me a cuddle.** Vieni ad abbracciarmi.

to **cuddle** VERB
▷ *see also* **cuddle** NOUN
abbracciare[13]

cue NOUN
la stecca *fem* (PL le stecche) *(for snooker, pool)*

culottes NOUN PL
la gonna pantalone *fem* (PL le gonne pantalone)

culture NOUN
la cultura *fem*

cunning ADJECTIVE
1 furbo (FEM furba) *(person)*

2 ingegnoso (FEM ingegnosa)
□ a cunning plan un piano ingegnoso

cup NOUN
1 la tazza *fem*
□ a cup of coffee una tazza di caffè
2 la coppa *fem (trophy)*

cupboard NOUN
1 l' armadio *masc (anywhere)*
2 la credenza *fem (in kitchen)*

to **cure** VERB
▷ *see also* **cure** NOUN
guarire[51]

cure NOUN
▷ *see also* **cure** VERB
la cura *fem*

curious ADJECTIVE
curioso (FEM curiosa)

curl NOUN
il ricciolo *masc*

curly ADJECTIVE
riccio (FEM riccia, MASC PL ricci, FEM PL ricce)
□ curly hair capelli ricci

currant NOUN
■ **currants** uva passa *fem sing*
■ **a currant bun** un panino con l'uva passa

currency NOUN
la valuta *fem*
□ foreign currency valuta estera

current NOUN
▷ *see also* **current** ADJECTIVE
la corrente *fem*

current ADJECTIVE
▷ *see also* **current** NOUN
1 attuale (FEM attuale)
□ The current situation is unacceptable. La situazione attuale è inaccettabile.
2 corrente (FEM corrente)
□ the current financial year l'anno finanziario corrente

current account NOUN
il conto corrente *masc*

current affairs NOUN PL
l' attualità *fem sing*
□ She presents a current affairs programme. Presenta un programma d'attualità.

curriculum NOUN
il programma *masc* (PL i programmi)

curriculum vitae NOUN
il curriculum vitae *masc* (PL i curriculum vitae)

curry NOUN
1 il piatto al curry *masc (dish)*
■ **to go out for a curry** andare[6E] al ristorante indiano
2 il curry *masc (spice)*
□ a spoonful of curry un cucchiaio di curry

curse NOUN
la maledizione *fem*

cursor NOUN
il cursore *masc*

curtain NOUN
la tenda *fem*
- **to draw the curtains** tirare [68] le tende

cushion NOUN
il cuscino *masc*

custard NOUN
la crema pasticciera *fem*

custody NOUN
l' affidamento *masc (of children)*
- **to be in custody** essere [47ᴱ] in arresto

custom NOUN
l' usanza *fem*

customer NOUN
il/la cliente *masc/fem*

customs NOUN PL
la dogana *fem*
- **to go through customs** passare [68] la dogana

customs officer NOUN
il doganiere *masc*

cut NOUN
▷ *see also* **cut** VERB
il taglio *masc*

to **cut** VERB
▷ *see also* **cut** NOUN
tagliare [25]
- **to cut oneself** tagliarsi [25ᴱ]

to **cut down** VERB
1 abbattere [1] *(tree)*
2 ridurre [85]
□ I'm cutting down on coffee. Sto riducendo il caffè.

to **cut off** VERB
tagliare [25]
□ The electricity has been cut off. L'elettricità è stata tagliata.
- **We've been cut off.** *(while phoning)* È caduta la linea.

to **cut out** VERB
1 spegnersi [105ᴱ]
□ The engine cut out at the traffic lights. Il motore si è spento al semaforo.
2 ritagliare [25]
□ I'll cut the article out of the paper. Ritaglierò l'articolo dal giornale.

to **cut up** VERB
sminuzzare [68] *(vegetables, meat)*

cutback NOUN
il taglio *masc*

□ There have been many cutbacks in public services. Ci sono stati molti tagli nei servizi pubblici.

cute ADJECTIVE
carino (FEM carina)

cutlery NOUN
le posate *fem pl*

cut-price ADJECTIVE
a prezzo ridotto

cutting NOUN
1 il ritaglio *masc (from newspaper)*
2 la talea *fem (from plant)*

CV NOUN
il curriculum vitae *masc* (PL i curriculum vitae)

cyberbullying NOUN
il bullismo informatico *masc*

cybercafé NOUN
il cybercaffè *masc* (PL i cybercaffè)

cyberspace NOUN
il ciberspazio *masc*

to **cycle** VERB
▷ *see also* **cycle** NOUN
andare [6ᴱ] in bicicletta
□ I cycle to school. Vado a scuola in bicicletta.

cycle NOUN
▷ *see also* **cycle** VERB
la bicicletta *fem*
□ a cycle ride un giro in bicicletta
- **cycle path** pista ciclabile

cycling NOUN
- **The roads round here are ideal for cycling.** Le strade qua attorno sono l'ideale per andare in bicicletta.

cyclist NOUN
il/la ciclista *masc/fem*

cylinder NOUN
il cilindro *masc*

Cyprus NOUN
Cipro *fem*

Czech NOUN
▷ *see also* **Czech** ADJECTIVE
1 il ceco *masc*
la ceca *fem (person)*
- **the Czechs** i cechi
2 il ceco *masc (language)*

Czech ADJECTIVE
▷ *see also* **Czech** NOUN
ceco (FEM ceca, MASC PL cechi, FEM PL ceche)
- **the Czech Republic** la Repubblica ceca

Dd

dad NOUN
il papà *masc* (PL i papà)
  □ I'll ask Dad. Lo chiederò al papà.

daddy NOUN
il papà *masc* (PL i papà)

daffodil NOUN
il trombone *masc*

daft ADJECTIVE
sciocco (FEM sciocca, MASC PL sciocchi, FEM PL sciocche)

daily ADJECTIVE
  ▷ *see also* **daily** ADVERB
quotidiano (FEM quotidiana)
  □ It's part of my daily routine. Fa parte del mio tran tran quotidiano.
  ■ **a daily paper** un quotidiano

daily ADVERB
  ▷ *see also* **daily** ADJECTIVE
ogni giorno
  □ The pool is open daily from nine until six. La piscina è aperta ogni giorno dalle nove alle diciotto.

dairy NOUN
la latteria *fem*

dairy products NOUN PL
i latticini *masc pl*

daisy NOUN
la margherita *fem*

dam NOUN
la diga *fem*

damage NOUN
  ▷ *see also* **damage** VERB
i danni *masc pl*
  □ The storm did a lot of damage. La tempesta ha causato molti danni.

to damage VERB
  ▷ *see also* **damage** NOUN
danneggiare [58]

damn NOUN
  ▷ *see also* **damn** ADJECTIVE
  ■ **I don't give a damn!** Me ne frego!
  ■ **Damn!** Maledizione!

damn ADJECTIVE
  ▷ *see also* **damn** NOUN
  ■ **It's a damn nuisance!** Che gran seccatura!

damp ADJECTIVE
umido (FEM umida)

dance NOUN
  ▷ *see also* **dance** VERB
1 il ballo *masc*
  □ The last dance was a waltz. L'ultimo ballo era un valzer.
2 la danza *fem*
  □ It's a Scottish dance. È una danza scozzese.

to dance VERB
  ▷ *see also* **dance** NOUN
ballare [68]
  ■ **to go dancing** andare [6^E] a ballare

dancer NOUN
il ballerino *masc*
la ballerina *fem*

dandruff NOUN
la forfora *fem*

Dane NOUN
il/la danese *masc/fem*
  ■ **the Danes** i danesi

danger NOUN
il pericolo *masc*
  ■ **in danger** in pericolo
  ■ **to be in danger of** rischiare [17] di
  □ We were in danger of missing the plane. Rischiavamo di perdere l'aereo.

dangerous ADJECTIVE
pericoloso (FEM pericolosa)

Danish ADJECTIVE
  ▷ *see also* **Danish** NOUN
danese (FEM danese)

Danish NOUN
  ▷ *see also* **Danish** ADJECTIVE
il danese *masc (language)*

Danish pastry NOUN
il dolcetto di pasta sfoglia *masc*

to dare VERB
1 osare [68]
  □ I didn't dare tell my parents. Non osavo dirlo ai miei genitori.
2 sfidare [68]
  □ I dare you! Ti sfido a farlo!
  ■ **I dare say...** Penso... □ I dare say it'll be okay. Penso che andrà bene.

daring ADJECTIVE
audace (FEM audace)

dark ADJECTIVE
  ▷ *see also* **dark** NOUN
1 buio (FEM buia, MASC PL bui, FEM PL buie)
  □ It's getting dark. Si sta facendo buio.

2 scuro

□ a dark green sweater un maglione verde scuro

3 bruno

□ He's tall, dark and handsome. È alto, bruno e bello.

dark NOUN

▷ *see also* **dark** ADJECTIVE

il buio *masc*

■ **after dark** quando fa buio

dark glasses NOUN PL

gli occhiali scuri *masc pl*

darkness NOUN

l' oscurità *fem*

darling NOUN

caro (FEM cara)

dart NOUN

la freccetta *fem*

■ **to play darts** giocare [18] a freccette

to **dash** VERB

▷ *see also* **dash** NOUN

1 precipitarsi [56ᴱ]

□ They dashed to the window. Si sono precipitati alla finestra.

2 scappare [68ᴱ]

□ I've got to dash! Devo scappare!

dash NOUN

▷ *see also* **dash** VERB

1 il goccio *masc*

□ a dash of vinegar un goccio d'aceto

2 il trattino *masc (punctuation mark)*

dashboard NOUN

il cruscotto *masc*

data NOUN PL

i dati *masc pl*

database NOUN

il database *masc* (PL i database)

data processing NOUN

l' elaborazione elettronica dei dati *fem*

date NOUN

1 la data *fem*

□ my date of birth la mia data di nascita

■ **What's the date today?** Quanti ne abbiamo oggi?

▸ **LANGUAGE TIP** Word for word, this means 'How many of them do we have today?'

■ **out of date 1** *(document, product)* scaduto

2 *(technology, idea)* superato

■ **up to date** *(dictionary, book)* aggiornato

2 l' appuntamento *masc*

□ I have a date with Mark. Ho un appuntamento con Mark.

3 il dattero *masc (fruit)*

daughter NOUN

la figlia *fem*

daughter-in-law NOUN

la nuora *fem*

dawn NOUN

l' alba *fem*

day NOUN

1 il giorno *masc*

□ every day ogni giorno □ during the day di giorno

■ **the day after tomorrow** dopodomani

■ **the day before yesterday** l'altroieri

■ **a day off** un giorno di ferie

■ **a day return** un biglietto giornaliero di andata e ritorno

2 la giornata *fem*

□ It's a nice day. È una bella giornata.

dead ADJECTIVE

▷ *see also* **dead** ADVERB

morto (FEM morta)

□ He was dead. Era morto.

■ **to be shot dead** essere [47ᴱ] colpito a morte

■ **to be a dead loss** non valere [118] niente

dead ADVERB

▷ *see also* **dead** ADJECTIVE

assolutamente

□ You're dead right! Hai assolutamente ragione!

■ **dead on time** in perfetto orario

dead end NOUN

il vicolo cieco *masc*

deadline NOUN

la scadenza *fem*

□ We'll never meet the deadline. Ci sarà impossibile rispettare la scadenza.

deaf ADJECTIVE

sordo (FEM sorda)

deafening ADJECTIVE

assordante (FEM assordante)

deal NOUN

▷ *see also* **deal** VERB

1 l' affare *masc*

□ It's a good deal. È un buon affare.

■ **It's a deal!** Affare fatto!

2 l' accordo *masc*

□ He made a deal with the kidnappers. Ha fatto un accordo con i rapitori.

■ **a great deal of** molto □ a great deal of money molto denaro

to **deal** VERB

▷ *see also* **deal** NOUN

dare [30] le carte

□ It's your turn to deal. Tocca a te dare le carte.

to **deal with** VERB

occuparsi [56ᴱ] di

□ He promised to deal with it. Ha promesso di occuparsene.

dealer NOUN

■ **a drug dealer** uno spacciatore

■ **an antique dealer** un antiquario

dealt VERB ▷ *see* **deal**

dear ADJECTIVE

caro (FEM cara)

d

■ **Dear Paul** Caro Paul
■ **Dear Mrs Smith** Gentile Signora Smith
■ **Dear Sir/Madam** Egregio Signore/Gentile Signora
■ **Oh dear!** Oh Dio!

death NOUN
la morte *fem*
□ I was bored to death. Mi annoiavo a morte.

death penalty NOUN
la pena di morte *fem*

debate NOUN
▷ *see also* **debate** VERB
il dibattito *masc*

to **debate** VERB
▷ *see also* **debate** NOUN
discutere [37]

debt NOUN
il debito *masc*
□ He's still paying off his debts. Sta ancora pagando i debiti.
■ **to be in debt** essere [47ᴱ] indebitato

decade NOUN
il decennio *masc*

decaffeinated ADJECTIVE
decaffeinato (FEM decaffeinata)

decay NOUN
▷ *see also* **decay** VERB
■ **tooth decay** la carie

to **decay** VERB
▷ *see also* **decay** NOUN
cariarsi [17ᴱ] *(teeth)*
■ **a decaying mansion** una villa in rovina

to **deceive** VERB
ingannare [68]

December NOUN
dicembre
□ in December in dicembre

decent ADJECTIVE
decente (FEM decente)

to **decide** VERB
1 decidere [31]
□ I decided to write to her. Ho deciso di scriverle. □ He decided not to go. Ha deciso di non andare.
2 decidersi [31ᴱ]
□ I can't decide. Non so decidermi.

to **decide on** VERB
scegliere [95]

decimal ADJECTIVE
decimale (FEM decimale)
□ the decimal system il sistema decimale
■ **decimal point** virgola

decision NOUN
la decisione *fem*
■ **to make a decision** prendere [77] una decisione

decisive ADJECTIVE
risoluto (FEM risoluta) *(person)*

deck NOUN
1 il ponte di coperta *masc (of ship)*
2 il piano *masc (of bus)*
■ **a deck of cards** un mazzo di carte

deck chair NOUN
la sedia a sdraio *fem*

to **declare** VERB
dichiarare [68]

to **decline** VERB
1 calare [68ᴱ]
□ The birth rate is declining. Il tasso di natalità sta calando.
2 declinare [68]
□ He declined the invitation. Ha declinato l'invito.

to **decorate** VERB
1 decorare [68] *(cake)*
2 pitturare [68] *(paint)*
3 tappezzare [68] *(wallpaper)*

decrease NOUN
▷ *see also* **decrease** VERB
la diminuzione *fem*
□ a decrease in the number of people out of work una diminuzione del numero dei disoccupati

to **decrease** VERB
▷ *see also* **decrease** NOUN
diminuire [51]
□ After two days I decreased the dose. Dopo due giorni ho diminuito la dose.

> **LANGUAGE TIP** When an auxiliary is needed to form past tenses use 'essere' when **diminuire** does not have an object.

□ The number has decreased Il numero è diminuito

dedicated ADJECTIVE
■ **a very dedicated teacher** un insegnante che ama molto il suo lavoro

to **deduct** VERB
detrarre [115]

deep ADJECTIVE
profondo (FEM profonda)
□ How deep is the lake? Quanto è profondo il lago?
■ **to take a deep breath** fare [49] un respiro profondo
■ **to be deep in debt** essere [47ᴱ] nei debiti fino al collo

deeply ADVERB
estremamente
□ deeply depressed estremamente depresso

deer NOUN
1 il cervo *masc (red deer)*
2 il daino *masc (fallow deer)*
3 il capriolo *masc (roe deer)*

> **LANGUAGE TIP** There is no general word in Italian for 'deer'.

defeat NOUN
▷ *see also* **defeat** VERB
la sconfitta *fem*

to **defeat** VERB
▷ *see also* **defeat** NOUN
sconfiggere [98]

defect NOUN
il difetto *masc*

defence NOUN
la difesa *fem*

to **defend** VERB
difendere [33]

defender NOUN
il difensore *masc*

defense NOUN (US)
la difesa *fem*

to **define** VERB
definire [51]

definite ADJECTIVE
1 preciso (FEM precisa)
□ I haven't got any definite plans. Non ho un programma preciso.
2 definitivo (FEM definitiva)
□ It's too soon to give a definite answer. È troppo presto per dare una risposta definitiva.
3 sicuro (FEM sicura)
□ Maybe we'll go to Spain, but it's not definite. Forse andremo in Spagna, ma non è sicuro.
4 categorico (FEM categorica, MASC PL categorici, FEM PL categoriche)
□ He was definite about it. È stato categorico a riguardo.
5 netto (FEM netta)
□ It's a definite improvement. È un netto miglioramento.

definitely ADVERB
decisamente
□ He's definitely the best player. È decisamente il miglior giocatore.
■ **Yes, definitely!** Sicuramente!
■ **Definitely not!** No di certo!

definition NOUN
la definizione *fem*

defriend VERB
cancellare [68] dagli amici
□ Her sister has defriended her on Facebook. Sua sorella l'ha cancellata dagli amici su Facebook.

degree NOUN
1 il grado *masc*
□ a temperature of thirty degrees una temperatura di trenta gradi
2 la laurea *fem*
□ a degree in English una laurea in inglese

DID YOU KNOW...?
Italian degrees on average take 4 to 5 years. Exams are both oral and written. In their final exam students are faced by examiners who ask questions about the thesis they have written on a chosen subject.

to **delay** VERB
▷ *see also* **delay** NOUN
rimandare [68]
□ We decided to delay our departure. Decidemmo di rimandare la partenza.
■ **Don't delay!** Non perdere tempo!
■ **to be delayed** subire [51] un ritardo
□ Our flight was delayed. Il nostro volo ha subito un ritardo.

delay NOUN
▷ *see also* **delay** VERB
il ritardo *masc*
□ a delay of twenty minutes un ritardo di venti minuti
■ **without delay** immediatamente

to **delete** VERB
cancellare [68]

deliberate ADJECTIVE
intenzionale (FEM intenzionale)

deliberately ADVERB
intenzionalmente

delicate ADJECTIVE
delicato (FEM delicata)

delicatessen NOUN
la salumeria *fem*

delicious ADJECTIVE
squisito (FEM squisita)

delight NOUN
il piacere *masc*

delighted ADJECTIVE
contentissimo (FEM contentissima)
□ He'll be delighted to see you. Sarà contentissimo di vederti.

delightful ADJECTIVE
1 delizioso (FEM deliziosa)
□ Lucy is a delightful child. Lucy è una bambina deliziosa.
2 incantevole (FEM incantevole)
□ Thank you for a delightful evening. Grazie per l'incantevole serata.

to **deliver** VERB
consegnare [14]
□ They delivered the parcel this morning. Mi hanno consegnato il pacco stamattina.
■ **to deliver a baby** far [49] nascere un bambino

delivery NOUN
la consegna *fem*
□ Allow 28 days for delivery. Calcola 28 giorni per la consegna.

to **demand** VERB
▷ *see also* **demand** NOUN
pretendere [112]
□ I demand an explanation. Pretendo una spiegazione.

demand NOUN
▷ *see also* **demand** VERB
la richiesta *fem*

d

demanding ADJECTIVE
1   impegnativo (FEM impegnativa)
    □ It's a very demanding job. È un lavoro molto impegnativo.
2   esigente (FEM esigente)
    □ a demanding child un bambino esigente

demo NOUN
la manifestazione *fem*

democracy NOUN
la democrazia *fem*

democratic ADJECTIVE
democratico (FEM democratica, MASC PL democratici, FEM PL democratiche)

to **demolish** VERB
demolire [51]

to **demonstrate** VERB
1   dimostrare [68]
    □ You have to demonstrate that you are reliable. Devi dimostrare di essere affidabile.
2   fare [49] una dimostrazione di
    □ She demonstrated the technique. Ha fatto una dimostrazione della tecnica.
3   manifestare [68]
    □ They demonstrated outside the court. Hanno manifestato fuori dal tribunale.

demonstration NOUN
la dimostrazione *fem*

demonstrator NOUN
il/la dimostrante *masc/fem*

denial NOUN
■ an official denial una smentita ufficiale

denied VERB ▷ see deny

denim NOUN
■ a denim jacket una giacca di jeans

denims NOUN PL
i blue jeans *masc pl*

Denmark NOUN
la Danimarca *fem*

dense ADJECTIVE
1   denso (FEM densa)
    □ Dense smoke prevented them from entering the building. Un fumo denso impediva loro di entrare nell'edificio.
2   ottuso (FEM ottusa)
    □ He's so dense! È così ottuso!

dent NOUN
    ▷ see also dent VERB
l' ammaccatura *fem*

to **dent** VERB
    ▷ see also dent NOUN
ammaccare [18]

dental ADJECTIVE
■ dental treatment cure dentistiche *fem pl*
■ a dental appointment un appuntamento dal dentista

dental floss NOUN
il filo interdentale *masc*

dentist NOUN
il/la dentista *masc/fem*
    □ Faith is a dentist. Faith fa la dentista.

to **deny** VERB
negare [76]

deodorant NOUN
il deodorante *masc*

to **depart** VERB
partire [41E]

department NOUN
il reparto *masc*
    □ the toy department il reparto giocattoli
■ the English department 1 *(in school)* i professori di inglese 2 *(in university)* l'istituto di inglese

department store NOUN
il grande magazzino *masc*

departure NOUN
la partenza *fem*
    □ after his departure dopo la sua partenza

departure lounge NOUN
la sala d'attesa *fem*

to **depend** VERB
dipendere [8E]
    □ It depends... Dipende...
■ to depend on dipendere [8E] da □ The price depends on the quality. Il prezzo dipende dalla qualità.
■ depending on a seconda di □ depending on the weather a seconda del tempo

to **deport** VERB
deportare [68]

deposit NOUN
1   l' acconto *masc*
    □ You have to pay a deposit. Devi pagare un acconto.
2   la cauzione *fem*
    □ You get the deposit back when you return the bike. Quanto riporti la bici ti ridanno la cauzione.

deposit account NOUN
il conto di deposito *masc*

depressed ADJECTIVE
depresso (FEM depressa)

depressing ADJECTIVE
deprimente (FEM deprimente)

depth NOUN
la profondità *fem* (PL le profondità)

to **descend** VERB
scendere [96E]
    □ We descended to the cellar. Scendemmo in cantina.
■ to descend on invadere [55] □ Tourists descend on the village every summer. Il paese è invaso ogni estate dai turisti.
■ to be descended from discendere [96E] da

to **describe** VERB
descrivere [99]

description NOUN
la descrizione *fem*

desert NOUN
il deserto *masc*

desert island NOUN
l' isola deserta *fem*

to **deserve** VERB
meritare [68]

design NOUN
▷ *see also* **design** VERB
1 il modello *masc*
  □ a new design of lawnmower un nuovo modello di tagliaerba
2 il design *masc* (PL i design)
  □ The design of the plane makes it safer. Il design rende più sicuro l'aereo.
3 la progettazione *fem*
  □ a design fault un difetto di progettazione
  □ garden design progettazione di giardini
4 il disegno *masc*
  □ a geometric design un disegno geometrico

to **design** VERB
▷ *see also* **design** NOUN
1 disegnare [14]
  □ She designed the dress herself. Ha disegnato lei stessa il vestito.
2 elaborare [68]
  □ We will design an exercise plan specially for you. Elaboreremo un programma di esercizi apposta per te.

designer NOUN
lo/la stilista *masc/fem (of clothes)*
  ■ **a furniture designer** un designer di mobili *masc*, una designer di mobili *fem*
  ■ **designer clothes** abiti firmati

  > LANGUAGE TIP Word for word, this means 'signed clothes'.

desire NOUN
▷ *see also* **desire** VERB
il desiderio *masc*

to **desire** VERB
▷ *see also* **desire** NOUN
desiderare [68]

desk NOUN
1 la scrivania *fem (in office)*
2 il banco *masc* (PL i banchi) *(in school, hotel)*

desktop NOUN
il desktop *masc* (PL i desktop) *(computer)*

despair NOUN
la disperazione *fem*
  ■ **to be in despair** essere [47ᴱ] disperato

desperate ADJECTIVE
disperato (FEM disperata)
  □ a desperate situation una situazione disperata
  ■ **to get desperate** essere [47ᴱ] sull'orlo della disperazione
  ■ **to be desperate for** volere [123] disperatamente

desperately ADVERB
1 estremamente
  □ We're desperately worried. Siamo estremamente preoccupati.
2 disperatamente
  □ He was desperately trying to persuade her. Stava tentando disperatamente di convincerla.

to **despise** VERB
disprezzare [68]

despite PREPOSITION
malgrado

dessert NOUN
il dessert *masc* (PL i dessert)

destination NOUN
la destinazione *fem*

to **destroy** VERB
distruggere [79]

destruction NOUN
la distruzione *fem*

detail NOUN
il dettaglio *masc*
  □ I can't remember the details. Non ricordo i dettagli.

detailed ADJECTIVE
dettagliato (FEM dettagliata)

detective NOUN
l' investigatore *masc*
l' investigatrice *fem*
  □ a private detective un investigatore privato
  ■ **a detective story** un romanzo poliziesco

detention NOUN
  ■ **to get a detention** essere [47ᴱ] trattenuto a scuola

detergent NOUN
il detersivo *masc*

determined ADJECTIVE
determinato (FEM determinata)
  □ She's a very determined woman. È una donna molto determinata. □ She's determined to succeed. È determinata a riuscire.

detour NOUN
la deviazione *fem*

devaluation NOUN
la svalutazione *fem*

devastated ADJECTIVE
sconvolto (FEM sconvolta)
  □ I was devastated. Ero sconvolto.

devastating ADJECTIVE
1 devastante (FEM devastante)
  □ Unemployment has a devastating effect on people. La disoccupazione ha un effetto devastante sulle persone.
2 sconvolgente (FEM sconvolgente) *(news)*
  □ She received some devastating news. Ha ricevuto notizie sconvolgenti.

to **develop** VERB
sviluppare [68]

□ I'll get the film developed. Farò sviluppare la pellicola. □ Girls develop faster than boys. Le ragazze si sviluppano prima rispetto ai ragazzi.
■ **to develop into** trasformarsi [56ᴱ] in □ The argument developed into a fight. La discussione si trasformò in una lite.

developing ADJECTIVE
■ **a developing country** un paese in via di sviluppo

development NOUN
lo sviluppo *masc*
□ the latest developments gli ultimi sviluppi

device NOUN
il congegno *masc*

devil NOUN
il diavolo *masc*

to **devise** VERB
escogitare [68]

to **devote** VERB
dedicare [18]

devoted ADJECTIVE
devoto (FEM devota) *(husband, friend)*
■ **to be devoted to** essere [47ᴱ] molto attaccato a □ He's completely devoted to her. Le è estremamente attaccato.

diabetes NOUN SING
il diabete *masc*

diabetic ADJECTIVE
diabetico (FEM diabetica, MASC PL diabetici, FEM PL diabetiche)

diagonal ADJECTIVE
diagonale (FEM diagonale)

diagram NOUN
il diagramma *masc* (PL i diagrammi)

to **dial** VERB
formare [68] *(number)*

dialling tone (US **dialing tone**) NOUN
il segnale di libero *masc*

dialogue NOUN
il dialogo *masc* (PL i dialoghi)

diamond NOUN
il diamante *masc*
□ a diamond ring un anello con diamante
■ **diamonds** *(in cards)* quadri

diaper NOUN (US)
il pannolino *masc*

diarrhoea (US **diarrhea**) NOUN
la diarrea *fem*

diary NOUN
1 l' agenda *fem*
□ I've got her phone number in my diary. Ho il suo numero di telefono nella mia agenda.
2 il diario *masc*
□ Her diaries are being published. I suoi diari saranno pubblicati.

dice NOUN
1 il dado *masc*
□ Throw the dice. Getta i dadi.

2 il dadino *masc*
□ Cut the vegetables into dice. Tagliate le verdure a dadini.

dictation NOUN
il dettato *masc*

dictionary NOUN
il dizionario *masc*

did VERB ▷ *see* **do**

didn't = **did not**

to **die** VERB
morire [61ᴱ]
□ He died last year. È morto l'anno scorso.
□ I'm dying of boredom. Muoio di noia.
■ **to be dying to do something** morire [61] dalla voglia di fare qualcosa

to **die down** VERB
calmarsi [56ᴱ]
□ The wind died down. Il vento si calmò.

diesel NOUN
1 il gasolio *masc*
□ thirty litres of diesel trenta litri di gasolio
2 il diesel *masc* (PL i diesel)
□ Our car is a diesel. La nostra macchina è un diesel.

diet NOUN
▷ *see also* **diet** VERB, ADJECTIVE
1 l' alimentazione *fem*
□ a healthy diet un'alimentazione sana
2 la dieta *fem* *(slimming)*
□ I'm on a diet. Sono in dieta.

diet ADJECTIVE
▷ *see also* **diet** NOUN, VERB
dietetico (FEM dietetica, MASC PL dietetici, FEM PL dietetiche)
□ diet drinks bibite dietetiche
■ **diet yoghurt** yogurt magro

to **diet** VERB
▷ *see also* **diet** NOUN, ADJECTIVE
seguire [41] una dieta
□ I've been dieting for two months. Seguo una dieta da due mesi.

difference NOUN
la differenza *fem*
□ There's not much difference. Non c'è molta differenza.
■ **The new system has made a big difference.** Il nuovo sistema ha apportato un grosso miglioramento.
■ **It makes no difference.** È uguale.

different ADJECTIVE
diverso (FEM diversa)
□ London is different from Rome. Londra è diversa da Roma.

difficult ADJECTIVE
difficile (FEM difficile)

difficulty NOUN
la difficoltà *fem* (PL le difficoltà)

to **dig** VERB
1 scavare [68]

□ They're digging a hole in the road. Stanno scavando un buco nella strada.

2 zappare [68]

□ Dad's out digging the garden. Il papà è fuori a zappare il giardino.

to **dig up** VERB

1 sradicare [18]

□ The cat's dug up my plants. Il gatto ha sradicato le mie piante.

2 dissotterrare [68]

□ The police have dug up a body. La polizia ha dissotterrato un corpo.

3 tirar [68] fuori

□ They're trying to dig up evidence against him. Stanno cercando di tirar fuori delle prove contro di lui.

digestion NOUN
la digestione *fem*

digger NOUN
l' escavatore *masc*

digital ADJECTIVE
digitale (FEM digitale)

■ **a digital camera** una macchina fotografica digitale

■ **a digital radio** una radio digitale

■ **digital TV** TV digitale

dim ADJECTIVE

1 debole (FEM debole)

□ a dim light una luce debole

2 scarso (FEM scarsa)

□ The prospects are dim. Le prospettive sono scarse.

3 tonto (FEM tonta) *(person)*

dimension NOUN
la dimensione *fem*

to **diminish** VERB
diminuire [51]

> **LANGUAGE TIP** When an auxiliary is needed to form past tenses use 'essere' when **diminuire** does not have an object.

□ The threat of nuclear war has diminished. La paura di una guerra nucleare è diminuita.

din NOUN
il chiasso *masc*

diner NOUN (US)
la tavola calda *fem*

dinghy NOUN

■ **a rubber dinghy** un gommone

dining car NOUN
il vagone ristorante *masc* (PL i vagoni ristorante)

dining room NOUN
la sala da pranzo *fem*

dinner NOUN

1 la cena *fem (in the evening)*

□ Dinner is at seven o'clock. La cena è alle sette.

■ **to have dinner** cenare [68]

2 il pranzo *masc*

□ Some schools provide breakfast as well as dinner. In alcune scuole viene data sia la colazione che il pranzo. □ It's half past twelve – nearly dinner time! È mezzogiorno e mezza, quasi ora di pranzo!

■ **to have dinner** *(at midday)* pranzare [68]

□ They have dinner at school. Pranzano a scuola.

■ **the dinner hour** l'intervallo del pranzo

dinner jacket NOUN
lo smoking *masc* (PL gli smoking)

dinner party NOUN
la cena *fem*

dinner time NOUN
l' ora di pranzo *masc*

dinosaur NOUN
il dinosauro *masc*

dip NOUN

▷ *see also* **dip** VERB

1 la salsa *fem (for vegetables, crisps)*

2 la nuotatina *fem (swim)*

■ **to go for a dip** andare [6ᴱ] a fare una nuotatina

to **dip** VERB

▷ *see also* **dip** NOUN

1 immergere [54]

□ He dipped his hand in the water. Ha immerso la mano nell'acqua.

■ **He dipped a biscuit into his tea.** Ha inzuppato un biscotto nel tè.

2 scendere [96ᴱ]

□ The sun dipped below the horizon. Il sole è sceso sotto l'orizzonte.

diploma NOUN
il diploma *masc* (PL i diplomi)

diplomat NOUN
il diplomatico *masc* (PL i diplomatici)

diplomatic ADJECTIVE
diplomatico (FEM diplomatica, MASC PL diplomatici, FEM PL diplomatiche)

direct ADJECTIVE, ADVERB

▷ *see also* **direct** VERB

1 diretto (FEM diretta)

□ the most direct route la strada più diretta

2 direttamente

□ You can go direct, without changing at Crewe. Si può andarci direttamente senza cambiare a Crewe.

to **direct** VERB

▷ *see also* **direct** ADJECTIVE, ADVERB

1 dirigere [36]

□ Is that remark directed at me? È diretta a me questa osservazione?

2 essere [47ᴱ] il regista di *(film, programme)*

direct debit NOUN
l' addebito in conto corrente *masc*

direction NOUN
la direzione *fem*

□ We're going in the wrong direction. Stiamo andando nella direzione sbagliata.

■ **to ask somebody for directions** chiedere [19] a qualcuno la strada

> **LANGUAGE TIP** Word for word, this means 'to ask somebody the road'.

direct object NOUN
il complemento oggetto *masc*

director NOUN
1 il/la dirigente *masc/fem (of company)*
2 il/la regista *masc/fem (of film, programme)*

directory NOUN
1 l' elenco *masc* (PL gli elenchi) *(phone book)*
■ **directory enquiries** informazioni elenco abbonati
2 la directory *fem* (PL le directory) *(in computing)*

direct speech NOUN
il discorso diretto *masc*

dirt NOUN
la sporcizia *fem*

dirty ADJECTIVE
sporco (FEM sporca, MASC PL sporchi, FEM PL sporche)

□ dirty socks calzini sporchi
■ **to get dirty** sporcarsi [18ᴱ]
■ **a dirty trick** un brutto scherzo

disabled ADJECTIVE
disabile (FEM disabile)

disadvantage NOUN
lo svantaggio *masc*

to disagree VERB
non essere [47ᴱ] d'accordo

□ We always disagree. Non siamo mai d'accordo.
□ He disagrees with me. Non è d'accordo con me.

disagreement NOUN
il disaccordo *masc*

to disappear VERB
scomparire [7ᴱ]

disappearance NOUN
la scomparsa *fem*

□ the disappearance of the money la scomparsa del denaro

disappointed ADJECTIVE
deluso (FEM delusa)

disappointing ADJECTIVE
deludente (FEM deludente)

disappointment NOUN
la delusione *fem*

disaster NOUN
il disastro *masc*

disastrous ADJECTIVE
disastroso (FEM disastrosa)

disc NOUN
il disco *masc* (PL i dischi)

discipline NOUN
la disciplina *fem*

disc jockey NOUN
il/la disk jockey *masc/fem*

disco NOUN
la festa *fem*

to disconnect VERB
staccare [18]

□ If you don't pay the bill the phone will be disconnected. Se non paghi la bolletta ti staccheranno il telefono.

discount NOUN
1 la riduzione *fem*

□ a discount for students una riduzione per studenti
2 lo sconto *masc*

□ a twenty per cent discount uno sconto del venti per cento

to discourage VERB
scoraggiare [58]

■ **to get discouraged** scoraggiarsi [58ᴱ]

to discover VERB
scoprire [9]

to discriminate VERB
■ **to discriminate against** fare [49] discriminazioni ai danni di

discrimination NOUN
la discriminazione *fem*

to discuss VERB
■ **to discuss something** discutere [37] di qualcosa □ We discussed the topic at length. Abbiamo discusso a lungo dell'argomento.

discussion NOUN
la discussione *fem*

disease NOUN
la malattia *fem*

disgraceful ADJECTIVE
scandaloso (FEM scandalosa)

disguise NOUN
il travestimento *masc*

disguised ADJECTIVE
■ **to be disguised as** essere [47ᴱ] travestito da

disgusted ADJECTIVE
disgustato (FEM disgustata)

disgusting ADJECTIVE
disgustoso (FEM disgustosa)

dish NOUN
il piatto *masc*

□ a vegetarian dish un piatto vegetariano
□ Put the peas in a serving dish. Metti i piselli in un piatto da portata.
■ **to do the dishes** lavare [68] i piatti
■ **a satellite dish** un'antenna parabolica

dishonest ADJECTIVE
disonesto (FEM disonesta)

dish soap NOUN (US)
il detersivo liquido (per stoviglie) *masc*

dish towel NOUN (US)
lo strofinaccio dei piatti *masc*

dishwasher NOUN
la lavastoviglie *fem* (PL le lavastoviglie)

disinfectant NOUN
il disinfettante *masc*

disk NOUN
il disco *masc* (PL i dischi)
□ the hard disk il disco rigido
■ **the disk drive** il disk drive

diskette NOUN
il dischetto *masc*

to **dislike** VERB
▷ *see also* **dislike** NOUN
■ **I dislike it.** Non mi piace.
> LANGUAGE TIP Word for word, this means 'it does not please me'.

dislike NOUN
▷ *see also* **dislike** VERB
■ **to take a dislike to somebody** prendere [77] in antipatia qualcuno
■ **my likes and dislikes** ciò che mi piace e ciò che non mi piace

dismal ADJECTIVE
misero (FEM misera)
□ a dismal failure un misero fallimento

to **dismiss** VERB
1 scartare [68]
□ He dismissed the suggestion. Ha scartato il suggerimento.
2 licenziare [17] (*employee*)

disobedient ADJECTIVE
disubbidiente (FEM disubbidiente)

display NOUN
▷ *see also* **display** VERB
la vetrina *fem*
□ The assistant took the watch out of the display. Il commesso ha preso l'orologio dalla vetrina.
■ **to be on display** essere [47E] in mostra
■ **a firework display** uno spettacolo di fuochi d'artificio

to **display** VERB
▷ *see also* **display** NOUN
1 mostrare [68]
□ She proudly displayed her medal. Ha mostrato con orgoglio la sua medaglia.
2 esporre [73]
□ the watches displayed in the shop window gli orologi esposti in vetrina

disposable ADJECTIVE
usa e getta
□ a disposable razor un rasoio usa e getta
■ **a disposable nappy** un pannolino

to **disqualify** VERB
squalificare [18]

to **disrupt** VERB
interrompere [92]
□ The meeting was disrupted by protesters. La riunione è stata interrotta dai dimostranti.
■ **Train services are being disrupted by the strike.** Lo sciopero sta creando il caos nel trasporto ferroviario.

dissatisfied ADJECTIVE
insoddisfatto (FEM insoddisfatta)
□ a dissatisfied customer un cliente insoddisfatto
■ **to be dissatisfied with** non essere [47E] soddisfatto di □ We were dissatisfied with the service. Non eravamo soddisfatti del servizio.

to **dissolve** VERB
sciogliere [97]

distance NOUN
la distanza *fem*
□ a distance of forty kilometres una distanza di quaranta chilometri
■ **It's within walking distance.** Ci si arriva a piedi.
■ **in the distance** in lontananza

distant ADJECTIVE
lontano (FEM lontana)

distillery NOUN
la distilleria *fem*

distinction NOUN
la distinzione *fem*
■ **to make a distinction between** fare [49] una distinzione tra
■ **I got a distinction in my exam.** Ho ottenuto il massimo dei voti all'esame.

distinctive ADJECTIVE
tutto particolare (FEM tutta particolare)

to **distinguish** VERB
distinguere [39]

to **distract** VERB
distrarre [115]

to **distribute** VERB
distribuire [51]

district NOUN
1 il quartiere *masc* (*of town*)
2 il distretto *masc* (*of country*)

district attorney NOUN (US)
la pubblica accusa *fem*

to **disturb** VERB
disturbare [68]
□ I'm sorry to disturb you. Mi dispiace disturbarti.

ditch NOUN
▷ *see also* **ditch** VERB
il fosso *masc*

to **ditch** VERB
▷ *see also* **ditch** NOUN
mollare [68]
□ She's just ditched her boyfriend. Ha appena mollato il suo ragazzo.

dive NOUN
▷ *see also* **dive** VERB
il tuffo *masc*

to **dive** VERB
▷ *see also* **dive** NOUN
tuffarsi [56E]

diver NOUN
il tuffatore *masc*
la tuffatrice *fem*

diversion - dolphin

diversion NOUN
la deviazione *fem (for traffic)*

to **divide** VERB
1 dividere [40]
□ Divide the pastry in half. Dividete la pasta a metà.
2 dividersi [40E]
□ We divided into two groups. Ci siamo divisi in due gruppi.

diving NOUN
i tuffi *masc pl (sport)*

diving board NOUN
il trampolino *masc*

division NOUN
la divisione *fem*

divorce NOUN
il divorzio *masc*

divorced ADJECTIVE
divorziato (FEM divorziata)

Diwali NOUN
festa induista del Diwali

DIY NOUN (= do-it-yourself)
il bricolage *masc*
■ **to do DIY** fare [49] bricolage
■ **a DIY shop** un negozio di bricolage

dizzy ADJECTIVE
■ **to feel dizzy** avere [12] il capogiro

DJ NOUN
il/la DJ *masc/fem* (PL i/le DJ)

to **do** VERB
1 fare [49]
□ He does chemistry. Fa chimica. □ What are you doing this evening? Cosa fai stasera?
□ She did it by herself. L'ha fatto da sola.
□ Have you done your homework? Hai fatto i compiti? □ I want to do physics at university. Voglio fare fisica all'università.
■ **I could do with a holiday.** Avrei bisogno di una vacanza.
2 andare [6E]
□ She's doing well at school. Va bene a scuola.
■ **How are you doing?** Come va?
■ **How do you do?** Piacere.
3 andare [6E] bene
□ It's not very good, but it'll do. Non è ottimo, ma andrà bene.
■ **That'll do, thanks.** Basta, grazie.

▌ LANGUAGE TIP When used as an auxiliary in questions, 'do' is not translated.
□ Where does he live? Dove vive? □ What does your father do? Cosa fa tuo padre?
□ Where did you go for your holidays? Dove sei andato in vacanza?

▌ LANGUAGE TIP Use **non** in negative sentences for 'don't', 'didn't' etc.
□ I don't understand. Non capisco. □ She doesn't speak Italian. Non parla italiano. □ He didn't come. Non è venuto. □ Why didn't you come? Perché non sei venuto?

▌ LANGUAGE TIP When 'do' is used with 'yes' and 'no', it is not translated.
□ Do you speak English? — Yes, I do. Parli inglese? — Sì. □ Do you like horses? — No, I don't. Ti piacciono i cavalli? — No. □ Did you tell him? — Yes, I did. Gliel'hai detto? — Sì.
□ Did you like the film? — No, I didn't. Ti è piaciuto il film? — No.
■ **So do I.** Anch'io.
■ **Neither did I.** Neanch'io.

▌ LANGUAGE TIP Use **vero?** to check information.
□ You go swimming on Fridays, don't you? Vai in piscina venerdì, vero? □ You told him, didn't you? Gliel'hai detto, vero? □ It doesn't matter, does it? Non importa, vero?

to **do up** VERB
1 allacciare [13] *(shoes)*
2 abbottonare [68] *(shirt, cardigan)*
■ **Do up your zip!** Tirati su la lampo!
3 rimettere [59] a nuovo *(house, room)*

to **do without** VERB
fare [49] a meno di
□ I couldn't do without my computer. Non potrei fare a meno del computer.

dock NOUN
la darsena *fem*

doctor NOUN
il dottore *masc*
la dottoressa *fem*
□ a good doctor un bravo dottore

doctor's office NOUN (US)
lo studio medico *masc*

document NOUN
il documento *masc*

documentary NOUN
il documentario *masc*

to **dodge** VERB
schivare [68] *(attacker, blow)*

Dodgems® NOUN PL
gli autoscontri *masc pl*

does VERB ▷ see **do**

doesn't = does not

dog NOUN
il cane *masc*

do-it-yourself NOUN
il fai da te *masc*

dole NOUN
il sussidio di disoccupazione *masc*
■ **to be on the dole** ricevere [27] il sussidio di disoccupazione
■ **to go on the dole** fare [49] domanda per il sussidio di disoccupazione

doll NOUN
la bambola *fem*

dollar NOUN
il dollaro *masc*

dolphin NOUN
il delfino *masc*

domestic ADJECTIVE
1 nazionale (FEM nazionale)
   □ a domestic flight un volo nazionale
2 domestico (FEM domestica, MASC PL domestici, FEM PL domestiche)
   □ domestic chores faccende domestiche

dominoes NOUN PL
il domino *masc sing*
   ■ to have a game of dominoes fare [49] una partita a domino

to **donate** VERB
donare [68]
   □ He donated his collection to the museum. Ha donato la sua collezione al museo.

done VERB ▷ *see* **do**

done ADJECTIVE
pronto (FEM pronta)
   □ Is the pasta done? È pronta la pasta?

dongle NOUN
il dongle *masc* (PL i dongle) *(for computer)*

donkey NOUN
l' asino *masc*

donor NOUN
il donatore *masc*
la donatrice *fem*

don't = do not

to **doodle** VERB
scarabocchiare [17]

door NOUN
1 la porta *fem*
   □ the first door on the right la prima porta a destra
2 la portiera *fem (of car)*
3 lo sportello *masc (of train)*

doorbell NOUN
il campanello *masc*

doorman NOUN
il portiere *masc*

doorstep NOUN
la soglia *fem*

dormitory NOUN
1 il dormitorio *masc*
   □ the boys' dormitory il dormitorio dei ragazzi
2 la casa dello studente *(US: at university)*

dose NOUN
la dose *fem*

dosh NOUN
la grana *fem (money)*

dot NOUN
1 il puntino *masc (on letter i)*
2 il punto *masc (in email addresses)*
   ■ on the dot in punto

to **double** VERB
   ▷ *see also* **double** ADJECTIVE, ADVERB
raddoppiare [17]

double ADJECTIVE, ADVERB
   ▷ *see also* **double** VERB
doppio (FEM doppia)

   □ a double helping una porzione doppia
   ■ to cost double costare [68] il doppio
   ■ a double bed un letto matrimoniale
   ■ a double room una camera matrimoniale

double bass NOUN
il contrabbasso *masc*

to **double-click** VERB
   ■ to double-click on cliccare [18] due volte su

double-decker bus NOUN
l' autobus a due piani *masc* (PL gli autobus a due piani)

double glazing NOUN
i doppi vetri *masc pl*

doubles NOUN PL
il doppio *masc (in tennis)*
   □ to play mixed doubles fare un doppio misto

doubt NOUN
   ▷ *see also* **doubt** VERB
il dubbio *masc*
   ■ if in doubt... in caso di dubbio...
   ■ no doubt sicuramente □ as you no doubt know... come saprai sicuramente...

to **doubt** VERB
   ▷ *see also* **doubt** NOUN
dubitare [68] di
   □ I don't doubt her honesty. Non dubito della sua onestà.
   ■ I doubt it. Ne dubito.
   ■ to doubt that dubitare [68] che □ I doubt that he'll agree. Dubito che sarà d'accordo.

doubtful ADJECTIVE
poco convinto (FEM poco convinta)
   □ She sounds doubtful. Sembra poco convinta.
   ■ to be doubtful about doing something essere [47ᴱ] incerto se fare qualcosa □ I'm doubtful about going by myself. Sono incerto se andare da solo.
   ■ It's doubtful. Non è sicuro.

dough NOUN
la pasta *fem*

doughnut NOUN
il krapfen *masc* (PL i krapfen)
   □ a jam doughnut un krapfen con la marmellata

dove VERB ▷ *see* **dive**

down ADVERB, ADJECTIVE, PREPOSITION
1 giù
   □ His office is down on the first floor. Il suo ufficio è giù al primo piano.
   ■ They live just down the road. Abitano un po' più in giù.
   ■ down there laggiù
2 a terra
   □ He threw down his racket. Ha gettato a terra la racchetta.
   ■ to feel down sentirsi [41ᴱ] giù di morale
   ■ to be down *(computer)* non funzionare [68]

381

download – draw up

download NOUN
▷ see also **download** VERB
il file da scaricare masc

to **download** VERB
▷ see also **download** NOUN
scaricare [18]

downpour NOUN
l' acquazzone masc

downstairs ADVERB, ADJECTIVE
1 al piano di sotto
□ the people downstairs le persone che abitano al piano di sotto
2 al piano terra
□ the downstairs bathroom il bagno al piano terra

downtown ADVERB (US)
in città

to **doze** VERB
sonnecchiare [17]

to **doze off** VERB
appisolarsi [56ᴱ]

dozen NOUN
la dozzina fem
□ a dozen eggs una dozzina di uova □ two dozen due dozzine
■ **dozens** (lots) centinaia □ I've told you that dozens of times. Te l'ho detto centinaia di volte.

drab ADJECTIVE
triste (FEM triste) (clothes)

draft NOUN
1 la bozza fem (of letter, speech)
2 la corrente d'aria fem (US: draught)

to **drag** VERB
▷ see also **drag** NOUN
trascinare [68] (thing, person)
■ **to drag and drop a file** trascinare [68] un file

drag NOUN
▷ see also **drag** VERB
■ **It's a real drag!** È proprio una rompitura!
■ **in drag** travestito da donna □ He was in drag. Era travestito da donna.

dragon NOUN
il drago masc (PL i draghi)

drain NOUN
▷ see also **drain** VERB
lo scarico masc (PL gli scarichi)
□ The drains are blocked. Gli scarichi sono ostruiti.

to **drain** VERB
▷ see also **drain** NOUN
scolare [68]

draining board NOUN
il piano del lavello masc

drainpipe NOUN
il tubo di scarico masc

drama NOUN
1 il dramma masc (PL i drammi)
□ a TV drama un dramma televisivo

2 la recitazione fem
□ Drama is my favourite subject. La recitazione è la mia materia preferita.
■ **drama school** scuola d'arte drammatica

dramatic ADJECTIVE
1 straordinario (FEM straordinaria)
□ a dramatic improvement un miglioramento straordinario
■ **dramatic news** notizie sensazionali
2 drammatico (FEM drammatica, MASC PL drammatici, FEM PL drammatiche)
□ the dramatic arts le arti drammatiche

drank VERB ▷ see **drink**

drapes NOUN PL (US)
le tende fem pl

drastic ADJECTIVE
drastico (FEM drastica, MASC PL drastici, FEM PL drastiche)
■ **to take drastic action** agire [51] in modo drastico

draught NOUN
la corrente d'aria fem

> **LANGUAGE TIP** Word for word, this means 'current of air'.

■ **draught beer** birra alla spina

draughts NOUN SING
la dama fem

draw NOUN
▷ see also **draw** VERB
1 il pareggio masc
□ The game ended in a draw. L'incontro è finito in pareggio.
2 l' estrazione fem
□ The draw takes place on Saturday. L'estrazione avviene sabato.

to **draw** VERB
▷ see also **draw** NOUN
1 disegnare [14]
□ I can't draw. Non so disegnare.
■ **to draw a picture** fare [49] un disegno
■ **to draw a picture of somebody** fare [49] il ritratto a qualcuno
■ **to draw a line** tracciare [13] una linea □ He drew a line. Ha tracciato una linea.
2 pareggiare [58] (in game)
□ We drew two-all. Abbiamo pareggiato due a due.
3 tirare [68]
□ He drew her towards him. La tirò verso di sé.
■ **to draw the curtains** tirare [68] le tende
□ She's drawn the curtains. Ha tirato le tende.

to **draw on** VERB
fare [49] ricorso a
□ He drew on his own experience to write the book. Ha fatto ricorso alla propria esperienza per scrivere il libro.

to **draw up** VERB
compilare [68]

□ She drew up a list of priorities. Compilò un elenco di priorità.

drawback NOUN
l' inconveniente *masc*

drawer NOUN
il cassetto *masc*

drawing NOUN
il disegno *masc*

drawing pin NOUN
la puntina da disegno *fem*

drawing room NOUN
il salotto *masc*

drawn VERB ▷ *see* **draw**

dreadful ADJECTIVE
1 terribile (FEM terribile)
□ a dreadful mistake un terribile errore
2 orribile (FEM orribile)
□ The weather was dreadful. Il tempo era orribile. □ You look dreadful. Hai un aspetto orribile.
■ **I feel dreadful about it.** Me ne vergogno terribilmente.

to **dream** VERB
▷ *see also* **dream** NOUN
sognare [14]

dream NOUN
▷ *see also* **dream** VERB
il sogno *masc*

to **drench** VERB
■ **to get drenched** bagnarsi [14ᴱ] fino all'osso
LANGUAGE TIP Word for word, this means 'to get wet to the bone'.

dress NOUN
▷ *see also* **dress** VERB
il vestito *masc*

to **dress** VERB
▷ *see also* **dress** NOUN
1 vestirsi [41ᴱ]
□ I got up, dressed, and went downstairs. Mi alzai, mi vestii e scesi dabbasso.
■ **to dress somebody** vestire [41] qualcuno
■ **to get dressed** vestirsi [41ᴱ]
2 condire [51] (*salad*)

to **dress up** VERB
1 vestirsi [41ᴱ] bene
□ There's no need to dress up. Non c'è bisogno di vestirsi bene.
2 vestirsi [41ᴱ] in maschera
□ Children like dressing up. Ai bambini piace vestirsi in maschera.

dressed ADJECTIVE
vestito (FEM vestita)
□ I'm not dressed yet. Non sono ancora vestito.
■ **to be dressed in** indossare [68] □ She was dressed in a jumper and jeans. Indossava un maglione e un paio di jeans.

dresser NOUN
la credenza *fem* (*piece of furniture*)

dressing NOUN
il condimento *masc* (*for salad*)

dressing gown NOUN
la vestaglia *fem*

dressing table NOUN
la toilette *fem* (PL le toilette)

dress rehearsal NOUN
la prova generale *fem*

drew VERB ▷ *see* **draw**

dried ADJECTIVE
secco (FEM secca, MASC PL secchi, FEM PL secche)
□ dried flowers fiori secchi

drier NOUN
■ **a tumble drier** un asciugabiancheria
■ **a hair drier** un asciugacapelli

drift NOUN
▷ *see also* **drift** VERB
■ **a snow drift** un cumulo di neve

to **drift** VERB
▷ *see also* **drift** NOUN
1 andare [6ᴱ] alla deriva (*boat*)
■ **to drift into crime** scivolare [68ᴱ] nell'illegalità
2 accumularsi [56ᴱ] (*snow*)

drill NOUN
▷ *see also* **drill** VERB
1 il trapano *masc* (*tool*)
2 l' esercizio orale *masc*
□ a grammar drill un esercizio orale di grammatica

to **drill** VERB
▷ *see also* **drill** NOUN
■ **to drill a hole** fare [49] un buco con il trapano

to **drink** VERB
▷ *see also* **drink** NOUN
bere [15]
□ What would you like to drink? Cosa vuoi da bere? □ She drank her tea. Ha bevuto il suo tè.
□ He's drunk a lot. Ha bevuto molto.
■ **I don't drink.** Non bevo alcolici.

drink NOUN
▷ *see also* **drink** VERB
la bibita *fem*
□ a cold drink una bibita fresca
■ **a hot drink** una bevanda calda
■ **Would you like a drink?** Vuoi qualcosa da bere?
■ **to go out for a drink** andare [6ᴱ] fuori a bere qualcosa
■ **to have a drink** bere [15] qualcosa

drinking water NOUN
l' acqua potabile *fem*

drive NOUN
▷ *see also* **drive** VERB
1 il giro in macchina *masc*
■ **to go for a drive** andare [6ᴱ] a fare un giro in macchina

2 il vialetto *masc*
□ He parked his car in the drive. Ha parcheggiato la macchina nel vialetto.

to **drive** VERB
▷ *see also* **drive** NOUN
1 guidare [68] *(car)*
□ Can you drive? Sai guidare? □ He drove to Edinburgh. Ha guidato fino a Edimburgo.
2 andare [6ᴱ] in macchina *(travel by car)*
□ We never drive into the town centre. Non andiamo mai in macchina in centro.
3 portare [68] in macchina *(take by car)*
□ I'll drive you home. Ti porto a casa in macchina.
■ **to drive somebody mad** far [49] diventare matto qualcuno □ He drives her mad. La fa diventare matta.

driver NOUN
1 il guidatore *masc*
la guidatrice *fem*
□ He's a terrible driver. È un pessimo guidatore.
2 l' autista *masc/fem (of bus, taxi)*

driver's license NOUN (US)
la patente *fem*

driving instructor NOUN
l' istruttore di guida *masc*
l' istruttrice di guida *fem*

driving lesson NOUN
la lezione di guida *fem*

driving licence NOUN
la patente *fem*

driving test NOUN
l' esame di guida *masc*
■ **to take one's driving test** fare [49] l'esame di guida

drizzle NOUN
la pioggerellina *fem*

drop NOUN
▷ *see also* **drop** VERB
1 la goccia *fem* (PL le gocce)
□ Milk? — Just a drop. Latte? — Solo una goccia.
2 il calo *masc*
□ a drop in temperature un calo della temperatura

to **drop** VERB
▷ *see also* **drop** NOUN
1 diminuire [51ᴱ]
□ The temperature will drop tonight. La temperatura diminuirà stanotte.
2 cadere [16ᴱ]
□ The book dropped onto the floor. Il libro è caduto sul pavimento.
■ **I dropped the glass.** Mi è caduto il bicchiere.
3 lasciare [13]
□ Could you drop me at the station? Puoi lasciarmi alla stazione?

4 non fare [49] più
□ I'm going to drop chemistry. Ho intenzione di non fare più chimica.

drought NOUN
la siccità *fem*

drove VERB ▷ *see* **drive**

to **drown** VERB
annegare [76ᴱ]

drug NOUN
1 la medicina *fem (medicine)*
2 la droga *fem (illegal)*
□ hard drugs droghe pesanti □ soft drugs droghe leggere
■ **to take drugs** drogarsi [76ᴱ]
■ **the drugs squad** la squadra narcotici

drug addict NOUN
il/la tossicodipendente *masc/fem*

drug pusher NOUN
lo spacciatore *masc*
la spacciatrice *fem*

drug smuggler NOUN
il contrabbandiere di droga *masc*

drugstore NOUN (US)
negozio di generi vari e di articoli di farmacia con un bar

drum NOUN
il tamburo *masc (instrument)*
■ **a drum kit** una batteria
■ **to play the drums** suonare [68] la batteria

drum majorette NOUN
la majorette *fem* (PL le majorette)

drummer NOUN
il/la batterista *masc/fem (in rock group)*

drunk ADJECTIVE
l' ubriaco *masc* (PL gli ubriachi)
l' ubriaca *fem* (PL le ubriache)
■ **to get drunk** ubriacarsi [18ᴱ]

drunk VERB ▷ *see* **drink**

dry ADJECTIVE
▷ *see also* **dry** VERB
1 asciutto (FEM asciutta) *(clothes, paint)*
2 secco (FEM secca, MASC PL secchi, FEM PL secche)
□ It's been exceptionally dry this spring. Il clima è stato insolitamente secco in primavera.
■ **a long dry period** un lungo periodo senza pioggia

to **dry** VERB
▷ *see also* **dry** ADJECTIVE
1 asciugare [76]
□ She was drying a customer's hair. Stava asciugando i capelli ad una cliente.
2 far [49] asciugare
□ There's nowhere to dry clothes here. Qui non c'è posto per far asciugare i vestiti.
■ **to dry one's hair** asciugarsi [76ᴱ] i capelli

dry-cleaner's NOUN
il lavasecco *masc* (PL i lavasecco)

dryer NOUN
- **a tumble dryer** l' asciugabiancheria
- **a hair dryer** un asciugacapelli

DTP NOUN (= *desktop publishing*)
il desktop publishing *masc*

dubbed ADJECTIVE
doppiato (FEM doppiata) (*film*)

dubious ADJECTIVE
dubbioso (FEM dubbiosa)

duck NOUN
l' anatra *fem*

due ADJECTIVE, ADVERB
- **He's due to arrive tomorrow.** Lo attendiamo per domani.
- **The plane's due in half an hour.** L'aereo è atteso tra mezz'ora.
- **When's the baby due?** Quando deve nascere il bambino?
- **due to** a causa di □ The trip was cancelled due to bad weather. Il viaggio è stato annullato a causa del maltempo.

dug VERB ▷ *see* dig

dull ADJECTIVE
1 noioso (FEM noiosa)
   □ He's nice, but a bit dull. È simpatico, ma un po' noioso.
2 nuvoloso (FEM nuvolosa)
   □ a dull day una giornata nuvolosa

dumb ADJECTIVE
stupido (FEM stupida)
   □ I was so dumb! Che stupido sono stato!
- **a dumb thing** una stupidaggine □ That was a really dumb thing I did! Ho fatto proprio una stupidaggine!

dummy NOUN
il succhiotto *masc* (*for baby*)

dump NOUN
▷ *see also* dump VERB
1 la discarica *fem* (PL le discariche)
   □ I'll take this stuff to the dump. Porterò questa roba in discarica.
- **a rubbish dump** una discarica
2 il postaccio *masc*
   □ It's a real dump! È proprio un postaccio!

to **dump** VERB
▷ *see also* dump NOUN
1 mollare [68]
   □ We dumped our bags at the hotel. Abbiamo mollato i bagagli all'albergo.
2 gettare [68] (*rubbish*)
   □ 'no dumping' 'è vietato gettare rifiuti'

dungarees NOUN PL
la salopette *fem* (PL le salopette)

dungeon NOUN
la prigione sotterranea *fem*

duration NOUN
la durata *fem*

during PREPOSITION
durante

dusk NOUN
il crepuscolo *masc*

dust NOUN
▷ *see also* dust VERB
la polvere *fem*

to **dust** VERB
▷ *see also* dust NOUN
spolverare [68]

dustbin NOUN
il bidone della spazzatura *masc*

dustman NOUN
lo spazzino *masc*

dusty ADJECTIVE
polveroso (FEM polverosa)

Dutch ADJECTIVE
▷ *see also* Dutch NOUN
olandese (FEM olandese)

Dutch NOUN
▷ *see also* Dutch ADJECTIVE
l' olandese *masc* (*language*)
- **the Dutch** gli olandesi

Dutchman NOUN
- **a Dutchman** un olandese

Dutchwoman NOUN
- **a Dutchwoman** un'olandese

duty NOUN
il dovere *masc*
   □ It was his duty to tell the police. Era suo dovere dirlo alla polizia.
- **to be on duty** 1 (*policeman*) essere [47E] in servizio 2 (*doctor, nurse*) essere [47E] di turno

duty-free ADJECTIVE
esente da dazio (FEM esente da dazio)

duvet NOUN
il piumino *masc*

DVD NOUN
il DVD *masc* (PL i DVD)
- **a DVD player** un lettore DVD

dying VERB ▷ *see* die

dynamic ADJECTIVE
dinamico (FEM dinamica, MASC PL dinamici, FEM PL dinamiche)

dyslexia NOUN
la dislessia *fem*

d

Ee

each ADJECTIVE, PRONOUN

1 ogni (FEM+PL ogni)
   □ each day ogni giorno

2 ciascuno (FEM ciascuna)
   □ They have ten points each. Hanno dieci punti ciascuno. □ The girls have two each. Le ragazze ne hanno due ciascuna.

   LANGUAGE TIP Use a reflexive verb to translate 'each other'.

   □ They hate each other. Si odiano. □ We write to each other. Ci scriviamo.

eager ADJECTIVE
impaziente (FEM impaziente)
   □ He was eager to tell us about his experiences. Era impaziente di raccontarci le sue esperienze.

ear NOUN
l' orecchio masc (FEM PL le orecchie)

earache NOUN
   ■ to have earache avere [12] mal d'orecchi

early ADVERB, ADJECTIVE

1 presto
   □ I have to get up early. Devo alzarmi presto.
   ■ to have an early night andare [6ᴱ] a letto presto
   ■ to make an early start iniziare [17] presto
   ■ earlier prima □ I get up earlier on weekdays. Mi alzo prima durante la settimana. □ I saw him earlier. L'ho visto prima.

2 in anticipo
   □ I arrived early. Sono arrivato in anticipo.

3 primo (FEM prima)
   □ his early films i suoi primi film

to **earn** VERB
guadagnare [14]
   □ She earns five pounds an hour. Guadagna cinque sterline all'ora.

earnings NOUN PL
lo stipendio masc sing
   □ Average earnings rose last year. L'anno scorso lo stipendio medio è aumentato.

earring NOUN
l' orecchino masc

earth NOUN
la terra fem
   ■ the Earth la terra
   ■ What on earth...? Cosa diavolo...?

earthquake NOUN
il terremoto masc

easily ADVERB
facilmente

east ADVERB, ADJECTIVE
   ▷ see also **east** NOUN

1 ad est (to the east)
   ■ east of a est di □ It's east of London. È a est di Londra.

2 verso est (eastwards)
   □ We were travelling east. Andavamo verso est.

3 orientale (FEM orientale) (eastern)
   □ the east coast la costa orientale

east NOUN
   ▷ see also **east** ADVERB, ADJECTIVE
l' est masc
   □ in the east ad est

Easter NOUN
la Pasqua fem
   ■ an Easter egg un uovo di Pasqua

eastern ADJECTIVE
orientale (FEM orientale)
   □ France's eastern border il confine orientale della Francia
   ■ Eastern Europe l'Europa dell'est

easy ADJECTIVE
facile (FEM facile)
   □ It's easy to understand. È facile da capire.

easy chair NOUN
la poltrona fem

easy-going ADJECTIVE
   ■ to be easy-going avere [12] un buon carattere □ She's very easy-going. Ha un ottimo carattere.

to **eat** VERB
mangiare [58]
   □ Would you like something to eat? Vuoi mangiare qualcosa? □ We slowly ate our sandwiches. Abbiamo mangiato lentamente i nostri panini.

e-book NOUN
il libro elettronico masc

EC NOUN (= European Community)
la CE fem (= Comunità Europea)

e-card NOUN
la cartolina virtuale fem

ECB NOUN (= European Central Bank)
la BCE fem (= Banca centrale europea)

eccentric ADJECTIVE
eccentrico (FEM eccentrica, MASC PL eccentrici, FEM PL eccentriche)

echo NOUN
l' eco *masc* (PL gli echi)

eco-friendly ADJECTIVE
ecologico (FEM ecologica, MASC PL ecologici, FEM PL ecologiche)

ecological ADJECTIVE
ecologico (FEM ecologica, MASC PL ecologici, FEM PL ecologiche)

ecology NOUN
l' ecologia *fem*

e-commerce NOUN
il commercio elettronico *masc*

economic ADJECTIVE
economico (FEM economica, MASC PL economici, FEM PL economiche) *(growth, development)*

economical ADJECTIVE
1 economico (FEM economica, MASC PL economici, FEM PL economiche) *(method, machine)*
2 economo (FEM economa) *(person)*

economics NOUN
l' economia *fem*
□ He's doing economics at university. Fa economia all'università.

to **economize** VERB
fare [49] economia
□ We'll have to economize. Dovremo fare economia.
■ **to economize on something** risparmiare [17] su qualcosa

economy NOUN
l' economia *fem*

ecstasy NOUN
l' ecstasy *fem (drug)*
■ **to be in ecstasy** essere [47ᴱ] in estasi

eczema NOUN
l' eczema *masc*

edge NOUN
il bordo *masc*
□ on the edge of the desk sul bordo della scrivania
■ **on the edge of the town** ai margini della città
■ **to be on edge** essere [47ᴱ] nervoso
■ **to be on the edge of extinction** stare [108ᴱ] per estinguersi
■ **to have the edge over somebody** essere [47ᴱ] in vantaggio su qualcuno

edgy ADJECTIVE
nervoso (FEM nervosa)

Edinburgh NOUN
Edimburgo *fem*

editor NOUN
1 il redattore *masc*
la redattrice *fem (writer)*

□ the political editor il redattore della pagina politica
2 il direttore *masc*
la direttrice *fem (in charge of paper)*

> **LANGUAGE TIP** Be careful not to translate editor by editore.

educated ADJECTIVE
istruito (FEM istruita)

education NOUN
■ **She wants to complete her education.** Vuole completare gli studi.
■ **There should be more investment in education.** Si dovrebbero fare più investimenti nella scuola.

educational ADJECTIVE
educativo (FEM educativa) *(experience, toy)*

effect NOUN
l' effetto *masc*
□ special effects effetti speciali

effective ADJECTIVE
efficace (FEM efficace)

effectively ADVERB
1 efficacemente *(efficiently)*
2 in effetti *(in effect)*

efficient ADJECTIVE
1 efficiente (FEM efficiente)
□ She is very efficient. È molto efficiente.
2 efficace (FEM efficace)
□ It's a very efficient system. È un sistema molto efficace.

effort NOUN
lo sforzo *masc*
□ He made no effort to hide his disappointment. Non ha fatto alcuno sforzo per nascondere la sua delusione.
■ **It wasn't worth the effort.** Non ne valeva la pena.

e.g. ABBREVIATION (= *exempli gratia*)
es.

egg NOUN
l' uovo *masc* (FEM PL le uova)
□ a hard-boiled egg un uovo sodo □ scrambled eggs le uova strapazzate

egg cup NOUN
il portauovo *masc* (PL i portauovo)

eggplant NOUN (US)
la melanzana *fem*

Egypt NOUN
l' Egitto *masc*

eight NUMBER
otto
□ She's eight. Ha otto anni.

eighteen NUMBER
diciotto
□ She's eighteen. Ha diciotto anni.

eighteenth ADJECTIVE
diciottesimo (FEM diciottesima)
□ the eighteenth floor il diciottesimo piano
■ **the eighteenth of August** il diciotto agosto

eighth – emergency

eighth ADJECTIVE
ottavo (FEM ottava)
□ the eighth floor l'ottavo piano
■ **the eighth of August** l'otto agosto

eighty NUMBER
ottanta
□ My grandad's eighty. Mio nonno ha
ottant'anni.

Eire NOUN
la Repubblica d'Irlanda *fem*

either ADJECTIVE, CONJUNCTION, PRONOUN
neanche
□ I don't like milk, and I don't like eggs either.
Non mi piace il latte e neanche le uova.
□ I've never been to Spain. — I haven't
either. Non sono mai stato in Spagna. —
Neanch'io.
■ **either… or…** o… o… □ You can have either
ice cream or yoghurt. Puoi prendere o il gelato
o lo yogurt.
■ **I don't like either of them.** Non mi piace
né l'uno né l'altro.
■ **Take either of them.** Prendi quello che
vuoi.
■ **Do either of you smoke?** Uno di voi due
fuma?

elastic NOUN
l' elastico *masc*

elastic band NOUN
l' elastico *masc*

elbow NOUN
il gomito *masc*

elder ADJECTIVE
maggiore (FEM maggiore)
□ my elder sister la mia sorella maggiore

elderly ADJECTIVE
anziano (FEM anziana)

eldest ADJECTIVE
maggiore (FEM maggiore)
□ my eldest sister la maggiore delle mie
sorelle

to **elect** VERB
eleggere [57]

election NOUN
l' elezione *fem*

electric ADJECTIVE
elettrico (FEM elettrica, MASC PL elettrici, FEM PL
elettriche)
□ an electric fire un stufa elettrica
■ **electric chair** sedia elettrica

electrical ADJECTIVE
elettrico (FEM elettrica, MASC PL elettrici, FEM PL
elettriche)
■ **an electrical engineer** un elettrotecnico

electrician NOUN
l' elettricista *masc/fem*

electricity NOUN
l' elettricità *fem*

electronic ADJECTIVE
elettronico (FEM elettronico, MASC PL elettronici,
FEM PL elettroniche)

electronics NOUN SING
l' elettronica *fem*

elegant ADJECTIVE
elegante (FEM elegante)

elementary school NOUN (US)
la scuola elementare

elephant NOUN
l' elefante *masc*

elevator NOUN (US)
l' ascensore *masc*

eleven NUMBER
undici
□ She's eleven. Ha undici anni.

eleventh ADJECTIVE
undicesimo (FEM undicesima)
□ the eleventh floor l'undicesimo piano
■ **the eleventh of August** l'undici agosto

else ADVERB
altro
□ somebody else qualcun altro □ nobody else
nessun altro □ something else qualcos'altro
□ nothing else nient'altro
■ **somewhere else** da qualche altra parte
■ **or else** altrimenti □ Give me the money, or
else I'll shoot. Dammi i soldi, altrimenti sparo.

email NOUN
▷ see also **email** VERB
1 la posta elettronica *fem*
□ It's quicker by email. È più veloce tramite
posta elettronica.
2 il messaggio di posta elettronica *masc*
□ I'll send him an email. Gli manderò un
messaggio di posta elettronica.

to **email** VERB
▷ see also **email** NOUN
■ **to email somebody** mandare [68] un
messaggio di posta elettronica a qualcuno
□ He emailed me. Mi ha mandato un
messaggio di posta elettronica.

email address NOUN
l' indirizzo di posta elettronica *masc*

embankment NOUN
la massicciata *fem (of railway)*

embarrassed ADJECTIVE
imbarazzato (FEM imbarazzata)

embarrassing ADJECTIVE
imbarazzante (FEM imbarazzante)

embassy NOUN
l' ambasciata *fem*

to **embroider** VERB
ricamare [68]

embroidery NOUN
il ricamo *masc*

emergency NOUN
l' emergenza *fem*

□ This is an emergency! Questa è un'emergenza!
- **in an emergency** in caso di emergenza
- **an emergency exit** un'uscita di sicurezza
- **an emergency landing** un atterraggio di emergenza
- **the emergency services** i servizi di pronto intervento

to emigrate VERB
emigrare [68ᴱ]

emoticon NOUN
la faccina *fem*

emotion NOUN
l' emozione *fem*

emotional ADJECTIVE
1 emotivo (FEM emotiva)
□ She's very emotional. È molto emotiva.
- **to get emotional** commuoversi [62ᴱ]
□ He got very emotional at the farewell party. Si è molto commosso alla festa d'addio.
2 sentito (FEM sentita)
□ Euthanasia is a very emotional issue. L'eutanasia è una questione molto sentita.

emperor NOUN
l' imperatore *masc*

to emphasize VERB
sottolineare [68]
□ He emphasized the importance of the point. Ha sottolineato l'importanza della questione.

empire NOUN
l' impero *masc*

to employ VERB
dare [30] lavoro a
□ The factory employs six hundred people. La fabbrica dà lavoro a seicento persone.
- **to be employed** lavorare [68] □ Thousands of people are employed in tourism. Migliaia di persone lavorano nel settore turistico.

employee NOUN
il/la dipendente *masc/fem*

employer NOUN
il datore di lavoro *masc*
la datrice di lavoro *fem*

employment NOUN
l' impiego *masc*
□ It's difficult to find employment. È difficile trovare un impiego.
- **their place of employment** il loro posto di lavoro
- **employment agency** l' agenzia di collocamento

empty ADJECTIVE
▷ *see also* **empty** VERB
vuoto (FEM vuota)

to empty VERB
▷ *see also* **empty** ADJECTIVE
vuotare [68]

to encourage VERB
incoraggiare [58]

encouragement NOUN
l' incoraggiamento *masc*

encyclopedia NOUN
l' enciclopedia *fem*

end NOUN
▷ *see also* **end** VERB
1 la fine *fem*
□ the end of the film la fine del film
- **in the end** alla fine
2 l' estremità *fem* (PL le estremità)
□ at the other end of the table all'altra estremità del tavolo
- **at the end of the street** in fondo alla strada
- **for hours on end** per ore e ore
- **to come to an end** finire [51]

to end VERB
▷ *see also* **end** NOUN
finire [51]
□ What time does the film end? A che ora finisce il film?

> **LANGUAGE TIP** When an auxiliary is needed to form past tenses use **essere** when **finire** does not have an object.

to end up VERB
finire [51]
□ She ended up in prison. È finita in prigione.
- **He could have ended up a millionaire.** Avrebbe anche potuto diventare miliardario.

ending NOUN
il finale *masc*
□ I didn't like the ending. Non mi è piaciuto il finale.
- **a happy ending** un lieto fine

endless ADJECTIVE
interminabile (FEM interminabile)

enemy NOUN
il nemico *masc* (PL i nemici)
la nemica *fem* (PL le nemiche)

energetic ADJECTIVE
attivo (FEM attiva)
□ She's very energetic. È molto attiva.

energy NOUN
l' energia *fem*

engaged ADJECTIVE
1 occupato (FEM occupata) *(telephone, toilet)*
2 fidanzato (FEM fidanzata)
□ She's engaged to Brian. È fidanzata con Brian.
- **to get engaged** fidanzarsi [56ᴱ]

engaged tone NOUN
il segnale di occupato *masc*

engagement NOUN
il fidanzamento *masc*
- **an engagement ring** un anello di fidanzamento

engine NOUN
1 il motore *masc* *(of car)*
2 la locomotiva *fem* *(pulling train)*

engineer NOUN
l' ingegnere *masc*
■ **service engineer** il tecnico
engineering NOUN
l' ingegneria *fem*
England NOUN
l' Inghilterra *fem*
English ADJECTIVE
▷ *see also* **English** NOUN
inglese (FEM inglese)
□ English students gli studenti inglesi
■ **English people** gli inglesi
English NOUN
▷ *see also* **English** ADJECTIVE
l' inglese *masc (language)*
□ Do you speak English? Parli inglese?
□ the English teacher l'insegnante di inglese
Englishman NOUN
■ **an Englishman** un inglese
Englishwoman NOUN
■ **an Englishwoman** un'inglese
to **enjoy** VERB
■ **Did you enjoy the film?** Ti è piaciuto il film?

> LANGUAGE TIP Word for word, this means 'Did the film please you?'.

■ **to enjoy oneself** divertirsi [41ᴱ]
enjoyable ADJECTIVE
piacevole (FEM piacevole)
enlargement NOUN
l' ingrandimento *masc (of photo)*
enormous ADJECTIVE
enorme (FEM enorme)
enough ADJECTIVE
abbastanza
□ I didn't have enough money. Non avevo abbastanza soldi. □ I've had enough of his lies! Ne ho abbastanza delle sue bugie!
■ **That's enough.** Basta così.
to **enquire** VERB
■ **to enquire about something** informarsi [56ᴱ] su qualcosa
enquiry NOUN
l' inchiesta *fem*
□ There will be an enquiry into the accident. Ci sarà un'inchiesta sull'incidente.
■ **to make enquiries** chiedere [19] informazioni
to **enter** VERB
1 entrare [68ᴱ] in
□ There was a sudden silence when she entered the room. Ci fu un improvviso silenzio quando entrò nella stanza.
2 immettere [59]
□ They entered the name into the computer. Hanno immesso il nome nel computer.
■ **to enter a competition** partecipare [68] ad una gara

to **entertain** VERB
1 divertire [41]
□ He entertained us with his stories. Ci ha divertito con le sue storie.
2 intrattenere [113] *(guests)*
entertainer NOUN
l' intrattenitore *masc*
l' intrattenitrice *fem*
entertaining ADJECTIVE
divertente (FEM divertente)
enthusiasm NOUN
l' entusiasmo *masc*
enthusiast NOUN
l' appassionato *masc*
l' appassionata *fem*
□ She's a DIY enthusiast. È un'appassionata di bricolage.
enthusiastic ADJECTIVE
1 entusiasta (FEM entusiasta) *(person)*
2 entusiastico (FEM entusiastica, MASC PL entusiastici, FEM PL entusiastiche) *(response)*
entire ADJECTIVE
intero (FEM intera)
□ the entire world il mondo intero
entirely ADVERB
1 completamente
□ entirely new completamente nuovo
2 pienamente
□ I agree entirely. Sono pienamente d'accordo.
entrance NOUN
l' ingresso *masc*
■ **the entrance fee** il biglietto d'ingresso
■ **an entrance exam** un esame di ammissione
entry NOUN
l' ingresso *masc*
■ **'no entry'** 1 *(on door)* 'vietato l'ingresso'
2 *(on road sign)* 'divieto d'accesso'
■ **an entry form** un modulo d'iscrizione
entry phone NOUN
il citofono *masc*
envelope NOUN
la busta *fem*
envied VERB ▷ *see* **envy**
envious ADJECTIVE
invidioso (FEM invidiosa)
environment NOUN
l' ambiente *masc*
environmental ADJECTIVE
ambientale (FEM ambientale)
environmentally-friendly ADJECTIVE
ecologico (FEM ecologica, MASC PL ecologici, FEM PL ecologiche)
envy NOUN
▷ *see also* **envy** VERB
l' invidia *fem*
to **envy** VERB
▷ *see also* **envy** NOUN
invidiare [17]

epileptic NOUN
l' epilettico *masc*
l' epilettica *fem*

episode NOUN
l' episodio *masc*

equal ADJECTIVE
▷ *see also* **equal** VERB
1 uguale (FEM uguale)
□ equal numbers of men and women un numero uguale di uomini e donne □ Divide the mixture into three equal parts. Dividi l'impasto in tre parti uguali.
2 pari (FEM+PL pari)
□ Women demand equal rights at work. Le donne chiedono di avere pari diritti sul lavoro.
■ **to be on equal terms** essere [47ᴱ] su un piano di parità

to equal VERB
▷ *see also* **equal** ADJECTIVE
1 essere [47ᴱ] uguale a
□ Eight and twelve equals twenty. Otto più dodici è uguale a venti.
2 eguagliare [25]
□ This score has never been equalled. Questo punteggio non è stato mai eguagliato.

equality NOUN
l' uguaglianza *fem*

to equalize VERB
pareggiare [58] (in sport)

equator NOUN
l' equatore *masc*

to equip VERB
preparare [68]
□ Vocational courses equip you for a particular job. I corsi di formazione professionale preparano per un lavoro specifico.
■ **to equip somebody with something** fornire [51] qualcosa a qualcuno

equipment NOUN
l' attrezzatura *fem*
□ skiing equipment attrezzatura da sci

equipped ADJECTIVE
attrezzato (FEM attrezzata)
□ This caravan is equipped for four people. Questa roulotte è attrezzata per quattro persone.
■ **equipped with** dotato di □ All rooms are equipped with phones, computers and faxes. Tutte le stanze sono dotate di telefono, computer e fax.

equivalent NOUN
▷ *see also* **equivalent** ADJECTIVE
l' equivalente *masc*

equivalent ADJECTIVE
▷ *see also* **equivalent** NOUN
equivalente (FEM equivalente)

e-reader NOUN
l' e-reader *masc* (PL gli e-reader)

erratic ADJECTIVE
1 discontinuo (FEM discontinua) (*performance, service*)
2 incostante (FEM incostante) (*behaviour*)

error NOUN
l' errore *masc*

escalator NOUN
la scala mobile *fem*

escape NOUN
▷ *see also* **escape** VERB
la fuga *fem* (PL le fughe) (*from prison*)
■ **It was a narrow escape.** L'abbiamo scampata bella.

to escape VERB
▷ *see also* **escape** NOUN
scappare [68ᴱ]
□ A lion has escaped. È scappato un leone.
■ **to escape unhurt** rimanere [88ᴱ] illeso
□ The passengers escaped unhurt. I passeggeri sono rimasti illesi.
■ **to escape from prison** evadere [48ᴱ] di prigione

escort NOUN
la scorta *fem*
□ a police escort una scorta di polizia

Eskimo NOUN
l' eschimese *masc/fem*

especially ADVERB
1 soprattutto
□ It's very hot there, especially in the summer. Fa molto caldo lì, soprattutto d'estate.
2 particolarmente
□ especially difficult particolarmente difficile

essay NOUN
il tema *masc* (PL i temi)
□ a history essay un tema di storia

essential ADJECTIVE
essenziale (FEM essenziale)

estate NOUN
1 il complesso edilizio *masc*
□ I live on a new estate. Vivo in un nuovo complesso edilizio.
2 la tenuta *fem*
□ He's got a large estate in the country. Ha una grossa tenuta in campagna.

estate agent NOUN
l' agente immobiliare *masc/fem*

estate car NOUN
la station wagon *fem* (PL le station wagon)

to estimate VERB
calcolare [68]
□ They estimated it would take three weeks. Hanno calcolato che ci sarebbero volute tre settimane.

etc ABBREVIATION (= *et cetera*)
ecc.

Ethiopia NOUN
l' Etiopia *fem*

391

ethnic - everywhere

ethnic ADJECTIVE
1 etnico (FEM etnica, MASC PL etnici, FEM PL etniche)
   □ an ethnic minority una minoranza etnica
   ■ **ethnic cleansing** pulizia etnica
2 tipico (FEM tipica, MASC PL tipici, FEM PL tipiche)
   □ Our local Greek restaurant serves delicious
   ethnic food. Nel nostro ristorante greco locale
   fanno dei buonissimi piatti tipici.

e-ticket NOUN
   il biglietto elettronico *masc*

EU NOUN (= European Union)
   l' UE *fem* (= Unione europea)

euro NOUN
   l' euro *masc* (PL gli euro)

Europe NOUN
   l' Europa *fem*

European ADJECTIVE
   ▷ *see also* **European** NOUN
   europeo (FEM europea)

European NOUN
   ▷ *see also* **European** ADJECTIVE
   l' europeo *masc*
   l' europea *fem*

to **evacuate** VERB
   evacuare [68]

eve NOUN
   ■ **Christmas Eve** la vigilia di Natale
   ■ **New Year's Eve** Santo Stefano

even ADVERB
   ▷ *see also* **even** ADJECTIVE
   perfino
   □ I like all animals, even snakes. Mi piacciono
   tutti gli animali, perfino i serpenti.
   ■ **not even** neanche □ He didn't even say
   hello. Non ha neanche salutato.
   ■ **even if** anche se
   ■ **even though** anche se
   ■ **even more** ancora di più □ You'll have even
   more fun tomorrow. Domani vi divertirete
   ancora di più.

even ADJECTIVE
   ▷ *see also* **even** ADVERB
1 pari (FEM+PL pari)
   □ an even number un numero pari □ The
   scores are even. Sono a pari punteggio.
2 costante (FEM costante)
   □ an even temperature una temperatura
   costante
   ■ **an even surface** una superficie liscia

evening NOUN
   la sera *fem*
   □ in the evening di sera □ all evening tutta la
   sera
   ■ **Good evening!** Buona sera!
   ■ **evening class** il corso serale

event NOUN
1 l' avvenimento *masc*
   □ It was one of the most important events in
   his life. È stato uno degli avvenimenti più
   importanti della sua vita.
2 la gara *fem*
   □ two events in the Olympics due gare nelle
   Olimpiadi
   ■ **a sporting event** una manifestazione
   sportiva
   ■ **social events for the students** iniziative
   per gli studenti
   ■ **in the event of** in caso di

eventful ADJECTIVE
   movimentato (FEM movimentata)

eventual ADJECTIVE
   finale (FEM finale)
   □ the eventual outcome il risultato finale

   > **LANGUAGE TIP** Be careful not to translate
   > **eventual** by **eventuale**.

eventually ADVERB
   alla fine

   > **LANGUAGE TIP** Be careful not to translate
   > **eventually** by **eventualmente**.

ever ADVERB
1 mai
   □ Have you ever been to Germany? Sei mai
   stato in Germania? □ the best I've ever seen il
   migliore che abbia mai visto
2 sempre
   □ It will become ever more complex.
   Diventerà sempre più complicato.
   ■ **for the first time ever** per la prima volta in
   assoluto
   ■ **ever since** da quando □ ever since I met
   him da quando l'ho incontrato
   ■ **ever since then** da allora

every ADJECTIVE
   ogni (FEM+PL ogni)
   □ every pupil ogni scolaro □ every time ogni volta
   ■ **every one of** tutti □ Every one of the
   components was faulty. Tutti i componenti
   erano difettosi.
   ■ **every now and then** di tanto in tanto

everybody PRONOUN
   tutti
   □ Everybody makes mistakes. Tutti fanno
   errori.

everyone PRONOUN
   tutti
   □ Everyone makes mistakes. Tutti fanno errori.

everything PRONOUN
   tutto
   □ You've thought of everything! Hai pensato a
   tutto!

everywhere ADVERB
1 dappertutto
   □ I've looked everywhere. Ho cercato
   dappertutto.
2 ovunque
   □ everywhere you go ovunque tu vada

evil ADJECTIVE
cattivo (FEM cattiva)

ex NOUN
l' ex masc/fem (PL gli/le ex)
□ He's one of my exes. È uno dei miei ex.

exact ADJECTIVE
esatto (FEM esatta)

exactly ADVERB
esattamente
□ exactly the same esattamente uguale
■ **It's exactly ten o'clock.** Sono le dieci in punto.

to **exaggerate** VERB
esagerare [68]

exaggeration NOUN
l' esagerazione fem

exam NOUN
l' esame masc
□ a French exam un esame di francese □ the exam results i risultati degli esami
■ **to take an exam** fare [49] un esame

examination NOUN
l' esame masc
□ on closer examination dopo un esame più approfondito
■ **a medical examination** una visita medica

to **examine** VERB
1 controllare [68]
□ He examined her passport. Le ha controllato il passaporto.
2 visitare [68]
□ The doctor examined him. Il dottore l'ha visitato.
3 esaminare [68]
□ Experts are examining the wreckage of the plane. Gli esperti stanno esaminando il relitto dell'aereo.

examiner NOUN
l' esaminatore masc
l' esaminatrice fem

example NOUN
l' esempio masc
■ **for example** per esempio

excellent ADJECTIVE
eccellente (FEM eccellente)
□ Her results were excellent. I suoi risultati erano eccellenti.
■ **It was excellent fun.** È stato veramente divertente.

except PREPOSITION
tranne
□ everyone except me tutti tranne me
■ **except for** ad eccezione di
■ **except that** salvo che

exception NOUN
l' eccezione fem

exceptional ADJECTIVE
eccezionale (FEM eccezionale)

to **exchange** VERB
▷ see also **exchange** NOUN
scambiare [17]

exchange NOUN
▷ see also **exchange** VERB
lo scambio masc
□ I'd like to do an exchange with an Italian student. Vorrei fare uno scambio con uno studente italiano.
■ **in exchange** in cambio □ What will you give me in exchange? Cosa mi darai in cambio?
■ **exchange rate** tasso di cambio

excited ADJECTIVE
eccitato (FEM eccitata)

exciting ADJECTIVE
1 entusiasmante (FEM entusiasmante)
□ an exciting match una partita entusiasmante
2 appassionante (FEM appassionante)
□ an exciting story una storia appassionante
3 eccitante (FEM eccitante)
□ an exciting adventure un'avventura eccitante

excuse NOUN
▷ see also **excuse** VERB
la scusa fem

to **excuse** VERB
▷ see also **excuse** NOUN
■ **Excuse me!** 1 (to attract attention, apologize) Scusi! 2 (when you want to get past) Permesso!
■ **Excuse me?** Come, scusi?

to **execute** VERB
giustiziare [17] (prisoner)

execution NOUN
l' esecuzione fem

executive NOUN
il/la dirigente masc/fem

exercise NOUN
1 l' esercizio masc
□ page ten, exercise three pagina dieci, esercizio numero tre
■ **an exercise book** un quaderno
2 la ginnastica fem
■ **to take some exercise** fare [49] un po' di ginnastica

exercise bike NOUN
la cyclette fem (PL le cyclette)

exhaust NOUN
il tubo di scappamento masc

exhausted ADJECTIVE
esausto (FEM esausta)

exhaust fumes NOUN PL
i gas di scarico masc pl

exhaust pipe NOUN
il tubo di scappamento masc

exhibition NOUN
la mostra fem

exist - extinct

to **exist** VERB
esistere [10E]

exit NOUN
l' uscita *fem*

exotic ADJECTIVE
esotico (FEM esotica, MASC PL esotici, FEM PL esotiche)

to **expect** VERB
1 aspettare [68]
  □ I'm expecting him for dinner. Lo aspetto per cena. □ She's expecting a baby. Sta aspettando un bambino.
2 aspettarsi [56E]
  □ I didn't expect that from him. Non me l'aspettavo da lui. □ I didn't expect him to agree. Non mi aspettavo che fosse d'accordo.
3 pensare [68]
  □ I expect he'll be late. Penso che arriverà tardi. □ I expect so. Penso di sì.

expedition NOUN
la spedizione *fem*

to **expel** VERB
  ■ **to get expelled** essere [47E] espulso

expenses NOUN PL
le spese *fem pl*
  □ Can you claim this on expenses? Puoi metterlo tra le spese?

expensive ADJECTIVE
costoso (FEM costosa)

experience NOUN
  ▷ *see also* **experience** VERB
l' esperienza *fem*

to **experience** VERB
  ▷ *see also* **experience** NOUN
1 avere [12]
  □ They're experiencing some problems. Hanno qualche problema.
2 provare [68]
  □ He experienced fear and pain. Ha provato paura e dolore.

experienced ADJECTIVE
  ■ **an experienced teacher** un insegnante che ha esperienza

experiment NOUN
l' esperimento *masc*

expert NOUN
  ▷ *see also* **expert** ADJECTIVE
l' esperto *masc*
l' esperta *fem*

expert ADJECTIVE
  ▷ *see also* **expert** NOUN
esperto (FEM esperta)

to **expire** VERB
scadere [16E] *(passport, ticket)*

to **explain** VERB
spiegare [76]

explanation NOUN
la spiegazione *fem*

to **explode** VERB
esplodere [45E]

> **LANGUAGE TIP** When an auxiliary is needed to form past tenses use 'essere' when **esplodere** does not have an object.

to **exploit** VERB
sfruttare [68]

exploitation NOUN
lo sfruttamento *masc*

to **explore** VERB
esplorare [68] *(place)*

explorer NOUN
l' esploratore *masc*
l' esploratrice *fem*

explosion NOUN
l' esplosione *fem*

explosive ADJECTIVE
  ▷ *see also* **explosive** NOUN
esplosivo (FEM esplosiva)

explosive NOUN
  ▷ *see also* **explosive** ADJECTIVE
l' esplosivo *masc*

to **express** VERB
esprimere [46]
  ■ **to express oneself** esprimersi [46E]

expression NOUN
l' espressione *fem*

expressway NOUN (US)
l' autostrada che attraversa la città *fem*

extension NOUN
1 l' annesso *masc (of building)*
2 l' interno *masc (telephone)*
  □ Extension three one three seven, please. L'interno tre uno tre sette, per favore.
3 la proroga *fem*
  □ He's been given a six month extension. Gli hanno dato una proroga di sei mesi.

extensive ADJECTIVE
1 vasto (FEM vasta)
  □ The hotel is set in extensive grounds. L'albergo sorge su un vasto terreno.
2 approfondito (FEM approfondita)
  □ extensive research ricerche approfondite
  ■ **to get extensive coverage** *(in press)* essere [47E] trattato ampiamente
  ■ **extensive damage** danni ingenti *masc pl*

extensively ADVERB
molto
  □ He has travelled extensively. Ha viaggiato molto.

extent NOUN
l' entità *fem*
  □ the extent of the damage l'entità dei danni
  ■ **to some extent** in una certa misura

exterior ADJECTIVE
esterno (FEM esterna)

extinct ADJECTIVE
estinto (FEM estinta)

□ Dinosaurs are extinct. I dinosauri sono estinti.

■ **to become extinct** estinguersi [39ᴱ]

extinguisher NOUN
l' estintore *masc*

extortionate ADJECTIVE
esorbitante (FEM esorbitante)

extra ADJECTIVE, ADVERB
in più

□ an extra blanket una coperta in più

■ **to pay extra** pagare [76] extra

■ **to be extra** essere [47ᴱ] a parte □ Breakfast is extra. La colazione è a parte.

■ **Be extra careful!** Stai attentissimo!

■ **extra time** tempi supplementari *masc pl*
□ They won after extra time. Hanno vinto dopo i tempi supplementari.

extraordinary ADJECTIVE
straordinario (FEM straordinaria)

extravagant ADJECTIVE
sprecone (FEM sprecona) *(person)*

□ I'm not extravagant, but I do like nice clothes. Non sono sprecone, ma mi piacciono i vestiti eleganti.

▌ **LANGUAGE TIP** Be careful not to translate **extravagant** by **stravagante**.

extreme ADJECTIVE
estremo (FEM estrema)

extremely ADVERB
estremamente

extremist NOUN
l' estremista *masc/fem*

eye NOUN
▷ *see also* **eye** VERB
l' occhio *masc*

□ I've got green eyes. Ho gli occhi verdi.

■ **to keep an eye on something** tenere [113] d'occhio qualcosa

■ **to catch somebody's eye** attirare [68] l'attenzione di qualcuno

■ **to cry one's eyes out** piangere [71] a calde lacrime

to eye VERB
▷ *see also* **eye** NOUN
scrutare [68]

□ They eyed the parcel with interest.
Scrutavano il pacco con interesse.

eyebrow NOUN
il sopracciglio *masc* (FEM PL le sopracciglia)

eyelash NOUN
il ciglio *masc* (FEM PL le ciglia)

eyelid NOUN
la palpebra *fem*

eyeliner NOUN
l' eye-liner *masc* (PL gli eye-liner)

eye shadow NOUN
l' ombretto *masc*

eyesight NOUN
la vista *fem*

eyewitness NOUN
il/la testimone oculare *masc/fem*

Ff

fabric NOUN
la stoffa *fem*

fabulous ADJECTIVE
favoloso (FEM favolosa)

face NOUN
▷ *see also* **face** VERB
1 la faccia *fem* (PL le facce)
□ He was red in the face. Era rosso in faccia.
2 la parete *fem*
□ the north face of the mountain la parete nord della montagna
3 il quadrante *masc (of watch)*
■ **on the face of it** a prima vista
■ **to take something at face value** giudicare [18] qualcosa dalle apparenze
■ **in the face of these difficulties** di fronte a queste difficoltà

to **face** VERB
▷ *see also* **face** NOUN
1 essere [47ᴱ] di fronte a
□ They faced each other. Erano uno di fronte all'altro.
2 trovarsi [56ᴱ] di fronte a
□ They will face serious problems. Si troveranno di fronte a gravi problemi.
■ **Let's face it...** Diciamocelo chiaramente...

to **face up to** VERB
accettare [68]
□ He refuses to face up to his responsibilities. Rifiuta di accettare le proprie responsabilità.

Facebook® NOUN
▷ *see also* **Facebook** VERB
Facebook® *fem*

to **Facebook** VERB
▷ *see also* **Facebook** NOUN
messaggiare [58] su Facebook

face cloth NOUN
il guanto di spugna *masc*

facilities NOUN PL
le attrezzature *fem pl*
□ This school has excellent facilities. Questa scuola ha ottime attrezzature.
■ **The youth hostel has cooking facilities.** È possibile cucinare all'ostello.

fact NOUN
il fatto *masc*
□ He finally accepted the fact that she didn't love him any more. Alla fine ha accettato il fatto che lei non lo amasse più.
■ **facts and figures** fatti e cifre
■ **in fact** in effetti

factory NOUN
la fabbrica *fem* (PL le fabbriche)
□ a car factory una fabbrica di automobili
■ **factory farming** l'allevamento su scala industriale

> **LANGUAGE TIP** Be careful not to translate **factory** by **fattoria**.

to **fade** VERB
1 scolorirsi [51ᴱ]
□ My jeans have faded. I miei jeans si sono scoloriti.
2 svanire [51ᴱ]
□ Hopes of peace are fading. Sta svanendo ogni speranza di pace.

fag NOUN
la cicca *fem* (PL le cicche)

to **fail** VERB
▷ *see also* **fail** NOUN
1 non superare [68] *(exam)*
□ He failed his driving test. Non ha superato l'esame di guida.
2 essere [47ᴱ] bocciato *(fail to pass)*
□ A quarter of the students failed. Un quarto degli studenti sono stati bocciati.
3 non funzionare [68]
□ The brakes failed. I freni non hanno funzionato.
4 fallire [51ᴱ]
□ The plan failed. Il piano è fallito.
■ **to fail to do something** non riuscire [117ᴱ] a fare qualcosa □ They failed to reach the quarter-finals. Non sono riusciti a raggiungere i quarti di finale.

fail NOUN
▷ *see also* **fail** VERB
■ **D is a pass, E is a fail.** Con D si passa, con E si viene bocciati.
■ **without fail** senz'altro

failure NOUN
il fallimento *masc*
□ a complete failure un fallimento completo
■ **I feel a failure.** Mi sento un fallito.

faint ADJECTIVE
▷ *see also* **faint** VERB
debole (FEM debole)
□ His voice was very faint. La sua voce era

molto debole.

■ **I haven't the faintest idea.** Non ne ho la più pallida idea.

■ **to feel faint** sentirsi [41ᴱ] svenire

to **faint** VERB

▷ *see also* **faint** ADJECTIVE

svenire [120ᴱ]

fair ADJECTIVE

▷ *see also* **fair** NOUN

1 giusto (FEM giusta)

□ That's not fair! Non è giusto!

2 chiaro (FEM chiara)

□ people with fair skin le persone con la pelle chiara

3 discreto (FEM discreta)

□ I have a fair chance of winning. Ho discrete probabilità di vincere.

■ **That's a fair distance.** È una bella distanza.

fair NOUN

▷ *see also* **fair** ADJECTIVE

il parco dei divertimenti *masc* (PL i parchi dei divertimenti)

□ I won a furry dog at the fair. Ho vinto un cane di peluche al parco dei divertimenti.

■ **a trade fair** una fiera campionaria

fairground NOUN

il parco dei divertimenti *masc* (PL i parchi dei divertimenti)

fair-haired ADJECTIVE

biondo (FEM bionda)

fairly ADVERB

1 abbastanza

□ My car is fairly new. La mia macchina è abbastanza nuova.

2 equamente

□ The money was divided fairly. Il denaro è stato diviso equamente.

fairness NOUN

■ **in all fairness** per una questione di giustizia

□ In all fairness, I think we should check the facts. Per una questione di giustizia, penso che dovremmo appurare i fatti.

fairy NOUN

la fata *fem*

fairy tale NOUN

la favola *fem*

faith NOUN

1 la fiducia *fem*

□ They have lost faith in the government. Hanno perso fiducia nel governo.

■ **to put one's faith in** fidarsi [56ᴱ] di

2 la fede *fem (religion)*

faithful ADJECTIVE

fedele (FEM fedele)

faithfully ADVERB

■ **Yours faithfully...** Distinti saluti...

fake NOUN, ADJECTIVE

falso (FEM falsa)

□ The painting was a fake. Il quadro era un

falso. □ a fake banknote una banconota falsa

■ **a fake fur coat** una pelliccia sintetica

fall NOUN

▷ *see also* **fall** VERB

1 la caduta *fem*

□ She had a nasty fall. Ha fatto una brutta caduta.

2 autunno (US)

□ in the fall in autunno

to **fall** VERB

▷ *see also* **fall** NOUN

1 cadere [16ᴱ]

□ He tripped and fell. È inciampato e caduto.

□ She's fallen. È caduta.

■ **to fall in love** innamorarsi [56ᴱ]

2 calare [68ᴱ]

□ Prices are falling. I prezzi stanno calando.

to **fall apart** VERB

cadere [16ᴱ] a pezzi

to **fall behind** VERB

rimanere [88ᴱ] indietro

to **fall for** VERB

1 cascarci [18ᴱ]

□ They fell for it! Ci sono cascati!

2 prendersi [77ᴱ] una cotta per

□ Anne fell for him immediately. Anne si è subito presa una cotta per lui.

to **fall off** VERB

1 cadere [16ᴱ]

□ The exhaust fell off. È caduto il tubo di scarico.

2 diminuire [51ᴱ]

□ Unemployment has fallen off. La disoccupazione è diminuita.

to **fall out** VERB

litigare [76]

□ Sarah's fallen out with her boyfriend. Sarah ha litigato col suo ragazzo.

to **fall through** VERB

fallire [51ᴱ]

fallen VERB ▷ *see* **fall**

false ADJECTIVE

falso (FEM falsa)

□ a false alarm un falso allarme

■ **under false pretences** con l'inganno

■ **false teeth** dentiera

fame NOUN

la fama *fem*

familiar ADJECTIVE

familiare (FEM familiare)

□ The name sounded familiar to me. Il nome mi suonava familiare.

■ **to be familiar with something** conoscere [24] bene qualcosa □ I'm familiar with his work. Conosco bene i suoi lavori.

family NOUN

la famiglia *fem*

□ the Cooke family la famiglia Cooke

■ **a family doctor** un medico di famiglia

famine NOUN
la carestia *fem*

famous ADJECTIVE
famoso (FEM famosa)

fan NOUN
1 il tifoso *masc*
la tifosa *fem*
□ the England fans i tifosi inglesi
2 l' ammiratore *masc*
l' ammiratrice *fem*
□ I'm one of his greatest fans. Sono uno dei
suoi più grandi ammiratori.
3 il patito *masc*
la patita *fem*
□ She's a jazz fan. È una patita di jazz.
4 il ventaglio *masc*
□ a silk fan un ventaglio di seta
■ an electric fan un ventilatore

fanatic NOUN
il fanatico *masc* (PL i fanatici)
la fanatica *fem* (PL le fanatiche)

to **fancy** VERB
■ to fancy something avere [12] voglia di
qualcosa
■ to fancy doing something aver [12] voglia
di fare qualcosa
■ He fancies her. Lei gli piace.

fancy dress NOUN
il costume *masc*
■ a fancy dress ball un ballo in maschera

fantastic ADJECTIVE
fantastico (FEM fantastica, MASC PL fantastici,
FEM PL fantastiche)

far ADJECTIVE, ADVERB
lontano (FEM lontana)
□ Is it far? È lontano? □ It's not far from
London. Non è lontano da Londra.
■ It's far from easy. Non è affatto facile.
■ How far is it? Quanto dista?
■ How far have you got? A che punto sei
arrivato?
■ at the far end of in fondo a
■ far better molto meglio
■ as far as I know per quanto ne so
■ so far fino ad ora

fare NOUN
la tariffa *fem*
□ Railway fares are very high. Le tariffe
ferroviarie sono molto alte.
■ He didn't have the bus fare, so he
walked. Non aveva i soldi per il biglietto
dell'autobus, e così è andato a piedi.
■ I spent a lot on taxi fares. Ho speso molto
per il taxi.
■ full fare la tariffa intera

Far East NOUN
l' Estremo Oriente *masc*

farm NOUN
la fattoria *fem*

farmer NOUN
1 il coltivatore *masc* (growing crops)
2 l' allevatore *masc* (raising animals)
■ a farmers' market un mercato per la
vendita diretta di prodotti agricoli

farmhouse NOUN
la fattoria *fem*

farming NOUN
l' agricoltura *fem*
□ organic farming agricoltura biologica
■ sheep farming l'allevamento di pecore

fascinating ADJECTIVE
affascinante (FEM affascinante)

fashion NOUN
la moda *fem*
■ in fashion di moda

fashionable ADJECTIVE
alla moda

fast ADJECTIVE, ADVERB
veloce (FEM veloce)
□ a fast car una macchina veloce
■ fast food il fast food
■ to be fast (watch) andare [6ᴱ] avanti
■ fast asleep profondamente addormentato

fastidious ADJECTIVE
pignolo (FEM pignola)

> **LANGUAGE TIP** Be careful not to translate
> fastidious by fastidioso.

fat ADJECTIVE
▷ see also **fat** NOUN
grasso (FEM grassa)
□ She thinks she's too fat. Pensa di essere
troppo grassa.

WORD POWER
You can use a number of other words
instead of **fat**:
overweight sovrappeso
□ an overweight child un bambino
sovrappeso
plump grassoccio
□ a plump girl una ragazza grassoccia
big grasso
□ a big woman una donna grassa

---

fat NOUN
▷ see also **fat** ADJECTIVE
il grasso *masc*
□ It's very high in fat. Contiene molti grassi.

fatal ADJECTIVE
1 mortale (FEM mortale)
□ a fatal accident un incidente mortale
2 fatale (FEM fatale)
□ a fatal mistake un errore fatale

father NOUN
il padre *masc*
□ my father mio padre
■ Father Christmas Babbo Natale

father-in-law NOUN
il suocero *masc*

faucet NOUN (US)
il rubinetto *masc*

fault NOUN
1 la colpa *fem*
□ It wasn't my fault. Non è stata colpa mia.
2 il difetto
□ He has his faults, but I still like him. Ha i suoi difetti, ma mi piace lo stesso.
■ **a technical fault** un guasto tecnico

faulty ADJECTIVE
difettoso (FEM difettosa)

favour (US **favor**) NOUN
il favore *masc*
□ Could you do me a favour? Potresti farmi un favore?
■ **to be in favour of something** essere [47ᴱ] a favore di qualcosa

favourite (US **favorite**) ADJECTIVE
▷ *see also* **favourite** NOUN
preferito (FEM preferita)
□ my favourite writer il mio scrittore preferito

favourite (US **favorite**) NOUN
▷ *see also* **favourite** ADJECTIVE
il favorito *masc*
la favorita *fem*
□ It's my favourite. È il mio favorito.

fax NOUN
▷ *see also* **fax** VERB
il fax *masc* (PL i fax)

to **fax** VERB
▷ *see also* **fax** NOUN
spedire [51] via fax *(letter, document)*
■ **to fax somebody something** spedire [51] via fax qualcosa a qualcuno □ I'll fax you the document. Ti spedirò via fax il documento.

fear NOUN
▷ *see also* **fear** VERB
la paura *fem*

to **fear** VERB
▷ *see also* **fear** NOUN
temere [27]

feather NOUN
la piuma *fem*

feature NOUN
la caratteristica *fem* (PL le caratteristiche)

February NOUN
febbraio
□ in February in febbraio

fed VERB ▷ *see* **feed**

fed up ADJECTIVE
■ **to be fed up with something** essere [47ᴱ] stufo di qualcosa

to **feed** VERB
1 dar [30] da mangiare a
□ Have you fed the cat? Hai dato da mangiare al gatto?

2 mantenere [113]
□ He worked hard to feed his family. Lavorava sodo per mantenere la famiglia.

to **feel** VERB
1 sentire [41]
□ I didn't feel much pain. Non sentivo molto dolore.
2 sentirsi [41ᴱ]
□ I don't feel well. Non mi sento bene. □ I felt lonely. Mi sentivo solo.
■ **to feel hungry** avere [12] fame
■ **to feel cold** avere [12] freddo
■ **to feel like doing something** aver [12] voglia di fare qualcosa □ I don't feel like going out tonight. Non ho voglia di uscire stasera.
■ **Do you feel like an ice cream?** Hai voglia di un gelato?

feeling NOUN
1 la sensazione *fem*
□ a burning feeling una sensazione di bruciore
2 il sentimento
□ He was afraid of hurting my feelings. Aveva paura di urtare i miei sentimenti.
■ **What are your feelings about it?** Cosa ne pensi?

feet NOUN PL ▷ *see* **foot**

fell VERB ▷ *see* **fall**

fellow ADJECTIVE
■ **fellow students** compagni di studio

felt VERB ▷ *see* **feel**

felt-tip pen NOUN
il pennarello *masc*

female ADJECTIVE
▷ *see also* **female** NOUN
1 femmina (FEM femmina)
□ Two of the puppies were female. Due dei cuccioli erano femmina.
2 femminile (FEM femminile)
□ the female sex il sesso femminile
■ **female MPs** le parlamentari
■ **female students** le studentesse

female NOUN
▷ *see also* **female** ADJECTIVE
la femmina *fem (animal)*

feminine ADJECTIVE
femminile (FEM femminile)

feminist NOUN
la femminista *fem*

fence NOUN
lo steccato *masc*

fern NOUN
la felce *fem*

ferocious ADJECTIVE
feroce (FEM feroce)

ferry NOUN
il traghetto *masc*
■ **a ferry crossing** una traversata
■ **the ferry terminal** il terminal dei traghetti

fertile ADJECTIVE
fertile (FEM fertile)

fertilizer NOUN
il fertilizzante *masc*

festival NOUN
il festival *masc* (PL i festival)
□ a jazz festival un festival di musica jazz

to **fetch** VERB
1 andare [6ᴱ] a prendere
□ Fetch the bucket. Vai a prendere il secchio.
2 essere [47ᴱ] venduto per
□ His painting fetched five thousand pounds.
Il suo quadro è stato venduto per cinquemila
sterline.

fever NOUN
la febbre *fem*
□ He's got a high fever. Ha la febbre alta.
■ **fever pitch** il colmo □ Excitement has reached
fever pitch. L'eccitazione ha raggiunto il colmo.

few ADJECTIVE, PRONOUN
pochi (FEM poche) *(not many)*
□ He has few friends. Ha pochi amici.
■ **a few** *(some)* alcuni □ a few of them alcuni
di loro □ I invited a few friends. Ho invitato
alcuni amici.
■ **quite a few people** un bel po' di gente

fewer ADJECTIVE
meno
□ There were fewer people than yesterday.
C'era meno gente di ieri.

fiancé NOUN
il fidanzato *masc*

fiancée NOUN
la fidanzata *fem*

fiction NOUN
la narrativa *fem*

field NOUN
il campo *masc*
□ a field of wheat un campo di grano
■ **field sports** la caccia e la pesca

fierce ADJECTIVE
1 feroce (FEM feroce)
□ a fierce dog un cane feroce
2 spietato (FEM spietata)
□ There's fierce competition between them.
C'è una concorrenza spietata tra loro.
3 violento (FEM violenta)
□ a fierce attack un violento attacco

fifteen NUMBER
quindici
□ I'm fifteen. Ho quindici anni.

fifteenth ADJECTIVE
quindicesimo (FEM quindicesima)
■ **the fifteenth of August** il quindici agosto

fifth ADJECTIVE
quinto (FEM quinta)
□ the fifth floor il quinto piano
■ **the fifth of August** il cinque agosto

fifty NUMBER
cinquanta
□ He's fifty. Ha cinquant'anni.

fifty-fifty ADJECTIVE, ADVERB
a metà
□ They split the money fifty-fifty. Hanno diviso
a metà i soldi.
■ **a fifty-fifty chance** una probabilità su due

fight NOUN
▷ see also **fight** VERB
1 la rissa *fem*
□ There was a fight in the pub. C'è stata una
rissa al pub.
■ **to have a fight with somebody** *(quarrel)*
litigare [76] con qualcuno □ She had a fight
with her best friend. Ha litigato con la sua
migliore amica.
2 la lotta *fem*
□ the fight against cancer la lotta contro il cancro
3 l' incontro *masc (boxing match)*

to **fight** VERB
▷ see also **fight** NOUN
1 azzuffarsi [56ᴱ]
□ The fans started fighting. I tifosi hanno
cominciato ad azzuffarsi.
2 litigare [76] *(quarrel)*
□ They fight sometimes, but they're good
friends. A volte litigano ma sono buoni amici.
3 lottare [68] contro
□ She always fought racism. Ha sempre
lottato contro il razzismo.
4 lottare [68]
□ Let us fight for peace. Lottiamo per la pace.
5 scontrarsi [56ᴱ]
□ The demonstrators fought with the police.
I dimostranti si sono scontrati con la polizia.

to **fight back** VERB
reagire [51]
□ The attackers ran away when the man fought
back. Gli assalitori sono scappati quando
l'uomo ha reagito.

fighting NOUN
la rissa *fem*
□ Fighting broke out outside the pub. È scoppiata
una rissa fuori dal pub.

figure NOUN
1 la cifra *fem*
□ Can you give me the exact figures? Puoi
darmi le cifre esatte?
2 figura
□ She's got a good figure. Ha una bella figura.
3 linea
□ I have to watch my figure. Devo stare
attenta alla linea.
4 personaggio
□ an important political figure un importante
personaggio politico
■ **a figure of speech** una figura retorica

file NOUN
▷ see also **file** VERB
1 la pratica *fem* (PL le pratiche)

□ There was stuff in that file that was private. C'erano delle cose riservate in quella pratica.
■ **The police have a file on him.** È schedato dalla polizia.
2 la cartella fem
□ She put the photocopy into her file. Ha messo la fotocopia nella sua cartella.
3 la lima fem
□ a nail file una lima per unghie
4 il file masc (PL i file) (on computer)

to **file** VERB
▷ see also **file** NOUN
1 raccogliere [21] (documents)
2 limare [68]
□ She was filing her nails. Si stava limando le unghie.

to **fill** VERB
riempire [86]
□ She filled the glass with water. Ha riempito il bicchiere d'acqua.

to **fill in** VERB
1 riempire [86]
□ Fill this form in, please. Riempia questo modulo, per favore.
2 mettere [59] al corrente
□ I'll fill you in on what's been happening. Ti metterò al corrente su quello che succede.

to **fill up** VERB
■ **Fill it up.** (car) Mi faccia il pieno.

film NOUN
1 il film masc (PL i film) (movie)
2 il rullino masc
□ I need a 36 exposure film. Vorrei un rullino da 36 foto.

film star NOUN
il divo del cinema masc
la diva del cinema fem

filthy ADJECTIVE
sudicio (FEM sudicia, MASC PL sudici, FEM PL sudice)

final ADJECTIVE
▷ see also **final** NOUN
1 ultimo (FEM ultima)
□ a final attempt un ultimo tentativo
2 definitivo (FEM definitiva)
□ a final decision una decisione definitiva
■ **...and that's final!** ...e basta! □ I'm not going and that's final! Non ci vado e basta!

final NOUN
▷ see also **final** ADJECTIVE
la finale fem
□ Murray is in the final. Murray è in finale.

finally ADVERB
1 infine
□ Finally, I would like to say... Vorrei dire, infine...
2 alla fine
□ They finally decided to leave. Alla fine hanno deciso di partire.

to **find** VERB
trovare [68]

□ I can't find the exit. Non riesco a trovare l'uscita. □ I've found it. L'ho trovato.

to **find out** VERB
scoprire [9]
■ **to find out about** 1 informarsi [56ᴱ] su
□ Find out as much as possible about the town. Informati il più possibile sulla città.
2 (discover) scoprire [9]

fine ADJECTIVE
▷ see also **fine** NOUN
1 bene
□ How are you? — Fine, thanks! Come stai? — Bene, grazie! □ I feel fine. Mi sento bene. □ It'll be ready tomorrow. — That's fine, thanks. Sarà pronto domani. — Va bene, grazie.
2 ottimo (FEM ottima)
□ He's a fine musician. È un ottimo musicista.
3 bello (FEM bella)
□ The weather is fine today. Oggi il tempo è bello.
4 sottile (FEM sottile)
□ She's got very fine hair. Ha i capelli molto sottili.

fine NOUN
▷ see also **fine** ADJECTIVE
la multa fem

finger NOUN
il dito masc (FEM PL le dita)
□ a ring on every finger un anello su ogni dito
■ **my little finger** il mignolo

fingernail NOUN
l' unghia fem

finish NOUN
▷ see also **finish** VERB
la fine fem
□ from start to finish dall'inizio alla fine

to **finish** VERB
▷ see also **finish** NOUN
finire [51]
□ I've finished! Ho finito! □ Have you finished eating? Hai finito di mangiare?

to **finish with** VERB
chiudere [20] con
□ She's finished with her boyfriend. Ha chiuso con il suo ragazzo.

Finland NOUN
la Finlandia fem

Finn NOUN
il/la finlandese masc/fem

Finnish ADJECTIVE
▷ see also **Finnish** NOUN
finlandese (FEM finlandese)

Finnish NOUN
▷ see also **Finnish** ADJECTIVE
il finlandese masc (language)

fir NOUN
l' abete masc

fire – fit

fire NOUN
▷ *see also* **fire** VERB
1 il fuoco *masc* (PL i fuochi)
□ He made a fire to warm himself up. Ha acceso un fuoco per scaldarsi.
■ **to be on fire** essere [47ᴱ] in fiamme
2 l' incendio *masc*
□ The house was destroyed by a fire. La casa è stata distrutta da un incendio.

to **fire** VERB
▷ *see also* **fire** NOUN
1 sparare [68]
□ She fired at him. Gli ha sparato.
■ **to fire a gun** fare [49] fuoco
2 licenziare [17]
□ He was fired from his job. È stato licenziato.

fire alarm NOUN
l' allarme antincendio *masc* (PL gli allarmi antincendio)

fire brigade NOUN
i vigili del fuoco *masc pl*

fire department NOUN (US)
i vigili del fuoco *masc pl*

fire engine NOUN
l' autopompa *fem*

fire escape NOUN
la scala di sicurezza *fem*

fire exit NOUN
l' uscita di sicurezza *fem*

fire extinguisher NOUN
l' estintore *masc*

fire fighter NOUN
il pompiere *masc*

fireman NOUN
il pompiere *masc*

fireplace NOUN
il caminetto *masc*

fire station NOUN
la caserma dei vigili del fuoco *fem*

fireworks NOUN PL
i fuochi d'artificio *masc pl*

firm ADJECTIVE
▷ *see also* **firm** NOUN
1 non troppo maturo (FEM matura) *(fruit, vegetables)*
□ firm tomates pomodori non troppo maturi
2 rigido (FEM rigida)
□ a firm mattress un materasso rigido
3 saldo (FEM salda)
□ a firm grip una presa salda
4 netto (FEM netta)
□ a firm refusal un netto rifiuto
5 deciso
■ **to be firm with somebody** essere [47ᴱ] deciso con qualcuno

firm NOUN
▷ *see also* **firm** ADJECTIVE
la ditta *fem*

first ADJECTIVE, NOUN, ADVERB
1 primo (FEM prima)
□ the first of September il primo settembre
□ Rachel came first. Rachel è arrivata prima.
■ **at first** all'inizio □ It was difficult at first. All'inizio è stato difficile.
2 prima
□ I want to get a job, but first I have to pass my exams. Voglio trovare un lavoro, ma prima devo passare gli esami.
■ **first of all** innanzitutto

first aid NOUN
il pronto soccorso *masc*
□ a first aid kit una cassetta del pronto soccorso

first-class ADJECTIVE
1 di prima classe
□ a first-class ticket un biglietto di prima classe
2 eccellente (FEM eccellente)
□ a first-class meal un pranzo eccellente
■ **a first-class stamp** un francobollo per posta prioritaria

firstly ADVERB
in primo luogo

first name NOUN
il nome di battesimo *masc*

fish NOUN
▷ *see also* **fish** VERB
il pesce *masc*
□ I caught three fish. Ho pescato tre pesci.
□ I don't like fish. Non mi piace il pesce.
■ **fish and chips** pesce impanato e patatine

to **fish** VERB
▷ *see also* **fish** NOUN
pescare [18]

fisherman NOUN
il pescatore *masc*

fish fingers (US **fish sticks**) NOUN
i bastoncini di pesce *masc pl*

fishing NOUN
la pesca *fem*
■ **a fishing boat** un peschereccio
■ **a fishing rod** la canna da pesca

fishing tackle NOUN
l' attrezzatura da pesca *fem*

fishmonger's NOUN
la pescheria *fem*

fish sticks NOUN PL (US)
i bastoncini di pesce *masc pl*

fist NOUN
il pugno *masc*

fit ADJECTIVE
▷ *see also* **fit** VERB, NOUN
in forma
□ He felt relaxed and fit. Si sentiva rilassato e in forma.
■ **to be fit to play** *(sport)* essere [47ᴱ] in condizione di giocare

■ **They're not fit to govern.** Non sono in grado di governare.

■ **Only two of the bikes were fit for the road.** Solo due bici erano utilizzabili.

■ **The water wasn't fit to drink.** L'acqua non era potabile.

fit NOUN
▷ *see also* **fit** ADJECTIVE, VERB

■ **to have a fit** 1 *(epileptic)* avere [12] un attacco epilettico 2 *(be angry)* andare [6ᴱ] su tutte le furie

to fit VERB
▷ *see also* **fit** ADJECTIVE, NOUN
andare [6ᴱ] bene *(clothes, shoes)*
□ Does it fit? Ti va bene?
installare [68]
□ It doesn't cost much to fit an alarm. Non costa molto installare un allarme.

to fit in VERB
inserire [51]
□ She fitted the key in to the lock. Ha inserito la chiave nella serratura.

■ **The doctor can't fit you in today.** Il dottore non ha tempo di vederla oggi.
corrispondere [90]
□ That story doesn't fit in with what he told us. La storia non corrisponde a quanto ci ha detto.
ambientarsi [56ᴱ]
□ She fitted in well at her new school. Si è ambientata bene nella nuova scuola.

fitness NOUN
la buona forma fisica *fem*

fitted carpet NOUN
la moquette *fem* (PL le moquette)

fitted kitchen NOUN
la cucina componibile *fem*

fitting room NOUN
il camerino *masc (in shop)*

five NUMBER
cinque
□ He's five. Ha cinque anni.

to fix VERB
aggiustare [68]
□ Can you fix my bike? Puoi aggiustarmi la bici?
fissare [68]
□ Let's fix a date for the party. Fissiamo una data per la festa. □ She fixed the picture to the wall. Ha fissato il quadro al muro.
preparare [68]
□ I'm fixing lunch. Sto preparando da mangiare.

to fix up VERB
fissare [68]
□ I've fixed up an appointment. Ho fissato un appuntamento.
sistemare [68]
□ I've fixed up Paul's old room. Ho sistemato la vecchia camera di Paul.

fixed ADJECTIVE
fisso (FEM fissa)
□ fixed prices prezzi fissi
■ **at a fixed time** ad un'ora stabilita

fizzy ADJECTIVE
gassato (FEM gassata)

flabby ADJECTIVE
flaccido (FEM flaccida)

flag NOUN
la bandiera *fem*

flame NOUN
la fiamma *fem*

flamingo NOUN
il fenicottero *masc*

flan NOUN
1 la torta *fem*
□ a raspberry flan una torta di lamponi
2 lo sformato *masc*
□ a cheese and onion flan uno sformato di formaggio e cipolla

flannel NOUN
1 il guanto di spugna *masc (facecloth)*
2 la flanella *fem (material)*

to flap VERB
battere [1] *(wings)*

flash NOUN
▷ *see also* **flash** VERB
il flash *masc* (PL i flash) *(of camera)*
■ **a flash of lightning** un lampo
■ **in a flash** in un baleno

to flash VERB
▷ *see also* **flash** NOUN
lampeggiare [58]
□ A light was flashing. Una luce stava lampeggiando.
■ **A lorry driver flashed him.** Un camionista gli ha lampeggiato coi fari.
■ **They flashed a torch in his face.** Gli hanno puntato una torcia in faccia.

flask NOUN
il thermos® *masc* (PL i thermos) *(vacuum flask)*

flat ADJECTIVE
▷ *see also* **flat** NOUN
piatto (FEM piatta)
□ a flat surface una superficie piatta
■ **flat shoes** scarpe basse
■ **I've got a flat tyre.** Ho una gomma a terra.

flat NOUN
▷ *see also* **flat** ADJECTIVE
l' appartamento *masc*

to flatter VERB
1 adulare [68]
□ She was just flattering me. Mi stava solo adulando.
2 donare [68] a
□ clothes that flatter you vestiti che ti donano

flattered ADJECTIVE
lusingato (FEM lusingata)

flavour (us **flavor**) NOUN
1 il sapore *masc*
  □ a very strong flavour un sapore molto forte
2 il gusto *masc*
  □ Which flavour ice cream would you like? Che gusto di gelato vuoi?

flavouring (us **flavoring**) NOUN
l' aroma *masc*

flew VERB ▷ *see* fly

flexible ADJECTIVE
flessibile (FEM flessibile)

to **flick** VERB
dare [30] un colpetto a
  □ He flicked the horse with his whip. Ha dato un colpetto al cavallo con la frusta.
  ■ He flicked a mosquito off his leg. Ha cacciato via una zanzara dalla gamba con un colpetto.
  ■ to flick through a book sfogliare [25] un libro

to **flicker** VERB
tremolare [68] *(light)*

flight NOUN
il volo *masc*
  □ What time is the flight to Paris? A che ora è il volo per Parigi?
  ■ a flight of stairs una rampa di scale

flight attendant NOUN
l' assistente di volo *masc/fem*

to **fling** VERB
gettare [68]
  □ He flung the dictionary onto the floor. Ha gettato il dizionario sul pavimento.

to **float** VERB
galleggiare [58]

flock NOUN
  ■ a flock of sheep un gregge di pecore
  ■ a flock of birds uno stormo di uccelli

flood NOUN
  ▷ *see also* flood VERB
1 l' inondazione *fem*
  □ The rain has caused serious floods. La pioggia ha causato gravi inondazioni.
2 la marea *fem*
  □ a flood of letters una marea di lettere

to **flood** VERB
  ▷ *see also* flood NOUN
allagare [76]
  □ The river has flooded the village. Il fiume ha allagato il paese.

flooding NOUN
l' inondazione *fem*

floor NOUN
1 il pavimento *masc*
  □ a tiled floor un pavimento a piastrelle
  ■ on the floor per terra
2 il piano *masc*
  □ the ground floor il piano terra

flop NOUN
il fiasco *masc* (PL i fiaschi)
  □ The film was a flop. Il film è stato un fiasco.

floppy disk NOUN
il floppy disk *masc* (PL i floppy disk)

Florence NOUN
Firenze

florist NOUN
il fioraio *masc*
la fioraia *fem*

flour NOUN
la farina *fem*

to **flow** VERB
scorrere [26E]

flower NOUN
  ▷ *see also* flower VERB
il fiore *masc*
  □ a bunch of flowers un mazzo di fiori

to **flower** VERB
  ▷ *see also* flower NOUN
fiorire [41E]

flower bed NOUN
l' aiuola *fem*

flown VERB ▷ *see* fly

flu NOUN
l' influenza *fem*

fluent ADJECTIVE
  ■ He speaks fluent French. Parla il francese correntemente.

flung VERB ▷ *see* fling

flush NOUN
  ▷ *see also* flush VERB
1 il rossore *masc*
  □ There was a slight flush on his cheeks. C'era un leggero rossore sulle sue guance.
2 lo sciacquone *masc*
  □ He heard the flush of a toilet. Ha sentito il rumore di uno sciacquone.

to **flush** VERB
  ▷ *see also* flush NOUN
arrossire [51E]
  □ Irene flushed with embarrassment. Irene è arrossita per l'imbarazzo.
  ■ to flush the toilet tirare [68] l'acqua

flute NOUN
il flauto *masc*

fly NOUN
  ▷ *see also* fly VERB
la mosca *fem* (PL le mosche)

to **fly** VERB
  ▷ *see also* fly NOUN
1 volare [68] *(plane, bird)*
2 andare [6E] in aereo
  □ He flew from London to Glasgow. È andato in aereo da Londra a Glasgow.

foal NOUN
il puledro *masc*

focus NOUN
  ▷ *see also* focus VERB

il centro *masc*

□ He was the focus of attention. Era al centro dell'attenzione.

to **focus** VERB
▷ *see also* **focus** NOUN
mettere [59] a fuoco *(camera, binoculars)*

■ **to focus on something** concentrarsi [56ᴱ] su qualcosa

focus group NOUN
il gruppo di discussione *masc*

fog NOUN
la nebbia *fem*

foggy ADJECTIVE
■ **It's foggy.** C'è nebbia.
■ **a foggy day** una giornata nebbiosa
■ **I haven't the foggiest idea.** Non ne ho la più pallida idea.

foil NOUN
la carta stagnola *fem*

fold NOUN
▷ *see also* **fold** VERB
la piega *fem* (PL le pieghe)

to **fold** VERB
▷ *see also* **fold** NOUN
piegare [76]

□ He folded the newspaper in half. Ha piegato a metà il giornale.

■ **to fold one's arms** incrociare [13] le braccia

folder NOUN
la cartella *fem*

folding ADJECTIVE
pieghevole (FEM pieghevole)

to **follow** VERB
seguire [41]

□ You go first and I'll follow. Vai tu per primo, io ti seguo. □ I follow him on Twitter. Lo seguo su Twitter.

to **follow up** VERB
seguire [41]

□ The police are following up several leads. La polizia sta seguendo diverse piste.

follower NOUN
il/la seguace *masc/fem*

□ How do I get more followers on Twitter? Come faccio ad ottenere più follower su Twitter?

following ADJECTIVE
seguente (FEM seguente)

fond ADJECTIVE
■ **to be fond of somebody** voler [123] bene a qualcuno

food NOUN
il cibo *masc*

□ I left some food for the cat. Ho lasciato un po' di cibo per il gatto.

■ **We need to buy some food.** Dobbiamo comprare qualcosa da mangiare.

■ **Italian food is very popular.** La cucina italiana è molto popolare.

food poisoning NOUN
l' intossicazione alimentare *fem*

food processor NOUN
il tritatutto elettrico *masc* (PL i tritatutto elettrici)

fool NOUN
lo sciocco *masc*
la sciocca *fem*

foot NOUN
1 il piede *masc*
□ She's got big feet. Ha i piedi grandi.
■ **on foot** a piedi

DID YOU KNOW...?
In Italy measurements are in metres and centimetres rather than feet and inches. A foot is about 30 centimetres.

□ Dave is six foot tall. Dave è alto circa un metro e ottanta.
2 la zampa *fem* (of animal)

football NOUN
1 il calcio *masc*
□ I like playing football. Mi piace giocare a calcio.
2 il pallone *masc*
□ Paul threw the football to me. Paul mi ha lanciato il pallone.

footballer NOUN
il calciatore *masc*
la calciatrice *fem*

football player NOUN
il calciatore *masc*
la calciatrice *fem*

football pools NOUN
il totocalcio *masc*

footpath NOUN
il sentiero *masc*

footprint NOUN
l' orma *fem*

footstep NOUN
il passo *masc*

for PREPOSITION
1 per
□ a present for me un regalo per me □ the train for London il treno per Londra □ He worked in France for two years. Ha lavorato in Francia per due anni. □ What for? Per cosa?
■ **What did he do that for?** Perché lo ha fatto?
■ **What's it for?** A che cosa serve?

LANGUAGE TIP When the perfect tense is used with 'for' to describe actions or states that started in the past and are still going on, use **da** with the present tense of the Italian verb.

□ He's been learning Italian for two years. Studia italiano da due anni. □ They've been here for ages. Sono qui da moltissimo tempo.
2 da
■ **It's time for lunch.** È ora di mangiare.

to **forbid** VERB
proibire [51]
■ **to forbid somebody to do something** proibire [51] a qualcuno di fare qualcosa

forbidden ADJECTIVE
vietato (FEM vietata)

force NOUN
▷ see also **force** VERB
la forza fem
□ the use of force l'uso della forza
■ UN forces le forze dell'ONU
■ in force (law) in vigore

to **force** VERB
▷ see also **force** NOUN
costringere [100] (person)

forecast NOUN
■ the weather forecast le previsioni del
tempo

foreground NOUN
il primo piano masc

forehead NOUN
la fronte fem

foreign ADJECTIVE
straniero (FEM straniera)
□ foreign countries paesi stranieri

foreigner NOUN
lo straniero masc
la straniera fem

foreign exchange NOUN
la valuta estera fem

to **foresee** VERB
prevedere [78]
□ He had foreseen the problem. Aveva previsto
il problema.

forest NOUN
la foresta fem

forever ADVERB
1 per sempre
□ yours forever tuo per sempre
■ Those days are gone forever. Quei giorni
non torneranno più.
2 sempre
□ She's forever complaining. Si lamenta
sempre.

forgave VERB ▷ see **forgive**

to **forge** VERB
falsificare [18]
□ She forged his signature. Ha falsificato la sua
firma.

forged ADJECTIVE
falso (FEM falsa)
□ forged documents documenti falsi

to **forget** VERB
dimenticare [18]
□ I've forgotten his name. Ho dimenticato il
suo nome. □ I'm sorry, I forgot! Scusa, me ne
sono dimenticato!
■ If that's what you're hoping, you can
forget it! Se questo è quello che speri puoi
scordartelo!

to **forgive** VERB
perdonare [68]

□ In the end he forgave me. Alla fine mi ha
perdonato.
■ to forgive somebody for doing
something perdonare [68] qualcuno di aver
fatto qualcosa

forgot, forgotten VERB ▷ see **forget**

fork NOUN
1 la forchetta fem
□ Mix it with a fork. Mescolalo con una
forchetta.
2 il bivio masc
□ Take the left fork. Al bivio volta a sinistra.

form NOUN
1 il modulo masc
■ to fill in a form riempire [86] un modulo
2 la forma fem
□ I'm against all forms of hunting. Sono
contrario a qualsiasi forma di caccia.
■ in top form in gran forma
3 la classe fem
□ He's in my form. È in classe con me.

formal ADJECTIVE
1 ufficiale (FEM ufficiale)
□ a formal dinner una cena ufficiale
2 formale (FEM formale)
□ formal language lingua formale
■ formal clothes abiti da cerimonia
■ His formal education ended when he was
16. Ha smesso di andare a scuola a 16 anni.

former ADJECTIVE
ex (FEM+PL ex)
□ a former pupil un ex alunno

formerly ADVERB
in passato

fort NOUN
il forte masc

forth ADVERB
■ to go back and forth andare [6ᴱ] avanti
e indietro
■ and so forth e così via

forthcoming ADJECTIVE
prossimo (FEM prossima)
□ It will be discussed at the forthcoming
meeting. Verrà discusso nella prossima
riunione.

fortnight NOUN
quindici giorni masc pl

LANGUAGE TIP Word for word, this means
'fifteen days'.
□ for a fortnight per quindici giorni

fortunate ADJECTIVE
■ It's fortunate that I remembered the
map. È una fortuna che mi sia ricordato della
cartina.

fortunately ADVERB
fortunatamente

fortune NOUN
la fortuna fem

f

□ It cost a fortune. È costato una fortuna. □ He made his fortune. Ha fatto fortuna.

■ **to tell somebody's fortune** predire [35] il futuro a qualcuno

forty NUMBER
quaranta

□ He's forty. Ha quarant'anni.

forward ADVERB
▷ see also **forward** VERB
avanti

to **forward** VERB
▷ see also **forward** ADVERB
inoltrare [68] (letter)

forward slash NOUN
la barra fem

to **foster** VERB
avere [12] in affidamento

□ She has fostered more than fifteen children. Ha avuto in affidamento più di quindici bambini.

foster child NOUN
il bambino in affidamento masc

fought VERB ▷ see **fight**

foul ADJECTIVE
▷ see also **foul** NOUN
1 orribile (FEM orribile)

□ The weather was foul. Il tempo era orribile.
2 disgustoso (FEM disgustosa)

□ It smells foul. Ha un odore disgustoso.
3 pessimo (FEM pessima)

□ Brenda is in a foul mood. Brenda è di pessimo umore.

foul NOUN
▷ see also **foul** ADJECTIVE
il fallo masc (in sport)

found VERB ▷ see **find**

to **found** VERB
fondare [68]

foundations NOUN PL
le fondamenta fem pl

fountain NOUN
la fontana fem

fountain pen NOUN
la penna stilografica fem (PL le penne stilografiche)

four NUMBER
quattro

□ She's four. Ha quattro anni.

fourteen NUMBER
quattordici

□ I'm fourteen. Ho quattordici anni.

fourteenth ADJECTIVE
quattordicesimo (FEM quattordicesima)

□ the fourteenth floor il quattordicesimo piano
■ **the fourteenth of July** il quattordici luglio

fourth ADJECTIVE
quarto (FEM quarta)

□ the fourth floor il quarto piano
■ **the fourth of July** il quattro luglio

fox NOUN
la volpe fem

fragile ADJECTIVE
fragile (FEM fragile)

frame NOUN
la cornice fem

□ a silver frame una cornice d'argento
■ **frames** la montatura fem sing □ glasses with plastic frames occhiali con la montatura di plastica

France NOUN
la Francia fem

frantic ADJECTIVE
frenetico (FEM frenetica, MASC PL frenetici, FEM PL frenetiche)

□ There was frantic activity backstage. C'era un'attività frenetica dietro le quinte.
■ **to go frantic** perdere [69] la testa □ I was going frantic. Stavo perdendo la testa.
■ **to be frantic with worry** essere [47E] fuori di sé dalla preoccupazione

fraud NOUN
1 la truffa fem

□ He was jailed for fraud. È stato messo in prigione per truffa.
2 l' impostore masc

□ You're a fraud! Sei un impostore!

freckles NOUN PL
le lentiggini fem pl

free ADJECTIVE
▷ see also **free** VERB
1 gratuito (FEM gratuita)

□ a free brochure un opuscolo gratuito
■ **a free gift** un omaggio
2 libero (FEM libera)

□ Is this seat free? È libero questo posto?

to **free** VERB
▷ see also **free** ADJECTIVE
liberare [68]

freedom NOUN
la libertà fem (PL le libertà)

free kick NOUN
il calcio di punizione masc (PL i calci di punizione)

to **freeze** VERB
1 gelare [68E]

□ The lake froze last winter. Il lago è gelato lo scorso inverno.
2 congelare [68] (food)

freezer NOUN
il freezer masc (PL i freezer)

freezing ADJECTIVE
■ **It's freezing!** Si gela!
■ **I'm freezing!** Sono congelato!
■ **3 degrees below freezing** tre gradi sotto zero
■ **freezing point** il punto di congelamento

freight NOUN
la merce fem
■ **a freight train** (US) un treno merci

French ADJECTIVE
▷ *see also* **French** NOUN
francese (FEM francese)

French NOUN
▷ *see also* **French** ADJECTIVE
il francese *masc*
□ I can speak French. Parlo il francese. □ the French teacher l'insegnante di francese
■ **the French** i francesi

French beans NOUN
i fagiolini *masc pl*

French fries NOUN
le patate fritte *fem pl*

French loaf NOUN
il filoncino *masc*

Frenchman NOUN
■ **a Frenchman** un francese

French windows NOUN
la porta finestra *fem sing*

Frenchwoman NOUN
■ **a Frenchwoman** una francese

frequent ADJECTIVE
frequente (FEM frequente)

fresh ADJECTIVE
fresco (FEM fresca, MASC PL freschi, FEM PL fresche)
□ Is the fish fresh? Il pesce è fresco?
■ **I need some fresh air.** Ho bisogno di un po' d'aria.
■ **a teacher fresh from college** un insegnante appena uscito dall'università
■ **fresh water** acqua dolce

to **freshen up** VERB
rinfrescarsi [18ᴱ]

freshwater ADJECTIVE
d'acqua dolce
□ a freshwater fish un pesce d'acqua dolce

to **fret** VERB
preoccuparsi [56ᴱ]

Friday NOUN
il venerdì *masc* (PL i venerdì)
■ **on Friday** venerdì □ I saw her on Friday. L'ho vista venerdì.
■ **on Fridays** di venerdì □ I go swimming on Fridays. Vado in piscina di venerdì.

fridge NOUN
il frigo *masc* (PL i frighi)
■ **a fridge magnet** un magnete per il frigorifero

fried ADJECTIVE
fritto (FEM fritta)
□ fried chicken pollo fritto
■ **a fried egg** un uovo al tegame

friend NOUN
▷ *see also* **friend** VERB
l' amico *masc* (PL gli amici)
l' amica *fem* (PL le amiche)
□ He's a friend of mine. È un mio amico.

to **friend** VERB
▷ *see also* **friend** NOUN
aggiungere [5] tra gli amici

□ I've friended her on Facebook. L'ho aggiunta tra gli amici su Facebook.

friendly ADJECTIVE
1 cordiale (FEM cordiale) *(person)*
2 accogliente (FEM accogliente) *(place)*

friendship NOUN
l' amicizia *fem*

fright NOUN
lo spavento *masc*
■ **to get a fright** spaventarsi [56ᴱ]

to **frighten** VERB
fare [49] paura a
□ Horror films frighten him. I film dell'orrore gli fanno paura.

frightened ADJECTIVE
■ **to be frightened** avere [12] paura

frightening ADJECTIVE
spaventoso (FEM spaventosa)

fringe NOUN
la frangia *fem* (PL le frange)
□ I want my fringe cut. Vorrei che mi tagliasse la frangia.

Frisbee® NOUN
il Frisbee® *masc* (PL i Frisbee)

fro ADVERB
■ **to go to and fro** andare [6ᴱ] avanti e indietro

frog NOUN
la rana *fem*

from PREPOSITION
da

  LANGUAGE TIP The preposition comes at the beginning of the Italian question.

□ Where do you come from? Da dove vieni?
□ The hotel is one kilometre from the beach. L'albergo è ad un chilometro dalla spiaggia.
■ **Who's it from?** *(letter, card)* Chi lo manda?
■ **I'm from Wales.** Sono gallese.

front NOUN
▷ *see also* **front** ADJECTIVE
il davanti *masc*
□ the front of the house il davanti della casa
■ **in front of** davanti a □ She sits in front of me in class. È seduta davanti a me in classe.
■ **at the front of the train** in testa al treno

front ADJECTIVE
▷ *see also* **front** NOUN
1 primo (FEM prima)
□ the front row la prima fila
2 davanti (FEM+PL davanti)
□ the front seats of the car i sedili davanti della macchina
■ **the front door** la porta d'ingresso
■ **the front room** il salotto

frontier NOUN
la frontiera *fem*

frost NOUN
il gelo *masc*

frosting NOUN (US)
la glassa *fem*

frosty ADJECTIVE
gelido (FEM gelida)
▢ one frosty morning una mattinata gelida
▢ They gave him a frosty reception. Gli hanno riservato un'accoglienza gelida.

to **frown** VERB
aggrottare [68] le sopracciglia

froze, frozen VERB ▷see **freeze**

frozen ADJECTIVE
congelato (FEM congelata)

fruit NOUN
la frutta fem
▢ Would you like some fruit? Vuoi della frutta?
■ **fruit juice** succo di frutta
■ **fruit salad** macedonia

fruit machine NOUN
la slot-machine fem (PL le slot-machine)

frustrated ADJECTIVE
frustrato (FEM frustrata)

to **fry** VERB
friggere [52]

frying pan NOUN
la padella fem

fuel NOUN
il carburante masc
▢ The plane ran out of fuel. L'aereo ha finito il carburante.

to **fulfil** VERB
realizzare [68]
▢ He fulfilled his dream. Ha realizzato il suo sogno.
■ **to fulfil a promise** mantenere [113] una promessa

full ADJECTIVE
1 pieno (FEM piena)
▢ The tank's full. Il serbatoio è pieno.
■ **full name** il nome completo e il cognome
■ **full board** pensione completa
2 sazio (FEM sazia)
▢ I'm full. Sono sazio.
■ **full information** tutte le informazioni
■ **at full speed** a tutta velocità

full stop NOUN
il punto masc (punctuation mark)

full-time ADJECTIVE, ADVERB
a tempo pieno

fully ADVERB
completamente

fumes NOUN PL
le esalazioni fem pl
▢ poisonous fumes esalazioni velenose
■ **exhaust fumes** gas di scarico

fun ADJECTIVE
▷see also **fun** NOUN
1 simpatico (FEM simpatica, MASC PL simpatici, FEM PL simpatiche) (person)
2 bello (FEM bella) (evening, time)

fun NOUN
▷see also **fun** ADJECTIVE
■ **to have fun** divertirsi [41ᴱ]

■ **It's fun!** È divertente!
■ **Have fun!** Divertiti!
■ **for fun** per divertimento
■ **to make fun of somebody** prendere [77] in giro qualcuno

funds NOUN PL
i fondi masc pl
■ **to raise funds** raccogliere [21] fondi

funeral NOUN
il funerale masc

funfair NOUN
il luna park masc (PL i luna park)

funny ADJECTIVE
1 divertente (FEM divertente)
▢ It was so funny I couldn't stop laughing. Era così divertente che non riuscivo a smettere di ridere.
2 strano (FEM strana)
▢ There's something funny about him. Ha qualcosa di strano.

fur NOUN
1 la pelliccia fem (PL le pellicce)
■ **a fur coat** una pelliccia
2 il pelo masc
▢ the cat's fur il pelo del gatto

furious ADJECTIVE
furioso (FEM furiosa)

furniture NOUN
i mobili masc pl
▢ The furniture is new. I mobili sono nuovi.
■ **a piece of furniture** un mobile

further ADVERB, ADJECTIVE
1 più lontano
▢ London is further from here than Oxford. Londra è più lontana da qui rispetto a Oxford.
■ **How much further is it?** Quanto manca ancora da qui?
■ **any further** più ▢ I can't walk any further. Non riesco a camminare più.
2 ulteriore (FEM ulteriore)
▢ Please write to us if you need any further information. Ci scriva se ha bisogno di ulteriori informazioni.

further education NOUN
i corsi di formazione masc pl

fuse NOUN
il fusibile masc

fuss NOUN
le storie fem pl
▢ What's all the fuss about? Cosa sono tutte queste storie?

fussy ADJECTIVE
difficile (FEM difficile)
▢ She is very fussy about her food. Fa la difficile per il cibo.
■ **I'm not fussy.** Per me è lo stesso.

future NOUN
il futuro masc

Gg

to gain VERB
guadagnare [14]
□ What do you hope to gain by this? Cosa speri di guadagnarci?
■ **to gain experience** fare [49] esperienza □ I gained experience by working there. Ho fatto esperienza lavorando lì.
■ **to gain speed** acquistare [68] velocità
■ **to gain weight** aumentare [68] di peso
■ **to gain on somebody** avvicinarsi [68ᴱ] a qualcuno

gallery NOUN
la galleria fem
□ an art gallery una galleria d'arte

to gamble VERB
▷ see also **gamble** NOUN
1 giocare [18]
□ He gambled at the casino. Giocava al casinò.
2 puntare [68]
□ Few firms want to gamble on new products. Poche ditte vogliono puntare su prodotti nuovi.

gamble NOUN
▷ see also **gamble** VERB
il rischio masc
□ It's a gamble. È un rischio.

gambler NOUN
il giocatore d'azzardo masc
la giocatrice d'azzardo fem

gambling NOUN
il gioco d'azzardo masc

game NOUN
1 il gioco masc (PL i giochi)
□ The children were playing a game. I bambini stavano facendo un gioco.
2 la partita fem
□ a game of football una partita di calcio □ a game of cards una partita a carte
3 la selvaggina fem
□ There's game on the menu. C'è selvaggina nel menù.

gamer NOUN
l' appassionato di video giochi masc
l' appassionata di video giochi fem (on computer)

games console NOUN
la console dei videogame fem (PL le console dei videogame)

gaming NOUN
il giocare al computer masc

gang NOUN
1 la banda fem (of thieves, troublemakers)
2 la comitiva fem (of friends)

to gang up VERB
■ **to gang up on somebody** fare [49] comunella contro qualcuno

gangster NOUN
il gangster masc (PL i gangster)

gap NOUN
1 il buco masc (PL i buchi)
□ There's a gap in the hedge. C'è un buco nella siepe.
2 l' intervallo masc
□ a gap of four years un intervallo di quattro anni

gap year NOUN
l' anno sabbatico masc

garage NOUN
1 il garage masc (PL i garage) (of house)
2 l' officina fem (for repairs)
3 la stazione di servizio fem (petrol station)

garbage NOUN (US)
1 la spazzatura fem
□ garbage can bidone della spazzatura
■ **garbage collection** raccolta dei rifiuti
2 le fesserie fem pl
□ That's garbage. Sono fesserie.

garbage collector NOUN (US)
il netturbino masc

garden NOUN
il giardino masc
□ a lovely garden un bel giardino

garden centre NOUN
il vivaio masc

gardener NOUN
il giardiniere masc
□ He's a gardener. Fa il giardiniere.

gardening NOUN
il giardinaggio masc

gardens NOUN PL
il giardino pubblico masc sing

garlic NOUN
l' aglio masc

garment NOUN
l' indumento masc

gas NOUN
1 il gas masc (PL i gas)

□ a gas leak una fuga di gas
■ **a gas cooker** una cucina a gas
■ **a gas cylinder** una bombola del gas
■ **a gas fire** una stufa a gas
2 la benzina *fem* (us: *petrol*)
□ I'll stop and get gas. Mi fermerò a fare benzina.
■ **a tank of gas** un pieno di benzina

gasoline NOUN (US)
la benzina *fem*

gas station NOUN (US)
la stazione di servizio *fem*

gate NOUN
1 il cancello *masc* (*of garden, field*)
2 l' uscita *fem* (*at airport*)

gateau NOUN
la torta *fem*

to **gather** VERB
1 riunirsi [51E] (*meet*)
2 raccogliere [21] (*information, material, things*)
■ **to gather speed** acquistare [68] velocità

gave VERB ▷ *see* **give**

gay ADJECTIVE
omosessuale (FEM omosessuale)

to **gaze** VERB
■ **to gaze at** fissare [68] □ He was gazing at her. La stava fissando.

GCSE NOUN (= *General Certificate of Secondary Education*)
il diploma di istruzione secondaria *masc*

gear NOUN
1 la marcia *fem* (PL le marce)
□ He left the car in gear. Ha lasciato la macchina in marcia.
■ **in first gear** in prima
2 l' attrezzatura *fem*
□ camping gear attrezzatura da campeggio
■ **sports gear** (*in football*) la divisa

gear box NOUN
la scatola del cambio *fem*

gear lever NOUN
la leva del cambio *fem*

gearshift NOUN (US)
la leva del cambio *fem*

geese NOUN PL ▷ *see* **goose**

gel NOUN
il gel *masc* (PL i gel)
□ hair gel gel per capelli

gem NOUN
la gemma *fem*

Gemini NOUN
i Gemelli *masc pl*
□ I'm Gemini. Sono dei Gemelli.

gender NOUN
il genere *masc* (*of noun*)

gene NOUN
il gene *masc*

general NOUN
▷ *see also* **general** ADJECTIVE
il generale *masc*

general ADJECTIVE
▷ *see also* **general** NOUN
generale (FEM generale)
□ a general improvement un miglioramento generale
■ **in general** in generale
■ **general election** elezioni politiche *fem pl*

general knowledge NOUN
la cultura generale *fem*

generally ADVERB
in genere
□ It's generally true that... In genere è vero che...
■ **generally speaking...** parlando in generale...

general practitioner NOUN
il medico di famiglia *masc* (PL i medici di famiglia)

generation NOUN
la generazione *fem*
□ the younger generation la nuova generazione

generator NOUN
il generatore *masc*

generous ADJECTIVE
generoso (FEM generosa)
□ That's very generous of you. È molto generoso da parte tua.

genetic ADJECTIVE
genetico (FEM genetica, MASC PL genetici, FEM PL genetiche)

genetically-modified ADJECTIVE
geneticamente modificato (FEM modificata)

genetics NOUN
la genetica *fem*

Geneva NOUN
Ginevra

genius NOUN
il genio *masc*

Genoa NOUN
Genova

gentle ADJECTIVE
1 dolce (FEM dolce) (*person, voice*)
2 leggero (FEM leggera) (*wind, push*)
□ I gave him a gentle push. Gli ho dato una leggera spinta.

LANGUAGE TIP Be careful not to translate **gentle** by gentile.

gentleman NOUN
il signore *masc*

gently ADVERB
1 dolcemente (*speak, smile*)
2 lievemente (*touch*)

gents NOUN SING
la toilette degli uomini *fem* (PL le toilette degli uomini)
□ Where's the gents, please? Dov'è la toilette degli uomini, per favore?
■ **'gents'** (*on sign*) 'uomini'

g

411

genuine ADJECTIVE
1 vero (FEM vera)
□ These are genuine diamonds. Questi sono diamanti veri.
2 sincero (FEM sincera)
□ She's a very genuine person. È una persona molto sincera.

geography NOUN
la geografia fem

germ NOUN
il germe masc

German ADJECTIVE
▷ see also **German** NOUN
tedesco (FEM tedesca, MASC PL tedeschi, FEM PL tedesche)

German NOUN
▷ see also **German** ADJECTIVE
1 il tedesco masc
la tedesca fem (person)
■ the Germans i tedeschi
2 il tedesco masc (language)
□ our German teacher il nostro insegnante di tedesco

German measles NOUN
la rosolia fem

German shepherd NOUN
il cane lupo masc

> LANGUAGE TIP Word for word, this means 'wolf dog'.

Germany NOUN
la Germania fem

gesture NOUN
il gesto masc
□ She made a threatening gesture. Ha fatto un gesto minaccioso.
■ a mere gesture un gesto simbolico

to **get** VERB

> LANGUAGE TIP There are several ways of translating 'get'. Scan the examples for one similar to what you want to say.

1 ricevere [27]
□ I got lots of presents. Ho ricevuto molti regali. □ He got first prize. Ha ricevuto il primo premio. □ The book's gotten good reviews. Il libro ha ricevuto buone critiche.
2 ottenere [113]
□ Jackie got good exam results. Jackie ha ottenuto un buon risultato all'esame.
3 prendere [77]
□ They've got the thief. Hanno preso il ladro. □ I'm getting the bus into town. Prendo l'autobus per andare in città.
4 capire [51]
□ I don't get the joke. Non capisco lo scherzo.
5 arrivare [68E]
□ He should get here soon. Dovrebbe arrivare presto. □ How do you get to the cinema? Come si arriva al cinema?

6 andare [6E] a cercare
□ Quick, get help! Svelto, vai a cercare aiuto!
7 procurare [68]
■ to get something for somebody procurare [68] qualcosa a qualcuno □ The shop got the book for me. La libreria mi ha procurato il libro.
■ I'll get it! 1 (phone) Rispondo io! 2 (door) Vado io!
■ to have got (own) avere [12] □ How many have you got? Quanti ne hai?

> LANGUAGE TIP When 'got' is used colloquially without 'have', it is translated by the present tense in Italian.

□ You got any identification? Ha un documento di identificazione?
■ to get something done farsi [49E] fare qualcosa □ I got my hair cut. Mi sono fatto tagliare i capelli.

> LANGUAGE TIP 'to have got to' is translated by dovere.

□ I've got to tell him. Devo dirglielo.

> LANGUAGE TIP 'to get' + an adjective is often translated by a specific verb in Italian.

□ to get old invecchiare
□ to get angry arrabbiarsi
□ to get tired stancarsi
■ It's getting late. Si sta facendo tardi.

to **get ahead** VERB
■ to get ahead of somebody superare [68] qualcuno

to **get around** VERB
superare [68] (problem)

to **get away** VERB
1 andare [6E] via
□ What time can you get away? A che ora puoi andare via?
2 scappare [68E]
□ One of the burglars got away. Uno dei ladri è scappato.

to **get away with** VERB
■ to get away with it passarla [68] liscia
□ You won't get away with it. Non riuscirai a passarla liscia.

to **get back** VERB
1 tornare [68E]
□ What time did you get back? A che ora sei tornato?
2 riavere [12] indietro
□ He got his money back. Ha riavuto indietro i suoi soldi.

to **get down** VERB
1 scendere [96E]
□ Get down from there! Scendi da lì!
2 buttare [68] giù
□ His constant grumbling really gets me down. Il suo continuo brontolare mi butta proprio giù.

3 annotare [68]

□ He spoke so fast I couldn't get it all down. Parlava così veloce che non sono riuscito ad annotare tutto.

to **get in** VERB

1 rientrare [68E]

□ What time did you get in last night? A che ora sei rientrato ieri sera?

2 arrivare [68E]

□ The train gets in at half past three. Il treno arriva alle tre e mezza.

to **get into** VERB

salire [93E] in

□ Sharon got into the car. Sharon è salita in macchina.

to **get off** VERB

1 scendere [96E] da

□ Isobel got off the train. Isobel è scesa dal treno.

2 andare [6E] via da

□ He managed to get off early from work yesterday. Ieri è riuscito ad andar via presto dal lavoro.

to **get on** VERB

1 montare [68E] su

□ Phyllis got on the bus. Phyllis è montata sull'autobus.

2 andare [6E] d'accordo

□ We got on really well. Andavamo molto d'accordo.

■ **How are you getting on?** Come va?

to **get out** VERB

1 scendere [96E]

□ She got out of the car. È scesa dalla macchina.

2 tirare [68] fuori

□ She got the map out. Ha tirato fuori la cartina.

to **get over** VERB

1 rimettersi [59E] da

□ It took her a long time to get over the illness. Ci è voluto molto tempo perché si rimettesse dalla malattia.

2 superare [68]

□ He managed to get over the problem. È riuscito a superare il problema.

to **get round to** VERB

trovare [68] il tempo per

□ I'll get round to it eventually. Prima o poi troverò il tempo per farlo.

to **get together** VERB

trovarsi [56E]

□ Could we get together this evening? Possiamo trovarci questa sera?

to **get up** VERB

alzarsi [56E]

□ What time do you get up? A che ora ti alzi?

ghetto NOUN

il ghetto *masc*

ghetto blaster NOUN

il maxistereo portatile *masc* (PL i maxistereo portatili)

ghost NOUN

il fantasma *masc* (PL i fantasmi)

□ ghost story storia di fantasmi

giant ADJECTIVE

▷ *see also* **giant** NOUN

gigante (FEM gigante)

giant NOUN

▷ *see also* **giant** ADJECTIVE

il gigante *masc*

gift NOUN

il regalo *masc*

□ a lovely gift un bel regalo

■ **to have a gift for something** essere [47E] portato per qualcosa □ Dave's got a gift for painting. Dave è portato per la pittura.

gifted ADJECTIVE

di talento

□ Janice is a gifted dancer. Janice è una ballerina di talento.

■ **one of the most gifted artists** uno degli artisti più dotati

gift shop NOUN

il negozio di articoli da regalo *masc*

gift token NOUN

il buono omaggio *masc* (PL i buoni omaggio)

gift-wrapped ADJECTIVE

impacchettato (FEM impacchettata)

gig NOUN

1 lo spettacolo *masc* (*performance*)

2 il giga *masc* (PL i giga) (*gigabyte*)

gigantic ADJECTIVE

gigantesco (FEM gigantesca, MASC PL giganteschi, FEM PL gigantesche)

to **giggle** VERB

ridacchiare [17]

gin NOUN

il gin *masc* (PL i gin)

ginger NOUN

▷ *see also* **ginger** ADJECTIVE

lo zenzero *masc*

ginger ADJECTIVE

▷ *see also* **ginger** NOUN

rossiccio (FEM rossiccia, MASC PL rossicci, FEM PL rossicce)

□ She's got ginger hair. Ha i capelli rossicci.

ginger ale NOUN

la bibita gassata allo zenzero *fem*

giraffe NOUN

la giraffa *fem*

girl NOUN

1 la bambina *fem*

□ a five-year-old girl una bambina di cinque anni

2 la ragazza *fem*

□ an English girl una ragazza inglese

g

3 la femmina *fem*
□ They've got a girl and two boys. Hanno una femmina e due maschi.

girlfriend NOUN
1 la ragazza *fem*
□ Paul's girlfriend is called Lee. La ragazza di Paul si chiama Lee.
2 l' amica *fem* (PL le amiche)
□ She often went out with her girlfriends. Usciva spesso con le sue amiche.

to **give** VERB
dare [30]

> **LANGUAGE TIP** dare is used with the preposition 'a'.

■ **to give somebody something** dare [30] qualcosa a qualcuno □ I gave my sister some money. Ho dato dei soldi a mia sorella.

> **LANGUAGE TIP** When 'give' is followed by a pronoun, use an indirect pronoun in Italian.

□ He gave me ten pounds. Mi ha dato dieci sterline. □ He gave it to me. Me l'ha dato.

■ **to give somebody a present** fare [49] un regalo a qualcuno

> **LANGUAGE TIP** Word for word, this means 'to make a present to somebody'.

□ They gave their teacher a present. Hanno fatto un regalo alla maestra.

■ **to give way** *(in car)* dare [30] la precedenza

to **give away** VERB
1 dar [30] via
□ We have six copies to give away. Abbiamo sei copie da dare via.
2 tradire [51]
□ Her accent gave her away. Il suo accento l'ha tradita.

to **give back** VERB
tornare [68]
□ I gave the book back to him. Gli ho tornato il libro.

to **give in** VERB
1 cedere [27]
□ His Mum gave in and let him go out. Sua madre ha ceduto e lo ha lasciato uscire.
2 arrendersi [83ᴇ]
□ I give in. Mi arrendo.

to **give out** VERB
distribuire [51]
□ He gave out leaflets in the street. Distribuiva manifestini per strada.

to **give up** VERB
lasciar [13] perdere
□ I couldn't do it, so I gave up. Non sono riuscito a farlo, così ho lasciato perdere.

■ **to give oneself up** arrendersi [83ᴇ] □ He gave himself up. Si è arreso.

■ **to give up doing something** smettere [59] di fare qualcosa □ He gave up smoking. Ha smesso di fumare.

given VERB ▷ see give

glad ADJECTIVE
contento (FEM contenta)

glamorous ADJECTIVE
affascinante (FEM affascinante) *(person)*

to **glance** VERB
▷ see also **glance** NOUN
■ **to glance at** dare [30] un'occhiata a □ Peter glanced at his watch. Peter ha dato un'occhiata all'orologio.

glance NOUN
▷ see also **glance** VERB
l' occhiata *fem*
□ We exchanged glances. Ci siamo scambiati un'occhiata.

■ **at first glance** a prima vista
■ **at a glance** a colpo d'occhio

to **glare** VERB
■ **to glare at somebody** fulminare [68] qualcuno con lo sguardo

glaring ADJECTIVE
■ **a glaring mistake** un errore palese

glass NOUN
1 il bicchiere *masc*
□ a glass of milk un bicchiere di latte
2 il vetro *masc*
□ a glass door una porta di vetro

glasses NOUN PL
gli occhiali *masc pl*
□ He wears glasses. Porta gli occhiali.

to **gleam** VERB
brillare [68]
□ Her eyes gleamed with excitement. Le brillavano gli occhi dall'eccitazione.

glider NOUN
l' aliante *masc*

gliding NOUN
il volo con l'aliante *masc*
□ My hobby is gliding. Il mio hobby è il volo con l'aliante.

glimpse NOUN
■ **to catch a glimpse of somebody** intravedere [119] qualcuno

to **glitter** VERB
luccicare [18]

global ADJECTIVE
mondiale (FEM mondiale)
□ on a global scale su scala mondiale
■ **a global view** una visione globale

global warming NOUN
il riscaldamento dell'atmosfera terrestre *masc*

globe NOUN
il globo *masc*

gloomy ADJECTIVE
tetro (FEM tetra)
□ a huge gloomy church un'enorme chiesa tetra
■ **She's been feeling gloomy recently.** Ultimamente si sente giù.

glorious ADJECTIVE
splendido (FEM splendida)

glove NOUN
il guanto masc
□ a pair of gloves un paio di guanti

glove compartment NOUN
il vano portaoggetti masc

to **glow** VERB
fare [49] luce (cigarette, fire)
■ **to glow with health** sprizzare [68] salute da tutti i pori

glue NOUN
▷ see also **glue** VERB
la colla fem

to **glue** VERB
▷ see also **glue** NOUN
incollare [68]

GM ADJECTIVE (= genetically-modified)
■ **GM foods** alimenti geneticamente modificati

GMO ABBREVIATION (= genetically-modified organism)
l' organismo geneticamente modificato masc

go NOUN
▷ see also **go** VERB
■ **to have a go at doing something** provare [68] a fare qualcosa
■ **Whose go is it?** A chi tocca?

to **go** VERB
▷ see also **go** NOUN
1 andare [6E]
□ I'm going to the cinema tonight. Vado al cinema stasera. □ My car won't go. La mia macchina non va. □ How did it go? Com'è andata? □ We went home. Siamo andati a casa.
■ **to go for a walk** andare [6] a fare una passeggiata □ He went for a walk. È andato a fare una passeggiata.
■ **to go past something** passare [68] accanto a qualcosa
2 andare [6E] via
□ Where's Judy? — She's gone. Dov'è Judy? — È andata via. □ I'm going now. Adesso vado via.
■ **to be going to**

> **LANGUAGE TIP** Use the future tense in Italian to say what you're going to do, or what's going to happen.

□ I'm going to do it tomorrow. Lo farò domani. □ It's going to be difficult. Sarà difficile.

to **go after** VERB
rincorrere [26E]
□ Quick, go after them! Veloce, rincorrili!

to **go ahead** VERB
proseguire [41]
□ The show went ahead as planned. Lo spettacolo proseguì come previsto.

■ **to go ahead with** mettere [59] in atto
□ We'll go ahead with your suggestion. Metteremo in atto il tuo suggerimento.

to **go around** VERB
■ **There's a rumour going around that...** Corre voce che...

to **go away** VERB
andarsene [6E]
□ Go away! Vattene!

to **go back** VERB
ritornare [68E]
□ We went back to the same place. Siamo ritornati allo stesso posto.

to **go by** VERB
passare [68E]
□ Two policemen went by. Sono passati due poliziotti.

to **go down** VERB
scendere [96E]
□ He went down the stairs. Ha sceso le scale.
□ The price of computers has gone down. Il prezzo dei computer è sceso.
■ **to go down with** (illness) beccarsi [18E]
□ My brother's gone down with flu. Mio fratello si è beccato l'influenza.

to **go for** VERB
1 scegliere [95]
□ I think I'll go for a casual look. Penso che sceglierò un look casual.
2 attaccare [18]
□ The dog went for me. Il cane mi ha attaccato.
■ **Go for it!** Forza!

to **go in** VERB
entrare [68E]
□ They all went in. Sono entrati tutti.

to **go off** VERB
1 andarsene [6E]
□ They went off after lunch. Se ne sono andati dopo pranzo.
■ **to go off with something** portare [68] via qualcosa
■ **I've gone off the idea.** L'idea non mi piace più.
2 scoppiare [17E]
□ The bomb went off at ten o'clock. La bomba è scoppiata alle 10.
■ **The gun went off by accident.** È partito un colpo accidentalmente.
3 suonare [68]
□ My alarm goes off at seven. La sveglia suona alle sette.
4 spegnersi [105E]
□ All the lights went off. Si sono spente tutte le luci.
5 andare [6E] a male
□ This milk has gone off. Il latte è andato a male.

g

to **go on** VERB

1 succedere [110ᴱ]

□ What's going on? Cosa succede?

2 durare [68ᴱ]

□ The concert went on until eleven o'clock. Il concerto è durato fino alle undici.

3 continuare [68]

□ He went on reading. Ha continuato a leggere.

■ **to go on about something** non finirla [51] più che qualcosa

■ **Go on!** Forza! □ Go on, tell me! Forza, dimmelo!

to **go out** VERB

1 uscire [117ᴱ]

□ I went out with Steven last night. Ieri sera sono uscita con Steven.

■ **to be going out with somebody** stare [108ᴱ] insieme a qualcuno □ I've been going out with him for two months. Sono due mesi che stiamo insieme.

■ **to go out for a meal** andare [6ᴱ] a mangiare fuori

2 spegnersi [105ᴱ]

□ Suddenly, the lights went out. Improvvisamente si sono spente le luci.

to **go past** VERB

passare [68ᴱ] vicino a

□ The bus goes past the school. L'autobus passa vicino alla scuola.

to **go round** VERB

1 visitare [68]

□ We want to go round the museum. Vogliamo visitare il museo.

■ **to go round to somebody's house** andare [6ᴱ] da qualcuno □ We're all going round to Paul's house. Andiamo tutti da Paul.

2 essere [47ᴱ] in circolazione

□ There's a bug going round. C'è un virus in circolazione.

■ **Is there enough food to go round?** C'è abbastanza da mangiare per tutti?

to **go through** VERB

1 passare [68ᴱ]

□ I know what you're going through. So cosa stai passando.

2 leggere [57] da cima a fondo

□ I went through his essay with him. Ho letto il suo tema da cima a fondo assieme a lui.

3 riesaminare [68] da cima a fondo

□ They went through the plan again. Hanno riesaminato il piano da cima a fondo.

4 frugare [76] tra

□ Someone had gone through her things. Qualcuno aveva frugato tra le sue cose.

to **go up** VERB

salire [93ᴱ]

□ She went up the stairs. Ha salito le scale.

□ The price has gone up. Il prezzo è salito.

■ **to go up in flames** andare [6ᴱ] in fiamme

to **go with** VERB

andare [6ᴱ] con

□ Does this blouse go with that skirt? Questa camicia va con quella gonna?

goal NOUN

1 il gol *masc* (PL i gol)

□ He scored the first goal. Ha segnato il primo gol.

2 l' obiettivo *masc*

□ His goal is to become the world champion. Il suo obiettivo è quello di diventare campione del mondo.

goalkeeper NOUN

il portiere *masc*

goat NOUN

la capra *fem*

□ goat's cheese formaggio di capra

god NOUN

il dio *masc* (PL gli dei)

□ I believe in God. Credo in Dio.

goddaughter NOUN

la figlioccia *fem* (PL le figliocce)

godfather NOUN

il padrino *masc*

godmother NOUN

la madrina *fem*

godson NOUN

il figlioccio *masc*

goggles NOUN PL

la maschera *fem sing*

gold NOUN

l' oro *masc*

□ a gold necklace una collana d'oro

goldfish NOUN

il pesce rosso *masc*

gold-plated ADJECTIVE

placcato oro (FEM placcata oro)

golf NOUN

il golf *masc*

■ **a golf club** una mazza da golf

■ **a golf course** un campo da golf

gone VERB ▷ see go

good ADJECTIVE

1 bello (FEM bella)

□ It's a very good film. È un film molto bello.

LANGUAGE TIP Use **bel** before a masculine noun starting with a consonant.

□ a good film un bel film

LANGUAGE TIP Use **bell'** before a masculine noun starting with a vowel.

□ a good pay rise un bell'aumento

LANGUAGE TIP Use **bello** before a masculine noun starting with impure s, gn, pn, ps, x, y or z.

□ a good salary un bello stipendio

LANGUAGE TIP Use **bei** before a plural masculine noun starting with a consonant.

□ good books bei libri

> **LANGUAGE TIP** Use **begli** before a plural masculine noun starting with a vowel, or with impure s, gn, pn, ps, x, y or z.

□ good salaries begli stipendi

WORD POWER

You can use a number of other words instead of **good** to mean 'great':

excellent eccellente
□ an excellent dinner una cena eccellente
fantastic fantastico
□ a fantastic holiday una vacanza fantastica
great fantastico
□ a great actor un attore fantastico
super fantastico
□ a super idea un'idea fantastica

---

2 gentile (FEM gentile)

□ They were very good to me. Sono stati molto gentili con me. □ That's very good of you. È molto gentile da parte tua.

3 bravo (FEM brava)

□ He's the best in the class. È il più bravo della classe.

■ **to be good at something** essere [47E] bravo in qualcosa □ Jane's very good at maths. Jane è molto brava in matematica.

4 buono (FEM buona)

□ Be good! Sii buono! □ They make very good soup here. Qui fanno una minestra molto buona.

> **LANGUAGE TIP** Use **buon** before a masculine noun starting with a consonant or a vowel.

□ a good number un buon numero □ a good friend un buon amico

> **LANGUAGE TIP** Use **buono** before a masculine noun starting with impure s, gn, pn, ps, x, y or z.

□ a good rucksack un buono zaino

> **LANGUAGE TIP** Use **buon'** before a feminine noun starting with a vowel.

□ Good idea! Buon'idea!

■ **Good morning!** Buongiorno!
■ **Good afternoon!** Buon pomeriggio!
■ **Good evening!** Buona sera!
■ **Good night!** Buona notte!
■ **Have a good journey!** Buon viaggio!
■ **Good!** Bene!

■ **to feel good** sentirsi [41E] bene □ I'm feeling really good today. Oggi mi sento proprio bene.

■ **to be good for somebody** far [49] bene a qualcuno □ Vegetables are good for you. La verdura ti fa bene.

■ **It's no good complaining.** Non vale la pena lamentarsi.

■ **for good** per sempre □ The theatre has closed for good. Il teatro ha chiuso per sempre.

■ **as good as** praticamente □ as good as new praticamente nuovo

goodbye EXCLAMATION
arrivederci

Good Friday NOUN
il venerdì santo masc

good-looking ADJECTIVE
bello (FEM bella)

good-natured ADJECTIVE
di buon carattere

goods NOUN PL
la merce fem
□ faulty goods merce difettosa
■ **a goods train** un treno merci

google VERB
cercare [18] con Google
□ Why not google it? Perché non lo cerchiamo con Google?

goose NOUN
l' oca fem (PL le oche)
□ a flock of geese un branco di oche

gooseberry NOUN
l' uva spina fem

gorgeous ADJECTIVE
stupendo (FEM stupendo)

gorilla NOUN
il gorilla masc (PL i gorilla)

gospel NOUN
il vangelo masc

gossip NOUN
▷ see also **gossip** VERB
1 i pettegolezzi masc pl
□ It's just gossip. Sono solo pettegolezzi.
■ **Tell me the gossip!** Dimmi le ultime!
2 il pettegolo masc
la pettegola fem (person)

to **gossip** VERB
▷ see also **gossip** NOUN
chiacchierare [68]
□ They were always gossiping. Chiacchieravano in continuazione.

got VERB ▷ see **get**

gotta VERB = **have got to**

gotten VERB (US) ▷ see **get**

government NOUN
il governo masc

GP NOUN (= general practitioner)
il medico di famiglia masc (PL i medici di famiglia)

GPS NOUN
il GPS masc (PL i GPS) (global positioning system)
■ **a GPS device** un GPS

to **grab** VERB
afferrare [68]
□ He grabbed my arm. Mi ha afferrato il braccio.
■ **to grab something from somebody** strappare [68] qualcosa di mano a qualcuno

417

graceful – grave

graceful ADJECTIVE
aggraziato (FEM aggraziata) *(person, movements)*

grade NOUN
1 il livello *masc*
□ **the grade II exam** un esame di secondo livello
2 il voto *masc (mark)*

grade crossing NOUN (US)
il passaggio a livello *masc* (PL i passaggi a livello)

grade school NOUN (US)
la scuola elementare *fem*

gradual ADJECTIVE
graduale (FEM graduale)

gradually ADVERB
gradualmente

graduate NOUN
▷ *see also* **graduate** VERB
il laureato *masc*
la laureata *fem*

to **graduate** VERB
▷ *see also* **graduate** NOUN
laurearsi [56ᴱ]
□ **He graduated from London University last year.** Si è laureato alla London University l'anno scorso.
■ **to graduate from high school** diplomarsi [56ᴱ]

graffiti NOUN PL
i graffiti *masc pl*

grain NOUN
1 il chicco *masc* (PL i chicchi)
□ **a grain of rice** un chicco di riso
■ **a grain of truth** un briciolo di verità
2 i cereali *masc pl*
□ **grain producers** produttori di cereali

gram NOUN
il grammo *masc*

grammar NOUN
la grammatica *fem*
□ **a grammar book** un libro di grammatica

grammar school NOUN
il liceo *masc*

grammatical ADJECTIVE
grammaticale (FEM grammaticale)

gramme NOUN
il grammo *masc*

grand ADJECTIVE
sontuoso (FEM sontuosa)
□ **Her house is very grand.** La sua casa è molto sontuosa.
■ **We had a grand time.** Ce la siamo proprio spassata.
■ **a grand total of two thousand pounds** una somma complessiva di duemila sterline

grandchild NOUN
il/la nipote *masc/fem*

granddad NOUN
il nonno *masc*

granddaughter NOUN
la nipote *fem*

grandfather NOUN
il nonno *masc*

grandma NOUN
la nonna *fem*

grandmother NOUN
la nonna *fem*

grandpa NOUN
il nonno *masc*

grandparents NOUN PL
i nonni *masc pl*

grand piano NOUN
il pianoforte a coda *masc*

grandson NOUN
il nipote *masc*

granny NOUN
la nonna *fem*

grant NOUN
▷ *see also* **grant** VERB
1 la sovvenzione *fem*
□ **a grant to restore the church** una sovvenzione per il restauro della chiesa
2 la borsa di studio *fem*
□ **Some students get grants.** Alcuni studenti ottengono delle borse di studio.

to **grant** VERB
▷ *see also* **grant** NOUN
concedere [27]
□ **He grants few interviews.** Concede poche interviste.
■ **to take somebody for granted** non rendersi [83] conto di quanto qualcuno sia importante
■ **to take something for granted** dare [30] qualcosa per scontato

grapefruit NOUN
il pompelmo *masc*

grapes NOUN PL
l' uva *fem sing*
□ **a bunch of grapes** un grappolo d'uva

graph NOUN
il grafico *masc* (PL i grafici)

graphics NOUN
la grafica *fem*

to **grasp** VERB
afferrare [68]

grass NOUN
l' erba *fem*
□ **Keep off the grass.** Vietato calpestare l'erba.

grasshopper NOUN
la cavalletta *fem*

to **grate** VERB
grattugiare [58]

grateful ADJECTIVE
grato (FEM grata)

grave NOUN
la tomba *fem*

gravel NOUN
la ghiaia *fem*

graveyard NOUN
il cimitero *masc*

gravy NOUN
il sugo della carne *masc*

gray ADJECTIVE (US)
grigio (FEM grigia, MASC PL grigi, FEM PL grigie)
□ a gray suit un vestito grigio
■ **to go gray** ingrigirsi [51ᴱ]

grease NOUN
il grasso *masc*

greasy ADJECTIVE
grasso (FEM grassa)
□ He has greasy hair. Ha i capelli grassi.

great ADJECTIVE
1 grande (FEM grande)
□ a great oak tree una grande quercia
■ **He took great care to explain clearly.**
Ha cercato in ogni modo di dare una
spiegazione chiara.
■ **a great many** moltissimi
2 fantastico (FEM fantastica, MASC PL fantastici,
FEM PL fantastiche)
□ That's great! È fantastico!

WORD POWER
You can use a number of other words
instead of **great** to mean 'good':
amazing eccezionale
□ an amazing view una vista eccezionale
fabulous favoloso
□ a fabulous idea un'idea favolosa
terrific fantastico
□ a terrific party una festa fantastica
wonderful meraviglioso
□ a wonderful day una giornata meravigliosa

Great Britain NOUN
la Gran Bretagna *fem*

great-grandfather NOUN
il bisnonno *masc*

great-grandmother NOUN
la bisnonna *fem*

Greece NOUN
la Grecia *fem*

greedy ADJECTIVE
1 ingordo (FEM ingorda)
□ Don't be greedy. Leave some cake for Helen.
Non essere ingordo. Lascia un po' di torta per
Helen.
2 avido (FEM avida) *(for money)*
□ to be greedy for power avere sete di potere

Greek ADJECTIVE
▷ *see also* **Greek** NOUN
greco (FEM greca, MASC PL greci, FEM PL greche)

Greek NOUN
▷ *see also* **Greek** ADJECTIVE

1 il greco *masc*
la greca *fem (person)*
■ **the Greeks** i greci
2 il greco *masc (language)*

green ADJECTIVE
▷ *see also* **green** NOUN
verde (FEM verde)
□ a green car una macchina verde
■ **the Green Party** i Verdi

green NOUN
▷ *see also* **green** ADJECTIVE
il verde *masc*
□ dark green verde scuro
■ **greens** la verdura
■ **the Green Party** i Verdi

green belt NOUN
la cintura di verde *fem*

green card NOUN
la carta verde *fem*

greengrocer NOUN
il fruttivendolo *masc*
■ **to go to the greengrocer's** andare [6ᴱ]
dal fruttivendolo

greenhouse NOUN
la serra *fem*
■ **the greenhouse effect** l'effetto serra
■ **greenhouse gas** il gas responsabile
dell'effetto serra

Greenland NOUN
la Groenlandia *fem*

to **greet** VERB
salutare [68]
□ He greeted me with a kiss. Mi ha salutata con
un bacio.
■ **to greet something with** accogliere [21]
qualcosa con

greetings NOUN PL
i saluti *masc pl*
□ Greetings from London! Saluti da Londra!
■ **'Season's greetings'** *(on card)* 'Buone Feste'

greetings card NOUN
il biglietto d'auguri *masc*

grew VERB ▷ *see* **grow**

grey (US gray) ADJECTIVE
grigio (FEM grigia, MASC PL grigi, FEM PL grigie)
□ a grey suit un completo grigio
■ **to go grey** ingrigirsi [51ᴱ]

grey-haired ADJECTIVE
dai capelli grigi

grid NOUN
1 la rete *fem*
□ a grid of streets una rete di strade
2 la grata *fem (made of metal)*

grief NOUN
il dolore *masc*

to **grieve** VERB
■ **to grieve over** piangere [71] □ She was
grieving over the death of her husband. Stava
piangendo la morte di suo marito.

g

■ **The family is still grieving.** La famiglia è ancora in lutto.

■ **I need time to grieve.** Ho bisogno di tempo per piangere la sua morte.

grill NOUN
▷ *see also* **grill** VERB
la griglia *fem (of cooker)*

■ **a mixed grill** una grigliata mista

to **grill** VERB
▷ *see also* **grill** NOUN
cucinare [68] alla griglia

grim ADJECTIVE
deprimente (FEM deprimente)
□ Parts of the city are very grim. Alcune parti della città sono molto deprimenti.

to **grin** VERB
▷ *see also* **grin** NOUN
fare [49] un gran sorriso
□ Dave grinned at me. Dave mi fece un gran sorriso.

grin NOUN
▷ *see also* **grin** VERB
il sorriso smagliante *masc*

to **grind** VERB
1 macinare [68] *(coffee, pepper)*
□ Have you ground the coffee? Hai macinato il caffè?
2 tritare [68] *(us: meat)*

to **grip** VERB
afferrare [68]

gripping ADJECTIVE
avvincente (FEM avvincente)

grit NOUN
la ghiaia *fem*

to **groan** VERB
▷ *see also* **groan** NOUN
gemere [27]
□ He groaned with pain. Gemette dal dolore.

groan NOUN
▷ *see also* **groan** VERB
il gemito *masc*

grocer NOUN
il/la negoziante di generi alimentari *masc/fem*

groceries NOUN PL
i generi alimentari *masc pl*
□ a shop selling groceries un negozio che vende generi alimentari

■ **a bag of groceries** una borsa di roba da mangiare

■ **to get some groceries** fare [49] un po' di spesa

grocer's NOUN
il negozio di alimentari *masc*

grocery store NOUN
il negozio di alimentari *masc* (PL i negozi di alimentari)

groom NOUN
lo sposo *masc*

□ the groom and his best man lo sposo e il suo testimone

to **grope** VERB
■ **to grope for something** cercare [18] qualcosa a tentoni □ He groped for the light switch. Cercò a tentoni l'interruttore della luce.

gross ADJECTIVE
1 lordo (FEM lorda)
□ gross interest interesse lordo
2 disgustoso (FEM disgustosa)
□ It was really gross! È stato veramente disgustoso!
3 obeso (FEM obesa) *(fat)*

grossly ADVERB
decisamente
□ We're grossly underpaid. Siamo decisamente sottopagati.

ground VERB ▷ *see* **grind**

ground NOUN
▷ *see also* **ground** ADJECTIVE
1 la terra *fem*
□ The ground's wet. La terra è bagnata.
■ **on the ground** per terra
■ **to get off the ground** 1 *(scheme)* prendere [77] il via 2 *(plane)* decollare [68]
2 il campo *masc*
□ a football ground un campo di calcio
■ **grounds** motivo *masc sing* □ We've got grounds for complaint. Abbiamo motivo di lamentarci.

ground ADJECTIVE
▷ *see also* **ground** NOUN, VERB
■ **ground coffee** caffè macinato
■ **ground meat** carne macinata

ground floor NOUN
il pianterreno *masc*
■ **on the ground floor** al pianterreno

group NOUN
il gruppo *masc*

to **grow** VERB
1 crescere [28E]
□ Haven't you grown! Come sei cresciuto!
■ **to grow a beard** farsi [49E] crescere la barba □ I'm growing a beard. Mi sto facendo crescere la barba. □ He grew a moustache. Si è fatto crescere i baffi.
2 aumentare [68E] *(number)*
3 coltivare [68]
□ He grew vegetables in his garden. Coltivava ortaggi in giardino. □ Lettuce was grown by the Romans. Gli antichi romani coltivavano l'insalata.

to **grow out of** VERB
1 non entrare [68E] più in *(clothes)*
□ He's grown out of his jacket. Non entra più nella giacca.
2 perdere [69] *(habit)*

to **grow up** VERB
crescere [28E]

□ I grew up in Rome. Sono cresciuto a Roma.
■ **Oh, grow up!** Non fare il bambino!

to **growl** VERB
ringhiare [17]

grown VERB ▷ *see* **grow**

growth NOUN
la crescita *fem*
□ economic growth crescita economica

grub NOUN
1 il bruco *masc* (PL i bruchi) *(insect)*
2 qualcosa da mangiare
□ Get yourself some grub. Prenditi qualcosa da mangiare.

grudge NOUN
il rancore *masc*
■ **to have a grudge against somebody** serbare [68] rancore a qualcuno

gruesome ADJECTIVE
orrendo (FEM orrenda)

guarantee NOUN
▷ *see also* **guarantee** VERB
la garanzia *fem*
□ a five-year guarantee una garanzia di cinque anni □ It's still under guarantee. È ancora in garanzia.

to **guarantee** VERB
▷ *see also* **guarantee** NOUN
garantire [51]
□ I can't guarantee he'll come. Non posso garantire che venga.

to **guard** VERB
▷ *see also* **guard** NOUN
fare [49] la guardia a
□ They guarded the palace. Facevano la guardia al palazzo.

guard NOUN
▷ *see also* **guard** VERB
1 la guardia *fem*
■ **security guard** guardia giurata
■ **to catch somebody off guard** prendere [77] qualcuno alla sprovvista
2 il capotreno *masc (on train)*

guard dog NOUN
il cane da guardia *masc*

to **guess** VERB
▷ *see also* **guess** NOUN
1 indovinare [68]
□ Can you guess what it is? Indovina cos'è!
■ **Guess what!** Sai l'ultima!
2 supporre [73]
□ I guess so. Suppongo di sì.

guess NOUN
▷ *see also* **guess** VERB
la supposizione *fem*
□ It's just a guess. È solo una supposizione.
■ **Have a guess!** Prova a indovinare!

guest NOUN
l' ospite *masc/fem*

□ We have guests staying with us. Abbiamo degli ospiti da noi.

guest house NOUN
la pensione *fem*

guide NOUN
la guida *fem (book, person)*
■ **the Guides** le Giovani esploratrici

guidebook NOUN
la guida *fem*

guide dog NOUN
il cane per ciechi *masc*

guilty ADJECTIVE
colpevole (FEM colpevole)
□ She was found guilty. È stata riconosciuta colpevole.
■ **to feel guilty** sentirsi [41ᴱ] in colpa □ He felt guilty about lying to her. Si sentiva in colpa per averle mentito.
■ **to have a guilty conscience** avere [12] la coscienza sporca

guinea pig NOUN
la cavia *fem*

guitar NOUN
la chitarra *fem*

gum NOUN
la gomma *fem*
□ I'm chewing gum. Sto masticando una gomma.
■ **gums** le gengive □ My gums are bleeding. Le gengive mi sanguinano.

gun NOUN
1 la pistola *fem (handgun)*
2 il fucile *masc (rifle)*

gunpoint NOUN
■ **at gunpoint** sotto la minaccia delle armi

gust NOUN
■ **gust of wind** raffica di vento

guy NOUN
il tipo *masc*
□ Who's that guy? Chi è quel tipo?

gym NOUN
la palestra *fem*
□ I go to the gym every day. Vado in palestra ogni giorno.
■ **gym classes** un corso di ginnastica

gymnast NOUN
il/la ginnasta *masc/fem*

gymnastics NOUN
la ginnastica *fem*

gym shoes NOUN
le scarpe da ginnastica *fem pl*

gypsy NOUN
lo zingaro *masc*
la zingara *fem*

Hh

habit NOUN
l' abitudine *fem*

to **hack** VERB
■ **to hack into a system** inserirsi [51ᴱ] illegalmente in un sistema

hacker NOUN
il pirata informatico *masc* (PL i pirati informatici)

had VERB ▷ *see* **have**

haddock NOUN
l' eglefino *masc*

hadn't = had not

hail NOUN
▷ *see also* **hail** VERB
la grandine *fem*

to **hail** VERB
▷ *see also* **hail** NOUN
grandinare [68ᴱ]
□ It's hailing. Grandina.

hair NOUN
1 i capelli *masc pl*
□ Her hair is lovely. Ha dei bei capelli.
■ **to have one's hair cut** farsi [49ᴱ] tagliare i capelli
2 il pelo *masc* (*of animal*)

hairbrush NOUN
la spazzola *fem*

haircut NOUN
il taglio *masc*
□ a nice haircut un bel taglio
■ **to have a haircut** farsi [49ᴱ] tagliare i capelli

hairdresser NOUN
il parrucchiere *masc*
la parrucchiera *fem*
□ at the hairdresser's dal parrucchiere

hair dryer NOUN
l' asciugacapelli *masc* (PL gli asciugacapelli)

hair gel NOUN
il gel *masc* (PL i gel)

hairgrip NOUN
la molletta *fem*

hair spray NOUN
la lacca *fem* (PL le lacche)

hair straighteners NOUN PL
la piastra per capelli *fem sing*

hairstyle NOUN
la pettinatura *fem*

hairy ADJECTIVE
peloso (FEM pelosa)

half NOUN
▷ *see also* **half** ADJECTIVE, ADVERB
la metà *fem* (PL le metà)
□ half of the cake metà torta □ I can do the job in half the time. Posso fare il lavoro in metà del tempo.
■ **Half the time I don't know what he's talking about.** Spesso non so di che cosa stia parlando.
■ **two and a half** due e mezzo
■ **half an hour** mezz'ora
■ **half past ten** dieci e mezza
■ **half a kilo** mezzo chilo
■ **to cut something in half** tagliare [25] qualcosa a metà
■ **One and two halves, please.** Un biglietto intero e due ridotti, per favore.

half ADJECTIVE, ADVERB
▷ *see also* **half** NOUN
mezzo (FEM mezza)
□ a half chicken mezzo pollo □ He was half asleep. Era mezzo addormentato.
■ **She half expected him to refuse.** Era quasi convinta che avrebbe rifiutato.

half-hour NOUN
la mezz'ora *fem*

half-price ADJECTIVE, ADVERB
a metà prezzo
□ I bought it half-price. L'ho comprato a metà prezzo.

half-term NOUN
la vacanza di metà trimestre *fem*

half-time NOUN
l' intervallo *masc*

halfway ADVERB
1 a metà strada
□ halfway between Oxford and London a metà strada tra Oxford e Londra
2 a metà
□ halfway through the film a metà del film

hall NOUN
1 l' ingresso *masc*
□ He hung his coat in the hall. Ha appeso il cappotto nell'ingresso.
2 la sala *fem*
□ a concert hall una sala concerti
■ **village hall** sala comunale a disposizione del pubblico

Hallowe'en NOUN
la vigilia di Ognissanti *fem*

hallway NOUN
l' ingresso *masc*

halt NOUN
▷ *see also* **halt** VERB
■ **to come to a halt** fermarsi [56E]

to **halt** VERB
▷ *see also* **halt** NOUN
arrestare [68]
□ The government failed to halt economic decline. Il governo non è riuscito ad arrestare il declino economico.

halves NOUN PL ▷ *see* **half**

ham NOUN
il prosciutto *masc*
□ a ham sandwich un panino al prosciutto

hamburger NOUN
l' hamburger *masc* (PL gli hamburger)

hammer NOUN
il martello *masc*

hamster NOUN
il criceto *masc*

hand NOUN
▷ *see also* **hand** VERB
1 la mano *fem*
□ Wash your hands! Lavati le mani!
2 la lancetta *fem (of clock)*
■ **on the one hand..., on the other hand...** da un lato..., dall'altro...

to **hand** VERB
▷ *see also* **hand** NOUN
passare [68]
□ He handed me the book. Mi ha passato il libro.

to **hand in** VERB
consegnare [14]
□ He handed his exam paper in. Ha consegnato il compito scritto.

to **hand out** VERB
distribuire [51]
□ The teacher handed out the books. L'insegnante ha distribuito i libri.

to **hand over** VERB
consegnare [14]
□ She handed the keys over to me. Mi ha consegnato le chiavi.

handbag NOUN
la borsetta *fem*

handball NOUN
1 la pallamano *fem*
□ We played handball. Giocavamo a pallamano.
2 il fallo di mano *masc (in football)*

handbook NOUN
il manuale *masc*

handcuffs NOUN PL
le manette *fem pl*

handkerchief NOUN
il fazzoletto *masc*

handle NOUN
▷ *see also* **handle** VERB
1 la maniglia *fem*
□ the door handle la maniglia della porta
2 il manico *masc* (PL i manici)
□ a knife with a plastic handle un coltello con il manico di plastica

to **handle** VERB
▷ *see also* **handle** NOUN
1 occuparsi [56E] di
□ Kath handled the travel arrangements. Kath si è occupata dell'organizzazione del viaggio.
2 gestire [51]
□ It was a difficult situation, but he handled it well. Era una situazione difficile, ma l'ha gestita bene.
3 trattare [68]
□ She's good at handling children. Sa come trattare i bambini.
■ **'handle with care'** 'fragile'

handlebars NOUN PL
il manubrio *masc sing*

handmade ADJECTIVE
fatto a mano (FEM fatta a mano)

handsome ADJECTIVE
bello (FEM bella)
□ My father's very handsome. Mio padre è proprio un bell'uomo.

handwriting NOUN
la scrittura *fem*

handy ADJECTIVE
1 pratico (FEM pratica, MASC PL pratici, FEM PL pratiche)
□ This knife's very handy. Questo coltello è molto pratico.
2 a portata di mano
□ Have you got a pen handy? Hai una penna a portata di mano?
■ **to come in handy** tornare [68E] utile □ The money came in very handy. Il denaro è tornato molto utile.

to **hang** VERB
1 appendere [8]
□ He hung the painting on the wall. Ha appeso il quadro al muro.
2 pendere [8]
□ There was a red bulb hanging from the ceiling. C'era una lampadina rossa che pendeva dal soffitto.
3 impiccare [18]
□ In the past criminals were hanged. In passato i criminali venivano impiccati.

to **hang around** VERB
1 gironzolare [68] *(loiter)*
2 restare [68E] ad aspettare *(wait)*

to **hang on** VERB
aspettare [68]
□ Hang on a minute please. Aspetta un momento per favore.

h

to **hang up** VERB
1 appendere [8] *(clothes)*
2 riattaccare [18] *(phone)*
  ■ **to hang up on somebody** mettere [59] giù il ricevitore a qualcuno

hanger NOUN
la gruccia *fem* (PL le grucce) *(for clothes)*

hang-gliding NOUN
il deltaplano *masc*

hangover NOUN
i postumi della sbornia *masc pl*
  □ I woke up with a hangover. Mi sono svegliato coi postumi della sbornia.

Hanukkah NOUN
Hanukkah

to **happen** VERB
succedere [110ᴱ]
  □ What happened? Cos'è successo?
  ■ **as it happens** per combinazione
  ■ **Do you happen to know if...** Sai per caso se...

happily ADVERB
1 felicemente
  □ He's happily married. È felicemente sposato.
  ■ **... and they lived happily ever after.** ... e vissero felici e contenti.
2 fortunatamente
  □ Happily, everything went well. Fortunatamente tutto è andato bene.

happiness NOUN
la felicità *fem*

happy ADJECTIVE
1 felice (FEM felice)
  □ Janet looks happy. Janet sembra felice.

WORD POWER

You can use a number of other words instead of **happy** to mean 'glad':
cheerful allegro
  □ a cheerful song una canzone allegra
delighted contentissimo
  □ I'm delighted. Sono contentissimo.
glad contento
  □ I'm glad you're here. Sono contenta che tu sia qui.

---

2 soddisfatto (FEM soddisfatta)
  □ I'm very happy with your work. Sono molto soddisfatto del tuo lavoro.
  ■ **Happy birthday!** Buon compleanno!
  ■ **a happy ending** un lieto fine

harassment NOUN SING
  ■ **sexual harassment** molestie sessuali *fem pl*

harbour (US **harbor**) NOUN
il porto *masc*

hard ADJECTIVE, ADVERB
1 duro (FEM dura)
  □ This cheese is very hard. Questo formaggio è proprio duro.

---

2 difficile (FEM difficile)
  □ This exercise is too hard for me. Quest'esercizio è troppo difficile per me.
  ■ **to work hard** lavorare [68] sodo
  ■ **hard cash** il denaro in contanti
  ■ **to be hard up** essere [47ᴱ] a corto di soldi

hard disk NOUN
il disco rigido *masc* (PL i dischi rigidi)

hardly ADVERB
appena
  □ I hardly know you. Ti conosco appena.
  ■ **I've got hardly any money.** Ho pochissimo denaro.
  ■ **hardly ever** quasi mai
  ■ **hardly anything** quasi niente

hare NOUN
la lepre *fem*

to **harm** VERB
  ▷ *see also* **harm** NOUN
  ■ **to harm somebody** far [49] male a qualcuno
  ■ **to harm something** danneggiare [58] qualcosa

harm NOUN
  ▷ *see also* **harm** VERB
  □ It might do more harm than good. Potrebbe fare più male che bene.
  ■ **There's no harm trying.** Tentar non nuoce.

harmful ADJECTIVE
dannoso (FEM dannosa)

harmless ADJECTIVE
innocuo (FEM innocua)

harsh ADJECTIVE
1 severo (FEM severa)
  □ harsh punishment una punizione severa
2 sgradevole (FEM sgradevole)
  □ She's got a very harsh voice. Ha una voce molto sgradevole.

has VERB ▷ *see* **have**

hashtag NOUN
l' hashtag *masc* (PL gli hashtag) *(on Twittter)*

hasn't = **has not**

hat NOUN
il cappello *masc*

to **hate** VERB
odiare [17]

hatred NOUN
l' odio *masc*

haunted ADJECTIVE
  ■ **a haunted castle** un castello infestato dagli spiriti

to **have** VERB
1 avere [12]
  □ Do you have any brothers or sisters? Hai fratelli o sorelle? □ He has one brother and two sisters. Ha un fratello e due sorelle. □ I had no idea you were here. Non avevo idea che fossi qui.

LANGUAGE TIP When translating perfect tenses remember that some Italian verbs take **avere** and others take **essere**. When a verb has an object the auxiliary is always **avere**.

□ I've seen that film. Ho visto quel film. □ If you had phoned me I'd have come round. Se mi avessi telefonato sarei venuto.

LANGUAGE TIP When the Italian verb takes **essere**, the past participle agrees with the subject of the sentence.

□ They've arrived. Sono arrivati. □ Has he ever been to Paris? È mai stato a Parigi? □ Has she gone? È andata via?

LANGUAGE TIP Reflexive verbs always take **essere**.

□ Lucy has hurt herself. Lucy si è fatta male.

LANGUAGE TIP The reply to a question containing 'to have' either has no verb in Italian, or the verb in full.

□ Have you read that book? — Yes, I have. Hai letto quel libro? — Sì, l'ho letto. □ Has he told you? — No, he hasn't. Te l'ha detto? — No.
- **You've done it, haven't you?** Lo hai fatto, vero?
- **to have got** avere [12] □ He's got blue eyes. Ha gli occhi azzurri. □ Have you got any brothers or sisters? Hai fratelli o sorelle?

2 fare [49]
□ He's already had breakfast. Ha già fatto colazione. □ We're going to have a party. Faremo una festa.

3 prendere [77]
□ I'll have a coffee. Prendo un caffè.
- **to have to do something** dover [42] fare qualcosa □ She had to do it. Ha dovuto farlo.
- **She has got to do it.** Deve farlo.
- **to have one's hair cut** farsi [49ᴱ] tagliare i capelli
- **to have a look** dare [30] un'occhiata

haven't = have not

hay NOUN
il fieno *masc*

hay fever NOUN
la febbre da fieno *fem*

hazelnut NOUN
la nocciola *fem*

he PRONOUN
lui
□ He loves dogs. Lui ama i cani.

LANGUAGE TIP 'he' is often not translated.
□ 'Come here,' he said. 'Vieni qui,' disse.

LANGUAGE TIP **lui** is the pronoun used in spoken and informal written Italian. The more formal word for 'he' is **egli**.

head NOUN
▷ *see also* **head** VERB
1 la testa *fem*
□ Mind your head! Attento alla testa! □ He

lost his head and started screaming. Ha perso la testa e ha cominciato a gridare.
- **I've got no head for figures.** Sono negato per la matematica.
- **Heads or tails? — Heads.** Testa o croce? — Testa.
- **to keep one's head** mantenere [113] la calma □ She always manages to keep her head in difficult situations. Riesce sempre a mantenere la calma nelle situazioni difficili.

2 il/la preside *masc/fem (of school)*
- **a head of state** un capo di stato

to head VERB
▷ *see also* **head** NOUN
essere [47ᴱ] in cima a
□ She headed the list. Era in cima all'elenco.
- **to head the ball** colpire [51] la palla di testa
- **to head for...** dirigersi [36ᴱ] verso... □ They headed for the church. Si sono diretti verso la chiesa.

headache NOUN
il mal di testa *masc*
□ I've got a headache. Ho mal di testa.

headlight NOUN
il faro *masc*

headline NOUN
il titolo *masc*

headmaster NOUN
il preside *masc*

headmistress NOUN
la preside *fem*

head office NOUN
la sede centrale *fem*

headphones NOUN PL
la cuffia *fem*

headquarters NOUN PL
la sede centrale *fem sing (of organization)*

head teacher NOUN
il/la preside *masc/fem*

head waiter NOUN
il capocameriere *masc*

to heal VERB
guarire [51ᴱ]

LANGUAGE TIP When an auxiliary is needed to form past tenses use 'essere' when **guarire** does not have an object.
□ The wound healed. La ferita è guarita.

health NOUN
la salute *fem*
□ She's in good health. È in buona salute.
- **the Department of Health** il Ministero della Sanità

healthy ADJECTIVE
sano (FEM sana)

heap NOUN
il mucchio *masc*
□ a heap of stones un mucchio di sassi
- **heaps of time** un sacco di tempo

to **hear** VERB
sentire [41]
□ I didn't hear anything. Non ho sentito niente.
□ She can't hear very well. Non sente molto
bene. □ Can you hear me? Mi senti?
■ **to hear about something** sentir [41]
parlare di qualcosa
■ **to hear from somebody** ricevere [27]
notizie da qualcuno

heart NOUN
il cuore *masc*
□ heart trouble disturbi di cuore
■ **the ace of hearts** l'asso di cuori
■ **to learn something by heart** imparare [68]
qualcosa a memoria

heart attack NOUN
l' infarto *masc*
■ **to have a heart attack** avere [12] un infarto

heartbroken ADJECTIVE
■ **to be heartbroken** avere [12] il cuore
infranto

heart failure NOUN
l' arresto cardiaco *masc*

heat NOUN
▷ *see also* **heat** VERB
il calore *masc*
□ the heat of the sun il calore del sole
■ **Take the pan off the heat.** Togli la pentola
dal fuoco.

to **heat** VERB
▷ *see also* **heat** NOUN
scaldare [68]
□ Heat gently for five minutes. Scaldare a fuoco
lento per cinque minuti.

to **heat up** VERB
riscaldare [68]

heater NOUN
1 la stufa *fem*
□ I had the heater on. Avevo la stufa accesa.
■ **an electric heater** una stufa elettrica
■ **a water heater** uno scaldaacqua
2 il riscaldamento *masc (in car)*
□ Could you put on the heater? Puoi
accendere il riscaldamento?

heather NOUN
l' erica *fem*

heating NOUN
il riscaldamento *masc*

heaven NOUN
il paradiso *masc*

heavily ADVERB
1 molto
□ It rained heavily in the night. Ha piovuto
molto durante la notte. □ He drinks heavily.
Beve molto.
2 pesantemente
□ She sat down heavily on the sofa. Si è
seduta pesantemente sul divano.

■ **He's a heavily built man.** È un uomo di
corporatura robusta.

heavy ADJECTIVE
1 pesante (FEM pesante)
□ This bag's very heavy. Questa borsa è molto
pesante.
2 forte (FEM forte)
□ heavy rain forte pioggia
■ **to be a heavy drinker** essere [47E] un forte
bevitore

he'd = he would, he had

hedge NOUN
la siepe *fem*

hedgehog NOUN
il riccio *masc*

heel NOUN
1 il tacco *masc* (PL i tacchi)
□ high heels tacchi alti
2 il tallone *masc (part of foot)*

height NOUN
l' altezza *fem*

heir NOUN
l' erede *masc*

heiress NOUN
l' erede *fem*

held VERB ▷ *see* hold

helicopter NOUN
l' elicottero *masc*

hell NOUN
l' inferno *masc*
□ He'll go to hell. Andrà all'inferno.
■ **Hell!** Porca miseria!
■ **It's a hell of a mess!** È un casino!

he'll = he will, he shall

hello EXCLAMATION
1 ciao *(to somebody you address as 'tu')*
2 salve *(also to somebody you address as 'lei')*
3 pronto *(on the phone)*

helmet NOUN
il casco *masc* (PL i caschi)

to **help** VERB
▷ *see also* **help** NOUN
aiutare [68]
□ Can you help me? Mi puoi aiutare? □ I'll help
you carry it. Ti aiuto a portarlo.
■ **Help yourself!** Serviti pure!
■ **I couldn't help laughing.** Non ho potuto
fare a meno di ridere.

help NOUN
▷ *see also* **help** VERB
l' aiuto *masc*

help desk NOUN
il servizio assistenza *masc* (PL i servizi
assistenza)
■ **an IT help desk** un servizio di assistenza
informatica

helpful ADJECTIVE
1 disponibile (FEM disponibile)

□ The staff are always helpful. Il personale è sempre disponibile.

2 utile (FEM utile)

□ He gave me some helpful advice. Mi ha dato dei consigli utili.

helpline NOUN
il servizio di assistenza telefonica *masc*

■ **a customer helpline** un servizio assistenza clienti □ Why don't you ring the customer helpline? Perché non telefoni al servizio assistenza clienti?

hen NOUN
la gallina *fem*

her ADJECTIVE
▷ *see also* **her** PRONOUN
1 il suo *masc* (PL i suoi)

□ her address il suo indirizzo □ her parents i suoi genitori

2 la sua *fem* (PL le sue)

□ her house la sua casa □ her best friends le sue migliori amiche

3 suo *masc* (PL suoi)

□ Sarah and her father Sarah e suo padre

4 sua *fem* (PL sue)

□ her aunt sua zia

> **LANGUAGE TIP** 'her' is often not translated.
□ She's lost her wallet. Ha perduto il portafoglio. □ with her hands in her pockets con le mani in tasca □ She took off her coat. Si è tolta il cappotto. □ She washed her hair this morning. Si è lavata i capelli stamattina.

her PRONOUN
▷ *see also* **her** ADJECTIVE
1 la

□ I saw her. L'ho vista. □ Look at her! Guardala!

2 le *(to her)*

□ I gave her a book. Le ho dato un libro.

3 lei

> **LANGUAGE TIP** lei is used after a preposition.
□ I'm going with her. Vado con lei. □ I'm older than her. Sono più vecchio di lei.

herb NOUN
l' erba aromatica *fem* (PL le erbe aromatiche) *(for cooking)*

here ADVERB
qui

□ I live here. Vivo qui.

■ **here is** ecco □ Here he is! Eccolo qui!

■ **here are** ecco □ Here are the books. Ecco i libri.

heritage NOUN

■ **cultural heritage** il patrimonio culturale

hero NOUN
l' eroe *masc*

heroin NOUN
l' eroina *fem (drug)*

■ **heroin addict** l' eroinomane *masc/fem*

heroine NOUN
l' eroina *fem (of novel)*

hers PRONOUN

> **LANGUAGE TIP** The Italian pronoun agrees with the noun it is replacing.
1 il suo (PL i suoi)

□ my dog and hers il mio cane e il suo □ my parents and hers i miei genitori e i suoi

2 la sua *fem* (PL le sue)

□ My car is older than hers. La mia macchina è più vecchia della sua. □ my friends and hers le mie amiche e le sue

3 suo *masc* (PL suoi) *(her property)*

□ Whose is this? — It's hers. Di chi è questo? — È suo.

4 sua *fem* (PL sue) *(her property)*

□ Is that car hers? È sua quella macchina?

■ **a friend of hers** una sua amica

herself PRONOUN
1 si

> **LANGUAGE TIP** A verb + 'herself' is often translated by a reflexive verb in Italian.
□ She's hurt herself. Si è fatta male. □ She looked at herself in the mirror. Si è guardata allo specchio.

2 lei *(emphatic use)*

□ She did it herself. L'ha fatto lei.

3 sé *(following preposition)*

□ She talked about herself. Ha parlato di sé.

■ **by herself** da sola □ She doesn't like travelling by herself. Non le piace viaggiare da sola.

he's = **he is, he has**

to **hesitate** VERB
esitare [68]

heterosexual ADJECTIVE
eterosessuale (FEM eterosessuale)

hi EXCLAMATION
1 ciao *(to somebody you address as 'tu')*

2 salve *(also to somebody you address as 'lei')*

hiccup NOUN
il problemino *masc*

□ The project is on course, despite one or two hiccups. Il programma è in atto nonostante uno o due problemini.

■ **to have hiccups** avere [12] il singhiozzo

to **hide** VERB
1 nascondere [64]

□ Paula hid the present. Paula ha nascosto il regalo.

2 nascondersi [64E]

□ He hid behind a bush. Si è nascosto dietro ad un cespuglio.

hideous ADJECTIVE
orribile (FEM orribile)

hi-fi NOUN
l' hi-fi *masc* (PL gli hi-fi)

high ADJECTIVE, ADVERB

1 alto (FEM alta)

□ The wall's two metres high. Il muro è alto due metri. □ Prices are higher in Germany. I prezzi sono più alti in Germania. □ The plane flew high over the mountains. L'aereo volava alto sulle montagne.

■ **to be high in something** avere [12] un alto contenuto di qualcosa □ It's very high in fat. Ha un altissimo contenuto di grassi.

2 forte (FEM forte)

□ There's high unemployment in Europe. C'è una forte disoccupazione in Europa.

3 acuto (FEM acuta)

□ She's got a very high voice. Ha una voce molto acuta.

■ **to be high** (on drugs) essere [47ᴱ] fatto
■ **the high season** l'alta stagione
■ **the high street** la via principale

high-heeled ADJECTIVE
con i tacchi alti

high jump NOUN
il salto in alto masc

highlight NOUN
▷ see also highlight VERB

1 il clou masc (PL i clou)

□ the highlight of the evening il clou della serata

2 il momento più bello masc

□ the highlight of the holiday il momento più bello della vacanza

to highlight VERB
▷ see also highlight NOUN
mettere [59] in evidenza

highlighter NOUN
l' evidenziatore masc

high-rise ADJECTIVE
■ **a high-rise building** un palazzone

high school NOUN
la scuola secondaria fem

to hijack VERB
dirottare [68]

hijacker NOUN
il dirottatore masc
la dirottatrice fem

hike NOUN
l' escursione a piedi fem

hiking NOUN
■ **to go hiking** fare [49] escursioni a piedi

hilarious ADJECTIVE
spassosissimo (FEM spassosissima)

hill NOUN
la collina fem

hill-walking NOUN
■ **to go hill-walking** fare [49] passeggiate in collina

him PRONOUN

1 lo

□ I saw him. L'ho visto. □ Look at him! Guardalo!

2 gli (to him)

□ I gave him a book. Gli ho dato un libro.

3 lui

LANGUAGE TIP lui is used after a preposition.

□ I'm going with him. Vado con lui. □ I'm older than him. Sono più vecchio di lui.

himself PRONOUN

1 si

LANGUAGE TIP A verb + 'himself' is often translated by a reflexive verb in Italian.

□ He's hurt himself. Si è fatto male. □ He was looking at himself in the mirror. Si guardava allo specchio.

2 lui (emphatic use)

□ He did it himself. L'ha fatto lui.

3 sé (following preposition)

□ He talked about himself. Ha parlato di sé.

■ **by himself** da solo □ He doesn't like travelling by himself. Non gli piace viaggiare da solo.

Hindu ADJECTIVE
indù (FEM+PL indù)

hint NOUN
▷ see also hint VERB

■ **to give a hint** dare [30] un'indicazione □ Give me a hint. Dammi un'indicazione.

■ **to drop a hint** lasciar [13] capire □ He dropped a hint that he was leaving. Ha lasciato capire che stava partendo.

■ **to take a hint** capire [51] l'antifona □ I told him I was a bit tired, but he didn't take the hint. Gli ho detto che ero un po' stanca, ma non ha capito l'antifona.

■ **a hint of garlic** una puntina d'aglio

to hint VERB
▷ see also hint NOUN
lasciar [13] intendere

□ He hinted I might get the job. Ha lasciato intendere che avrei potuto ottenere il lavoro.

hip NOUN
il fianco masc (PL i fianchi)

□ She put her hands on her hips. Si è messa le mani sui fianchi.

hippie NOUN

1 l' hippy masc (PL gli hippy)
2 la hippy (PL le hippy)

hippo NOUN
l' ippopotamo masc

to hire VERB
▷ see also hire NOUN

1 noleggiare [58]

□ We hired a car. Abbiamo noleggiato una macchina.

2 assumere [11]

□ They hired a lawyer. Hanno assunto un avvocato.

hire NOUN
▷ *see also* **hire** VERB
il noleggio *masc*
■ **car hire** noleggio dell'auto
■ **for hire** a noleggio
■ **a hire car** un'auto a noleggio

his ADJECTIVE
▷ *see also* **his** PRONOUN
1 il suo *masc* (PL i suoi)
□ his address il suo indirizzo □ his parents i suoi genitori
2 la sua *fem* (PL le sue)
□ his house la sua casa □ his opinions le sue opinioni
3 suo *masc* (PL suoi)
□ Joe and his father Joe e suo padre
4 sua *fem* (PL sue)
□ his aunt sua zia

LANGUAGE TIP 'his' is often not translated.
□ He took off his coat. Si è tolto il cappotto.
□ He's washing his hair. Si sta lavando i capelli.

his PRONOUN
▷ *see also* **his** ADJECTIVE

LANGUAGE TIP The Italian pronoun agrees with the noun it is replacing.
1 il suo *masc* (PL i suoi)
□ my dog and his il mio cane e il suo □ my parents and his i miei genitori e i suoi
2 la sua *fem* (PL le sue)
□ My car is older than his. La mia macchina è più vecchia della sua. □ my shoes and his le mie scarpe e le sue
3 suo *masc* (PL suoi) *(his property)*
□ Whose is this? — It's his. Di chi è questo? — È suo.
4 sua *fem* (PL sue) *(his property)*
□ Is that car his? È sua quella macchina?
■ **a friend of his** un suo amico

history NOUN
la storia *fem*

to **hit** VERB
▷ *see also* **hit** NOUN
1 colpire [51]
□ He hit the ball. Ha colpito la palla.
■ **to hit the target** colpire [51] il bersaglio
2 picchiare [17]
□ Andrew hit him. Andrew l'ha picchiato.
3 urtare [68]
□ He was hit by a car. È stato urtato da una macchina.
■ **to hit it off with somebody** andare [6ᴱ] d'accordo con qualcuno

hit NOUN
▷ *see also* **hit** VERB
il successo *masc*
□ the band's latest hit l'ultimo successo del complesso

hitch NOUN
l' intoppo *masc*

□ There's been a slight hitch. C'è stato un piccolo intoppo.

to **hitchhike** VERB
fare [49] autostop

hitchhiker NOUN
l' autostoppista *masc/fem*

hitchhiking NOUN
l' autostop *masc*

hit man NOUN
il sicario *masc*

HIV-negative ADJECTIVE
sieronegativo (FEM sieronegativa)

HIV-positive ADJECTIVE
sieropositivo (FEM sieropositiva)

hobby NOUN
l' hobby *masc* (PL gli hobby)

hockey NOUN
l' hockey *masc*

to **hold** VERB
1 tenere [113]
□ He was holding her in his arms. La teneva tra le braccia.
2 tenere [113] in braccio
□ She was holding the baby. Teneva in braccio il bambino. □ He held the pistol in his right hand. Teneva la pistola con la mano destra.
3 contenere [113]
□ It holds ten litres. Contiene dieci litri.
■ **Hold the line!** *(on the phone)* Resti in linea!
■ **Hold it!** Fermati!
■ **to get hold of something** procurarsi [56ᴱ] qualcosa

to **hold on** VERB
aspettare [68]
□ Hold on, I'm coming! Aspettami, arrivo!
■ **Hold on!** *(on the phone)* Resti in linea!

to **hold on to** VERB
1 tenersi [113ᴱ] stretto a
□ Hold on to the rail. Tieniti stretto alla ringhiera.
2 conservare [68]
□ He managed to hold on to his job. È riuscito a conservare il posto di lavoro.

to **hold up** VERB
1 alzare [68]
□ Peter held up his hand. Peter ha alzato la mano.
2 trattenere [113]
□ I was held up at the office. Sono stato trattenuto in ufficio.
3 rapinare [68] *(bank)*

hold-up NOUN
1 la rapina *fem*
□ A bank clerk was injured in the hold-up. Un impiegato di banca è rimasto ferito nella rapina.
2 l' intoppo *masc*
□ No one explained the reason for the hold-up. Nessuno ha spiegato i motivi dell'intoppo.

h

429

3 l' ingorgo *masc* (PL gli ingorghi)
□ a hold-up on the motorway un ingorgo sull'autostrada

hole NOUN
il buco *masc* (PL i buchi)

holiday NOUN
1 la vacanza *fem*
□ the school holidays le vacanze scolastiche
■ **on holiday** in vacanza
2 la festa *fem*
□ Next Monday is a holiday. Lunedì prossimo è festa.
3 le ferie *fem pl* (time off work)
□ He took a day's holiday. Ha preso un giorno di ferie.

holiday home NOUN
la seconda casa per le vacanze *fem*

Holland NOUN
l'Olanda

hollow ADJECTIVE
cavo (FEM cava)

holly NOUN
l' agrifoglio *masc*

holy ADJECTIVE
santo (FEM santa)

home NOUN, ADVERB
la casa *fem*
□ at home a casa □ I'll be home at five o'clock. Sarò a casa alle cinque.
■ **Make yourself at home.** Fai come se fossi a casa tua.
■ **to get home** arrivare [68] a casa

home address NOUN
l' indirizzo di casa *fem*

homeland NOUN
la patria *fem*

homeless ADJECTIVE, NOUN
il senzatetto *masc*
■ **the homeless** i senzatetto

home match NOUN
la partita in casa *fem*

homeopathy NOUN
l' omeopatia *fem*

home page NOUN
l' home page *fem* (PL le home page)

homesick ADJECTIVE
■ **to be homesick** avere [12] nostalgia di casa

homework NOUN
i compiti *masc pl*
□ Have you done your homework? Hai fatto i compiti?

homosexual ADJECTIVE
omosessuale (FEM omosessuale)

honest ADJECTIVE
onesto (FEM onesta)
□ an honest man un uomo onesto
■ **To be honest...** Onestamente...
■ **Tell me your honest opinion.** Dimmi cosa ne pensi sinceramente.

honestly ADVERB
onestamente
□ Did you honestly think we wouldn't notice? Pensavi onestamente che non l'avremmo notato?

honesty NOUN
l' onestà *fem*

honey NOUN
il miele *masc*
□ a pot of honey un vaso di miele
■ **Hi honey, I'm here!** Ciao cara, sono qui!

honeymoon NOUN
il viaggio di nozze *masc*

honour (US **honor**) NOUN
l' onore *masc*
□ I would consider it an honour. Sarebbe un onore per me.

honours degree NOUN
la laurea *fem*
■ **to get an honours degree** laurearsi [56ᴱ]

hood NOUN
1 il cappuccio *masc*
□ a coat with a hood un cappotto con il cappuccio
2 il cofano *masc* (US: of car)

hook NOUN
1 il gancio *masc*
□ He hung the painting on the hook. Ha appeso il quadro al gancio.
2 l' amo *masc*
□ He felt a fish pull at his hook. Ha sentito che un pesce abboccava all'amo.
■ **to take the phone off the hook** staccare [18] il ricevitore

hooligan NOUN
il teppista *masc*

hooray EXCLAMATION
urrà!

Hoover® NOUN
l' aspirapolvere *masc* (PL gli aspirapolvere)

to hoover VERB
passare [68] l'aspirapolvere

to hop VERB
1 saltellare [68] (animal)
2 saltellare [68] su un piede (person)

to hope VERB
▷ see also **hope** NOUN
sperare [68]
□ I hope he comes. Spero che venga. □ I hope so. Spero di sì. □ I hope not. Spero di no.

hope NOUN
▷ see also **hope** VERB
la speranza *fem*
■ **to give up hope** abbandonare [68] le speranze

hopeful ADJECTIVE
1 ottimista (FEM ottimista)
□ I'm hopeful. Sono ottimista.
■ **He's hopeful of winning.** Conta di vincere.
2 incoraggiante (FEM incoraggiante)

□ The prospects look hopeful. Le prospettive sembrano incoraggianti.

hopefully ADVERB
■ **Hopefully he'll make it in time.** Si spera che arrivi in tempo.

hopeless ADJECTIVE
1 impossibile (FEM impossibile)

□ a hopeless task un compito impossibile
2 inutile

□ It's hopeless to try and change her mind. È inutile cercare di farle cambiare idea.

■ **They feel hopeless about job prospects.** Sentono di non avere prospettive di lavoro.

■ **to be hopeless at something** essere [47E] completamente negato per qualcosa

■ **a hopeless case** un caso disperato

horizon NOUN
l' orizzonte *masc*

horizontal ADJECTIVE
orizzontale (FEM orizzontale)

horn NOUN
1 il clacson *masc* (PL i clacson)

□ He sounded the horn. Ha suonato il clacson.
2 il corno *masc* (of animal)

horoscope NOUN
l' oroscopo *masc*

horrible ADJECTIVE
orribile (FEM orribile)

to **horrify** VERB
lasciare [13] inorridito

□ I was horrified by the news. La notizia mi ha lasciato inorridito.

horrifying ADJECTIVE
spaventoso (FEM spaventosa)

horror NOUN
1 l' orrore *masc*

□ To my horror I discovered I was locked out. Ho scoperto con orrore di essere rimasto chiuso fuori.
2 il terrore *masc*

□ She has a horror of spiders. Ha il terrore dei ragni.

■ **a horror film** un film dell'orrore

horse NOUN
il cavallo *masc*

horse-racing NOUN
l' ippica *fem*

horseshoe NOUN
il ferro di cavallo *masc*

hose NOUN
il tubo di gomma *masc*

hosepipe NOUN
il tubo di gomma *masc*

hospital NOUN
l' ospedale *masc*

hospitality NOUN
l' ospitalità *fem*

host NOUN
1 l' ospite *masc*

□ We thanked our hosts. Abbiamo ringraziato i nostri ospiti.
2 il mucchio *masc*

□ a host of problems un mucchio di problemi

hostage NOUN
l' ostaggio *masc*

■ **to take somebody hostage** prendere [77] qualcuno in ostaggio

hostel NOUN
l' ostello *masc*

□ youth hostel ostello della gioventù

hostess NOUN
1 l' ospite *fem*

□ We thanked our hostess. Abbiamo ringraziato la nostra ospite.
2 l' hostess *fem* (PL le hostess) (on plane)

hostile ADJECTIVE
ostile (FEM ostile)

hot ADJECTIVE
1 caldo (FEM calda)

□ a hot bath un bagno caldo □ I'm hot. Ho caldo. □ It's hot today. Fa caldo oggi.
2 piccante

□ Indian food's too hot for me. Il cibo indiano è troppo piccante per me.

hot dog NOUN
l' hot-dog *masc* (PL gli hot-dog)

hotel NOUN
l' albergo *masc* (PL gli alberghi)

hour NOUN
l' ora *fem*

□ a quarter of an hour un quarto d'ora □ two and a half hours due ore e mezza □ half an hour mezz'ora

■ **They work long hours.** Hanno una giornata lavorativa molto lunga.

hourly ADJECTIVE, ADVERB
■ **There are hourly buses.** Ci sono autobus ogni ora.

■ **to be paid hourly** essere [47E] pagato all'ora

house NOUN
la casa *fem*

□ at his house a casa sua

housewife NOUN
la casalinga *fem* (PL le casalinghe)

housework NOUN
i lavori di casa *masc pl*

hovercraft NOUN
l' hovercraft *masc* (PL gli hovercraft)

how ADVERB
come

□ How are you? Come stai? □ How do you say 'apple' in Italian? Come si traduce 'apple' in italiano?

■ **How many?** Quanti?
■ **How much?** Quanto?
■ **How old are you?** Quanti anni hai?
■ **How far is it to Edinburgh?** Quanto dista Edimburgo?

h

■ **How long have you been here?** Da quanto tempo sei qui?
■ **How long does it take?** Quanto tempo ci vuole?

however CONJUNCTION
tuttavia

to **howl** VERB
1 ululare [68]
□ The dog howled all night. Il cane ha ululato tutta la notte.
2 urlare [68]
□ He howled with pain. Urlava dal dolore.

HTML NOUN
l' HTML *masc*

to **hug** VERB
▷ *see also* **hug** NOUN
abbracciare [13]

hug NOUN
▷ *see also* **hug** VERB
■ **to give somebody a hug** abbracciare [13] qualcuno

huge ADJECTIVE
enorme (FEM enorme)

to **hum** VERB
canticchiare [17]

human ADJECTIVE
umano (FEM umana)
■ **a human being** un essere umano

humble ADJECTIVE
umile (FEM umile)

humour (US **humor**) NOUN
l' umorismo *masc*
■ **to have a sense of humour** avere [12] il senso dell'umorismo

hundred NUMBER
■ **a hundred** cento

> LANGUAGE TIP When 'hundred' follows any number except one, -**cento** is added to the number.

□ three hundred boys and five hundred girls trecento ragazzi e cinquecento ragazze
■ **hundreds of people** centinaia di persone

hung VERB ▷ *see* **hang**

Hungary NOUN
l'Ungheria

hunger NOUN
la fame *fem*

hungry ADJECTIVE
■ **to be hungry** avere [12] fame □ I'm not hungry. Non ho fame.

to **hunt** VERB
1 dare [30] la caccia a
□ They hunt foxes. Danno la caccia alle volpi.
2 cercare [18]
□ The police are hunting the killer. La polizia sta cercando il killer.
■ **to hunt for something** cercare [18]

qualcosa □ I hunted everywhere for that book. Ho cercato quel libro dappertutto.

hunting NOUN
la caccia *fem*
□ fox hunting caccia alla volpe
■ **to go hunting** andare [6ᴱ] a caccia

hurdle NOUN
l' ostacolo *masc*
■ **the 100 metres hurdles** i 100 metri ad ostacoli

hurricane NOUN
l' uragano *masc*

to **hurry** VERB
▷ *see also* **hurry** NOUN
affrettarsi [56ᴱ]
□ Sharon hurried back home. Sharon si affrettò a tornare a casa.
■ **Hurry up!** Sbrigati!

hurry NOUN
▷ *see also* **hurry** VERB
la fretta *fem*
□ There's no hurry. Non c'è fretta.
■ **to be in a hurry** avere [12] fretta
■ **to do something in a hurry** fare [49] qualcosa in fretta

to **hurt** VERB
▷ *see also* **hurt** ADJECTIVE
1 fare [49] male
□ That hurts. Fa male.
■ **to hurt somebody** fare [49] male a qualcuno □ You're hurting me! Mi fai male! □ Have you hurt yourself? Ti sei fatto male? □ My leg hurts. Mi fa male la gamba.
2 ferire [51]
□ His criticisms really hurt me. Le sue critiche mi hanno proprio ferito.

hurt ADJECTIVE
▷ *see also* **hurt** VERB
ferito (FEM ferita)
□ Is he badly hurt? È ferito gravemente?
■ **to get hurt** farsi [49ᴱ] male □ Nobody got hurt. Nessuno si è fatto male.

husband NOUN
il marito *masc*

hut NOUN
la capanna *fem*

hybrid ADJECTIVE
ibrido (FEM ibrida)
□ a hybrid car un'auto ibrida

hymn NOUN
l' inno *masc*

hypermarket NOUN
l' ipermercato *masc*

hypertext NOUN
l' ipertesto *masc*

hyphen NOUN
il trattino *masc*

h

I PRONOUN
io
□ Ann and I Ann ed io
LANGUAGE TIP 'I' is often not translated.
□ I love cats. Amo i gatti.

ice NOUN
il ghiaccio *masc*
□ a sheet of ice una lastra di ghiaccio

iceberg NOUN
l' iceberg *masc* (PL gli iceberg)

icebox NOUN (US)
il frigorifero *masc*

ice cream NOUN
il gelato *masc*
□ a vanilla ice cream un gelato alla vaniglia

ice cube NOUN
il cubetto di ghiaccio *masc*

ice hockey NOUN
l' hockey su ghiaccio *masc*

Iceland NOUN
l' Islanda *fem*

ice lolly NOUN
il ghiacciolo *masc*

ice rink NOUN
la pista di pattinaggio su ghiaccio *fem*

ice-skating NOUN
il pattinaggio su ghiaccio *masc*
■ **to go ice-skating** andare [6ᴱ] a pattinare sul ghiaccio

icing NOUN
la glassa *fem (on cake)*
■ **icing sugar** zucchero a velo

icon NOUN
l' icona *fem*

icy ADJECTIVE
1 gelido (FEM gelida)
□ an icy wind un vento gelido
2 ghiacciato
□ The roads are icy. Le strade sono ghiacciate.

I'd = I had, I would

idea NOUN
l' idea *fem*

ideal ADJECTIVE
ideale (FEM ideale)

identical ADJECTIVE
identico (FEM identica, MASC PL identici, FEM PL identiche)

identification NOUN
1 il documento d'identità *masc*
□ Have you got any identification? Ha un documento d'identità?
2 l' individuazione *fem*
□ the identification of genes l'individuazione dei geni
3 l' identificazione *fem*
□ the identification of bodies l'identificazione dei corpi

to identify VERB
1 individuare [68]
□ We have identified the problem. Abbiamo individuato il problema.
2 identificare [18]
□ The police have identified the body. La polizia ha identificato il corpo.

identity NOUN
l' identità *fem*

identity card NOUN
la carta d'identità *fem*

DID YOU KNOW...?
All Italians have an identity card.

idiom NOUN
l' espressione idiomatica *fem*

idiot NOUN
l' idiota *masc/fem*

idiotic ADJECTIVE
idiota (FEM idiota)

idle ADJECTIVE
■ **It's just idle gossip.** Sono solo chiacchiere futili.
■ **I asked out of idle curiosity.** L'ho chiesto per pura curiosità.
■ **to be idle** *(person)* non avere [12] niente da fare

i.e. ABBREVIATION *(= id est)*
cioè

if CONJUNCTION
se
□ You can have it if you like. Puoi prenderlo se vuoi. □ If I were you... Se fossi in te...
■ **if only** se solo □ If only I had more money! Se solo avessi più denaro!
■ **if not** altrimenti □ Are you coming? If not, I'll go with Mark. Vieni? Altrimenti vado con Mark.
■ **if so** allora □ Are you coming? If so, I'll wait. Vieni? Allora ti aspetto.

i

ignorant – improvement

ignorant ADJECTIVE
ignorante (FEM ignorante)

to **ignore** VERB
ignorare [68]

ill ADJECTIVE
ammalato (FEM ammalata)
□ He's seriously ill. È gravemente ammalato.
■ **to be taken ill** ammalarsi [56ᴱ] □ She was taken ill. Si è ammalata.
■ **ill at ease** a disagio

I'll = I will

illegal ADJECTIVE
illegale (FEM illegale)

illegible ADJECTIVE
illeggibile (FEM illeggibile)

ill feeling NOUN
il rancore masc

illness NOUN
la malattia fem

illusion NOUN
l' illusione fem

illustration NOUN
l' illustrazione fem

I'm = I am

image NOUN
l' immagine fem
□ The company has changed its image. La società ha cambiato immagine.

imagination NOUN
l' immaginazione fem
□ She has no imagination. Non ha immaginazione.

to **imagine** VERB
immaginare [68]

to **imitate** VERB
imitare [68]

imitation NOUN
l' imitazione fem
■ **imitation leather** finta pelle

immediate ADJECTIVE
immediato (FEM immediata)

immediately ADVERB
immediatamente

immigrant NOUN
l' immigrato masc
l' immigrata fem

immigration NOUN
l' immigrazione fem

immoral ADJECTIVE
immorale (FEM immorale)

impartial ADJECTIVE
imparziale (FEM imparziale)

impatience NOUN
l' impazienza fem

impatient ADJECTIVE
impaziente (FEM impaziente)
□ She was impatient to get back home. Era impaziente di tornare a casa.

■ **to get impatient** spazientirsi [51ᴱ] □ People are getting impatient. La gente si sta spazientendo.

impatiently ADVERB
con impazienza

impersonal ADJECTIVE
impersonale (FEM impersonale)

to **implement** VERB
attuare [68]
□ It'll take a few months to implement the plan. Ci vorranno alcuni mesi per attuare il piano.

to **imply** VERB
insinuare [68]
□ Are you implying I did it on purpose? Stai insinuando che l'ho fatto apposta?

importance NOUN
l' importanza fem

important ADJECTIVE
importante (FEM importante)

to **impose** VERB
imporre [73]

impossible ADJECTIVE
impossibile (FEM impossibile)

to **impress** VERB
1 colpire [51]
□ what impressed him most quello che l'ha colpito di più □ He really impressed me! Mi ha veramente colpito!
2 fare [49] buona impressione su
□ a group of students trying to impress their teacher un gruppo di studenti che cercavano di fare buona impressione sull'insegnante

impressed ADJECTIVE
colpito (FEM colpita)
□ I'm impressed! Sono colpito!

> **LANGUAGE TIP** Be careful not to translate **impressed** by **impressionato**.

impression NOUN
l' impressione fem
□ I was under the impression that... Avevo l'impressione che...

impressive ADJECTIVE
1 notevole (FEM notevole)
□ an impressive achievement un risultato notevole
2 imponente (FEM imponente) (building)

to **improve** VERB
migliorare [68]
□ He's improved his technique. Ha migliorato la tecnica.

> **LANGUAGE TIP** When an auxiliary is needed to form past tenses use **essere** when **migliorare** does not have an object.

□ My Italian improved a lot. Il mio italiano è migliorato molto.

improvement NOUN
il miglioramento masc

in PREPOSITION, ADVERB

1 in

□ **in the house** in casa □ **in the country** in campagna □ **in town** in città □ **in two thousand and two** nel duemila due □ **I did it in 3 hours.** L'ho fatto in tre ore. □ **in English** in inglese

■ **in time** in tempo

2 a

□ **in school** a scuola □ **in hospital** all'ospedale □ **in London** a Londra □ **It was written in pencil.** Era scritto a matita.

3 di

□ **the best pupil in the class** il migliore studente della classe □ **at six in the morning** alle sei del mattino □ **an increase in accidents** un aumento degli incidenti

■ **to be in** *(at home, work)* esserci [47ᴱ] □ **He wasn't in.** Non c'era.

■ **to ask somebody in** invitare [68] qualcuno ad entrare □ **Why don't you ask John in?** Perché non inviti John ad entrare?

■ **the boy in the blue shirt** il ragazzo con la camicia azzurra

■ **I'll see you in three weeks.** Ci vediamo tra tre settimane.

■ **You look good in that dress.** Quel vestito ti sta bene.

■ **in here** qui dentro

■ **in the rain** sotto la pioggia

■ **one person in ten** una persona su dieci

■ **in writing** per iscritto

■ **the in thing** la cosa che va di moda

inaccurate ADJECTIVE

inesatto (FEM inesatta)

inadequate ADJECTIVE

inadeguato (FEM inadeguata)

incentive NOUN

l' incentivo *masc*

□ **There's no incentive to work.** Non c'è alcun incentivo a lavorare.

inch NOUN

il pollice *masc*

> **DID YOU KNOW...?**
> In Italy measurements are in metres and centimetres rather than feet and inches. An inch is about 2.5 centimetres.

incident NOUN

l' incidente *masc*

□ **a minor incident** un piccolo incidente

inclined ADJECTIVE

■ **I'm inclined to agree with you.** Credo di essere d'accordo con te.

■ **Nobody seemed inclined to argue with Steve.** Nessuno sembrava propenso a litigare con Steve.

■ **He was inclined to self-pity.** Tendeva ad autocommiserarsi.

to **include** VERB

comprendere [77]

□ **Service is not included.** Il servizio non è compreso.

including PREPOSITION

compreso

□ **two hundred pounds, including tax** duecento sterline tasse comprese

inclusive ADJECTIVE

tutto compreso

□ **The inclusive price is two hundred pounds.** Il prezzo tutto compreso è di duecento sterline.

■ **inclusive of VAT** IVA compresa

income NOUN

il reddito *masc*

□ **low income families** famiglie a basso reddito

income tax NOUN

l' imposta sul reddito *masc*

incompetent ADJECTIVE

incompetente (FEM incompetente)

incomplete ADJECTIVE

incompleto (FEM incompleta)

inconsistent ADJECTIVE

incostante (FEM incostante)

□ **Your work this year has been very inconsistent.** Il tuo rendimento quest'anno è stato incostante.

■ **to be inconsistent with** essere [47ᴱ] in contraddizione con

inconvenience NOUN

il disturbo *masc*

□ **I don't want to cause any inconvenience.** Non vorrei dare disturbo.

inconvenient ADJECTIVE

■ **Is it an inconvenient time for you?** Ti è scomodo a quest'ora?

incorrect ADJECTIVE

1 inesatto (FEM inesatta)

□ **The information he gave me was incorrect.** Le informazioni che mi ha dato erano inesatte.

2 scorretto (FEM scorretta)

□ **incorrect posture** postura scorretta

increase NOUN

▷ *see also* **increase** VERB

l' aumento *masc*

□ **an increase in road accidents** un aumento degli incidenti stradali □ **a salary increase** un aumento di stipendio

to **increase** VERB

▷ *see also* **increase** NOUN

aumentare [68]

□ **They've increased the price.** Hanno aumentato il prezzo.

> **LANGUAGE TIP** When an auxiliary is needed to form past tenses use 'essere' when **aumentare** does not have an object.

□ **The number increased.** Il numero è aumentato.

i

incredible ADJECTIVE
incredibile (FEM incredibile)

indecisive ADJECTIVE
indeciso (FEM indecisa) *(person)*

indeed ADVERB
1 veramente
□ It's very hard indeed. È veramente molto difficile.
2 certamente
□ Know what I mean? — Indeed I do. Sai cosa intendo? — Certamente.
■ **Thank you very much indeed!** Grazie infinite!

independence NOUN
l' indipendenza *fem*

independent ADJECTIVE
indipendente (FEM indipendente)
□ **two independent studies** due studi indipendenti
■ **an independent school** una scuola privata

index NOUN
l' indice *masc*
□ Look in the index. Guarda nell'indice.

index finger NOUN
l' indice *masc*

India NOUN
l' India *fem*

Indian ADJECTIVE
▷ *see also* **Indian** NOUN
indiano (FEM indiana)

Indian NOUN
▷ *see also* **Indian** ADJECTIVE
l' indiano *masc*
l' indiana *fem*
■ **American Indians** gli indiani d'America

to **indicate** VERB
1 indicare [18]
□ This indicates a change in US policy. Questo indica un cambiamento della politica statunitense.
2 mettere [59] la freccia *(when driving)*

indigestion NOUN
■ **I've got indigestion.** Ho qualcosa sullo stomaco.

individual ADJECTIVE
▷ *see also* **individual** NOUN
individuale (FEM individuale)

individual NOUN
▷ *see also* **individual** ADJECTIVE
l' individuo *masc*

indoor ADJECTIVE
coperto (FEM coperta)
□ an indoor swimming pool una piscina coperta

indoors ADVERB
dentro
□ They're indoors. Sono dentro.

industrial ADJECTIVE
industriale (FEM industriale)

industrial estate NOUN
la zona industriale *fem*

industry NOUN
l' industria *fem*
□ the oil industry l'industria petrolifera
■ **the tourist industry** il turismo

inefficient ADJECTIVE
inefficiente (FEM inefficiente)

inevitable ADJECTIVE
inevitabile (FEM inevitabile)

inexpensive ADJECTIVE
poco costoso (FEM poco costosa)

inexperienced ADJECTIVE
inesperto (FEM inesperta)

infant school NOUN
la scuola elementare *fem*

infection NOUN
l' infezione *fem*
□ an ear infection un'infezione all'orecchio
■ **a throat infection** un'angina

infectious ADJECTIVE
infettivo (FEM infettiva)

infinitive NOUN
l' infinito *masc*

infirmary NOUN
l' ospedale *masc*

inflatable ADJECTIVE
gonfiabile (FEM gonfiabile)

inflation NOUN
l' inflazione *fem*

influence NOUN
▷ *see also* **influence** VERB
l' influenza *fem*
□ He's a bad influence on her. Ha una cattiva influenza su di lei.

to **influence** VERB
▷ *see also* **influence** NOUN
influenzare [68]

influenza NOUN
l' influenza *fem*

to **inform** VERB
informare [68]
□ Nobody informed me. Nessuno mi ha informato.

informal ADJECTIVE
■ **informal language** linguaggio colloquiale
■ **an informal visit** una visita non ufficiale
■ **an informal party** una festa tra amici
■ **'informal dress'** 'non è richiesto l'abito da sera'

information NOUN
l' informazione *fem*
□ Where did you get this information? Dove hai avuto questa informazione? □ Could you give me some information about... Potrebbe darmi qualche informazione su...
┃ LANGUAGE TIP informazione is often used in the plural.

□ For further information contact the number below. Per ulteriori informazioni contattate il numero sottostante.

■ **a piece of information** un'informazione

information office NOUN
l' ufficio informazioni *masc* (PL gli uffici informazioni)

infuriating ADJECTIVE
estremamente irritante (FEM irritante)

ingenious ADJECTIVE
ingegnoso (FEM ingegnosa)

ingredient NOUN
l' ingrediente *masc*

inhabitant NOUN
l' abitante *masc/fem*

inhaler NOUN
l' inalatore *masc*

to **inherit** VERB
ereditare [68]

initials NOUN PL
le iniziali *fem pl*

initiative NOUN
l' iniziativa *fem*

to **inject** VERB
iniettare [68]

■ **to inject with** fare [49] un'iniezione di
□ They injected me with antibiotics. Mi hanno fatto un'iniezione di antibiotici.

■ **to inject oneself** farsi [49ᴱ] un'iniezione
□ He needs to inject himself twice a day. Deve farsi un'iniezione due volte al giorno.

injection NOUN
l' iniezione *fem*
□ The doctor gave me an injection. Il dottore mi ha fatto un'iniezione.

to **injure** VERB
ferire [51]

injured ADJECTIVE
ferito (FEM ferita)

injury NOUN
la ferita *fem*
□ a serious injury una ferita grave

injury time NOUN
i minuti di recupero *masc pl*

injustice NOUN
l' ingiustizia *fem*

ink NOUN
l' inchiostro *masc*

in-laws NOUN PL
1 la famiglia del marito *fem (husband's family)*
2 la famiglia della moglie *fem (wife's family)*

inn NOUN
la locanda *fem*

inner ADJECTIVE
1 interno (FEM interna)
□ an inner office un ufficio interno
2 profondo (FEM profonda)
□ her inner sense of security il suo profondo senso di sicurezza

■ **the inner city** i quartieri in degrado del centro

inner tube NOUN
la camera d'aria *fem*

innocent ADJECTIVE
innocente (FEM innocente)

inquest NOUN
l' inchiesta ufficiale *fem*

to **inquire** VERB
domandare [68]
□ 'What's wrong?' he inquired. 'Cosa c'è che non va?', domandò.

■ **to inquire about something** informarsi [56ᴱ] su qualcosa

inquiries office NOUN
l' ufficio informazioni *masc* (PL gli uffici informazioni)

inquiry NOUN
l' inchiesta *fem*
□ There will be an inquiry into the accident. Ci sarà un'inchiesta sull'incidente.

■ **to make inquiries** chiedere [19] informazioni

inquisitive ADJECTIVE
curioso (FEM curiosa)

insane ADJECTIVE
pazzo (FEM pazza)

inscription NOUN
l' iscrizione *fem (on stone, plaque)*

insect NOUN
l' insetto *masc*

insect repellent NOUN
l' insettifugo *masc* (PL gli insettifughi)

insensitive ADJECTIVE
insensibile (FEM insensibile)

to **insert** VERB
inserire [51]

inside NOUN
▷ *see also* **inside** ADVERB, PREPOSITION
l' interno *masc*

inside ADVERB, PREPOSITION
▷ *see also* **inside** NOUN
dentro
□ Come inside! Vieni dentro!
■ **inside the house** in casa
■ **inside out** alla rovescia □ He put his jumper on inside out. Si è messo il maglione alla rovescia.

inside lane NOUN
la corsia di marcia *fem*

insincere ADJECTIVE
falso (FEM falsa)

to **insist** VERB
1 insistere [10]
□ I didn't want to, but he insisted. Non volevo, ma ha insistito.

■ **to insist on doing something** insistere [10] per fare qualcosa □ She insisted on paying. Ha insistito per pagare.

2 sostenere [113]
□ He insisted that he was innocent. Sosteneva di essere innocente.

inspector NOUN
l' ispettore *masc*
l' ispettrice *fem*
■ **the ticket inspector** il controllore

to **install** VERB
installare [68]

instalment (US **installment**) NOUN
la puntata *fem* (*of serial*)
■ **to pay in instalments** pagare [76] a rate

instance NOUN
il caso *masc*
□ in many instances in molti casi
■ **for instance** per esempio

instant ADJECTIVE
▷ *see also* **instant** NOUN
immediato (FEM immediata)
□ It was an instant success. È stato un successo immediato.
■ **instant coffee** caffè solubile

instant NOUN
▷ *see also* **instant** ADJECTIVE
l' istante *masc*

instantly ADVERB
immediatamente

instead PREPOSITION, ADVERB
■ **instead of** invece di □ We played tennis instead of going swimming. Abbiamo giocato a tennis invece di andare a nuotare.
■ **He went instead of Peter.** È andato al posto di Peter.
■ **The pool was closed, so we played tennis instead.** La piscina era chiusa e così abbiamo giocato a tennis.

instinct NOUN
l' istinto *masc*

institute NOUN
l' istituto *masc*

institution NOUN
l' istituzione *fem*

to **instruct** VERB
■ **to instruct somebody to do something** ordinare [68] a qualcuno di fare qualcosa □ She instructed us to wait outside. Ci ha ordinato di aspettare fuori.

instructions NOUN PL
le istruzioni *fem pl*

instructor NOUN
l' istruttore *masc*
l' istruttrice *fem*
□ my driving instructor il mio istruttore di guida
■ **a skiing instructor** un maestro di sci

instrument NOUN
lo strumento *masc*
□ Do you play an instrument? Suoni qualche strumento?

insufficient ADJECTIVE
insufficiente (FEM insufficiente)

insulin NOUN
l' insulina *fem*

insult NOUN
▷ *see also* **insult** VERB
l' insulto *masc*

to **insult** VERB
▷ *see also* **insult** NOUN
insultare [68]

insurance NOUN
l' assicurazione *fem*
□ his car insurance la sua assicurazione della macchina
■ **an insurance policy** una polizza di assicurazione

intelligent ADJECTIVE
intelligente (FEM intelligente)

to **intend** VERB
■ **to intend to do something** avere [12] intenzione di fare qualcosa □ I intend to do languages at university. Ho intenzione di fare lingue all'università.

intense ADJECTIVE
1 intenso (FEM intensa)
□ intense heat calore intenso
2 vivo (FEM viva)
□ intense interest vivo interesse

intensive ADJECTIVE
intensivo (FEM intensiva)

intention NOUN
l' intenzione *fem*

intercom NOUN
l' interfono *masc*

interest NOUN
▷ *see also* **interest** VERB
l' interesse *masc*
□ She has a wide range of interests. Ha moltissimi interessi. □ 5% interest un interesse del 5%
■ **to lose interest** perdere [69] l'interesse
■ **to have no interest in** non interessarsi [56ᴱ] di

to **interest** VERB
▷ *see also* **interest** NOUN
interessare [68]
■ **to be interested in something** interessarsi [56ᴱ] di qualcosa □ I'm not interested in politics. Non mi interesso di politica.

interest-free ADJECTIVE
senza interessi

interesting ADJECTIVE
interessante (FEM interessante)

interest rate NOUN
il tasso di interesse *masc*

interior NOUN
l' interno *masc*

interior designer NOUN
l' arredatore *masc*
l' arredatrice *fem*

intermediate ADJECTIVE
intermedio (FEM intermedia)

internal ADJECTIVE
interno (FEM interna)

international ADJECTIVE
internazionale (FEM internazionale)

internet NOUN
Internet *masc*
□ on the internet su Internet

internet café NOUN
il Internet cafè *masc* (PL i Internet cafè)

internet user NOUN
l' utente Internet *masc/fem*

to **interpret** VERB
1 tradurre [85] *(for speaker)*
2 interpretare [68] *(law, theory)*

interpreter NOUN
l' interprete *masc/fem*

to **interrupt** VERB
interrompere [92]

interruption NOUN
l' interruzione *fem*

interval NOUN
l' intervallo *masc*

interview NOUN
▷ *see also* **interview** VERB
1 l' intervista *fem (on TV, radio)*
2 il colloquio *masc (for job)*

to **interview** VERB
▷ *see also* **interview** NOUN
intervistare [68]
□ I was able to interview one of the actors.
Ho potuto intervistare uno degli attori.
■ **to be interviewed for a job** avere [12]
un colloquio di lavoro

interviewer NOUN
l' intervistatore *masc*
l' intervistatrice *fem*

intimate ADJECTIVE
intimo (FEM intima)

into PREPOSITION
in
□ I'm going into town. Vado in città.
□ Translate it into Italian. Traducilo in italiano.
□ He got into the car. È salito in macchina.
■ **He walked into a lamppost.** Ha battuto
contro un lampione.

intranet NOUN
■ **the intranet** Intranet *masc*

to **introduce** VERB
1 presentare [68]
□ He introduced me to his parents. Mi ha
presentato ai suoi genitori.
2 introdurre [85]
□ A new system is to be introduced. Verrà
introdotto un nuovo sistema.

introduction NOUN
1 l' introduzione *fem*
□ the introduction of the new system
l'introduzione del nuovo sistema
2 la presentazione *fem*
□ a letter of introduction una lettera di
presentazione

intruder NOUN
l' intruso *masc*
l' intrusa *fem*

intuition NOUN
l' intuito *masc*

to **invade** VERB
invadere [55]

invalid NOUN
▷ *see also* **invalid** ADJECTIVE
l' invalido *masc*
l' invalida *fem*

invalid ADJECTIVE
▷ *see also* **invalid** NOUN
non valido (FEM valida)

to **invent** VERB
inventare [68]

invention NOUN
l' invenzione *fem*

inventor NOUN
l' inventore *masc*
l' inventrice *fem*

investigation NOUN
l' indagine *fem*

investment NOUN
l' investimento *masc*

invigilator NOUN
l' addetto alla sorveglianza in sede d'esame
masc

invisible ADJECTIVE
invisibile (FEM invisibile)

invitation NOUN
l' invito *masc*

to **invite** VERB
invitare [68]
□ You're invited to a party at Claire's house.
Sei invitato ad una festa a casa di Claire.

to **involve** VERB
1 comportare [68]
□ It involves a lot of work. Comporta un sacco
di lavoro.
2 coinvolgere [91]
□ We won't involve him. Non lo
coinvolgeremo.
■ **to be involved in something** essere [47E]
coinvolto in qualcosa □ I don't want to be
involved in the argument. Non voglio essere
coinvolto nella discussione.
■ **She was involved in politics.** Si occupava
di politica.
■ **to be involved with somebody** avere [12]
una relazione con qualcuno □ She was
involved with Ben. Aveva una relazione con Ben.

iPad® NOUN
l' iPad® *masc* (PL gli iPad)

iPhone® NOUN
l' iPhone® *masc* (PL gli iPhone)

iPod® NOUN
l' iPod® *masc* (PL gli iPod)

IQ NOUN (= *intelligence quotient*)
il QI *masc* (= *quoziente d'intelligenza*)

Iran NOUN
l' Iran *masc*

Iraq NOUN
l' Iraq *masc*

Iraqi ADJECTIVE
▷ *see also* **Iraqi** NOUN
iracheno (FEM irachena)

Iraqi NOUN
▷ *see also* **Iraqi** ADJECTIVE
l' iracheno *masc*
l' irachena *fem*

Ireland NOUN
l' Irlanda *fem*

Irish ADJECTIVE
▷ *see also* **Irish** NOUN
irlandese (FEM irlandese)

Irish NOUN
▷ *see also* **Irish** ADJECTIVE
l' irlandese *masc (language)*
■ **the Irish** gli irlandesi

Irishman NOUN
■ **an Irishman** un irlandese

Irishwoman NOUN
■ **an Irishwoman** un'irlandese

iron NOUN
▷ *see also* **iron** VERB
1 il ferro *masc*
□ **an iron gate** un cancello di ferro
2 il ferro da stiro *masc (for clothes)*

to **iron** VERB
▷ *see also* **iron** NOUN
stirare [68]

ironic ADJECTIVE
ironico (FEM ironica, MASC PL ironici, FEM PL
ironiche)
□ **an ironic remark** un commento ironico

ironing NOUN
■ **to do the ironing** stirare [68]
■ **I hate ironing.** Odio stirare.

ironing board NOUN
la tavola da stiro *fem*

ironmonger's NOUN
la ferramenta *fem*

irrelevant ADJECTIVE
1 non pertinente (FEM pertinente)
□ **He gave irrelevant answers.** Ha dato
risposte non pertinenti.
■ **That's irrelevant.** Non c'entra.
2 non importante (FEM importante)
□ **If he has the qualifications, his age is**

irrelevant. Se ha le qualifiche la sua età non è
importante.

irresponsible ADJECTIVE
irresponsabile (FEM irresponsabile)

irritating ADJECTIVE
irritante (FEM irritante)

is VERB ▷ *see* **be**

Islam NOUN
l' Islam *masc*

Islamic ADJECTIVE
islamico (FEM islamica, MASC PL islamici, FEM PL
islamiche)
□ **Islamic countries** paesi islamici

island NOUN
l' isola *fem*

isle NOUN
■ **the Isle of Man** l'isola di Man
■ **the Isle of Wight** l'isola di Wight

isn't = **is not**

isolated ADJECTIVE
isolato (FEM isolata)

ISP NOUN (= *Internet Service Provider*)
il provider *masc* (PL i provider)

Israel NOUN
l' Israele *masc*

Israeli ADJECTIVE
▷ *see also* **Israeli** NOUN
israeliano (FEM israeliana)

Israeli NOUN
▷ *see also* **Israeli** ADJECTIVE
l' israeliano *masc*
l' israeliana *fem*

issue NOUN
▷ *see also* **issue** VERB
1 la questione *fem*
□ **a controversial issue** una questione
controversa
■ **to make an issue of something** fare [49]
un problema di qualcosa
2 il numero *masc (of magazine)*
□ **the March issue** il numero di marzo

to **issue** VERB
▷ *see also* **issue** NOUN
rilasciare [13]
□ **He issued a statement yesterday.** Ieri ha
rilasciato una dichiarazione.
■ **Staff will be issued with new uniforms.**
Al personale verranno consegnate nuove
uniformi.

it PRONOUN

LANGUAGE TIP When the subject of the
sentence, 'it' is not translated.
□ **Where's my book? — It's on the table.** Dov'è
il mio libro? — È sul tavolo. □ **It's raining.**
Piove. □ **It's Friday tomorrow.** Domani è
venerdì. □ **Who is it? — It's me.** Chi è? — Sono
io.

LANGUAGE TIP Use a plural verb when
telling the time.

□ It's six o'clock. Sono le sei.

> **LANGUAGE TIP** When the object of the sentence, 'it' is translated by **lo** or **la**, depending on whether the noun referred to is masculine or feminine.

□ It's a good film. Did you see it? È un bel film. Lo hai visto? □ There's a croissant left. Do you want it? C'è ancora una brioche. La vuoi?

> **LANGUAGE TIP** ne is the translation for 'of it' and is used when the Italian verb takes **di**.

□ I'm sure of it. Ne sono sicuro. □ They don't know anything about it. Non ne sanno nulla. □ I doubt it. Ne dubito.

■ **Have you told him about the party? — Yes I told him about it yesterday.** Gli hai detto della festa? — Sì, gliel'ho detto ieri.

Italian ADJECTIVE
> ▷ see also **Italian** NOUN
italiano (FEM italiana)

Italian NOUN
> ▷ see also **Italian** ADJECTIVE
1 l' italiano masc
l' italiana fem (person)
■ **the Italians** gli italiani
2 l' italiano masc (language)
□ Can you speak Italian? Parli italiano? □ our Italian teacher il nostro insegnante di italiano

italics NOUN PL
il corsivo masc sing
□ in italics in corsivo

Italy NOUN
l' Italia fem
□ Do you like Italy? Ti piace l'Italia?

to **itch** VERB
prudere [27]

itchy ADJECTIVE
■ **My arm is itchy.** Ho prurito al braccio.

it'd = it had, it would
item NOUN
1 l' articolo masc
□ a collector's item un articolo da collezione
2 l' oggetto masc
□ the first item he bought il primo oggetto che ha comprato
3 la voce fem
□ He checked the items on his bill. Ha controllato le voci del conto.
4 il punto masc
□ the next item on the agenda il prossimo punto all'ordine del giorno
■ **an item of news** una notizia

itinerary NOUN
l' itinerario masc

it'll = it will

its ADJECTIVE
il suo (FEM la sua, MASC PL i suoi, FEM PL le sue)
□ The party has concluded its annual conference. Il partito ha concluso la sua conferenza annuale.

> **LANGUAGE TIP** 'its' is often not translated.

□ The dog is losing its hair. Il cane sta perdendo il pelo.

it's = it is, it has

itself PRONOUN
1 si
□ The dog has hurt itself. Il cane si è fatto male. □ The heating switches itself off. Il riscaldamento si spegne da solo.
2 stesso
□ life itself la vita stessa
■ **by itself** da solo
■ **in itself** di per sé □ It's not a problem in itself. Non è un problema di per sé.

I've = I have

i

Jj

jab NOUN
> *see also* **jab** VERB
la puntura *fem*

to **jab** VERB
> *see also* **jab** NOUN
conficcare [18]
□ She jabbed the needle into my arm. Mi ha conficcato l'ago nel braccio.

jack NOUN
1 il cric *masc* (PL i cric)
□ The jack's in the boot. Il cric è nel bagagliaio.
2 il fante *masc* (in cards)

jacket NOUN
la giacca *fem* (PL le giacche)
□ a wool jacket una giacca di lana
■ **jacket potatoes** patate cotte in forno

jackpot NOUN
il primo premio *masc*
□ He won the jackpot. Ha vinto il primo premio.
■ **to hit the jackpot** fare [49] centro

jail NOUN
> *see also* **jail** VERB
la prigione *fem*
■ **to go to jail** andare [6ᴱ] in prigione

to **jail** VERB
> *see also* **jail** NOUN
mandare [68] in prigione

jam NOUN
> *see also* **jam** VERB
la marmellata *fem*
□ strawberry jam marmellata di fragole
■ **a traffic jam** un ingorgo

to **jam** VERB
> *see also* **jam** NOUN
bloccare [18]
□ Crowds jammed the city centre. La folla ha bloccato il centro.
■ **Twenty people jammed into the tiny office.** Venti persone erano ammassate nel piccolo ufficio.

jam jar NOUN
il vasetto da marmellata *masc*

jammed ADJECTIVE
bloccato (FEM bloccata)
□ The window's jammed. La finestra è bloccata.

jam-packed ADJECTIVE
pieno zeppo (FEM piena zeppa)
□ The hall was jam-packed. La sala era piena zeppa.

janitor NOUN
il custode *masc*

January NOUN
gennaio
□ in January in gennaio

Japan NOUN
il Giappone *masc*

Japanese ADJECTIVE
> *see also* **Japanese** NOUN
giapponese (FEM giapponese)

Japanese NOUN
> *see also* **Japanese** ADJECTIVE
il giapponese *masc* (language)
■ **the Japanese** i giapponesi

jar NOUN
il vasetto *masc*
□ a jar of honey un vasetto di miele

jaundice NOUN
l' itterizia *fem*

javelin NOUN
il giavellotto *masc*

jaw NOUN
la mascella *fem*

jazz NOUN
il jazz *masc*

jealous ADJECTIVE
geloso (FEM gelosa)

jeans NOUN PL
i jeans *masc pl*

to **jeer** VERB
fischiare [17]

Jehovah's Witness NOUN
il/la testimone di Geova *masc/fem*

Jell-o® NOUN (US)
la gelatina *fem*

jelly NOUN
1 la gelatina *fem*
□ fruit jelly gelatina di frutta
2 la marmellata *fem* (US: jam)

jellyfish NOUN
la medusa *fem*

jersey NOUN
la maglia *fem* (jumper)

Jesus NOUN
Gesù

jet NOUN
il jet *masc* (PL i jet)

jet lag NOUN
■ **to be suffering from jet lag** essere [47ᴱ] scombussolato per il cambiamento di fuso orario

jetty NOUN
l' imbarcadero *masc*

Jew NOUN
l' ebreo *masc*
l' ebrea *fem*
■ **the Jews** gli ebrei

jewel NOUN
il gioiello *masc*

jeweller (US **jeweler**) NOUN
il gioielliere *masc*

jeweller's shop (US **jeweler's shop**) NOUN
la gioielleria *fem*

jewellery (US **jewelry**) NOUN
i gioielli *masc pl*

Jewish ADJECTIVE
1 ebreo (FEM ebrea)
  □ He's Jewish. È ebreo.
2 ebraico (FEM ebraica, MASC PL ebraici, FEM PL ebraiche)
  □ a Jewish festival una festività ebraica

jigsaw NOUN
il puzzle *masc* (PL i puzzle)

job NOUN
1 il lavoro *masc*
  □ a part-time job un lavoro part-time
  □ You've done a good job! Hai fatto un ottimo lavoro!
2 il compito *masc*
  □ It's not my job to make the tea. Fare il tè non è compito mio.

job centre NOUN
l' ufficio di collocamento *masc*

jobless ADJECTIVE
disoccupato (FEM disoccupata)

jockey NOUN
il fantino *masc*

to **jog** VERB
fare [49] jogging

jogging NOUN
il jogging *masc*
■ **to go jogging** andare [6ᴱ] a fare jogging

john NOUN (US)
il gabinetto *masc*

to **join** VERB
1 iscriversi [99ᴱ] a
  □ I'm going to join the ski club. Ho intenzione di iscrivermi ad uno sci club.
2 raggiungere [5]
  □ I'll join you later. Ti raggiungo più tardi.
  ■ **Hi Tony, come and join us!** Ciao Tony, siediti qui con noi!

■ **Do you mind if I join you?** Posso venire con voi?
■ **Will you join me for a coffee?** Vieni a bere un caffè?
3 collegare [76]
  □ The car parks are joined by a footpath. I parcheggi sono collegati da un sentiero.

to **join in** VERB
partecipare [68]

joiner NOUN
il falegname *masc*

joint NOUN
1 l' articolazione *fem*
  □ I've got pains in my joints. Mi fanno male le articolazioni.
  ■ **a joint of pork** un pezzo di maiale da arrosto
2 lo spinello *masc* (drugs)

joke NOUN
▷ see also **joke** VERB
1 lo scherzo *masc*
  □ It was only a joke. Era solo uno scherzo.
2 la barzelletta *fem*
  ■ **to tell a joke** raccontare [68] una barzelletta

to **joke** VERB
▷ see also **joke** NOUN
scherzare [68]
  □ You must be joking! Stai scherzando!

jolly ADJECTIVE, ADVERB
1 allegro (FEM allegra) (person)
  ■ **a jolly party** una bella festa
2 molto
  □ You were jolly unlucky. Sei stato molto sfortunato.

Jordan NOUN
la Giordania *fem*

to **jot down** VERB
annotare [68] (address, phone number)

jotter NOUN
il blocchetto per appunti *masc*

journalism NOUN
il giornalismo *masc*

journalist NOUN
il/la giornalista *masc/fem*

journey NOUN
il viaggio *masc*
  □ a five-hour journey un viaggio di cinque ore
  ■ **My journey to school takes half an hour.** Ci vuole una mezz'ora per andare a scuola.
  ■ **to go on a journey** fare [49] un viaggio

joy NOUN
la gioia *fem*

joystick NOUN
il joystick *masc* (PL i joystick)

judge NOUN
▷ see also **judge** VERB
il giudice *masc*

j

to **judge** VERB
▷ *see also* **judge** NOUN
giudicare [18]

judo NOUN
il judo *masc*

jug NOUN
la brocca *fem* (PL le brocche)

juggler NOUN
il giocoliere *masc*

juice NOUN
il succo *masc* (PL i succhi)
■ **orange juice** succo d'arancia

July NOUN
luglio
▢ in July in luglio

jumble NOUN
il miscuglio *masc*
▢ **a meaningless jumble of words** un miscuglio di parole senza senso

jumble sale NOUN
la vendita di beneficenza di roba usata *fem*

to **jump** VERB
saltare [68]
▢ **They jumped over the wall.** Hanno saltato oltre il muro.
■ **You made me jump!** Mi hai spaventato!

jumper NOUN
il maglione *masc*

junction NOUN
l' incrocio *masc* (of roads)

June NOUN
giugno
▢ in June in giugno

jungle NOUN
la giungla *fem*

junior ADJECTIVE, NOUN
■ **a junior minister** un sottosegretario
■ **He's three years my junior.** Ha tre anni meno di me.

junior school NOUN
la scuola elementare *fem*

junk NOUN
la robaccia *fem*
▢ **The attic's full of junk.** La soffitta è piena di robaccia.
■ **to eat junk food** mangiare [58] porcherie
■ **a junk shop** un rigattiere

junk mail NOUN
la posta spazzatura *fem*

jury NOUN
la giuria *fem*

just ADVERB
1 proprio
▢ **I did it just now.** L'ho fatto proprio adesso.
■ **just now** (at the moment) in questo momento ▢ **I'm rather busy just now.** In questo momento sono molto occupato.
2 appena
▢ **just in time** appena in tempo ▢ **He's just arrived.** È appena arrivato. ▢ **We had just enough money.** Il denaro ci è bastato appena.
3 solo
▢ **I just thought that...** Pensavo solo che...
■ **Just a minute!** Aspetta un attimo!
■ **just about** quasi
■ **just after Christmas** poco dopo Natale
■ **I'm just coming!** Arrivo subito!

justice NOUN
la giustizia *fem*

to **justify** VERB
giustificare [18]

Kk

kangaroo NOUN
il canguro *masc*

karaoke NOUN
il karaoke *masc*

karate NOUN
il karate *masc*

kebab NOUN
lo spiedino *masc*
□ a lamb kebab uno spiedino di agnello

keen ADJECTIVE
1 entusiasta (FEM entusiasta)
□ He doesn't seem very keen. Non sembra molto entusiasta.
2 attento e interessato (FEM attenta e interessata)
□ She's a keen student. È una studentessa attenta e interessata.
■ **I'm not very keen on maths.** Non mi piace molto la matematica.
■ **He's keen on her.** Lei gli piace molto.
■ **to be keen on doing something** avere [12] una gran voglia di fare qualcosa

to **keep** VERB
1 tenere [113]
□ You can keep it. Lo puoi tenere. □ The noise kept him awake. Il rumore lo teneva sveglio.
2 stare [108ᴱ]
□ Keep still! Stai fermo! □ Keep quiet! Stai zitto!
3 continuare [68]
□ Keep straight on. Continua dritto.
■ **I keep forgetting my keys.** Continuo a dimenticare le chiavi.
■ **Keep trying!** Prova ancora!
■ **'keep out'** 'vietato l'ingresso'
■ **'keep off the grass'** 'non calpestare l'erba'

to **keep back** VERB
1 tenere [113] da parte
□ Keep back some strawberries to decorate the cake. Tieni da parte qualche fragola per guarnire la torta.
2 nascondere [64]
□ I'm sure she's keeping something back. Sono sicuro che sta nascondendo qualcosa.

to **keep on** VERB
continuare [68]
□ The car keeps on breaking down. La macchina continua a rompersi.

to **keep up** VERB
star [108ᴱ] dietro a
□ Matthew walks so fast I can't keep up. Matthew cammina così veloce che non riesco a stargli dietro.

keep-fit NOUN
la ginnastica *fem*
□ I go to keep-fit classes. Vado ad un corso di ginnastica.

kennel NOUN
il canile *masc*

kept VERB ▷ *see* **keep**

kerosene NOUN (US)
il cherosene *masc*

ketchup NOUN
il ketchup *masc*

kettle NOUN
il bollitore *masc*

key NOUN
▷ *see also* **key** ADJECTIVE
1 la chiave *fem*
□ a bunch of keys un mazzo di chiavi
2 il tasto *masc* (of computer)

key ADJECTIVE
▷ *see also* **key** NOUN
chiave (FEM+PL chiave)
□ Yes, this is a key point. Sì, è un punto chiave.

keyboard NOUN
la tastiera *fem*

key ring NOUN
il portachiavi *masc* (PL i portachiavi)

kick NOUN
▷ *see also* **kick** VERB
il calcio *masc*

to **kick** VERB
▷ *see also* **kick** NOUN
■ **to kick somebody** dare [30] un calcio a qualcuno □ He kicked me. Mi ha dato un calcio. □ He kicked the ball hard. Ha dato un forte calcio alla palla.
■ **to kick off** dare [30] il calcio d'inizio (in football)

kick-off NOUN
■ **The kick-off is at 10 o'clock.** La partita inizia alle dieci.

kid NOUN
▷ *see also* **kid** VERB

k

1 il bambino *masc*
la bambina *fem*
□ One of the kids was crying. Uno dei bambini stava piangendo.
2 il figlio *masc*
la figlia *fem*
□ They've got three kids. Hanno tre figli.
■ **a gang of kids on motorbikes** una banda di ragazzi in motorino

to **kid** VERB
▷ *see also* **kid** NOUN
scherzare [68]

to **kidnap** VERB
rapire [51]

kidney NOUN
1 il rene *masc*
□ He's got kidney trouble. Ha disturbi ai reni.
2 il rognone *masc*
□ I don't like kidneys. Non mi piace il rognone.

to **kill** VERB
uccidere [31]
□ She killed her husband. Ha ucciso suo marito. □ Sixteen people were killed in the accident. Nell'incidente sono rimaste uccise sedici persone.
■ **He was killed in a car accident.** È morto in un incidente stradale.
■ **Luckily, nobody was killed.** Fortunatamente non ci sono state vittime.
■ **to kill oneself** uccidersi [31ᴱ] □ He killed himself. Si è ucciso.

killer NOUN
1 l' assassino *masc*
l' assassina *fem*
□ The police are searching for the killer. La polizia sta cercando l'assassino.
■ **Meningitis can be a killer.** Si può morire di meningite.
2 il/la killer *masc/fem* (PL i/le killer) (*hitman*)

kilo NOUN
il chilo *masc*
□ £5 a kilo cinque sterline al chilo

kilometre (US **kilometer**) NOUN
il chilometro *masc*

kilt NOUN
il kilt *masc* (PL i kilt)

kind ADJECTIVE
▷ *see also* **kind** NOUN
gentile (FEM gentile)
■ **to be kind to somebody** essere [47ᴱ] gentile con qualcuno
■ **Thank you for being so kind.** Grazie mille.

kind NOUN
▷ *see also* **kind** ADJECTIVE
la specie *fem*
□ It's a kind of sausage. È una specie di salsiccia.

kindergarten NOUN
l' asilo *masc*

kindly ADVERB
gentilmente
□ They kindly offered to lend me some money. Si sono offerti gentilmente di prestarmi del denaro.
■ **'Don't worry,' she said kindly.** 'Non preoccuparti,' disse con dolcezza.
■ **Kindly refrain from smoking.** Si prega di non fumare.

kindness NOUN
la gentilezza *fem*

king NOUN
il re *masc* (PL i re)

kingdom NOUN
il regno *masc*

kiosk NOUN
il chiosco *masc* (PL i chioschi) (*small shop*)
■ **a telephone kiosk** una cabina telefonica

kipper NOUN
l' aringa affumicata *fem* (PL le aringhe affumicate)

kiss NOUN
▷ *see also* **kiss** VERB
il bacio *masc*

to **kiss** VERB
▷ *see also* **kiss** NOUN
1 baciare [13]
□ He kissed her passionately. L'ha baciata appassionatamente.
2 baciarsi [13ᴱ]
□ They kissed. Si sono baciati.

kit NOUN
1 la roba *fem*
□ I've forgotten my gym kit. Ho dimenticato la roba da ginnastica.
2 il kit *masc* (PL i kit)
□ a tool kit un kit di attrezzi □ a sewing kit un kit da cucito
■ **a first aid kit** una cassetta del pronto soccorso
■ **a puncture repair kit** l'attrezzatura per riparare la gomma
■ **a drum kit** una batteria

kitchen NOUN
la cucina *fem*
□ a fitted kitchen una cucina componibile □ the kitchen units gli elementi della cucina □ a kitchen knife un coltello da cucina

kite NOUN
l' aquilone *masc*
LANGUAGE TIP Word for word, this means 'big eagle'.

kitten NOUN
il gattino *masc*
LANGUAGE TIP Word for word, this means 'little cat'.

knee NOUN
il ginocchio *masc* (PL le ginocchia)

k

□ I've hurt my knee. Mi sono fatto male al ginocchio.

■ **to be on one's knees** essere [47ᴱ] in ginocchio

to **kneel** VERB
inginocchiarsi [17ᴱ]

knew VERB ▷ *see* **know**

knickers NOUN
gli slip *masc pl*

■ **a pair of knickers** un paio di slip

knife NOUN
il coltello *masc*

□ a sharp knife un coltello affilato

to **knit** VERB
lavorare [68] a maglia

knitting NOUN

■ **I like knitting.** Mi piace lavorare a maglia.

knives NOUN PL ▷ *see* **knife**

knock NOUN

▷ *see also* **knock** VERB
il colpo *masc*

to **knock** VERB

▷ *see also* **knock** NOUN
bussare [68]

□ Someone's knocking at the door. Qualcuno sta bussando alla porta.

to **knock down** VERB
investire [41]

□ She was knocked down by a car. È stata investita da una macchina.

to **knock out** VERB

1 eliminare [68]

□ They were knocked out early in the tournament. Sono stati eliminati all'inizio del torneo.

2 stordire [51]

□ They knocked out the watchman. Hanno stordito il guardiano.

knot NOUN
il nodo *masc*

■ **to tie a knot in something** fare [49] un nodo a qualcosa

to **know** VERB

LANGUAGE TIP Use **sapere** for knowing facts, **conoscere** for knowing people and places.

1 sapere [94]

□ Yes, I know. Sì, lo so. □ I don't know. Non so. □ I don't know any German. Non so una parola di tedesco. □ He knows a lot about cars. Sa molte cose sulle macchine. □ How should I know? Come vuoi che lo sappia? □ You never know! Non si sa mai! □ I knew it. Lo sapevo.

■ **to know that** sapere [94] che

2 conoscere [24]

□ I know her. La conosco. □ I know Rome well. Conosco bene Roma.

■ **to get to know somebody** conoscere [24] qualcuno

know-all NOUN
il sapientone *masc*
la sapientona *fem*

□ He's such a know-all! È un gran sapientone!

know-how NOUN
il know-how *masc*

knowledge NOUN
la conoscenza *fem*

knowledgeable ADJECTIVE

■ **to be knowledgeable about something** essere [47ᴱ] ben informato su qualcosa

known VERB ▷ *see* **know**

Koran NOUN
il Corano *masc*

Korea NOUN
la Corea *fem*

kosher ADJECTIVE
kasher (FEM+PL kasher)

k

Ll

lab NOUN
il laboratorio *masc*
- a lab technician un tecnico di laboratorio

label NOUN
▷ *see also* **label** VERB
l' etichetta *fem*

to **label** VERB
▷ *see also* **label** NOUN
■ **to be labelled** essere [47ᴱ] etichettato

laboratory NOUN
il laboratorio *masc*

Labour (US **Labor**) NOUN
il/la laburista *masc/fem*
- the Labour Party il partito laburista

labour (US **labor**) NOUN
■ **the labour market** il mercato del lavoro
■ **to be in labour** avere [12] le doglie

labourer (US **laborer**) NOUN
il manovale *masc (construction worker)*
■ **a farm labourer** un bracciante agricolo

lace NOUN
1 il laccio *masc*
- a pair of laces un paio di lacci
2 il pizzo *masc*
- a lace collar un colletto di pizzo

lack NOUN
la mancanza *fem*
- He got the job, despite his lack of experience.
Ha ottenuto il lavoro nonostante la mancanza
d'esperienza.

lacquer NOUN
la lacca *fem* (PL le lacche)

lad NOUN
il ragazzo *masc*

ladder NOUN
la scala a pioli *fem*

lady NOUN
la signora *fem*
- Ladies and gentlemen... Signore e signori...
■ **What can I do for you, young lady?** Cosa
posso fare per te, cara?
■ **the ladies** la toilette delle signore

ladybird (US **ladybug**) NOUN
la coccinella *fem*

to **lag behind** VERB
restare [68ᴱ] indietro

lager NOUN
la birra chiara *fem*

■ **a can of lager** una lattina di birra

laid VERB ▷ *see* **lay**

laid-back ADJECTIVE
tranquillo e rilassato (FEM tranquilla e
rilassata)
- his laid-back attitude il suo atteggiamento
tranquillo e rilassato

lain VERB ▷ *see* **lie**

lake NOUN
il lago *masc* (PL i laghi)

lamb NOUN
l' agnello *masc*
- a lamb chop una cotoletta d'agnello

lame ADJECTIVE
1 zoppo (FEM zoppa)
- She was lame in one leg. Era zoppa da un
piede.
2 zoppicante (FEM zoppicante)
- a lame excuse una scusa zoppicante

lamp NOUN
la lampada *fem*

lamppost NOUN
il lampione *masc*

land NOUN
▷ *see also* **land** VERB
la terra *fem*
- people who work on the land la gente che
lavora la terra

to **land** VERB
▷ *see also* **land** NOUN
atterrare [68ᴱ]
- The plane landed at 5 o'clock. L'aereo è
atterrato alle cinque.

landing NOUN
1 l' atterraggio *masc (of plane)*
2 il pianerottolo *masc (of staircase)*
■ **a landing strip** una pista d'atterraggio

landlady NOUN
la padrona di casa *fem*

landline NOUN
il telefono fisso *masc*

landlord NOUN
1 il padrone di casa *masc (of rented property)*
2 il proprietario *masc (of pub)*

landmark NOUN
il punto di riferimento *masc*
- Big Ben is a London landmark. La torre del
Big Ben è un punto di riferimento a Londra.

landscape NOUN
il paesaggio *masc*
lane NOUN
1 la stradina *fem*
□ a country lane una stradina di campagna
2 la corsia *fem*
□ the outside lane la corsia esterna
language NOUN
la lingua *fem*
□ a foreign language una lingua straniera
■ **to use bad language** dire [35] parolacce
lap NOUN
il giro *masc*
□ I ran ten laps. Ho fatto dieci giri di corsa.
■ **Andrew was sitting on his mother's lap.**
Andrew era seduto in braccio a sua madre.
laptop NOUN
il computer portatile *masc* (PL i computer portatili)
larder NOUN
la dispensa *fem*
large ADJECTIVE
1 grande (FEM grande)
□ a large house una casa grande
2 grosso (FEM grossa)
□ a large amount una grossa cifra
■ **a large, cheerful woman** un donnone allegro
■ **a large number of people** molte persone
largely ADVERB
in gran parte
laser NOUN
il laser *masc* (PL i laser)
lass NOUN
la ragazza *fem*
last ADJECTIVE, ADVERB
▷ *see also* **last** VERB
1 scorso (FEM scorsa)
□ last Friday venerdì scorso
2 ultimo (FEM ultima)
□ the last time l'ultima volta □ He arrived last.
È arrivato ultimo.
3 per l'ultima volta
□ I've lost my bag. — When did you see it last?
Ho perso la borsa. — Dove l'hai vista per l'ultima volta?
■ **last night 1** ieri notte □ I couldn't sleep
last night. Ieri notte non sono riuscito a dormire. **2** ieri sera □ I got home at midnight
last night. Ieri sera sono arrivata a casa a mezzanotte.
■ **at last** finalmente
to **last** VERB
▷ *see also* **last** ADJECTIVE, ADVERB
durare [68ᴱ]
□ The concert lasts two hours. Il concerto dura due ore.
lastly ADVERB
infine

□ Lastly I'd like to mention... Infine vorrei accennare a...
late ADJECTIVE, ADVERB
1 tardi
□ Hurry up or you'll be late! Sbrigati o farai tardi!
□ I went to bed late. Sono andato a letto tardi.
2 in ritardo
□ I'm often late for school. Arrivo spesso in ritardo a scuola.
■ **to arrive late** arrivare [68ᴱ] in ritardo
■ **in the late afternoon** nel tardo pomeriggio
■ **in late May** verso la fine di maggio
lately ADVERB
ultimamente
□ I haven't seen him lately. Ultimamente non l'ho visto.
later ADVERB
più tardi
□ I'll do it later. Lo farò più tardi.
■ **See you later!** Ci vediamo dopo!
latest ADJECTIVE
ultimo (FEM ultima)
□ their latest album il loro ultimo album
■ **at the latest** al più tardi □ by ten o'clock at
the latest alle dieci al più tardi
Latin NOUN
il latino *masc*
□ I do Latin. Studio latino.
Latin America NOUN
l' America Latina *fem*
Latin American ADJECTIVE
sudamericano (FEM sudamericana)
latter ADJECTIVE, NOUN
l' ultimo *masc*
l' ultima *fem*
□ the latter part of the match l'ultima parte della partita
■ **the former..., the latter...** il primo...,
il secondo...
laugh NOUN
▷ *see also* **laugh** VERB
la risata *fem*
□ with a laugh con una risata
■ **It was a good laugh.** È stato molto divertente.
to **laugh** VERB
▷ *see also* **laugh** NOUN
ridere [84]
■ **to laugh at somebody** ridere [84] di qualcuno
to **launch** VERB
lanciare [13]
□ They're about to launch the new model.
Stanno per lanciare il nuovo modello.
launderette® NOUN
la lavanderia a gettone *fem*
Laundromat® NOUN (US)
la lavanderia a gettone *fem*

I

laundry NOUN
il bucato *masc*
□ She does my laundry. Mi fa lei il bucato.

lavatory NOUN
il gabinetto *masc*

lavender NOUN
la lavanda *fem*

law NOUN
la legge *fem*
□ It's against the law. È contro la legge.
■ **law and order** l'ordine pubblico

law court NOUN
il tribunale *masc*

lawn NOUN
il prato all'inglese *masc*

lawnmower NOUN
il tagliaerba *masc* (PL i tagliaerba)

law school NOUN (US)
la facoltà di legge *fem* (PL le facoltà di legge)

lawyer NOUN
l' avvocato *masc*

to **lay** VERB
■ **LANGUAGE TIP** 'lay' is also the past of 'to lie'.
1 mettere [59]
□ She laid the baby in her cot. Ha messo la bambina nel suo lettino.
2 posare [68]
□ He laid a sheet of newspaper on the floor. Ha posato un foglio di giornale sul pavimento.
■ **to lay the table** apparecchiare [17] la tavola
□ I haven't laid the table yet. Non ho ancora apparecchiato la tavola.

to **lay off** VERB
licenziare [17]
□ My father's been laid off. Mio padre è stato licenziato.
■ **Lay off me!** Piantala!

to **lay on** VERB
1 fornire [51]
□ They laid on extra buses. Hanno fornito autobus supplementari.
2 organizzare [68]
□ They laid on a lunch. Hanno organizzato un pranzo.

lay-by NOUN
la piazzola di sosta *fem*

layer NOUN
lo strato *masc*

layout NOUN
la disposizione *fem* (of house)

lazy ADJECTIVE
pigro (FEM pigra)

lead (1) NOUN
▷ see also **lead** VERB
1 il filo *masc* (cable)
2 il guinzaglio *masc*
□ Dogs must be kept on a lead. I cani devono essere tenuti al guinzaglio.

3 il vantaggio *masc*
■ **to be in the lead** essere [47ᴱ] in vantaggio

lead (2) NOUN
il piombo *masc*
□ a lead pipe un tubo di piombo

to **lead** VERB
▷ see also **lead** NOUN
1 portare [68]
□ the street that leads to the station la strada che porta alla stazione □ The incident led to serious trouble. L'incidente ha portato a problemi seri.
2 guidare [68]
□ He led the party for five years. Ha guidato il partito per cinque anni.
■ **to lead the way** fare [49] strada

to **lead away** VERB
condurre [85] via

leaded petrol NOUN
la benzina con piombo *fem*

leader NOUN
il capo *masc*

lead-free ADJECTIVE
■ **lead-free petrol** benzina verde

lead singer NOUN
il/la cantante solista *masc/fem*

leaf NOUN
la foglia *fem*

leaflet NOUN
il dépliant *masc* (PL i dépliant)

league NOUN
il campionato *masc*
□ They are at the top of the league. Sono in testa al campionato.
■ **the Premier League** la prima divisione

leak NOUN
▷ see also **leak** VERB
1 la fuga *fem* (PL le fughe)
□ a gas leak una fuga di gas
2 la perdita *fem*
□ a leak in the radiator una perdita del radiatore

to **leak** VERB
▷ see also **leak** NOUN
perdere [69]
□ The pipe is leaking. Il tubo perde.

to **lean** VERB
appoggiare [58]
□ He leaned the ladder against the wall. Ha appoggiato la scala al muro.
■ **to be leaning against something** essere [47ᴱ] appoggiato a qualcosa

to **lean forward** VERB
piegarsi [76ᴱ] in avanti

to **lean on** VERB
1 appoggiarsi [76ᴱ]
□ She leant on his arm. Si appoggiò al suo braccio.
2 spingere [106]

□ She leant on him to contribute. Lo ha spinto a contribuire.

to **lean out** VERB
sporgersi [107ᴱ]
□ She leant out of the window. Si è sporta dal finestrino.

to **lean over** VERB
chinarsi [56ᴱ]
□ Don't lean over too far. Non chinarti troppo.

to **leap** VERB
▷ see also **leap** NOUN
saltare [68ᴱ]
□ He leapt out of his chair when his team scored. È saltato in piedi quando la sua squadra ha segnato.

leap NOUN
▷ see also **leap** VERB
il salto *masc*
□ a leap in the dark un salto nel buio

leap year NOUN
l' anno bisestile *masc*

to **learn** VERB
imparare [68]
□ I'm learning to ski. Sto imparando a sciare.

learner NOUN
■ She's a quick learner. Impara in fretta.

learner driver NOUN
il/la principiante *masc/fem*

least ADJECTIVE, PRONOUN, ADVERB
1 minimo (FEM minima)
□ I haven't the least idea. Non ne ho la minima idea. □ It's the least I can do. È il minimo che possa fare.
2 meno
□ Go for the ones with least fat. Scegli quelli con meno grassi. □ the least expensive hotel l'albergo meno costoso □ It takes the least time. È quello per cui ci vuole meno tempo. □ History is the subject I like the least. La storia è la materia che mi piace di meno.
3 ultimo (FEM ultima)
□ That's the least of my worries. È l'ultima delle mie preoccupazioni.
■ at least almeno □ At least nobody was hurt. Almeno nessuno si è fatto male.

leather NOUN
la pelle *fem*
□ a black leather jacket una giacca di pelle nera

leave NOUN
▷ see also **leave** VERB
1 il permesso *masc (from work)*
2 la licenza *fem (from army)*
□ My brother is on leave. Mio fratello è in licenza.

to **leave** VERB
▷ see also **leave** NOUN
1 lasciare [13]
□ Don't leave your wallet in the car. Non lasciare il portafoglio in macchina.

2 partire [41ᴱ]
□ The bus leaves at eight. L'autobus parte alle otto. □ They left yesterday. Sono partiti ieri.
3 partire [41ᴱ] da
□ We leave London at six o'clock. Partiamo da Londra alle sei.
4 andare [6ᴱ] via
□ She's just left. È appena andata via.
■ to leave home andarsene [6ᴱ] di casa
□ She left home when she was sixteen. Se n'è andata di casa quando aveva sedici anni.
■ to leave somebody alone lasciare [13] in pace qualcuno □ Leave me alone! Lasciami in pace!

to **leave behind** VERB
dimenticare [18]
□ I left my umbrella behind. Ho dimenticato l'ombrello.

to **leave out** VERB
escludere [3]
□ I felt left out. Mi sentivo proprio escluso.

leaves NOUN PL ▷ see **leaf**

Lebanon NOUN
il Libano *masc*

lecture NOUN
▷ see also **lecture** VERB
1 la conferenza *fem*
□ a public lecture una conferenza pubblica
2 la lezione *fem (at university)*

to **lecture** VERB
▷ see also **lecture** NOUN
1 insegnare [14]
□ She lectures at the technical college. Insegna all'istituto tecnico.
2 rimproverare [68]
□ He's always lecturing us. Ci rimprovera sempre.

lecturer NOUN
il/la docente *masc/fem*

led VERB ▷ see **lead**

leek NOUN
il porro *masc*

left VERB ▷ see **leave**

left ADJECTIVE, ADVERB
▷ see also **left** NOUN
1 sinistro (FEM sinistra)
□ my left hand la mia mano sinistra
2 a sinistra
□ Turn left at the traffic lights. Volta a sinistra al semaforo.
■ I haven't got any money left. Non ho più denaro.
■ Is there any tea left? C'è ancora del tè?

left NOUN
▷ see also **left** ADJECTIVE, ADVERB
la sinistra *fem*
■ on the left a sinistra

left-hand ADJECTIVE
■ the left-hand side il lato sinistro

451

left-handed ADJECTIVE
mancino (FEM mancina)

left-luggage office NOUN
il deposito bagagli *masc*

leg NOUN
la gamba *fem*
□ She's broken her leg. Si è rotta la gamba.
■ **a leg of lamb** una coscia d'agnello

legal ADJECTIVE
legale (FEM legale)

leggings NOUN PL
i fuseaux *masc pl*

leisure NOUN
■ **leisure time** tempo libero
■ **leisure activities** attività ricreative

leisure centre NOUN
il centro ricreativo pubblico *masc* (PL i centri ricreativi pubblici)

lemon NOUN
il limone *masc*

lemonade NOUN
la limonata *fem*

to lend VERB
prestare [68]
□ I can lend you some money. Posso prestarti del denaro. □ He lent me £10. Mi ha prestato dieci sterline.

length NOUN
la lunghezza *fem*
■ **It's about a metre in length.** È lungo circa un metro.

lens NOUN
1 la lente *fem (of microscope)*
2 l' obiettivo *masc (of camera)*
■ **contact lenses** lenti a contatto

Lent NOUN
la Quaresima *fem*

lent VERB ▷ see **lend**

lentil NOUN
la lenticchia *fem*

Leo NOUN
il Leone *masc*
□ I'm Leo. Sono del Leone.

lesbian NOUN
la lesbica *fem* (PL le lesbiche)

less ADJECTIVE, PRONOUN, ADVERB
meno
□ A bit less, please. Un po' meno, per favore.
□ It's less than a kilometre from here. È a meno di un chilometro da qui. □ less than half meno della metà
■ **less and less** sempre meno

lesson NOUN
la lezione *fem*
□ an English lesson una lezione d'inglese

to let VERB
1 lasciare [13]
■ **to let somebody do something** lasciar [13]

fare qualcosa a qualcuno □ Let me go! Lasciami andare!
■ **to let somebody know something** far [49] sapere qualcosa a qualcuno □ I'll let you know the date as soon as possible. Ti farò sapere la data prima possibile.
■ **to let in** far [49] entrare □ They wouldn't let me in. Non mi hanno fatto entrare.
2 affittare [68]
□ 'to let' 'affittasi'

   LANGUAGE TIP When making suggestions, use the **-iamo** form of the Italian verb.
□ Let's go to the cinema! Andiamo al cinema!
□ Let's have a break! — Yes, let's. Facciamo una pausa! — Va bene.

to let down VERB
deludere [32]
□ I won't let you down. Non ti deluderò.

letter NOUN
la lettera *fem*

letter bomb NOUN
la lettera esplosiva *fem*

letterbox NOUN
1 la buca delle lettere sulla porta *fem* (PL le buche delle lettere sulla porta)
2 la cassetta per la posta *fem (in entrance hall)*

lettuce NOUN
la lattuga *fem* (PL le lattughe)

leukaemia (US **leukemia**) NOUN
la leucemia *fem*

level ADJECTIVE
▷ see also **level** NOUN
piano (FEM piana)
□ a level surface una superficie piana

level NOUN
▷ see also **level** ADJECTIVE
il livello *masc*
□ The level of the river is rising. Il livello del fiume sta salendo.

level crossing NOUN
il passaggio a livello *masc* (PL i passaggi a livello)

lever NOUN
la leva *fem*

liable ADJECTIVE
■ **He's liable to panic.** È facile che si lasci prendere dal panico.

liar NOUN
il bugiardo *masc*
la bugiarda *fem*

liberal ADJECTIVE
liberale (FEM liberale)
□ liberal views vedute liberali
■ **the Liberal Democrats** i liberaldemocratici

liberation NOUN
la liberazione *fem*

Libra NOUN
la Bilancia *fem*
□ I'm Libra. Sono della Bilancia.

librarian NOUN
il bibliotecario *masc*
la bibliotecaria *fem*

library NOUN
la biblioteca *fem* (PL le biblioteche)

Libya NOUN
la Libia *fem*

licence (US **license**) NOUN
la patente *fem*
□ He lost his licence for a year. Gli hanno ritirato la patente per un anno.
■ **a television licence** un abbonamento alla TV

license plate NOUN (US)
la targa *fem* (PL le targhe)

to **lick** VERB
leccare [18]

lid NOUN
il coperchio *masc (of box, pan)*

lie NOUN
▷ *see also* **lie** VERB
la bugia *fem*
■ **to tell a lie** dire [35] una bugia

to **lie** VERB
▷ *see also* **lie** NOUN
1 mentire [41] *(tell untruths)*
□ I know she's lying. So che sta mentendo.
□ You lied to me! Mi hai mentito!
2 essere [47E] disteso *(be lying down)*
□ He was lying on the sofa. Era disteso sul divano. □ He had lain there for hours. È rimasto disteso lì per ore.

to **lie down** VERB
distendersi [112E]
□ Why not go and lie down? Perché non vai a distenderti?
■ **to be lying down** essere [47E] disteso

lie-in NOUN
■ **to have a lie-in** rimanere [88E] a letto

lieutenant NOUN
il tenente *masc*

life NOUN
la vita *fem*
□ all my life tutta la vita
■ **life insurance** assicurazione sulla vita
■ **life jacket** giubbotto di salvataggio
■ **life sentence** ergastolo

lifebelt NOUN
il salvagente *masc*

lifeboat NOUN
la scialuppa di salvataggio *fem*

lifeguard NOUN
il bagnino *masc*

life-saving NOUN
il salvataggio *masc*
□ I've done a course in life-saving. Ho fatto un corso di salvataggio.

lifestyle NOUN
lo stile di vita *masc*

to **lift** VERB
▷ *see also* **lift** NOUN
sollevare [68]
□ It's too heavy, I can't lift it. È troppo pesante, non riesco a sollevarlo.

lift NOUN
▷ *see also* **lift** VERB
1 l' ascensore *masc*
□ The lift isn't working. L'ascensore non funziona.
2 il passaggio *masc*
□ He gave me a lift to the cinema. Mi ha dato un passaggio al cinema.

light ADJECTIVE
▷ *see also* **light** NOUN, VERB
1 leggero (FEM leggera)
□ a light jacket una giacca leggera □ a light meal un pasto leggero
2 chiaro (FEM chiara)
□ a light blue sweater una maglia azzurro chiaro

light NOUN
▷ *see also* **light** ADJECTIVE, VERB
la luce *fem*
□ He switched on the light. Ha acceso la luce.
□ He switched off the light. Ha spento la luce.
■ **Have you got a light?** Ha da accendere?
■ **the traffic lights** il semaforo *masc sing*

to **light** VERB
▷ *see also* **light** ADJECTIVE, NOUN
accendere [2]
□ She lit the candles on the cake. Ha acceso le candeline sulla torta.

light bulb NOUN
la lampadina *fem*

lighter NOUN
l' accendino *masc*

lighthouse NOUN
il faro *masc*

lightning NOUN SING
i fulmini *masc pl*
□ thunder and lightning tuoni e fulmini
■ **a flash of lightning** un fulmine

to **like** VERB
▷ *see also* **like** PREPOSITION
LANGUAGE TIP When saying what you like, remember that the Italian verb **piacere** is impersonal. This means that instead of saying what you like, you say what is pleasing to you. If this is singular the verb is singular, if it is plural the verb is plural.
□ I like Tom. Tom mi piace. □ I don't like dogs. Non mi piacciono i cani. □ I like riding. Mi piace cavalcare. □ How did you like the trip? Ti è piaciuto il viaggio?
LANGUAGE TIP When 'would like' means 'want' it is translated by the conditional of **volere**.

□ I'd like an orange juice, please. Vorrei un'aranciata, per favore. □ I'd like to wash my hands. Vorrei lavarmi le mani. □ He'd like to leave. Vorrebbe andarsene.
■ Would you like...? Vuoi...? □ Would you like to come? Vuoi venire?
■ What would you like? Cosa vuoi?

like PREPOSITION
▷ *see also* **like** VERB
come
□ a city like Paris una città come Parigi
□ What was Turkey like? Com'era la Turchia?
■ What's the weather like? Che tempo fa?
■ It's a bit like salmon. Assomiglia un po' al salmone.
■ It's fine like that. Così va bene.
■ Do it like this. Fallo così.
■ something like that qualcosa del genere
■ to look like somebody assomigliare [25] a qualcuno □ You look like my brother. Assomigli a mio fratello.
■ What does she look like? Che aspetto ha?

likely ADJECTIVE
probabile (FEM probabile)
□ That's not very likely. Non è molto probabile.
■ She's not likely to come. È difficile che venga.

lily of the valley NOUN
il mughetto *masc*

lime NOUN
la limetta *fem (fruit)*
■ lime green giallo-verdino

limit NOUN
il limite *masc*
□ The speed limit is 70 mph. Il limite di velocità è di settanta miglia all'ora.

limousine NOUN
la limousine *fem* (PL le limousine)

to **limp** VERB
▷ *see also* **limp** NOUN
zoppicare [18]

limp NOUN
▷ *see also* **limp** VERB
■ to have a limp zoppicare [18]

line NOUN
▷ *see also* **line** VERB
1 la linea *fem*
□ a straight line una linea retta □ our best-selling line la linea che vendiamo di più
■ to draw a line under something dimenticare [18] qualcosa □ I want to draw a line under the experience. Voglio dimenticare quell'esperienza.
2 la fila *fem*
□ a line of people una fila di persone
■ to stand in line (US) stare [108ᴱ] in fila
3 la riga *fem* (PL le righe)
□ He wrote a few lines. Ha scritto qualche riga.

■ a railway line una linea ferroviaria
■ a phone line una linea telefonica
■ Hold the line, please. Attenda in linea, per favore.
■ It's a very bad line. La comunicazione è disturbata.

to **line** VERB
▷ *see also* **line** NOUN
rivestire [41]
□ Line the tin with greaseproof paper. Rivesti la tortiera con carta oleata.
■ Crowds lined the street. C'erano molte persone ai bordi della strada.
■ The street was lined with trees. La strada era alberata.

to **line up** VERB
mettersi [59ᴱ] in fila
□ Line up in twos. Mettetevi in fila per due.

linen NOUN
il lino *masc*
□ a linen jacket una giacca di lino

liner NOUN
la nave di linea *fem*

lining NOUN
la fodera *fem (of coat, jacket)*

link NOUN
▷ *see also* **link** VERB
il collegamento *masc*
□ the link between smoking and cancer il collegamento tra fumo e cancro □ There's a link to another site. C'è un collegamento ad un altro sito.
■ cultural links rapporti culturali

to **link** VERB
▷ *see also* **link** NOUN
collegare [76]

lino NOUN
il linoleum *masc*

lion NOUN
il leone *masc*

lioness NOUN
la leonessa *fem*

lip NOUN
il labbro *masc* (FEM PL le labbra)
■ red lips labbra rosse

to **lip-read** VERB
leggere [57] le labbra

lipstick NOUN
il rossetto *masc*

liqueur NOUN
il liquore *masc*

liquid NOUN, ADJECTIVE
liquido (FEM liquida)

liquidizer NOUN
il frullatore *masc*

list NOUN
▷ *see also* **list** VERB
la lista *fem*

to **list** VERB
▷ *see also* **list** NOUN
elencare [18]

to **listen** VERB
ascoltare [68]
□ Listen to this! Ascolta!

listener NOUN
l' ascoltatore *masc*
l' ascoltatrice *fem*

lit VERB ▷ *see* **light**

liter NOUN (US)
il litro *masc*

literally ADVERB
letteralmente
□ It was literally impossible to find a seat. Era letteralmente impossibile trovare un posto.

literature NOUN
la letteratura *fem*

litre (US **liter**) NOUN
il litro *masc*

litter NOUN SING
i rifiuti *masc pl*
■ **a litter bin** un cestino dei rifiuti

little ADJECTIVE
▷ *see also* **little** NOUN
1 piccolo (FEM piccola)
□ a little girl una bambina piccola

WORD POWER
You can use a number of other words instead of **little** to mean 'small':
miniature in miniatura
□ a miniature car un'automobile in miniatura
minute minuscolo
□ a minute piece un pezzettino minuscolo
tiny minuscolo
□ a tiny kitchen una cucina minuscola

---

2 poco (FEM poca)
□ It makes little difference. Fa poca differenza.
□ We've got very little time. Abbiamo molto poco tempo.

little NOUN
▷ *see also* **little** ADJECTIVE
poco
□ Little is known about his childhood. Si sa poco della sua infanzia. □ It's changed very little. È cambiato molto poco.
■ **a little** un po' □ How much would you like? — Just a little. Quanto ne vuoi? — Solo un po'.
□ We've still got a little time. Abbiamo ancora un po' di tempo.
■ **little by little** a poco a poco

live ADJECTIVE
▷ *see also* **live** VERB
vivo (FEM viva)
□ I'm against tests on live animals. Sono

contrario agli esperimenti su animali vivi.
■ **a live broadcast** una trasmissione in diretta
■ **a live concert** un concerto dal vivo

to **live** VERB
▷ *see also* **live** ADJECTIVE
1 vivere [122ᴱ]
□ I live with my grandmother. Vivo con mia nonna. □ How can people live like that? Come si può vivere così?
2 abitare [68]
□ Where do you live? Dove abiti? □ I live in Hull. Abito a Hull.

to **live together** VERB
convivere [122ᴱ]

lively ADJECTIVE
vivace (FEM vivace)
□ She's got a lively personality. È una persona vivace.

liver NOUN
il fegato *masc*

lives NOUN ▷ *see* **life**

living NOUN
■ **to make a living** guadagnarsi [14ᴱ] da vivere
■ **What does she do for a living?** Come si guadagna da vivere?
■ **living standards** il tenore di vita *masc sing*

living room NOUN
il salotto *masc*

lizard NOUN
la lucertola *fem*

load NOUN
▷ *see also* **load** VERB
il carico *masc* (PL i carichi)
□ a heavy load un pesante carico
■ **loads of** un sacco di □ They've got loads of money. Hanno un sacco di soldi.
■ **a load of rubbish** un mucchio di sciocchezze □ You're talking a load of rubbish! Stai dicendo un mucchio di sciocchezze!

to **load** VERB
▷ *see also* **load** NOUN
caricare [18]
□ I can't load the program. Non riesco a caricare il programma.

loaf NOUN
la pagnotta *fem*

loan NOUN
▷ *see also* **loan** VERB
il prestito *masc*

to **loan** VERB
▷ *see also* **loan** NOUN
dare [30] in prestito

to **loathe** VERB
detestare [68]
□ I loathe her. La detesto.

loaves NOUN ▷ *see* **loaf**

lobster NOUN
l' astice *masc*
■ **a spiny lobster** un'aragosta

local ADJECTIVE
locale (FEM locale)
  □ the local paper il giornale locale
  ■ **local anaesthetic** l'anestesia locale
  ■ **a local call** una chiamata urbana

local authority NOUN
l' autorità locale fem

loch NOUN
il lago masc (PL i laghi)

lock NOUN
  ▷ see also **lock** VERB
la serratura fem (of door)

to lock VERB
  ▷ see also **lock** NOUN
chiudere [20] a chiave
  □ Make sure you lock your door. Non dimenticare di chiudere la porta a chiave.

to lock out VERB
chiudere [20] fuori
  □ The door slammed and I was locked out. La porta si è chiusa di colpo e sono rimasto chiuso fuori.

locker NOUN
l' armadietto masc
  □ left-luggage lockers armadietti per deposito bagagli

locker room NOUN
lo spogliatoio masc

locket NOUN
il medaglione portaritratti masc

lodger NOUN
il/la pensionante masc/fem

loft NOUN
la soffitta fem

log NOUN
il ciocco masc (PL i ciocchi) (piece of wood)

to log in VERB
registrarsi [56E]

to log off VERB
scollegarsi [76E]

to log on VERB
registrarsi [56E] (to computer)
  ■ **to log on to the Net** collegarsi [76E] in rete

to log out VERB
scollegarsi [76E]

logical ADJECTIVE
logico (FEM logica, MASC PL logici, FEM PL logiche)

lollipop NOUN
il lecca lecca masc (PL i lecca lecca)

lolly NOUN
  ■ **an ice lolly** un ghiacciolo

London NOUN
Londra
  □ I'm from London. Sono di Londra.

Londoner NOUN
il/la londinese masc/fem

loneliness NOUN
la solitudine fem

lonely ADJECTIVE
1 solo (FEM sola) (person)
  □ I sometimes feel lonely. Qualche volta mi sento solo.
2 isolato (FEM isolata) (place)
  □ a lonely cottage una villetta isolata

lonesome ADJECTIVE
  ■ **to feel lonesome** sentirsi [41E] solo

long ADJECTIVE, ADVERB
  ▷ see also **long** VERB
lungo (FEM lunga, MASC PL lunghi, FEM PL lunghe)
  □ She's got long hair. Ha i capelli lunghi.
  □ The room is six metres long. La stanza è lunga sei metri.
  ■ **a long time** molto tempo □ It takes a long time. Ci vuole molto tempo. □ I've been waiting a long time. Aspetto da molto tempo.
  ■ **as long as** sempre che □ I'll come as long as it's not too expensive. Verrò, sempre che non costi troppo.
  ■ **How long did you stay there?** Per quanto tempo sei rimasto lì?
  ■ **How long is the flight?** Quanto dura il volo?
  ■ **How long will it take?** Quanto ci vorrà?

  LANGUAGE TIP Sentences with 'how long' and the perfect tense are translated by an Italian verb in the present tense.

  □ How long have you been here? Da quanto sei qui? □ How long has he been learning Italian? Da quanto studia l'italiano?

to long VERB
  ▷ see also **long** ADJECTIVE, ADVERB
  ■ **to long to do something** morire [61E] dalla voglia di fare qualcosa

long-distance ADJECTIVE
  ■ **a long-distance call** una chiamata interurbana

longer ADVERB
  ▷ see also **long** ADJECTIVE, ADVERB
  ■ **no longer** non... più □ They're no longer going out together. Non escono più insieme.
  □ I can't stand it any longer. Non lo sopporto più.

loo NOUN
il gabinetto masc

look NOUN
  ▷ see also **look** VERB
l' occhiata fem
  □ Have a look at this! Dai un'occhiata a questo!
  ■ **I don't like the look of it.** Non mi piace per niente.

to look VERB
  ▷ see also **look** NOUN
1 guardare [68]
  ■ **to look at something** guardare [68] qualcosa □ Look at the picture on page three. Guardate la figura a pagina tre.
2 sembrare [68E]

□ She looks surprised. Sembra sorpresa.
□ That cake looks nice. La torta sembra buona.

■ **Look out!** Attento!

■ **to look like somebody** assomigliare [25] a qualcuno □ He looks like his brother. Assomiglia a suo fratello.

■ **What does she look like?** Che aspetto ha?

to **look after** VERB
occuparsi [56ᴱ] di
□ I look after my little sister. Mi occupo della mia sorellina.

to **look for** VERB
cercare [18]
□ I'm looking for my passport. Sto cercando il mio passaporto.

to **look forward to** VERB
non veder [119] l'ora di

> LANGUAGE TIP Word for word, this means 'I can't see the time to'.

□ I'm looking forward to meeting you. Non vedo l'ora di incontrarti.

■ **I'm looking forward to the holidays.** Non vedo l'ora che arrivino le vacanze.

■ **Looking forward to hearing from you...** Aspettando tue notizie...

to **look round** VERB
1 voltarsi [56ᴱ]
□ I shouted and he looked round. Ho gridato e lui si è voltato.
2 dare [30] un'occhiata
□ I'm just looking round. Sto solo dando un'occhiata.

■ **to look round an exhibition** visitare [68] una mostra

to **look up** VERB
cercare [18]
□ If you don't know a word, look it up in the dictionary. Se non conosci qualche parola cercala sul dizionario.

loose ADJECTIVE
largo (FEM larga, MASC PL larghi, FEM PL larghe)
□ a loose shirt una camicia larga

■ **a loose screw** una vite allentata

■ **loose change** spiccioli masc pl

lord NOUN
il signore masc (feudal)

■ **the House of Lords** la Camera dei Lord

■ **Good Lord!** Mio Dio!

lorry NOUN
il camion masc (PL i camion)

■ **a lorry driver** un/una camionista □ He's a lorry driver. Fa il camionista.

to **lose** VERB
perdere [69]
□ I've lost my purse. Ho perso il portamonete.
□ They lost the match. Hanno perso la partita.

■ **to get lost** perdersi [69ᴱ] □ I was afraid I'd

get lost. Avevo paura di perdermi.

■ **to lose weight** dimagrire [51ᴱ]

loser NOUN
il/la perdente masc/fem

■ **to be a bad loser** non saper [94] perdere

loss NOUN
la perdita fem

lost VERB ▷ see lose

lost ADJECTIVE
perso (FEM persa)
□ I realized I was lost. Ho capito che mi ero perso.

lost property office (US **lost-and-found**)
NOUN
l' ufficio oggetti smarriti masc

lot NOUN

■ **a lot** molto □ She talks a lot. Parla molto.
□ Do you like football? — Not a lot. Ti piace il calcio? — Non molto.

■ **a lot of** molto □ I drink a lot of coffee. Bevo molto caffè. □ We saw a lot of interesting things. Abbiamo visto molte cose interessanti.

■ **lots of** molto □ He's got lots of friends. Ha molti amici. □ She's got lots of self-confidence. Ha molta fiducia in se stessa.

■ **That's the lot.** È tutto.

lottery NOUN
la lotteria fem

■ **to win the lottery** vincere [121] alla lotteria

loud ADJECTIVE
forte (FEM forte)

loudly ADVERB
forte

loudspeaker NOUN
l' altoparlante masc

lousy ADJECTIVE
pessimo (FEM pessima)
□ The food's lousy. Il cibo è pessimo.

■ **I feel lousy.** Sto da cani.

love NOUN
▷ see also **love** VERB
l' amore masc
□ true love vero amore

■ **to be in love** essere [47ᴱ] innamorato
□ She's in love with Paul. È innamorata di Paul.

■ **to fall in love** innamorarsi [56ᴱ]

■ **to make love** fare [49] l'amore

■ **Give Gloria my love.** Salutami Gloria.

■ **Love,...** (in letter) Con affetto,...

to **love** VERB
▷ see also **love** NOUN
1 amare [68]
□ I love you. Ti amo.
2 voler [123] bene a
□ Everybody loves her. Tutti le vogliono bene.

■ **I love chocolate.** Mi piace molto la cioccolata.

■ **I'd love to...** Mi piacerebbe molto... □ I'd love to come. Mi piacerebbe molto venire.

■ **Would you like to come? — I'd love to.**
Vuoi venire? — Mi piacerebbe molto.

love affair NOUN
la relazione *fem*

lovely ADJECTIVE
1 bello (FEM bella)
□ What a lovely surprise! Che bella sorpresa!
□ They've got a lovely house. Hanno una bella casa.
2 buonissimo (FEM buonissima)
□ Is your meal okay? — Yes, it's lovely. Ti piace il pranzo? — Sì, è buonissimo.
3 delizioso (FEM deliziosa)
□ She's a lovely person. È una persona deliziosa.
■ **Have a lovely time!** Divertiti!

lover NOUN
l' amante *masc/fem*

low ADJECTIVE, ADVERB
basso (FEM bassa)
□ That plane is flying very low. Quell'aereo vola molto basso. □ in the low season in bassa stagione

to **lower** VERB
abbassare [68]
□ They have lowered interest rates. Hanno abbassato i tassi d'interesse.

lower ADJECTIVE
inferiore (FEM inferiore)
□ a lower standard un livello inferiore
■ **the lower sixth** biennio conclusivo della scuola secondaria

low-fat ADJECTIVE
magro (FEM magra)

loyalty NOUN
la lealtà *fem*

loyalty card NOUN
la carta fedeltà *fem* (PL le carte fedeltà) (of shop)

lozenge NOUN
la pastiglia *fem* (for throat)

luck NOUN
la fortuna *fem*
■ **Good luck!** Buona fortuna!
■ **Bad luck!** Che sfortuna!
■ **Just my luck!** La mia solita sfortuna!

luckily ADVERB
fortunatamente

lucky ADJECTIVE
fortunato (FEM fortunata)
□ He's lucky, he's got a job. È fortunato. Ha un lavoro.
■ **Black cats are lucky in Britain.** I gatti neri

portano fortuna in Gran Bretagna.
■ **That was lucky!** Per fortuna!
■ **a lucky horseshoe** un ferro di cavallo portafortuna

luggage NOUN
i bagagli *masc pl*
□ My luggage was left behind. Hanno dimenticato i miei bagagli.

lukewarm ADJECTIVE
tiepido (FEM tiepida)

lump NOUN
1 il pezzo *masc* (piece)
2 il bernoccolo *masc*
□ He's got a lump on his forehead. Ha un bernoccolo sulla fronte.

lump sum NOUN
la somma forfettaria *fem*

lunatic NOUN
il pazzo *masc*
la pazza *fem*
□ He's an absolute lunatic. È completamente pazzo.

lunch NOUN
il pranzo *masc*
■ **to have lunch** pranzare [68] □ We have lunch at 12 00. Pranziamo a mezzogiorno.

luncheon voucher NOUN
il buono pasto *masc* (PL i buoni pasto)

lung NOUN
il polmone *masc*
□ lung cancer il cancro ai polmoni

luscious ADJECTIVE
succoso (FEM succosa) (fruit)

lush ADJECTIVE
lussureggiante (FEM lussureggiante)

lust NOUN
il desiderio *masc*

Luxembourg NOUN
il Lussemburgo *masc*

luxurious ADJECTIVE
lussuoso (FEM lussuosa)

  LANGUAGE TIP Be careful not to translate **luxurious** by **lussurioso**.

luxury NOUN
il lusso *masc*
□ It was luxury! È stato un vero lusso!
□ a luxury hotel un albergo di lusso

  LANGUAGE TIP Be careful not to translate **luxury** by **lussuria**.

lying VERB ▷ see **lie**

lyrics NOUN PL
le parole *fem pl*

Mm

mac NOUN
l' impermeabile *masc*

macaroni NOUN SING
i maccheroni *masc pl*

machine NOUN
1 la macchina *fem*
□ It's a complicated machine. È una macchina complicata.
2 la lavatrice *fem*
□ I put clothes in the machine. Ho messo i vestiti in lavatrice.

machine gun NOUN
la mitragliatrice *fem*

machinery NOUN SING
i macchinari *masc pl*
□ The machinery in the factory was outdated. I macchinari della fabbrica erano superati.

mackerel NOUN
lo sgombro *masc*

mad ADJECTIVE
1 pazzo (FEM pazza)
□ You're mad! Tu sei pazzo!
■ **to go mad** impazzire [51ᴱ] □ Have you gone mad? Sei impazzito?
■ **to be mad about** andare [6ᴱ] matto per □ He's mad about football. Va matto per il calcio.
■ **mad cow disease** morbo della mucca pazza
2 furioso (FEM furiosa)
□ She'll be mad when she finds out. Sarà furiosa quando lo scoprirà.

madam NOUN
la signora *fem*
□ How may I help you Madam? La signora desidera?

made VERB ▷ *see* make

madly ADVERB
■ **They're madly in love.** Sono follemente innamorati.

madman NOUN
il pazzo *masc*

madness NOUN
la pazzia *fem*
□ It's absolute madness. È pura pazzia.

magazine NOUN
la rivista *fem*

> **LANGUAGE TIP** Be careful not to translate **magazine** by **magazzino**.

maggot NOUN
il baco *masc* (PL i bachi)

magic NOUN
▷ *see also* **magic** ADJECTIVE
la magia *fem*

magic ADJECTIVE
▷ *see also* **magic** NOUN
1 magico (FEM magica, MASC PL magici, FEM PL magiche)
□ a magic potion una pozione magica
2 miracoloso (FEM miracolosa)
□ There's no magic solution. Non ci sono soluzioni miracolose.
3 fantastico (FEM fantastica, MASC PL fantastici, FEM PL fantastiche)
□ It was magic! È stato fantastico!

magician NOUN
1 l' illusionista *masc/fem* (entertainer)
2 il mago *masc* (PL i maghi) (in stories)

magnet NOUN
la calamita *fem*

magnificent ADJECTIVE
1 magnifico (FEM magnifica, MASC PL magnifici, FEM PL magnifiche)
□ a magnificent view una vista magnifica
2 grosso (FEM grossa)
□ It is a magnificent achievement. È un grosso risultato.

magnifying glass NOUN
la lente d'ingrandimento *fem*

maid NOUN
1 la cameriera *fem* (in hotel)
2 la domestica *fem* (PL le domestiche) (in house)
■ **an old maid** una vecchia zitella

maiden name NOUN
il nome da ragazza *masc*

mail NOUN
▷ *see also* **mail** VERB
la posta *fem*
□ by mail per posta

to **mail** VERB
▷ *see also* **mail** NOUN
1 spedire [51] per posta
□ He mailed me the contract. Mi ha spedito il contratto per posta.
2 imbucare [18]
□ I forgot to mail the letter. Ho dimenticato di imbucare la lettera.

mailbox NOUN (US)
la cassetta delle lettere *fem*

mailing list NOUN
la mailing list *fem* (PL le mailing list)

mailman NOUN (US)
il postino *masc*

main ADJECTIVE
principale (FEM principale)
□ the main points i punti principali

mainly ADVERB
principalmente

main road NOUN
la strada principale *fem*

to **maintain** VERB
1 mantenere [113]
□ They want to maintain standards. Vogliono mantenere un certo livello.
2 sostenere [113]
□ She had always maintained her innocence. Aveva sempre sostenuto la propria innocenza.

maintenance NOUN
1 la manutenzione *fem*
□ car maintenance la manutenzione della macchina
2 gli alimenti *masc pl*
□ His father has to pay maintenance. Suo padre deve pagare gli alimenti.

maize NOUN
il granturco *masc*

majesty NOUN
la maestà *fem*

major ADJECTIVE
1 grosso (FEM grossa)
□ Drugs are a major problem. La droga è un grosso problema.
2 importante (FEM importante)
□ a major new film un importante nuovo film

Majorca NOUN
Maiorca

majority NOUN
la maggioranza *fem*
□ the majority of our products la maggioranza dei nostri prodotti

make NOUN
▷ *see also* **make** VERB
la marca *fem* (PL le marche)

to **make** VERB
▷ *see also* **make** NOUN
1 fare [49]
□ I'd like to make a phone call. Vorrei fare una telefonata. □ I make my bed every morning. Mi faccio il letto ogni mattina. □ What time do you make it? Che ora fai? □ It's well made. È ben fatto.
2 fabbricare [18]
□ It was made in Italy. È stato fabbricato in Italia.
3 guadagnare [14]

□ He makes a lot of money. Guadagna un sacco di soldi.
4 arrivare [68ᴱ] a
□ We made Exeter by seven o'clock. Siamo arrivati ad Exeter alle sette.
■ **to make somebody do something** obbligare [76] qualcuno a fare qualcosa
□ My mother makes me do my homework. Mia madre mi obbliga a fare i compiti.
■ **to make do with** accontentarsi [56ᴱ] di
□ You'll have to make do with a cheaper alternative. Dovrai accontentarti di qualcosa che costi meno.
■ **Sorry, I can't make it to the party.** Mi dispiace, ma non riesco a venire alla festa.
■ **I make the total cost £1200.** Penso che il costo complessivo sia di milleduecento sterline.

to **make off** VERB
svignarsela [56ᴱ]

to **make out** VERB
1 decifrare [68]
□ I can't make out the address on the label. Non riesco a decifrare l'indirizzo sull'etichetta.
2 capire [51]
□ I can't make her out at all. Non riesco proprio a capirla.
3 voler [123] far credere
□ They're making out it was my fault. Vogliono far credere che sia colpa mia.
■ **to make a cheque out to somebody** intestare [68] un assegno a qualcuno

to **make up** VERB
1 inventare [68]
□ He made up the whole story. Ha inventato tutta la storia.
2 fare [49] la pace
□ They had a quarrel, but soon made up. Hanno litigato, ma hanno subito fatto la pace.
3 truccarsi [18ᴱ]
□ She spends hours making herself up. Passa delle ore a truccarsi.
■ **Women make up thirteen per cent of the police force.** Il tredici percento del corpo di polizia è formato da donne.

to **make up for** VERB
compensare [68]
□ Money can't make up for the stress I've suffered. Il denaro non può compensare lo stress che ho subito.

to **make up to** VERB
■ **I'll make it up to you somehow.** La ricompenserò in qualche modo.

makeover NOUN
il rifacimento *masc (di casa)*
■ **to have a makeover** *(di persona)* rifarsi [49ᴱ] il look

maker NOUN
il produttore *masc*

□ Italy's biggest car maker il più grosso produttore di automobili in Italia

make-up NOUN
il trucco *masc*
■ **to put on one's make-up** truccarsi [18ᴱ]
□ She put on her make-up. Si è truccata.

male ADJECTIVE
maschio (MASC PL maschi)
□ Most football players are male. Quasi tutti i giocatori di calcio sono maschi.
■ **Sex: Male** Sesso: Maschile
■ **a male nurse** un infermiere
■ **a male chauvinist** un maschilista

mall NOUN
il centro commerciale *masc*

Malta NOUN
Malta

mammoth ADJECTIVE
▷ *see also* **mammoth** NOUN
mostruoso (FEM mostruosa)
□ a mammoth task un lavoro mostruoso

mammoth NOUN
▷ *see also* **mammoth** ADJECTIVE
il mammut *masc* (PL i mammut)

man NOUN
l' uomo *masc* (PL gli uomini)

to manage VERB
1 riuscire [117ᴱ]
□ I managed to pass the exam. Sono riuscito a passare l'esame.
2 farcela [56]
□ Can you manage? Ce la fai?
■ **Can you manage a bit more?** Posso mettertene ancora un po'?
3 arrangiarsi [58ᴱ]
□ We haven't got much money, but we manage. Non abbiamo molto denaro, ma ci arrangiamo.
4 dirigere [36]
□ She manages a big store. Dirige un grande negozio.

manageable ADJECTIVE
accettabile (FEM accettabile)
□ It was a manageable task. Era un compito accettabile.

management NOUN
la gestione *fem*
□ The restaurant is under new management. Il ristorante ha una nuova gestione.
■ **management and workers** dirigenti e lavoratori

manager NOUN
1 il direttore *masc*
la direttrice *fem*
□ I complained to the manager. Mi sono lamentato con il direttore.
2 il commissario tecnico *masc* (PL i commissari tecnici)

□ the England manager il commissario tecnico dell'Inghilterra

manageress NOUN
la direttrice *fem*

mandarin NOUN
il mandarino *masc*

mango NOUN
il mango *masc* (PL i manghi)

maniac NOUN
1 il maniaco *masc* (PL i maniaci)
la maniaca *fem* (PL le maniache)
□ a dangerous maniac un pericoloso maniaco
2 il pazzo *masc*
la pazza *fem*
□ He drives like a maniac. Guida come un pazzo.

to manipulate VERB
manipolare [68]
□ She used her position to manipulate people. Usava la sua posizione per manipolare le persone.
■ **He tried to manipulate the situation.** Ha cercato di pilotare la situazione a proprio vantaggio.

man-made ADJECTIVE
artificiale (FEM artificiale)

manner NOUN
il modo *masc*
□ She was behaving in an odd manner. Si comportava in modo strano.
■ **a confident manner** un modo di fare molto sicuro
■ **good manners** buona educazione *fem sing*
■ **Her manners are appalling.** Non conosce le buone maniere.
■ **It's bad manners to speak with your mouth full.** È da maleducati parlare con la bocca piena.

manpower NOUN
la manodopera *fem*

mansion NOUN
la casa signorile *fem*

mantelpiece NOUN
il caminetto *masc*

manual NOUN
il manuale *masc*

to manufacture VERB
fabbricare [18]

manufacturer NOUN
il produttore *masc*

manure NOUN
il concime *masc*

manuscript NOUN
il manoscritto *masc*

many ADJECTIVE, PRONOUN
molti *masc pl* (FEM PL molte)
□ He hasn't got many friends. Non ha molti amici.

m

461

- **many people** molta gente
- **How many?** Quanti? □ How many do you want? Quanti ne vuoi?
- **too many** troppi □ Sixteen people? That's too many. Sedici persone? Sono troppe.
- **so many** tanti □ He told so many lies. Ha detto tante bugie.
- **as many as** quanti □ Take as many as you like. Prendine quanti ne vuoi.

map NOUN
1 la carta geografica *fem* (PL le carte geografiche)
  □ a map of Egypt una carta geografica dell'Egitto
2 la cartina *fem*
  □ maps and guide books cartine e guide
  - **a map of the city** una pianta della città

marathon NOUN
la maratona *fem*

marble NOUN
il marmo *masc*
  □ a marble statue una statua di marmo

March NOUN
marzo
  □ in March in marzo

to **march** VERB
  ▷ *see also* **march** NOUN
1 sfilare [68]
  □ The demonstrators marched along the main street. I dimostranti sfilavano sulla via principale.
2 marciare [13]
  □ The soldiers marched 50 miles. I soldati hanno marciato per cinquanta miglia.

march NOUN
  ▷ *see also* **march** VERB
la marcia *fem* (PL le marce)

mare NOUN
la cavalla *fem*

margarine NOUN
la margarina *fem*

margin NOUN
il margine *masc*

marijuana NOUN
la marijuana *fem*

marina NOUN
la marina *fem* (*for leisure craft*)

marital status NOUN
lo stato civile *masc*

mark NOUN
  ▷ *see also* **mark** VERB
1 il voto *masc*
  □ I get good marks for French. Prendo bei voti in francese.
2 il segno *masc*
  □ There were red marks all over his back. Aveva segni rossi su tutta la schiena.
3 la macchia *fem*
  □ You've got a mark on your shirt. Hai una macchia sulla camicia.

to **mark** VERB
  ▷ *see also* **mark** NOUN
1 correggere [82]
  □ The teacher hasn't marked my homework yet. Il professore non mi ha ancora corretto il compito.
2 segnare [14]
  □ Mark its position on the map. Segna il posto in cui si trova sulla cartina.

to **mark down** VERB
ribassare [68]
  □ The shirts were marked down at the beginning of the week. Le camicie sono state ribassate all'inizio della settimana.

market NOUN
il mercato *masc*
  - **market research** indagini di mercato *fem pl*

marketing NOUN
il marketing *masc*

marketplace NOUN
la piazza del mercato *fem*

marmalade NOUN
la marmellata d'arance *fem*

  LANGUAGE TIP Word for word, this means 'orange jam'.

maroon ADJECTIVE
bordeaux (FEM+PL bordeaux)

  LANGUAGE TIP Be careful not to translate **maroon** by **marrone**.

marriage NOUN
il matrimonio *masc*
  - **marriage certificate** il certificato di matrimonio

married ADJECTIVE
sposato (FEM sposata)

marrow NOUN
la zucca *fem* (PL le zucche) (*vegetable*)
  - **bone marrow** il midollo osseo

to **marry** VERB
sposare [68]
  □ He wants to marry her. Vuole sposarla.
  - **to get married** sposarsi [56ᴱ] □ My sister's getting married in June. Mia sorella si sposa in giugno.

marvellous (US **marvelous**) ADJECTIVE
stupendo (FEM stupenda)
  □ The weather was marvellous. Il tempo era stupendo.

marzipan NOUN
il marzapane *masc*

mascara NOUN
il mascara *masc* (PL i mascara)

masculine ADJECTIVE
maschile (FEM maschile)

to **mash** VERB
schiacciare [13] (*vegetables, fruit*)

mashed potatoes NOUN
il purè di patate *masc sing*

mask NOUN
la maschera *fem*

masked ADJECTIVE
mascherato (FEM mascherata)

mass NOUN
1 la massa *fem*
   □ a mass of books and papers una massa di libri e carte
2 la messa *fem*
   □ Sunday mass messa della domenica

massage NOUN
il massaggio *masc*

massive ADJECTIVE
enorme (FEM enorme)

to **master** VERB
impadronirsi [51ᴱ] di
   □ She soon mastered the technique. Si è impadronita rapidamente della tecnica.

masterpiece NOUN
il capolavoro *masc*

mat NOUN
il tappetino *masc (doormat)*
   ■ **a table mat** una tovaglietta all'americana

match NOUN
   ▷ *see also* **match** VERB
1 la partita *fem*
   □ Are you going to the match? Vai alla partita?
2 il fiammifero *masc*
   □ a box of matches una scatola di fiammiferi

to **match** VERB
   ▷ *see also* **match** NOUN
1 intonarsi [56ᴱ] con
   □ The jacket matches the trousers. La giacca si intona con i pantaloni.
2 far [49] corrispondere
   □ Match the pictures to the titles. Fai corrispondere le immagini ai titoli.

matching ADJECTIVE
intonato (FEM intonata)

mate NOUN
l' amico *masc (PL gli amici)*
   □ He always goes on holiday with his mates. Va sempre in vacanza con i suoi amici.

material NOUN
1 la stoffa *fem*
   □ The curtains are made of thin material. Le tende sono fatte di una stoffa sottile.
2 il materiale *masc*
   □ I'm collecting material for my project. Sto raccogliendo materiale per la mia ricerca.
   ■ **raw materials** materie prime

maths (US **math**) NOUN
la matematica *fem*

matron NOUN
l' infermiera capo *fem (PL le infermiere capo)*

matter NOUN
   ▷ *see also* **matter** VERB
la questione *fem*

□ It's a matter of life and death. È una questione di vita o di morte.
   ■ **What's the matter?** Cosa c'è che non va?
   ■ **as a matter of fact** per dire la verità

to **matter** VERB
   ▷ *see also* **matter** NOUN
importare [68ᴱ]
   □ It doesn't matter. Non importa.
   ■ **Today or tomorrow? — Whenever, it doesn't matter.** Oggi o domani? — Quando vuoi, è uguale.
   ■ **It matters a lot to me.** È molto importante per me.

mattress NOUN
il materasso *masc*

mature ADJECTIVE
maturo (FEM matura)

maximum NOUN, ADJECTIVE
il massimo *masc*
la massima *fem*

May NOUN
maggio
   □ in May in maggio
   ■ **May Day** il primo maggio

may VERB

   LANGUAGE TIP 'may' is usually translated by **potere**.

   □ May I smoke? Posso fumare? □ It may rain. Potrebbe piovere.
   ■ **Are you going to the party? — I don't know, I may...** Vai alla festa? — Non so, forse...
   ■ **He may come.** Può darsi che venga.
   ■ **They may have thought you were joking.** Forse hanno pensato che scherzassi.

maybe ADVERB
forse

mayonnaise NOUN
la maionese *fem*

mayor NOUN
il sindaco *masc (PL i sindaci)*

maze NOUN
il labirinto *masc*

me PRONOUN
1 mi
   □ Excuse me! Mi scusi! □ Could you lend me your pen? Puoi prestarmi la penna? □ Look at me! Guardami!
2 me
   □ Come with me! Vieni con me!
   ■ **without me** senza di me
   ■ **It's me.** Sono io.

meal NOUN
il pasto *masc*
   □ before meals prima dei pasti
   ■ **Enjoy your meal!** Buon appetito!

mealtime NOUN
   ■ **at mealtimes** all'ora dei pasti

to **mean** VERB
▷ see also **mean** ADJECTIVE
1 significare [18]
□ What does 'trap' mean? Cosa significa 'trap'? □ You mean a lot to me. Significhi molto per me.
2 intendere [112]
□ That's not what I meant. Non era quello che intendevo. □ Do you mean me? Intendi me?
3 volere [123]
□ I didn't mean to hurt you. Non volevo farti del male.
■ **Do you really mean it?** Parli sul serio?
■ **He means what he says.** Parla sul serio.

mean ADJECTIVE
▷ see also **mean** VERB
1 avaro (FEM avara)
□ He's too mean to buy presents. È troppo avaro per comprare regali.
2 meschino (FEM meschina)
□ That's a really mean thing to say! Che cosa meschina da dire!
3 cattivo (FEM cattiva)
□ You're being mean to me. Sei cattivo con me.

meaning NOUN
il significato masc

means NOUN SING
il mezzo masc
□ He'll do it by any possible means. Lo farà con ogni mezzo possibile.
■ **a means of transport** un mezzo di trasporto
■ **by means of** per mezzo di
■ **Can I come? — By all means!** Posso venire? — Ma certamente!

meant VERB ▷ see **mean**

meanwhile ADVERB
nel frattempo

measles NOUN SING
il morbillo masc

to **measure** VERB
misurare [68]
□ They regularly measure pollution levels. Misurano regolarmente il grado di inquinamento.

measurements NOUN PL
le misure fem pl
□ Are you sure the measurements are correct? Sei sicuro che le misure siano giuste?

meat NOUN
la carne fem
□ I don't eat meat. Non mangio carne.

Mecca NOUN
la Mecca fem

mechanic NOUN
il meccanico masc (PL i meccanici)

medal NOUN
la medaglia fem

medallion NOUN
il medaglione masc

media NOUN PL
■ **the media** i mass media

median strip NOUN PL (US)
la banchina spartitraffico fem (PL le banchine spartitraffico)

medical ADJECTIVE
▷ see also **medical** NOUN
medico (FEM medica, MASC PL medici, FEM PL mediche)
□ medical treatment cure mediche fem pl

medical NOUN
▷ see also **medical** ADJECTIVE
la visita medica fem (PL le visite mediche)
□ He had his medical last week. Ha fatto una visita medica la settimana scorsa.

medicine NOUN
la medicina fem

Mediterranean ADJECTIVE
mediterraneo (FEM mediterranea)

medium ADJECTIVE
medio (FEM media)
□ Small, medium or large? Piccola, media o grande?
■ **a medium size town** una città di dimensioni medie

to **meet** VERB
1 incontrare [68]
□ I met Paul in town. Ho incontrato Paul in città.
2 incontrarsi [56ᴱ]
□ We met by chance. Ci siamo incontrati per caso.
3 trovarsi [56ᴱ]
□ I'm going to meet my friends at the swimming pool. Mi trovo con i miei amici in piscina.
4 andare [6ᴱ] a prendere
□ I'll meet you at the station. Vengo a prenderti in stazione.
5 conoscere [24]
□ Come and meet my dad. Vieni a conoscere mio padre.
■ **Pleased to meet you.** Piacere di conoscerla.

to **meet up** VERB
incontrarsi [56ᴱ]
□ They arranged to meet up with the others at eight o'clock. Hanno stabilito di incontrarsi con gli altri alle otto.

meeting NOUN
1 l' incontro masc
□ their first meeting il loro primo incontro
2 la riunione fem
□ a business meeting una riunione di lavoro

meg NOUN
il mega masc (PL i mega) (megabyte)

mega ADJECTIVE
■ **He's mega rich.** È straricco.

melody NOUN
la melodia *fem*

melon NOUN
il melone *masc*

to **melt** VERB
1 sciogliere [97]
□ Melt sixty grams of butter in a saucepan. Sciogliete sessanta grammi di burro in una casseruola.
2 sciogliersi [97ᴱ]
□ The snow is melting. La neve si sta sciogliendo.

member NOUN
1 il membro *masc*
□ a member of NATO un membro della NATO
■ **a member of the public** un privato cittadino *masc*, una privata cittadina *fem*
2 il socio *masc (of club)*
□ 'members only' 'riservato ai soci'
■ **a Member of Parliament** un deputato *masc*, una deputata *fem*

membership NOUN
l' iscrizione *fem*
□ I'm going to apply for membership. Farò domanda d'iscrizione.

membership card NOUN
la tessera *fem*

memento NOUN
il ricordo *masc*

memorial ADJECTIVE
▷ *see also* **memorial** NOUN
■ **a memorial service** una funzione commemorativa

memorial NOUN
▷ *see also* **memorial** ADJECTIVE
■ **a war memorial** un monumento ai caduti

to **memorize** VERB
imparare [68] a memoria

memory NOUN
1 la memoria *fem*
□ I've got a terrible memory. Ho una pessima memoria.
2 il ricordo *masc*
□ happy memories bei ricordi

memory card NOUN
la scheda di memoria *fem*

memory stick NOUN
la pennetta USB *fem*

men NOUN PL ▷ *see* **man**

to **mend** VERB
aggiustare [68]

meningitis NOUN
la meningite *fem*

mental ADJECTIVE
mentale (FEM mentale)
□ a mental illness una malattia mentale

mentality NOUN
la mentalità *fem* (PL le mentalità)

to **mention** VERB
1 parlare [68] di
□ He didn't mention it to me. Non me ne ha parlato.
2 accennare [68] a
□ She didn't mention her unpleasant experience. Non ha accennato alla sua spiacevole esperienza.
3 dire [35]
□ I mentioned she might come later. Ho detto che poteva passare più tardi.
■ **Thank you! — Don't mention it!** Grazie! — Di niente!

menu NOUN
il menù *masc* (PL i menù)
□ a set menu un menù a prezzo fisso

merchant NOUN
il/la commerciante *masc/fem*
□ a wine merchant un commerciante di vini

merchant navy NOUN
la marina mercantile *fem*

mercy NOUN
la pietà *fem*

mere ADJECTIVE
semplice (FEM semplice)
□ It's a mere formality. È una semplice formalità.
■ **a mere five percent** solo il cinque per cento
■ **the merest** il minimo □ the merest hint of criticism il minimo accenno di critica

meringue NOUN
la meringa *fem* (PL le meringhe)

merry ADJECTIVE
■ **Merry Christmas!** Buon Natale!

merry-go-round NOUN
la giostra *fem*

mess NOUN
1 il disordine *masc*
■ **to be a mess** essere [47ᴱ] in disordine □ My hair's a mess, it needs cutting. Ho i capelli in disordine: devo tagliarli.
2 il guaio *masc*
□ I'll be in a mess if I fail the exam. Sarò in un bel guaio se non passerò l'esame.

to **mess about** VERB
trafficare [18]
□ Don't mess about with my computer! Non trafficare con il mio computer!
■ **I didn't do much at the weekend, just messed about with friends.** Non ho fatto granché per il fine settimana, sono stato con degli amici.

to **mess up** VERB
incasinare [68]
□ You've messed up my CDs! Hai incasinato i miei CD!

465

m

■ **I messed up my chemistry exam.** Mi è andato male l'esame di chimica.

message NOUN
▷ *see also* **message** VERB
il messaggio *masc*

to **message** VERB
▷ *see also* **message** NOUN
messaggiare [58]
□ She messaged me on Facebook. Mi ha messaggiato su Facebook.

messenger NOUN
il messaggero *masc*
la messaggera *fem*

messy ADJECTIVE
pasticcione (FEM pasticciona)
□ She's such a messy person! È una persona talmente pasticciona!
■ **Painting can be a messy activity.** Dipingere è un'attività con cui ci si può sporcare molto.
■ **Her writing is very messy.** Ha una scritturaccia.

met VERB ▷ *see* **meet**

metal NOUN
il metallo *masc*

meter NOUN
1 il parchimetro *masc (parking meter)*
2 il contatore *masc (for gas, electricity)*
3 il metro *masc (US: metre)*

method NOUN
il metodo *masc*

Methodist NOUN
il/la metodista *masc/fem*

metre NOUN
il metro *masc*

metric ADJECTIVE
metrico (FEM metrica, MASC PL metrici, FEM PL metriche)

Mexico NOUN
il Messico *masc*

to **miaow** VERB
miagolare [68]

mice NOUN ▷ *see* **mouse**

microblog NOUN
il microblog *masc (PL i microblog)*

microblogging site NOUN
il sito di microblogging *masc*

microchip NOUN
il microcircuito integrato *masc*

microphone NOUN
il microfono *masc*

microscope NOUN
il microscopio *masc*

microwave NOUN
il forno a microonde *masc*

mid ADJECTIVE
■ **in mid May** a metà maggio
■ **He's in his mid twenties.** Avrà circa venticinque anni.

midday NOUN
il mezzogiorno *masc*

middle NOUN
▷ *see also* **middle** ADJECTIVE
■ **in the middle** in mezzo   □ In the middle let's put... E in mezzo mettiamo...
■ **in the middle of** in mezzo a   □ The car was in the middle of the road. La macchina era in mezzo alla strada.
■ **The potatoes were still raw in the middle.** Le patate erano ancora crude dentro.
■ **She was in the middle of her exams.** Era sotto esame.
■ **in the middle of the night** nel cuore della notte

middle ADJECTIVE
▷ *see also* **middle** NOUN
di mezzo
□ the middle seat il sedile di mezzo
■ **the middle finger** il medio
■ **middle name** secondo nome

middle-aged ADJECTIVE
di mezza età

Middle Ages NOUN PL
■ **the Middle Ages** il Medioevo

middle-class ADJECTIVE
borghese (FEM borghese)

Middle East NOUN
il Medio Oriente *masc*

middle name NOUN
il secondo nome *masc*

midge NOUN
il moscerino *masc*

midnight NOUN
la mezzanotte *fem*

midwife NOUN
l' ostetrica *fem (PL le ostetriche)*

might VERB

> LANGUAGE TIP 'might' is often translated by the conditional of **potere**.

□ We might go to Spain next year. Potremmo andare in Spagna il prossimo anno.   □ She might not have understood. Potrebbe non aver capito.   □ He might come later. Forse potrebbe arrivare più tardi.
■ **I suppose you might as well come with us.** Tanto vale che tu venga con noi, suppongo.

migraine NOUN
l' emicrania *fem*

mike NOUN
il microfono *masc*

Milan NOUN
Milano *fem*

mild ADJECTIVE
1 mite (FEM mite)
□ The winters are quite mild. Gli inverni sono abbastanza miti.

■ **It's very mild today.** Oggi non fa affatto freddo.
2 delicato (FEM delicata)
□ a mild flavour un sapore delicato
■ **mild soap** sapone neutro

mile NOUN
il miglio *masc* (FEM PL le miglia)

> **DID YOU KNOW...?**
> In Italy distances are expressed in kilometres. A mile is about 1.6 kilometres.

■ **We walked for miles!** Abbiamo fatto chilometri a piedi!

military ADJECTIVE
militare (FEM militare)

milk NOUN
▷ *see also* **milk** VERB
il latte *masc*
□ tea with milk tè con il latte

to **milk** VERB
▷ *see also* **milk** NOUN
mungere [5]

milk chocolate NOUN
il cioccolato al latte *masc*

milkman NOUN
il lattaio *masc*

milk shake NOUN
il frappé *masc* (PL i frappé)

mill NOUN
il mulino *masc*
□ an old mill un vecchio mulino
■ **a woollen mill** un lanificio
■ **a pepper mill** un macinapepe

millennium NOUN PL
il millennio *masc*

millimetre (US **millimeter**) NOUN
il millimetro *masc*

million NOUN
il milione *masc*
□ two million pounds due milioni di sterline

millionaire NOUN
il miliardario *masc*
la miliardaria *fem*

to **mimic** VERB
imitare [68]

mince NOUN
la carne macinata *fem*
□ lean mince carne macinata magra

mince pie NOUN
il tortino natalizio *masc*

to **mind** VERB
▷ *see also* **mind** NOUN
1 fare [49] attenzione a
□ Mind you don't fall. Fa' attenzione a non cadere.
■ **Mind the step!** Attenzione al gradino!
2 occuparsi [56E] di
□ Could you mind the baby this afternoon? Puoi occuparti del bambino questo pomeriggio?

3 guardare [68]
□ Could you mind my bags for a few minutes? Può guardarmi le borse per qualche minuto?
■ **Do you mind if I open the window? — No, I don't mind.** Le dispiace se apro la finestra? — Faccia pure.
■ **I don't mind getting up early.** Non mi dispiace alzarmi presto.
■ **I don't mind the noise.** Il rumore non mi dà fastidio.
■ **Never mind!** Non fa niente!

mind NOUN
▷ *see also* **mind** VERB
la mente *fem*
□ What have you got in mind? Che cos'hai in mente? □ It never crossed my mind. Non mi ha mai sfiorato la mente.
■ **to make up one's mind** decidere [31]
□ I haven't made up my mind yet. Non ho ancora deciso.
■ **to change one's mind** cambiare [17] idea
□ He's changed his mind. Ha cambiato idea.
■ **to bear something in mind** tener [113] presente □ I'll bear that in mind. Lo terrò presente.
■ **Are you out of your mind?** Sei impazzito?
■ **It'll keep your mind off the exam.** Ti distrarrà dall'esame.
■ **She's got a mind of her own.** Pensa con la sua testa.

mine PRONOUN
▷ *see also* **mine** NOUN

> **LANGUAGE TIP** The Italian pronoun agrees with the noun it is replacing.

1 il mio *masc* (PL i miei)
□ Is this your coat? — No, mine's black. È tuo questo cappotto? — No, il mio è nero. □ Your marks are better than mine. I tuoi voti sono migliori dei miei.
2 la mia *fem* (PL le mie)
□ Is this your scarf? — No, mine's red. È tua questa sciarpa? — No, la mia è rossa. □ Her shoes are nicer than mine. Le sue scarpe sono più belle delle mie.
3 mio *masc* (PL miei) (my property)
□ That book's mine. Quel libro è mio.
■ **He's a friend of mine.** È un mio amico.
4 mia *fem* (PL mie) (my property)
□ These pencils are mine. Queste matite sono mie.
■ **She's a friend of mine.** È una mia amica.

mine NOUN
▷ *see also* **mine** PRONOUN
1 la miniera *fem*
□ a coal mine una miniera di carbone
2 la mina *fem*
□ unexploded mines mine inesplose

miner NOUN
il minatore *masc*

mineral ADJECTIVE
minerale (FEM minerale)

mineral water NOUN
l' acqua minerale *fem*

miniature ADJECTIVE
in miniatura

minibus NOUN
il pulmino *masc*

minicab NOUN
il taxi *masc* (PL i taxi)

Minidisc® NOUN
il minidisco *masc* (PL i minidischi)

minimum ADJECTIVE, NOUN
il minimo *masc*
la minima *fem*

miniskirt NOUN
la minigonna *fem*

minister NOUN
1 il ministro *masc*
  □ the Education Minister il ministro della Pubblica Istruzione
2 il pastore *masc* (of church)

ministry NOUN
il ministero *masc*

mink NOUN
il visone *masc*
  □ a mink coat una pelliccia di visone

minor ADJECTIVE
1 secondario (FEM secondaria, MASC PL secondari, FEM PL secondarie)
  □ a minor problem un problema secondario
2 piccolo (FEM piccola)
  □ a minor operation una piccola operazione

minority NOUN
la minoranza *fem*

mint NOUN
1 la mentina *fem*
  □ Would you like a mint? Vuoi una mentina?
2 la menta *fem* (herb)
  ■ **mint sauce** la salsa alla menta

minus PREPOSITION
1 meno
  □ sixteen minus three sedici meno tre □ I got a B minus for my French. Ho ricevuto B meno in francese.
  ■ **minus two degrees** due gradi sotto zero
2 ma senza
  □ I found my wallet, minus the money. Ho ritrovato il mio portafoglio, ma senza il denaro.

minute NOUN
  ▷ *see also* **minute** ADJECTIVE
  il minuto *masc*
  □ ten minutes dieci minuti

minute ADJECTIVE
  ▷ *see also* **minute** NOUN
  minuscolo (FEM minuscola)
  □ Her flat is minute. Il suo appartamento è minuscolo.
  ■ **a minute amount** una quantità minima

miracle NOUN
il miracolo *masc*

mirror NOUN
1 lo specchio *masc*
  □ She looked at herself in the mirror. Si è guardata allo specchio.
2 lo specchietto *masc*
  □ She got in the car and adjusted the mirror. È entrata in macchina e ha regolato lo specchietto.

to misbehave VERB
comportarsi [56ᴱ] male

miscellaneous ADJECTIVE
vario (FEM varia)
  □ miscellaneous items articoli vari

mischief NOUN
  ■ **She's always up to mischief.** Ne combina sempre una.
  ■ **full of mischief** birichino

mischievous ADJECTIVE
birichino (FEM birichina)

miser NOUN
l' avaro *masc*
l' avara *fem*

miserable ADJECTIVE
infelice (FEM infelice)
  □ a miserable life una vita infelice
  ■ **to feel miserable** essere [47ᴱ] giù di morale
  ■ **miserable weather** brutto tempo
  ■ **a miserable failure** un fiasco

misery NOUN
1 la tristezza *fem*
  □ All that money brought nothing but misery. Tutto quel denaro non ha portato che tristezza.
2 la lagna *fem*
  □ She's a real misery. È proprio una lagna.

misfortune NOUN
la sfortuna *fem*

mishap NOUN
la disavventura *fem*
  □ a minor mishap una piccola disavventura
  ■ **without mishap** senza incidenti

to misjudge VERB
1 giudicare [18] male
  □ I may have misjudged him. Posso averlo giudicato male.
2 valutare [68] male
  □ She misjudged the bend. Ha valutato male la curva.

to mislay VERB
smarrire [51]

to mislead VERB
trarre [115] in inganno

misleading ADJECTIVE
fuorviante (FEM fuorviante)

misprint NOUN
l' errore di stampa *masc*

Miss NOUN
> la signorina *fem*
> □ Miss Peters wants to see you. La signorina Peters vuole vederla.

> **DID YOU KNOW...?**
> When 'Miss' is used to address a secondary school teacher, it is translated by **professoressa**. **Maestra** would be used for a primary school teacher.

miss NOUN
> ▷*see also* **miss** VERB
> ■ He decided to give the film a miss. Ha deciso di non andare a vedere quel film.
> ■ We had a near miss. Per poco non ci è successo un incidente.

to **miss** VERB
> ▷*see also* **miss** NOUN
1 perdere [69]
> □ Hurry or you'll miss the bus. Affrettati o perderai l'autobus. □ It's too good an opportunity to miss. È un'opportunità da non perdere assolutamente.
2 mancare [18]
> □ He missed the target. Ha mancato il bersaglio.
3 saltare [68]
> □ You've missed a page. Hai saltato una pagina.
4 sentire [41] la mancanza di
> □ I miss my family. Sento la mancanza della mia famiglia.

to **miss out** VERB
> saltare [68]
> □ What about Sally? You've missed her out. E Sally? L'hai saltata.

missing ADJECTIVE
> mancante (FEM mancante)
> □ the missing link l'anello mancante
> ■ to be missing 1 *(thing)* mancare [18ᴱ]
> 2 *(person)* mancare [18ᴱ] all'appello
> ■ a missing person un disperso

missionary NOUN
> il missionario *masc*
> la missionaria *fem*

mist NOUN
> la foschia *fem*

mistake NOUN
> ▷*see also* **mistake** VERB
> l' errore *masc*
> □ a spelling mistake un errore di ortografia
> □ There must be some mistake. Dev'esserci un errore. □ He makes a lot of mistakes. Fa molti errori.
> ■ by mistake per sbaglio

to **mistake** VERB
> ▷*see also* **mistake** NOUN
> scambiare [17]
> □ He mistook me for my sister. Mi ha scambiato per mia sorella.

mistaken ADJECTIVE
> ■ to be mistaken sbagliarsi [25ᴱ] □ If you think I'm going to pay, you're mistaken. Se pensi che ho intenzione di pagare ti sbagli.

mistakenly ADVERB
> erroneamente

mistletoe NOUN
> il vischio *masc*

mistook VERB ▷*see* **mistake**

mistress NOUN
1 l' amante *fem*
> □ He's got a mistress. Ha un'amante.
2 la professoressa *fem*
> □ our English mistress la nostra professoressa di inglese

mistrust NOUN
> la diffidenza *fem*
> □ a mistrust of politicians una diffidenza nei confronti dei politici

misty ADJECTIVE
> nebbioso (FEM nebbiosa)

to **misunderstand** VERB
> fraintendere [112]
> □ Maybe I misunderstood you. Forse ho frainteso.

misunderstanding NOUN
> il fraintendimento *masc*
> □ I think there's been some misunderstanding. Penso che ci sia stato un fraintendimento.

misunderstood VERB ▷*see* **misunderstand**

mix NOUN
> ▷*see also* **mix** VERB
> il misto *masc*
> □ a mix of science fiction and comedy un misto di fantascienza e commedia
> ■ a cake mix un preparato per torte

to **mix** VERB
> ▷*see also* **mix** NOUN
1 mescolare [68]
> □ Mix the flour with the sugar. Mescolate la farina con lo zucchero.
2 unire [51]
> □ He's mixing business with pleasure. Unisce l'utile al dilettevole.
3 legare [76]
> □ He doesn't mix much. Non lega molto con gli altri.
> ■ to mix with frequentare [68] □ I like mixing with all sorts of people. Mi piace frequentare persone di tutti i tipi.

to **mix up** VERB
> confondere [23]
> □ He mixed up the bookings. Ha confuso le prenotazioni.

mixed ADJECTIVE
1 misto (FEM mista)
> □ a mixed grill una grigliata mista

469

2 contrastante (FEM contrastante)
□ I've got mixed feelings about it. Ho dei sentimenti contrastanti a riguardo.
3 variabile (FEM variabile)
□ The weather was mixed. C'era tempo variabile.

mixed up ADJECTIVE
1 disorientato (FEM disorientata)
□ I'm getting mixed up. Sono disorientato.
2 confuso (FEM confusa)
□ a mixed up teenager un adolescente confuso

■ **to be mixed up with** avere [12] a che fare con □ He's mixed up with drug dealers. Ha a che fare con degli spacciatori.

■ **to get something mixed up** scambiare [17] qualcosa □ He got their names mixed up. Ha scambiato i loro nomi.

mixer NOUN
il frullatore *masc*

mixture NOUN
il miscuglio *masc*
□ a mixture of spices un miscuglio di spezie

mix-up NOUN
la confusione *fem*

to moan VERB
lamentarsi [56E]
□ She's always moaning about something. Ha sempre qualcosa di cui lamentarsi.

mobile ADJECTIVE
▷ *see also* **mobile** NOUN
■ **She's ninety, but still mobile.** Ha novant'anni ma riesce ancora a camminare.

mobile NOUN
▷ *see also* **mobile** ADJECTIVE
il cellulare *masc*
□ You can get me on my mobile. Mi puoi trovare sul cellulare.

mobile home NOUN
la grande roulotte *fem*

mobile phone NOUN
il telefono cellulare *masc*
■ **a mobile phone mast** un ripetitore per telefoni cellulari

to mock VERB
▷ *see also* **mock** ADJECTIVE
canzonare [68]

mock ADJECTIVE
▷ *see also* **mock** VERB
■ **a mock exam** una simulazione d'esame

mod cons NOUN PL
■ **with all mod cons** con tutti i comfort

model NOUN, ADJECTIVE
▷ *see also* **model** VERB
1 il modello *masc*
□ It's the basic model. È il modello base.
2 il modellino *masc*
□ a model of the castle un modellino del castello
■ **a model railway** un trenino in miniatura

3 la modella *fem*
□ She's a famous model. È una modella famosa.

to model VERB
▷ *see also* **model** NOUN, ADJECTIVE
indossare [68]

modem NOUN
il modem *masc* (PL i modem)

moderate ADJECTIVE
moderato (FEM moderata)
□ His views are quite moderate. Ha opinioni abbastanza moderate.
■ **a moderate amount of** un po' di □ I do a moderate amount of exercise. Faccio un po' di ginnastica.

modern ADJECTIVE
moderno (FEM moderna)

to modernize VERB
modernizzare [68]

modest ADJECTIVE
modesto (FEM modesta)

to modify VERB
modificare [18]

moist ADJECTIVE
1 umido (FEM umida)
□ Sow the seeds in moist soil. Piantate i semi nel terreno umido.
2 soffice (FEM soffice)
□ This cake is very moist. Questa torta è molto soffice.

moisture NOUN
l' umidità *fem*

moisturizer NOUN
la crema idratante *fem*

moldy ADJECTIVE (US)
ammuffito (FEM ammuffita)

mole NOUN
1 il neo *masc*
□ I've got a mole on my back. Ho un neo sulla schiena.
2 la talpa *fem* (animal, spy)

moment NOUN
il momento *masc*
□ any moment now da un momento all'altro

momentous ADJECTIVE
di grande importanza

monarch NOUN
il monarca *masc* (PL i monarchi)

monarchy NOUN
la monarchia *fem*

monastery NOUN
il monastero *masc*

Monday NOUN
il lunedì *masc* (PL i lunedì)
■ **on Monday** lunedì □ I saw her on Monday. L'ho vista lunedì.
■ **on Mondays** di lunedì □ I go swimming on Mondays. Vado in piscina di lunedì.

money NOUN
i soldi *masc pl*

□ I need to change some money. Devo cambiare dei soldi.

mongrel NOUN
il bastardo *masc*
□ My dog's a mongrel. Il mio cane è un bastardo.

monk NOUN
il monaco *masc* (PL i monaci)

monkey NOUN
la scimmia *fem*

monkey nut NOUN
la nocciolina americana *fem*

monopoly NOUN
il monopolio *masc*
□ a state monopoly un monopolio di stato
■ **to play Monopoly**® giocare [18] a Monopoli®

monster NOUN
il mostro *masc*

month NOUN
il mese *masc*
□ last month il mese scorso

monthly ADJECTIVE
mensile (FEM mensile)

mood NOUN
l' umore *masc*
□ He was in a bad mood. Era di cattivo umore.

moody ADJECTIVE
1 lunatico (FEM lunatica, MASC PL lunatici, FEM PL lunatiche)
□ He's moody and unpredictable. È lunatico e imprevedibile.
2 malinconico (FEM malinconica, MASC PL malinconici, FEM PL malinconiche)
□ moody lyrics parole malinconiche

moon NOUN
la luna *fem*
□ There's a full moon tonight. Stanotte c'è la luna piena.
■ **She's over the moon about it.** È al settimo cielo.

moor NOUN
▷ *see also* **moor** VERB
la brughiera *fem*

to **moor** VERB
▷ *see also* **moor** NOUN
ormeggiare [58]

mop NOUN
il mocio® *masc*

moped NOUN
il motorino *masc*

moral NOUN
la morale *fem*
□ The moral of the story is... La morale della storia è...
■ **morals** moralità *fem sing*

morale NOUN
il morale *masc*
□ Morale was low. Il morale era basso.

more ADJECTIVE, PRONOUN, ADVERB
1 più
□ There isn't any more. Non ce n'è più.
2 di più
□ It costs a lot more. Costa molto di più.
3 ancora
□ A bit more? Ancora un po'? □ Is there any more? Ce n'è ancora? □ It'll take a few more days. Ci vorrà ancora qualche giorno.
■ **more than** più di □ I spent more than ten pounds. Ho speso più di dieci sterline. □ He's more intelligent than me. È più intelligente di me.
■ **more or less** più o meno
■ **more than ever** più che mai
■ **more and more** sempre più □ I got more and more depressed. Ero sempre più depresso. □ more and more often sempre più spesso

moreover ADVERB
inoltre

Mormon NOUN
il/la mormone *masc/fem*

morning NOUN
la mattina *fem*
□ at seven o'clock in the morning alle sette di mattina
■ **I'll do it first thing in the morning.** Lo farò domani mattina appena mi sveglio.
■ **this morning** stamattina
■ **the morning papers** i giornali del mattino

Moscow NOUN
Mosca
□ He's in Moscow. È a Mosca.

Moslem NOUN, ADJECTIVE
il mussulmano *masc*
la mussulmana *fem*

mosque NOUN
la moschea *fem*

mosquito NOUN
la zanzara *fem*
□ a mosquito bite una puntura di zanzara

mosquito repellent NOUN
l' insettifugo *masc* (PL gli insettifughi)

most ADJECTIVE, PRONOUN, ADVERB
di più
□ the thing she most feared la cosa che temeva di più □ He's the one who talks most. Lui è quello che parla di più.
■ **the most** il più □ the most expensive restaurant il ristorante più caro
■ **He won the most votes.** Ha avuto più voti degli altri.
■ **most of** gran parte di □ I know most of them. Conosco gran parte di loro. □ most of the time gran parte del tempo □ I did most of the work. Ho fatto gran parte del lavoro.
■ **most people** quasi tutti □ Most people go

out on Friday night. Quasi tutti escono venerdì sera.

■ **at the most** al massimo □ two hours at the most due ore al massimo

■ **to make the most of** sfruttare [68] al massimo □ He made the most of his holiday. Ha sfruttato al massimo la vacanza.

mostly ADVERB
in genere

□ The teachers are mostly quite nice. In genere gli insegnanti sono abbastanza gentili.

MOT NOUN
la revisione *fem*

□ My car has failed its MOT. La mia macchina non ha passato la revisione.

moth NOUN
1 la falena *fem (butterfly)*
2 la tarma *fem (clothes moth)*

mother NOUN
la madre *fem*

□ my mother mia madre

■ **mother tongue** madrelingua

mother-in-law NOUN
la suocera *fem*

Mother's Day NOUN
la festa della mamma *fem*

> **DID YOU KNOW…?**
> Mother's Day in Italy is the second Sunday in May, while in Britain it is the fourth Sunday of Lent.

motionless ADJECTIVE
immobile (FEM immobile)

motivated ADJECTIVE
motivato (FEM motivata)

□ He's highly motivated. È fortemente motivato.

motivation NOUN
la motivazione *fem*

motive NOUN
1 il movente *masc*
□ the motive for the killing il movente dell'omicidio
2 l' intenzione *fem*
□ for the best of motives con la migliore delle intenzioni

■ **an ulterior motive** un secondo fine

motor NOUN
il motore *masc*

□ a boat with a motor una barca a motore

motorbike NOUN
la motocicletta *fem*

motorboat NOUN
il motoscafo *masc*

motorcycle NOUN
la motocicletta *fem*

motorcyclist NOUN
il/la motociclista *masc/fem*

motorist NOUN
l' automobilista *masc/fem*

motor mechanic NOUN
il meccanico *masc* (PL i meccanici)

motor racing NOUN
le corse automobilistiche *fem pl*

motorway NOUN
l' autostrada *fem*

□ on the motorway in autostrada

> **DID YOU KNOW…?**
> In Italy you have to pay a toll on motorways.

mouldy (US **moldy**) ADJECTIVE
ammuffito (FEM ammuffita)

to mount VERB
1 organizzare [68]
□ They're mounting a publicity campaign. Stanno organizzando una campagna pubblicitaria.
2 aumentare [68E]
□ Tension is mounting. La tensione sta aumentando.

to mount up VERB
1 accumularsi [56E]
□ Letters and bills mounted up while we were on holiday. Lettere e fatture si sono accumulate mentre eravamo in vacanza.
2 aumentare [68E]
□ My savings are mounting up gradually. I miei risparmi aumentano a poco a poco.

mountain NOUN
la montagna *fem*

■ **in the mountains** in montagna

■ **mountain rescue** soccorso alpino

mountain bike NOUN
la mountain bike *fem* (PL le mountain bike)

mountaineer NOUN
l' alpinista *fem*

mountaineering NOUN
l' alpinismo *masc*

■ **to go mountaineering** fare [49] alpinismo

mountainous ADJECTIVE
montagnoso (FEM montagnosa)

mouse NOUN
1 il topo *masc (animal)*
2 il mouse *masc* (PL i mouse) *(of computer)*

mouse mat NOUN
il tappetino del mouse *masc*

mouse pad NOUN
il tappetino del mouse *masc*

mousse NOUN
1 la mousse *fem* (PL le mousse)
□ chocolate mousse mousse di cioccolata
2 la schiuma *fem (for hair)*

moustache NOUN
i baffi *masc pl*

mouth NOUN
la bocca *fem* (PL le bocche)

mouthful NOUN
1 il boccone *masc (of food)*
2 la sorsata *fem (of liquid)*

mouth organ NOUN
l' armonica a bocca *fem* (PL le armoniche a bocca)

mouthwash NOUN
il colluttorio *masc*

move NOUN
▷ *see also* **move** VERB
1 la mossa *fem*
□ That was a good move! Bella mossa!
■ **It's your move.** Tocca a te giocare.
2 il trasloco *masc* (PL i traslochi)
□ our move from Oxford to Luton il nostro trasloco da Oxford a Luton
■ **Get a move on!** Sbrigati!

to move VERB
▷ *see also* **move** NOUN
1 muoversi [62ᴱ]
□ Don't move! Non muovetevi!
2 spostare [68]
□ Could you move your stuff please? Può spostare le sue cose per favore?
3 traslocare [18]
□ We're moving in July. Traslochiamo in luglio.
4 avanzare [68ᴱ]
□ The car was moving very slowly. La macchina avanzava molto lentamente.
5 commuovere [62]
□ The book moved me deeply. Il libro mi ha commossa profondamente.

to move away VERB
andarsene [6ᴱ]
□ Our neighbours are moving away. I nostri vicini se ne vanno.

to move back VERB
ritornare [68ᴱ]
□ They had no intention of moving back to Britain. Non avevano intenzione di ritornare in Gran Bretagna.

to move in VERB
arrivare [68ᴱ]
□ When are the new neighbours moving in? Quando arrivano i nuovi vicini?

to move on VERB
cambiare [17]
□ I felt it was time to move on. Sentii che era arrivato il momento di cambiare.
■ **Let's move on to the next question.** Passiamo alla prossima domanda.
■ **The policeman told them to move on.** Il poliziotto ha ordinato loro di andare via.

to move over VERB
spostarsi [56ᴱ]
□ Could you move over a bit? Puoi spostarti un po'?

movement NOUN
1 il movimento *masc*
□ a sudden movement un movimento brusco
2 lo spostamento *masc*
□ He was asked to account for his movements. Gli è stato chiesto di rendere conto dei suoi spostamenti.

movie NOUN
il film *masc* (PL i film)
■ **the movies** il cinema

moving ADJECTIVE
1 in movimento
□ a moving bus un autobus in movimento
2 commovente
□ a moving story una storia commovente

to mow VERB
tagliare [25]
□ I sometimes mow the lawn. A volte taglio l'erba del prato.

mower NOUN
il tagliaerba *masc* (PL i tagliaerba)

mown VERB ▷ *see* **mow**

MP NOUN
il deputato *masc*
la deputata *fem*

MP3 player NOUN
il lettore MP3 *masc*

MP4 player NOUN
il lettore MP4 *masc*

mph ABBREVIATION (= *miles per hour*)

> **DID YOU KNOW...?**
> Speeds in Italy are measured in kilometres per hour. 50 mph is about 80 km/h.

Mr NOUN
il signor *masc*

Mrs NOUN
la signora *fem*

MS NOUN (= *multiple sclerosis*)
la sclerosi multipla *fem*
□ She's got MS. Ha la sclerosi multipla.

Ms NOUN
la signora *fem*

MSc NOUN
il Master in scienze naturali *masc*
□ She's got an MSc. Ha un Master in scienze naturali.

much ADJECTIVE, PRONOUN, ADVERB
molto (FEM molta)
□ I feel much better now. Ora mi sento molto meglio. □ I haven't got much money. Non ho molto denaro. □ Have you got a lot of luggage? — No, not much. Ha molto bagaglio? — No, non molto.
■ **very much** moltissimo □ I enjoyed myself very much. Mi sono divertito moltissimo.
■ **Thank you very much.** Mille grazie.
■ **how much** quanto □ How much is it? Quanto costa?
■ **too much** troppo □ They give us too much homework. Ci danno troppi compiti.
■ **so much** così tanto □ I like it so much. Mi piace così tanto.

mud NOUN
il fango *masc*

muddle NOUN
il disordine *masc*
■ **in a muddle** in disordine □ The photos are in a muddle. Le foto sono in disordine.

to **muddle up** VERB
confondere [23]
□ He muddles me up with my sister. Mi confonde con mia sorella.
■ **to get muddled up** essere [47**E**] confuso
□ I'm getting muddled up. Sono confuso.

muddy ADJECTIVE
fangoso (FEM fangosa)

muffler NOUN (US)
la marmitta *fem*

mug NOUN
▷ see also **mug** VERB
la tazza *fem*
□ a mug of coffee una tazza di caffè
■ **a beer mug** un boccale

to **mug** VERB
▷ see also **mug** NOUN
aggredire [51]
□ He was mugged in the city centre. È stato aggredito in centro.

mugger NOUN
lo scippatore *masc*

mugging NOUN
l' aggressione *fem*

muggy ADJECTIVE
■ It's muggy today. Oggi c'è afa.

multiple ADJECTIVE
multiplo (FEM multipla)
□ multiple injuries ferite multiple

multiple choice test NOUN
gli esercizi a scelta multipla *masc pl*

multiple sclerosis NOUN
la sclerosi multipla *fem*

to **multiply** VERB
moltiplicare [18]

multi-storey car park NOUN
il parcheggio a più piani *masc*

mum NOUN
la mamma *fem*
□ I'll ask mum. Chiederò alla mamma. □ my mum la mia mamma

mummy NOUN
1 la mamma *fem*
□ I want my mummy. Voglio la mia mamma.
2 la mummia *fem (Egyptian)*

mumps NOUN SING
gli orecchioni *masc pl*

Munich NOUN
Monaco di Baviera *fem*

murder NOUN
▷ see also **murder** VERB
l' omicidio *masc*

□ a terrible murder un terribile omicidio
■ **the murder weapon** l'arma del delitto
■ **She gets away with murder.** Se la cava sempre.

to **murder** VERB
▷ see also **murder** NOUN
assassinare [68]

murderer NOUN
l' assassino *masc*
l' assassina *fem*

muscle NOUN
il muscolo *masc*

muscular ADJECTIVE
muscoloso (FEM muscolosa)
□ He's got muscular legs. Ha gambe muscolose.

museum NOUN
il museo *masc*

mushroom NOUN
il fungo *masc* (PL i funghi)

music NOUN
la musica *fem*

musical ADJECTIVE
▷ see also **musical** NOUN
1 musicale (FEM musicale)
□ a musical instrument uno strumento musicale
2 portato per la musica
□ I'm not musical. Non sono portato per la musica.

musical NOUN
▷ see also **musical** ADJECTIVE
la commedia musicale *fem*

music centre NOUN
lo stereo compatto *masc* (PL gli stereo compatti)

musician NOUN
il/la musicista *masc/fem*

Muslim NOUN, ADJECTIVE
il mussulmano *masc*
la mussulmana *fem*

mussel NOUN
la cozza *fem*

must VERB
▷ see also **must** NOUN

> LANGUAGE TIP 'must' is often translated by dovere.

□ I must do it. Devo farlo. □ You mustn't forget to send her a card. Non devi dimenticare di mandarle una cartolina. □ There must be some problem. Dev'esserci qualche problema. □ You must come again next year. Devi assolutamente tornare il prossimo anno.
■ **You must be joking!** Stai scherzando!

must NOUN
▷ see also **must** VERB
■ **to be a must** essere [47**E**] d'obbligo □ For a wedding champagne is a must. Per un matrimonio lo champagne è d'obbligo.

mustard NOUN
la senape *fem*

mustn't = must not

to **mutter** VERB
borbottare [68]

mutton NOUN
la carne di montone *fem*

mutual ADJECTIVE
reciproco (FEM reciproca, MASC PL reciproci, FEM PL reciproche)
  □ The feeling was mutual. Il sentimento era reciproco.
  ■ **a mutual friend** un amico comune

my ADJECTIVE
1 il mio *masc* (PL i miei)
  □ my friend il mio amico □ my parents i miei genitori
2 la mia *fem* (PL le mie)
  □ my car la mia macchina □ my opinions le mie opinioni
3 mio *masc* (PL miei)
  □ my father mio padre
4 mia *fem* (PL mie)
  □ my aunt mia zia
  ▌ LANGUAGE TIP 'my' is not always translated.
  □ I've lost my wallet. Ho perduto il portafoglio.
  □ with my hands in my pockets con le mani in tasca
  ■ **I want to wash my hair.** Voglio lavarmi i capelli.

■ **I've hurt my foot.** Mi sono fatto male ad un piede.

myself PRONOUN
1 mi
  ▌ LANGUAGE TIP A verb + 'myself' is often translated by a reflexive verb in Italian.
  □ I've hurt myself. Mi sono fatto male.
  □ I looked at myself in the mirror. Mi sono guardato allo specchio.
2 me
  □ a beginner like myself un principiante come me
3 io
  □ I made it myself. L'ho fatto io.
  ■ **by myself** da solo □ I don't like travelling by myself. Non mi piace viaggiare da solo.

mysterious ADJECTIVE
misterioso (FEM misteriosa)

mystery NOUN
il mistero *masc*
  □ It's a mystery! È un mistero!
  ■ **a murder mystery** un romanzo giallo
  ▌ LANGUAGE TIP Word for word, this means 'a yellow novel'.

myth NOUN
il mito *masc*
  □ a Greek myth un mito greco
  ■ **That's a myth.** È una credenza falsa.

mythology NOUN
la mitologia *fem*

m

Nn

naff ADJECTIVE
kitsch (FEM+PL kitsch)

to nag VERB
tormentare [68]
□ She's always nagging me. Mi tormenta in continuazione.

nail NOUN
1 il chiodo *masc*
□ He hammered a nail into the wall. Ha piantato un chiodo nel muro.
2 l' unghia *fem*
□ She bites her nails. Si mangia le unghie.

nail brush NOUN
lo spazzolino per unghie *masc*

nail file NOUN
la limetta per unghie *fem*

nail polish NOUN
lo smalto per unghie *masc*

nail scissors NOUN PL
le forbicine per unghie *fem pl*

nail varnish NOUN
lo smalto per unghie *masc*

nail varnish remover NOUN
l' acetone *masc*

naked ADJECTIVE
nudo (FEM nuda)

name NOUN
il nome *masc*
□ his real name il suo vero nome
■ **What's your name?** Come ti chiami?

nanny NOUN
la bambinaia *fem*

nap NOUN
il pisolino *masc*
□ She has a nap in the afternoon. Fa un pisolino di pomeriggio.

napkin NOUN
il tovagliolo *masc*

Naples NOUN
Napoli *fem*

nappy NOUN
il pannolino *masc*

narrow ADJECTIVE
stretto (FEM stretta)

narrow-minded ADJECTIVE
■ **to be narrow-minded** essere [47ᴱ] di idee ristrette

nasty ADJECTIVE
1 brutto (FEM brutta)
□ a nasty cold un brutto raffreddore
2 cattivo (FEM cattiva)
□ a nasty smell un cattivo odore
■ **a nasty look** un'occhiataccia □ He gave me a nasty look. Mi ha dato un'occhiataccia.

nation NOUN
la nazione *fem*

national ADJECTIVE
nazionale (FEM nazionale)

national anthem NOUN
l' inno nazionale *masc*

National Health Service NOUN
il servizio sanitario nazionale *masc*

nationalism NOUN
il nazionalismo *masc*

nationalist NOUN, ADJECTIVE
il/la nazionalista *masc/fem*

nationality NOUN
la nazionalità *fem* (PL le nazionalità)

National Lottery NOUN
la lotteria nazionale *fem*

national park NOUN
il parco nazionale *masc* (PL i parchi nazionali)

native ADJECTIVE
natale (FEM natale)
□ my native country il mio paese natale
■ **native language** lingua madre □ English isn't their native language. L'inglese non è la loro lingua madre.
■ **a Native American** un discendente di tribù dell'America settentrionale

naturalist NOUN
lo studioso di scienze naturali *masc*
la studiosa di scienze naturali *fem*

naturally ADVERB
naturalmente
□ Naturally, we were very disappointed. Naturalmente siamo rimasti molto delusi.
■ **Her hair's naturally curly.** È riccia naturale.

nature NOUN
la natura *fem*
□ the ambitious nature of the project la natura ambiziosa del progetto
■ **nature study** l'osservazione della natura *fem*

naughty ADJECTIVE
cattivo (FEM cattiva)
□ Naughty girl! Cattiva!

navy NOUN
la marina *fem*
□ He's in the navy. È in marina.

navy-blue ADJECTIVE
blu scuro (FEM blu scura)
□ a navy-blue skirt una gonna blu scuro

near ADJECTIVE, PREPOSITION, ADVERB
1 vicino (FEM vicina)
□ It's quite near. È abbastanza vicino. □ It's very near to the school. È molto vicino alla scuola. □ Where's the nearest service station? Dov'è la stazione di servizio più vicina? □ The nearest shops were three kilometres away. I negozi più vicini erano a tre chilometri di distanza. □ Is there a bank near here? C'è una banca qui vicino?
■ **That was a near miss.** C'è mancato poco.
2 vicino a
□ I live near Liverpool. Abito vicino a Liverpool.

nearby ADJECTIVE, ADVERB
1 vicino (FEM vicina)
□ a nearby village un paese vicino
2 qui vicino
□ There's a supermarket nearby. C'è un supermercato qui vicino.

nearly ADVERB
quasi
□ Dinner's nearly ready. La cena è quasi pronta. □ I'm nearly fifteen. Ho quasi quindici anni.
■ **I nearly missed the train.** Per poco non ho preso il treno.

neat ADJECTIVE
1 ordinato (FEM ordinata)
□ Everything was clean and neat. Era tutto pulito e ordinato.
2 stupendo (FEM stupenda) (US: *great*)

neatly ADVERB
con cura
□ neatly folded piegato con cura

necessarily ADVERB
■ **not necessarily** non necessariamente

necessary ADJECTIVE
necessario (FEM necessaria)

necessity NOUN
la necessità *fem* (PL le necessità)

neck NOUN
il collo *masc*
□ a V-neck sweater un maglione con il collo a V
■ **a stiff neck** un torcicollo

necklace NOUN
la collana *fem*

to **need** VERB
▷ *see also* **need** NOUN
aver [12] bisogno di
□ I need you. Ho bisogno di te.

■ **You don't need to go.** Non c'è bisogno che tu vada.
■ **You needn't worry.** Non devi preoccuparti.

need NOUN
▷ *see also* **need** VERB
il bisogno *masc*
□ There's no need to book. Non c'è bisogno di prenotare.
■ **to be in need of** avere [12] bisogno di
LANGUAGE TIP Word for word, this means 'to have need of'.
□ It's in need of a wash. Ha bisogno di una lavata.

needle NOUN
l' ago *masc*
□ used needles aghi già usati

negative NOUN
▷ *see also* **negative** ADJECTIVE
la negativa *fem (of photo)*

negative ADJECTIVE
▷ *see also* **negative** NOUN
negativo (FEM negativa)
□ He's got a very negative attitude. Ha un atteggiamento molto negativo.

neglected ADJECTIVE
trascurato (FEM trascurata)
□ The garden is neglected. Il giardino è trascurato.

to **negotiate** VERB
negoziare [17]

negotiations NOUN PL
le trattative *fem pl*

neighbour (US **neighbor**) NOUN
il vicino *masc*
la vicina *fem*

neighbourhood (US **neighborhood**) NOUN
il quartiere *masc*

neither ADJECTIVE, CONJUNCTION, PRONOUN
1 nessuno dei due
□ Carrots or peas? — Neither, thanks. Vuoi carote o piselli? — Nessuno dei due, grazie. □ Neither of them is coming. Non viene nessuno dei due.
2 neanche
□ I don't like him. — Neither do I! Non mi è simpatico. — Neanche a me! □ I've never been to Spain. — Neither have I. Non sono mai stato in Spagna. — Neanch'io.
■ **neither… nor…** né… né… □ Neither Sarah nor Tamsin is coming to the party. Alla festa non vengono né Sarah né Tamsin.

neon NOUN
il neon *masc*
□ a neon light una luce al neon

nephew NOUN
il nipote *masc (di zii)*

nerve NOUN
1 il nervo *masc*

□ She sometimes gets on my nerves. Certe volte mi dà ai nervi.

2 la faccia tosta *fem*

□ He's got a nerve! Ha una bella faccia tosta!

nerve-racking ADJECTIVE
snervante (FEM snervante)

nervous ADJECTIVE
teso (FEM tesa)

□ I bite my nails when I'm nervous. Quando sono teso mi mangio le unghie. □ I'm a bit nervous about the exams. Sono un po' tesa per gli esami.

■ **a nervous breakdown** un esaurimento nervoso

nest NOUN
il nido *masc*

Net NOUN
la Rete *fem*

□ on the Net in Rete

■ **to surf the Net** navigare [76] in Internet

net NOUN
▷ *see also* **net** ADJECTIVE
la rete *fem*

□ a fishing net una rete da pesca

net ADJECTIVE
▷ *see also* **net** NOUN
netto (FEM netta)

netball NOUN
la pallacanestro *fem*

Netherlands NOUN PL
i Paesi Bassi *masc pl*

network NOUN
la rete *fem*

neurotic ADJECTIVE
nevrotico (FEM nevrotica, MASC PL nevrotici, FEM PL nevrotiche)

never ADVERB
mai

□ Have you ever been to Germany? — No, never. Sei mai stato in Germania? — No, mai. □ Never leave valuables in your car. Non lasciare mai oggetti di valore in macchina.

■ **Never again!** Mai più!

■ **Never mind.** Non fa niente.

new ADJECTIVE
nuovo (FEM nuova)

□ her new boyfriend il suo nuovo ragazzo

■ **new moon** luna nuova

newcomer NOUN
il nuovo arrivato *masc*
la nuova arrivata *fem*

news NOUN SING

1 le notizie *fem pl*

□ good news buone notizie □ It was nice to have your news. Mi ha fatto piacere avere tue notizie.

2 la notizia *fem*

□ That's wonderful news! Che bella notizia!

3 il telegiornale *masc*

□ I watch the news every evening. Guardo il telegiornale ogni sera.

4 il giornale radio *masc*

□ I listen to the news every morning. Ascolto il giornale radio ogni mattina.

newsagent NOUN
il giornalaio *masc*

news dealer NOUN (US)
il giornalaio *masc*

newspaper NOUN
il giornale *masc*

newsreader NOUN
il/la giornalista *masc/fem*

New Year NOUN
l' anno nuovo *masc*

□ to celebrate New Year festeggiare l'anno nuovo

■ **Happy New Year!** Buon anno!

■ **New Year's Day** Capodanno

■ **New Year's Eve** la vigilia di Capodanno

■ **a New Year's Eve party** un veglione di Capodanno

New Zealand NOUN
la Nuova Zelanda *fem*

New Zealander NOUN
il/la neozelandese *masc/fem*

next ADJECTIVE, ADVERB, PREPOSITION

1 prossimo (FEM prossima)

□ next Saturday sabato prossimo □ the next time la prossima volta

■ **Next please!** Avanti il prossimo!

2 dopo

□ What did you do next? Cos'hai fatto dopo? □ What happened next? Cos'è successo dopo? □ the next day il giorno dopo

3 accanto

□ the next room la stanza accanto

■ **next to** accanto a □ next to the bank accanto alla banca

■ **next door** della porta accanto □ the girl next door la ragazza della porta accanto

■ **They live next door.** Abitano nella casa accanto.

NHS NOUN (= National Health Service)
il servizio sanitario nazionale *masc*

nice ADJECTIVE

1 simpatico (FEM simpatica, MASC PL simpatici, FEM PL simpatiche)

□ Your parents are very nice. I tuoi genitori sono molto simpatici.

2 gentile (FEM gentile)

□ She was always very nice to me. È sempre stata gentile con me.

3 carino (FEM carina)

□ That's a nice dress! Che vestito carino! □ It was nice of you to remember me. Sei stata carina a ricordarti di me.

4 buono (FEM buona)

□ This pasta is very nice. Questa pasta è molto buona.

5 bello (FEM bella)

□ Pisa is a nice town. Pisa è una bella città. □ nice weather bel tempo □ It's a nice day. È una bella giornata. □ a nice cup of coffee una bella tazza di caffè

WORD POWER

You can use a number of other words instead of **nice** to mean 'pretty':

attractive attraente

□ an attractive boy un ragazzo attraente

beautiful bello

□ a beautiful painting un bel quadro

lovely bello

□ a lovely surprise una bella sorpresa

pretty carino

□ a pretty girl una ragazza carina

■ **Have a nice time!** Divertiti!

nickname NOUN

il soprannome *masc*

niece NOUN

la nipote *fem (di zii)*

Nigeria NOUN

la Nigeria *fem*

night NOUN

1 la notte *fem*

□ I want a room for two nights. Vorrei una camera per due notti.

■ **at night** di notte

2 la sera *fem*

□ We went to a party last night. Ieri sera siamo andati ad una festa.

nightdress NOUN

la camicia da notte *fem* (PL le camicie da notte)

nightie NOUN

la camicia da notte *fem* (PL le camicie da notte)

nightlife NOUN

la vita notturna *fem*

nightmare NOUN

l' incubo *masc*

□ The whole trip was a nightmare. Il viaggio è stato un vero incubo.

night shift NOUN

il turno di notte *masc*

nightshirt NOUN

la camicia da notte *fem* (PL le camicie da notte)

nil NOUN

lo zero *masc*

□ We won one-nil. Abbiamo vinto uno a zero.

nine NUMBER

nove

□ She's nine. Ha nove anni.

nineteen NUMBER

diciannove

□ She's nineteen. Ha diciannove anni.

nineteenth NUMBER

diciannovesimo

□ the nineteenth floor il diciannovesimo piano

■ **the nineteenth of July** il diciannove luglio

ninety NUMBER

novanta

ninth ADJECTIVE

nono (FEM nona)

□ the ninth floor il nono piano

■ **the ninth of August** il nove agosto

no ADVERB, ADJECTIVE

1 no

□ Are you coming? — No. Vieni? — No. □ Would you like some more? — No thank you. Ne vuoi ancora? — No grazie.

2 non

□ There's no hot water. Non c'è acqua calda. □ There are no trains on Sundays. La domenica non ci sono treni.

■ **I've got no idea.** Non ne ho la minima idea.

■ **no one** nessuno □ Who's going with you? — No one. Chi ti accompagna? — Nessuno. □ There was no one in the office. In ufficio non c'era nessuno.

■ **No way!** Neanche per sogno!

■ **'no smoking'** 'vietato fumare'

nobody PRONOUN

nessuno

□ Who's going with you? — Nobody. Chi ti accompagna? — Nessuno. □ There was nobody in the office. In ufficio non c'era nessuno. □ Nobody likes him. Non è simpatico a nessuno.

to nod VERB

fare [49] un cenno col capo

noise NOUN

il rumore *masc*

□ Please make less noise. Per favore fate meno rumore.

noisy ADJECTIVE

rumoroso (FEM rumorosa)

□ the noisiest city in the world la città più rumorosa del mondo

to nominate VERB

candidare [68]

none PRONOUN

nessuno

□ How many sisters have you got? — None. Quante sorelle hai? — Nessuna. □ None of my friends wanted to come. Nessuno dei miei amici è voluto venire.

■ **There's none left.** Non ce n'è più.

■ **There are none left.** Non ce ne sono più.

nonsense NOUN

le sciocchezze *fem pl*

□ She talks a lot of nonsense. Dice un sacco di sciocchezze. □ Nonsense! Che sciocchezze!

n

non-smoker NOUN
il non fumatore *masc*
la non fumatrice *fem*
■ **to be a non-smoker** non fumare [68]

non-smoking ADJECTIVE
■ **non-smoking area** settore riservato ai non fumatori
■ **Smoking or non-smoking?** Fumatori o non fumatori?

non-stop ADJECTIVE, ADVERB
1 diretto (FEM diretta)
□ a non-stop flight un volo diretto □ We flew non-stop. Abbiamo preso un volo diretto.
2 ininterrottamente
□ He talks non-stop. Parla ininterrottamente.

noodles NOUN PL
1 i tagliolini *masc pl (Italian)*
2 gli spaghetti cinesi *masc pl (Chinese)*

noon NOUN
il mezzogiorno *masc*

nor CONJUNCTION
neanche
□ I haven't seen him. — Nor have I. Non l'ho visto. — Neanch'io. □ I didn't like the film. — Nor did I. Il film non mi è piaciuto. — Neanche a me.
■ **neither... nor** né... né □ neither the cinema nor the swimming pool né il cinema né la piscina

normal ADJECTIVE
normale (FEM normale)

normally ADVERB
normalmente

north NOUN, ADVERB, ADJECTIVE
1 il nord *masc*
□ in the north al nord
2 verso nord
□ We were travelling north. Viaggiavamo verso nord.
■ **north of** a nord di □ It's north of London. È a nord di Londra.
3 settentrionale
□ the north coast la costa settentrionale

North America NOUN
l' America del Nord *fem*

northbound ADJECTIVE
diretto a nord (FEM diretta a nord)

northeast NOUN
il nord-est *masc*

northern ADJECTIVE
settentrionale (FEM settentrionale)
□ Northern Europe l'Europa settentrionale

Northern Ireland NOUN
l' Irlanda del nord *fem*

North Pole NOUN
il Polo nord *masc*

North Sea NOUN
il mare del Nord *masc*

northwest NOUN
il nord-ovest *masc*

Norway NOUN
la Norvegia *fem*

Norwegian ADJECTIVE
▷ *see also* **Norwegian** NOUN
norvegese (FEM norvegese)

Norwegian NOUN
▷ *see also* **Norwegian** ADJECTIVE
1 il/la norvegese *masc/fem (person)*
2 il norvegese *masc (language)*

nose NOUN
il naso *masc*
■ **to have a nose job** rifarsi [49ᴱ] il naso

nosebleed NOUN
l' emorragia nasale *fem* (PL le emorragie nasali)

nosy ADJECTIVE
■ **She's very nosy.** È una vera ficcanaso.

not ADVERB
1 no
□ Are you coming or not? Vieni o no? □ I hope not. Spero di no.
2 non
□ I'm not sure. Non sono sicuro. □ He isn't coming. Non viene. □ Have you finished? — Not yet. Hai finito? — Non ancora.
■ **not at all** non... affatto □ I'm not at all sure. Non sono affatto sicuro.
■ **Thank you very much. — Not at all.** Grazie infinite. — Di niente.

note NOUN
1 l' appunto *masc*
□ Remember to take notes. Ricordati di prendere appunti.
2 la nota *fem*
□ I'll drop her a note. Le lascerò una nota.
3 il biglietto *masc*
□ a five pound note un biglietto da cinque sterline

to **note down** VERB
prendere [77] nota di
□ I noted down the main points. Ho preso nota dei punti principali.

notebook NOUN
il blocchetto per appunti *masc*

note pad NOUN
il bloc notes *masc* (PL i bloc notes)

notepaper NOUN
la carta da lettere *fem*

nothing PRONOUN
niente
□ nothing special niente di speciale □ He does nothing. Non fa niente. □ He ate nothing. Non ha mangiato niente.

to **notice** VERB
▷ *see also* **notice** NOUN
accorgersi [4ᴱ]

notice NOUN
▷ *see also* **notice** VERB

1 l' avviso *masc*
□ There's a notice on the board about the trip. In bacheca c'è un avviso a proposito del viaggio.
□ 'until further notice' 'fino a nuovo avviso'
2 il preavviso *masc*
□ He was transferred without notice. È stato trasferito senza preavviso.
■ **to hand in one's notice** dare [30] le dimissioni □ She handed in her notice yesterday. Ha dato le dimissioni ieri.
■ **a warning notice** un avvertimento
■ **Don't take any notice of him!** Non far caso a lui!

notice board NOUN
la bacheca *fem* (PL le bacheche)

nought NOUN
lo zero *masc*

noun NOUN
il nome *masc*

novel NOUN
il romanzo *masc*

novelist NOUN
il romanziere *masc*
la romanziera *fem*

November NOUN
novembre
□ in November in novembre

now ADVERB, CONJUNCTION
ora
□ What are you doing now? Cosa fai ora?
■ **just now** in questo momento □ I'm very busy just now. In questo momento sono molto occupato.
■ **I did it just now.** L'ho appena fatto.
■ **by now** ormai □ It should be ready by now. Ormai dovrebbe essere pronto.
■ **from now on** d'ora in poi
■ **now and then** ogni tanto

nowhere ADVERB
da nessuna parte
□ nowhere else da nessun'altra parte

nuclear ADJECTIVE
nucleare (FEM nucleare)
□ nuclear power energia nucleare

nude ADJECTIVE, NOUN
nudo (FEM nuda)

nudist NOUN
il/la nudista *masc/fem*

nuisance NOUN
1 la seccatura *fem*
□ It's a real nuisance. È una vera seccatura.
2 lo scocciatore *masc*
la scocciatrice *fem*
□ You're a nuisance! Sei uno scocciatore!

numb ADJECTIVE
■ **numb with cold** intirizzito dal freddo

number NOUN
il numero *masc*
□ They live at number five. Abitano al numero cinque. □ What's your phone number? Qual è il tuo numero di telefono? □ You've got the wrong number. Ha sbagliato numero.
■ **a large number of people** moltissima gente

number plate NOUN
la targa *fem* (PL le targhe) *(on car)*

nun NOUN
la suora *fem*

nurse NOUN
l' infermiere *masc*
l' infermiera *fem*

nursery NOUN
1 il vivaio *masc (for plants)*
2 l' asilo *masc (for children)*

nursery rhyme NOUN
la filastrocca *fem* (PL le filastrocche)

nursery school NOUN
la scuola materna *fem*

nursery slope NOUN
la pista da sci per principianti *fem*

nut NOUN
1 la noce *fem (walnut)*
2 la nocciola *fem (hazelnut)*
3 la nocciolina *fem (peanut)*

> LANGUAGE TIP In Italian there is no general word for 'nut'.

■ **nuts** frutta secca *fem sing*
4 il dado *masc (made of metal)*
■ **He's nuts.** È pazzo.

nutmeg NOUN
la noce moscata *fem*

nutritious ADJECTIVE
nutriente (FEM nutriente)

nutter NOUN
■ **He's a nutter.** È completamente matto.

n

Oo

oak NOUN
la quercia *fem* (PL le querce)

oar NOUN
il remo *masc*

oats NOUN PL
l' avena *fem*

obedient ADJECTIVE
ubbidiente (FEM ubbidiente)

to **obey** VERB
ubbidire [51]
■ **to obey the rules** rispettare [68] il regolamento

object NOUN
▷ see also **object** VERB
l' oggetto *masc*

to **object** VERB
▷ see also **object** NOUN
obiettare [68]
□ A lot of people objected to the proposal. Molti hanno obiettato alla proposta.

objection NOUN
l' obiezione *fem*

objective ADJECTIVE, NOUN
l' obiettivo *masc*

oblong ADJECTIVE
rettangolare (FEM rettangolare)

oboe NOUN
l' oboe *masc* (PL gli oboe)

obscene ADJECTIVE
osceno (FEM oscena)

observant ADJECTIVE
■ **You're very observant!** Hai molto spirito di osservazione!

> **LANGUAGE TIP** Be careful not to translate observant by osservante.

to **observe** VERB
osservare [68]

obsessed ADJECTIVE
■ **He's obsessed with westerns.** Ha una fissazione per i film western.

obsession NOUN
la fissazione *fem*
□ It's getting to be an obsession with you. Sta diventando una fissazione per te.

obsolete ADJECTIVE
sorpassato (FEM sorpassata)

obstacle NOUN
l' ostacolo *masc*

obstinate ADJECTIVE
ostinato (FEM ostinata)

to **obstruct** VERB
bloccare [18]
□ A lorry was obstructing the traffic. Un camion bloccava il traffico.

to **obtain** VERB
ottenere [113]

obvious ADJECTIVE
ovvio (FEM ovvia)

obviously ADVERB
ovviamente
□ Obviously I'd be sorry if we didn't go. Ovviamente mi dispiacerebbe non andarci.
■ **She was obviously tired.** Si vedeva che era stanca.
■ **Obviously not!** Certo che no!

occasion NOUN
l' occasione *fem*
■ **on several occasions** in varie occasioni

occasionally ADVERB
ogni tanto

occupation NOUN
la professione *fem*

to **occupy** VERB
occupare [68]
□ The toilet was occupied. Il bagno era occupato.

to **occur** VERB
succedere [110E]
□ The accident occurred yesterday. L'incidente è successo ieri.
■ **to occur to somebody** venire [120E] in mente a qualcuno □ It occurred to me that... Mi è venuto in mente che...

> **LANGUAGE TIP** Be careful not to translate to occur by occorrere.

ocean NOUN
l' oceano *masc*

o'clock ADVERB
■ **It's one o'clock.** È l'una.

> **LANGUAGE TIP** Except for one o'clock, use the plural article and a plural verb when telling the time.

■ **at four o'clock** alle quattro
■ **It's five o'clock.** Sono le cinque.

October NOUN
ottobre *masc*
□ in October in ottobre

o

odd ADJECTIVE
1 strano (FEM strana)
   □ That's odd! Che strano!
2 dispari (FEM+PL dispari)
   □ an odd number un numero dispari
   ■ **odd jobs** lavori occasionali
of PREPOSITION
   di
   □ a boy of ten un bambino di dieci anni □ a kilo of oranges un chilo di arance □ It's made of wood. È di legno.
   ■ **There were three of us.** Eravamo in tre.
   ■ **a friend of mine** un mio amico
   ■ **the 14th of May** il quattordici maggio
   ■ **That's very kind of you.** È molto gentile da parte tua.
off ADJECTIVE, ADVERB, PREPOSITION
1 spento (FEM spento) (heating, light, TV)
   □ The lights are off. Le luci sono spente.
2 chiuso (FEM chiusa) (tap, gas)
   □ Are you sure the tap is off? Sei sicuro che il rubinetto sia chiuso?
   ■ **to be off sick** essere [47ᴱ] assente per malattia
   ■ **a day off** un giorno di ferie □ She took a day off work to go to the wedding. Ha preso un giorno di ferie per andare al matrimonio.
   ■ **I've got tomorrow off.** Domani ho un giorno libero.
   ■ **She's off school today.** Oggi non è a scuola.
   ■ **I must be off now.** Ora devo andare.
   ■ **I'm off.** Io me ne vado.
   ■ **10% off** sconto del 10%
   ■ **It's just off Baker Street.** È una trasversale di Baker Street.
   ■ **Sorry, the lasagne is off.** Mi dispiace, le lasagne sono terminate.
   ■ **The match is off.** La partita non si gioca più.
offence (US **offense**) NOUN
   il reato masc
offensive ADJECTIVE
   offensivo (FEM offensiva)
offer NOUN
   ▷ see also **offer** VERB
   l' offerta fem
   □ 'on special offer' 'in offerta speciale'
to **offer** VERB
   ▷ see also **offer** NOUN
1 offrire [66]
   □ Can I offer you a drink? Posso offrirti qualcosa da bere?
2 offrirsi [66ᴱ]
   □ He offered to help me. Si è offerto di aiutarmi.
office NOUN
   l' ufficio masc
   ■ **office hours** orario d'ufficio

officer NOUN
   l' ufficiale masc (in the army)
   ■ **a police officer** un agente di polizia
official ADJECTIVE
   ufficiale (FEM ufficiale)
off-licence NOUN
   la rivendita di alcolici fem
off-peak ADVERB
1 in bassa stagione
   □ It's cheaper to go on holiday off-peak. Costa meno andare in vacanza in bassa stagione.
2 al di fuori dell'ora di punta
   □ Train tickets are cheaper off-peak. I biglietti ferroviari sono più economici al di fuori dell'ora di punta.
offside ADJECTIVE
   fuorigioco (FEM+PL fuorigioco)
often ADVERB
   spesso
   □ It often rains. Spesso piove.
   ■ **How often?** Ogni quanto? □ How often do you go to the gym? Ogni quanto vai in palestra?
to **oil** VERB
   ▷ see also **oil** NOUN
   lubrificare [18]
oil NOUN
   ▷ see also **oil** VERB
1 l' olio masc (for salad)
2 il petrolio masc (crude oil)
oil rig NOUN
   la piattaforma petrolifera fem
oil slick NOUN
   la chiazza di petrolio fem
oil well NOUN
   il pozzo petrolifero masc
ointment NOUN
   la pomata fem
okay EXCLAMATION, ADJECTIVE
   va bene
   □ Is that okay? Va bene? □ I'll do it tomorrow, if that's okay with you. Lo faccio domani, se per te va bene.
   ■ **Are you okay?** Tutto ok?
   ■ **The film was okay.** Il film non era male.
old ADJECTIVE
   vecchio (FEM vecchia, MASC PL vecchi, FEM PL vecchie)
   □ My grandfather is very old. Mio nonno è molto vecchio. □ He's older than me. È più vecchio di me.
   ■ **an old man** un vecchio
   ■ **old people** gli anziani
   ■ **How old are you?** Quanti anni hai?
   ■ **He's ten years old.** Ha dieci anni.
   ■ **my older brother** il mio fratello maggiore
   ■ **She's two years older than me.** Ha due anni più di me.

old age pensioner – open

old age pensioner NOUN
il pensionato *masc*
la pensionata *fem*

old-fashioned ADJECTIVE
1 fuori moda *(clothes)*
2 all'antica
  □ My parents are rather old-fashioned. I miei sono un po' all'antica.

olive NOUN
l' oliva *fem*

olive oil NOUN
l' olio d'oliva *fem*

olive tree NOUN
l' olivo *masc*

Olympic ADJECTIVE
olimpico (FEM olimpica, MASC PL olimpici, FEM PL olimpiche)
  ■ **the Olympics** le Olimpiadi

on PREPOSITION, ADVERB
▷ *see also* **on** ADJECTIVE
1 su
  □ on the table sul tavolo □ on an island su un'isola
2 a
  □ on the left a sinistra □ on TV alla TV
  ■ **on foot** a piedi □ It's about ten minutes on foot. A piedi ci vogliono circa dieci minuti.
3 in
  □ I go to school on my bike. Vado a scuola in bicicletta. □ on holiday in vacanza

  LANGUAGE TIP When used with dates and days 'on' is generally not translated.

  □ on June twentieth il venti giugno □ on my birthday il giorno del mio compleanno □ on Christmas Day il giorno di Natale □ on Friday venerdì
  ■ **on Fridays** di venerdì
  ■ **He's on drugs.** È un tossicodipendente.
  ■ **She was on antibiotics for a week.** Ha preso antibiotici per una settimana.
  ■ **Is the party still on?** Si fa sempre la festa?
  ■ **I've got a lot on this weekend.** Questo fine settimana sono molto impegnata.
  ■ **The coffee is on the house.** Il caffè lo offre la casa.
  ■ **What is he on about?** Cosa va dicendo?

on ADJECTIVE
▷ *see also* **on** PREPOSITION, ADVERB
1 acceso (FEM accesa) *(light, TV, heating)*
  □ I left the light on. Ho lasciato la luce accesa.
2 aperto (FEM aperta) *(tap, gas)*
  □ Leave the tap on. Lascia il rubinetto aperto.
3 in funzione
  □ Is the dishwasher on? È in funzione la lavastoviglie?
  ■ **What's on at the cinema?** Cosa danno al cinema?

once ADVERB
una volta

  LANGUAGE TIP Word for word, this means 'one time'.

  □ once more ancora una volta □ I've been to Italy once before. Sono già stato in Italia una volta. □ once a week una volta alla settimana
  ■ **Once upon a time…** C'era una volta…
  ■ **once in a while** una volta ogni tanto
  ■ **once and for all** una volta per tutte
  ■ **at once** immediatamente

one NUMBER, PRONOUN
1 uno (FEM una)
  □ I've got one brother and one sister. Ho un fratello e una sorella. □ I need a smaller one. Me ne serve uno più piccolo.
  ■ **The big ones cost more.** Quelli grandi costano di più.
2 si *(impersonal)*
  □ One never knows. Non si sa mai.
  ■ **this one** questo □ Which foot? — This one. Che piede? — Questo.
  ■ **that one** quello □ Which bag is yours? — That one. Qual è la tua borsa? — Quella.

oneself PRONOUN
1 si

  LANGUAGE TIP A verb + 'oneself' is often translated by a reflexive verb in Italian.

  □ One asks oneself how it could happen. Ci si chiede come sia potuto succedere.
2 da solo *masc* (FEM da sola)
  □ It's quicker to do it oneself. Si fa più in fretta a farlo da solo.

one-way ADJECTIVE
1 a senso unico
  □ a one-way street una strada a senso unico
2 di sola andata
  □ a one-way ticket un biglietto di sola andata

onion NOUN
la cipolla *fem*

online ADJECTIVE, ADVERB
on line
  □ an online catalogue un catalogo on line
  ■ **to be online** essere [47ᴱ] in Internet

only ADVERB, ADJECTIVE, CONJUNCTION
solo
  □ only ten pounds solo dieci sterline □ We only want to stay for one night. Vorremmo stare solo una notte.
  ■ **only child** figlio unico □ She's an only child. È figlia unica.

onwards ADVERB
in poi
  □ from July onwards da luglio in poi

open ADJECTIVE
▷ *see also* **open** VERB
aperto (FEM aperta)

□ The shop's open on Sunday morning.
Il negozio è aperto la domenica mattina.
■ **in the open air** all'aperto

to **open** VERB
▷ see also **open** ADJECTIVE
1 aprire [9]
□ What time do the shops open? A che ora aprono i negozi?
2 aprirsi [9ᴱ]
□ The door opens automatically. La porta si apre automaticamente.

opening hours NOUN PL
l' orario di apertura *fem*

opera NOUN
l' opera *fem (music)*

to **operate** VERB
1 funzionare [68]
□ I don't know how the system operates. Non so come funziona il sistema.
2 far [49] funzionare
□ Can you operate the video? Sai far funzionare il videoregistratore?
3 operare [68] *(perform surgery)*
■ **to operate on someone** operare [68] qualcuno

operation NOUN
l' operazione *fem*
□ a minor operation una piccola operazione
■ **to have an operation** essere [47ᴱ] operato

operator NOUN
il/la centralinista *masc/fem*

opinion NOUN
l' opinione *fem*
■ **in my opinion** secondo me
■ **What's your opinion?** Cosa ne pensi?

opinion poll NOUN
il sondaggio d'opinione *masc*

opponent NOUN
l' avversario *masc*
l' avversaria *fem*

opportunity NOUN
l' opportunità *fem* (PL le opportunità)
□ I've never had the opportunity to go to Spain. Non ho mai avuto l'opportunità di andare in Spagna.

opposing ADJECTIVE
avversario (FEM avversaria)
□ the opposing team la squadra avversaria

opposite ADJECTIVE, ADVERB, PREPOSITION
1 opposto (FEM opposta)
□ It's in the opposite direction. È nella direzione opposta.
2 di fronte
□ They live opposite. Abitano di fronte.
3 di fronte a
□ the girl sitting opposite me la ragazza seduta di fronte a me
■ **the opposite sex** l'altro sesso

opposition NOUN
1 l' opposizione *fem*
□ The plan met considerable opposition.
Il progetto ha incontrato una notevole opposizione.
2 la squadra avversaria *fem*
□ What are the opposition like? Com'è la squadra avversaria?

optician NOUN
l' ottico *masc* (PL gli ottici)

optimist NOUN
l' ottimista *masc/fem*
□ I'm an optimist. Sono ottimista.

optimistic ADJECTIVE
ottimista (FEM ottimista)
□ Let's be optimistic. Cerchiamo di essere ottimisti.

option NOUN
1 la scelta *fem*
□ I've got no option. Non ho scelta.
2 la materia facoltativa *fem*
□ I'm doing geology as my option. Come materia facoltativa studio geologia.

optional ADJECTIVE
facoltativo (FEM facoltativa)

or CONJUNCTION
1 o
□ Would you like tea or coffee? Vuoi del tè o del caffè?
2 altrimenti
□ Hurry up or you'll miss the bus. Sbrigati, altrimenti perdi l'autobus.
■ **not... or...** né... né... □ I don't eat meat or fish. Non mangio né carne né pesce. □ She can't dance or sing. Non sa né ballare né cantare.

oral ADJECTIVE
▷ see also **oral** NOUN
orale (FEM orale)
□ an oral exam un esame orale

oral NOUN
▷ see also **oral** ADJECTIVE
l' orale *masc*
□ I've got my Italian oral soon. Tra poco avrò l'orale d'italiano.

orange NOUN
▷ see also **orange** ADJECTIVE
l' arancia *fem* (PL le arance)
■ **an orange juice** un succo d'arancia

orange ADJECTIVE
▷ see also **orange** NOUN
arancione (FEM+PL arancione)
□ an orange jumper un maglione arancione

orchard NOUN
il frutteto *masc*

orchestra NOUN
l' orchestra *fem*

o

order NOUN

▷ *see also* **order** VERB

1 l' ordine *masc*

□ in alphabetical order in ordine alfabetico

2 l' ordinazione *fem*

□ The waiter took our order. Il cameriere ha preso la nostra ordinazione.

■ **an order form** un modulo d'ordine

■ **in order to** per □ He does it in order to earn money. Lo fa per guadagnare qualcosa.

■ **'out of order'** 'guasto'

to **order** VERB

▷ *see also* **order** NOUN

ordinare [68]

□ We ordered steak and chips. Abbiamo ordinato bistecca e patatine. □ Are you ready to order? Volete ordinare?

to **order about** VERB

dare [30] ordini

□ He tries to order me about. Cerca di darmi ordini.

ordinary ADJECTIVE

1 come tanti (FEM come tante)

□ an ordinary day una giornata come tante

□ He's just an ordinary guy. È uno come tanti.

2 normale

□ It has 25 calories less than ordinary ice cream. Ha 25 calorie in meno rispetto ad un gelato normale.

organ NOUN

l' organo *masc*

organic ADJECTIVE

biologico (FEM biologica, MASC PL biologici, FEM PL biologiche) *(fruit, vegetables)*

> **LANGUAGE TIP** Word for word, this means 'biological'.

organization NOUN

l' organizzazione *fem*

to **organize** VERB

organizzare [68]

origin NOUN

l' origine *fem*

original ADJECTIVE

originale (FEM originale)

originally ADVERB

in origine

Orkneys NOUN PL

le Orcadi *fem pl*

ornament NOUN

il soprammobile *masc (on shelf, mantelpiece)*

orphan NOUN

l' orfano *masc*

l' orfana *fem*

ostrich NOUN

lo struzzo *masc*

> **LANGUAGE TIP** Be careful not to translate **ostrich** by **ostrica**.

other ADJECTIVE, PRONOUN

altro (FEM altra, MASC PL altri, FEM PL altre)

□ Have you got these jeans in other colours? Avete questi jeans in altri colori?

■ **the other one** l'altro □ This one? — No, the other one. Questo? — No, l'altro.

■ **the others** gli altri □ The others are going but I'm not. Gli altri ci vanno ma io no.

otherwise ADVERB, CONJUNCTION

1 altrimenti

□ Note down the number, otherwise you'll forget it. Scrivili il numero, altrimenti te lo dimentichi.

2 a parte ciò

□ I'm tired, but otherwise I'm fine. Sono stanco, ma a parte ciò sto bene.

ought VERB

> **LANGUAGE TIP** 'ought' is usually translated by the conditional of **dovere**.

□ I ought to phone my parents. Dovrei telefonare ai miei. □ You ought not to do that. Non dovresti farlo. □ He ought to win. Dovrebbe vincere lui.

ounce NOUN

l' oncia *fem* (PL le once)

> **DID YOU KNOW...?**
> In Italy measurements are in grams and kilograms. One ounce is about 30 grams.

our ADJECTIVE

1 il nostro (FEM la nostra, MASC PL i nostri, FEM PL le nostre)

□ our dog il nostro cane □ our neighbours i nostri vicini □ our school la nostra scuola □ our opinions le nostre opinioni

2 nostro (FEM nostra, MASC PL nostri, FEM PL nostre)

□ our father nostro padre □ our aunt nostra zia

> **LANGUAGE TIP** 'our' is not always translated.

□ We took off our coats. Ci siamo tolti i cappotti. □ We washed our hair. Ci siamo lavati i capelli.

ours PRONOUN

> **LANGUAGE TIP** The Italian pronoun agrees with the noun it is replacing.

1 il nostro (FEM la nostra, MASC PL i nostri, FEM PL le nostre)

□ Your garden is much bigger than ours. Il vostro giardino è molto più grande del nostro. □ Our teachers are strict. — Ours are too. I nostri professori sono severi. — Anche i nostri. □ Your house is big, ours is much smaller. Casa tua è grande, la nostra è molto più piccola.

2 nostro (FEM nostra, MASC PL nostri, FEM PL nostre) *(our property)*

□ Whose is this? — It's ours. Di chi è questo? — È nostro. □ Those tickets are ours. Quei

O

biglietti sono nostri. ▫ That car is ours. Quella macchina è nostra.

■ **He is a friend of ours.** È un nostro amico.
■ **She is a friend of ours.** È una nostra amica.

ourselves PRONOUN

1 ci

> **LANGUAGE TIP** A verb + 'ourselves' is often translated by a reflexive verb in Italian.

▫ We really enjoyed ourselves. Ci siamo divertiti moltissimo.

2 noi *(emphatic use)*

▫ We built our garage ourselves. Il garage l'abbiamo costruito noi.

■ **by ourselves** da soli ▫ We don't like travelling by ourselves. Non ci piace viaggiare da soli.

out ADVERB

▷ *see also* **out** ADJECTIVE

fuori

▫ It's cold out. Fuori fa freddo. ▫ a night out with my friends una serata fuori con gli amici ▫ That's out of the question. Questo è fuori discussione.

■ **out of town** fuori città ▫ He's out of town this week. Questa settimana è fuori città.
■ **She's out.** È uscita.
■ **She's out for the afternoon.** Starà via tutto il pomeriggio.
■ **to drink out of a bottle** bere [15] dalla bottiglia
■ **out of curiosity** per curiosità
■ **to be out of something** aver [12] finito qualcosa ▫ We're out of milk. Abbiamo finito il latte.
■ **in nine cases out of ten** in nove casi su dieci
■ **three kilometres out of town** a tre chilometri dalla città
■ **out of work** senza lavoro
■ **'way out'** 'uscita'
■ **'now out on DVD'** 'ora su DVD'

out ADJECTIVE

▷ *see also* **out** ADVERB

1 spento (FEM spenta)

▫ The lights are out. Le luci sono spente.

2 eliminato (FEM eliminata)

▫ Liverpool are out. Il Liverpool è stato eliminato.

outbreak NOUN

1 l' insorgenza *fem*

▫ an outbreak of cholera l'insorgenza del colera

2 lo scoppio *masc*

▫ the outbreak of war lo scoppio della guerra

outcome NOUN

il risultato *masc*

outdoor ADJECTIVE

■ **an outdoor swimming pool** una piscina scoperta
■ **outdoor activities** attività all'aperto

outdoors ADVERB

all'aria aperta

outgoing ADJECTIVE

estroverso (FEM estroversa)

▫ She's very outgoing. È molto estroversa.

outing NOUN

la gita *fem*

■ **to go on an outing** andare [6ᴱ] in gita

outline NOUN

1 l' abbozzo *masc*

▫ This is an outline of the plan. Questo è un abbozzo del progetto.

2 il contorno *masc*

▫ the outline of the building il contorno dell'edificio

outlook NOUN

la visione *fem*

▫ It changed my outlook on life. Ha cambiato la mia visione della vita.

outrageous ADJECTIVE

1 scandaloso (FEM scandalosa)

▫ Her behaviour was outrageous. Il suo comportamento è stato scandaloso.

2 esorbitante (FEM esorbitante)

▫ The prices they charge are outrageous. Hanno prezzi esorbitanti.

outset NOUN

l' inizio *masc*

▫ at the outset all'inizio

outside ADJECTIVE, NOUN

▷ *see also* **outside** ADVERB, PREPOSITION

esterno (FEM esterna)

▫ the outside walls le mura esterne ▫ the outside of the house l'esterno della casa

outside ADVERB, PREPOSITION

▷ *see also* **outside** ADJECTIVE, NOUN

1 fuori

▫ It's very cold outside. Fa molto freddo fuori.

2 fuori di

▫ outside the school fuori della scuola

■ **outside school hours** al di fuori dell'orario scolastico

outsize ADJECTIVE

■ **outsize clothes** abiti per taglie forti

outskirts NOUN PL

la periferia *fem*

■ **on the outskirts of town** in periferia

outstanding ADJECTIVE

eccellente (FEM eccellente)

oval ADJECTIVE

ovale (FEM ovale)

oven NOUN

il forno *masc*

over ADJECTIVE

▷ *see also* **over** PREPOSITION, ADVERB

finito (FEM finita)

▫ I'll be happy when the exams are over. Sarò contento quando gli esami saranno finiti.

o

487

over PREPOSITION, ADVERB
▷ *see also* **over** ADJECTIVE
1 sopra
□ There's a mirror over the washbasin. Sopra il lavandino c'è uno specchio.
2 oltre
□ The ball went over the wall. La palla è andata oltre il muro. □ It's over twenty kilos. Pesa oltre venti chili.
3 durante
□ over the summer durante l'estate □ over Christmas durante il periodo natalizio
4 dall'altra parte di
□ The shop is over the road. Il negozio è dall'altra parte della strada.
5 su
□ I spilled coffee over my shirt. Mi sono versato del caffè sulla camicia.
■ **over here** qua
■ **over there** là
■ **all over Scotland** in tutta la Scozia

overall ADJECTIVE, ADVERB
nel complesso
□ What was your overall impression? Nel complesso che impressione ti ha fatto?
□ Overall I was disappointed. Nel complesso sono rimasto deluso.

overalls NOUN PL
la tuta da lavoro *fem*

overcast ADJECTIVE
coperto (FEM coperta) (*sky*)

to **overcharge** VERB
fare [49] pagare troppo
□ They overcharged us for the meal. Ci hanno fatto pagare troppo per il pranzo.

overdone ADJECTIVE
troppo cotto (FEM troppo cotta)

overdose NOUN
l' overdose *fem* (PL le overdose)

to **overestimate** VERB
sopravvalutare [68]

overhead projector NOUN
la lavagna luminosa *fem*

to **overlook** VERB
1 dare [30] su
□ The hotel overlooked the beach. L'albergo dava sulla spiaggia.
2 trascurare [68]
□ He had overlooked one important problem. Aveva trascurato un problema importante.

overseas ADVERB
all'estero

oversight NOUN
la svista *fem*

to **oversleep** VERB
non svegliarsi [25ᴱ] in tempo
□ I overslept. Non mi sono svegliato in tempo.

to **overtake** VERB
sorpassare [68]

overtime NOUN
lo straordinario *masc*
■ **to work overtime** fare [49] lo straordinario

overweight ADJECTIVE
sovrappeso (FEM+PL sovrappeso)

to **owe** VERB
dovere [42]
□ How much do I owe you? Quanto le devo?

owing to PREPOSITION
a causa di
□ owing to bad weather a causa del maltempo

owl NOUN
il gufo *masc*

own ADJECTIVE
▷ *see also* **own** VERB
■ **This is my own recipe.** È una mia ricetta.
■ **He can't trust his own judgement.** Non si può fidare del proprio giudizio.
■ **of my own** tutto per me □ a room of my own una camera tutta per me
■ **on his own** da solo
■ **on their own** da soli

to **own** VERB
▷ *see also* **own** ADJECTIVE
possedere [101]
□ everything I own tutto ciò che possiedo
■ **The golf course is owned by a Japanese company.** Il campo da golf appartiene ad una società giapponese.

to **own up** VERB
confessare [68]

owner NOUN
il proprietario *masc*
la proprietaria *fem*

oxygen NOUN
l' ossigeno *masc*

oyster NOUN
l' ostrica *fem* (PL le ostriche)

ozone NOUN
l' ozono *masc*
■ **the ozone layer** lo strato d'ozono

O

Pp

PA NOUN (= personal assistant)
la segretaria di direzione fem
■ **the PA system** l'impianto di amplificazione

pace NOUN
il passo masc
□ He was walking at a brisk pace. Camminava a passo spedito.

Pacific NOUN
■ **the Pacific** il Pacifico

pacifier NOUN (US)
il succhiotto masc

to **pack** VERB
▷ see also **pack** NOUN
fare [49] i bagagli
□ I'll help you pack. Ti aiuto a fare i bagagli.
■ **to pack one's case** fare [49] la valigia □ I've packed my case. Ho fatto la valigia.
■ **Pack it in!** Piantala!

pack NOUN
▷ see also **pack** VERB
1 il pacco masc (PL i pacchi)
□ He was carrying a heavy pack. Portava un grosso pacco.
2 la confezione fem
□ a six-pack una confezione da sei
■ **an information pack** una serie di opuscoli informativi
■ **a pack of cigarettes** una stecca di sigarette
■ **a pack of cards** un mazzo di carte

package NOUN
il pacco masc (PL i pacchi)
□ a small package un piccolo pacco
■ **a package holiday** un viaggio organizzato

packed ADJECTIVE
affollato (FEM affollata)
□ The cinema was packed. Il cinema era affollato.

packed lunch NOUN
il pranzo al sacco masc

packet NOUN
1 il pacchetto masc
□ a packet of cigarettes un pacchetto di sigarette
2 il sacchetto masc
□ a packet of crisps un sacchetto di patatine

pad NOUN
il bloc-notes masc (PL i bloc-notes)

to **paddle** VERB
▷ see also **paddle** NOUN

1 sguazzare [68] (in water)
2 pagaiare [68] (in a boat)

paddle NOUN
▷ see also **paddle** VERB
la pagaia fem (oar)
■ **to go for a paddle** sguazzare [68] nell'acqua

padlock NOUN
il lucchetto masc

Padua NOUN
Padova fem

page NOUN
▷ see also **page** VERB
la pagina fem
□ on page three a pagina tre

to **page** VERB
▷ see also **page** NOUN
chiamare [68] col cercapersone

paid VERB ▷ see pay

paid ADJECTIVE
pagato (FEM pagata)
□ three weeks' paid holiday tre settimane di ferie pagate

pail NOUN
il secchio masc

pain NOUN
1 il dolore masc
□ a terrible pain un dolore insopportabile
■ **I've got a pain in my stomach.** Mi fa male lo stomaco.
■ **to be in pain** soffrire [66] □ She's in a lot of pain. Soffre molto.
2 il/la rompiscatole masc/fem
□ He's a real pain. È un gran rompiscatole.

painful ADJECTIVE
doloroso (FEM dolorosa)

painkiller NOUN
l' analgesico masc (PL gli analgesici)

paint NOUN
▷ see also **paint** VERB
la vernice fem

to **paint** VERB
▷ see also **paint** NOUN
1 verniciare [13]
□ He decided to paint it green. Ha deciso di verniciarlo di verde.
2 dipingere [34]
□ When did he paint the picture? Quando ha dipinto il quadro?

P

■ **He painted her portrait.** Le ha fatto il ritratto.

paintbrush NOUN
il pennello masc

painter NOUN
1 l' imbianchino masc
□ The painter is coming tomorrow to redecorate the house. Domani viene l'imbianchino per ridipingere la casa.
2 il pittore masc
la pittrice fem
□ a famous 13th century painter un famoso pittore del tredicesimo secolo

painting NOUN
1 il quadro masc
□ a painting by Picasso un quadro di Picasso
2 la pittura fem
□ My hobby is painting. Il mio hobby è la pittura.

pair NOUN
il paio masc (FEM PL le paia)
□ a pair of shoes un paio di scarpe □ a pair of scissors un paio di forbici
■ **in pairs** a coppie □ We work in pairs. Lavoriamo a coppie.

pajamas NOUN PL (US)
il pigiama masc
□ my pajamas il mio pigiama

Pakistan NOUN
il Pakistan masc

Pakistani ADJECTIVE
▷ see also **Pakistani** NOUN
pachistano (FEM pachistana)

Pakistani NOUN
▷ see also **Pakistani** ADJECTIVE
il pachistano masc
la pachistana fem

pal NOUN
l' amico masc (PL gli amici)
l' amica fem (PL le amiche)

palace NOUN
il palazzo masc

pale ADJECTIVE
pallido (FEM pallida)
□ She's very pale. È molto pallida.
■ **pale pink** rosa pallido
■ **pale blue** celeste
■ **pale green** verdolino

Palestine NOUN
la Palestina fem

Palestinian ADJECTIVE
▷ see also **Palestinian** NOUN
palestinese (FEM palestinese)

Palestinian NOUN
▷ see also **Palestinian** ADJECTIVE
il/la palestinese masc/fem

palm NOUN
il palmo masc (of hand)

■ **a palm tree** una palma
■ **Palm Sunday** la domenica delle Palme

pamphlet NOUN
il dépliant masc (PL i dépliant)

pan NOUN
la pentola fem

pancake NOUN
la crêpe fem (PL le crêpe)

pandemic NOUN
la pandemia fem
□ a flu pandemic una pandemia di influenza

panic NOUN
▷ see also **panic** VERB
il panico masc (PL i panici)

to **panic** VERB
▷ see also **panic** NOUN
farsi [49E] prendere dal panico
□ He panicked when he saw the blood. Quando ha visto il sangue si è fatto prendere dal panico.
■ **Don't panic!** Non agitarti!

panther NOUN
la pantera fem

panties NOUN PL
le mutandine fem pl

pants NOUN PL
1 le mutande fem pl
□ bra and pants reggiseno e mutande
2 i pantaloni masc pl (US: trousers)

pantyhose NOUN (US)
il collant masc (PL i collant)

paper NOUN
1 la carta fem
□ a paper towel una salvietta di carta □ a paper hankie un fazzoletto di carta
■ **paper clip** graffetta
2 il giornale masc
□ I saw an advert in the paper. Ho visto un annuncio sul giornale.
■ **an exam paper** una prova scritta

paperback NOUN
il tascabile masc (book)

> **LANGUAGE TIP** Word for word, this means 'one you can put into your pocket'.

paper boy NOUN
il ragazzo che recapita i giornali a domicilio masc

paper girl NOUN
la ragazza che recapita i giornali a domicilio fem

paper round NOUN
il giro di distribuzione dei giornali masc

paperweight NOUN
il fermacarte masc (PL i fermacarte)

paperwork NOUN
le pratiche fem pl
□ I've got a lot of paperwork to do. Ho un sacco di pratiche da sbrigare.

parachute NOUN
il paracadute masc

parade NOUN
la sfilata *fem*

paradise NOUN
il paradiso *masc*

paraffin NOUN
la paraffina *fem*
■ **a paraffin lamp** una lampada a petrolio

paragraph NOUN
il paragrafo *masc*

parallel ADJECTIVE
parallelo (FEM parallela)

paralysed ADJECTIVE
paralizzato (FEM paralizzata)

paramedic NOUN
il paramedico *masc* (PL i paramedici)

parcel NOUN
il pacco *masc* (PL i pacchi)

pardon NOUN
▷ *see also* **pardon** VERB
■ **Pardon?** Prego?

to **pardon** VERB
▷ *see also* **pardon** NOUN
scusare [68]

parent NOUN
1 il padre *masc (father)*
2 la madre *fem*
□ She changed when she became a parent. È cambiata quando è diventata madre.
■ **my parents** i miei genitori

  LANGUAGE TIP Be careful not to translate **parent** by parente.

Paris NOUN
Parigi *fem*

Parisian NOUN
il parigino *masc*
la parigina *fem*

park NOUN
▷ *see also* **park** VERB
il parco *masc* (PL i parchi)
□ a walk in the park una passeggiata al parco
■ **a national park** un parco nazionale
■ **a theme park** un parco a tema
■ **a car park** un parcheggio

to **park** VERB
▷ *see also* **park** NOUN
parcheggiare [58]
□ Where can I park my car? Dove posso parcheggiare la macchina?

parking NOUN
■ **Parking is difficult in the city centre.** È difficile trovare un posto per la macchina in centro.
■ **'no parking'** 'divieto di sosta'

parking lot NOUN (US)
il parcheggio *masc*

parking meter NOUN
il parchimetro *masc*

parking ticket NOUN
la multa per sosta vietata *fem*

parliament NOUN
il parlamento *masc*

parole NOUN
■ **on parole** in libertà vigilata

parrot NOUN
il pappagallo *masc*

parsley NOUN
il prezzemolo *masc*

part NOUN
▷ *see also* **part** VERB
1 la parte *fem*
□ The first part of the play was boring. La prima parte della commedia era noiosa.
□ She got a part in the film. Ha ottenuto una parte nel film.
■ **to take part in something** partecipare [68] a qualcosa □ A lot of people took part in the demonstration. Alla manifestazione ha partecipato molta gente.
■ **in part exchange** in pagamento parziale
2 il pezzo *masc*
■ **spare parts** pezzi di ricambio
3 la riga *fem* (US: *parting*)

to **part** VERB
▷ *see also* **part** NOUN
separarsi [56ᴱ]
□ They are parting after six years. Si stanno separando dopo sei anni.
■ **to part with something** separarsi [56ᴱ] da qualcosa □ I hate to part with this lamp. Mi dispiace separarmi da questa lampada.

particular ADJECTIVE
particolare (FEM particolare)
■ **to place particular emphasis on something** dare [30] particolare importanza a qualcosa
■ **nothing in particular** nulla di particolare

particularly ADVERB
particolarmente

parting NOUN
la riga *fem* (PL le righe) *(in hair)*

partly ADVERB
in parte

partner NOUN
il/la partner *masc/fem* (PL i/le partner)

part-time ADJECTIVE, ADVERB
part time (FEM+PL part time)
□ a part-time job un lavoro part time □ She works part-time. Lavora part time.

party NOUN
1 la festa *fem*
□ a birthday party una festa di compleanno
2 il partito *masc*
□ the Conservative Party il partito conservatore
3 la comitiva *fem*
□ a party of tourists una comitiva di turisti

pass NOUN
▷ *see also* **pass** VERB

pass – pattern

1 il passaggio *masc (in football)*
   □ a brilliant pass un bel passaggio
2 il valico *masc* (PL i valichi)
   □ The pass was blocked with snow. Il valico era bloccato dalla neve.
   ■ **to get a pass** *(in exam)* avere [12] la sufficienza □ I got six passes. Ho avuto la sufficienza in sei materie.
   ■ **a bus pass** un tesserino dell'autobus

to **pass** VERB
   ▷ *see also* **pass** NOUN
   1 passare [68ᴱ]
   □ Could you pass me the salt, please? Mi passi il sale, per favore?

   | **LANGUAGE TIP** Use **essere** to form past tenses when **passare** does not have an object.

   □ The time has passed quickly. Il tempo è passato molto in fretta. □ I hope I'll pass the exam. Spero di passare l'esame.
   2 passare [68ᴱ] davanti a
   □ I pass his house on my way to school. Andando a scuola passo davanti a casa sua.

to **pass out** VERB
   svenire [120ᴱ]

passage NOUN
   1 il brano *masc*
   □ Read the passage carefully. Leggi attentamente il brano.
   2 il passaggio *masc (corridor)*

passenger NOUN
   il passeggero *masc*
   la passeggera *fem*

passion NOUN
   la passione

passive ADJECTIVE
   passivo (FEM passiva)
   ■ **passive smoking** fumo passivo

Passover NOUN
   la Pasqua ebraica *fem*

passport NOUN
   il passaporto *masc*
   □ passport control il controllo passaporti

password NOUN
   la parola d'ordine *fem*

past ADVERB, PREPOSITION
   ▷ *see also* **past** NOUN
   oltre
   □ It's on the right, just past the station. È sulla destra, appena oltre la stazione.
   ■ **to go past** passare [68ᴱ] □ The bus went past without stopping. L'autobus è passato senza fermarsi.
   ■ **The bus goes past our house.** L'autobus passa davanti a casa nostra.
   ■ **It's half past ten.** Sono le dieci e mezza.
   ■ **It's quarter past nine.** Sono le nove e un quarto.
   ■ **It's ten past eight.** Sono le otto e dieci.
   ■ **It's past midnight.** È mezzanotte passata.

past NOUN
   ▷ *see also* **past** ADVERB, PREPOSITION
   il passato *masc*
   □ She lives in the past. Vive nel passato.

pasta NOUN
   la pasta *fem*

paste NOUN
   la colla *fem (glue)*

pasteurized ADJECTIVE
   pastorizzato (FEM pastorizzata)

pastime NOUN
   il passatempo *masc*

pastry NOUN
   la pasta *fem*

patch NOUN
   la toppa *fem*
   □ jackets with patches on the elbows giacche con le toppe sui gomiti
   ■ **a patch of land** un appezzamento
   ■ **a patch of grass** un pezzetto di prato
   ■ **a bald patch** una calvizie incipiente
   ■ **a bad patch** un periodaccio

patched ADJECTIVE
   rattoppato (FEM rattoppata)
   □ a pair of patched jeans un paio di jeans rattoppati

pâté NOUN
   il pâté *masc* (PL i pâté)

path NOUN
   il sentiero *masc*

pathetic ADJECTIVE
   1 penoso (FEM penosa)
   □ his pathetic excuses le sue scuse penose
   2 patetico (FEM patetica, MASC PL patetici, FEM PL patetiche)
   □ a pathetic sight uno spettacolo patetico

patience NOUN
   1 la pazienza *fem*
   □ He hasn't got much patience. Non ha molta pazienza.
   2 il solitario *masc*
   □ She was playing patience. Stava facendo un solitario.

patient NOUN, ADJECTIVE
   il/la paziente *masc/fem*

patio NOUN
   l'area pavimentata *fem (in garden)*

patriotic ADJECTIVE
   patriottico (FEM patriottica, MASC PL patriottici, FEM PL patriottiche)

patrol NOUN
   la pattuglia *fem*
   ■ **on patrol** di pattuglia

patrol car NOUN
   l'autopattuglia *fem*

pattern NOUN
   1 lo schema *masc* (PL gli schemi)
   □ The three attacks follow the same pattern. Le tre aggressioni seguono lo stesso schema.

P

2 il motivo *masc*
  □ a geometric pattern un motivo geometrico
  ■ **a sewing pattern** un cartamodello
pause NOUN
  la pausa *fem*
pavement NOUN
  il marciapiede *masc*

  > **LANGUAGE TIP** Be careful not to translate **pavement** by **pavimento**.

paw NOUN
  la zampa *fem*
pay NOUN
  ▷ *see also* **pay** VERB
  la paga *fem*
  ■ **a pay slip** un foglio paga
  ■ **pay phone** cabina telefonica
to **pay** VERB
  ▷ *see also* **pay** NOUN
  pagare [76]
  □ They pay me more on Sundays. La domenica mi pagano di più. □ Can I pay by cheque? Posso pagare con un assegno? □ I paid by credit card. Ho pagato con la carta di credito.
  ■ **to pay for something** pagare [76] qualcosa
  □ I paid fifty pounds for it. L'ho pagato cinquanta sterline.
  ■ **I'll pay you back tomorrow.** Ti restituisco i soldi domani.
  ■ **to pay attention** prestare [68] attenzione
  □ I wasn't paying attention to the teacher. Non prestavo attenzione all'insegnante.
  ■ **Don't pay any attention to him!** Non dargli retta!
  ■ **to pay somebody a visit** andare [6ᴱ] a trovare qualcuno □ Let's pay Paul a visit. Andiamo a trovare Paul.
payable ADJECTIVE
  ■ **Who shall I make the cheque payable to?** A chi devo intestare l'assegno?
payment NOUN
  il pagamento *masc*
payphone NOUN
  il telefono pubblico *masc*
PC NOUN
  il personal computer *masc* (PL i personal computer)
PE NOUN (= *physical education*)
  l' educazione fisica *fem*
pea NOUN
  il pisello *masc*
peace NOUN
  la pace *fem*
  ■ **peace talks** i negoziati di pace
  ■ **a peace treaty** un trattato di pace
peaceful ADJECTIVE
1 tranquillo (FEM tranquilla)
  □ a peaceful afternoon un pomeriggio tranquillo
2 pacifico (FEM pacifica, MASC PL pacifici, FEM PL pacifiche)

  □ a peaceful demonstration una manifestazione pacifica
peach NOUN
  la pesca *fem* (PL le pesche)
peacock NOUN
  il pavone *masc*
peak NOUN
1 la cima *fem* (of mountain)
2 l' apice *masc*
  □ His career was at its peak. La sua carriera era all'apice.
  ■ **peak season** l'alta stagione
peak rate NOUN
  la tariffa ore di punta *fem* (for phone)
peanut NOUN
  la nocciolina americana *fem*
  □ a packet of peanuts un pacchetto di noccioline americane
peanut butter NOUN
  il burro di arachidi *masc*
pear NOUN
  la pera *fem*
pearl NOUN
  la perla *fem*
pebble NOUN
  il ciottolo *masc*
peckish ADJECTIVE
  ■ **to feel peckish** avere [12] un languorino
peculiar ADJECTIVE
  strano (FEM strana)
  □ He's a peculiar person. È un tipo strano.
  □ It tastes peculiar. Ha un sapore strano.
pedal NOUN
  il pedale *masc*
pedestrian NOUN
  il pedone *masc*
  □ cyclists and pedestrians ciclisti e pedoni
pedestrian crossing NOUN
  l' attraversamento pedonale *masc*
pedestrianized ADJECTIVE
  ■ **a pedestrianized street** una via pedonalizzata
pedestrian precinct NOUN
  la zona pedonale *fem*
pedigree ADJECTIVE
  di razza
  □ a pedigree dog un cane di razza
pee NOUN
  ■ **to have a pee** fare [49] la pipì
peek NOUN
  ■ **to have a peek at** dare [30] una sbirciatina a □ I had a peek at his diary. Ho dato una sbirciatina al suo diario.
peel NOUN
  ▷ *see also* **peel** VERB
1 la buccia *fem* (PL le bucce)
  □ apple peel buccia di mela
2 la scorza *fem*
  □ orange peel scorza d'arancio

P

493

peel – perform

to **peel** VERB
▷ see also **peel** NOUN
1 sbucciare [13]
□ Shall I peel the potatoes? Sbuccio le patate?
2 spellarsi [56ᴱ]
□ My nose is peeling. Mi si sta spellando il naso.

peg NOUN
1 l' attaccapanni masc (PL gli attaccapanni) (for clothes)
2 la molletta fem (for washing)
■ **a tent peg** un picchetto

Pekinese NOUN
il pechinese masc (dog)

pellet NOUN
il pallino masc (for gun)

pelvis NOUN
il bacino masc

pen NOUN
la penna fem
□ I haven't got a pen. Non ho una penna.
■ **a pen name** uno pseudonimo

penalty NOUN
1 la pena fem
□ The penalty is life imprisonment. La pena è l'ergastolo.
■ **the death penalty** la pena di morte
2 il calcio di rigore masc (in football)
■ **a penalty shoot-out** i rigori

pence NOUN PL
i penny masc pl
□ 24 pence ventiquattro penny

pencil NOUN
la matita fem
□ in pencil a matita

pencil case NOUN
il portamatite masc (PL i portamatite)

pencil sharpener NOUN
il temperamatite masc (PL i temperamatite)

pendant NOUN
il pendaglio masc

pen-friend NOUN
l' amico di penna masc (PL gli amici di penna)
l' amica di penna fem (PL le amiche di penna)

penguin NOUN
il pinguino masc

penicillin NOUN
la penicillina fem

penis NOUN
il pene masc

penitentiary NOUN (US)
il penitenziario masc

penknife NOUN
il temperino masc

penny NOUN
il penny masc (PL i penny)

pension NOUN
la pensione fem

pensioner NOUN
il pensionato masc
la pensionata fem

pentathlon NOUN
il pentathlon masc

people NOUN PL
1 la gente fem sing
□ a lot of people un sacco di gente

> **LANGUAGE TIP** Use a singular verb with gente.

□ The people were nice. La gente era simpatica.
2 le persone fem pl
□ six people sei persone □ several people diverse persone
■ **How many people are there in your family?** Quanti siete in famiglia?
■ **Italian people** gli italiani
■ **People say that...** Si dice che...

pepper NOUN
1 il pepe masc
□ Pass the pepper, please. Mi passi il pepe, per favore?
2 il peperone masc
□ a green pepper un peperone verde

peppermint NOUN
la caramella alla menta fem
□ Would you like a peppermint? Vuoi una caramella alla menta?

per PREPOSITION
a
□ per day al giorno □ per week alla settimana
□ 30 miles per hour trenta miglia all'ora
■ **per annum** all'anno
■ **per cent** per cento □ fifty per cent cinquanta per cento

percussion NOUN
le percussioni fem pl
□ I play percussion. Suono le percussioni.

perfect ADJECTIVE
▷ see also **perfect** NOUN
perfetto (FEM perfetta)
□ That's perfect! Perfetto!

perfect NOUN
▷ see also **perfect** ADJECTIVE
■ **the perfect** il passato composto

perfectly ADVERB
perfettamente

to **perform** VERB
1 compiere [22]
□ He performed many acts of bravery. Ha compiuto molti atti di coraggio.
2 rappresentare [68]
□ This play was first performed in 1890. Questa commedia è stata rappresentata per la prima volta nel 1890.
■ **to perform a task** svolgere [91] un compito
■ **to perform brilliantly** (team) fornire [51] un'ottima prestazione

P

performance NOUN
1 lo spettacolo *masc*
  □ The performance lasts two hours. Lo spettacolo dura due ore.
2 l' interpretazione *fem*
  □ his performance as Hamlet la sua interpretazione di Amleto
3 la prestazione *fem*
  □ the team's disappointing performance la deludente prestazione della squadra

perfume NOUN
il profumo *masc*

perhaps ADVERB
forse
  □ Perhaps he's ill. Forse è malato.

period NOUN
1 il periodo *masc*
  □ for a limited period per un periodo limitato
2 l' epoca *fem*
  □ the Victorian period l'epoca vittoriana
3 le mestruazioni *fem pl*
  □ I'm having my period. Ho le mestruazioni.
4 la lezione *fem*
  □ Each period lasts forty minutes. Ogni lezione dura quaranta minuti.
5 il punto *masc (US: full stop)*
  □ Comma or period? Virgola o punto?

perm NOUN
la permanente *fem*
  □ She's got a perm. Ha la permanente.

permanent ADJECTIVE
permanente (FEM permanente)
  □ a permanent ban un divieto permanente
  ■ a permanent job un lavoro fisso

permission NOUN
il permesso *masc*
  □ You'll have to ask permission. Dovrai chiedere il permesso.

permit NOUN
il permesso *masc*
  □ a work permit un permesso di lavoro
  ■ a fishing permit una licenza di pesca

Persian ADJECTIVE
persiano (FEM persiana)
  □ a Persian cat un gatto persiano

persistent ADJECTIVE
tenace (FEM tenace)

person NOUN
la persona *fem*

personal ADJECTIVE
personale (FEM personale)
  □ a personal opinion un'opinione personale

personal assistant NOUN
la segretaria di direzione *fem*

personal column NOUN
la colonna dei piccoli annunci *fem*

personality NOUN
la personalità *fem* (PL le personalità)

personally ADVERB
personalmente
  □ Personally I don't agree. Personalmente non sono d'accordo.

personal stereo NOUN
il walkman® *masc* (PL i walkman)

personnel NOUN
il personale *masc*

perspiration NOUN
la traspirazione *fem*

to persuade VERB
convincere [121]
  □ She persuaded me to go with her. Mi ha convinto ad andare con lei.

pessimist NOUN
il/la pessimista *masc/fem*

pessimistic ADJECTIVE
pessimista (FEM pessimista)

pest NOUN
1 l' insetto nocivo *masc*
  □ garden pests gli insetti nocivi del giardino
2 il/la rompiscatole *masc/fem*
  □ He's a real pest! È un gran rompiscatole!

to pester VERB
tormentare [68]
  □ He's always pestering me. Mi tormenta in continuazione.

pet NOUN
l' animale domestico *masc* (PL gli animali domestici)
  □ Have you got any pets? Hai qualche animale domestico?
  ■ the teacher's pet il cocco dell'insegnante

petition NOUN
la petizione *fem*

petrified ADJECTIVE
terrorizzato (FEM terrorizzata)
  □ I was petrified. Ero terrorizzato.

petrol NOUN
la benzina *fem*
  □ They spend a lot on petrol. Spendono molto per la benzina.
  ■ unleaded petrol la benzina verde
  ■ a petrol pump un distributore di benzina
  LANGUAGE TIP Be careful not to translate petrol by petrolio.

petrol station NOUN
la stazione di servizio *fem*

petrol tank NOUN
il serbatoio della benzina *masc*

phantom NOUN
il fantasma *masc* (PL i fantasmi)

pharmacy NOUN
la farmacia *fem*

pheasant NOUN
il fagiano *masc*

philosophy NOUN
la filosofia *fem*

P

phobia NOUN
la fobia *fem*

to **phone** VERB
▷ *see also* **phone** NOUN
telefonare [68]
□ I'll phone the station. Telefono alla stazione.
■ **to phone back** richiamare [68]

phone NOUN
▷ *see also* **phone** VERB
1 il telefono *masc*
■ **by phone** per telefono
■ **to be on the phone** essere [47ᴱ] al telefono
□ She's on the phone at the moment. In questo momento è al telefono.
2 il cellulare *masc (mobile)*
□ I've lost my phone. Ho perso il cellulare.

phone bill NOUN
la bolletta del telefono *fem*

phone book NOUN
l' elenco telefonico *masc* (PL gli elenchi telefonici)

phone box NOUN
la cabina telefonica *fem* (PL le cabine telefoniche)

phone call NOUN
la telefonata *fem*
□ to make a phone call fare una telefonata

phonecard NOUN
la scheda telefonica *fem* (PL le schede telefoniche)

phone number NOUN
il numero di telefono *masc*

photo NOUN
la foto *fem* (PL le foto)
■ **to take a photo** fare [49] una foto □ I took a photo of the bride and groom. Ho fatto una foto agli sposi.

photocopy NOUN
▷ *see also* **photocopy** VERB
la fotocopia *fem*

to **photocopy** VERB
▷ *see also* **photocopy** NOUN
fotocopiare [17]

photograph NOUN
▷ *see also* **photograph** VERB
la fotografia *fem*

to **photograph** VERB
▷ *see also* **photograph** NOUN
fotografare [68]

photographer NOUN
il fotografo *masc*
la fotografa *fem*
□ She's a photographer. Fa la fotografa.

photography NOUN
la fotografia *fem*
□ My hobby is photography. Il mio hobby è la fotografia.

Photoshop® NOUN
▷ *see also* **Photoshop** VERB
Photoshop® *masc*

to **Photoshop** VERB
▷ *see also* **Photoshop** NOUN
photoshoppare [68]

phrase NOUN
la frase *fem*

phrase book NOUN
il manuale di conversazione *masc*

physical ADJECTIVE
▷ *see also* **physical** NOUN
fisico (FEM fisica, MASC PL fisici, FEM PL fisiche)

physical NOUN (US)
▷ *see also* **physical** ADJECTIVE
la visita medica *fem*

physicist NOUN
il fisico *masc*
□ a nuclear physicist un fisico nucleare

physics NOUN
la fisica *fem*
□ She teaches physics. Insegna fisica.

physiotherapist NOUN
il/la fisioterapista *masc/fem*

physiotherapy NOUN
la fisioterapia *fem*

pianist NOUN
il/la pianista *masc/fem*

piano NOUN
il pianoforte *masc*

pick NOUN
▷ *see also* **pick** VERB
il piccone *masc*
□ pick and shovel pala e piccone
■ **Take your pick!** Scegli quello che vuoi!
  LANGUAGE TIP Use 'quella' if what you may pick is feminine, and 'quelli' or 'quelle' if it is plural.

to **pick** VERB
▷ *see also* **pick** NOUN
1 scegliere [95]
□ I picked the biggest piece. Ho scelto il pezzo più grosso.
2 cogliere [21]
□ I picked some strawberries. Ho colto un po' di fragole.
■ **to pick on somebody** prendersela [77ᴱ] con qualcuno □ She's always picking on me. Se la prende sempre con me.

to **pick out** VERB
scegliere [95]
□ I like them all – it's difficult to pick one out. Mi piacciono tutti, è difficile sceglierne uno.

to **pick up** VERB
1 prendere [77]
□ We'll come to the airport to pick you up. Veniamo a prenderti all'aeroporto.
2 raccogliere [21]

P

□ Could you help me pick up the toys? Mi aiuti a raccogliere i giocattoli?

3 imparare [68]

□ I picked up some Spanish during my holiday. Ho imparato un po' di spagnolo in vacanza.

4 prendersi [77ᴱ]

□ They picked up a nasty infection. Si sono presi una brutta infezione.

pickpocket NOUN
il borseggiatore *masc*
la borseggiatrice *fem*

picnic NOUN
il picnic *masc* (PL i picnic)
■ **to have a picnic** fare [49] un picnic

picture NOUN
▷ *see also* **picture** VERB

1 l' illustrazione *fem*
□ Children's books have lots of pictures. Ci sono molte illustrazioni nei libri per bambini.

2 la foto *fem* (PL le foto)
□ My picture was in the paper. C'era la mia foto sul giornale.

3 il quadro *masc*
□ There were pictures on the walls. C'erano dei quadri alle pareti.
■ **to paint a picture of something** dipingere [34] qualcosa

4 il disegno *masc*
□ a nice picture un bel disegno
■ **to draw a picture of something** disegnare [14] qualcosa
■ **the pictures** il cinema *masc sing* □ Shall we go to the pictures? Andiamo al cinema?

to picture VERB
▷ *see also* **picture** NOUN
immaginare [68]
□ I can just picture it! Me lo immagino!

picturesque ADJECTIVE
pittoresco (FEM pittoresca, MASC PL pittoreschi, FEM PL pittoresche)

pie NOUN

1 la torta *fem*
□ an apple pie una torta di mele

2 il pasticcio in crosta *masc* (*savoury*)

piece NOUN
il pezzo *masc*
□ A small piece, please. Un pezzo piccolo, per favore.
■ **a piece of furniture** un mobile
■ **a piece of advice** un consiglio
■ **a 10p piece** una moneta da dieci penny

pie chart NOUN
il grafico a torta *masc* (PL i grafici a torta)

Piedmont NOUN
il Piemonte

pier NOUN
il pontile *masc*

to pierce VERB
perforare [68]
□ A bullet pierced his chest. Un proiettile gli ha perforato il petto.
■ **to have one's ears pierced** farsi [49ᴱ] fare i buchi alle orecchie

pierced ADJECTIVE
■ **to have pierced ears** avere [12] i buchi per gli orecchini □ I've got pierced ears. Ho i buchi per gli orecchini.

piercing NOUN
il piercing *masc* (PL i piercing)
□ She has several piercings. Ha diversi piercing.

pig NOUN
il maiale *masc*

pigeon NOUN
il piccione *masc*

piggyback NOUN
■ **to give a piggyback** portare [68] a cavalluccio □ I can't give you a piggyback, you're too heavy. Non posso portarti a cavalluccio, sei troppo pesante.

piggy bank NOUN
il salvadanaio *masc*

pigtail NOUN
la treccia *fem* (PL le trecce)

pile NOUN
la pila *fem*
□ piles of dirty dishes C'erano pile di piatti sporchi in cucina.

piles NOUN PL
le emorroidi *fem pl*

pile-up NOUN
il tamponamento a catena *masc*

pill NOUN
la pillola *fem*
■ **to be on the pill** prendere [77] la pillola

pillar NOUN
il pilastro *masc*
□ marble pillars pilastri di marmo

pillar box NOUN
la buca delle lettere *fem* (PL le buche delle lettere)

pillow NOUN
il guanciale *masc*

pilot NOUN
il/la pilota *masc/fem*
□ He's a pilot. Fa il pilota.

pilot light NOUN
la fiamma pilota *fem*

pimple NOUN
il brufolo *masc*

PIN NOUN (= *personal identification number*)
il numero di codice segreto *masc*

pin NOUN
▷ *see also* **pin** VERB
lo spillo *masc*
□ fastened with a pin fissato con uno spillo
■ **pins and needles** il formicolio □ I've got pins and needles. Ho un formicolio.

497

P

to **pin** VERB
▷ see also **pin** NOUN
appuntare [68]
□ They pinned a notice on the board. Hanno appuntato un avviso in bacheca.

pinafore NOUN
il grembiule masc

pinball NOUN
il flipper masc
□ They're playing pinball. Giocano a flipper.
■ **a pinball machine** un flipper

to **pinch** VERB
1 pizzicare [18]
□ He pinched me! Mi ha pizzicato!
2 fregare [76]
□ Who's pinched my pen? Chi mi ha fregato la penna?

pine NOUN
il pino masc

pineapple NOUN
l' ananas masc (PL gli ananas)

pink ADJECTIVE
rosa (FEM+PL rosa)

pint NOUN
la pinta fem

> **DID YOU KNOW...?**
> In Italy measurements are in litres and centilitres. A pint is about the same as 0.6 litres.

■ **a pint of beer** una birra grande
■ **half a pint of beer** una birra piccola
■ **to have a pint** bere [15] una birra
■ **to go out for a pint** uscire [117ᴱ] a bere una birra

pipe NOUN
1 il tubo masc
□ a plastic pipe un tubo di plastica
2 la pipa fem
□ He smokes a pipe. Fuma la pipa.
■ **the pipes** la cornamusa fem sing □ He plays the pipes. Suona la cornamusa.

pirate NOUN
il pirata masc (PL i pirati)

pirated ADJECTIVE
piratato (FEM piratata)
□ a pirated CD un CD piratato

Pisces NOUN
i Pesci masc pl
□ I'm Pisces. Sono dei Pesci.

pitch NOUN
▷ see also **pitch** VERB
il campo masc
□ a football pitch un campo di calcio

to **pitch** VERB
▷ see also **pitch** NOUN
1 lanciare [13]
□ He pitched the bottle into the lake. Ha lanciato la bottiglia nel lago.

2 piantare [68]
□ We pitched our tent near the beach. Abbiamo piantato la tenda vicino alla spiaggia.

pity NOUN
▷ see also **pity** VERB
la compassione fem
■ **to feel pity for somebody** provare [68] compassione per qualcuno
■ **What a pity!** Che peccato!

to **pity** VERB
▷ see also **pity** NOUN
compatire [51]
□ I don't hate him, I pity him. Non lo odio, lo compatisco.

pizza NOUN
la pizza fem

place NOUN
▷ see also **place** VERB
il posto masc
□ It's a quiet place. È un posto tranquillo.
□ There are a lot of interesting places to visit. Ci sono tanti posti interessanti da vedere.
□ a university place un posto all'università
■ **to change places** scambiarsi [17ᴱ] di posto
■ **to take place** avere [12] luogo □ Elections will take place on November 25th. Le elezioni avranno luogo il 25 novembre.
■ **at your place** a casa tua □ Shall we meet at your place? Ci incontriamo a casa tua?

to **place** VERB
▷ see also **place** NOUN
posare [68]
□ He placed his hand on hers. Ha posato la mano sulla sua.

placement NOUN
lo stage masc (PL gli stage)
■ **to do a work placement** fare [49] uno stage

plain ADJECTIVE
1 in tinta unita
□ a plain tie una cravatta in tinta unita
2 semplice (FEM semplice)
□ a plain white blouse una camicetta bianca, semplice
■ **in plain clothes** in borghese

plain chocolate NOUN
il cioccolato fondente masc

plait NOUN
la treccia fem (PL le trecce)

plan NOUN
▷ see also **plan** VERB
1 il programma masc (PL i programmi)
□ What are your plans for the holidays? Che programmi hai per le vacanze?
■ **to make plans** fare [49] progetti
■ **according to plan** come previsto
□ Everything went according to plan. È andato tutto come previsto.

2 la piantina *fem*

□ a plan of the campsite una piantina del campeggio

to **plan** VERB

▷ *see also* **plan** NOUN

1 progettare [68]

□ We're planning a trip to Rome. Stiamo progettando un viaggio a Roma.

2 organizzare [68]

□ Plan your revision carefully. Organizza bene il ripasso.

■ **to plan to do something** avere [12] intenzione di fare qualcosa □ I'm planning to get a job. Ho intenzione di trovare un lavoro.

plane NOUN

l' aereo *masc*

□ by plane in aereo

planet NOUN

il pianeta *masc* (PL i pianeti)

planning NOUN

■ **The trip needs careful planning.** Bisogna organizzare bene il viaggio.

■ **planning permission** permesso di costruzione

■ **family planning** pianificazione familiare

to **plant** VERB

▷ *see also* **plant** NOUN

piantare [68]

plant NOUN

▷ *see also* **plant** VERB

1 la pianta *fem*

□ I water my plants every week. Annaffio le piante ogni settimana.

2 la fabbrica *fem* (PL le fabbriche)

□ a chemical plant una fabbrica chimica

plaque NOUN

1 la targa *fem* (PL le targhe) *(commemorative)*

2 la placca *fem* *(on teeth)*

plaster NOUN

1 il cerotto *masc*

□ Have you got a plaster, by any chance? Hai un cerotto, per caso?

2 il gesso *masc*

■ **Her leg's in plaster.** Ha una gamba ingessata.

plastic NOUN

▷ *see also* **plastic** ADJECTIVE

la plastica *fem*

□ It's made of plastic. È di plastica.

plastic ADJECTIVE

▷ *see also* **plastic** NOUN

di plastica

□ a plastic bag un sacchetto di plastica

plate NOUN

il piatto *masc*

platform NOUN

1 il binario *masc*

□ at platform four al binario quattro

2 la banchina *fem*

□ They were waiting on the platform. Aspettavano sulla banchina.

3 il palco *masc* (PL i palchi)

□ The soloist had just left the platform. Il solista aveva appena lasciato il palco.

play NOUN

▷ *see also* **play** VERB

1 la commedia *fem*

□ a play by Shakespeare una commedia di Shakespeare

■ **to put on a play** mettere [59] in scena una commedia

2 il gioco *masc*

□ work and play lavoro e gioco

to **play** VERB

▷ *see also* **play** NOUN

1 giocare [18]

□ He's playing with his friends. Sta giocando con gli amici.

2 giocare [18] contro

□ Italy will play Scotland next month. Il mese prossimo l'Italia giocherà contro la Scozia.

3 giocare [18] a

□ I play hockey. Gioco a hockey. □ Can you play pool? Sai giocare a biliardo?

4 suonare [68]

□ I play the guitar. Suono la chitarra.

5 ascoltare [68]

□ She's always playing that record. Ascolta sempre quel disco.

6 recitare [68] il ruolo di

□ I want to play Cleopatra. Voglio recitare il ruolo di Cleopatra.

to **play down** VERB

minimizzare [68] su

□ He played down his illness. Ha minimizzato sulla sua malattia.

to **play up** VERB

1 fare [49] i capricci

□ The car's playing up. La macchina fa i capricci.

2 far [49] male

□ My leg's playing up. La gamba mi fa male.

player NOUN

il giocatore *masc*

la giocatrice *fem*

■ **a football player** un calciatore

■ **a piano player** un pianista

■ **a saxophone player** un sassofonista

playful ADJECTIVE

giocherellone (FEM giocherellona)

playground NOUN

1 il cortile per la ricreazione *masc* *(at school)*

2 il campo giochi *masc* *(in park)*

playgroup NOUN

l' asilo *masc*

playing card NOUN

la carta da gioco *fem*

499

playing field NOUN
il campo sportivo *masc*

playtime NOUN
la ricreazione *fem*

playwright NOUN
il commediografo *masc*
la commediografa *fem*

pleasant ADJECTIVE
piacevole (FEM piacevole)

please EXCLAMATION
per favore
□ Two coffees, please. Due caffè, per favore.
■ **Yes please.** Sì, grazie.

pleased ADJECTIVE
contento (FEM contenta)
□ My mother's not going to be very pleased.
Mia madre non sarà molto contenta. □ It's
beautiful: she'll be pleased with it. È bellissimo,
ne sarà contenta.
■ **Pleased to meet you!** Piacere!

pleasure NOUN
il piacere *masc*

plenty PRONOUN
abbastanza
□ I've got plenty. Ne ho abbastanza.
■ **I've got plenty to do.** Ho un sacco di cose
da fare.
■ **plenty of** un sacco di □ We've got plenty
of time. Abbiamo un sacco di tempo.
■ **I've got plenty of money.** Ho soldi a
sufficienza.

pliers NOUN PL
le pinze *fem pl*

plot NOUN
▷ *see also* **plot** VERB
1 la trama *fem*
□ a complicated plot una trama complicata
2 il complotto *masc*
□ a plot against the president un complotto
contro il presidente
■ **a vegetable plot** un orticello

to plot VERB
▷ *see also* **plot** NOUN
complottare [68]

plug NOUN
1 la spina *fem*
□ The plug is faulty. La spina è difettosa.
2 il tappo *masc* (for sink, bath)

to plug in VERB
attaccare [18]
□ Is the iron plugged in? È attaccato il ferro da
stiro?

plum NOUN
la prugna *fem*

plumber NOUN
l' idraulico *masc* (PL gli idraulici)
□ He's a plumber. Fa l'idraulico.

plump ADJECTIVE
grassoccio (FEM grassoccia, MASC PL grassocci,
FEM PL grassocce)

to plunge VERB
tuffarsi [56ᴱ]
□ She plunged into the pool. Si è tuffata nella
piscina.

plural NOUN
il plurale *masc*

plus CONJUNCTION, ADJECTIVE
1 più
□ 4 plus 3 quattro più tre
2 e
□ three children plus a dog tre bambini e un cane
■ **I got B plus for my essay.** Ho ricevuto B più
nel tema.

p.m. ADVERB (= post meridiem)
■ **at eight p.m.** alle otto di sera
■ **at two p.m.** alle quattordici

pneumonia NOUN
la polmonite *fem*

poached ADJECTIVE
■ **a poached egg** un uovo affogato
LANGUAGE TIP Word for word, this means
'drowned egg'.

pocket NOUN
la tasca *fem* (PL le tasche)
□ He had his hands in his pockets. Aveva le
mani in tasca.

pocket calculator NOUN
la calcolatrice tascabile *fem*

pocket money NOUN
la paghetta *fem*
□ £8 a week pocket money una paghetta
settimanale di otto sterline

podcast NOUN
il podcast *masc* (PL i podcast)
□ to download a podcast scaricare un podcast

poem NOUN
la poesia *fem*

poet NOUN
la poeta *fem*
la poetessa *fem*

poetry NOUN
la poesia *fem*

point NOUN
▷ *see also* **point** VERB
1 il punto *masc*
□ a point on the horizon un punto all'orizzonte
□ They scored five points. Hanno segnato cinque
punti. □ At that point, we decided to leave. A
quel punto abbiamo deciso di andarcene.
■ **a point of view** un punto di vista
■ **to get to the point** arrivare [68ᴱ] al punto
2 l' osservazione *fem*
□ He made some interesting points. Ha fatto
delle osservazioni interessanti.
3 la punta *fem*

□ a pencil with a sharp point una matita con la punta

4 la virgola *fem (in decimals)*

□ two point five (2.5) due virgola cinque (2,5)

■ **to get somebody's point** capire [51] ciò che qualcuno vuole dire □ Yes, I get your point. Sì, capisco ciò che vuoi dire.

■ **That's a good point!** Giusto!

■ **There's no point.** È inutile. □ There's no point waiting. È inutile aspettare.

■ **What's the point?** Perché? □ What's the point of leaving so early? Perché partire così presto?

to **point** VERB

▷ *see also* **point** NOUN

indicare [18] col dito

□ Don't point! Non indicare col dito!

■ **to point at somebody** indicare [18] qualcuno col dito □ She pointed at Anne. Ha indicato Anne col dito.

■ **to point a gun at somebody** puntare [68] una pistola contro qualcuno

to **point out** VERB

1 indicare [18]

□ The guide pointed out Big Ben to us. La guida ci ha indicato il Big Ben.

2 far [49] presente

□ She pointed out our mistakes. Ci ha fatto presente i nostri errori.

■ **I'd like to point out that...** Vorrei far notare che...

pointless ADJECTIVE

inutile (FEM inutile)

□ It's pointless to argue. È inutile discutere.

poison NOUN

▷ *see also* **poison** VERB

il veleno *masc*

to **poison** VERB

▷ *see also* **poison** NOUN

avvelenare [68]

poisonous ADJECTIVE

1 velenoso (FEM velenosa)

□ poisonous snakes serpenti velenosi

2 tossico (FEM tossica, MASC PL tossici, FEM PL tossiche)

□ poisonous fumes vapori tossici

to **poke** VERB

■ **He poked me in the eye.** Mi ha ficcato un dito nell'occhio.

poker NOUN

il poker *masc*

□ I play poker. Gioco a poker.

Poland NOUN

la Polonia *fem*

polar bear NOUN

l' orso bianco *masc* (PL gli orsi bianchi)

Pole NOUN

il polacco *masc*

la polacca *fem*

pole NOUN

1 il palo *masc*

□ a telegraph pole un palo del telegrafo

■ **a tent pole** un paletto per la tenda

■ **a ski pole** una racchetta da sci

2 il polo *masc*

□ the earth's poles i poli terrestri

■ **the North Pole** il polo nord

■ **the South Pole** il polo sud

pole vault NOUN

il salto con l'asta *masc*

police NOUN PL

la polizia *fem sing*

□ We called the police. Abbiamo chiamato la polizia.

police car NOUN

l' auto della polizia *fem* (PL le auto della polizia)

policeman NOUN

il poliziotto *masc*

police station NOUN

il comando di polizia *masc*

policewoman NOUN

la donna poliziotto *fem* (PL le donne poliziotto)

polio NOUN

il polio *masc*

Polish ADJECTIVE

polacco (FEM polacca, MASC PL polacchi, FEM PL polacche)

polish NOUN

▷ *see also* **polish** VERB

1 il lucido *masc*

□ shoe polish lucido per scarpe

2 la cera *fem (for furniture)*

to **polish** VERB

▷ *see also* **polish** NOUN

lucidare [68] *(shoes, furniture)*

polite ADJECTIVE

educato (FEM educata)

politely ADVERB

educatamente

politeness NOUN

l' educazione *fem*

□ out of politeness per educazione

political ADJECTIVE

politico (FEM politica, MASC PL politici, FEM PL politiche)

politician NOUN

il politico *masc* (PL i politici)

politics NOUN PL

la politica *fem*

□ I'm not interested in politics. Non m'interesso di politica.

poll NOUN

il sondaggio *masc*

□ A recent poll revealed that... Un recente sondaggio ha rivelato che...

pollen NOUN

il polline *masc*

P

to **pollute** VERB
inquinare [68]

polluted ADJECTIVE
inquinato (FEM inquinata)

pollution NOUN
l' inquinamento masc

polo neck NOUN
il maglione dolcevita masc

polo-necked ADJECTIVE
■ a polo-necked sweater un maglione dolcevita

polo shirt NOUN
la polo fem (PL le polo)

polythene bag NOUN
il sacchetto di plastica masc

pond NOUN
1 lo stagno masc (natural)
2 il laghetto masc (artificial)

pony NOUN
il pony masc (PL i pony)
■ to go pony trekking fare [49] un'escursione a cavallo

ponytail NOUN
1 la coda di cavallo fem
□ She's got a ponytail. Ha la coda di cavallo.
2 il codino masc (man's)

poodle NOUN
il barboncino masc

pool NOUN
▷ see also **pool** VERB
1 la pozza fem
□ a pool of blood una pozza di sangue
2 lo stagno masc (pond)
3 la piscina fem (swimming bath)
4 il biliardo masc
□ Let's play pool. Giochiamo a biliardo.
■ the pools il totocalcio
■ to do the pools giocare [18] la schedina

to **pool** VERB
▷ see also **pool** NOUN
mettere [59] insieme

poor ADJECTIVE
1 povero (FEM povera)
□ a poor family una famiglia povera □ Poor David, he's very unlucky! Povero David, è proprio sfortunato!
■ the poor i poveri
2 mediocre (FEM mediocre)
□ a poor mark un voto mediocre

poorly ADJECTIVE
■ to be poorly sentirsi [41ᴱ] poco bene

pop ADJECTIVE
▷ see also **pop** VERB
pop (FEM+PL pop)
□ a pop group un gruppo pop

to **pop** VERB
▷ see also **pop** ADJECTIVE

1 scoppiare [17ᴱ]
□ The balloon popped. Il pallone è scoppiato.
2 mettere [59]
□ He popped a sweet into his mouth. Si è messo una caramella in bocca.
3 fare [49] un salto
□ I'll just pop to the toilet. Farò un salto alla toilette. □ I'm just popping round to John's. Faccio un salto da John.

to **pop up** VERB
apparire [7ᴱ]

popcorn NOUN
il popcorn masc

Pope NOUN
■ the Pope il Papa

poppy NOUN
il papavero masc

Popsicle® NOUN (US)
il ghiacciolo masc

popular ADJECTIVE
1 in voga
□ This is a very popular style. Questo stile è molto in voga.
2 popolare (FEM popolare)
□ the popular press la stampa popolare □ He's the most popular politician in France. È il personaggio politico più popolare in Francia.
■ Madame Tussaud's is very popular with tourists. Madame Tussaud piace molto ai turisti.
3 simpatico (FEM simpatica, MASC PL simpatici, FEM PL simpatiche)
□ She's a very popular girl. È molto simpatica a tutti.

population NOUN
la popolazione fem

porch NOUN
la veranda fem

pork NOUN
la carne di maiale fem
□ I don't eat pork. Non mangio carne di maiale.
■ a pork chop una braciola di maiale

porn NOUN
▷ see also **porn** ADJECTIVE
la pornografia fem

porn ADJECTIVE
▷ see also **porn** NOUN
porno (FEM+PL porno)

pornographic ADJECTIVE
pornografico (FEM pornografica, MASC PL pornografici, FEM PL pornografiche)

pornography NOUN
la pornografia fem

porridge NOUN
il porridge masc

port NOUN
il porto masc

portable ADJECTIVE
portatile (FEM portatile)
□ a portable TV una TV portatile

porter NOUN
1 il portiere *masc (in hotel)*
2 il facchino *masc (at station)*

portion NOUN
la porzione *fem*

portrait NOUN
il ritratto *masc*

Portugal NOUN
il Portogallo *masc*

Portuguese ADJECTIVE
▷ *see also* **Portuguese** NOUN
portoghese (FEM portoghese)

Portuguese NOUN
▷ *see also* **Portuguese** ADJECTIVE
il portoghese *masc (language)*
■ **the Portuguese** i portoghesi

posh ADJECTIVE
1 di lusso
□ **a posh hotel** un albergo di lusso
2 snob (FEM+PL snob)
□ **posh people** gente snob

position NOUN
la posizione *fem*
□ **an uncomfortable position** una posizione scomoda

positive ADJECTIVE
1 positivo (FEM positiva)
□ **a positive attitude** un atteggiamento positivo
2 sicuro (FEM sicura)
□ **I'm positive.** Ne sono sicuro.

possession NOUN
il possesso *masc*
□ **in possession of** in possesso di
■ **one's possessions** le sue cose □ **Have you got all your possessions?** Hai tutte le tue cose?

possibility NOUN
la possibilità *fem* (PL le possibilità)
□ **the possibility of a strike** la possibilità di uno sciopero
■ **It's a possibility.** È possibile.

possible ADJECTIVE
possibile (FEM possibile)
□ **as soon as possible** al più presto possibile

possibly ADVERB
forse
□ **Are you coming to the party? — Possibly.** Vieni alla festa? — Forse.
■ **...if you possibly can.** ...se ti è possibile.
■ **I can't possibly come.** Non posso proprio venire.

to post VERB
▷ *see also* **post** NOUN
1 imbucare [18]
□ **I've got some cards to post.** Devo imbucare delle cartoline.
2 postare [68] *(on website)*
□ **She posted the message on Facebook.** Ha postato il messaggio su Facebook.

■ **She posted it on my wall.** Me l'ha attaccato al muro.

post NOUN
▷ *see also* **post** VERB
1 la posta *fem*
□ **by post** per posta □ **Is there any post for me?** C'è posta per me?
2 il palo *masc*
□ **The ball hit the post.** Il pallone ha colpito il palo.
3 il post *masc* (PL i post) *(on social network, blog)*

postage NOUN
l' affrancatura *fem*

postbox NOUN
la buca delle lettere *fem* (PL le buche delle lettere)

postcard NOUN
la cartolina *fem*

postcode NOUN
il codice postale *masc*

poster NOUN
1 il poster *masc* (PL i poster)
□ **I've got posters on my bedrooms walls.** Ho dei poster sulle pareti di camera mia.
2 il manifesto *masc*
□ **There are posters all over town.** Ci sono manifesti in tutta la città.

postman NOUN
il postino *masc*
□ **He's a postman.** Fa il postino.

postmark NOUN
il timbro postale *masc*

post office NOUN
l' ufficio postale *masc*

to postpone VERB
rinviare [17]
□ **The match has been postponed.** La partita è stata rinviata.

postwoman NOUN
la postina *fem*
□ **She's a postwoman.** Fa la postina.

pot NOUN
1 la pentola *fem*
□ **a pot of soup** una pentola di zuppa
■ **pots and pans** le pentole
2 il vasetto *masc*
□ **a pot of jam** un vasetto di marmellata
■ **a pot plant** una pianta in vaso
3 l' erba *fem (marijuana)*
□ **to smoke pot** fumare erba

potato NOUN
la patata *fem*
■ **mashed potatoes** il purè di patate *masc sing*
■ **a baked potato** una patata cotta al forno con la buccia
■ **potato chips** (US: *crisps*) le patatine

potential NOUN
▷ *see also* **potential** ADJECTIVE
■ **He has great potential.** È promettente.

P

503

potential - precisely

potential ADJECTIVE
▷ see also **potential** NOUN
potenziale (FEM potenziale)
□ a potential problem un problema potenziale

pothole NOUN
la buca fem (PL le buche)

pottery NOUN
la ceramica fem

pound NOUN
▷ see also **pound** VERB
1 la libbra fem
■ **a pound of carrots** mezzo chilo di carote
2 la sterlina fem
□ twenty pounds venti sterline □ a pound coin una moneta da una sterlina

to **pound** VERB
▷ see also **pound** NOUN
battere [1] forte
□ My heart was pounding. Mi batteva forte il cuore.

to **pour** VERB
1 versare [68]
□ She poured some water into the pan. Ha versato dell'acqua nella pentola. □ She poured him a drink. Gli ha versato da bere. □ Shall I pour you a cup of tea? Ti verso del tè?
2 diluviare [17]
□ It's pouring. Sta diluviando.
■ **in the pouring rain** sotto una pioggia torrenziale

poverty NOUN
la povertà fem

powder NOUN
la polvere fem
□ white powder polvere bianca
■ **face powder** cipria
■ **powder room** toilette delle signore

power NOUN
1 il potere masc
□ They were in power for 18 years. Sono stati al potere per diciotto anni.
2 la corrente fem
□ The power's off. La corrente è staccata.
3 l' energia fem
□ nuclear power energia nucleare □ solar power energia solare

power cut NOUN
l' interruzione di corrente fem

powerful ADJECTIVE
potente (FEM potente)

power point NOUN
la presa di corrente fem

power station NOUN
la centrale elettrica fem (PL le centrali elettriche)

practical ADJECTIVE
pratico (FEM pratica, MASC PL pratici, FEM PL pratiche)
□ a practical suggestion un consiglio pratico
□ She's very practical. È una tipa molto pratica.

practically ADVERB
praticamente
□ It's practically impossible. È praticamente impossibile.

practice NOUN
l' allenamento masc
□ football practice allenamento di calcio
□ I'm out of practice. Sono fuori allenamento.
■ **piano practice** esercizi al piano
■ **in practice** in pratica □ In practice it's more difficult. In pratica è più difficile.
■ **a medical practice** uno studio medico

to **practise** (US **practice**) VERB
1 esercitarsi [56E]
□ I ought to practise more. Dovrei esercitarmi di più.
2 esercitarsi [56E] a
□ I practise the flute every evening. Mi esercito al flauto ogni sera.
3 fare [49] pratica di
□ I practised my Italian when I was on holiday. Ho fatto pratica d'italiano quand'ero in vacanza.
4 allenarsi [56E]
□ The team practises on Thursdays. La squadra si allena di giovedì.

practising (US **practicing**) ADJECTIVE
praticante (FEM praticante)
□ She's a practising Catholic. È cattolica praticante.

pram NOUN
la carrozzina fem

prawn NOUN
il gamberetto masc

prawn cocktail NOUN
il cocktail di gamberetti masc (PL i cocktail di gamberetti)

to **pray** VERB
pregare [76]

prayer NOUN
la preghiera fem

precaution NOUN
la precauzione fem

preceding ADJECTIVE
precedente (FEM precedente)

precinct NOUN
■ **a shopping precinct** un centro commerciale
■ **a pedestrian precinct** una zona pedonale

precious ADJECTIVE
prezioso (FEM preziosa)

precise ADJECTIVE
preciso (FEM precisa)
□ at that precise moment in quel preciso istante

precisely ADVERB
precisamente
□ Precisely! Precisamente!
■ **at 10 a.m. precisely** alle dieci precise

to **predict** VERB
predire [35]
predictable ADJECTIVE
prevedibile (FEM prevedibile)
prefect NOUN
studente con funzioni disciplinari
to **prefer** VERB
preferire [51]
□ Which would you prefer? Quale preferisci?
□ I prefer chemistry to maths. Preferisco la
chimica alla matematica.
preference NOUN
la preferenza fem
pregnant ADJECTIVE
incinta fem
□ She's six months pregnant. È incinta di sei
mesi.
prehistoric ADJECTIVE
preistorico (FEM preistorica, MASC PL preistorici,
FEM PL preistoriche)
prejudice NOUN
il pregiudizio masc
□ There's a lot of racial prejudice. Ci sono molti
pregiudizi razziali.
prejudiced ADJECTIVE
■ **to be prejudiced against somebody**
essere [47ᴱ] prevenuto contro qualcuno
premature ADJECTIVE
prematuro (FEM prematura)
□ a premature baby un neonato prematuro
premier NOUN
il primo ministro masc
□ the Australian premier il primo ministro
australiano
■ **the Premier League** la prima divisione
premises NOUN PL
i locali masc pl
□ They're moving to new premises. Si
trasferiscono in nuovi locali.
premonition NOUN
il presentimento masc
preoccupied ADJECTIVE
tutto preso (FEM tutta presa)
□ They're preoccupied with the forthcoming
wedding. Sono tutti presi dall'imminente
matrimonio.

> **LANGUAGE TIP** Be careful not to translate
> **preoccupied** by preoccupato.

prep NOUN
i compiti masc pl
□ history prep compiti di storia
preparation NOUN
la preparazione fem
□ months of preparation mesi di preparazione
■ **in preparation for** in vista di
■ **preparations** i preparativi □ preparations
for the Queen's visit i preparativi per la visita
della regina

to **prepare** VERB
preparare [68]
□ Teachers have to prepare lessons in the
evening. La sera gli insegnanti devono
preparare le lezioni.
■ **to prepare for something** fare [49] i
preparativi per qualcosa □ We're preparing
for our skiing holiday. Stiamo facendo i
preparativi per le vacanze in montagna.
prepared ADJECTIVE
■ **to be prepared to do something** essere
[47ᴱ] pronto a fare qualcosa □ I'm prepared to
help you. Sono pronto ad aiutarti.
prep school NOUN
la scuola privata fem
Presbyterian NOUN
il presbiteriano masc
la presbiteriana fem
to **prescribe** VERB
prescrivere [99]
prescription NOUN
la ricetta medica fem (PL le ricette mediche)
presence NOUN
la presenza fem
□ presence of mind presenza di spirito
present ADJECTIVE
▷ see also **present** NOUN, VERB
1 attuale (FEM attuale)
□ the present situation la situazione attuale
2 presente (FEM presente)
□ He wasn't present at the meeting. Non era
presente alla riunione.
■ **the present tense** il presente
■ **the present perfect** il passato composto
present NOUN
▷ see also **present** ADJECTIVE, VERB
1 il regalo masc
■ **to give somebody a present** fare [49] un
regalo a qualcuno □ He gave me a lovely
present. Mi ha fatto un bel regalo.
2 il presente masc
□ the past and the present il passato e il presente
■ **for the present** per il momento
■ **at present** al momento
to **present** VERB
▷ see also **present** ADJECTIVE, NOUN
■ **to present somebody with something**
consegnare [14] qualcosa a qualcuno □ The
Mayor presented the winner with a medal. Il
sindaco ha consegnato una medaglia al
vincitore.
■ **if the opportunity presents itself** se si
presenterà l'opportunità
presenter NOUN
il presentatore masc
la presentatrice fem
presently ADVERB
1 tra poco

□ You'll feel better presently. Tra poco ti sentirai meglio.
2 al momento
□ They're presently on tour. Al momento sono in tournée.

president NOUN
il presidente *masc*

press NOUN
▷ *see also* **press** VERB
■ **the press** la stampa

to **press** VERB
▷ *see also* **press** NOUN
1 premere [27]
□ Don't press so hard! Non premere così forte!
2 stirare [68]
□ She was pressing her blouse. Si stava stirando la camicetta.
■ **They pressed me to stay.** Hanno insistito perché restassi.

press conference NOUN
la conferenza stampa *fem*

pressed ADJECTIVE
■ **to be pressed for time** avere [12] poco tempo

press-up NOUN
■ **to do press-ups** fare [49] flessioni sulle braccia

pressure NOUN
▷ *see also* **pressure** VERB
la pressione *fem*
■ **to be under pressure** essere [47E] sotto pressione □ He's been under a lot of pressure recently. Ultimamente è stato molto sotto pressione.
■ **a pressure group** un gruppo di pressione

to **pressure** VERB
▷ *see also* **pressure** NOUN
fare [49] pressioni su
□ My parents are pressuring me to stay on at school. I miei fanno pressioni su di me perché continui gli studi.

to **pressurize** VERB
■ **to pressurize somebody to do something** fare [49] pressione su qualcuno perché faccia qualcosa

prestige NOUN
il prestigio *masc*

prestigious ADJECTIVE
prestigioso (FEM prestigiosa)

presumably ADVERB
presumibilmente

to **presume** VERB
presumere [11]
□ I presume so. Presumo di sì. □ I presume he'll come. Presumo che venga.

to **pretend** VERB
■ **to pretend to do something** fare [49] finta di fare qualcosa □ He pretended to be asleep. Ha fatto finta di dormire.

pretty ADVERB
▷ *see also* **pretty** ADJECTIVE
piuttosto
□ The weather was pretty awful. Il tempo era piuttosto brutto.
■ **pretty much** praticamente □ It's pretty much the same. È praticamente la stessa cosa.

pretty ADJECTIVE
▷ *see also* **pretty** ADVERB
carino (FEM carina)
□ She's very pretty. È molto carina.
■ **pretty weather** (US) bel tempo

to **prevent** VERB
impedire [51]
■ **to prevent somebody from doing something** impedire [51] a qualcuno di fare qualcosa □ The police prevented the protesters from entering the building. La polizia ha impedito ai dimostranti di entrare nell'edificio.
■ **to prevent something happening again** fare [49] in modo che qualcosa non si ripeta

previous ADJECTIVE
precedente (FEM precedente)

previously ADVERB
precedentemente

prey NOUN
la preda *fem*
□ Tourists are easy prey. I turisti sono una facile preda.
■ **a bird of prey** un uccello rapace

price NOUN
il prezzo *masc*
□ I'll ask the price. Chiederò il prezzo.
■ **to go up in price** aumentare [68E]
□ Petrol went up in price last week. La benzina è aumentata la settimana scorsa.
■ **to come down in price** calare [68E] di prezzo

price list NOUN
il listino prezzi *masc*

to **prick** VERB
pungere [80]
□ I've pricked my finger. Mi sono punto un dito.

pride NOUN
1 l' orgoglio *masc*
□ wounded pride orgoglio ferito
2 la superbia *fem*
□ His pride may be his downfall. La superbia potrebbe essere la sua rovina.

priest NOUN
il prete *masc*

primary ADJECTIVE
principale (FEM principale)
□ the primary reason for my choice la principale ragione della mia scelta

primary school NOUN
la scuola elementare *fem*

prime ADJECTIVE
principale (FEM principale)
□ my prime concern la mia preoccupazione principale

prime minister NOUN
il primo ministro *masc*

primitive ADJECTIVE
primitivo (FEM primitiva)

prince NOUN
il principe *masc*
□ the Prince of Wales il principe di Galles

princess NOUN
la principessa *fem*

principal ADJECTIVE
▷ see also **principal** NOUN
principale (FEM principale)

principal NOUN
▷ see also **principal** ADJECTIVE
il/la preside *masc/fem*

principle NOUN
il principio *masc*
■ **on principle** per principio

print NOUN
▷ see also **print** VERB
1 la foto *fem* (PL le foto)
□ colour prints foto a colori
2 l' impronta digitale *fem*
□ The policeman took his prints. Il poliziotto gli ha preso le impronte digitali.
3 la stampa *fem*
□ a framed print una stampa incorniciata
■ **in small print** a caratteri piccoli

to **print** VERB
▷ see also **print** NOUN
1 stampare [68]
□ It was printed in Hong Kong. È stato stampato ad Hong Kong.
2 scrivere [99] in stampatello
□ Please print your name and address. Per favore, scrivi il tuo nome ed indirizzo in stampatello.

printer NOUN
la stampante *fem*

priority NOUN
1 la priorità *fem* (PL le priorità)
□ the government's priority la priorità del governo
■ **my first priority** la mia priorità
2 la precedenza *fem*
■ **to take priority over something** avere [12] la precedenza su qualcosa □ My family takes priority over my work. La mia famiglia ha la precedenza sul lavoro.

prison NOUN
il carcere *masc*
■ **to send somebody to prison for five years** condannare [68] qualcuno a cinque anni di carcere
■ **a prison officer** un agente di custodia

prisoner NOUN
1 il detenuto *masc*
la detenuta *fem*
□ Prisoners have to share cells. I detenuti devono dividere le celle.
2 il prigioniero *masc*
la prigioniera *fem* (prisoner of war)

privacy NOUN
la privacy *fem*

private ADJECTIVE
privato (FEM privata)
□ a private school una scuola privata
■ **private property** la proprietà privata
■ **'private'** (on envelope) 'riservato'

private eye NOUN
l' investigatore privato *masc*

to **privatize** VERB
privatizzare [68]

privilege NOUN
il privilegio *masc*

prize NOUN
il premio *masc*
□ She won first prize. Ha vinto il primo premio.

prize-giving NOUN
la premiazione *fem*

prizewinner NOUN
il vincitore *masc*
la vincitrice *fem*

pro NOUN
■ **the pros and cons** i pro e i contro □ We weighed up the pros and cons. Abbiamo valutato i pro e i contro.

probability NOUN
la probabilità *fem* (PL le probabilità)

probable ADJECTIVE
probabile (FEM probabile)

probably ADVERB
probabilmente

problem NOUN
il problema *masc* (PL i problemi)
□ No problem! Non c'è problema!
■ **What's the problem?** Che cosa c'è?

to **proceed** VERB
1 procedere [27]
□ Work was proceeding normally. Il lavoro procedeva normalmente.
2 recarsi [18E]
□ Please proceed to gate thirty-two. Vi preghiamo di recarvi all'uscita trentadue.
■ **to proceed to do something** cominciare [13] a fare qualcosa □ He then proceeded to tell me the whole story. Quindi cominciò a raccontarmi tutta la storia.

proceeds NOUN PL
il ricavato *masc sing*
□ the proceeds from the concert il ricavato del concerto

process NOUN
il processo *masc*

□ the peace process il processo di pace
■ **We're in the process of painting the kitchen.** Stiamo ridipingendo la cucina.

procession NOUN
la processione *fem*

to **produce** VERB
produrre [85]

producer NOUN
il produttore *masc*
la produttrice *fem*

product NOUN
il prodotto *masc*

production NOUN
1 la produzione *fem*
□ They're increasing production. Stanno aumentando la produzione.
■ **the production line** la catena di lavorazione
2 la rappresentazione *fem*
□ a production of 'Hamlet' una rappresentazione di 'Amleto'

profession NOUN
la professione *fem*

professional NOUN
▷ *see also* **professional** ADJECTIVE
il/la professionista *masc/fem*

professional ADJECTIVE
▷ *see also* **professional** NOUN
professionista (FEM professionista)
□ a professional musician un musicista professionista
■ **a very professional piece of work** un lavoro da professionista

professionally ADVERB
■ **She sings professionally.** È una cantante professionista.

professor NOUN
il/la docente *masc/fem*

profit NOUN
il guadagno *masc*
□ a profit of ten thousand pounds un guadagno di diecimila sterline

profitable ADJECTIVE
redditizio (FEM redditizia, MASC PL redditizi, FEM PL redditizie)

program NOUN
▷ *see also* **program** VERB
■ **a computer program** un programma per computer

to **program** VERB
▷ *see also* **program** NOUN
programmare [68]

programme (US program) NOUN
il programma *masc* (PL i programmi)

programmer NOUN
il programmatore *masc*
la programmatrice *fem*
□ She's a programmer. Fa la programmatrice.

progress NOUN
il progresso *masc*
□ That's progress! Questo è il progresso!
■ **to make progress** fare [49] progressi
□ You're making progress! Stai facendo progressi!

to **prohibit** VERB
vietare [68]
□ Smoking is prohibited. È vietato fumare.

project NOUN
▷ *see also* **project** VERB
1 il piano *masc*
□ a development project un piano di sviluppo
2 la ricerca *fem* (PL le ricerche)
□ a project on the greenhouse effect una ricerca sull'effetto serra

to **project** VERB
▷ *see also* **project** NOUN
1 prevedere [78]
□ A population rise of five per cent is projected. È previsto un aumento della popolazione del cinque per cento.
2 proiettare [68] *(film)*

projector NOUN
il proiettore *masc*

promenade NOUN
il lungomare *masc* (PL i lungomare)

promise NOUN
▷ *see also* **promise** VERB
la promessa *fem*
□ He made me a promise. Mi ha fatto una promessa.
■ **It's a promise!** Promesso!

to **promise** VERB
▷ *see also* **promise** NOUN
promettere [59]
□ She promised to write. Ha promesso di scrivere.

promising ADJECTIVE
promettente (FEM promettente)
□ a promising player un giocatore promettente

to **promote** VERB
■ **to be promoted** avere [12] una promozione
□ She was promoted after six months. Ha avuto una promozione dopo sei mesi.

promotion NOUN
la promozione *fem*

prompt ADJECTIVE, ADVERB
▷ *see also* **prompt** VERB
1 sollecito (FEM sollecita)
□ a prompt reply una risposta sollecita
2 puntuale (FEM puntuale)
□ He's always very prompt. È sempre puntualissimo.
3 in punto
□ at eight o'clock prompt alle otto in punto

to **prompt** VERB
▷ *see also* **prompt** ADJECTIVE, ADVERB
■ **to prompt somebody to do something** spingere [106] qualcuno a fare qualcosa

promptly ADVERB
puntualmente
□ We left promptly at seven. Siamo partiti puntualmente alle sette.

pronoun NOUN
il pronome *masc*

to **pronounce** VERB
pronunciare [13]
□ How do you pronounce that word? Come si pronuncia quella parola?

pronunciation NOUN
la pronuncia *fem*

proof NOUN
la prova *fem*

proper ADJECTIVE
1 vero (FEM vera)
□ We didn't have a proper lunch. Non abbiamo mangiato un vero pranzo.
2 adatto (FEM adatta)
□ You have to have the proper equipment. Bisogna avere l'attrezzatura adatta.
3 corretto (FEM corretta)
□ This is the proper way to do it. Questo è il modo corretto per farlo.
■ **at the proper time** all'ora giusta □ If you had come at the proper time... Se fossi venuto all'ora giusta...

properly ADVERB
1 come si deve
□ You're not doing it properly. Non lo stai facendo come si deve.
2 in modo adeguato
□ Dress properly for your interview. Vestiti in modo adeguato per il colloquio.

property NOUN
1 la proprietà *fem* (PL le proprietà)
■ **'private property'** 'proprietà privata'
2 la casa *fem*
□ a new property una nuova casa
■ **The value of property in the area is rising.** Il valore degli immobili della zona sta salendo.

proportional ADJECTIVE
proporzionale (FEM proporzionale)
■ **proportional representation** rappresentanza proporzionale

proposal NOUN
la proposta *fem*

to **propose** VERB
proporre [73]
□ What do you propose to do? Cosa proponi di fare?
■ **to propose to somebody** fare [49] una proposta di matrimonio a qualcuno

to **prosecute** VERB
perseguire [41] a norma di legge
□ 'Shoplifters will be prosecuted' 'I taccheggiatori saranno perseguiti a norma di legge'

prospect NOUN
la prospettiva *fem*
□ His future prospects are good. Ha delle buone prospettive.

prospectus NOUN
il prospetto *masc*

prostitute NOUN
la prostituta *fem*
■ **a male prostitute** un prostituto

to **protect** VERB
proteggere [79]

protection NOUN
la protezione *fem*

protein NOUN
la proteina *fem*

protest NOUN
▷ *see also* **protest** VERB
la protesta *fem*
□ He ignored their protests. Ha ignorato le loro proteste. □ a protest march una manifestazione di protesta

to **protest** VERB
▷ *see also* **protest** NOUN
protestare [68]

Protestant NOUN
▷ *see also* **Protestant** ADJECTIVE
il/la protestante *masc/fem*

Protestant ADJECTIVE
▷ *see also* **Protestant** NOUN
protestante (FEM protestante)

protester NOUN
il/la dimostrante *masc/fem*

proud ADJECTIVE
fiero (FEM fiera)
□ Her parents are proud of her. I suoi sono fieri di lei.

to **prove** VERB
dimostrare [68]
□ The police couldn't prove it. La polizia non è riuscita a dimostrarlo.

proverb NOUN
il proverbio *masc*

to **provide** VERB
fornire [51]
■ **to provide somebody with something** fornire [51] qualcosa a qualcuno □ They provided us with maps. Ci hanno fornito delle cartine.

to **provide for** VERB
mantenere [113]
□ He can't provide for his family any more. Non è più in grado di mantenere la famiglia.

provided CONJUNCTION
sempre che
□ He'll play, provided he's fit. Giocherà, sempre che sia in forma.

prowler NOUN
■ **There was a prowler in the garden.** C'era un tipo sospetto che si aggirava in giardino.

P

509

prune NOUN
la prugna secca fem (PL le prugne secche)

to **pry** VERB
impicciarsi[13ᴱ]
□ He's always prying into other people's business. S'impiccia sempre degli affari altrui.

pseudonym NOUN
lo pseudonimo masc

psychiatrist NOUN
lo/la psichiatra masc/fem

psychological ADJECTIVE
psicologico (fem psicologica, masc PL psicologici, fem PL psicologiche)

psychologist NOUN
lo psicologo masc (PL gli psicologi)
la psicologa fem (PL le psicologhe)

psychology NOUN
la psicologia fem

PTO ABBREVIATION (= please turn over)
vedi retro

pub NOUN
il pub masc (PL i pub)

public NOUN
▷ see also **public** ADJECTIVE
■ **the public** il pubblico □ open to the public aperto al pubblico
■ **in public** in pubblico

public ADJECTIVE
▷ see also **public** NOUN
pubblico (fem pubblica, masc PL pubblici, fem PL pubbliche)
□ a public place un luogo pubblico
■ **to be in the public eye** essere[47ᴱ] un personaggio in vista

publican NOUN
il gestore di un pub masc

public holiday NOUN
la festa nazionale fem

publicity NOUN
la pubblicità fem

public opinion NOUN
l' opinione pubblica fem

public school NOUN
la scuola superiore privata fem

public transport NOUN
i mezzi pubblici masc pl

to **publish** VERB
pubblicare[18]

publisher NOUN
la casa editrice fem (company)

pudding NOUN
il dessert masc (PL i dessert)
□ What's for pudding? Cosa c'è per dessert?
■ **a rice pudding** un budino di riso
■ **black pudding** il sanguinaccio

puddle NOUN
la pozzanghera fem

puff pastry NOUN
la pasta sfoglia fem

to **pull** VERB
tirare[68]
□ She pulled my hair. Mi ha tirato i capelli.
□ Pull! Tira!
■ **to pull the trigger** premere[27] il grilletto
■ **to pull a muscle** stirarsi[56] un muscolo
■ **You're pulling my leg!** Mi stai prendendo in giro!
■ **Pull yourself together!** Datti una mossa!

to **pull down** VERB
demolire[51]
□ The old school was pulled down last year. L'anno scorso hanno demolito la vecchia scuola.

to **pull in** VERB
fermarsi[56ᴱ]
□ She pulled in at the side of the road. Si fermò a lato della strada.

to **pull out** VERB
1 spostarsi[56ᴱ] sulla destra (in Great Britain)
□ The car pulled out to overtake. L'auto si è spostata sulla destra per sorpassare.
2 ritirarsi[56ᴱ]
□ She pulled out of the tournament. Si è ritirata dal torneo.

to **pull through** VERB
cavarsela[56ᴱ]
□ They think he'll pull through. Pensano che se la caverà.

to **pull up** VERB
fermarsi[56ᴱ]
□ A black car pulled up beside me. Una macchina nera si è fermata accanto a me.

pullover NOUN
il pullover masc (PL i pullover)

pulse NOUN
il polso masc
□ The nurse took his pulse. L'infermiera gli ha tastato il polso.

pulses NOUN PL
i legumi secchi masc pl

pump NOUN
▷ see also **pump** VERB
1 la pompa fem
□ a bicycle pump una pompa di bicicletta
■ **a petrol pump** un distributore di benzina
2 la scarpa da ginnastica fem
□ She was wearing black pumps. Indossava scarpe da ginnastica nere.

to **pump** VERB
▷ see also **pump** NOUN
pompare[68] (water, blood)
■ **to pump up** gonfiare[17]

pumpkin NOUN
la zucca fem (PL le zucche)

punch NOUN
▷ see also **punch** VERB
il pugno masc

to punch VERB
▷ see also **punch** NOUN
1 dare [30] un pugno a
□ He punched me! Mi ha dato un pugno!
2 forare [68]
□ He forgot to punch my ticket. Si è dimenticato di forarmi il biglietto.

punctual ADJECTIVE
puntuale (FEM puntuale)

punctuation NOUN
la punteggiatura fem

puncture NOUN
■ **to have a puncture** forare [68] □ I had a puncture on the motorway. Ho forato sull'autostrada.

LANGUAGE TIP Be careful not to translate **puncture** by **puntura**.

to punish VERB
punire [51]

punishment NOUN
la punizione fem

punk NOUN, ADJECTIVE
il/la punk masc/fem (PL i/le punk)

pupil NOUN
l' allievo masc
l' allieva fem

puppet NOUN
il burattino masc

puppy NOUN
il cucciolo masc

to purchase VERB
acquistare [68]

pure ADJECTIVE
puro (FEM pura)
□ pure orange juice puro succo d'arancia
□ He's doing pure maths. Fa matematica pura.

purple ADJECTIVE
viola (FEM+PL viola)

purpose NOUN
lo scopo masc
□ What is the purpose of these changes? Qual è lo scopo di questi cambiamenti? □ his purpose in life lo scopo della sua vita
■ **on purpose** apposta □ He did it on purpose. L'ha fatto apposta.

to purr VERB
fare [49] le fusa

purse NOUN
1 il portamonete masc (PL i portamonete)
□ I've got ten pounds in my purse. Ho dieci sterline nel portamonete.
2 la borsa fem (US: handbag)

to pursue VERB
1 proseguire [41] (career)
2 inseguire [41] (person, vehicle)

pursuit NOUN
1 la ricerca fem
□ the pursuit of success la ricerca del successo

2 l' attività fem (PL le attività)
□ outdoor pursuits attività all'aperto

push NOUN
▷ see also **push** VERB
la spinta fem
■ **to give somebody a push** dare [30] una spinta a qualcuno □ He gave me a push. Mi ha dato una spinta.

to push VERB
▷ see also **push** NOUN
spingere [106]
■ **to push somebody to do something** spingere [106] qualcuno a fare qualcosa □ My parents are pushing me to go to university. I miei mi spingono ad andare all'università.
■ **to push drugs** spacciare [13] droga
■ **Push off!** Sparisci!
■ **Don't push your luck!** Non tirare troppo la corda!
■ **to push one's way through** farsi [49^E] largo □ I pushed my way through to the front. Mi sono fatto largo fino ad arrivare davanti.

to push around VERB
dare [30] ordini a
□ He likes pushing people around. Gli piace dare ordini a tutti.

to push on VERB
andare [6^E] avanti
□ I've got a lot to do, so I must push on. Ho molto da fare, quindi devo andare avanti.

pushchair NOUN
il passeggino masc

pushed ADJECTIVE
■ **to be pushed for** essere [47^E] a corto di □ I'm a bit pushed for money. Sono un po' a corto di denaro.
■ **I'm pushed for time today.** Oggi non ho un minuto di tempo.

pusher NOUN
lo spacciatore masc
la spacciatrice fem

push-up NOUN
la flessione sulle braccia fem
■ **to do push-ups** fare [49] flessioni sulle braccia

to put VERB
mettere [59]
□ Where shall I put my things? Dove metto le mie cose? □ She's putting the baby to bed. Sta mettendo a letto il bambino.

to put across VERB
riuscire [117^E] a comunicare
□ He finds it hard to put his ideas across. Trova difficile riuscire a comunicare le proprie idee.

to put aside VERB
tenere [113] da parte
□ Can you put this aside for me till tomorrow? Me lo può tenere da parte fino a domani?

to **put away** VERB
1 riporre [73]
  □ Can you put away the dishes, please?
  Ti dispiace riporre i piatti?
2 mettere [59] dentro *(in prison)*
  □ I hope they put him away for a long time.
  Spero che lo mettano dentro per un bel pezzo.

to **put back** VERB
1 rimettere [59] a posto
  □ Put it back when you've finished with it.
  Rimettilo a posto quando hai finito.
2 rinviare [17]
  □ The meeting's been put back. La riunione è
  stata rinviata.
3 mettere [59] indietro
  □ Remember to put your watch back. Ricorda
  di mettere indietro l'orologio.

to **put down** VERB
1 posare [68]
  □ I'll put these bags down for a minute. Poso
  un attimo queste borse.
2 buttare [68] giù
  □ I've put down a few ideas. Ho buttato giù
  alcune idee.
3 far [49] abbattere
  □ We had our dog put down. Abbiamo fatto
  abbattere il cane.

to **put in** VERB
presentare [68]
  □ He's put in a request for an assistant. Ha
  presentato richiesta per avere un assistente.
  ■ **to put in a lot of work** lavorare [68] sodo

to **put off** VERB
1 spegnere [105]
  □ Shall I put the light off? Spengo la luce?
2 rimandare [68]
  □ I keep putting it off. Continuo a rimandarlo.
3 distrarre [115]
  □ Stop putting me off! Smettila di distrarmi!
4 scoraggiare [58]
  □ He's not easily put off. Non si lascia
  scoraggiare facilmente.

to **put on** VERB
1 mettersi [59E]
  □ I'll put my coat on. Mi metto il cappotto.
2 accendere [2]
  □ Shall I put the heating on? Accendo il
  riscaldamento?
3 mettere [59] in scena
  □ We're putting on 'Bugsy Malone'. Stiamo
  mettendo in scena 'Bugsy Malone'.
  ■ **She's not ill: she's just putting it on.** Non
  è malata, sta solo facendo finta.
4 mettere [59] a cuocere
  □ I'll put the potatoes on. Metto a cuocere le
  patate.
5 ingrassare [68E] di

□ I put on four pounds. Sono ingrassata di due
chili.
  ■ **to put on weight** ingrassare [68E] □ He's
  put on a lot of weight. È ingrassato parecchio.

to **put out** VERB
1 spegnere [105]
  □ It took them five hours to put out the fire. Ci
  sono volute cinque ore per spegnere l'incendio.
2 tendere [112]
  □ He smiled and put out his hand. Ha sorriso
  tendendo la mano.
  ■ **to be put out** essere [47E] seccato □ He's a
  bit put out that nobody came. È un po'
  seccato che non sia venuto nessuno.

to **put through** VERB
passare [68]
  □ Can you put me through to the manager?
  Mi passa il direttore, per favore?
  ■ **I'm putting you through.** Le dò la
  comunicazione.

to **put up** VERB
1 appendere [8]
  □ The poster's great. I'll put it up on my wall.
  Il poster è fantastico, lo appendo alla parete.
2 montare [68]
  □ We put up our tent in a field. Abbiamo
  montato la tenda in un prato.
3 aumentare [68]
  □ They've put up the price. Hanno aumentato
  il prezzo.
4 ospitare [68]
  □ A friend will put me up for the night. Un
  amico mi ospita per la notte.
5 alzare [68]
  □ If you have any questions, put up your hand.
  Se avete domande alzate la mano.
  ■ **to put up with something** sopportare [68]
  qualcosa □ I'm not going to put up with it.
  Non ho intenzione di sopportarlo.
  ■ **to put up for sale** mettere [59] in vendita
  □ They're going to put their house up for sale.
  Metteranno in vendita la casa.

puzzle NOUN
il puzzle *masc* (PL i puzzle)

puzzled ADJECTIVE
perplesso (FEM perplessa)
  □ You look puzzled! Hai un'aria perplessa!

puzzling ADJECTIVE
sconcertante (FEM sconcertante)

pyjamas NOUN PL
il pigiama *masc sing*
  □ They were already in their pyjamas. Erano già
  in pigiama.
  ■ **a pair of pyjamas** un pigiama

pyramid NOUN
la piramide *fem*

Pyrenees NOUN PL
i Pirenei *masc pl*

Qq

quaint ADJECTIVE
pittoresco (FEM pittoresca, MASC PL pittoreschi, FEM PL pittoresche) *(house)*

qualification NOUN
1 la qualifica *fem* (PL le qualifiche)
□ what qualifications do they require? Che qualifiche richiedono?
■ **vocational qualifications** qualifiche professionali
2 il titolo di studio *masc*
□ He left school without any qualifications. Ha lasciato la scuola senza alcun titolo di studio.

qualified ADJECTIVE
1 abilitato (FEM abilitata)
□ a qualified teacher un insegnante abilitato
2 diplomato (FEM diplomata)
□ a qualified nurse un'infermiera diplomata
■ **to be well qualified** *(for job)* avere [12] tutti i requisiti necessari

to qualify VERB
1 ottenere [113] l'abilitazione
□ She has qualified as a teacher. Ha ottenuto l'abilitazione all'insegnamento.
2 qualificarsi [18E]
□ We didn't qualify for the finals. Non ci siamo qualificati per le finali.

quality NOUN
la qualità *fem*
□ good-quality paper carta di buona qualità

quantity NOUN
la quantità *fem* (PL le quantità)

quarantine NOUN
la quarantena *fem*
□ in quarantine in quarantena

quarrel NOUN
▷ see also **quarrel** VERB
la lite *fem*
□ after their last quarrel dopo la loro ultima lite
■ **to have a quarrel** litigare [76] □ We had a quarrel. Abbiamo litigato.

to quarrel VERB
▷ see also **quarrel** NOUN
litigare [76]

quarry NOUN
la cava *fem*

quart NOUN
■ **a quart** due pinte

quarter NOUN
1 il quarto *masc*
□ three quarters tre quarti □ a quarter of an hour un quarto d'ora □ a quarter past ten le dieci e un quarto
■ **a quarter to eleven** le dieci e tre quarti
■ **a quarter of ten** (US) le nove e tre quarti
2 la moneta da venticinque centesimi *fem* (US: *coin*)

quarter-finals NOUN PL
i quarti di finale *masc pl*

quartet NOUN
il quartetto *masc*
□ a string quartet un quartetto di archi

quay NOUN
la banchina *fem*

queasy ADJECTIVE
■ **to feel queasy** avere [12] la nausea

queen NOUN
la regina *fem*
□ Queen Elizabeth la regina Elisabetta □ the queen of hearts la regina di cuori

query NOUN
▷ see also **query** VERB
la domanda *fem*

to query VERB
▷ see also **query** NOUN
mettere [59] in dubbio
□ No one queried my decision. Nessuno ha messo in dubbio la mia decisione.
■ **They queried the bill.** Hanno chiesto spiegazioni sul conto.

to question VERB
▷ see also **question** NOUN
interrogare [76]
□ He was questioned by the police. È stato interrogato dalla polizia.

question NOUN
▷ see also **question** VERB
1 la domanda *fem*
□ Can I ask a question? Posso fare una domanda?
2 la questione *fem*
□ That's a difficult question. È una questione difficile.
■ **It's out of the question.** È fuori discussione.

question mark NOUN
il punto di domanda *masc*

questionnaire – quote

questionnaire NOUN
il questionario *masc*

queue NOUN
▷ *see also* **queue** VERB
la fila *fem*
□ We were standing in a queue outside the cinema. Eravamo in fila fuori dal cinema.

to **queue** VERB
▷ *see also* **queue** NOUN
fare[49] la fila
□ We had to queue for tickets. Abbiamo dovuto fare la fila per i biglietti.

quick ADJECTIVE, ADVERB
veloce (FEM veloce)
□ a quick lunch un pranzo veloce □ It's quicker by train. È più veloce in treno.
■ **Be quick!** Fa' presto!
■ **She's a quick learner.** Impara presto.

quickly ADVERB
velocemente

quiet ADJECTIVE
1 silenzioso (FEM silenziosa)
□ You're very quiet today. Sei molto silenzioso oggi. □ The engine's very quiet. Il motore è molto silenzioso.
2 tranquillo (FEM tranquilla)
□ a quiet little town una cittadina tranquilla □ a quiet weekend un tranquillo fine settimana
■ **Be quiet!** Fate silenzio!
■ **Quiet!** Silenzio!

quietly ADVERB
1 piano
□ 'She's dead,' he said quietly. 'È morta,' disse piano.
2 senza far rumore
□ He quietly opened the door. Ha aperto la porta senza far rumore.

quilt NOUN
il piumino *masc*

to **quit** VERB
1 lasciare[13]
□ I quit my job last week. Ho lasciato il lavoro la settimana scorsa.
■ **I've been given notice to quit.** Mi hanno dato lo sfratto.
2 smettere[59]
□ I've quit smoking. Ho smesso di fumare.

quite ADVERB
1 piuttosto
□ It's quite warm today. Fa piuttosto caldo oggi. □ It's quite a long way. È piuttosto lontano.
■ **quite a lot** un bel po' □ It costs quite a lot. Costa un bel po'. □ quite a lot of money un bel po' di denaro
■ **I've been there quite a lot.** Ci sono stato un bel po' di volte.
■ **There were quite a few people there.** C'era un bel po' di gente.
2 abbastanza
□ I quite liked the film, but... Il film mi è piaciuto abbastanza, ma...
■ **How was the film? — Quite good.** Com'era il film? — Non era male.
3 del tutto
□ I'm not quite sure. Non sono del tutto sicuro.
4 proprio
□ It was quite a shock. È stato proprio uno shock. □ It's not quite the same. Non è proprio lo stesso.

quiz NOUN
il quiz *masc* (PL i quiz)

quota NOUN
la quota *fem*

quotation NOUN
1 la citazione *fem*
□ a quotation from Shakespeare una citazione da Shakespeare
2 il preventivo *masc*
□ I asked the firm to give me a quotation. Ho chiesto alla ditta di farmi un preventivo.

quotation marks NOUN PL
le virgolette *fem pl*

quote NOUN
▷ *see also* **quote** VERB
1 la citazione *fem*
□ a Shakespeare quote una citazione da Shakespeare
2 il preventivo *masc*
□ Can you give me a quote? Può farmi un preventivo?
■ **quotes** virgolette *fem pl* □ in quotes tra virgolette

to **quote** VERB
▷ *see also* **quote** NOUN
citare[68]

Rr

rabbi NOUN
il rabbino *masc*

rabbit NOUN
il coniglio *masc*
■ **a rabbit hutch** una conigliera

rabies NOUN SING
la rabbia *fem*
□ a dog with rabies un cane con la rabbia

race NOUN
▷ *see also* **race** VERB
1 la gara *fem*
□ a cycle race una gara ciclistica
2 la corsa *fem*
□ a race against time una corsa contro il tempo
3 la razza *fem*
□ students of all races studenti di tutte le razze
■ **race relations** rapporti interrazziali
■ **the human race** il genere umano

to **race** VERB
▷ *see also* **race** NOUN
correre [26]
□ We raced to catch the bus. Abbiamo corso per prendere l'autobus.
■ **I'll race you!** Facciamo a gara!

racecourse NOUN
l' ippodromo *masc*

racehorse NOUN
il cavallo da corsa *masc*

racer NOUN
1 la bicicletta da corsa *fem*
□ a red racer una bicicletta da corsa rossa
2 il corridore *masc (person)*

racetrack NOUN
la pista *fem*

racial ADJECTIVE
razziale (FEM razziale)
□ racial discrimination discriminazione razziale

racing car NOUN
la macchina da corsa *fem*

racing driver NOUN
il corridore automobilistico *masc* (PL i corridori automobilistici)

racism NOUN
il razzismo *masc*

racist ADJECTIVE, NOUN
razzista (FEM razzista)

rack NOUN
1 il portabagagli *masc* (PL i portabagagli) *(in train)*
2 il portapacchi *masc* (PL i portapacchi) *(on car)*
3 l' appendiabiti *masc* (PL gli appendiabiti) *(for clothes)*
4 la rastrelliera *fem (for bikes)*

racket NOUN
1 il baccano *masc (noise)*
2 la racchetta *fem (tennis racket)*

racquet NOUN
la racchetta *fem*

radar NOUN
il radar *masc* (PL i radar)

radiation NOUN
la radiazione *fem*

radiator NOUN
il radiatore *masc*

radio NOUN
la radio *fem* (PL le radio)
■ **on the radio** alla radio
■ **a radio station** una stazione radio

radioactive ADJECTIVE
radioattivo (FEM radioattiva)

radio-controlled ADJECTIVE
radiocomandato (FEM radiocomandata)

radish NOUN
il ravanello *masc*

raffle NOUN
la lotteria di beneficenza *fem*

raft NOUN
la zattera *fem*

rag NOUN
lo straccio *masc*
□ dressed in rags vestito di stracci

rage NOUN
la rabbia *fem*
□ He was trembling with rage. Tremava dalla rabbia.
■ **mad with rage** arrabbiatissimo
■ **to be in a rage** essere [47ᴱ] furioso
■ **It's all the rage.** Fa furore.

raid NOUN
▷ *see also* **raid** VERB
1 la rapina *fem*
□ a bank raid una rapina in banca
2 il raid *masc* (PL i raid)
□ a police raid un raid della polizia

to **raid** VERB
▷ see also **raid** NOUN
1 rapinare [68] (bank)
2 fare [49] un raid in
   □ The police raided a club in Soho. La polizia ha fatto un raid in una discoteca di Soho.

rail NOUN
1 il corrimano masc
   □ He climbed the stairs, holding the rail. Salì le scale tenendosi al corrimano.
2 il parapetto masc
   □ He leaned over the rail. Si è sporto dal parapetto.
3 la rotaia fem (for train)
   □ between the rails tra le rotaie
   ■ by rail in treno
   ■ a rail strike uno sciopero dei treni
4 l' appendiabiti masc (PL gli appendiabiti) (for clothes)

railcard NOUN
la tessera di riduzione ferroviaria fem

railroad NOUN (US)
la ferrovia fem

railway NOUN
la ferrovia fem
   ■ a railway line una linea ferroviaria
   ■ the railway station la stazione ferroviaria

rain NOUN
▷ see also **rain** VERB
la pioggia fem (PL le piogge)
   □ in the rain sotto la pioggia

to **rain** VERB
▷ see also **rain** NOUN
piovere [72]

rainbow NOUN
l' arcobaleno masc

raincoat NOUN
l' impermeabile masc

rainfall NOUN
la piovosità fem

rainforest NOUN
la foresta pluviale fem

rainy ADJECTIVE
piovoso (FEM piovosa)

to **raise** VERB
1 sollevare [68]
   □ He raised his hand. Ha sollevato la mano.
2 migliorare [68]
   □ They want to raise standards in schools. Vogliono migliorare il livello qualitativo delle scuole.
3 far [49] sorgere (doubts, suspicions)
   ■ to raise money raccogliere [21] fondi

raisins NOUN PL
l' uvetta fem sing

rake NOUN
il rastrello masc

rally NOUN
1 il raduno masc

□ a pre-election rally un raduno pre-elettorale
2 il rally masc (PL i rally)
   □ a rally driver un pilota di rally
3 lo scambio masc (in tennis)

ram NOUN
▷ see also **ram** VERB
il montone masc

to **ram** VERB
▷ see also **ram** NOUN
cozzare [68] contro

Ramadan NOUN
il Ramadan masc

rambler NOUN
l' escursionista masc/fem

ramp NOUN
la rampa d'accesso fem

ran VERB ▷ see **run**

ranch NOUN
il ranch masc (PL i ranch)

random ADJECTIVE
   ■ a random selection una selezione effettuata a caso
   ■ at random a caso

rang VERB ▷ see **ring**

range NOUN
▷ see also **range** VERB
la gamma fem
   □ There's a wide range of colours. C'è una vasta gamma di colori.
   ■ a range of subjects diverse materie
   ■ It's out of my price range. Non è alla mia portata.
   ■ a range of mountains una catena di montagne

to **range** VERB
▷ see also **range** NOUN
   ■ to range from... to andare [6ᴱ] da... a
   □ Tickets range from £4 to £20. I prezzi vanno dalle quattro alle venti sterline.

rank NOUN
▷ see also **rank** VERB
il grado masc
   □ the rank of captain il grado di capitano
   ■ a taxi rank un posteggio di taxi

to **rank** VERB
▷ see also **rank** NOUN
classificare [18]

ransom NOUN
il riscatto masc

rap NOUN
il rap masc (music)
   ■ There was a rap on the door. Hanno bussato alla porta.

rape NOUN
▷ see also **rape** VERB
lo stupro masc

to **rape** VERB
▷ see also **rape** NOUN
stuprare [68]

rapids NOUN PL
le rapide *fem pl*

rapist NOUN
lo stupratore *masc*

rare ADJECTIVE
1 raro (FEM rara)
  □ a rare disease una malattia rara
2 al sangue *(meat)*

rash NOUN
  ▷ *see also* **rash** ADJECTIVE
  l' eritema *masc* (PL gli eritemi)
  □ I've got a rash on my chest. Ho un eritema sul petto.

rash ADJECTIVE
  ▷ *see also* **rash** NOUN
  avventato (FEM avventata)

rasher NOUN
  ■ a rasher of bacon una fettina di pancetta

raspberry NOUN
  il lampone *masc*

rat NOUN
  il ratto *masc*
  □ a huge rat un ratto enorme
  ■ rat race la corsa al successo

rate NOUN
  ▷ *see also* **rate** VERB
1 la tariffa *fem*
  □ reduced rates for students tariffe ridotte per gli studenti
2 il tasso *masc*
  □ a high rate of interest un alto tasso d'interesse
3 la velocità *fem* (PL le velocità)
  □ at a slow rate a bassa velocità

to rate VERB
  ▷ *see also* **rate** NOUN
  considerare [68]
  □ He was rated the best. Era considerato il migliore.

rather ADVERB
  piuttosto
  □ I was rather disappointed. Ero piuttosto deluso.
  ■ rather a lot molto □ I've got rather a lot of homework to do. Ho molti compiti da fare.
  ■ I'd rather preferirei □ I'd rather stay in tonight. Preferirei stare a casa, stasera.

rattle NOUN
  il sonaglio *masc (baby's)*

rattlesnake NOUN
  il serpente a sonagli *masc*

to rave VERB
  ▷ *see also* **rave** VERB
  farneticare [18]
  □ She cried and raved for weeks. Ha urlato e farneticato per settimane.
  ■ to rave about essere [47ᴱ] assolutamente entusiasta di □ They raved about the film. Erano assolutamente entusiasti del film.

rave NOUN
  ▷ *see also* **rave** VERB
  il rave *masc* (PL i rave)

raven NOUN
  il corvo *masc*

ravenous ADJECTIVE
  ■ to be ravenous avere [12] una fame da lupi

raving ADJECTIVE
  ■ raving mad matto da legare

raw ADJECTIVE
  crudo (FEM cruda)
  □ raw carrots carote crude
  ■ to get a raw deal essere [47ᴱ] bidonato
  ■ raw materials materie prime

razor NOUN
  il rasoio *masc*
  □ disposable razors rasoi usa e getta
  ■ a razor blade una lametta da barba

RE NOUN *(= religious education)*
  la religione *fem*

reach NOUN
  ▷ *see also* **reach** VERB
  ■ out of reach fuori portata
  ■ Keep medicine out of reach of children. Non lasciare medicinali alla portata dei bambini.
  ■ within easy reach of in prossimità di □ The hotel is within easy reach of the town centre. L'albergo è in prossimità del centro.

to reach VERB
  ▷ *see also* **reach** NOUN
1 arrivare [68ᴱ] a
  □ We reached the hotel at seven o'clock. Siamo arrivati all'albergo alle sette.
  □ Eventually they reached a decision. Alla fine hanno preso una decisione.
2 contattare [68]
  □ We need to be able to reach him in an emergency. Dobbiamo essere in grado di contattarlo in caso di emergenza.
  ■ He reached for his gun. Ha fatto per prendere la pistola.

to react VERB
  reagire [51]

reaction NOUN
  la reazione *fem*

reactor NOUN
  il reattore *masc*

to read VERB
  leggere [57]
  □ I read a lot. Leggo molto.

to read out VERB
  leggere [57] a voce alta

reader NOUN
  il lettore *masc*
  la lettrice *fem*

readily ADVERB
  prontamente

reading - recipe

reading NOUN
la lettura *fem*
□ reading and writing lettura e scrittura
■ **I like reading.** Mi piace leggere.

ready ADJECTIVE
pronto (FEM pronta)
□ She was always ready to help. Era sempre pronta ad aiutare.
■ **to get ready** prepararsi [56^E]
■ **to get something ready** preparare [68] qualcosa

real ADJECTIVE
vero (FEM vera)
□ He wasn't a real policeman. Non era un vero poliziotto.
■ **in real life** in realtà
■ **in real time** in tempo reale

real estate NOUN (US)
i beni immobili *masc pl*

realistic ADJECTIVE
realistico (FEM realistica, MASC PL realistici, FEM PL realistiche)

reality NOUN
la realtà *fem* (PL le realtà)

reality star NOUN
la star del reality *fem*

reality TV NOUN
la reality TV *fem*

reality TV show NOUN
il reality *masc*

to realize VERB
rendersi [83^E] conto
□ I realized he was lying. Mi sono reso conto che mentiva.
■ **to realize something** rendersi [83^E] conto di qualcosa □Once they realized their mistake... Dopo che si erano resi conto del loro errore...

really ADVERB
1 davvero
□ I'm learning German. — Really? Sto studiando tedesco. — Davvero?
2 proprio
□ She's really nice. È proprio simpatica.
□ I really don't like Tom. Tom non mi piace proprio.
■ **Did he hurt you? — Not really.** Ti ha fatto male? — Non è niente di grave.

Realtor® NOUN (US)
l' agente immobiliare *masc/fem*

rear ADJECTIVE
▷ *see also* **rear** NOUN
posteriore (FEM posteriore)
□ the rear wheel la ruota posteriore

rear NOUN
▷ *see also* **rear** ADJECTIVE
il retro *masc*
□ the rear of the building il retro dell'edificio
■ **at the rear of the train** in coda al treno

reason NOUN
la ragione *fem*
□ for security reasons per ragioni di sicurezza

reasonable ADJECTIVE
1 ragionevole (FEM ragionevole)
□ Be reasonable! Sii ragionevole!
2 discreto (FEM discreta)
□ He wrote a reasonable essay. Ha fatto un tema discreto.

reasonably ADVERB
■ **reasonably well** discretamente □ The team played reasonably well. La squadra ha giocato discretamente.
■ **reasonably priced accommodation** alloggi a prezzi ragionevoli

to reassure VERB
rassicurare [68]

reassuring ADJECTIVE
rassicurante (FEM rassicurante)

rebel NOUN
▷ *see also* **rebel** VERB
il/la ribelle *masc/fem*

to rebel VERB
▷ *see also* **rebel** NOUN
ribellarsi [56^E]

rebellious ADJECTIVE
ribelle (FEM ribelle)

receipt NOUN
la ricevuta *fem*

to receive VERB
ricevere [27]

receiver NOUN
la cornetta *fem*
□ She picked up the receiver. Ha sollevato la cornetta.

recent ADJECTIVE
recente (FEM recente)
□ recent events avvenimenti recenti
■ **in recent weeks** nelle ultime settimane

recently ADVERB
di recente
□ I haven't seen him recently. Non l'ho visto di recente.

reception NOUN
1 la reception *fem* (PL le reception)
□ Please leave your key at reception. Si prega di lasciare le chiavi alla reception.
2 il ricevimento *masc*
□ The reception will be at a big hotel. Il ricevimento si terrà in un grande albergo.
3 l' accoglienza *fem*
□ He got a cool reception. Ha ricevuto un'accoglienza fredda.

receptionist NOUN
il/la receptionist *masc/fem* (PL i/le receptionist)

recession NOUN
la recessione *fem*

recipe NOUN
la ricetta *fem*

to **reckon** VERB
pensare [68]
□ What do you reckon? Cosa ne pensi?

reclining ADJECTIVE
■ **reclining seat** sedile reclinabile *masc*

recognizable ADJECTIVE
riconoscibile (FEM riconoscibile)

to **recognize** VERB
riconoscere [24]

to **recommend** VERB
consigliare [25]
□ What do you recommend? Che cosa ci consiglia?

to **reconsider** VERB
riconsiderare [68]

record NOUN
▷ *see also* **record** VERB
1 il record *masc* (PL i record)
□ the world record il record mondiale □ in record time a tempo di record
■ **a record holder** un primatista
2 il disco *masc* (PL i dischi)
□ one of my favourite records uno di miei dischi preferiti
3 la traccia *fem* (PL le tracce)
□ There is no record of your booking. Non c'è traccia della vostra prenotazione.
■ **to keep a record of something** tenere [113] nota di qualcosa
■ **to have a criminal record** avere [12] precedenti penali
■ **records** archivio □ I'll check in the records. Controllo in archivio.

to **record** VERB
▷ *see also* **record** NOUN
registrare [68]

recorded delivery NOUN
■ **to send something recorded delivery** spedire [51] qualcosa per raccomandata

recorder NOUN
il flauto dolce *masc*
■ **to play the recorder** suonare [68] il flauto dolce

recording NOUN
la registrazione *fem*

to **recover** VERB
riprendersi [77ᴱ]
□ It took her half an hour to recover. Le ci è voluta mezz'ora per riprendersi.

> **LANGUAGE TIP** Be careful not to translate **recover** by **ricoverare**.

recovery NOUN
la ripresa *fem*

rectangle NOUN
il rettangolo *masc*

rectangular ADJECTIVE
rettangolare (FEM rettangolare)

to **recycle** VERB
riciclare [68]

recycling NOUN
il riciclaggio *masc*

red ADJECTIVE
rosso (FEM rossa)
□ a red light un semaforo rosso
■ **to go through a red light** passare [68ᴱ] col rosso

Red Cross NOUN
la Croce Rossa *fem*

redcurrant NOUN
il ribes rosso *masc*
□ redcurrant jelly marmellata di ribes rosso
■ **redcurrants** ribes rosso *masc sing*

to **redecorate** VERB
1 tinteggiare [58] di nuovo (*repaint*)
2 tappezzare [68] di nuovo (*repaper*)

red-haired ADJECTIVE
dai capelli rossi

red-handed ADJECTIVE
■ **to catch somebody red-handed** prendere [77] qualcuno con le mani nel sacco

redhead NOUN
il rosso *masc*

to **redo** VERB
rifare [49]

red tape NOUN
la burocrazia *fem*

to **reduce** VERB
ridurre [85]
□ at a reduced price a prezzo ridotto
■ **'reduce speed now'** 'rallentare'

reduction NOUN
la riduzione *fem*
□ reductions in staff riduzioni di personale
■ **'huge reductions!'** 'ribassi!'

redundancy NOUN
il licenziamento *masc*
■ **a redundancy payment** un'indennità di licenziamento

redundant ADJECTIVE
■ **to be made redundant** essere [47ᴱ] licenziato

reed NOUN
la canna di palude *fem*

reel NOUN
il rocchetto *masc*

to **refer** VERB
■ **to refer to** fare [49] accenno a □ He referred to my letter. Ha fatto accenno alla mia lettera.

referee NOUN
l' arbitro *masc*

reference NOUN
il riferimento *masc*
□ With reference to... In riferimento a...
■ **a reference number** un numero di riferimento
■ **references** (*for job*) referenze *fem pl*
■ **a reference book** un testo di consultazione

to **refill** VERB
riempire [86] di nuovo

refinery NOUN
la raffineria *fem*

to **reflect** VERB
riflettere [87]

reflection NOUN
il riflesso *masc*

reflex NOUN
il riflesso *masc*

reflexive ADJECTIVE
riflessivo (FEM riflessiva)
□ a reflexive verb un verbo riflessivo

refresher course NOUN
il corso di aggiornamento *masc*

refreshing ADJECTIVE
1 rinfrescante (FEM rinfrescante) (drink)
2 piacevole (FEM piacevole) (change)

refreshments NOUN PL
i rinfreschi *masc pl*

refrigerator NOUN
il frigorifero *masc*

to **refuel** VERB
rifornirsi [51ᴱ] di carburante

refuge NOUN
il rifugio *masc*

refugee NOUN
il profugo *masc* (PL i profughi)
la profuga *fem* (PL le profughe)

refund NOUN
▷ see also **refund** VERB
il rimborso *masc*

to **refund** VERB
▷ see also **refund** NOUN
rimborsare [68]

refusal NOUN
il rifiuto *masc*

to **refuse** VERB
▷ see also **refuse** NOUN
rifiutare [68]

refuse NOUN
▷ see also **refuse** VERB
i rifiuti *masc pl*
■ **refuse collection** la raccolta dei rifiuti

to **regain** VERB
■ **to regain control** riacquistare [68] il controllo
■ **to regain consciousness** riprendere [77] conoscenza

regard NOUN
▷ see also **regard** VERB
■ **with regard to** riguardo a
■ **regards** saluti □ Give my regards to Alice. Saluti a Alice.
■ **with kind regards** cordiali saluti

to **regard** VERB
▷ see also **regard** NOUN
■ **to regard something as** considerare [68] qualcosa come
■ **as regards** per quel che riguarda

regarding PREPOSITION
riguardante

□ the laws regarding alcohol le leggi riguardanti gli alcolici

regardless ADVERB
■ **to carry on regardless** continuare [68] come se niente fosse

regiment NOUN
il reggimento *masc*

region NOUN
la regione *fem*

regional ADJECTIVE
regionale (FEM regionale)

register NOUN
▷ see also **register** VERB
il registro *masc*
□ the hotel register il registro dell'albergo
■ **to call the register** fare [49] l'appello

to **register** VERB
▷ see also **register** NOUN
iscriversi [99ᴱ] (enrol)
□ We have to register tomorrow. Dobbiamo iscriverci domani.
■ **He registered the birth of his son.** Ha denunciato all'anagrafe la nascita del figlio.

registered ADJECTIVE
■ **a registered letter** un'assicurata

registration NOUN
1 l' iscrizione *fem*
□ registration of voters iscrizione alle liste elettorali dei votanti
2 l' appello *masc* (at school)
□ the first lesson after registration la prima lezione dopo l'appello

registration number NOUN
il numero di targa *masc*

regret NOUN
▷ see also **regret** VERB
il rimpianto *masc*

to **regret** VERB
▷ see also **regret** NOUN
pentirsi [41ᴱ]
□ Try it, you won't regret it! Provalo, non te ne pentirai!
■ **to regret doing something** rimpiangere [71] di aver fatto qualcosa

regular ADJECTIVE
1 regolare (FEM regolare)
□ at regular intervals a intervalli regolari
■ **to take regular exercise** fare [49] moto regolarmente
2 abituale (FEM abituale)
□ He's a regular customer. È un cliente abituale.
3 medio (FEM media)
□ a regular portion of fries una porzione media di patatine fritte

regularly ADVERB
regolarmente

regulation NOUN
la norma *fem*
□ safety regulations norme di sicurezza

rehearsal NOUN
la prova *fem*
■ **the dress rehearsal** la prova generale

to **rehearse** VERB
provare [68]

reindeer NOUN
la renna *fem*

reins NOUN PL
le redini *fem pl*

to **reject** VERB
scartare [68] *(idea, suggestion)*

relapse NOUN
la ricaduta *fem*

related ADJECTIVE
imparentato (FEM imparentata)
□ We're related. Siamo imparentati.
■ **The two events were not related.** Non c'è alcun rapporto tra i due avvenimenti.

relation NOUN
1 il/la parente *masc/fem*
□ He's a distant relation. È un lontano parente.
2 il rapporto *masc*
□ It has no relation to reality. Non ha nessun rapporto con la realtà.
■ **in relation to** con riferimento a

relationship NOUN
1 il rapporto *masc*
□ We have a good relationship. Abbiamo un bel rapporto.
2 la relazione *fem (with partner)*
□ I'm not in a relationship at the moment. Al momento non ho una relazione.

relative NOUN
il/la parente *masc/fem*

relatively ADVERB
relativamente

to **relax** VERB
rilassarsi [56ᴱ]

relaxation NOUN
il relax *masc*

relaxed ADJECTIVE
rilassato (FEM rilassata)

relaxing ADJECTIVE
rilassante (FEM rilassante)

relay NOUN
▷ *see also* **relay** VERB
■ **a relay race** una corsa a staffetta

to **relay** VERB
▷ *see also* **relay** NOUN
trasmettere [59]

to **release** VERB
▷ *see also* **release** NOUN
1 rimettere [59] in libertà *(prisoner)*
2 rendere [83] noto *(news, report)*
3 far [49] uscire *(record, DVD)*

release NOUN
▷ *see also* **release** VERB
la liberazione *fem*
□ the release of Nelson Mandela

la liberazione di Nelson Mandela
■ **the band's latest release** l'ultimo disco del gruppo

relegated ADJECTIVE
■ **to be relegated** essere [47ᴱ] retrocesso

relevant ADJECTIVE
1 pertinente (FEM pertinente)
□ Make sure that what you say is relevant. Cerca di dire qualcosa di pertinente.
■ **Education should be relevant to real life.** L'istruzione dovrebbe avere un riscontro nella vita reale.
2 del caso
□ They passed all relevant information to the police Hanno passato tutte le informazioni del caso alla polizia.
■ **That's not relevant.** Questo non c'entra.
LANGUAGE TIP Be careful not to translate **relevant** by rilevante.

reliable ADJECTIVE
affidabile (FEM affidabile)

relief NOUN
il sollievo *masc*
□ That's a relief! Che sollievo!

to **relieve** VERB
alleviare [17]

relieved ADJECTIVE
sollevato (FEM sollevata)

religion NOUN
la religione *fem*

religious ADJECTIVE
religioso (FEM religiosa)

reluctant ADJECTIVE
■ **to be reluctant to do something** essere [47ᴱ] restio a fare qualcosa

reluctantly ADVERB
a malincuore

to **rely on** VERB
contare [68] su
□ I'm relying on you. Conto su di te.

to **remain** VERB
restare [68ᴱ]
■ **to remain silent** restare [68ᴱ] in silenzio

remaining ADJECTIVE
■ **the remaining ingredients** il resto degli ingredienti

remains NOUN PL
i resti *masc pl*
□ the remains of the picnic i resti del picnic
□ human remains resti umani
■ **Roman remains** le rovine romane

remake NOUN
il remake *masc* (PL i remake)

remark NOUN
▷ *see also* **remark** VERB
il commento *masc*

to **remark** VERB
▷ *see also* **remark** NOUN
osservare [68]

remarkable ADJECTIVE
straordinario (FEM straordinaria, MASC PL straordinari, FEM PL straordinarie)

remarkably ADVERB
straordinariamente

to **remarry** VERB
risposarsi [56ᴱ]

remedy NOUN
il rimedio masc

to **remember** VERB
ricordarsi [56ᴱ]

> **LANGUAGE TIP** Word for word, this means 'to remind oneself'.

□ I can't remember his name. Non mi ricordo come si chiama. □ Remember to post that letter. Ricordati di imbucare la lettera. □ I don't remember saying that. Non mi ricordo di aver detto una cosa del genere.

to **remind** VERB
ricordare [68]

□ The scenery here reminds me of Scotland. Il paesaggio mi ricorda la Scozia. □ Remind me to speak to Daniel. Ricordami di parlare a Daniel.

remnant NOUN
■ **the remnants of the defeated army** ciò che restava dell'esercito sconfitto

remorse NOUN
il rimorso masc

remote ADJECTIVE
isolato (FEM isolata)
□ a remote village un paesino isolato

remote control NOUN
il telecomando masc

remotely ADVERB
vagamente
□ nobody remotely resembling this description nessuno che corrispondesse neanche vagamente alla descrizione
■ **It is remotely possible that...** C'è una remota possibilità che...

removable ADJECTIVE
staccabile (FEM staccabile)

removal NOUN
1 l'asportazione fem
□ the removal of a small lump in her breast l'asportazione di un piccolo nodulo al seno
2 il trasloco masc (PL i traslochi)
■ **a removal van** un furgone per traslochi

to **remove** VERB
togliere [114]
□ Please remove your bag from my seat. Le dispiace togliere la borsa dal mio sedile?

rendezvous NOUN
l'appuntamento masc

to **renew** VERB
rinnovare [68] (passport, licence)

renewable ADJECTIVE
rinnovabile (FEM rinnovabile)

to **renovate** VERB
restaurare [68]

renowned ADJECTIVE
rinomato (FEM rinomata)

rent NOUN
▷ see also **rent** VERB
l'affitto masc

to **rent** VERB
▷ see also **rent** NOUN
1 affittare [68] (house)
2 noleggiare [58] (car, bike)

rental NOUN
il noleggio masc

rental car NOUN
la macchina a nolo fem

to **reorganize** VERB
riorganizzare [68]

rep NOUN
il/la rappresentante masc/fem

repaid VERB ▷ see **repay**

to **repair** VERB
▷ see also **repair** NOUN
aggiustare [68]
■ **to get something repaired** fare [49] aggiustare qualcosa □ I got the washing machine repaired. Ho fatto aggiustare la lavatrice.

repair NOUN
▷ see also **repair** VERB
la riparazione fem

to **repay** VERB
rimborsare [68]
■ **I don't know how I can ever repay you.** Come potrò mai ricompensarti?

repayment NOUN
■ **debt repayment** il rimborso del debito
■ **mortgage repayments** le rate del mutuo

to **repeat** VERB
▷ see also **repeat** NOUN
ripetere [1]

repeat NOUN
▷ see also **repeat** VERB
la replica fem (PL le repliche)
□ There are too many repeats on TV. Ci sono troppe repliche in TV.

repeatedly ADVERB
ripetutamente

repellent NOUN
■ **insect repellent** l'insettifugo

repetitive ADJECTIVE
ripetitivo (FEM ripetitiva)

to **replace** VERB
1 rimpiazzare [68]
□ Computers have replaced typewriters. I computer hanno rimpiazzato le macchine da scrivere.
2 riattaccare [18] (receiver)

replay NOUN
▷ see also **replay** VERB
la partita di spareggio fem

r

to **replay** VERB
▷ *see also* **replay** NOUN
1 rigiocare [18] *(match)*
2 riascoltare [68] *(record, tape)*

replica NOUN
la replica *fem* (PL le repliche)

reply NOUN
▷ *see also* **reply** VERB
la risposta *fem*

to **reply** VERB
▷ *see also* **reply** NOUN
rispondere [90]

report NOUN
▷ *see also* **report** VERB
1 la relazione *fem*
□ the committee's report la relazione della commissione
2 l' articolo *masc*
□ There's a report in today's paper. C'è un articolo sul giornale di oggi.
3 la pagella *fem* (at school)
□ He got a terrible report. Ha ricevuto una bruttissima pagella.
■ **a report card** una pagella

to **report** VERB
▷ *see also* **report** NOUN
1 denunciare [13]
□ I reported the theft to the police. Ho denunciato il furto alla polizia.
2 presentarsi [56ᴱ]
□ Report to reception when you arrive. Si presenti alla reception al suo arrivo.

to **report back** VERB
riferire [51] *(comment, verdict)*
■ **I'll report back as soon as I hear anything.** Appena ho notizie glielo faccio sapere.

reporter NOUN
il/la reporter *masc/fem* (PL i/le reporter)

to **represent** VERB
rappresentare [68]

representative ADJECTIVE
rappresentativo (FEM rappresentativa)

reproduction NOUN
la riproduzione *fem*

reptile NOUN
il rettile *masc*

republic NOUN
la repubblica *fem* (PL le repubbliche)

repulsive ADJECTIVE
ripugnante (FEM ripugnante)

reputable ADJECTIVE
degno di fiducia (FEM degna di fiducia)

reputation NOUN
la reputazione *fem*

request NOUN
▷ *see also* **request** VERB
la richiesta *fem*

to **request** VERB
▷ *see also* **request** NOUN
richiedere [19]

to **require** VERB
richiedere [19]
□ What qualifications are required? Che qualifiche si richiedono?

requirement NOUN
il requisito *masc*
□ What are the requirements for the job? Quali sono i requisiti necessari per il lavoro?
■ **entry requirements** i criteri d'ammissione

to **rescue** VERB
▷ *see also* **rescue** NOUN
salvare [68]

rescue NOUN
▷ *see also* **rescue** VERB
1 il salvataggio *masc*
□ a rescue operation un'operazione di salvataggio
2 il soccorso *masc*
□ a mountain rescue team una squadra di soccorso alpino
■ **to come to somebody's rescue** venire [120ᴱ] in aiuto di qualcuno

research NOUN
1 la ricerca *fem*
□ He's doing research. Fa ricerca.
2 le ricerche *fem pl*
□ She's doing some research in the library. Sta facendo delle ricerche in biblioteca.

resemblance NOUN
la somiglianza *fem*

to **resent** VERB
■ **to resent somebody** provare [68] risentimento nei confronti di qualcuno
■ **I resent being dependent on her.** Non sopporto di dipendere da lei.

resentful ADJECTIVE
pieno di risentimento (FEM piena di risentimento)
■ **to feel resentful towards somebody** essere [47] pieno di risentimento nei confronti di qualcuno

reservation NOUN
1 la prenotazione *fem*
□ I've got a reservation for two nights. Ho una prenotazione per due notti.
2 la riserva *fem*
□ I've got reservations about it. Ho delle riserve a riguardo.

reserve NOUN
▷ *see also* **reserve** VERB
la riserva *fem*

to **reserve** VERB
▷ *see also* **reserve** NOUN
riservare [68]
□ I'd like to reserve a table. Vorrei riservare un tavolo.

reserved ADJECTIVE
riservato (FEM riservata)

reservoir NOUN
il bacino idrico *masc* (PL i bacini idrici)

resident – retired

resident NOUN
l' abitante *masc/fem*
□ local residents gli abitanti della zona

residential ADJECTIVE
residenziale (FEM residenziale)
□ a residential area una zona residenziale

to **resign** VERB
dare [30] le dimissioni

resistance NOUN
la resistenza *fem*

to **resit** VERB
ripresentarsi [56ᴱ] a
□ I'm resitting the exam in December. Mi ripresento all'esame in dicembre.

resolution NOUN
1 il buon proposito *masc*
□ Have you made any New Year resolutions? Hai fatto dei buoni propositi per l'anno nuovo?
2 la risoluzione *fem*
□ a UN resolution una risoluzione dell'ONU

resort NOUN
la località turistica *fem* (PL le località turistiche)
■ a seaside resort una stazione balneare
■ a ski resort una stazione sciistica
■ as a last resort come ultima risorsa

resource NOUN
la risorsa *fem*

respect NOUN
▷ see also **respect** VERB
il rispetto *masc*
□ I have tremendous respect for Dean. Ho un grandissimo rispetto per Dean.
■ in some respects sotto certi aspetti

to **respect** VERB
▷ see also **respect** NOUN
rispettare [68]

respectable ADJECTIVE
1 rispettabile (FEM rispettabile)
□ a respectable family una famiglia rispettabile
2 discreto (FEM discreta)
□ My marks were respectable. I miei voti erano discreti.

respectively ADVERB
rispettivamente

responsibility NOUN
la responsabilità *fem* (PL le responsabilità)

responsible ADJECTIVE
responsabile (FEM responsabile)
■ to be responsible for something essere [47ᴱ] responsabile di qualcosa
■ a responsible job un posto di responsabilità

rest NOUN
▷ see also **rest** VERB
1 il riposo *masc*
□ five minutes' rest cinque minuti di riposo
■ to have a rest riposarsi [56ᴱ]
2 il resto *masc*
□ I'll do the rest. Faccio io il resto. □ the rest of the money il resto dei soldi

■ the rest of them gli altri □ The rest of them went swimming. Gli altri sono andati a nuotare.

to **rest** VERB
▷ see also **rest** NOUN
1 riposare [68]
□ She's resting in her room. È in camera sua a riposare.
2 non affaticare [18]
□ He has to rest his knee. Non deve affaticare il ginocchio.
3 appoggiare [58]
□ I rested my bike against the window. Ho appoggiato la bici alla finestra.

restaurant NOUN
il ristorante *masc*
■ the restaurant car il vagone ristorante

restful ADJECTIVE
riposante (FEM riposante)

restless ADJECTIVE
irrequieto (FEM irrequieta)

restoration NOUN
il restauro *masc*

to **restore** VERB
1 ripristinare [68]
□ They restored order. Hanno ripristinato l'ordine.
■ to restore somebody's confidence fare [49] riacquistare fiducia a qualcuno
2 restaurare [68]
□ The picture has been restored. Il quadro è stato restaurato.

to **restrict** VERB
limitare [68]

rest room NOUN (US)
la toilette *fem* (PL le toilette)

result NOUN
▷ see also **result** VERB
il risultato *masc*
□ an excellent result un risultato eccellente
■ as a result di conseguenza □ ...and as a result, morale is low. ...e di conseguenza il morale è basso.

to **result** VERB
▷ see also **result** NOUN
■ to result in causare [68] □ Many accidents result in head injuries. Molti incidenti causano delle lesioni craniche.
■ The enquiry resulted in her being sacked. L'inchiesta ha portato al suo licenziamento.

to **resume** VERB
riprendere [77]
□ They've resumed work. Hanno ripreso il lavoro.

résumé NOUN (US)
il curriculum vitae *masc* (PL i curriculum vitae)

to **retire** VERB
andare [6ᴱ] in pensione

retired ADJECTIVE
in pensione
□ a retired teacher un insegnante in pensione

retirement NOUN
- **since his retirement** da quando è andato in pensione

to **retrace** VERB
- **to retrace one's steps** ritornare[68E] sui propri passi

return NOUN
▷ *see also* **return** VERB
1 il ritorno *masc*
□ **on our return** al nostro ritorno
- **the return journey** il viaggio di ritorno
- **a return match** una partita di ritorno
  LANGUAGE TIP Word for word, this means 'a ticket to go and come back'.
□ A return to Bangor, please. Vorrei un biglietto di andata e ritorno per Bangor.
2 il biglietto di andata e ritorno *masc*
- **in return** in cambio □ ...and I help her in return. ...e io in cambio aiuto lei.
- **in return for** in cambio di
- **Many happy returns!** Cento di questi giorni!
3 invio *(key)*
□ Hit return. Premere invio.

to **return** VERB
▷ *see also* **return** NOUN
1 tornare[68E]
□ I've just returned from Rome. Sono appena tornato da Roma.
2 restituire[51]
□ She borrows my things and doesn't return them. Prende le mie cose e poi non le restituisce.

retweet NOUN
▷ *see also* **retweet** VERB
il retweet *masc* (PL i retweet)

to **retweet** VERB
▷ *see also* **retweet** NOUN
retwittare[68]

reunion NOUN
la riunione *fem*

to **reuse** VERB
riutilizzare[68]

to **reveal** VERB
rivelare[68]

revenge NOUN
la vendetta *fem*
□ This is my revenge. Questa è la mia vendetta.
- **to take revenge** vendicarsi[18E]

to **reverse** VERB
▷ *see also* **reverse** ADJECTIVE
1 fare[49] retromarcia
□ He reversed without looking. Ha fatto retromarcia senza guardare.
2 invertire[41]
□ They are trying to reverse this trend. Stanno cercando di invertire la tendenza.
- **to reverse one's decision** tornare[68E] sulla propria decisione
- **to reverse the charges** fare[49] una telefonata a carico del destinatario

reverse ADJECTIVE
▷ *see also* **reverse** VERB
inverso (FEM inversa)
□ in reverse order in ordine inverso
- **in reverse gear** in retromarcia

review NOUN
▷ *see also* **review** VERB
la recensione *fem*
□ The book got good reviews. Il libro ha avuto recensioni favorevoli.
- **to be under review** essere[47E] preso in esame

to **review** VERB
▷ *see also* **review** NOUN
fare[49] la recensione di

to **revise** VERB
ripassare[68]
□ I haven't started revising yet. Non ho ancora cominciato a ripassare.
- **to revise one's opinion** cambiare[17] idea

revision NOUN
il ripasso *masc*

to **revive** VERB
rianimare[68]
□ The nurses tried to revive him. Gli infermieri cercarono di rianimarlo.

revolting ADJECTIVE
disgustoso (FEM disgustosa)

revolution NOUN
la rivoluzione *fem*

revolutionary ADJECTIVE
rivoluzionario (FEM rivoluzionaria)

revolver NOUN
il revolver *masc* (PL i revolver)

reward NOUN
la ricompensa *fem*

rewarding ADJECTIVE
gratificante (FEM gratificante)
□ a rewarding job un lavoro gratificante

to **rewind** VERB
riavvolgere[91]

rheumatism NOUN
il reumatismo *masc*

Rhine NOUN
- **the Rhine** il Reno

rhinoceros NOUN
il rinoceronte *masc*

Rhone NOUN
- **the Rhone** il Rodano

rhubarb NOUN
il rabarbaro *masc*

rhythm NOUN
il ritmo *masc*

rib NOUN
la costola *fem*

ribbon NOUN
il nastro *masc*

rice NOUN
il riso *masc*
- **rice pudding** il budino di riso

r

rich ADJECTIVE
ricco (FEM ricca, MASC PL ricchi, FEM PL ricche)
■ **the rich** i ricchi

to **rid** VERB
liberare [68]
□ an attempt to rid the house of mice un tentativo di liberare la casa dai topi
■ **to get rid of** sbarazzarsi [56ᴱ] di

to **ride** VERB
▷ see also **ride** NOUN
cavalcare [18]
□ I'm learning to ride. Sto imparando a cavalcare.
■ **to ride a horse** cavalcare [18]
■ **to ride a bike** andare [6ᴱ] in bicicletta □ Can you ride a bike? Sai andare in bicicletta? □ He rode to school on his new bike. È andato a scuola con la bici nuova.
■ **to ride the bus** (US) prendere [77] l'autobus

ride NOUN
▷ see also **ride** VERB
■ **to go for a ride** **1** (on horse) andare [6ᴱ] a fare una cavalcata **2** (on bike) andare [6ᴱ] a fare un giro in bicicletta
■ **It's a short bus ride to the town centre.** In autobus al centro non è lontano.

rider NOUN
1 il cavallerizzo masc
la cavallerizza fem
□ She's a good rider. È una buona cavallerizza.
2 il/la ciclista masc/fem (cyclist)

ridiculous ADJECTIVE
ridicolo (FEM ridicola)

riding NOUN
l' equitazione fem
■ **to go riding** fare [49] equitazione
■ **a riding school** una scuola d'equitazione

rifle NOUN
il fucile masc

rig NOUN
■ **an oil rig** una piattaforma petrolifera

right ADJECTIVE, ADVERB
▷ see also **right** NOUN
1 giusto (FEM giusta)
□ It isn't the right size. Non è la taglia giusta.
2 esatto (FEM esatta)
□ Do you have the right time? Hai l'ora esatta? □ the right answer la risposta esatta □ That's right! Esatto!
■ **to be right** (person) avere [12] ragione
□ You were right! Avevi ragione!
3 bene
□ Did I pronounce it right? L'ho pronunciato bene? □ Right! Let's get started. Bene, cominciamo! □ It's not right to behave like that. Non sta bene fare così.
■ **to do the right thing** fare [49] bene □ I think you did the right thing. Secondo me hai fatto bene.
4 destro (FEM destra)

□ my right hand la mano destra
5 a destra
□ Turn right at the traffic lights. Al semaforo gira a destra.
■ **right away** subito □ I'll do it right away. Lo faccio subito.

right NOUN
▷ see also **right** ADJECTIVE, ADVERB
1 il diritto masc
□ You've got no right to do that. Non hai diritto di farlo.
■ **to have right of way** (person) avere [12] la precedenza
2 la destra fem
■ **on the right** a destra

right angle NOUN
l' angolo retto masc

right-hand ADJECTIVE
destro (FEM destra)
□ the right-hand side il lato destro
■ **to be on the right-hand side** essere [47ᴱ] sulla destra

right-handed ADJECTIVE
■ **I'm right-handed.** Scrivo con la destra.

rightly ADVERB
1 giustamente
□ She rightly decided that he was lying. Concluse, giustamente, che lui mentiva.
2 bene
□ If I remember rightly. Se mi ricordo bene.

rim NOUN
l' orlo masc
□ the rim of a cup l'orlo di una tazza
■ **rims** montatura fem sing □ glasses with wire rims occhiali con montatura metallica

ring NOUN
▷ see also **ring** VERB
1 l' anello masc
□ He gave her a silver ring. Le ha regalato un anello d'argento.
■ **a wedding ring** una fede
2 il cerchio masc
□ They were sitting in a ring. Erano seduti in cerchio.
3 lo squillo masc (of phone, bell)
□ He answered at the first ring. Ha risposto al primo squillo.
■ **to give somebody a ring** telefonare [68] a qualcuno

to **ring** VERB
▷ see also **ring** NOUN
1 telefonare [68]
□ Your mother rang this morning. Stamattina ha telefonato tua madre. □ Several friends have rung to congratulate me. Mi hanno telefonato diversi amici per congratularsi.
■ **to ring somebody** telefonare [68] a qualcuno
2 squillare [68]
□ The phone's ringing. Sta squillando il telefono.

■ **to ring the bell** suonare [68] il campanello
■ **to ring back** richiamare [68] □ I'll ring back later. Richiamerò più tardi.
■ **to ring up** telefonare [68]

ring binder NOUN
il classificatore ad anelli *masc*

ring road NOUN
la circonvallazione *fem*

ringtone NOUN
la suoneria *fem*

rink NOUN
la pista di pattinaggio *fem*

to **rinse** VERB
sciacquare [68]

riot NOUN
▷ *see also* **riot** VERB
la sommossa *fem*
■ **police in riot gear** polizia in tenuta antisommossa

to **riot** VERB
▷ *see also* **riot** NOUN
fare [49] una sommossa

to **rip** VERB
strappare [68]
□ I accidentally ripped the envelope. Senza volere ho strappato la busta.
■ **I've ripped my jeans.** Mi si sono strappati i jeans.

to **rip off** VERB
pelare [68]
□ The hotel ripped us off. All'albergo ci hanno pelato.

to **rip up** VERB
strappare [68]
□ He read the note and then ripped it up. Ha letto il biglietto e poi l'ha strappato.

ripe ADJECTIVE
maturo (FEM matura)

rip-off NOUN
■ **It's a rip-off!** È un furto!

rise NOUN
▷ *see also* **rise** VERB
l' aumento *masc*

to **rise** VERB
▷ *see also* **rise** NOUN
1 aumentare [68ᴱ]
□ Prices have risen. I prezzi sono aumentati.
2 sorgere [102ᴱ] *(sun)*
■ **to rise to one's feet** alzarsi [56ᴱ] in piedi
□ He rose to his feet. Si alzò in piedi.

riser NOUN
■ **to be an early riser** essere [47ᴱ] mattutino

risk NOUN
▷ *see also* **risk** VERB
il rischio *masc*
■ **to take risks** correre [26] dei rischi
■ **It's at your own risk.** È a tuo rischio e pericolo.

to **risk** VERB
▷ *see also* **risk** NOUN
rischiare [17]

risky ADJECTIVE
rischioso (FEM rischiosa)

rival NOUN
▷ *see also* **rival** ADJECTIVE, VERB
il/la rivale *masc/fem*

rival ADJECTIVE
▷ *see also* **rival** NOUN, VERB
1 rivale (FEM rivale)
□ a rival gang una banda rivale
2 concorrente (FEM concorrente)
□ a rival company una ditta concorrente

to **rival** VERB
▷ *see also* **rival** ADJECTIVE, NOUN
competere [1] con
□ Florida rivals Spain as a holiday destination. La Florida compete con la Spagna come destinazione turistica.

rivalry NOUN
la rivalità *fem* (PL le rivalità)

river NOUN
il fiume *masc*
□ across the river dall'altra parte del fiume
■ **the river bank** l'argine *masc*

Riviera NOUN
■ **the French Riviera** la Costa Azzurra
■ **the Italian Riviera** la riviera ligure

road NOUN
la strada *fem*

road accident NOUN
l' incidente stradale *masc*

road map NOUN
la carta stradale *fem*

road rage NOUN
l' aggressività al volante *fem*

road sign NOUN
il cartello stradale *masc*

roadworks NOUN PL
i lavori stradali *masc pl*

roast ADJECTIVE
arrosto (FEM+PL arrosto)
□ roast chicken pollo arrosto
■ **roast pork** arrosto di maiale
■ **roast beef** arrosto di manzo

to **rob** VERB
derubare [68]
□ I've been robbed. Sono stato derubato.
■ **to rob somebody of something** rubare [68] qualcosa a qualcuno □ He was robbed of his wallet. Gli hanno rubato il portafoglio.
■ **to rob a bank** svaligiare [58] una banca

robber NOUN
il rapinatore *masc*
la rapinatrice *fem*
□ armed robbers rapinatori armati

robbery NOUN
1 la rapina *fem* (in bank, shop)
■ **a bank robbery** una rapina in banca
■ **an armed robbery** una rapina a mano armata

r

527

2 il furto *masc*
  □ robberies on trains furti sui treni

robin NOUN
  il pettirosso *masc*

robot NOUN
  il robot *masc* (PL i robot)

rock NOUN
  ▷ *see also* **rock** VERB
1 la roccia *fem* (PL le rocce)
  □ I sat on a rock. Mi sono seduto su una roccia.
  ■ **Morale was at rock bottom.** Il morale era a terra.
  ■ **Prices have hit rock bottom.** I prezzi sono scesi tantissimo.
2 il sasso *masc*
  □ The crowd started to throw rocks. La folla cominciò a lanciare sassi.
3 il rock *masc*
  □ a rock concert un concerto rock
  ■ **rock and roll** il rock and roll
  ■ **a stick of rock** un bastoncino di zucchero

to rock VERB
  ▷ *see also* **rock** NOUN
1 far [49] oscillare
  □ The tremor rocked the building. Il terremoto ha fatto oscillare l'edificio.
2 cullare [68] *(baby)*

rockery NOUN
  il giardino roccioso *masc*

rocket NOUN
  il razzo *masc*

rocking chair NOUN
  la sedia a dondolo *fem*

rocking horse NOUN
  il cavallo a dondolo *masc*

rod NOUN
  la canna da pesca *fem*

rode VERB ▷ *see* **ride**

role NOUN
  il ruolo *masc*

role play NOUN
  il gioco di ruolo *masc* (PL i giochi di ruolo)
  ■ **to do a role play** fare [49] un gioco di ruolo

roll NOUN
  ▷ *see also* **roll** VERB
1 il rotolo *masc*
  □ a toilet roll un rotolo di carta igienica
  ■ **a roll of film** un rullino fotografico
2 il panino *masc*
  □ a cheese roll un panino al formaggio
  ■ **roll call** *(at school)* l'appello

to roll VERB
  ▷ *see also* **roll** NOUN
  rotolare [68]
  □ The ball rolled into the net. La palla rotolò in rete.

to roll out VERB
  spianare [68] *(pastry)*

to roll up VERB
  rimboccare [18] *(sleeves)*

roller NOUN
  il bigodino *masc* *(for hair)*

to roller-blade VERB
  pattinare [68]

Rollerblades® NOUN PL
  i pattini in linea *masc pl*

rollercoaster NOUN
  le montagne russe *fem pl*

roller skates NOUN PL
  i pattini a rotelle *masc pl*

roller-skating NOUN
  il pattinaggio a rotelle *masc*

rolling pin NOUN
  il mattarello *masc*

Roman ADJECTIVE, NOUN
  il romano *masc*
  la romana *fem*
  □ the Roman empire l'impero romano
  ■ **the Romans** i romani

Roman Catholic NOUN
  il cattolico *masc*
  la cattolica *fem*

romance NOUN
1 l' amore *masc*
  □ a holiday romance un amore estivo
2 il fascino *masc*
  □ the romance of Paris il fascino di Parigi
3 il romanzo rosa *masc* (PL i romanzi rosa)
  □ She writes romances. Scrive romanzi rosa.

Romania NOUN
  la Romania *fem*

Romanian ADJECTIVE
  rumeno (FEM rumena)

romantic ADJECTIVE
  romantico (FEM romantica, MASC PL romantici, FEM PL romantiche)

Rome NOUN
  Roma *fem*

roof NOUN
  il tetto *masc*
  □ a sloping roof un tetto spiovente

roof rack NOUN
  il portapacchi *masc* (PL i portapacchi)

room NOUN
1 la stanza *fem*
  □ the biggest room in the house la stanza più grande della casa
2 la camera *fem* *(bedroom)*
  □ She's in her room. È in camera sua.
  ■ **a single room** una camera singola
  ■ **a double room** una camera matrimoniale
3 la sala *fem*
  □ the music room la sala musica
4 il posto *masc*
  □ There's no room for that box. Non c'è posto per quella scatola.

roommate NOUN
  il compagno di stanza *masc*
  la compagna di stanza *fem*

r

room service NOUN
il servizio in camera *masc*

root NOUN
▷ *see also* **root** VERB
la radice *fem*

to **root** VERB
▷ *see also* **root** NOUN
mettere [59] radici

to **root around** VERB
rovistare [68]

to **root out** VERB
eliminare [68]
□ They want to root out corruption. Vogliono eliminare la corruzione.

rope NOUN
la corda *fem*

to **rope** VERB
legare [76]
□ The climbers were roped together. I rocciatori erano legati assieme.

to **rope in** VERB
tirar [68] dentro
□ I was roped in to help with the refreshments. Mi hanno tirato dentro a dare una mano con i rinfreschi.

rose VERB ▷ *see* **rise**

rose NOUN
la rosa *fem*

to **rot** VERB
1 marcire [51ᴱ]
□ The wood had rotted. Il legno era marcito.
2 cariare [17]
□ Sugar rots your teeth. Lo zucchero caria i denti.

rotten ADJECTIVE
marcio (FEM marcia, MASC PL marci, FEM PL marce)
□ a rotten apple una mela marcia
■ **rotten weather** tempo da cani
■ **That's a rotten thing to do.** Che carognata!
■ **to feel rotten** sentirsi [41ᴱ] da cani

rough ADJECTIVE, ADVERB
1 ruvido (FEM ruvida)
□ My hands are rough. Ho le mani ruvide.
2 violento (FEM violenta)
□ Rugby's a rough sport. Il rugby è uno sport violento.
3 poco raccomandabile
□ It's a rough area. È una zona poco raccomandabile.
4 mosso (FEM mossa)
□ The sea was rough. Il mare era mosso.
5 approssimativo (FEM approssimativa)
□ I've got a rough idea. Ne ho un'idea approssimativa.
■ **to feel rough** sentirsi [41ᴱ] poco bene
■ **to sleep rough** dormire [41] per strada □ A lot of people sleep rough in London. A Londra tanta gente dorme per strada.

roughly ADVERB
pressapoco
□ It weighs roughly twenty kilos. Pesa pressapoco venti chili.
■ **Roughly chop the vegetables.** Tagliare le verdure a pezzi grossi.

round ADJECTIVE, ADVERB, PREPOSITION
▷ *see also* **round** NOUN
1 rotondo (FEM rotonda)
□ a round table un tavolo rotondo
2 intorno a
□ We were sitting round the table. Eravamo seduti intorno al tavolo.
■ **a round number** una cifra tonda
■ **round the corner** dietro l'angolo
■ **to go round to somebody's house** andare [6ᴱ] a casa di qualcuno
■ **to have a look round** dare [30] un'occhiata in giro
■ **to go round a museum** visitare [68] un museo
■ **round here** da queste parti □ Is there a chemist's round here? C'è una farmacia da queste parti?
■ **all round** tutt'intorno □ There were vineyards all round. Tutt'intorno c'erano delle vigne.
■ **all year round** tutto l'anno
■ **round about** circa □ It costs round about £100. Costa circa cento sterline.
■ **round about eight o'clock** verso le otto

round NOUN
▷ *see also* **round** ADJECTIVE, ADVERB, PREPOSITION
1 il round *masc* (PL i round) *(in boxing)*
□ He was knocked out in the tenth round. È andato al tappeto al decimo round.
2 il giro *masc*
□ another round of talks un altro giro di consultazioni
3 la fettina *fem*
□ a few rounds of cucumber alcune fettine di cetriolo
■ **to buy a round of drinks** *(in pub)* offrire [66] un giro
■ **I think it's my round.** Tocca a me offrire da bere.
■ **a round of golf** una partita di golf
■ **a round of sandwiches** un tramezzino

to **round off** VERB
terminare [68]
□ They rounded off the meal with liqueurs. Hanno terminato il pranzo con dei liquori.

to **round up** VERB
1 fare [49] una retata *(suspects)*
2 arrotondare [68] *(sum, number)*

roundabout NOUN
1 la rotatoria *fem* *(at junction)*
2 la giostra *fem* *(in fairground)*

r

529

rounders NOUN
  gioco per bambini simile al baseball
round trip NOUN (US)
  l' andata e ritorno *masc*
route NOUN
  l' itinerario *masc*
  □ a different route un itinerario diverso
  ■ **a bus route** un percorso dell'autobus
routine NOUN
  ▷ *see also* **routine** ADJECTIVE
  ■ **my daily routine** le mie occupazioni
  quotidiane
routine ADJECTIVE
  ▷ *see also* **routine** NOUN
  di routine
  □ a routine check un controllo di routine
row (1) NOUN
  la fila *fem*
  □ a row of houses una fila di case □ in the front
  row in prima fila □ five times in a row cinque
  volte di fila
row (2) NOUN
1 il baccano *masc*
  □ What's that terrible row? Cos'è quel
  baccano?
2 il litigio *masc*
  □ their latest row il loro ultimo litigio
  ■ **to have a row** litigare [76] □ They've had a
  row. Hanno litigato.
to **row (3)** VERB
  remare [68] *(in boat)*
rowboat NOUN (US)
  la barca a remi *fem* (PL le barche a remi)
rowing NOUN
  il canottaggio *masc*
  □ I like rowing. Mi piace il canottaggio.
  ■ **a rowing boat** una barca a remi
royal ADJECTIVE, NOUN
  reale (FEM reale)
  ■ **the royals** i reali
to **rub** VERB
  sfregare [76]
  □ She gently rubbed the stain. Ha sfregato
  leggermente la macchia. □ She rubbed her
  eyes. Si sfregò gli occhi.
to **rub out** VERB
  cancellare [68]
rubber NOUN
1 la gomma *fem*
  □ rubber soles suole di gomma
2 la gomma da cancellare *fem* (eraser)
  □ You'll need a pencil and a rubber. Occorre
  una matita e una gomma da cancellare.
  ■ **a rubber band** un elastico
rubber plant NOUN
  il ficus *masc* (PL i ficus)
rubbish NOUN
  ▷ *see also* **rubbish** ADJECTIVE

1 le immondizie *fem pl*
  □ The rubbish is collected on Mondays. Le
  immondizie vengono portate via di lunedì.
  □ He threw the bottle in the rubbish. Ha
  buttato la bottiglia nelle immondizie.
  ■ **the rubbish bin** la pattumiera
2 le porcherie *fem pl*
  □ They eat a lot of rubbish. Mangiano molte
  porcherie.
3 le sciocchezze *fem pl*
  □ Don't talk rubbish! Non dire sciocchezze!
  □ That's a load of rubbish! Tutte sciocchezze!
rubbish ADJECTIVE
  ▷ *see also* **rubbish** NOUN
  ■ **They're a rubbish team!** È una squadra che
  non vale niente!
rubbish dump NOUN
  la discarica *fem* (PL le discariche)
rucksack NOUN
  lo zaino *masc*
rude ADJECTIVE
1 maleducato (FEM maleducata)

    LANGUAGE TIP Word for word, this means
    'badly brought up'.

  □ It's rude to interrupt. È maleducato
  interrompere. □ He was very rude to me. È
  stato molto maleducato nei miei confronti.
2 volgare (FEM volgare)
  □ a rude joke una barzelletta sporca
  ■ **a rude word** una parolaccia
rug NOUN
1 il tappeto *masc* (carpet)
2 la coperta *fem* (blanket)
rugby NOUN
  il rugby *masc*
ruin NOUN
  ▷ *see also* **ruin** VERB
  la rovina *fem*
  □ the ruins of the castle le rovine del castello
to **ruin** VERB
  ▷ *see also* **ruin** NOUN
  rovinare [68]
rule NOUN
  ▷ *see also* **rule** VERB
  la regola *fem*
  ■ **as a rule** di regola
  ■ **It's against the rules.** È contro il
  regolamento.
to **rule** VERB
  ▷ *see also* **rule** NOUN
  governare [68]
  □ He has ruled the country since 1996.
  Governa il paese dal 1996.
to **rule out** VERB
  escludere [3]
ruler NOUN
  il righello *masc*
rum NOUN
  il rum *masc*

rumour (us **rumor**) NOUN
■ **There's a rumour that...** Corre voce che...
▌ LANGUAGE TIP Be careful not to translate **rumour** by **rumore**.

rump steak NOUN
la bistecca di girello *fem*

run NOUN
▷ *see also* **run** VERB
1 la corsa *fem*
■ **to go for a run** andare [6ᴱ] a correre □ I go for a run every morning. Vado a correre ogni mattina.
■ **to be on the run** essere [47ᴱ] latitante
□ The criminals are still on the run. I criminali sono ancora latitanti.
2 il punto *masc (in cricket)*
3 la pista *fem (ski run)*
■ **in the long run** alla lunga

to **run** VERB
▷ *see also* **run** NOUN
1 correre [26]
□ He was running towards her. Correva verso di lei. □ I ran five kilometres. Ho corso cinque chilometri.
■ **to run a marathon** partecipare [68] ad una maratona
2 dirigere [36]
□ He runs a large company. Dirige una grossa società.
3 organizzare [68]
□ They run music courses in the holidays. Organizzano corsi di musica durante le vacanze.
4 portare [68] *(in car)*
□ I can run you to the station. Ti porto io alla stazione.
■ **to leave the tap running** lasciare [13] il rubinetto aperto
■ **to run a bath** preparare [68] il bagno

to **run away** VERB
scappare [68ᴱ]
□ They ran away before the police came. Sono scappati prima che arrivasse la polizia.

to **run out** VERB
finire [51ᴱ]
□ The supplies have run out. Le provviste sono finite.
■ **to run out of** rimanere [88ᴱ] senza □ We ran out of money. Siamo rimasti senza soldi.

to **run over** VERB
investire [41]
■ **to get run over** essere [47ᴱ] investito

rung VERB ▷ *see* **ring**

runner NOUN
il corridore *masc*

runner beans NOUN PL
i fagiolini *masc pl*

runner-up NOUN
il secondo arrivato *masc*
la seconda arrivata *fem*

running NOUN
1 la corsa *fem (sport)*
□ running shoes scarpe da corsa
2 la gestione *fem (management)*
□ the running of the business la gestione della ditta
■ **running costs** costi d'esercizio *masc pl*
3 l' organizzazione *fem*
□ They're involved in the running of the competition. Partecipano all'organizzazione della gara.
■ **to be out of the running** non essere [47ᴱ] più in lizza

run-up NOUN
■ **in the run-up to Christmas** nel periodo che precede Natale

runway NOUN
la pista *fem*

rural ADJECTIVE
rurale (FEM rurale)

to **rush** VERB
▷ *see also* **rush** NOUN
1 affrettarsi [56ᴱ]
□ There's no need to rush. Non c'è bisogno di affrettarsi.
2 precipitarsi [56ᴱ]
□ Everyone rushed outside. Tutti si precipitarono fuori.

rush NOUN
▷ *see also* **rush** VERB
la fretta *fem*
□ There's no rush. Non c'è fretta.
■ **in a rush** in fretta
■ **to be in a rush** avere [12] fretta

rush hour NOUN
l' ora di punta *fem*

rusk NOUN
la fetta biscottata *fem*

Russia NOUN
la Russia *fem*

Russian NOUN
▷ *see also* **Russian** ADJECTIVE
1 il russo *masc*
la russa *fem (person)*
■ **the Russians** i russi
2 il russo *masc (language)*

Russian ADJECTIVE
▷ *see also* **Russian** NOUN
russo (FEM russa)

rust NOUN
la ruggine *fem*

rusty ADJECTIVE
arrugginito (FEM arrugginita)

ruthless ADJECTIVE
spietato (FEM spietata)

rye NOUN
la segale *fem*
■ **rye bread** il pane di segale

Ss

Sabbath NOUN
1 il sabato *masc (Jewish)*
2 la domenica *fem (Christian)*

sack NOUN
  ▷ *see also* **sack** VERB
  il sacco *masc (PL i sacchi)*
  □ a sack of potatoes un sacco di patate
  ■ **to get the sack** essere [47ᴱ] licenziato

to sack VERB
  ▷ *see also* **sack** NOUN
  licenziare [17]

sacred ADJECTIVE
  sacro *(FEM sacra)*

sacrifice NOUN
  il sacrificio *masc*

sad ADJECTIVE
  triste *(FEM triste)*

saddle NOUN
  la sella *fem*

saddlebag NOUN
  la bisaccia *fem (PL le bisacce)*

sadly ADVERB
1 tristemente
  □ 'She's gone,' he said sadly. 'Se n'è andata,'
  disse tristemente.
2 sfortunatamente
  □ Sadly, it was too late. Sfortunatamente era
  troppo tardi.

safe NOUN
  ▷ *see also* **safe** ADJECTIVE
  la cassaforte *fem (PL le casseforti)*

safe ADJECTIVE
  ▷ *see also* **safe** NOUN
1 sicuro *(FEM sicura)*
  □ This car isn't safe. Questa macchina non è
  sicura.
  ■ **Don't worry, it's perfectly safe.** Non
  preoccuparti, non c'è alcun pericolo.
  ■ **safe to drink** potabile □ Is the water safe to
  drink? È potabile l'acqua?
2 al sicuro
  □ You're safe now. Ora sei al sicuro.
  ■ **to feel safe** sentirsi [41ᴱ] al sicuro

safety NOUN
  la sicurezza *fem*
  ■ **safety belt** cintura di sicurezza
  ■ **a safety pin** una spilla da balia

Sagittarius NOUN
  il Sagittario *masc*
  □ I'm Sagittarius. Sono del Sagittario.

Sahara NOUN
  ■ **the Sahara desert** il Deserto del Sahara

said VERB ▷ *see* **say**

sail NOUN
  ▷ *see also* **sail** VERB
  la vela *fem*

to sail VERB
  ▷ *see also* **sail** NOUN
  salpare [68ᴱ]
  □ The boat sails at eight o'clock. Il battello
  salpa alle otto.
  ■ **to sail round the world** fare [49] il giro del
  mondo a vela

sailing NOUN
  la vela *fem (sport)*
  ■ **to go sailing** fare [49] vela
  ■ **a sailing ship** un veliero

sailor NOUN
  il marinaio *masc*

saint NOUN
  il santo *masc*
  la santa *fem*

sake NOUN
  ■ **for the sake of the children** per il bene dei
  bambini
  ■ **for the sake of argument** a titolo d'esempio
  ■ **For goodness sake!** Per amor del cielo!

salad NOUN
  l' insalata *fem*
  □ green salad insalata verde
  ■ **salad dressing** il condimento

salami NOUN SING
  il salame *masc*

salary NOUN
  lo stipendio *masc*

sale NOUN
1 la vendita *fem*
  □ the sale of the company la vendita della
  ditta □ on sale in vendita
  ■ **for sale** in vendita □ The house is for sale.
  La casa è in vendita.
  ■ **'for sale'** 'vendesi'
2 i saldi *masc pl*
  □ There's a sale on at Harrods. Da Harrods ci
  sono i saldi.

sales assistant NOUN
  il commesso *masc*
  la commessa *fem*
sales clerk NOUN (US)
  il commesso *masc*
  la commessa *fem*
salesman NOUN
1 il rappresentante di commercio *masc (sales rep)*
2 il commesso *masc (assistant)*
  ■ **a car salesman** un rivenditore di auto
sales rep NOUN
  il/la rappresentante di commercio *masc/fem*
saleswoman NOUN
1 la rappresentante di commercio *fem (sales rep)*
2 la commessa *fem (assistant)*
salmon NOUN
  il salmone *masc*
salon NOUN
  il salone *masc*
  □ hair salon il salone da parrucchiere
  ■ **beauty salon** istituto di bellezza
saloon car NOUN
  la berlina *fem*
salt NOUN
  il sale *masc*
salty ADJECTIVE
  salato (FEM salata)
to **salute** VERB
  fare [49] il saluto militare *(soldier)*
same ADJECTIVE
1 stesso (FEM stessa)
  □ the same model lo stesso modello □ It's not the same. Non è lo stesso. □ It's all the same to me. Per me fa lo stesso.
2 uguale (FEM uguale)
  □ They're exactly the same. Sono esattamente uguali.
sample NOUN
  il campione *masc*
  □ a free sample of perfume un campione gratuito di profumo
sand NOUN
  la sabbia *fem*
  □ sand dune duna di sabbia
sandal NOUN
  il sandalo *masc*
sandwich NOUN
  il sandwich *masc* (PL i sandwich)
  ■ **sandwich course** corso di formazione professionale
sang VERB ▷ *see* sing
sanitary napkin NOUN (US)
  l' assorbente igienico *masc* (PL gli assorbenti igienici)
sanitary towel NOUN
  l' assorbente igienico *masc* (PL gli assorbenti igienici)

sank VERB ▷ *see* sink
Santa Claus NOUN
  Babbo Natale
sarcastic ADJECTIVE
  sarcastico (FEM sarcastica, MASC PL sarcastici, FEM PL sarcastiche)
Sardinia NOUN
  la Sardegna *fem*
sat VERB ▷ *see* sit
satchel NOUN
  la cartella *fem*
satellite NOUN
  il satellite *masc*
  □ satellite television televisione via satellite
  ■ **a satellite dish** un'antenna parabolica
satisfactory ADJECTIVE
  soddisfacente (FEM soddisfacente)
satisfied ADJECTIVE
  soddisfatto (FEM soddisfatta)
satnav NOUN
  il navigatore satellitare *masc*
  □ Have you got satnav? Hai il navigatore satellitare?
Saturday NOUN
  il sabato *masc*
  ■ **on Saturday** sabato □ I saw her on Saturday. L'ho vista sabato.
  ■ **on Saturdays** di sabato □ I go swimming on Saturdays. Vado in piscina di sabato.
sauce NOUN
  la salsa *fem*
saucepan NOUN
  la pentola *fem*
saucer NOUN
  il piattino *masc*

    LANGUAGE TIP Word for word, this means 'little plate'.

Saudi Arabia NOUN
  l' Arabia Saudita *fem*
sauna NOUN
  la sauna *fem*
sausage NOUN
  la salsiccia *fem* (PL le salsicce)
  ■ **a sausage roll** un involtino di pasta sfoglia con salsiccia
to **save** VERB
1 mettere [59] da parte
  □ I've saved fifty pounds already. Ho già messo da parte cinquanta sterline.
2 risparmiare [17]
  □ I saved money by staying in hostels. Ho risparmiato alloggiando negli ostelli. □ It saved us time. Ci ha fatto risparmiare tempo.
3 salvare [68]
  □ She saved his life. Gli ha salvato la vita.
4 memorizzare [68]
  □ I saved the file onto a diskette. Ho memorizzato il file su un dischetto.

S

save up – school

to **save up** VERB
risparmiare [17]
□ I'm saving up for a bike. Sto risparmiando per comprare una bici.

savings NOUN PL
i risparmi *masc pl*
□ She spent all her savings on a computer. Ha speso tutti i risparmi per comprare un computer.

savoury (US **savory**) ADJECTIVE
salato (FEM salata)

> **LANGUAGE TIP** Word for word, this means 'salted'.

□ Is it sweet or savoury? È dolce o salato?

saw VERB ▷ see **see**

saw NOUN
la sega *fem* (PL le seghe)

sax NOUN
il sax *masc* (PL i sax)

saxophone NOUN
il sassofono *masc*

to **say** VERB
dire [35]
□ What did he say? Cos'ha detto? □ David said he'd come. David ha detto che sarebbe venuto.
■ **to say again** ripetere [1] □ Could you say that again? Potresti ripetere?
■ **It goes without saying that...** Va da sé che...

saying NOUN
il detto *masc*

scale NOUN
1 la scala *fem*
□ a large-scale map una carta geografica dettagliata
2 la portata *fem*
□ the scale of the problem la portata del problema

scales NOUN PL
la bilancia *fem sing*
■ **bathroom scales** la bilancia pesapersone *sing*

scampi NOUN PL
gli scampi *masc pl*

scandal NOUN
lo scandalo *masc*
□ It caused a scandal. Ha fatto scandalo.

Scandinavia NOUN
la Scandinavia *fem*

Scandinavian ADJECTIVE
scandinavo (FEM scandinava)

scar NOUN
la cicatrice *fem*

scarce ADJECTIVE
scarso (FEM scarsa)

scarcely ADVERB
appena
□ I scarcely knew him. Lo conoscevo appena.

scare NOUN
▷ see also **scare** VERB
lo spavento *masc*
□ We had a scare. Ci siamo presi uno spavento.
■ **a bomb scare** un allarme per sospetta presenza di una bomba

to **scare** VERB
▷ see also **scare** NOUN
spaventare [68]
□ You scared me! Mi hai spaventato!

scarecrow NOUN
lo spaventapasseri *masc* (PL gli spaventapasseri)

scared ADJECTIVE
■ **to be scared** aver [12] paura □ Are you scared of him? Hai paura di lui?
■ **to be scared stiff** essere [47ᴱ] mezzo morto di paura

scarf NOUN
1 la sciarpa *fem (woollen)*
2 il foulard *masc* (PL i foulard) *(silk)*

scary ADJECTIVE
■ **to be scary** fare [49] paura □ It was really scary. Faceva veramente paura.
■ **a scary film** un film del brivido

scene NOUN
la scena *fem*
□ It was an amazing scene. È stata una scena incredibile.
■ **the scene of the crime** il luogo del delitto
■ **to make a scene** fare [49] una scenata

scenery NOUN
il paesaggio *masc*

scent NOUN
il profumo *masc*

schedule NOUN
▷ see also **schedule** VERB
il programma *masc* (PL i programmi)
□ a busy schedule un programma fitto d'impegni
■ **on schedule** in orario
■ **to be behind schedule** essere [47ᴱ] in ritardo sulla tabella di marcia

to **schedule** VERB
▷ see also **schedule** NOUN
fissare [68]
□ The meeting is scheduled for Monday. La riunione è fissata per lunedì.

scheduled flight NOUN
il volo di linea *masc*

scheme NOUN
il progetto *masc*
□ a road-widening scheme un progetto di ampliamento della strada

scholarship NOUN
la borsa di studio *fem*

school NOUN
la scuola *fem*

schoolbook NOUN
il libro scolastico *masc* (PL i libri scolastici)

schoolboy NOUN
lo scolaro *masc*

schoolchildren NOUN
gli scolari *masc/fem pl*

schoolgirl NOUN
la scolara *fem*

science NOUN
la scienza *fem*

science fiction NOUN
la fantascienza *fem*

scientific ADJECTIVE
scientifico (FEM scientifica, MASC PL scientifici, FEM PL scientifiche)

scientist NOUN
lo scienziato *masc*
la scienziata *fem*

scissors NOUN PL
le forbici *fem pl*

to **scoff** VERB
ridere [84]
□ My friends scoffed at the idea. I miei amici hanno riso dell'idea.

scone NOUN
la focaccina da tè *fem*

scooter NOUN
1 lo scooter *masc* (PL gli scooter)
□ He was riding a scooter. Era in sella ad uno scooter.
2 il monopattino *masc* (for children)

score NOUN
▷ see also **score** VERB
il punteggio *masc*
□ The score was three nil. Il punteggio era tre a zero.
■ **scores of** molti □ scores of times molte volte

to **score** VERB
▷ see also **score** NOUN
1 segnare [14]
□ He scored a goal. Ha segnato una rete.
2 tenere [113] il punteggio
□ Who's going to score? Chi tiene il punteggio?
■ **to score six out of ten** totalizzare [68] un punteggio di sei su dieci

Scorpio NOUN
lo Scorpione *masc*
□ I'm Scorpio. Sono dello Scorpione.

Scot NOUN
lo/la scozzese *masc/fem*

Scotch tape® NOUN (US)
lo scotch® *masc*

Scotland NOUN
la Scozia *fem*

Scots ADJECTIVE
scozzese (FEM scozzese)
□ a Scots accent un accento scozzese

Scotsman NOUN
lo scozzese *masc*

Scotswoman NOUN
la scozzese *fem*

Scottish ADJECTIVE
scozzese (FEM scozzese)
■ **the Scottish Parliament** il Parlamento scozzese

scout NOUN
il boy-scout *masc* (PL i boy-scout)

scrambled eggs NOUN PL
le uova strapazzate *fem pl*

scrap NOUN
▷ see also **scrap** VERB
il pezzo *masc*
□ a scrap of paper un pezzo di carta
■ **There wasn't a scrap of evidence.** Non c'era la benché minima prova.
■ **to sell for scrap** vendere [27] come ferrovecchio
■ **scrap iron** ferraglia
■ **to get into a scrap** azzuffarsi [56E] □ He got into a scrap with a bigger boy. Si è azzuffato con un ragazzo più grande.

to **scrap** VERB
▷ see also **scrap** NOUN
scartare [68]
□ In the end the plan was scrapped. Alla fine il progetto venne scartato.

scrapbook NOUN
l' album *masc* (PL gli album)

to **scratch** VERB
▷ see also **scratch** NOUN
1 grattarsi [56E]
□ He scratched his head. Si è grattato la testa.
2 graffiare [17]
□ The cat scratched me. Il gatto mi ha graffiato.

scratch NOUN
▷ see also **scratch** VERB
il graffio *masc* (on skin)
■ **to start from scratch** cominciare [13] da zero
■ **a scratch card** un gratta e vinci®

scream NOUN
▷ see also **scream** VERB
il grido *masc* (FEM PL le grida)

to **scream** VERB
▷ see also **scream** NOUN
gridare [68]

screen NOUN
lo schermo *masc*

screen saver NOUN
lo screensaver *masc* (PL gli screensaver)

screw NOUN
la vite *fem*

screwdriver NOUN
il cacciavite *masc*

S

535

scribble - section

to **scribble** VERB
scribacchiare [17]

to **scrub** VERB
sfregare [76]

sculpture NOUN
la scultura *fem*

sea NOUN
il mare *masc*

seafood NOUN
i frutti di mare *masc pl*

> **LANGUAGE TIP** Word for word, this means 'fruits of the sea'.

seagull NOUN
il gabbiano *masc*

seal NOUN
▷ *see also* **seal** VERB
1 la foca *fem* (PL le foche) (*animal*)
2 il sigillo *masc* (*on envelope*)

to **seal** VERB
▷ *see also* **seal** NOUN
sigillare [68]

seaman NOUN
il marinaio *masc*

to **search** VERB
▷ *see also* **search** NOUN
1 perquisire [51]
   □ The police searched him for drugs. La polizia l'ha perquisito alla ricerca di droga.
2 perlustrare [68]
   □ They searched the woods for the little girl. Hanno perlustrato i boschi alla ricerca della bambina.
   ■ **to search for** cercare [18] □ They're searching for the missing climbers. Stanno cercando gli alpinisti dispersi.

search NOUN
▷ *see also* **search** VERB
la ricerca *fem* (PL le ricerche)
   □ The search was abandoned. La ricerca fu abbandonata.
   ■ **She went in search of Paul.** È andata a cercare Paul.

search engine NOUN
il motore di ricerca *masc*

search party NOUN
la squadra di ricerca *fem*

seashore NOUN
la riva del mare *fem*

seasick ADJECTIVE
   ■ **to be seasick** avere [12] il mal di mare

seaside NOUN
il mare *masc*
   □ at the seaside al mare
   ■ **seaside resort** la località balneare

season NOUN
▷ *see also* **season** VERB
la stagione *fem*
   □ out of season fuori stagione

   ■ **during the holiday season** nel periodo delle vacanze
   ■ **a season ticket** una tessera d'abbonamento

to **season** VERB
▷ *see also* **season** NOUN
condire [51]
   □ Season with salt and pepper. Condite con sale e pepe.

seat NOUN
1 il sedile *masc*
   □ on the back seat of the car sul sedile posteriore della macchina
   ■ **Please take a seat.** Si accomodi.
2 il posto *masc*
   □ Are there any seats left? Ci sono ancora posti?
3 il seggio *masc*
   □ The party won thirty seats. Il partito ha ottenuto trenta seggi.

seat belt NOUN
la cintura di sicurezza *fem*

seaweed NOUN
le alghe *fem pl*

second ADJECTIVE, NOUN
il secondo *masc*
la seconda *fem*
   ■ **to come second** arrivare [68ᴱ] secondo
   ■ **to travel second class** viaggiare [58] in seconda classe
   ■ **the second of March** il due marzo
   ■ **to have second thoughts** ripensarci [68]

secondary school NOUN
la scuola secondaria *fem*

second-class ADJECTIVE, ADVERB
   ■ **second-class citizen** cittadino di serie B
   ■ **to send a letter second-class** mandare [68] una lettera per posta ordinaria

secondhand ADJECTIVE
di seconda mano

secondly ADVERB
   ■ **firstly..., secondly...** in primo luogo..., in secondo luogo...

secret ADJECTIVE
▷ *see also* **secret** NOUN
segreto (FEM segreta)
   □ a secret mission una missione segreta

secret NOUN
▷ *see also* **secret** ADJECTIVE
il segreto *masc*
   □ Can you keep a secret? Sai tenere un segreto?
   ■ **in secret** in segreto

secretary NOUN
la segretaria *fem*

secretly ADVERB
segretamente

section NOUN
la sezione *fem*

security NOUN
la sicurezza _fem_
□ They have improved airport security. Hanno migliorato la sicurezza dell'aeroporto.
■ **to have no job security** non avere [12] la garanzia del posto di lavoro
■ **a security guard** una guardia giurata

sedan NOUN (US)
la berlina _fem_

to **see** VERB
vedere [119]
□ I can't see anything. Non vedo niente.
□ I saw him yesterday. L'ho visto ieri. □ Have you seen that film? Hai visto quel film?
■ **See you!** Ci vediamo!
■ **See you soon!** A presto!

to **see to** VERB
occuparsi [56ᴱ] di
□ The shower isn't working. Can you see to it please? La doccia non funziona. Se ne può occupare, per favore?

seed NOUN
il seme _masc_
□ sunflower seeds semi di girasole

to **seek** VERB
cercare [18]
□ people seeking work le persone che cercano lavoro □ They are seeking a solution. Stanno cercando una soluzione. □ He sought to calm them down. Ha cercato di tranquillizzarli.
■ **to seek help** chiedere [19] aiuto

to **seem** VERB
sembrare [68ᴱ]
□ That seems like a good idea. Mi sembra una buona idea.
■ **It seems that...** Pare che... □ It seems she's getting married. Pare che si sposi.

seen VERB ▷ see **see**

seesaw NOUN
l' altalena a bilico _masc_

see-through ADJECTIVE
trasparente (FEM trasparente)

seldom ADVERB
raramente

to **select** VERB
selezionare [68]

selection NOUN
la selezione _fem_

self-assured ADJECTIVE
sicuro di sé (FEM sicura di sé)

self-catering ADJECTIVE
■ **self-catering apartment** appartamento con cucina

self-centred (US **self-centered**) ADJECTIVE
egocentrico (FEM egocentrica, MASC PL egocentrici, FEM PL egocentriche)

self-confidence NOUN
la fiducia in se stesso _fem_

self-conscious ADJECTIVE
1 impacciato (FEM impacciata)
□ She was very self-conscious at first. All'inizio era molto impacciata.
2 complessato (FEM complessata)
□ She was self-conscious about her height. Era complessata per la statura.

self-contained ADJECTIVE
indipendente (FEM indipendente)

self-control NOUN
l' autocontrollo _masc_

self-defence (US **self-defense**) NOUN
la difesa personale _fem_
□ self-defence classes corso di difesa personale
■ **She killed him in self-defence.** L'ha ucciso per legittima difesa.

self-discipline NOUN
l' autodisciplina _fem_

self-employed ADJECTIVE
■ **to be self-employed** lavorare [68] in proprio
■ **the self-employed** i lavoratori autonomi

selfish ADJECTIVE
egoista (FEM egoista)

self-respect NOUN
la dignità _fem_

self-service ADJECTIVE
self-service (FEM+PL self-service)

to **sell** VERB
vendere [27]
□ They're selling the house. Stanno vendendo la casa. □ He sold his car to Tom. Ha venduto la macchina a Tom.
■ **Do you sell stamps?** Avete francobolli?

to **sell off** VERB
svendere [27]

to **sell out** VERB
andare [6ᴱ] esaurito
□ The tickets sold out in three hours. I biglietti sono andati esauriti in tre ore.

sell-by date NOUN
la data di scadenza _fem_

Sellotape® NOUN
lo scotch® _masc_

semi NOUN
la villa bifamiliare _fem_

semicircle NOUN
il semicerchio _masc_

semicolon NOUN
il punto e virgola _masc_

semi-final NOUN
la semifinale _fem_

semi-skimmed milk NOUN
il latte parzialmente scremato _masc_

to **send** VERB
1 spedire [51]
□ Have you sent the letter? Hai spedito la lettera?

send back - sequence

2 mandare[68]
□ She sent me a birthday card. Mi ha mandato un biglietto d'auguri.

to **send back** VERB
rispedire[51]

to **send off** VERB
1 spedire[51]
□ We sent off your order. Abbiamo spedito il suo ordine.
2 espellere[44] *(player)*
□ He was sent off. L'hanno espulso.

to **send off for** VERB
ordinare[68] per posta
■ **I'll send off for a brochure.** Mi farò spedire un depliant.

to **send out** VERB
inviare[55]
□ She sent out a hundred invitations. Ha inviato cento inviti.
■ **to send out for** farsi[49ᴱ] portare □ Let's send out for a pizza. Facciamoci portare una pizza.

sender NOUN
il/la mittente *masc/fem*

senior ADJECTIVE, NOUN
di grado superiore
□ senior management i dirigenti di grado superiore
■ **She's five years my senior.** Ha cinque anni più di me.
■ **senior pupils** gli studenti delle classi superiori

senior citizen NOUN
il pensionato *masc*
la pensionata *fem*

senior school NOUN
il liceo *masc*

sensational ADJECTIVE
sensazionale (FEM sensazionale)

sense NOUN
1 il senso *masc*
□ It makes sense. Ha senso. □ It doesn't make sense. Non ha senso. □ the five senses i cinque sensi
■ **sense of humour** senso dell'umorismo
■ **a keen sense of smell** un olfatto finissimo
2 il buonsenso *masc*
□ Have a bit of sense! Un po' di buonsenso, via!

senseless ADJECTIVE
1 insensato (FEM insensata)
□ acts of senseless violence atti di violenza insensata
2 privo di sensi (FEM priva di sensi)
□ She fell senseless to the ground. Cadde a terra priva di sensi.

sensible ADJECTIVE
ragionevole (FEM ragionevole)
□ Be sensible! Sii ragionevole! □ It would

be sensible to check first. Sarebbe meglio controllare prima.

▎**LANGUAGE TIP** Be careful not to translate **sensible** by **sensibile**.

sensitive ADJECTIVE
sensibile (FEM sensibile)

sensuous ADJECTIVE
sensuale (FEM sensuale)

sent VERB ▷ *see* **send**

sentence NOUN
▷ *see also* **sentence** VERB
1 la frase *fem*
□ He wrote a sentence. Ha scritto una frase.
2 la condanna *fem*
□ the death sentence la condanna a morte
□ He served a long sentence. Ha scontato una lunga condanna.
■ **He got a life sentence.** Ha avuto l'ergastolo.

to **sentence** VERB
▷ *see also* **sentence** NOUN
■ **to sentence somebody to life imprisonment** condannare[68] qualcuno all'ergastolo
■ **to sentence somebody to death** condannare[68] a morte qualcuno

sentimental ADJECTIVE
sentimentale (FEM sentimentale)

separate ADJECTIVE
▷ *see also* **separate** VERB
1 separato (FEM separata)
□ They have separate rooms. Hanno camere separate.
2 diverso (FEM diversa)
□ on separate occasions in diverse occasioni
3 altro (FEM altra)
□ I wrote it on a separate sheet. L'ho scritto su un altro foglio di carta.

to **separate** VERB
▷ *see also* **separate** ADJECTIVE
1 separare[68]
□ The police tried to separate the two groups. La polizia ha cercato di separare i due gruppi.
2 separarsi[56ᴱ]
□ They separated seven years ago. Si sono separati sette anni fa.

separately ADVERB
separatamente

separation NOUN
la separazione *fem*

September NOUN
settembre
□ in September in settembre

sequel NOUN
il seguito *masc*

sequence NOUN
1 la serie *fem*
□ a sequence of events una serie di avvenimenti

2 l' ordine *masc*
- **in sequence** in ordine
3 la sequenza *fem (in film)*

sergeant NOUN
il sergente *masc*

serial NOUN
il serial *masc* (PL i serial)

series NOUN
la serie *fem* (PL le serie)

serious ADJECTIVE
1 serio (FEM seria)
□ You're looking very serious. Hai un'aria molto seria.
- **Are you serious?** Parli sul serio?
2 grave (FEM grave)
□ a serious illness una grave malattia

seriously ADVERB
seriamente
□ We'll have to think about it seriously. Dovremo pensarci seriamente.
- **No, but seriously...** No, scherzi a parte...
- **to take somebody seriously** prendere [77] sul serio qualcuno
- **seriously injured** gravemente ferito

sermon NOUN
il sermone *masc*

servant NOUN
il domestico *masc* (PL i domestici)
la domestica *fem* (PL le domestiche)

to **serve** VERB
▷ *see also* **serve** NOUN
1 servire [41]
□ Dinner is served. La cena è servita.
- **It's Murray's turn to serve.** È Murray al servizio.
2 scontare [68] *(sentence)*
- **to serve time** essere [47ᴱ] in prigione
- **It serves you right.** Ben ti sta.

serve NOUN
▷ *see also* **serve** VERB
il servizio *masc (in tennis)*

server NOUN
il server *masc* (PL i server)

to **service** VERB
▷ *see also* **service** NOUN
revisionare [68] *(car)*

service NOUN
▷ *see also* **service** VERB
1 il servizio *masc*
□ Service is included. Il servizio è compreso.
□ the postal service il servizio postale
2 la revisione *fem (of car)*
3 la funzione *fem (religious)*
- **the armed services** le forze armate

service area NOUN
l' area di servizio *masc*

service charge NOUN
il servizio *masc*
□ There's no service charge. Il servizio è compreso.

serviceman NOUN
il militare *masc*

service station NOUN
la stazione di servizio *fem*

serviette NOUN
il tovagliolo *masc*

session NOUN
la sessione *fem*

set NOUN
▷ *see also* **set** VERB
1 la serie *fem* (PL le serie)
□ a set of calculations una serie di calcoli
- **a set of keys** una serie completa di chiavi
- **The sofa and chairs are sold only as a set.**
Il divano e le poltrone non si possono vendere separatamente.
- **a chess set** un gioco di scacchi
- **a train set** un trenino elettrico
2 il set *masc* (PL i set)
□ She was leading five-one in the first set. Conduceva il primo set cinque a uno.

to **set** VERB
▷ *see also* **set** NOUN
1 mettere [59]
□ I set the alarm for seven o'clock. Ho messo la sveglia alle sette.
2 stabilire [51]
□ The world record was set last year. Il record mondiale è stato stabilito l'anno scorso.
3 tramontare [68]
□ The sun was setting. Il sole stava tramontando.
- **to be set** *(novel, film)* essere [47ᴱ] ambientato □ The film is set in Morocco. Il film è ambientato in Marocco.
- **to set sail** salpare [68ᴱ]
- **to set the table** apparecchiare [17] la tavola

to **set off** VERB
partire [41ᴱ]
□ We set off after breakfast. Siamo partiti dopo colazione.

to **set out** VERB
partire [41ᴱ]
□ We set out for London at nine o'clock. Siamo partiti per Londra alle nove.

settee NOUN
il divano *masc*

settings NOUN PL
le impostazioni *fem pl*

to **settle** VERB
1 risolvere [89]
□ That should settle the problem. Questo dovrebbe risolvere il problema.
2 saldare [68]
□ I'll settle the bill tomorrow. Salderò il conto domani.

to **settle down** VERB
sistemarsi [56ᴱ]

□ I want to settle down and start a family. Voglio sistemarmi e metter su famiglia.
□ Things will settle down. Le cose si sistemeranno.

to **settle in** VERB
ambientarsi [56ᴱ]

to **settle on** VERB
decidere [31] per

seven NUMBER
sette
□ She's seven. Ha sette anni.

seventeen NUMBER
diciassette
□ He's seventeen. Ha diciassette anni.

seventeenth ADJECTIVE
diciassettesimo (FEM diciassettesima)
□ the seventeenth floor il diciassettesimo piano
■ **the seventeenth of August** il diciassette agosto

seventh ADJECTIVE
settimo (FEM settima)
□ the seventh floor il settimo piano
■ **the seventh of August** il sette agosto

seventy NUMBER
settanta

several ADJECTIVE, PRONOUN
diversi *masc*
diverse *fem*
□ several times diverse volte

to **sew** VERB
cucire [41]
□ She was sewing. Cuciva. □ It was sewn by hand. Era cucito a mano.

to **sew up** VERB
rammendare [68]

sewing NOUN
■ **I like sewing.** Mi piace cucire.
■ **a sewing machine** una macchina da cucire

sewn VERB ▷ *see* sew

sex NOUN
il sesso *masc*
□ the opposite sex il sesso opposto
■ **to have sex with somebody** avere [12] rapporti sessuali con qualcuno
■ **sex education** educazione sessuale

sexism NOUN
il sessismo *masc*

sexist ADJECTIVE
sessista (FEM sessista)

sexual ADJECTIVE
sessuale (FEM sessuale)
□ sexual discrimination la discriminazione sessuale □ sexual harassment molestie sessuali

sexuality NOUN
la sessualità *fem*

sexy ADJECTIVE
sexy (FEM+PL sexy)

shabby ADJECTIVE
trasandato (FEM trasandata)

shade NOUN
1 l' ombra *fem*
□ It was thirty five degrees in the shade. C'erano trentacinque gradi all'ombra.
2 la tonalità *fem* (PL le tonalità)
□ a beautiful shade of blue una bella tonalità d'azzurro

shadow NOUN
l' ombra *fem*
■ **the shadow cabinet** il governo ombra

to **shake** VERB
1 scuotere [100]
□ Donald shook his head. Donald scosse il capo.
2 tremare [68]
□ He was shaking with cold. Tremava di freddo.
■ **to shake hands with somebody** stringere [109] la mano a qualcuno □ They shook hands. Si strinsero la mano.

shaken ADJECTIVE
scosso (FEM scossa)
□ I was feeling a bit shaken. Ero un po' scosso.

shaky ADJECTIVE
1 incerto (FEM incerta)
□ The team got off to a shaky start. La partita ha avuto un avvio incerto per la squadra.
2 tremante (FEM tremante)
□ He answered in a shaky voice. Ha risposto con voce tremante.
■ **to feel shaky** sentirsi [41ᴱ] debole

shall VERB
> LANGUAGE TIP 'shall I' and 'shall we' are translated by the present tense.
□ Shall I shut the window? Chiudo la finestra?
□ Shall we ask him to come with us? Gli chiediamo di venire con noi?
> LANGUAGE TIP When 'shall' means 'will', it is translated by the future tense.
□ I shall know more next week. Ne saprò qualcosa di più la prossima settimana.

shallow ADJECTIVE
poco profondo (FEM poca profonda)

shambles NOUN SING
il disastro *masc*
□ It's a complete shambles. È un disastro totale.

shame NOUN
la vergogna *fem*
□ I'd die of shame! Morirei di vergogna!
■ **What a shame!** Che peccato!
■ **It's a shame that...** È un peccato che...

shampoo NOUN
lo shampoo *masc* (PL gli shampoo)

shandy NOUN
la birra con gazzosa *fem*

shan't = shall not

shape NOUN
la forma *fem*
□ a strange shape una strana forma
■ **to be in good shape** *(person)* essere [47ᴱ] in forma

share NOUN
▷ *see also* **share** VERB
1 la parte *fem*
□ a fair share una parte equa
2 l' azione *fem*
□ They've got shares in IBM. Hanno delle azioni della IBM.
3 la quota *fem*
□ He refused to pay his share of the bill. Ha rifiutato di pagare la sua quota del conto.

to **share** VERB
▷ *see also* **share** NOUN
dividere [40]
□ I share the room with Helen. Divido la stanza con Helen.

to **share out** VERB
distribuire [51]
□ They shared the sweets out among the children. Hanno distribuito i dolci ai bambini.

shark NOUN
lo squalo *masc*

sharp ADJECTIVE
1 affilato (FEM affilata)
□ Be careful, that knife's sharp! Stai attento, quel coltello è affilato!
2 brusco e notevole (FEM brusca e notevole)
□ a sharp rise in prices un brusco e notevole aumento dei prezzi
3 sveglie (FEM sveglia, MASC PL svegli, FEM PL sveglie)
□ She's very sharp. È molto sveglia.
■ **at two o'clock sharp** alle due in punto
■ **a sharp bend** una curva a gomito

to **shave** VERB
▷ *see also* **shave** NOUN
farsi [49ᴱ] la barba

 LANGUAGE TIP Word for word, this means 'to do one's beard'.
□ He's shaving. Si fa la barba.
■ **to shave one's legs** depilarsi [56ᴱ] le gambe

shave NOUN
▷ *see also* **shave** VERB
■ **I need a shave.** Devo farmi la barba.
■ **That was a close shave!** Ce la siamo cavata per un pelo!

shaver NOUN
■ **electric shaver** rasoio elettrico

shaving cream NOUN
la crema da barba *fem*

shaving foam NOUN
la schiuma da barba *fem*

she PRONOUN
lei

□ She was fifteen then. Allora lei aveva quindici anni.
 LANGUAGE TIP 'she' is often not translated.
□ She's very tall. È molto alta.
 LANGUAGE TIP lei is the pronoun used in spoken and informal written Italian. The more formal word for 'she' is ella.

shed NOUN
la rimessa *fem*

she'd = she had, she would

sheep NOUN
la pecora *fem*

sheepdog NOUN
il cane da pastore *masc*

sheer ADJECTIVE
puro (FEM pura)
□ It's sheer greed. È pura avidità.

sheet NOUN
il lenzuolo *masc* (FEM PL le lenzuola)
□ cotton sheets lenzuola di cotone
■ **a sheet of paper** un foglio di carta

shelf NOUN
1 la mensola *fem* (on wall)
2 il ripiano *masc* (in cupboard)

shell NOUN
1 la conchiglia *fem* (on beach, snail)
2 il guscio *masc*
□ an egg shell un guscio d'uovo
3 la granata *fem*
□ an unexploded shell una granata inesplosa

she'll = she will

shellfish NOUN
i frutti di mare *masc pl*

shell suit NOUN
la tuta di acetato *fem*

shelter NOUN
il riparo *masc*
■ **to take shelter** mettersi [59ᴱ] al riparo
■ **a bus shelter** una pensilina d'autobus

shelves NOUN PL ▷ *see* **shelf**

shepherd NOUN
il pastore *masc*
□ a shepherd with his dog un pastore con il suo cane

sheriff NOUN
lo sceriffo *masc*

sherry NOUN
lo sherry *masc* (PL gli sherry)

she's = she is, she has

Shetland Islands NOUN PL
le isole Shetland *fem pl*

shield NOUN
lo scudo *masc*

shift NOUN
▷ *see also* **shift** VERB
il turno *masc*
□ the night shift il turno di notte
■ **to do shift work** fare [49] i turni

S

541

shift – shoplifting

to **shift** VERB
▷ *see also* **shift** NOUN
spostare [68]
□ I couldn't shift the wardrobe on my own. Non riuscivo a spostare l'armadio da solo.
□ Shift yourself! Spostati!

shifty ADJECTIVE
1 losco (FEM losca, MASC PL loschi, FEM PL losche)
□ He looked shifty. Aveva un'aria losca.
2 sfuggente (FEM sfuggente) *(eyes)*

shin NOUN
lo stinco *masc* (PL gli stinchi)

to **shine** VERB
splendere [27]
□ The sun was shining. Splendeva il sole.

shiny ADJECTIVE
lucido (FEM lucida)

ship NOUN
la nave *fem*

shipbuilding NOUN
la costruzione navale *fem*

shipwreck NOUN
il naufragio *masc*

shipwrecked ADJECTIVE
■ **to be shipwrecked** fare [49] naufragio

shipyard NOUN
il cantiere navale *masc*

shirt NOUN
la camicia *fem* (PL le camicie)

to **shiver** VERB
rabbrividire [51E]

shock NOUN
▷ *see also* **shock** VERB
1 lo shock *masc* (PL gli shock)
□ The news came as a shock. La notizia è stata uno shock.
2 la scossa *fem*
□ I got a shock when I touched the switch. Quando ho toccato l'interruttore ho preso la scossa.
■ **an electric shock** una scossa elettrica

to **shock** VERB
▷ *see also* **shock** NOUN
1 scioccare [18]
□ They were shocked by the news. Erano scioccati dalla notizia.
2 scandalizzare [68]
□ After twenty years in the police nothing shocks him. Dopo vent'anni di lavoro in polizia non lo scandalizza più niente.

shocked ADJECTIVE
scioccato (FEM scioccata)

shocking ADJECTIVE
1 scandaloso (FEM scandalosa)
□ It's shocking! È scandaloso!
2 vergognoso (FEM vergognosa)
□ a shocking waste uno spreco vergognoso
3 orribile (FEM orribile)

□ The weather was shocking. Il tempo era orribile.

shoe NOUN
la scarpa *fem*
□ shoe polish lucido per scarpe □ shoe shop negozio di scarpe

shoelace NOUN
il laccio di scarpa *masc*

shone VERB ▷ *see* **shine**

shook VERB ▷ *see* **shake**

to **shoot** VERB
1 colpire [51]
□ He was shot by a sniper. È stato colpito da un cecchino.
■ **to shoot somebody dead** colpire [51] a morte qualcuno
2 fucilare [68]
□ He was shot at dawn. È stato fucilato all'alba.
3 sparare [68]
□ Don't shoot! Non sparare! □ He shot himself with a revolver. Si è sparato con un revolver.
■ **to shoot at somebody** sparare [68] a qualcuno
4 girare [68]
□ The film was shot in Prague. Il film è stato girato a Praga.
5 tirare [68]
■ **to shoot wide** tirare [68] a vuoto
6 sfrecciare [13]
□ A car shot past me. Una macchina mi è sfrecciata accanto.
■ **to shoot an arrow** scoccare [18] una freccia

shooting NOUN
1 gli spari *masc pl*
□ They heard shooting. Hanno sentito degli spari.
■ **a shooting** una sparatoria
2 la caccia *fem*
□ shooting and fishing la caccia e la pesca

shop NOUN
▷ *see also* **shop** VERB
il negozio *masc*
□ a sports shop un negozio di articoli sportivi
■ **the workers on the shop floor** gli operai

to **shop** VERB
▷ *see also* **shop** NOUN
fare [49] shopping
□ They shop in expensive stores. Fanno shopping in negozi costosi.

shop assistant NOUN
il commesso *masc*
la commessa *fem*

shopkeeper NOUN
il/la negoziante *masc/fem*

shoplifting NOUN
il taccheggio *masc*

shopping NOUN
la spesa *fem*
□ Can you get the shopping from the car? Puoi prendere la spesa dalla macchina?
■ **I love shopping.** Adoro fare shopping.
■ **a shopping bag** una borsa per la spesa
■ **a shopping centre** un centro commerciale

shop window NOUN
la vetrina *fem*

shore NOUN
la riva *fem*
□ boats on the shore barche sulla riva
■ **on shore** a terra

short ADJECTIVE
1 corto (FEM corta)
□ a short skirt una gonna corta □ short hair capelli corti
■ **to be short of something** essere [47ᴱ] a corto di qualcosa
2 breve (FEM breve)
□ a short break una breve pausa □ It was a great holiday, but too short. È stata una bella vacanza, ma troppo breve.
3 basso (FEM bassa)
□ She's quite short. È piuttosto bassa.
■ **at short notice** con poco preavviso
■ **in short** per farla breve □ In short, the answer is no. Per farla breve, la risposta è no.

shortage NOUN
la scarsità *fem* (PL le scarsità)

short cut NOUN
la scorciatoia *fem*

shorthand NOUN
la stenografia *fem*

short list NOUN
la rosa dei candidati *fem*

shortly ADVERB
tra poco

shorts NOUN PL
gli shorts *masc pl*

short-sighted ADJECTIVE
miope (FEM miope)

short story NOUN
il racconto *masc*

shot VERB ▷ see shoot

shot NOUN
1 lo sparo *masc*
□ He said he heard a shot. Ha detto di aver sentito uno sparo.
2 la foto *fem* (PL le foto)
□ a shot of Edinburgh castle una foto del castello di Edimburgo
3 l' iniezione *fem*
□ They gave him shots. Gli hanno fatto delle iniezioni.
■ **to have a shot at doing something** provare [68] a fare qualcosa
■ **He had only one shot at goal.** Ha avuto solo una possibilità di segnare.

shotgun NOUN
il fucile da caccia *masc*

should VERB
LANGUAGE TIP 'should' is usually translated by the conditional of **dovere**.
□ You should take more exercise. Dovresti fare più moto. □ He should be there by now. A quest'ora dovrebbe essere arrivato. □ That shouldn't be too hard. Non dovrebbe essere troppo difficile. □ I should have told you before. Avrei dovuto dirtelo prima.
■ **I should go if I were you.** Se fossi in te ci andrei.
■ **I should be so lucky!** Sarebbe bello!

shoulder NOUN
la spalla *fem*
□ broad shoulders spalle larghe
■ **a shoulder bag** una borsa a tracolla

shoulder blade NOUN
la scapola *fem*

shouldn't = should not

to **shout** VERB
▷ see also **shout** NOUN
urlare [68]
□ Don't shout! Non urlare! □ 'Go away!' he shouted. 'Vattene!' urlò.

shout NOUN
▷ see also **shout** VERB
l' urlo *masc* (FEM PL le urla)

shovel NOUN
la pala *fem*

show NOUN
▷ see also **show** VERB
1 lo spettacolo *masc*
□ We're seeing a show this evening. Stasera andiamo a vedere uno spettacolo.
■ **a fashion show** una sfilata di moda
■ **the motor show** il salone dell'automobile
2 il programma *masc* (PL i programmi) *(on TV)*
□ He's now got his own show. Ora ha un suo programma.
3 la dimostrazione *fem*
□ a show of strength una dimostrazione di forza

to **show** VERB
▷ see also **show** NOUN
1 mostrare [68]
■ **to show somebody something** mostrare [68] qualcosa a qualcuno □ He showed me his flat. Mi ha mostrato il suo appartamento.
□ Have you shown the article to your boss? Hai mostrato l'articolo al tuo capo?
2 dimostrare [68]
□ She showed great courage. Ha dimostrato un gran coraggio.
■ **It shows.** Si vede. □ I've never been riding before. — It shows. Non sono mai andato a cavallo prima d'ora. — Si vede.

S

to **show off** VERB
mettersi [59ᴱ] in mostra

to **show up** VERB
presentarsi [56ᴱ]
□ He showed up late as usual. Si è presentato in ritardo, come al solito.

show business NOUN
il mondo dello spettacolo masc

shower NOUN
1 la doccia fem (PL le docce) (in bathroom)
■ **to have a shower** fare [49] la doccia
2 il rovescio masc (of rain)

showerproof ADJECTIVE
impermeabile (FEM impermeabile)

showing NOUN
la proiezione fem (of film)

shown VERB ▷ see show

show-off NOUN
l' esibizionista masc/fem

shrank VERB ▷ see shrink

to **shriek** VERB
strillare [68]

shrimps NOUN PL
i gamberetti masc pl

to **shrink** VERB
restringersi [109ᴱ]
□ My sweater shrank in the wash. Il mio maglione si è ristretto durante il lavaggio. □ All my jumpers have shrunk. Mi si sono ristretti tutti i maglioni.

Shrove Tuesday NOUN
il martedì grasso masc

to **shrug** VERB
■ **to shrug one's shoulders** fare [49] spallucce

shrunk VERB ▷ see shrink

to **shudder** VERB
rabbrividire [51ᴱ]

to **shuffle** VERB
strascicare [18] i piedi
□ She shuffled along the corridor. Strascicava i piedi lungo il corridoio.
■ **to shuffle the cards** mescolare [68] le carte

to **shut** VERB
chiudere [20]
□ What time do the shops shut? A che ora chiudono i negozi?

to **shut down** VERB
chiudere [20] i battenti
□ The cinema shut down last year. Il cinema ha chiuso i battenti l'anno scorso.

to **shut off** VERB
spegnere [105]

to **shut up** VERB
stare [108ᴱ] zitto
□ Shut up! Stai zitto!

shutters NOUN PL
le imposte fem pl

shuttle NOUN
la navetta fem

shuttlecock NOUN
il volano masc

shy ADJECTIVE
timido (FEM timida)

Sicily NOUN
la Sicilia fem

sick ADJECTIVE
1 malato (FEM malata)
□ She looks after her sick mother. Si occupa della madre malata.
2 di cattivo gusto
□ That's really sick! È veramente di cattivo gusto!
■ **to be sick** vomitare [68] □ I was sick twice last night. Ho vomitato due volte, ieri notte.
■ **I feel sick.** Ho la nausea.
■ **to be sick of something** averne [12] abbastanza di qualcosa □ I'm sick of your lies. Ne ho abbastanza delle tue bugie.

sickening ADJECTIVE
nauseante (FEM nauseante)

sick leave NOUN
il congedo per malattia masc

sickness NOUN
la malattia fem

sick note NOUN
1 la giustificazione per assenza fem (for pupil)
2 il certificato di malattia masc (for employee)

sick pay NOUN
indennità di malattia o infortunio

side NOUN
1 il lato masc
□ on the wrong side of the road sul lato sbagliato della strada
■ **a side entrance** un ingresso laterale
2 il bordo masc
□ at the side of the road sul bordo della strada
■ **by the side of the lake** sulla riva del lago
3 il fianco masc (PL i fianchi)
□ She was lying on her side. Era sdraiata su un fianco. □ side by side fianco a fianco
4 la parte fem
□ I'm on your side Sto dalla tua parte.
■ **to take sides with somebody** schierarsi [56ᴱ] con qualcuno
5 la squadra fem
□ Leeds was the stronger side. Il Leeds era la squadra più forte.

sideboard NOUN
la credenza fem

side-effect NOUN
l' effetto collaterale masc

side street NOUN
la traversa fem

sidewalk NOUN (US)
il marciapiede masc

sideways ADVERB
di lato
□ I took a step sideways. Ho fatto un passo di lato.
■ **sideways on** di profilo

sieve NOUN
il setaccio *masc*

sigh NOUN
▷ *see also* **sigh** VERB
il sospiro *masc*

to **sigh** VERB
▷ *see also* **sigh** NOUN
sospirare [68]

sight NOUN
1 la vista *fem*
□ My sight is failing. La vista mi sta calando.
■ **to know somebody by sight** conoscere [24] di vista qualcuno
■ **in sight** visibile
■ **Keep out of sight!** Non farti vedere!
2 lo spettacolo *masc*
□ It was an amazing sight. Era uno spettacolo incredibile.
■ **the sights** le attrazioni turistiche
■ **to see the sights of London** visitare [68] Londra

sightseeing NOUN
■ **to go sightseeing** fare [49] un giro turistico

sign NOUN
▷ *see also* **sign** VERB
1 il cartello *masc*
□ There was a big sign saying 'private'. C'era un grande cartello con la scritta 'privato'.
■ **a road sign** un segnale stradale
2 il segno *masc*
□ There's no sign of improvement. Non c'è alcun segno di miglioramento. □ What sign are you? Di che segno sei?

to **sign** VERB
▷ *see also* **sign** NOUN
firmare [68]
□ Sign here, please. Firmi qui, per favore.

to **sign up** VERB
iscriversi [99ᴱ]
■ **to sign up for** iscriversi [99ᴱ] a

signal NOUN
▷ *see also* **signal** VERB
il segnale *masc*

to **signal** VERB
▷ *see also* **signal** NOUN
■ **to signal to somebody** fare [49] segno a qualcuno

signature NOUN
la firma *fem*
□ a petition containing one thousand signatures una petizione con mille firme

signature tune NOUN
la sigla musicale *fem*

significance NOUN
l' importanza *fem*

significant ADJECTIVE
1 importante (FEM importante)
□ a significant development uno sviluppo importante
2 notevole (FEM notevole)
□ a significant improvement un miglioramento notevole

sign language NOUN
il linguaggio dei segni *masc*

signpost NOUN
l' indicatore stradale *masc*

silence NOUN
il silenzio *masc*

silent ADJECTIVE
silenzioso (FEM silenziosa)

silicon NOUN
il silicio *masc*
LANGUAGE TIP Be careful not to translate **silicon** by silicone.

silicon chip NOUN
il chip *masc* (PL i chip)

silicone NOUN
il silicone *masc*

silk NOUN
la seta *fem*
□ a silk scarf un foulard di seta

silky ADJECTIVE
di seta

silly ADJECTIVE
sciocco (FEM sciocca, MASC PL sciocchi, FEM PL sciocche)

silver NOUN
l' argento *masc*
□ a silver medal una medaglia d'argento

similar ADJECTIVE
simile (FEM simile)

simple ADJECTIVE
1 semplice (FEM semplice)
□ The answer is simple. La risposta è semplice.
■ **the simple past** il passato semplice
2 sprovveduto (FEM sprovveduta)
□ He's a bit simple. È un po' sprovveduto.

simply ADVERB
semplicemente

simultaneous ADJECTIVE
simultaneo (FEM simultanea)

sin NOUN
▷ *see also* **sin** VERB
il peccato *masc*

to **sin** VERB
▷ *see also* **sin** NOUN
peccare [18]

since PREPOSITION, ADVERB, CONJUNCTION
1 da
□ since Christmas da Natale □ since then da allora

545

sincere – sixteen

LANGUAGE TIP When describing a state or action that started in the past and is still continuing, translate 'since' by **da** and use the present tense of the Italian verb.

□ I've been here since the beginning of June. Sono qua dall'inizio di giugno. □ We've been waiting for him since three o'clock. Siamo qui ad aspettarlo dalle tre.

2 da allora
□ I haven't seen him since. Non lo vedo da allora.
■ **ever since** da allora

3 da quando
□ I haven't seen her since she left. Non l'ho più vista da quando è partita.

4 dato che
□ Since you're tired, let's stay at home. Dato che sei stanco restiamo a casa.

sincere ADJECTIVE
sincero (FEM sincera)

sincerely ADVERB
■ **Yours sincerely...** Distinti saluti...

to sing VERB
cantare [68]
□ She sang in the school choir. Cantava nel coro della scuola. □ He has sung in the choir for two years. Canta nel coro da due anni.

singer NOUN
il/la cantante masc/fem

singing NOUN
il canto masc

single ADJECTIVE
▷ see also **single** NOUN
1 singolo (FEM singola)
□ a single room una camera singola
2 solo (FEM sola)
□ She hadn't said a single word. Non aveva detto una sola parola.
■ **a single bed** un letto a una piazza
■ **in single file** in fila indiana
3 single (FEM+PL single)
□ a single mother una madre single
■ **a single parent** un genitore che alleva i figli da solo
■ **a single parent family** una famiglia con un solo genitore

single NOUN
▷ see also **single** ADJECTIVE
1 il biglietto di sola andata masc

LANGUAGE TIP Word for word, this means 'a ticket only for going'.

□ A single to Oxford, please. Un biglietto di sola andata per Oxford, per favore.
2 il singolo masc
□ a CD single un CD singolo

singles NOUN PL
il singolare masc sing
□ the women's singles il singolare femminile

singular NOUN
il singolare masc

□ in the singular al singolare

sinister ADJECTIVE
sinistro (FEM sinistra)

sink NOUN
▷ see also **sink** VERB
1 il lavello masc (in kitchen)
2 il lavandino masc (in bathroom)

to sink VERB
▷ see also **sink** NOUN
affondare [68]
□ The ship sank. La nave è affondata.
□ The ship was sunk in the war. La nave venne affondata durante la guerra.

sir NOUN
il signore masc

siren NOUN
la sirena fem

sister NOUN
1 la sorella fem
□ This is my sister. Questa è mia sorella.
2 l' infermiera caposala fem (PL le infermiere caposala)
□ She's a sister at the hospital. È infermiera caposala all'ospedale.

sister-in-law NOUN
la cognata fem

to sit VERB
essere [47ᴱ] seduto
□ He was sitting in front of me. Era seduto davanti a me. □ We sat in the front row. Eravamo seduti in prima fila.
■ **to sit an exam** sostenere [113] un esame

to sit down VERB
sedersi [101ᴱ]
□ He sat down at his desk. Si sedette alla scrivania.

sitcom NOUN
la situation comedy fem (PL le situation comedy)

site NOUN
1 il luogo masc (PL i luoghi)
□ the site of the disaster il luogo del disastro
2 il campeggio masc (for tents)
3 il sito masc (website)
■ **to visit a site** visitare [68] un sito
■ **an archaeological site** una zona archeologica

sitting room NOUN
il soggiorno masc

situated ADJECTIVE
■ **to be situated** essere [47ᴱ] situato

situation NOUN
la situazione fem

six NUMBER
sei
□ He's six. Ha sei anni.

sixteen NUMBER
sedici
□ He's sixteen. Ha sedici anni.

sixteenth ADJECTIVE
sedicesimo (FEM sedicesima)
□ the sixteenth floor il sedicesimo piano
■ **the sixteenth of August** il sedici agosto

sixth ADJECTIVE
sesto (FEM sesta)
□ the sixth floor il sesto piano
■ **the sixth of August** il sei agosto
■ **sixth form** ultimi due anni della scuola
superiore

sixty NUMBER
sessanta

size NOUN
1 la grandezza fem
□ plates of various sizes piatti di varia
grandezza
■ **to be the size of** essere [47^E] grande come
□ Leeds is about the size of Florence. Leeds è
grande più o meno come Firenze.
2 la taglia fem
□ What size do you take? Che taglia porti?
3 il numero masc (of shoes)

to skate VERB
pattinare [68]

skateboard NOUN
lo skateboard masc (PL gli skateboard)

skateboarding NOUN
■ **I like skateboarding.** Mi piace andare sullo
skateboard.

skates NOUN PL
i pattini masc pl

skating NOUN
il pattinaggio masc
■ **to go skating** fare [49] pattinaggio
■ **figure skating** pattinaggio artistico
■ **skating rink** pista di pattinaggio

skeleton NOUN
lo scheletro masc

sketch NOUN
▷ see also **sketch** VERB
l' abbozzo masc
■ **sketch pad** blocco per schizzi

to sketch VERB
▷ see also **sketch** NOUN
abbozzare [68] (picture)

to ski VERB
▷ see also **ski** NOUN
sciare [55]

ski NOUN
▷ see also **ski** VERB
lo sci masc (PL gli sci)
■ **ski boots** scarponi da sci
■ **ski lift** impianto di risalita
■ **ski pants** pantaloni da sci
■ **ski pass** ski pass
■ **ski pole** bastoncino da sci
■ **ski slope** pista da sci
■ **ski suit** tuta da sci

to skid VERB
scivolare [68^E]

skier NOUN
lo sciatore masc
la sciatrice fem

skiing NOUN
lo sci masc (sport)
■ **to go skiing** andare [6^E] a sciare
■ **to go on a skiing holiday** fare [49] una
vacanza sulla neve

skilful (US skillful) ADJECTIVE
abile (FEM abile)

skill NOUN
la abilità fem (PL le abilità)
□ It requires a lot of skill. Richiede molta
abilità.

skilled ADJECTIVE
■ **a skilled worker** un operaio specializzato

skimmed milk NOUN
il latte scremato masc

skimpy ADJECTIVE
1 succinto (FEM succinta) (clothes)
2 frugale (FEM frugale) (meal)

skin NOUN
la pelle fem
■ **skin cancer** cancro della pelle

skinhead NOUN
il/la skinhead masc/fem (PL gli/le skinhead)

skinny ADJECTIVE
magro (FEM magra)

skin-tight ADJECTIVE
aderente (FEM aderente)

skip NOUN
▷ see also **skip** VERB
la benna fem

to skip VERB
▷ see also **skip** NOUN
saltare [68]
□ You should never skip breakfast. Non si
dovrebbe mai saltare la colazione.
■ **to skip school** marinare [68] la scuola

skirt NOUN
la gonna fem

skittles NOUN PL
i birilli masc pl

to skive VERB
fare [49] il lavativo
□ She's skiving as usual. Come al solito fa la
lavativa.
■ **to skive off school** marinare [68] la scuola

skull NOUN
1 il cranio masc (of someone alive)
2 il teschio masc (of skeleton)

sky NOUN
il cielo masc

Skype® NOUN
▷ see also **Skype** VERB
Skype® masc

to **Skype** VERB
▷ see also **Skype** NOUN
fare [49] Skype

skyscraper NOUN
il grattacielo *masc*

slack ADJECTIVE
1 allentato (FEM allentata) (*rope*)
2 negligente (FEM negligente) (*person*)

to **slag off** VERB
sputtanare [68]

to **slam** VERB
sbattere [1]
□ She slammed the door. Ha sbattuto la porta.

slang NOUN
il gergo *masc*

slap NOUN
▷ see also **slap** VERB
lo schiaffo *masc*

to **slap** VERB
▷ see also **slap** NOUN
dare [30] uno schiaffo a

slate NOUN
1 l' ardesia *fem*
□ a slate roof un tetto d'ardesia
2 la tegola d'ardesia *fem*
□ a missing slate una tegola d'ardesia mancante

sledge NOUN
la slitta *fem*

sledging NOUN
■ to go sledging andare [6E] in slitta

sleep NOUN
▷ see also **sleep** VERB
il sonno *masc*
□ a couple of hours' sleep un paio di ore di sonno
■ to walk in one's sleep camminare [68] nel sonno
■ to go to sleep addormentarsi [56E]

to **sleep** VERB
▷ see also **sleep** NOUN
dormire [41]
□ I couldn't sleep last night. Ieri notte non riuscivo a dormire. □ The baby slept during the journey. Il bambino ha dormito lungo il tragitto.

to **sleep around** VERB
andare [6E] a letto con tutti

to **sleep in** VERB
dormire [41] fino a tardi

to **sleep together** VERB
avere [12] rapporti sessuali

to **sleep with** VERB
andare [6E] a letto con

sleeping bag NOUN
il sacco a pelo *masc* (PL i sacchi a pelo)

sleeping car NOUN
il vagone letto *masc* (PL i vagoni letto)

sleeping pill NOUN
il sonnifero *masc*

sleepy ADJECTIVE
■ to feel sleepy essere [47E] assonnato
■ a sleepy little village un paesino tranquillo

sleet NOUN
il nevischio *masc*

sleeve NOUN
1 la manica *fem* (PL le maniche) (*of shirt, coat*)
2 la copertina *fem* (*of record*)

sleigh NOUN
lo slittino *masc*

slept VERB ▷ see **sleep**

slice NOUN
▷ see also **slice** VERB
la fetta *fem*

to **slice** VERB
▷ see also **slice** NOUN
affettare [68]

slick NOUN
▷ see also **slick** ADJECTIVE
■ an oil slick una chiazza di petrolio

slick ADJECTIVE
▷ see also **slick** NOUN
impeccabile (FEM impeccabile)
□ a slick performance una performance impeccabile

to **slide** VERB
▷ see also **slide** NOUN
scivolare [68E]

slide NOUN
▷ see also **slide** VERB
1 lo scivolo *masc*
□ some swings and a slide alcune altalene ed uno scivolo
2 la diapositiva *fem*
□ He showed us his slides. Ci ha mostrato le sue diapositive.
3 il fermacapelli *masc* (PL i fermacapelli) (*for hair*)

slight ADJECTIVE
■ a slight problem un piccolo problema
■ a slight improvement un leggero miglioramento

slightly ADVERB
leggermente
□ They are slightly more expensive. Sono leggermente più costosi.

slim ADJECTIVE
▷ see also **slim** VERB
magro (FEM magra)

to **slim** VERB
▷ see also **slim** ADJECTIVE
dimagrire [51]
□ She's trying to slim. Sta cercando di dimagrire.
■ I'm slimming. Sono a dieta.

sling NOUN
▷ see also **sling** VERB
la fascia a tracolla *fem*

to **sling** VERB
▷ *see also* **sling** NOUN
buttare [68]
□ He slung his bag onto the floor. Ha buttato la borsa sul pavimento.

slip NOUN
▷ *see also* **slip** VERB
1 lo sbaglio *masc*
□ There must be no slips. Non ci devono essere sbagli.
2 la sottoveste *fem*
□ a white slip una sottoveste bianca
■ **a slip of paper** un pezzo di carta
■ **a slip of the tongue** un lapsus
■ **slip road** rampa di accesso

to **slip** VERB
▷ *see also* **slip** NOUN
scivolare [68ᴱ]
□ He slipped on the ice. È scivolato sul ghiaccio.

to **slip up** VERB
fare [49] un errore

slipper NOUN
la pantofola *fem*

slippery ADJECTIVE
scivoloso (FEM scivolosa)

slip-up NOUN
lo sbaglio *masc*

slope NOUN
il pendio *masc*
□ a steep slope un pendio ripido

sloppy ADJECTIVE
trascurato (FEM trascurata)

slot NOUN
1 la fessura *fem*
□ Put the money in the slot. Inserite il denaro nella fessura.
2 lo spazio *masc* (*in programme*)

slot machine NOUN
la slot-machine *fem* (PL le slot-machine)

slow ADJECTIVE, ADVERB
lento (FEM lenta)
□ a slow lorry un camion lento
■ **in slow motion** al rallentatore
■ **to go slow** andare [6ᴱ] piano □ Go slower! Vai più piano!
■ **The clock's slow.** L'orologio è indietro.

to **slow down** VERB
rallentare [68]
> **LANGUAGE TIP** Use **essere** to form past tenses when **rallentare** does not have an object.

slowly ADVERB
lentamente

slug NOUN
la lumaca *fem* (PL le lumache)

slum NOUN
il quartiere povero *masc*

slush NOUN
la fanghiglia *fem*

sly ADJECTIVE
scaltro (FEM scaltra)
□ She's sly! È scaltra!
■ **a sly smile** un sorriso sornione

smack NOUN
▷ *see also* **smack** VERB
il ceffone *masc*

to **smack** VERB
▷ *see also* **smack** NOUN
dare [30] un ceffone a

small ADJECTIVE
piccolo (FEM piccola)
□ a small car una macchina piccola

WORD POWER
You can use a number of other words instead of **small** to mean 'little':
miniature in miniatura
□ a miniature garden un giardino in miniatura
minute minuscolo
□ a minute piece un pezzettino minuscolo
tiny minuscolo
□ a tiny kitchen una cucina minuscola

■ **small change** spiccioli *masc pl*
■ **small talk** chiacchiere *fem pl*

smart ADJECTIVE
1 elegante (FEM elegante)
□ a smart navy blue suit un elegante vestito blu
2 intelligente (FEM intelligente)
□ He thinks he's smarter than Sarah. Pensa di essere più intelligente di Sarah.

smart card NOUN
la smart card *fem* (PL le smart card)

smart phone NOUN
lo smart phone *masc* (PL gli smart phone)

smash NOUN
▷ *see also* **smash** VERB
lo scontro *masc*

to **smash** VERB
▷ *see also* **smash** NOUN
1 rompere [92]
□ They smashed the windows. Hanno rotto le finestre.
2 rompersi [92ᴱ]
□ The glass smashed. Il bicchiere si è rotto.
■ **to smash into tiny pieces** andare [6ᴱ] in frantumi

smashing ADJECTIVE
formidabile (FEM formidabile)
□ I think he's smashing. Io lo trovo formidabile.

smell NOUN
▷ *see also* **smell** VERB
l' odore *masc*

□ a nice smell un buon odore
■ **the sense of smell** l'odorato
to **smell** VERB
▷ see also **smell** NOUN
1 puzzare [68]
□ That dog smells! Quel cane puzza!
■ **to smell of something** avere [12] odore di qualcosa □ It smells of petrol. Ha odore di benzina.
2 sentire [41] odore di
□ I can smell gas. Sento odore di gas.
smelly ADJECTIVE
puzzolente (FEM puzzolente)
smile NOUN
▷ see also **smile** VERB
il sorriso masc
to **smile** VERB
▷ see also **smile** NOUN
sorridere [84]
smiley NOUN
la faccina fem
smoke NOUN
▷ see also **smoke** VERB
il fumo masc
to **smoke** VERB
▷ see also **smoke** NOUN
fumare [68]
■ **to stop smoking** smettere [59] di fumare
smoker NOUN
il fumatore masc
la fumatrice fem
smoking NOUN
■ **Smoking is bad for you.** Il fumo fa male.
■ **'no smoking'** 'vietato fumare'
smooth ADJECTIVE
1 liscio (FEM liscia, MASC PL lisci, FEM PL lisce)
□ It keeps your skin soft and smooth. Mantiene la pelle morbida e liscia.
2 melliflup (FEM melliflua)
□ He's too smooth for my liking. È troppo melliflup per i miei gusti.
smudge NOUN
la sbavatura fem
smug ADJECTIVE
compiaciuto (FEM compiaciuta)
to **smuggle** VERB
contrabbandare [68]
□ They smuggle arms and drugs. Contrabbandano armi e droga.
■ **to smuggle in** far [49] entrare illegalmente
■ **to smuggle out** far [49] uscire illegalmente
smuggler NOUN
il contrabbandiere masc
la contrabbandiera fem
smuggling NOUN
il contrabbando masc
smutty ADJECTIVE
sconcio (FEM sconcia, MASC PL sconci, FEM PL sconce)

□ a smutty magazine un giornale sconcio
■ **smutty jokes** barzellette sporche fem pl
snack NOUN
lo spuntino masc
■ **to have a snack** fare [49] uno spuntino
snack bar NOUN
lo snack bar masc (PL gli snack bar)
snail NOUN
la lumaca fem (PL le lumache)
snake NOUN
il serpente masc
to **snap** VERB
spezzare [68ᴱ] di netto
□ The branch snapped. Il ramo si è spezzato di netto.
■ **to snap one's fingers** schioccare [18] le dita
snapshot NOUN
la foto fem (PL le foto)
to **snarl** VERB
ringhiare [17]
to **snatch** VERB
■ **to snatch something from somebody** strappare [68] qualcosa a qualcuno □ He snatched the keys from my hand. Mi ha strappato di mano le chiavi.
■ **My bag was snatched.** Mi hanno scippato.
to **sneak** VERB
■ **to sneak a look at something** dare [30] una sbirciatina a qualcosa
■ **to sneak in** entrare [68ᴱ] di nascosto
■ **to sneak out** uscire [117ᴱ] di nascosto
■ **to sneak up on** avvicinarsi [56ᴱ] senza far rumore
sneaker NOUN (US)
la scarpa da ginnastica fem
to **sneeze** VERB
starnutire [51]
to **sniff** VERB
1 tirare [68] su col naso
□ Stop sniffing! Smettila di tirare su col naso!
2 annusare [68]
□ The dog sniffed my hand. Il cane mi ha annusato la mano.
■ **to sniff glue** sniffare [68] colla
snob NOUN
lo/la snob masc/fem (PL gli/le snob)
snooker NOUN
il biliardo masc
snooze NOUN
il pisolino masc
■ **to have a snooze** fare [49] un pisolino
to **snore** VERB
russare [68]
snow NOUN
▷ see also **snow** VERB
la neve fem
to **snow** VERB
▷ see also **snow** NOUN

nevicare [18]

□ It's snowing. Nevica.

snowball NOUN

la palla di neve *fem*

snowflake NOUN

il fiocco di neve *masc* (PL i fiocchi di neve)

snowman NOUN

il pupazzo di neve *masc*

so CONJUNCTION, ADVERB

1 così

□ It was raining, so I got wet. Pioveva, e così mi sono bagnato. □ It was so heavy! Era così pesante! □ He was talking so fast I couldn't understand. Parlava così in fretta che non capivo. □ That's not so. Non è così.

2 allora

□ So, have you always lived here? Allora, sei sempre vissuto qui?

■ **So what?** E con questo?

■ **How's your father? — Not so good.** Come sta tuo padre? — Non tanto bene.

■ **so much** tanto □ I love you so much. Ti voglio tanto bene. □ I've got so much work. Ho tanto lavoro.

■ **so many** tanti □ I've got so many things to do today. Ho così tante cose da fare oggi.

■ **so do I** anch'io □ I love horses. — So do I. Adoro i cavalli. — Anch'io.

■ **so have we** anche noi □ I've been waiting for an hour. — So have we. È un'ora che aspetto. — Anche noi.

■ **I think so.** Penso di sì.

■ **I hope so.** Lo spero.

■ **so far** finora □ It's been easy so far. Finora è stato facile.

■ **so far so good** fin qui tutto bene

■ **ten or so people** circa una decina di persone

■ **at five o'clock or so** verso le cinque

to **soak** VERB

mettere [59] in ammollo

□ Soak it in cold water. Mettilo in ammollo nell'acqua fredda.

■ **to soak up the sun** rosolarsi [56^E] al sole

soaked ADJECTIVE

bagnato fradicio (FEM bagnata fradicia)

soaking ADJECTIVE

zuppo (FEM zuppa)

□ Your shoes are soaking. Hai le scarpe zuppe.

soap NOUN

1 il sapone *masc* (to wash with)

2 la soap opera *fem* (PL le soap opera) (on TV)

soap powder NOUN

il detersivo in polvere *masc*

to **sob** VERB

singhiozzare [68]

sober ADJECTIVE

sobrio (FEM sobria, MASC PL sobri, FEM PL sobrie)

to **sober up** VERB

smaltire [51] la sbornia

soccer NOUN

il calcio *masc*

□ a game of soccer una partita di calcio

■ **a soccer player** un calciatore

social ADJECTIVE

sociale (FEM sociale)

□ social problems problemi sociali

■ **social media** i social media

socialism NOUN

il socialismo *masc*

socialist NOUN

▷ see also **socialist** ADJECTIVE

il/la socialista *masc/fem*

socialist ADJECTIVE

▷ see also **socialist** NOUN

socialista (FEM socialista)

social networking site NOUN

il social network *masc* (PL i social network)

social security NOUN

la previdenza sociale *fem*

■ **to be on social security** ricevere [27] sussidi dalla previdenza sociale

social worker NOUN

l' assistente sociale *masc/fem*

society NOUN

1 la società *fem* (PL le società)

□ a multi-cultural society una società multiculturale

2 l' associazione *fem*

□ a literary society un'associazione letteraria

sociology NOUN

la sociologia *fem*

sock NOUN

il calzino *masc*

socket NOUN

la presa di corrente *fem*

soda NOUN

il selz *masc* (PL i selz)

soda pop NOUN (US)

la gassosa *fem*

sofa NOUN

il divano *masc*

soft ADJECTIVE

1 morbido (FEM morbida)

□ a nice soft towel un asciugamano bello morbido

2 soffice (FEM soffice)

□ The mattress is too soft. Il materasso è troppo soffice.

■ **to be soft on somebody** essere [47^E] indulgente con qualcuno

■ **soft cheeses** formaggi a pasta molle

■ **a soft drink** una bibita analcolica

■ **soft drugs** droghe leggere

■ **a soft option** la scelta più facile

software NOUN

il software *masc*

soggy ADJECTIVE
molliccio (FEM molliccia, MASC PL mollicci, FEM PL mollicce)

soil NOUN
la terra fem

solar ADJECTIVE
solare (FEM solare)
■ **solar panel** pannello solare
■ **solar power** energia solare

sold VERB ▷ see **sell**

soldier NOUN
il soldato masc

sold out ADJECTIVE
esaurito (FEM esaurita)
□ The tickets are all sold out. I biglietti sono tutti esauriti.

solicitor NOUN
1 l' avvocato masc (for lawsuits)
2 il notaio masc (for wills, property)

solid ADJECTIVE
solido (FEM solida)
□ a solid wall un muro solido
■ **solid gold** oro massiccio
■ **for three solid hours** per tre ore filate

solo NOUN
l' assolo masc
□ a guitar solo un assolo di chitarra

solution NOUN
la soluzione fem

to **solve** VERB
risolvere [89]

some ADJECTIVE, PRONOUN
1 del masc
della fem
□ some bread del pane □ some beer della birra

> LANGUAGE TIP Use **dello** before a masculine noun if it starts with gn, pn, ps, x, y, z or s + another consonant.

□ some yoghurt dello yogurt

> LANGUAGE TIP Use **dell'** before nouns starting with vowels.

□ some salad dell'insalata
■ **some of it** un po' □ I only took some of it. Ne ho preso solo un po'.
■ **Would you like some coffee? — No thanks, I've got some.** Vuoi del caffè? — No grazie, ne ho.
2 alcuni masc pl
alcune fem pl
□ You have to be careful with mushrooms: some are poisonous. Bisogna stare attenti con i funghi, alcuni sono velenosi.
■ **some of them** alcuni □ I only sold some of them. Ne ho venduto solo alcuni.
■ **some people** alcuni
■ **some day** un giorno □ Some day you'll understand. Un giorno capirai.

somebody PRONOUN
qualcuno

somehow ADVERB
in un modo o nell'altro
□ I'll do it somehow. Lo farò, in un modo o nell'altro.
■ **Somehow I don't think he believed me.** Qualcosa mi dice che non mi ha creduto.

someone PRONOUN
qualcuno

someplace ADVERB (US)
da qualche parte
□ I've left my keys someplace. Ho lasciato le chiavi da qualche parte.

something PRONOUN
qualcosa
□ something special qualcosa di speciale □ Wear something warm. Mettiti qualcosa di pesante.
■ **His name is Peter or something.** Si chiama Peter o qualcosa del genere.
■ **...or something like that** ...o giù di lì □ It cost a hundred pounds, or something like that. È costato cento sterline o giù di lì.
■ **It would be really something!** Non sarebbe mica male!

sometime ADVERB
1 un giorno o l'altro
□ I want to go to Spain sometime. Voglio andare in Spagna un giorno o l'altro.
2 uno di questi giorni
□ Come and see us sometime. Vieni a trovarci uno di questi giorni.
■ **sometime last month** il mese scorso

sometimes ADVERB
a volte
□ Sometimes I think he hates me. A volte ho l'impressione che mi detesti.

somewhere ADVERB
da qualche parte
□ I've left my keys somewhere. Ho lasciato le chiavi da qualche parte.
■ **I'd like to go on holiday, somewhere exotic.** Vorrei andare in vacanza, in qualche località esotica.

son NOUN
il figlio masc

song NOUN
la canzone fem

son-in-law NOUN
il genero masc

soon ADVERB
presto
□ very soon prestissimo
■ **soon afterwards** poco dopo
■ **as soon as possible** il più presto possibile

sooner ADVERB
prima

□ Can't you come a bit sooner? Non puoi venire un po' prima?
  ■ **sooner or later** prima o poi
  ■ **the sooner the better** prima è meglio è

soot NOUN
la fuliggine *fem*

soppy ADJECTIVE
sentimentale (FEM sentimentale)

soprano NOUN
il/la soprano *masc/fem*

sorcerer NOUN
lo stregone *masc*

sore ADJECTIVE
▷ *see also* **sore** NOUN
  ■ **It's sore.** Mi fa male.
  ■ **a sore point** un punto delicato

sore NOUN
▷ *see also* **sore** ADJECTIVE
la piaga *fem* (PL le piaghe)

sorry ADJECTIVE
  ■ **Sorry!** Scusi!
  ■ **Sorry?** Come, scusa?
  ■ **I'm very sorry.** Mi dispiace tanto.
  ■ **I'm sorry I'm late.** Scusa il ritardo.
  ■ **You'll be sorry!** Te ne pentirai!
  ■ **to feel sorry for somebody** dispiacersi [70E] per qualcuno

sort NOUN
▷ *see also* **sort** VERB
il tipo *masc*
□ What sort of bike have you got? Che tipo di bici hai?

to sort VERB
▷ *see also* **sort** NOUN
suddividere [40E]
□ They are sorted into three groups. Sono suddivisi in tre gruppi.

to sort out VERB
1 riordinare [68] *(things)*
2 risolvere [89] *(problem)*

so-so ADVERB
così così
□ How are you feeling? — So-so. Come ti senti? — Così così.

sought VERB ▷ *see* **seek**

soul NOUN
l' anima *fem*

sound NOUN
▷ *see also* **sound** VERB, ADJECTIVE, ADVERB
1 il rumore *masc*
□ Don't make a sound! Non fare rumore!
□ the sound of footsteps il rumore di passi
2 il suono *masc*
□ the speed of sound la velocità del suono
  ■ **sound effects** effetti sonori
3 l' audio *masc*
□ Can I turn the sound down? Posso abbassare l'audio?

to sound VERB
▷ *see also* **sound** NOUN, ADJECTIVE, ADVERB
sembrare [68E]
□ That sounds interesting. Mi sembra interessante. □ It sounds as if she's doing well at school. Sembra che stia andando bene a scuola. □ That sounds like a good idea. Sembra una buona idea.

sound ADJECTIVE, ADVERB
▷ *see also* **sound** NOUN, VERB
buono (FEM buona)
□ Julian gave me some sound advice. Julian mi ha dato un buon consiglio.
  ■ **sound asleep** profondamente addormentato

soundtrack NOUN
la colonna sonora *fem*

soup NOUN
la minestra *fem*

sour ADJECTIVE
acido (FEM acida)

south NOUN, ADJECTIVE, ADVERB
1 il sud *masc*
□ the South of France il sud della Francia
□ South Wales il Galles del sud
  ■ **in the south** a sud
  ■ **south of** a sud di □ It's south of London. È a sud di Londra.
2 verso sud
□ We were travelling south. Viaggiavamo verso sud.
3 meridionale
□ the south coast la costa meridionale

South Africa NOUN
il Sudafrica *masc*

South America NOUN
il Sudamerica *masc*

South American NOUN
▷ *see also* **South American** ADJECTIVE
il sudamericano *masc*
la sudamericana *fem*

South American ADJECTIVE
▷ *see also* **South American** NOUN
sudamericano (FEM sudamericana)

southbound ADJECTIVE
diretto a sud (FEM diretta a sud)

south-east NOUN
il sud-est *masc*

southern ADJECTIVE
meridionale (FEM meridionale)
□ the southern part of the island la zona meridionale dell'isola □ Southern England l'Inghilterra meridionale

South Pole NOUN
il Polo sud *masc*

south-west NOUN
il sud-ovest *masc*

souvenir NOUN
il souvenir *masc* (PL i souvenir)
□ a souvenir shop un negozio di souvenir

Soviet ADJECTIVE
sovietico (FEM sovietica, MASC PL sovietici, FEM PL sovietiche)

soya NOUN
la soia *fem*

soy sauce NOUN
la salsa di soia *fem*

space NOUN
lo spazio *masc*
□ There isn't enough space. Non c'è abbastanza spazio. □ in the space of a few minutes nello spazio di pochi minuti
■ a parking space un parcheggio

spacecraft NOUN
il veicolo spaziale *masc*

spade NOUN
la pala *fem*
□ spade and fork pala e forcone
■ **spades** picche □ the ace of spades l'asso di picche

Spain NOUN
la Spagna *fem*

spam NOUN
lo spam *masc*

Spaniard NOUN
lo spagnolo *masc*
la spagnola *fem*

spaniel NOUN
lo spaniel *masc* (PL gli spaniel)

Spanish ADJECTIVE
▷ see also **Spanish** NOUN
spagnolo (FEM spagnola)

Spanish NOUN
▷ see also **Spanish** ADJECTIVE
lo spagnolo *masc* (language)
■ **the Spanish** gli spagnoli

to **spank** VERB
sculacciare [13]

spanner NOUN
la chiave fissa *fem*

spare ADJECTIVE
▷ see also **spare** VERB, NOUN
di scorta
□ spare batteries pile di scorta
■ **Any spare change, please?** Ha qualche spicciolo, per favore?
■ **a spare part** un pezzo di ricambio
■ **a spare room** una camera degli ospiti
■ **spare time** il tempo libero
■ **the spare wheel** la ruota di scorta

to **spare** VERB
▷ see also **spare** ADJECTIVE, NOUN
■ **Can you spare a moment?** Hai un attimo di tempo?
■ **I can't spare the time.** Non ho tempo.

■ **They've got no money to spare.** Non hanno poi tanti soldi.
■ **We arrived with time to spare.** Siamo arrivati un po' in anticipo.

spare NOUN
▷ see also **spare** ADJECTIVE, VERB
l'altro *masc*
l'altra *fem*
□ I've lost my key. — Have you got a spare? Ho perso la chiave. — Ne hai un'altra?

sparkling ADJECTIVE
frizzante (FEM frizzante)
□ sparkling wine vino frizzante

sparrow NOUN
il passero *masc*

spat VERB ▷ see **spit**

to **speak** VERB
parlare [68]
□ Do you speak English? Parli inglese? □ Have you spoken to him? Gli hai parlato? □ I've spoken to him about it. Gliene ho parlato. □ I spoke to her yesterday. Le ho parlato ieri. □ She spoke to him about it. Gliene ha parlato.
■ **Speaking!** (on phone) Sono io! □ Could I speak to Alison? — Speaking! Posso parlare con Alison? — Sono io!

to **speak out** VERB
parlare [68]
□ He finally decided to speak out. Alla fine si è deciso a parlare.

speaker NOUN
1 l'altoparlante *masc* (loudspeaker)
2 l'oratore *masc*
l'oratrice *fem* (person)

special ADJECTIVE
speciale (FEM speciale)

specialist NOUN
lo/la specialista *masc/fem*

speciality NOUN
la specialità *fem* (PL le specialità)

to **specialize** VERB
specializzarsi [56ᴱ]

specially ADVERB
1 specialmente
□ It can be very cold here, specially in January. Qui può fare molto freddo, specialmente in gennaio.
■ **not specially** non particolarmente □ Do you like opera? — Not specially. Ti piace l'opera? — Non particolarmente.
2 apposta
□ It's specially designed for teenagers. È concepito apposta per i giovani.

species NOUN
la specie *fem* (PL le specie)

specific ADJECTIVE
1 specifico (FEM specifica, MASC PL specifici, FEM PL specifiche)

□ certain specific issues certi problemi specifici

2 preciso (FEM precisa, MASC PL precisi, FEM PL precise)

□ Could you be more specific? Puoi essere più preciso?

specifically ADVERB

1 appositamente

□ It's specifically designed for teenagers. È appositamente concepito per i giovani.

2 specificamente

□ In Britain, or more specifically in England... In Gran Bretagna, o più specificamente in Inghilterra...

3 chiaramente

□ I specifically said that... Avevo chiaramente detto che...

specs NOUN PL
gli occhiali masc pl

spectacles NOUN PL
gli occhiali masc pl

spectacular ADJECTIVE
fantastico (FEM fantastica, MASC PL fantastici, FEM PL fantastiche)

spectator NOUN
lo spettatore masc
la spettatrice fem

speech NOUN
il discorso masc

□ He made a speech. Ha fatto un discorso.

speechless ADJECTIVE

■ to be speechless rimanere [88ᴱ] senza parole

speed NOUN
la velocità fem (PL le velocità)

□ at top speed ad alta velocità

■ a ten-speed bike una bicicletta a dieci marce

to **speed up** VERB
accelerare [68]

speedboat NOUN
il motoscafo masc

speeding NOUN
l' eccesso di velocità masc

□ He was fined for speeding. Ha preso la multa per eccesso di velocità.

speed limit NOUN
il limite di velocità masc

■ to break the speed limit superare [68] il limite di velocità

speedometer NOUN
il tachimetro masc

to **spell** VERB
▷ see also spell NOUN

■ How do you spell your name? Come si scrive il tuo nome?

■ Can you spell that please? Come si scrive?

■ I can't spell. Faccio errori di ortografia.

spell NOUN
▷ see also spell VERB
l' incantesimo masc

■ to cast a spell on somebody fare [49] un incantesimo a qualcuno

■ to be under somebody's spell essere [47ᴱ] stregato da qualcuno

spelling NOUN
l' ortografia fem

□ a spelling mistake un errore di ortografia

■ My spelling is terrible. Faccio molti errori di ortografia.

to **spend** VERB

1 spendere [8]

□ They spend an enormous amount of money on advertising. Spendono grosse cifre per la pubblicità.

2 trascorrere [26]

□ He spent a month in France. Ha trascorso un mese in Francia.

■ to spend time on dedicare [18] del tempo a

□ He spends a lot of time on his hobbies. Dedica un sacco di tempo ai suoi hobby.

spice NOUN
la spezia fem

spicy ADJECTIVE
speziato (FEM speziata)

spider NOUN
il ragno masc

to **spill** VERB

1 rovesciare [13ᴱ]

□ He spilled coffee on his trousers. S'è rovesciato il caffè sui pantaloni.

2 fuoriuscire [117ᴱ]

□ Oil is spilling from the tanker. Il petrolio sta fuoriuscendo dalla petroliera.

to **spin** VERB

1 girare [68]

□ He spun the wheel sharply. Ha girato il volante bruscamente.

2 filare [68]

□ She spins wool from her own sheep. Fila la lana delle sue pecore.

3 centrifugare [76] (washing)

spinach NOUN
gli spinaci masc pl

□ The spinach is delicious. Gli spinaci sono ottimi.

spin doctor NOUN
il curatore d'immagine masc
la curatrice d'immagine fem

spin drier NOUN
la centrifuga fem (PL le centrifughe)

spine NOUN
la colonna vertebrale fem

spinster NOUN
la zitella fem

spire NOUN
la guglia fem

spirit NOUN
1 lo spirito *masc*
 □ the human spirit lo spirito umano
2 il coraggio *masc*
 □ Everyone admired her spirit. Tutti ammiravano il suo coraggio.

spirit level NOUN
 la livella a bolla *fem*

spirits NOUN
 i superalcolici *masc pl*
 □ I don't drink spirits. Non bevo superalcolici.
 ■ **to be in good spirits** essere [47ᴱ] su di morale

spiritual ADJECTIVE
 spirituale (FEM spirituale)

spit NOUN
 ▷ *see also* **spit** VERB
 lo sputo *masc*

to **spit** VERB
 ▷ *see also* **spit** NOUN
 sputare [68]
 □ They spat at me. Mi hanno sputato addosso.

to **spit out** VERB
 sputare [68]
 □ It tasted horrible and I spat it out. Aveva un saporaccio e l'ho sputato.

spite NOUN
 ▷ *see also* **spite** VERB
 ■ **in spite of** malgrado
 ■ **out of spite** per dispetto

to **spite** VERB
 ▷ *see also* **spite** NOUN
 fare [49] dispetto a
 □ He just did it to spite me. L'ha fatto solo per farmi dispetto.

spiteful ADJECTIVE
 dispettoso (FEM dispettosa)

to **splash** VERB
 ▷ *see also* **splash** NOUN
1 schizzare [68]
 □ Don't splash me! Non schizzarmi!
2 spruzzare [68]
 □ He splashed water on his face. Si spruzzò acqua sul viso.

splash NOUN
 ▷ *see also* **splash** VERB
 il tonfo *masc*
 □ I heard a splash. Ho sentito un tonfo.
 ■ **a splash of colour** un tocco di colore

splendid ADJECTIVE
 splendido (FEM splendida)

splint NOUN
 la stecca *fem* (PL le stecche)

splinter NOUN
 la scheggia *fem* (PL le schegge)

to **split** VERB
1 spaccare [18]
 □ He split the wood with an axe. Spaccava la legna con l'ascia.

2 spaccarsi [18ᴱ]
 □ The ship split in two. La nave s'è spaccata in due.
3 dividere [40]
 □ They decided to split the profits. Hanno deciso di dividere i guadagni.

to **split up** VERB
 separarsi [56ᴱ]

to **spoil** VERB
1 rovinare [68]
 □ Don't let it spoil your holiday! Non lasciare che ti rovini la vacanza!
2 viziare [17]
 □ They like to spoil their grandchildren. A loro piace viziare i nipoti.

spoilsport NOUN
 il/la guastafeste *masc/fem*

spoke VERB ▷ *see* **speak**

spoke NOUN
 il raggio *masc*

spoken VERB ▷ *see* **speak**

spokesman NOUN
 il portavoce *masc* (PL i portavoce)

spokeswoman NOUN
 la portavoce *fem* (PL le portavoce)

sponge NOUN
 la spugna *fem*
 □ a wet sponge una spugna bagnata
 ■ **sponge bag** nécessaire *masc*
 ■ **sponge cake** pan di Spagna

sponsor NOUN
 ▷ *see also* **sponsor** VERB
 lo sponsor *masc* (PL gli sponsor)

to **sponsor** VERB
 ▷ *see also* **sponsor** NOUN
 sponsorizzare [68]
 □ The tournament was sponsored by local firms. Il torneo è stato sponsorizzato da imprese locali.
 ■ **She got her friends to sponsor her.** Ha chiesto ai suoi amici di contribuire alla colletta.

spontaneous ADJECTIVE
 spontaneo (FEM spontanea)

spooky ADJECTIVE
 sinistro (FEM sinistra)
 □ The house has a spooky atmosphere. La casa ha un'atmosfera sinistra.

spoon NOUN
 il cucchiaio *masc*

sport NOUN
 lo sport *masc* (PL gli sport)
 □ I'm not interested in sport. Lo sport non mi interessa.
 ■ **sports bag** la sacca sportiva
 ■ **sports car** l'auto sportiva
 ■ **sports jacket** la giacca sportiva
 ■ **Go on, be a sport!** Dai, sii buono!

sportsman NOUN
 lo sportivo *masc*

sportswear NOUN
l' abbigliamento sportivo *masc*

sportswoman NOUN
la sportiva *fem*

sporty ADJECTIVE
sportivo (FEM sportiva)

spot NOUN
▷ *see also* **spot** VERB
1 la macchia *fem*
□ There's a spot on your shirt. Hai una macchia sulla camicia.
2 il pallino *masc*
□ a red dress with white spots un vestito rosso a pallini bianchi
3 il brufolo *masc*
□ He's covered in spots. È pieno di brufoli.
4 il posto *masc*
□ It's a lovely spot for a picnic. È un posto ideale per un picnic.
■ **on the spot** 1 immediatamente
□ They offered her the job on the spot. Le hanno offerto immediatamente il lavoro.
2 sul posto □ Troops are on the spot. Le truppe sono sul posto.
■ **a spot check** un controllo senza preavviso

to **spot** VERB
▷ *see also* **spot** NOUN
notare [68]
□ I spotted a mistake. Ho notato un errore.

spotless ADJECTIVE
immacolato (FEM immacolata)

spotlight NOUN
il riflettore *masc*

spotty ADJECTIVE
brufoloso (FEM brufolosa)

spouse NOUN
il/la coniuge *masc/fem*

to **sprain** VERB
▷ *see also* **sprain** NOUN
slogarsi [76ᴱ]
□ She's sprained her ankle. S'è slogata una caviglia.

sprain NOUN
▷ *see also* **sprain** VERB
la slogatura *fem*

spray NOUN
▷ *see also* **spray** VERB
lo spray *masc* (PL gli spray)

to **spray** VERB
▷ *see also* **spray** NOUN
spruzzare [68]
□ She sprayed perfume on my hand. Mi ha spruzzato del profumo sulla mano.
■ **Graffiti was sprayed on the wall.** C'erano dei graffiti sul muro.

spread NOUN
▷ *see also* **spread** VERB

■ **cheese spread** formaggio da spalmare
■ **chocolate spread** cioccolata da spalmare

to **spread** VERB
▷ *see also* **spread** NOUN
1 spalmare [68]
□ Spread the cream over the cake. Spalma la panna montata sulla torta.
2 diffondersi [23ᴱ]
□ The news spread rapidly. La notizia si diffuse rapidamente.

to **spread out** VERB
1 sparpagliarsi [25ᴱ]
□ The soldiers spread out across the field. I soldati si sparpagliarono nel campo.
2 spiegare [76]
□ He spread the map out on the table. Ha spiegato la cartina sul tavolo.

spreadsheet NOUN
il foglio di calcolo *masc* (PL i fogli di calcolo)

spring NOUN
▷ *see also* **spring** ADJECTIVE
1 la primavera *fem*
□ in spring in primavera □ last spring la scorsa primavera
2 la molla *fem*
□ a broken spring una molla rotta
3 la sorgente *fem*
□ water from a spring acqua di sorgente

spring ADJECTIVE
▷ *see also* **spring** NOUN
primaverile (FEM primaverile)
□ spring weather tempo primaverile

spring-cleaning NOUN
le pulizie di primavera *fem pl*

spring onion NOUN
la cipollina *fem*

springtime NOUN
la primavera *fem*

sprinkler NOUN
l' irrigatore *masc*

sprint NOUN
▷ *see also* **sprint** VERB
lo sprint *masc* (PL gli sprint)
□ in a sprint finish con uno sprint finale
■ **the women's 100 metres sprint** i cento metri piani femminili

to **sprint** VERB
▷ *see also* **sprint** NOUN
fare [49] una corsa
□ She sprinted for the bus. Ha fatto una corsa per prendere l'autobus.

sprinter NOUN
il/la velocista *masc/fem*

sprouts NOUN PL
■ **Brussels sprouts** cavoletti di Bruxelles

spun VERB ▷ *see* **spin**

spy NOUN
la spia *fem*

to **spy on** VERB
spiare [55]

spying NOUN
lo spionaggio *masc*

to **squabble** VERB
bisticciare [13]
□ Stop squabbling! Smettetela di bisticciare!

square NOUN
▷ *see also* **square** ADJECTIVE
1 il quadrato *masc*
□ a square and a triangle un quadrato e un triangolo
2 la piazza *fem*
□ the main square la piazza principale

square ADJECTIVE
▷ *see also* **square** NOUN
quadrato (FEM quadrata)
□ a square table un tavolo quadrato □ two square metres due metri quadrati
■ It's two metres square. Misura due metri per due.

squash NOUN
▷ *see also* **squash** VERB
1 lo squash *masc (sport)*
■ a squash court un campo da squash
■ a squash racket una racchetta da squash
2 la zucca *fem (vegetable)*
■ orange squash sciroppo di arancia

to **squash** VERB
▷ *see also* **squash** NOUN
schiacciare [13]
□ You're squashing me. Mi stai schiacciando.

to **squeak** VERB
1 scricchiolare [68]
□ The door squeaked as it opened. La porta scricchiolò aprendosi.
2 lanciare [13] un gridolino
□ She squeaked with delight. Ha lanciato un gridolino di gioia.

to **squeeze** VERB
1 spremere [58]
□ Squeeze two large lemons. Spremete due grossi limoni.
2 stringere [109]
□ She squeezed my hand. Mi ha stretto la mano.
■ The thieves squeezed through a tiny window. I ladri si sono introdotti attraverso una finestrella.
■ I can squeeze you in at two o'clock. Le posso dare un appuntamento alle due.

to **squint** VERB
▷ *see also* **squint** NOUN
strizzare [68] gli occhi

squint NOUN
▷ *see also* **squint** VERB
lo strabismo *masc*
■ to have a squint essere [47ᴱ] strabico

squirrel NOUN
lo scoiattolo *masc*

to **stab** VERB
accoltellare [68]

stable NOUN
▷ *see also* **stable** ADJECTIVE
la stalla *fem*

stable ADJECTIVE
▷ *see also* **stable** NOUN
1 stabile (FEM stabile)
□ a stable relationship una relazione stabile
2 stazionario (FEM stazionaria, MASC PL stazionari, FEM PL stazionarie)
□ The injured man is in a stable condition. Le condizioni del ferito sono stazionarie.

stack NOUN
la pila *fem*
□ a stack of CDs una pila di CD
■ stacks of un sacco di □ They've got stacks of money. Hanno un sacco di soldi.

stadium NOUN
lo stadio *masc*

staff NOUN
il personale *masc*

staffroom NOUN
la sala professori *fem*

stage NOUN
▷ *see also* **stage** VERB
1 la fase *fem*
□ at this stage in the negotiations in questa fase dei negoziati
2 la tappa *fem*
□ the final stage of their tour la tappa conclusiva della loro tournée
3 il palco *masc* (PL i palchi)
□ She went on stage and did her act. È salita sul palco e ha fatto il suo show.
■ to go on the stage fare [49] del teatro

to **stage** VERB
▷ *see also* **stage** NOUN
1 organizzare [68] *(event)*
2 mettere [59] in scena *(play, show)*

to **stagger** VERB
barcollare [68]

stain NOUN
▷ *see also* **stain** VERB
la macchia *fem*
□ a large stain una grande macchia

to **stain** VERB
▷ *see also* **stain** NOUN
macchiare [17]

stainless steel NOUN
l' acciaio inossidabile *masc*

stain remover NOUN
lo smacchiatore *masc*

stair NOUN
il gradino *masc*

□ He left the bag on the bottom stair. Ha lasciato la borsa sul primo gradino.

staircase NOUN
la scala *fem*

stairs NOUN PL
le scale *fem pl*

□ a flight of stairs una rampa di scale

stale ADJECTIVE
■ **stale bread** pane raffermo

stalemate NOUN
il punto morto *masc*

□ The negotiations have reached a stalemate. I negoziati sono arrivati ad un punto morto.

stall NOUN
la bancarella *fem (in market)*

■ **the stalls** *(in theatre)* la platea

stamina NOUN
la resistenza fisica *fem*

stammer NOUN
■ **He's got a stammer.** È balbuziente.

stamp NOUN
▷ *see also* **stamp** VERB
1 il francobollo *masc*

□ I collect stamps. Faccio collezione di francobolli.

■ **a stamp album** un album per francobolli
2 il timbro *masc*

□ an official stamp un timbro ufficiale

LANGUAGE TIP Be careful not to translate **stamp** by **stampa**.

to **stamp** VERB
▷ *see also* **stamp** NOUN
timbrare [68]

□ He looked at her ticket, and stamped it. Le ha guardato il biglietto e l'ha timbrato.

■ **to stamp one's feet** battere [1] i piedi
□ The audience stamped their feet. Il pubblico batteva i piedi.

stamped ADJECTIVE
■ **stamped addressed envelope** busta già affrancata per la risposta

stand NOUN
▷ *see also* **stand** VERB
lo stand *masc* (PL gli stand)

□ our stand at the trade fair il nostro stand alla fiera

to **stand** VERB
▷ *see also* **stand** NOUN
1 stare [108E] in piedi

LANGUAGE TIP Word for word, this means 'to be on one's feet'.

□ He was standing by the door. Stava in piedi vicino alla porta.
2 essere [47E] situato

□ The house stands on top of a hill. La casa è situata in cima ad una collina.
3 sopportare [68]

□ I can't stand this noise. Non sopporto questo chiasso.

to **stand down** VERB
farsi [49E] da parte

to **stand for** VERB
1 essere [47E] l'abbreviazione di

□ 'BT' stands for 'British Telecom'. 'BT' è l'abbreviazione di 'British Telecom'.
2 tollerare [68]

□ I won't stand for it any more! Non ho intenzione di tollerarlo oltre!

to **stand in for** VERB
sostituire [51]

to **stand out** VERB
spiccare [18]

to **stand up** VERB
alzarsi [56E] in piedi

to **stand up for** VERB
difendere [33]

□ Stand up for your rights! Difendi i tuoi diritti!

standard ADJECTIVE
▷ *see also* **standard** NOUN
1 standard (FEM+PL standard)

□ standard English inglese standard
2 di serie *(accessories)*

standard NOUN
▷ *see also* **standard** ADJECTIVE
il livello qualitativo *masc*

□ The standard is very high. Il livello qualitativo è molto alto.

■ **She's got high standards.** È molto esigente.
■ **standard of living** tenore di vita

standard lamp NOUN
la lampada a stelo *fem*

stand-by ticket NOUN
il biglietto stand-by *masc*

standpoint NOUN
il punto di vista *masc*

stands NOUN PL
la tribuna *fem sing*

stank VERB ▷ *see* **stink**

staple NOUN
▷ *see also* **staple** ADJECTIVE, VERB
il punto metallico *masc* (PL i punti metallici)

to **staple** VERB
▷ *see also* **staple** ADJECTIVE, NOUN
cucire [41] con punti metallici

staple ADJECTIVE
▷ *see also* **staple** NOUN, VERB
principale (FEM principale)

□ Rice is their staple food. Il loro alimento principale è il riso.

stapler NOUN
la cucitrice *fem*

star NOUN
▷ *see also* **star** VERB
la stella *fem*

□ the moon and stars la luna e le stelle
■ **a TV star** una star della TV
■ **the stars** l'oroscopo

to **star** VERB
▷ see also **star** NOUN
avere [12] come protagonista
□ The film stars Sharon Stone. Il film ha come protagonista Sharon Stone.

■ …starring Johnny Depp …con Johnny Depp
■ to star in a film essere [47ᴱ] protagonista di un film

to **stare** VERB
guardare [68] fisso

stark ADVERB
■ stark naked completamente nudo

start NOUN
▷ see also **start** VERB
l' inizio masc
□ It's not much, but it's a start. Non è molto ma è pur sempre un inizio.

■ to make a start cominciare [13] □ Shall we make a start? Cominciamo?
■ for a start per cominciare □ For a start you need to check all the names. Per cominciare devi controllare tutti i nomi.

to **start** VERB
▷ see also **start** NOUN
1 iniziare [17]
□ What time does it start? A che ora inizia?
■ to start doing something iniziare [17] a fare qualcosa
2 avviare [17]
□ He wants to start his own business. Vuole avviare un'attività in proprio.
3 lanciare [13]
□ She started a campaign against drugs. Ha lanciato una campagna contro la droga.
4 far [49] partire
□ He couldn't start the car. Non riusciva a far partire la macchina.
5 partire [41ᴱ]
□ The car wouldn't start. La macchina non partiva.

to **start off** VERB
mettersi [59ᴱ] in viaggio
□ We started off first thing in the morning. Ci siamo messi in viaggio di buon mattino.

starter NOUN
l' antipasto masc

to **starve** VERB
morire [61ᴱ] di fame
□ People are starving. La gente muore di fame.
■ I'm starving! Ho una fame da lupo!

state NOUN
▷ see also **state** VERB
1 lo stato masc
□ It's an independent state. È uno stato indipendente.
2 le condizioni fem pl
□ He was in no state to drive. Non era in condizioni di guidare.

■ to be in a state of shock essere [47ᴱ] sotto shock
■ to be in a real state (person) essere [47ᴱ] tutto agitato
■ the States gli Stati Uniti

to **state** VERB
▷ see also **state** NOUN
dichiarare [68]
□ He stated his intention to resign. Ha dichiarato di essere intenzionato a dimettersi.
■ Please state your name and address. Fornisca nome e indirizzo.

stately home NOUN
la dimora signorile fem

statement NOUN
1 la dichiarazione fem
□ He made a statement to the police. Ha fatto una dichiarazione alla polizia.
2 l' affermazione fem
□ I found this statement vague and unclear. Ho trovato vaga e poco chiara l'affermazione.
3 l' estratto conto masc (bank statement)
■ a bank statement un estratto conto bancario

station NOUN
la stazione fem
■ the bus station la stazione degli autobus
■ the police station il commissariato di polizia
■ a radio station una stazione radiofonica

stationer's NOUN
la cartoleria fem

station wagon NOUN (US)
la station wagon fem

statue NOUN
la statua fem

status NOUN
lo stato civile masc

stay NOUN
▷ see also **stay** VERB
il soggiorno masc
□ my stay in Italy il mio soggiorno in Italia

to **stay** VERB
▷ see also **stay** NOUN
1 restare [68ᴱ]
□ Stay here! Resta qui!
2 stare [108ᴱ]
□ She's staying with friends. Sta presso amici.
3 alloggiare [58]
□ Where are you staying? Dove alloggi?
■ to stay the night passare [68ᴱ] la notte

to **stay in** VERB
restare [68ᴱ] a casa

to **stay up** VERB
rimanere [88ᴱ] alzato
□ We stayed up till midnight. Siamo rimasti alzati fino a mezzanotte.

steady ADJECTIVE
1 regolare (FEM regolare)

□ a steady income un reddito regolare
2 **fermo** (FEM ferma)

□ You need a steady hand for this job. Ci vuole mano ferma per fare questo lavoro.
3 **fisso** (FEM fissa)

□ a steady job un lavoro fisso
■ **steady progress** progresso costante
■ **Steady on!** Calma!

steak NOUN
la bistecca fem (PL le bistecche)

to **steal** VERB
rubare [68]

□ Thieves stole the statue. I ladri hanno rubato la statua. □ My car was stolen last week. Mi hanno rubato la macchina la settimana scorsa.

steam NOUN
▷ see also **steam** VERB
il vapore masc

□ a steam engine una locomotiva a vapore

to **steam** VERB
▷ see also **steam** NOUN
cuocere [29] a vapore (vegetables)

to **steam up** VERB
appannarsi [56E] (windows)

steel NOUN
l' acciaio masc

steep ADJECTIVE
ripido (FEM ripida)

steeple NOUN
il campanile masc

to **steer** VERB
guidare [68]

□ My father let me steer the car. Mio padre mi ha lasciato guidare la macchina. □ He steered us into the nearest seats. Ci ha guidati fino ai posti più vicini.

steering wheel NOUN
il volante masc

step NOUN
▷ see also **step** VERB
1 il passo masc

□ He took a step forward. Fece un passo in avanti.
2 il gradino masc

□ She tripped over the step. Ha inciampato sul gradino.

to **step** VERB
▷ see also **step** NOUN
fare [49] un passo

□ I tried to step forward. Ho cercato di fare un passo in avanti.
■ **Step this way, please.** Da questa parte, per favore.

to **step aside** VERB
farsi [49E] da parte

to **step back** VERB
indietreggiare [58]

to **step up** VERB
intensificare [18]

stepbrother NOUN
il fratellastro masc

stepdaughter NOUN
la figliastra fem

stepfather NOUN
il patrigno masc

stepladder NOUN
la scala a libretto fem

stepmother NOUN
la matrigna fem

stepsister NOUN
la sorellastra fem

stepson NOUN
il figliastro masc

stereo NOUN
lo stereo masc (PL gli stereo)

sterling ADJECTIVE
■ **pound sterling** lira sterlina

stew NOUN
lo spezzatino masc

steward NOUN
lo steward masc (PL gli steward)

stewardess NOUN
la hostess fem (PL le hostess)

stick NOUN
▷ see also **stick** VERB
il bastone masc

□ walking stick bastone da passeggio

to **stick** VERB
▷ see also **stick** NOUN
1 attaccare [18]

□ Stick the stamps on the envelope. Attacca i francobolli sulla busta.
2 attaccarsi [18E]

□ The rice stuck to the pan. Il riso s'è attaccato.
3 ficcare [18]

□ He picked up the papers and stuck them in his briefcase. Ha raccolto i documenti e li ha ficcati nella valigetta.
■ **I can't stick it any longer.** Non ne posso più.

to **stick by** VERB
rimanere [88E] al fianco di

□ She always stuck by him. È sempre rimasta al suo fianco.

to **stick out** VERB
1 tirare [68] fuori

□ The little girl stuck out her tongue. La bambina tirò fuori la lingua.
2 spiccare [18]

□ It sticks out because of the colour. Spicca a causa del colore.

to **stick up for** VERB
battersi [1E] per

sticker NOUN
l' autoadesivo masc

561

sticky – stop

sticky ADJECTIVE
1 appiccicoso (FEM appiccicosa)
   □ My hands are sticky. Ho le mani appiccicose.
2 adesivo (FEM adesiva)
   □ a sticky label un'etichetta adesiva

stiff ADJECTIVE, ADVERB
rigido (FEM rigida)
   □ stiff material stoffa rigida
   ■ **to have a stiff neck** avere [12] il torcicollo
   ■ **to feel stiff** sentirsi [41ᴱ] indolenzito
   ■ **to be bored stiff** essere [47ᴱ] annoiato a morte
   ■ **to be frozen stiff** essere [47ᴱ] congelato
   ■ **to be scared stiff** essere [47ᴱ] morto di paura

still ADVERB
   ▷ see also **still** ADJECTIVE
1 ancora
   □ I still haven't finished! Non ho ancora finito!
   □ Are you still in bed? Sei ancora a letto?
   □ better still meglio ancora
2 ciò nonostante
   □ She knows I don't like it, but she still does it. Sa che non mi piace, ma ciò nonostante lo fa lo stesso.
3 in fondo
   □ Still, it's the thought that counts. In fondo è il pensiero che conta.

still ADJECTIVE
   ▷ see also **still** ADVERB
fermo (FEM ferma)
   □ Keep still! Stai fermo!
   ■ **still mineral water** acqua minerale naturale
   ■ **a still life** una natura morta

sting NOUN
   ▷ see also **sting** VERB
la puntura fem
   □ a bee sting una puntura d'ape

to **sting** VERB
   ▷ see also **sting** NOUN
pungere [80]
   □ I got stung by a wasp. Mi ha punto una vespa.

stingy ADJECTIVE
avaro (FEM avara)

to **stink** VERB
   ▷ see also **stink** NOUN
puzzare [68]
   □ The room stank of cigarettes. La stanza puzzava di fumo.

stink NOUN
   ▷ see also **stink** VERB
la puzza fem

to **stir** VERB
mescolare [68]
   □ Stir the mixture well. Mescolare bene l'impasto.

to **stir up** VERB
1 fomentare [68] (ill feeling)
2 provocare [18] (trouble)

to **stitch** VERB
   ▷ see also **stitch** NOUN
cucire [41]

stitch NOUN
   ▷ see also **stitch** VERB
il punto masc
   □ I had five stitches. Mi hanno messo cinque punti.

stock NOUN
   ▷ see also **stock** VERB
1 la scorta fem
   □ a small stock of medicines una piccola scorta di medicine
   ■ **in stock** disponibile □ Yes, we've got your size in stock. Sì, abbiamo la sua taglia.
   ■ **out of stock** esaurito □ I'm sorry, they're out of stock. Mi dispiace, sono esauriti.
2 il brodo masc
   □ chicken stock brodo di pollo

to **stock** VERB
   ▷ see also **stock** NOUN
vendere [27]
   □ Do you stock camping stoves? Vendete fornellini da campeggio?

to **stock up** VERB
fare [49] provvista
   □ I must stock up on candles. Devo fare provvista di candele.

stock cube NOUN
il dado da brodo masc

stock exchange NOUN
la Borsa fem

stockings NOUN PL
le calze fem pl
   □ a pair of stockings un paio di calze

stock market NOUN
il mercato azionario masc

stole, stolen VERB ▷ see **steal**

stomach NOUN
lo stomaco masc (PL gli stomachi)
   ■ **to have stomach ache** avere [12] mal di stomaco

stone NOUN
1 la pietra fem
   □ a stone wall un muro di pietra
2 il nocciolo masc
   □ a peach stone un nocciolo di pesca
   DID YOU KNOW...?
   In Italy weight is expressed in kilos. A stone is about 6.3 kg.

stood VERB ▷ see **stand**

stool NOUN
lo sgabello masc

to **stop** VERB
   ▷ see also **stop** NOUN
fermarsi [56ᴱ]

□ The bus doesn't stop there. L'autobus non si ferma lì.

■ **Stop that!** Smettila!

■ **to stop doing something** smettere [59] di fare qualcosa □ I must stop smoking. Devo smettere di fumare.

■ **to stop somebody doing something** impedire [51] a qualcuno di fare qualcosa

■ **to stop to do something** fermarsi [56ᴱ] per fare qualcosa □ He stopped to look at the view. Si è fermato per guardare il panorama.

stop NOUN
▷ see also **stop** VERB
la fermata fem

□ a bus stop una fermata d'autobus

stopwatch NOUN
il cronometro masc

store NOUN
▷ see also **store** VERB
1 il negozio masc

□ a furniture store un negozio di mobili
2 la scorta fem

□ my secret store of biscuits la mia scorta segreta di biscotti

■ **to lie in store for somebody** aspettare [68] qualcuno □ We had no idea what lay in store for us. Non avevamo idea di cosa ci aspettasse.

to store VERB
▷ see also **store** NOUN
conservare [68]

storey (US **story**) NOUN
il piano masc

□ a three-storey building un palazzo a tre piani

storm NOUN
1 la tempesta fem

□ Their boat sank in a storm. La barca è affondata durante una tempesta.
2 il temporale masc

□ There was a power cut because of the storm. C'è stato un blackout a causa del temporale.

stormy ADJECTIVE
tempestoso (FEM tempestosa)

story NOUN
la storia fem

stove NOUN
1 la cucina fem

□ an electric stove una cucina elettrica
2 il fornello masc

□ a camping stove un fornello da campeggio

straight ADJECTIVE, ADVERB
1 dritto (FEM dritta)

□ a straight road una strada dritta
■ **a straight line** una linea retta
2 liscio (FEM liscia, MASC PL lisci, FEM PL lisce)

□ straight hair capelli lisci
3 eterosessuale (FEM eterosessuale)

□ I'm sure he's straight. Sono sicura che sia eterosessuale.
4 subito

□ I'll come straight back. Torno subito.
■ **straight away** subito
■ **straight on** sempre dritto

straightforward ADJECTIVE
1 semplice (FEM semplice)

□ The question seemed straightforward enough. La questione sembrava abbastanza semplice.
2 onesto (FEM onesta)

□ She's a very straightforward girl. È una ragazza molto onesta.

strain NOUN
▷ see also **strain** VERB
la pressione fem

□ She is under considerable strain. È molto sotto pressione.

■ **It was a strain.** È stata dura.

to strain VERB
▷ see also **strain** NOUN
1 sforzare [68] (eyes)
2 mettere [59] sotto pressione

□ The volume of flights is straining the air traffic control system. Il gran numero di voli sta mettendo sotto pressione il sistema di controllo del traffico aereo.

■ **to strain one's back** farsi [49ᴱ] male alla schiena

■ **to strain a muscle** farsi [49ᴱ] uno strappo muscolare

strained ADJECTIVE
■ **a strained muscle** uno strappo muscolare

stranded ADJECTIVE
■ **to be stranded** rimanere [88ᴱ] bloccato

strange ADJECTIVE
strano (FEM strana)

stranger NOUN
lo sconosciuto masc
la sconosciuta fem

LANGUAGE TIP Word for word, this means 'unknown person'.

□ Don't speak to strangers. Non parlare con gli sconosciuti.

■ **I'm a stranger here.** Non sono del posto.

to strangle VERB
strangolare [68]

strap NOUN
1 la tracolla fem

□ the strap of her bag la tracolla della borsa
2 il cinturino masc

□ I need a new strap for my watch. Ho bisogno di un cinturino nuovo per l'orologio.
3 la spallina fem

□ a top with narrow straps un top con le spalline strette

straw NOUN
1 la paglia fem

□ a straw hat un cappello di paglia

2 la cannuccia *fem* (PL le cannucce)
□ He drank with a straw. Ha bevuto con la cannuccia.
■ **That's the last straw!** Questa è la goccia che fa traboccare il vaso!

strawberry NOUN
la fragola *fem*

stray ADJECTIVE
randagio (FEM randagia, MASC PL randagi, FEM PL randage)
□ a stray cat un gatto randagio

stream NOUN
il ruscello *masc*

street NOUN
la strada *fem*
□ a narrow street una strada stretta
■ **a street plan** una cartina della città

street car NOUN (US)
il tram *masc* (PL i tram)

streetlamp NOUN
il lampione *masc*

streetwise ADJECTIVE
■ **to be streetwise** sapersela [94ᴱ] cavare
■ **a streetwise kid** un ragazzo smaliziato

strength NOUN
la forza *fem*

to stress VERB
▷ *see also* **stress** NOUN
sottolineare [68]
□ I would like to stress that... Vorrei sottolineare che...

stress NOUN
▷ *see also* **stress** VERB
1 lo stress *masc*
□ a stress-related illness una malattia legata allo stress
■ **I'm under stress.** Sono sotto pressione.
2 l' accento *masc*
□ The stress is on the first syllable. L'accento cade sulla prima sillaba.

stretch NOUN
▷ *see also* **stretch** VERB
1 il pezzo *masc*
□ a stretch of road un pezzo di strada
2 l' esercizio di stretching *masc*
□ We'll begin with a few stretches. Cominceremo con qualche esercizio di stretching.

to stretch VERB
▷ *see also* **stretch** NOUN
1 stiracchiarsi [17ᴱ]
□ The dog woke up and stretched. Il cane s'è svegliato e s'è stiracchiato.
2 allargarsi [76ᴱ]
□ My sweater stretched when I washed it. Il maglione s'è allargato durante il lavaggio.
3 tendere [112]
□ They stretched a rope between two trees. Hanno teso una corda tra due alberi.

to stretch out VERB
1 distendersi [112ᴱ]
□ There wasn't enough room to stretch out. Non c'era abbastanza spazio per distendersi.
2 allungare [76]
□ She stretched out an arm and grabbed me. Ha allungato un braccio per afferrarmi.

stretcher NOUN
la barella *fem*

stretchy ADJECTIVE
elastico (FEM elastica, MASC PL elastici, FEM PL elastiche)

strict ADJECTIVE
severo (FEM severa)

strike NOUN
▷ *see also* **strike** VERB
lo sciopero *masc*
■ **to be on strike** essere [47ᴱ] in sciopero
■ **to go on strike** scioperare [68]

to strike VERB
▷ *see also* **strike** NOUN
1 fare [49] sciopero
□ They decided to strike. Hanno deciso di fare sciopero.
2 colpire [51]
□ He struck the ball hard. Ha colpito forte la palla. □ They fear the killer may strike again. Temono che il killer possa colpire di nuovo.
3 suonare [68]
□ The clock struck three. L'orologio ha suonato le tre.
■ **to strike a match** accendere [2] un fiammifero

striker NOUN
1 lo/la scioperante *masc/fem*
□ The strikers wanted more money. Gli scioperanti volevano più soldi.
2 l' attaccante *masc/fem*
□ the Manchester striker l'attaccante del Manchester

striking ADJECTIVE
notevole (FEM notevole)
□ a striking resemblance una notevole somiglianza

string NOUN
1 lo spago *masc*
□ a piece of string un pezzo di spago
2 la corda *fem* (of violin, guitar)
3 la serie *fem* (PL le serie)
□ a string of victories una serie di vittorie

string bean NOUN
il fagiolino *masc*

to strip VERB
▷ *see also* **strip** NOUN
spogliarsi [25ᴱ]

strip NOUN
▷ *see also* **strip** VERB
1 la striscia *fem* (PL le strisce)
□ a strip of material una striscia di stoffa

2 la divisa *fem*

□ the Manchester strip la divisa del Manchester

strip cartoon NOUN
il fumetto *masc*

stripe NOUN
la striscia *fem* (PL le strisce)

striped ADJECTIVE
a righe

□ a striped skirt una gonna a righe

stripper NOUN
lo/la spogliarellista *masc/fem*

stripy ADJECTIVE
a righe

to **stroke** VERB
▷ *see also* **stroke** NOUN
accarezzare [68]

stroke NOUN
▷ *see also* **stroke** VERB
l' ictus *masc* (PL gli ictus)

□ He had a stroke. Ha avuto un ictus.

■ **a stroke of luck** un colpo di fortuna

stroll NOUN
■ **to go for a stroll** andare [6ᴱ] a fare due passi

stroller NOUN (US)
il passeggino *masc*

strong ADJECTIVE
forte (FEM forte)

□ She's stronger than me. Lei è più forte di me.

■ **Punctuality isn't my strong point.** La puntualità non è il mio forte.

strongly ADVERB
■ **We recommend strongly that...** Raccomandiamo vivamente di...

■ **to smell strongly of something** avere [12] un forte odore di qualcosa

■ **strongly built** robusto

■ **I don't feel strongly about it.** Per me fa lo stesso.

struck VERB ▷ *see* **strike**

to **struggle** VERB
▷ *see also* **struggle** NOUN
1 divincolarsi [56ᴱ]

□ He struggled, but he couldn't escape. Si divincolò ma non riuscì a liberarsi.

2 lottare [68]

□ He struggled to get custody of his daughter. Ha lottato per ottenere la custodia della figlia.

■ **They struggle to pay their bills.** Riescono a stento a pagare le bollette.

struggle NOUN
▷ *see also* **struggle** VERB
la lotta *fem*

□ a violent struggle una lotta violenta

■ **It was a struggle.** È stata dura.

stub NOUN
il mozzicone *masc* (cigarette)

to **stub out** VERB
spegnere [105]

stubborn ADJECTIVE
testardo (FEM testarda)

stuck VERB ▷ *see* **stick**

stuck ADJECTIVE
bloccato (FEM bloccata)

■ **to get stuck** rimanere [88ᴱ] bloccato

□ We got stuck in a traffic jam. Siamo rimasti bloccati nel traffico.

stuck-up ADJECTIVE
presuntuoso (FEM presuntuosa)

stud NOUN
1 l' orecchino *masc* (earring)

□ gold studs orecchini d'oro

2 il tacchetto *masc* (in football boots)

student NOUN
lo studente *masc*
la studentessa *fem*

studio NOUN
lo studio *masc*

□ a TV studio uno studio televisivo

■ **a studio flat** un monolocale

to **study** VERB
studiare [17]

stuff NOUN
la roba *fem*

□ Have you got all your stuff? Hai tutta la tua roba?

■ **I need some stuff for hay fever.** Mi serve qualcosa per il raffreddore da fieno.

stuffy ADJECTIVE
■ **It's stuffy in here.** Si soffoca qui dentro.

to **stumble** VERB
inciampare [68]

stung VERB ▷ *see* **sting**

stunk VERB ▷ *see* **stink**

stunned ADJECTIVE
sbalordito (FEM sbalordita)

stunning ADJECTIVE
fantastico (FEM fantastica, MASC PL fantastici, FEM PL fantastiche)

stunt NOUN
1 la trovata *fem*

□ a publicity stunt una trovata pubblicitaria

2 la scena pericolosa *fem*

□ He performed his own stunts. Ha girato personalmente le scene pericolose.

stuntman NOUN
lo stuntman *masc* (PL gli stuntman)

stupid ADJECTIVE
stupido (FEM stupida)

to **stutter** VERB
▷ *see also* **stutter** NOUN
balbettare [68]

stutter NOUN
▷ *see also* **stutter** VERB
■ **He's got a stutter.** È balbuziente.

style NOUN
lo stile *masc*

□ That's not his style. Non è nel suo stile.

subject NOUN
1 l' argomento *masc*
   □ The subject of my project is the internet. L'argomento della mia ricerca è Internet.
2 la materia *fem*
   □ What's your favourite subject? Quale materia preferisci?
3 il soggetto *masc (of sentence)*

subjunctive NOUN
il congiuntivo *masc*

submarine NOUN
il sottomarino *masc*

subscription NOUN
l' abbonamento *masc (to magazine)*
   ■ **to take out a subscription** abbonarsi [56ᴱ]

subsequently ADVERB
in seguito

to **subsidize** VERB
sovvenzionare [68]

subsidy NOUN
la sovvenzione *fem*

substance NOUN
la sostanza *fem*

substitute NOUN
   ▷ see also **substitute** VERB
1 il sostituto *masc*
   □ He's looking for a substitute. Sta cercando un sostituto.
   ■ **There's no substitute for personal contact.** Non c'è niente di meglio dei contatti personali.
2 la riserva *fem (in sport)*
   □ A substitute came on in the 71ˢᵗ minute. È entrata una riserva al 71° minuto.

to **substitute** VERB
   ▷ see also **substitute** NOUN
sostituire [51]
   □ They substituted gas for coal. Hanno sostituito il carbone con il gas.

subtitled ADJECTIVE
sottotitolato (FEM sottotitolata)

subtitles NOUN PL
i sottotitoli *masc pl*

subtle ADJECTIVE
sottile (FEM sottile)

to **subtract** VERB
sottrarre [115]

suburb NOUN
il sobborgo *masc (PL i sobborghi)*
   □ a London suburb un sobborgo di Londra
   ■ **in the suburbs** in periferia □ They live in the suburbs. Abitano in periferia.

suburban ADJECTIVE
periferico (FEM periferica, MASC PL periferici, FEM PL periferiche)
   □ a suburban street una via periferica
   ■ **a suburban shopping centre** un centro commerciale fuori città

subway NOUN
1 il sottopassaggio *masc (for pedestrians)*
2 la metropolitana *fem (train)*

to **succeed** VERB
riuscire [117ᴱ]
   ■ **to succeed in doing something** riuscire [117ᴱ] a fare qualcosa □ They succeeded in persuading her. Sono riusciti a persuaderla.
   ■ **The plan did not succeed.** Il piano è fallito.

success NOUN
il successo *masc*

successful ADJECTIVE
riuscito (FEM riuscita)
   □ a successful attempt un tentativo riuscito
   ■ **to be successful in doing something** riuscire [117] a fare qualcosa
   ■ **a successful lawyer** un avvocato affermato

successfully ADVERB
con successo

successive ADJECTIVE
consecutivo (FEM consecutiva)
   □ He was the winner for a second successive year. Ha vinto per il secondo anno consecutivo.

such ADJECTIVE, ADVERB
così
   □ such nice people gente così simpatica
   □ such a lot così tanto □ such a lot of work così tanto lavoro
   ■ **It was such a waste of time.** Era una tale perdita di tempo.
   ■ **such a thing** una cosa del genere □ I wouldn't dream of doing such a thing. Non mi sognerei di fare una cosa del genere.
   ■ **such as** come □ hot countries such as India paesi caldi come l'India
   ■ **There's no such thing.** Non esiste.
   ■ **He's not an expert as such, but...** Non è un vero e proprio esperto, però...

such-and-such ADJECTIVE
tale (FEM tale)
   □ such-and-such a place il tale posto

to **suck** VERB
succhiare [17]
   □ She sucks her thumb. Si succhia il pollice.

sudden ADJECTIVE
improvviso (FEM improvvisa)
   □ a sudden change un cambiamento improvviso
   ■ **all of a sudden** all'improvviso

suddenly ADVERB
improvvisamente

suede NOUN
la pelle scamosciata *fem*
   □ a suede jacket una giacca di pelle scamosciata

to **suffer** VERB
soffrire [66]
   ■ **to suffer from something** soffrire [66] di

qualcosa □ I suffer from hay fever. Soffro di raffreddore da fieno.

to **suffocate** VERB
soffocare [18]

sugar NOUN
lo zucchero *masc*

to **suggest** VERB
1 proporre [73]
□ She suggested going out for a pizza. Ha proposto di andare a mangiare la pizza.
2 consigliare [25]
□ I suggested they set off early. Ho consigliato loro di partire presto.
3 insinuare [68]
□ What are you trying to suggest? Cosa vuoi insinuare?

suggestion NOUN
la proposta *fem*

suicide NOUN
il suicidio *masc*
□ a case of attempted suicide un caso di tentato suicidio
■ **to commit suicide** suicidarsi [56ᴱ]

suicide bomber NOUN
l' attentatore suicida *masc*
l' attentatrice suicida *fem*

suit NOUN
▷ *see also* **suit** VERB
1 l' abito *masc (man's)*
2 il tailleur *masc* (PL i tailleur) *(woman's)*

to **suit** VERB
▷ *see also* **suit** NOUN
1 andare [6ᴱ] bene
□ What time would suit you? A che ora ti andrebbe bene? □ That suits me fine. Per me va benissimo.
2 stare [108ᴱ] bene a
□ That dress really suits you. Quel vestito ti sta benissimo.
■ **Suit yourself!** Fa' come ti pare!

suitable ADJECTIVE
1 conveniente (FEM conveniente)
□ a suitable time un'ora conveniente
2 adatto (FEM adatta)
□ suitable clothing vestiti adatti

suitcase NOUN
la valigia *fem* (PL le valigie)

suite NOUN
la suite *fem* (PL le suite)
□ a suite at the Paris Hilton una suite all'Hilton di Parigi
■ **a bedroom suite** *(furniture)* una camera da letto
■ **a three-piece suite** un divano e due poltrone

to **sulk** VERB
fare [49] il broncio

sulky ADJECTIVE
imbronciato (FEM imbronciata)

sultana NOUN
■ **sultanas** l'uva sultanina *sing*

sum NOUN
1 la somma *fem*
□ a sum of money una somma di denaro
2 l' addizione *fem*
□ We do sums. Facciamo le addizioni.

to **sum up** VERB
riassumere [11]
□ To sum up... Per riassumere...

to **summarize** VERB
riassumere [11]

summary NOUN
il riassunto *masc*

summer NOUN
▷ *see also* **summer** ADJECTIVE
l' estate *fem*
□ in the summer d'estate □ last summer l'estate scorsa

summer ADJECTIVE
▷ *see also* **summer** NOUN
estivo (FEM estiva)
□ summer clothes abiti estivi □ the summer holidays le vacanze estive

summertime NOUN
l' estate *fem*

summit NOUN
1 il vertice *masc*
□ the NATO summit in Rome il vertice della NATO a Roma
2 la cima *fem*
□ Yes, we reached the summit. Sì, abbiamo raggiunto la cima.

sun NOUN
il sole *masc*
□ in the sun al sole

to **sunbathe** VERB
prendere [77] il sole

sun block NOUN
la protezione solare totale *fem*

sunburn NOUN
la scottatura *fem*

sunburnt ADJECTIVE
scottato dal sole (FEM scottata dal sole)
□ sunburn shoulders spalle scottate dal sole
■ **to get sunburnt** scottarsi [56ᴱ]

Sunday NOUN
la domenica *fem*
■ **on Sunday** domenica □ I saw her on Sunday. L'ho vista domenica.
■ **on Sundays** di domenica □ I go swimming on Sundays. Vado in piscina di domenica.

Sunday school NOUN
la scuola di catechismo *fem*

sunflower NOUN
il girasole *masc*

sung VERB ▷ *see* sing

sunglasses NOUN PL
gli occhiali da sole *masc pl*

sunk VERB ▷ *see* **sink**

sunlight NOUN
la luce solare *fem*

sunny ADJECTIVE
■ **It's sunny.** C'è il sole.
■ **a sunny day** una bella giornata

sunrise NOUN
l' alba *fem*
□ before sunrise prima dell'alba

sunroof NOUN
il tettuccio apribile *masc*

sunscreen NOUN
la crema solare protettiva *fem*

sunset NOUN
il tramonto *masc*

sunshine NOUN
il sole *masc*
□ six hours of sunshine sei ore di sole □ in the sunshine al sole

sunstroke NOUN
l' insolazione *fem*
■ **to get sunstroke** prendere [77] un'insolazione

suntan NOUN
l' abbronzatura *fem*
□ her usual suntan la sua solita abbronzatura
■ **a suntan lotion** una lozione abbronzante
■ **suntan oil** olio abbronzante

super ADJECTIVE
fantastico (FEM fantastica, MASC PL fantastici, FEM PL fantastiche)

superb ADJECTIVE
magnifico (FEM magnifica, MASC PL magnifici, FEM PL magnifiche)

supermarket NOUN
il supermercato *masc*

supernatural ADJECTIVE
soprannaturale (FEM soprannaturale)

superstitious ADJECTIVE
superstizioso (FEM superstiziosa)

to **supervise** VERB
vigilare [68]

supervisor NOUN
1 il/la sorvegliante *masc/fem*
□ a supervisor in the factory un sorvegliante della fabbrica
2 il capocommesso *masc*
la capocommessa *fem (in shop)*
□ He's a supervisor in a big store. È capocommesso in un grande magazzino.

supper NOUN
la cena *fem*

supplement NOUN
il supplemento *masc*

to **supply** VERB
▷ *see also* **supply** NOUN
fornire [51]

■ **to supply somebody with something**
fornire [51] qualcosa a qualcuno □ The centre supplied us with all the equipment. Il centro ci ha fornito tutta l'attrezzatura.

supply NOUN
▷ *see also* **supply** VERB
1 la provvista *fem*
□ a supply of paper una provvista di carta
2 la fornitura *fem*
□ the water supply la fornitura dell'acqua
■ **supplies** rifornimenti
■ **medical supplies** medicinali

supply teacher NOUN
il/la supplente *masc/fem*

to **support** VERB
▷ *see also* **support** NOUN
1 appoggiare [58]
□ My friends have always supported me. I miei amici mi hanno sempre appoggiato.
2 tifare [68] per
□ What team do you support? Per quale squadra tifi?
3 mantenere [113]
□ She had to support five children. Ha dovuto mantenere cinque figli.

> **LANGUAGE TIP** Be careful not to translate **to support** by **sopportare**.

support NOUN
▷ *see also* **support** VERB
l' appoggio *masc*

supporter NOUN
1 il tifoso *masc*
la tifosa *fem*
□ a Leeds supporter un tifoso del Leeds
2 il/la simpatizzante *masc/fem*
□ a supporter of the Labour Party un simpatizzante del partito Laburista
3 il sostenitore *masc*
la sostenitrice *fem*
□ a supporter of reform un sostenitore della riforma

to **suppose** VERB
supporre [73]
□ I suppose he's late. Suppongo che sia in ritardo.
■ **I suppose so.** Credo di sì.
■ **He's supposed to...** Dovrebbe... □ He's supposed to leave on Sunday. Dovrebbe partire domenica.
■ **You're not supposed to smoke in the toilet.** Non è consentito fumare nel bagno.
■ **It's supposed to be...** Sembra che...
□ It's supposed to be the best hotel in the city. Sembra che sia il miglior albergo della città.

supposing CONJUNCTION
■ **supposing that** mettiamo che □ Supposing you won the lottery... Mettiamo che tu vinca alla lotteria...

to **suppress** VERB
reprimere [46]

surcharge NOUN
il sovrapprezzo *masc*

sure ADJECTIVE
sicuro (FEM sicura)
□ Are you sure? Sei sicuro?
■ **Sure!** Certo!
■ **to make sure that** assicurarsi [56E] che
□ I'm going to make sure the door's locked.
Voglio assicurarmi che la porta sia chiusa a
chiave.

surely ADVERB
■ **Surely you don't believe that?** Non ci
crederai davvero?

to **surf** VERB
▷ *see also* **surf** NOUN
fare [49] surf
■ **to surf the net** navigare [76] in Internet

surf NOUN
▷ *see also* **surf** VERB
la spuma *fem*

surface NOUN
la superficie *fem*

surfboard NOUN
la tavola da surf *fem*

surfing NOUN
il surf *masc (sport)*
■ **to go surfing** fare [49] surf

surgeon NOUN
il chirurgo *masc* (PL i chirurghi)

surgery NOUN
l' ambulatorio *masc*
□ surgery hours orario di ambulatorio

surname NOUN
il cognome *masc*

surprise NOUN
la sorpresa *fem*

surprised ADJECTIVE
sorpreso (FEM sorpresa)
□ I was surprised to see him. Ero sorpreso di
vederlo.

surprising ADJECTIVE
sorprendente (FEM sorprendente)

to **surrender** VERB
▷ *see also* **surrender** NOUN
arrendersi [83E]

surrender NOUN
▷ *see also* **surrender** VERB
la resa *fem*

to **surround** VERB
circondare [68]

surroundings NOUN PL
■ **in beautiful surroundings** in una
bellissima posizione

survey NOUN
▷ *see also* **survey** VERB
l' indagine *fem*

□ They did a survey of a thousand students.
È stata fatta un'indagine su un campione di
mille studenti.

to **survey** VERB
▷ *see also* **survey** NOUN
1 condurre [85] un'indagine su
□ They have surveyed a number of
companies. Hanno condotto un'indagine su
diverse società.
2 esaminare [68]
□ He surveyed the room. Ha esaminato la
stanza.
3 fare [49] un rilevamento di
□ They have surveyed the area. Hanno fatto
un rilevamento della zona.

surveyor NOUN
1 il perito geometra *masc (of buildings)*
2 l' agrimensore *masc (of land)*

survivor NOUN
il/la superstite *masc/fem*
□ There were no survivors. Non ci sono stati
superstiti.

to **suspect** VERB
▷ *see also* **suspect** NOUN
sospettare [68]

suspect NOUN
▷ *see also* **suspect** VERB
il sospetto *masc*
la sospetta *fem*

to **suspend** VERB
sospendere [8]

suspenders NOUN (US)
le bretelle *fem pl (braces)*

suspense NOUN
1 l' attesa *fem*
□ The suspense was terrible. L'attesa era
terribile.
2 la suspense *fem*
□ a film with lots of suspense un film ricco di
suspense

suspension NOUN
la sospensione *fem*

suspicious ADJECTIVE
1 sospettoso (FEM sospettosa)
□ He was suspicious at first. All'inizio era
sospettoso.
2 sospetto (FEM sospetta)
□ suspicious behaviour un comportamento
sospetto

to **swallow** VERB
inghiottire [51]

swam VERB ▷ *see* **swim**

swan NOUN
il cigno *masc*

to **swap** VERB
1 scambiare [17]
□ He swapped the vouchers for tickets. Ha
scambiato i voucher con i biglietti.

S

swat – swing

2 fare [49] scambio

□ Do you want to swap? Vuoi fare scambio?

to swat VERB
schiacciare [13]

to sway VERB
oscillare [68]

to swear VERB

1 giurare [68]

□ I swear I didn't know. Giuro che non lo sapevo. □ He swore he wouldn't do it again. Ha giurato che non l'avrebbe rifatto.

2 imprecare [18]

□ He swore under his breath. Ha imprecato sottovoce.

swearword NOUN
la parolaccia *fem* (PL le parolacce)

> **LANGUAGE TIP** Word for word, this means 'bad word'. The endings -**accio**, -**accia**, -**acci** or -**acce** imply something bad.

sweat NOUN
▷ *see also* **sweat** VERB
il sudore *masc*

to sweat VERB
▷ *see also* **sweat** NOUN
sudare [68]

sweater NOUN
il maglione *masc*

sweatshirt NOUN
la felpa *fem*

sweaty ADJECTIVE
sudato (FEM sudata)

Swede NOUN
lo/la svedese *masc/fem*

swede NOUN
la rapa svedese *fem* (vegetable)

Sweden NOUN
la Svezia *fem*

Swedish ADJECTIVE
▷ *see also* **Swedish** NOUN
svedese (FEM svedese)

Swedish NOUN
▷ *see also* **Swedish** ADJECTIVE
lo svedese *masc*

to sweep VERB
spazzare [68]

□ She swept the floor. Ha spazzato il pavimento.

sweet NOUN
▷ *see also* **sweet** ADJECTIVE

1 la caramella *fem*

□ a bag of sweets un sacchetto di caramelle

2 il dolce *masc*

□ Are you going to have a sweet? Prendi il dolce?

sweet ADJECTIVE
▷ *see also* **sweet** NOUN

1 dolce (FEM dolce)

□ a sweet wine un vino dolce

2 carino (FEM carina)

□ That was really sweet of you. È stato molto carino da parte tua.

■ **sweet and sour pork** maiale in agrodolce

sweetcorn NOUN
il mais *masc*

sweltering ADJECTIVE

■ **It was sweltering.** Faceva un caldo soffocante.

swept VERB ▷ *see* **sweep**

to swerve VERB
sterzare [68]

□ I swerved to avoid the cyclist. Ho sterzato per evitare il ciclista.

swim NOUN
▷ *see also* **swim** VERB
la nuotata *fem*

□ Let's go for a swim. Andiamo a fare una nuotata.

to swim VERB
▷ *see also* **swim** NOUN
nuotare [68]

□ Can you swim? Sai nuotare? □ I swam for an hour. Ho nuotato per un'ora. □ I've never swum in the sea. Non ho mai nuotato nel mare.

■ **to go swimming** andare [6E] a nuotare
■ **to swim across...** attraversare... [68] a nuoto □ She swam across the river. Ha attraversato il fiume a nuoto.

swimmer NOUN
il nuotatore *masc*
la nuotatrice *fem*

swimming NOUN
il nuoto *masc*

□ swimming and cycling il nuoto ed il ciclismo
■ **Do you like swimming?** Ti piace nuotare?
■ **a swimming cap** una cuffia da bagno
■ **a swimming costume** un costume da bagno
■ **swimming trunks** calzoncini da bagno

swimming pool NOUN
la piscina *fem*

swimsuit NOUN
il costume da bagno *masc*

swine flu NOUN
l'influenza suina *fem*

swing NOUN
▷ *see also* **swing** VERB
l'altalena *fem*

□ a slide and some swings uno scivolo e alcune altalene
■ **a mood swing** un cambiamento d'umore

to swing VERB
▷ *see also* **swing** NOUN
dondolare [68]

□ A large key swung from his belt. Dalla cintura gli dondolava una grossa chiave.
■ **to swing round** rigirarsi [56E] □ The canoe

English-Italian

suddenly swung round. La canoa si rigirò all'improvviso.

■ **He swung the bag over his shoulder.** Si mise la borsa sulla spalla.

■ **The gate swung shut.** Il cancello si è chiuso.

Swiss ADJECTIVE
▷ *see also* **Swiss** NOUN
svizzero (FEM svizzera)

Swiss NOUN
▷ *see also* **Swiss** ADJECTIVE
lo svizzero *masc*

■ **the Swiss** gli svizzeri

switch NOUN
▷ *see also* **switch** VERB
l' interruttore *masc*

to **switch** VERB
▷ *see also* **switch** NOUN
cambiare [17]
□ We switched partners. Abbiamo cambiato partner.

to **switch off** VERB
spegnere [105] *(TV, engine, machine)*

to **switch on** VERB
accendere [2] *(TV, engine, machine)*

Switzerland NOUN
la Svizzera *fem*

swollen ADJECTIVE
gonfio (FEM gonfia, MASC PL gonfi, FEM PL gonfie)
□ My ankle is swollen. Ho una caviglia gonfia.

to **swop** VERB
1 scambiare [17]
□ He swopped the vouchers for tickets. Ha scambiato i voucher con i biglietti.
2 fare [49] scambio
□ Do you want to swop? Vuoi fare scambio?

sword NOUN
la spada *fem*

swore, sworn VERB ▷ *see* **swear**

to **swot** VERB
▷ *see also* **swot** NOUN
sgobbare [68]

■ **to swot for an exam** sgobbare [68] per un esame

swot NOUN
▷ *see also* **swot** VERB
lo sgobbone *masc*
la sgobbona *fem*

swum VERB ▷ *see* **swim**

swung VERB ▷ *see* **swing**

syllabus NOUN
il programma *masc* (PL i programmi)

symbol NOUN
il simbolo *masc*

sympathetic ADJECTIVE
comprensivo (FEM comprensiva)
□ I told my teacher and she was sympathetic. L'ho detto all'insegnante e lei è stata comprensiva.

  LANGUAGE TIP Be careful not to translate **sympathetic** by **simpatico**.

to **sympathize** VERB
■ **to sympathize with somebody** capire [51] qualcuno

sympathy NOUN
la compassione *fem*

symptom NOUN
il sintomo *masc*

syringe NOUN
la siringa *fem* (PL le siringhe)

system NOUN
il sistema *masc* (PL i sistemi)

S

Tt

table NOUN
il tavolo *masc*
□ It's on the table. È sul tavolo.
■ **to lay the table** apparecchiare [17] la tavola

tablecloth NOUN
la tovaglia *fem*

tablespoon NOUN
il cucchiaio *masc*
□ a tablespoonful of sugar un cucchiaio di zucchero

tablet NOUN
1 la pastiglia *fem* (medicine)
2 il tablet *masc* (PL i tablet) (computer)

table tennis NOUN
il ping-pong *masc*

tabloid NOUN
il tabloid *masc* (PL i tabloid)

tackle NOUN
▷ see also **tackle** VERB
1 il contrasto *masc* (in football)
2 il placcaggio *masc* (in rugby)
■ **fishing tackle** l'attrezzatura da pesca

to **tackle** VERB
▷ see also **tackle** NOUN
1 contrastare [68] (in football)
2 placcare [18] (in rugby)
■ **to tackle a problem** affrontare [68] un problema

tact NOUN
il tatto *masc*

tactful ADJECTIVE
pieno di tatto (FEM piena di tatto)

tactics NOUN PL
la tattica *fem sing*

tactless ADJECTIVE
privo di tatto (FEM priva di tatto) (person)
■ **a tactless remark** un'osservazione indelicata

tadpole NOUN
il girino *masc*

tag NOUN
l'etichetta *fem*

tail NOUN
la coda *fem* (of animal)
■ **Heads or tails?** Testa o croce?
■ **the tail end** la fine

tail coat NOUN
la marsina *fem*

tailor NOUN
il sarto *masc*

to **take** VERB
1 prendere [77]
□ He took a plate out of the cupboard. Ha preso un piatto dall'armadietto.
2 portare [68]
□ Don't forget to take your camera. Non scordarti di portare la macchina fotografica.
□ He goes to London every week, but he never takes me. Va a Londra tutte le settimane ma non mi porta mai con sé.
3 volerci [123E]
□ It takes about an hour. Ci vuole circa un'ora.
□ It won't take long. Non ci vorrà molto. □ It takes a lot of money to do that. Ci vogliono un sacco di soldi per farlo.
4 sopportare [68]
□ He can't take being criticized. Non sopporta di essere criticato.
5 fare [49]
□ Have you taken your driving test yet? Hai già fatto l'esame di guida? □ He took a photograph. Ha fatto una fotografia.

to **take after** VERB
assomigliare [25] a
□ She takes after her mother. Assomiglia a sua madre.

to **take apart** VERB
■ **to take something apart** smontare [68] qualcosa

to **take away** VERB
1 portare [68] via
□ They took away all his belongings. Gli hanno portato via tutte le sue cose.
■ **hot meals to take away** i piatti pronti da asporto
2 togliere [114]
□ She was afraid her children would be taken away from her. Temeva che le togliessero i bambini.
3 sottrarre [115]
□ You need to take this amount away from the total. Devi sottrarre questa cifra dal totale.
■ **sixteen take away three** sedici meno tre

to **take back** VERB
1 riportare [68]

□ I took it back to the shop. L'ho riportato al negozio.

2 ritirare [68]

□ I take it all back! Ritiro tutto quello che ho detto!

to take down VERB
prendere [77] nota di

□ He took down the details. Ha preso nota dei particolari.

to take in VERB

1 capire [51]

□ I didn't really take it in. Non avevo capito bene.

2 abbindolare [68]

□ They were taken in by his story. Si sono lasciati abbindolare dalla sua storia.

to take off VERB

1 decollare [68]

□ The plane took off twenty minutes late. L'aereo ha decollato con venti minuti di ritardo.

2 levarsi [56ᴱ]

□ Take your coat off. Levati il cappotto.

to take out VERB
tirare [68] fuori

□ He opened his wallet and took out some money. Ha aperto il portafoglio e ha tirato fuori dei soldi.

■ **to take somebody out to...** portare [68] qualcuno a... □ He took her out to the theatre. L'ha portata a teatro.

to take over VERB
assumere [11] il controllo di

□ They took over the company last year. Hanno assunto il controllo della società l'anno scorso.

■ **I'll take over now.** Ti dò il cambio.

■ **to take over from somebody** subentrare [68ᴱ] a qualcuno

takeaway NOUN

1 il piatto pronto (da asporto) masc (food)

2 la tavola calda con piatti pronti (da asporto) fem (restaurant)

taken VERB ▷ see take

takeoff NOUN
il decollo masc

talcum powder NOUN
il talco masc

tale NOUN
il racconto masc

talent NOUN
il talento masc

□ He's got a lot of talent. Ha molto talento.

■ **to have a talent for** essere [47ᴱ] portato per □ He's got a real talent for languages. È molto portato per le lingue.

talented ADJECTIVE
di talento

□ She's a talented pianist. È una pianista di talento.

talk NOUN
▷ see also **talk** VERB

1 la conversazione fem

■ **to have a talk about** parlare [68] di □ I had a talk with my Mum about it. Ne ho parlato con mia mamma.

■ **to give a talk on** fare [49] un intervento su □ She gave a talk on ancient Egypt. Ha fatto un intervento sull'antico Egitto.

2 le chiacchiere fem pl

□ It's just talk. Sono solo chiacchiere.

■ **a talk show** un talk show

to talk VERB
▷ see also **talk** NOUN
parlare [68]

□ What did you talk about? Di che cosa avete parlato?

■ **to talk something over with somebody** discutere [37] qualcosa con qualcuno □ I'll talk it over with Tom. Ne discuterò con Tom.

talkative ADJECTIVE
loquace (FEM loquace)

tall ADJECTIVE
alto (FEM alta)

■ **to be two metres tall** essere [47ᴱ] alto due metri

tame ADJECTIVE
addomesticato (FEM addomesticata) (animal)

tampon NOUN
il tampone masc

tan NOUN
l' abbronzatura fem

tangerine NOUN
il mandarino masc

tangle NOUN
il groviglio masc

□ a tangle of wires un groviglio di fili

tank NOUN

1 il serbatoio masc (for fuel)

■ **a fish tank** un acquario

2 il carro armato masc

□ The army sent in its tanks. L'esercito ha inviato i carri armati.

tanker NOUN
l' autocisterna fem (lorry)

■ **an oil tanker** una petroliera

to tantalize VERB
tormentare [68]

tap NOUN
▷ see also **tap** VERB

1 il rubinetto masc

□ the hot tap il rubinetto dell'acqua calda

2 il colpetto masc

□ a tap on the door un colpetto alla porta

to tap VERB
▷ see also **tap** NOUN
dare [30] un colpetto a

□ I tapped him on the shoulder. Gli ho dato un colpetto sulla spalla.

tap-dancing – teaching assistant

tap-dancing NOUN
il tip tap *masc*

to **tape** VERB
▷ *see also* **tape** NOUN
registrare [68]
□ Did you tape the film last night? Hai registrato il film di ieri sera?

tape NOUN
▷ *see also* **tape** VERB
1 il nastro *masc*
□ adhesive tape nastro adesivo
2 la cassetta *fem (audio)*

tape deck NOUN
la piastra di registrazione *fem*

tape measure NOUN
il metro a nastro *masc*

tape recorder NOUN
il registratore a cassette *masc*

target NOUN
▷ *see also* **target** VERB
1 il bersaglio *masc*
□ The bullet hit the target. Il proiettile ha colpito il bersaglio.
2 l' obiettivo *masc*
□ He achieved his target. Ha raggiunto il suo obiettivo.

to **target** VERB
▷ *see also* **target** NOUN
puntare [68] su
□ They target childless couples. Puntano sulle coppie senza figli.

Tarmac® NOUN
l' asfalto *masc*

tart NOUN
la crostata *fem*

tartan ADJECTIVE
scozzese (FEM scozzese)
□ a tartan scarf una sciarpa scozzese

task NOUN
il compito *masc*
□ a difficult task un compito difficile

taste NOUN
▷ *see also* **taste** VERB
1 il sapore *masc*
□ It's got a really strange taste. Ha un sapore veramente strano.
■ **Would you like a taste?** Vuoi assaggiare?
2 il gusto *masc*
□ a joke in bad taste uno scherzo di cattivo gusto

to **taste** VERB
▷ *see also* **taste** NOUN
1 assaggiare [58]
□ Would you like to taste it? Vuoi assaggiare?
■ **You can taste the garlic in it.** Si sente il sapore dell'aglio.
2 sapere [94]
□ It tastes of fish. Sa di pesce.

tasteful ADJECTIVE
di buon gusto

tasteless ADJECTIVE
1 insipido (FEM insipida)
□ The soup was tasteless. La minestra era insipida.
2 di cattivo gusto
□ a tasteless remark un'osservazione di cattivo gusto

tasty ADJECTIVE
saporito (FEM saporita)

tattoo NOUN
il tatuaggio *masc*

taught VERB ▷ *see* **teach**

Taurus NOUN
il Toro *masc*
□ I'm Taurus. Sono del Toro.

tax NOUN
1 la tassa *fem*
□ the tax on cigarettes la tassa sulle sigarette
2 le tasse *fem pl*
□ Nobody wants to pay more tax. Nessuno vuole pagare più tasse.
■ **tax disc** il bollo

taxi NOUN
il taxi *masc* (PL i taxi)

taxi driver NOUN
il/la tassista *masc/fem*

taxi rank NOUN
il posteggio di taxi *masc* (PL i posteggi di taxi)

TB NOUN (= *tuberculosis*)
la tubercolosi *fem*

tea NOUN
1 il tè *masc* (PL i tè)
□ Would you like some tea? Vuoi del tè?
□ a cup of tea una tazza di tè
■ **tea leaves** le foglie di tè
2 la cena *fem (evening meal)*
□ We're having sausages for tea. Per cena abbiamo salsicce.

tea bag NOUN
la bustina di tè *fem*

tea break NOUN
la pausa per il tè *fem*

to **teach** VERB
insegnare [14]
□ She teaches physics. Insegna fisica.
□ My sister taught me to swim. Mia sorella mi ha insegnato a nuotare.
■ **That'll teach you!** Così impari!

teacher NOUN
l' insegnante *masc/fem*
□ my English teacher il mio insegnante di inglese
■ **He's the teacher's pet.** È il cocco della maestra.

teaching assistant NOUN
l' insegnante di sostegno *masc/fem*

tea cloth NOUN
  lo strofinaccio *masc* (PL gli strofinacci)

team NOUN
  la squadra *fem*

teapot NOUN
  la teiera *fem*

tear (1) NOUN
  la lacrima *fem*
  □ a few tears qualche lacrima
  ■ **to burst into tears** scoppiare [17ᴱ]
  a piangere

tear (2) NOUN
  ▷ *see also* **tear** VERB
  lo strappo *masc*
  □ There was a tear in the sleeve. C'era uno
  strappo sulla manica.

to **tear** VERB
  ▷ *see also* **tear** NOUN
1 strappare [68]
  □ Be careful or you'll tear the page. Stai
  attento o strapperai la pagina. □ He tore his
  jacket. Gli si è strappata la giacca. □ I've torn
  my jeans. Mi si sono strappati i jeans.
2 strapparsi [56ᴱ]
  □ It won't tear, it's very strong. Non si strappa,
  è molto resistente.

to **tear up** VERB
  strappare [68]
  □ He tore the letter up. Ha strappato la
  lettera.

tear gas NOUN
  il gas lacrimogeno *masc*

to **tease** VERB
1 tormentare [68]
  □ Stop teasing that poor animal! Smettila di
  tormentare quella povera bestia!
2 prendere [77] in giro

    LANGUAGE TIP Word for word, this means
    'to take into a circle'.

  □ He's teasing you. Ti sta prendendo in giro.
  □ I was only teasing. Ti stavo solo prendendo
  in giro.

teaspoon NOUN
  il cucchiaino *masc*

    LANGUAGE TIP Word for word, this means
    'little spoon'.

  □ a teaspoonful of sugar un cucchiaino di
  zucchero

teatime NOUN
  ■ **at teatime** all'ora del tè
  ■ **Teatime!** A tavola!

tea towel NOUN
  lo strofinaccio *masc* (PL gli strofinacci)

technical ADJECTIVE
  tecnico (FEM tecnica, MASC PL tecnici, FEM PL
  tecniche)

technical college NOUN
  l' istituto tecnico *masc* (PL gli istituti tecnici)

technician NOUN
  il tecnico *masc* (PL i tecnici)

technique NOUN
  la tecnica *fem* (PL le tecniche)

techno NOUN
  la musica techno *fem*

technological ADJECTIVE
  tecnologico (FEM tecnologica, MASC PL
  tecnologici, FEM PL tecnologiche)

technology NOUN
  la tecnologia *fem*

teddy bear NOUN
  l' orsacchiotto *masc*

teenage ADJECTIVE
1 per ragazzi
  □ a teenage magazine una rivista per ragazzi
2 adolescente (FEM adolescente)
  □ She has two teenage daughters. Ha due
  figlie adolescenti.

teenager NOUN
  l' adolescente *masc/fem*

teens NOUN PL
  ■ **She's in her teens.** È un'adolescente.

tee-shirt NOUN
  la maglietta *fem*

teeth NOUN PL ▷ *see* **tooth**

to **teethe** VERB
  mettere [59] i denti

teetotal ADJECTIVE
  astemio (FEM astemia, MASC PL astemi, FEM PL
  astemie)

telecommunications NOUN PL
  le telecomunicazioni *fem pl*

teleconference NOUN
  la teleconferenza *fem*

telephone NOUN
  il telefono *masc*
  ■ **a telephone call** una telefonata
  ■ **the telephone directory** l'elenco
  telefonico
  ■ **a telephone number** un numero di
  telefono

telesales NOUN PL
  la vendita per telefono *fem*

telescope NOUN
  il telescopio *masc*

television NOUN
  la televisione *fem*
  ■ **on television** alla televisione
  ■ **television licence** l'abbonamento alla
  televisione

television set NOUN
  il televisore *masc*

teleworking NOUN
  il telelavoro *masc*

to **tell** VERB
  dire [35]
  ■ **to tell lies** dire [35] bugie

t

575

■ **to tell somebody something** dire [35]
qualcosa a qualcuno □ Did you tell your
mother? L'hai detto a tua madre? □ I told him I
was going on holiday. Gli ho detto che andavo
in vacanza. □ Who told you? Chi te l'ha detto?

■ **to tell somebody to do something** dire
[35] a qualcuno di fare qualcosa □ He told me
to wait. Mi ha detto di aspettare.

■ **to tell a story** raccontare [68] una storia

■ **I can't tell the difference between them.**
Non riesco a distinguerli uno dall'altro.

■ **You can tell he's not serious.** Si vede che
sta scherzando.

to **tell off** VERB
sgridare [68]

telly NOUN
la tivù *fem* (PL le tivù)

temper NOUN
il carattere *masc*

□ He's got a terrible temper. Ha un pessimo
carattere.

■ **to be in a bad temper** essere [47ᴱ] in collera

■ **to lose one's temper** arrabbiarsi [17ᴱ]
□ I lost my temper. Mi sono arrabbiato.

temperature NOUN
la temperatura *fem*

■ **to have a temperature** avere [12] la febbre

temple NOUN
il tempio *masc*

temporary ADJECTIVE
temporaneo (FEM temporanea)

to **tempt** VERB
tentare [68]

□ I'm very tempted! Sono proprio tentato!

■ **to tempt somebody to do something**
cercare [18] di indurre qualcuno a fare
qualcosa

temptation NOUN
la tentazione *fem*

tempting ADJECTIVE
allettante (FEM allettante)

ten NUMBER
dieci

□ She's ten. Ha dieci anni.

tenant NOUN
l' inquilino *masc*
l' inquilina *fem*

to **tend** VERB

■ **to tend to do something** avere [12] la
tendenza a fare qualcosa

tender ADJECTIVE
tenero (FEM tenera)

tennis NOUN
il tennis *masc*

■ **a tennis ball** una pallina da tennis

■ **a tennis court** un campo da tennis

■ **a tennis racket** una racchetta da tennis

■ **tennis shoes** le scarpe da tennis

tennis player NOUN
il/la tennista *masc/fem*

tenor NOUN
il tenore *masc*

tenpin bowling NOUN
il bowling *masc*

tense ADJECTIVE
▷ see also **tense** NOUN
teso (FEM tesa)

tense NOUN
▷ see also **tense** ADJECTIVE
il tempo *masc*

■ **the present tense** il presente

tension NOUN
la tensione *fem*

tent NOUN
la tenda *fem*

■ **a tent peg** un picchetto da tenda

■ **a tent pole** un montante da tenda

tenth ADJECTIVE
decimo (FEM decima)

□ the tenth floor il decimo piano

■ **the tenth of August** il dieci agosto

term NOUN
1 il quadrimestre *masc*

□ It's nearly the end of term. È quasi la fine del
quadrimestre.

2 il termine *masc*

□ a short-term solution una soluzione a breve
termine

■ **to be on good terms with** essere [47ᴱ] in
buoni rapporti con

■ **to come to terms with** accettare [68]
□ He has come to terms with his disability.
Ha accettato la propria invalidità.

terminal ADJECTIVE
▷ see also **terminal** NOUN
terminale (FEM terminale)

terminal NOUN
▷ see also **terminal** ADJECTIVE

■ **a computer terminal** un terminale

■ **an air terminal** un terminal

terminally ADVERB

■ **the terminally ill** i malati terminali

terrace NOUN
la terrazza *fem*

□ We were sitting on the terrace. Eravamo
seduti in terrazza.

■ **Our house is in a terrace.** Abitiamo in una
casa a schiera.

■ **the terraces** (*in stadium*) le gradinate

terraced ADJECTIVE

■ **a terraced house** una casa a schiera

terrible ADJECTIVE
terribile (FEM terribile)

□ a terrible nightmare un incubo terribile

■ **to feel terrible** sentirsi [41ᴱ] malissimo

terribly ADVERB
1 terribilmente
  □ I'm terribly sorry. Mi spiace terribilmente.
2 moltissimo
  □ He suffered terribly. Ha sofferto moltissimo.
terrific ADJECTIVE
fantastico (FEM fantastica, MASC PL fantastici, FEM PL fantastiche)
  □ That's terrific! Fantastico!
  ■ **You look terrific!** Stai benissimo!
terrified ADJECTIVE
terrorizzato (FEM terrorizzata)
  □ I was terrified. Ero terrorizzata.
terrorism NOUN
il terrorismo *masc*
terrorist NOUN
il/la terrorista *masc/fem*
  □ a group of terrorists un gruppo di terroristi
  ■ **a terrorist attack** un attentato terroristico
to **test** VERB
  ▷ *see also* **test** NOUN
1 provare [68]
  □ Test the water with your wrist. Prova l'acqua con il polso.
2 sperimentare [68]
  □ The drug was tested on rats. La medicina è stata sperimentata sui ratti.
  ■ **to test something out** testare [68] qualcosa
3 interrogare [76]
  □ He tested us on the new vocabulary. Ci ha interrogato sui nuovi vocaboli.
  ■ **to be tested for drugs** essere [47ᴱ] sottoposto all'antidoping
  ■ **to test positive for** risultare [68ᴱ] positivo al test di
test NOUN
  ▷ *see also* **test** VERB
1 l'esperimento *masc*
  □ nuclear tests esperimenti nucleari □ tests on animals esperimenti sugli animali
2 l'analisi *fem* (PL le analisi)
  □ They're going to do some more tests. Devono fare altre analisi.
  ■ **to have a blood test** fare [49] le analisi del sangue
3 il compito in classe *masc*
  □ We've got an English test tomorrow. Abbiamo un compito in classe di inglese domani.
  ■ **a driving test** un esame di guida
test match NOUN
la partita internazionale *fem*
test tube NOUN
la provetta *fem*
tetanus NOUN
il tetano *masc*
  ■ **tetanus injection** l'antitetanica

textbook NOUN
il libro di testo *masc*
textiles NOUN PL
i tessuti *masc pl (fabrics)*
Thames NOUN
il Tamigi *masc*
than CONJUNCTION
1 di
  □ She's taller than me. È più alta di me.
  □ more than once più d'una volta
2 che
  □ I've got more CDs than tapes. Ho più CD che cassette.
to **thank** VERB
ringraziare [17]
  □ Don't forget to write and thank them. Mi raccomando, scrivi per ringraziarli.
  ■ **thank you** grazie
  ■ **thank you very much** grazie mille
thanks EXCLAMATION
grazie
that ADJECTIVE
  ▷ *see also* **that** PRONOUN, CONJUNCTION, ADVERB
quel (FEM quella)
  □ that day quel giorno □ that time quella volta
    LANGUAGE TIP Use **quell'** when the word following starts with a vowel.
  □ that man quell'uomo □ that university quell'università
    LANGUAGE TIP Use **quello** when the word following starts with gn, pn, ps, x, y, z or s + another consonant.
  □ that rucksack quello zaino
  ■ **that one** quello là □ Do you like this photo? — No, I prefer that one. Ti piace questa foto? — No, preferisco quella là.
that PRONOUN
  ▷ *see also* **that** ADJECTIVE, CONJUNCTION, ADVERB
1 quello (FEM quella) *(demonstrative)*
  □ What's that? Cos'è quello? □ Who's that? Chi è quello?
  ■ **Is that you?** Sei tu?
2 che *(in relative clause)*
  □ the man that we saw l'uomo che abbiamo visto
  ■ **the man that we spoke to** l'uomo con cui abbiamo parlato
that CONJUNCTION
  ▷ *see also* **that** ADJECTIVE, PRONOUN, ADVERB
che
  □ He thought that Henry was ill. Credeva che Henry fosse malato. □ I know that she likes chocolate. So che le piace la cioccolata.
that ADVERB
  ▷ *see also* **that** ADJECTIVE, PRONOUN, CONJUNCTION
così
  □ It was that big. Era grande così. □ It's not that difficult. Non è poi così difficile.

thatched ADJECTIVE
■ **a thatched cottage** un cottage con il tetto di paglia

the ARTICLE

> **LANGUAGE TIP** Use **il** before a masculine noun, **la** before a feminine noun and **l'** before nouns starting with vowels. If a masculine noun starts with gn, pn, ps, x, y, z or s + another consonant, use **lo**.

□ the boy il ragazzo □ the girl la ragazza □ the murderer l'assassino □ the rucksack lo zaino

> **LANGUAGE TIP** For plural nouns use **i** for masculine and **le** for feminine. If a masculine plural noun starts with a vowel or gn, pn, ps, x, y, z or s + another consonant use **gli**.

□ the knives i coltelli □ the forks le forchette □ the friends gli amici □ the spaghetti gli spaghetti

> **LANGUAGE TIP** 'the' is sometimes not translated.

□ on the internet su Internet □ paid by the hour pagato a ore

theatre (US **theater**) NOUN
il teatro *masc*

theft NOUN
il furto *masc*

their ADJECTIVE
1 il loro *masc* (PL i loro)
□ their money il loro denaro □ their parents i loro genitori
2 la loro *fem* (PL le loro)
□ their house la loro casa □ their girlfriends le loro ragazze

> **LANGUAGE TIP** 'their' is sometimes not translated.

□ They took off their coats. Si sono tolti il cappotto. □ They washed their hair. Si sono lavati i capelli. □ Someone has left their bag here. Qualcuno ha lasciato qui la borsa.

theirs PRONOUN

> **LANGUAGE TIP** The Italian pronoun agrees with the noun it is replacing.

1 il loro *masc* (PL i loro) (*their one*)
□ Our garden is smaller than theirs. Il nostro giardino è più piccolo del loro.
2 la loro *fem* (PL le loro) (*their one*)
□ It's not our car, it's theirs. Non è la nostra macchina, è la loro.
3 loro (*their property*)
□ Is this car theirs? È loro questa macchina?
■ **a friend of theirs** un loro amico

them PRONOUN
1 li *masc* (FEM le)

> **LANGUAGE TIP** Use **li** or **le** when 'them' is the direct object of the verb in the sentence.

□ I didn't see them. Non li ho visti. □ I'm looking for the tickets, have you seen them? Sto cercando i biglietti, li hai visti? □ Where are the sweets, have you eaten them? Dove sono le caramelle? Le hai mangiate?
2 loro

> **LANGUAGE TIP** Use **loro** when 'them' means 'to them'.

□ I gave them some brochures. Ho dato loro alcuni depliant.

> **LANGUAGE TIP** **loro** is also used after prepositions.

□ Sally came with them. Sally è venuta con loro. □ It's for them. È per loro.

theme NOUN
il tema *masc* (PL i temi)

theme park NOUN
il parco dei divertimenti a tema *masc* (PL i parchi dei divertimenti a tema)

themselves PRONOUN
1 si

> **LANGUAGE TIP** A verb + 'themselves' is often translated by a reflexive verb in Italian.

□ Did they hurt themselves? Si sono fatti male?
2 loro (*following an English preposition*)
□ beginners like themselves dei principianti come loro
■ **They built it themselves.** L'hanno costruito da soli.
■ **by themselves** da soli □ They never travel by themselves. Non viaggiano mai da soli.

then ADVERB, CONJUNCTION
1 poi
□ I get dressed, then I have breakfast. Mi vesto e poi faccio colazione.
2 allora
□ My pen's run out. — Use a pencil then! È finita la penna. — Allora usa una matita! □ There was no electricity then. Allora non c'era l'elettricità.
■ **now and then** ogni tanto

therapy NOUN
la terapia *fem*

there ADVERB
1 lì
□ Put it there, on the table. Mettilo lì sul tavolo.
■ **over there** là
■ **in there** là dentro
■ **on there** là sopra
■ **up there** lassù
■ **down there** laggiù
■ **There he is!** Eccolo!
2 ci
□ He went there on Friday. Ci è andato venerdì.
■ **there is** c'è □ There's a factory near my house. Vicino a casa mia c'è una fabbrica.
■ **there are** ci sono □ There are two apples each. Ci sono due mele per ciascuno.

■ **There's been a lot of rain.** È piovuto molto.

therefore ADVERB
perciò

there's = there is, there has

thermometer NOUN
il termometro masc

Thermos® NOUN
il thermos® masc (PL i thermos)

these ADJECTIVE, PRONOUN
questi (FEM queste)

□ these shoes queste scarpe □ I want these!
Voglio questi!

■ **these ones** questi qui masc (FEM queste qui)
□ These ones are very interesting. Questi qui
sono molto interessanti.

they PRONOUN
loro

□ Who are they? Chi sono loro?

  LANGUAGE TIP 'they' is often not translated.
□ They were watching TV. Guardavano la TV.
□ They're horrible. Sono bruttissimi.

■ **They say that...** Si dice che...

  LANGUAGE TIP loro is the pronoun used in
  spoken and informal written Italian. The
  more formal words for 'they' are essi and
  esse.

they'd = they had, they would
they'll = they will
they're = they are
they've = they have

thick ADJECTIVE
spesso (FEM spessa)

□ It's very thick. È molto spesso.

■ **The walls are one metre thick.** I muri
hanno uno spessore di un metro.

tonto (FEM tonta)

□ He's a bit thick. È un po' tonto.

thief NOUN
il ladro masc
la ladra fem

thigh NOUN
la coscia fem (PL le cosce)

thin ADJECTIVE
sottile (FEM sottile)

□ a thin slice una fettina sottile
magro (FEM magra)

□ She's very thin. È molto magra.

WORD POWER

You can use a number of other words
instead of **thin** to mean 'skinny':

skinny magro

□ She's too skinny. È troppo magra.

slim magro

□ a slim girl una ragazza magra

---

thing NOUN
la cosa fem

□ Where shall I put my things? Dove metto le
mie cose?

2 il coso masc

□ What's that thing called? Come si chiama
quel coso?

■ **You poor thing!** Poverino!

to **think** VERB
pensare [68]

□ What do you think of it? Cosa ne pensi?
□ Think carefully before you reply. Pensaci
bene prima di rispondere. □ What are you
thinking about? A cosa stai pensando? □ Have
you thought about it? Ci hai pensato? □ I think
so. Penso di sì.

■ **I don't think so.** Non credo.

■ **think tank** gruppo di esperti

■ **I'll think it over.** Ci penserò su.

third ADJECTIVE, NOUN
il terzo masc
la terza fem

□ the third time la terza volta □ I came third.
Sono arrivato terzo. □ a third of the population
un terzo della popolazione

■ **the third of March** il tre marzo

thirdly ADVERB
in terzo luogo

Third World NOUN
il terzo mondo masc

thirst NOUN
la sete

thirsty ADJECTIVE

■ **to be thirsty** avere [12] sete

  LANGUAGE TIP Word for word, this means
  'to have thirst'.

thirteen NUMBER
tredici

□ I'm thirteen. Ho tredici anni.

thirteenth ADJECTIVE
tredicesimo (FEM tredicesima)

□ the thirteenth floor il tredicesimo piano

■ **the thirteenth of March** il tredici marzo

thirty NUMBER
trenta

this ADJECTIVE, PRONOUN
questo (FEM questa)

□ this man quest'uomo □ this apple questa
mela □ What's this? Cos'è questo?

■ **this one** questo qui □ Pass me that pen. —
This one? Passami quella penna. — Questa qui?

■ **This is Gavin speaking.** Sono Gavin. (on the
phone)

thistle NOUN
il cardo masc

thorough ADJECTIVE
1 minuzioso (FEM minuziosa)

□ a thorough check un controllo minuzioso
2 meticoloso (FEM meticolosa)

□ She's very thorough. È molto meticolosa.

t

thoroughly ADVERB
1 meticolosamente
 □ I checked the car thoroughly. Ho controllato la macchina meticolosamente.
2 bene
 □ Mix the ingredients thoroughly. Mescolare bene gli ingredienti.
3 moltissimo
 □ I thoroughly enjoyed myself. Mi sono divertito moltissimo.

those ADJECTIVE
 ▷ see also **those** PRONOUN
1 quei (FEM quelle)
 □ those days quei giorni □ those pages quelle pagine
2 quegli masc

> **LANGUAGE TIP** Use **quegli** when the word following starts with a vowel, gn, pn, ps, x, y, z or s + another consonant.

 □ those students quegli studenti
 ■ **those ones** quelli lì □ Pass me those books. — Those ones? Passami quei libri. — Quelli lì?

those PRONOUN
 ▷ see also **those** ADJECTIVE
 quelli (FEM quelle)
 □ I want those! Voglio quelli!

though CONJUNCTION
 anche se
 □ Though it's raining... Anche se piove...
 □ He's nice, though not very bright. È simpatico, anche se non è molto sveglio.

thought VERB ▷ see **think**

thought NOUN
1 il pensiero masc
 □ It was a nice thought, thank you. È stato un pensiero carino, grazie.
2 l' idea fem
 □ I've just had a thought. Ho un'idea.

thoughtful ADJECTIVE
1 pensieroso (FEM pensierosa)
 □ She had a thoughtful expression on her face. Aveva un'espressione pensierosa.
2 premuroso (FEM premurosa)
 □ a thoughtful and caring man un uomo premuroso ed attento

thoughtless ADJECTIVE
 poco delicato (FEM poco delicata)
 □ It was thoughtless of her. È stato poco delicato da parte sua.

thousand NUMBER
 ■ **a thousand** mille □ a thousand pounds mille sterline

> **LANGUAGE TIP** When 'thousand' follows any number except one, -**mila** is added to the number.

 □ three thousand boys and five thousand girls tremila ragazzi e cinquemila ragazze
 ■ **thousands of people** migliaia di persone

thousandth ADJECTIVE, NOUN
 il millesimo masc
 la millesima fem

thread NOUN
 il filo masc

threat NOUN
 la minaccia fem (PL le minacce)

to **threaten** VERB
 minacciare [13]
 ■ **to threaten to do something** minacciare [13] di fare qualcosa

three NUMBER
 tre
 □ She's three. Ha tre anni.

three-dimensional ADJECTIVE
 tridimensionale (FEM tridimensionale)

three-piece suite NOUN
 un divano e due poltrone

threw VERB ▷ see **throw**

thrifty ADJECTIVE
 parsimonioso (FEM parsimoniosa)

thrill NOUN
 l' emozione fem
 □ It was a great thrill to see my team win. Che emozione vedere vincere la mia squadra!

thrilled ADJECTIVE
 ■ **I was thrilled.** Ero felicissimo.

thriller NOUN
 il thriller masc (PL i thriller)

thrilling ADJECTIVE
 entusiasmante (FEM entusiasmante)
 □ a thrilling match una partita entusiasmante

throat NOUN
 la gola fem
 ■ **to have a sore throat** avere [12] il mal di gola

to **throb** VERB
 ■ **My arm's throbbing.** Ho delle fitte al braccio.
 ■ **a throbbing pain** un dolore pulsante

throne NOUN
 il trono masc

through PREPOSITION, ADJECTIVE
1 attraverso
 □ through the crowd attraverso la folla
 ■ **to go through Crewe** passare [68ᴱ] per Crewe
 ■ **to look through a telescope** guardare [68] con un telescopio
 ■ **to walk through the woods** attraversare [68] i boschi
 ■ **a through train** un treno diretto
 ■ **'no through road'** 'strada senza uscita'
2 tramite
 □ I know her through my sister. La conosco tramite mia sorella.

throughout PREPOSITION
 ■ **throughout Britain** in tutta la Gran Bretagna
 ■ **throughout the year** per tutto l'anno

to **throw** VERB
1 lanciare [13]
□ He threw the ball to me. Mi ha lanciato la palla.
2 sconcertare [68]
□ That really threw him. L'ha veramente sconcertato.
■ **to throw a party** dare [30] una festa

to **throw away** VERB
buttare [68] via
□ He threw it away. Lo ha buttato via.

to **throw out** VERB
buttare [68] fuori

to **throw up** VERB
vomitare [68]

thug NOUN
il teppista masc

thumb NOUN
il pollice masc

thumbtack NOUN (US)
la puntina da disegno fem

to **thump** VERB
picchiare [17]

thunder NOUN
il tuono masc

thunderstorm NOUN
il temporale masc

thundery ADJECTIVE
temporalesco (FEM temporalesca, MASC PL temporaleschi, FEM PL temporalesche)

Thursday NOUN
il giovedì masc (PL i giovedì)
■ **on Thursday** giovedì □ I saw her on Thursday. L'ho vista giovedì.
■ **on Thursdays** di giovedì □ I go swimming on Thursdays. Vado in piscina di giovedì.

thyme NOUN
il timo masc

Tiber NOUN
il Tevere masc

tick NOUN
▷ see also **tick** VERB
1 il visto masc
□ Put a tick in the appropriate box. Metti un visto nell'apposita casella.
2 il ticchettio masc
□ the loud tick of the alarm clock il forte ticchettio della sveglia
■ **in a tick** in un attimo

to **tick** VERB
▷ see also **tick** NOUN
fare [49] un segno accanto a
□ Tick the right answer. Fai un segno accanto alla risposta esatta.

to **tick off** VERB
1 spuntare [68]
□ He ticked the names off the list. Ha spuntato i nomi dalla lista.

2 sgridare [68]
□ She ticked me off for being late. Mi ha sgridato per il ritardo.

ticket NOUN
1 il biglietto masc
□ the man inspecting the tickets l'uomo che controlla i biglietti
2 la multa per sosta vietata fem (for parking)

ticket inspector NOUN
il controllore masc

ticket office NOUN
la biglietteria fem

to **tickle** VERB
fare [49] il solletico

ticklish ADJECTIVE
■ **to be ticklish** soffrire [66] il solletico

tide NOUN
la marea fem
□ high tide alta marea □ low tide bassa marea

tidy ADJECTIVE
▷ see also **tidy** VERB
ordinato (FEM ordinata)

to **tidy** VERB
▷ see also **tidy** ADJECTIVE
mettere [59] in ordine
□ Go and tidy your room. Vai a mettere in ordine la tua camera.

to **tidy up** VERB
riordinare [68]

tie NOUN
▷ see also **tie** VERB
1 la cravatta fem
□ a red tie una cravatta rossa
2 il pareggio masc
□ The match ended in a tie. La partita è finita in pareggio.

to **tie** VERB
▷ see also **tie** NOUN
1 legare [76]
□ He tied the handles of the bag together. Ha legato assieme i manici della borsa.
■ **to tie a knot** fare [49] un nodo
2 pareggiare [58]
□ They tied three-all. Hanno pareggiato tre a tre.

to **tie up** VERB
legare [76]

tiger NOUN
la tigre fem

tight ADJECTIVE
1 stretto (FEM stretta)
□ This dress is a bit tight. Questo vestito è un po' stretto.
2 attillato (FEM attillata)
□ tight jeans jeans attillati

to **tighten** VERB
tendere [112]
□ He tightened the rope. Ha teso la corda.
■ **to tighten one's grip** stringere [109] la presa

■ **to tighten security** aumentare [68] la sicurezza

tightly ADVERB
stretto

■ **to hold something tightly** tenere [113] stretto qualcosa □ She held his hand tightly. Gli tenne stretta la mano.

■ **tightly closed** saldamente chiuso

tights NOUN PL
i collant *masc pl*

tile NOUN
1 la tegola *fem*
□ roofs with red tiles tetti con le tegole rosse
2 la piastrella *fem*
□ black and white tiles piastrelle bianche e nere

tiled ADJECTIVE
1 di tegole
□ a tiled roof un tetto di tegole
2 piastrellato (FEM piastrellata)
□ tiled walls pareti piastrellate

till NOUN
▷ *see also* **till** PREPOSITION
la cassa *fem*
□ Pay at the till. Pagare alla cassa.

till PREPOSITION
▷ *see also* **till** NOUN
fino a
□ I waited till ten o'clock. Ho aspettato fino alle dieci.

■ **not... till** non... prima di □ It won't be ready till next week. Non sarà pronto prima della settimana prossima.

■ **till now** finora

■ **till then** fino ad allora

time NOUN
1 l' ora *fem*
□ What time is it? Che ora è? □ What time do you get up? A che ora ti alzi? □ It was two o'clock, Italian time. Erano le due, ora italiana.
2 il tempo *masc*
□ I haven't got time. Non ho tempo. □ a long time molto tempo

■ **Have you lived here for a long time?** È da tanto che abiti qui?

■ **in time** in tempo □ just in time appena in tempo □ We arrived in time for lunch. Siamo arrivati in tempo per il pranzo.
3 la volta *fem*
□ this time questa volta □ two at a time due alla volta □ How many times? Quante volte?

■ **at times** certe volte

■ **two times two is four** due per due fa quattro

■ **to be on time** essere [47ᴱ] puntuale

■ **He never arrives on time.** Non è mai puntuale.

■ **in no time** prestissimo □ It will be ready in no time. Sarà pronto prestissimo.

■ **from time to time** di tanto in tanto

■ **for the time being** per il momento

■ **in a week's time** tra una settimana

■ **any time now** da un momento all'altro

■ **Come and see us any time.** Vieni a trovarci quando vuoi.

■ **to have a good time** divertirsi [41ᴱ] □ Did you have a good time? Vi siete divertiti?

■ **to take time out** assentarsi [56ᴱ]

■ **a time limit** un limite di tempo

time off NOUN
il tempo libero *masc*

timer NOUN
il contaminuti *masc* (PL i contaminuti)

time scale NOUN
i tempi d'esecuzione *masc pl*

time-share NOUN
la casa in multiproprietà *fem*

timetable NOUN
1 l' orario *masc*
□ the train timetable l'orario dei treni
2 il programma *masc* (PL i programmi)
□ the subjects on the timetable le materie in orario

time zone NOUN
il fuso orario *masc*

tin NOUN
1 il barattolo *masc*
□ a tin of beans un barattolo di fagioli

■ **a biscuit tin** una scatola per biscotti
2 lo stagno *masc (metal)*

tin foil NOUN
la carta stagnola *fem*

tinned ADJECTIVE
in scatola
□ tinned peaches pesche in scatola

tin opener NOUN
l' apriscatole *masc* (PL gli apriscatole)

tinsel NOUN
i fili argentati *masc pl*

tinted ADJECTIVE
colorato (FEM colorata) *(glasses, window)*

tiny ADJECTIVE
minuscolo (FEM minuscola)

tip NOUN
▷ *see also* **tip** VERB
1 la mancia *fem* (PL le mance)
□ He didn't leave a tip. Non ha lasciato la mancia.
2 il consiglio *masc*
□ a useful tip un buon consiglio
3 la punta *fem*
□ It's on the tip of my tongue. Ce l'ho sulla punta della lingua.
4 la discarica *fem* (PL le discariche)
□ I took the old sofa to the tip. Ho portato il vecchio divano in discarica.

■ **This place is a complete tip!** Che porcile!

to **tip** VERB
▷ see also **tip** NOUN
1 vuotare [68]
□ She tipped the leftovers in the bin. Ha vuotato gli avanzi nella pattumiera.
2 dare [30] la mancia a
□ He tipped the waiter. Ha dato la mancia al cameriere.
■ **to tip back** inclinare [68] all'indietro
□ She tipped back her head. Ha inclinato la testa all'indietro.

tipsy ADJECTIVE
brillo (FEM brilla)

tiptoe NOUN
■ **on tiptoe** in punta di piedi

tired ADJECTIVE
stanco (FEM stanca)
□ I'm tired. Sono stanco.
■ **to be tired of** essere [47ᴱ] stufo di □ I'm tired of waiting. Sono stufa di aspettare.

tiring ADJECTIVE
stancante (FEM stancante)

tissue NOUN
1 il tessuto masc
□ muscle tissue tessuto muscolare
2 il fazzolettino di carta masc
□ She blew her nose on a tissue. Si è soffiata il naso con un fazzolettino di carta.

tissue paper NOUN
la carta velina fem

title NOUN
il titolo masc
□ author and title autore e titolo

title role NOUN
il ruolo principale masc

to PREPOSITION
1 a
□ I go to school. Vado a scuola. □ ready to go pronto a partire
■ **from... to...** da... a... □ from nine o'clock to half past three dalle nove alle tre e mezza
2 da
□ He's been to the doctor. È stato dal medico. □ Let's go to Anne's house. Andiamo da Anne. □ something to drink qualcosa da bere □ I've got things to do. Ho da fare. □ It's easy to remember. È facile da ricordare.
3 in
□ We're going to Portugal. Andiamo in Portogallo.
4 fino a
□ Count to ten! Conta fino a dieci!
5 per
□ the train to London il treno per Londra □ I did it to help you. L'ho fatto per aiutarti. □ She's too young to go to school. È troppo piccola per andare a scuola.
■ **to be kind to** essere [47ᴱ] gentile con

■ **the key to the front door** la chiave della porta d'ingresso
■ **It's difficult to say.** È difficile dirlo.

toad NOUN
il rospo masc

toadstool NOUN
il fungo velenoso masc (PL i funghi velenosi)

toast NOUN
1 il pane tostato masc
□ a piece of toast una fetta di pane tostato
2 il brindisi masc (PL i brindisi)
■ **to drink a toast to somebody** brindare [68] a qualcuno

toaster NOUN
il tostapane masc (PL i tostapane)

toastie NOUN
il toast masc (PL i toast)

tobacco NOUN
il tabacco masc

tobacconist's NOUN
la tabaccheria fem

toboggan NOUN
lo slittino masc

tobogganing NOUN
■ **to go tobogganing** andare [6ᴱ] in slittino

today ADVERB
oggi

toddler NOUN
bambino che impara a camminare

toe NOUN
il dito del piede masc (FEM PL le dita del piede)
LANGUAGE TIP Word for word, this means 'foot finger'.

toffee NOUN
la caramella mou fem (PL le caramelle mou)

together ADVERB
insieme
□ Are they still together? Stanno ancora insieme?

toilet NOUN
la toilette fem (PL le toilette)
□ Where's the toilet? Dov'è la toilette?

toilet bag NOUN
il nécessaire da toilette masc

toilet paper NOUN
la carta igienica fem

toiletries NOUN PL
gli articoli da toilette masc pl

toilet roll NOUN
il rotolo di carta igienica masc

token NOUN
■ **as a token of our respect** come segno di rispetto
■ **a token gesture** un gesto simbolico
■ **a gift token** un buono omaggio

told VERB ▷ see **tell**

tolerant ADJECTIVE
tollerante (FEM tollerante)

toll NOUN
il pedaggio *masc*

tomato NOUN
il pomodoro *masc*

tomboy NOUN
il maschiaccio *masc*
□ She's a tomboy. È un maschiaccio.

tomorrow ADVERB
domani
□ See you tomorrow. Ci vediamo domani.
■ **the day after tomorrow** dopodomani

ton NOUN
la tonnellata *fem*

tongue NOUN
la lingua *fem*
■ **to say something tongue in cheek** dire [35] qualcosa ironicamente

tonic NOUN
l' acqua tonica *fem*
□ a bottle of tonic una bottiglia di acqua tonica
■ **a gin and tonic** un gin tonic

tonight ADVERB
1 stasera
□ Are you going out tonight? Esci stasera?
2 stanotte
□ I'll sleep well tonight. Stanotte dormirò bene.

tonsillitis NOUN
la tonsillite *fem*

tonsils NOUN PL
le tonsille *fem pl*

too ADVERB, ADJECTIVE
1 anche
□ My sister came too. È venuta anche mia sorella.
2 troppo
□ The water's too hot. L'acqua è troppo calda.
□ We arrived too late. Siamo arrivati troppo tardi.
■ **too much** troppo
■ **too many** troppi
■ **Too bad!** Tanto peggio!

took VERB ▷ *see* **take**

tool NOUN
l' attrezzo *masc*
□ a tool box una cassetta degli attrezzi

tooth NOUN
il dente *masc*

toothache NOUN
il mal di denti *masc*

toothbrush NOUN
lo spazzolino da denti *masc*

toothpaste NOUN
il dentifricio *masc*

top NOUN
▷ *see also* **top** ADJECTIVE
1 la cima *fem*
□ at the top of the page in cima alla pagina
□ from top to bottom da cima a fondo

2 il coperchio *masc (of jar)*
3 il tappo *masc (of bottle)*
4 la maglia *fem*
□ a cotton top una maglia di cotone
■ **a bikini top** il pezzo di sopra di un bikini
■ **on top of** sopra □ on top of the cupboard sopra l'armadio
■ **There's a surcharge on top of that.** In più c'è un sovrapprezzo.

top ADJECTIVE
▷ *see also* **top** NOUN
grande (FEM grande)
□ a top surgeon un grande chirurgo
■ **a top model** una top model
■ **top marks** ottimi voti *masc pl* □ He always gets top marks in Italian. Ha sempre degli ottimi voti in italiano.
■ **the top floor** l'ultimo piano

top hat NOUN
il cilindro *masc*

topic NOUN
l' argomento *masc*
□ The essay can be on any topic. Per il tema si può scegliere un argomento qualunque.

topical ADJECTIVE
d'attualità
□ a topical issue un problema d'attualità

topless ADJECTIVE
■ **to go topless** mettersi [59ᴱ] in topless

top-secret ADJECTIVE
top secret (FEM+PL top secret)

torch NOUN
la torcia elettrica *fem* (PL le torce elettriche)

tore, torn VERB ▷ *see* **tear**

tortoise NOUN
la tartaruga *fem* (PL le tartarughe)

torture NOUN
▷ *see also* **torture** VERB
la tortura *fem*

to **torture** VERB
▷ *see also* **torture** NOUN
torturare [68]

Tory NOUN
il conservatore *masc*
la conservatrice *fem*
□ the Tories i conservatori

to **toss** VERB
1 lanciare [13]
□ She tossed me a can of beer. Mi ha lanciato una lattina di birra.
2 mescolare [68]
□ Toss the salad in the dressing. Mescola l'insalata con il condimento.
■ **to toss pancakes** far [49] saltare le crêpes
■ **Shall we toss for it?** Facciamo a testa o croce?

total ADJECTIVE
▷ *see also* **total** NOUN
totale (FEM totale)

total NOUN
▷ see also **total** ADJECTIVE
il totale *masc*

totally ADVERB
completamente

touch
▷ see also **touch** VERB
■ **at the touch of a button** premendo un bottone
■ **to get in touch with somebody** mettersi [59ᴱ] in contatto con qualcuno
■ **to keep in touch with somebody** tenersi [113ᴱ] in contatto con qualcuno □ I'll keep in touch with Ann. Mi terrò in contatto con Ann.
■ **I haven't kept in touch with Hilary.** Non sono rimasta in contatto con Hilary.
■ **Keep in touch!** Fatti vivo!
■ **to lose touch** perdersi [69ᴱ] di vista
■ **to lose touch with somebody** perdere [69] di vista qualcuno

to **touch** VERB
▷ see also **touch** NOUN
1 toccare [18]
□ Don't touch that! Non toccare!
2 commuovere [62]
□ The story touched me deeply. La storia mi ha commosso profondamente.

touchdown NOUN
l' atterraggio *masc*

touched ADJECTIVE
commosso (FEM commossa)
□ I was really touched. Ero veramente commosso.

touching ADJECTIVE
commovente (FEM commovente)

touchline NOUN
la linea laterale *fem (on football pitch)*

touchpad NOUN
il touchpad *masc* (PL i touchpad)

touchy ADJECTIVE
suscettibile (FEM suscettibile)

tough ADJECTIVE
1 duro (FEM dura)
□ It was tough, but I managed okay. È stata dura ma ce l'ho fatta. □ The meat is tough. La carne è dura. □ He thinks he's a tough guy. Crede di essere un duro.
2 resistente (FEM resistente)
□ tough leather gloves guanti di pelle resistenti
■ **Tough luck!** Tanto peggio!

to **tour** VERB
▷ see also **tour** NOUN
visitare [68]
□ She is touring the country. Sta visitando il paese.
■ **The band is touring Europe.** Il complesso è in tournée in Europa.

tour NOUN
▷ see also **tour** VERB
1 il giro *masc*
□ a tour of the city un giro della città
■ **a package tour** un viaggio organizzato
2 la tournée *fem* (PL le tournée)
□ on tour in tournée
■ **to go on tour** fare [49] una tournée

tour guide NOUN
la guida turistica *fem* (PL le guide turistiche)

tourism NOUN
il turismo *masc*

tourist NOUN
il/la turista *masc/fem*
□ There were lots of tourists. C'erano molti turisti.
■ **tourist information office** l'ufficio informazioni turistiche

tournament NOUN
il torneo *masc*

tour operator NOUN
l' operatore turistico *masc* (PL gli operatori turistici)

towards (US **toward**) PREPOSITION
1 verso
□ He came towards me. È venuto verso di me.
2 nei confronti di
□ my feelings towards him i miei sentimenti nei suoi confronti

towel NOUN
l' asciugamano *masc*

tower NOUN
la torre *fem*
□ the towers of the castle le torri del castello

tower block NOUN
il palazzone *masc*

town NOUN
la città *fem* (PL le città)
□ a town plan una piantina della città
■ **the town centre** il centro

town hall NOUN
il municipio *masc* (PL i municipi)

town planning NOUN
l' urbanistica *fem*

tow truck NOUN
il carro attrezzi *masc* (PL i carri attrezzi)

toy NOUN
il giocattolo *masc*
□ a toy shop un negozio di giocattoli
■ **a toy car** un'automobilina

trace NOUN
▷ see also **trace** VERB
la traccia *fem* (PL le tracce)
□ There was no trace of the robbers. Non c'era traccia dei ladri.

to **trace** VERB
▷ see also **trace** NOUN
1 rintracciare [13]

□ The police are trying to trace witnesses. La polizia sta cercando di rintracciare i testimoni.
2 ricalcare [18] *(map, picture)*

tracing paper NOUN
la carta da ricalco *fem*

track NOUN
1 il sentiero *masc*
□ a mountain track un sentiero di montagna
2 il binario *masc*
□ A woman fell onto the tracks. Una donna è caduta sui binari.
3 la pista *fem*
□ two laps of the track due giri di pista
4 il pezzo *masc (song)*
□ This is my favourite track. Questo è il mio pezzo preferito.
5 la traccia *fem* (PL le tracce)
□ They followed the tracks for miles. Hanno seguito le tracce per miglia.

to **track down** VERB
trovare [68]
□ The police never tracked down the killer. La polizia non ha mai trovato l'assassino.

tracksuit NOUN
la tuta da ginnastica *fem*

tractor NOUN
il trattore *masc*

trade NOUN
▷ *see also* **trade** VERB
1 il commercio *masc*
□ the arms trade il commercio di armi
■ **free trade** il libero scambio
■ **a trade agreement** un accordo commerciale
2 il mestiere *masc*
□ to learn a trade imparare un mestiere

to **trade** VERB
▷ *see also* **trade** NOUN
1 commerciare [13]
□ They have traded with France for centuries. Commerciano con la Francia da secoli.
2 scambiare [17] *(swap)*
■ **They traded insults**. Si sono insultati a vicenda.

trade fair NOUN
la fiera campionaria *fem*

trade union NOUN
il sindacato *masc*

trade unionist NOUN
il/la sindacalista *masc/fem*

tradition NOUN
la tradizione *fem*

traditional ADJECTIVE
tradizionale (FEM tradizionale)

traffic NOUN
il traffico *masc*
□ heavy traffic traffico pesante

traffic circle NOUN (US)
la rotonda *fem*

traffic jam NOUN
l' ingorgo stradale *masc* (PL gli ingorghi stradali)

traffic lights NOUN PL
il semaforo *masc sing*

traffic warden NOUN
il vigile urbano *masc*

tragedy NOUN
la tragedia *fem*

tragic ADJECTIVE
tragico (FEM tragica, MASC PL tragici, FEM PL tragiche)

trailer NOUN
1 il rimorchio *masc*
□ a car and trailer un'auto con rimorchio
2 il trailer *masc* (PL i trailer) *(of film)*
3 la roulotte *fem* (PL le roulotte) *(US: caravan)*
□ They live in a trailer. Vivono in una roulotte.
■ **a trailer park** (US) un accampamento

train NOUN
▷ *see also* **train** VERB
il treno *masc*

to **train** VERB
▷ *see also* **train** NOUN
1 allenarsi [56ᴱ]
■ **to train for a race** allenarsi [56ᴱ] per una gara
■ **to train as a teacher** fare [49] tirocinio come insegnante
2 addestrare [68] *(animal)*

trained ADJECTIVE
qualificato (FEM qualificata)
□ highly trained workers operai altamente qualificati
■ **She's a trained nurse.** È infermiera diplomata.

trainee NOUN
l' apprendista *masc/fem*
□ a trainee plumber un apprendista idraulico
■ **She's a trainee.** Sta facendo il tirocinio.

trainer NOUN
1 l' allenatore *masc*
l' allenatrice *fem (of team)*
2 l' addestratore *masc*
l' addestratrice *fem (of animals)*
■ **a language trainer** un/un'insegnante di lingua

trainers NOUN PL
le scarpe da ginnastica *fem pl*

training NOUN
1 la formazione *fem*
□ a training course un corso di formazione
2 l' allenamento *masc*
□ He strained a muscle in training. Si è fatto uno strappo durante l'allenamento.

tram NOUN
il tram *masc* (PL i tram)

tramp NOUN
il vagabondo *masc*
la vagabonda *fem*

trampoline NOUN
il trampolino *masc*

tranquillizer NOUN
il tranquillante *masc*

□ She's on tranquillizers. Prende tranquillanti.

transfer NOUN
▷ *see also* **transfer** VERB
1 il trasferimento *masc*

□ a bank transfer un trasferimento bancario

■ **the transfer of power** il passaggio di potere

2 la decalcomania *fem (with design)*

to **transfer** VERB
▷ *see also* **transfer** NOUN
trasferire [51]

transfusion NOUN
la trasfusione *fem*

transistor NOUN
il transistor *masc* (PL i transistor)

transit NOUN
il transito *masc*

□ in transit in transito

transit lounge NOUN
la sala di transito *fem*

to **translate** VERB
tradurre [85]

translation NOUN
la traduzione *fem*

translator NOUN
il traduttore *masc*
la traduttrice *fem*

transparent ADJECTIVE
trasparente (FEM trasparente)

transplant NOUN
il trapianto *masc*

□ a heart transplant un trapianto cardiaco

transport NOUN
▷ *see also* **transport** VERB
1 il trasporto *masc*

□ rail transport il trasporto ferroviario

2 il mezzo di trasporto *masc*

□ Have you got your own transport? Hai un tuo mezzo di trasporto?

■ **public transport** i trasporti pubblici

to **transport** VERB
▷ *see also* **transport** NOUN
trasportare [68]

trap NOUN
▷ *see also* **trap** VERB
la trappola *fem*

to **trap** VERB
▷ *see also* **trap** NOUN
catturare [68]

□ They trapped rabbits. Catturavano conigli usando delle trappole.

■ **to be trapped** rimanere [88ᴱ] intrappolato

□ Six people were trapped in the burning building. Sei persone sono rimaste intrappolate nell'edificio in fiamme.

trash NOUN (US)
la spazzatura *fem*

□ I'll take out the trash. Porto fuori la spazzatura.

■ **the trash can** il secchio della spazzatura

trashy ADJECTIVE
scadente (FEM scadente)

□ a trashy film un film scadente

traumatic ADJECTIVE
traumatico (FEM traumatica, MASC PL traumatici, FEM PL traumatiche)

to **travel** VERB
▷ *see also* **travel** NOUN
viaggiare [58]

□ I prefer to travel by train. Preferisco viaggiare in treno.

■ **We travelled over 800 kilometres.** Abbiamo fatto più di ottocento chilometri.

■ **to travel round the world** girare [68] il mondo

■ **News travels fast!** Le notizie volano!

travel NOUN
▷ *see also* **travel** VERB

■ **Air travel is cheap these days.** Viaggiare in aereo non costa molto di questi tempi.

■ **travel insurance** l'assicurazione di viaggio

travel agency NOUN
l'agenzia di viaggi *fem*

travel agent NOUN
l'agente di viaggio *masc/fem*

traveller (US **traveler**) NOUN
il viaggiatore *masc*
la viaggiatrice *fem*

traveller's cheque NOUN
il traveller's cheque *masc* (PL i traveller's cheque)

travelling (US **traveling**) NOUN
■ **I love travelling.** Adoro viaggiare.

travel sickness NOUN
1 il mal d'auto *masc (in car)*
2 il mal d'aria *masc (in plane)*

tray NOUN
il vassoio *masc* (PL i vassoi)

to **tread** VERB
calpestare [68]

■ **to tread on something** calpestare [68] qualcosa □ He trod on a piece of glass. Ha calpestato un pezzo di vetro.

■ **He trod on her foot.** Le ha pestato un piede.

treasure NOUN
il tesoro *masc*

treat NOUN
▷ *see also* **treat** VERB
1 il regalo *masc*

□ as a birthday treat come regalo di compleanno

2 la sorpresa *fem*

□ They're taking her out to dinner as a treat. Per farle una sorpresa la portano fuori a cena.

■ **to give somebody a treat** fare [49] una sorpresa a qualcuno

3 la leccornia *fem (to eat)*

to **treat** VERB

▷ *see also* **treat** NOUN

1 trattare [68]

□ The hostages were well treated. Gli ostaggi sono stati trattati bene.

2 curare [68]

□ She was treated for a head wound. Le hanno curato una ferita alla testa.

■ **to treat somebody to something** offrire [66] qualcosa a qualcuno

■ **I'll treat you!** Offro io!

treatment NOUN

1 la cura *fem*

□ an effective treatment for eczema una cura efficace per l'eczema

2 il trattamento *masc*

□ We don't want any special treatment. Non vogliamo un trattamento di favore.

to **treble** VERB

▷ *see also* **treble** ADVERB

triplicare [18]

treble ADVERB

▷ *see also* **treble** VERB

il triplo

□ He now earns treble what he did. Guadagna il triplo rispetto a prima.

tree NOUN

l' albero *masc*

to **tremble** VERB

tremare [68]

tremendous ADJECTIVE

1 fantastico (FEM fantastica, MASC PL fantastici, FEM PL fantastiche)

□ He was a tremendous person. Era una persona fantastica.

2 strepitoso (FEM strepitosa)

□ a tremendous success un successo strepitoso

LANGUAGE TIP Be careful not to translate **tremendous** by **tremendo**.

trend NOUN

la moda *fem*

□ the latest trend l'ultima moda

■ **There's a trend towards part-time employment.** Il lavoro part-time è sempre più diffuso.

trendy ADJECTIVE

trendy (FEM+PL trendy)

trial NOUN

1 il processo *masc*

□ the witnesses at the trial i testimoni del processo

2 la prova *fem*

□ a trial period un periodo di prova

triangle NOUN

il triangolo *masc*

tribe NOUN

la tribù *fem* (PL le tribù)

trick NOUN

▷ *see also* **trick** VERB

il trucco *masc* (PL i trucchi)

□ It's not easy, there's a trick to it. Non è facile, c'è un trucco per farlo.

■ **to play a trick on somebody** giocare [18] un tiro a qualcuno

to **trick** VERB

▷ *see also* **trick** NOUN

imbrogliare [25]

tricky ADJECTIVE

difficile (FEM difficile)

tricycle NOUN

il triciclo *masc*

trifle NOUN

la zuppa inglese *fem*

LANGUAGE TIP Word for word, this means 'English soup'.

□ Trifle or ice cream? Zuppa inglese o gelato?

■ **a trifle...** un po'... □ That seems a trifle ambitious. Sembra un po' ambizioso.

to **trim** VERB

▷ *see also* **trim** NOUN, ADJECTIVE

1 spuntare [68] *(hair)*

2 tagliare [25] *(grass)*

trim NOUN

▷ *see also* **trim** VERB, ADJECTIVE

■ **to have a trim** farsi [49ᴱ] spuntare i capelli

trim ADJECTIVE

▷ *see also* **trim** VERB, NOUN

snello (FEM snella)

□ a trim figure una figura snella

trip NOUN

▷ *see also* **trip** VERB

il viaggio *masc*

■ **to go on a trip** fare [49] un viaggio □ Have a good trip! Buon viaggio!

■ **a day trip** una gita di un giorno

to **trip** VERB

▷ *see also* **trip** NOUN

inciampare [68]

triple ADJECTIVE

triplo (FEM tripla)

triplets NOUN PL

■ **to have triplets** avere [12] tre gemelli

trivial ADJECTIVE

insignificante (FEM insignificante)

LANGUAGE TIP Be careful not to translate **trivial** by **triviale**.

trod, trodden VERB ▷ *see* **tread**

trolley NOUN

il carrello *masc*

trombone NOUN

il trombone *masc*

troops NOUN PL
le truppe *fem pl*

trophy NOUN
il trofeo *masc*

tropical ADJECTIVE
tropicale (FEM tropicale)

to **trot** VERB
trottare [68]

trouble NOUN
il problema *masc* (PL i problemi)
▢ The trouble is, it's expensive. Il problema è
che costa troppo.
■ **to be in trouble** essere [47ᴱ] nei guai
■ **What's the trouble?** Cosa c'è che non va?
■ **stomach trouble** disturbi gastrici *masc pl*
■ **to take a lot of trouble over something**
mettere [59] molto impegno in qualcosa

troublemaker NOUN
l' attaccabrighe *masc/fem* (PL gli attaccabrighe)

trousers NOUN PL
i pantaloni *masc pl*

trout NOUN
la trota *fem*

truant NOUN
■ **to play truant** marinare [68] la scuola

truck NOUN
il camion *masc* (PL i camion)

truck driver NOUN
il/la camionista *masc/fem*

trucker NOUN (US)
il/la camionista *masc/fem*

true ADJECTIVE
vero (FEM vera)
▢ That can't be true! Non può essere vero!
■ **to come true** avverarsi [56ᴱ] ▢ I hope my
dream will come true. Spero che il mio sogno si
avveri.

truly ADVERB
veramente
▢ It was a truly remarkable victory. È stata
veramente una vittoria straordinaria.
■ **Yours truly...** Distinti saluti...

trumpet NOUN
la tromba *fem*

trunk NOUN
1 il tronco *masc* (PL i tronchi)
▢ a tree trunk un tronco d'albero
2 la proboscide *fem* (of elephant)
3 il baule *masc* (luggage)
4 il bagagliaio *masc* (US: boot)
▢ Put it in the trunk. Mettilo nel portabagagli.
■ **swimming trunks** i calzoncini da bagno

trust NOUN
▷ see also **trust** VERB
la fiducia *fem*

to **trust** VERB
▷ see also **trust** NOUN
fidarsi [56ᴱ] di

▢ Don't you trust me? Non ti fidi di me?
▢ Trust me! Fidati di me!

trusting ADJECTIVE
fiducioso (FEM fiduciosa)

truth NOUN
la verità *fem*

truthful ADJECTIVE
sincero (FEM sincera)

try NOUN
▷ see also **try** VERB
il tentativo *masc*
▢ his third try il suo terzo tentativo
■ **to have a try** provare [68]
■ **to give something a try** provare [68]
qualcosa
■ **It's worth a try.** Vale la pena di tentare.

to **try** VERB
▷ see also **try** NOUN
1 tentare [68]
▢ I tried, but failed. Ho tentato, ma non ci
sono riuscito. ▢ You must try harder. Devi
tentare ancora.
■ **to try to do something** provare [68] a fare
qualcosa
■ **to try again** ritentare [68]
2 assaggiare [58] (taste)
▢ Would you like to try some? Vuoi
assaggiare?

to **try on** VERB
provare [68] (clothes)

to **try out** VERB
provare [68] (machine, system)

T-shirt NOUN
la maglietta *fem*

tube NOUN
1 il tubetto *masc*
▢ a tube of toothpaste un tubetto di
dentifricio
2 il tubo *masc*
▢ a cardboard tube un tubo di cartone
■ **the Tube** la metropolitana di Londra

tuberculosis NOUN
la tubercolosi *fem*

Tuesday NOUN
il martedì *masc* (PL i martedì)
■ **on Tuesday** martedì ▢ I saw her on
Tuesday. L'ho vista martedì.
■ **on Tuesdays** di martedì ▢ I go swimming
on Tuesdays. Vado in piscina di martedì.
■ **Shrove Tuesday** martedì grasso

tug-of-war NOUN
il tiro alla fune *masc*

tuition NOUN
le lezioni *fem pl*
■ **private tuition** le lezioni private

tulip NOUN
il tulipano *masc*

t

to **tumble** VERB
fare [49] un capitombolo
□ He tumbled down the steps. Ha fatto un capitombolo giù dalle scale.

tumble dryer NOUN
l' asciugatrice *fem*

tummy NOUN
la pancia *fem* (PL le pance)
■ **tummy ache** il mal di pancia

tuna NOUN
il tonno *masc*

tune NOUN
la melodia *fem*
□ a familiar tune una melodia familiare
■ **to play in tune** essere [47ᴱ] accordato
■ **to sing out of tune** stonare [68]

Tunisia NOUN
la Tunisia *fem*

tunnel NOUN
il tunnel *masc* (PL i tunnel)

Turin NOUN
Torino *fem*

Turk NOUN
il turco *masc*
la turca *fem*
■ **the Turks** i turchi

Turkey NOUN
la Turchia *fem*

turkey NOUN
il tacchino *masc*

Turkish ADJECTIVE
▷ *see also* **Turkish** NOUN
turco (FEM turca, MASC PL turchi, FEM PL turche)

Turkish NOUN
▷ *see also* **Turkish** ADJECTIVE
il turco *masc (language)*

turn NOUN
▷ *see also* **turn** VERB
1 la svolta *fem*
□ Take the next turn left. Prendi la prossima svolta a sinistra.
■ **'no left turn'** 'divieto di svolta a sinistra'
2 il turno *masc*
■ **to take turns** fare [49] a turno
■ **It's my turn!** Tocca a me!

to **turn** VERB
▷ *see also* **turn** NOUN
1 girare [68]
□ Turn right at the lights. Al semaforo gira a destra.
2 diventare [68ᴱ]
□ When he's drunk he turns nasty. Quando è ubriaco diventa cattivo.
■ **It's turned cold.** La temperatura è scesa.
■ **to turn into** trasformarsi [56ᴱ] in □ The holiday turned into a nightmare. La vacanza si è trasformata in un incubo.

to **turn back** VERB
tornare [68ᴱ] indietro
□ We turned back. Siamo tornati indietro.

to **turn down** VERB
1 rifiutare [68]
□ He turned down the offer. Ha rifiutato l'offerta.
2 abbassare [68]
□ Shall I turn the heating down? Abbasso il riscaldamento?

to **turn off** VERB
1 spegnere [105]
□ I'll turn off the radio. Spegnerò la radio.
2 chiudere [20]
□ You haven't turned off the tap. Non hai chiuso il rubinetto.

to **turn on** VERB
1 accendere [2]
□ Shall I turn on the light? Accendo la luce?
2 aprire [9]
□ She turned on the tap. Ha aperto il rubinetto.

to **turn out** VERB
risultare [68ᴱ]
□ It turned out to be a mistake. È risultato essere un errore. □ It turned out that she was right. È risultato che aveva ragione lei.

to **turn round** VERB
1 girare [68] *(car)*
2 voltarsi [56ᴱ] *(person)*

to **turn up** VERB
1 arrivare [68ᴱ]
□ She never turned up. Non è mai arrivata.
2 saltare [68ᴱ] fuori
□ The painting turned up in London. Il dipinto è saltato fuori a Londra.
3 alzare [68]
□ Can you turn up the volume? Puoi alzare il volume?

turning NOUN
la svolta *fem*
□ We took the wrong turning. Non abbiamo preso la svolta giusta.
■ **a turning point** una svolta decisiva

turnip NOUN
la rapa *fem*

turquoise ADJECTIVE
turchese (FEM turchese)

turtle NOUN
la testuggine *fem*

Tuscany NOUN
la Toscana *fem*

tutor NOUN
l' insegnante privato *masc*
l' insegnante privata *fem*

tuxedo NOUN (US)
lo smoking *masc* (PL gli smoking)

TV NOUN
la TV *fem* (PL le TV)

tweet NOUN
  ▷ *see also* **tweet** VERB
  il post su Twitter *masc*

to **tweet** VERB
  ▷ *see also* **tweet** NOUN
  scrivere [99] su Twitter

tweezers NOUN PL
  la pinzetta *fem*

twelfth ADJECTIVE
  dodicesimo (FEM dodicesima)
  □ the twelfth floor il dodicesimo piano
  ■ **the twelfth of August** il dodici agosto

twelve NUMBER
  dodici
  □ She's twelve. Ha dodici anni.

twentieth ADJECTIVE
  ventesimo (FEM ventesima)
  □ the twentieth floor il ventesimo piano
  ■ **the twentieth of May** il venti maggio

twenty NUMBER
  venti
  □ He's twenty. Ha vent'anni.
  ■ **in twenty fourteen** nel
  duemilaquattordici

twice ADVERB
  due volte
  □ I tried twice. Ho provato due volte.
  ■ **twice as much** il doppio

twin NOUN
  il gemello *masc*
  □ my twin brother mio fratello gemello
  ■ **twin beds** i letti gemelli
  ■ **a twin room** una camera con due letti

twinned ADJECTIVE
  gemellato (FEM gemellata)
  □ Nottingham is twinned with Minsk.
  Nottingham è gemellata con Minsk.

to **twist** VERB
1 attorcigliare [17] *(hair)*
  ■ **to twist one's ankle** slogarsi [76ᴱ] la
  caviglia
2 travisare [68]
  □ You're twisting my words. Stai travisando
  le mie parole.

twit NOUN
  il cretino *masc*
  la cretina *fem*

two NUMBER
  due
  □ She's two. Ha due anni.

type NOUN
  ▷ *see also* **type** VERB
  il tipo *masc*
  □ What type of camera have you got? Che tipo
  di macchina fotografica hai?

to **type** VERB
  ▷ *see also* **type** NOUN
  battere [1] a macchina

typewriter NOUN
  la macchina da scrivere *fem*

typical ADJECTIVE
  tipico (FEM tipica, MASC PL tipici, FEM PL tipiche)
  □ That's just typical! Tipico!

tyre (US **tire**) NOUN
  lo pneumatico *masc*
  ■ **tyre pressure** la pressione dei pneumatici

Uu

UFO NOUN (= *Unidentified Flying Object*)
l' ufo *masc* (PL gli ufo)

ugh EXCLAMATION
puah!

ugly ADJECTIVE
brutto (FEM brutta)

UK NOUN (= *United Kingdom*)
il Regno Unito *masc*

ulcer NOUN
l' ulcera *fem*
  □ a stomach ulcer un'ulcera allo stomaco
  ■ a mouth ulcer un'afta

Ulster NOUN
l' Ulster *masc*

ultimate ADJECTIVE
supremo (FEM suprema)
  □ the ultimate challenge la sfida suprema
  ■ the ultimate in luxury il massimo del lusso

ultimately ADVERB
in fin dei conti
  □ Ultimately, it's your decision. In fin dei conti, la decisione è tua.

umbrella NOUN
l' ombrello *masc*

umpire NOUN
1 l' arbitro *masc* (*in cricket*)
2 il giudice di gara *masc* (*in tennis*)

UN NOUN (= *United Nations*)
l' ONU *fem*

unable ADJECTIVE
  ■ to be unable to do something non poter [74] fare qualcosa □ He was unable to come. Non è potuto venire.

unacceptable ADJECTIVE
inaccettabile (FEM inaccettabile)

unanimous ADJECTIVE
unanime (FEM unanime)

unattended ADJECTIVE
incustodito (FEM incustodita)
  □ Please do not leave your luggage unattended. Non lasciare il bagaglio incustodito.

unavoidable ADJECTIVE
inevitabile (FEM inevitabile)

unaware ADJECTIVE
  ■ to be unaware of non essere [47ᴱ] a conoscenza di □ She was unaware of the

regulations. Non era a conoscenza del regolamento.
  ■ She was unaware she was being filmed. Non si era resa conto di essere filmata.

unbearable ADJECTIVE
insopportabile (FEM insopportabile)

unbeatable ADJECTIVE
imbattibile (FEM imbattibile)

unbelievable ADJECTIVE
incredibile (FEM incredibile)

unborn ADJECTIVE
  ■ the unborn child il feto

unbreakable ADJECTIVE
infrangibile (FEM infrangibile)

uncanny ADJECTIVE
strano (FEM strana)
  □ That's uncanny! È strano!
  ■ an uncanny resemblance una rassomiglianza stupefacente

uncertain ADJECTIVE
incerto (FEM incerto)
  □ The future is uncertain. L'avvenire è incerto.

uncivilized ADJECTIVE
incivile (FEM incivile)

uncle NOUN
lo zio *masc* (PL gli zii)

uncomfortable ADJECTIVE
1 scomodo (FEM scomoda)
  □ an uncomfortable position una posizione scomoda
2 a disagio
  □ He makes me feel uncomfortable. Mi fa sentire a disagio.

unconscious ADJECTIVE
svenuto (FEM svenuta)

uncontrollable ADJECTIVE
irrefrenabile (FEM irrefrenabile)

unconventional ADJECTIVE
1 anticonformista (FEM anticonformista) (*person*)
2 poco convenzionale (FEM poco convenzionale) (*technique*)

under PREPOSITION
sotto
  □ The cat's under the table. Il gatto è sotto il tavolo. □ the tunnel under the Channel il tunnel sotto la Manica
  ■ under there lì sotto □ What's under there? Cosa c'è lì sotto?

■ **children under ten** bambini al di sotto dei dieci anni

■ **under twenty people** meno di venti persone

under-age ADJECTIVE

■ **He's under-age.** È minorenne.

undercover ADJECTIVE, ADVERB
1 segreto (FEM segreta)

□ an undercover agent un agente segreto
2 in incognito

□ She was working undercover. Agiva in incognito.

underdog NOUN

■ **Inter were the underdogs.** L'Inter era la squadra sfavorita.

to **underestimate** VERB
sottovalutare [68]

to **undergo** VERB
sottoporsi [73ᴱ] a

underground ADJECTIVE, ADVERB
▷see also **underground** NOUN
1 sotterraneo (FEM sotterranea)

□ an underground car park un parcheggio sotterraneo
2 sottoterra

□ Moles live underground. Le talpe vivono sottoterra.

■ **to go underground** (political group, terrorist) entrare [68ᴱ] in clandestinità

underground NOUN
▷see also **underground** ADJECTIVE, ADVERB
la metropolitana fem

to **underline** VERB
sottolineare [68]

underneath PREPOSITION, ADVERB
sotto

□ underneath the carpet sotto la moquette □ I got out of the car and looked underneath. Sono sceso dalla macchina e ho guardato sotto.

underpaid ADJECTIVE
sottopagato (FEM sottopagata)

underpants NOUN PL
le mutande da uomo fem pl

underpass NOUN
il sottopassaggio masc

undershirt NOUN (US)
1 la canottiera fem (sleeveless)
2 la maglietta fem (with short sleeves)

underskirt NOUN
la sottogonna fem

to **understand** VERB
capire [51]

□ Do you understand? Capisci? □ I don't understand the question. Non ho capito la domanda.

■ **Is that understood?** È chiaro?

understanding ADJECTIVE
comprensivo (FEM comprensiva)

understood VERB ▷see **understand**

undertaker NOUN
l' impresario di pompe funebri masc

underwater ADJECTIVE, ADVERB
1 subacqueo (FEM subacquea)

□ underwater photography fotografia subacquea
2 sott'acqua

□ a sequence filmed underwater una scena girata sott'acqua

underwear NOUN
la biancheria intima fem

▎ LANGUAGE TIP Word for word, this means 'intimate linen'.

underwent VERB ▷see **undergo**

to **undo** VERB
1 sbottonare [68]

□ She undid her coat. Si è sbottonata il cappotto.
2 sciogliere [97]

□ I can't undo the knot. Non riesco a sciogliere il nodo.

■ **Your laces are undone.** Hai le scarpe slacciate.

to **undress** VERB
spogliarsi [25ᴱ]

uneconomic ADJECTIVE
poco redditizio (FEM poco redditizia)

unemployed ADJECTIVE
disoccupato (FEM disoccupata)

■ **the unemployed** i disoccupati

unemployment NOUN
la disoccupazione fem

unexpected ADJECTIVE
inatteso (FEM inattesa)

unexpectedly ADVERB
inaspettatamente

unfair ADJECTIVE
ingiusto (FEM ingiusta)

unfamiliar ADJECTIVE
sconosciuto (FEM sconosciuta)

□ I heard an unfamiliar voice. Ho sentito una voce sconosciuta.

unfashionable ADJECTIVE
fuori moda

unfit ADJECTIVE
fuori forma

□ I'm really unfit at the moment. Al momento sono proprio fuori forma.

■ **to be unfit for work** essere [47ᴱ] inabile al lavoro

to **unfold** VERB
spiegare [76]

□ She unfolded the map. Ha spiegato la cartina.

unforgettable ADJECTIVE
indimenticabile (FEM indimenticabile)

unfortunately ADVERB
sfortunatamente

to **unfriend** VERB
cancellare [68] dagli amici

□ Her sister has unfriended her on Facebook.
Sua sorella l'ha cancellata dagli amici su
Facebook.

unfriendly ADJECTIVE
antipatico (FEM antipatica, MASC PL antipatici,
FEM PL antipatiche)

□ The waiters are a bit unfriendly. I camerieri
sono un po' antipatici.

ungrateful ADJECTIVE
ingrato (FEM ingrata)

unhappy ADJECTIVE
infelice (FEM infelice)

□ He was very unhappy as a child. Da bambino
era molto infelice.

■ **to look unhappy** avere [12] l'aria triste

unhealthy ADJECTIVE
malaticcio (FEM malaticcia, MASC PL malaticci,
FEM PL malaticce)

□ an unhealthy girl una ragazza malaticcia

■ **He's unhealthy and depressed.** Non sta
bene ed è depresso.

■ **an unhealthy diet** una dieta poco
equilibrata

uni NOUN
l' università fem (PL le università)

□ He's at uni. È all'università.

uniform NOUN
▷ see also **uniform** ADJECTIVE
l' uniforme fem

■ **school uniform** la divisa scolastica

uniform ADJECTIVE
▷ see also **uniform** NOUN
uniforme (FEM uniforme)

uninhabited ADJECTIVE
disabitato (FEM disabitata)

union NOUN
il sindacato masc

□ Do you belong to a union? Appartieni ad un
sindacato?

Union Jack NOUN
la bandiera del Regno Unito fem

unique ADJECTIVE
unico (FEM unica)

unit NOUN
l' unità fem (PL le unità)

□ a unit of measurement un'unità di misura

■ **a kitchen unit** un elemento componibile
della cucina

United Kingdom NOUN
il Regno Unito masc

United Nations NOUN
le Nazioni Unite fem pl

United States NOUN PL
gli Stati Uniti masc pl

universe NOUN
l' universo masc

university NOUN
l' università fem (PL le università)

unleaded petrol NOUN
la benzina verde fem

unless CONJUNCTION
se non

□ We won't get there in time unless we leave
earlier. Se non partiamo prima non arriveremo
in tempo. □ unless I am mistaken... se non mi
sbaglio...

unlike PREPOSITION
a differenza di

□ Unlike Tom, I really enjoy flying. Io, a
differenza di Tom, adoro viaggiare in aereo.

unlikely ADJECTIVE
poco probabile (FEM poco probabile)

□ He's unlikely to come. È poco probabile che
venga.

unlisted ADJECTIVE (US)
■ **an unlisted number** un numero che non è
sull'elenco del telefono

to **unload** VERB
scaricare [18]

to **unlock** VERB
aprire [9]

□ He unlocked the car door. Ha aperto la
portiera.

unlucky ADJECTIVE
■ **to be unlucky** 1 (person) non avere [12]
fortuna 2 (number, thing) portare [68] sfortuna

unmarried ADJECTIVE
non sposato (FEM non sposata)

□ an unmarried couple una coppia non sposata

■ **an unmarried mother** una ragazza madre

unnatural ADJECTIVE
poco naturale (FEM poco naturale)

unnecessary ADJECTIVE
non necessario (FEM non necessaria)

unofficial ADJECTIVE
ufficioso (FEM ufficiosa)

□ unofficial figures cifre ufficiose

■ **an unofficial strike** uno sciopero non
autorizzato

to **unpack** VERB
1 disfare [38]

□ I unpacked my suitcase. Ho disfatto la
valigia.

■ **I haven't unpacked my clothes yet.** Non
ho ancora tolto i vestiti dalla valigia.
2 disfare [38] le valigie

□ I went to my room to unpack. Sono andato
in camera mia a disfare le valigie.

unpleasant ADJECTIVE
1 spiacevole (FEM spiacevole)

□ an unpleasant situation una situazione
spiacevole
2 sgradevole (FEM sgradevole)

□ an unpleasant smell un odore sgradevole

3 antipatico (fem antipatica, masc pl antipatici, fem pl antipatiche) (person)

to **unplug** verb
staccare [18] la presa di
◻ She's unplugged the TV. Ha staccato la presa della TV.

unpopular adjective
impopolare (fem impopolare)

unpredictable adjective
imprevedibile (fem imprevedibile)

unreal adjective
1 irreale (fem irreale)
◻ an unreal situation una situazione irreale
2 falso (fem falsa)
◻ unreal expectations false aspettative
3 incredibile (fem incredibile)
◻ It was unreal! Era incredibile!

unrealistic adjective
non realistico (fem non realistica)

unreasonable adjective
irragionevole (fem irragionevole)
◻ Her attitude was completely unreasonable. Il suo atteggiamento era del tutto irragionevole.

unreliable adjective
inaffidabile (fem inaffidabile)
◻ It's a nice car, but unreliable. È una bella macchina ma inaffidabile.

to **unroll** verb
srotolare [68]

unsatisfactory adjective
poco soddisfacente (fem poco soddisfacente)

to **unscrew** verb
svitare [68]

unshaven adjective
non rasato (fem non rasata)

unskilled adjective
■ an unskilled worker un operaio non specializzato

unstable adjective
instabile (fem instabile)

unsteady adjective
malsicuro (fem malsicura)

unsuccessful adjective
fallito (fem fallita)
◻ an unsuccessful artist un artista fallito
■ The attempt was unsuccessful. Il tentativo fallì.

unsuitable adjective
non adatto (fem non adatta)

untidy adjective
1 in disordine (place)
2 disordinato (fem disordinata) (person)

to **untie** verb
1 sciogliere [97]
◻ He couldn't untie the knots. Non riusciva a sciogliere i nodi.
2 slegare [76] (animal, person)

until preposition, conjunction
fino a

◻ I waited until ten o'clock. Ho aspettato fino alle dieci.
■ It won't be ready until next week. Non sarà pronto prima della settimana prossima.
■ until now finora ◻ It's never been a problem until now. Non è mai stato un problema, finora.
■ until then fino ad allora ◻ Until then I'd never been to Italy. Fino ad allora non ero mai stato in Italia.

unusual adjective
1 insolito (fem insolita)
◻ an unusual shape una forma insolita
2 raro (fem rara)
◻ It's unusual to get snow at this time of year. È raro che nevichi in questa stagione.

unwilling adjective
■ He was unwilling to help me. Non era disposto ad aiutarmi.

to **unwind** verb
1 rilassarsi [56ᴱ]
◻ I need time to unwind. Ho bisogno di tempo per rilassarmi.
2 srotolare [68]
◻ He unwound the rope. Ha srotolato la fune.

unwise adjective
imprudente (fem imprudente)

to **unwrap** verb
aprire [9]
◻ Then we unwrapped the presents. Poi abbiamo aperto i regali.

up preposition, adverb
su
◻ up on the hill su in collina
■ up here quassù
■ up there lassù
■ up north su al nord
■ to be up essersi [47ᴱ] alzato ◻ We were up at six. Ci siamo alzati alle sei. ◻ He's not up yet. Non si è ancora alzato.
■ What's up? Che c'è?
■ What's up with her? Che cos'ha?
■ to go up salire [93ᴱ] ◻ The bus went up the hill. L'autobus salì su per la collina.
■ to go up to somebody avvicinarsi [56ᴱ] a qualcuno ◻ She came up to me. Mi si avvicinò.
■ up to fino a ◻ to count up to fifty contare fino a cinquanta ◻ up to three hours fino a tre ore
■ up to now finora
■ It's up to you. Sta a te decidere.
■ up to date **1** moderno ◻ the most up-to-date factories le fabbriche più moderne
2 aggiornato ◻ an up-to-date timetable un orario aggiornato
■ to bring somebody up-to-date on something aggiornare [68] qualcuno su qualcosa

u

upbringing NOUN
l' educazione *fem*

uphill ADJECTIVE
■ **It was an uphill struggle.** È stata dura.

to **upload** VERB
caricare [18]

upper ADJECTIVE
superiore (FEM superiore)
□ on the upper floor al piano superiore

upper sixth NOUN
ultimo anno della scuola superiore

upright ADJECTIVE
■ **to stand upright** stare [108ᴱ] dritto

upset NOUN
▷ *see also* **upset** ADJECTIVE, VERB
■ **to have a stomach upset** avere [12] lo
stomaco scombussolato

upset ADJECTIVE
▷ *see also* **upset** NOUN, VERB
turbato (FEM turbata)
□ She's still upset. È ancora turbata.
■ **to have an upset stomach** avere [12] lo
stomaco scombussolato
■ **to get upset** prendersela [77ᴱ] □ Don't get
upset. Non te la prendere.

to **upset** VERB
▷ *see also* **upset** NOUN, ADJECTIVE
■ **to upset somebody** turbare [68] qualcuno
□ You'll only upset her if you mention it.
Riuscirai solo a turbarla menzionandolo.
■ **Don't upset yourself.** Non te la prendere.

upside down ADVERB
alla rovescia
□ The painting was hung upside down. Il
quadro era appeso alla rovescia.

upstairs ADVERB
di sopra
□ Where's your coat? — It's upstairs. Dov'è il
tuo cappotto? — È di sopra. □ He went
upstairs to bed. È andato di sopra a coricarsi.

uptight ADJECTIVE
nervoso (FEM nervosa)

upwards ADVERB
verso l'alto

urgent ADJECTIVE
urgente (FEM urgente)

urine NOUN
l' urina *fem*

URL NOUN
l' indirizzo Internet *masc*

US NOUN (= United States)
gli Stati Uniti *masc pl*

us PRONOUN
1 ci
□ They helped us. Ci hanno aiutato.
2 noi
LANGUAGE TIP Use **noi** after a preposition.
□ Why don't you come with us? Perché non

vieni con noi?

USA NOUN (= United States of America)
gli USA *masc pl*

USB stick NOUN
la pennetta USB *fem*

use NOUN
▷ *see also* **use** VERB
l' uso *masc*
□ 'directions for use' 'istruzioni per l'uso'
■ **It's no use...** È inutile... □ It's no use
shouting, she's deaf. È inutile gridare, è sorda.

to **use** VERB
▷ *see also* **use** NOUN
usare [68]
□ a used car una macchina usata

LANGUAGE TIP 'used to' + verb is usually
translated by the Italian imperfect.

□ I used to live in London. Una volta abitavo a
Londra. □ I didn't use to like maths when I
was at school. La matematica non mi piaceva
quando andavo a scuola.
■ **to be used to something** essere [47ᴱ]
abituato a qualcosa
■ **to be used to doing something** essere
[47ᴱ] abituato a fare qualcosa □ He wasn't
used to driving on the right. Non era abituato
a guidare sulla destra. □ Don't worry, I'm
used to it. Non preoccuparti, ci sono abituato.

to **use up** VERB
finire [51]
□ We've used up all the paint. Abbiamo finito
tutta la vernice.

useful ADJECTIVE
utile (FEM utile)

useless ADJECTIVE
1 inutile (FEM inutile)
□ It's useless! È inutile!
2 impedito (FEM impedita)
□ I'm useless at tennis! A tennis sono un
impedito!

user NOUN
l' utente *masc/fem*

user-friendly ADJECTIVE
di facile uso

username NOUN
il nome utente *masc* (PL i nomi utente)
□ What's your username? Qual è il tuo nome
utente?

usual ADJECTIVE
solito (FEM solita)
■ **as usual** come al solito

usually ADVERB
di solito

utility room NOUN
la stanza adibita a lavanderia *fem*

U-turn NOUN
l' inversione a U *fem* (by driver)

vacancy NOUN
1 il posto vacante *masc (job)*
□ There were no vacancies. Non c'erano posti vacanti.
■ **They have vacancies for programmers.** Cercano programmatori.
2 la camera disponibile *fem (in hotel)*
■ **'no vacancies'** 'completo'
▌ **LANGUAGE TIP** Be careful not to translate **vacancy** by **vacanza**.

vacant ADJECTIVE
libero (FEM libera)

vacation NOUN (US)
la vacanza *fem*

to **vaccinate** VERB
vaccinare [68]

to **vacuum** VERB
▷ *see also* **vacuum** NOUN
passare [68] l'aspirapolvere in
□ to vacuum the lounge passare l'aspirapolvere nel salotto

vacuum NOUN
▷ *see also* **vacuum** VERB
il vuoto *masc*
□ His departure left a vacuum. La sua partenza ha lasciato un vuoto.

vacuum cleaner NOUN
l' aspirapolvere *masc*

vagina NOUN
la vagina *fem*

vague ADJECTIVE
vago (FEM vaga)

vain ADJECTIVE
1 vano (FEM vana)
□ a vain hope una speranza vana
2 vanitoso (FEM vanitosa)
□ He's very vain. È molto vanitoso.
■ **in vain** invano

Valentine card NOUN
il biglietto di auguri per San Valentino *masc*

Valentine's Day NOUN
il San Valentino *masc*

valid ADJECTIVE
valido (FEM valida)

valley NOUN
la valle *fem*

valuable ADJECTIVE
1 di valore
□ a valuable painting un quadro di valore

2 prezioso (FEM preziosa)
□ valuable help un aiuto prezioso

valuables NOUN PL
gli oggetti di valore *masc pl*

value NOUN
il valore *masc*
■ **value added tax** l'imposta sul valore aggiunto

van NOUN
il furgone *masc*

vandal NOUN
il vandalo *masc*

vandalism NOUN
il vandalismo *masc*

to **vandalize** VERB
rovinare [68]

vanilla NOUN
la vaniglia *fem*

to **vanish** VERB
sparire [104ᴱ]

variable ADJECTIVE
variabile (FEM variabile)

varied ADJECTIVE
vario (FEM varia, MASC PL vari, FEM PL varie)

variety NOUN
la varietà *fem* (PL le varietà)

various ADJECTIVE
vario (FEM varia, MASC PL vari, FEM PL varie)
□ We visited various villages. Abbiamo visitato vari paesini.

to **vary** VERB
variare [17]

vase NOUN
il vaso *masc*

VAT NOUN
l' IVA *fem*

VCR NOUN (= *video cassette recorder*)
il videoregistratore *masc*

VDU NOUN (= *visual display unit*)
il videoterminale *masc*

veal NOUN
la carne di vitello *fem*

vegan NOUN
il vegetaliano *masc*
la vegetaliana *fem*

vegetable NOUN
la verdura *fem*
□ vegetable soup minestra di verdura

vegetarian ADJECTIVE

v

▷ *see also* **vegetarian** NOUN
vegetariano (FEM vegetariana)

vegetarian NOUN
▷ *see also* **vegetarian** ADJECTIVE
il vegetariano *masc*
la vegetariana *fem*

vehicle NOUN
il veicolo *masc*

vein NOUN
la vena *fem*

velvet NOUN
il velluto *masc*

vending machine NOUN
il distributore automatico *masc*

Venetian blind NOUN
la veneziana *fem*

Venice NOUN
Venezia *fem*

verb NOUN
il verbo *masc*

verdict NOUN
la sentenza *fem*

vertical ADJECTIVE
verticale (FEM verticale)

vertigo NOUN
le vertigini *fem pl*
□ I get vertigo. Mi vengono le vertigini.

very ADVERB
molto
□ very tall molto alto □ not very interesting
non molto interessante
■ **very much** moltissimo

vest NOUN
1 la canottiera *fem*
□ a thermal vest una canottiera termica
2 il gilè *masc* (PL i gilè) (US: *waistcoat*)

vet NOUN
il veterinario *masc*
la veterinaria *fem*

via PREPOSITION
passando per
□ We went to Rome via London. Siamo andati
a Roma passando per Londra.

vicar NOUN
il pastore *masc*

vice NOUN
1 il vizio *masc*
□ vices and virtues vizi e virtù
2 la morsa *fem*
□ held in a vice stretto in una morsa

vice versa ADVERB
viceversa

vicious ADJECTIVE
1 brutale (FEM brutale)
□ a vicious attack un attacco brutale
2 cattivo (FEM cattiva) (*dog, person*)
■ **a vicious circle** un circolo vizioso

victim NOUN
la vittima *fem*
□ He was the victim of a mugging. È stato

vittima di un'aggressione.

victory NOUN
la vittoria *fem*

to **video** VERB
▷ *see also* **video** NOUN
1 registrare [68] (*from TV*)
□ I'll video the programme. Registrerò il
programma.
2 filmare [68] (*with camera*)

video NOUN
▷ *see also* **video** VERB
1 la videocassetta *fem*
□ She lent me a video. Mi ha prestato una
videocassetta.
2 il videoregistratore *masc*
□ Have you got a video? Hai il
videoregistratore?
■ **a video camera** una videocamera
■ **a video recorder** un videoregistratore
■ **a video shop** un videonoleggio

video game NOUN
il videogioco *masc* (PL i videogiochi)

videophone NOUN
il videofonino *masc*

Vietnam NOUN
il Vietnam *masc*

Vietnamese ADJECTIVE
vietnamita (FEM vietnamita)

view NOUN
▷ *see also* **view** VERB
1 la vista *fem*
□ There's an amazing view. C'è una vista
fantastica.
2 l'avviso *masc*
□ in my view a mio avviso

to **view** VERB
▷ *see also* **view** NOUN
considerare [68]
□ How do you view this development? Come
consideri questo sviluppo?

viewer NOUN
il telespettatore *masc*
la telespettatrice *fem*

viewpoint NOUN
il punto di vista *masc*

vile ADJECTIVE
disgustoso (FEM disgustosa)

villa NOUN
la villa *fem*

village NOUN
il paese *masc*

villain NOUN
il/la malvivente *masc/fem*
■ **the villain** (*of film, story*) il cattivo

vine NOUN
la vite *fem*

vinegar NOUN
l'aceto *masc*

vineyard NOUN
il vigneto *masc*

viola NOUN
la viola fem

violence NOUN
la violenza fem

violent ADJECTIVE
violento (FEM violenta)

violin NOUN
il violino masc

violinist NOUN
il/la violinista masc/fem

viral ADJECTIVE
virale (FEM virale)
□ The video has gone viral in a few hours. Il filmato è diventato virale in poche ore.

virgin NOUN
la vergine fem

Virgo NOUN
la Vergine fem
□ I'm Virgo. Sono della Vergine.

virtual ADJECTIVE
■ It's a virtual certainty. È praticamente una certezza.

virtual reality NOUN
la realtà virtuale fem

virus NOUN
il virus masc (PL i virus)

visa NOUN
il visto masc (in passport)

vise NOUN (US)
la morsa fem

visible ADJECTIVE
visibile (FEM visibile)

visit NOUN
▷ see also **visit** VERB
la visita fem

to **visit** VERB
▷ see also **visit** NOUN
1 andare [6ᴱ] a trovare
□ I visited my grandmother last week. Sono andato a trovare mia nonna la settimana scorsa.
2 visitare [68]
□ We'd like to visit the castle. Ci piacerebbe visitare il castello.

visitor NOUN
il visitatore masc
la visitatrice fem
□ important visitors visitatori importanti
■ to have a visitor avere [12] una visita

visual ADJECTIVE
visivo (FEM visiva)

to **visualize** VERB
immaginare [68]

vital ADJECTIVE
d'importanza vitale
□ vital information informazioni d'importanza vitale
■ It's vital to sterilize the equipment. È essenziale sterilizzare l'attrezzatura.

vitamin NOUN

la vitamina fem

vivid ADJECTIVE
vivo (FEM viva) (colour)
■ to have a vivid imagination avere [12] una fervida immaginazione

vocabulary NOUN
il vocabolario masc

vocational ADJECTIVE
professionale (FEM professionale)
■ vocational training formazione professionale

vodka NOUN
la vodka fem

voice NOUN
la voce fem
□ I heard voices. Sentivo delle voci.

voice mail NOUN
il servizio di messaggeria vocale masc

volcano NOUN
il vulcano masc

volleyball NOUN
la pallavolo fem

voltage NOUN
il voltaggio masc

voluntary ADJECTIVE
1 volontario (FEM volontaria, MASC PL volontari, FEM PL volontarie)
□ voluntary contributions contributi volontari
2 facoltativo (FEM facoltativa)
□ Attendance is voluntary. La frequenza è facoltativa.
■ to do voluntary work fare [49] volontariato

volunteer NOUN
▷ see also **volunteer** VERB
il volontario masc
la volontaria fem

to **volunteer** VERB
▷ see also **volunteer** NOUN
■ to volunteer to do something offrirsi [66ᴱ] volontario per fare qualcosa

to **vomit** VERB
vomitare [68]

to **vote** VERB
▷ see also **vote** NOUN
votare [68]

vote NOUN
▷ see also **vote** VERB
1 il voto masc
□ They won by two votes. Hanno vinto per due voti.
2 la votazione fem
□ Now let's take a vote. Passiamo ora alla votazione.

voucher NOUN
il buono masc
□ a gift voucher un buono acquisto

vowel NOUN
la vocale fem

vulgar ADJECTIVE
volgare (FEM volgare)

Ww

wafer NOUN
la cialda *fem*

wage NOUN
la paga *fem*
□ a low wage una paga bassa
■ **the minimum wage** il salario minimo garantito
■ **wages** la paga *fem sing* □ He collected his wages. Ha ritirato la paga.

wage packet NOUN
la busta paga *fem* (PL le buste paga)

waist NOUN
la vita *fem*
□ He put his arm round her waist. Le ha messo un braccio attorno alla vita.

waistcoat NOUN
il gilè *masc* (PL i gilè)

to **wait** VERB
aspettare [68]
□ How long have you been waiting? Da quanto tempo stai aspettando?
■ **to wait for something** aspettare [68] qualcosa
■ **to wait for somebody** aspettare [68] qualcuno □ I'll wait for you. Ti aspetto. □ Wait for me! Aspettami!
■ **to keep somebody waiting** fare [49] aspettare qualcuno □ They kept us waiting for hours. Ci hanno fatto aspettare per delle ore.
■ **I can't wait for the holidays.** Non vedo l'ora che arrivino le vacanze.
■ **I can't wait to see him again.** Non vedo l'ora di rivederlo.
■ **to wait on somebody** *(waiter)* servire [41] qualcuno

to **wait up** VERB
■ **to wait up for somebody** rimanere [88E] alzato ad aspettare qualcuno □ Don't wait up for me. Non rimanere alzato ad aspettarmi.

waiter NOUN
il cameriere *masc*

waiting list NOUN
la lista d'attesa *fem*

waiting room NOUN
la sala d'attesa *fem*

waitress NOUN
la cameriera *fem*

to **wake** VERB
1 svegliarsi [25E]
□ I woke at six o'clock. Mi sono svegliato alle sei.
2 svegliare [25]
□ Please would you wake me at seven o'clock? Mi può svegliare alle sette, per favore? □ I was woken at seven. Mi hanno svegliato alle sette.

to **wake up** VERB
1 svegliarsi [25E]
□ He's just woken up. Si è appena svegliato.
2 svegliare [25]
□ Don't wake him up! Non svegliarlo!

Wales NOUN
il Galles *masc*
□ the Prince of Wales il Principe di Galles

to **walk** VERB
▷ *see also* **walk** NOUN
1 camminare [68]
□ They walked in silence for a while. Hanno camminato in silenzio per un po'. □ We walked 10 kilometres. Abbiamo camminato per dieci chilometri.
2 andare [6E] a piedi
□ Are you walking or going by bus? Ci vai a piedi o in autobus?
■ **to walk the dog** portare [68] fuori il cane
■ **to walk out on somebody** abbandonare [68] qualcuno □ He walked out on his wife. Ha abbandonato la moglie.
■ **He walked out of the meeting.** Ha abbandonato la riunione.

walk NOUN
▷ *see also* **walk** VERB
la passeggiata *fem*
□ We went for a walk. Abbiamo fatto una passeggiata.
■ **It's 10 minutes' walk from here.** Ci vogliono dieci minuti a piedi da qui.

walkie-talkie NOUN
il walkie-talkie *masc* (PL i walkie-talkie)

walking NOUN
l' escursionismo *masc*
□ I did some walking in the Alps last summer. Ho fatto escursionismo sulle Alpi, l'estate scorsa.

walking shoes NOUN
le scarpe per camminare *fem pl*

walking stick NOUN
il bastone da passeggio *masc*

Walkman® NOUN
il Walkman® *masc* (PL i Walkman)

wall NOUN
il muro *masc*

wallet NOUN
il portafoglio *masc*

wallpaper NOUN
la carta da parati *fem*

walnut NOUN
la noce *fem*

to **wander** VERB
■ **to wander around** gironzolare [68] □ I just wandered around for a while. Ho gironzolato per un po'.

to **want** VERB
volere [123]
□ Do you want some cake? Vuoi un po' di torta?
■ **to want to do something** volere [123] fare qualcosa □ What do you want to do tomorrow? Che cosa vuoi fare domani?
■ **He is wanted by the police.** È ricercato dalla polizia.

war NOUN
la guerra *fem*

ward NOUN
il reparto *masc* (in hospital)

warden NOUN
il guardiano *masc*

wardrobe NOUN
l' armadio *masc*

warehouse NOUN
il magazzino *masc*

warm ADJECTIVE
▷ see also **warm** VERB
1 caldo (FEM calda)
□ warm water acqua calda □ It's warm in here. Fa caldo qui. □ I'm too warm. Ho troppo caldo.
2 caloroso (FEM calorosa)
□ a warm welcome una calorosa accoglienza

to **warm** VERB
▷ see also **warm** ADJECTIVE
scaldare [68]
□ She warmed her hands by the fire. Si è scaldata le mani vicino al fuoco.

to **warm up** VERB
1 riscaldare [68]
□ I'll warm up some lasagne for you. Ti riscaldo delle lasagne.
2 fare [49] riscaldamento (in gym)
□ Spend the first five minutes warming up. Innanzitutto, fai cinque minuti di riscaldamento.

to **warn** VERB
avvertire [41]

□ Well, I warned you! Beh, ti avevo avvertito!
■ **to warn somebody not to do something** consigliare [25] a qualcuno di non fare qualcosa

warning NOUN
l' avvertimento *masc*

warning light NOUN
la spia luminosa *fem*

warning triangle NOUN
il triangolo *masc*

Warsaw NOUN
Varsavia *fem*

wart NOUN
la verruca *fem* (PL le verruche)

was VERB ▷ see be

wash NOUN
▷ see also **wash** VERB
■ **to have a wash** lavarsi [56ᴱ]
■ **to give something a wash** lavare [68] qualcosa

to **wash** VERB
▷ see also **wash** NOUN
1 lavare [68]
□ I'll wash the dishes. Lavo io i piatti.
2 lavarsi [56ᴱ]
□ He washed his hands. Si è lavato le mani.
□ Have you washed your hair? Ti sei lavata i capelli?

to **wash away** VERB
spazzare [68] via

to **wash up** VERB
lavare [68] i piatti

washbasin NOUN
il lavandino *masc*

washcloth NOUN
il guanto di spugna *masc*

washing NOUN
il bucato *masc*
■ **to do the washing** fare [49] il bucato
■ **dirty washing** roba da lavare

washing machine NOUN
la lavatrice *fem*

washing powder NOUN
il detersivo in polvere per bucato *masc*

washing-up NOUN
■ **to do the washing-up** fare [49] i piatti

washing-up liquid NOUN
il detersivo liquido per stoviglie *masc*

wasn't = was not

wasp NOUN
la vespa *fem*

waste NOUN
▷ see also **waste** VERB
1 lo spreco *masc* (PL gli sprechi)
□ It's such a waste! È un tale spreco!
■ **It's a waste of time.** È tempo sprecato.
2 scorie
□ nuclear waste scorie nucleari
■ **the waste pipe** il tubo di scarico

w

601

to **waste** VERB
▷ see also **waste** NOUN
sprecare [18]
□ I don't like wasting money. Non mi piace sprecare i soldi.
■ **to waste time** perdere [69] tempo
□ There's no time to waste. Non c'è tempo da perdere.

wastepaper basket NOUN
il cestino per la cartaccia *masc*

watch NOUN
▷ see also **watch** VERB
l' orologio *masc*
□ He was wearing an expensive watch. Portava un orologio costoso.

to **watch** VERB
▷ see also **watch** NOUN
1 guardare [68]
□ I was watching TV. Stavo guardando la TV.
2 sorvegliare [25]
□ The police were watching the house. La polizia sorvegliava la casa.
■ **Watch out!** Attento!

water NOUN
▷ see also **water** VERB
l' acqua *fem*
□ a glass of water un bicchiere d'acqua

to **water** VERB
▷ see also **water** NOUN
annaffiare [17]
□ She's watering the geraniums. Sta annaffiando i gerani.

to **water down** VERB
1 annacquare [68] *(wine)*
2 indebolire [51] *(suggestions, rules)*

waterfall NOUN
la cascata *fem*

water heater NOUN
lo scaldabagno *masc*

watering can NOUN
l' annaffiatoio *masc*

watermelon NOUN
il cocomero *masc*

waterproof ADJECTIVE
impermeabile (FEM impermeabile)

water-skiing NOUN
lo sci nautico *masc*

water tank NOUN
il serbatoio d'acqua *masc* (PL i serbatoi d'acqua)

wave NOUN
▷ see also **wave** VERB
1 l' onda *fem*
□ He was knocked over by a big wave. È stato gettato a terra da una grossa onda.
2 il cenno *masc (of the hand)*
□ a friendly wave un cenno amichevole
■ **to give somebody a wave** salutare [68] qualcuno con la mano

to **wave** VERB
▷ see also **wave** NOUN
fare [49] un cenno con la mano
□ He waved at me. Mi ha fatto un cenno con la mano.
■ **to wave goodbye** salutare [68] con la mano

wavy ADJECTIVE
ondulato (FEM ondulata)
□ a wavy line una linea ondulata
■ **wavy hair** i capelli mossi

wax NOUN
la cera *fem*

way NOUN
1 il modo *masc*
□ She looked at me in a strange way. Mi ha guardato in modo strano.
2 la strada *fem*
□ I don't know the way. Non so la strada.
■ **Do you know the way to the hotel?** Sai come arrivare all'albergo?
■ **on the way** per strada
■ **He lost it on the way to school.** Lo ha perso andando a scuola.
3 la parte *fem*
□ Which way is it? Da che parte è? □ The supermarket is this way. Il supermercato è da questa parte.
■ **in a way** in un certo senso
■ **a way of life** uno stile di vita
■ **It's a long way.** È lontano.
■ **He's on his way.** Sta arrivando.
■ **'way in'** 'entrata'
■ **'way out'** 'uscita'
■ **by the way...** a proposito...

we PRONOUN
noi
□ We aren't so lucky. Noi non siamo così fortunati.
▌ LANGUAGE TIP 'we' is often not translated.
□ We'll arrive tomorrow. Arriveremo domani.

weak ADJECTIVE
debole (FEM debole)

wealthy ADJECTIVE
ricco (FEM ricca, MASC PL ricchi, FEM PL ricche)

weapon NOUN
l' arma *fem*

to **wear** VERB
portare [68]
□ She was wearing a black coat. Portava un cappotto nero.
■ **She was wearing black.** Era vestita di nero.
□ He wore black trousers and a T-shirt. Portava pantaloni neri ed una maglietta.
■ **This is the first time I've worn these shoes.** È la prima volta che metto queste scarpe.

to **wear off** VERB
svanire [51ᴱ]

□ The feeling soon wore off. Presto la sensazione svanì.

to **wear out** VERB
1 consumare [68]
   □ He's worn out his shoes. Ha consumato le scarpe.
2 stancarsi [18ᴱ] tanto
   □ Don't wear yourself out! Non stancarti tanto!

weather NOUN
il tempo *masc*
   □ What's the weather like? Che tempo fa?

weather forecast NOUN
le previsioni del tempo *fem pl*

weather man NOUN
il meteorologo *masc* (PL i meteorologi)

web NOUN
■ **the web** il Web

web address NOUN
l' indirizzo Internet *masc*

web browser NOUN
il browser *masc* (PL i browser)

webcam NOUN
la webcam *fem* (PL le webcam)

webmaster NOUN
il webmaster *masc* (PL i webmaster)

web page NOUN
la pagina Web *fem*

website NOUN
il sito Internet *masc*

webzine NOUN
la rivista web *fem*

we'd = we had, we would

wedding NOUN
il matrimonio *masc*
   ■ **a wedding anniversary** un anniversario di matrimonio
   ■ **a wedding dress** un abito da sposa

wedding ring NOUN
la fede *fem*

> **LANGUAGE TIP** Word for word, this means 'faith'.

Wednesday NOUN
il mercoledì *masc* (PL i mercoledì)
   ■ **on Wednesday** mercoledì □ I saw her on Wednesday. L'ho vista mercoledì.
   ■ **on Wednesdays** di mercoledì □ I go swimming on Wednesdays. Vado in piscina di mercoledì.

weed NOUN
   ▷ see also **weed** VERB
l' erbaccia *fem* (PL le erbacce)
   □ The garden's full of weeds. Il giardino è pieno di erbacce.

to **weed** VERB
   ▷ see also **weed** NOUN
diserbare [68]

week NOUN
la settimana *fem*

□ in a week's time tra una settimana
   ■ **a week on Friday** venerdì a otto

weekday NOUN
il giorno feriale *masc*
   ■ **on weekdays** durante la settimana

weekend NOUN
il fine settimana *masc* (PL i fine settimana)
   □ last weekend l'altro fine settimana

to **weep** VERB
piangere [71]
   □ She wept for hours. Pianse per ore.

to **weigh** VERB
pesare [68]
   □ How much do you weigh? Quanto pesi?
   ■ **to weigh oneself** pesarsi [56ᴱ]

to **weigh down** VERB
appesantire [51]

to **weigh up** VERB
valutare [68]

weight NOUN
il peso *masc*
   □ the weight of the load il peso del carico
   ■ **to lose weight** dimagrire [51ᴱ]
   ■ **to put on weight** ingrassare [68ᴱ]
   ■ **to do weight training** fare [49] pesi

weightlifter NOUN
il sollevatore di pesi *masc*

weightlifting NOUN
il sollevamento pesi *masc*

weird ADJECTIVE
strano (FEM strana)

welcome NOUN
   ▷ see also **welcome** VERB
l' accoglienza *fem*
   ■ **a warm welcome** un'accoglienza calorosa
   ■ **Welcome!** Benvenuto!

to **welcome** VERB
   ▷ see also **welcome** NOUN
1 accogliere [21]
   □ Everyone was there to welcome me. Erano tutti lì ad accogliermi.
2 apprezzare [68]
   □ They did not welcome the suggestion. Non hanno apprezzato il suggerimento.
   ■ **Thank you! — You're welcome!** Grazie! — Di niente!

well ADJECTIVE, ADVERB
   ▷ see also **well** NOUN
1 bene
   □ You did that really well. L'hai fatto proprio bene.
   ■ **to do well** andare [6ᴱ] bene □ She's doing really well at school. Va molto bene a scuola.
   ■ **to be well** stare [108ᴱ] bene □ I'm not very well. Non sto molto bene.
   ■ **Get well soon!** Guarisci presto!
   ■ **Well done!** Bravo!
2 beh
   □ It's enormous! Well, quite big anyway.

w

well – wheat intolerance

È gigantesco! Beh, diciamo molto grande.
■ **as well** anche □ We worked hard, but we had some fun as well. Abbiamo lavorato sodo ma ci siamo anche divertiti. □ We went to Verona as well as Venice. Siamo stati a Venezia e anche a Verona.

well NOUN
▷ *see also* **well** ADJECTIVE, ADVERB
il pozzo *masc*

we'll = we will

well-behaved ADJECTIVE
beneducato (FEM beneducata)

well-dressed ADJECTIVE
elegante (FEM elegante)

wellingtons NOUN PL
gli stivali di gomma *masc pl*

well-known ADJECTIVE
famoso (FEM famosa)
□ a well-known film star un famoso divo del cinema

well-off ADJECTIVE
benestante (FEM benestante)

Welsh ADJECTIVE
▷ *see also* **Welsh** NOUN
gallese (FEM gallese)
■ the Welsh Assembly il parlamento gallese

Welsh NOUN
▷ *see also* **Welsh** ADJECTIVE
il gallese *masc (language)*
■ the Welsh i gallesi

Welshman NOUN
il gallese *masc*

Welshwoman NOUN
la gallese *fem*

went VERB ▷ *see* go

wept VERB ▷ *see* weep

were VERB ▷ *see* be

we're = we are

weren't = were not

west NOUN, ADVERB, ADJECTIVE
1 l' ovest *masc*
□ in the west ad ovest
■ west of a ovest di □ Stroud is west of Oxford. Stroud è a ovest di Oxford.
2 verso ovest
□ We were travelling west. Andavamo verso ovest.
3 occidentale (FEM occidentale)
□ the west coast la costa occidentale
■ the West Country il sud-ovest dell'Inghilterra

westbound ADJECTIVE
diretto ad ovest (FEM diretta ad ovest)

western NOUN
▷ *see also* **western** ADJECTIVE
il western *masc* (PL i western)

western ADJECTIVE
▷ *see also* **western** NOUN
occidentale (FEM occidentale)

□ the western coast of Scotland la costa occidentale della Scozia

West Indian ADJECTIVE
▷ *see also* **West Indian** NOUN
caraibico (FEM caraibica, MASC PL caraibici, FEM PL caraibiche)
□ the West Indian team la squadra caraibica
□ the West Indian community la comunità caraibica

West Indian NOUN
▷ *see also* **West Indian** ADJECTIVE
il caraibico *masc*
la caraibica *fem*

West Indies NOUN
i Caraibi *masc pl*

wet ADJECTIVE
bagnato (FEM bagnata)
□ wet clothes abiti bagnati
■ to get wet bagnarsi [14ᴱ]
■ dripping wet gocciolante
■ wet weather tempo piovoso
■ It was wet all week. È piovuto tutta la settimana.

wet blanket NOUN
il/la guastafeste *masc/fem* (PL i/le guastafeste)

wet suit NOUN
la muta subacquea *fem*

we've = we have

whale NOUN
la balena *fem*

what ADJECTIVE, PRONOUN
1 che
□ What subjects are you studying? Che materie studi? □ What colour is it? Di che colore è? □ What a mess! Che disordine!
2 quale
□ What's the capital of Finland? Qual è la capitale della Finlandia? □ What's her telephone number? Qual è il suo numero di telefono?
3 che cosa
□ Tell me what you did. Dimmi che cosa hai fatto. □ What are you doing? Che cosa fai? □ What did you say? Che cos'hai detto? □ What is it? Che cos'è? □ What's the matter? Che cosa c'è? □ What happened? Che cos'è successo?
4 quello che (FEM quella che)
□ I saw what happened. Ho visto quello che è successo. □ I heard what he said. Ho sentito quello che ha detto.
■ **What?** **1** Come? *(what did you say?)*
2 Cosa? *(what do you want?)* **3** Cosa? *(surprised)*

wheat NOUN
il grano *masc*

wheat intolerance NOUN
l' intolleranza al glutine *fem*

wheel NOUN
la ruota *fem*
 □ the front wheel la ruota davanti
 ■ **a wheel clamp** un morsetto bloccaruota
 ■ **the steering wheel** il volante
wheelchair NOUN
la sedia a rotelle *fem*
when ADVERB, CONJUNCTION
quando
 □ When did he go? Quando è partito? □ She was reading when I came in. Quando sono entrato stava leggendo.
where ADVERB, CONJUNCTION
dove
 □ Where do you live? Dove abiti? □ Where are you going? Dove vai?
whether CONJUNCTION
se
 □ I don't know whether to go or not. Non so se andare o no.
which PRONOUN, ADJECTIVE
1 quale
 □ Which would you like? Quale vuoi? □ Which of these are yours? Quali di questi sono tuoi?
 ■ **Which one?** Quale? □ I know his sister.
 — Which one? Conosco sua sorella. — Quale?
2 che
 □ Which flavour do you want? Che gusto vuoi?
 □ the CD which is playing now il CD che stiamo ascoltando
while CONJUNCTION
 ▷ *see also* **while** NOUN
mentre
 □ You hold the torch while I look inside. Tieni la pila mentre io guardo dentro. □ Isobel is very dynamic, while Kay is more laid-back. Isobel è molto attiva mentre Kay è più tranquilla.
while NOUN
 ▷ *see also* **while** CONJUNCTION
 ■ **a while** un po' di tempo
 ■ **after a while** dopo un po'
 ■ **a while ago** poco fa □ He was here a while ago. Era qui poco fa.
 ■ **for a while** per un po' □ I lived in London for a while. Ho abitato a Londra per un po'.
 ■ **quite a while** tanto tempo □ I haven't seen him for quite a while. È da tanto tempo che non lo vedo.
whip NOUN
 ▷ *see also* **whip** VERB
la frusta *fem*
to **whip** VERB
 ▷ *see also* **whip** NOUN
1 frustare [68] *(horse)*
2 montare [68]
 □ Whip the cream. Montate la panna.
3 sbattere [1]
 □ Whip the egg whites. Sbattete gli albumi.

whipped cream NOUN
la panna montata *fem*
whisk NOUN
 ▷ *see also* **whisk** VERB
il frullino *masc*
to **whisk** VERB
 ▷ *see also* **whisk** NOUN
1 trascinare [68]
 □ He was whisked away in a police car. È stato trascinato via in una macchina della polizia.
2 sbattere [1]
 □ Whisk the yolks with the sugar. Sbattete i tuorli e lo zucchero.
whiskers NOUN PL
i baffi *masc pl*
whisky (US **whiskey**) NOUN
il whisky *masc* (PL i whisky)
to **whisper** VERB
sussurrare [68]
whistle NOUN
 ▷ *see also* **whistle** VERB
1 il fischietto *masc (thing)*
2 il fischio *masc (noise)*
 ■ **The referee blew his whistle.** L'arbitro ha fischiato.
to **whistle** VERB
 ▷ *see also* **whistle** NOUN
fischiare [17]
white ADJECTIVE
bianco (FEM bianca, MASC PL bianchi, FEM PL bianche)
 □ He's got white hair. Ha i capelli bianchi.
 ■ **white wine** vino bianco
 ■ **white bread** pane bianco
 ■ **white coffee** caffellatte
 ■ **a white man** un bianco
 ■ **white people** i bianchi
whiteboard NOUN
la lavagna bianca *fem*
 ■ **an interactive whiteboard** una lavagna interattiva
Whitsun NOUN
la Pentecoste *fem*
who PRONOUN
1 chi
 □ Who said that? Chi l'ha detto? □ Who is it? Chi è?
2 che
 □ the man who saw us l'uomo che ci ha visto
 □ the man who spoke to him l'uomo che gli ha parlato
whole ADJECTIVE
 ▷ *see also* **whole** NOUN
intero (FEM intera)
 □ the whole class la classe intera □ a whole box of chocolates un'intera scatola di cioccolatini
 ■ **the whole afternoon** tutto il pomeriggio
 ■ **the whole world** tutto il mondo

w

whole NOUN

▷ *see also* **whole** ADJECTIVE

■ **the whole of** tutto □ the whole of August tutto agosto □ The whole of Wales was affected. Tutto il Galles è stato colpito.

■ **on the whole** nel complesso

wholemeal ADJECTIVE
integrale (FEM integrale)

□ wholemeal bread pane integrale

wholewheat ADJECTIVE (US)
integrale (FEM integrale)

□ wholewheat bread pane integrale

whom PRONOUN

1 chi

□ Whom did you see? Chi hai visto?

2 cui

□ the man to whom I spoke l'uomo con cui ho parlato

whose PRONOUN

1 di chi

□ Whose is this? Di chi è questo? □ I know whose it is. Io lo so di chi è. □ Whose book is this? Di chi è questo libro?

2 il cui
la cui

□ the girl whose picture was in the paper la ragazza la cui foto era sul giornale

why ADVERB
perché

□ Why did you do it? Perché l'hai fatto? □ That's why he did it. Ecco perché l'ha fatto.

wicked ADJECTIVE

1 cattivo (FEM cattiva)

□ a wicked deed un gesto cattivo

2 un po' malizioso (FEM un po' maliziosa)

□ She has a wicked sense of humour. Ha un senso dell'umorismo un po' malizioso.

wicket NOUN
la porta *fem (in cricket)*

wide ADJECTIVE, ADVERB

1 largo (FEM larga, MASC PL larghi, FEM PL larghe)

□ a wide road una strada larga

2 ampio (FEM ampia, MASC PL ampi, FEM PL ampie)

□ a wide choice un'ampia scelta

■ **wide open** spalancato □ The door was wide open. La porta era spalancata.

■ **wide awake** completamente sveglio

widow NOUN
la vedova *fem*

widower NOUN
il vedovo *masc*

width NOUN
la larghezza *fem*

wife NOUN
la moglie *fem*

wig NOUN
la parrucca *fem (PL le parrucche)*

wild ADJECTIVE

1 selvatico (FEM selvatica, MASC PL selvatici, FEM PL selvatiche)

□ a wild animal un animale selvatico

2 pazzo (FEM pazza)

□ She's a bit wild. È un po' pazza.

wild card NOUN
il carattere jolly *masc*

wildlife NOUN
la natura *fem*

will NOUN

▷ *see also* **will** VERB

1 il testamento *masc*

□ He made a will. Ha fatto testamento.

2 la volontà *fem*

□ a strong will una forte volontà

will VERB

▷ *see also* **will** NOUN

| **LANGUAGE TIP** When 'will' + verb refers to the future, it can be translated both by the future tense of the Italian verb, and by the present.

□ I will finish it tomorrow. Lo finirò domani. □ It won't take long. Non ci vorrà molto. □ She'll love that card. Quel biglietto le piacerà moltissimo. □ Will you do it? — No, I won't. Lo farai? — No. □ Will you help me? Mi aiuti? □ I won't go there again. Lì non ci ritorno.

| **LANGUAGE TIP** When 'will' + verb refers to the present, it is translated by the present tense of the Italian verb.

□ I'll show you your room. Ti mostro la tua stanza. □ I'll give you a hand. Ti dò una mano. □ Will you be quiet! Fai silenzio! □ That will be the postman. Dev'essere il postino.

| **LANGUAGE TIP** When 'won't' means 'refuses to' it is translated by the present tense of **volere**.

□ She won't listen to me. Non mi vuol dar retta.

willing ADJECTIVE

■ **to be willing to do something** essere [47ᴱ] disposto a fare qualcosa

to **win** VERB

▷ *see also* **win** NOUN
vincere [121]

□ Did you win? Hai vinto? □ He won a medal. Ha vinto una medaglia.

■ **to win the lottery** vincere [121] alla lotteria

win NOUN

▷ *see also* **win** VERB
la vittoria *fem*

wind NOUN

▷ *see also* **wind** VERB
il vento *masc*

□ a strong wind un vento forte

■ **a wind farm** una centrale eolica

■ **a wind instrument** uno strumento a fiato

■ **wind power** l'energia eolica
■ **a wind turbine** una pala eolica

to **wind** VERB
  ▷ see also **wind** NOUN
1 avvolgere [91]
  □ He wound the rope round a tree. Ha avvolto la fune attorno ad un albero.
2 snodarsi [56ᴱ] (road, river)

to **wind up** VERB
1 chiudere [20]
  □ The company will be wound up. La società verrà chiusa.
2 finire [51ᴱ]
  □ He'll wind up in jail. Finirà in prigione.

windmill NOUN
  il mulino a vento masc

window NOUN
1 la finestra fem
  □ the kitchen window la finestra della cucina
2 il finestrino masc
  □ He wound down the window. Ha abbassato il finestrino.
3 il vetro masc
  □ a broken window un vetro rotto
  ■ **a window pane** un vetro
  ■ **a shop window** una vetrina

window box NOUN
  la cassetta per i fiori fem

window cleaner NOUN
  il/la lavavetri masc/fem (PL i/le lavavetri)

windscreen NOUN
  il parabrezza masc (PL i parabrezza)

windscreen wiper NOUN
  il tergicristalli masc (PL i tergicristalli)

windshield NOUN (US)
  il parabrezza masc (PL i parabrezza)

windshield wiper NOUN (US)
  il tergicristalli masc (PL i tergicristalli)

windsurfing NOUN
  il windsurf masc

windy ADJECTIVE
  ventoso (FEM ventosa)
  □ a windy day una giornata ventosa
  ■ **It's windy.** C'è vento.

wine NOUN
  il vino masc
  □ white wine vino bianco □ red wine vino rosso □ a glass of wine un bicchiere di vino □ a wine glass un bicchiere da vino
  ■ **a wine bar** un bar
  ■ **the wine list** la carta dei vini
  ■ **a wine tasting** una degustazione dei vini

wing NOUN
  l' ala fem (PL le ali)

to **wink** VERB
  ■ **to wink at somebody** fare [49] l'occhiolino a qualcuno

winner NOUN
  il vincitore masc
  la vincitrice fem

winning ADJECTIVE
  vincitore (FEM vincitrice, MASC PL vincitori, FEM PL vincitrici)
  □ the winning team la squadra vincitrice
  ■ **the winning goal** il gol della vittoria
  ■ **the winning post** il traguardo

winter NOUN
  ▷ see also **winter** ADJECTIVE
  l' inverno masc
  □ in winter d'inverno □ last winter lo scorso inverno

winter ADJECTIVE
  ▷ see also **winter** NOUN
  invernale (FEM invernale)
  □ winter clothes vestiti invernali □ winter sports sport invernali

to **wipe** VERB
  pulire [51]
  ■ **to wipe one's feet** pulirsi [51ᴱ] i piedi

to **wipe out** VERB
  spazzare [68] via

to **wipe up** VERB
  asciugare [76]

wire NOUN
  il filo masc
  □ copper wire filo di rame □ electrical wire filo elettrico □ the telephone wire il filo del telefono

wireless ADJECTIVE
  wireless (FEM+PL wireless)
  □ wireless technology la tecnologia wireless

wisdom tooth NOUN
  il dente del giudizio masc

wise ADJECTIVE
  saggio (FEM saggia, MASC PL saggi, FEM PL sagge)

to **wish** VERB
  ▷ see also **wish** NOUN
  volere [123]
  □ I wish to make a complaint. Voglio sporgere reclamo. □ I wish you were here! Come vorrei che tu fossi qui!
  ■ **I wish you'd told me!** Se solo me l'avessi detto!
  ■ **to wish for something** desiderare [68] qualcosa
  ■ **to wish somebody happy birthday** augurare [68] buon compleanno a qualcuno

wish NOUN
  ▷ see also **wish** VERB
1 la voglia fem
  □ She had no wish for conversation. Non aveva alcuna voglia di conversare.
2 il desiderio masc
  □ Make a wish. Esprimi un desiderio.
  ■ 'best wishes' 'tanti auguri'
  ■ 'with best wishes, Jo' 'cari saluti, Jo'

W

wit NOUN
lo spirito *masc*
□ his intelligence and wit la sua intelligenza e il suo spirito
■ **to be at one's wits' end** non sapere [94] più cos'altro fare □ I'm at my wits' end! Non so più cos'altro fare!

with PREPOSITION
1 con
□ Come with me. Vieni con me. □ a woman with blue eyes una donna con gli occhi azzurri
2 a casa di
□ We stayed with friends. Siamo stati a casa di amici.
3 di
□ green with envy verde d'invidia □ He was shaking with fear. Tremava di paura. □ Fill the jug with water. Riempi la brocca d'acqua.

within PREPOSITION
1 all'interno di
□ communication within the organization la comunicazione all'interno dell'organizzazione
2 entro
□ within the week entro questa settimana
■ **within easy reach** vicino □ The shops are within easy reach. I negozi sono vicini.

without PREPOSITION
senza
□ without a coat senza il cappotto □ without speaking senza parlare

witness NOUN
il/la testimone *masc/fem*
□ There were no witnesses. Non c'erano testimoni.
■ **the witness box** il banco dei testimoni
■ **the witness stand** (US) il banco dei testimoni

witty ADJECTIVE
spiritoso (FEM spiritosa)

wives NOUN ▷ *see* **wife**

woke, woken VERB ▷ *see* **wake**

wolf NOUN
il lupo *masc*

woman NOUN
la donna *fem*
□ a man and two women un uomo e due donne
■ **a woman doctor** una dottoressa

won VERB ▷ *see* **win**

to **wonder** VERB
chiedersi [19ᴱ]
□ I wonder why she said that. Mi chiedo perché l'abbia detto.
■ **I wonder what that means.** Chissà cosa vuol dire.

wonderful ADJECTIVE
meraviglioso (FEM meravigliosa)

won't = will not

wood NOUN
1 il legno *masc*
□ It's made of wood. È di legno.
2 il bosco *masc* (PL i boschi)
□ We went for a walk in the wood. Siamo andati a passeggiare nel bosco.

wooden ADJECTIVE
di legno
□ a wooden chair una sedia di legno

woodwork NOUN
la falegnameria *fem (school subject)*

wool NOUN
la lana *fem*

word NOUN
la parola *fem*
□ The word 'ginseng' is Chinese. La parola 'ginseng' è cinese.
■ **in other words** in altri termini
■ **to have a word with somebody** parlare [68] con qualcuno □ Can I have a word with you? Posso parlarti?

word processing NOUN
l' elaborazione testi *fem*

word processor NOUN
il word processor *masc* (PL i word processor)

wore VERB ▷ *see* **wear**

work NOUN
▷ *see also* **work** VERB
il lavoro *masc*
□ She's looking for work. Sta cercando lavoro.
■ **It's hard work.** È faticoso.
■ **to be off work** essere [47ᴱ] in congedo
■ **to be out of work** essere [47ᴱ] disoccupato

to **work** VERB
▷ *see also* **work** NOUN
1 lavorare [68]
□ She works in a shop. Lavora in un negozio.
□ They are working hard. Lavorano sodo.
2 funzionare [68]
□ The heating isn't working. Il riscaldamento non funziona. □ My plan worked perfectly. Il mio piano ha funzionato a meraviglia.

to **work out** VERB
1 fare [49] ginnastica
□ I work out twice a week. Faccio ginnastica due volte alla settimana.
2 andare [6ᴱ] bene
□ I hope it will all work out. Spero che tutto vada bene.
3 capire [51]
□ I just couldn't work it out. Non riuscivo proprio a capire.
■ **It works out at £10 each.** Fanno dieci sterline a testa.

worker NOUN
il lavoratore *masc*
la lavoratrice *fem*
□ a good worker un bravo lavoratore
■ **a factory worker** un operaio

work experience NOUN
1 l' esperienza lavorativa *fem*
  □ They have little work experience. Hanno poca esperienza lavorativa.
2 il tirocinio *masc*
  □ I'm doing work experience in a factory. Faccio tirocinio in una fabbrica.

working class ADJECTIVE
operaio (FEM operaia)
  □ a working class family una famiglia operaia
  ■ **I'm working class.** Vengo da una famiglia operaia.

workman NOUN
l' operaio *masc*

works NOUN SING
la fabbrica *fem*

worksheet NOUN
la scheda *fem* (at school)

workshop NOUN
il laboratorio *masc*
  □ a drama workshop un laboratorio teatrale

workstation NOUN
la stazione di lavoro *fem*

world NOUN
il mondo *masc*
  □ the world champion il campione del mondo
  ■ **the World Wide Web** il Web

worm NOUN
il verme *masc*

worn VERB ▷ *see* wear

worn ADJECTIVE
logoro (FEM logora)
  □ The carpet is a bit worn. La moquette è un po' logora.
  ■ **worn out 1** logoro □ worn out shoes scarpe logore **2** sfinito □ I'm worn out! Sono sfinito!

worried ADJECTIVE
preoccupato (FEM preoccupata)
  □ I was worried about my job. Ero preoccupato per il mio lavoro.
  ■ **to look worried** avere [12] l'aria preoccupata

to **worry** VERB
preoccuparsi [56ᴱ]
  □ Don't worry! Non preoccuparti!

worse ADJECTIVE, ADVERB
1 peggiore (FEM peggiore)
  □ It was even worse than mine. Era anche peggiore del mio.
2 peggio
  □ I'm feeling worse. Mi sento peggio.
  ■ **to get worse** peggiorare [68ᴱ] □ In March the weather will get worse. In marzo il tempo peggiorerà.
  ■ **He is now worse off than before.** Ora è in condizioni peggiori di prima.

to **worship** VERB
adorare [68]

worst ADJECTIVE
  ▷ *see also* **worst** NOUN
  ■ **the worst** il peggiore □ the worst student in the class il peggior studente della classe
  ■ **my worst enemy** il mio peggior nemico

worst NOUN
  ▷ *see also* **worst** ADJECTIVE
il peggio *masc*
  □ The worst of it is that... Il peggio è che...
  ■ **at worst** alla peggio
  ■ **if the worst comes to the worst** nel peggiore dei casi

worth ADJECTIVE
  ■ **to be worth** valere [118ᴱ] □ It's worth a lot of money. Vale un sacco di soldi. □ How much is it worth? Quanto vale?
  ■ **It's worth it.** Ne vale la pena. □ Is it worth it? Ne vale la pena? □ It's not worth it. Non ne vale la pena.

would VERB

  ⎮ **LANGUAGE TIP** 'would you like' is translated by **volere**, or by the conditional of **piacere**.
  □ Would you like a biscuit? Vuoi un biscotto?
  □ Would you like to go and see a film? Ti piacerebbe andare al cinema?

  ⎮ **LANGUAGE TIP** When 'would you' + verb is used to ask somebody to do something it can be translated by the imperative.
  □ Would you close the door please? Chiudi la porta per favore.

  ⎮ **LANGUAGE TIP** When 'would' + verb indicates the conditional it is translated by the conditional of the Italian verb.
  □ It wouldn't cost much. Non costerebbe tanto. □ He'd probably do it. Probabilmente lo farebbe. □ If you asked him he'd do it. Se glielo chiedessi lo farebbe. □ If you had asked him he would have done it. Se glielo avessi chiesto lo avrebbe fatto.

  ⎮ **LANGUAGE TIP** In indirect speech the perfect conditional of the Italian verb is used.
  □ I said I would do it. Ho detto che l'avrei fatto.
  ■ **I'd like...** Mi piacerebbe... □ I'd like to go to America. Mi piacerebbe andare in America.

  ⎮ **LANGUAGE TIP** When 'wouldn't' means 'refused to' it is translated by the past tense of **volere**.
  □ He wouldn't lend me the money. Non mi ha voluto prestare i soldi.

wouldn't = would not

wound NOUN
  ▷ *see also* **wound** VERB
la ferita *fem*

to **wound** VERB
  ▷ *see also* **wound** NOUN
ferire [51]

609

wound – WWW

wound VERB ▷see **wind**

to **wrap** VERB
incartare [68]
□ She's wrapping her Christmas presents. Sta incartando i regali di Natale.
■ **Can you wrap it for me please?** Mi può fare una confezione regalo, per favore?

to **wrap up** VERB
avvolgere [91]

wrapping paper NOUN
la carta da regalo *fem*

wreck NOUN
▷ see also **wreck** VERB
1 il rottame *masc*
□ That car is a wreck! Quella macchina è un rottame!
2 l' incidente *masc* (US)
□ He was killed in a car wreck. È rimasto ucciso in un incidente automobilistico.
■ **to be a complete wreck** essere [47ᴱ] distrutto □ After the exams I was a complete wreck. Dopo gli esami ero distrutto.

to **wreck** VERB
▷ see also **wreck** NOUN
1 distruggere [79]
□ The explosion wrecked the whole house. L'esplosione ha completamente distrutto la casa.
2 rovinare [68]
□ The trip was wrecked by bad weather. Il brutto tempo ha rovinato la gita.

wreckage NOUN
1 i rottami *masc pl*
□ the wreckage of the coach i rottami della corriera
2 le macerie *fem pl*
□ the wreckage of the building le macerie dell'edificio

wrestler NOUN
il lottatore *masc*

wrestling NOUN
la lotta libera *fem*

wrinkled ADJECTIVE
1 pieno di rughe (FEM piena di rughe)
□ I'm old and wrinkled. Sono vecchio e pieno di rughe.
2 stropicciato (FEM stropicciata)
□ His suit was wrinkled. Il suo vestito era stropicciato.

wrist NOUN
il polso *masc*

to **write** VERB
scrivere [99]
□ I was writing a letter. Stavo scrivendo una lettera. □ Have you written the letter? Hai scritto la lettera? □ He wrote me a letter last week. Mi ha scritto una lettera la settimana scorsa.
■ **to write to somebody** scrivere [99] a qualcuno

to **write down** VERB
1 annotare [68]
□ I wrote down the address. Ho annotato l'indirizzo.
2 scrivere [99]
□ Can you write it down for me? Me lo può scrivere?

writer NOUN
lo scrittore *masc*
la scrittrice *fem*

writing NOUN
la scrittura *fem*
□ I can't read your writing. Non riesco a leggere la tua scrittura.
■ **in writing** per iscritto

written VERB ▷see **write**

wrong ADJECTIVE, ADVERB
sbagliato (FEM sbagliata)
□ The information they gave us was wrong. Ci hanno dato le informazioni sbagliate.
□ the wrong answer la risposta sbagliata
■ **You've got the wrong number.** Ha sbagliato numero.
■ **to be wrong** sbagliarsi [25ᴱ] □ You're wrong about that. Ti sbagli.
■ **to do something wrong** sbagliare [25]
□ You've done it wrong. Hai sbagliato.
■ **to go wrong** andare [6ᴱ] male □ The robbery went wrong and they got caught. La rapina è andata male e li hanno presi.
■ **Lying is wrong.** Non si dicono le bugie.
■ **What's wrong?** Cosa c'è che non va?
■ **Something must be wrong.** Dev'esserci qualcosa che non va.
■ **What's wrong with her?** Cos'ha?

wrote VERB ▷see **write**

WWW NOUN (= World Wide Web)
il Web *masc*

Xx

Xerox® NOUN
▷ *see also* **xerox** VERB
la fotocopiatrice *fem*

to **xerox** VERB
▷ *see also* **Xerox** NOUN
fotocopiare [17]

Xmas NOUN
il Natale *masc*

to **X-ray** VERB
▷ *see also* **X-ray** NOUN
fare [49] una radiografia a

□ They X-rayed my arm. Mi hanno fatto
una radiografia al braccio.

X-ray NOUN
▷ *see also* **X-ray** VERB
la radiografia *fem*

■ **to have an X-ray** farsi [49ᴱ] fare una
radiografia

■ **X-rays** raggi X

xylophone NOUN
lo xilofono *masc*

Yy

yacht NOUN
lo yacht *masc* (PL gli yacht)

yard NOUN
1 la iarda *fem*

> **DID YOU KNOW...?**
> In Italy measurements are in metres rather than yards. A yard is slightly less than a metre.

2 il cortile *masc*
□ a small yard behind the house un piccolo cortile dietro alla casa
3 il giardino *masc (US: garden)*

to **yawn** VERB
▷ *see also* **yawn** NOUN
sbadigliare [25]

yawn NOUN
▷ *see also* **yawn** VERB
lo sbadiglio *masc*

year NOUN
l' anno *masc*
□ last year l'anno scorso
■ **to be 15 years old** avere [12] quindici anni
■ **an eight-year-old child** un bambino di otto anni
■ **She's in year eleven.** È in quinta.

to **yell** VERB
▷ *see also* **yell** NOUN
urlare [68]

yell NOUN
▷ *see also* **yell** VERB
l' urlo *masc*

> **LANGUAGE TIP** The plural of **urlo** is usually **le urla**.

yellow ADJECTIVE
giallo (FEM gialla)

yes ADVERB
sì
□ Do you like it? — Yes. Ti piace? — Sì.

yesterday ADVERB
ieri

yet ADVERB
1 ancora *(still)*
□ A settlement might yet be possible. È ancora possibile trovare un accordo.
■ **not yet** non ancora □ It's not finished yet. Non è ancora finito.
■ **as yet** per ora □ There's no news as yet. Per ora non ci sono notizie.

2 già *(already)*
□ Have you told your parents yet? Lo hai già detto ai tuoi genitori?

to **yield** VERB (US)
dare [30] la precedenza

yob NOUN
il teppista *masc*

yoghurt NOUN
lo yogurt *masc* (PL gli yogurt)

yolk NOUN
il tuorlo *masc*

you PRONOUN
1 tu *(informal: 1 person)*
□ It's you! Sei tu!
2 te *(following preposition)*
□ I'll come with you. Vengo con te.
3 ti *(object)*
□ I told you what I thought. Ti ho detto quello che pensavo.
4 voi *(plural)*
□ I'd like to come with you. Vorrei venire con voi. □ all of you tutti voi
5 vi *(plural, object)*
□ I'll take you to the station. Vi porto in stazione.
6 lei *(polite singular)*
□ You're a good teacher. Lei è una brava insegnante. □ This is for you. Questo è per lei.
7 la *(polite singular, direct object)*
□ I'll call you later. La chiamo più tardi.
8 le *(polite singular, indirect object)*
□ As I was telling you... Come le stavo dicendo...
9 si *(one)*
□ I doubt it, but you never know. Ne dubito, ma non si sa mai.

> **LANGUAGE TIP** 'you' is sometimes not translated.

□ Where are you going? Dove andate?

young ADJECTIVE
giovane (FEM giovane)
□ You're too young. Sei troppo giovane.
■ **young people** i giovani
■ **young children** bambini piccoli
■ **younger** più giovane □ He's younger than me. È più giovane di me.
■ **my younger brother** il mio fratello minore
■ **my youngest brother** il mio fratello minore

■ **the youngest** **1** *(masculine)* il più giovane
□ He's the youngest. È il più giovane.
2 *(feminine)* la più giovane □ She's the
youngest in the class. È la più giovane della
classe.

■ **She is the youngest competitor.** È la
concorrente più giovane.

your ADJECTIVE
1 il tuo (PL i tuoi)
la tua (PL le tue) *(familiar form)*
□ your address il tuo indirizzo □ your parents
i tuoi genitori □ your pen la tua penna
2 tuo (PL tuoi)
tua (PL tue)
□ your father tuo padre □ your mother tua
madre
3 il vostro (PL i vostri)
la vostra (PL le vostre)
□ Children, give these letters to your parents.
Ragazzi, date queste lettere ai vostri genitori.
□ Children, give these letters to your mothers.
Ragazzi, date queste lettere alle vostre madri.
4 vostro (PL vostri)
vostra (PL vostre)
□ your father vostro padre □ your mother
vostra madre
5 il suo (PL i suoi)
la sua (PL le sue) *(polite form)*
□ Your ticket, madam. Il suo biglietto, signora.
□ Your car, madam. La sua macchina, signora.
6 suo (PL suoi)
sua (PL sue)
□ your father suo padre □ your mother sua
madre

> **LANGUAGE TIP** 'your' is not always
> translated.

□ Wash your hands. Lavati le mani.
□ Remember to take your umbrella, sir. Non
dimentichi di prendere l'ombrello.

yours PRONOUN

> **LANGUAGE TIP** The Italian pronoun agrees
> with the noun it is replacing.

1 il tuo (PL i tuoi)
la tua (PL le tue) *(familiar form)*
□ My garden is smaller than yours. Il mio
giardino è più piccolo del tuo. □ That bag's
not mine, it's yours. Questa borsa non è la
mia, è la tua.
2 tuo (PL tuoi)
tua (PL tue) *(your property)*
□ Is this yours? È tuo questo?
■ **a friend of yours** un tuo amico □ Is this
bag yours? È tua questa borsa?
3 il vostro (PL i vostri)
la vostra (PL le vostre)

□ our parents and yours i nostri genitori ed i
vostri □ My car is older than yours. La mia
macchina è più vecchia della vostra.
4 vostro (PL vostre)
vostra (PL vostre) *(your property)*
□ Is that dog yours? È vostro quel cane? □ Is
that car yours? È vostra quella macchina?
5 il suo (PL i suoi)
la sua (PL le sue) *(polite form)*
□ my luggage and yours il mio bagaglio ed il
suo □ My house is smaller than yours. La mia
casa è più piccola della sua.
6 suo (PL suoi)
sua (PL sue) *(your property)*
□ Excuse me, madam. Is this yours? Mi scusi
signora. È suo questo? □ Is that car yours, sir?
È sua quella macchina, signore?

yourself PRONOUN
1 ti *(familiar form)*

> **LANGUAGE TIP** A verb + 'yourself' is often
> translated by a reflexive verb in Italian.

□ Have you looked at yourself in the mirror?
Ti sei guardato allo specchio?
2 te *(familiar form, following an English
preposition)*
□ a beginner like yourself un principiante
come te
3 si *(polite form)*

> **LANGUAGE TIP** A verb + 'yourself' is often
> translated by a reflexive verb in Italian.

□ Did you enjoy yourself, sir? Si è divertito,
signore?
4 lei *(polite form, following an English preposition)*
□ an important person like yourself una
persona importante come lei
■ **by yourself** da solo □ Do you like travelling
by yourself? Ti piace viaggiare da solo?

yourselves PRONOUN
1 vi

> **LANGUAGE TIP** A verb + 'yourselves' is often
> translated by a reflexive verb in Italian.

□ Have you looked at yourselves in the mirror?
Vi siete guardati allo specchio?
2 voi *(following an English preposition)*
□ important people like yourselves persone
importanti come voi
■ **by yourselves** da soli □ Do you like
travelling by yourselves? Vi piace viaggiare da
soli?

youth NOUN
■ **in my youth** quand'ero giovane

youth club NOUN
il circolo giovanile *masc*

youth hostel NOUN
l' ostello della gioventù *masc*

Zz

zany ADJECTIVE
un po' pazzo (FEM un po' pazza)

zebra NOUN
la zebra *fem*

zebra crossing NOUN
il passaggio pedonale *masc* (PL i passaggi pedonali)

zero NOUN
lo zero *masc*

Zimbabwe NOUN
lo Zimbabwe *masc*

Zimmer frame® NOUN
il deambulatore *masc*

zip NOUN
▷ *see also* **zip** VERB
la cerniera lampo *fem* (PL le cerniere lampo)

> **LANGUAGE TIP** Word for word, this means 'the lightning fastener'.

□ The zip's stuck. La cerniera lampo è inceppata.

to **zip** VERB
▷ *see also* **zip** NOUN
1 sfrecciare [13ᴱ]

□ A car zipped past me. Una macchina mi è sfrecciata accanto.

2 zippare [68] *(file)*

zip code NOUN (US)
il codice postale *masc*

zipper NOUN (US)
la cerniera lampo *fem*

zit NOUN (US)
il brufolo *masc*

zodiac NOUN
lo zodiaco *masc*

zone NOUN
la zona *fem*

zoo NOUN
lo zoo *masc* (PL gli zoo)

to **zoom** VERB
sfrecciare [13ᴱ]

□ The police car zoomed by very close to him. La macchina della polizia gli è sfrecciata accanto vicinissima.

zoom lens NOUN
lo zoom *masc* (PL gli zoom)

zucchini NOUN SING (US)
la zucchina *fem*

□ potatoes and zucchini patate e zucchine